Online Research and Reference Aids

Whether you want to investigate the ideas behind a thought-provoking topic or conduct in-depth research for a paper, our Online Research and Reference Aids can help you refine your research skills, find the information you need on the Web, and use that information effectively. You can access these resources directly or through the links on the companion Web site for *The American Promise*, Third Edition, at **bedfordstmartins.com/roark**.

DocLinks
bedfordstmartins.com/doclinks

Annotated links with single-click access to primary documents online. Search by topic, date, or textbook chapter.

HistoryLinks
bedfordstmartins.com/historylinks

Annotated links to history-related Web sites, including those containing image galleries, maps, and audio and video clips for supplementing research. Search by date, subject, medium, keyword, or specific textbook chapter.

A Student's Online Guide to History Reference Sources
bedfordstmartins.com/benjamin

A collection of links to history-related electronic reference sources such as databases, indexes, and journals, plus contact information for state, provincial, local, and professional history organizations. Based on the appendix to Jules Benjamin's *A Student's Guide to History*, Ninth Edition.

Research and Documentation Online
bedfordstmartins.com/resdoc

Clear advice on how to integrate primary and secondary sources into research papers and cite sources correctly.

The St. Martin's Tutorial on Avoiding Plagiarism
bedfordstmartins.com/plagiarismtutorial

An online tutorial that reviews the consequences of plagiarism and explains what sources to acknowledge, how to keep good notes, how to organize research, and how to integrate sources appropriately. Includes exercises on integrating sources and recognizing acceptable summaries.

bedfordstmartins.com/history

ELIZABETH ECKFORD TURNED AWAY FROM ENTERING CENTRAL HIGH SCHOOL IN LITTLE ROCK BY ARKANSAS NATIONAL GUARD TROOPS UNDER ORDERS FROM GOVERNOR ORVAL FAUBUS IN SEPTEMBER 1957   Francis Miller/Time Life Pictures/Getty Images nation "the last best hope of Earth." Kept alive by countless sacrifices, that hope has been marred by compromises, disappointments, and denials, but it lives still. We believe that *The American Promise*, Third Edition, with its increased attention to making history come alive, will help students become aware of the legacy of hope bequeathed to them by previous generations of Americans stretching back nearly four centuries, a legacy that is theirs to preserve and build on.

Features

From the beginning, readers have proclaimed this textbook a visual feast, richly illustrated in ways that extend and reinforce the narrative. The third edition furthers this benefit by nearly doubling the number of **illustrations** to more than 750. Many in full color and large enough to study in detail, these illustrations are contemporaneous with the period of the chapter in which they appear. In our effort to make history tangible and memorable, we expanded and enriched the art program's acclaimed use of **artifacts** and added **all-new embedded artifacts**—100 small images of material culture— from boots and political buttons to guns and sewing machines— folded into the lines of the narrative. These, combined with full-page **chapter-opening artifacts** and other captioned artifacts throughout, emphasize the importance of material culture in the study of the past and enrich the historical account. Similarly, within our **new illustrated chapter chronologies** we placed thumbnail-size images from the chapter to reinforce the narrative and stimulate students' power of recall. A striking **new design** highlights the illustration program and makes the most of our **comprehensive captions** while enticing students to delve deeper into the text itself.

Our highly regarded **map program** offers more maps than any other U.S. survey text— over 170 maps in all (20 more than in the previous edition). Each chapter offers, on average, four **full-size maps** showing major developments in a wide range of areas, from environmental and technological issues to political, social, cultural,

and diplomatic matters. New increased attention to Native Americ and to the West in particular, and they cove varied topics as zones of empire in eighteenth-century North America; Indian war in the West, 1777–1781; western mining, 1848–1890; urban riots, 1965–1968; and the election of 2000. In addition, each chapter includes two to three **spot maps,** small, single-concept maps embedded in the narrative to strengthen students' grasp of crucial issues. Unique to *The American Promise,* new spot maps in the third edition highlight such topics as Spanish missions in California, frontier land opened by Indian removal in the 1830s, the Mexican cession, the Battle of Glorieta Pass, the Samoan Islands, selected Indian relocations from 1950 to 1970, the Cuban missile crisis, contemporary Liberia, con-

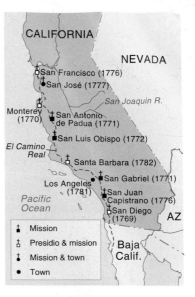

Spanish Missions in California

temporary Israel, and the recent conflict in Afghanistan. Another unique feature is our brief **Atlas of the Territorial Growth of the United States,** a series of full-color maps at the end of each volume that reveal the changing cartography of the nation.

Imaginative and effective pedagogy remains a hallmark of our text. All chapters are constructed to preview, reinforce, and review the narrative in the most memorable and engaging means possible. To prepare students for the reading to come, each chapter begins with a **new chapter outline** to accompany the vivid **opening vignette** that invites students into the narrative with lively accounts of individuals or groups who embody the central themes of the chapter. Each vignette ends with a **narrative overview** of all of the chapter's main topics. New vignettes in this edition include, among others, Roger Williams being banished from Puritan Massachusetts, runaway slave William Gould enlisting in the Union navy, Native American boarding school students celebrating Indian Citizenship Day, Henry Ford putting America on wheels, Colonel Paul Tibbets dropping the bomb on Hiroshima, Phyllis Schlafly promoting conservatism, and Colin Powell adjusting to the post–cold war world. To further

...students as they read, major sections within each chapter have **introductory paragraphs** that preview the subsections that follow. Throughout each chapter, **two-tiered running heads** with dates and topical headings remind students where the sections they are reading fall chronologically, and **call-outs** reinforce key points. In addition, **new thematic chronologies** reinforce and extend points in the narrative, and a **new Glossary of Historical Vocabulary** makes history even more accessible. To help students understand the role of geography in American history and to teach them how to read maps and how map content relates to chapter content, we include twice as many of our popular **map exercises** as in the last edition—now two per chapter.

MAP 7.2 **Loyalist Strength and Rebel Support**
he exact number of loyalists can never be known. No one could have made an accurate count at the time; in addition, political allegiance often shifted with the winds. This map shows the regions of loyalist strength on which the British relied—most significantly the lower Hudson valley and the Carolina Piedmont.

EADING THE MAP: Which forces were stronger, those loyal to Britain or those rebelling? (Consider size of areas, centers of population, and vital port locations.) What areas were contested? If the contested areas ultimately sided with the British, how would the balance of power change?

CONNECTIONS: Who was more likely to be a loyalist, and why? How many loyalists left the United States? Where did they go?

OR MORE HELP ANALYZING THIS MAP, see the map activity for this chapter in the Online Study Guide at bedfordstmartins.com/roark.

At the end of each chapter, an annotated and **illustrated chapter chronology** reviews important events, and a **conclusion** critically reexamines central ideas and provides a bridge to the next chapter.

An enriched array of special features reinforces the narrative and offers teachers more points of departure for assignments and discussion. By providing two entirely new types of features (on 41 topics) in this edition, we supply a widened variety of choices to spark students' interest while helping them understand that history is both a body of knowledge and an ongoing process of investigation. The two new types of boxed features we added are designed to expand and deepen students' understanding of the American story and make it come alive for them. The **new American Places** feature brings history home to students through a brief essay in each chapter on an American locale related to the

discussion at hand— such as Jamestown, the California Mission Trail, Lowell National His-

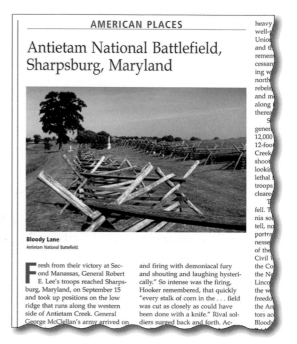

AMERICAN PLACES

Antietam National Battlefield, Sharpsburg, Maryland

Bloody Lane
Antietam National Battlefield.

Fresh from their victory at Second Manassas, General Robert E. Lee's troops reached Sharpsburg, Maryland, on September 15 and took up positions on the low ridge that runs along the western side of Antietam Creek. General George McClellan's army arrived on and firing with demoniacal fury and shouting and laughing hysterically." So intense was the firing, Hooker remembered, that quickly "every stalk of corn in the . . . field was cut as closely as could have been done with a knife." Rival soldiers surged back and forth. Ac-

toric Park, Antietam National Battlefield, the Lower East Side Tenement Museum, and Alcatraz Island—that students can visit today in person and on the Web. Too often, written history seems to float detached from the landscape in which events occurred, untouched by the powerful influences of place. By discussing the history of specific historical sites and describing what visitors today will find there, we hope to illustrate that history is rooted in both time *and* place and provide students with a tangible, and thus memorable, bridge to the past. This feature concludes with a cross-reference to our **new PlaceLinks** feature on the book's companion Web site (at bedfordstmartins.com/roark) for virtual visits to each described site and to other sites throughout the United States.

Because we understand that students need help making connections with historical geographies outside the United States as well, we complement attention to international topics in the narrative with twelve essays in our **new Beyond America's Borders** feature. Essays as varied as "American Tobacco and European Consumers," "Back to Africa: The United States and Liberia," "Transnational Feminisms," and "Jobs in a Globalizing Era" challenge students to consider the effects of transnational connections. These essays seek to widen students' perspectives, to help them see that this country did not develop in isolation. This broader notion of American history will help students understand more fully the complex development of their nation's history and help prepare them to live in the world.

Fresh topics in our three enduring special features further enrich this edition. Each **Documenting the American Promise** feature juxtaposes three or four primary documents to dramatize the human dimension of major events and show varying perspectives on a topic or issue. Feature introductions and document headnotes contextualize the sources, and Questions for Analysis and Debate promote critical thinking about primary sources. New topics in this edition include "Missionaries Report on California Missions," "Families Divide over the Revolution," "Young Women Homesteaders and the Promise of the West," and "Voices of Protest." Illustrated **Historical Questions** essays pose and interpret specific questions of continuing interest so as to demonstrate the depth and variety of possible answers, thereby countering the belief of many beginning students that historians simply gather facts and string them together into a chronological narrative. New questions in this edition include "How Long Did the Seven Years' War Last in Indian Country?" and "Social Darwinism: Did Wealthy Industrialists Practice What They Preached?" The **Promise of Technology** essays examine the ramifications—positive and negative—of technological developments in American society and culture. New topics in this edition include "Stoves Transform Cooking," "C.S.S. *H. L. Hunley:* The First Successful Submarine," "Artificial Limbs: Filling the 'Empty Sleeve,'" and "Solar Energy."

Textual Changes

In our ongoing effort to offer a comprehensive text that braids all Americans into the national narrative, we give particular attention to diversity and the influence of class, religion, race, ethnicity, gender, and region. For example, increased coverage of the West and its peoples from the beginnings of American history means fresh material throughout the text and a new post–Civil War chapter, "The West in the Gilded Age." We also give more coverage to the environment, Native Americans, Mexicans, Latinos, Chinese workers, and other topics often related to the history of the West. We enriched the discussion of pre-Columbian America in chapter 1 (the prologue in the second edition) with more discussion of Native Americans on the eve of European contact, to complement the chapter's introduction to the process—and limits—of historical investigation.

To strengthen coverage and increase clarity and accessibility, we reorganized certain chapters. In particular, reorganization in the chapters on antebellum America and the Gilded Age provides clearer themes with smoother transitions and better places the West in the national narrative. We also provide stronger post-1945 chapters, reorganized to make themes more compelling and chronology clearer. These post-1945 chapters also include a fresh array of voices, pay greater attention to the West and related topics, and, of course, provide up-to-date coverage of the George W. Bush administration, the Middle East, and the war on terrorism.

Staying abreast of current scholarship is of perennial concern to us, and this edition reflects that keen interest. We incorporated a wealth of new scholarship into the third edition in myriad ways to benefit students. Readers will note that we made good use of the latest works on a number of topics, such as Spanish borderlands, Native Americans in the Seven Years' War, the role of political wives in the early Republic, the social history of the gold rush, the active participation of blacks in their own liberation during the Civil War, mining and commercial farming in the Gilded Age West, race and Americanization, Mexican migration into the American Southwest and how this compares to black migration into the North, the story of the atomic bomb, the black civil rights struggle in global context, and the rise of contemporary conservatism.

Supplements

Developed with our guidance and thoroughly revised to reflect the changes in the third edition, the comprehensive collection of print and electronic resources accompanying the textbook provide a aids. Again, we learned much from the book's community of adopters, and we broadened the scope of the supplements to create a learning package that responds to the real needs of instructors and students. Cross-references in the textbook to the groundbreaking Online Study Guide and to the primary source reader signal the tight integration of the core text with the supplements.

For Students

Reading the American Past: Selected Historical Documents, **Third Edition.** Edited by Michael P. Johnson (Johns Hopkins University), one of the authors of *The American Promise,* and designed to complement the textbook, *Reading the American Past* provides a broad selection of over 150 primary source documents, as well as editorial apparatus to help students understand the sources. Emphasizing the important social, political, and economic themes of U.S. history courses, 31 new documents (one per chapter) were added to provide a multiplicity of perspectives on environmental, western, ethnic, and gender history and to bring a global dimension to the anthology.

Online Study Guide at bedfordstmartins.com/ roark. The popular Online Study Guide for *The American Promise* is a free and uniquely personalized learning tool to help students master themes and information presented in the textbook and improve their historical skills. Assessment quizzes let students evaluate their comprehension and pro-

vide them with customized plans for further study through a variety of activities. Instructors can monitor students' progress through the online Quiz Gradebook or receive e-mail updates.

NEW *Maps in Context: A Workbook for American History.* Written by historical cartography expert Gerald A. Danzer (University of Illinois, Chicago), this skill-building workbook helps students comprehend essential connections between geographic literacy and historical understanding. Organized to correspond to the typical U.S. history survey course, *Maps in Context* presents a wealth of map-centered projects and convenient pop quizzes that give students hands-on experience working with maps.

NEW *History Matters: A Student Guide to U.S. History Online.* This new resource, written by Alan Gevinson, Kelly Schrum, and Roy Rosenzweig (all of George Mason University), provides an illustrated and annotated guide to 250 of the most useful Web sites for student research in U.S. history as well as advice on evaluating and using Internet sources. This essential guide is based on the acclaimed "History Matters" Web site developed by the American History Social Project and the Center for History and New Media.

Telecourse Guide for *Shaping America: U.S. History to 1877.* This guide by Kenneth G. Alfers (Dallas County Community College District) is designed for students using *The American Promise* in conjunction with the Dallas TeleLearning telecourse *Shaping America* (see p. xviii). Lesson overviews, assignments, objectives, and focus points provide structure for distance learners, while enrichment ideas, suggested readings, and brief primary sources extend the unit lessons. Practice tests help students evaluate their mastery of the material. *Note:* The telecourse and guide for *Transforming America: U.S. History since 1877* will be available in fall 2005.

Bedford Series in History and Culture. Over 70 titles in this highly praised series combine first-rate scholarship, historical narrative, and important primary documents for undergraduate courses. Each book is brief, inexpensive, and focused on a specific topic or period. Package discounts are available.

Historians at Work Series. Brief enough for a single assignment yet meaty enough to provoke thoughtful discussion, each volume in this series examines a single historical question by combining unabridged selections by distinguished historians, each with a different perspective on the issue, with helpful learning aids. Package discounts are available.

PlaceLinks at bedfordstmartins.com/roark. Extending the goals of the "American Places" textbook feature, PlaceLinks provides access to over 100 Web sites about locations in all fifty states, such as specific monuments, parks, and museums, that connect students to the places where history happened.

DocLinks at bedfordstmartins.com/doclinks. This Web site provides over 750 annotated Web links to online primary documents, including links to speeches, legislation, treaties, social commentary, Supreme Court decisions, essays, travelers' accounts, personal narratives and testimony, newspaper articles, visual artifacts, songs, and poems. Students and teachers alike can search documents by topic, date, or specific chapter of *The American Promise*. Links can be selected and stored for later use or published to a unique Web address.

HistoryLinks at bedfordstmartins.com/history links. Recently updated, HistoryLinks directs instructors and students to over 500 carefully selected and annotated links to history-related Web sites, including those containing image galleries, maps, and audio and video clips for supplementing lectures or assignments. Users can browse these Internet starting points by date, subject, medium, keyword, or specific chapter in *The American Promise*. Instructors can assign these links as the basis for homework assignments or research projects, or students can use them in their own history research. Links can be selected and stored for later use or published to a unique Web address.

A Student's Online Guide to History Reference Sources at bedfordstmartins.com/benjamin. This Web site provides links to history-related databases, indexes, and journals, plus contact information for state, provincial, local, and professional history organizations.

Research and Documentation Online at bedfordstmartins.com/resdoc. This Web site provides clear advice on how to integrate primary and secondary sources into research papers, how to cite sources correctly, and how to format in MLA, APA, *Chicago,* or CBE style.

The St. Martin's Tutorial on Avoiding Plagiarism at bedfordstmartins.com/plagiarismtutorial. This online tutorial reviews the consequences of plagiarism and explains what sources to acknowledge, how to keep good notes, how to organize research, and how to integrate sources appropriately. The tutorial includes exercises to help students practice integrating sources and recognize acceptable summaries.

Critical Thinking Modules at bedfordstmartins .com/historymodules. This Web site offers over two dozen online modules for interpreting maps, audio, visual, and textual sources, centered on events covered in the U.S. history survey. An online guide correlates modules to textbook chapters and to books in the Bedford Series in History and Culture.

For Instructors

Instructor's Resource Manual. This popular manual by Sarah E. Gardner (Mercer University) offers both experienced and first-time instructors tools for presenting textbook material in exciting and engaging ways—annotated chapter outlines, lecture strategies, discussion starters, and film and video recommendations. The new edition includes in-class activities on analyzing visual sources and primary documents from the textbook, as well as a chapter-by-chapter guide to all of the supplements available with *The American Promise*. An extensive guide for first-time teaching assistants and sample syllabi are also included.

Transparencies. This set of over 160 full-color acetate transparencies includes all full-size maps and many other images from the textbook to help instructors present lectures and teach students important map-reading skills.

Book Companion Site at bedfordstmartins.com/ roark. The companion Web site gathers all the electronic resources for *The American Promise*, including the Online Study Guide and related Quiz Gradebook, at a single Web address, providing convenient links to lecture, assignment, and research materials such as PowerPoint chapter outlines, DocLinks, HistoryLinks, and Map Central.

Computerized Test Bank. This test bank by Bradford Wood (Eastern Kentucky University) and Peter Lau (University of Rhode Island) provides easy-to-use software to create tests. Over 80 exercises are provided per chapter, including multiple-choice, fill-in-the-blank, map analysis, short essay, and full-length essay questions. Instructors can customize quizzes, add or edit both questions and answers, as well as export questions and answers to a variety of formats, including WebCT and Blackboard. The disc includes correct answers and essay outlines.

Instructor's Resource CD-ROM. This disc provides instructors with ready-made and customizable PowerPoint multimedia presentations built around chapter outlines, maps, figures, and selected images from the textbook. The disc also includes images in jpeg format, an electronic version of the *Instructor's Resource Manual,* outline maps in pdf format for quizzing or handouts, and quick start guides to the Online Study Guide.

Map Central at bedfordstmartins.com/mapcentral. Map Central is a searchable database of over 750 maps from Bedford/St. Martin's history texts for classroom presentation and over 50 basic political and physical outline maps for quizzing or handouts.

Using the Bedford Series in History and Culture in the U.S. History Survey at bedfordstmartins .com/usingseries. This online guide helps instructors integrate volumes from the highly regarded Bedford Series in History and Culture into their U.S. history survey course. The guide not only correlates themes from each series book with the survey course but also provides ideas for classroom discussions.

Blackboard Course Cartridge and **WebCT e-Pack.** Blackboard and WebCT content are available for this book.

Videos and Multimedia. A wide assortment of videos and multimedia CD-ROMs on various topics in American history is available to qualified adopters. Also available are segments from the telecourse *Shaping America.*

***The American Promise* via Telecourse.** We are pleased to announce that *The American Promise* has been selected as the textbook for the award-winning U.S. history telecourse *Shaping America* and the forthcoming *Transforming America* telecourse by Dallas TeleLearning, the LeCroy Center, Dallas County Community College District. Guides for students and instructors fully integrate the narrative of *The American Promise* into each telecourse. The telecourse package for *Shaping America: U.S. History to 1877,* updated for *The American Promise,* Third Edition, will be available for examination in fall 2004. The telecourse package for *Transforming America: U.S. History since 1877* will premiere in fall 2005. For more information on these distance-learning opportunities, visit the Dallas TeleLearning Web site at http://telelearning.dcccd.edu, e-mail tlearn@dcccd.edu, or call 972-669-6650.

Acknowledgments

We gratefully acknowledge all of the helpful suggestions from those who have read and taught from the previous editions of *The American Promise,* and we hope that our many classroom collaborators will be pleased to see their influence in the third edition. In particular, we wish to thank the talented scholars and teachers who gave generously of their time and knowledge to review this book; their critiques and suggestions contributed greatly to the published work: Eric Arnesen, *University of Illinois, Chicago;* Carl H. Boening, *Shelton State Community College;* Tommy L. Bynum, *Georgia Perimeter College;* Lawrence Cebula, *Missouri Southern State College;* Michael Connolly, *Tidewater Community College;* Gary Darden, *Rutgers University;* David Engerman, *Brandeis University;* Maurine W. Greenwald, *University of Pittsburgh;* David Igler, *University of Utah;* Peter F. Lau, *University of Rhode Island;* Charles H. Martin, *University of Texas, El Paso;* April Masten, *State University of New York, Stony Brook;* Jim R. McClellan, *Northern Virginia Community College;* Constance McGovern, *Frostburg State University;* Karen Merrill, *Williams College;* Peggy Renner, *Glendale Community College;* Steven Reschly, *Truman State University;* Leo Ribuffo, *The George Washington University;* Christine Sears, *University of Delaware;* Michael Sherry, *Northwestern University;* Steven Stoll, *Yale University;* Diana Turk, *New York University;* Elliott West, *University of Arkansas;* Jon A. Whitfield, *Central Texas College, Fort Knox;* Thomas Winn, *Austin Peay State University;* and Thomas Zeiler, *University of Colorado at Boulder.*

A project as complex as this requires the talents of many individuals. First, we would like to acknowledge our families for their support, forbearance, and toleration of our textbook responsibilities. Pembroke Herbert and Sandi Rygiel of Picture Research Consultants, Inc., contributed their unparalleled knowledge, soaring imagination, and diligent research to make possible the extraordinary illustration program. Susan Dawson at the Ohio State University provided helpful research assistance.

We would also like to thank the many people at Bedford/St. Martin's who have been crucial to this project. No one contributed more than senior editor Heidi L. Hood, who managed the entire revision and oversaw the development of each chapter. The results of her dedication to excellence and commitment to creating the best textbook imaginable are evident on every page. We thank as well executive editor Elizabeth Welch, senior editor Louise Townsend, and freelance editor Ellen Kuhl for their help with the manuscript. Thanks also go to editorial assistant Elizabeth Harrison, who provided unflagging assistance and who coordinated the supplements. We are also grateful to Jane Knetzger, director of development for history, and Mary Dougherty, executive editor, for their support and guidance. For their imaginative and tireless efforts to promote the book, we want to thank Jenna Bookin Barry, marketing manager, and Amanda Byrnes, marketing associate. With great skill and professionalism, Karen Baart, senior production editor, pulled together the many pieces related to copyediting, design, and typesetting, with the able assistance of Amy Derjue and Anne True and the guidance of managing editor Elizabeth Schaaf and assistant managing editor John Amburg. Senior production supervisor Joe Ford oversaw the manufacturing of the book. Designer and page makeup artist Wanda Kossak, copyeditor Patricia Herbst, and proofreaders Janet Cocker and Mary Lou Wilshaw-Watts attended to the myriad details that help make the book shine. Maro Riofrancos provided an outstanding index. Associate new media editor Bryce Sady and new media production coordinator Coleen O'Hanley made sure that *The American Promise* remains at the forefront of technological support for students and instructors. Editorial director Denise Wydra provided helpful advice throughout the course of the project. Finally, Joan E. Feinberg, president, and Charles H. Christensen, former president, took a personal interest in *The American Promise* from the start and guided all editions through every stage of development.

PROGRESSIVE PARTY CAMPAIGN SOUVENIR
This colorful cotton bandana, a campaign novelty from the 1912 presidential race, celebrates the Progressive Party and its candidate Theodore Roosevelt. The progressive reform movement, growing out of the crises of the 1890s, emerged full-blown in the first decades of the twentieth century. Progressives challenged laissez-faire liberalism and argued for government action to counter the power of big business and ensure greater social justice. Theodore Roosevelt, whose presidency set the tone for the era, became so closely associated with progressivism that when he failed to win the Republican nomination in 1912, his followers formed a new Progressive Party proclaiming, as the bandana notes, "We Want Our Teddy Back." Accepting the nomination, Roosevelt announced that he felt "as fit as a bull moose," giving the new party a mascot. But progressivism was more than one man or one party. A movement that ran from the grass roots to the White House, it included not only members of the short-lived Progressive Party, but Democrats and Republicans as well, who had in common a belief in government activism that would reshape the liberal state of the twentieth century.

Collection of Janice L. and David J. Frent.

Progressivism from the Grass Roots to the White House

1890–1916

I N THE SUMMER OF 1889, a young woman leased the upper floor of a dilapidated mansion on Chicago's West Side in the heart of a burgeoning immigrant population of Italians, Russian Jews, and Greeks. Watching the preparations, neighbors scratched their heads, wondering why the well-dressed woman, who surely could afford a better house in a better neighborhood, chose to live on South Halsted Street. Yet the house built by Charles Hull precisely suited the needs of Jane Addams.

For Addams, personal action marked the first step in the search for solutions to the social problems fostered by urban industrialism. Her object was twofold: She wanted to help her immigrant neighbors, and she wanted to offer an opportunity for educated women like herself to find meaningful work. As she later wrote in her autobiography, *Twenty Years at Hull-House* (1910), "I gradually became convinced that it would be a good thing to rent a house in a part of the city where many primitive and actual needs are found, in which young women who had been given over too exclusively to study might restore a balance of activity along traditional lines and learn of life from life itself." Addams's emphasis on the reciprocal relationship between the social classes made Hull House different from other philanthropic enterprises. She wished to do things with, not just for, Chicago's poor.

In the next decade, Hull House expanded from one rented floor in the old brick mansion to some thirteen buildings housing a remarkable variety of activities. Bathrooms in the basement were converted into public baths, a coffee shop and restaurant sold take-out food to working women too tired to cook after their long shifts, and a nursery and kindergarten provided care for neighborhood children. Hull House offered classes, lectures, art exhibits, musical instruction, and college extension courses. It boasted a gymnasium, a theater, a manual training workshop, a labor museum, and the first public playground in Chicago.

But Hull House was more than a group of buildings. From the first, it attracted an extraordinary set of reformers. Some stayed for decades, as did Julia Lathrop before she went to Washington, D.C., in 1912 to head the Children's Bureau. Others, like Gerard Swope, who later became president of the General Electric Company, came for only a short while. Most had jobs, paid room and board, and devoted time to research and reform. The people

- **Grassroots Progressivism**
  Civilizing the City
  Progressives and the Working Class

- **Progressivism: Theory and Practice**
  Reform Darwinism, Pragmatism, and Social Engineering
  Progressive Government: City and State

- **Progressivism Finds a President: Theodore Roosevelt**
  The Square Deal
  Roosevelt the Reformer
  Roosevelt and Conservation
  Roosevelt the Diplomat

- **Progressivism Stalled**
  The Troubled Presidency of William Howard Taft
  Progressive Insurgency and the Election of 1912

- **Woodrow Wilson and Progressivism at High Tide**
  Wilson's Reforms: Tariff, Banking, and the Trusts
  Wilson, Reluctant Progressive

- **The Limits of Progressive Reform**
  Radical Alternatives
  Progressivism for White Men Only

- **Conclusion: The Transformation of the Liberal State**

Jane Addams

Jane Addams was twenty-nine years old when she founded Hull House on South Halsted Street in Chicago. Graduates of the Rockford Female Seminary, she and her college roommate, Ellen Gates Starr, established America's premier social settlement. Her desire to live among the poor and her insistence that settlement house work benefited educated women like herself as well as her immigrant neighbors separated her from the charity workers who had come before her and marked the distance from philanthropy to progressive reform.

Jane Addams Memorial Collection, Special Collection, University Library, University of Illinois at Chicago.

who lived at Hull House were among the first to investigate the problems of the city with scientific precision. Armed with statistics, they launched campaigns to improve housing, end child labor, fund playgrounds, mediate between labor and management, and lobby for protective legislation.

Addams quickly learned that it was impossible to deal with urban problems without becoming involved in political action. Her determination to clean up the garbage on Halsted Street led her into politics. Piles of decaying garbage overflowed the street's wooden trash bins, breeding flies and disease. Investigation revealed that the contract to pick up the trash was a political plum awarded by the local ward boss to a contractor who felt under no obligation to provide adequate service. To end the graft, Addams got herself appointed garbage inspector. Out on the streets at six in the morning, she rode atop the garbage wagon to make sure it made its rounds. When the ward boss removed her, she squared off against him. After backing several unsuccessful political campaigns to oust the boss, Addams realized that bossism was a symptom and not the cause of urban blight. Recognizing that bosses stayed in power by providing jobs and services to their constituents, she moved instead to sponsor legislation to help her neighbors. Eventually her struggle to aid the urban poor led her not only to city hall but on to the state capitol and to Washington, D.C. Addams became a strong advocate of woman **suffrage**, arguing that city women needed the ballot, not the broom, to keep their neighborhoods clean.

Under Jane Addams's leadership, Hull House, the premier settlement house in the United States, became a "spearhead for reform," part of a broader movement that contemporaries called **progressivism**. The transition from personal action to political activism that Addams personified became one of the hallmarks of this reform period, which lasted from the 1890s to World War I.

By the 1890s it had become clear to many Americans that the **laissez-faire** approach of government toward business no longer worked. The classical **liberalism** of the nation's Founders, with its emphasis on opposition to the tyranny of centralized government, had not reckoned on the enormous private wealth and power of the Gilded Age's Rockefellers and Morgans. The injunction that government stay out of the marketplace made it impossible to curb the excesses of the huge corporations. As the gap between rich and poor widened in the 1890s, issues of social justice also challenged traditional notions of laissez-faire liberalism. The violence and militance of the 1890s—labor strikes, farmers' revolt, suffrage rallies, the antilynching campaign—eloquently testified to the growing polarities in society. Yet a laissez-faire state only exacerbated the inequalities of class, race, and gender. With women denied basic political and economic rights, southern blacks threatened by lynching and intimidation, and courts privileging private property over personal rights, laissez-faire liberalism effectively prevented the country from addressing issues of social justice and ameliorating the inequities of urban industrial capitalism. A generation of progressive reformers demanded government intervention to guarantee a more equitable society. The willingness to use the government to promote change and to counterbalance the power of private interests redefined liberalism in the twentieth century.

Faith in activism in both the political and the private realms formed a common thread that

Hull House Playground
Settlement houses worked hard to provide opportunities for neighborhood youth. Hull House opened Chicago's first children's playground, shown here, in 1894 to provide supervised recreation in a safe, clean alternative to filthy tenement alleys. Reformers believed that access to playgrounds and parks would instill qualities of morality and citizenship in the city's children. As Jacob Riis testified, "A boy robbed of his chance to play will not be an honest and effective citizen."

Jane Addams Memorial Collection, Special Collection, University Library, University of Illinois at Chicago.

Grassroots Progressivism

Much of progressive reform began at the grassroots level and percolated upward into local, state, and eventually national politics as reformers attacked the social problems fostered by urban industrialism. While reform flourished in many different settings across the country, urban problems inspired the progressives' greatest efforts. In their zeal to "civilize the city," reformers founded settlement houses, professed a new Christian **social gospel**, and campaigned against vice and crime in the name of "social purity." Allying with the working class, they sought to better the lot of sweatshop garment workers and to end child labor. Their reform efforts often began on the local level but ended up being debated in state legislatures, in Congress, and in the Oval Office. From Hull House to the White House, progressivism became a major political force in the first decade of the twentieth century.

Civilizing the City

Progressives attacked the problems of the city on many fronts. The settlement house movement attempted to bridge the distance between the classes. The social gospel called for the churches to play a new role in social reformation. And the **social purity movement** campaigned to clean up vice, particularly prostitution.

The settlement house movement, begun in England, came to the United States in 1886 with the opening of the University Settlement House in New York City. The needs of poor urban neighborhoods provided the impetus for these social settlements. In 1893, Lillian Wald, a nurse attending medical school in New York, went to care for a woman living in a dilapidated tenement. The experience led Wald to leave medical school and recruit several other nurses to move to New York City's Lower East Side "to live in the neighborhood as nurses, identify ourselves with it socially, and . . . contribute to it our citizenship." Expanded in 1895, the Henry Street settlement pioneered public health nursing. Although Wald herself was Jewish, she insisted that the Henry Street settlement remain independent of religious ties, making it different from the avowedly religious English settlements.

Women, particularly college-educated women like Jane Addams and Lillian Wald, formed the backbone of the settlement house movement. Eager to use their knowledge, educated women

united an otherwise diverse group of progressive reformers with a variety of schemes for the betterment of society. A sense of Christian mission inspired some. Others, frightened by the political tensions of the 1890s, feared social upheaval and sought to remove some of the worst evils of urban industrialism—tenements, child labor, and harsh working conditions. Progressives shared a growing concern about the power of wealthy individuals and corporations and a strong dislike of the **trusts**. But often they feared the new immigrants at the opposite end of the economic ladder and sought to control and Americanize them. Along with moral fervor, a belief in technical expertise and scientific principles infused progressivism and made the cult of efficiency part and parcel of the movement. All of these elements—uplift and efficiency, social justice and social control—came together in the Progressive Era and characterized the progressive movement both at the grassroots level in the cities and states and in the presidencies of Theodore Roosevelt and Woodrow Wilson.

AMERICAN PLACES

Jane Addams Hull-House Museum, Chicago, Illinois

The Jane Addams Hull-House Museum, administered by the University of Illinois at Chicago, is located at 800 South Halsted Street in Chicago. Built by Charles J. Hull in 1856, the two-story brick mansion is decorated with a white wooden cupola and classic Greek columns. After the Chicago fire of 1871, the "better classes" moved to other parts of the city, and the area attracted a large population of Italian, Greek, and Jewish immigrants. The run-down mansion sat in the midst of factories and tenements in 1889 when Jane Addams and her college roommate, Ellen Gates Starr, leased the drawing room and the upper floor to found the Hull House social settlement.

From the first, Jane Addams put her personal stamp on the social settlement, or settlement house, movement. Hull House attracted women who sought to put their education to work for the betterment of society, and it became the first social settlement in which residents of both sexes lived under one roof.

Addams intended Hull House to serve as a living room for her tenement neighbors. Its educative function worked in both directions: for the benefit of her poor neighbors, who used it as a clubhouse, day nursery, union meeting hall, and a place to relax; but also to educate the privileged classes who came to live at Hull House or attended lectures by prominent speakers who stopped by on their trips to Chicago. In this way Hull House functioned as a bridge between the classes, introducing the well-off to the poor in a personal, homelike setting.

With no set program or political theory to advance, Addams sought to help her neighbors where she could. In the process, she and other Hull House workers pioneered an impressive list of firsts for Chicago: the first public playground, the first public baths, the first public gymnasium, the first citizenship preparation classes, the first public kitchen, the first community theater, the first college extension courses, the first free art exhibits, the first public swimming pool, and the first Boy Scout troop.

Residents at Hull House paid their own way and put their talents to work in the service of their neighbors by investigating urban problems—truancy, poor sanitation, infectious diseases, drug traffic, and infant mortality. Their meticulous research led to the first factory laws in Illinois and to Chicago's first model tenement code. Illinois' first factory inspector, Florence Kelley, came from Hull House, as did Alzina Stevens, Chicago's first probation officer, and Julia Lathrop, the head of the federal government's Children's Bureau.

By grounding their investigations in concern for the lives of their immigrant neighbors, the residents of Hull House put a human face on urban statistics. Their work helped

---

Settlement houses gave college-educated women a place to use their talents in the service of society. In the process, settlement house women created a new profession—social work.

found themselves blocked from medicine, law, and the clergy (fewer than 1,500 women practiced law in 1900, and women constituted only 6 percent of the medical profession). Settlement houses gave college-educated women a place to use their talents in the service of society. Largely due to women's efforts, settlements like Hull House grew in number from six in 1891 to more than four hundred in 1911. (See "American Places," above.) In the process, settlement house women created a new profession—social work.

Some churches along with the settlement houses confronted urban social problems by enunciating a new social gospel, one that saw its mission not simply to reform individuals but to reform society. The social gospel offered a powerful corrective to the **gospel of wealth**, as outlined by Andrew Carnegie, with its belief that riches somehow signaled divine favor. Washington Gladden, a prominent social gospel minister, challenged that view when he urged Congregationalists to turn down a gift from John D. Rockefeller, arguing that it was "tainted money." In place of the gospel of wealth, the clergy exhorted their congregations to put Christ's teachings to work in their daily lives. For Walter Rauschenbusch, a Baptist minister change public attitudes about poverty, challenging the notion that the poor were drunken, vicious, or lazy and turning the private troubles of the urban poor into public issues. Hull House became a "spearhead for reform," an integral part of the progressive movement, championing the belief that the nation had a responsibility to address poverty, living conditions, and the health and welfare of working people.

By 1907, the Hull House settlement included a two-block complex of thirteen buildings. Jane Addams lived at Hull House until her death in 1935. During her lifetime, she worked to advance the cause of social justice, writing ten books and over 200 articles and delivering hundreds of speeches. She fought for women's right to vote, helped found the National Association for the Advancement of Colored People (NAACP), organized labor unions, and presided over the Women's International League for Peace and Freedom. In 1931, Addams received the Nobel Peace Prize. Thousands of mourners attended her funeral in the Hull House courtyard in 1935 to pay their respects to "Saint Jane." Hull House continued to function as a

The Jane Addams Hull-House Museum
Jane Addams Hull-House Museum.

social settlement until 1963, when the University of Illinois purchased the property. Plans to demolish Hull House set off a public protest that led to its designation as a National Historic Landmark in 1967.

Today the Jane Addams Hull-House Museum includes two of the original buildings, the Hull Mansion and the Residents' Dining Hall.

The mansion contains furnishings, paintings, and photographs—many belonging to Addams—as well as exhibits that re-create the history of this world-famous settlement and the work of its residents.

For Web links related to this site and other American Places, see "PlaceLinks" at bedfordstmartins.com/roark.

---

working in New York's tough Hell's Kitchen neighborhood, the social gospel grew out of the depression of the 1890s, which left thousands of people unemployed. "They wore down our threshold and they wore away our hearts," he later wrote. "One could hear human virtue cracking and crumbling all around." In *Christianity and the Social Crisis* (1907), Rauschenbusch called for the church to play a new role in promoting social justice.

Ministers also played an active role in the social purity movement, the campaign to attack vice. To end the "social evil," as reformers euphemistically called prostitution, the social purity movement brought together ministers who wished to stamp out sin, doctors concerned

about the spread of venereal disease, and women reformers determined to fight the double standard that made it acceptable for men to engage in premarital and extramarital sex but punished women who strayed. Together, they waged campaigns to close red-light districts in cities across the country and lobbied for the Mann Act, passed in 1910, which made it illegal to transport women across state lines for "immoral purposes." On the state level, they struck at venereal disease by securing legislation to require a blood test for syphilis before marriage.

Attacks on alcohol went hand in hand with the push for social purity. The **temperance** campaign launched by the Woman's Christian

Temperance Union (WCTU) heated up in the early twentieth century. The Anti-Saloon League, formed in 1895 under the leadership of **Protestant** clergy, campaigned for an end to the sale of liquor. Reformers pointed to links between drinking, prostitution, wife and child abuse, unemployment, and industrial accidents. The powerful liquor lobby fought back, spending liberally in election campaigns, fueling the charge that liquor corrupted the political process.

An element of **nativism** (dislike of foreigners) ran through the movement for prohibition, as it did in a number of progressive reforms. The Irish, the Italians, and the Germans were among the groups stigmatized by temperance reformers for their drinking. Progressives often failed to see the important role the tavern played in many ethnic communities. Unlike the American saloon, an almost exclusively male domain, the tavern was often a family retreat. German

Americans of all ages socialized at beer gardens after church on Sunday. Even though most workers toiled six days a week and had only Sunday for recreation and relaxation, some progressives campaigned on the local level to enforce the Sunday closing of taverns. To deny the working class access to alcohol, these progressives pushed for state legislation to outlaw the sale of liquor; by 1912, seven states were "dry."

Progressives' efforts to civilize the city, whether by launching social settlements or campaigning against prostitution and alcohol, demonstrated their willingness to take action, their belief that environment, not heredity alone, determined human behavior, and their optimism that conditions could be corrected through government action without radically altering America's economy or institutions. All of these attitudes characterized the progressive movement.

Progressives and the Working Class

Day-to-day contact with their neighbors made settlement house workers particularly sympathetic to labor unions. When Mary Kenney O'Sullivan complained that her bookbinders' union met in a dirty, noisy saloon, Jane Addams invited the union to meet at Hull House. And during the Pullman strike in 1894, Hull House residents organized strike relief and lent their

prestige and financial resources. "Hull-House has been so unionized," grumbled one Chicago businessman, "that it has lost its usefulness and become a detriment and harm to the community." But to the working class, the support of middle-class reformers marked a significant gain.

Attempts to forge a cross-class alliance became institutionalized in 1903 with the creation of the Women's Trade Union League (WTUL). The WTUL brought together women workers and middle-class "allies." Its goal was to organize working women into unions under the auspices of the American Federation of Labor (AFL). However, the AFL provided little more than lip service to the organization of women workers. As one working woman confided, "The men think that the girls should not get as good work as the men and should not make half as much money as a man." When it came to women, the AFL's main concern seemed to be to protect men from female competition. Samuel Gompers, president of the AFL, endorsed the principle of equal pay for equal work, shrewdly observing that it would help male workers more than women, since many employers hired women precisely because they could be paid less and otherwise would hire men. Given the AFL's attitude, it was not surprising that the money and leadership to organize women came largely from wealthy allies in the WTUL.

The league's most notable success came in 1909 in the "uprising of twenty thousand." In November, hundreds of women employees of the Triangle Shirtwaist Company in New York City went on strike to protest low wages, dangerous and demeaning working conditions, and management's refusal to recognize their union, the International Ladies' Garment Workers Union (ILGWU). In support of the walkout, the ILGWU called for a general strike of all garment workers. An estimated 20,000 workers, most of them teenage girls and many of them Jewish and Italian immigrants, walked off the job and stayed out on strike through the winter, picketing in the bitter cold. More than 600 were arrested, and many were sent to jail for "streetwalking," a move by the authorities to try to break the strike by impugning the morals of the striking women. By the time the strike ended in February 1910, the workers had won important demands in many shops. But they lost their bid to gain recognition for their union. The solidarity shown by the women workers proved to be the strike's greatest achievement. As Clara Lemlich, one of the strike's leaders, exclaimed, "They used to say that you couldn't even organize women. They wouldn't come to union meetings. They were 'temporary' workers. Well we showed them!"

The WTUL made enormous contributions to the strike. The league provided volunteers for the picket lines, posted more than $29,000 in bail, protested police brutality, organized a parade of 10,000 strikers, took part in the arbitration conference, arranged mass meetings, appealed for funds, and generated publicity for the strike. Under the leadership of the WTUL, women from every class of society, from J. P. Morgan's daughter Anne to **socialists** on New York's Lower East Side, joined the strikers in a dramatic demonstration of cross-class alliance.

But despite its demonstration of solidarity, the uprising of the twenty thousand failed to change the dangerous conditions faced by women workers. In March 1911, a little over a year after the shirtwaist makers' strike ended, fire alarms sounded at the Triangle Shirtwaist factory. The building, full of lint and combustible cloth, went up in flames in minutes and burned to rubble in half an hour. A WTUL member described the scene below on the street: "Two young girls whom I knew to be working in the vicinity came rushing toward me, tears were running from their eyes and they were white and shaking as they caught me by the arm. 'Oh,' shrieked one of them, 'they are jumping. Jumping from ten stories up! They are going through the air like bundles of clothes.'"

The terrified Triangle workers had little choice but to jump. One door was blocked by flames, and the other had been locked so that workers leaving the building could be searched to prevent pilfering. The lucky ones made it out on the elevator or by climbing to the roof where they escaped to a neighboring building. For the rest, the building proved a deathtrap. The flimsy, rusted fire escape collapsed under the weight of fleeing workers, killing dozens. Trapped, 54 workers jumped from the ninth-floor windows, only to smash to their deaths on the sidewalk. Of 500 workers, 146 died and scores of others were injured. The owners of the Triangle firm were later tried for negligence, but they avoided conviction when authorities determined that the fire had been started by a careless smoker. The Triangle Shirtwaist Company reopened in another firetrap within weeks.

Outraged and overwhelmed by the catastrophe, Rose Schneiderman, a leading WTUL organizer, made a bitter speech at the memorial service for the dead Triangle workers. "I would

Women Strikers
The "uprising of the 20,000" pitted garment workers against their employers in a strike that lasted throughout the bitter winter of 1909–10. The strikers, primarily young women from the Jewish and Italian immigrant communities, joined the International Ladies' Garment Workers Union and proved that women could be unionized and mount an effective strike. The Women's Trade Union League, a cross-class alliance of working women and middle-class "allies," contributed money and offered moral support to the strikers.
ILGWU Archives, Labor-Management Documentation Center, Cornell University.

be a traitor to those poor burned bodies if I came here to talk good fellowship," she told her audience. "We have tried you good people of the public and we have found you wanting. . . . I know from my experience it is up to the working people to save themselves . . . by a strong working class movement."

The Triangle fire tested severely the bonds of the cross-class alliance. Along with Schneiderman, WTUL leaders experienced a growing sense of futility. It seemed not enough to organize and to strike. Increasingly, the WTUL turned its efforts to lobbying for protective legislation—laws that would limit hours and regulate working conditions for women workers.

> By the time the strike ended in February 1910, the workers had won important demands in many shops. The solidarity shown by the women proved to be the strike's greatest achievement.

14. Viewing the unfortunates at the M

Triangle Fire Morgue

After the Triangle fire on March 26, 1911, New York City set up a makeshift morgue at the end of Manhattan's Charities Pier. There the remains of more than a hundred young women and two dozen young men were laid out in coffins for their friends and relatives to identify. Victims who had jumped to their deaths from the ninth-floor windows or leaped down the elevator shaft could be easily recognized. Those trapped in the building were burned beyond recognition. A ring, a charred shoe, a melted hair comb often provided the only clues to the identity of a sister, a daughter, or a sweetheart. In the *New York Evening Journal* (right), a survivor recounted the horror inside when the girls discovered that one of the two doors leading out of the building was locked, barring their escape. In the trial that followed the fire, the owners of the Triangle Shirtwaist Company avoided penalty when their skillful lawyer challenged the credibility of witnesses like the woman in the news story, who testified that one door had been locked to keep girls from pilfering.

UNITE Archives, Kheel Center, Cornell University, Ithaca, NY 14853-3901.

Advocates of protective legislation won a major victory in 1908 when the U.S. Supreme Court, in *Muller v. Oregon*, reversed its previous rulings and upheld an Oregon law that limited to ten the hours women could work in a day. A mass of sociological evidence put together by Florence Kelley of the National Consumers' League and Josephine Goldmark of the WTUL and presented by Goldmark's brother-in-law, lawyer Louis Brandeis, demonstrated the ill effects of long hours on the health and safety of women. The "Brandeis brief" convinced the Court that long hours endangered women and therefore the entire race. The Court's ruling set a precedent, but one that separated the well-being of women workers from that of men by arguing that women's reproductive role justified special treatment. Later generations of women fighting for equality would question the effectiveness of this strategy and argue that it ultimately closed good jobs to women. But the WTUL greeted protective legislation as a first step in the attempt to ensure the safety not just of women but of all workers.

The National Consumers' League (NCL), like the WTUL, fostered cross-class alliance. Its work also extended beyond the United States (see "Beyond America's Borders," page 756). When Florence Kelley took over the leadership of the NCL in 1899, she urged middle-class women to boycott stores and exert pressure for decent wages and working conditions for women employees, primarily saleswomen. But like the WTUL, the National Consumers' League turned increasingly to protective legislation to achieve its goals. Frustrated by the reluctance of the private sector to respond to the need for reform, progressives turned to government at all levels. Critics would later charge that the progressives assumed too easily that government regulation could best solve social problems.

Progressivism: Theory and Practice

Progressive reformers developed a theoretical basis for their activist approach by countering **social Darwinism** with a dynamic new **reform Darwinism** and by championing the uniquely American philosophy of pragmatism. Progressives emphasized action and experimentation. No longer was the universe seen as a massive, slow-moving machine, but as a system amenable to tinkering by human intelligence. Unchecked admiration for speed and productivity also inspired enthusiasm for **scientific management** and a new cult of efficiency. These varied strands of progressive theory found practical application in state and local politics, where reformers challenged traditional laissez-faire government.

Reform Darwinism, Pragmatism, and Social Engineering

The active, interventionist approach of the progressives directly challenged social Darwinism, with its insistence that the world operated on the principle of survival of the fittest and that human beings stood powerless in the face of the law of natural selection. Without abandoning the evolutionary framework of Darwinism, a new group of sociologists argued that evolution could be advanced more rapidly if men and women used their intellects to alter the environment. Dubbed "reform Darwinism," the new sociological theory condemned laissez-faire, insisting that the liberal state should play a more active role in solving social problems. Reform Darwinism provided a rationale for attacking social ills and became the ideological basis for progressive reform.

In their pursuit of reform, progressives were influenced by the work of two philosophers, William James and John Dewey, who argued for a new test for truth. They insisted that there were no eternal truths and that the real worth of any idea lay in its consequences. They called their relativistic philosophy pragmatism. Dewey put his theories to the test in the classroom of his laboratory school at the University of Chicago. A pioneer in American education, he emphasized process rather than content and encouraged child-centered schools where students would learn by doing. By championing social experimentation, the American pragmatists provided an important impetus for progressive reform.

Efficiency and *expertise* became watchwords in the progressive vocabulary. The journalist and critic Walter Lippmann, in *Drift and Mastery* (1914), a classic statement of the progressive agenda, called for skilled technocrats to use scientific techniques to control social change, substituting social engineering for aimless drift. Progressive reformers' emphasis on expertise inevitably fostered a kind of elitism. Whereas **Populists** had called for a greater voice for the masses, progressivism, for all its emphasis on social justice, insisted that experts be put in charge.

At its extreme, the application of expertise and social engineering took the form of scientific management, which by elevating productivity and efficiency alienated the working class. Frederick Winslow Taylor pioneered "systematized shop management." After dropping out of Harvard after a nervous breakdown, Taylor went to work as a machinist at Midvale Steel in Philadelphia in the 1880s. Obsessed with making men and machines produce more and faster, he carefully timed workers with his stopwatch and attempted to break their work down into its simplest components, one repetitious action after another, on the theory that productivity would increase if tasks were reduced to their simplest parts. Workers hated the monotony of systematized shop management and argued that it led to the speedup—pushing workers to produce more in less time and for less pay. But advocates of "Taylorism" included progressives like Louis Brandeis, who applauded the increased productivity and efficiency of Taylor's system.

Progressive Government: City and State

The politicians who became premier progressives were generally the followers, not the leaders, in a movement already well advanced at the grassroots level. Yet they left their stamp on the movement. Tom Johnson made Cleveland, Ohio,

> Whereas Populists had called for a greater voice of the masses, progressivism, for all its emphasis on social justice, insisted that experts be put in charge.

Protecting the World's Workers: The National Consumers' League

The United States was not alone in wrestling with the problems accompanying urban industrialism. In western Europe, particularly Germany and England where industrial development occurred even more rapidly than in the United States, concern for the welfare of the industrial workforce led beginning in the 1890s to the elaboration of statutes designed to protect workers' safety and general welfare. America lagged behind. "In no country of the first rank is this legislation so weak as in the United States," observed John Graham Brooks, the first president of the National Consumers' League. Compared to European workers, he concluded, American workers' lives were barely touched by protective legislation. But progressive associations in the United States slowly began to work on issues of protection, and with the help of their cross-Atlantic connections eventually inspired the formation of additional groups in Europe to fight for similar measures.

The National Consumers' League (NCL) that Brooks headed drew on European models of factory inspection and legislation that sought to promote better working conditions for laborers. Like the social settlement movement, another significant European import, the consumers' league movement in the United States soon outstripped its European counterparts, largely thanks to the college-educated women who also gave the American settlement house movement its unique stamp. While Brooks and other men served as its officers (largely honorific posts), women formed the backbone of the National Consumers' League.

The league began on the grassroots level. In 1888, New York City garment worker and union organizer Leonora O'Reilly invited some of the city's prominent women to a meeting of the New York Working Women's Society, where they heard an appeal to help their "toiling and down-trodden sisters." The group appointed a committee to make and circulate a list of "such shops as deal justly with their employees" so that women consumers could patronize shops that met minimum standards. Begun as a genteel boycott among New York City women alarmed at the conditions of women in the garment trades, the Consumers' League of New York took shape in 1891, led by philanthropist Josephine Shaw Lowell. Lowell liked to portray the league's work as part of a historical continuum in women's activism, tracing its roots back to colonial women's patriotic refusal to buy British goods in the Revolutionary War era.

Taking as its motto "Investigate, agitate, legislate," the New York league affixed a "white label" to goods made in shops that met its standards for wages, work hours, and safety. Women shoppers were urged to "look for the white label" before buying. To determine which shops merited the label, consumers' league inspectors explored working conditions in cramped sweatshops, canneries, laundries, and department stores. They collected masses of data on women's wages, budgets, health, employment, and living standards. And they used the tactics of exposure and muckraking to bring to the nation's attention the grim realities of women's working conditions.

The movement spread rapidly. By 1896, 64 consumers' leagues had formed in 20 states, primarily in the Northeast and Midwest. In 1898 the national scope of the movement was recognized with the founding of the National Consumers' League. Membership in the NCL peaked in 1916, when it claimed 15,000 members in 43 states.

The most prominent woman in the NCL was Florence Kelley, who left Hull House in 1899 to become

a model of progressive reform; Robert La Follette turned Wisconsin into a laboratory for progressivism; and Hiram Johnson ended the domination of the Southern Pacific Railroad in California politics.

Progressivism burst forth at every level of government in 1900, but nowhere more forcefully than in Cleveland, Ohio, with the election of Thomas Lofton Johnson mayor. A self-made millionaire by age forty, Johnson had made his the salaried executive secretary of the newly formed NCL, a post she held for two decades. Kelley grew up in Philadelphia the daughter of a Republican congressman nicknamed William "Pig Iron" Kelley because of his support for the protective tariff benefiting Pennsylvania's iron and steel industry. When she was a young girl her father reportedly told her, "My generation has created industry, and your generation must humanize it." Kelley along with other highly educated and public-spirited women of the Progressive period eagerly took on the task of civilizing capitalism.

After graduating from Cornell University in 1882, Kelley traveled to Europe to study law and government at the University of Zurich. There she became an ardent socialist, married a Russian medical student, and had three children. In 1891 she left her abusive husband and moved into Chicago's Hull House. She soon established herself as an expert on tenement labor. In 1893, reform governor John Peter Altgeld named Kelley Illinois's chief factory inspector, making her the first woman in the United States to head a state labor department. Kelley developed a formidable reputation as a champion of better working conditions. And, as an active member of Chicago's consumers' league, she spearheaded the campaign against sweatshops.

At the NCL, Kelley helped propel the league from consumer pressure tactics to political action, sometimes with influence from

Florence Kelley, 1905

Florence Kelley left Hull House in 1899 to become the salaried executive secretary of the National Consumers' League head-quartered in New York City. While men like John Graham Brooks held offices (largely honorific) in the organization, Kelley and other highly educated women made up the backbone of the NCL, demonstrating the significant role women played in inter-national progressive reform. Until her death in 1932, Kelley used the NCL to cam-paign for shorter hours and better working conditions for America's workingwomen.

Rare Books & Manuscripts, Columbia University in the City of New York.

abroad. By 1902, the league main-tained a separate lobbying agency to fight for an end to child labor. After hearing convincing arguments from British delegates at the 1908 interna-tional consumers league congress in Geneva, Kelley led the NCL to push for minimum wage legislation. Working with women like Maud Nathan (a prominent figure in inter-national women's circles), Mary

Kingsbury Simkhovitch of New York's Greenwich House, and Pauline and Josephine Goldmark and their brother-in-law Louis Brandeis, the NCL also mounted a legal defense campaign on behalf of state statutes limiting the maximum hours of women wage earners. Their efforts paid off in 1908 when in *Muller v. Oregon* the Supreme Court ruled constitutional the regulation of women's working hours—a land-mark decision in which, for the first time, the Court acknowledged that an individual's right to form con-tracts did not rule out setting limits on working hours.

Such successes, along with the international ties of many NCL ac-tivists, helped the league spin off a number of European sister organiza-tions. By 1910, league-inspired affili-ates had formed in France, Belgium, Germany, and Switzerland. Revers-ing the trend for progressive reform measures to cross the Atlantic from Europe to America, the National Consumers' League reached beyond America's borders as European con-sumer organizations borrowed American tactics to help protect workers.

BIBLIOGRAPHY

Josephine Goldmark, *Impatient Crusader: Florence Kelley's Life Story* (1976).
Daniel T. Rodgers, *Atlantic Crossings: So-cial Politics in a Progressive Age* (1998).
Kathryn Kish Sklar, *Florence Kelley and the Nation's Work: The Rise of Women's Political Culture, 1830–1900* (1995).
Landon R.Y. Storrs, *Civilizing Capitalism: The National Consumers' League, Wom-en's Activism, and Labor Standards in the New Deal Era* (2000).

money in the street railroad business in Detroit, where he had clashed frequently with reform mayor Hazen Pingree. Johnson turned his back on business in 1899 and moved to Cleveland, where he determined to seek election as a reform

mayor. "I embarked on this new field for purely selfish motives," he later wrote. A flamboyant man who craved power and acclaim, Johnson pledged during the campaign to reduce the streetcar fare from five cents to three cents. His

Tom Johnson

Tom Johnson, the reform mayor of Cleveland, Ohio, from 1901 to 1909, is shown here campaigning in Cleveland's Wade Park in 1908. For more than seven years, Mayor Johnson fought for a three-cent streetcar fare, winning the support of the working class and angering the business interests who ran the city's streetcars. To get this low fare, Johnson finally instituted municipal ownership of the transit system. The three-cent token was a campaign novelty distributed during Johnson's bid for reelection in 1907.

The Western Reserve Historical Society, Cleveland, Ohio.

election touched off a seven-year war between advocates of the lower fare, who believed that workers paid a disproportionate share of their meager earnings for transportation, and the streetcar moguls, who argued that they couldn't meet costs with the lower fare. When Johnson responded by building his own streetcar line, his foes tore up the tracks and blocked him with court injunctions and legal delays. At the prompting of his opponents, the Ohio legislature sought to limit Johnson's mayoral power by revoking the charters of every city in the state, replacing home rule with central control from the state capital, Columbus.

During his tenure as mayor, Johnson fought for home rule and fair taxation even as he called for greater **democracy** through the use of the initiative, referendum, and recall—devices that allowed voters to have a direct say in legislative and judicial matters. Frustrated in his attempt to bring the streetcar industry to heel, he successfully championed municipal ownership of street railways and public utilities, a tactic that progressives called "gas and water socialism." The city bought the streetcar system and instituted the three-cent fare. Under Johnson's administration, Cleveland became, in the words of journalist Lincoln Steffens, the "best governed city in America."

In Wisconsin, Robert M. La Follette, who as a young congressional representative had supported William McKinley, converted to the progressive cause early in the 1900s. An astute politician, La Follette capitalized on the grassroots movement for reform to launch his long political career, first as governor (1901–1905) and later as a U.S. senator (1906–1925). A graduate of the University of Wisconsin, La Follette brought scientists and professors into his administration and used the university, only a few blocks from the statehouse in Madison, as a resource in drafting legislation. As governor he lowered railroad rates, raised railroad taxes, improved education, preached conservation, established factory regulation and workers' compensation, instituted the first direct primary in the country, and inaugurated the first state income tax. Under his leadership, Wisconsin earned the title "laboratory of democracy."

A fiery orator, "Fighting Bob" La Follette united his supporters around issues that transcended party loyalties. This emphasis on reform characterized progressivism, which attracted followers from both major parties. Democrats like Tom Johnson and Republicans like Robert La Follette could lay equal claim to the label "progressive."

West of the Rockies, progressivism arrived somewhat later and found a champion in Hiram Johnson of California, who served as governor from 1911 to 1917 and as U.S. senator from 1917 to 1945. Since the 1870s, California politics had been dominated by the Southern Pacific Railroad, a corporation so rapacious that novelist Frank Norris called it "the Octopus." Johnson ran for governor in 1910 on the promise to "kick the Southern Pacific out of politics." With the support of the reform wing of the Republican Party, he handily won. *Efficiency* and *rationalization* became the watchwords of Hiram Johnson's administration. He promised to "return the government to the people"—to give them honest public service untarnished by corruption and corporate influence. As governor he introduced the direct primary; supported the initiative, referendum, and recall; strengthened the state's railroad commission; supported conservation; and signed an employer's liability law.

Who benefited most from Johnson's progressivism? California's entrepreneurs—large farmers, independent oil producers, and other rising businessmen who could make money more easily once Johnson curtailed the influence of the Southern Pacific. A vigorous, compelling personality with a reputation for a towering temper, Hiram Johnson proved an able governor. In 1912 he could boast that by regulating the Southern Pacific Railroad he had saved shippers more than $2 million.

✕

Progressivism Finds a President: Theodore Roosevelt

On September 6, 1901, President William McKinley was shot twice by Leon Czolgosz, an **anarchist**, while attending the Pan-American Exposition in Buffalo, New York. Eight days later, McKinley died. When news of his assassination reached his friend and political mentor Mark Hanna, Hanna is said to have growled, "Now that damned cowboy is president." He was speaking of Vice President Theodore Roosevelt, the colorful hero of San Juan Hill, who had indeed punched cattle in the Dakotas in the 1880s.

At age forty-two, Roosevelt was the youngest man ever to move into the White House. A patrician by birth and an activist by temperament, Roosevelt brought to the job enormous talent and energy. As president he would use that energy to strengthen the power of the federal government, putting business on notice that it could no longer count on laissez-faire to give it free rein.

The Square Deal

The "absolutely vital question" facing the country, Roosevelt wrote to a friend in 1901, was "whether or not the government has the power to control the trusts." The Sherman Antitrust Act of 1890 had been badly weakened by a conservative Supreme Court and by attorneys general more willing to use it against labor unions than against **monopolies**. To determine if the law had any teeth left, Roosevelt, in one of his first acts as president, ordered his attorney general to begin a secret antitrust investigation of the Northern Securities Company. He chose a good target. Northern Securities, formed by a controversial merger, monopolized railroad traffic in the

> The "absolutely vital question" facing the country, Roosevelt wrote a friend in 1901, was "whether or not the government has the power to control the trusts."

Northwest and to many small investors and farmers symbolized corporate high-handedness.

Five months later, in February 1902, Wall Street rocked with the news that the government had filed an antitrust suit against Northern Securities. As one newspaper editor sarcastically observed, "Wall Street is paralyzed at the thought that a President of the United States would sink so low as to try to enforce the law." An indignant J. P. Morgan, who had created Northern Securities, demanded to know why he had not been consulted. "If we have done anything wrong," he told the president, "send your man to my man and they can fix it up." Roosevelt, amused, later noted that Morgan "could not help regarding me as a big rival operator." In a sense, that was just what Roosevelt intended. Roosevelt's thunderbolt put Wall Street on notice that the money men were dealing with a president who demanded to be treated as an equal and who was willing to use government to control business. Perhaps sensing the new mood, the Supreme Court, in a significant turnaround, upheld the Sherman Act and called for the dissolution of Northern Securities in 1904.

"Hurrah for Teddy the Trustbuster," cheered the papers. Roosevelt went on to use the Sherman Act against forty-three trusts, including such giants as the American Tobacco Company, Du Pont, and Standard Oil. Always the moralist, he insisted on a "rule of reason." He would punish "bad" trusts (those that broke the law) and leave "good" ones alone. In practice, he preferred regulation to antitrust suits. In 1903, he pressured Congress to pass the Elkins Act, outlawing railroad rebates (money returned to a shipper to guarantee repeat business). And he created the new cabinet-level Department of Commerce and Labor with a subsidiary Bureau of Corporations to act as a corporate watchdog.

In his handling of the anthracite coal strike in 1902,

Roosevelt as a Giant Killer

In this political cartoon from 1904, President Theodore Roosevelt is "Jack the Giant Killer," taking on the Wall Street titans. To the right of the president looms J. P. Morgan with his hand out. To the left stands James J. Hill, builder of the Great Northern Railroad. The cartoon was published after Roosevelt brought antitrust proceedings against the Northern Securities Company, a railroad combination put together by Morgan that included Hill's Great Northern Railroad. Roosevelt's unprecedented action earned him a reputation as a "trustbuster," but in fact he favored government regulation of big business. His activist presidency used government to counter the power of big business. As the cartoonist clearly shows, the government was seen as small indeed when Roosevelt took his stand. Library of Congress.

Roosevelt again demonstrated his willingness to assert the moral and political authority of the presidency, this time to mediate between labor and management. In May, 147,000 coal miners in

Theodore Roosevelt

Described aptly by a contemporary observer as "a steam engine in trousers," Theodore Roosevelt at forty-two was the youngest president to occupy the White House. He brought to the office energy, intellect, and activism in equal measure. Roosevelt boasted that he used the presidency as a "bully pulpit"—a forum from which he advocated reforms ranging from trust-busting to conservation.
Library of Congress.

Pennsylvania went out on strike. Most of the miners were Slavic immigrants organized by the United Mine Workers (UMW) under the leadership of a young Irishman, John Mitchell. The UMW demanded a reduction in the workday from twelve to ten hours, an equitable system of weighing each miner's output, and a 10 percent wage increase, along with recognition of the union.

When asked about the appalling conditions in the mines that had led to the strike, George Baer, the mine operators' spokesman, scoffed, "The miners don't suffer, why they can't even speak English." Buttressed by social Darwinism, Baer observed that "God in his infinite wisdom" had placed "the rights and interests of the laboring man" in the hands of the capitalists, not "the labor agitators." His Olympian confidence rested on the fact that six eastern railroads owned over 70 percent of the anthracite mines. With the power of the railroads behind them, Baer and the mine owners refused to budge.

The strike dragged on through the summer and into the fall. Hoarding and profiteering drove the price of coal from $2.50 to $6.00 a ton. Coal heated nearly every house, school, and hospital in the Northeast, and as winter approached, coal shortages touched off near riots in the nation's big cities. In the face of mounting tension, Roosevelt did what no president had ever done. He stepped in to mediate, issuing a personal invitation to representatives from both sides to meet in Washington in October. At the meeting, Baer and the mine owners refused to talk with the union representatives, insulting both the president and the attorney general. Angered by the "wooden-headed obstinacy and stupidity" of management, Roosevelt threatened to seize the mines and run them with federal troops. This was a powerful bluff that called into question not only the supremacy of private property but also the rule of law. The specter of federal troops being used to operate the mines quickly brought management around. At the prompting of J. P. Morgan, the mine owners agreed to arbitration. In the end, the miners won a reduction in hours and a wage increase, but the owners succeeded in preventing formal recognition of the UMW.

Taken together, Roosevelt's actions in the Northern Securities case and the anthracite coal strike marked a dramatic departure from the presidential passivity of his predecessors in the Gilded Age. Roosevelt demonstrated conclusively that government intended to act as a force independent of big business. Pleased with his

role in the anthracite strike, he announced that all he had tried to do was give labor and capital a "square deal."

The phrase "Square Deal" became his slogan in the 1904 election campaign. To win the presidency in his own right, Roosevelt moved to wrest control of the Republican Party from party boss Mark Hanna, the only man who stood between him and the nomination. Roosevelt adroitly used patronage to win supporters. Even before Hanna died of typhoid fever in 1904, Roosevelt was the undisputed leader of the party. In the presidential election of 1904, he swept into office with the largest popular majority—57.9 percent—any candidate had polled to that time.

Breaker Boys

When anthracite miners declared a strike in 1902, child labor was common in the mines of Pennsylvania. "Breaker boys," some as young as seven years old, picked over coal moving on a conveyor belt to remove rock and stone. The boys in this photograph are taking a short rest during their twelve-hour workday. Their unsmiling faces bear testimony to the difficulty and danger of their work. A committee investigating child labor found more than 10,000 children illegally employed in the Pennsylvania coalfields.
Brown Brothers.

Roosevelt the Reformer

"Tomorrow I shall come into my office in my own right," Roosevelt is said to have remarked on the eve of his election. "Then watch out for me!" Roosevelt's stunning victory gave him a mandate for reform. He would need all the popularity and political savvy he could muster, however, to guide his reform measures through Congress. The Senate remained controlled by a staunchly **conservative** Republican "old guard," with many senators on the payrolls of the corporations Roosevelt sought to curb. Roosevelt's pet project remained railroad regulation. The Elkins Act prohibiting rebates had not worked. No one could stop big shippers like Standard Oil from wringing concessions from the railroads. The Interstate Commerce Commission (ICC), created in 1887 to regulate the railroads, had been largely stripped of its powers by the Supreme Court. In the face of a widespread call for railroad reform, Roosevelt determined that the only solution lay in giving the ICC real power to set rates and prevent discriminatory practices. But the right to determine the price of goods or services was an age-old prerogative of private enterprise, and one that business had no intention of yielding to government.

To ensure passage of the Hepburn Act, which would increase the power of the ICC, Roosevelt worked skillfully behind the scenes. At first, he allied himself with insurgent progressives; then, when they could not muster the needed votes, he switched sides and succeeded in getting the Republican old guard to accept a compromise. In its final form, the Hepburn Act, passed in May 1906, gave the ICC power to set rates subject to court review. Committed progressives like La Follette judged the law a defeat for reform.

Die-hard conservatives branded it a "piece of populism." Both sides exaggerated. The law left the courts too much power and failed to provide adequate means for the ICC to determine rates, but its passage was a landmark in federal control of private industry. For the first time, a government commission had the power to investigate private business records and to set rates.

Passage of the Hepburn Act marked the high point of Roosevelt's presidency. In a serious political blunder, Roosevelt had announced on the eve of his election in 1904 that he would not run again. By 1906, his term was starting to run out and his influence on Congress and his party was waning. He became a "lame duck" at the very moment he was enjoying his greatest public popularity and was eager to press for more reform.

Always an apt reader of the public temper, Roosevelt witnessed a growing appetite for reform fed by the revelations of corporate and political wrongdoing and social injustice that filled the papers and boosted the sales of popular periodicals. (See "The Promise of Technology," page 764.) Roosevelt, who wielded publicity like a weapon in his pursuit of reform, counted many of the new investigative journalists, such as Jacob Riis, among his friends. But he warned them against going too far like the allegorical character in *Pilgrim's Progress* who was so busy raking muck that he took no notice of higher things. Roosevelt's criticism gave the American vocabulary a new word, *muckraker*, which journalists soon appropriated as a title of honor.

Muckraking, as Roosevelt was keenly aware, had been of enormous help in securing progressive legislation. In the spring of 1906, publicity generated by the muckrakers about poisons in patent medicines goaded the Senate, with Roosevelt's backing, into passing a pure food and drug bill. Opponents in the House of Representatives hoped to keep the legislation locked up in committee. There it would have

THE JUNGLE

UPTON SINCLAIR

The Jungle

Novelist Upton Sinclair, a lifelong socialist, wrote *The Jungle* to expose the evils of capitalism. But readers were more horrified by the unsanitary conditions he described in the meatpacking industry, where the novel's hapless hero saw rats, filth, and diseased animals processed into potted beef. It was rumored that after reading the book, President Theodore Roosevelt could no longer stomach sausage for breakfast. The president immediately ordered a thorough study of conditions in the meatpacking industry. The public outcry surrounding *The Jungle* contributed to the enactment of pure food and drug legislation and a federal meat inspection law. Sinclair ruefully remarked, "I aimed at the public's heart, but I hit them in the stomach."

By permission of the Houghton Library, Harvard University.

died, were it not for publication of Upton Sinclair's novel *The Jungle* (1906), with its sensational account of filthy conditions in meatpacking plants. A massive public outcry led to the passage of a tough Pure Food and Drug Act and a Meat Inspection Act.

In the waning years of his administration, Roosevelt moved farther to the left, allying with the more progressive elements of the Republican Party. In speech after speech, he attacked "malefactors of great wealth." Styling himself a "radical," he claimed credit for leading the "ultra conservative" party of McKinley to a position of "progressive conservatism and conservative radicalism."

When an economic panic developed in the fall of 1907, business interests quickly blamed the president. The panic of 1907 proved to be severe but short. As he had done in 1895, J. P. Morgan stepped in to avert disaster, this time switching funds from one bank to another to prop up weak institutions. For his services, he claimed the Tennessee Coal and Iron Company, an independent steel business that had long been coveted by his U.S. Steel Corporation. Morgan dispatched his lieutenants to Washington, where they told Roosevelt that the sale of the company would aid the economy "but little benefit" U.S. Steel. Willing to take the word of a gentleman, Roosevelt tacitly agreed not to institute antitrust proceedings against U.S. Steel. But, as Roosevelt later learned, Morgan and his men had been less than candid. The acquisition of Tennessee Coal and Iron for a price below market value greatly strengthened U.S. Steel and undercut the economy of the Southeast. This episode later gave rise to the charge that Roosevelt had acted as a tool of the Morgan interests.

The charge of collusion between business and government underscored the extent to which business leaders like Morgan and his partner George W. Perkins found federal regulation preferable to unbridled competition or harsher state measures. During the Progressive Era, enlightened business leaders cooperated with government in the hope of avoiding antitrust prosecution. Convinced that regulation and not trust-busting offered the best way to deal with big business, Roosevelt never acknowledged that his regulatory policies fostered an alliance between business and government that today is called corporate liberalism. Despite his harsh attacks on "malefactors of great wealth," Roosevelt's actions in the panic of 1907 demonstrated the president's indebtedness to Morgan,

who still functioned as the national bank and would continue to do so until passage of the Federal Reserve Act six years later.

Roosevelt and Conservation

In at least one area, Roosevelt was well ahead of his time. Robert La Follette, who thought Roosevelt a lukewarm progressive and found much to criticize in his presidency, hailed as Roosevelt's "greatest work" his efforts in the conservation of natural resources. When Roosevelt took office, some 45 million acres of land remained as government reserves. He more than tripled that number to 150 million acres, buying land and creating national parks and wildlife preserves by executive order. To conserve natural resources, he fought not only western cattle barons, lumber kings, and mining interests but also powerful leaders in Congress, including Speaker of the House Joseph Cannon, who was determined to spend "not one cent for scenery."

As the first president to have lived and worked in the West—as a rancher in the Dakotas—Roosevelt came to the White House convinced of the need for better management of the nation's rivers and forests. During the 1890s, concern for the wanton exploitation of natural resources led Congress to pass legislation giving the president the power to "reserve" forest land from commercial development by executive proclamation. During his presidency, Roosevelt did not hesitate to wield that power. He placed the nation's conservation policy in the hands of scientifically trained experts like his chief forrester, Gifford Pinchot. Pinchot fought for the principle of managed use. He desired not so much to remove land from commercial use, but to use the power of the federal government to effect long-term planning and the rational management of the nation's resources. Unlike preservationists, who wished to leave the land in its natural state, Roosevelt, Pinchot,

> Roosevelt's regulatory policies fostered an alliance between business and government that today is called corporate liberalism.

and the conservationists advocated efficient use of natural resources. Willing to permit grazing, lumbering, and the development of hydroelectric power, conservationists fought private interests only when they felt business acted irresponsibly or threatened to monopolize water and electric power.

Flash Photography and the Birth of Photojournalism

The camera was not new at the turn of the twentieth century. Americans had eagerly imported the technology developed by Frenchman L. J. M. Daguerre to make portraits called daguerreotypes as early as the 1840s. By the 1880s, the invention of dry plates had simplified photography, and by the 1890s, Americans could purchase a Kodak camera marketed by George Eastman. But for Jacob Riis, who wished to document the horrors of tenement life, photography was useless because it required daylight or careful studio lighting. Riis, a progressive reformer and journalist who covered the police beat for the *New York Tribune*, never thought of buying a camera. He could only rudely sketch the dim hovels, the criminal nightlife, and the windowless tenement rooms of New York. Then came the breakthrough. "One morning scanning my newspaper at the breakfast table," he wrote, "I put it down with an outcry. . . . There it was, the thing I had been looking for all these years. . . . A way had been discovered . . . to take pictures by flashlight. The darkest corner might be photographed that way."

The new technology involved a pistol lamp that fired magnesium cartridges to provide light for instantaneous photography. Armed with the new flash pistols, Riis and a band of amateur photographers soon set out to shine light in the dark corners of New York. "Our party carried terror wherever it went," Riis later recounted. "The spectacle of strange men invading a house in the midnight hours armed with [flash] pistols which they shot off recklessly was hardly reassuring . . . and it was not to be wondered at if the tenants bolted through the windows and down fire-escapes."

Unhappy with the photographers he hired to follow him on his nighttime forays into the slums, Riis determined to try his own hand at taking pictures and laid out $25 for his first photographic equipment in 1888. It consisted of a four-by-five-inch wooden box camera, glass plates, a tripod, a safety lantern, flash pistols, developing trays, and a printing frame. He soon replaced the pistols with a newer flash technology developed in 1887 that used magnesium powder blown through an alcohol flame. Riis carried a frying pan in which to ignite the powder, observing, "It seemed more homelike."

Flash photography was dangerous. The pistol lamp cartridges contained highly explosive chemicals that could seriously burn the photographer. The newer technology employing magnesium powder also proved risky. Riis once blew the flash into his own eyes, and only his glasses saved him from being blinded. Nor was Riis the only one in peril. When he photographed the residents of a tenement on "Blind Man's Alley," he set the place on fire when he ignited the flash. He later claimed the tenement, nicknamed the "Dirty Spoon," was so filthy it wouldn't burn. He was able to douse the flames without his blind subjects ever realizing their danger.

Riis turned his photographs into slides that he used to illustrate his lectures on tenement life. They helped spread his message, but not until *Scribner's* magazine printed his story entitled "How the Other Half Lives" in December 1889 did he begin to develop a mass audience. The article, illustrated with line drawings of Riis's photographs, became the basis for his best-selling book of the same title published in 1890.

Preservationists like John Muir, the founder of the Sierra Club, believed the wilderness needed to be protected from all commercial exploitation. Muir soon clashed with Roosevelt. After a devastating earthquake in 1906, San Francisco sought federal approval for a project that would supply fresh water and electric power to the city. The plan called for building a dam that would flood the spectacular Hetch Hetchy Valley in Yosemite National Park. Muir, who had played a central role in establishing Yosemite as a national park, fiercely opposed

Jacob Riis and Baxter Court

Jacob Riis (to the right), a Danish immigrant who knew the squalor of New York's lodging houses and slums from his early days in the city, vigorously campaigned for tenement reform. He warned slumlords (some of them prominent New Yorkers) that their greed bred crime and disease and might provoke class warfare. Flash photography enabled Riis to expose the dark alleys and tenements of New York. He took his camera (much like the one pictured in the inset) into Baxter Street Court, then recorded these observations: "I counted the other day the little ones, up to ten years old in a . . . tenement that for a yard has a . . . space in the center with sides fourteen or fifteen feet long, just enough for a row of ill-smelling [water] closets . . . and a hydrant. . . . There was about as much light in the 'yard' as in the average cellar. . . . I counted one hundred twenty eight [children] in forty families."

Riis portrait: National Portrait Gallery, Smithsonian Institution/Art Resource, NY; Baxter Street courtyard: The Jacob A. Riis Collection, #108 Museum of the City of New York; camera: George Eastman House.

How the Other Half Lives made photographic history. It contained, along with Riis's text and the line drawings that had appeared in *Scribner's*, seventeen halftone prints of Riis's photographs. Riis's text and pictures shined the light on New York's darkest corners—vagrants in filthy lodging houses; "street arabs," homeless boys who lived by their wits on the streets; the saloons and dives of lower New York; evil-smelling tenement yards; stifling sweatshops.

For the first time, unposed action pictures taken with a flash documented social conditions. Riis's pioneering photojournalism shocked the nation and led not only to tenement reform but also to the development of city playgrounds, neighborhood parks, and child labor laws.

Roosevelt and Pinchot, who saw the Hetch Hetchy project as a progressive victory because it would place control of the water supply in the hands of the municipal government and not private developers. After a protracted publicity battle, Roosevelt and the conservationists prevailed, although preservationists won many converts to the cause of saving the vanishing wilderness and launched what would become the modern environmentalist movement.

The Newlands Reclamation Act of 1902 also drew criticism. It established a Reclamation

Bureau within the Department of the Interior and provided federal funding for irrigation projects. Rather than aiding small farmers, as the act's framer originally intended, the legislation encouraged the growth of large-scale farming. Yet the growing involvement of the federal government in the management of water resources, a critical issue in the West, marked another victory for the policy of federal intervention that characterized progressivism and marked the end of laissez-faire liberalism.

In 1907, Congress put the brakes on Roosevelt's conservation program through a law limiting his power to create forest reserves in six western states. In the days leading up to the law's passage, Roosevelt feverishly created twenty-one new reserves and enlarged eleven more. And when Congress denied Pinchot the right to withdraw hydroelectric power sites from private use, he managed to save 2,500 by designating them "ranger stations." Roosevelt backed him up, even though the subterfuge involved stretching the law considerably. Firm in his commitment to conservation, Roosevelt never wavered. Today, the six national parks, sixteen national monuments, and fifty-one wildlife refuges that he created stand witness to his substantial accomplishments as a conservationist (Map 21.1).

Roosevelt the Diplomat

Roosevelt took a keen interest in shaping foreign policy and worked to buttress the United States's newly won place among world leaders. A fierce proponent of America's interests abroad, he believed that Congress was inept in foreign affairs, and he relied on executive power to effect a vigorous foreign policy, sometimes stretching the powers of the presidency beyond legal limits in his pursuit of American interests. A man who relished military discipline and viewed life as a constant conflict for supremacy, Roosevelt believed that "civilized nations" should police the world and hold "backward" countries in line. In

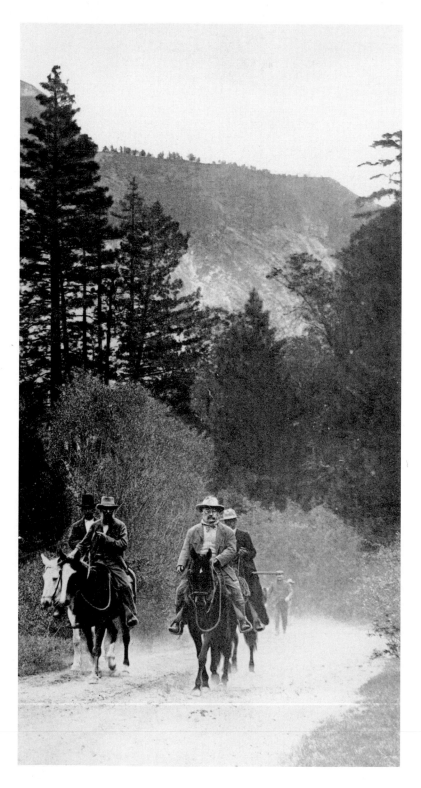

Roosevelt and Muir in Yosemite
In 1903, President Roosevelt took a camping trip to Yosemite, California, with John Muir, naturalist and founder of the Sierra Club. Roosevelt's experience as a rancher in the Dakotas made him the first president to have experienced firsthand the trans-Mississippi West. As president, he acted vigorously to protect the beauty and resources of the West for posterity, using executive power to set aside more than a hundred million acres in government reserves and to create six national parks. Roosevelt and Muir later clashed over the flooding of the Hetch Hetchy Valley in Yosemite. Muir upheld the preservationist position; Roosevelt, a conservationist, advocated managed use.
Theodore Roosevelt Collection, Harvard College Library.

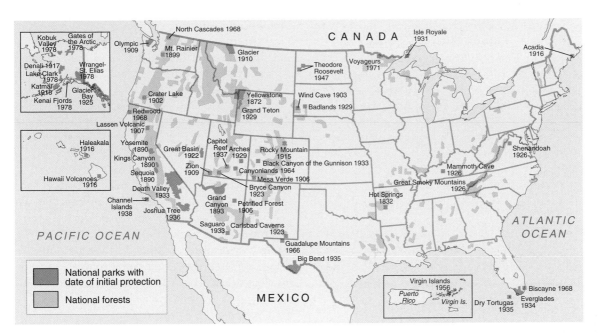

MAP 21.1 National Parks and Forests

The national park system in the West began with Yellowstone in 1872. Grand Canyon, Yosemite, Kings Canyon, and Sequoia followed in the 1890s. During his presidency, Theodore Roosevelt added six parks—Crater Lake, Wind Cave, Petrified Forest, Lassen Volcanic, Mesa Verde, and Zion.

READING THE MAP: Collectively, do national parks or national forests contain larger tracts of land? According to the map, how many national parks were created before 1910? How many were created after 1910?

CONNECTIONS: How do conservation and preservation differ? Why did Theodore Roosevelt believe conservation was important? What principle guided the national land use policy of the Roosevelt administration?

FOR MORE HELP ANALYZING THIS MAP, see the map activity for this chapter in the Online Study Guide at bedfordstmartins.com/roark.

his relations with the European powers, he relied on military strength and diplomacy, a combination he aptly described with the aphorism "Speak softly but carry a big stick."

In the Caribbean, Roosevelt jealously guarded the U.S. sphere of influence defined in the **Monroe Doctrine**. In 1902, he risked war to keep Germany from intervening in Venezuela when that country's dictator borrowed money in Europe and could not repay it. Roosevelt issued an ultimatum to the German kaiser, warning him to stay out of Latin American affairs or face war with the United States. The matter was eventually settled by arbitration.

Roosevelt's proprietary attitude toward the Western Hemisphere became evident in the case of the Panama Canal. A firm advocate of naval power and an astute naval strategist, Roosevelt had long been a supporter of a canal linking the Caribbean and the Pacific, which, by enabling ships to move quickly from the Atlantic to the

Pacific, would effectively double the navy's power. Having decided on a route across the Panamanian isthmus (a narrow strip of land connecting North and South America), then a part of Colombia, Roosevelt in 1902 offered the Colombian government a one-time sum of $10 million and an annual rent of $250,000. When the government in Bogotá refused to accept the offer, Roosevelt became incensed at what he called the "homicidal corruptionists" in Colombia for trying to "blackmail" the United States. The result was an uprising in Panama in 1903 arranged by New York investors. The U.S. government aided and protected the "revolution" by placing the warship *Nashville* off the isthmus, and the State Department recognized the new government of Panama within twenty-four hours. The Panamanians promptly accepted the $10 million, and the building got under way (Map 21.2). The canal would take eleven years and $375 million to complete; it opened in 1914.

The Roosevelt Corollary in Action

In the wake of the Panama affair, the confrontation with Germany over Venezuela, and yet another default on a European debt, this time in the Dominican Republic, Roosevelt announced in 1904 what became known as the Roosevelt Corollary to the Monroe Doctrine: The United States would not intervene in Latin America as long as nations there conducted their affairs with "decency." But the United States would step in if any Latin American nation proved guilty of "brutal wrongdoing," such as defaulting on debts owed to European nations. The Roosevelt Corollary in effect made the United States the policeman of the Western Hemisphere and served notice to the European powers to keep out. To ensure the payment of debts, Roosevelt immediately put the corollary into practice by intervening in Costa Rica and by taking over the customhouse in the Dominican Republic.

In Asia, Roosevelt inherited the Open Door policy initiated by Secretary of State John Hay in 1899, which was designed to ensure U.S. commercial entry into China. As Britain, France, Russia, Japan, and Germany raced to secure Chinese trade and territory, Roosevelt was tempted to use force to enter the fray and gain economic or possibly territorial concessions. As a

Theodore Roosevelt and the Big Stick

In this political cartoon from 1904, President Theodore Roosevelt, dressed in his Rough Rider uniform and carrying his "big stick," turns the Caribbean into a Yankee pond. The Roosevelt Corollary to the Monroe Doctrine did exactly that. Granger Collection.

FOR MORE HELP ANALYZING THIS IMAGE, see the visual activity for this chapter in the Online Study Guide at bedfordstmartins.com/roark.

THE BIG STICK IN THE CARIBBEAN SEA

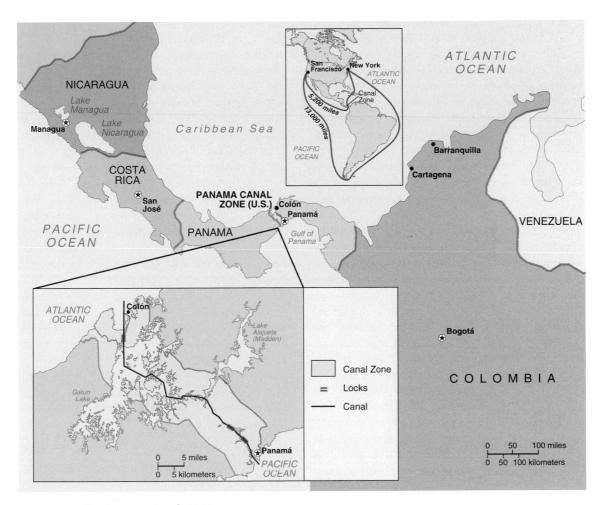

MAP 21.2 The Panama Canal, 1914

The Panama Canal, completed in 1914, bisected the isthmus in a series of massive locks and dams. As Theodore Roosevelt had planned, the canal greatly strengthened the navy by allowing ships to move from the Atlantic to the Pacific in a matter of days.

READING THE MAP: How long was the trip from New York to San Francisco before the Panama Canal was built? And after? Geographically, why is Panama a likely site for a canal?

CONNECTIONS: How did Roosevelt's desire for a canal lead to independence for Panama? How did canal benefit the U.S. navy?

FOR MORE HELP ANALYZING THIS MAP, see the map activity for this chapter in the Online Study Guide at bedfordstmartins.com/roark.

result of victory in the Spanish-American War, the United States already enjoyed a foothold in the region by virtue of its control of the Philippines. Realizing that Americans would not support an aggressive Asian policy, Roosevelt sensibly held back.

In his relations with Europe, Roosevelt sought to establish the United States, fresh from its victory over Spain, as a rising force in world affairs. When tensions flared between France

and Germany in Morocco in 1905, Roosevelt was invited to mediate at a conference in Algeciras, Spain, where he worked to maintain a balance of power that helped neutralize German ambitions. His skillful mediation of the dispute gained him a reputation as an astute player on the world stage and demonstrated the United States's new presence in world affairs.

Roosevelt earned the Nobel Peace Prize in 1906 for his role in negotiating an end to the

Russo-Japanese War, which had broken out when the Japanese invaded Chinese Manchuria, threatening Russia's sphere of influence in the area. Once again, Roosevelt sought to maintain a balance of power, in this case working to curb Japanese expansionism. Roosevelt admired the Japanese, judging them "the most dashing fighters in the world," but he did not want Japan to become too strong in Asia. He presided over the peace conference at Portsmouth, New Hampshire, where he was able to prevent Japan from dominating Manchuria. However, he had no qualms about initiating the Taft-Katsura agreement, granting Japan control of the sovereign nation of Korea in exchange for a pledge that Japan would not threaten the Philippines.

Roosevelt fumed when the United States's good relations with Japan were jeopardized in 1906 by discriminatory legislation in California calling for segregated public schools for "Orientals." Roosevelt smoothed over the incident by negotiating a "Gentleman's Agreement" in 1907 whereby he reversed the segregation order in exchange for voluntary restrictions on Japanese immigration to the United States. This informal arrangement allowed the Japanese to save face while also placating nativist sentiment in California.

> Once in office, Taft proved a perfect tool in the hands of Republicans who yearned for a return to the days of a less active executive.

To demonstrate America's naval power and counter Japan's growing bellicosity, Roosevelt dispatched the Great White Fleet, sixteen of the navy's most up-to-date battleships, on a "goodwill mission" around the world. U.S. relations with Japan improved, and in the 1908 Root-Takahira agreement the two nations pledged to maintain the Open Door and support the status quo in the Pacific. Roosevelt's show of American force constituted a classic example of his dictum "Speak softly but carry a big stick." Political cartoonists delighted in caricaturing the president wielding a cudgel in foreign affairs, and the American public seemed to relish the image.

Progressivism Stalled

Roosevelt retired from the presidency in 1909 at age fifty and went on safari to shoot big game in Africa. He turned the White House over to his handpicked successor, William Howard Taft, a lawyer who had served as governor general of the Philippines. In the presidential election of 1908, Taft soundly defeated the perennial Democratic candidate, William Jennings Bryan. But Taft's popular majority amounted to only half of Roosevelt's record win in 1904. On the eve of his inauguration, Taft showed little enthusiasm about his triumph and little zest for the future. In fact, the presidency for Taft proved an ordeal. As a symptom of his discomfort in office, his weight ballooned from an already hefty 297 pounds to over 350 pounds.

Any man would have found it difficult to follow in Roosevelt's footsteps, but Taft proved hopelessly ill suited to the task. A genial man with a talent for law, Taft had no experience in elective office, no feel for politics, no ability to compromise, and no nerve for controversy. His ambitious wife coveted the office and urged him to seek it. He would have been better off listening to his mother, who warned, "Roosevelt is a good fighter and enjoys it, but the malice of politics would make you miserable." Her words proved prophetic. Taft's presidency was marked by a progressive stalemate, a bitter break with Roosevelt, and a schism in the Republican Party.

The Troubled Presidency of William Howard Taft

Once in office, Taft proved a perfect tool in the hands of Republicans who yearned for a return to the days of a less active executive. A lawyer by training and instinct, Taft believed that it was up to the courts, not the president, to arbitrate social issues. Roosevelt had carried presidential power to a new level, often castigating the judiciary and flouting the separation of powers. Taft the legalist found it difficult to condone such actions. Wary of the progressive insurgents in his own party and without Roosevelt to guide him, Taft relied increasingly on conservatives in the Republican Party. As a progressive senator lamented, "Taft is a ponderous and amiable man completely surrounded by men who know exactly what they want."

Taft's troubles began on the eve of his inaugural when he called a special session of Congress to deal with the tariff, which had grown unconscionably high under Republican rule. Roosevelt had been too politically astute to tackle the troublesome tariff issue, even though he knew that rates needed to be lowered. Taft, with his stubborn courage, blundered into the fray. The House of Representatives passed a modest downward revision and, to make up for lost revenue, imposed a small inheritance tax. Led by Senator Nelson Aldrich of Rhode Island, the conservative Senate struck down the tax and added more than eight hundred crippling amendments to the tariff. The Payne-Aldrich bill that emerged actually raised the tariff, benefiting big business and trusts at the expense of consumers. As if paralyzed, Taft neither fought for changes nor vetoed the measure. On a tour of the Midwest in 1909, he was greeted with jeers when he claimed, "I think the Payne bill is the best bill that the Republican Party ever passed." In the eyes of a growing number of Americans, his praise of the tariff made him either a fool or a liar.

Taft's legalism got him into hot water in the area of conservation as well. He refused to endorse his predecessor's methods of bending the law to protect the nation's resources. He undid Roosevelt's work to preserve hydroelectric power sites when he learned that they had been improperly designated as ranger stations. And when Gifford Pinchot publicly denounced Taft's secretary of the interior, Richard Ballinger, as a tool of western land-grabbers, Taft fired Pinchot, touching off a storm of controversy that damaged Taft and alienated Roosevelt.

Talk of substituting Roosevelt on the ticket in 1912 grew as Republican progressives became increasingly dissatisfied with Taft's policies. In June 1910, Roosevelt returned to New York, where he received a hero's welcome and attracted a stream of visitors and reporters seeking his advice and opinions. Hurt, Taft kept his distance. By late summer, Roosevelt had taken sides with the progressive insurgents in his party. "Taft is utterly hopeless as a leader," Roosevelt confided to his son as he set out on a speaking tour of the West. Reading the mood of the country, Roosevelt began to sound more and more like a candidate.

With the Republican Party divided, the Democrats swept the congressional elections of 1910. Branding the Payne-Aldrich tariff "the mother of trusts," they captured a majority in the House of Representatives and won several key governorships. The revitalized Democratic Party could look to new leaders, among them the progressive governor of New Jersey, Woodrow Wilson.

The new Democratic majority in the House, working with progressive Republicans in the Senate, achieved a number of key reforms, including legislation to regulate mine and railroad safety, to create a Children's Bureau in the

William Howard Taft
William Howard Taft had little aptitude for politics. When Theodore Roosevelt tapped him as his successor in 1908, Taft had never held an elected office. A legalist by training and temperament, Taft moved congenially in the conservative circles of the Republican Party. His actions dismayed progressives and eventually led Roosevelt to challenge him for the presidency in 1912. The break with Roosevelt saddened and embittered Taft, who heartily disliked the presidency and was glad to leave it.
Library of Congress.

Department of Labor, and to establish an eight-hour day for federal workers. Two significant constitutional amendments—the Sixteenth Amendment, which provided for a modest graduated income tax, and the Seventeenth Amendment, which called for the direct election of senators (formerly chosen by state legislatures)—went to the states, where they would later win ratification in 1913. While Congress rode the high tide of progressive reform, Taft sat on the sidelines.

In foreign policy, too, Taft had a difficult time following in Roosevelt's footsteps. In the

Taft's "Dollar Diplomacy"

Caribbean, he pursued a policy of "dollar diplomacy," championing commercial goals rather than the strategic aims that Roosevelt had advocated. He provoked anti-American feeling by attempting to force commercial treaties on Nicaragua and Honduras and by dispatching the U.S. marines to Nicaragua and the Dominican Republic in 1912.

In Asia, Taft's foreign policy proved equally inept. He openly avowed his intent to promote in China "active intervention to secure for . . . our capitalists opportunity for profitable investment." Lacking Roosevelt's understanding of power politics, Taft naively believed that he could substitute "dollars for bullets." He never recognized that an aggressive commercial policy could not exist without military might. As a result, dollar diplomacy was doomed to failure.

Taft was forced to recognize the limits of dollar diplomacy when revolution broke out in Mexico in 1911. Under pressure to protect American investment, which amounted to more than $4 billion, he mobilized troops along the border. But in the end, with no popular support for a war with Mexico, he fell back on diplomatic pressure to salvage American interests.

Always a legalist at heart, Taft hoped to encourage world peace through the use of a world court and arbitration. He unsuccessfully sponsored a series of arbitration treaties that Roosevelt, who prized national honor more than international law, vehemently opposed. By 1910, Roosevelt had become a vocal critic of Taft's foreign policy, which he dismissed as "maudlin folly."

The final breach between Taft and Roosevelt came in 1911, when Taft's attorney general filed an antitrust suit against U.S. Steel. In its brief against the corporation, the government cited Roosevelt's agreement with the Morgan interests in the 1907 acquisition of Tennessee Coal and Iron by the steel giant. The incident greatly embarrassed Roosevelt by making it clear that he either had been hoodwinked or had acted as a tool of Wall Street. Thoroughly enraged, Roosevelt lambasted Taft's "archaic" antitrust policy and hinted that he might be persuaded to run for president again.

Progressive Insurgency and the Election of 1912

In February 1912, Roosevelt challenged Taft for the Republican nomination, announcing, "My hat is in the ring." But for all his popularity, Roosevelt no longer controlled the party machinery. Taft, with uncharacteristic strength, refused to step aside. As he bitterly told a journalist, "Even a rat in a corner will fight." Roosevelt took advantage of newly passed primary election laws and ran in thirteen states, winning 278 delegates to Taft's 48. But at the Chicago convention, Taft's bosses refused to seat the Roosevelt delegates. Fistfights broke out on the convention floor as Taft won renomination on the first ballot. Crying robbery, Roosevelt's supporters bolted the party.

Seven weeks later, in the same Chicago auditorium, the hastily organized Progressive Party met to nominate Roosevelt. Few Republican officeholders joined the new party, but the advance guard of progressivism turned out in full force. Amid a thunder of applause, Jane Addams seconded Roosevelt's nomination. Full of reforming zeal, the delegates chose Roosevelt and Hiram Johnson to head the new party and approved the most ambitious platform since the Populists' in 1892. Planks called for woman suffrage, the direct election of senators, presidential primaries, conservation of natural resources, an end to child labor, minimum wages for women, workers' compensation, social security, and a federal income tax.

Roosevelt arrived in Chicago to accept the nomination and announced that he felt "as strong as a bull moose," giving the new party a nickname and a mascot. But for all the excitement and the cheering, the new Progressive Party was doomed, and the candidate knew it. The people may have supported the party, but the politicians, even insurgents like La Follette, stayed within the Republican fold. "I am under no illusion about it," Roosevelt confessed to a friend. "It is a forlorn hope." But he had gone too far to turn back. He led the Bull Moose Party into the fray, exhorting his followers in ringing biblical tones, "We shall not falter, we stand at Armageddon and do battle for the Lord."

The Democrats, delighted at the split in the Republican ranks, smelled victory for the first time since 1892. Their convention turned into a bitter fight for the nomination. After forty-six ballots, Woodrow Wilson became the party's nominee. Wilson's career in politics was nothing

Wilson Ribbon

Woodrow Wilson's political career was meteoric, propelling him from the presidency of Princeton University to the presidency of the United States in three years. As governor of New Jersey from 1910 to 1912, Wilson turned against the Democratic machine that had backed him and made a reputation as a champion of progressive reform. With the Republicans divided in 1912, the Democrats turned to Wilson to lead their party, nominating him on the forty-sixth ballot. In those days, prospective candidates generally did not attend the nominating convention. The ribbon in the photograph belonged to a member of the Democratic National Committee who traveled to Wilson's summer home in Sea Girt, New Jersey, on August 7, 1912, to inform Wilson officially of his nomination for president.

Collection of Janice L. and David J. Frent.

short of meteoric. Elected governor of New Jersey in 1910, after only eighteen months in office the former professor of political science and president of Princeton University found himself running for president of the United States.

Voters in 1912 could choose among three candidates, each claiming to be a progressive. That the term could stretch to cover all three underscored major disagreements in progressive thinking about the relation between business and government. Taft, in spite of his trust-busting, was generally viewed as the candidate of the old guard. The real contest for the presidency was between Roosevelt and Wilson and the two political philosophies summed up in their respective campaign slogans: "The New Nationalism" and "The New Freedom."

The New Nationalism expressed Roosevelt's belief in federal planning and regulation. He accepted the inevitability of big business but demanded that government act as "a steward of the people" to regulate the giant corporations. Roosevelt called for an increase in the power of the federal government, a decrease in the power of the courts, and an active role for the president. As political theorist Herbert Croly pointed out in his influential book *The Promise of American Life* (1909), Roosevelt hoped to use an active federal government to promote social justice and democracy, replacing the laissez-faire policies of the old liberal state with a new form of liberalism.

Wilson, schooled in the Democratic principles of limited government and **states' rights**, set a markedly different course with his New Freedom. Tutored in economics by *Muller v. Oregon* lawyer Louis Brandeis, who railed against the "curse of bigness," Wilson promised to use antitrust legislation to get rid of big corporations and to give small businesses and farmers better opportunities in the marketplace.

Wilson and Roosevelt fought it out, and the energy and enthusiasm of the Bull Moosers made the race seem closer than it really was. In the end, the Republican vote was split while the Democrats remained united. No candidate claimed a majority in the race. Wilson captured a bare 42 percent of the popular vote, polling fewer votes than Bryan had received when he lost to Taft in 1908. Roosevelt and his Bull Moose Party won 27 percent of the vote, an unprecedented tally for a new party. Taft came in third with 23 percent. But in the electoral college, Wilson won a decisive 435, with 88 going to Roosevelt and only 8 to Taft (Map 21.3). The

MAP 21.3 The Election of 1912

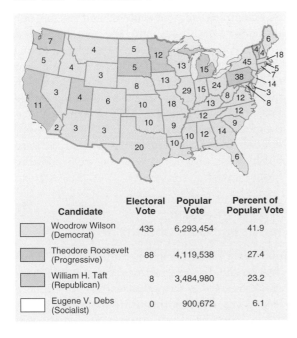

Candidate	Electoral Vote	Popular Vote	Percent of Popular Vote
Woodrow Wilson (Democrat)	435	6,293,454	41.9
Theodore Roosevelt (Progressive)	88	4,119,538	27.4
William H. Taft (Republican)	8	3,484,980	23.2
Eugene V. Debs (Socialist)	0	900,672	6.1

Novelty Postcards of the Election of 1912
These postcards picture the mascot of each party with a moving spring for a tail—the Democrats' donkey, the Progressives' bull moose, and the Republicans' elephant. The hat shown with Roosevelt comes from his phrase "My hat is in the ring," signifying his challenge to incumbent William Howard Taft. Taft's Grand Old Party (GOP) elephant is shown with a steamroller. Many critics charged that Taft won the Republican nomination from Roosevelt in 1912 by steamrolling the party's convention. The caption asks "Has He Got Enough Steam?" In a more obscure reference, Woodrow Wilson is pictured with "The New Jersey Mosquito," and the caption asks "Will He Get Stung?"
Collection of Janice L. and David J. Frent.

Bull Moose Party essentially collapsed after Roosevelt's defeat. It had always been, in the words of one astute observer, "a house divided against itself and already mortgaged."

Woodrow Wilson and Progressivism at High Tide

Born in Virginia and raised in Georgia, Woodrow Wilson became the first southerner to be elected president since James K. Polk in 1844 and only the second Democrat to occupy the White House since Reconstruction. Democrats who anticipated a wild celebration when Wilson took office soon had their hopes dashed. The son of a Presbyterian minister, Wilson was a teetotaler more given to Scripture than to celebration. He called instead for a day of prayer.

This lean, ascetic man with an otherworldly gaze was, as one biographer conceded, a man whose "political convictions were never as fixed as his ambition." Although he owed his governorship to the Democratic machine, he quickly turned his back on the bosses and put New Jersey in the vanguard of progressivism. A year into his term, Wilson had his eye on the presidency. Always able to equivocate, Wilson proved rarely able to compromise. He brought to the White House a gift for oratory, a stern will, and a set of fixed beliefs. His tendency to turn differences of opinion into personal hatreds would impair his leadership and damage his presidency. Fortunately for Wilson, he came to power with a Democratic Congress eager to do his bidding.

Although he opposed big government in his campaign, Wilson viewed himself as the only leader who could speak for the country. He was prepared to work on the base built by Roosevelt to strengthen presidential power, exerting leadership and working through his party in Congress to accomplish the Democratic agenda. Before he was finished, Wilson presided over progressivism at high tide and lent his support not only to the platform of the Democratic Party but to many of the Progressive Party's social reforms as well.

Wilson's Reforms: Tariff, Banking, and the Trusts

In March 1913, Wilson became the first president since John Adams to go to Capitol Hill and speak directly to Congress, calling for tariff reform. "The object of the tariff," Wilson told Congress, "must be effective competition." Eager to topple the high tariff, the Democratic House of Representatives hastily passed the Underwood tariff, which lowered rates by 15 percent. To compensate for lost revenue, Congress approved a moderate federal income tax, made possible by ratification of the Sixteenth Amendment a month earlier. In the Senate, lobbyists for industries quietly went to work to get the tariff raised, but Wilson rallied public opinion by attacking the "industrious and insidious lobby." In the harsh glare of publicity, the Senate passed the Underwood tariff, which earned praise as "the most honest tariff since the Civil War."

Wilson next turned his attention to banking. The panic of 1907 dramatically testified to the failure of the banking system. That year, Roosevelt, like President Grover Cleveland before him, had to turn to J. P. Morgan to avoid economic catastrophe. But by the time Wilson came to office, Morgan's legendary power was coming under close scrutiny. In 1913, Arsène Pujo, a Democratic senator from Louisiana, headed a committee to investigate the "money trust," calling J. P. Morgan himself to testify. The Pujo committee uncovered an alarming concentration of banking power. J. P. Morgan and Company and its affiliates held 341 directorships in 112 corporations, controlling assets of more than $22 billion. The sensational findings created a mandate for banking reform.

The Federal Reserve Act of 1913 marked the most significant piece of domestic legislation of Wilson's presidency. It established a national banking system composed of twelve regional banks, privately controlled but regulated and supervised by a Federal Reserve Board appointed by the president. It gave the United States its first efficient banking and currency system and, at the same time, provided for a larger degree of government control over banking than had ever existed. The new system made currency more elastic and credit adequate for the needs of business and agriculture. It did not, however, attempt to take control of the boom and bust cycles in the U.S. economy, which would produce another major depression in the 1930s.

Wilson, flushed with success, tackled the trust issue next. When Congress reconvened in January 1914, Wilson supported the introduction of the Clayton Antitrust Act to outlaw "unfair competition"—practices such as price discrimination and interlocking directorates (directors from one corporation sitting on the board of another). By spelling out which practices were unfair, Wilson hoped to guide business activity

back to healthy competition without resorting to regulation. Despite a grandiose preamble that stated, "The labor of human beings is not a commodity or article of commerce," the Clayton Act did not improve labor's position. Although AFL president Samuel Gompers hailed the act as the "Magna Carta of labor," the conservative courts continued to issue injunctions and to use antitrust legislation against labor unions.

In the midst of the fight for the Clayton Act, Wilson, at the prompting of Louis Brandeis, changed course and threw his support behind the creation of the Federal Trade Commission (FTC), precisely the kind of federal regulatory agency that Roosevelt had advocated in his New Nationalism platform. The FTC, created in 1914, had not only wide investigatory powers but the authority to prosecute corporations for "unfair trade practices" and to enforce its judgments by issuing "cease and desist" orders. Along with the Clayton Act, Wilson's antitrust program worked to regulate rather than to break up big business.

By the fall of 1914, Wilson had exhausted the stock of ideas that made up the New Freedom. He alarmed progressives by declaring that the progressive movement had fulfilled its mission and that the country needed "a time of healing." Disgruntled progressives also disapproved of Wilson's conservative appointments. Having fought provisions in the Federal Reserve Act that would give bankers control, Wilson promptly named a banker, Paul Warburg, as the first chief of the Federal Reserve Board. Appointments to the new FTC also went to conservative businessmen. The progressive penchant for efficiency and expertise helps explain Wilson's choices. Believing that experts in the field could best understand the complex issues at stake, Wilson appointed bankers to oversee the banks and businessmen to regulate business.

> Before he was finished, Wilson presided over progressivism at high tide and championed not only the platform of the Democratic Party but many of the Progressive Party's social reforms as well.

Wilson, Reluctant Progressive

Progressives watched in dismay as Wilson repeatedly obstructed or obstinately refused to endorse further progressive reforms. He failed to support labor's demand for an end to court injunctions against labor unions. He twice threatened to veto legislation providing for farm credits on nonperishable crops. He refused to

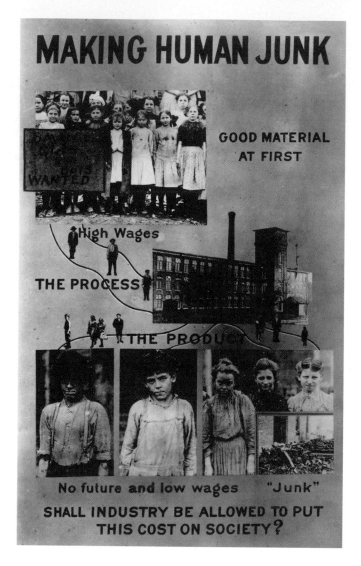

Progressive Poster Condemning Child Labor
This poster attacks child labor, borrowing the convention of the business flowchart to portray graphically how industries employing children are "making human junk." Progressives' concern for the plight of poor children won them the label "child savers." Although activists worked hard to enact federal legislation prohibiting child labor in 1916, the Supreme Court declared the law unconstitutional two years later on the grounds that Congress had no right to regulate manufacturing within states. What does this poster emphasize most in its appeal to end child labor—concern for children or for society?
Library of Congress.

In the face of Wilson's obstinacy, reform might have ended in 1913 had not politics intruded. In the congressional elections of 1914, the Republican Party, no longer split by Roosevelt's Bull Moose faction, won substantial gains. Democratic strategists, with their eyes on the 1916 presidential race, recognized that Wilson needed to pick up support in the Midwest and the West by capturing votes from former Bull Moose progressives.

Wilson responded belatedly to this political pressure by lending his support to reform in the months leading up to the election of 1916. In a sharp about-face, he cultivated union labor, farmers, and social reformers. To please labor, he appointed Louis Brandeis to the Supreme Court. To woo farmers, he threw his support behind legislation to obtain rural credits. And he won support from advanced progressives like Jane Addams by supporting workers' compensation and the Keating-Owen child labor law, which outlawed the regular employment of children younger than sixteen. When a railroad strike threatened in the months before the election, Wilson practically ordered Congress to establish an eight-hour day at ten-hour pay on the railroads. He had moved a long way from his position in 1912 to embrace many of the social reforms championed by Theodore Roosevelt. (See "Documenting the American Promise," page 777.) As Wilson boasted, the Democrats had "opened their hearts to the demands of social justice" and had "come very near to carrying out the platform of the Progressive Party." Wilson's shift toward reform, along with his claim that he had kept the United States out of the war in Europe, helped him win reelection in 1916.

The Limits of Progressive Reform

While progressivism called for a more active role for the liberal state, at heart it was a movement that sought reforms designed to preserve American institutions and stem the tide of more radical change. Its basic conservatism can be seen by comparing it to more radical movements of the era—socialism, radical labor, and birth control—and by looking at the groups progressive reform left behind, including women and African Americans.

support child labor legislation or woman suffrage. Wilson used the rhetoric of the New Freedom to justify his actions, claiming that his administration would condone "special privileges to none." But in fact his stance often reflected the interests of his small-business constituency.

The Issue of Child Labor

By the early years of the twentieth century, as many as four million children between the ages of ten and fifteen toiled long hours for little pay. They worked in the depths of coal mines, in the searing heat of glass factories, in canneries and textile mills, in cotton fields—wherever employers coveted small size and nimble fingers. Progressive reformers, often called "child savers," attempted to curb exploitation of children under the age of fourteen in sweatshops, mines, and mills across America. But they ran into solid opposition not only from employers, who had a vested interest in the cheap labor children performed, but also from parents, who counted on the meager wages of their children. In rural America, no one questioned parents' right to put children to hard tasks in the fields and on the farm. Similarly, immigrants from rural Italy, Germany, or Russia could see no harm in putting children to work in factories or sweatshops in America's industrial cities and viewed it as the parents' prerogative to command their children's wages. Progressives found themselves up against stiff opposition.

DOCUMENT 1
Lewis W. Parker, Testimony before the Congressional Committee on Labor, 1914

Not just immigrants but old-stock Americans relied on child labor, particularly in the South, where entire families of poor whites left the land to work side by side in the textile mills. On May 22, 1914, a South Carolina mill owner testified before the House of Representatives Committee on Labor on why child labor was necessary in the South.

It is not possible for a man who has been working on a farm who is an adult—after the age of 21 years, for instance—to become a skilled employee in a cotton mill. His fingers are knotted and gnarled; he is slow in action, whereas activity is required in working in the cotton mills. Therefore, as a matter of necessity, the adult of the family had to come to the cotton mill as an unskilled employee, and it was the children of the family who became the skilled employees in the cotton mills. For that reason it was the children who had to support the families for the time being. I have seen instances in which a child of 12 years of age, working in the cotton mills, is earning one and one-half times as much as his father of 40 or 50 years of age.

DOCUMENT 2
Florence Kelley, Testimony before the Congressional Committee on Labor, 1914

Progressives countered these arguments with poignant testimony about the plight of young workers and the failure of the states to enforce the law. At the same 1914 committee hearings, reformer Florence Kelley described her experiences investigating child labor practices in Illinois.

. . . I was at one time chief inspector of factories and workshops in the State of Illinois. I found great numbers of children working at night—working illegally. The superintendent of a glass-bottle company told me himself that this occurred once when he was rushed with work: A widow had come to him bringing two little boys, one still in kilts [baby skirts worn by small boys] and one in knee breeches. She told him that their father had just been killed on the railroad, and that they were penniless; and she wanted the older little boy to go to work in the glassworks, where he would get 40 cents a day. The superintendent was pressed for boys, and said, "I won't take the bigger fellow alone, but if you will take the baby back home and put him into knee pants, and then bring them both back in trousers, I will take them both." She did so, and those two little fellows, aged 9 and 7 years, began their work on the night shift.

DOCUMENT 3
Lowell Mellett, Interview with Reuben Dagenhart, 1923

Despite heavy odds against them, progressives achieved victory in 1916 when the National Child Labor Committee finally convinced Congress and President Woodrow Wilson to enact the Keating-Owen bill forbidding the regular employment of children under sixteen. The child savers' victory proved short-lived, however. Powerful business interests and a Supreme Court sympathetic to their views took advantage of the waning fervor for reform, and in 1918 in Hammer v. Dagenhart, *the Court struck down the child labor law on the grounds that Congress could not regulate manufacturing within states. This decision made it legal for the chief plaintiff in the case, Roland Dagenhart, to continue having his young sons, aged thirteen and seven, work in a North Carolina cotton mill. It also protected the boys' "constitutional right" to continue to work at the mill, where they put in*

(continued)

twelve-hour days and sometimes worked night shifts as well.

Ironically, one of the plaintiffs in the Dagenhart case had a very negative view of its outcome. In 1923, reporter Lowell Mellett tracked down Reuben Dagenhart, one of the boys in whose favor the Supreme Court had ruled six years earlier. In an article published in Labor *in November 1923, Mellett recounted his meeting with Dagenhart.*

I found him at his home in Charlotte. He is about the size of the office boy—weighs 105 pounds, he told me. But he is a married man with a child. He is 20 years old.

"What benefit," I asked him, "did you get out of the suit which you won in the United States Supreme Court?"

"You mean the suit the Fidelity Manufacturing Company won? (It was the Fidelity Company for which the Dagenharts were working.) I don't see that I got any benefit. I guess I'd been alot better off if they hadn't won it. . . .

"Look at me! A hundred and five pounds, a grown man and no education. I may be mistaken, but I think the years I've put in in the cotton mills have stunted my growth. They kept me from getting any schooling. I had to stop school after the third grade and now I need the education I didn't get."

"How was your growth stunted?"

"I don't know—the dust and the lint, maybe. But from 12 years old on, I was working 12 hours a day—from 6 in the morning till 7 at night, with time out for meals. And sometimes I worked nights besides. Lifting a hundred pounds and I only weighed 65 pounds myself."

He explained that he and his sister worked together, "on section," spinning. They each made about a dollar a day, though later he worked up to where he could make $2. His father made $15 a week and infant John, at the time the suit was brought, was making close to $1 a day.

"Just what did you and John get out of that suit, then?"

"Why, we got some automobile rides when them big lawyers from the North was down here. Oh, yes, and they brought both of us a coca-cola! That's all we got out of it."

"What did you tell the judge when you were in court?"

"Oh, John and me never was in court! Just Paw was there. John and me was just little kids in short pants. I guess we wouldn't have looked like much in court. We were working in the mill while the case was going on. But Paw went up to Washington."

Reuben hasn't been to school, but his mind has not been idle.

"It would have been a good thing for all the kids in this state if that law they passed had been kept. . . . I know one thing. I ain't going to let them put my kid sister in the mill. . . . She's only 15 and she's crippled and I bet I stop that!"

Despite the efforts of committed reformers, child labor persisted into the 1920s, immune from federal law and condoned by states reluctant to exercise their authority against the force of private money and growing public indifference.

SOURCE: Documents 1 and 2, House of Representatives Hearings before the Committee on Labor (1914), 93, 35–36; document 3, *Labor*, November 17, 1923.

Radical Alternatives

The year 1900 marked the birth of the Social Democratic Party in America, later called simply the Socialist Party. Like the progressives, the socialists were middle class and native-born. They had broken with the older, more militant Socialist Labor Party precisely because of its dogmatic approach and immigrant constituency. The new group of socialists proved eager to appeal to a broad mass of Americans.

The Socialist Party chose as its standard-bearer Eugene V. Debs, whose experience in the Pullman strike of 1894 convinced him that "there is no hope for the toiling masses of my country-men, except by the pathways mapped out by Socialism." Debs's brand of socialism, which owed as much to the social gospel as to the theories of Karl Marx, advocated cooperation over competition and urged men and women to liberate themselves from "the barbarism of private ownership and wage slavery." Roosevelt labeled Debs a "mere inciter to murder and preacher of applied anarchy." Debs, for his part, pointed to the conservatism that underlay Roosevelt's fiery rhetoric. In the 1912 election, Debs indicted both old parties as "Tweedledee and Tweedledum," each dedicated to the preservation of capitalism and the continuation of the wage system. The Socialist Party alone, he argued, was the "revolutionary party of the working class." Debs would run for president five times, in every election (except 1916) from 1900 to 1920. His best showing came in 1912, when he polled 6 percent of the popular vote, capturing almost a million votes.

Farther to the left of the socialists stood the Industrial Workers of the World (IWW), nicknamed the Wobblies. In 1905, Debs, along with Western Federation of Miners leader William Dudley "Big Bill" Haywood, created the IWW, "one big union" dedicated to organizing the most destitute segment of the workforce, the unskilled workers disdained by Samuel Gompers's AFL—western miners, migrant farmworkers, lumbermen, and immigrant textile workers. Haywood, a craggy-faced miner with one eye (he had lost the other in a childhood accident), was a charismatic leader and a proletarian intellectual. Debs in-

sisted that change could come from ballots, not bullets, but the IWW unhesitatingly advocated direct action, sabotage, and the general strike—tactics designed to trigger a workers' uprising. The IWW never had more than 10,000 members at any one time, although possibly as many as 100,000 workers belonged to the union at one time or another in the early twentieth century. Nevertheless, the IWW's influence on the country extended far beyond its numbers.

The movement for birth control during the Progressive Era was another example of a cross-class alliance in which middle-class women made common cause with the working class. The leading advocates of birth control from 1914 to 1920 came from the ranks of anarchists, feminists, and socialists. Radicals such as the anarchist Emma Goldman were among the first to champion birth control, which they saw as a way to improve the plight of the workers, urging

---

"We Want Debs"

Eugene Victor Debs, shown in the train window wearing a bow tie, poses with Socialist Party campaign workers on a whistle-stop tour during the presidential campaign of 1912. Arguing that Roosevelt and Wilson were as alike as "Tweedledee and Tweedledum," Debs saw the Socialist Party as the only hope for the working class. Over a million voters agreed and cast their votes for him in 1912.

Photo: Brown Brothers; button: Collection of Janice L. and David J. Frent.

working-class women to quit producing recruits for the factory and the army.

Margaret Sanger, a nurse and social activist, promoted birth control as a movement for social change. Sanger, the daughter of a radical Irish father and a mother who died at age fifty after bearing eleven children, coined the term *birth control* in 1915 and launched a movement with broad social implications. Sanger and her followers saw birth control not only as a sexual and medical reform but also as a means to alter social and political power relationships and to alleviate human misery.

Although birth control became a public issue only in the early twentieth century, the birthrate in the United States had been falling consistently throughout the nineteenth century. The average number of children per family dropped from 7.0 in 1800 to 3.6 by 1900. The desire for family limitation was widespread, and in this sense, birth control was nothing new. But the open advocacy of *contraception*, the use of artificial means to prevent pregnancy, seemed to many people both new and shocking. Theodore Roosevelt fulminated against birth control as "race suicide," warning that the "white" population was declining while immigrants and "undesirables" continued to breed.

Convinced that women needed to be able to control their pregnancies but unsure of the best

Margaret Sanger's Brownsville Birth Control Clinic

Margaret Sanger opened the first birth control clinic in the United States in the Brownsville section of Brooklyn in 1916. During the nine days it operated before police shut it down, more than four hundred women visited the clinic. Here they are shown waiting patiently in line with their baby carriages. Sanger published her flyers in English, Yiddish, and Italian, and her clinic attracted immigrant women, proving that Italian Catholics and Russian Jews wanted birth control information as much as their middle- and upper-class Protestant counterparts did. What does the picture say about which women sought birth control, married or single women?

Sophia Smith Collection, Smith College.

Inez Mullholland Leads Washington Suffrage Parade
In 1913 when women marched on Washington, D.C., to demand the vote, the mass march was a novel tactic. Many worried that women would not be physically able to march the full distance. Ambulances stood by to tend to any who fainted along the way. Led by Inez Hayes Mullholland riding a white horse, the women proved neither faint nor faint-hearted. Incoming president Woodrow Wilson refused even to acknowledge their protest in his inaugural address the following day.
Brown Brothers.

methods to do so, Sanger traveled to Europe in 1913 to learn more about contraceptive techniques. On her return, she promoted birth control in her newspaper, *The Woman Rebel*. Social purity laws passed in the 1870s made it illegal to distribute either information on birth control or contraceptive devices, classing both as "obscene." The post office confiscated Sanger's magazine and brought charges against her. Facing arrest, she fled to Europe only to return in 1916 something of a national celebrity. In her absence, birth control had become linked with free speech and had been taken up as a liberal cause. Under public pressure, the government dropped the charges against Sanger, who undertook a nationwide tour to publicize the birth control cause.

Sanger then turned to direct action, opening the nation's first birth control clinic in the Brownsville section of Brooklyn, New York, in October 1916. Located in the heart of a Jewish and Italian immigrant neighborhood, the clinic attracted 464 clients in the nine days it remained open. On the tenth day, police shut down the clinic and threw Sanger in jail. By then she had become a national figure, and the cause she championed had gained legitimacy, if not legal-

ity. After World War I, the birth control movement would become much less radical as Sanger turned to medical doctors for support and mouthed the racist theories of the eugenics movement. But in its infancy, the movement Sanger led was part of a radical vision for reforming the world that made common cause with the socialists and the IWW in challenging the limits of progressive reform.

Progressivism for White Men Only

The day before President Woodrow Wilson's inauguration in March 1913, more than five thousand demonstrators marched in Washington to demand the vote for women. A rowdy crowd on hand to celebrate the Democrats' triumph heckled the marchers, as did the police. "If my wife were where you are," a burly cop told one suffragist, "I'd break her head." But for all the marching, Wilson, who didn't believe that a "lady" should vote, pointedly ignored woman suffrage in his inaugural address the next day.

The march served as a reminder that the political gains of progressivism were not spread equally in the population. As the twentieth century dawned, women still could not vote in most states. Increasingly, however, woman suffrage had become an international movement. In Great Britain, Emmeline Pankhurst and her daughters Cristabel and Sylvia promoted a new, militant suffragism. They seized the spotlight in a series of marches, mass meetings, and acts of civil disobedience, which sometimes escalated into riots, violence, and arson.

Alice Paul, a Quaker social worker who had visited England and participated in suffrage activism there, returned to the United States in 1910 in time to plan the mass march on the eve of Wilson's inauguration and to lobby for a federal amendment to give women the vote. Paul's dramatic tactics alienated many in the National American Woman Suffrage Association (NAWSA). In 1916, Paul founded the militant National Woman's Party (NWP), which became the radical voice of the suffrage movement, advocating direct action such as mass marches and civil disobedience. Paul and her followers rejected the state-by-state strategy of the NAWSA and continued to press for a constitutional suffrage amendment, called by its supporters the Susan B. Anthony amendment.

The NAWSA, spurred by the actions of Paul and her followers, gained new direction after Carrie Chapman Catt became president in 1915. Catt revitalized the organization with a carefully crafted "winning plan" designed to achieve suffrage in six years. While Paul and her NWP held a six-month vigil outside the White House—holding banners that read "Mr. Wilson, What Will You Do for Woman Suffrage?"—Catt led a centrally directed effort that worked on several levels. In states where women already voted, Catt lobbied for a federal constitutional amendment. Where state referenda could be won, she launched campaigns to maintain the suffrage momentum. Catt's strategy was to "keep so much 'suffrage noise' going all over the country that neither the enemy [n]or friends will discover where the real battle is." Catt's "winning plan" worked effectively, taking only four years instead of the six Catt had predicted to ratify a constitutional amendment for woman suffrage.

World War I would provide the final impetus for woman suffrage. Paul and the NWP refused to work for the war, insisting "democracy should begin at home." In contrast, Catt seized the mantle of patriotism, arguing that there was no conflict between fighting for suffrage and aiding the war effort. When the Nineteenth Amendment became part of the U.S. Constitution in August 1920, the victory belonged both to Catt and to Paul. For without the militancy of the NWP, the NAWSA would not have seemed so moderate and respectable.

Women weren't the only group left out in progressive reform. Progressivism, as it was practiced in the West and South, was tainted with racism and sought to limit the rights of African and Asian Americans. Anti-Asian bigotry in the West had led to a renewal of the Chinese Exclusion Act in 1902. At first, California governor Hiram Johnson stood up against the strong anti-Asian prejudice of his state; then in 1913 he caved in to near unanimous pressure and signed the Alien Land Law, which barred Japanese immigrants from purchasing land in California. His support of the legislation amounted to little more than cynical demagoguery. As Johnson well knew, the law was largely symbolic—ineffectual in practice because Japanese children born in the United States were U.S. citizens and property could be purchased in their names. Progressive politicians like Johnson, dedicated to democracy and opposed to special interests, proved willing to lay aside their principles and condone nativism and racism in order to maintain their popularity with voters.

South of the Mason-Dixon line, the progressives' racism targeted African Americans. Progressives preached the disfranchisement of black voters as a "reform." During the bitter electoral fights that had pitted Populists against Democrats in the 1890s, the party of white supremacy held on to power by means of votes purchased or coerced from African Americans. Southern progressives proposed to "reform" the electoral system by eliminating black voters. Beginning in 1890 with Mississippi, southern states curtailed the African American vote through devices such as poll taxes (fees required for voting) and literacy tests. Not coincidentally, these measures also denied access to poor, illiterate whites likely to vote Populist. The racist intent of southern voting legislation became especially clear after 1900. With the Populist threat gone, states resorted to the grandfather clause, a legal provision that allowed men who failed a literacy test to vote if their grandfathers had cast a ballot. Grandfathering permitted nearly all southern white men to vote and

> Progressivism, as it was practiced in the West and South, was tainted with racism and sought to limit the rights of African and Asian Americans.

excluded nearly all blacks, whose grandparents had most likely been slaves and never voted.

The Progressive Era also witnessed the rise of **Jim Crow** laws to segregate public facilities (Jim Crow was the name of a character in a popular minstrel song). The new railroads precipitated segregation in the South where it had rarely existed before, at least on paper. Blacks traveling by train were restricted to Jim Crow coaches even when they paid the first-class fare. Soon separate waiting rooms, separate bathrooms, and separate dining facilities for blacks sprang up across the South. In courtrooms in Mississippi, blacks were even required to swear on a separate Bible.

In the face of this growing repression, Booker T. Washington, the preeminent black leader of the day, urged caution and restraint. A former slave, Washington had opened the Tuskegee Institute in Alabama in 1881 to teach vocational skills to African Americans. He emphasized education and economic progress for his race and urged African Americans to put aside issues of political and social equality. In an 1895 speech in Atlanta, which came to be known as the "Atlanta Compromise," he stated, "In all things that are purely social we can be as separate as the fingers, yet one as the hand in all things essential to mutual progress." Washington's accommodationist policy appealed to whites in all sections, who elevated "the wizard of Tuskegee" to the role of national spokesman for African Americans.

The year after Washington proclaimed the Atlanta Compromise, the Supreme Court upheld the legality of racial segregation, affirming in *Plessy v. Ferguson* (1896) the constitutionality of the doctrine of "separate but equal." Blacks could be segregated in separate schools, restrooms, and other facilities, as long as the facilities were "equal" to those provided for whites. In actuality, facilities for blacks rarely proved equal. In the North, where racism of a different sort led to a clamor for legislation to restrict immigration, support for African American equality found few advocates. And with anti-Asian bigotry strong in the West, the doctrine of "white

Booker T. Washington and Theodore Roosevelt Dine at the White House
When Theodore Roosevelt invited Booker T. Washington to the White House in 1901, he stirred up a hornet's nest of controversy that continued into the election of 1904. This Republican campaign piece gives the meeting a positive slant, showing Roosevelt and Washington sitting under a portrait of Abraham Lincoln, a symbol of the party's historic commitment to African Americans. Can you tell from this illustration that Washington is African American? Democrats portrayed the meeting in a very different light; their campaign buttons pictured Washington with darker skin and implied that Roosevelt favored "race mingling."
Collection of Janice L. and David J. Frent.

supremacy" found increasing support in all sections of the country.

When Theodore Roosevelt invited Booker T. Washington to dine at the White House in 1901, a storm of racist criticism erupted. One southern editor fumed that the White House "had been painted black." But Roosevelt summoned Washington to talk politics and patronage, not African American rights. Busy tearing apart Mark Hanna's Republican machine, Roosevelt wanted Washington's counsel in selecting black Republicans for party posts in the South. The president remained more interested in his own political fortunes than in those of African Americans. His attitude became obvious in the Brownsville incident in 1906, when he dishonorably discharged three companies of black soldiers because he suspected (although there was no proof) that they were shielding the murderer of a white saloonkeeper killed in a shootout in the Texas town.

When Woodrow Wilson became president, he brought with him southern attitudes toward race and racial segregation. At the prompting of his wife, he instituted segregation in the federal workforce, especially the post office, and approved segregated drinking fountains and restrooms in the nation's capital. When critics attacked the policy, Wilson insisted that segregation was "in the interest of the Negro."

Faced with intolerance and open persecution, educated blacks in the North rebelled against the conservative leadership of Booker T. Washington. In *The Souls of Black Folk* (1903), Harvard graduate W. E. B. Du Bois attacked the "Tuskegee Machine," comparing Booker T. Washington to a political boss who used his influence to silence his critics and reward his followers. Du Bois founded the Niagara movement in 1905, calling for universal male suffrage, civil rights, and leadership by a black intellectual elite. In 1909, the Niagara movement helped found the National Association for the Advancement of Colored People (NAACP), a coalition of blacks and whites who sought legal and political rights for African Americans through the courts. Like many progressive reform coalitions, the NAACP attracted a diverse group—social workers, socialists, and black intellectuals. In the decades that followed, the NAACP came to represent the future for African Americans, while Booker T. Washington, who died in 1915, represented the past.

Conclusion: The Transformation of the Liberal State

Progressivism was never a radical movement. Its goal remained the reform of the existing system—by government intervention if necessary, but without uprooting any of the traditional American political, economic, or social institutions. As Theodore Roosevelt, the bellwether of the movement, insisted, "The only true conservative is the man who resolutely sets his face toward the future." Roosevelt was such a man, and progressivism was such a movement. But although progressivism was never radical, neither was it the laissez-faire liberalism of the previous century. Progressives' willingness to use the power of the federal government to regulate business and achieve a measure of social justice redefined liberalism in the twentieth century, tying it to the expanded power of the state.

Progressivism contained many paradoxes. A diverse coalition of individuals and interests, the progressive movement began at the grass roots but left as its legacy a stronger presidency and unprecedented federal involvement in the economy and social welfare. A movement that believed in social justice, progressivism often promoted social control. And while progressives called for greater democracy, they worshipped experts and efficiency.

But whatever its inconsistencies and limitations, progressivism took action to deal with the problems posed by urban industrialism. Progressivism saw grassroots activists address social problems on the local and state levels and search for national solutions to the problems of urban industrialism. By increasing the power of the presidency and expanding the power of the state, progressives worked to bring about greater social justice and to achieve a better balance between government and business. Jane Addams and Theodore Roosevelt could lay equal claim to the movement that redefined liberalism and launched the liberal state of the twentieth century. War on a global scale would provide progressivism with yet another challenge even before it had completed its ambitious agenda.

FOR ADDITIONAL FIRSTHAND ACCOUNTS OF THIS PERIOD, see Chapter 21 in Michael Johnson, ed., *Reading the American Past*, Third Edition.

TO ASSESS YOUR MASTERY OF THE MATERIAL IN THIS CHAPTER, see the Online Study Guide at bedfordstmartins.com/roark.

FOR WEB LINKS RELATED TO TOPICS IN THIS CHAPTER, see "HistoryLinks," "DocLinks," and "PlaceLinks" at bedfordstmartins.com/roark.

CHRONOLOGY

1889 • Jane Addams opens Hull House in Chicago.

1895 • Booker T. Washington enunciates "Atlanta Compromise," supporting separation of blacks and whites.

• Protestant clergy found Anti-Saloon League.

1896 • U.S. Supreme Court upholds doctrine of "separate but equal" in *Plessy v. Ferguson.*

1899 • Florence Kelley heads National Consumers' League (NCL).

1900 • Socialist Party founded with Eugene V. Debs as standard-bearer.

• Tom Johnson elected mayor of Cleveland, Ohio.

• Robert M. La Follette elected governor of Wisconsin.

1901 • Theodore Roosevelt succeeds to presidency following assassination of William McKinley.

1902 • U.S. government files antitrust lawsuit against Northern Securities Company.

• Roosevelt brings labor and management to bargaining table in anthracite coal strike.

• Dispute between United States and Germany over Venezuelan debt ends in arbitration.

1903 • Women's Trade Union League (WTUL) founded, bringing together women workers and middle-class "allies."

• United States begins construction of Panama Canal.

• Congress passes Elkins Act, outlawing railroad rebates.

• W. E. B. Du Bois challenges Booker T. Washington in his book *The Souls of Black Folk.*

1904 • Roosevelt wins presidential election in landslide.

• Roosevelt Corollary to Monroe Doctrine effectively makes the United States "policeman" of the Western Hemisphere.

1905 • Big Bill Haywood, calling for labor to adopt radical measures in its struggle against capitalism, founds Industrial Workers of the World (IWW).

• W. E. B. Du Bois founds the Niagara movement, calling for suffrage and civil rights for blacks.

• Roosevelt mediates dispute between Germans and French over access to trade in Morocco at the Algeciras conference in Spain.

• Taft-Katsura Agreement gives Japan control over Korea.

1906 • Congress passes Pure Food and Drug Act and Meat Inspection Act.

• Roosevelt urges investigative reporters not to resort to "muckraking." Journalists appropriate the term for exposé writing, calling themselves *muckrakers.*

• Congress passes Hepburn Act to regulate railroads and strengthen Interstate Commerce Commission.

• Roosevelt dishonorably discharges three companies of African American soldiers in Brownsville, Texas, without proof of their guilt.

• Roosevelt receives Nobel Peace Prize for mediating Russo-Japanese War.

1907 • Panic on Wall Street.

• Barred by Congress from creating any more federal reserves in six western states, Roosevelt hastily adds 21 before law goes into effect.

• Roosevelt signs "Gentleman's Agreement" with Japan restricting immigration.

• Social gospel minister Walter Rauschenbusch publishes *Christianity and the Social Crisis.*

1908 • In *Muller v. Oregon*, U.S. Supreme Court upholds Oregon state law limiting women's working hours to ten a day.

• In the Root-Takahira agreement, the United States and Japan agree to maintain Open Door policy in the Pacific.

• William Howard Taft elected president.

1909 • "Uprising of twenty thousand" in New York City, a garment workers' strike, backed by the WTUL.

• Herbert Croly publishes *The Promise of American Life.*

• National Association for the Advancement of Colored People (NAACP) formed.

• Taft defends Payne-Aldrich tariff.

1910 • Hiram Johnson elected governor of California.

• Woodrow Wilson elected governor of New Jersey.

• Congress passes Mann Act to limit traffic in women across state lines.

• Jane Addams publishes *Twenty Years at Hull-House.*

1911 • Triangle fire in New York City kills 146 workers.

• Taft launches antitrust suit against U.S. Steel.

1912 • Taft sends marines into Nicaragua and the Dominican Republic.

• Republicans nominate incumbent William Howard Taft.

• Theodore Roosevelt runs for president on Progressive Party ticket.

• Democrat Woodrow Wilson elected president.

- Socialist Eugene V. Debs garners 6 percent of the presidential vote.

1913
- Suffragists march on eve of Wilson's inauguration to demand the vote.
- Congress passes Federal Reserve Act, establishing national banking system under government control.
- Sixteenth Amendment (income tax) and Seventeenth Amendment (direct election of senators) ratified.

1914
- Wilson signs legislation establishing Federal Trade Commission (FTC).
- Congress passes Clayton Antitrust Act, outlawing "unfair competition."
- Panama Canal opens.

- Walter Lippmann publishes *Drift and Mastery*, statement of progressive belief in scientific expertise.

1915
- Carrie Chapman Catt takes over leadership of national woman suffrage movement.

1916
- Alice Paul launches National Woman's Party.
- Margaret Sanger opens first U.S. birth control clinic, in Brooklyn, New York.
- Congress passes Keating-Owen bill, outlawing child labor.
- Woodrow Wilson elected to a second term.

1918
- In *Hammer v. Dagenhart*, U.S. Supreme Court strikes down Keating-Owen child labor law.

BIBLIOGRAPHY

General

Sean Dennis Cashman, *America in the Age of the Titans: The Progressive Era and World War I* (1988).
Alan Dawley, *Struggles for Justice: Social Responsibility and the Liberal State* (1991).
Vincent P. DeSantis, *The Shaping of Modern America, 1877–1920* (2nd ed., 1989).
Steven Diner, *A Very Different Age: Americans of the Progressive Era* (1998).
Glenda Elizabeth Gilmore, ed., *Who Were the Progressives?* (2002).
Linda K. Kerber, Alice Kessler-Harris, and Katherine Kish Sklar, *U.S. History as Women's History* (1995).
Nell Irvin Painter, *Standing at Armageddon: The United States, 1877–1919* (1987).
Daniel Rogers, *Atlantic Crossings: Social Politics in a Progressive Age* (1998).

Grassroots Progressivism

Joyce Antler, *Lucy Sprague Mitchell* (1987).
Karen J. Blair, *The Clubwoman as Feminist: True Womanhood Redefined, 1868–1914* (1980).
Paul Boyer, *Urban Masses and Moral Order in America, 1820–1920* (1978).
Mina Carson, *Settlement Folk: Social Thought and the American Settlement Movement, 1885–1930* (1990).
Robert M. Crunden, *Ministers of Reform: The Progressive Achievement in American Civilization, 1889–1920* (1982).
Doris Groshen Daniels, *Always a Sister: The Feminism of Lillian D. Wald* (1989).
Allen F. Davis, *American Heroine: The Life and Legend of Jane Addams* (1973).
Nancy Schrom Dye, *As Equals and as Sisters: Feminism, Unionism, and the Women's Trade Union League of New York* (1980).
John H. Ehrenreich, *The Altruistic Imagination: A History of Social Work and Social Policy in the United States* (1985).
Jean Bethke Elshtain, *Jane Addams and the Dream of American Democracy* (2002).

Ellen Fitzpatrick, *Endless Crusade: Women, Social Scientists, and Progressive Reform* (1990).
Lynn D. Gordon, *Gender and Higher Education in the Progressive Era* (1989).
Alice Kessler Harris, *Out to Work: A History of Wage-Earning Women in the United States* (1982).
Melvin Holli, *The American Mayor: The Best and Worst Big-City Leaders* (1999).
Michael B. Katz, *In the Shadow of the Poorhouse: A Social History of Welfare in America* (1986).
Seth Koven and Sonya Michel, eds., *Mothers of a New World: Maternalist Politics and the Origins of the Welfare State* (1993).
Rivka Lissak, *Pluralism and Progressives: Hull House and the New Immigrants, 1890–1919* (1989).
Kathleen McCarthy, ed., *Lady Bountiful Revisited: Women, Philanthropy, and Power* (1990).
Robyn Muncy, *Creating a Female Dominion in American Reform* (1991).
Elizabeth Payne, *Reform, Labor, and Feminism: Margaret Dreier Robins and the Women's Trade Union League* (1988).
David Pivar, *The Purity Crusade: Sexual Morality and Social Control* (1973).
Anne Firor Scott, *Natural Allies: Women's Associations in American History* (1991).
Peter R. Shergold, *Working-Class Life: The "American Standard" in Comparative Perspective, 1899–1913* (1982).
Beatrice Siegel, *Lillian Wald of Henry Street* (1983).
Kathryn Kish Sklar, *Florence Kelley and the Nation's Work: The Rise of Women's Political Culture, 1830–1900* (1995).
Barbara Miller Solomon, *In the Company of Educated Women* (1985).
Landon R. Y. Storre, *Civilizing Capitalism: The National Consumers' League, Women's Activism, and Labor Standards in the New Deal Era* (2000).
David Stradling, *Smokestacks and Progressives: Environmentalists, Engineers, and Air Quality in America, 1881–1951* (1999).
David Von Drehle, *Triangle: The Fire That Changed America* (2003).
Barbara Mayer Wertheimer, *We Were There: The Story of Working Women in America* (1977).
Harold S. Wilson, *"McClure's Magazine" and the Muckrakers* (1970).

Progressive Politics and Diplomacy

Donald E. Anderson, *William Howard Taft* (1973).

Norman Birnbaum, *After Progress: American Social Reform and European Socialism in the Twentieth Century* (2001).

John Morton Blum, *The Republican Roosevelt* (2nd ed., 1977).

H. W. Brands, *T. R.: The Last Romantic* (1997).

John D. Buenker, *Urban Liberalism and Progressive Reform* (1973).

David Mark Chalmers, *The Muckrake Years* (1980).

James Chace, *1912: Wilson, Roosevelt, Taft and Debs—the Election that Changed the Country* (2004).

Kendrick A. Clements, *The Presidency of Woodrow Wilson* (1992).

Michael L. Collins, *That Damned Cowboy: Theodore Roosevelt and the American West, 1883–1898* (1989).

John Milton Cooper Jr., *The Warrior and the Priest: Woodrow Wilson and Theodore Roosevelt* (1983).

Louis Filler, *Muckraking and Progressivism in the American Tradition* (rev. ed., 1996).

Lewis L. Gould, *Reform and Regulation: American Politics from Roosevelt to Wilson* (2nd ed., 1986).

Lewis L. Gould, *The Presidency of Theodore Roosevelt* (1991).

William H. Harbaugh, *The Life and Times of Theodore Roosevelt* (rev. ed., 1982).

Samuel P. Hays, *Conservation and the Gospel of Efficiency* (1959).

Matthew Frye Jacobson, *Barbarian Virtues: The United States Encounters Foreign Peoples at Home and Abroad, 1876–1917* (2000).

James Kloppenberg, *Uncertain Victory: Social Democracy and Progressivism in European and American Thought, 1870–1920* (1986).

Gabriel Kolko, *The Triumph of Conservatism* (1963).

William A. Link, *The Paradox of Southern Progressivism, 1880–1930* (1992).

Richard Coke Lower, *A Bloc of One: The Political Career of Hiram W. Johnson* (1993).

Richard L. McCormick, *From Realignment to Reform: Political Change in New York State* (1981).

Richard L. McCormick, *The Party Period and Public Policy* (1986).

Edmund Morris, *Theodore Rex* (2001).

Spencer Olin Jr., *California's Prodigal Sons: Hiram Johnson and the Progressives, 1911–1917* (1968).

Eric Rauchway, *Murdering McKinley: The Making of Theodore Roosevelt's America* (2003).

Emily S. Rosenberg, *Spreading the American Dream: American Economic and Cultural Expansion, 1890–1945* (1982).

Alan R. Sadovnik and Susan F. Semel, eds., *Founding Mothers and Others: Women Educational Leaders during the Progressive Era* (2002).

Judith Sealander, *Grand Plans: Business Progressivism and Social Change in Ohio's Miami Valley, 1890–1919* (1988).

Ted Steinberg, *Down to Earth: Nature's Role in American History* (2002).

Phillipa Strum, *Louis D. Brandeis* (1984).

David P. Thelen, *Robert M. La Follette and the Insurgent Spirit* (1985).

Nancy C. Unger, *Fighting Bob La Follette: The Righteous Reformer* (2000).

Michael A. Weatherson and Hal W. Bochin, *Hiram Johnson, Political Revivalist* (1995).

James Weinstein, *The Corporate Ideal in the Liberal State, 1900–1918* (1969).

Robert H. Wiebe, *The Search for Order, 1877–1920* (1967).

James Wright, *The Progressive Yankees* (1987).

Clarence E. Wunderlin Jr., *Visions of a New Industrial Order: Social Science and Labor Theory in America's Progressive Era* (1992).

James Harvey Young, *Securing the Federal Food and Drug Act of 1906* (1989).

Radical Alternatives

Mary Jo Buhl, *Women and American Socialism, 1870–1920* (1981).

Ellen Chesler, *Woman of Valor: Margaret Sanger and the Birth Control Movement in America* (1993).

Melvyn Dubofsky, *"Big Bill" Haywood* (1987).

Melvyn Dubofsky, *We Shall Be All: A History of the Industrial Workers of the World* (2nd ed., 1988).

Leslie Fishbein, *Rebels in Bohemia: The Radicals of the Masses, 1911–1917* (1982).

David J. Goldberg, *A Tale of Three Cities: Labor Organization and Protest in Paterson, Passaic, and Lawrence, 1916–1921* (1988).

Anthony Lukas, *Big Trouble: A Murder in a Small Western Town Sets Off a Struggle for the Soul of America* (1998).

Janice Jacqueline Miller, *Challenge from the Left: The Socialist Press and the Progressive Reform Movement, 1900–1917* (1989).

Bruno Ramirez, *When Workers Fight: The Politics of Industrial Relations in the Progressive Era, 1898–1916* (1978).

Salvatore Salerno, *Red November, Black November: Culture and Community in the Industrial Workers of the World* (1989).

Nick Salvatore, *Eugene V. Debs: Citizen and Socialist* (1982).

Ann Huber Tripp, *The IWW and the Paterson Silk Strike of 1913* (1987).

Alice Wexler, *Emma Goldman: An Intimate Life* (1984).

Race Relations and Woman Suffrage

Sara M. Evans, *Born for Liberty: A History of Women in America* (1989).

Kevin K. Gaines, *Uplifting the Race: Black Leadership, Politics, and Culture in the Twentieth Century* (1996).

Glenda Elizabeth Gilmore, *Gender and Jim Crow: Women and the Politics of White Supremacy in North Carolina, 1896–1920* (1996).

Louis R. Harlan, *Booker T. Washington: The Making of a Black Leader, 1856–1901* (1972).

Louis R. Harlan, *Booker T. Washington: The Wizard of Tuskegee, 1901–1915* (1983).

Evelyn Higginbotham, *Righteous Discontent: The Women's Movement in the Black Baptist Church, 1880–1920* (1993).

Charles F. Kellogg, *NAACP: A History of the National Association for the Advancement of Colored People, 1909–1920* (1967).

Jack Temple Kirby, *Darkness at the Dawning: Race and Reform in the Progressive South* (1972).

Elisabeth Lasch-Quinn, *Black Neighbors: Race and the Limits of Reform in the American Settlement House Movement, 1890–1945* (1993).

David Levering Lewis, *W. E. B. Du Bois: Biography of a Race, 1868–1919* (1993).

Alessandra Lorini, *Rituals of Race: American Public Culture and the Search for Racial Democracy* (1999).

Christine Lunardini, *From Equal Suffrage to Equal Rights: Alice Paul and the National Woman's Party, 1910–1928* (1986).

Neil R. McMillen, *Dark Journey: Black Mississippians in the Age of Jim Crow* (1989).

Joel Williamson, *The Crucible of Race* (1984).

GAS MASK

Prior to World War I, poison gas was considered uncivilized. But desperate fighting eroded old moral boundaries. On April 22, 1915, the Germans used poison gas for the first time in battle, and after that soldiers faced death by chemical weapons as well as by artillery, rifles, mortars, machine guns, hand grenades, tanks, airplanes, bayonets, and flamethrowers. The Allies condemned the German innovation as diabolic, but they quickly developed research programs of their own, and for the remainder of the fighting poison gas warfare increased. Gas caused a large number of casualties early on, but the growing use of improved gas masks meant deaths from gas declined sharply. Despite the crude appearance of this gas mask, filter respirators (using charcoal or antidote chemicals) proved highly effective. While some 50,300 American soldiers were killed in action during the war, fewer than 1,500 died from gas. But those who were gassed and survived were often disabled and likely to die young.

22

World War I: The Progressive Crusade at Home and Abroad

1914–1920

W HEN THE UNITED STATES entered World War I against Germany and its allies in 1917, it had neither a grand army nor a commander to lead one. But President Woodrow Wilson quickly tapped Major General John "Black Jack" Pershing, a ramrod-straight West Point graduate, to command the American Expeditionary Force (AEF) on the battlefields of France. Pershing had much to recommend him: He fought Apaches in the West in the 1880s, led a company of African American soldiers up San Juan Hill in 1898 (hence his nickname "Black Jack"), overcame fierce resistance in the Philippine jungles in the first decade of the twentieth century, and headed Wilson's Punitive Expedition into Mexico in 1916 and 1917 in pursuit of the revolutionary bandit Pancho Villa. Pershing's courage and resilience had been severely tested in 1915 when he suffered the irretrievable loss of his wife and three daughters in a fire at their home in San Francisco.

On June 13, 1917, Pershing and his officer corps arrived in France, where huge crowds shouted "Vive l'Amérique!" and greeted the Americans as saviors. Three years of savage warfare had bled France white and pushed the war-weary nation to the breaking point. But Pershing knew that it would be months before America's disorganized war effort succeeded in supplying a steady stream of "doughboys," as American troops would be called. Pershing, who was responsible for organizing, training, and supplying this inexperienced force that eventually numbered more than 2 million, sought to put his own stamp on the AEF. "The standards for the American Army will be those of West Point," he declared. "The upright bearing, attention to detail, uncomplaining obedience to instruction required of the cadet will be required of every officer and soldier of our armies in France." Hard and relentless, Pershing more than once chewed out an exhausted soldier for having mud on his boots and his collar unbuttoned.

Pershing found himself waging two wars, one against the Germans and the other against America's allies, as he constantly rebuffed French and British efforts to siphon off his soldiers into their badly depleted divisions on the front lines. Having seen too much of Europe's trench warfare, where enemies dug in, pounded one another with artillery, and squandered thousands of lives in hopeless assaults, Pershing insisted on keeping American soldiers under his own command. He believed that the Americans could break

- **Woodrow Wilson and the World**
  Taming the Americas
  The European Crisis
  The Ordeal of American Neutrality
  The United States Enters the War

- **Over There**
  The Call to Arms
  The War in France

- **The Crusade for Democracy at Home**
  The Progressive Stake in the War
  Women, War, and the Battle for Suffrage
  The Struggle over National Purpose

- **A Compromised Peace**
  Wilson's Fourteen Points
  The Paris Peace Conference
  The Fight for the Treaty

- **Democracy at Risk**
  Economic Hardship and Labor Upheaval
  The Red Scare
  The Great Migrations of African Americans and Mexicans
  Postwar Politics and the Election of 1920

- **Conclusion: Troubled Crusade**

Pershing Button

A steely-eyed and determined General John J. Pershing stares out at the viewer while surrounded by the flags of the Allied nations. The words circling the button declare that the Allies fight in the "cause of liberty," echoing President Woodrow Wilson's insistence that American democratic ideals were universal and could be achieved internationally through U.S. participation in the war.
Collection of Janice L. and David J. Frent.

the impasse by relying on the rifle and rapid movement tactics taught at West Point to create "open warfare," an American style of warfare. But as a disgusted British journalist observed, "After eight months . . . you haven't really fired a damned shot!"

By the summer of 1918, Americans had still seen only limited action, and when the Allied armies began preparing a massive attack against the Germans, Ferdinand Foch, head of the French army, rushed to Pershing's headquarters to "insist" once again that American troops merge with his decimated divisions. Pershing responded: "Marshal Foch, you may insist all you please, but . . . our army will fight . . . only as an independent American Army." Foch stormed out, and Pershing readied his army to strike at the German forces dug in at Saint-Mihiel and to begin what he was certain would be a victory march to Berlin. Assembling his officers, Pershing praised them for what they were about to do—break the stalemet of trench warfare. But American troops would be attacking fortifications the German army had spent years constructing. Indeed, American troops met a storm of machine-gun and artillery fire, and it took forty days and 100,000 casualties for the Americans to reach the German border, something Pershing had thought his soldiers could do in a few days. Nevertheless, fresh American troops helped destroy the German will to continue the war. In November 1918, Berlin asked for an immediate armistice, and the "Great War," as participants called the conflict, ended.

Pershing's stubborn effort to protect the autonomy of his army was only part of America's tortuous struggle to identify its interests in World War I and to maintain its national independence. When Wilson entered the White House, he believed that war was an affliction that modern diplomacy would eventually eradicate. He proclaimed America's absolute neutrality when war erupted in Europe in 1914. By standing apart, Wilson explained, America could offer "impartial mediation" and broker a healing peace. But trade and principle soon entangled the United States in Europe's troubles. When the nation was finally drawn into the war in 1917, Wilson sought to rescue America's grand purpose. Clinging to his battered ideals, he hoped that America's participation would uplift both the United States and the entire world.

At home, the war helped reformers finally achieve their goals of national prohibition and woman **suffrage**, but war also promoted a vicious attack on Americans' civil liberties. Hyperpatriotism meant intolerance, repression, and vigilante violence. Overseas, American troops under Pershing helped win the war in 1918, and in 1919 Wilson sailed for Europe to secure a just peace. Unable to dictate a settlement to the victors, Wilson accepted disappointing compromises. Upon his return to the United States he met a crushing defeat that marked the end of Wilsonian internationalism. Crackdowns on dissenters, immigrants, racial and ethnic minorities, and unions signaled the end of the **Progressive** Era at home.

Woodrow Wilson and the World

Shortly after winning election to the presidency in 1912, Woodrow Wilson confided to a friend: "It would be an irony of fate if my administration had to deal with foreign affairs." Indeed, Wilson had based his life and career on domestic concerns, seldom venturing far from home and traveling abroad only on brief vacations. As president of Princeton University and then governor of New Jersey, he had remained rooted in local affairs. In his campaign for the presidency, Wilson spoke passionately about domestic reform but hardly mentioned foreign affairs.

But Wilson could not avoid the world and the rising tide of militarism, **nationalism**, and violence that beat against American shores. America's own economic needs also compelled the nation outward. Moreover, Wilson was drawn abroad by his own progressive political principles. He believed that the United States had a moral duty to set an example in international affairs by championing national self-determination, peaceful free trade, and political **democracy**. "We have no selfish ends to serve," he proclaimed. "We desire no conquest, no dominion. . . . We are but one of the champions of the rights of mankind." Yet, as president Wilson revealed, he was as ready as any American president to apply military solutions to problems of foreign policy.

Taming the Americas

When he took office, Wilson sought to distinguish his foreign policy from that of his Republican predecessors. To Wilson, Theodore Roosevelt's "big stick" and William Howard Taft's "dollar diplomacy" appeared a crude flexing of military and economic muscle. To counter such arrogance, Wilson appointed William Jennings Bryan as secretary of state. A pacifist on religious grounds, Bryan immediately turned his attention to making agreements with thirty nations for the peaceful settlement of disputes.

But Wilson and Bryan, like Roosevelt and Taft, also believed that the **Monroe Doctrine** gave the United States special rights and responsibilities in the Western Hemisphere. Issued in 1823 to warn Europeans not to attempt to **colonize** the New World again, the doctrine had become a cloak for American domination. Wilson thus authorized the 1912 occupation of Nicaragua by U.S. marines to thwart a radical revolution that threatened American property. In 1915, he sent marines into Haiti to quell lawlessness and to protect American interests, and in 1916 he followed a similar course in the Dominican Republic. Almost everywhere in the Western Hemisphere, U.S. military intervention paved the way for the firm financial control of American banks and corporations. All the while, Wilson believed that American actions were promoting order and democracy. "I am going to teach the South American Republics to elect good men!" he declared. He did not mention protecting the Panama Canal and American investments (Map 22.1).

Wilson's most serious and controversial involvement in Latin America came in Mexico. Just weeks before Wilson was elected, General Victoriano Huerta seized power by violent means. Most European nations promptly recognized Huerta as the new Mexican president, but Wilson balked, declaring that he would not support a "government of butchers." In April 1914,

"Pancho" Villa and General Pershing
In 1914, Mexican revolutionary Francisco "Pancho" Villa (center) and American general John J. Pershing (right) posed genially as allies in the struggle to overthrow the dictatorial ruler of Mexico, Victoriano Huerta. Soon afterward, Villa and Pershing became adversaries. After Villa's raid across the New Mexico border in 1915 to punish Americans for aiding his revolutionary rivals, Pershing pursued Villa into Mexico.
© Bettmann/Corbis.

when Huerta refused to apologize for briefly detaining American sailors in Tampico, Wilson sent 800 marines to seize the port of Veracruz to prevent the unloading of a large shipment of arms for Huerta, who was by then involved in a civil war of his own. After brief resistance, Huerta fled to Spain, and the United States welcomed a more compliant government.

Wilson was not able to subdue Mexico that easily, however. A rebellion erupted among desperately poor farmers who believed that the new government, aided by American business interests, had betrayed the revolution's promise to help the common people. In January 1916, the rebel army, commanded by Francisco "Pancho" Villa, seized a train carrying gold to Texas from an American-owned mine deep within Mexico and killed the seventeen American engineers aboard. Another band of Villa's men crossed the border on March 9 for a predawn raid on

U.S. Intervention in Mexico, 1916–1917

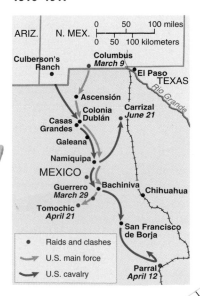

| | | 0   50   100 miles |
| | | 0 50 100 kilometers |
ARIZ. N. MEX.
Culberson's Ranch
Columbus *March 9*
El Paso
TEXAS
Ascensión
Colonia Dublán
Carrizal *June 21*
Casas Grandes
Galeana
Namiquipa
MEXICO
Guerrero *March 29*
Bachiniva
Chihuahua
Tomochic *April 21*
San Francisco de Borja
Parral *April 12*
Rio Grande

• Raids and clashes
→ U.S. main force
→ U.S. cavalry

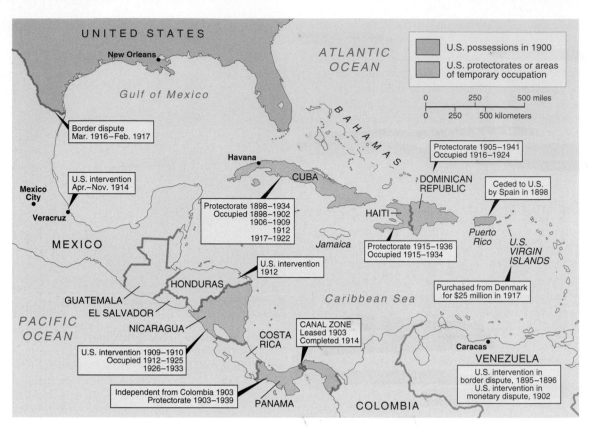

MAP 22.1   U.S. Involvement in Latin America and the Caribbean, 1895–1941
Victory against Spain in 1898 made Puerto Rico an American possession and Cuba a protectorate. The United States also gained control over the Panama Canal. The nation proved quick to protect expanding economic interests with military force by propping up friendly, though not necessarily democratic, governments.

Columbus, New Mexico, that cost several more lives and left the town in flames. (See "American Places," page 793.) Wilson promptly dispatched 12,000 troops, led by General John J. Pershing, who years earlier had chased the Apache chief Geronimo through the same Mexican desert. Unlike Geronimo, the wily Villa avoided capture, and in January 1917 Wilson recalled Pershing so that he might prepare the army for the possibility of fighting in the Great War.

The European Crisis

Before 1914, Europe had enjoyed decades of peace, but just beneath the surface lay the potentially destructive forces of nationalism and **imperialism**. The consolidation of the German and Italian states into unified nations and the similar ambition of Russia to create a "Pan-Slavic" union initiated new rivalries throughout Europe. As the conviction spread that colonial possessions were a mark of national greatness, competition expanded onto the world stage. Most ominously, Germany's efforts under Kaiser Wilhelm II to challenge Great Britain's world supremacy by creating an empire abroad, industrial muscle at home, and a mighty navy threatened the balance of power and thus the peace.

European nations sought to avoid an explosion with a complex web of military and diplomatic alliances. By 1914, Germany, Austria-Hungary, and Italy (the Triple Alliance) stood opposed to Great Britain, France, and Russia (the Triple Entente, also known as "the Allies"). But in their effort to prevent war through a balance of power, Europeans had actually magnified the possibility of large-scale conflict by creating trip wires along the boundaries of two heavily armed power blocs (Map 22.2). Treaties, some of them secret, obligated members of the alliances to come to the aid of another member if attacked.

The fatal sequence started in southeastern Europe, in the Balkans. On June 28, 1914, in the

AMERICAN PLACES

Pancho Villa State Park, Columbus, New Mexico

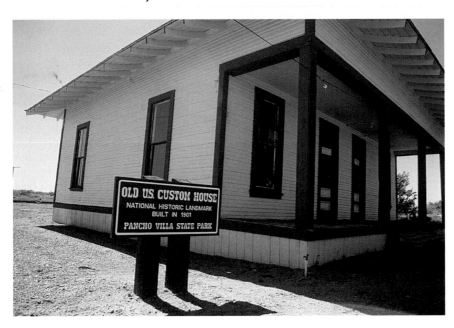

Old U.S. Custom House, Pancho Villa State Park
Courtesy of Pancho Villa State Park, New Mexico Energy, Minerals, and Natural Resources Department.

Before dawn on March 9, 1916, General Francisco "Pancho" Villa and some 400 to 500 troops ("Villistas") raced across the Mexican border on horseback and attacked the village and U.S. military camp at Columbus, New Mexico. At the time, Villa was locked in a fierce civil war in Mexico. Between 1913 and 1917, Woodrow Wilson meddled almost continuously in Mexican affairs, first supporting the wild revolutionary Villa, and then by 1916 Villa's chief rival,

the dignified Venustiano Carranza. Villa figured that his raid would draw U.S. troops across the border and that an American invasion of Mexico would weaken Carranza's claim to authority. The Villistas stayed in Columbus for less than two hours, but they burned much of the village and killed 18 Americans before disappearing into the vastness of the Mexican interior. Wilson took Villa's bait, and General "Black Jack" Pershing, who would later command American forces

in France during World War I, launched his fruitless eleven-month chase of Villa into Mexico.

Pancho Villa State Park in Columbus, New Mexico, sits in the Chihuahuan Desert just east of the Continental Divide, only three miles from the border with Mexico. Several buildings dating from the time of Villa's raid still stand in Columbus. The adobe Hoover Hotel was the site of some of the fiercest fighting. American troops set up a machine gun on the street in front of the hotel and both Villistas and U.S. citizens died fighting there. The Columbus railroad depot has been restored and today houses a private museum. Within the park, the old 1901 U.S. Customs House serves as the visitor center and contains exhibits describing the colorful histories of Pancho Villa, the Columbus raid of 1916, and Pershing's Punitive Expedition. Although Camp Furlong lies in ruins, visitors to Columbus can get a feel for the camp through the park's display of vehicles similar to those employed by Pershing and his men: a 1916 four-wheel-drive truck, a 1915 Jeffery Quad armored personnel carrier, and two Dodge touring cars—a 1916 model that was Pershing's choice for a personal staff car and a 1915 model that was sprayed by gunfire as one Columbus family fled the Villistas. The park also contains nature trails and a botanical garden with more than 30 kinds of cacti.

FOR WEB LINKS RELATED TO THIS SITE AND OTHER AMERICAN PLACES, see "PlaceLinks" at bedfordstmartins.com/roark.

Bosnian city of Sarajevo, a Bosnian Serb terrorist assassinated Archduke Franz Ferdinand, heir to the Austro-Hungarian throne. The next day, Austria declared war on Serbia, holding it accountable for the killing. The elaborate **alliance system** meant that the war could not

remain local. Russia announced that it would back the Serbs. Compelled to support Austria-Hungary, Germany on August 6 declared war on Russia and on France. In response, Great Britain, upholding its pact with France, declared war on Germany. Within weeks, Europe was engulfed in

MAP 22.2   European Alliances after the Outbreak of World War I
With Germany and the Austro-Hungarian Empire wedged between their Entente rivals, and all parties fully armed, Europe was poised for war when the Archduke Franz Ferdinand of Austria was assassinated in Sarajevo in July 1914.

war. The conflict became a world war when Japan, seeing an opportunity to rid itself of imperialist competition in China, joined the cause against Germany.

Recognizing that the war would devastate the civilization he knew, England's foreign secretary, Edward Grey, announced: "The lamps are going out all over Europe. We shall not see them lit again in our lifetime." Indeed, the evenly matched alliances would fight a long, exhausting, and bloody war lasting more than four years, at a cost of 8.5 million soldiers' lives—an entire generation of young men. A war that started with a solitary murder proved impossible to stop.

The Ordeal of American Neutrality

When news of the outbreak of war reached the United States, Woodrow Wilson announced that it was a European matter that had

> When news of the outbreak of war reached the United States, Woodrow Wilson announced that it was a European matter that had nothing to do with America.

nothing to do with America. "Again and ever," he declared, "I thank heaven for the Atlantic Ocean." Because the war engaged no vital American interest and involved no significant principle, Wilson said, the United States would remain neutral and continue normal relations with the warring nations. The United States had traditionally insisted on the broadest possible definition of neutral rights. In the American view, "free ships made free goods"—that is, neutral nations were entitled to trade freely with all nations at war, to send their ships safely through the open seas, and to demand the safe passage of their citizens on the merchant and passenger ships of all belligerents. More was involved than just this belief. In the year before Europe went to war, the American economy had started to slide into a recession that wartime disruption of European trade could drastically worsen.

Although Wilson proclaimed neutrality, his sympathies, like those of many Americans, lay with Great Britain and France. Americans shared with the English a language, a culture, and a commitment to **liberty**. Germany, in contrast, was a monarchy with strong militaristic traditions. The German ruler, Kaiser Wilhelm II, proved a cartoonist's dream. The British portrayed him as personally responsible for the war's atrocities, and before long American newspapers were labeling him "the Mad Dog of Europe" and "the Beast of Berlin." Still, Wilson insisted on neutrality, in part because he feared the conflict's effects on the United States as a nation of immigrants, millions of whom had only recently come from countries now at war. As he told the German ambassador, "We definitely have to be neutral, since otherwise our mixed populations would wage war on each other."

Great Britain was the first to test America's neutrality. Britain's powerful fleet controlled the seas and quickly set up a blockade of Germany. The United States vigorously protested, but Britain refused to give up its naval advantage. Although the blockade bruised American feelings, it had little economic impact on the United States. Between 1914 and the spring of 1917, while trade with Germany dwindled to the vanishing point, war-related exports to Britain—food, clothing, steel, and munitions—escalated by some 400 percent, enough to pull the American economy out of its prewar slump. Although the British blockade of German ports clearly violated American neutrality, the Wilson administration gradually and reluctantly acquiesced, thus beginning the fateful process of alienation from Germany.

Germany retaliated with a submarine blockade of British ports. This terrifying new form of combat by *Unterseebooten*, or U-boats, threatened traditional rules of war. Unlike surface warships that could harmlessly stop and search freighters and prevent them from entering a war zone, submarines relied on surprising and sinking their quarry. And once they sank a ship, the tiny, cramped U-boats could not possibly pick up any survivors. Britain portrayed the submarine as an outlaw weapon that violated notions of how a "civilized" nation should fight. Nevertheless, in February 1915, Germany announced that it intended to sink on sight enemy ships en route to the British Isles. On May 7, 1915, a German U-boat torpedoed the British passenger liner *Lusitania*, killing 1,198 passengers, 128 of them U.S. citizens.

The attack seemed to confirm what anti-German propaganda claimed: that the Germans

were by nature barbaric and uncivilized. American newspapers featured drawings of drowning women and children, and some editorials demanded war. Most Americans, however, did not want to break relations with Germany. Some pointed out that the German embassy had warned prospective passengers that the *Lusitania* carried millions of rounds of ammunition and so was a legitimate target. Secretary of State Bryan resisted the hysteria and declared that a ship carrying war materiel "should not rely on passengers to protect her from attack—it would be like putting women and children in front of an army." He argued that Wilson should instead warn American citizens that they traveled on ships of belligerent countries at their own risk.

Sinking of the *Lusitania*, 1915

Wilson sought a middle course that would retain his commitment to peace and neutrality without condoning German attacks on passenger ships. On May 10, he distanced himself from the proponents of American intervention by declaring that "there is such a thing as a man being too proud to fight," which caused former president Theodore Roosevelt, who urged war, to label him a "flub dub and mollycoddle." But Wilson also rejected Bryan's position. Any further destruction of ships, Wilson warned, would be regarded as "deliberately unfriendly" and might lead the United States to break diplomatic relations with Germany. Wilson essentially demanded that Germany abandon unrestricted submarine warfare. Rather than support the president, Bryan resigned, predicting that he had placed the United States on a colli-

Construction of a German U-boat

Even in drydock, this German submarine looks menacing. Deadly and stealthy, U-boats became known as "Assassins of the Seas." German submarines reached their peak of power in the summer of 1917, when nearly 150 patrolled the Atlantic, seeking both Allied warships and merchant vessels. But predator turned prey when the Allies developed SONAR (a kind of underwater radar), the depth-charge (a container filled with explosives that detonates deep under the sea), mines (used in the relatively confined English Channel), and the convoy system. One consequence of Allied advances against the menace of the U-boat was that the entire American Expeditionary Force arrived in Europe with the loss of only one ship.

Bibliothek fur Zeitgeschichte Stuttgart.

sion course with Germany. Wilson's replacement for Bryan was far from neutral. Two weeks after taking over the State Department, Robert Lansing announced that "the German Government is utterly hostile to all nations with democratic institutions." Because of Germany's "ambition for world dominance," it "must not be permitted to win this war or even to break even."

When Germany, anxious not to provoke the United States any further, apologized for the civilian deaths on the *Lusitania* and offered an indemnity, tensions momentarily subsided. After the sinking of the English steamer *Sussex* in 1916, at the cost of two more American lives, the German government quickly acted to head off war by promising no more submarine attacks without warning and without provisions for the safety of civilians. Observers celebrated the success of Wilson's middle-of-the-road strategy that steered a course between Roosevelt's aggressiveness and Bryan's pacificism.

Wilson's diplomacy proved helpful in his bid for reelection in 1916. Still, he was no shoo-in, for controversies over neutrality, intervention in Mexico, and the government's role in regulating the economy gave Wilson's able Republican opponent, Charles Evans Hughes—an associate justice of the Supreme Court and former governor of New York—a good chance. The Democratic Party ran Wilson under the slogan "He kept us out of war," but Wilson shied away from the claim, recognizing that any "little German lieutenant can push us into the war at any time by some calculated outrage." Ultimately, Wilson's case for neutrality appealed to the majority in favor of peace. Wilson won, but only by the razor-thin margins of 600,000 popular and 23 electoral votes.

The United States Enters the War

Step by step, the United States backed away from "absolute neutrality" and grew more forthrightly pro-Allied (that is, pro–Triple Entente). The consequence of protesting the German blockade of Great Britain but accepting the British blockade of Germany was that by 1916 the United States was supplying the Allies with 40 percent of their war material. When France and Britain ran short of money to pay for American goods and asked for loans, some Americans objected.

> Step by step, the United States backed away from "absolute neutrality" and grew more forthrightly pro-Allied.

Wilson himself argued that "Loans by American bankers to any foreign government which is at war are inconsistent with the true spirit of neutrality." But rather than jeopardize America's wartime prosperity, Wilson relaxed his objections, and billions of dollars in loans kept American goods flowing to Britain and France.

In January 1917, the German military high command persuaded the kaiser that the country could no longer afford to allow neutral shipping to reach Great Britain while the enemy blockade gradually starved Germany. The German government chose to resume unrestricted submarine warfare and sink without warning any ship, enemy and neutral, found in the waters off Great Britain. The German military understood that the decision would probably bring the United States into the war but gambled that the submarines would strangle the British economy and allow the kaiser's armies to win a military victory in France before American troops began arriving in Europe.

Theodore Roosevelt and most of Wilson's advisers demanded an immediate declaration of war, but Wilson continued to hope for a negotiated peace and only broke off diplomatic relations with Germany. Then on February 25, 1917, British authorities informed Wilson of a secret telegram sent by the German foreign secretary, Arthur Zimmermann, to the German minister in Mexico. It promised that in the event of war between Germany and the United States, Germany would see that Mexico regained its "lost provinces" of Texas, New Mexico, and Arizona if Mexico would declare war against the United States. Wilson angrily responded to the Zimmermann telegram by asking Congress to approve a policy of "armed neutrality" that would allow merchant ships to fight back against any attackers. Wilson stated privately that this wicked attempt to penetrate the Western Hemisphere finally convinced him that the war was, indeed, a defense of democracy against autocratic German aggression.

In March, German submarines sank five American vessels in the sea lanes to Britain, killing 66 Americans. After agonizing over the probable consequences, on April 2 the president asked Congress to issue a declaration of war. No longer too proud to fight, Wilson accused Germany of "warfare against all mankind." Still, he called for a "war without hate" and insisted that the destruction of Germany was not the goal of the United States. Rather, America fought to "vindicate the principles of peace and justice";

he promised that in a world made "safe for democracy," a reconstructed Germany would find its proper place. On April 6, 1917, by majorities of 373 to 50 in the House and 82 to 6 in the Senate, Congress voted to declare war.

Wilson did not overlook the tragic difference between those lofty aims and the brutal means chosen to achieve them. He spoke despairingly to a friend just prior to his appearance before Congress: "Once lead this people into war, and they'll forget there ever was such a thing as tolerance. To fight you must be brutal and ruthless, and the spirit of ruthless brutality will infect Congress, the courts, the policeman on the beat, the man in the street."

Over There

The American Expeditionary Force that eventually carried 2 million troops to Europe, by far the largest military venture the United States had ever undertaken on foreign soil, was trained to be morally upright as well as fiercely effective. Imbued with a sense of democratic mission, some doughboys found the adventure exhilarating and maintained their idealism to the end. The majority, however, saw little that was gallant in rats, lice, and poison gas, and—despite the progressives' hopes—little to elevate the human soul in a landscape of utter destruction and death.

"Men Wanted for the United States Army"

The exuberant soldiers swarming over this overloaded truck are so thrilled with their task of recruiting new men that they managed to display the flag backward. Their urgency reflects the fact that when America declared war in April 1917 its army numbered barely 120,000, roughly the size of the army of Chile. Unwilling to trust voluntary enlistments, Wilson's war message to Congress included an endorsement of "the principle of universal liability to service," in other words, a draft. Congress quickly obliged with a conscription bill, and within months, nearly 10 million American men had registered for the draft. When the war ended, 2 million men had volunteered for military service and 3 million had been drafted.

Brown Brothers.

The Call to Arms

When America entered the war, Britain and France were nearly exhausted after almost three years of conflict. Hundreds of thousands of soldiers had perished; morale and food supplies were dangerously low. One of the Allied powers, Russia, was in turmoil. In March 1917, a revolution had forced Czar Nicholas II to abdicate, and eight months later in a separate peace with Germany the Bolshevik revolutionary government removed Russia from the war. On May 18, 1917, to meet the demand for fighting men, Wilson signed a sweeping Selective Service Act, authorizing a **draft** of all young men into the armed forces. In contrast to the Civil War, this draft prohibited enlistment bounties and personal substitutes, while it sanctioned deferments on the basis of family responsibility. **Conscription** soon transformed a tiny volunteer armed force of 80,000 men, spread thinly around the United States and in outposts from the Caribbean to China, into a vast army and navy. Although almost 350,000 inductees either failed to report or claimed conscientious objector status, the draft boards eventually inducted 2.8 million men into the armed services, in addition to the 2 million who volunteered.

Progressives in the government were determined that the training camps that transformed raw recruits into fighting men would have the highest moral and civic purposes. Medical examinations, along with recently developed sociological and psychological testing, took the measure of American youth. The shocking news that almost 30 percent of those drafted were rejected on physical grounds acted as a stimulus to the public health and physical education movements. Secretary of War Newton D. Baker, whose outlook had been shaped by reform crusades as progressive mayor of Cleveland, created a Commission on Training Camp Activities staffed by YMCA workers and veterans of the settlement house and playground movements. The Military Draft Act of 1917 prohibited prostitution and alcohol near training camps. An army pamphlet asked soldiers to stop thinking about sex, explaining that a "man who is thinking below the belt is not efficient." Instead, military training included games, singing, and college extension courses. Baker de-

> The shocking news that almost 30 percent of those drafted were rejected on physical grounds acted as a stimulus to the public health and physical education movements.

scribed military camps as "national universities—training schools to which the flower of American youth is being sent" to provide them with an "invisible armor" of education, comradeship, and moral fitness.

Wilson's selection of Pershing to command the AEF recognized the need for hard professionalism in the leadership, not the sort of romantic patriotism that had given amateurs like Theodore Roosevelt the chance to command combat troops in the Spanish-American War. Pershing, described by one observer as "lean, clean, keen," gave progressives confidence that he would carry out his duties with the level-headed efficiency required of modern war on a vast scale. When Pershing and the wide-eyed troops of the AEF marched through Paris on the Fourth of July 1917, just a week after the first troopship landed, grateful French citizens showered them with flowers. At the statue of the hero who symbolized France's aid to the American Revolution, an officer stepped out and proclaimed in an inspired phrase that summed up the spirit of the occasion, "Lafayette, we are here!"

The War in France

At the front, the AEF discovered a desperate situation. The three-year-old war had degenerated into a stalemate of armies dug defensively into hundreds of miles of trenches across France. Huddling in the mud among the corpses and rats, soldiers were separated from the enemy by only a few hundred yards of "no-man's-land." When ordered "over the top," troops raced desperately toward the enemy's trenches, only to be entangled in barbed wire, enveloped in poison gas, and mowed down by machine guns. Commanders were slow to recognize the futility of their tactics even after the deadly standoff at the Battle of the Somme in 1916, the bloodiest battle of the war. After a three-day assault in which French and British forces lost 600,000 dead and wounded and the Germans 500,000, the Allies were able to advance their trenches only a few meaningless miles across devastated land.

Still, American troops hurried to France only to wait while Pershing assessed the situation, and they saw almost no combat in 1917. Instead, they continued to train and used much of their free time to explore places that most of them otherwise could never have hoped to see. True to the crusader image, American officials allowed only uplifting tourism. Paris temptations were off-limits, and French premier Georges Clemenceau's offer to supply American troops with licensed prostitutes was declined with the half-serious remark that if Wilson found out he would stop the war.

The sightseeing ended abruptly in March 1918. The Brest-Litovsk treaty signed that month by Germany and the Bolsheviks officially took Russia out of the war, and the Germans launched a massive offensive aimed at French ports on the Atlantic. After six thousand cannons let loose the heaviest barrage in history, a million German soldiers smashed a hole in the French and British lines at a cost of 250,000 casualties on each side. Paris became gripped by the greatest terror of the war when shells fired eighty miles away by "Big Bertha" cannons began falling on the city. Pershing, who believed the right moment for U.S. action had finally come, visited Foch to ask for the "great honor" of becoming "engaged in the greatest battle in history." Foch agreed to Pershing's terms of a separate American command and in May assigned a combined army and marine force to the central sector.

Once committed, the Americans remained true to their way of war. In May and June, at Cantigny and then at Château-Thierry, the eager but green Americans checked the German advance with a series of dashing assaults (Map 22.3). Then they headed toward the forest stronghold of Belleau Wood. The American force, with the Fifth and Sixth Marine Regiments in the lead, made its way against streams of refugees and retreating Allied soldiers who cried that the Germans had won: "La guerre est finie!" (The war is over!) A French officer commanded the marines to turn and retreat with them, but the American commander replied sharply, "Retreat, hell. We just got here." After charging through a wheat field against withering machine-gun fire, the marines plunged into a hand-to-hand forest battle of stalking and ambush. Victory came hard, but a German report praised the enemy's spirit, noting that "the Americans' nerves are not yet worn out." Indeed, it was German morale that was on the verge of cracking.

MAP 22.3   The American Expeditionary Force, 1918
In the last year of the war, the AEF joined the French army on the western front to counterattack the final German offensive and pursue the retreating enemy until surrender.

READING THE MAP: Across which rivers did the Germans advance in 1918? Where did the armistice line of November 11, 1918, lie in relation to the stabilized front of 1915–1917? Through which countries did the armistice line run?

CONNECTIONS: What events paved the way for the American Expeditionary Force to join the combat in 1918? What characteristic(s) differentiated American troops from other Allied forces and helped them achieve victory?

FOR MORE HELP ANALYZING THIS MAP, see the map activity for this chapter in the Online Study Guide at bedfordstmartins.com/roark.

In the summer of 1918, the Allies launched a massive counteroffensive that would end the war. A quarter of a million American troops joined in the rout of German forces along the Marne River. In September, more than a million Americans took part in the assault that threw the Germans back from positions along the Meuse River. By November, German survivors were

Life in the Trenches

These U.S. soldiers in a rat-infested trench either tensely look out for danger or slump in exhausted sleep. They offer a glimpse of the reality of the Great War, minus the noise, stench, and danger. This trench is dry for the moment, but with the rains came mud so deep that wounded men drowned in it. By the time American doughboys arrived in Europe, troops had faced one another for more than three years, burrowed into a double line of trenches, protected by barbed wire, machine gun nests, and mortars, backed by heavy artillery. Trenches with millions of inhabitants stretched from French ports on the English channel all the way to Switzerland. Nothing could make living in such holes anything better than miserable, but a decent shave with a Gillette safety razor, a pair of dry boots, and a set of checkers offered doughboys temporary relief. Inevitably, however, whistles would blow that ended the boredom, fatigue, and discomfort of trench life and sent soldiers "over the top," streaming toward enemy lines.

FOR MORE HELP ANALYZING THIS IMAGE, see the visual activity for this chapter in the Online Study Guide at bedfordstmartins.com/roark.

Photo: Imperial War Museum; shaving kit and boots: Collection of Colonel Stuart S. Corning Jr./Picture Research Consultants, Inc.

---

trudging northward. Soon, a revolt against the German government sent Kaiser Wilhelm II fleeing to Holland. On November 11, 1918, a delegation from the newly established German republic met with the French high command in a railroad car in Compiègne to sign an armistice that brought the fighting to an end.

The adventure of the AEF was brief, bloody, and victorious. When Germany had resumed unrestricted U-boat warfare in 1917, it was gambling that it could defeat Britain and France before the Americans could raise and train an army and ship it to France. The German military had miscalculated. Of the 2 million American troops in Europe, 1.3 million saw at least some action. By the end, 112,000 soldiers of the AEF had perished from wounds and disease. Another 230,000 Americans suffered casualties but survived, many of them with permanent physical and psychological disabilities. Poison gas accounted for almost 30 percent of all AEF casualties. Only the Civil War, which lasted much longer, had been more costly in American lives. European nations, however, suffered much greater losses: 2.2 million Germans, 1.9 million Russians, 1.4 million French, and 900,000 Britons. Where they had fought, the landscape was as blasted and barren as the moon.

The Crusade for Democracy at Home

Despite Wilson's fears that entering the war would lead to brutal intolerance at home, many progressives hoped that war would improve the quality of American life as well as free Europe from its bondage to tyranny and militarism. Progressive enthusiasm powered the mobilization of industrial and agricultural production behind the war effort. Moreover, labor shortages caused by workers entering the military provided new opportunities in the booming wartime economy. With labor at a premium, unionized workers gained higher pay and shorter hours. They were joined by women taking jobs formerly reserved for men. To instill loyalty in a public whose ancestry was rooted in all the belligerent nations, Wilson launched a campaign to foster patriotism. The campaign included the creation of a government agency to promote official propaganda, indoctrination in the schools, and parades, rallies, films, and other forms of patriotic expression. But with stimulation of patriotism also came suppression of dissent. When the government launched a harsh assault on civil liberties, mobs gained license to attack those whom they considered disloyal. Increasingly, the progressive ideals of rational progress and free expression took a beating as the nation undertook its crusade for democracy.

The Progressive Stake in the War

The idea of the war as an agent of social improvement fanned the old zeal of the progressive movement. The Wilson administration realized that Washington would have to assert greater control to mobilize the nation's human and physical resources. The nation's capital soon bristled with hastily created agencies charged with managing the war effort. Bernard Baruch headed the central planning authority, the War Industries Board (WIB), created to stimulate and direct industrial production. At once a wealthy southern gentleman, a Jewish Wall Street stockbroker, and a reform Democrat, Baruch could speak to many constituencies. Shrewdly, he brought industrial management and labor together into a team that produced everything from boots to bullets and made American troops the best equipped soldiers in the world.

Herbert Hoover, a self-made millionaire engineer, headed the Food Administration.

Sober and tireless, he led remarkably successful "Hooverizing" campaigns for "meatless" Mondays and "wheatless" Wednesdays and other means of conserving resources. Guaranteed high prices, the American heartland not only supplied the needs of U.S. citizens and armed forces but also became the breadbasket of America's allies. Even the First Family, including Wilson's second wife, Edith Galt, did its part with a White House "victory garden" and sheep put to graze on the White House lawn in the absence of the gardeners, who had moved on to new work in the war effort.

Other wartime agencies abounded: The Railroad Administration directed railroad traffic, the Fuel Administration coordinated the coal industry and other fuel suppliers, the Shipping Board organized the merchant marine, and the National War Labor Policies Board resolved labor disputes. Their successes gave progressives reason to believe that the Wilson administration would mediate between business and government and encourage harmony in the public interest. Buoyed by these developments, influential voices like those of philosopher-educator John Dewey and journalist-critic Walter Lippmann cheered the war as a means of promoting progressive reform. Some progressives, however, stubbornly refused to accept the argument that war and reform marched together. Wisconsin senator Robert La Follette kept up a steady drumbeat of opposition to the war and claimed that Wilson's promises of peace and democracy were a case of "the blind leading the blind," at home and abroad.

Industrial leaders were encouraged that, in achieving feats of production and efficiency, wartime agencies helped corporate profits triple. Some working people also had cause to celebrate. Mobilization meant high prices for farmers and plentiful jobs in the new war industries (Figure 22.1). Aware that increased industrial production required peaceful labor relations and the avoidance of strikes, the National War Labor Policies Board and other agencies enacted the eight-hour day, a living minimum wage, and **collective bargaining** rights in some industries that had long resisted them. Wages rose sharply during the war (as did prices), and the American Federation of Labor (AFL) saw its membership soar from 2.7 million to more than 5 million.

> The idea of the war as an agent of social improvement fanned the old zeal of the progressive movement.

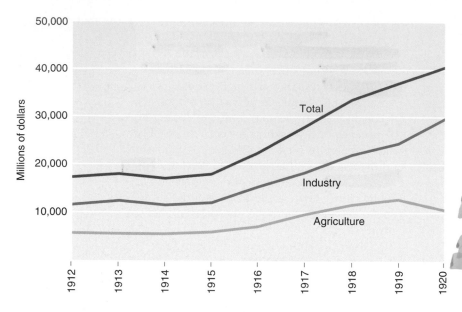

Agriculture: cash receipts.
Industry: includes mining, electric power, manufacturing, construction, and communications.

FIGURE 22.1 Industrial Wages, 1912–1920
With help from unions and progressive reformers, wage workers gradually improved their economic condition. The entry of millions of young men into the armed forces caused labor shortages and led to a rapid surge in wages.

After long insisting that health was a private matter, Congress bowed to the patriotic cause of providing death and disability insurance for the armed forces.

The war also provided a huge boost to the stalled moral crusade to ban alcohol. Before the war, prohibitionists had campaigned to ban the manufacture and sale of alcoholic beverages, and by 1917, nineteen states had gone dry. Liquor's opponents could now cite the war as a reason for national prohibition, for banning alcohol would make the cause of democracy powerful and pure. At the same time, shutting down the distilleries would save millions of bushels of grain that could feed the United States and its allies. "Shall the many have food or the few drink?" the drys asked. Prohibitionists added a patriotic twist by arguing that closing breweries with German names like Schlitz, Pabst, and Anheuser-Busch would deal a blow to the kaiser and the German cause. Swept along by these arguments, Congress in December 1917 passed the Eighteenth Amendment, which banned the manufacture, transportation, and sale of alcohol; after swift ratification by the states, the amendment went into effect on January 1, 1920.

Women, War, and the Battle for Suffrage

Women had made real strides during the Progressive Era, but war presented new opportunities. When Theodore Roosevelt told young men that the war was the "Great Adventure" of the age, young women listened too. More than 25,000 women served in France. About half were nurses; the others drove ambulances, ran canteens for the Red Cross and YMCA, worked with French civilians in devastated areas, and acted as war correspondents. Like men, women struggled against disillusionment and depression. One

U.S. Army Medical Corps Contract Surgeon's Uniform
Before the war ended, some 25,000 American women made it to France, all as volunteers. Ex-president Theodore Roosevelt proclaimed war the "Great Adventure," and some women were eager to share in it. About half became nurses, where as one said, they dealt with "a sea of stretchers, a human carpet." Women also drove ambulances, acted as social workers, and ran canteens for the Red Cross and the YMCA. One YMCA worker, Mary Baldwin, hoped that a few hours in her canteen would "make life, and even death, easier 'out there.'" A handful of female physicians worked as contract surgeons for the U.S. army. Dr. Loy McAfee wore this uniform in France.
National Museum of American History, Smithsonian Institution, Washington, D.C.

woman explained: "Over in America, we thought we knew something about the war . . . but when you get here the difference is [like the one between] studying the laws of electricity and being struck by lightning."

At home, long-standing barriers against hiring women fell when millions of working men became soldiers and few new immigrant workers made it across the Atlantic. The new Women's Bureau of the Department of Labor along with the Women's Trade Union League (WTUL) helped open jobs to women, often against the opposition of the major trade organization, the AFL. For the first time, tens of thousands of women found work with the railroads and in defense plants as welders, metalworkers, and heavy machine operators, jobs traditionally reserved for men. Between 1910 and 1920, the number of women clerks doubled. Before the war ended, more than a million women found work in war industries. "This is the women's age," exaggerated Margaret Dreier Robins, president of the WTUL. "At last . . . women are coming into the labor and festival of life on equal terms with men."

The most dramatic advance for women came in the political arena. Since the Seneca Falls convention of 1848, where women voiced their first formal demand for the ballot, the struggle for woman suffrage had inched forward. Adopting a state-by-state approach, suffragists had achieved some success in the West; but by 1910, only four small western states had adopted woman suffrage (Map 22.4). Elsewhere, voting rights for women met strong hostility and defeat. After 1910, suffrage leaders added a federal campaign to amend the Constitution to the traditional state-by-state strategy for suffrage. Their powerful and well-organized federal campaign targeted Congress and the president.

The radical wing of the suffragists, led by the indomitable Alice Paul, picketed the White House, where they unfurled banners that proclaimed: "America Is Not a Democracy. Twenty Million Women Are Denied the Right to Vote." They chained themselves to fences and went to jail, where many engaged in hunger strikes. "They seem bent on making their cause as obnoxious as possible," Woodrow Wilson declared. His wife, Edith, detested the idea of "masculinized" voting women. But membership in the mainstream organization, the National American Woman Suffrage Association, led by Carrie

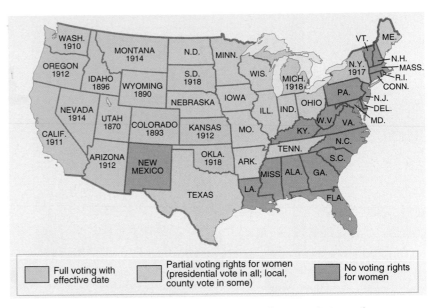

MAP 22.4   Women's Voting Rights before the Nineteenth Amendment
The long campaign for women's voting rights reversed the pioneer epic that ran from east to west. Suffrage rolled eastward from its first successes in the new democratic West toward the entrenched, male-dominated public life of the Northeast and the South.

READING THE MAP: What was the first state to grant woman suffrage? How many states extended full voting rights to women before the World War I years (1914–1918)? During World War I?

CONNECTIONS: Suffragists redirected their focus during World War I. What strategies did they use during the war? In which states was the struggle for woman suffrage fiercest, and why?

FOR MORE HELP ANALYZING THIS MAP, see the map activity for this chapter in the Online Study Guide at bedfordstmartins.com/roark.

Chapman Catt, soared to some 2 million members. NAWSA even accepted African American women in its ranks, although not on an equal basis. Seeing the handwriting on the wall, the Republican and Progressive parties endorsed woman suffrage in time for the 1916 election.

In 1918, Wilson gave his support to suffrage, calling the amendment "vital to the winning of the war." He praised women's wartime contributions and conceded that it would be wrong not to reward the "partnership of suffering and sacrifice" with a "partnership of privilege and right." By linking the drive for a constitutional amendment to the wartime emphasis on national unity, the advocates of woman suffrage finally triumphed. In 1919, Congress passed the Nineteenth Amendment, granting women the vote, and by August 18, 1920, it was ratified by the required

> By linking the drive for a constitutional amendment to the wartime emphasis on national unity, the advocates of woman suffrage finally triumphed.

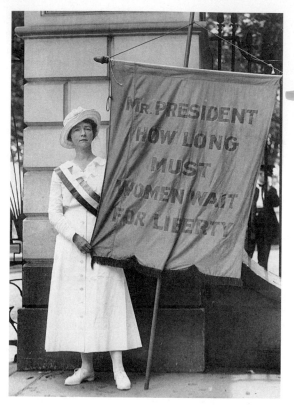

Picketing the White House for the Vote
Here Mrs. William L. Colt pickets Woodrow Wilson's home to demand women's right to vote. Because of such direct pressure and in recognition of women's service in the defense industry at home and in France as nurses and Red Cross workers, Wilson finally pledged support for the suffrage amendment. A gentleman from the old school, he believed women could tame men's aggressive tendencies, and he hoped that women's moderating influence would help make the Great War the war to end all wars.
© Bettmann/Corbis.

two-thirds of the states. As Carrie Chapman Catt later recalled, "to get that word, male, out of the Constitution, cost the women of the country fifty-two years of campaigning." But rather than woman suffrage being the end of the long road to women's full equality, as some suffragists contended, it proved to be only the beginning.

The Struggle over National Purpose

When Congress finally committed the nation to war, most peace advocates rallied around the flag. Several business and civic leaders who had been antiwar created the League to Enforce Peace in support of Wilson's insistence that military force had become the only means to peaceful ends. In a similar shift in view, the Carnegie Endowment for International Peace adopted new stationery with the heading "Peace through Victory" and issued a resolution saying that "the most effectual means of promoting peace is to prosecute the war against the Imperial German Government."

Only a handful of reformers resisted the tide of conversion from pacifism to patriotism. Soon after the guns began booming in 1914, a group of professional women, led by settlement house leader Jane Addams and economics professor Emily Greene Balch, denounced what Addams described as "the pathetic belief in the regenerative results of war." The Women's Peace Party that emerged in 1915 and its foreign affiliates in the Women's International League for Peace and Freedom (WILPF) led the struggle to persuade governments to negotiate peace and spare dissenters from harsh punishment. It proved to be discouraging, unpopular work, and after America entered the conflict, advocates for peace were routinely labeled cowards and traitors, their efforts crushed by the steamroller of conformity.

Wilson's major strategy for fending off criticism of the war was to stir up patriotic fervor. In 1917, the president created the Committee on Public Information (CPI) under the direction of George Creel, a muckraking journalist who thumped for the war like a cheerleader at the big game. He sent "Four-Minute Men," a squad of 75,000 volunteers, around the country to give brief pep talks and distribute millions of press releases that described successes on the battlefields and in the factories. (See "Documenting the American Promise," page 806.) Everywhere, posters, pamphlets, and cartoons depicted brave American soldiers and sailors defending freedom and democracy against the "evil Hun." (The derogatory nickname "Hun" was often applied to Germans, particularly German soldiers, during both world wars.)

America turned out to help Creel's campaign. The film industry cranked out reels of melodrama about battle-line and home-front heroes and induced audiences to hiss at the German kaiser. A musical, *The Kaiser: The Beast of Berlin*, opened on Broadway in 1918. Colleges and universities generated war propaganda in the guise of scholarship, and some added courses depicting the war as a culmination of the age-old struggle for civilization. When Professor James McKeen Cattell of Columbia University in New York urged that America should seek peace with Germany short of victory, university president Nicholas Murray Butler fired him on the grounds that "what had been folly is now treason."

A firestorm of anti-German passion swept the nation. Campaigns with the slogan "100% American" enlisted ordinary people to sniff out disloyalty. German, the most widely taught foreign language in 1914, practically disappeared from the high school and college curriculum. Anger mounted against German-born Americans, including Karl Muck, conductor of the Boston Symphony Orchestra, and the renowned violinist Fritz Kreisler, who were driven from the concert stage. *The Saturday Evening Post,* one of America's most popular magazines, declared that it was time to rid the country of "the scum of the melting pot." The rabid attempt to

D. W. Griffith's *Hearts of the World*

Hollywood joined in the government's efforts to work up war rage against the "brutal Huns," as Germans were often called. In a film made for the British and French governments by America's leading filmmaker, D. W. Griffith, a hulking German is about to whip a defenseless farm woman (Lillian Gish, one of the nation's favorite stars) innocently carrying potatoes from a field. When the film premiered in Washington, D.C., in 1918, Mrs. Woodrow Wilson wrote Griffith pleading with him to cut or soften the violent whipping scene. Her plea was one of the few acts coming from the nation's capital that sought to moderate the hate campaign.

Library of Congress.

punish Germans reached its extreme with the lynching of Robert Prager, a baker in Collinsville, Illinois. In the atmosphere of mob rule, it was enough that Prager was German-born and had **socialist** leanings, even though he had not opposed American participation in the war. Persuaded by the defense lawyer who praised what he called a "patriotic murder," the jury at the trial of the killers took only twenty-five minutes to acquit.

As hysteria increased, absurdity mingled with cruelty. In Montana, a school board barred a history text that had good things to say about medieval Germany. Menus across the nation changed German toast to French toast and sauerkraut to liberty cabbage. In Milwaukee, vigilantes mounted a machine gun outside the Pabst Theater to prevent the staging of Schiller's *Wilhelm Tell,* a powerful protest against tyranny. One vigilant citizen claimed to see a periscope in the Great Lakes, and the fiancée of one of the war's leading critics, caught dancing on the dunes of Cape Cod, was held on suspicion of signaling to German submarines.

The Wilson administration's zeal in suppressing dissent contrasted sharply with its war aims of defending democracy. Undermining the First Amendment, in the name of self-defense, the Espionage Act (June 1917), the Trading with the Enemy Act (October 1917), and the Sedition Act (May 1918) gave the government sweeping powers to punish any opinion or activity it considered "disloyal, profane, scurrilous, or abusive" to the American flag or uniform. When Postmaster General Albert Burleson blocked mailing privileges for publications he considered disloyal, a number of independent-minded journals were forced to close down, including the leading literary magazine *Seven Arts.* Of the fifteen hundred individuals eventually charged with sedition, all but a dozen had merely spoken words the government found objectionable. One of them was Eugene V. Debs, the leader of the Socialist Party, who was convicted under the Espionage Act for speeches condemning the war as a capitalist plot and sent to the Atlanta penitentiary.

The president hoped that national commitment to the war would subdue partisan politics. He could not legitimately repress his Republican rivals, however, and they found many opportunities to use the war as a weapon against the Democrats. The trick was to oppose Wilson's conduct of the war but not the war itself. For example, Republicans outshouted Wilson on the

For and Against World War I

World War I became a battle-ground of loyalties as well as of guns. Through the Committee on Public Information (CPI), the Wilson administration developed the art of propaganda far beyond anything known before. The CPI promoted the war by organizing rallies and parades, blanketing the country with posters and cartoons, publishing a daily official bulletin, and mobilizing 75,000 volunteers to give speeches to hometown audiences. Only a few conscientious objectors, socialists, and disillusioned idealists were left to argue that war could not produce democracy but would instead destroy many lives and perhaps cherished values of progress and reform as well.

DOCUMENT 1
A "Four-Minute Man" Speech

The Committee on Public Information recruited volunteers in local communities to carry the official version of the war directly to their neighbors. Called "Four-Minute Men" because their speeches were supposed to last only four minutes, these enthusiasts spoke from carefully crafted scripts. The following example indicates how the speakers encouraged audiences to buy war bonds by rousing their indignation against the Germans.

While we are sitting here tonight enjoying a picture show, do you realize that thousands and thousands of Belgians, people just like ourselves, are languishing in slavery under Prussian masters? . . .

Prussian "Schrecklichkeit" (the deliberate policy of terrorism) leads to almost unbelievable besotten brutality. The German soldiers—their letters are reprinted—were often forced against their wills, they themselves weeping, to carry out unspeakable orders against defenseless old men, women, and children, so that "respect" might grow for German "efficiency." For instance, at Dinant the wives and children of 40 men were forced to witness the execution of their husbands and fathers.

Now, then, do you want to take the slightest chance of meeting Prussianism here in America?

If not, then you'll have to help in summoning all the resources of this country for the giant struggle. For resources will win the war.

Here's the way you can help save our resources. Instead of throwing money away on unnecessary things, buy Thrift Stamps, 25 cents, and War-Savings-Stamps, $4.12, worth $5 in five years, 4 percent compound interest. They're good as government money; like a mortgage on the U.S.A.

SOURCE: James R. Mock and Cedric Larson, excerpt (pp. 123–24) from *Words That Won the War.* Copyright © 1939 by Princeton University Press. Reprinted with permission of Princeton University Press. All rights reserved.

DOCUMENT 2
John S. P. Tatlock, "Why America Fights Germany," 1918

To influence public opinion, the War Department enlisted journalists and professors to write a series of "war information pamphlets." In the following example, history professor John S. P. Tatlock of Stanford University describes the sort of invasion that could be expected if the German hordes were not checked.

Now let us picture what a sudden invasion of the United States by these Germans would mean; sudden, because their settled way is always to attack suddenly. First they set themselves to capture New York City. While their fleet blockades the harbor and shells the city and the forts from far at sea, their troops land somewhere near and advance toward the city in order to cut its rail communications, starve it into surrender and then plunder it. One body of from 50,000 to 100,000 men lands, let us suppose, at Barnegat Bay, New Jersey, and advances without meeting resistance, for the brave but small American army is scattered elsewhere. They pass through Lakewood, a station on the Central Railroad of New Jersey. They first demand wine for the officers and beer for the men. Angered to find that an American town does not contain large quantities of either, they pillage and burn the post office and most of the hotels and stores. Then they demand $1,000,000 from the residents. One feeble old woman tries to conceal $20 which she has been hoarding in her desk drawer; she is taken out and hanged (to save a cartridge). Some of the teachers in two district schools meet a fate which makes them envy her. The Catholic priest and Methodist minister are thrown into a pig-sty, while the German soldiers look on and laugh. Some of the officers quarter themselves in a handsome house on the edge of the town, insult the ladies of the family, and destroy and defile the contents of the house. By this time some of the soldiers have managed to get drunk . . .

and then hell breaks loose. Robbery, murder and outrage run riot. Fifty leading citizens are lined up against the First National Bank building, and shot. Most of the town and the beautiful pinewoods are burned, and then the troops move on to treat New Brunswick in the same way—if they get there.

This is not just a snappy story. It is not fancy. The general plan of campaign against America has been announced repeatedly by German military men. And every horrible detail is just what the German troops have done in Belgium and France.

SOURCE: John S. P. Tatlock, "Why America Fights Germany," War Information Series pamphlet no. 15, War Department, 1918.

DOCUMENT 3
Jane Addams,
Address at Carnegie Hall,
New York City, July 9, 1915

True to her belief in reason, not force, the leader of the settlement house movement, Jane Addams, helped form the Women's Peace Party in 1915. Soon afterward, she participated in the Hague Conference of Women in Holland and then, with a group of the delegates, visited the capitals of six warring nations to urge the leaders of those countries to seek peaceful resolution of the conflict. In this address to a New York City audience, Addams spoke about the conclusions she had drawn from her tour of Europe.

The first thing which was striking is this, that the same causes and reasons for the war were heard everywhere. Each warring nation solemnly assured you it is fighting under the impulse of self-defense. . . .

In each of the warring nations there is this other point of similarity.

Generally speaking, we heard everywhere that this war was an old man's war; that the young men who were dying, the young men who were doing the fighting, were not the men who wanted the war, and were not the men who believed in the war; that somewhere in church and state, somewhere in the high places of society, the elderly people, the middle-aged people, had established themselves and had convinced themselves that this was a righteous war. . . .

I quote a letter published in the *Cambridge Magazine* at Cambridge University and written by a young man who had gone to the front. . . .

". . . Just when the younger generation was beginning to take its share in the affairs of the world, and was hoping to counteract the Victorian influences of the older generation, this war has come to silence us,—permanently or temporarily as the case may be. Meanwhile, the old men are having field days on their own. In our name, and for our sakes as they pathetically imagine, they are doing their very utmost, it would seem, to perpetuate, by their appeals to hate, intolerance and revenge, those very follies which have produced the present conflagration." . . .

It seemed to me . . . that the older men believed more in abstractions, shall I say; that when they talked of patriotism, when they used certain theological or nationalistic words, these meant more to them than they did to the young men; that the young men had come to take life much more from the point of view of experience . . . and when they went to the trenches and tested it out, they concluded that it did not pay, that it was not what they wanted to do with their lives.

Perhaps the most shocking impression left upon one's mind is this, that in the various countries the tem-

per necessary for continuing the war is worked up and fed largely by the things which have occurred in the war itself. . . .

Let us say that there are two groups of boys in a boys' club, and I have much experience of that sort in boys' clubs to draw upon. If one says, "We did this because the other fellows did that," you will simply have to say, "I won't go into the rights and wrongs of this, but this thing must stop, because it leads nowhere and gets nowhere." . . .

. . . And what it needs, it seems to me, and to many of us, is a certain touch of human nature. . . . When you find that you can't talk to a woman on any subject, however remote from the war, without finding at once that she is in the deepest perplexity,—that while she is carrying herself bravely and going on with her accustomed activities because she thinks thereby that she is serving her country, her heart is being torn all the time,—it is borne in upon you that at last human nature must revolt. . . . Then men must see the horrible things which have happened; they will have to soberly count up the loss of life, and the debt they have settled upon themselves for years to come.

SOURCE: Jane Addams, "The Revolt against War," *Survey*, July 17, 1915.

DOCUMENT 4
Diary of an Anonymous
American Soldier, 1918

Encouraged by civilian and military officials to make their crusade in Europe an enlightening experience, many soldiers recorded their impressions in diaries and letters. In the case of one anonymous

(continued)

soldier, the task became so absorbing that it eventually found its way into print as Wine, Women, and War: A Diary of Disillusionment *(1926). As time in combat dragged on, the diarist changed his tone and looked critically at war aims and their probable outcome.*

25 August 1918: Base Hospital at Neuilly. Has the Lord ordained that from hideous mangling of flesh beautiful things should come? . . . Can't evade it—there is sublimity in war. Man made in mold of divinity, and more than a flavor of his origin still clinging to his soul. The cheer of these lads, their quiet grave resignation, too beautiful for marring touch of praise. . . .

One comes away from this eddy of human wreckage, a little sick at heart. But one presently forgets the bodies shattered, the faces marred, the freshness of lives become stale and useless, and remembers only that "God fulfills himself in many ways." The singular evangelism of blood. . . .

18 October 1918: Three hundredth day from Hoboken! Damned cold. Shivering, fingers numb as lead, and not even November yet. . . . Race between Kaiser and my pants still on. Vital interest in early termination of conflict! Each day another seam opens or another button drops from fatigue—and can't keep pants up by merely gritting teeth. Each morning,

scan communiques first—then breeches. Strain beginning to tell.

After the war problems of readjustment, hitherto kept in background, going to make all sorts of trouble. League of Nations, not mere imaginative sentimental Utopia, but only practicable solution of world in chaos. . . . The real victors in this war will be determined 10 or 20 years afterwards, and they will be the nation who will be the best able to face the growing discontent of a disillusioned people, to ward off impending famine, and to save their people from the appalling consequences of the universal bankruptcy to which Europe is speeding every day with increasing pace.

Vast amount of nonsense about Germany. Silly idea of demanding huge indemnities, and in same breath refusing to allow access to raw material, i.e., ask tree to give fruit, but shut off sun and air. . . . Either slaughter entire Teutonic race, or take them back and try to make something of them. No middle ground. No sense hating Germans. Only proper object for hate, to anyone with brains God gave little snails, is an idea. And can't destroy ideas, or crush them, or punish them. Can only substitute good ideas for bad ones.

This life hard on illusions. Not many left. A hell of a way from best

of all possible worlds, and man certainly a son-of-a-bitch when he puts his mind to it. But hope not to travel too far along road on which so many realists stub their silly toes, of believing there is no angel worth mentioning in poor, complex human heart. Heaven and hell both there.

SOURCE: Anonymous, *Wine, Women, and War: A Diary of Disillusionment* (New York, 1926).

QUESTIONS FOR ANALYSIS AND DEBATE

1. What did the Committee on Public Information mean by "Prussianism"? In what ways did the committee suppose it might be present in American life?

2. How likely were Americans to be convinced by Professor Tatlock's warning of a German invasion? What estimate does Tatlock seem to be making of the general awareness and intelligence of the American public?

3. How plausible is Jane Addams's contention that war is the disastrous result of old men's abstractions that are later refuted by young men's experience?

4. Does the anonymous diarist become more at peace with the world, or less, as a result of his war experience? Why?

---

nation's need to mobilize for war but then complained that Wilson's War Industries Board was a tyrannical agency that crushed free enterprise. Such attacks appealed to widely diverse business, labor, and patriotic groups. As the war progressed, Republicans gathered power against the coalition of Democrats and progressives that had narrowly reelected Wilson in 1916.

Wilson erred when he attempted to make the off-year congressional elections of 1918 a referendum on his leadership. Instead, amid criti-

cism of the White House for playing politics with the war, Republicans gained a narrow majority in both House and Senate. The end of Democratic control of Congress not only suspended any possibility of further domestic reform but also meant that the United States would advance toward military victory with authority divided between a Democratic presidency and a Republican Congress likely to contest Wilson's plans for international cooperation.

A Compromised Peace

Wilson decided to reaffirm his noble war ideals by announcing his peace aims before the end of hostilities was in sight. He hoped the victorious Allies would rally around his generous ideas, but he soon discovered that his plan for international democracy did not receive eager acceptance. The leaders of England, France, and Italy understood that Wilson's principles jeopardized their own postwar plans for the acquisition of enemy territory, new colonial empires, and reparations. He also faced strong opposition at home from those who feared that his ardor for international cooperation would undermine American sovereignty.

Wilson's Fourteen Points

On January 8, 1918, nine months after the United States entered the war, President Wilson delivered a speech to Congress that revealed his vision of a liberal peace. Wilson's Fourteen Points provided a blueprint for a new democratic world order. The first five points affirmed basic liberal ideals: "open covenants of peace, openly arrived at," that is, an end to secret treaties; freedom of the seas in war and peace; removal of economic barriers to free trade; reduction of weapons of war; and recognition of the rights of colonized peoples. The next eight points supported the right to self-determination of European peoples who had been dominated by Germany or its allies. Wilson's final point called for a "general association of nations"—a League of Nations—to provide "mutual guarantees of political independence and territorial integrity to great and small states alike." The insistence on a League of Nations reflected Wilson's lifelong dream of a "parliament of man." Only such an organization, he believed, could justify the war and secure a lasting peace. Wilson concluded his speech by pledging that the United States would welcome Germany into the family of "peace-loving nations" if it would renounce its militarism and imperialism.

The Fourteen Points roused popular enthusiasm in the United States and every Allied country. Armed with such public support, Wilson felt confident that he could prevail against undemocratic forces at the peace table. During the final year of the war, he pressured the Allies to accept the Fourteen Points as the basis of the settlement. If necessary, Wilson was willing to speak over the heads of government leaders directly to the people and so expand his role as spokesman for American citizens to the champion of all the world's people. The Allies had won the war; Wilson would win the peace.

The Paris Peace Conference

From January 18 to June 28, 1919, the eyes of the world focused on Paris. There, powerful men wrestled with difficult problems. Inspired by his sense of mission, Wilson decided to attend the peace conference in person, as head of the U.S. delegation. No other American president had ever gone to Europe while in office, but Wilson believed he owed it to the American soldiers. "It is now my duty," he announced, "to play my full part in making good what they gave their life's blood to obtain." A dubious British diplomat retorted that Wilson was drawn to Paris "as a debutante is entranced by the prospect of her first ball." The decision to leave the country at a time when his political opponents were sharply contesting his leadership was risky enough, but his stubborn refusal to include prominent Republicans in the delegation proved foolhardy and eventually cost him his dream of a new world order with America at its center.

The peace venture began well. Huge crowds cheered the American president's motorcade on its way to Paris. After four terrible years of war, Europeans looked on Wilson as someone who would create a safer, more decent world. However, when the conference convened at Louis XIV's magnificent palace at Versailles, Wilson encountered a very different reception. Representing the Allies were the decidedly unidealistic David Lloyd George of Britain, Georges Clemenceau of France, and Vittorio Orlando of Italy. To the Allied leaders, Wilson was a naive and impractical moralist whose desire to reconcile former foes within a new international democratic order showed how little he understood hard European realities. The French premier claimed that Wilson "believed you could do everything by formulas" and "empty theory." Disparaging the Fourteen Points, he added, "God himself was con-

> Wilson's Fourteen Points provided a blueprint for a new democratic world order.

> To the Allied leaders, Wilson was a naive and impractical moralist whose desire to reconcile former foes within a new international democratic order showed how little he understood hard European realities.

Leaders of the Paris Peace Conference
The three leaders in charge of putting the world back together after the Great War—from left to right, David Lloyd George, prime minister of Great Britain; Georges Clemenceau, premier of France; and U.S. president Woodrow Wilson—amiably and confidently stride toward the peace conference at the palace of Versailles. Clemenceau is caught offering animated instruction to Wilson, whom he considered naively idealistic. Indeed, in an unguarded moment, Clemenceau expressed his contempt for the entire United States as a country that was unique in having passed directly from barbarism to decadence without an intervening period of civilization. Walking silently alongside, Lloyd George maintains the poker face that helped keep his views carefully guarded throughout the conference.
Gamma Liaison.

tent with ten commandments." The Allies wanted to fasten blame for the war on Germany, totally disarm it, and make it pay so dearly that it would never threaten its neighbors again. The French demanded retribution in the form of territory containing some of Germany's richest mineral resources. And the British made it clear that they were not about to give up the powerful weapon of naval blockade for the vague principle of the freedom of the seas.

Wilson was forced to make drastic compromises. In return for French moderation of territorial claims, he agreed to support Article 231 of the peace treaty, assigning war guilt to Germany. Though saved from permanently losing Rhineland territory to the French, Germany was outraged at being singled out as the instigator of the war and saddled with more than $33 billion in damages. Many Germans felt that their nation had been betrayed. After agreeing to an armistice on the belief that peace terms would be based on Wilson's generous Fourteen Points, they faced hardship and humiliation instead.

Wilson had better success in establishing the principle of self-determination. But from the beginning, he had been vague about what self-determination actually meant. "When I gave utterance to those words," he admitted, "I said them without the knowledge that nationalities existed, which are coming to us day after day." Secretary of State Robert Lansing knew that the "phrase is simply loaded with dynamite." Lansing wondered, "What unit has he in mind? Does he mean a race, a territorial area, or a community?" Lansing believed that the notion of self-determination "will raise hopes which can never be realized. It will, I fear, cost thousands of lives. In the end it is bound to be discredited, to be called the dream of an idealist who failed to realize the danger until it was too late."

Yet on the basis of self-determination, the conference redrew the map of Europe and parts of the rest of the world. Portions of the Austro-Hungarian Empire were ceded to Italy, Poland, and Romania, and the remainder was reassembled into Austria, Hungary, Czechoslovakia, and Yugoslavia—independent republics with boundaries determined according to concentrations of ethnic groups. More arbitrarily, the Ottoman Empire was carved up into small mandates (including Palestine) run by local leaders but under the control of France and Great Britain. The conference reserved the mandate system for those regions it deemed insufficiently "civilized" or advanced to have full independence. Thus, with varying degrees of danger from ethnic and nationalist rivalries, each reconstructed nation faced the challenge of making a new democratic government work (Map 22.5). Many of today's bitterest disputes—in the Balkans and Iraq, between Greece and Turkey, between Arabs and Jews—have roots in the decisions made in Paris in 1919.

Wilson hoped that self-determination would also be the fate of Germany's colonies in Asia and Africa. But the Allies who had taken over the colonies during the war would go no further than allowing the League of Nations a mandate to administer them. Technically, the mandate system rejected imperialism, but in reality it was an attempt to avoid outright imperialism while

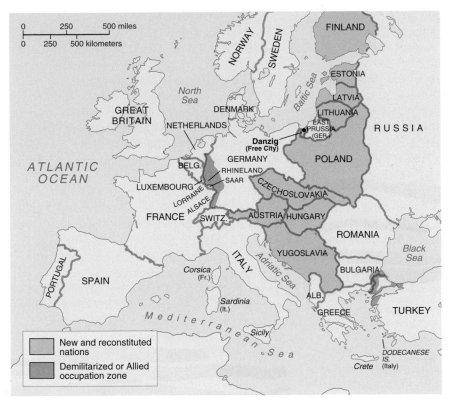

MAP 22.5   Europe after World War I
The post–World War I settlement redrew boundaries to create new nations based on ethnic groupings. This left within defeated Germany and Russia bitter peoples who resolved to recover territory that the new arrangements took from their homelands.

still allowing Europeans to maintain control. While denying Germany its colonies, the Allies retained their own colonial empires.

The cause of democratic equality suffered another setback when the peace conference refused to endorse Japan's proposal for a clause in the treaty proclaiming the principle of racial equality. Wilson's belief in the superiority of whites, as well as his apprehension about how white Americans would respond to such a declaration, led him to oppose the clause. To soothe hurt feelings, Wilson agreed to grant Japan a mandate over the Shantung Peninsula in northern China, which had formerly been controlled by Germany. The gesture mollified Japan's moderate leaders, but the military faction preparing to take over the country used bitterness toward racist Western colonialism to build support for expanding Japanese power throughout Asia.

The issue that was closest to Wilson's heart was finding a new way of managing international relations, an idea sketched out in his Fourteen Points. In Wilson's view, war had finally discredited the old strategy of balance of power. Instead, he proposed a League of Nations that would provide **collective security** and order. The League would establish rules of international conduct and resolve conflicts between

nations through rational and peaceful means. When the Allies agreed to the League, Wilson was overjoyed. He believed that the League would rectify the errors his colleagues had forced on him in Paris. The League would solidify and extend the noble work he had begun.

To many Europeans and Americans whose hopes had been stirred by Wilson's lofty aims, the Versailles treaty came as a bitter disappointment. Wilson's admirers were shocked that the president dealt in compromise like any other politician. But without Wilson's presence, the treaty that was signed on June 28, 1919, surely would have been more vindictive. Wilson returned home in July 1919 consoled that, despite his many frustrations, he had gained what he most wanted—creation of the League of Nations. In Wilson's judgment, "We have completed in the least time possible the greatest work that four men have ever done."

The Fight for the Treaty

The tumultuous reception Wilson received when he arrived home persuaded him, probably correctly, that the American people supported the treaty. On July 10, 1919, the president submitted the treaty to the Senate, warning that failure to ratify it would "break the heart of the world." By then, however, criticism of the treaty was mounting, especially from Americans convinced that their countries of ethnic origin had not been given fair treatment. Irish Americans, Italian Americans, and German Americans launched especially sharp attacks. Even Wilson's supporters worried that the president's concessions at Versailles had jeopardized the treaty's capacity to provide a generous plan for rebuilding Europe and to guarantee world peace.

Some of the most potent critics were found in the Senate. Bolstered by a slight Republican majority in Congress, a group of Republican "irreconcilables," which included such powerful **isolationist** senators as Hiram Johnson of California and William Borah of Idaho, con-

demned the treaty for entangling the United States in world affairs. A larger group of Republicans did not object to American participation in world politics but feared that membership in the League of Nations would jeopardize the nation's independence. No Republican, in any case, was eager to hand Wilson and the Democrats a foreign policy victory with the 1920 presidential election little more than a year away.

At the center of Republican opposition was Wilson's archenemy, Senator Henry Cabot Lodge of Massachusetts. Lodge's hostility was in part purely personal. "I never thought I could hate a man as much as I hate Wilson," he once admitted. But in addition to seeking Wilson's personal humiliation and defeat, Lodge raised cogent objections to the treaty and the League. Lodge was no isolationist, but he thought that too much of the Fourteen Points was a "general bleat about virtue being better than vice." Like his friend Theodore Roosevelt, who died in January 1919, Lodge expected the United States's economic might and strong army and navy to propel the nation into a major role in world affairs. But he insisted that membership in the League of Nations, which would require collective action to maintain peace, threatened the nation's freedom of choice in foreign relations.

To undermine public support for Wilson, Lodge used his position as chairman of the Senate Foreign Relations Committee to air every sort of complaint. Out of the committee hearings came several amendments, or "reservations," that sought to limit the consequences of American membership in the League. For example, several reservations required approval of both House and Senate before the United States could participate in League-sponsored economic sanctions or military action.

Eventually, it became clear that ratification of the treaty depended on acceptance of the Lodge reservations. Democratic senators, who overwhelmingly supported the treaty, urged Wilson to accept Lodge's terms, arguing that they left the essentials of the treaty intact. Wilson, however, insisted that the reservations cut "the very heart out of the treaty." He expressed personal hatred as well. "*Lodge* reservations?" he thundered. "Never! I'll never consent to adopt any policy with which that impossible name is so prominently identified."

With the treaty about to be reported from the Foreign Relations Committee to the full Senate with reservations attached, Wilson decided to take his case directly to the people. On

Pro-League Poster

Woodrow Wilson's faith in international cooperation through the League of Nations struck a chord among a majority of Americans. To them, the League represented an extension of progressivism's conviction that humans could achieve democracy, human rights, and peace through just and effective government. In this poster announcing a rally to support the League, the victorious international community employs the League to lock up German militarism and end the threat of world war.

By Special Permission of Manuscripts Division, University of Minnesota Libraries, Minneapolis.

September 3, 1919, he set out by train on the most ambitious speaking tour ever undertaken by a president. Already exhausted by the peace conference and further debilitated by his fight with Lodge, Wilson went despite the objections of his doctors. He enjoyed some early success, but on September 25 in Pueblo, Colorado, Wilson collapsed and had to return to Washington. There he suffered a massive stroke that partially paralyzed him. From his bedroom, Wilson sent messages through his wife and cabinet instructing Democrats in the Senate to hold firm against any and all reservations. If the Senate approved the treaty with reservations, he said, he would not sign it. In the end, Wilson commanded enough loyalty to ensure a vote against the Lodge reservations. But when the treaty without reservations came before the Senate in March 1920, the combined opposition of the Republican irreconcilables and Republican reservationists left Wilson six votes short of the two-thirds majority needed for passage.

The nations of Europe went about organizing the League of Nations at Geneva, Switzerland, but the United States never became a member. Whether American membership could have prevented the world war that began in Europe in 1939 is highly unlikely, but America's failure to join certainly weakened the League from the start. In refusing to accept relatively minor compromises with Senate moderates, Wilson lost his treaty and American membership in the League. Would the Europeans have accepted reservations by the Americans? Lloyd George claimed later that they had always expected that they might have to. Brought low by their feud, Woodrow Wilson and Henry Cabot Lodge both died in 1924, never seeing international order or security, never knowing the whirlwind of resentment and violence that would eventually follow the Great War's failure to make the world safe for democracy.

Democracy at Risk

The defeat of Wilson's idealistic hopes for international democracy was the crowning blow to those progressives who had hoped that the war could serve as a vehicle for reform at home. The reaction that followed included an urge to demobilize swiftly. In the process, servicemen, defense workers, and farmers lost their war-related jobs and much of their economic security. The combination of displaced veterans returning home, a stalled economy, and leftover wartime patriotism looking for a new cause was so volatile that it could hardly fail to explode. Wartime anti-German passion was quickly succeeded by antiradicalism, a fevered campaign broad enough to ensnare unionists, socialists, dissenters, and African Americans and Mexicans who had committed no offense but to seek to escape rural poverty.

> Wartime anti-German passion was quickly succeeded by antiradicalism, a fevered campaign broad enough to ensnare unionists, socialists, dissenters, African Americans, and Mexicans.

Economic Hardship and Labor Upheaval

With the armistice came an urgent desire to return the United States to a peacetime economy. In response, the government abruptly abandoned its wartime controls on the economy and almost overnight canceled millions of dollars in orders for war materiel. In a matter of months, more than three million soldiers were mustered out of the military with only $60 and a one-way ticket home. When war production ceased and veterans flooded the job market, unemployment rose sharply. At the same time, consumers went on a postwar spending spree and inflation soared. In 1919, prices rose an astonishing 75 percent over prewar levels, and in 1920, though inflation slowed, prices rose another 28 percent.

Most of the gains workers had made during the war evaporated. Freed from wartime control, business turned against the eight-hour day and attacked labor unions. Workers fought back rather than sitting back and watching inflation eat up their paychecks and bosses destroy their unions. The year 1919 witnessed nearly 3,600 strikes involving 4 million workers. The most spectacular strike occurred in February 1919 in Seattle, where shipyard workers had been put out of work by demobilization. When a coalition of the radical International Workers of the World (IWW) and the moderate American Federation of Labor (AFL) called a general strike, the largest work stoppage in American history shut down the city. Newspapers across the nation echoed claims in the *Seattle Times* that the walkout was "a Bolshevik effort to start a revolution" engineered by "Seattle labor criminals." An effort to deport strike leaders failed because they were citizens, not aliens, but the suppression of the strike by Seattle's anti-union mayor, Ole Hanson, cost the AFL much of the support it had gained during the war and contributed to the destruction of the IWW soon afterward.

A strike by Boston policemen in the fall of 1919 brought out postwar hostility toward labor militancy in the public sector. Though they were paid less than pick-and-shovel laborers and had received no raise since before the war, the police won little sympathy. Once the officers stopped walking their beats, looters sacked the city. After two days of near anarchy only slightly tamed by a volunteer police force of Harvard students and recently discharged soldiers, Massachusetts governor Calvin Coolidge called in the National Guard to restore order. The public, yearning for peace and security in the wake of war, welcomed Coolidge's anti-union assurance that "there is no

"The Warrior's Return"

About 16,000 Native Americans served in the U.S. armed forces during World War I. This magazine cover offers a romanticized reconstruction of one homecoming. The young soldier, still in uniform and presumably fresh from France, rides his painted pony to the tepee of his parents, where they proudly welcome the brave warrior. Their tepee even has a star, a national symbol that families with sons in the military displayed on their homes. The painting sought to demonstrate that all Americans, even those on the margins of national life, were sufficiently assimilated and loyal to join the national sacrifice to defeat the enemy.

Picture Research Consultants & Archives.

right to strike against the public safety by anybody, anywhere, any time."

Labor strife climaxed in the grim steel strike of 1919. Steelworkers had serious grievances, but for decades the industry had succeeded in beating back all their efforts to unionize. In 1919, however, the AFL, still led by its founding father, Samuel Gompers, decided it was time to try again. It had little choice given the industry's plan to revert to seven-day weeks, twelve-hour days, and weekly wages of about $20. Having loyally backed the government's war effort, the AFL expected federal support for unionization. When Gompers began to recruit union members, however, he learned that he faced the steel barons alone. Following the refusal of U.S. Steel and Bethlehem Steel to negotiate, Gompers called for a strike; 350,000 workers in fifteen states walked out in September 1919. The steel industry hired 30,000 strikebreakers (many of them African Americans) and convinced the public that the strikers were radicals bent on subverting the Republic. State and federal troops protected scabs who crossed picket lines. In January 1920, after eighteen striking workers had been killed, the strike collapsed. That devastating defeat initiated a sharp decline in the fortunes of the labor movement, a trend that would continue for almost twenty years.

The Red Scare

Suppression of labor strikes was one manifestation of a general fear of internal subversion that swept the nation in 1919. The "Red scare" (red refers to the color of the Bolshevik flag), which far outstripped the assault on civil liberties during the war, had homegrown causes: the postwar recession, labor unrest, and the difficulties of reintegrating millions of returning veterans. But unsettling events abroad also added to Americans' anxieties. Russian bolshevism became even more menacing in March 1919 when the new Soviet leaders created the Comintern, a worldwide association of Communist leaders intent on fomenting revolution in capitalist countries. (See "Beyond America's Borders," page 816.) A Communist revolution in the United States was extremely unlikely, but a flurry of isolated terrorist acts in 1919, most notably thirty-eight bombs mailed to prominent Americans, convinced edgy Americans that revolutionaries were at the door. Fear, anger, and uncertainty led swiftly to a hunt for terrorists. Arguing that "there could be no nice distinctions

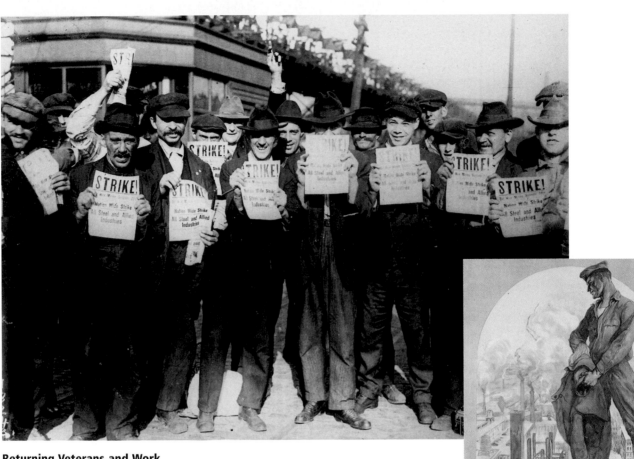

Returning Veterans and Work

After the triumphal parades ended, attention turned to the question of what the heroes would do at home. The Department of Labor poster tries to convey a strong image of purposefulness and prosperity by portraying a soldier in front of a booming industrial landscape. The U.S. Employment Service had little to offer veterans beyond posters, however, and unions were unprepared to cope with the massive numbers of former soldiers who needed retraining. As workplace conditions deteriorated, the largest number of strikes in the nation's history broke out in 1919.

Library of Congress; © Bettmann/Corbis.

After the Welcome Home–
a JOB!
U.S. EMPLOYMENT SERVICE *Dep't of Labor*

drawn between the theoretical ideals of the radicals and their actual violations of our national laws," Attorney General A. Mitchell Palmer led an assault on alleged conspirators. Targeting men and women who harbored what Palmer considered ideas that could lead to violence, even though they may not have done anything illegal, the Justice Department sought to purge the supposed enemies of America.

In January 1920, Palmer ordered a series of raids that netted 6,000 alleged subversives. Though the revolutionary conspiracies he expected to uncover did not turn up, and the three pistols he confiscated did not amount to an armory, Palmer nevertheless ordered 500 noncitizen suspects deported. His action came in the midst of a campaign against the most notorious radical alien, Russian-born Emma Goldman. Before the war, Goldman's passionate support of labor strikes, women's rights, and birth control had made her a leading symbol of outspoken disrespect for mainstream opinion. Finally, after a stay in prison for attacking military conscription, she was ordered deported by the fervent young director of the Radical Division of the Justice Department, J. Edgar Hoover. In December 1919, as Goldman and 250 others boarded a ship for exile in Russia, the defiant

Bolshevism

One month before Woodrow Wilson asked Congress for a declaration of war against Germany, revolutionary forces in Russia overthrew Czar Nicolas II and installed a democratic government. The March 1917 revolution removed the last despot among the Allies fighting Germany and bolstered Wilson's confidence that the war really was a clear-cut fight between "democracy and autocracy." The American president embraced the revolution, declaring that Russia "is a fit partner for a league of honour."

In November 1917, however, Russia experienced a second revolution. Marxist radicals calling themselves Bolsheviks seized control and made their leader, Vladimir Ilyich Lenin, ruler of Russia, which after 1922 was known as the Soviet Union. Lenin scoffed at the idea that the Allies were fighting for democracy and insisted that greedy capitalists were waging war for international dominance. In March 1918, Lenin shocked Wilson and the Allies when Russia signed a separate peace with Germany and withdrew from the war. The Allies, still locked in a desperate struggle with Germany, cried betrayal and feared that vast numbers of German soldiers fighting on the eastern front would turn to confront exhausted Allied troops on the western front.

Britain and France, prodded by British leader Winston Churchill who declared that "the Bolshevik infant should be strangled in its cradle,"

urged the United States to join them in sending troops to Russia where they would support Russian democrats against the new revolutionary socialist regime. Wilson hesitated before committing troops to a civil war in Russia. He told his trusted advisor, Colonel House, "I've been sweating blood over the question of what is right and feasible to do in Russia." Several prominent Americans spoke out against American intervention. Senator William Borah of Idaho declared: "The Russian people have the same right to establish a Socialist state as we have to establish a republic." But Wilson concluded that the Bolsheviks were a dictatorial party that came to power through a violent coup that denied Russians political choice. Moreover, if anti-Bolshevik forces succeeded, Wilson figured, they might bring Russia back into the war against Germany. By September 1918, on the pretext of helping 60,000 trapped Czechoslovakians return to the West to fight the Germans, Wilson had ordered 14,000 American troops to Russia to join British and French forces there. When the Allies defeated Germany in November 1918, the continued presence of Western troops in Russia could no longer be defended as part of the war with Germany. Clearly, American, British, and French troops were fighting to overthrow Lenin and annul the Bolshevik Revolution. But the Bolsheviks (who by this time called themselves Communists) prevailed,

and American troops withdrew from Russia in June 1919, after the loss of more than 200 American lives.

The Bolshevik regime dedicated itself not only to ending capitalism in Russia but also to overthrowing capitalist and imperialist regimes everywhere. Clearly, Lenin's imagined future jeopardized Wilson's proposed liberal new world order. Wilson withheld diplomatic recognition from the Soviet Union (a policy that persisted until 1934) and joined the Allies in an economic boycott to bring down the Bolshevik government. Unbowed, Lenin promised that his party would "incite rebellion among all the peoples now oppressed," and revolutionary agitation became central to Soviet foreign policy. Communist revolutions erupted in Bavaria and Hungary following the end of World War I. Although short-lived, the Communist regimes sent shock waves throughout the West. In 1919, moreover, a Russian official claimed that monies sent to Europe to foment rebellion were "nothing compared to the funds transmitted to New York for the purpose of spreading bolshevism in the United States." American attention shifted from revolutionaries in Europe to revolutionaries at home. The Red scare was on.

Having failed to make the world "safe for democracy," the Wilson administration set out to make democracy safe in America. Attorney General A. Mitchell Palmer perceived a "blaze of Revolution sweeping over every American institution of law and order . . . licking the altars of churches . . . crawling into the sacred corners of American homes." The government launched an all-out attack on the Communist ("Red") menace (see page 814). But rather than looking on the Bolshevik success as monstrous, a few Americans saw Russia as the world's best hope, especially after the Versailles treaty shattered Wilson's grand plans for the peace. Some traveled to Russia and wrote rapturously about the society that promised economic and social justice and the end of the exploitation of workers by capitalist bosses.

Nevertheless, the vast majority of Americans were no more drawn to communism than to czarism. When disgruntled socialists founded the American Communist Party in 1919, the new party attracted only a handful of members. And they spent most of their time arguing the fine points of doctrine, not manufacturing bombs. But in 1919, a few radicals did resort to bombs. "Bolshevism means chaos, wholesale murder, the complete destruction of civilization," one observer declared, and the nation responded by bullying and terrorizing even mild dissenters. Workers seeking better wages and conditions, women and African Americans demanding equal rights, and others who pushed for change found the government hurling the epithet "Red" at anyone who opposed the status quo. Beatings, jailings, and deportation often followed. But with the sailing of the "Soviet Ark" that deported Emma Goldman and other radicals out of the country on December 21, 1919, the hysteria subsided.

The Bolshevik Revolution in Russia had endless consequences. It initiated a brutal reign of terror in the Soviet Union that lasted more than seven decades. It also set up a polarity in international politics that lasted nearly as long. In a very real sense, the cold war that set the United States and the Soviet Union at each others' throats after World War Two began in 1917. America's abortive military intervention against the

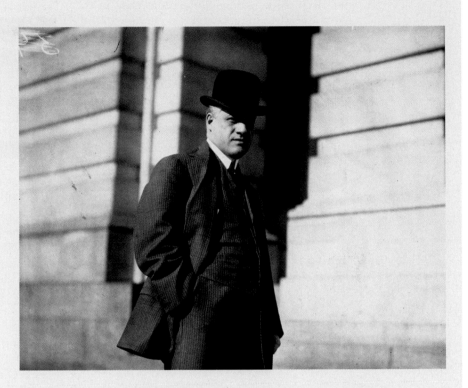

Attorney General A. Mitchell Palmer
On January 2, 1920, Attorney General A. Mitchell Palmer ordered hundreds of federal agents to 33 American cities to smash the alleged Bolshevik conspiracy. Led by J. Edgar Hoover, the agents arrested more than 6,000 individuals on charges of plotting to overthrow the government. Palmer revealed much more about himself than about those arrested when he said, "Out of the sly and crafty eyes of many of them leap cupidity, cruelty, insanity, and crime; from their lopsided faces, sloping brows, and misshapen features may be recognized the unmistakable criminal type."
Library of Congress.

Bolshevik regime and the Bolsheviks' call for worldwide revolution convulsed relations from the very beginning. In the United States, the Red scare's rabid antiradicalism did significant damage to American values. Commitment to the protection of dissent succumbed to irrational anticommunism. Even mild reform became tarred with the brush of Bolshevism. Although the Red scare withered as quickly as it sprouted, the habit of crushing dissent in the name of security lived on. Years later, when Americans' anxiety mounted and confidence waned once again,

witch hunts against radicalism would again haunt American democracy.

BIBLIOGRAPHY

Peter G. Boyle, *American-Soviet Relations: From the Russian Revolution to the Fall of Communism* (1993).

Gordon A. Craig, *Europe since 1815* (1961).

Thomas Fleming, *The Illusion of Victory: America in World War I* (2003).

John Gaddis, *Russia, the Soviet Union, and the United States* (1978).

N. Gordon Levin Jr., *Woodrow Wilson and World Politics: America's Response to War and Revolution* (1968).

Ted Morgan, *Reds: McCarthyism in Twentieth-Century America* (2004).

rebel turned on the gangplank to thumb her nose at a jeering crowd and disappeared onto the deck. Anticipating timid conformity in the next decade, one observer remarked, "With Prohibition coming in and Emma Goldman goin' out, 'twill be a dull country."

The effort to rid the country of alien radicals was matched by efforts to crush troublesome citizens. Law enforcement officials and vigilante groups joined hands in several cities and towns to rid themselves of so-called Reds. On Armistice Day, November 11, 1919, events reached their grimmest in Centralia, Washington, a rugged lumber town home to one of only two IWW halls left in the state. Intimidated by a menacing crowd gathered in front of the hall, nervous IWW members opened fire, killing three people. Three IWW members were arrested and later convicted of murder, but another, an ex-soldier, was carried off by a mob who castrated him and then, after hanging him from a bridge, riddled his body with bullets. His death was officially ruled a suicide.

Public institutions joined the attack on civil liberties. Local libraries removed dissenting books. Schools and colleges fired unorthodox teachers. Police shut down radical newspapers. State legislatures refused to seat elected representatives who professed socialist ideas, and in 1919, Congress removed its lone socialist representative, Victor Berger, on the grounds that he was a threat to national safety. That same year, the Supreme Court provided a formula for restricting free speech. In upholding the conviction of socialist Charles Schenck for publishing a pamphlet urging resistance to the draft during wartime (*Schenck v. United States*), Justice Oliver Wendell Holmes, writing for the Court, established a "clear and present danger" test. Such utterances as Schenck's during a time of national peril, Holmes wrote, were equivalent to shouting "Fire!" in a crowded theater. But Schenck's pamphlet spoke softly in the open air, not in a crowded theater, and had little power to provoke a public firmly opposed to its message.

In time, the Red scare lost credibility. The lack of any real radical menace became clear after newspaper headlines carried Attorney General Palmer's warning that radicals were planning to celebrate the Bolshevik Revolution with a nationwide wave of violence on May 1, 1920. Officials responded by calling out state militia, fortifying public buildings and churches, mobilizing bomb squads, even placing machine-gun nests at major city intersections. When May 1 came and went without a single disturbance, the public mood turned from fear to scorn. The Red scare collapsed in its excesses.

The Great Migrations of African Americans and Mexicans

Before the Red scare lost steam, the government raised alarms about the loyalty of African Americans. A Justice Department investigation concluded that Reds were fomenting racial unrest among blacks. While the report was wrong about Bolshevik influence, it was correct in identifying a new stirring among African Americans, a new assertiveness borne of participation in the war effort and in a massive migration out of the South.

In 1900, nine of every ten blacks still lived in the South, where disfranchisement, segregation, and violence dominated their lives. Thirty-five years after **emancipation**, African Americans had made little progress toward full citizenship. The majority of black men continued to toil in agriculture as dirt-poor tenants or sharecroppers, or they worked for wages of sixty cents a day. Black women worked in the homes of

Emma Goldman Is Deported

In the fall of 1919, federal agents arrested hundreds of "Bolsheviks" they considered a "menace to law and order." On December 6, 1919, anarchist Emma Goldman, seen here hiding her face, was escorted to detention on Ellis Island, which had welcomed millions of immigrants over the years. Two weeks later, Goldman and 248 others were put on the aging troopship *Buford* and deported to Soviet Russia. Some of this crowd (and much of America) was happy to see "Red Emma" and her friends sent, as the State Department said, "whence they came."
© Bettmann / Corbis.

If You are a Stranger in the City

If you want a job   If you want a place to live
If you are having trouble with your employer
If you want information or advice of any kind
CALL UPON

The CHICAGO LEAGUE ON URBAN
CONDITIONS AMONG NEGROES
3719 South State Street

Telephone Douglas 9098   T. ARNOLD HILL, Executive Secretary

No charges—no fees. We want to help YOU

SELF-HELP

1. Do not loaf. Get a job at once.
2. Do not live in crowded rooms. Others can be obtained.
3. Do not carry on loud conversations in street cars and public places.
4. Do not keep your children out of school.
5. Do not send for your family until you get a job.
6. Do not think you can hold your job unless you are industrious, sober, efficient and prompt.

Cleanliness and fresh air are necessary for good health. In case of sickness send immediately for a good physician. Become an active member in some church as soon as you reach the city.

Issued by

African Americans Migrate North

In 1912, this southern family arrived in its new home in an unnamed northern city. Dressed in their Sunday best, they carried the rest of what they owned in two suitcases. Several factors combined to prompt the massive African American migration out of the South. To the burden of racism was added the steady erosion of opportunities to make a living. In the 1920s, many rural blacks lost work when boll weevils drastically reduced the cotton crop. Then mechanization and government programs to support crop prices by reducing acreage drove many more people off the land.

In Chicago, the young Urban League sought to ease the transition of southern blacks to life in the North. As the card suggests, new arrivals—mostly rural, agricultural people—faced a raft of difficulties, including finding work in factories, places to live in a confusing, congested city, and getting along with their northern employers. Other Urban League cards advised hard work, sobriety, cleanliness, finding a church, getting children into school, and speaking softly in public places.

Photograph: Photographs and Prints Division, Schomburg Center for Research in Black Culture, New York Public Library, Astor, Lenox and Tilden Foundations; card: Special Collections, The University Library, University of Illinois at Chicago.

---

whites as domestics for $2 or less a week. Whites remained committed to keeping blacks down. "If we own a good farm or horse, or cow, or bird-dog, or yoke of oxen," a black Mississippian observed in 1913, "we are harassed until we are bound to sell, give away, or run away, before we can have any peace in our lives."

The First World War provided African Americans with the opportunity to escape the South's cotton fields and kitchens. Just as production demands in northern factories were increasing, the war deprived companies of their traditional sources of labor—immigrants and white male workers. War caused the number of European immigrants to fall from more than a million in 1914 to 31,000 in 1918. In addition, war channeled some 5 million American workers into military service. When acute labor shortages caused northern industries to turn to black labor, labor recruiters, newspapers, and word of mouth spread the news that north-

> The First World War provided African Americans with the opportunity to escape the South's cotton fields and kitchens.

ern factories had jobs for African Americans. Young black men, who made up the bulk of the early migrants, found work in steel mills, shipyards, munitions plants, railroad yards, and mines. From 1915 to 1920, a half million blacks (approximately 10 percent of the South's black population) boarded trains bound for Philadelphia, Detroit, Cleveland, Chicago, St. Louis, and other industrial cities.

> By 1940, more than one million blacks had left the South, profoundly changing their own lives and the course of the nation's history.

Opportunities differed from city to city. In Detroit, for example, blacks found work in automobile factories. Ford and other companies established strong relations with urban black churches, which acted as recruiters for the labor-strapped industry. Workers at Ford wore badges to get in the gates, and black men were so proud of their jobs that they wore their badges to church on Sunday. Thousands of migrants wrote home to tell family and friends about their experiences in the North. One man announced proudly that he had recently been promoted to "first assistant to the head carpenter." He added, "I should have been here twenty years ago. I just begin to feel like a man. . . . My children are going to the same school with the whites and I don't have to [h]umble to no one. I have registered—will vote the next election and there ain't any 'yes sir'—it's all yes and no and Sam and Bill."

But the North was not the promised land. Black men stood on the lowest rungs of the labor ladder. Jobs of any kind proved scarce for black women. Limited by both race and sex, most worked as domestic servants as they did in the South. The existing black middle classes sometimes shunned the less educated, less sophisticated rural Southerners crowding into northern cities. Many whites, fearful of losing jobs and status, lashed out against the new migrants. Savage race riots ripped through two dozen northern cities. The worst occurred on a hot July night in 1917 when a mob of whites invaded a section of East St. Louis, Illinois, crowded with blacks who had been recruited to help break a strike. The mob murdered at least thirty-nine people and left most of the black district in flames. In 1918, the nation witnessed ninety-six lynchings of blacks, some of them returning war veterans still in uniform.

African Americans in the military also suffered from racial violence. The most disastrous episode occurred in August 1917 when a group of armed black soldiers went to Houston, Texas, to avenge incidents of harassment by the police. In the clash that followed, thirteen whites, including several policemen, and one black soldier were killed. With vengeful swiftness that denied any appeal, a military court had thirteen of the black soldiers hanged and sentenced forty-one others to life imprisonment. (See "Historical Question," page 822.)

While the North was not the promised land, it was better than the South. Most migrants stayed and encouraged friends and family to follow. By 1940, more than one million blacks had left the South, profoundly changing their own lives and the course of the nation's history. The rising black population in the North led to the emergence of black enclaves, "cities within cities," such as Harlem in New York and the South Side of Chicago. These assertive communities provided a solid foundation for black protest and political organization in the years ahead. Indeed, drawing strength from these black urban communities, the NAACP evolved from an interracial organization to a largely black organization, funded by its growing black membership.

At virtually the same moment that black Americans streamed into northern cities, another migration was under way in the American Southwest. Between 1910 and 1920, the Mexican-born population in the United States soared from 222,000 to 478,000. Mexican immigration was the result of developments on both sides of the border. At the turn of the century the Mexican dictator Porfirio Díaz initiated land policies that decimated poor farmers. When the Mexicans revolted against Díaz in 1910, initiating a ten-year civil war that eventually claimed the lives of one to two million people, the trickle of migration became a flood. North of the border, the Chinese Exclusion Act of 1882, then the disruption of World War I, cut off the supply of cheap foreign labor and caused western employers in the expanding rail, mining, construction, and agricultural industries to look south to Mexico for workers.

As a result of Americans' racial stereotyping of Mexicans—a U.S. government economist described them as "docile, patient, usually orderly in camp, fairly intelligent under competent supervision, obedient and cheap"—Mexicans were considered excellent prospects for manual labor but not for citizenship. Employers tried to dampen racial fears by stressing that the immigrants were only temporary residents, no lasting threat. "Like a pigeon," a spokesman for the California Farm Bureau Federation said, "he goes back to roost." Even after the revelation of the Zimmermann telegram, when the *Los Angeles Times* denounced Germany's "proposed alliance with Mexico" and accused recent Mexican migrants of "treason and sedition within our own gates," the need for laborers trumped **nativist** sentiment. And in 1917, when anti-immigration advocates convinced Congress to do something about foreigners coming into the United States, the restrictive legislation bowed to southwestern industry and exempted Mexicans. By 1920, ethnic Mexicans made up some three-fourths of California's farm laborers. They were also crucial to the Texas economy, comprising 75 percent of laborers in the cotton fields and in construction.

Like immigrants from Europe and black migrants from the South, Mexicans in the American Southwest dreamed of a better life. And like the others, they found both opportunity and disappointment. Wages were better than in Mexico, but life in the fields, mines, and factories was hard, and living conditions—in box cars or labor camps or urban barrios—often dismal. Signs that read "No Mexicans Allowed" increased rather than declined. Mexicanas nurtured families, but many women also worked for wages. Thousands of women, for example, picked cotton, sometimes dragging hundred-pound cotton sacks with a baby perched on top. *Los recien llegados* (the recent arrivals) encountered mixed reactions among Mexican Americans, some of whom had lived in the Southwest for a century or more. One Mexican American expressed the ambivalence: "We are all Mexicans anyway because the *gueros* [Anglos] treat us all alike," he declared, but he also called for immigration quotas because the recent arrivals drove down wages and incited white prejudice that affected all ethnic Mexicans. *Los recien llegados* also harbored mixed feelings, sometimes calling Mexican Americans *pochos* (faded or bleached ones).

Despite this friction, large-scale immigration into the Southwest meant a resurgence of the Mexican cultural presence, which in time became the basis for greater solidarity and political action for the ethnic Mexican population. Shortly after World War I, Mexican Americans began organizing, a development that culminated with the formation of the League of United Latin American Citizens (LULAC) in Texas in 1929.

> Like immigrants from Europe and black migrants from the South, Mexicans in the American Southwest dreamed of a better life.

Mexican Women Arriving in El Paso, 1911

These new arrivals, carrying bundles and wearing traditional shawls, try to get their bearings on arriving in El Paso, Texas—the Ellis Island for Mexican immigrants. Perhaps they are looking for a family member who preceded them, or perhaps they are alone and calculating their next step. In any case, these women were part of the first modern wave of Mexican immigration to the United States. Women like these found work at home taking in sewing, laundry, and boarders and in the cotton and sugar-beet fields, canneries, and restaurants of the Southwest. Whatever their work, their journey across the border proved life changing.

Courtesy of the Rio Grande Historical Collections, New Mexico State University Library, Las Cruces, New Mexico.

Postwar Politics and the Election of 1920

Two thousand miles away in Washington, D.C., President Woodrow Wilson, bedridden and paralyzed, stubbornly ignored the mountain of domestic troubles—labor strikes, the Red scare, race riots, immigration backlash—and insisted that the 1920 election would be a "solemn referendum" on the League of Nations. Dutifully, the Democratic nominees for president, James M. Cox, three-time governor of Ohio, and for vice president, the New York aristocrat Franklin

What Did the War Mean to African Americans?

When the United States entered the First World War, some black leaders remembered the crucial role of African American soldiers in the Civil War. They rejoiced that military service would again offer blacks a chance to demonstrate their patriotism and prove themselves as citizens. Others believed that black Americans had long ago demonstrated their worth. They instead saw the war as an opportunity to force the nation to pay its debt to African Americans.

A month after America entered the war, the National Association for the Advancement of Colored People (NAACP) approved a series of resolutions, most of them written by W. E. B. Du Bois, known for his bold dissent against the white power structure. The NAACP demanded that the principle of consent of the governed be extended "not only to the smaller nations of Europe but among the natives of Asia and Africa, the Western Indies, and the Negroes of the United States." It declared that black Americans would support the war but added, "absolute loyalty in arms and civil duties need not for a moment lead us to abate our just complaints and just demands." Still, Du Bois in an editorial in the NAACP's journal *Crisis* urged blacks to "close ranks" and to temporarily "forget our special

grievances" until the nation had won the war. The enemy of the moment, Du Bois insisted, was German "military despotism." Unchecked, that despotism "spells death to the aspirations of Negroes and all darker races for equality, freedom, and democracy."

While African Americans remained skeptical about President Wilson's claim that the United States was fighting to make the world safe for democracy, most nevertheless followed Du Bois's advice and supported the war effort. On the first day of registration for military service, more than 700,000 black men signed in at their draft boards. By war's end, 370,000 blacks had been inducted, some 31 percent of the total number of blacks registered. The figure for whites was 26 percent.

During training, black recruits suffered the same prejudices that they had encountered in civilian life. Rigidly segregated, they were usually assigned to labor battalions. They faced crude abuse and miserable conditions. One base in Virginia that trained blacks as cargo handlers quartered troops in tents without floors or stoves and provided no changes of clothes, no blankets for the winter, and no facilities for bathing. Only several deaths from disease and exposure moved the authorities to make conditions barely tolerable.

When black soldiers began arriving in Europe, white commanders made a point of maintaining racial distinctions. A special report from the headquarters of the American commander, General John J. Pershing, advised the French that their failure to draw the color line threatened Franco-American relations. They should resist the urge, the report declared, to accept blacks as equals or to thank them for their efforts, for fear of "spoiling the Negroes."

Under such circumstances, German propagandists raised some painful questions. One leaflet distributed by the Germans to black troops reminded them that they lacked the rights that whites enjoyed and that they were segregated and often lynched. "Why, then, fight the Germans," the leaflet asked, "only for the benefit of the Wall Street robbers and to protect the millions they have loaned to the British, French, and Italians?" Why, indeed?

Black soldiers hoped to prove a point. While at first they worked mainly as laborers and stevedores, before long they had their chance to fight. In February 1918, General Pershing received an urgent call from the French for help on the front lines. Determined not to lose command over the white troops he valued the most, Pershing sent black soldiers—the 369th, 370th, 371st, and 372nd Regiments of the 92nd Division—to the front, where they were integrated into units of the French army. In 191 days spent in battle—longer than the time spent by any other American outfit—the

Delano Roosevelt, campaigned on Wilson's international ideals. The Republican Party chose a very different sort of candidate: handsome, gregarious Warren Gamaliel Harding, senator from Ohio. Harding's rise in Ohio politics was a trib-

ute to his amiability and ability to connect with the common folk rather than to any political commitment. On the two most heated domestic political issues of the day—woman suffrage and prohibition—Harding showed little knowledge

African American Machine Gun Company
The members of this company from the 370th Regiment of the Illinois National Guard, shown early in their training, exemplify the proud determination of black soldiers to prove their worth in battle. Once in France, the 370th encountered resistance from American commanders reluctant to use combat-ready black troops for anything but hard labor behind the lines. When desperation in the face of a German offensive in the spring of 1918 gave them the chance to fight with French units, the 370th showed its mettle by receiving more medals for valor than any other unit in the American armed forces. Black soldiers recognized the irony of having to gain respect as Americans by serving with the French.
William Gladstone.

369th Regiment won the most medals of any American combat unit, more than one hundred Croix de Guerre, crosses given by the French for gallantry in war. In June 1918, the French high command paid its highest respect by asking the Americans to send all the black troops they could spare.

When the battle-scarred survivors of the 92nd Division returned home, they marched proudly past cheering crowds in Manhattan and Chicago. Black spokesmen proclaimed a new era for black Americans. In May 1919, Du Bois argued that it was time for

African Americans to collect what was due them. "We return *from fighting*," Du Bois declared. "We *return fighting*. Make way for Democracy. We saved it in France, and by the Great Jehovah, we will save it in the U.S.A., or know the reason why."

Reasons soon presented themselves. Segregation remained entrenched, and its defenders continued to hold power in Congress and in the White House. Postwar recession left blacks "the last hired, the first fired." Whites scapegoated blacks and launched race riots across the nation. The willingness of blacks to stand

their ground demonstrated a new resolve, but it also meant more suffering from escalating violence. Nor did the armed services continue to offer new opportunities. Until the late 1940s, after the next world war, the American military remained not only segregated but also almost devoid of black officers. Discrimination extended even beyond the ultimate sacrifice. When the organizers of a trip to France for parents of soldiers lost in the First World War announced that the boat would be segregated, black mothers felt honor bound to decline the offer to visit the cemeteries where their sons lay.

It took decades for the nation to recognize the sacrifice and heroism of black soldiers in France. In 1991, as the nation cheered U.S. success in the Gulf War, a Defense Department investigating team, though insisting it had found no evidence of discrimination in the fact that none of the 127 Medals of Honor awarded during World War I had gone to blacks, declared that the time had come to correct an "administrative oversight." For leading a charge on September 28, 1918, up a German-held hill that cost him and 40 percent of his company their lives, Corporal Freddie Stowers would receive the Medal of Honor—until then the only one attained by an African American in the world wars. The slain soldier's elderly sister, who had survived seventy-three years to accept the award for her hero brother, could take solace that recognition came under the command of General Colin Powell, the first black chairman of the Joint Chiefs of Staff.

or conviction, but eventually he voted for them in a nod to grassroots sentiment.

Harding found the winning formula when he declared that "America's present need is not heroics, but healing; not nostrums [questionable remedies] but normalcy." But what was "normalcy"? Harding explained: "By 'normalcy' I don't mean the old order but a regular steady order of things. I mean normal procedure, the natural way, without excess." The urbane *New*

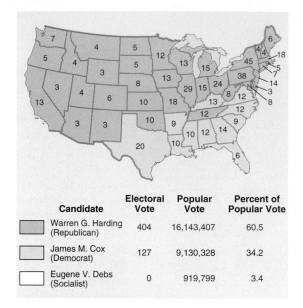

Candidate	Electoral Vote	Popular Vote	Percent of Popular Vote
Warren G. Harding (Republican)	404	16,143,407	60.5
James M. Cox (Democrat)	127	9,130,328	34.2
Eugene V. Debs (Socialist)	0	919,799	3.4

MAP 22.6   The Election of 1920

York Times understood the word's appeal, observing, "Mr. Harding is not writing for the super-fine weighers of verbs and adjectives but for the men and women who see in his expressions their own ideas."

Eager to put wartime crusades and postwar strife behind them, voters responded by giving Harding the largest presidential victory ever: 60.5 percent of the popular vote and 76 percent of the electoral vote (Map 22.6). On his coattails rode Republican majorities in both houses of Congress. Once in office, the Hardings threw open the White House gates, which had been closed since the declaration of war in 1917. Their welcome brought throngs of visitors and lifted the national pall, signaling a new era of easygoing good cheer.

Conclusion: Troubled Crusade

America's experience in the war that raged from 1914 to 1918 was exceptional. For much of the world, the Great War produced great destruction, acres of blackened fields and ruined factories and millions of casualties. But in the United States, war and prosperity marched hand in hand. America emerged from World War I with the strongest economy in the world and a position of international preeminence.

Still, the nation paid a heavy price both at home and abroad. American soldiers and sailors encountered unprecedented horrors—submarines, poison gas, machine guns—and more than 100,000 died. General Pershing recognized and honored their sacrifice. "I pay supreme tribute to our officers and soldiers of the line. When I think of their heroism, their patience under hardships, their unflinching spirit of offensive action, I am filled with emotions which I am unable to express." Rather than redeeming their sacrifice, however, as Wilson promised, the peace that followed the armistice tarnished it. At home, war brought prosperity, but rather than permanently improving working conditions, advancing public health, and spreading educational opportunity, as progressives had hoped, the war threatened to undermine the achievements of the previous two decades. Moreover, rather than promoting American democracy, the war bred fear, intolerance, and repression that led to a crackdown on dissent and a demand for conformity. Reformers could count only woman suffrage as a permanent victory.

Woodrow Wilson had promised more than anyone could deliver. Progressive hopes of extending democracy and **liberal** reform nationally and internationally were dashed. In 1920, a bruised and disillusioned society stumbled into a new decade. The era coming to an end had called on Americans to crusade and sacrifice. Now whoever could promise them peace, prosperity, and a good time would have the best chance to win their hearts.

FOR ADDITIONAL FIRSTHAND ACCOUNTS OF THIS PERIOD, see Chapter 22 in Michael Johnson, ed., *Reading the American Past,* Third Edition.

TO ASSESS YOUR MASTERY OF THE MATERIAL IN THIS CHAPTER, see the Online Study Guide at bedfordstmartins.com/roark.

FOR WEB LINKS RELATED TO TOPICS IN THIS CHAPTER, see "HistoryLinks," "DocLinks," and "PlaceLinks" at bedfordstmartins.com/roark.

CHRONOLOGY

1914
- **April.** Attempting to impose democracy on Mexico, President Woodrow Wilson sends marines to occupy the port of Veracruz.
- **June 28.** Assassination of Archduke Franz Ferdinand of Austria in Sarajevo starts chain of events leading to World War I.
- **July 28.** Austria declares war on Serbia.
- **August 6.** All-out conflict erupts when Germany declares war on Russia and France; in response, Great Britain declares war on Russia.

1915
- German submarine sinks British liner *Lusitania*, with loss of 1,198 lives, including 128 Americans.
- Settlement house reformer Jane Addams helps form Women's Peace Party to seek peaceful resolution of war.

1916
- General John J. Pershing leads military expedition into Mexico in pursuit of rebel leader Francisco "Pancho" Villa.
- Wilson wins reelection by narrow margin.

1917
- Intercepted telegram from German foreign secretary, Arthur Zimmermann, promising aid to Mexico for war against the United States prompts Wilson to ask Congress to approve "armed neutrality" policy.
- **April 6.** Congress votes to declare war on Germany.
- Wilson creates Committee on Public Information to promote U.S. war aims.
- Selective Service Act authorizes military draft that brings 2.8 million men into armed services; in addition, 2 million volunteer.
- Congress passes Espionage Act, first of three laws limiting First Amendment rights.
- Resentment against blacks migrating northward in search of work ignites race riot in East St. Louis, Illinois.
- **August.** Armed action by black soldiers against racial discrimination in Houston results in execution of 13 of the soldiers and life sentences for 41 more.

- Bolshevik revolutionary government ends Russian participation in war by arranging for a separate peace with Germany.

1918
- **January 8.** President Wilson gives Fourteen Points speech, outlining his plan for peace.
- **May–June.** U.S. marines succeed in their first major combat with Germans at Cantigny and Château-Thierry.
- **September.** American forces deployed to support Russian efforts to undo Bolshevik Revolution.
- **November 11.** Armistice signed ending World War I.

1919
- **January.** Paris peace conference begins; President Wilson heads the U.S. delegation.
- **June.** Versailles peace treaty signed.
- **September.** Wilson undertakes speaking tour to rally support for ratification of Versailles treaty and League of Nations; his ill health in Colorado ends the tour.
- Postwar recession and end of wartime support for labor unions lead to wave of strikes.

1919–1920
- As part of the Red scare, Attorney General A. Mitchell Palmer leads effort to rid country of radicals and aliens.

1920
- **January 1.** Prohibition begins, following ratification of Eighteenth Amendment.
- Steel strike ends without settlement, dealing organized labor its greatest blow.
- Senate votes against ratification of Versailles peace treaty.
- **August 18.** Nineteenth Amendment ratified, granting women the vote.
- **November.** Warren G. Harding elected president.

BIBLIOGRAPHY

General Works

Byron Farwell, *Over There: The United States in the Great War, 1917–1918* (1999).

Niall Ferguson, *The Pity of War: Explaining World War I* (1999).

Thomas Fleming, *The Illusion of Victory: America in World War I* (2003).

Paul Fussell, *The Great War and Modern Memory* (1975).

Ellis W. Hawley, *The Great War and the Search for a Modern Order: A History of the American People and Their Institutions, 1917–1933* (1979).

Derek Heater, *National Self-Determination: Woodrow Wilson and His Legacy* (1994).

John Keegan, *The First World War* (1999).

David Kennedy, *Over Here: The First World War and American Society* (1980).

Nell Painter, *Standing at Armageddon: The United States, 1877–1919* (1987).

Robert D. Schulzinger, *American Diplomacy in the Twentieth Century* (1984).

David Steigerwald, *Wilsonian Idealism in America* (1994).

David Stevenson, *The First World War and International Politics* (1988).

J. M. Winter, *The Experience of World War I* (1989).

Neil A. Wynn, *From Progressivism to Prosperity: World War I and American Society* (1986).

Robert H. Zieger, *America's Great War: World War I and the American Experience* (2000).

Woodrow Wilson and the World

Kendrick A. Clement, *Woodrow Wilson, World Statesman* (1987).

Patrick Devlin, *Too Proud to Fight: Woodrow Wilson's Neutrality* (1974).

Modris Eksteins, *Rites of Spring: The Great War and the Birth of the Modern Age* (1990).

John S. D. Eisenhower, *Intervention! The United States and the Mexican Revolution, 1913–1917* (1993).

Lloyd C. Gardner, *Safe for Democracy: The Anglo-American Response to Revolution, 1913–1923* (1987).

James Joll, *The Origins of the First World War* (1992).

Friedrich Katz, *The Life and Times of Pancho Villa* (1998).

Burton I. Kaufman, *Efficiency and Expansion: Foreign Trade Organization in the Wilson Administration, 1913–1921* (1974).

Thomas Knock, *To End All Wars: Woodrow Wilson and the Quest for a New World Order* (1992).

Gordon N. Levin, *Woodrow Wilson and World Politics: America's Response to War and Revolution* (1970).

Margaret Olwen Macmillan, *Paris 1919: Six Months That Changed the World* (2002).

Charles L. May Jr., *The End of Order: Versailles, 1919* (1980).

George L. Mosse, *Fallen Soldiers: Reshaping the Memory of the World Wars* (1991).

Mary A. Renda, *Taking Haiti: Military Occupation and the Culture of U.S. Imperialism, 1915–1940* (2001).

Emily S. Rosenberg, *Financial Missionaries to the World: The Politics and Culture of Dollar Diplomacy, 1890–1930* (1999).

Martin J. Sklar, *The United States as a Developing Country: Studies in U.S. History in the Progressive Era and the 1920s* (1992).

Ralph A. Stone, *The Irreconcilables: The Fight against the League of Nations* (1970).

Barbara W. Tuchman, *The Guns of August* (1962).

Arthur Walworth, *Wilson and His Peacemakers: American Diplomacy at the Paris Peace Conference, 1919* (1986).

William C. Widenor, *Henry Cabot Lodge and the Search for an American Foreign Policy* (1980).

Over There

Michael C. C. Adams, *The Great Adventure: Male Desire and the Coming of World War I* (1990).

Gerald Astor, *The Right to Fight: A History of African Americans in the Military* (1998).

Arthur E. Barbeau and Florette Henri, *The Unknown Soldiers: Black American Troops in World War I* (1974).

Thomas A. Britten, *American Indians in World War I: At Home and at War* (1997).

John Whiteclay Chambers II, *To Raise an Army: The Draft Comes to Modern America* (1987).

Edward M. Coffman, *The War to End All Wars: The American Military Experience in World War I* (1968).

Kenneth J. Hagan, *This People's Navy: The Making of American Sea Power* (1990).

Lee Kennett, *The First Air War, 1914–1918* (1990).

Albert Marrin, *The Yanks Are Coming* (1986).

Bernard C. Nalty, *Strength for the Fight: A History of Black Americans in the Military* (1986).

Gerald Wilson Patton, *War and Race: The Black Officer in the American Military, 1915–1941* (1981).

G. Kurt Piehler, *Remembering War the American Way* (1995).

Gene Smith, *Until the Last Trumpet Sounds: The Life of General of the Armies John J. Pershing* (1998).

Donald Smythe, *Pershing, General of the Armies* (1986).

David F. Trask, *The AEF and Coalition Warmaking, 1917–1918* (1993).

William S. Triplet, *A Youth in the Meuse-Argonne: A Memoir, 1917–1918* (2000).

Frank E. Vandiver, *Black Jack: The Life and Times of John J. Pershing*, 2 vols. (1977).

Russell F. Weigley, *The American Way of War: A History of United States Military Strategy and Policy* (1977).

Stanley Weintraub, *A Stillness Heard round the World: The End of the Great War, November 1918* (1985).

The Crusade for Democracy at Home

Daniel Beaver, *Newton D. Baker and the American War Effort, 1917–1919* (1966).

William T. Breen, *Uncle Sam at Home: Civilian Mobilization, Wartime Federalism, and the Council of National Defense, 1917–1919* (1984).

Jean Conner, *The National War Labor Board: Stability, Social Justice, and the Voluntary State in World War I* (1983).

Richard Cork, *The Bitter Truth: Avant-Garde Art and the Great War* (1994).

Nancy F. Cott, *The Grounding of American Feminism* (1987).

Robert D. Cuff, *The War Industries Board: Business-Government Relations during World War I* (1973).

Leslie Midkiff DeBauche, *Reel Patriotism: The Movies and World War I* (1997).

Marc A. Eisner, *From Warfare State to Welfare State: World War I, Compensatory State Building, and the Limits of the Modern Order* (2000).

Carrie A. Foster, *The Women and the Warriors: The U.S. Section of the Women's International League for Peace and Freedom, 1915–1946* (1995).

Maurine Weiner Greenwald, *Women, War, and Work: The Impact of World War I on Women Workers in the United States* (1980).

Margaret Randolph Higonnet, Jane Jenson, Sonya Michel, and Margaret Collins Weitz, eds., *Behind the Lines: Gender and the Two World Wars* (1987).

C. Roland Marchand, *The American Peace Movement and Social Reform* (1973).

John F. McClymer, *War and Welfare: Social Engineering in America, 1890–1925* (1980).

Marian J. Morton, *Emma Goldman and the American Left* (1992).

Paul L. Murphy, *World War I and the Origin of Civil Liberties in the United States* (1979).

George H. Nash, *The Life of Herbert Hoover*, vol. 2, *The Humanitarian, 1914–1917*, vol. 3, *Master of Emergences, 1917–1918* (c. 1983–c. 1996).

Ronald Schaffer, *America in the Great War: The Rise of the War Welfare State* (1991).

Barbara J. Steinson, *American Women's Activism in World War I* (1982).

Cass Sunstein, *Democracy and the Problem of Free Speech* (1993).

Rosalyn Terborg-Penn, *African American Women in the Struggle for the Vote, 1850–1920* (1998).

Stephen Vaughn, *Holding Fast the Inner Lines: Democracy, Nationalism, and the Committee for Public Information* (1980).

Susan Zeiger, *In Uncle Sam's Service: Women with the AEF, 1917–1919* (1999).

Disappointment and Reaction

Casey N. Blake, *Beloved Community: The Cultural Criticism of Randolph Bourne, Van Wyck Brooks, Waldo Frank and Lewis Mumford* (1990).

Peter G. Boyle, *American-Soviet Relations: From the Russian Revolution to the Fall of Communism* (1993).

David Brody, *Labor in Crisis: The Steel Strike of 1919* (1965).

Elizabeth Clark-Lewis, *Living In, Living Out: African American Domestics in Washington, D.C., 1910–1940* (1994).

Melvyn Dubofsky, *We Shall Be All: A History of the Industrial Workers of the World* (1969, 1988).

Melvyn Dubofsky, *The State and Labor in Modern America* (1994).

Mario T. Garcia, *Mexican Americans: Leadership, Ideology, and Identity, 1930–1960* (1989).

James R. Grossman, *Land of Hope: Chicago, Black Southerners, and the Great Migration* (1989).

David G. Gutierrez, *Walls and Mirrors: Mexican Americans, Mexican Immigrants, and the Politics of Ethnicity* (1995).

David Levering Lewis, *W. E. B. Du Bois: Biography of a Race, 1868–1919* (1993).

Carole Marks, *Farewell—We're Good and Gone: The Great Black Migration* (1989).

Joseph A. McCartin, *Labor's Great War: The Struggle for Industrial Democracy and the Origins of Modern American Labor Relations, 1912–1921* (1977).

Robert K. Murray, *Red Scare: A Study in National Hysteria, 1919–1920* (1955).

William Pencak, *For God and Country* (1989).

Richard Polenberg, *Fighting Faiths: The Abrams Case, the Supreme Court, and Free Speech* (1987).

William G. Ross, *Forging New Freedoms: Nativism, Education, and the Constitution, 1917–1927* (1994).

Vicki Ruiz, *From out of the Shadows: Mexican Women in Twentieth-Century America* (1998).

Francis Russell, *A City in Terror: 1919, the Boston Police Strike* (1975).

George J. Sanchez, *Becoming Mexican American: Ethnicity, Culture, and Identity in Chicano Los Angeles, 1900–1945* (1993).

Richard Severo and Lewis Milford, *The Wages of War: When America's Soldiers Came Home—from Valley Forge to Vietnam* (1989).

Joe William Trotter Jr., ed., *The Great Migration in Historical Perspective* (1991).

William Tuttle Jr., *Race Riot: Chicago and the Red Summer of 1919* (1970).

MODEL T FORD

Nothing symbolized the 1920s more than automobiles. Americans drove millions of them—Briscoes, Dodges, Lexingtons, Cadillacs, Maxwells, and especially Model T Fords. When Henry Ford introduced the Model T in 1908, Americans thought of automobiles as toys of the rich, far too costly for average people. By the 1920s, millions of Americans owned Fords, and their lives were never the same. Oklahoma humorist Will Rogers claimed that Henry Ford "changed the habits of more people than Caesar, Mussolini, Charlie Chaplin, Clara Bow, Xerxes, Amos 'n Andy, and Bernard Shaw." One of novelist Booth Tarkington's characters expressed some reservation about automobiles: "With all their speed forward, they may be a step backward in civilization." But most Americans loved their automobiles and sped away into the future.

National Museum of American History, Smithsonian Institution, Behring Center.

23

From New Era to Great Depression

1920–1932

A MERICANS IN THE 1920s cheered Henry Ford as an authentic American folk hero. When the decade began, he had already produced 6,000,000 automobiles; by 1927, the figure reached 15,000,000. In 1920, one car rolled off the Ford assembly line every minute; in 1925, one appeared every ten seconds. In 1920, a Ford car cost $845; in 1928, the price was less than $300, within range of most of the country's skilled workingmen. Henry Ford put America on wheels, and in the eyes of most Americans he was a good and honest man whose simple virtues were reflected in the car he made: basic, inexpensive, and reliable. He became the embodiment of American industry and free enterprise, the greatest example of its promise and achievement. But like the age in which he lived, Henry Ford was many-sided, more complex and contradictory than this simple image suggests.

Born in 1863 on a farm in Dearborn, Michigan, Ford hated the drudgery of farmwork and loved tinkering with machines. At sixteen, he fled rural life for Detroit, where he became a journeyman machinist and experimented with internal combustion engines. In 1893, he put together one of the first successful gasoline-driven carriages in the United States. His ambition, he said, was to "make something in quantity." The product he chose reflected American restlessness, the desire to be on the move. "Everybody wants to be someplace he ain't," Ford declared. "As soon as he gets there he wants to go right back." In 1903, with $28,000 from a few backers, Ford gathered twelve workers in a 250-by-50-foot shed and created the Ford Motor Company.

Ford's early cars were custom-made one at a time. By 1914, his cars were being built along a continuously moving assembly line; workers bolted on parts brought to them by cranes and conveyor belts. Ford made only one kind of car, the Model T, which became synonymous with mass production. Ford conceived of his product as the "universal car," a boxlike black vehicle that was cheap, easy to drive, and simple to repair. His reward was dominance over the market. Throughout the rapid expansion of the automotive industry, the Ford Motor Company remained the industry leader, peaking in 1925 when it outsold all its rivals combined (Map 23.1).

Nobody entertained grander or more contradictory visions of the new America he had helped to create than Henry Ford himself. When he began his rise, **progressive** critics were vilifying the industrial giants of the nineteenth century as "robber barons" who lived in luxury while reducing their workers to wage slaves. Ford, however, identified with the common folk and sought to claim his place as benefactor of Americans yearning to be free and mobile.

- **The New Era**
  A Business Government
  Promoting Prosperity and Peace Abroad
  Automobiles, Mass Production, and Assembly-Line Progress
  Consumer Culture

- **The Roaring Twenties**
  Prohibition
  The New Woman
  The New Negro
  Mass Culture
  The Lost Generation

- **Resistance to Change**
  Rejecting the "Huddled Masses"
  The Rebirth of the Ku Klux Klan
  The Scopes Trial
  Al Smith and the Election of 1928

- **The Great Crash**
  Herbert Hoover: The Great Engineer
  The Distorted Economy
  The Crash of 1929
  Hoover and the Limits of Individualism

- **Life in the Depression**
  The Human Toll
  Denial and Escape
  Working-Class Militancy

- **Conclusion: Dazzle and Despair**

Henry and Edsel

In this 1924 photograph, Henry Ford looks fondly at his first car while his son, Edsel, stands next to the ten millionth Model T. Edsel, the Fords' only child, remained unspoiled by his father's enormous wealth. Forsaking college, he entered the family business out of high school. Serious, disciplined, and an acute observer, he realized by the mid-1920s that General Motors's more advanced Chevrolet was about to surpass the Model T. Henry Ford stubbornly refused to change his automobile, insisting that the "Model T is the most perfect car in the world." Under Edsel's leadership, however, the Ford Motor Company moved beyond the plain, boxy, black, and fabulously successful Model T.

Henry Ford Museum and Greenfield Village.

farm and the small town. Although the nation prospered as a whole, the new wealth widened the gap between rich and poor. While millions admired urban America's sophisticated new style and consumer products, others condemned postwar society for its vulgar materialism. A great outpouring of artistic talent led, ironically, to incessant critiques of America's artistic barrenness. The Ku Klux Klan and some other champions of an idealized older America resorted to violence and harassment as well as words when they chastised the era's "new women," "new Negroes," and surging immigrant populations.

The public, disillusioned with the outcome of World War I, no longer thrilled to the Christian moralism and idealism that had fueled the crusades of progressives. In the twenties, Ford and businessmen like him replaced political reformers such as Theodore Roosevelt and Woodrow Wilson as the exemplars of progress. The U.S. Chamber of Commerce crowed, "The American businessman is the most influential person in the nation." Social justice gave way to individual advancement. At the center of it all, President Calvin Coolidge spoke in praise of those in power when he declared, "The business of America is business." The fortunes of the era rose, and then crashed, according to the values and practices of the business community.

Ford's automobile plants made him a billionaire, but their highly regimented assembly lines reduced Ford workers to near robots. On the cutting edge of modern technology, Ford nevertheless remained nostalgic about rural values. His pet project was to revive the past in Greenfield Village, a museum outside Detroit, where he relocated buildings from a bygone era, including his parents' farmhouse. With its exhibits of homespun family life and crafts, Greenfield Village contrasted poignantly with the roaring, racing Ford plant farther along the Detroit River at River Rouge. In the factory toiled the African American and immigrant workers left out of Ford's village idyll. Yet all would be well, Ford insisted, if Americans remained loyal to the virtues of an agrarian past and somehow managed to be modern and scientific at the same time.

Tension between traditional values and modern conditions lay at the heart of the conflicted 1920s. For the first time, according to the census of 1920, more Americans lived in urban than in rural areas, yet nostalgia idealized the

The New Era

The rejection of the progressive call for government intervention and regulation in favor of the revival of free-enterprise individualism was one of several factors that made the 1920s a time of contradiction and ambivalence. Once Woodrow Wilson left the White House, the energy generated by the crusade in Europe flowed away from civic reform and toward private economic endeavor and personal creativity. The rise of a free-wheeling economy and a heightened sense of individualism caused Secretary of Commerce Herbert Hoover to declare that America had entered a "New Era." But the complexity of the 1920s finds expression in other labels attached to the age. Some terms focus on the decade's high-spirited energy and cultural changes: Roaring Twenties, Jazz Age, Flaming Youth, Age of the Flapper. Others echo the rising importance of money—Dollar Decade, Golden Twenties, Prosperity Decade—or reflect the sinister side of

MAP 23.1 Auto Manufacturing

By the mid-1920s, the massive coal and steel industries of the Midwest had made the region the center of the new automobile industry. A major road-building program by the federal government carried the thousands of new cars produced each day to every corner of the country.

READING THE MAP: How many states had factories involved with the manufacture of automobiles? In what regions was auto manufacture concentrated?

CONNECTIONS: On what related industries did auto manufacture depend? How did the integration of the automobile into everyday life affect American society?

FOR MORE HELP ANALYZING THIS MAP, see the map activity for this chapter in the Online Study Guide at bedfordstmartins.com/roark.

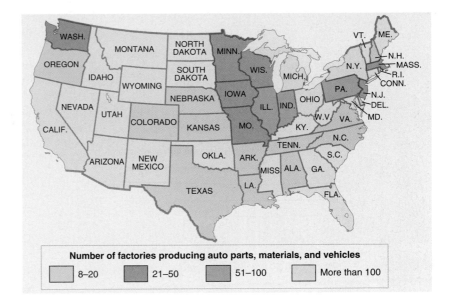

Number of factories producing auto parts, materials, and vehicles

8–20	21–50
51–100	More than 100

gangster profiteering—Lawless Decade. Still others emphasize the lonely confusion of a Lost Generation and the stress and anxiety of the Aspirin Age.

America in the twenties was many things, but there was no getting around the truth of Calvin Coolidge's insight: The business of America was business. Politicians and diplomats tipped their hats to businessmen and proclaimed business the heart of American civilization. Average men and women bought into the idea that business and its wonderful products were what made America great, as they snatched up the unprecedented flood of new consumer items American factories sent forth.

A Business Government

Republicans controlled the White House from 1921 to 1933. The first of the three Republican presidents was Warren Gamaliel Harding, the Ohio senator who in his 1920 campaign called for a "return to normalcy," by which he meant the end of public crusades and a return to private pursuits. Harding, who had few qualifications for the presidency, promised a government run by the best minds, and he chose some men of real stature for his cabinet. Charles Evan Hughes, former associate justice of the Supreme Court and Republican presidential candidate in 1916, became secretary of state. Henry C. Wallace, the leading champion of scientific agriculture,

was tapped for secretary of agriculture. Herbert Hoover, the self-made millionaire and former head of the wartime Food Administration, became secretary of commerce and, according to one wag who testified to Hoover's ambition and energy, assistant secretary of everything else. But wealth also counted. Most significantly, Harding answered the call of **conservatives** to name Andrew Mellon, one of the richest men in America, secretary of the treasury. And friendship counted, too. Harding loyally handed out jobs to his old "Ohio gang" for whom friendship was their only qualification. This curious combination of merit and cronyism made for a disjointed administration in which a few "best minds" debated national needs, while much less qualified men looked for ways to advance their own interests.

When Harding was elected in 1920 in a landslide over Democratic opponent James Cox (see chapter 22, Map 22.6), the national unemployment rate hit 20 percent, the highest ever suffered up to that point. Farmers fared the worst, as their bankruptcy rate increased tenfold and real farm income fell far below wartime levels. Seeking to return the country to prosperity, Harding pushed several measures to aid American enterprise—high tariffs to protect American businesses (the Fordney-McCumber

> Politicians and diplomats tipped their hats to businessmen and proclaimed business the heart of American civilization.

reactionary/progressive (handwritten)

Republican Campaign Decal

Stern and determined, these 1920 Republican candidates seek to persuade voters that they can put an end to radical and alien disruption and restore old-fashioned American values. Warren G. Harding, the Washington insider from the traditional Republican stronghold of Ohio, promises to get the country "back to normal." His running mate, Calvin Coolidge, the Massachusetts governor who gained national fame by crushing the Boston police strike, appears as the exemplar of "law and order."

Collection of Janice L. and David J. Frent.

tariff in 1922 raised duties to unprecedented heights), price supports for agriculture, and the dismantling of wartime government control over industry in favor of unregulated private business. "Never before, here or anywhere else," the U.S. Chamber of Commerce said proudly, "has a government been so completely fused with business."

Harding's policies to boost American enterprise made him a very popular president, but ultimately the small-town congeniality and trusting ways that had made his career possible did him in. The affable Harding resisted admitting for as long as he could that certain of his friends in the "Ohio gang" were involved in lawbreaking. In the end, three of Harding's appointees would go to jail and others would be indicted. When Interior Secretary Albert Fall was convicted of accepting bribes of more than $400,000 for leasing oil reserves on public land in Teapot Dome, Wyoming, "Teapot Dome" became a lasting label for political corruption.

Baffled about how to deal with "my Goddamned friends," Harding in the summer of 1923 set off on a trip to Alaska to escape his troubles. But the president found no rest and his health declined. On August 2, 1923, a shocked nation learned of the fifty-eight-year-old Harding's sudden death from a heart attack.

Vice President Calvin Coolidge was vacationing at his family's farmhouse in Plymouth Notch, Vermont, when he was wakened during the night with the news of Harding's death. The family gathered in the parlor where, by the flickering light of an oil lamp, Coolidge's father, a justice of the peace, swore his son in as president. This rustic drama had the intended effect of calming a nation confronting the death of a president and continuing scandal in Washington. A spare, solemn man, steeped in old-fashioned Yankee morality, the new president basked in the public's acceptance of him as a savior.

Coolidge once expressed his belief that "the man who builds a factory builds a temple, the man who works there worships there." Reverence for free enterprise meant that Coolidge rarely stirred in the White House and discouraged others in his administration from taking initiatives that would expand government. With his approval, Secretary of the Treasury Andrew Mellon concentrated on reducing the government's control over the economy. Tax cuts for corporations and wealthy individuals reduced government tax revenue by about half. New rules for the Federal Trade Commission severely limited its power to regulate business. Even the most active cabinet member, Secretary of Commerce Herbert Hoover, shied away from exerting governmental authority over the economy, preferring instead to encourage trade associations that would keep business honest and efficient through voluntary cooperation.

Coolidge found a staunch ally in the Supreme Court. For many years the Court had opposed federal regulation of hours, wages, and working conditions on the grounds that such legislation was the proper concern of the states. Early in the Coolidge years, the Court found ways to curtail a state's ability to regulate business as well. The Court showed its partiality toward management by ruling against **closed shops**, businesses where only union members could be employed, while confirming the right of owners to form exclusive trade associations. In 1923, the Court declared unconstitutional the District of Columbia's minimum-wage law for women, asserting that the law interfered with the freedom of employer and employee to make labor contracts. On a broad front, the Court and the president attacked government intrusion in the free market, even when the prohibition of government regulation threatened the welfare of workers.

The election of 1924 confirmed the defeat of the progressive principle that the state should take a leading role in ensuring the general welfare. To oppose Coolidge, the Democrats nominated John W. Davis, a corporate lawyer whose conservative views differed little from Republican principles. Only the Progressive Party and its presidential nominee, Senator Robert La Follette of Wisconsin, offered a genuine alternative. In the showdown, the Republicans, who focused their attack on "Fighting Bob" La Follette, coined the slogan "Coolidge or Chaos." La Follette's fervent pledges to champion the progressive tradition of support for labor unions, regulation of business, and protection of civil liberties failed to rouse the public. By this time, most Americans had turned their backs on what they considered labor radicalism and reckless reform. Coolidge managed to capture more votes than his two opponents put together, and conservative Republicans strengthened their majorities in both houses of Congress. The 1924 election proved that Coolidge was right when he declared, "This is a business country, and it wants a business government." What was true of the government's relationship to business at home was also true abroad.

Promoting Prosperity and Peace Abroad

After directing the Senate's successful effort to deny American membership in the League of Nations, Henry Cabot Lodge boasted, "We have torn Wilsonism up by the roots." But repudiation of Wilsonian internationalism and rejection of **collective security** offered through the League of Nations did not mean that the United States retreated into **isolationism.** The United States emerged from World War I with its economy intact and enjoyed a decade of stunning growth. Deep economic involvement in the world and the continuing chaos in Europe made withdrawal impossible. Corporate chieftain Owen Young observed: "Whether the United States will sit in the court of great economic movements throughout the world is not a question which the Senate, or even all of our people combined can decide. We are there . . . inescapably there." New

Coolidge Posing as a Farmer
After the labor wars subsided, the image of Coolidge as the enforcer of law and order gave way to the softer image of "Silent Cal." Though he knew the ways of farming from his youth, the hay and pitchfork are mere props for playing the political game. Coolidge's gleaming dress shoes and the official car with Secret Service men in the background give the game away and show that traditional rural imagery had become nostalgic window dressing for the New Era of wealth and power.
Brown Brothers.

York replaced London as the center of world finance, and the United States became the world's chief creditor. American banks poured billions into war-torn Europe's economic recovery. Europe not only absorbed American loans and products but encountered a flood of American popular culture in the form of fashion, style, and Hollywood motion pictures.

One of the Republicans' most ambitious foreign policy initiatives was the Washington Disarmament Conference that convened in 1921 to establish a global balance of naval power. Secretary of State Charles Evans Hughes shaped the Five-Power Naval Treaty, which was signed in 1922, that committed Britain, France, Japan, Italy, and the United States to a proportional reduction of naval forces. The treaty resulted in the scrapping of more than two million tons of warships, by far the world's greatest success in disarmament. This effort gained President Harding

> The election of 1924 confirmed the defeat of the progressive principle that the state should take a leading role in ensuring the general welfare.

popular acclaim for safeguarding the peace without reopening the contentious issue of whether the United States should join the League. By fostering international peace, he also helped make the world a safer place for American trade.

A second major effort on behalf of world peace came in 1928 when American secretary of state Frank Kellogg joined French foreign minister Aristide Briand to produce the Kellogg-Briand pact. Eventually, nearly fifty nations signed the solemn pledge to renounce war and settle international disputes peacefully. The nation's signature, most Americans hoped, would inoculate it from the foolishness of Wilson's notion of a progressive, uplifting war.

But Republican administrations preferred private sector diplomacy to state action. With the blessing of the White House, a team of American financiers led by the Chicago banker Charles Dawes swung into action when Germany suspended its war reparation payments in 1923. Impoverished, Germany was staggering under the massive bill of $33 billion presented by the victorious Allies in the Versailles treaty. When Germany failed to meet its annual payment, France sought to enforce the treaty by occupying Germany's industrial Ruhr Valley, creating the worst international crisis since the war. In 1924, American corporate leaders produced the Dawes Plan, which halved Germany's annual reparation payments, initiated fresh American loans to Germany, caused the French to retreat from the Ruhr, and got money flowing again in Germany's financial markets. Although the United States failed to join the League and rarely participated in big-power politics, it continued to exercise significant economic and diplomatic influence abroad. These Republican successes overseas helped to fuel prosperity at home.

Automobiles, Mass Production, and Assembly-Line Progress

The automobile industry emerged as the largest single manufacturing industry in the nation. Aided by the federal government's decision to spend more on roads than on anything else, cars, trucks, and buses surged past the railroads by the end of the 1920s as the primary haulers of passengers and freight. Henry Ford made a shrewd decision when he located his company

Detroit and the Automobile Industry in the 1920s

in Detroit. Key materials for the automobile—steel, oil, glass, and rubber—were manufactured in Pennsylvania, Ohio, Indiana, and Illinois, making transportation of these goods convenient (see Map 23.1). The keystone of the American economy, the automobile industry not only employed hundreds of thousands of workers directly but also brought whole industries into being—filling stations, garages, fast-food restaurants, and "guest cottages" (motels). The need for tires, glass, steel, highways, oil, and refined gasoline for automobiles provided millions of related jobs (see "American Places," page 836). By 1929, one American in four found employment directly or indirectly in the automobile industry. "Give us our daily bread" was no longer addressed to the Almighty, one commentator quipped, but to Detroit.

Automobiles altered the face of America. Cars changed where people lived, what work they did, how they spent their leisure, even how they thought. Hundreds of small towns declined or died within the decade, largely because the automobile enabled rural people to bypass them in favor of more distant cities and towns. The one-room schoolhouse and the crossroads church began to vanish from the landscape. Urban streetcars began to disappear as workers moved from the cities to the suburbs and commuted to work along crowded highways. Nothing shaped modern America more than the automobile. And efficient mass production made the automobile revolution possible.

Mass production by the assembly-line technique had become standard in almost every factory, from automobiles to meatpacking to cigarettes. Moreover, Ford's assembly-line success also renewed interest in the **scientific management** movement, pioneered by steel industry engineer Frederick Winslow Taylor at the end of the nineteenth century (see chapter 21). In an effort to improve efficiency, corporations reduced assembly-line work to the simplest, most repetitive tasks. They also established specialized divisions—procurement, production, marketing, and employee relations—each with its own team of professionally trained managers. Such changes on the assembly line and in manage-

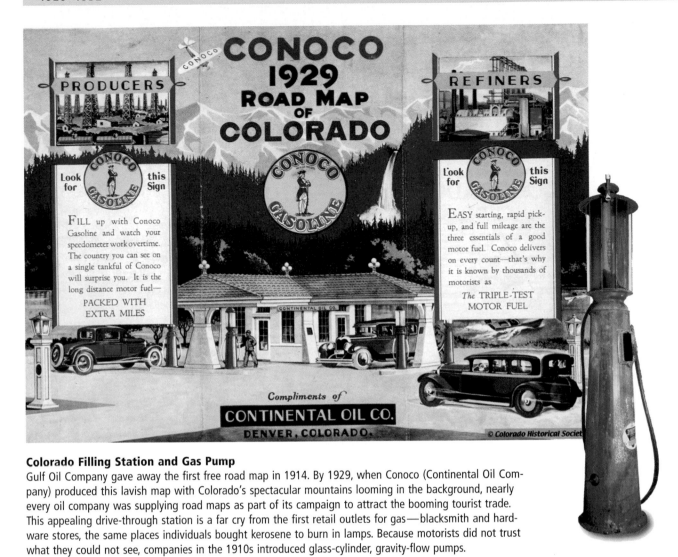

Colorado Filling Station and Gas Pump
Gulf Oil Company gave away the first free road map in 1914. By 1929, when Conoco (Continental Oil Company) produced this lavish map with Colorado's spectacular mountains looming in the background, nearly every oil company was supplying road maps as part of its campaign to attract the booming tourist trade. This appealing drive-through station is a far cry from the first retail outlets for gas—blacksmith and hardware stores, the same places individuals bought kerosene to burn in lamps. Because motorists did not trust what they could not see, companies in the 1910s introduced glass-cylinder, gravity-flow pumps.
Courtesy, Colorado Historical Society.

FOR MORE HELP ANALYZING THIS IMAGE, see the visual activity for this chapter in the Online Study Guide at bedfordstmartins.com/roark.

ment, along with technological advances, significantly boosted overall efficiency. Between 1922 and 1929, productivity in manufacturing increased 32 percent. Average wages, however, increased only 8 percent. As assembly lines became standard, laborers lost many of the skills in which they had once taken pride, but corporations reaped great profits from these changes.

Scientific management also led industries to develop programs beneficial to workers that came to be called **welfare capitalism.** With the help of industrial psychologists and labor consultants, some businesses improved safety and sanitation inside factories and instituted paid va-

cations and contributory pension plans. Welfare capitalism purposely encouraged loyalty to the company and discouraged traditional labor unions. Not wanting to relive the chaotic strikes of 1919, industrialists sought to eliminate reasons for workers to join unions. One labor organizer in the steel industry bemoaned the success of welfare capitalism. "So many workmen here had been lulled to sleep by the company union, the welfare plans, the social organizations fostered by the employer," he declared, "that they had come to look upon the employer as their protector, and had believed vigorous trade union organization unnecessary for their welfare."

AMERICAN PLACES

East Texas Oil Museum, Kilgore, Texas

Re-created Kilgore Street in the East Texas Oil Museum

East Texas Oil Museum.

The automobile revolution of the 1920s ran on petroleum. Wildcatters (individuals who drilled for oil in unlikely areas) fanned out over the Southwest seeking to fill the urgent need. In 1930, they found oil in East Texas, an oil field that became the largest in the lower forty-eight states. The town of Kilgore stands at the center of the vast East Texas Oil Field, and within months of oil's discovery there, wells began sprouting up all over town. By 1931, Kilgore looked like a pin cushion with more than 1,100 wells within the city limits. One oil-crazy Kilgore citizen even drilled a well through the floor of the town's bank. East Texas's most successful wildcatter was H. L.

Hunt, who brought in more than 900 successful wells and thus became one of the country's richest men.

The East Texas Oil Museum, which stands on the campus of Kilgore College in Kilgore, Texas, re-creates the discovery of oil and its production in the early 1930s. Visitors can walk down a re-created street of Kilgore and relive the lives of wildcatters and roughnecks (oil-field workers) who swarmed into the area. A roadster is mired in knee-high mud on Main Street, and a mule-drawn wagon struggles to get through. Along the street are the businesses that catered to the tough oilmen. The museum also depicts the process of drilling for oil with a simulated 3,800-foot elevator ride through multiple layers of rock to the rich deposits deep inside the earth. A film shows historical footage of the chaotic early days of oil drilling—gushers like that at Hunt's Daisy Bradford #3; the building boom that occurred when more than 10,000 people rushed to the tiny town of 500; and the day when the governor ordered the National Guard out to keep peace between the roughnecks, oil speculators, and town folks. Outside the museum an old drilling rig stands as a monument to the courage and fortitude of East Texas's oil pioneers and to the East Texas Oil Field, which continues to produce oil today.

FOR WEB LINKS RELATED TO THIS SITE AND OTHER AMERICAN PLACES, see "PlaceLinks" at bedfordstmartins.com/roark.

Consumer Culture

Mass production's success fueled corporate profits and national economic prosperity. Despite a brief postwar recession, the economy grew spectacularly during the 1920s. Per capita income increased by a third, the cost of living stayed the same, and unemployment remained low. But the rewards of the economic boom were not evenly distributed. Americans who labored with their hands inched ahead, while white, urban Americans in the middle and upper classes enjoyed significantly more spending money and more leisure time to spend it (Figure 23.1). Mass production of a broad range of wonderful new products—automobiles, radios, refrigerators, electric irons, washing machines—produced a consumer goods revolution. (See "The Promise of Technology," page 838.)

In this new era of abundance, more people than ever conceived of the American dream in terms of the things they could acquire. No better guide exists to how the business boom and business values of the 1920s affected average Americans than the classic *Middletown* (1929). Sociologists Robert and Helen Lynd visited the small city of Muncie, Indiana, to compile data on its secular and spiritual life. At the end of five years of study, the Lynds determined that Muncie was, above all, "a culture in which everything hinges on money." Faced with technological and organizational change beyond their comprehension, many citizens had lost confidence in their ability to play an effective role in civic affairs. Instead, they deferred to the supposed expertise of leaders in politics and economics and even in child rearing and so found themselves relegated to the role of more passive consumers.

The pied piper of these disturbing changes, according to the Lynds, was the rapidly expanding business of advertising, which stimulated the desire for new products and "pounded away" at the traditional values of thrift and saving. Newspapers, magazines, radios, and billboards told Americans what they had to have in order to be popular, secure, and successful. The advertising industry linked the possession of material goods to the fulfillment of every spiritual and emotional

> Mass production of a broad range of new products—automobiles, radios, refrigerators, electric irons, washing machines—produced a consumer goods revolution.

FIGURE 23.1 Production of Consumer Goods, 1920–1930

Transportation, communications, and entertainment changed the lives of consumers in the 1920s. Labor-saving devices for the home were popular, but the vastly greater sales of automobiles and radios showed that consumerism was powerful in moving people's attention beyond their homes.

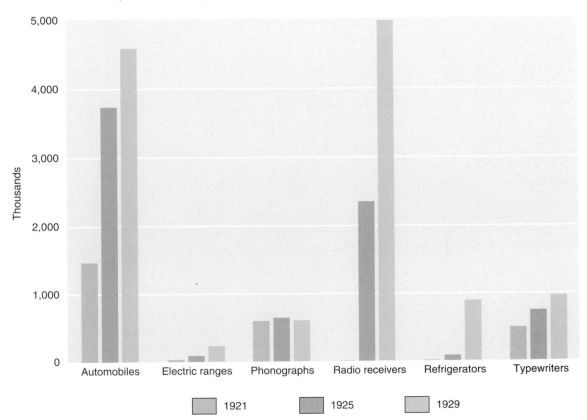

Better Living through Electricity

In the 1920s, after forty years of technical development, prophecies that electricity would be a bearer of leisure and culture seemed about to come true. Thomas Edison, America's greatest inventor of electric marvels, cheerfully predicted that electrified homes would free women from household drudgery. Warming to his subject, Edison suggested that some women might then be able to develop their minds as highly as men. Perpetual light might eliminate the need for sleep. Perhaps, he concluded, someone might even invent electrical means for communicating with the dead.

Edison's hard-driving protégé Samuel Insull led in expanding electricity from commercial to domestic use. Insull's Chicago-based Commonwealth Edison Company, with General Electric and Westinghouse close behind, provided the power to increase the number of homes with electricity from 14 percent in 1910 to 70 percent in 1930. Now the lights that had shown exclusively on the privileged could also shine on average Americans and their aspirations—as long as they lived in the cities.

A barrage of advertising— General Electric alone raised its annual budget from $2 million to $12 million between 1922 and 1930— fanned Americans' expectations of a better life. Without sooty gaslights, their houses would be easier to maintain, and electric vacuum cleaners would lessen whatever toil was still necessary. Electric refrigerators would keep a wide array of food available for elegant entertaining, electric washers and irons would facilitate high fashion, and radios would bring knowledge and music into comfortable, air-conditioned homes. One General Electric ad cheerily announced that, nowadays, "nobody works but ol' man river." Chiding foolish backwardness, other ads insisted that "any woman who turns the wringer [on a hand-operated clothes washer] . . . who cooks in a hot stuffy kitchen is doing work which electricity will do for a few cents per day." Rather than struggling with wringers and scrub boards, women could relax and listen to the radio "soap operas" sponsored by the makers of the laundry detergents foaming in their automatic washers.

Yet, despite $555 million in utility revenues by 1928, the promise of an idyllic electric future was hard to keep. Because electric companies saw little profit in running lines into sparsely settled rural areas, country folk lacked access. And the urban poor could not afford to buy into the fully wired paradise. Most city homes, for example, stayed with iceboxes until the late 1930s because they were considerably cheaper to buy and use than electric refrigerators. Freezers were so much more expensive that, although the advantages of frozen food were known in the 1920s, their use was limited to hotels and ocean liners until the late 1940s. Television, another invention of the 1920s, remained undeveloped for lack of financial support, and air conditioning was rarely used because the very people in the hottest parts of the country who needed it most were least able to afford it.

To the extent that electric appliances found a place in American homes, they did not bear out utopian dreams of leisure. The gleaming new devices fostered expectations of higher standards of cleanliness that housewives could meet only by operating their appliances early and often. In some affluent homes, the burden was lightened by servants who used the appliances. But the number of domestic servants was declining because the booming 1920s economy offered better-paying work

need. Americans increasingly defined and measured their social status, and indeed their personal worth, on the yardstick of material possessions. Happiness itself rode on owning a car and choosing the right cigarettes and toothpaste.

By the 1920s, the United States had achieved the physical capacity to satisfy Americans' material wants. The economic problem shifted from production to consumption: Who would buy the goods flying off American assembly lines? One solution was to expand America's markets in in offices and factories—including those that manufactured electric appliances. Electricity boosters, however, remained unfazed until the end of the decade.

The gap between technology's promises and real life was magnified by the 1929 stock market crash and ensuing depression, which shattered many consumer dreams. While the means to pay for electricity dwindled, the collapse of Insull's electric empire revealed a tangle of fraud and corruption. Insull was indicted and vilified as the bearer of technology's false hopes. Ironically, in the face of such woes, one of the most popular electric inventions, the radio, provided old-fashioned reassurance. In the 1930s, families that had been lured from their traditional closeness around the hearth by central heating and electric light in every room huddled around technology's electronic hearth—the radio—to hear President Franklin Roosevelt pledge protection of their homes and basic values in his fireside chats (see chapter 24). Once prosperity returned, they were assured, the promise of a bright electric future would be renewed.

Hard times eventually eased, and sales of new appliances soared again. But surveys showed that the hours people spent taking care of their households remained essentially the same as before the advent of electricity. Only in the boom years after World War II would electricity begin to deliver on its promise.

Westinghouse

The "COMPLETELY BALANCED" Electric Refrigerator

A PRODUCT OF TWELVE YEARS' SCIENTIFIC RESEARCH BY THE WESTINGHOUSE ENGINEERING STAFF

Westinghouse
Advertisements like this one from a 1931 issue of *The Saturday Evening Post* often presented the promise of electricity in terms of its almost magical powers. The illustrator, Rockwell Kent, makes the generating plant in the background puny in comparison with the superhuman reflector of lightning and the fireball next to her. As a result, the "completely balanced" electric refrigerator seems a marvel created out of nature by divine genius. Still, scientists and managers at the corporate giant Westinghouse gladly accepted credit.
Picture Research Consultants & Archives.

foreign countries, and government and business joined in that effort. Another solution to the problem of consumption was to expand the market at home.

Henry Ford had realized early on what became accepted truth in the 1920s: "Mass production requires mass consumption." Understanding that automobile workers not only produced cars but would buy them if they made enough money, Ford in 1914 raised wages in his factories to $5 a day, more than twice the going rate. High wages made for workers who were more loyal

Lucky Strike

Smoking cigarettes promised instant maturity, sophistication, and worldlinesss—and, as revealed in this 1929 advertisement for the popular brand Lucky Strike, a svelte figure. Any woman seeking to remain attractive by avoiding matronly extra pounds could just reach for her Luckies. In the 1920s, Americans smoked billions of cigarettes each year, and they could puff Luckies confident that because they were "toasted," they were "purified." How did smokers know that they ran no health risk? Because precisely 20,679 physicians said so! How has cigarette advertising changed? How has it remained the same? Gaslight Advertising Archives.

and more exploitable, and high wages returned as profits when workers bought Fords.

Not all industrialists were as far-seeing as Ford. The wages of many workers barely edged upward; many people's incomes were too puny to satisfy the growing addiction to consumer goods. Business supplied the solution: Americans could realize their dreams through credit. Installment buying—a little money down, a payment each month—allowed people to purchase expensive items they could not otherwise afford or purchase items before saving the necessary money. As one newspaper announced, "The first

responsibility of an American to his country is no longer that of a citizen, but of a consumer." During the 1920s, America's motto became spend, not save, and replace, rather than make do. American culture had shifted.

The Roaring Twenties

By the beginning of the decade, psychoanalyst Sigmund Freud had become a household name. Most Americans were spared the complexity of his pioneering work in the psychology of the unconscious by learning about his therapies in popular magazines that stressed self-fulfillment. Still, people realized that Freud offered a way of looking at the world that was as radically different and important to the twentieth century as Charles Darwin's theory of evolution had been to the century before.

In the twenties, much to Freud's disgust, the American media turned his therapeutic wisdom about the sexual origins of behavior on its head. If it is wrong to deny that we are sexual beings, some reasoned, then the key to health and fulfillment must lie in following impulse freely. Those who doubted this reasoning were simply "repressed."

The new ethic of personal freedom excited a significant number of Americans to seek pleasure without guilt in a whirl of activity that earned the decade the name "Roaring Twenties." Prohibition made lawbreakers of millions of otherwise decent folks. Flappers and "new women" challenged traditional gender boundaries. Other Americans, inhibited by conscience or concern for appearances, enjoyed the "Roaring Twenties" at a safe distance through the words and images of vastly expanded mass communication. Motion pictures, radio, and magazines marketed celebrities. In the freedom of America's big cities, particularly New York, a burst of creativity produced a "New Negro," who confounded and disturbed white Americans. And a "lost generation" of writers, profoundly disillusioned with mainstream America's cultural direction, fled the country.

Prohibition

Republicans generally sought to curb the powers of government and liberate private initiative, but the twenties witnessed a great exception to this rule when the federal government implemented one of the last reforms of the Progressive Era, the Eighteenth Amendment, which banned the manufacture and sale of alcohol and took effect in January 1920 (see chapter 22, page 802). Drying up the rivers of liquor that Americans consumed, supporters of prohibition declared, would boost production, eliminate crime, and lift the nation's morality. Women particularly lent support to prohibition because heavy drinking was closely associated with domestic violence and poverty. Charged with enforcing prohibition, the Treasury Department put more than 3,000 agents in the field, and in 1925 alone, they smashed more than 172,000 illegal stills.

Treasury agents succeeded in lowering the consumption of alcohol, but they faced a staggering task. Local resistance was intense. In 1929, an agent in Indiana reported, "Conditions in most important cities very bad. Lax and corrupt public officials great handicap . . . prevalence of drinking among minor boys and the . . . middle or better class of adults." (See "Historical Question," page 842.) The "speakeasy," a place where men (and, increasingly, women) drank publicly, became a common feature of the urban landscape. There, bootleggers, so named a century before because they put bottles in their tall boots to sneak past tax collectors, provided whiskey smuggled from Canada, tequila from Mexico, and liquor concocted in makeshift stills. Otherwise upright people discovered the thrill of breaking the law. One dealer, trading on common knowledge that whiskey still flowed in the White House, distributed cards advertising himself as the "President's Bootlegger."

Eventually, serious criminals took over the liquor trade. They made bootlegging a highly organized big business. Although Alphonse "Al" Capone's business cards listed his occupation as "secondhand furniture dealer," Capone became the era's most notorious gang lord by establishing a bootlegging empire in Chicago that reputedly grossed more than $60 million in a single year. During the first four years of prohibition, Chicago witnessed over 200 gang-related killings as rival mobs struggled for control of the lucrative liquor trade. The most notorious event came on St. Valentine's Day, 1929, when Capone's Italian-dominated mob machine-gunned seven members of a rival Irish gang. Federal authorities finally sent Capone to prison for income tax evasion, but by then he had achieved hero status in the eyes of some immigrant youth eager to escape poor ethnic ghettos as Capone had done. Capone was a gangster, but he was also a resourceful entrepreneur and successful businessman.

Gang-war slayings generated by enforcement of the Eighteenth Amendment prompted demands for its repeal. In 1931, a panel of distinguished experts reported to President Hoover that prohibition, which Hoover had once called "a great social and economic experiment," had failed. The social and political costs of prohibition outweighed the benefits. Prohibition caused ordinary citizens to disrespect the law, corrupted the police, and demoralized the judiciary. In 1933, after thirteen years, the nation ended prohibition.

The New Woman

Of all the changes in American life in the 1920s, none sparked more heated debates than the alternatives offered to the traditional roles of women. Increasing numbers of women worked and went to college. Older gender hierarchies and norms shook under the onslaught of the changes in American society. Even mainstream magazines like *Ladies' Home Journal* and *Saturday Evening Post* offered radical challenges to Victorian notions of female propriety. The *Post* began publishing stories early in the decade about young, college-educated women who drank gin cocktails, smoked cigarettes, wore skimpy dresses and dangly necklaces, daringly rolled their stockings at the knee, swore like sailors, and enjoyed sex. Before the Great War, the "new woman" dwelt in New York City's bohemian Greenwich Village, but afterward the mass media brought her into middle-class America's living rooms.

Politically, women entered uncharted territory in the 1920s. The Nineteenth Amendment, ratified in 1920, granted women the vote and set off wild speculation about how women would exercise their new right. **Feminists** expected women to reshape the political landscape. Women quickly began pressuring Congress to pass laws that especially concerned women, including measures to protect women in factories, grant federal aid to schools, and promote disarmament. Black women activists lobbied particularly for federal courts to assume jurisdiction over the crime of lynching, but white Southerners crushed the effort. Women achieved a measure of victory in 1921 when Congress enacted the Sheppard-Towner Act, which extended federal assistance to states seeking to reduce shockingly high infant mortality rates. Rather

Was Prohibition a Bad Idea?

Americans have always been fond of alcohol. By the 1830s, the average adult was consuming a yearly total of 14 gallons of hard liquor, mostly whiskey and rum. Alarm over what one historian has called the "alcoholic republic" eventually produced two unique developments. First, the United States became the world's only society ever to outlaw its most popular intoxicant. Second, to accomplish that feat, Americans passed the only constitutional amendment to be subsequently repealed.

At the end of the nineteenth century, prohibitionists challenged the thousands of saloons that were springing up alongside factories and in immigrant neighborhoods. Prominent dry champion Reverend Mark Matthews raged against the saloon, "the most fiendish, corrupt and hell-soaked institution that ever crawled out of the slime of the eternal pit." To back up such claims, the Anti-Saloon League produced statistics and scientific studies of drunkenness, vividly portraying horror stories of its destructive results. A powerful coalition against alcohol emerged. Because saloons were mostly male preserves—awash with gambling and prostitution as well as beer—they roused strong resistance from advocates for women and children, who suffered most of the saloons' bad side effects. Prohibition also became linked to nativism and anti-Catholicism when old-line Yankees and old-time Protestants backed efforts to ban saloons frequented by Irish and German Catholics. Mobilization for World War I added another boost when the army insisted soldiers remain pure in spirit and free of drink. Many industrialists advocated prohibition because efficiency experts advised that alcohol was the enemy of a productive workplace and thus of a successful war effort. With such broad support, the prohibition amendment was easily ratified in 1919.

Prohibition enjoyed some success. At the start of the Jazz Age, saloons disappeared from American street corners, and Americans emerged from prohibition drinking less than before. The annual per person consumption of alcoholic beverages declined from 2.60 gallons per capita just before prohibition to 0.97 gallons in 1934, the year after prohibition ended. Down as well were arrests for drunken disorder, along with alcohol-related deaths and psychoses.

Nonetheless, the "noble experiment," as Herbert Hoover called prohibition, became the butt of jokes. To critics, prohibition was a ridiculous violation of human nature by puritanical busybodies. H. L. Mencken, a cynical journalist who appreciated the German beer halls in his native Baltimore, jeered that given the depth of human depravity, society would be safer if people were drunk all the time.

An avalanche of other objections helped overthrow prohibition. As gangsters moved into bootlegging and bodies began to pile up, the public became convinced that prohibition was more about crime than about redemption. Believers in individual and **states' rights** joined the clamor by opposing the federal government's attempt to control private behavior. And even the most committed "drys" found it difficult to claim that prohibition was a noble experiment once the Ku Klux Klan used it as a justification for a brutal campaign against minorities. At the head of the parade to repeal the Eighteenth Amendment marched a group of practical businessmen. By 1930, several of them pushed for repeal of prohibition, convinced that

than the beginning of women's political success, however, the act marked the high tide of women's influence in the 1920s.

A number of factors helped to dilute women's political influence. Most important, women, like men, held a wide range of political views. In addition, male domination of both political parties, the rarity of female candidates, and lack of experience in voting, especially among recent immigrants, kept many women away from the polls. In the South, poll taxes, residency requirements, literacy tests, as well as outright terrorism, continued to decimate the vote of African Americans, men and women alike. Some women, deeply anxious about shifting gender roles, refused to join in political activity at all.

banning alcohol was more likely to produce an unruly lower class, angry over losing their saloons, than a sober and docile workforce as they had once believed.

The repeal of prohibition in 1933 set off a rush of profit seekers, including gangsters who converted their bootlegging empires into legitimate businesses. Heavy advertising campaigns, along with story lines on radio and in the movies, promoted drinking and smoking as signs of sophistication and success. Making the old vices respectable and glamorous helped reverse the decline in drinking; by the 1970s, Americans had reached the pre-prohibition levels of consumption. By 1996, 52 percent of the population, or 111 million persons, used alcohol; of these, 32 million were part of a new binge-drinking trend and about 11 million were alcoholics. A quarter of the alcoholics also abused drugs.

Alarm over substance abuse in the latter part of the twentieth century led to sharply divided action. Memory of the prohibition fiasco prevented any serious consideration of outlawing alcohol use except by minors; rescue of the expanding number of alcoholics was left mainly to the self-help of Alcoholics Anonymous (AA), a private group founded in 1935, two years after prohibition

Prohibition Action
Prohibition agents sometimes entertained appreciative audiences. The wastefulness of pouring 900 gallons of perfectly good wine down a drain in Los Angeles amuses some spectators and troubles others. Of course, those who had an interest in drinking despite the law could witness the disposal of bootleg alcohol serenely confident that they could easily find more.
Corbis.

ended. Other drugs, however, were strictly prohibited. Efforts culminated in the Anti–Drug Abuse Acts of 1986 and 1988, which set mandatory minimum sentences for using as well as dealing controlled substances and established the nation's first "drug czar" to coordinate several federal agencies in a "war on drugs."

This new approach to the drug problem created problems of its own.

Ten years after passage of the first Anti–Drug Abuse Act, the United States stood out in the world as the country with the largest proportion of its population in jail. The number of newly admitted prisoners, most of them in on drug charges, rose by 120 percent between 1986 and 1996, bringing the total incarcerated to a record 1 million, at an estimated increase in cost from $45.6 billion to $93.8 billion. By 2000, the number of persons behind bars in America for nonviolent drug offenses alone, a disproportionate percentage of them black and Hispanic, exceeded the prison population of all European nations combined. Yet, despite the crackdown and a corresponding wave of antidrug propaganda, an estimated 25 million Americans continued to use hard drugs, and double that number smoked marijuana.

The unwelcome ghost of prohibition has hovered confusingly around subsequent efforts to crack down on the abuse of drugs. The Eighteenth Amendment was repealed on the grounds that outlawing drink had been a spectacular failure that bred disrespect for the law. America today, however, has suffered an even greater defeat, for unlike prohibition the current war on drugs has not produced a decline in the use of forbidden substances.

Moreover, rather than forming a solid voting bloc, feminists divided. Some argued for women's right to special protection; others demanded equal protection. The radical National Woman's Party fought for an Equal Rights Amendment, which the party put before Congress in 1923. The amendment made all forms of discrimination against women illegal: "Men and women shall have equal rights throughout the United States. . . ." The more moderate League of Women Voters feared that the amendment's wording threatened state laws that provided women special protection, such as barring women from night work and preventing them from working on certain machines. The Equal Rights Amendment went down to defeat, and

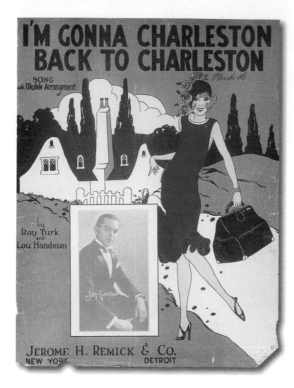

Charleston Flapper

The music to this popular 1920s tune portrays the kind of postadolescent girl who was making respectable families frantic. Flappers scandalized their middle-class parents by ripping up the old moral codes. This saucy young woman wears the latest fashion and clearly suffers from what one critic called "the intoxication of rouge." She's kicking up her high heels in anticipation of doing the Charleston, one of those modern dances the *Catholic Telegraph* of Cincinnati denounced: "The music is sensuous, the embracing of partners—the female only half dressed—is absolutely indecent; and the motions—they are such as may not be described, with any respect for propriety, in a family newspaper."

Picture Research Consultants & Archives.

> Rather than forming a solid voting block, feminists divided. Some argued for women's right to special protection; others demanded equal protection.

women who stuck with a progressive agenda were forced to act within a network of private agencies and reform associations to advance the causes of birth control, legal equality for minorities, and the end of child labor.

Economically, women's relationship to paid work changed. More women worked for pay—approximately one in four by 1930—but they clustered in "women's jobs." The proportion of women working in manufacturing fell, while the number of women working as secretaries, stenographers, typists, and office clerks skyrocketed. Women almost monopolized the occupations of librarian, nurse, elementary school teacher, and telephone operator. Women also represented 40 percent of salesclerks by 1930. More female white-collar workers meant fewer women were interested in protective legislation for women; "new women" wanted salaries and opportunities equal to men's.

Increased earnings gave working women more buying power and a special relationship with the new **consumer culture**. A stereotype of the new earning and spending young women soon emerged in which women spent freely on clothes and cosmetics. The flapper, so called because of the short-lived fad of wearing unbuckled galoshes, was a woman who had short "bobbed" hair and wore lipstick and rouge. She favored the latest styles—dresses with short skirts and drop waists, bare arms, and no petticoats—and she danced all night to wild jazz.

The new woman both reflected and propelled the modern birth control movement as well. Margaret Sanger, the crusading pioneer for contraception during the Progressive Era, restated her principal conviction in 1920: "No woman can call herself free until she can choose consciously whether she will or will not be a mother." By shifting strategy in the twenties, Sanger successfully courted the conservative American Medical Association, linked birth control with the eugenics movement, which advocated limiting reproduction among "undesirable" groups, and thus made contraception a respectable subject for discussion.

Flapper style and values spread from coast to coast through films, novels, magazines, and advertisements. New women challenged older American certainties of **separate spheres** for women and men, the double standard of sexual conduct, and Victorian ideas of proper female appearance and behavior. While the majority of American women in the 1920s were decidedly not radical new women, all women, even those who remained at home, felt the great changes of the era. The greater availability of birth control, for example, meant that married couples could be sexually active and still control family size.

The New Negro

The 1920s witnessed the emergence not only of a "new woman" but of a "New Negro" as well. And both new identities riled conservatives and reactionaries. African Americans who challenged the caste system that confined dark-skinned Americans to the lowest levels of society confronted whites who insisted that race relations would not change. Cheers for black soldiers quickly faded after their return from the First World War, and African Americans soon faced grim days of race riots and economic hardship (see chapter 22).

Still, a sense of optimism remained strong among African Americans. In New York City, hope and talent came together to form an exceptionally dynamic moment in black history. Poor blacks from the South, as well as sophisticated immigrants from the West Indies, poured into Harlem in uptown Manhattan. New York City's black population increased 115 percent (from 152,000 to 327,000) in the 1920s, while white population increased only 20 percent. Similar demographic changes occurred on a smaller scale throughout the urban North. Overcrowding and unsanitary housing accompanied this black population explosion, but so too did a new self-consciousness and self-confidence that fed into political activity.

During the 1920s, the prominent African American intellectual W. E. B. Du Bois and the National Association for the Advancement of Colored People (NAACP) aggressively pursued the passage of a federal antilynching law to counter mob violence against blacks in the South. Many poor urban blacks, however, disillusioned with mainstream politics, turned for new leadership to a Jamaican-born visionary named Marcus Garvey. Garvey regularly mounted a soapbox at 135th Street and Lenox Avenue in New York City to urge African Americans to rediscover the heritage of Africa, take pride in their own culture and achievements, and maintain racial purity by avoiding **miscegenation**. He denounced the NAACP for its reliance on white funding, its acceptance of white members, and the prominence of light-skinned blacks like Du Bois within its membership. In 1917, Garvey launched the Universal Negro Improvement Association (UNIA) to help African Americans gain economic and political independence entirely outside white society. After the war, the UNIA gained thousands of new members and in 1919 created its own shipping company, the Black Star Line, to support the migration of black Americans to Africa (a movement known as "Back to Africa"). Garvey knew how to inspire followers, but he was no businessman, and the enterprise was a massive economic failure. In 1927, the federal government pinned charges of illegal practices on Garvey and deported him to

Jamaica. Nevertheless, the issues Garvey raised about racial pride, black identity, and the search for equality persisted, and his legacy remains at the center of **black nationalist** thought.

During this active time, an extraordinary mix of black artists, sculptors, novelists, musicians, and poets made Harlem their home. They introduced to the world a "New Negro," as Howard University scholar Alain Locke put it in 1925 in a book by that name, who rose from the ashes of slavery and segregation to proclaim African Americans' creative genius. The emergence of the New Negro came to be known as the Harlem Renaissance. Harlem became home to African American intellectuals, artists, and social leaders who deliberately set out to create a distinctive African American culture that drew on their identities as Americans and Africans. Building on the independence and pride displayed by black soldiers during the war, they sought to defeat the fresh onslaught of racial discrimination and violence with poems, paintings, and plays. "We younger Negro artists . . . intend to express our individual dark-skinned selves without fear or shame," Langston Hughes, a determined young black poet, said of the Harlem Renaissance. "If white people are pleased, we are glad. If they are not, it doesn't matter. We know we are beautiful. And ugly, too."

The Harlem Renaissance produced dazzling talent. Black writer James Weldon Johnson, who in 1903 had written the Negro national anthem, "Lift Every Voice," wrote "God's Trombones" (1927), in which he expressed the wisdom and beauty of black folktales from the South. Zora Neale Hurston focused on those tales as an anthropology student at Barnard College. Her masterpiece, a novel called *Their Eyes Were Watching God* (1937), explores the complex passions of black people in a southern community. Langston Hughes, Claude McKay, and Countee Cullen wrote poetry conveying the vitality of life in Harlem. Black painters, led by Aaron Douglas, linked African art, from which European modernist artists had begun taking inspiration, to the concept of the New Negro. In bold, colorful scenes, Douglas combined biblical and African myths in ways that expressed a powerful

> Harlem became home to African American intellectuals, artists, and social leaders who deliberately set out to create a distinctive African American culture that drew on their identities as Americans and Africans.

Noah's Ark

Kansas-born painter Aaron Douglas expressed the Harlem Renaissance visually. When Douglas arrived in New York City in 1925, he quickly attracted the attention of W. E. B. Du Bois, who believed that the arts could manifest the African American soul. At Du Bois's urging, Douglas sought ways of integrating the African cultural heritage with American experience. This depiction of an African Noah commanding the loading of the ark displays a technique that became closely associated with African American art: strong silhouetted figures awash in misty color, indicating a connection between Christian faith and the vital, colorful origins of black Americans in a distant, mythologized African past.

Fisk University Art Galleries.

> Thousands of movie palaces sprang up in cities across the country. Admission was cheap, and in the dark, Americans of all classes could savor the same ideal of the good life.

the Cotton Club through delivery doors and could not use the restrooms, which were for whites only. The vigor and optimism of the Harlem Renaissance left a powerful legacy for black Americans, but the creative burst did little in the short run to dissolve the prejudice of a white society not yet prepared to allow African Americans equal opportunities.

Mass Culture

By the late 1920s, jazz had captured the nation. Americans who clung to symphonic music as the epitome of high culture might still call jazz "jungle music," but jazz giants such as Louis Armstrong, Jelly Roll Morton, Duke Ellington, and King Oliver, accompanied by singers such as Ma Rainey, Bessie Smith, and Ethel Waters, entertained huge audiences. Jazz was only one of the entertainment choices of Americans, however. In the twenties, popular culture, like consumer goods, was mass-produced and -consumed. Since politics was undemanding and uninteresting, Americans looked elsewhere for excitement. The proliferation of movies, radios, music, and sports meant that they found plenty to do, and in doing the same things, they helped create a national culture.

Nothing offered such escapist delights as the movies. Starting with the construction of the Regent Theatre in New York City in 1913, thousands of movie palaces, some of them larger and more ornate than European opera houses, sprang up in cities across the country. Admission was cheap, and in the dark, Americans of all classes could savor the same ideal of the good life. Blacks and whites, however, still entered theaters through separate entrances and sat separately.

The center of the film industry moved in the 1920s from makeshift sound stages in New York City to Hollywood, California, where producers found open space and endless sunshine. A new breed of entrepreneur, the movie mogul, soon discovered the successful formula of combining opulence, sex, and adventure. By 1929, Hollywood was drawing more than 80 million people to the movies in a single week, as many as lived in the entire country. Rudolph Valentino, described as "catnip to women," and Clara Bow, the "It Girl" (everyone knew what *it* was), became household names. "America's Sweetheart," Mary Pickford, and her real-life husband, Douglas Fairbanks, offered more wholesome adventure. Comedy made the closest connection

cultural heritage for African Americans.

Despite such vibrancy, for most whites, Harlem remained a separate black ghetto known to them only for its lively nightlife. Fashionable whites crowded into Harlem's nightclubs, the most famous of which was the Cotton Club, a gangster-owned speakeasy. There, whites believed, they could hear "real" jazz, a relatively new musical form, in its "natural" surroundings. In reality, black performers hired to entertain strictly white audiences had to enter

Heroes and Heroines

Two kinds of women look up adoringly at two kinds of 1920s heroes. A wholesome image is seen to the left on this 1927 cover of *People Popular Monthly* magazine. The healthy outdoor girl, smartly turned out in her raccoon coat and pennant, flatters a naive college football hero but remains in control. At the right, the pale, sensitive Vilma Banky kneels imploringly before the hypnotic gaze of the movies' greatest heartthrob, Rudolph Valentino. The 1926 movie poster titillates with ambivalence: Is the pale heroine beseeching her kidnapper to release her? Or is she swooning with desire as the sheik begins to disrobe?

Magazine: Picture Research Consultants & Archives; poster: Billy Rose Theatre Collection, The New York Public Library at Lincoln Center.

with audiences, however, especially in calling sympathetic attention to the pitfalls and absurdity ordinary people experienced. Most loved of all the comics was Charlie Chaplin, whose famous character, the wistful tramp, showed an endearing inability to cope with the rules and complexities of modern life.

Americans also found heroes in sports. Baseball, professionalized since 1869 and segregated into white and black leagues, solidified its place as the national pastime in the 1920s (Figure 23.2). It remained essentially a game played by and for the working class, an outlet for raw energy with a tinge of rebelliousness. In George Herman "Babe" Ruth, baseball had the most cherished free spirit of the time. An incorrigible whose parents sent him to reform school at age eight, Ruth mixed his record-setting home runs with rowdy escapades, satisfying the view that sports offered a way to break out of the ordinariness of everyday life.

The public also fell in love with a young boxer from the grim mining districts of Colorado. As a teenager, Jack Dempsey had made his living hanging around saloons betting he could beat anyone in the house. When he took the heavyweight crown just after World War I, he was revered as America's equalizer, a stand-in for the average American who felt increasingly confined by bureaucracy and machine-made culture. In Philadelphia in 1926, a crowd of 125,000 fans saw challenger Gene Tunney carve up and defeat the people's champ.

Football, essentially a college sport, held greater sway with the upper classes. The most famous coach, Knute Rockne of Notre Dame, celebrated football for its life lessons of hard work and teamwork. Let the professors make learning as interesting and significant as football, Rockne advised, and the problem of getting youth to learn would disappear. But in keeping with the times, football moved toward a more commercial spectacle. The gridiron's greatest hero, Harold "Red" Grange, the "Galloping Ghost," a quiet, straitlaced son of the prairies, led the way by going from stardom at the University of Illinois to the Chicago Bears in the new professional football league.

The decade's hero worship reached its zenith in the celebration of Charles Lindbergh, a young pilot who set out on May 20, 1927, from Long Island in his specially built single-engine plane, *The Spirit of St. Louis*, to become the first person to fly nonstop across the Atlantic. Thirty-three hours later, Lindbergh landed in the midst of a wildly cheering crowd at the Paris airport. Newspapers tagged Lindbergh the "Lone Eagle"—the perfect hero for an age that celebrated individual accomplishment. "Charles Lindbergh," one journalist proclaimed, "is the stuff out of which have been made the pioneers that opened up the wilderness. His are the qualities which we, as a people, must nourish." Lindbergh realized, however, that technical and organizational complexity was fast reducing chances for solitary achievement. To make the point about a new sort of heroism, he entitled his book about the flight *We* (1927) to include the machine that made it all possible.

Another machine—the radio—became important to mass culture in the 1920s. The nation's first licensed radio station, KDKA in Pittsburgh, began broadcasting in 1920, and soon American airwaves buzzed with news, sermons, soap operas, sports, comedy, and music. Americans isolated in the high plains laughed at the latest jokes from New York. For the first time, citizens were able to listen to the voices of political candidates without leaving home. Because they could now reach prospective customers in their own homes, advertisers bankrolled the new medium's rapid growth. Between 1922 and 1929,

Movie Attendance

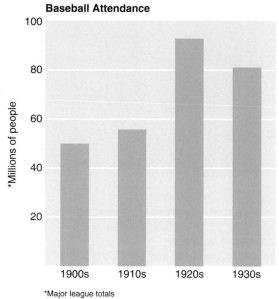

Baseball Attendance

*Major league totals

FIGURE 23.2 Movie and Baseball Attendance
America's favorite pastimes, movies and baseball, served as a fever chart for the economy. The percentage of national income spent by spectators of movies and major league baseball remained nearly constant during the interwar years; the rise and fall of weekly movie attendance and seasonal baseball attendance mirrored the rise and fall of prosperity.

the number of radio stations in the United States increased from 30 to 606. In those seven short years, homes with radios jumped from 60,000 to a staggering 10,250,000.

Radio added to the spread of popular music, especially jazz. Young people particularly welcomed jazz's energetic style and its suggestion of freedom and sexual openness. Jazz provided the sounds for the rebellious mood of youth, who for the first time in the 1920s became a social class distinct in itself. As the traditional bonds of community, religion, and family loosened, the young felt less pressure to imitate their elders and more freedom to develop their own culture. An increasing number of college students helped the "rah-rah" style of college life become a fad, promoted in movies, songs, and advertisements. The collegiate set was the vanguard of the decade's "flaming youth."

The Lost Generation

Some writers and artists felt alienated from America's mass-culture society, which they found shallow, anti-intellectual, and materialistic. Adoration of silly movie stars and other favorites of popular culture disgusted them. Moreover, they believed that business culture and business values blighted nearly every aspect of American life. To their minds, Henry Ford made a poor hero. Young, white, and mostly college educated, these expatriates, as they came to be called, felt embittered by the war and renounced the progressives who had promoted it as a crusade. For them, Europe—not Hollywood or Harlem—seemed the place to seek their renaissance.

The American-born writer Gertrude Stein, long established in Paris, remarked famously as the young exiles gathered around her, "They are the lost generation." Most of the expatriates, however, believed to the contrary that they had finally found themselves. The cost of living in Paris was low and the culture receptive to free expression. Far from the complications of home and steady work, the expatriates helped launch the most creative period in American art and literature in the twentieth century.

The novelist whose spare, clean style best exemplified the expatriate efforts to make art mirror basic reality was Ernest Hemingway. Hemingway's experience in the war convinced him that the world in which he was raised, with its Christian moralism and belief in progress, was bankrupt. His code of honor dismissed creeds, ideologies, and patriotism as pious attempts to cover up the fact that life is a losing battle with death. Hemingway expressed his ideal of macho courage, "grace under pressure," with unflinching directness in his novel *The Sun Also Rises* (1926). The central characters discover little to sustain them on a journey through Spain and France except their own animal ability to appreciate sensual experience and endure suffering. Admirers found the novel's terse language

and hard lessons perfect expressions of a world stripped of illusions.

Many writers who remained in America were exiles in spirit. Before the war, intellectuals had eagerly joined progressive, even radical, reform movements that sought social uplift and regeneration. Afterward, they were more likely to act as lonely critics of American cultural barrenness and vulgarity. With prose dripping with scorn for conventional values, novelist Sinclair Lewis in *Main Street* (1920) and *Babbitt* (1922) satirized his native Midwest as a cultural wasteland. Humorists like James Thurber created outlandish characters to poke fun at American stupidity and inhibitions. And southern writers, led by William Faulkner, railed against the South's reputation as a literary desert by exploring the dark undercurrents of that region's grim class and race heritage. But worries about alienation surfaced as well. Although he gained fame and wealth as chronicler of flaming youth, F. Scott Fitzgerald spoke sadly in *This Side of Paradise* (1920) of a disillusioned generation "grown up to find all Gods dead, all wars fought, all faiths in man shaken."

Resistance to Change

Large areas of the country did not share in the wealth of the 1920s and had little confidence that they would anytime soon. By the end of the decade, 40 percent of the nation's farmers were landless, and 90 percent of rural homes had no indoor plumbing, gas, or electricity. Rural America had known a troubled relationship with urban America since the nineteenth century, but wariness and distrust turned to despair in 1920s when the census reported that the majority of the population had shifted from the country to the city (Map 23.2). Urban domination over the nation's political and cultural life and sharply rising economic disparity drove rural Americans in often ugly, reactionary directions.

The cities seemed to stand for everything rural areas stood against. Rural America imagined itself as solidly Anglo-Saxon (despite the presence of millions of African Americans in the South and Mexican Americans, Native Americans, and Asian Americans in the West), and the cities seemed to be filling up with immigrants—swarthy, different, and potentially dangerous foreigners. Rural America was the home

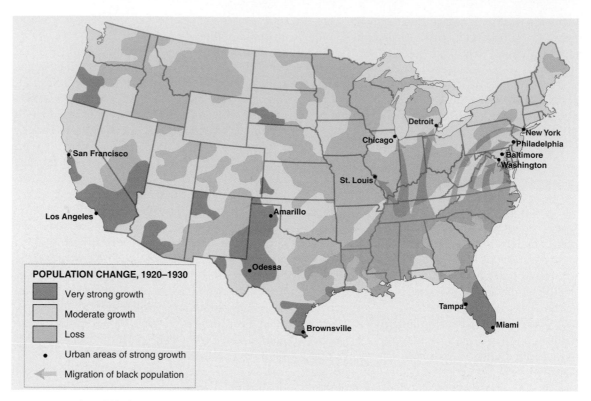

MAP 23.2   The Shift from Rural to Urban Population, 1920–1930
The movement of whites and Hispanics toward urban and agricultural opportunity made Florida, the West, and the Southwest the regions of fastest population growth. In contrast, large numbers of blacks left the rural South to find a better life in the North. Because almost all migrating blacks went from the countryside to cities in distant parts of the nation, while white and Hispanic migrants tended to move shorter distances toward familiar places, the population shift brought more drastic overall change to blacks than to whites and Hispanics.

READING THE MAP: Which states held the areas of strongest growth? To which cities did southern blacks predominantly migrate?
CONNECTIONS: What conditions in the countryside made the migration to urban areas appealing to many rural Americans? In what social and cultural ways did rural America view itself as different from urban America?

FOR MORE HELP ANALYZING THIS MAP, see the map activity for this chapter in the Online Study Guide at bedfordstmartins.com/roark.

of old-time **Protestant** religion, and the cities teamed with Catholics, Jews, liberal Protestants, and atheists. Rural America championed old-fashioned moral standards—abstinence, self-denial, and regenerative suffering—while the cities spawned every imaginable vice. America had changed. Once the "backbone of the republic," rural Americans had become poor country cousins. In the 1920s, frustrated rural people sought to regain their country by helping to push through prohibition, dam the flow of immigrants, revive the Ku Klux Klan, defend the

Bible as literal truth, and defeat an urban Roman Catholic for president.

Rejecting the "Huddled Masses"

Before the war, when about a million immigrants arrived each year, some Americans warned that the nation was about to drown in an "invasion" of unassimilable foreigners. War against Germany and its allies expanded **nativist** and antiradical sentiment. After the war, large-scale immigration resumed (another 800,000 immigrants arrived in

1921) at a moment when industrialists no longer needed new factory laborers. African American and Mexican migration had relieved labor shortages. Moreover, union leaders feared that millions of poor immigrants would undercut their efforts to organize American workers. Rural America's God-fearing Protestants were particularly alarmed that most of the immigrants were Catholic, Jewish, or atheist. In 1921, Congress responded by very nearly slamming shut the open door to immigrants.

In 1924, Congress passed an even tougher immigrant restriction measure, the Johnson-Reid Act. The 1924 law limited the number of immigrants to no more than 161,000 a year and gave each European nation a quota based on 2 percent of the number of people from that country listed in the U.S. census of 1890. The act revealed the fear and bigotry that fueled anti-immigration legislation. It cut immigration by more than 80 percent, but it squeezed some nationalities more than others. Backers of Johnson-Reid openly declared that America had become the "garbage can and the dumping ground of the world," and they manipulated quotas to ensure entry only to "good" immigrants. By basing quotas on the 1890 census, in which western Europeans predominated, the law effectively reversed the trend toward immigration from southern and eastern Europe, which by 1914 had amounted to 75 percent of the yearly total. For example, the Johnson-Reid Act allowed Great Britain 62,458 entries, but Russia could send only 1,992.

Rural Americans, who had most likely never laid eyes on a Polish packing-house worker, a Slovak coal miner, or an Armenian sewing-machine operator, strongly supported the 1924 law, as did industrialists and labor leaders. The immigrants' few defenders were congressmen who represented urban, ethnic ghettos. No one championed immigrants more fiercely than New York City representative (and later mayor) Fiorello La Guardia, who had an Italian father and a Jewish mother and was an Episcopalian.

The 1924 law reaffirmed the 1880s legislation barring Chinese immigrants and added Japanese and other Asians to the list of the excluded. But it left open immigration from the Western Hemisphere, and during the 1920s, some 500,000 Mexicans crossed the border. Farm interests preserved Mexican immigration because of their value in southwestern agriculture. The immigration restriction laws of the 1920s provided the basic framework for immigration policy until the 1960s. They marked the end of an

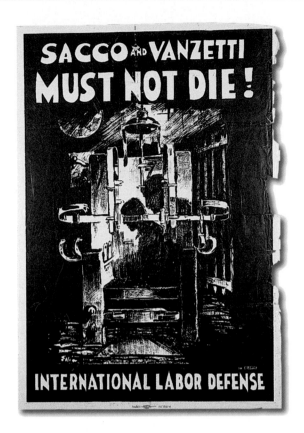

Sacco and Vanzetti Poster
This grim poster sought to galvanize support for pardoning the shoemaker Nicola Sacco and the fish peddler Bartolomeo Vanzetti. The shadows of the convicted men are cast on the electric chair, the sinister device that summoned the two men to their doom. In the 1920s, Sacco and Vanzetti became symbols of the suffering of immigrants, the working class, and political radicals. On August 23, 1927, the state of Massachusetts executed them both. Deportation and mob violence were the typical weapons used against alien radicals and others deemed dangerously un-American.
Collection of Janice L. and David J. Frent.

era, the denial of the Statue of Liberty's open-armed welcome to Europe's "huddled masses yearning to breathe free."

Antiforeign hysteria climaxed in the trial of two **anarchist** immigrants from Italy, Nicola Sacco and Bartolomeo Vanzetti. Arrested in 1920 for robbery and murder in South Braintree, Massachusetts, the men were sentenced to death by a judge who openly referred to them as "anarchist bastards." In response to doubts about the fairness of the verdict, the governor of Massachusetts named a review committee of establishment notables, including the presidents of Harvard University and Massachusetts Institute of Technology. The panel found the trial judge guilty of a "grave breach of official decorum" but refused to recommend a motion for retrial. When Massachusetts executed Sacco and Vanzetti on August 23, 1927, 50,000 mourners followed the caskets in the rain, convinced that the men had died because they were immigrants and radicals, not because they were murderers.

> The Klan's secrecy, uniforms, and rituals helped counter a sense of insignificance among people outside the new world of cities and corporations.

The Rebirth of the Ku Klux Klan

The nation's sour, antiforeign mood struck a responsive chord in members of the Ku Klux Klan. The Klan first appeared in the South during Reconstruction to thwart black freedom and expired with the reestablishment of white supremacy. In 1915, the Klan revived soon after D. W. Griffith's blockbuster film *Birth of a Nation* celebrated earlier Klan racist violence as heroic and necessary. Launched at Stone Mountain, Georgia, the new Klan swiftly spread beyond the South and extended its targets beyond black Americans. Under a banner proclaiming "100 percent Americanism," the new Klan organized a network of local societies across the country. The Klan promised to defend family, morality, and traditional American values against the threat posed by blacks, immigrants, radicals, feminists, Catholics, and Jews.

So widespread was the sense of cultural dislocation in rural America that the Klan quickly attracted some 3 to 4 million members—women as well as

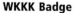

WKKK Badge
Some half a million women were members of Women of the Ku Klux Klan (WKKK). Young girls could join the female youth auxiliary, the Tri-K for Girls. Klanswomen fit perfectly within the organization because it proclaimed itself the defender of the traditional virtues of pure womanhood and decent homes. This badge from Harrisburg, Pennsylvania, advertises the local WKKK's support for a home for needy and orphan children. Klanswomen also joined in boycotts of businesses owned by Jews and others whom they did not consider "100% American."
Collection of Janice L. and David J. Frent.

men. Women members worked for prohibition, strong public schools, and traditional morality. By the mid-1920s, the Klan had spread throughout the nation, virtually controlling Indiana and influencing politics in Illinois, California, Oregon, Texas, Louisiana, Oklahoma, and Kansas. The Klan's secrecy, uniforms, and rituals helped counter a sense of insignificance among people outside the new world of cities and corporations. At the same time, the Klan appealed to the vengeful and brutal side of human nature, enabling its hooded members to beat and intimidate their victims anonymously with little fear of consequences. The Klan offered a certain counterfeit dignity for old-stock, Protestant, white Americans who felt passed over.

Eventually, social changes, along with lawless excess, brought the Klan down. Immigration restrictions eased the worry about invading foreigners, and sensational wrongdoing by Klan leaders cost it the support of traditional moralists. Grand Dragon David Stephenson of Indiana, for example, went to jail for the kidnap and rape of a woman who subsequently committed suicide. Yet the social grievances, economic problems, and religious anxieties of the countryside and small towns remained, ready to be ignited by other incidents.

The Scopes Trial

In 1925 in a steamy Tennessee courtroom, old-time religion and the new spirit of science went head to head. The confrontation occurred after several southern states passed legislation in the early twenties against the teaching of Charles Darwin's theory of evolution in the public schools. **Fundamentalist** Protestants insisted that the Bible's creation story be taught as the literal truth. In answer to a clamor from scientists and civil liberties organizations for a challenge to the law, John Scopes, a young biology teacher in Dayton, Tennessee, offered to test his state's ban on teaching evolution. When the state of Tennessee brought Scopes to trial in the summer of 1925, Clarence Darrow, a brilliant defense lawyer from Chicago, volunteered to defend him. Darrow, an avowed agnostic, took on the prosecution's William Jennings Bryan, three-time Democratic nominee for president, symbol of rural America, and fervent fundamentalist, who was eager to defeat the proposition that humans had evolved from apes.

The Scopes trial quickly degenerated into a media circus, despite the serious issues it raised.

The first trial to be covered live on radio, it attracted an avid nationwide audience. Most of the reporters from big-city papers who converged on Dayton were hostile to Bryan, none more so than the cynical H. L. Mencken, who painted Bryan as a sort of Darwinian missing link ("a sweating anthropoid," a "gaping primate"). When, under relentless questioning by Darrow, Bryan declared on the witness stand that he did indeed believe the world was created in six days and that Jonah had lived in the belly of a whale, his humiliation in the eyes of most urban observers was complete. Nevertheless, the Tennessee court upheld the law in defiance of modern intellectual consensus and punished Scopes with a $100 fine. Although fundamentalism won the battle, it lost the war. Mencken had the last word in a merciless obituary for Bryan, who died just weeks after the trial ended. Portraying the "monkey trial" as a battle between the country and the city, Mencken flayed Bryan as a "charlatan, a mountebank, a zany without shame or dignity," motivated solely by "hatred of the city men who had laughed at him for so long."

As Mencken's acid prose indicated, Bryan's humiliation was not purely a victory of reason and science. It also revealed the disdain urban people felt for country people and the values they clung to. The Ku Klux Klan revival and the Scopes trial dramatized and inflamed divisions between city and country, intellectuals and the unlettered, the privileged and the poor, the scoffers and the faithful.

Al Smith and the Election of 1928

The presidential election of 1928 brought many of the most significant developments of the 1920s—prohibition, immigration, religion, and the clash of rural and urban values—into sharp focus. Republicans emphasized the economic success of their party's pro-business government. But both parties generally agreed that the American economy was basically sound, so the campaign turned on social issues that divided Americans. Tired of the limelight, Calvin Coolidge chose not to seek reelection, and the Republicans turned to Herbert Hoover, the energetic secretary of commerce and the leading public symbol of 1920s prosperity.

The Democrats nominated four-time governor of New York, Alfred E. Smith. A New Yorker by birth, bearing, and accent, Smith adopted "The Sidewalks of New York" as a campaign theme song and seemed to represent all that rural Americans feared and resented. A child of immigrants, Smith got his start in politics with the help of Tammany Hall, New York City's Irish-dominated political machine, the epitome of big-city corruption in many minds. He believed that immigration quotas were wrong, and he spoke out against restriction. He signed New York State's anti-Klan bill and condemned the decade's growing intolerance. Smith also opposed prohibition, believing that it was a nativist attack on immigrant customs. When Smith supposedly asked reporters in 1922, "Wouldn't you like to have your foot on the rail and blow the foam off some suds?" prohibition forces dubbed him "Alcohol Al."

> The presidential election of 1928 brought prohibition, immigration, religion, and the clash of rural and urban values into sharp focus.

Hoover Campaign Poster

Herbert Hoover's 1928 campaign poster effectively illustrated his message: Republican administrations in the 1920s had produced middle-class prosperity, complete with a house in the suburbs and the latest automobile. To remind voters that Hoover as secretary of commerce had promoted industry that made the suburban dream possible, the poster displays smoking chimneys at a discrete distance. The poster gives no hint that this positive message would give way to outright religious bigotry in the campaign against the Democrat (and Catholic) Al Smith.
Collection of Janice L. and David J. Frent.

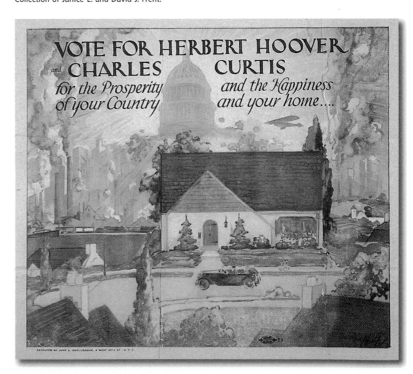

Smith's greatest vulnerability in the heartland, however, was his religion. He was the first Catholic to run for president. A Methodist bishop in Virginia denounced Roman Catholicism as "the Mother of ignorance, superstition, intolerance and sin" and begged Protestants not to vote for a candidate who represented "the kind of dirty people that you find today on the sidewalks of New York." An editorial in the *Baptist and Commoner* argued that the election of Smith "would be granting the Pope the right to dictate to this government what it should do." The editorial further claimed that edicts from the White House would proclaim that "Protestants are now living in adultery because they were not married by a priest."

Hoover, who neatly combined the images of morality, efficiency, service, and prosperity, won the election by a landslide (Map 23.3). He received 58 percent of the vote, taking all but eight states, and gained 444 electoral votes to Smith's 87. The Republicans' most notable success came in the previously solid Democratic South, where Smith's religion, views on prohibition, and big-city persona allowed them to take four states. Smith carried the deep South, where the Democratic Party's identification with white supremacy prevailed. The only dark cloud over the Republican victory was the party's reduced support in the cities and among discontented farmers. The nation's largest cities voted Democratic in a striking reversal of 1924, indicating the rising strength of ethnic minorities, including Smith's fellow Catholics.

The Great Crash

At his inauguration in 1929, Herbert Hoover told the American people, "given a chance to go forward with the policies of the last eight years, we shall soon with the help of God be in sight of the day when poverty will be banished from this nation." Those words came back to haunt Hoover, for in eight short months the Roaring Twenties came to a crashing halt. The prosperity Hoover touted collapsed with the stock market, and the nation ended nearly three decades of barely interrupted economic growth and fell into the most serious economic depression of all time. Hoover and his reputation were among the first casualties, along with the reverence for business that had been the hallmark of the New Era.

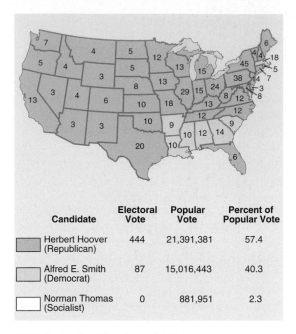

Candidate	Electoral Vote	Popular Vote	Percent of Popular Vote
Herbert Hoover (Republican)	444	21,391,381	57.4
Alfred E. Smith (Democrat)	87	15,016,443	40.3
Norman Thomas (Socialist)	0	881,951	2.3

MAP 23.3   The Election of 1928

Herbert Hoover: The Great Engineer

When Herbert Hoover became president in 1929, he possessed credentials that seemed perfect for the leader of a prosperous business nation. He personified America's rags-to-riches ideal, having risen from poor Iowa orphan to one of the world's most successful mining engineers by the time he was thirty. His success in managing efforts to feed civilian victims of the fighting during World War I won him acclaim as the "Great Humanitarian" and led Woodrow Wilson to name him head of the Food Administration once the United States entered the war. During the 1920s, Hoover's reputation soared even higher when he proved himself an especially effective secretary of commerce in the Harding and Coolidge administrations.

But Hoover was no old-fashioned pro-business advocate like most of the men who gathered in Washington during the 1920s. He belonged to the progressive wing of his party, and as early as 1909 he declared, "The time when the employer could ride roughshod over his labor is disappearing with the doctrine of '*laissez-faire*' on which it is founded." He urged a limited business-government partnership that would actively manage the sweeping changes Americans experienced. "A new era and new forces have come into our economic life and our setting among nations of the world," he declared in 1928. "These forces demand of us constant study and effort if prosperity, peace, and contentment shall be maintained." In his thoughtful book *American Individualism* (1922), Hoover sketched a picture of individualism that was as much cooperative, mutual, and responsible as it was "rugged." He candidly described flaws in American capitalism and turned to his cooperative brand of individual effort to address them. When Hoover entered the White House, he brought a reform agenda: "We want to see a nation built of home owners and farm owners. We want to see their savings protected. We want to see them in steady jobs. We want to see more and more of them insured against death and accident, unemployment and old age. We want them all secure."

But Hoover also had ideological and political liabilities. Principles that appeared to most observers as strengths in the prosperous 1920s—individual self-reliance, industrial self-management, and a limited federal government—became straitjackets when economic catastrophe struck at the end of the decade. Moreover, Hoover had never held an elected public office, he had a poor political touch, and he seemed overly stiff in his starched white color and was too thin-skinned to be an effective politician. Hoover realized that despite these shortcomings most Americans considered him "a sort of superman" able to solve any problem. Prophetically, he confided to a friend his fear that "If some unprecedented calamity should come upon the nation . . . I would be sacrificed to the unreasoning disappointment of a people who expected too much." The distorted national economy set the stage for the calamity Hoover so feared.

The Distorted Economy

In the spring of 1929, the United States basked in the sunshine of a false paradise. Although America had become the world's leading economy, it had done little to help the international economic community after the First World War. European countries, devastated by the war, could not get the aid they needed for full recovery. Rather than stepping in to help rebuild Europe's shattered economy, the Harding and Coolidge administrations demanded that European nations repay their war loans. In addition, to further boost American business, the United States enacted tariffs that prevented

other nations from selling their goods to Americans. Foreign nations thus had less money to buy American goods, which were pouring out in record abundance. In a move that could work only in the short run, American banks propped up the nation's export trade by extending credit to foreign customers. Debt piled onto debt in an absurd pyramid. By the end of the decade, the United States had acquired most of the world's gold in return for its exports.

The domestic economy was also in trouble. The distribution of wealth was badly skewed. Farmers continued to suffer from low prices and chronic indebtedness; the average income of families working the land amounted to only $240 per year during the 1920s. Industrial workers, though enjoying a slight rise in wages during the decade, failed to keep up with productivity and corporate profits. Overall, nearly two-thirds of all American families lived on less than the $2,000 per year that economists estimated would "supply only basic necessities." In sharp contrast, the top 1 percent received 15 percent of the nation's income, an amount equal to that received by the bottom 42 percent of the population. The Coolidge administration worsened the deepening inequality by cutting taxes on the wealthy.

> Ideological principles that appeared as strengths in the prosperous 1920s—individual self-reliance, industrial self-management, and a limited federal government—became straitjackets when economic catastrophe struck.

By 1929, the inequality of wealth produced a serious problem in consumption. The rich, brilliantly portrayed in F. Scott Fitzgerald's novel *The Great Gatsby* (1925), gave the era much of its eye-popping glitter with their lavish spending; but they could absorb only a tiny fraction of the nation's output. Ordinary folk, on whom the system ultimately depended, were unable to take up the slack. For a time, the new device of installment buying—buying on credit—kept consumer demand up; by the end of the decade, four out of five automobiles and two out of three radios were bought on credit. But personal indebtedness rose to an all-time high that could not be sustained.

Signs of economic trouble began to appear at mid-decade. A slowdown of new construction after 1925 indicated that the rate of business expansion had decreased. Faltering automobile sales signaled that, with nearly 30 million cars already on the road, demand had been met and producers would begin to cut back production and lay off workers. Banks followed suit. Between 1921 and 1928, as investment and loan opportunities faded, 5,000 banks failed. Still, the boom seemed to roar on, muffling the sounds of economic distress just beneath the surface.

The Crash of 1929

Even as the economy faltered, America's faith in it remained unshaken. Hoping for yet bigger slices of the economic pie, Americans speculated wildly in the stock market on Wall Street. Between 1924 and 1929, the values of stocks listed on the New York Stock Exchange increased by more than 400 percent. Buying stocks on margin—that is, putting up only part of the money at the time of purchase—grew rampant. Many people got rich this way, but those who bought on credit could finance their loans only if their stock increased in value. Thus, the stock market became dependent on uninterrupted expansion. Speculators could not imagine that the market might fall and they would be forced to meet their margin loans with cash they did not have.

> The stock market became dependent on uninterrupted expansion. Speculators could not imagine that the market might fall and they would be forced to meet their margin loans with cash they did not have.

When stock purchased on margin rose to about 20 percent of the total by the summer of 1929, Hoover urged Richard Whitney, the head of the New York Stock Exchange, to tighten requirements. But Whitney, who later went to prison for embezzlement, gave only empty promises. Spokesmen from prestigious banks and investment houses assured Hoover that all was well. The prudent Hoover, however, rejected the optimistic advice and decided to sell some of his own stocks, saying: "The only trouble with capitalism is capitalists. They're too damned greedy."

Finally, in the autumn of 1929, the market hesitated. Sniffing danger, investors nervously began to sell their overvalued stock. The dip quickly became a rush, building to panic on October 24, the day that came to be known as Black Thursday. Brokers jammed the stock exchange and overflowed into the street. Stirred by the cries of "Sell! Sell!" outside their windows, the giants of finance gathered in the offices of J. P. Morgan Jr., son of the nineteenth-century Wall Street lion, to plot ways of restoring confidence. They injected $100 million of their assets to bolster the market and issued brave declara-

Black Friday

Edward Laning, a mural painter who lost his personal fortune in the stock market crash, gained a measure of revenge in this melodramatic version of panic on the floor of the New York Stock Exchange. The painting shows Exchange president Richard Whitney standing in the center as stock prices fall and brokers collapse around him. A few years later, Whitney went to prison for stealing from other people's accounts to cover his own losses. Why do you suppose the painter placed an American flag so prominently in this mural? Laning later achieved fame for the murals he painted to adorn buildings on Ellis Island and the New York Public Library.
Collection of John P. Axelrod.

tions of faith. But more panic selling came on Black Tuesday, October 29, the day the market suffered a greater fall than ever before. In the next six months, the stock market lost six-sevenths of its total value.

It was once thought that the crash alone caused the Great Depression. It did not. In 1929, the national and international economies were already riddled with severe problems. But the dramatic losses in the stock market crash and the fear of risking what was left acted as a great brake on economic activity. The collapse on Wall Street shattered the New Era's aggressive confidence that America would enjoy perpetually expanding prosperity.

Hoover and the Limits of Individualism

At first, Americans expressed relief that Herbert Hoover resided in the White House when the "bright bubble broke." One observer declared that no previous president "would have been so well prepared as Hoover." Hoover had no use for conservative wisdom that preached that the government should do nothing during economic downturns. He believed that "we should use the powers of government to cushion the situation" by preventing future financial panics and mitigating the hardships of farmers and the unemployed. Hoover was no do-nothing president, but there were limits to his activism.

To keep the stock market collapse from ravaging the entire economy, Hoover in November 1929 called a White House conference of business and labor leaders and urged them to join in a voluntary plan for recovery: Businesses would forge ahead with their pre-crash investment plans, maintain production, and keep their workers on the job; labor would accept the status quo and withdraw demands for improvements in wages, hours, or conditions. Within a few months, however, the bargain fell apart. As demand for their products declined, industrialists cut production, sliced wages, and laid off workers. Poorly paid or unemployed workers could not buy much, and their decreased spending led to further cuts in production and further loss of jobs. Thus began the terrible spiral of economic decline.

To deal with the problems of rural America, Hoover got Congress in 1929 to pass the Agricultural Marketing Act. The act created the Farm Board, which used its budget of $500 million to buy up agricultural surpluses and thus, it was hoped, raise prices. Although the Farm Board bought one-third of the nation's wheat supply in 1930, conditions worsened. To help end the decline, Hoover joined conservatives in urging protective tariffs on agricultural goods, and, with his approval, the Hawley-Smoot tariff of 1930 established the highest rates in history. In early 1930, Congress authorized $420 million for public works projects to give the unemployed jobs and create more purchasing power. In three years, the Hoover administration nearly doubled federal public works expenditures.

But with each year of Hoover's term, the economy declined. Tariffs did not end the suffering of farmers because foreign nations retaliated with increased tariffs of their own that further crippled American farmers' ability to sell abroad. Hoover's response to hard-pressed industry was more generous. In keeping with his previous efforts to promote cooperation between business and government, in 1932 Hoover sponsored the Reconstruction Finance Corporation (RFC), a federal agency empowered to lend government funds to endangered banks and corporations. The theory was **trickle-down economics**: Pump money into the economy at the top, and in the long run the people at the bottom would benefit. Or as one wag put it, "feed the sparrows by feeding the horses." In the end, very little of what critics of the RFC called a "millionaires' dole" trickled down to the poor.

And the poor multiplied. Hundreds of thousands of additional workers lost their jobs each month. By 1932, an astounding one-quarter of the American workforce—more than 12 million men and women—were unemployed. There was no direct federal assistance, and state services and private charities were swamped. Cries grew louder for the federal government to give hurting people relief.

In responding, Hoover revealed the limits of his conception of government's proper role. He compared direct federal aid to the needy to the "dole" in England, which he thought destroyed the moral fiber of the chronically unemployed. In 1931, he called on the Red Cross to distribute government-owned agricultural surpluses to the hungry. In 1932, he relaxed his principles further to offer small federal loans, not gifts, to the states to help them in their relief efforts. But these concessions were no more than Band-Aids on deep wounds. Hoover's circumscribed philosophy of legitimate government action proved vastly inadequate to the problems of restarting the economy and ending human suffering.

Life in the Depression

In 1930, the nation realized that prosperity would not soon return. Suffering on a massive scale set in, and despair settled over the land. Men and women hollow-eyed with hunger grew increasingly bewildered and angry in the face of cruel contradictions. They saw agricultural surpluses pile up in the countryside and knew that their children were going to bed hungry. They saw factories standing idle and knew that they and millions of others were willing to work. The gap between the American people and leaders who failed to resolve these contradictions widened as the depression deepened. By 1932, America's economic problems had created a dangerous social crisis.

The Human Toll

Statistics only hint at the human tragedy of the Great Depression. When Herbert Hoover took office in 1929, the American economy stood at its peak. When he left in 1933, it had reached its twentieth-century low (Figure 23.3). In 1929, national income was $88 billion. By 1933, it had declined to $40 billion. In 1929, unemployment was 3.1 percent, one and a half million workers. By 1933, unemployment stood at 25 percent, twelve and a half million workers. By 1932, more than nine thousand banks had shut their doors, and depositors had lost more than $2.5 billion. The nation's steel industry operated at only 12 percent of capacity.

Jobless, homeless victims wandered in search of work, and the tramp, or hobo, became one of the most visible figures of the decade. Young men and women unable to land their first job made up about half of the million-strong army of hoboes. Riding the rails or hitchhiking, the vagabonds tended to move southward and westward, toward the sun and opportunities, they hoped, for seasonal agricultural work. Other unemployed men and women, sick or less hopeful, huddled in doorways. Scavengers haunted alleys behind restaurants and picked over garbage dumps in search of food. In describing what he called the "American Earthquake," the writer Edmund Wilson told of an elderly woman who always took off her glasses to avoid seeing the maggots crawling over the garbage she ate. Starvation claimed its victims, but enervating, rampant malnutrition posed the greater threat. The Children's Bureau announced that one in five schoolchildren did not get enough to eat.

Rural poverty was most acute. Landless tenant farmers and sharecroppers, mainly in the South, came to symbolize how poverty crushed the human spirit. In 1930, eight and a half million people, three million of them black, lived in tenant and sharecropping families—amounting to one-quarter of the total southern population. Often illiterate, usually without cash incomes, they crowded into two- and three-room cabins lacking screens or even doors, without plumbing, electricity, running water, or sanitary wells. They subsisted—just barely—on salt pork, cornmeal, molasses, beans, peas, and whatever they could hunt or fish. All the diseases of dietary and vitamin deficiencies wracked them. When economist John Maynard Keynes was

> Jobless, homeless victims wandered in search of work, and the tramp, or hobo, became one of the most visible figures of the decade.

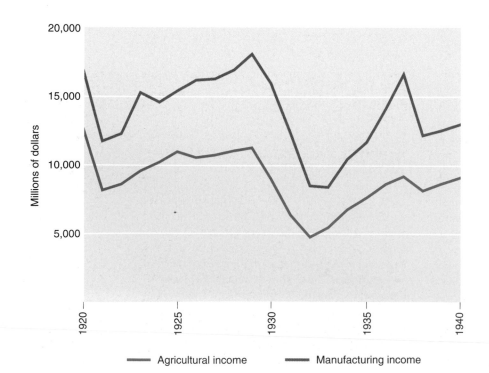

FIGURE 23.3   Manufacturing and Agricultural Income, 1920–1940
After economic collapse, recovery in the 1930s began under New Deal auspices. The sharp declines in 1937–1938, when federal spending was reduced, indicated that New Deal stimuli were still needed to restore manufacturing and agricultural income.

Millions of dollars

20,000
15,000
10,000
5,000

1920   1925   1930   1935   1940

—— Agricultural income   —— Manufacturing income

Unemployed Youth
Joblessness was frightening and humiliating. Brought up to believe that if you work hard, you get ahead, the unemployed had difficulty seeing failure to find work as anything other than personal failure. Many slipped into despair and depression. We can only imagine this young man's story. Utterly alone, sitting on a bench that might be his bed, his hat on the ground and his head in his hands, he looks emotionally battered and perhaps defeated. Whether he found work, joined the throngs of beggars and panhandlers on the streets, or cast his lot with the army of hoboes who rode the rails looking for something better is unknown.
Library of Congress.

Mexican Americans. During the relatively prosperous years of the 1920s, cheap agricultural labor from Mexico flowed legally across the U.S. border, welcomed by the large farmers. In the 1930s, however, public opinion turned on the newcomers, denouncing them as dangerous aliens who took jobs from Americans. Government officials, most prominently those in Los Angeles County, targeted all Mexican residents for deportation regardless of citizenship status. As many as half a million Mexicans and Mexican Americans were deported or fled to Mexico. Among them were children born in the United States, American citizens from the start who had never lived outside the country.

The depression deeply affected the American family. Young people postponed marriage; when they did marry, they produced so few children that demographers warned that, for the first time, the United States was on the verge of losing population. White women, who generally worked in light industry or low-paying service areas, did not lose their jobs as often as men who worked in steel, automobile, and other heavy in-

Deportation to Mexico
On March 9, 1932, 1,400 Mexicans and Mexican Americans crowded into this Los Angeles train station en route to Mexico. Men, women, and children, with their blankets, bundles, and suitcases, wait for the four trains that Los Angeles County chartered to carry them away. County officers estimated that transportation would cost $15,000, a sum that "would be recovered within six weeks in savings on charity." Perhaps sensitive to criticism, officials promised that "many of the Mexicans will be taken back to their home towns." Some of the deportees were American-born citizens who had never been south of the border.
Security Pacific National Bank Photograph Collection, Los Angeles Public Library.

asked whether anything like this degradation had existed before, he replied, "Yes, it was called the Dark Ages and it lasted four hundred years."

There was no federal assistance to meet this human catastrophe, only a patchwork of strapped charities and destitute state and local agencies. For a family of four without any income, the best the city of Philadelphia could do was provide $5.50 per week. That was not enough to live on but still comparatively generous. New York City, where the greatest number of welfare cases gathered, provided only $2.39 per week; and Detroit, devastated when the bottom fell out of the auto industry, allotted sixty cents a week before the city ran out of money altogether.

The deepening crisis roused old fears and caused some Americans to look for scapegoats. Among the most thoroughly scapegoated were

Unemployed men resented women workers, yet necessity drove women into the marketplace.

dustries. Unemployed men resented women workers. To lose one's job in America's business culture was devastating. After a decade of rising consumption and conflating consumption with self-worth, idle men fell prey to guilt and loss of self-respect. Both government and private employers discriminated against married women workers, but necessity continued to drive women into the marketplace during the depression. As a result, by 1940, some 25 percent more women were employed for wages than in 1930.

Denial and Escape

Under scrutiny, those who had presided over the economic collapse and now sought to lead the nation back to prosperity showed how little they knew about ordinary American society. Chief among the offenders was President Hoover himself. To express his confidence in prosperity, he favored formal dress and manners in the White House, and at dinner, with or without guests, a retinue of valets and waiters attended him. No one was starving, he calmly assured the American people. Contradicting the president's message were makeshift shantytowns, called "Hoovervilles," that sprang up on the edges of America's cities. Newspapers used as cover by those sleeping on the streets were "Hoover blankets." An empty pocket turned inside out was a "Hoover flag," and jackrabbits caught for food were "Hoover hogs." Innumerable bitter jokes circulated about the increasingly unpopular president. One told of Hoover asking for a nickel to telephone a friend. Flipping him a dime, an aide said, "Here, call them both."

While Hoover practiced denial, other Americans sought refuge from reality at the movies. Throughout the depression, between sixty and seventy-five million people (nearly two-thirds of the nation) managed to scrounge up enough change to fill the movie palaces every week. Box office successes typically capitalized on the hope that renewed prosperity lay just around the corner. Leading musicals—*Forty-Second Street* and *Gold Diggers of 1933*, for example—offered a variation on the old rags-to-riches story of the chorus girl who makes the most of her big break.

Grim conditions moved a few filmmakers to grapple with depression woes rather than escape them. Films such as King Vidor's *Our Daily*

Bread (1932) expressed compassion for the down-and-out. Gangster films such as *The Public Enemy* (1931) taught hard lessons about ill-gotten gains. Indeed, under the new production code of 1930, designed to protect public morals, all movies had to find some way to show that crime does not pay.

Despite Hollywood's efforts to keep Americans on the right side of the law, crime increased in the early 1930s. Away from the movie palaces, out in the countryside, the plight of people who had lost their farms to bank foreclosures led to the romantic idea that bank robbers were only getting back what banks had stolen from the poor. Woody Guthrie, the populist folk singer from Oklahoma, captured the public's tolerance for outlaws in his widely admired tribute to a murderous bank robber with a choirboy face, "The Ballad of Pretty Boy Floyd":

> Yes, as through this world I ramble,
> I see lots of funny men,
> Some will rob you with a six-gun,
> Some will rob you with a pen.
> But as through your life you'll travel,
> Wherever you may roam,
> You won't never see an outlaw drive
> A family from their home.

Working-Class Militancy

Members of the nation's working class—both employed and unemployed—bore the brunt of the economic collapse. In Chicago, working women received less than twenty-five cents an hour. Sawmill workers in the West got a nickel. Still, the labor movement, including the dominant American Federation of Labor (AFL), was slow to respond. During the 1920s, court injunctions curtailing the right of unions to organize and strike had hobbled organized labor. Early in the depression, William Green, head of the AFL, echoed Hoover when he argued that a dole would turn the worker into "a ward of the state." But by 1931, Green had turned militant. "I warn the people who are exploiting the workers," he shouted at the AFL's annual convention, "that they can drive them only so far before they will turn on them and destroy them. They are taking no account of the history of nations in which governments have been overturned. Revolutions grow out of the depths of hunger."

Like the labor leaders, the American people were slow to anger, then strong in protest. On the morning of March 7, 1932, several thousand unemployed autoworkers massed at the gates of Henry Ford's River Rouge factory in Dearborn, Michigan, to demand work. Ford sent out his private security forces, who told the demonstrators to disperse. The workers refused and began hurling rocks. Ford's army responded with tear gas and freezing water but quickly turned to gunfire, killing four demonstrators and wounding dozens more. An outraged public—forty thousand strong—turned out for the unemployed men's funerals, while editorials and protest rallies across the country denounced Ford's callous resort to violence.

Farmers, who desperately needed relief, mounted uprisings of their own. When Congress refused to guarantee farm prices that would at least equal the cost of production, some three thousand farmers, led by the charismatic Milo Reno, created the National Farmers' Holiday Association, so named because its members planned to force farmers to take a "holiday" from delivering produce to the public. Reno and his followers barricaded roads around Sioux City, Iowa, turned back farmers heading for market, and dumped thousands of gallons of milk in the ditches. Although the 1932 rebellion was short-lived and did not force a critical shortage of food, it raised general awareness of farm grievances. Farm militants had greater success with what they called "penny sales." When farmers defaulted on their mortgages and farms were put up for auction, neighbors packed the auctions and, after warning others not to bid, bought the foreclosed property for a few pennies and returned it to the bankrupt owners. Under this kind of pressure, some states suspended debts or reduced mortgages.

Resistance also took root in the fields of California. When landowners cut their laborers' already substandard wages, more than 50,000 farmworkers, most of them Mexicans, went on strike in 1933. About half of the workers won small wage increases. Surveying the strife mounting nationwide, John Simpson, president of the National Farmers Union, observed that "the biggest and finest crop of revolutions you ever saw is sprouting all over the country right now."

Hard times revived the left in America. The Great Depression—the massive failure of Western capitalism—brought **socialism** back to life and propelled the **Communist Party** to

its greatest size and influence in American history. Eventually, some 100,000 Americans—workers, intellectuals, college students—joined the Communist Party in the belief that only an overthrow of the capitalist system could save the victims of depression. In 1931, the party, through its National Miners Union, carried its convictions into Harlan County, Kentucky, to support a strike by brutalized coal miners. Newspapers and newsreels riveted the attention of the public with their graphic portrayals of the violence unleashed by mine owners' thugs against the strikers. Eventually, the owners beat the miners down, but the Communist Party emerged from the coalfields with a reputation as the most dedicated and fearless champion of the union cause.

The left also led the fight against racism. While both major parties refused to challenge the system of segregation in the South, the

Harlan County Coal Strike, 1931

"Scottsboro Boys"

Nine black youths, ranging in age from thirteen to twenty-one, stand in front of rifle-bearing National Guard troops called up by Alabama governor B. M. Miller, who feared a mob lynching after two white women accused the nine of rape in March 1931. In less than two weeks, an all-white jury heard flimsy evidence, convicted the nine of rape, and sentenced them to death. Although none was executed, all nine spent years in jail. Eventually, the state dropped charges against the youngest four and granted paroles to others. The last "Scottsboro Boy" left jail in 1950.

© Bettmann/Corbis.

Socialist Party, led by Norman Thomas, attacked the system of sharecropping that left many African Americans in poverty and near servitude. The Communist Party also took action. When nine young black men in Scottsboro, Alabama, were arrested on trumped-up rape charges in 1931, a team of lawyers sent by the party saved the defendants from the electric chair. The party also opposed the efforts of Alabama plantation owners to evict their black tenants. Although Communists were unable to force much change on the deeply entrenched southern way of life, their efforts briefly attracted new recruits to the party. From only about 50 black members in 1930, party totals rose to 10,000 by the end of the decade.

Radicals on the left often sparked action, but protests by moderate workers and farmers occurred on a far greater scale. Breadlines, soup kitchens, foreclosures, unemployment, and cold despair drove patriotic men and women to question American capitalism. "I am as conservative as any man could be," a Wisconsin farmer explained, "but any economic system that has in its power to set me and my wife in the streets, at my age—what can I see but red?"

Conclusion: Dazzle and Despair

In the aftermath of World War I, America turned its back on progressive crusades and embraced conservative Republican politics, the growing influence of corporate leaders, and business values. Changes in the nation's industrial economy—Henry Ford's automobile revolution, advertising, mass production—propelled fundamental change throughout society. Living standards rose, economic opportunity increased, and Americans threw themselves into private pleasures—gobbling up the latest household goods and fashions, attending baseball and football games and boxing matches, gathering around the radio, and going to the movies. As big cities came to dominate American life, the culture of youth and flappers became the leading edge of what one observer called a "revolution in manners and morals." The twenties were also a wildly creative and vital moment in American novels, art, and music. At home in Harlem and abroad in Paris, American high culture flourished.

For many Americans, however, none of the glamour and vitality had much meaning. Instead of seeking thrills at speakeasies, plunging into speculation on Wall Street, or escaping abroad, the vast majority struggled just to earn a decent living. Blue-collar America did not participate fully in white-collar prosperity. Rural America was almost entirely left out of the Roaring Twenties. Country folks, deeply suspicious and profoundly discontented, championed prohibition, revived the Klan, attacked immigration, and defended old-time Protestant religion.

Just as the dazzle of the Roaring Twenties hid divisions in society, extravagant prosperity masked structural flaws in the economy. The crash of 1929 and the depression that followed starkly revealed the economy's crises of consumption and international trade. Economic hard times swept high living off the front pages of the nation's newspapers. Different images emerged: hoboes hopping freight trains, strikers confronting police, malnourished sharecroppers staring blankly into the distance, empty apartment buildings alongside cardboard shantytowns, and mountains of food rotting in the sun while guards with shotguns chased away the hungry.

The depression shook up all quarters of American society. Everyone was hurt, but the poor were hurt most. As the laboring ranks sank into aching hardship, businessmen rallied around Herbert Hoover to proclaim that private enterprise would get the country moving again. But things fell apart, and Hoover faced increasingly determined and more radical opposition. Membership in the Socialist and Communist parties surged, and more and more Americans contemplated desperate measures. By 1932, the depression had nearly brought the nation to its knees. America faced its greatest crisis since the Civil War, and citizens demanded new leaders who would save them from the "Hoover Depression."

For additional firsthand accounts of this period, see Chapter 23 in Michael Johnson, ed., *Reading the American Past*, Third Edition.

To assess your mastery of the material in this chapter, see the Online Study Guide at bedfordstmartins.com/roark.

For Web links related to topics in this chapter, see "HistoryLinks," "DocLinks," and "PlaceLinks" at bedfordstmartins.com/roark.

CHRONOLOGY

1920
- Eighteenth Amendment, prohibiting sale of liquor, goes into effect.
- Nineteenth Amendment, granting women the vote, ratified.
- Station KDKA in Pittsburgh begins first regular commercial radio broadcasts.
- Membership in Marcus Garvey's Universal Negro Improvement Association surges.
- Republican Warren G. Harding elected president.

1921
- Congress passes Sheppard-Towner Act, providing federal funds to states to help reduce infant mortality.
- Congress passes immigration restriction law.

1922
- Fordney-McCumber Act sets protective tariffs at record heights.
- Five-Power Naval Treaty sharply reduces the number of warships in British, French, Japanese, Italian, and U.S. navies.

1923
- Equal Rights Amendment introduced in Congress.
- Calvin Coolidge succeeds to presidency when Harding dies in office.

1924
- Dawes Plan temporarily saves Europe from economic collapse and renewed military conflict.
- Calvin Coolidge elected president.
- Congress passes Johnson-Reid Act, limiting immigration to small annual quotas.

1925
- John Scopes convicted for violating Tennessee statute forbidding teaching of evolution.
- Alain Locke expresses cultural aspirations of Harlem Renaissance in *The New Negro*.

1926
- Ernest Hemingway publishes his novel *The Sun Also Rises*.

1927
- Charles Lindbergh becomes America's most famous hero by flying nonstop alone across Atlantic Ocean.
- Massachusetts executes Italian anarchist immigrants Nicola Sacco and Bartolomeo Vanzetti.
- Ford Motor Company produces its 15,000,000th automobile.

1928
- Kellogg-Briand pact renounces war as an instrument of foreign policy.
- Herbert Hoover defeats Alfred E. Smith in presidential election.

1929
- St. Valentine's Day massacre claims seven lives in Chicago as rival gangs seek control of the illegal liquor trade.
- Robert and Helen Lynd publish *Middletown*, their study of an average American small city.
- Congress passes the Agricultural Marketing Act to support prices of farm products.
- Stock market collapses in panicked selling of stock on Black Thursday, October 24, and on Black Tuesday, October 29.

1930
- Congress authorizes $420 million for public works projects to relieve the unemployed.
- Hawley-Smoot tariff passes, protecting agricultural goods from foreign competition.
- Farm Board buys one-third of the nation's wheat to support prices.

1931
- Communist Party lawyers ardently defend nine black men arrested in Scottsboro, Alabama.
- Communist Party gains reputation as defender of labor by championing coal miners' strike in Harlan County, Kentucky.

1932
- Thousands of demonstrators at Ford plant protest unemployment; security forces fire on crowd, killing four.
- Congress establishes the Reconstruction Finance Corporation to lend government funds to industries and banks.
- National Farmers' Holiday Association blocks roads and pours milk on ground to protest falling prices.

BIBLIOGRAPHY

General Works

Frederick Lewis Allen, *Only Yesterday: An Informal History of the Nineteen-Twenties* (1930).
Michael Bernstein, *The Great Depression* (1987).
Dorothy Brown, *Setting a Course: American Women in the 1920s* (1987).
Stanley Coben, *Rebellion against Victorianism: The Impetus for Cultural Change in 1920s America* (1991).
Nancy Cott, *The Grounding of Modern Feminism* (1987).
Robert Crunden, *From Self to Society: Transition in American Thought, 1919–1941* (1972).
Alan Dawley, *Struggles for Justice: Social Responsibility and the Liberal State* (1991).
Lynn Dumenil, *The Modern Temper: American Culture and Society in the 1920s* (1995).
David J. Goldberg, *Discontented America: The United States in the 1920s* (1999).
David M. Kennedy, *Freedom from Fear: The American People in Depression and War, 1929–1945* (1999).
William E. Leuchtenburg, *The Perils of Prosperity, 1914–1932* (1958).
Michael Parrish, *Anxious Decades: America in Prosperity and Depression, 1920–1941* (1992).

Mainstream Politics, 1920–1933

Kristi Andersen, *After Suffrage: Women in Partisan and Electoral Politics before the New Deal* (1996).
David Burner, *Herbert Hoover: A Public Life* (1979).
Kendrick A. Clements, *Hoover, Conservation, and Consumerism: Engineering the Good Life* (2000).
Warren I. Cohen, *Empire without Tears: America's Foreign Relations, 1921–1933* (1987).
Frank Costigliola, *Awkward Dominion: American Political, Economic, and Cultural Relations with Europe, 1919–1933* (1984).
Paula Elder, *Governor Alfred E. Smith: The Politician as Reformer* (1983).
Robert H. Ferrell, *The Strange Deaths of Warren Harding* (1996).
Donald R. McCoy, *Calvin Coolidge* (1967).
Frances Fox Piven and Richard A. Cloward, *Why Americans Don't Vote* (1988).
Emily S. Rosenberg, *Spreading the American Dream: American Economic and Cultural Expansion, 1890–1945* (1982).
Martin J. Sklar, *The United States as a Developing Country: Studies in U.S. History in the Progressive Era and the 1920s* (1992).
Joan Hoff Wilson, *Herbert Hoover: Forgotten Progressive* (1975).

Technology and Consumption

Susan Porter Benson, *Counter Cultures* (1986).
Douglas Brinkley, *Wheels for the World: Henry Ford, His Company, and a Century of Progress, 1903–2003* (2003).
Ruth Schwartz Cowan, *More Work for Mother: The Ironies of Household Technology from the Open Hearth to the Microwave* (1983).
James J. Flink, *The Automobile Age* (1988).
Louis Galambos and Joseph Pratt, *The Rise of the Corporate Commonwealth: U.S. Business and Public Policy in the Twentieth Century* (1988).
Kenneth T. Jackson, *Crabgrass Frontier: The Suburbanization of the United States* (1985).
Jill Jonnes, *Empires of Light: Edison, Tesla, and Westinghouse, and the Race to Electrify the World* (2003).

T. J. Jackson Lears, *Fables of Abundance: A Cultural History of Advertising in America* (1994).
Roland Marchand, *Advertising the American Dream: Making Way for Modernity, 1920–1940* (1985).
John Margolies, *Pump and Circumstances: Glory Days of the Gas Station* (1993).
David F. Noble, *America by Design: Science, Technology, and the Rise of Corporate Capitalism* (1977).

Labor

Irving Bernstein, *The Lean Years: A History of the American Worker, 1920–1933* (1960).
Lizabeth Cohen, *Making a New Deal: Industrial Workers in Chicago, 1919–1939* (1990).
Colin Gordon, *New Deals: Business, Labor, and Politics in America, 1920–1935* (1994).
Sanford M. Jacoby, *Employing Bureaucracy: Managers, Unions, and the Transformation of Work in American Industry, 1900–1945* (1985).
Stephen Meyer, *The Five Dollar Day* (1981).
John A. Salmond, *Gastonia 1929: The Story of the Loray Mill Strike* (1995).
Winifred Wandersee, *Women's Work and Family Values, 1920–1940* (1981).
Gerald Zahavi, *Workers, Managers, and Welfare Capitalism* (1988).
Robert H. Zieger, *Republicans and Labor, 1919–1929* (1969).

Rural and Small-Town Life

Michael L. Berger, *The Devil Wagon in God's Country: The Automobile and Social Change in Rural America, 1893–1929* (1979).
James N. Gregory, *American Exodus: The Dust Bowl Migration and Okie Culture in California* (1989).
Jack Temple Kirby, *Rural Worlds Lost: The American South, 1920–1960* (1987).
Donald Worster, *Dust Bowl: The Southern Plains in the 1930s* (1979).

Popular Culture

Thomas Cripps, *Slow Fade to Black: The Negro in American Film, 1900–1942* (1977).
Ann Douglas, *Mongrel Manhattan in the 1920s* (1994).
Ronald Edsforth, *Popular Culture and Political Change in Modern America* (1991).
Lewis Erenberg, *Steppin' Out: New York City Nightlife and the Transformation of American Culture, 1890–1930* (1981).
Paula S. Fass, *The Damned and the Beautiful: American Youth in the 1920s* (1977).
Jill Jonnes, *Hep-Cats, Narcs, and Pipe Dreams: A History of America's Romance with Illegal Drugs* (1996).
Lary May, *The Big Tomorrow: Hollywood and the Politics of the American Way* (2000).
Ray Robinson, *Rockne of Notre Dame: The Making of a Football Legend* (1999).
Steven J. Ross, *Working-Class Hollywood: Silent Film and the Shaping of Class in America* (2000).
Arnold Shaw, *The Jazz Age: Popular Music in the 1920s* (1987).
Susan Smulyan, *Selling Radio: The Commercialization of American Broadcasting, 1920–1934* (1994).

Education and Art

Charles C. Alexander, *Here the Country Lies: Nationalism and the Arts in Twentieth-Century America* (1980).

Malcolm Cowley, *Exile's Return* (1934).

Helen Lefkowitz Horowitz, *Campus Life: Undergraduate Cultures from the End of the Eighteenth Century to the Present* (1987).

Lary May, *Outside In: Minorities and the Transformation of American Education* (1989).

Elizabeth Hutton Turner, *American Artists in Paris, 1919–1929* (1988).

Resistance to Change

David H. Bennett, *The Party of Fear: From Nativist Movements to the New Right in American History* (1988).

Kathleen M. Blee, *Women of the Klan: Racism and Gender in the 1920s* (1991).

Roger Daniels, *Guarding the Golden Door: American Immigration Policy and Immigrants since 1882* (2004).

Lyle W. Dorsett, *Billy Sunday and the Redemption of Urban America* (1991).

Ray Ginger, *Six Days or Forever? Tennessee v. John Thomas Scopes* (1958).

Nancy MacLean, *Behind the Mask of Chivalry: The Making of the Second Ku Klux Klan* (1994).

George M. Marsden, *Fundamentalism and American Culture* (1980).

David M. Reimers, *Unwelcome Strangers: American Identity and the Turn against Immigration* (1998).

Daniel Joseph Singal, *The War Within: From Victorian to Modernist Thought in the South, 1919–1945* (1982).

Reform and Dissent

James R. Barrett, *William Z. Foster and the Tragedy of American Radicalism* (1999).

Milton Cantor, *The Divided Left: American Radicalism, 1900–1975* (1978).

Clarke Chambers, *Seedtime of Reform, 1918–1933* (1956).

John P. Diggins, *The Rise and Fall of the American Left* (1992).

Alex Keyssar, *Right to Vote: The Contested History of Democracy in the United States* (2000).

Davis Levering Lewis, *W. E. B. Du Bois: The Fight for Equality and the American Century, 1919–1963* (2000).

Thomas R. Pegram, *Battling Demon Rum: The Struggle for a Dry America, 1800–1933* (1998).

Nick Salvatore, *Eugene V. Debs: Citizen and Socialist* (1982).

David Thelen, *Robert M. La Follette and the Insurgent Spirit* (1976).

Race and Minorities

Rodolfo Acuna, *Occupied America: A History of Chicanos* (1980).

Francisco E. Balderrama and Raymond Rodriguez, *Decade of Betrayal: Mexican Repatriation in the 1930s* (1995).

William B. Barlow, *"Looking Up at Down": The Emergence of Blues Culture* (1989).

Dan T. Carter, *Scottsboro: A Tragedy of the Modern South* (1969).

Angela Davis, *Blues Legacies and Black Feminism: Gertrude "Ma" Rainey, Bessie Smith, and Billie Holiday* (1999).

George Hutchinson, *The Harlem Renaissance in Black and White* (1995).

David Levering Lewis, *When Harlem Was in Vogue* (1989).

Manning Marable, *W. E. B. Du Bois: Black Radical Democrat* (1986).

Donald L. Parman, *Indians and the American West in the Twentieth Century* (1994).

Judith Stein, *The World of Marcus Garvey* (1986).

Cheryl A. Wall, *Women of the Harlem Renaissance* (1995).

Henry Yu, *Thinking Orientals: Migration, Contact, and Exoticism in Modern America* (2001).

The Crash and Response

William J. Barber, *From New Era to New Deal: Herbert Hoover, the Economists, and American Economic Policy, 1921–1933* (1985).

John Kenneth Galbraith, *The Great Crash, 1929* (1961).

Robert McElvaine, *The Great Depression in America* (1984).

David P. Peeler, *Hope Among Us Yet: Social Criticism and Social Thought in the Depression Years* (1987).

Studs Terkel, *Hard Times: An Oral History of the Great Depression* (1979, 1986).

Tom Terrill and Jerrold Hirsch, *Such as Us* (1978).

T. H. Watkins, *The Hungry Years: America in an Age of Crisis, 1929–1939* (1999).

**FRANKLIN ROOSEVELT'S
MICROPHONE**

President Roosevelt used this microphone to broadcast his famous fireside
chats explaining New Deal programs to
ordinary Americans. These chats traveled on
airwaves into homes throughout the nation, reassuring
listeners that Washington cared about the suffering the Great Depres-
sion was spreading across the land. Shortly after the first chat in March 1933, a New Yorker, "a citizen
of little or no consequence" as he called himself, wrote the White House in gratitude for "the President's broadcast. I felt that he walked into my home, sat down and in plain and forceful language explained to me how he was tackling the job I and my fellow citizens gave him. . . . Such forceful, direct
and honest action commands the respect of all Americans, it is certainly deserving of it."

National Museum of American History, Smithsonian Institution, Behring Center.

24

The New Deal Experiment

1932–1939

I N THE DEPTHS OF THE GREAT DEPRESSION, a Pennsylvania mother with three small children appealed to the Hoover administration for help for her husband "who is a world war Veteran and saw active service in the trenches, became desperate and applied for Compensation or a pension from the Government and was turned down." With a weekly income of only $15.60, she declared, there ought to be "enough to pay all world war veterans a pension . . . and there by relieve a lot of suffering, and banish resentment that causes Rebellions and Bolshevism." She asked questions murmured by millions of other desperate Americans: "Oh why is it that it is always a bunch of overley rich, selfish, dumb ignorant money hogs that persist in being Senitors, legislatures, representitives? Where would they and their possessions be if it were not for the Common Soldier, the common laborer that is compelled to work for a starvation wage[?] . . . Right now our good old U.S.A. is sitting on a Seething Volcano."

This mother's plea echoed in the demands of tens of thousands of World War I veterans who gathered in Washington, D.C., during June and July 1932 to lobby for immediate payment of the pension (known as a "bonus"). The veterans came from every state and by nearly every means of transportation. The throng that congregated in a huge camp on the outskirts of Washington appeared "dusty, weary, and melancholy" to a Washington reporter who noted that the veterans included jobless "truck drivers and blacksmiths, steel workers and coal miners, stenographers and common laborers," in all "a fair cross section" of the nation: immigrants and natives; whites, blacks, and Indians. The "one absentee," a black civil rights leader observed, was "James Crow." Beneath the veterans' social and geographic diversity lay their shared economic suffering. They were all, one journalist wrote, "down at the heel."

Calling themselves Bonus Marchers or the Bonus Army, the veterans hoped their numbers, solidarity, and poverty would persuade Congress to give them the bonus they had been promised in 1924: $1 for every day they had been in uniform and a bit extra for time served overseas. Instead of cash payments, Congress decided to hand out promissory notes that veterans could not convert to cash until 1945. Bonus Marchers condemned this "tombstone bonus" that would not be paid until many of them were dead. As veterans from Utah and California emblazoned their truck, "We Done a Good Job in France, Now You Do a Good Job in America—We Need the Bonus."

The veterans had supporters in Congress but not in the White House. President Hoover opposed the payment of an expensive bonus that would

- **Franklin D. Roosevelt: A Patrician in Government**
  The Making of a Politician
  The Election of 1932

- **Launching the New Deal**
  The New Dealers
  Banking and Finance Reform
  Relief and Conservation Programs
  Agricultural Initiatives
  Industrial Recovery

- **Challenges to the New Deal**
  Resistance to Business Reform
  Casualties in the Countryside
  Politics on the Fringes

- **Toward a Welfare State**
  Relief for the Unemployed
  Empowering Labor
  Social Security and Tax Reform
  Neglected Americans and the New Deal

- **The New Deal from Victory to Deadlock**
  The Election of 1936
  Court Packing
  Reaction and Recession
  The Last of the New Deal Reforms

- **Conclusion: Achievements and Limitations of the New Deal** require the government to go into debt. Hoover refused to meet with representatives of the Bonus Army, who, his press secretary charged, were "communists or bums." The House of Representatives, controlled by Democrats, voted to pay the promised bonus of $2.4 billion, but the Senate, dominated by Hoover's fellow Republicans, rejected the bonus. Upon hearing of their defeat in the Senate, the Bonus Marchers did not confirm Republican fears of an enraged mob led by **Communists**. Instead, the disap-

pointed but patriotic veterans joined in singing "America," then slowly drifted back to their camp.

About 20,000 veterans remained in Washington, determined, as one of them proclaimed, "to stay here until 1945 if necessary to get our bonus." While the Bonus Army hunkered down in their shanties, Hoover feared the veterans would riot and spark uprisings throughout the country. He ordered General Douglas MacArthur to evict the Bonus Marchers from the city, but not to invade their camp.

On July 28, MacArthur led an attack force of five tanks and 500 soldiers armed with loaded weapons and fixed bayonets through the streets of Washington. Exceeding Hoover's orders, MacArthur pushed the Bonus Marchers back into their camp, where his soldiers torched the veterans' humble dwellings. While their camp burned, the Bonus Marchers raced away. MacArthur boasted that without his victory over the veterans, "I believe the institutions of our Government would have been severely threatened."

MacArthur's expulsion of the Bonus Army undermined public support for the beleaguered, fearful Hoover. When the Democrats' recently nominated presidential candidate, Franklin Delano Roosevelt, heard about the attack, he predicted that it "will elect me." Roosevelt's political instincts proved correct. Voters rejected Hoover, who seemed unsympathetic to the suffering the Great Depression inflicted on millions

Attack on the Bonus Marchers

Washington police, spearheaded by 500 army soldiers commanded by General Douglas MacArthur, participated in the attack on the Bonus Marchers. Soldiers lobbed tear gas grenades toward the Bonus Marchers, quickly breaking up skirmishes like the one shown here, then advanced into the veterans' camp and torched it. At the head of the mounted cavalry attacking the veterans was George S. Patton, who became a famous general in World War II. MacArthur's chief aide was Dwight D. Eisenhower, who subsequently commanded the Allied assault on Nazi Germany and became president. Eisenhower recalled later that he "told that dumb son-of-a-bitch [MacArthur] he had no business going down there" to destroy the Bonus Marchers' camp, in violation of Hoover's orders. Hoover, however, did not discipline MacArthur for his insubordination.
National Archives.

FOR MORE HELP ANALYZING THIS IMAGE, see the visual activity for this chapter in the Online Study Guide at bedfordstmartins.com/roark.

of Americans. In his inaugural address in March 1933, barely seven months after the expulsion of the Bonus Army, Roosevelt proclaimed a central theme of his personal style, his political temperament, and his public appeal by saying, "The only thing we have to fear is fear itself." Instead of succumbing to fear and suspicion, Roosevelt said, Americans should roll up their sleeves and find some way out of their present difficulties. Roosevelt's confidence that the government could somehow improve the lives of citizens energized **New Deal** policies and his presidency, the longest in American history.

When several thousand veterans reassembled in Washington to lobby again for the bonus a few months after Roosevelt's inauguration, the new president's hospitality contrasted with Hoover's hostility. Roosevelt arranged for the veterans to be housed in abandoned military barracks and fed at government expense while they lobbied for the bonus. He invited a delegation of veterans to the White House, where he chatted casually with them, explaining that he could not support the bonus because it was too expensive, although he was determined to help them and other victims of the depression. And, to the veterans' surprise and delight, Eleanor Roosevelt slogged through rain and mud to talk personally with the veterans, to express her sympathy, and to lead them in singing their favorite songs. As the veterans voluntarily left their encampment in Washington, one remarked, "Hoover sent the Army; Roosevelt sent his wife."

Unlike the Bonus Marchers, the tens of millions of other Americans suffering from the Great Depression did not flock to Washington to lobby the government. But like the Bonus Marchers, they appreciated Roosevelt's optimism and expressions of concern. Even more, they welcomed government help from Roosevelt's New Deal initiatives to provide relief for the needy, to speed economic recovery, and to reform basic economic and governmental institutions. Roosevelt's New Deal elicited bitter opposition from critics on the right and left and failed to satisfy fully its own goals of relief, recovery, and reform. But within the Democratic Party the New Deal energized a powerful political coalition that helped millions of Americans withstand the privations of the Great Depression and, in the process, made the federal government a major presence in the daily lives of most American citizens.

Franklin D. Roosevelt: A Patrician in Government

Unlike the millions of Americans in 1932 who had no work, little food, and still less hope, Franklin Roosevelt came from a wealthy and privileged background that contributed to his sunny optimism, self-confidence, and vitality. He constantly drew upon these personal qualities in his political career to bridge the economic, social, and cultural chasm that separated him from the struggles of ordinary Americans. During the twelve years he served as president (1933–1945), many elites came to hate him as a traitor to his class, while millions more Americans, especially the hardworking poor and dispossessed, revered him because he cared about them and their problems.

The Making of a Politician

Born in 1882, Franklin Delano Roosevelt grew up on his father's leafy estate at Hyde Park on the Hudson River, north of New York City. Insulated from the privations, uncertainties, and conflicts experienced by working people, Roosevelt was steeped at home and school in high-minded doctrines of public service and Christian duty to help the poor and weak. He prepared for a career in politics, hoping to follow in the political footsteps of his fifth cousin, Theodore Roosevelt. In 1905, when he married his distant cousin Eleanor Roosevelt, the president of the United States, Theodore Roosevelt, gave the bride away—an indication of Franklin Roosevelt's gilt-edged political and familial connections.

Unlike cousin Teddy, Franklin Roosevelt sought his political fortune in the Democratic Party. After a two-year stint in the New York legislature, he ascended to national office when Woodrow Wilson appointed him assistant secretary of the navy. In 1920, he catapulted to the second spot on the national Democratic ticket, as the vice presidential candidate of presidential nominee James M. Cox. Although the Republicans' Warren G. Harding trounced Cox in the general election (see chapter 23), Roosevelt's energetic campaigning convinced Democratic leaders that he had a bright future in national politics.

In the summer of 1921, however, his life took a painful detour. He became infected with the polio virus, which paralyzed both his legs. For the rest of his life, he could stand only with his legs encased in heavy steel braces and could walk a few awkward steps only by leaning on another person. Tireless physical therapy helped him regain his vitality and intense desire for high political office. But he had to recapture his political momentum mostly from a sitting position, although he studiously avoided being photographed in the wheelchair he used routinely.

After his polio attack, Roosevelt frequently visited a polio therapy facility at Warm Springs, Georgia. There, Roosevelt combined the health benefits of the soothing waters with political overtures to southern Democrats, which helped make him a rare political creature: a New Yorker from the Democratic Party's urban and immigrant wing with whom whites from the Democratic Party's entrenched southern wing felt comfortable.

Roosevelt's chance to return to political office came in 1928. New York's Democratic governor, Al Smith, decided to run for president and hoped to secure the state's electoral votes by encouraging Roosevelt to campaign to succeed him as governor. Smith lost both New York and the general election (see chapter 23), but Roosevelt squeaked out a narrow victory. As the newly elected governor of the nation's most populous state, Roosevelt was poised to showcase his leadership and his suitability for a presidential bid of his own. His activist policies following the 1929 stock market crash and the cascading economic woes of the Great Depression made his governorship a dress rehearsal for his subsequent actions as president.

> Roosevelt's activist policies following the 1929 stock market crash made his governorship a dress rehearsal for his subsequent actions as president.

Governor Roosevelt took immediate action. He believed government should intervene to protect citizens from economic hardships, rather than standing passively on the sidelines and waiting for the blind laws of supply and demand to improve the economy. Roosevelt's sympathy for the underdog contrasted with the traditional **laissez-faire** views of many **conservatives**— both Republicans and Democrats—that the depression represented the hard hand of the market winnowing the strong from the weak. For government to help the needy, according to conservatives, was wrong on at least two counts: It sapped individual initiative, the source of self-respect and economic hope for the poor; and it impeded the self-correcting forces of the market by rewarding the losers in the economic struggle

Roosevelt's Common Touch

In his campaign for reelection as governor of New York in 1930, Franklin Roosevelt boosted his vote total by 700,000 over his slender victory margin of 25,000 in 1928, and he became the first Democratic candidate for governor to win the vote outside New York City. Sensing that his presentation of himself as a good neighbor was responsible for much of his popularity, Roosevelt arranged to have a friendly chat outside polls in his hometown of Hyde Park with working-class voter Ruben Appel. In this photograph, Appel seems unaware that Roosevelt's standing was itself a feat of stagecraft. His legs rendered useless by polio, Roosevelt could remain upright only by using the strength he had developed in his arms and shoulders to prop himself up on his cane. Rare photos like this and a taboo against showing Roosevelt in his wheelchair kept the public from thinking of Roosevelt as a "cripple" and unfit for office, or in many cases from even realizing that he was disabled.

Franklin D. Roosevelt Library.

to survive. Roosevelt lacked a full-fledged counterargument to these conservative qualms, but he refused to allow them to hobble his government's efforts to provide short-term aid to the jobless and the hungry. "To these unfortunate citizens," he proclaimed, "aid must be extended by governments, not as a matter of charity but as a matter of social duty. . . . [No one should go] unfed, unclothed, or unsheltered."

The highlight of Roosevelt's efforts to relieve the economic hardships of New Yorkers was the Temporary Emergency Relief Administration (TERA), created in 1931. Until then, no state had ever provided so much help for the poor, some $20 million. TERA and Roosevelt's other initiatives as governor earned the gratitude of New Yorkers and the attention of national politicians.

To his supporters, Roosevelt seemed to be a leader determined to use the resources of government to attack the economic crisis without deviating from **democracy**—unlike **fascist** parties gaining strength in Europe—or from capitalism—unlike Communists in power in the Soviet Union. Roosevelt's ideas about precisely how to revive the economy were vague. A prominent journalist characterized Roosevelt in 1931 as "a kind of amiable boy scout . . . a pleasant man who, without any important qualifications for the office, would very much like to be president." Such sneering assessments did not much concern Roosevelt's numerous supporters, who appreciated his energy, his activism, and his belief that, as he put it, "The duty of the state towards its citizens is the duty of the servant to its master." Roosevelt's conviction that government could and should do something to help Americans climb out of the economic abyss propelled him into the front ranks of the national Democratic Party.

The Election of 1932

The Democrats who convened in Chicago in July 1932 to nominate their presidential candidate knew they had a good chance to recapture the White House. Many Americans blamed President Hoover, just then confronting the Bonus Marchers in Washington, for the nation's economic distress. Hoover's unpopularity gave the Democrats a historic opportunity. In 56 of the 72 years since Abraham Lincoln's election, the White House had been a Republican preserve. Now, with the nation gripped by the worst depression in its history, Democrats might reverse generations of Republican rule if they chose the right nominee.

Opposition to Republicans and hunger for office, but little else, united Democrats. Warring factions divided Democrats by region, religion, culture, and commitment to the status quo. Southern Democrats chaired powerful committees in Congress thanks to their continual reelection in the one-party South devoted to white supremacy. This southern, native-born, white, rural, **Protestant**, conservative wing of the Democratic Party found little common ground with the northern, immigrant, urban, disproportionately Catholic, **liberal** wing. Rural and small-town drys (supporters of prohibition) clashed with urban and foreign-born wets (opponents of prohibition). Eastern-establishment Democratic dignitaries shared few goals with angry farmers and factory workers. Nonetheless, this unruly coalition of constituencies finally agreed to nominate Franklin Roosevelt as their presidential candidate.

Roosevelt signaled his break with tradition as well as his energy and activism by flying to Chicago to appear before the Democratic conventioneers and accepting their nomination in person. He pledged his commitment to "the forgotten man at the bottom of the pyramid" and promised "bold, persistent experimentation" to find ways to help. Highlighting his differences with Hoover and Republicans, he proposed to lead the nation toward "liberal thought, . . . planned action, . . . enlightened international outlook, and . . . the greatest good to the greatest number of our citizens." He summarized his determination to govern decisively without being bound by "foolish traditions" by announcing, "I pledge you, I pledge myself, to a new deal for the American people."

Few details about what Roosevelt meant by a "new deal" emerged in the presidential campaign. He declared that "the people of America want more than anything else . . . two things; work . . . with all the moral and spiritual values that go with work . . . and a reasonable measure of security . . . for themselves and for their wives and children." He encouraged Americans to go into voting booths asking themselves one simple question: Should Hoover be reelected, or was it time for a change, a new deal? Voters answered that question in no uncertain terms.

Roosevelt won in a historic landslide (Map 24.1). He received 57 percent of popular votes, the first Democratic popular-vote majority since the election of Franklin Pierce in 1852. In the electoral college, Roosevelt amassed an 89 percent majority, carrying state after state that had voted Republican for years (Map 24.2). Roosevelt's coattails also swept Democrats into control of Congress by large margins. Voters' mandate for change could hardly have been more emphatic.

Roosevelt's victory represented the emergence of what came to be known as the New Deal coalition. Attracting support from farmers, factory workers, immigrants, city folk, African Americans, women, and **progressive** intellectuals, Roosevelt launched a realignment of the nation's political loyalties. The New Deal coalition dominated American politics throughout Roosevelt's presidency and remained powerful long after his death in 1945. United less by ideology or support for specific policies, voters in the New Deal coalition instead expressed their faith in Roosevelt's promise of a government that would, somehow, change things for the better. Nobody, including Roosevelt, knew exactly what the New Deal would change or whether the changes would revive the nation's ailing economy and improve Americans' lives. But Roosevelt and many others knew that the future of American capitalism and democracy was at stake.

> Attracting support from farmers, factory workers, immigrants, city folk, African Americans, women, and progressive intellectuals, Roosevelt launched a realignment of the nation's political loyalties.

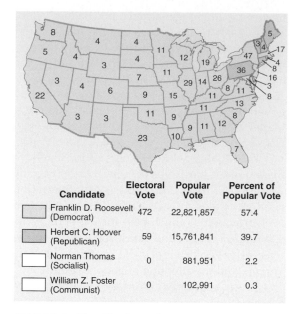

Candidate	Electoral Vote	Popular Vote	Percent of Popular Vote
Franklin D. Roosevelt (Democrat)	472	22,821,857	57.4
Herbert C. Hoover (Republican)	59	15,761,841	39.7
Norman Thomas (Socialist)	0	881,951	2.2
William Z. Foster (Communist)	0	102,991	0.3

MAP 24.1   The Election of 1932

Launching the New Deal

At noon on March 4, 1933, Americans gathered around their radios to hear the inaugural address of the newly elected president. Roosevelt began by asserting his "firm belief that the only thing we have to fear is fear itself—nameless, unreasoning, unjustified terror which paralyzes needed efforts to convert retreat into advance." Roosevelt promised "direct, vigorous action" in order "to wage war against the emergency" cre-

MAP 24.2   Electoral Shift, 1928–1932
Democratic victory in 1932 signaled the rise of a New Deal coalition within which women and minorities, many of them new voters, made the Democrats the majority party for the first time in the twentieth century.

READING THE MAP: How many states voted Democratic in 1928? How many states voted Republican in 1932? How many states shifted from Republican to Democratic between 1928 and 1932?

CONNECTIONS: What did Franklin Roosevelt's campaign slogans call for? What past programs did Roosevelt cite as influences? What factions within the Democratic Party opposed his candidacy in 1932, and why?

FOR MORE HELP ANALYZING THIS MAP, see the map activity for this chapter in the Online Study Guide at bedfordstmartins.com/roark.

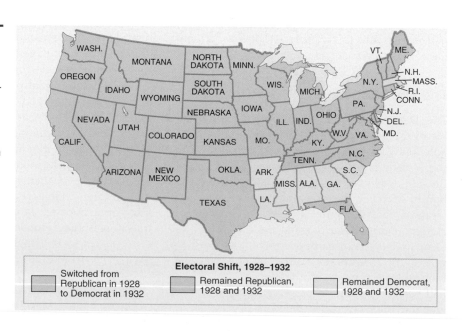

Electoral Shift, 1928–1932

Switched from Republican in 1928 to Democrat in 1932	Remained Republican, 1928 and 1932	Remained Democrat, 1928 and 1932

ated by "the dark realities" confronting "a stricken Nation in the midst of a stricken world." The first months of Roosevelt's administration, termed "the Hundred Days," fulfilled that promise in a whirlwind of government initiatives that launched the New Deal.

Roosevelt and his advisers had three interrelated objectives: to provide relief to the destitute, especially the one out of four Americans who were unemployed; to foster the economic recovery of farms and businesses, thereby creating jobs and reducing the need for relief; and to reform the government and economy in ways that would reduce the risk of devastating consequences in future economic slumps. The New Deal never fully achieved these goals of relief, recovery, and reform. But by aiming for them, Roosevelt's experimental programs enormously expanded government's role in the nation's economy and society.

The New Dealers

To design and implement the New Deal, Roosevelt needed ideas and people. As governor of New York, he frequently hosted private, informal conversations about social and economic policy with a small group of professors from Columbia University. Dubbed the "Brains Trust," these men and others continued to advise the new president about the problems faced by the nation and how to deal with them.

Hundreds of other reformers rushed to join the Roosevelt administration. Among the most important were two veterans of Roosevelt's New York governorship: Harry Hopkins and Frances Perkins. Hopkins, a tough-talking, soft-hearted social worker devoted to the **social gospel** of moral and material uplift of the downtrodden, administered New Deal relief efforts and served as one of the president's loyal confidants. Perkins, like Hopkins, embraced the social gospel tradition, having worked for a time in Jane Addams's Hull House in Chicago. Perkins also had extensive experience trying to improve working conditions in shops and factories, including directing New York's investigation of the 1911 Triangle Shirtwaist Factory fire that killed 146 women (see chapter 21). Roosevelt tapped Perkins to serve as secretary of labor, the first woman cabinet member in American history—an indication of her expertise and of the growing strength of women in the Democratic Party, which had an organized and active Women's Division.

No New Dealers were more important than the president and his wife, Eleanor. The gregarious president radiated charm and good cheer, giving the New Deal's bureaucratic regulations a benevolent human face. During his frequent informal news conferences, Roosevelt bantered with reporters and skillfully broadcast his plans and policies. Eleanor Roosevelt became the New Deal's unofficial ambassador. She served as her husband's eyes and ears—and legs—as she traveled throughout the nation connecting the corridors of power in Washington to Americans of all colors and creeds in church basements, meeting halls, and front parlors.

As Roosevelt's programs swung into action, many Americans benefited directly through jobs and relief or indirectly from economic improvements. In time, the millions of beneficiaries of the New Deal became grassroots New Dealers who expressed their appreciation by voting Democratic on election day. A signal success of the New Deal was to create a durable political coalition of Democrats that stretched from the Oval Office to the nation's fields and factories and that would reelect Roosevelt in 1936, 1940, and 1944.

As Roosevelt and his advisers developed plans to meet the economic emergency, their watchwords were *action, experiment,* and *improvise.* Without a sharply defined template for how to provide relief, recovery, and reform, they moved from ideas to policies as quickly as possible, hoping to identify ways to help people and to boost the economy. But underlying New Dealers' experimentation and improvisation were four guiding ideas.

First, Roosevelt and his advisers sought capitalist solutions to the economic crisis. They believed that the depression resulted from basic imbalances in the nation's capitalist economy, imbalances they wanted to correct. They had no desire to eliminate private property or impose **socialist** programs, such as public ownership of productive resources. Instead, they hoped to save the capitalist economy by remedying its flaws.

Second, Roosevelt's Brains Trust persuaded him that the greatest flaw of America's capi-

> The New Deal never fully achieved the goals of relief, recovery, and reform. But by aiming for them, Roosevelt's experimental programs enormously expanded government's role in the nation's economy and society.

> A signal success of the New Deal was to create a durable political coalition of New Deal Democrats that stretched from the Oval Office to the nation's fields and factories and re-elected Roosevelt in 1936, 1940, and 1944.

talist economy was underconsumption, the root cause of the current economic paralysis. Underconsumption, New Dealers argued, resulted from the gigantic productive success of capitalism. Factories and farms produced more than they could sell to consumers, causing factories to lay off workers and farmers to lose money on bumper crops. Workers without wages and farmers without profits shrank consumption and choked the economy. Somehow, the balance between consumption and production needed to be restored.

Third, New Dealers believed that the immense size and economic power of American corporations needed to be counterbalanced by government and by organization among workers and small producers. Unlike progressive trustbusters in Woodrow Wilson's administration, New Dealers did not seek to splinter big businesses. Huge businesses had developed for good economic reasons and were here to stay. Roosevelt and his advisers hoped to counterbalance big economic institutions and their quest for profits with government programs focused on protecting individuals and the public interest.

Fourth, New Dealers felt that government must somehow moderate the imbalance of wealth created by American capitalism. Wealth concentrated in a few hands reduced consumption by most Americans and thereby contributed to the current economic gridlock. In the long run, government needed to find a way to permit ordinary working people to share more fully in the

Eleanor Roosevelt Meeting Women Reporters

Even though about 80 percent of newspaper owners opposed the president and his wife, both Franklin and Eleanor Roosevelt had close rapport with the working press. Making the point that women had something important to contribute to public affairs and that the First Lady could be more than simply a White House hostess, Eleanor Roosevelt wrote a daily column, "My Day," and held regular news conferences to which only women reporters were admitted. She used the occasions to reinvigorate the commitment women had expressed in the Progressive Era to education, equal rights, decent working conditions, and child welfare.

Stock Montage.

Soup Kitchen

Chicago gangster Al Capone sponsored this soup kitchen for the unemployed in 1931. Before the New Deal, most relief for the jobless came from private sources, although very little came from mobsters like Capone. Notice that the people in line are all men, that they include both whites and blacks, and that they appear comparatively well dressed, suggesting that they had lost their jobs relatively recently. Why might a gangster like Capone offer free soup to the jobless?

National Archives.

fruits of the economy. In the short term, New Dealers sought to lend a helping hand to poor people who suffered from the maldistribution of wealth.

Roosevelt had outlined these guiding ideas during the presidential campaign, and they served as a creed among New Dealers. "Our task now," Roosevelt declared, "is . . . meeting the problem of underconsumption, . . . adjusting production to consumption, . . . [and] distributing wealth and products more equitably." Once Roosevelt took office, the New Dealers' creed guided their actions.

Banking and Finance Reform

Roosevelt wasted no time making good on his inaugural pledge for "action now." As he took the oath of office on March 4, the nation's banking system was on the brink of collapse. Since 1930 more than 5,000 banks had failed. Depositors who feared losing their savings withdrew their money from surviving banks, making them so shaky that the nation's governors had suspended almost all states' banking operations. Roosevelt immediately declared a four-day "bank holiday" in order to devise a plan to shore up banks and restore depositors' confidence. Working round the clock, New Dealers drafted the Emergency Banking Act, which gave the secretary of the treasury the power to decide which banks could be safely reopened and to release funds from the Reconstruction Finance Corporation (RFC) to bolster banks' assets. To secure the confidence of depositors, Congress passed the Glass-Steagall Banking Act, setting up the Federal Deposit Insurance Corporation (FDIC), which guaranteed bank customers that the federal government would reimburse them for deposits if their banks failed.

On Sunday night March 12, while the banks were still closed, Roosevelt broadcast the first of what became a series of "fireside chats." Speaking in a friendly, informal manner, Roosevelt addressed the millions of Americans who tuned their radios to hear the president explain these first New Deal initiatives. The new banking legislation, he said, made it "safer to keep your money in a reopened bank than under the mattress." With such plain talk, Roosevelt translated complex matters into common sense. This and subsequent fireside chats forged a direct connection—via radio waves—between Roosevelt and millions of Americans. Evidence of their link to Roosevelt piled up in the White House mail room: During Roosevelt's first week in office, Americans sent him almost half a million personal letters, an avalanche of correspondence from ordinary people that persisted throughout his presidency. Millions shared the views of a man from Paris, Texas, who wrote Roosevelt, "you are the one & only President that ever helped a Working Class of People. . . . Please help us some way I Pray to God for relief."

The banking legislation and fireside chat worked. Within a few days, most of the nation's major banks reopened, and they remained solvent as reassured depositors switched funds from their mattresses to their accounts (Figure 24.1). Some radical critics of the New Deal believed Roosevelt should have nationalized

the banks and made them a cornerstone of economic planning by the federal government. Instead, these first New Deal measures propped up the private banking system with federal funds and subjected banks to federal regulation and oversight. One adviser correctly identified the New Deal's goal, claiming, "Capitalism was saved in eight days," although the rescue operation took much longer to succeed.

In his inaugural address Roosevelt criticized financiers for their greed and incompetence. To prevent the fraud, corruption, insider trading, and other abuses that had tainted Wall Street and contributed to the crash of 1929, Roosevelt pressed Congress to regulate the stock market—like banks, a fundamental institution of American capitalism. Legislation in 1934 created the Securities and Exchange Commission (SEC) to oversee financial markets by licensing investment dealers, monitoring all stock transactions, and requiring corporate officers to make full disclosures about their companies. To head the SEC, Roosevelt named an abrasive and ravenously ambitious Wall Street trader, Joseph P. Kennedy, whose reputation had been clouded by questionable stock manipulations. When critics complained about Kennedy's selection, Roosevelt replied shrewdly, "Set a thief to catch a thief."

Kennedy proved to be a tough administrator who faced down threats by stockbrokers, some of them with things to hide. Cleaned up and regu-

Emergency Money

When bank failures in 1933 caused prudent depositors to withdraw their money from their accounts and hide it away, the resulting scarcity of currency paralyzed businesses. Store owners, service clubs, and communities created "emergency money" to keep the wheels of local commerce turning. Leiter's Pharmacy in Pismo Beach, California, for example, used clamshells for currency; other places issued buckskin and wooden dollars. Such improvisation demonstrates the collapse of the banking system and the creative solutions of some of its victims.

National Museum of American History, Smithsonian Institution, Behring Center.

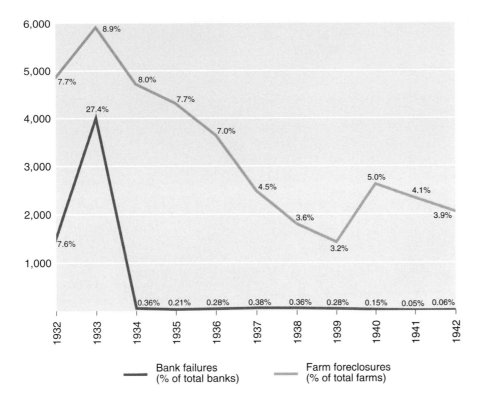

Bank failures
(% of total banks)   Farm foreclosures
(% of total farms)

lated, Wall Street slowly recovered, but the stock market stayed well below its frothy heights of the 1920s.

Relief and Conservation Programs

Patching up the nation's financial structure provided little relief for the hungry and unemployed. A poor man from Nebraska asked Eleanor Roosevelt "if the folk who was borned here in America . . . are this Forgotten Man, the President had in mind, [and] if we are this Forgotten Man then we are still Forgotten." Since its founding, the federal government had never assumed responsibility for needy people, except in moments of natural disaster or emergencies such as the Civil War. Instead, churches, private charities, county and municipal governments, and occasionally states assumed the burden of poor relief, usually with meager payments. To persuade Americans that the depression necessitated unprecedented federal relief efforts, Harry Hopkins dispatched investigators throughout the nation to describe the plight of impoverished Americans. Reports of families surviving on "bull-dog gravy"—a thin paste of lard, flour, and water—and of many others who lacked even that filtered back to Washington, along with news that working hours of tens of thou-

sands of workers had been cut back, reducing their wages to about $1.50 a day. As one New Yorker wrote the government, "We work, ten hours a day for six days. In the grime and dirt of a nation [for] . . . low pay [making us] . . . slaves—slaves of the depression!"

Such reports galvanized support for the Federal Emergency Relief Administration (FERA), which provided $500 million to feed the hungry and create jobs. Established in May 1933, FERA supported 4 to 5 million households with $20 or $30 a month. FERA also created jobs for the unemployed on thousands of public works projects, organized by Hopkins into the Civil Works Administration (CWA), which siphoned funds from other government agencies. Earning wages between forty and sixty cents an hour, laborers renovated schools, dug sewers, and rebuilt roads and bridges. In the five months it existed, CWA put paychecks worth over $800 million into the hands of previously jobless workers. FERA extended the scope of relief to include health and education, providing vaccinations and immunizations for millions and funding literacy classes.

The most popular work relief program was the Civilian Conservation Corps (CCC), established in March 1933. It offered unemployed young men a chance to earn wages while working

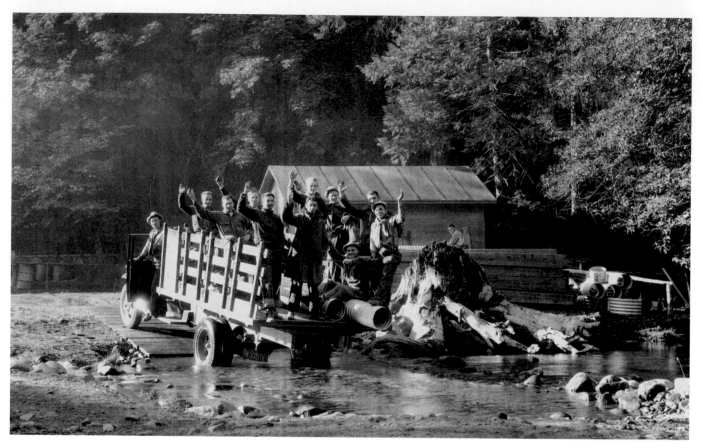

Civilian Conservation Corps Workers
No New Deal program was more popular among its participants and the general public than the Civilian Conservation Corps. It offered young men healthy outdoor work that got them out of the cities and eased their unemployment blues. To the public it showed that the New Deal would act against the depression in a way that would repair neglect of America's natural resources.
Forest Service Photo Collection.

> The CCC, CWA, and other work relief efforts replaced the stigma of welfare with the dignity of jobs.

to conserve natural resources, a long-standing interest of Roosevelt. Like the 3 million other young men who enlisted with CCC, Blackie Gold had been out of work and had to "beg for coal, [and] buy bread that's two, three days old" in order to help support his large family. After he joined the CCC, he earned $30 a month and was required to send all but $5 home to his family. By the end of the program in 1942, CCC workers had checked soil erosion, tamed rivers, and planted more than 2 billion trees. In the process, the CCC left a legacy of vast new recreation areas, along with roads that made them accessible to millions of people. Just as important, CCC, CWA, and other work relief efforts replaced the stigma of welfare with

the dignity of jobs. As one woman said, "We aren't on relief anymore. My husband is working for the Government."

The New Deal also sought to harness natural resources for hydroelectric power. Continuing a project begun under Hoover, the New Deal completed the colossal Hoover Dam across the Colorado River in Nevada, providing not only electricity but also flood control and irrigation water for Arizona and southern California (see "American Places," page 879).

The New Deal's most ambitious and controversial natural resources development project was the Tennessee Valley Authority (TVA), created in May 1933 to build dams along the Tennessee River to supply impoverished rural communities with cheap electricity (Map 24.3). TVA planned model towns for power station

AMERICAN PLACES

Hoover Dam, Nevada

When President Franklin Roosevelt dedicated the just-completed Boulder Dam in Nevada in September 1935, he noted that only four years earlier "the mighty waters of the Colorado [River] were running unused to the sea" but now the dam "translate[s] them into a great national possession." The massive dam—then the largest in the world—tamed the river to provide public services of flood control, hydroelectric power, and water for crops and people throughout the Southwest. From the neon glare of the Las Vegas strip to the suburban expanses of Phoenix and Los Angeles, Americans today switch on lights, water their lawns, and eat irrigated crops all made possible by the enormous concrete monolith that turned the wild river into a great national possession.

Construction began in 1931, when the project was called the Hoover Dam in honor of the president who was instrumental in pushing the long-contemplated dream into reality. By 1933, when Roosevelt became president, the first of some 4.3 million cubic yards of concrete had been poured, enough to pave a highway from San Francisco to New York. Before construction could begin, however, loose rock from the canyon walls had to be stripped away. This physically demanding and dangerous work was done by men

called "high-scalers." Climbing with ropes, the high-scalers—many of them former sailors and circus acrobats, plus some Native Americans—used jackhammers and dynamite to remove the loose rock. When they were finished, welders, "greasemen," blacksmiths, pipefitters, electricians, cement finishers, and others built the dam.

On-the-job accidents killed 96 of the dam workers. Others perished from heat exhaustion, pneumonia,

or heart trouble. After falling debris caused several deaths, workers took steps to protect their heads. They smeared coal tar on their cloth hats and let it harden, creating an early precursor to the hard hats now routinely worn at construction sites.

By 1933, New Dealers had officially renamed the dam Boulder Dam, and so it remained until 1947 when it was officially renamed Hoover Dam. At a cost of less than $200 million, the construction project provided jobs for over 4,000 men and inspired Americans with dramatic evidence of the creative potential of ambitious public works.

Today, a million people a year visit what Roosevelt called this "twentieth century marvel." They listen to the roar of water jetting through the spillway outlets and wander among the giant turbines that generate power for western homes and businesses. Admiring the modernist design, they can contemplate the human brains and brawn responsible for erecting such a massive structure—two years ahead of schedule—to turn the rampaging Colorado River into Lake Mead, which stretches over 100 miles. Tours conducted through the visitor center and exhibits at the nearby Boulder City/Hoover Dam Museum bring to life the history of the dam and the many people who helped harness the river's power.

FOR WEB LINKS RELATED TO THIS SITE AND OTHER AMERICAN PLACES, see "PlaceLinks" at bedfordstmartins.com/roark.

Hoover Dam
Hoover Dam National Historic Landmark.

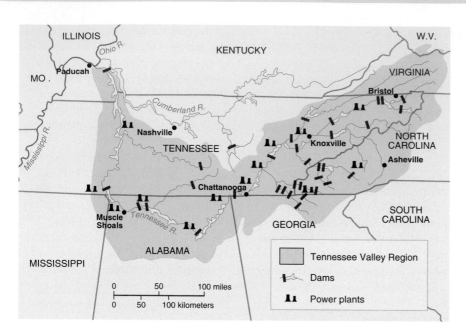

MAP 24.3   The Tennessee Valley Authority
The New Deal created the Tennessee Valley Authority to modernize a vast impoverished region with hydroelectric power dams and, at the same time, to reclaim eroded lands and preserve old folkways.

READING THE MAP: How many states were affected by the TVA? How many miles of rivers (approximately) were affected?
CONNECTIONS: What kinds of benefits—economic as well as social and cultural—did TVA programs bring to the region? How might the lives of a poor farming family in Alabama or Tennessee have changed after the mid-1930s owing to these programs?

FOR MORE HELP ANALYZING THIS MAP, see the map activity for this chapter in the Online Study Guide at bedfordstmartins.com/roark.

workers and new homes for farmers, who would benefit from electricity and flood control. The TVA also sought to preserve the region's culture with programs to encourage local crafts and folkways. The most ambitious example of New Deal enthusiasm for planning, TVA set out to demonstrate that a partnership between the federal government and local residents could overcome barriers of state governments and of private enterprises to make efficient use of abundant natural resources and break the ancient cycle of poverty. TVA never fully realized these utopian ends, especially because of bitter resistance from competing private power companies. It did, however, succeed in improving the lives of millions in the region with electric power, flood protection, soil reclamation, and jobs.

Agricultural Initiatives

Farmers had been mired in depression since the end of World War I. New Dealers diagnosed farmers' plight as a classic case of overproduction and underconsumption. Following age-old practices, farmers tried to compensate for low crop prices by growing more crops, hoping to boost their earnings by selling larger quantities. Instead, producing more pushed prices lower still. Farm income sank from a disastrously low $6 billion in 1929 to a catastrophically low $2 billion in 1932. The median annual income among farm families plunged to $167, barely one-tenth of the national average.

New Dealers sought to cut agricultural production, thereby raising crop prices and farmers' income. With more money in their pockets, farm families—who made up one-third of all Americans—would then buy more goods and thereby lift consumption in the entire economy. To reduce production, the Agricultural Adjustment Act (AAA) authorized the "domestic allotment plan," which paid farmers not to grow crops: Individual farmers who agreed not to plant crops on a portion of their fields (their "allotment") would receive a government payment compensating them for the crops they did not plant. Since crops were already in the ground by the time AAA passed in May 1933, drastic measures were necessary to reduce production immediately. While millions of Americans went to bed hungry, farmers slaughtered millions of cattle, hogs, sheep, and other livestock and destroyed millions of acres of crops in order to qualify for their allotment payments.

With the formation of the Commodity Credit Corporation, the federal government allowed farmers to hold their harvested crops off the market and wait for a higher price. In the meantime, the government stored the crop and gave farmers a "commodity loan" based on a favorable price. If the market price rose above that level, the farmer could repay the loan, sell the crop, and pocket the difference. If the market price never rose above the loan level, the farmer simply took the loan as payment, and the government kept the crop. In effect, commodity loans addressed the problem of underconsumption by making the federal government a major consumer of agricultural goods and reducing farmers' vulnerability to low prices. New Dealers also sponsored the Farm Credit Act (FCA) to provide long-term credit on mortgaged farm property, allowing debt-ridden farmers to avoid foreclosures that were driving thousands off their land.

Crop allotments, commodity loans, and mortgage credit made farmers major beneficiaries of the New Deal. Crop prices rose impressively, farm income jumped 50 percent by 1936, and FCA loans financed 40 percent of farm mortgage debt by the end of the decade. These gains were distributed fairly equally among farmers in the corn, hogs, and wheat region of the Midwest. In the South's cotton belt, however, landlords controlled the distribution of New Deal agricultural benefits and shamelessly rewarded themselves while denying benefits to many sharecroppers and tenant farmers—blacks and whites—by taking the land they had worked out of production and assigning it to the allotment program. Many such tenants and sharecroppers could no longer find work, and their privation worsened. (See "The Promise of Technology," page 882.)

The New Deal also brought the wonders of electric power to country folk, fulfilling an old progressive dream. When Roosevelt became president, 90 percent of rural Americans lacked electricity. Private electric companies refused to build transmission lines into the sparsely settled countryside when they had a profitable market in more accessible and densely populated urban areas. Beginning in 1935, the Rural Electrification Administration (REA) made low-cost loans available to local cooperatives for power plants and transmission lines to serve rural communities. Within ten years, the REA delivered electricity to nine out of ten farms, giving rural Americans access for the first time to modern conveniences that urban people had enjoyed for decades.

Industrial Recovery

Unlike farmers, industrialists cut production with the onset of the depression. Between 1929 and 1933, industrial production fell more than 40 percent. In a sense, industrialists voluntarily adopted the general strategy that the New Dealers used in agriculture: cutting production to balance low demand with low supply and

Sketch for a Federal Arts Program Mural
This sketch for a mural commissioned for Lenoir City, Tennessee, is typical of the Federal Arts Program's goal to memorialize significant moments of achievement in every region of the country. For rural folk, the sight of Rural Electrification Authority (REA) workers extending power lines was an exciting symbol of the New Deal. When the REA came into existence in 1935, less than 10 percent of the nation outside the cities had electricity. Ten years later the figure had risen to 90 percent, and the gulf of silence and darkness between town and country was successfully bridged.
Public Buildings Service, General Services Administration.

Mechanized Cotton Picking Waits Out the Depression

Cotton Picker
Courtesy of the Fogg Art Museum, Harvard University Art Museums. Gift of Bernarda Bryson Shahn.

In 1935, the Farmall tractor and the Rust cotton picker cut through a field of cotton, showing how mechanization could eliminate the backbreaking work of harvesting cotton by hand. Within ten years, tractors would displace horses as the main means of doing heavy farmwork. Success for mechanical cotton pickers, however, was longer in coming. Since the invention of the cotton gin in 1793, inventors had been trying to create a device that would make picking cotton as efficient as ginning it. The first patent for a crude mechanical picker was granted in 1850, and nearly two thousand more patents were issued before John Rust in 1931 demonstrated a machine that could pick more bales of cotton in a day than the average farmer in the deep South grew in a year.

Although the technology of mechanized cotton agriculture was available during the 1930s, few farmers used it. Why? One reason was the availability of ample cheap labor from poor tenants and sharecroppers. Another was landowning farmers' lack of money to invest in machinery during the hard times of the 1930s. By 1931, cotton prices had plunged to six cents a bale from a high of thirty-five cents in 1919, and New Deal agricultural policies were designed to reduce crop production, not increase it.

Not until the depression lifted during World War II, as the nation geared up for maximum production with a labor force reduced by millions of men and women in uniform, did economic circumstances begin to favor the widespread purchase and use of mechanical cotton pickers. During the 1940s and 1950s, large farms using the new mechanical cotton picker became dominant, shifting most cotton growing from the South to the West, where vast agricultural holdings were the rule. Displaced by the decline of King Cotton in the South, thousands of sharecroppers like the woman shown here migrated to the North in search of new jobs and a new life.

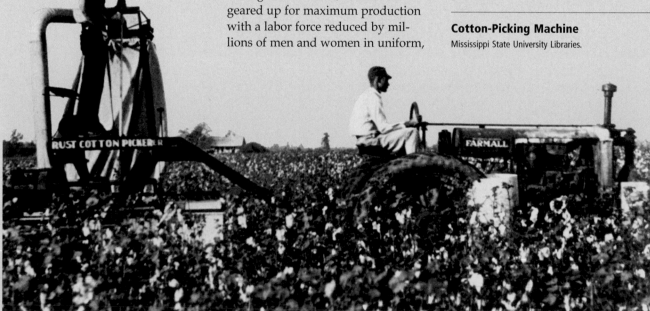

Cotton-Picking Machine
Mississippi State University Libraries.

thereby maintaining prices. But the industrialists' strategy created major economic and social problems for Roosevelt and his advisers, for declining industrial production meant that millions of working people lost their jobs. Unlike farmers, most working people lived in towns and cities and did not grow their own food—they literally needed jobs to eat. Mass unemployment also reduced consumer demand for industrial products, contributing to a downward spiral in both production and jobs, with no end in sight. Industries responded by reducing wages for employees who still had jobs, further depressing demand—a trend made worse by competition among industrial producers. New Dealers struggled to find a way to break this cycle of unemployment and underconsumption, a way consistent with corporate profits and capitalism.

The New Deal's National Industrial Recovery Act (NIRA) opted for a government-sponsored form of industrial self-government through the National Recovery Administration (NRA), established in June 1933. The NRA encouraged industrialists in every part of the economy to agree on rules—known as codes—to define fair working conditions, to set prices, and to minimize competition. The idea behind codes was to stabilize existing industries and maintain their workforces while avoiding what both industrialists and New Dealers termed "destructive competition" that forced employers to cut both wages and jobs. Industry after industry wrote elaborate codes addressing detailed features of production, pricing, and competition. In exchange for relaxing federal antitrust regulations that prohibited such business agreements, the NRA received a promise from participating businesses that they would recognize the right of working people to organize and engage in **collective bargaining**. To encourage consumers to patronize businesses participating in NRA codes, the New Deal mounted a public relations campaign that displayed the NRA's Blue Eagle in shop windows and on billboards throughout the nation.

New Dealers hoped that NRA codes would yield businesses with a social conscience, ensuring fair treatment for workers and consumers and promotion of the general economic welfare. Instead, NRA codes tended to strengthen conventional business practices. Large corporations wrote codes that served primarily the interests of corporate profits rather than the needs of workers or the welfare of the national economy. Many

Major Legislation of the New Deal's First Hundred Days

	Name of Act	Basic Provisions
March 9, 1933	Emergency Banking Act	Provided for reopening stable banks and authorizing RFC to supply funds
March 31, 1933	Civilian Conservation Corps Act	Provided jobs for unemployed youth
May 12, 1933	Agricultural Adjustment Act	Provided funds to pay farmers for not growing surplus crops
May 12, 1933	Federal Emergency Relief Act	Provided relief funds for the destitute
May 18, 1933	Tennessee Valley Authority Act	Set up authority for development of electric power and conservation
June 16, 1933	National Industrial Recovery Act	Specified cooperation among business, government, and labor in setting fair prices and working conditions
June 16, 1933	Glass-Steagall Banking Act	Created Federal Deposit Insurance Corporation (FDIC) to insure bank deposits

business leaders criticized NRA codes as heavy-handed government regulation of private enterprise. Some even claimed the NRA was a homegrown version of Benito Mussolini's corporate fascism taking shape in Italy. In reality, however, compliance with NRA codes was voluntary, and government enforcement efforts were weak to nonexistent. The NRA did little to reduce unemployment, raise consumption, or relieve the depression. In effect, the NRA represented a peace offering to business leaders by Roosevelt and his advisers, conveying the message that the New Deal did not intend to wage war against profits or private enterprise. The peace offering failed, however. Most corporate leaders became active and often bitter opponents of Roosevelt and the New Deal.

National Recovery Administration Quilt
The Blue Eagle of the National Recovery Administration, fiercely clutching a machine gear and lightning bolts, symbolized the government's determination to bring American industry around to a coordinated plan for recovery. The attempt to balance the interests of producers, workers, and consumers proved too much for the Blue Eagle. Yet, as this backcountry quilt indicates, the Blue Eagle was sometimes able to carry the spirit of cooperation far from the centers of industrial turmoil.
Franklin D. Roosevelt Library.

> Having enjoyed a long era of public adoration and political deference from Republicans, business leaders fulminated against New Deal efforts to reform or regulate what they considered their private concerns.

Challenges to the New Deal

The first New Deal initiatives engendered fierce criticism and political opposition. From the right, Republicans and business people charged that New Deal programs were too radical, undermining private property, economic stability, and democracy. Critics on the left faulted the New Deal for its failure to allay the human suffering caused by the depression and for its timidity in attacking corporate power and greed.

Resistance to Business Reform

Although New Deal programs rescued capitalism, business leaders criticized Roosevelt even though their prospects improved more steadily during the depression than did those of most other Americans. The hierarchical structure of concentrated corporate power that had developed during the boom years at the turn of the century avoided reform. The greatest wounds business leaders suffered were to their pride and political control. Resentful and fearful of regulation, taxes, and unions, they mounted stridently anti–New Deal campaigns. One editor called the president "Stalin Delano Roosevelt" and insisted that the New Deal was a "Raw Deal." Having enjoyed a long era of public adoration and political deference from Republicans, business leaders fulminated against New Deal efforts to reform or regulate what they considered their private concerns.

By 1935, two major business organizations, the National Association of Manufacturers and the Chamber of Commerce, had become openly anti–New Deal. Their critiques were amplified by the American Liberty League, founded in 1934, which decried the New Deal for betraying basic constitutional guarantees of freedom and individualism. To them, the AAA was a "trend toward fascist control of agriculture," relief programs marked "the end of democracy," and the NRA was a plunge into the "quicksand of visionary experimentation." Although the Liberty League's membership never exceeded 125,000, its well-financed publicity campaign widened the rift between Roosevelt and business people.

Economic planners who favored rational planning in the public interest and labor leaders who sought to influence wages and working conditions by organizing unions attacked the New Deal from the left. In their view, the NRA stifled enterprise by permitting **monopolistic** practices. They pointed out that industrial trade associations twisted NRA codes to suit their aims, thwarted competition, and engaged in price gouging. Labor leaders especially resented the NRA's willingness to allow businesses to form company-controlled unions while blocking workers from organizing genuine grassroots unions to bargain for themselves.

The Supreme Court stepped into this crossfire of criticisms in May 1935 and declared that the NRA unconstitutionally conferred powers reserved to Congress on an administrative agency staffed by government appointees. The

NRA lingered briefly, but its codes lost their authority. The failure of the NRA demonstrated the depth of many Americans' resistance to economic planning and the stubborn refusal of business leaders to yield to government regulations or reforms.

Casualties in the Countryside

The AAA weathered critical battering by champions of the old order better than the NRA. Allotment checks for keeping land fallow and crop prices high created loyalty among farmers with enough acreage to participate. As a white farmer in North Carolina declared, "I stand for the New Deal and Roosevelt. . . . The NRA, the AAA . . . and crop control." Agricultural processors and distributors, however, criticized the AAA. They objected that the program reduced the volume of crop production—the only source of their profits—while they paid a tax on processed crops that funded the very program that disadvantaged them. In 1936, the Supreme Court agreed with their contention that they were victims of an illegal attempt to tax one group (processors and distributors) to enrich another (farmers). Down but not out, the AAA rebounded from the Supreme Court ruling by eliminating the offending tax and funding allotment payments from general government revenues.

Protests stirred, however, among those who did not qualify for allotments. The Southern Farm Tenants Union argued passionately that the AAA enriched large farmers and impoverished small farmers who rented rather than owned their land. Landlords took out of production the land that tenants farmed, simultaneously qualifying themselves for government subsidies and relieving themselves of the need to employ tenants. One black sharecropper explained why only $75 a year from New Deal agricultural subsidies trickled down to her: "De landlord is landlord, de politicians is landlord, de judge is landlord, de shurf [sheriff] is landlord,

Black Sharecroppers
An unintended consequence of the New Deal plan to maintain farm prices by reducing acreage in production was the eviction of tenant farmers when the land they worked was unused. Champions of the tenant farmers, most notably the Southern Farm Tenants Union, protested in vain that federal crop subsidies should be shared between owners and those who usually worked the land. Often, however, sharecroppers like these were simply cast adrift, and lobbies for farm owners thwarted any governmental challenge. Tenant farmers' sad state continued until World War II provided opportunities for displaced tenants to escape to the cities.
Corbis.

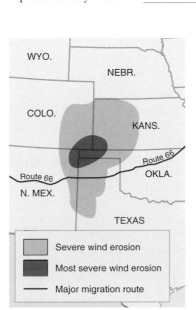

The Dust Bowl

ever'body is landlord, en we [sharecroppers] ain' got nothin'!" Such testimony showed that the AAA, like the NRA, tended to help most those who least needed help. Roosevelt's political dependence on southern Democrats caused him to avoid confronting such economic and racial inequities in the South's entrenched order.

Displaced tenants often joined the army of migrant workers who straggled across rural America during the 1930s, some to flee Plains dust storms. Many migrants came from Mexico to work Texas cotton, Michigan beans, Idaho sugar beets, and California crops of all kinds. But since people willing to take agricultural jobs usually

Okie Family
This tenant farmer worked land near Eagleton, Oklahoma, but became sick with pneumonia and lost his farm. The county he had lived in for fifteen years refused to give him WPA benefits because he briefly left the county after recovering from his illness. Accompanied by his five children, he pulled his earthly possessions in a toy wagon along a highway, looking for work. Such poor, jobless migrants were common along America's roads during the 1930s.
Library of Congress.

exceeded the jobs available, wages fell and native-born white migrants fought to reserve even these low-wage jobs for themselves. Hundreds of thousands of "Okie" migrants streamed out of the Dust Bowl of Oklahoma, Kansas, Texas, and Colorado, where chronic drought and harmful agricultural practices blasted crops and hopes. Parched, poor, and windblown, Okies—like the Joad family immortalized in John Steinbeck's novel *The Grapes of Wrath*—migrated to the lush fields and orchards of California, congregating in labor camps and hoping to find work and a future. But migrant laborers seldom found steady or secure work. As one Okie said, "When they need us they call us migrants, and when

we've picked their crop, we're bums and we got to get out."

Politics on the Fringes

Politically, the New Deal's staunchest opponents were in the Republican Party—organized, well-heeled, mainstream, and determined to challenge Roosevelt at every turn. But from the political fringes the New Deal also faced challenges, fueled by the hardship of the depression and the hope for a cure-all.

Socialists and Communists accused the New Deal of being the handmaiden of business elites and of rescuing capitalism from its self-inflicted crisis. Socialist author Upton Sinclair ran for governor of California in 1934 on a plan he called "End Poverty in California." Sinclair demanded that the state take ownership of idle factories and unused land and give them to cooperatives of working people, a first step toward what he envisioned as a "Cooperative Commonwealth" that would put the needs of people above profits. Although Sinclair received endorsements from intellectuals and labor leaders and considerable popular support, he lost the election, ending the most serious socialist electoral challenge to the New Deal.

Many other intellectuals and artists decided the time was ripe to advance the cause of more radical change, and they joined left-wing organizations, including the American Communist Party. The Communists eventually claimed about 30,000 members, the large majority of them immigrants, especially Scandinavians in the Midwest and eastern European Jews in major cities. Individual Communists worked to organize labor unions, protect the civil rights of black people, and help the destitute, but the party preached the overthrow of "bourgeois democracy" and the destruction of capitalism in favor of Soviet-style communism. Party spokesmen termed the NRA a "fascist slave program" and likened Roosevelt and the New Deal to Hitler and the Nazis. But heated talk about proletarian workers breaking their chains and rising in revolution against their bosses attracted few followers among the nation's millions of poor and unemployed. They wanted jobs and economic security within American capitalism and democracy, not violent revolution to establish a dictatorship of the Communist Party.

More powerful radical challenges to the New Deal sprouted from homegrown roots. Many Americans felt overlooked by New Deal programs that concentrated on finance, agriculture, and industry but did little to produce jobs or aid the poor. The merciless reality of the depression also continued to erode the security of people who still had a job but worried constantly about when they too might be pushed into the legions of the unemployed and penniless.

A Catholic priest in Detroit named Charles Coughlin spoke to, and for, many worried Americans in his weekly radio broadcasts, which reached a nationwide audience of 40 million. Father Coughlin expressed outrage at the suffering and inequities that he blamed on Communists, bankers, and "predatory capitalists" who, he claimed, were mostly Jews. In 1932,

Coughlin applauded Roosevelt's election and declared, "The New Deal is Christ's deal." But frustrated by Roosevelt's refusal to grant him influence, Coughlin turned against the New Deal for its failure to "drive the moneychangers from the temple" and end "want in the midst of plenty." Coughlin's message resonated with his radio audience, who inundated him with even more mail than Roosevelt received. Encouraged, Coughlin founded the National Union for Social Justice, or the Union Party, in 1935 and invited other dissidents to join him in a third-party challenge to Roosevelt in the 1936 presidential election. Tapping the popular appeal of anti-Semitism, Coughlin's Union Party called for an expanded money supply backed by silver so that the poor could be rescued from the "international bankers" responsible for the depression and coddled by Roosevelt.

Among those who answered Father Coughlin's call was Dr. Francis Townsend in Long Beach, California. Angry that many of his retired patients lived in misery, Townsend proposed in 1934 the creation of an Old Age Revolving Pension that would pay every American over age sixty a pension of $200 a month. In order to receive the pension, senior citizens had to agree to spend the entire amount within thirty days, thereby stimulating the economy. Townsend organized pension clubs with more than 2 million paying members and petitioned the federal government to enact his scheme. Had Townsend's plan been adopted, it would have required doubling taxes and spending half the nation's income to support the elderly, who comprised less than 10 percent of the population. When the major political parties rebuffed his impractical plan, Townsend merged his forces with Coughlin's Union Party in time for the 1936 election.

A more formidable challenge to the New Deal came from the ranks of the Democratic Party and from the region of its greatest strength. Huey Long, son of a backcountry Louisiana farmer, was elected governor of the state in 1928 with his slogan "Every man a king, but no one wears a crown." As governor, Long delivered on his promises to provide jobs and build roads, schools, and hospitals. Swaggering and bullying to get his way, Long delighted his grateful supporters, who elected him to the U.S. Senate in 1932 (see "Historical Question," page 888). As a freshman senator, Long introduced a sweeping "soak the rich" tax bill that would outlaw personal incomes of more than $1 million and in-

Huey Long: Demagogue or Champion of the Dispossessed?

From the time he was a small child, Huey Pierce Long was what one exasperated neighbor called a "pesterance." Defiant at school, artful at avoiding any disagreeable chores, ruthlessly driven to be the center of attention, Long got ahead with his intelligence and willingness to flout conventional rules. Though he spent only brief periods studying law at the University of Oklahoma and Tulane University, he cajoled a judge to convene a special bar examination, which he passed easily at the age of twenty-one. Declaring that he came out of that examination "running for office," Long rose swiftly from election as state railroad commissioner in 1918 to governor ten years later, dazzling the public with his brash style.

Louisiana's established leaders made white supremacy the cornerstone of their rule. Out of step with majority opinion on race, Long advanced his fortunes by appealing to class division—poor against rich, rural against urban, the humble against the elite—rather than white against black. He focused his reform program on a more equitable distribution of income and opportunity. At St. Martinsville, deep in swampy Cajun country, he asked, "Where are the schools that you have waited for your children to have, that have never come? Where are the roads and the highways that you sent your money to build . . . ? Where are the institutions to care for the sick and disabled?" When Long became governor, Louisiana had only 331 miles of paved roads outside the cities. It was also the most illiterate state in the nation. In 1893, when Long was born, 45 percent of those above the age of ten could not read; by 1920, the rate of illiteracy was still 22 percent, including 38 percent of all blacks.

Long articulated the grievances and hopes of the poor people of Louisiana. He also behaved ruthlessly to achieve his goals. After overcoming an **impeachment** effort in 1929, Long moved to consolidate his power. "I used to try to get things done by saying 'please,'" he said. "That didn't work and now I'm a dynamiter. I dynamite 'em out of my path." By 1930, Long completely dominated the state. Journalists around the country routinely referred to him as the "dictator of Louisiana." He made no effort to hide his power. Once an angry opponent thrust a volume in his face and shouted, "Maybe you've heard of this book. It's the constitution of the state of Louisiana." Long shrugged and said, "I'm the constitution here now." He bullied and bribed the state legislature into a rubber-stamp body that passed a series of laws giving him the power to count ballots and thus determine the outcome of elections. Every state employee knew that his or her job depended on loyalty to "the Kingfish," as Long liked to call himself.

His grasp on Louisiana firm, Long leaped into the national limelight by winning election to the U.S. Senate in 1932, where he quickly introduced a sweeping "soak-the-rich" tax bill that would have outlawed annual personal incomes of more than $1 million and inheritances of more than $5 million. Swift rejection by the Senate triggered his long-range strategy of becoming president by mobilizing the vast numbers of low-income Americans into a Share Our Wealth protest movement. Long's plan was to mount a presidential campaign in 1936 that would

heritances of more than $5 million. When the Senate summarily rejected his proposal, Long decided to run for president, mobilizing more than 5 million Americans behind his "Share Our Wealth" plan. Like Townsend's scheme, Long's program promised far more than it could deliver. Even if all wealth over a million dollars could have been converted to cash and confiscated, it would have paid for no more than 1 or 2 percent of the awards Long promised. Long did not linger over such troublesome details, predicting instead that he would become "your next President." Although the Share Our Wealth campaign died when Long was assassinated in 1935, his constituency and the wide appeal of a more equitable distribution of wealth persisted.

The challenges to the New Deal from Republicans as well as from more radical groups take enough votes from Roosevelt to tip the election to the Republican candidate. After four years of Republican failure to alleviate the depression with conservative policies, Long planned to sweep into the presidency in 1940, the savior of a suffering people.

The electoral showdown never came, however. On September 8, 1935, Carl Austin Weiss, a young physician enraged by the dishonor Long had visited on his family by removing his father from the Louisiana bench and suggesting black ancestry, fatally shot Long in a corridor of the Louisiana State House and was immediately gunned down by Long's bodyguards. The long lines of worn and ragged people passing by Long's coffin in the capitol and the smaller number of better-dressed mourners at Weiss's funeral testified to the split in Louisiana along class lines.

Long always answered charges that he was a dictator rather than a man of the people by insisting that the polite ways of conventional democratic rules could never cure the nation's deepest ills. Only forceful means, he insisted, could finally break the hold of the privileged and extend opportunity to everyone. He could point to real achievements in Louisiana. As promised, he taxed the oil companies and utilities that had run Louisiana for decades, and

Huey Long

Huey Long's ability to adapt his captivating stump-speech style to the radio made him the one rival politician who gave Roosevelt serious concern in the mid-1930s. Here Long is shown in 1932 campaigning in Arkansas in support of Hattie Carraway's bid for election to the U.S. Senate. Stigmatized as both a woman and a populist reformer, Carraway seemed a sure loser until Long crossed the border from Louisiana on her behalf. In a mere two weeks of speaking and pressing the flesh, Long brushed aside criticism that he was an interloper and boosted Carraway to victory as part of his crusade to share the wealth.

Corbis.

he funneled the revenue into programs to benefit those who had been left out. While he built monuments to his own vanity, Long also addressed many of the state's genuine social needs. At one time, Louisiana's road-building program was the biggest in the nation, and by 1935 the state had ten times more paved roads than when Long became governor. He made Louisiana State University a major institution of higher learning. He greatly expanded the state's pitiful public health facilities. For children, he provided free schoolbooks and new schools. For adults, he started night schools to combat illiteracy.

Disdainful both of Long and of those who turned to him, critics labeled Long a homegrown fascist and called him the "Messiah of the Rednecks." They compared him to Mussolini and Hitler and expressed relief that his life, and thus the damage he and the "rabble" who supported him could do, was cut short. Roosevelt recognized that the New Deal had to reach out to the "forgotten man," but Long reached farther to connect with neglected citizens. He gave Americans the only chance they ever had, for better or worse, to vote for a candidate with a broad national following who offered sweeping change comparable to that of parties on the radical right and left in other countries during the 1930s.

stirred Democrats to solidify their winning coalition. In 1934, in the midterm congressional elections—normally a time when a seated president loses support—Roosevelt sought to distance the New Deal from critics on the right and left. In the election, voters gave New Dealers a landslide victory. Democrats increased their majority in the House of Representatives and gained a two-thirds majority in the Senate.

Toward a Welfare State

The popular mandate for the New Deal revealed by the congressional elections persuaded Roosevelt to press ahead with bold new efforts of relief, recovery, and reform. Despite the initiatives of the Hundred Days, the depression still strangled the economy. Rumbles of discontent from Father Coughlin, Huey Long, and their

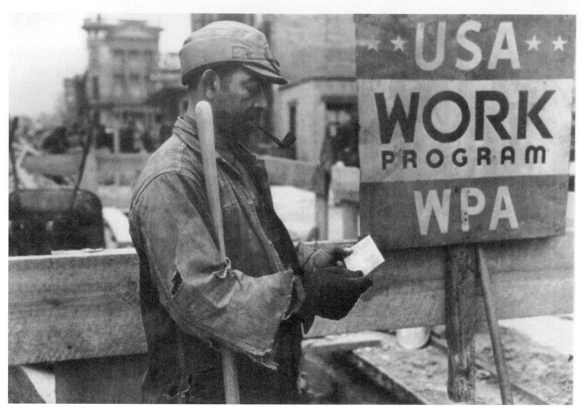

WPA Paycheck
WPA projects gave jobs and paychecks to millions of Americans who, like this man in Washington, D.C., dug ditches. Workers on New Deal public works projects also built the San Francisco–Oakland Bay Bridge, the Lincoln Tunnel in New York, and the Overseas Highway in the Florida Keys, as well as thousands of other bridges, roads, and buildings still in use today.
National Archives.

supporters showed that New Deal programs had fallen far short of their goals. In 1935, Roosevelt capitalized on his congressional majorities to enact major new programs that signaled the emergence of an American **welfare state**.

Taken together, these New Deal efforts stretched a safety net under the lives of ordinary Americans. Although many citizens remained unprotected, New Deal programs helped millions with jobs, relief, and government support. Knitting together the safety net was the idea that the federal government bore responsibility for the welfare of individual Americans. When individuals suffered because of economic and social forces beyond their control—as in the Great Depression—the federal government had the duty to provide them a measure of support and protection. The safety net of welfare programs tied the political loyalty of working people to the New Deal and the Democratic Party. As a North Carolina mill worker said, "Mr. Roosevelt is the only man we ever had in the White House who would understand that my boss is a sonofabitch."

Relief for the Unemployed

First and foremost, Americans still needed jobs. Since the private economy left 8 million people jobless by 1935, Roosevelt and his advisers launched a massive work relief program. Government handouts, Roosevelt declared, crippled recipients by inducing "spiritual and moral disintegration . . . destructive to the human spirit." Work relief—jobs—bolstered individuals' "self-respect, . . . self-confidence, . . . courage, and determination." With a congressional appropriation of nearly $5 billion—more than all government revenues in 1934—the New Deal created the Works Progress Administration (WPA) to give unemployed Americans government-funded jobs on public works projects. The WPA put millions of jobless citizens to work on roads, bridges, parks, public buildings, and more—projects that served public needs not otherwise being met. WPA paychecks pumped billions of dollars into the economy, boosting consumption along with what Roosevelt termed "the human spirit" of working people. In addition, Congress passed—over Roosevelt's veto—the bonus long-sought by the Bonus Marchers, giving veterans an average of $580, further stimulating the economy.

By 1936, WPA funds provided jobs for 7 percent of the nation's labor force. In effect, the WPA made the federal government the employer of last resort, creating useful jobs when the capitalist economy failed to do so. By the time the WPA ended in 1943—because mobilization for World War II created full employment—it had made major contributions to both relief and recovery. WPA jobs put 13 million men and women to work and gave them paychecks worth $10 billion.

About three out of four WPA jobs involved construction and renovation of the nation's physical infrastructure. WPA workers built 572,000 miles of country roads, 78,000 bridges, 67,000 miles of city streets, 40,000 public buildings, 8,000 parks, 350 airports, and much else. In addition to work with picks, shovels, hammers, nails, bricks, and mortar, the WPA gave jobs to 6,000 artists, musicians, actors, journalists, poets, and novelists. Artists painted murals in post offices and courthouses while writers penned travel guides and interviewed elderly former slaves. Actors in WPA theater groups attracted 60 million people to their performances, and more than 50 million Americans listened to concerts by WPA musicians. The WPA reached the most isolated corners of the nation; for example, WPA-funded librarians delivered books on horseback to remote cabins in Appalachia. WPA projects throughout the nation displayed tangible evidence of the New Deal's commitment to public welfare.

Empowering Labor

During the Great Depression, factory workers who managed to keep their jobs worried constantly about being laid off while their wages and working hours were cut. When workers tried to organize labor unions to protect themselves, municipal and state governments usually sided with employers. Since the Gilded Age, the state and federal governments had been far more effective at busting unions than busting **trusts**. The New Deal dramatically reversed the federal

government's stance toward unions. With legislation and political support, the New Deal encouraged an unprecedented wave of union organizing among the nation's working people. When the head of the United Mine Workers, John L. Lewis, told coal miners that "the President wants you to join a union," he exaggerated only a little. New Dealers believed unions would counterbalance the organized might of big corporations by defending working people, maintaining wages, and replacing the bloody violence that often accompanied strikes with economic peace and commercial stability.

> In addition to work with picks, shovels, hammers, nails, bricks, and mortar, the WPA gave jobs to 6,000 artists, musicians, actors, journalists, poets, and novelists.

Violent battles on the nation's streets and docks showed the determination of militant labor leaders to organize unions that would protect jobs as well as wages. In 1934, striking workers in Toledo, Minneapolis, San Francisco, and elsewhere were beaten and shot by police and the National Guard. In Congress, labor leaders lobbied for the National Labor Relations Act (NLRA), a bill sponsored by Senator Robert Wagner of New York that authorized the federal government to intervene in labor disputes and supervise the organization of labor unions. Justly considered a "Magna Carta for labor," the Wagner Act, as it came to be called, guaranteed workers the right to organize unions, putting the might of federal law behind the appeals of labor leaders. The Wagner Act created the National Labor Relations Board (NLRB) to sponsor and oversee elections for union representation. If the majority of workers at a company voted for a union, then the union became the sole bargaining agent for the entire workplace, and the employer was required to negotiate with the elected union leaders. Roosevelt signed the Wagner Act in July 1935, providing for the first time federal support for labor organization—the most important New Deal reform of the industrial order.

> Justly considered a "Magna Carta for labor," the Wagner Act guaranteed workers the right to organize unions, putting the might of federal law behind the appeals of labor leaders.

The achievements that flowed from the Wagner Act and renewed labor militancy were impressive. When Roosevelt became president in 1933, union membership—almost entirely composed of skilled workers in trade unions affiliated with the American Federation of Labor

Sit-Down Strikers

In 1937, workers occupied General Motors's Fisher Body plant in Flint, Michigan, demanding recognition of the United Auto Workers (UAW) as the sole bargaining agent for all GM workers. With nearly 250,000 workers producing about half of all American automobiles, General Motors fought the union with what a government committee termed an "industrial Cheka [Cheka was the Soviet Union's network of spies, later known as the KGB] . . . the most colossal supersystem of spies yet devised in any American corporation." Nonetheless, the Flint plant was a crucial choke point in the production of many popular GM cars, allowing the sit-down strikers to outmaneuver the spies and cut production to a trickle. After 44 days, the strikers won General Motors's recognition of the UAW, a landmark victory in industrial unionism.

Library of Congress.

(AFL)—stood at 3 million, down by half since the end of World War I. With the support of the Wagner Act, union membership expanded almost fivefold, to 14 million by the time of Roosevelt's death in 1945. By then, 30 percent of the workforce was unionized, the highest union representation in American history.

Most of the new union members were factory workers and unskilled laborers, many of them immigrants and African Americans. For decades, established AFL unions had no desire to organize factory and unskilled workers, who struggled along without unions. In 1935, under the aggressive leadership of the mine workers' John L. Lewis, and the head of the Amalgamated Clothing Workers, Sidney Hillman, a coalition of unskilled workers formed the Committee for Industrial Organization (CIO; later the Congress

of Industrial Organizations). The CIO, helped by the Wagner Act, mobilized organizing drives in major industries. The exceptional courage and organizing skill of labor militants, a few of them Communists, earned the CIO the leadership role in the campaign to organize the bitterly anti-union automobile and steel industries.

The bloody struggle by the CIO-affiliated United Auto Workers (UAW) to organize workers at General Motors climaxed in January 1937 when striking workers occupied the main assembly plant in Flint, Michigan, in a "sit-down" strike that slashed the plant's production of 15,000 cars a week to a mere 150. In desperation, General Motors obtained court injunctions against the sit-down strikers. But neither Roosevelt nor the Michigan governor would act to enforce the injunction. Stymied, General

Motors surrendered and agreed to make the UAW the sole bargaining agent for all the company's workers and to refrain from interfering with union activity. Having subdued the auto industry's leading producer, the UAW expanded its campaign until, after much violence, the entire industry was unionized when the Ford Motor Company capitulated to the union in 1941.

The CIO hoped to ride organizing success in auto plants to victory in the steel mills. But after unionizing the industry giant U.S. Steel, the CIO ran up against fanatic opposition from smaller steel firms. The climax came in May 1937 when a crowd of strikers gathered in a field outside Chicago to organize a picket line around Republic Steel. Without warning, police who had been sent to keep order charged the crowd, swinging clubs and firing their weapons, killing ten strikers and injuring scores. Following this debacle, the battered steelworkers halted their organizing campaign. In steel and other major industries, such as the stridently anti-union southern textile mills, organizing efforts stalled until after 1941, when military mobilization created labor shortages that gave workers greater bargaining power.

Social Security and Tax Reform

The single most important feature of the New Deal's emerging welfare state was Social Security. An ambitious, far-reaching, and permanent reform, Social Security was designed to provide a modest income to relieve the poverty of elderly people. Only about 15 percent of older Americans had private pension plans, and during the depression corporations and banks often failed to pay the meager pensions they had promised. Prompted by the popular but impractical panaceas of Dr. Townsend, Father Coughlin, and Huey Long, Roosevelt became the first president to advocate protection for the elderly.

The political struggle for Social Security highlighted class differences among Americans. Support for the measure came from a coalition of advocacy groups for the elderly and the poor, traditional progressives, leftists, social workers, and labor unions. Arrayed against them were economic conservatives, including the Liberty League, the National Association of Manufacturers, the Chamber of Commerce, and the American Medical Association. Enact the Social Security system, these conservatives and their representatives in the Republican Party warned, and the government will gain a whip hand over private property, destroy initiative, and reduce proud individuals to spineless loafers.

The large New Deal majority in Congress carried the day in August 1935. Yet the strong objections to federal involvement in matters traditionally left to individuals and local charities persuaded the framers of Social Security to strike an awkward balance among federal, state, and personal responsibility. The Social Security Act required that pensions for the elderly be funded not by direct government subsidies but instead by tax contributions from workers and their employers. Although this provision subtracted money from consumption—hindering economic recovery—it gave contributing workers a personal stake in the system and made it politically invulnerable. Social Security also created unemployment insurance, paid for by employers' contributions, that provided modest benefits for workers who lost their jobs. In a bow to traditional beliefs about local governments' responsibility for public assistance, Social Security also issued multi-million-dollar grants to the states to use to support dependent mothers and children, public health services, and the blind, providing desperately needed

Social Security Card

The Social Security Act required each working American who participated in the system to register with the government and obtain a unique number—the "SSN" familiar to every citizen today—inscribed on an identity card, making benefits portable from one job and one state to another. For the first time in the nation's history, millions of ordinary citizens were numbered, registered, and identified by a government bureaucracy, creating a personal, individualized connection between people and the federal government. Administering the massive agency needed to collect, monitor, and regulate this information and distribute the benefits that flowed from it gave government jobs to tens of thousands, providing security for government workers as well as for Social Security beneficiaries.

Picture Research Consultants & Archives.

> Millions of Americans—women, children, old folks, the unorganized, unskilled, uneducated, and unemployed—often fell through the New Deal's safety net.

relief. After a Supreme Court decision in 1937 upheld the right of Congress to require all citizens to pay for Social Security through federal taxes, the program was expanded to include benefits for dependent survivors of deceased recipients. Although the first Social Security check (for $41.30) was not issued until 1940, the system gave working people assurance that in the future, when they became too old to work, they would receive income from the government. This safety net protected ordinary working people from fears of a penniless and insecure old age.

Fervent opposition to Social Security struck New Dealers as evidence that the rich had learned little from the depression. Roosevelt had long felt contempt for the moneyed elite who ignored the sufferings of the poor. He looked for a way to redistribute wealth that would weaken conservative opposition, advance the cause of social equity, and defuse political challenges from Huey Long and Father Coughlin. In June 1935, as the Social Security Act was being debated, Roosevelt delivered a message to Congress outlining comprehensive tax reform. Charging that large fortunes put "great and undesirable concentration of control in [the hands of] relatively few individuals," Roosevelt urged a graduated tax on corporations, an inheritance tax, and an increase in maximum personal income taxes. Congress endorsed Roosevelt's basic principle by taxing those with higher incomes at a somewhat higher rate.

Neglected Americans and the New Deal

While the WPA and other work relief programs aided working people, the average unemployment rate for the 1930s stayed high—17 percent, about one of every six workers. Even many working people remained more or less untouched by New Deal benefits. Workers in industries that resisted unions received little help from the Wagner Act or the WPA. Tens of thousands of women in southern textile mills, for example, commonly received wages of less than ten cents an hour and were fired if they protested. Domestic workers—almost all of them women—and agricultural workers—many of them African, Hispanic, or Asian

Americans—were neither unionized nor eligible for Social Security. The safety net of New Deal programs provided the best protection for unionized workers in major industries, neglecting millions of other, less fortunate Americans. The patchwork of New Deal reforms erected a two-tier welfare state. In the top tier, organized workers were the greatest beneficiaries of New Deal initiatives. In the bottom tier, millions of neglected Americans—women, children, old folks, the unorganized, unskilled, uneducated, and

Mary McLeod Bethune
At the urging of Eleanor Roosevelt, Mary McLeod Bethune, a southern educational and civil rights leader, became director of the National Youth Administration's Division of Negro Affairs. The first black woman to head a federal agency, Bethune used her position to promote social change. Here Bethune takes her mission to the streets to protest the discriminatory hiring practices of the Peoples Drug Store chain in the nation's capital.
Moorland-Spingarn Research Center, Howard University.

Hispanic-American Alliance Banner

Between 1910 and 1940, when refugees from the Mexican revolution poured across the American border, the Hispanic-American Alliance and other such organizations sought to protect Mexican Americans' rights against nativist fears and hostility. In the years between the world wars, many alliance banners such as this one flew in opposition to the deportation of Mexican aliens, an attempt in 1926 to bar Mexican Americans from city jobs in Los Angeles, and the disproportionately high use of the death penalty against Mexicans convicted of crimes. Throughout these and other trials, the alliance steadfastly emphasized the desire of Mexican Americans to receive permanent status in the United States.
The Oakland Museum.

unemployed—often fell through the New Deal safety net.

The New Deal neglected few citizens more than African Americans. About half of black Americans in cities were jobless, double the unemployment rate among whites. In the rural South, where the vast majority of African Americans lived, conditions were worse. New Deal agricultural policies like the AAA favored landowners and often resulted in black sharecroppers and tenants being pushed off land they farmed. Disfranchisement by intimidation and legal subterfuge prevented southern blacks from protesting their plight at the ballot box. Protest risked vicious retaliation from local whites. After years of decline, lynching increased during the 1930s. In Alabama, the black "Scottsboro Boys" faced the death penalty in 1931 for a rape they did not commit (see chapter 23); in Georgia, radical black unionist Angelo Herndon received a sentence to the chain gang for trying to organize black workers. Only 11 of more than 10,000 WPA supervisors in the South were black, even though African Americans comprised about a third of the region's population. Up north, a riot in 1935 that focused on white-owned businesses in Harlem dramatized blacks' resentment and despair. Bitter critics charged that the New Deal's NRA stood for "Negro Run Around" or "Negroes Ruined Again."

Roosevelt responded to such criticisms with great caution since New Deal reforms required the political support of powerful conservative, segregationist, southern Democrats, who would be alienated by programs that aided blacks. A white Georgia relief worker expressed the common view that "Any Nigger who gets over $8 a week is a spoiled Nigger, that's all." Stymied by the political clout of entrenched white racism, New Dealers tried to attract political support from black leaders. Roosevelt's overtures to African Americans prompted northern black voters to shift in the 1934 elections from the Republican to the Democratic Party, helping elect New Deal Democrats.

Eleanor Roosevelt sponsored the appointment of Mary McLeod Bethune—the energetic cofounder of the National Council on Negro Women—as head of the Division of Negro Affairs in the National Youth Administration. The highest ranking black official in Roosevelt's administration, Bethune used her position to guide a small number of black professionals and civil rights activists to posts within New Deal agencies. Nicknamed the "Black Cabinet," these men and women comprised the first sizable representation of African Americans in white-collar posts in the federal government, and they ultimately helped about one in four African Americans get access to New Deal relief programs.

Despite these gains, by 1940 African Americans still suffered severe handicaps. Most of the 13 million black workers toiled at low-paying menial jobs, unprotected by the New Deal safety net. Infant mortality was 50 percent greater than for whites, and life expectancy was twelve years shorter. Making a mockery of the "separate but equal" doctrine, segregated black schools had less money and worse facilities than those of whites, and only 1 percent of black students earned college degrees. In southern states, there were no black police officers or judges and hardly any black lawyers, and vigilante violence against blacks went unpunished. To these problems of black Americans, the New Deal offered few remedies.

Hispanic Americans did no better. About a million Mexican Americans lived in the United States in the 1930s, most of them first- or second-generation immigrants who worked at stoop labor tending crops throughout the West. During the depression, field workers saw their low wages plunge lower still to about a dime an hour. Ten thousand Mexican American pecan shellers in San Antonio, Texas, earned only a nickel an hour. To preserve scarce jobs for U.S. citizens, the federal government choked off immigration from Mexico while state and local officials prohibited employment of aliens on work relief projects and summarily deported tens of thousands of Mexican Americans, many with their American-born children. Local white administrators of many New Deal programs throughout the West discriminated against Hispanics and other people of color. Even when Mexican Americans managed to join government work projects, they often received lower pay than their white counterparts, and less aid when out of a job. A New Deal study concluded that "The Mexican is . . . segregated from the rest of the community as effectively as the Negro . . . [by] poverty and low wages."

Asian Americans had similar experiences. Asian immigrants were still excluded from U.S. citizenship and in many states were not permitted to own land. Although by 1930 more than half of Japanese Americans had been born in the United States, they were still liable to discrimination. Even college-educated Asian Americans worked in family shops, restaurants, and laundries. One young Asian American expressed frustrations felt by many others: "I am a fruit-stand worker. I would much rather it were doctor or lawyer . . . but my aspirations [were] frustrated long ago by circumstances [and] I am only what I am, a professional carrot washer."

Native Americans—like blacks, Hispanics, and Asian Americans—suffered neglect from New Deal agencies. As a group, they remained the poorest of the poor. Since the Dawes Act of 1887, the federal government had encouraged Native Americans to assimilate, to abandon their Indian identities and adopt the cultural norms of the majority society. Under the leadership of the New Deal's commissioner of Indian affairs, John Collier, the New Deal's Indian Reorganization Act (IRA) of 1934 largely reversed that policy. Collier claimed that "the most interesting and important fact about Indians" was that they "do not expect much, often they expect nothing at all; yet they are able to be happy." Given such views, the IRA provided little economic aid to Native Americans, but it did restore their right to own land communally and to have greater control over their own affairs, including the right to vote on whether they should live under the IRA. In special elections in 1934 and 1935, 172 tribes with about 132,000 members opted to accept the IRA, and 73 tribes with about 63,000 members voted to reject it. The IRA brought little immediate benefit to Native Americans and remained a divisive issue for decades, but it did provide an important foundation for Indians' economic, cultural, and political resurgence a generation later.

John Collier Meets with Navajo Representatives
Commissioner of Indian Affairs John Collier receives a Navajo delegation protesting restrictions in the Indian Reorganization Act of 1934. The Navajos display a blanket made from the wool of their own sheep to protest limits on the number of sheep they could raise. Collier had crafted the act to revive Native American society by granting tribes an independent land base and many self-governing powers. However, his attempt to make the reservations economically viable through conservation measures, including restrictions on grass-devouring sheep, roused resistance by Indians who chose traditional ways of using resources. The tension between federal benevolence and Indian views of their own way of life has remained a painful issue.
Wide World Photos, Inc.

New Deal Needle Book

In the 1936 presidential campaign, Democrats distributed this sewing-needle book to celebrate New Deal achievements during Roosevelt's first term. Evoking Roosevelt's 1932 campaign theme song, "Happy Days Are Here Again," the illustrations on the needle book emphasize the return of harmony in agriculture, of booming factories providing plenty of jobs, and above all of "happiness restored" at home around the well-appointed dinner table. Notice that the working people in factories are faceless but the white-collar worker and the family are individualized sympathetically. The needle book signifies Democrats' attempt to mobilize women to vote in gratitude for the happiness supplied by Roosevelt and the New Deal. Like most campaign material, the needle book's claims for New Deal success exaggerated greatly.

Collection of Janice L. and David J. Frent.

The troubadour of working people, singer and songwriter Woody Guthrie, traveled the nation for eight years during the 1930s "by the thumb route . . . no job, no money, no home . . . no nothing." At night, he recalled, other rambling men told him "the story of their life, how it used to be," giving voice to experiences especially common among Americans neglected by the New Deal: "how the home went to pieces, how the young wife died or left, how the mother died in the insane asylum, how Dad tried twice to kill himself, and lay flat on his back for 18 months—and then crops got to where they wouldn't bring nothing, work in factories would kill a dog . . . work in the steel mills burned your system up . . . and—always, always [you] had to fight and argue and cuss and swear . . . to try to get a nickel more out of the rich bosses."

interests of the workers who produced the nation's wealth. But in 1935 the Soviet Union, worried about the threat of fascism in Europe, instructed Communists throughout the world to join hands with non-Communist progressives in a "Popular Front" to advance the fortunes of the working class. With varying degrees of enthusiasm, many radicals switched from opposing the New Deal to supporting its relief programs and encouragement of labor unions.

Roosevelt's conservative opponents reacted to the massing of New Deal force by intensifying their opposition to the welfare state. To Roosevelt, the situation seemed part of a drama that had played out since the nation's beginning, pitting a Hamiltonian faction of wealth and privilege against the heirs of Jefferson who, like Roosevelt himself, favored a more equitable distribution of wealth and opportunity.

The New Deal from Victory to Deadlock

To accelerate the sputtering economic recovery, Roosevelt shifted the emphasis of the New Deal in the mid-1930s. Instead of seeking cooperation from conservative business leaders, he decided to rely on the growing New Deal coalition to enact reforms over the strident opposition of Republicans and corporate interests.

Added to New Deal strength in farm states and big cities were some new allies on the left. Throughout Roosevelt's first term, socialists and Communists denounced the slow pace of change and accused the New Deal of failing to serve the

The Election of 1936

Roosevelt believed that the presidential election of 1936 would test his leadership and progressive ideals. The depression still had a stranglehold on the economy. Nearly 8 million remained jobless, and millions more were stuck in poverty. Conservative leaders believed that the New Deal's failure to lift the nation out of the depression indicated that Americans were ready for a change. Left-wing critics insisted that the New Deal had missed the opportunity to displace capitalism with a socialist economy and would lose votes to candidates who recommended more radical remedies.

Faces of the Depression

New Deal agencies dispatched dozens of photographers to document the lives of Americans during the 1930s. In thousands of pictures, the photographers captured the faces of the depression. Their photographs, the sources of the portraits shown here, demonstrate that, unlike the people shown on the New Deal sewing book, working Americans were not faceless drones but human individuals struggling to survive—whether dispossessed black sharecroppers in the South, Japanese American mothers and daughters in California produce fields, Mexican laborers in the Southwest, farmers in the Tennessee mountains, or Okie grannies, mothers, and children in California labor camps. As these portraits suggest, working people knew that, while the New Deal might provide welcome aid, they depended in the end on their own resourcefulness and the support of family and friends.

Library of Congress.

Republicans turned to the Kansas heartland to select Governor Alfred (Alf) Landon as their presidential nominee. A moderate who had supported some New Deal measures, Landon stressed mainstream Republican proposals to achieve a balanced federal budget and to ease the perils of illness and old age with old-fashioned neighborliness instead of faceless government bureaucracies like Social Security.

Roosevelt put his faith in the growing coalition of New Deal supporters, who he believed shared his conviction that the New Deal was the nation's liberator from a long era of privilege and wealth for a few and "economic slavery" for the rest. At the end of the campaign, Roosevelt struck a defiant pose before a thunderous crowd at Madison Square Garden, calling "the roll of honor of those who stood with us in 1932 and still stand with us today . . . men who never had a chance, women in sweatshops, [and] children at looms." Assailing his "old enemies . . . business and financial monopoly, speculation, reckless banking, [and] class antagonism," he proclaimed, "Never before in all our history have these forces been so united against one candidate as they stand today. They are unanimous in their hate for me—and I welcome their hatred." When the crowd's roar subsided, Roosevelt concluded: "I should like to have it said of my first Administration that in it the forces of selfishness and of lust for power met their match. I should like to have it said of my second Administration that in it these forces met their master."

Roosevelt triumphed spectacularly. He won 60.8 percent of the popular vote, 11 million more votes than Landon, the widest presidential margin to date. He carried the electoral votes of every state except Maine and Vermont. Third parties—including the Socialists and the Communists—fell pitifully short of the support they expected and never again mounted a significant challenge to the New Deal. Congressional results were equally lopsided, with Democrats outnumbering Republicans more than three to one in both houses.

Roosevelt's victory testified to the New Deal's mobilization of voters. For example, in nineteen northern cities where more than half the population was composed of first- and second-generation immigrants, Democratic votes more than doubled compared to 1932, while Republican voters increased by less than a third. In his inaugural address, Roosevelt pledged to use his mandate to help all citizens achieve a decent standard of living. He an-

nounced, "I see one third of a nation ill-housed, ill-clad, [and] ill-nourished," and he promised to devote his second term to alleviate their wants.

Court Packing

In the afterglow of his reelection triumph, Roosevelt pondered how to remove the remaining obstacles to New Deal reforms. He decided to target the Supreme Court. Laden with conservative justices appointed by Republican presidents, the Court had invalidated eleven New Deal measures as unconstitutional interferences with free enterprise. Now, Social Security, the Wagner Act, the Securities and Exchange Commission, and other New Deal innovations were moving toward an ominous rendezvous with the justices.

Roosevelt concluded that he must do something to ensure that the Supreme Court's "horse and buggy" notions did not dismantle

> To ensure that the Supreme Court did not dismantle the New Deal, Roosevelt proposed that one new justice be added for each existing judge who had already served for ten years and was over the age of seventy.

the New Deal. He proposed that one new justice be added for each existing judge who had already served for ten years and was over the age of seventy. In effect, the proposed law would give Roosevelt the power to pack the Court with up to six New Dealers who could outvote the elderly, conservative, Republican justices.

But the president had not reckoned with Americans' deeply rooted deference to the independent authority of the Supreme Court. More than two-thirds of Americans believed the Court should be free from political interference. Even New Deal supporters were disturbed by the "court-packing" scheme. The suggestion that individuals over seventy had diminished mental capacity also offended many elderly members of Congress. Although Roosevelt insisted that the bill was intended to improve the efficiency of an "overworked" Court, the real purpose was to make room for supporters of New Deal initiatives. A storm of public protest whipped up by conservatives prompted the heavily Democratic Senate to defeat the bill.

Although Roosevelt's court-packing plan failed, Supreme Court justices nonetheless got Roosevelt's message. After the furor abated, Chief Justice Charles Evans Hughes and fellow moderate Owen Roberts moderated their views enough to keep the Court from invalidating the Wagner Act and Social Security. Then the most conservative of the elderly justices—the "four horsemen of reaction," one New Dealer called them—retired. Roosevelt eventually named eight justices to the Court—more than any other president. His choice of liberals to fill vacancies on the Court ultimately gave safe passage to New Deal laws through the shoals of judicial review.

Reaction and Recession

Emboldened by their defeat of the court-packing plan, Republicans and southern Democrats rallied around their common conservatism to obstruct additional reforms. Arguments over whether the New Deal needed to be expanded and, if so, how, undermined consensus among reformers and sparked antagonism between Congress and the White House. The ominous rise of belligerent regimes in Germany, Italy, Japan, and elsewhere slowed reform as some Americans began to worry more about defending the nation than changing it. These developments impeded reform despite Roosevelt's 1936 landslide.

Roosevelt himself favored slowing the pace of the New Deal. He believed that existing New Deal measures had steadily boosted the economy and largely eliminated the depression crisis. In fact, the gross national product in 1937 briefly equaled the 1929 level, before drooping lower for the rest of the decade. Unemployment declined to 14 percent in 1937 but quickly spiked upward and stayed higher until 1940. Roosevelt's unwarranted optimism about the economic recovery persuaded him that additional deficit spending by the federal government was no longer necessary. He also worried that pump-priming deficits would cause inflation and reduce the value of hard-earned savings. Accordingly, Roosevelt moved cautiously toward a balanced budget by cutting funds for relief projects. He also urged the Federal Reserve to raise interest rates to discourage speculators from borrowing on easy terms.

Roosevelt's retrenchment soon backfired. Rather than preventing inflation, the reduction in deficit spending reversed the improving economy. Anxious about inflation, Roosevelt failed to consider how far the economy had to go before it would reach inflationary levels. Even at

> Roosevelt's unwarranted optimism about the economic recovery persuaded him that additional deficit spending by the federal government was no longer necessary.

the high-water mark of recovery in the summer of 1937, 7 million people lacked jobs. In the next few months, national income and production slipped backward so steeply that almost two-thirds of the economic gains since 1933 were lost by June 1938. Farm prices dropped 20 percent, and unemployment rose by more than 2 million.

This economic reversal hurt the New Deal politically. Conservatives argued that this recession proved New Deal measures produced only an illusion of progress. The way to weather the recession was to tax and spend less and wait for the natural laws of supply and demand to restore prosperity. Many New Dealers believed instead that the recession demonstrated anew the failure of free-enterprise orthodoxies. They insisted that the continuing depression showed the necessity of government intervention in the economy. They demanded that Roosevelt revive federal spending and redouble efforts to stimulate the economy. In 1938, Congress heeded such pleas and enacted a massive new program of federal spending.

The New Deal's ad hoc methods received support from new economic ideas advanced by the brilliant British economist John Maynard Keynes. In his influential work *The General Theory of Employment, Interest, and Money* (1936), Keynes made a sophisticated, theoretical argument in favor of practices that New Deal relief agencies had developed in a commonsense way. A nation's economy, Keynes declared, could not automatically reach its full potential in the complex, interdependent modern world. The depression had painfully illustrated that economic activity could become stalled at a level far short of a society's true potential. When that happened, only government intervention could pump enough money into the system to revive production, boost consumption, and restore prosperity.

Roosevelt never had the inclination or the time to follow his economic advisers into the thicket of **Keynesian** theory. But the recession scare of 1938 taught the president the Keynesian lesson that economic growth had to be carefully nurtured. Escape from the depression required a plan for large-scale spending to alleviate distress and stimulate economic growth.

The Last of the New Deal Reforms

From the moment he was sworn in, Roosevelt sought to expand the powers of the presidency. He believed that the president needed more authority to meet emergencies such as the depression and to administer the sprawling federal bureaucracy. Arguing the need for "efficiency," Roosevelt submitted an ambitious plan of executive reorganization to Congress in 1937. The bill failed, but in September 1938 Congress passed the Administrative Reorganization Act, which gave Roosevelt part of what he desired. With a Democratic majority in Congress, a now friendly Supreme Court, and the revival of deficit spending, the newly empowered White House seemed to be in a good position to move ahead with a revitalized New Deal.

Resistance to further reform was also on the rise, however. Conservatives argued that the New Deal had pressed government centralization too far and was bent on creating what later came to be known as the "imperial presidency." Even the New Deal's friends became weary of one emergency program after another, especially while economic woes still shadowed New Deal achievements. By the midpoint of Roosevelt's second term, restive members of Congress balked at new initiatives. Clearly, the New Deal was losing momentum, but enough energy remained for one last burst of reform.

The farm sector still had strong claims on New Deal attention in the face of drought, declining prices, and impoverished sharecroppers and tenants. In 1937, the Agriculture Department created the Farm Security Administration (FSA) to provide housing and loans to help tenant farmers become independent. But the FSA was starved for funds and ran up against the major farm organizations intent on serving their own interests. With only minor successes to show, the FSA petered out in the early 1940s. For those who owned farms, the New Deal offered renewed prosperity with a second Agricultural Adjustment Act (AAA) in 1938. To moderate price swings by regulating supply, the plan combined production quotas on five staple crops—cotton, tobacco, wheat, corn, and rice—with storage loans through its Commodity Credit Corporation. The most prosperous farmers benefited most, but the act's Federal Surplus Commodities Corporation added an element of charity by issuing food stamps so that the poor could obtain surplus food. The AAA of 1938 brought stability to American agriculture and ample food to most—but not all—tables.

Advocates for the urban poor also made modest gains after decades of neglect. New York senator Robert Wagner convinced Congress to pass the National Housing Act in 1937. By 1941, some 160,000 residences had been made available to poor people at affordable rents. The project did not come close to meeting the need for affordable housing, but for the first time the federal government took an active role in providing decent urban housing.

The last major piece of New Deal labor legislation, the Fair Labor Standards Act of June 1938, reiterated the New Deal pledge to provide workers with a decent standard of living. After lengthy haggling and compromise that revealed the waning strength of the New Deal, Congress finally agreed to intervene in the long-sacrosanct realm of worker contracts. The new law set wage and hours standards and at long last curbed the use of child labor. The minimum-wage level was modest—twenty-five cents an hour for a maximum of forty-four hours a week. And, in order to attract enough conservative votes, the act exempted merchant seamen, fishermen, domestic help, and farm laborers from these minimal wage and hours standards—relegating most white women and most African Americans to lower wages. Nevertheless, the Fair Labor Standards Act advanced Roosevelt's inaugural promise to improve the living standards of the poorest Americans.

The final New Deal reform effort failed to make much headway against the hidebound system of racial segregation. Although Roosevelt denounced lynching as murder, he would not jeopardize his vital base of southern political support by demanding antilynching legislation. In 1934 and 1935, Congress voted down attempts to make lynching a federal crime, and in 1938 the last antilynching bill of the decade died in a Senate filibuster. Laws to eliminate the poll tax—used to deny blacks the opportunity to vote—encountered the same overwhelming resistance. Although some African Americans received benefits from employment opportunities in northern relief projects and federal agencies, the New Deal refused to confront the injustice of racial segregation with the same vigor it brought to bear on economic hardship.

By the end of 1938, the New Deal had lost steam and encountered stiff opposition. As leg-

> Conservatives argued that the New Deal had pressed government centralization too far and was bent on creating what later came to be known as the "imperial presidency."

> The Fair Labor Standards Act reiterated the New Deal pledge to provide workers with a decent standard of living, setting wage and hours standards and at long last curbing the use of child labor.

islative initiative waned and programs played themselves out, the conservative tide rose. In the congressional elections of 1938, Republicans picked up seven seats in the Senate and eighty in the House, giving them more congressional influence than they had enjoyed since 1932. New Dealers could claim unprecedented and resounding achievements since 1933, but nobody needed reminding that those achievements had not ended the depression. In his annual message to Congress in January 1939, Roosevelt signaled a halt to New Deal reforms by speaking about preserving the progress already achieved, rather than extending it. He pointed to the threat posed by fascist aggressors in Europe and Asia, and he proposed defense expenditures that surpassed New Deal appropriations for relief and economic recovery.

Conclusion: Achievements and Limitations of the New Deal

The New Deal replaced the fear symbolized by Hoover's expulsion of the Bonus Army with Roosevelt's confidence, optimism, and energetic pragmatism. A growing majority of Americans agreed with Roosevelt that the federal government should help those in need, thereby strengthening the political coalition that propelled the New Deal. In the process of seeking relief for victims of the depression, recovery of the general economy, and basic reform of major economic institutions, the New Deal vastly expanded the size and influence of the federal government and changed the way the American people viewed Washington. New Dealers achieved significant victories such as Social Security, labor's right to organize, and guarantees that farm prices would be maintained through controls on production and marketing. New Deal measures marked the emergence of a welfare state, but its limited, two-tier character left many needy Americans with little aid.

Full-scale relief, recovery, and reform eluded New Deal programs. Even though millions of Americans benefited directly from the New Deal's alphabet soup of agencies and programs, both relief and recovery were limited and temporary. By 1940 the depression still proved distressingly durable. The most durable achievements of the New Deal were reforms that stabilized agriculture, encouraged the organization of labor unions, and created the safety net of Social Security and fair labor standards. But perhaps the most impressive achievement of the New Deal was what did not happen: Authoritarian governments and anticapitalist policies were common during the 1930s outside the United States, but they were shunned by the New Deal. The greatest economic crisis the nation had ever faced did not cause Americans to abandon democracy, as happened in Germany, where Adolf Hitler seized dictatorial power. Nor did the nation turn to radical alternatives such as socialism or communism.

Republicans and other conservatives claimed that the New Deal amounted to a form of socialism that threatened democracy and capitalism. But as Frances Perkins said, Franklin Roosevelt took capitalism as much for granted as he did his family. Rather than attack capitalism, he sought to save it, and he succeeded. That success also marked the limits of the New Deal's achievements. Like his cousin Teddy, Franklin Roosevelt understood that a strengthened national government was necessary to curb the destructive tendencies of concentrated economic power. A shift of authority toward the federal government, both Roosevelts believed, would allow capitalist enterprises to be balanced by the nation's democratic tradition. The New Deal stopped far short of challenging capitalism either by undermining private property or by imposing strict national planning.

New Dealers repeatedly described their programs as a kind of warfare against the economic adversities of the 1930s. In the next decade, with the depression only partly vanquished, the Roosevelt administration had to turn from the New Deal's war against economic crisis at home to participate in a worldwide conflagration to defeat the enemies of democracy abroad.

For additional firsthand accounts of this period, see Chapter 24 in Michael Johnson, ed., *Reading the American Past,* Third Edition.

To assess your mastery of the material in this chapter, see the Online Study Guide at bedfordstmartins.com/roark.

For Web links related to topics in this chapter, see "HistoryLinks," "DocLinks," and "PlaceLinks" at bedfordstmartins.com/roark.

CHRONOLOGY

1932 • Bonus Army marches on Washington and is routed by federal troops.

1933 • Democrat Franklin D. Roosevelt assumes presidency.

• **March–June.** New Deal established through passage of reform legislation of the Hundred Days.

• Roosevelt closes nation's banks for four-day "holiday" to allow time to stabilize banking system.

• Federal Emergency Relief Administration (FERA) provides relief for unemployed.

1934 • Securities and Exchange Commission (SEC) licenses and regulates stock exchanges.

• Upton Sinclair loses bid for governorship of California and the chance to enact his End Poverty in California work relief program.

• Wealthy conservatives of American Liberty League oppose New Deal.

• Dr. Francis Townsend devises Old Age Revolving Pension scheme to provide money to impoverished elderly.

• Congress passes Indian Reorganization Act.

1935 • Louisiana senator Huey Long assassinated.

• Legislation creates Works Progress Administration (WPA).

• Congress passes Wagner Act to guarantee workers the right to organize unions and bargain collectively.

• Committee for Industrial Organization (CIO) founded to provide union representation for unskilled workers.

• Social Security Act provides supplementary income for aged and retired persons.

• "Radio Priest" Father Charles Coughlin begins National Union for Social Justice.

1936 • John Maynard Keynes publishes *The General Theory of Employment, Interest, and Money,* providing theoretical justification for government deficit financing.

• Franklin Roosevelt elected to a second term by a landslide over Republican Alfred Landon.

1937 • CIO stages successful sit-down strike at General Motors plant in Flint, Michigan.

• Roosevelt's court-packing legislation defeated in Senate.

1937–1938 • Economic recession slows recovery from depression.

1938 • Second Agricultural Adjustment Act and Fair Labor Standards Act bring New Deal legislation to an end.

• Congress rejects administration's antilynching bill.

• Administrative Reorganization Act enlarges scope and power of presidency.

BIBLIOGRAPHY

General Works

Anthony Badger, *The New Deal: The Depression Years, 1933–1940* (1989).

Gary Dean Best, *The Retreat from Liberalism: Collectivists versus Progressives in the New Deal Years* (2002).

Alan Brinkley, *The End of Reform: New Deal Liberalism in Recession and War* (1995).

Laura Browder, *Rousing the Nation: Radical Culture in Depression America* (1998).

William H. Chafe, ed., *The Achievement of American Liberalism: The New Deal and Its Legacies* (2003).

Kenneth S. Davis, *FDR,* 4 vols. (1985–1993).

Ronald Edsforth, *The New Deal: America's Response to the Great Depression* (2000).

Steve Fraser and Gary Gerstle, eds., *The Rise and Fall of the New Deal Order* (1988).

David M. Kennedy, *Freedom from Fear: The American People in Depression and War, 1929–1945* (1999).

Alice Kessler-Harris, *In Pursuit of Equity: Women, Men, and the Quest for Economic Citizenship in Twentieth-Century America* (2001).

William E. Leuchtenburg, *The FDR Years: On Roosevelt and His Legacy* (1995).

Suzanne Mettler, *Dividing Citizens: Gender and Federalism in New Deal Public Policy* (1998).

Sidney M. Milkis and Jerome M. Mileur, eds., *The New Deal and the Triumph of Liberalism* (2002).

Harvard Sitkoff, ed., *Fifty Years Later: The New Deal Evaluated* (1985).

Gene Smiley, *Rethinking the Great Depression* (2002).

G. Edward White, *The Constitution and the New Deal* (2000).

The Roosevelt Leadership

Philip Abbott, *The Exemplary Presidency: Franklin D. Roosevelt and the American Political Tradition* (1990).

Blanche Wiesen Cook, *Eleanor Roosevelt*, 2 vols. (1992, 1999).

Matthew J. Dickinson, *Bitter Harvest: FDR, Presidential Power, and the Growth of the Presidential Branch* (1997).

Frank Friedel, *Franklin D. Roosevelt: A Rendezvous with Destiny* (1990).

Alonzo L. Hamby, *For the Survival of Democracy: Franklin Roosevelt and the World Crisis of the 1930s* (2004).

Davis W. Houk and Amos Kiewe, *FDR's Body Politics: The Rhetoric of Disability* (2003).

Marian C. McKenna, *Franklin Roosevelt and the Great Constitutional War: The Court-Packing Crisis of 1937* (2002).

Albert U. Romasco, *The Politics of Recovery: Roosevelt's New Deal* (1983).

Sean J. Savage, *Roosevelt: The Party Leader, 1932–1945* (1991).

Richard W. Steele, *Propaganda in an Open Society: The Roosevelt Administration and the Media, 1933–1941* (1985).

Geoffrey C. Ward, *A First-Class Temperament: The Emergence of Franklin Roosevelt* (1989).

Susan Ware, *Beyond Suffrage: Women in the New Deal* (1981).

Susan Ware, *Partner and I: Molly Dewson, Feminism, and New Deal Politics* (1987).

Economics and Planning

William J. Barber, *From New Era to New Deal: Herbert Hoover, the Economists, and American Economic Policy, 1921–1933* (1985).

Donald R. Brand, *Corporatism and the Rule of Law: A Study of the National Recovery Administration* (1988).

Mark Gelfand, *A Nation of Cities: The Federal Government and Urban America, 1933–1945* (1975).

Erwin C. Hargrove, *Prisoners of Myth: The Leadership of the Tennessee Valley Authority, 1933–1990* (1990).

Ellis Hawley, *The New Deal and the Problem of Monopoly: A Study in Economic Ambivalence* (1966).

Susan Estabrook Kennedy, *The Banking Crisis of 1933* (1973).

Mark Leff, *The Limits of Symbolic Reform: The New Deal and Taxation, 1933–1939* (1984).

Dean May, *From New Deal to New Economics* (1981).

Michael Parrish, *Securities Regulation and the New Deal* (1970).

Patrick D. Reagan, *Designing a New America: The Origins of New Deal Planning, 1890–1936* (1999).

Theodore Rosenof, *Economics in the Long Run: New Deal Theorists and Their Legacies, 1933–1993* (1997).

Landon R. Y. Stors, *Civilizing Capitalism: The National Consumers' League, Women's Activism, and Labor Standards in the New Deal Era* (2000).

Michael J. Webber, *New Deal Fat Cats: Business, Labor, and Campaign Finance in the 1936 Presidential Election* (2000).

Reform and Welfare

W. Andrew Achenbaum, *Shades of Gray: Old Age, American Values and Federal Policies since 1920* (1983).

Edward D. Berkowitz, *America's Welfare State: From Roosevelt to Reagan* (1991).

William R. Brock, *Welfare, Democracy, and the New Deal* (1987).

Floris Barnett Cash, *African American Women and Social Action: The Clubwomen and Volunteerism from Jim Crow to the New Deal, 1896–1936* (2001).

John A. Clausen, *Looking Back at the Children of the Great Depression* (1993).

Phoebe Cutler, *The Public Landscape of the New Deal* (1986).

Linda Gordon, *Pitied but Not Entitled: Single Mothers and the History of Welfare* (1994).

William Graebner, *A History of Retirement: The Meaning and Function of an American Institution, 1885–1978* (1980).

Kenneth J. Heineman, *A Catholic New Deal: Religion and Reform in Depression Pittsburg* (1999).

Roy Lubove, *The Struggle for Social Security, 1900–1935* (1968).

Paul E. Mertz, *New Deal Policy and Southern Rural Poverty* (1978).

James T. Patterson, *America's Struggle against Poverty, 1900–1980* (1981).

John Salmond, *The Civilian Conservation Corps, 1933–1942* (1967).

Bonnie Fox Schwartz, *The Civil Works Administration, 1933–1934* (1984).

Challenges to the New Deal

Alan Brinkley, *Voices of Protest: Huey Long, Father Coughlin, and the Great Depression* (1983).

Cecilia Bucki, *Bridgeport's Socialist New Deal, 1915–1936* (2001).

William Ivy Hair, *The Kingfish and His Realm* (1991).

Harvey Klehr, *The Heyday of American Communism* (1984).

Donald J. Lisio, *The President and Protest: Hoover, Conspiracy, and the Bonus Riot* (1974).

Leo P. Ribuffo, *The Old Christian Right: The Protestant Far Right from the Great Depression to the Cold War* (1983).

Clyde P. Weed, *The Nemesis of Reform: The Republican Party during the New Deal* (1994).

George Wolfskill, *The Revolt of the Conservatives: A History of the American Liberty League, 1934–1940* (1962).

Agriculture

David E. Conrad, *The Forgotten Farmers: The Story of the Share-Croppers in the New Deal* (1965).

Cletus E. Daniel, *Bitter Harvest: A History of California Farmworkers, 1870–1941* (1981).

David E. Hamilton, *From New Day to New Deal: American Farm Policy from Hoover to Roosevelt, 1928–1933* (1991).

Michael R. Grey, *New Deal Medicine: The Rural Health Programs of the Farm Security Administration* (1999).

Jack Temple Kirby, *Rural Worlds Lost: The American South, 1920–1960* (1987).

Richard Lowitt, *The New Deal and the West* (1984).

Labor

John Barnard, *Walter Reuther and the Rise of the Auto Workers* (1983).

Irving Bernstein, *A Caring Society: The New Deal, the Worker, and the Great Depression* (1985).

Lizbeth Cohen, *Making a New Deal: Industrial Workers in Chicago, 1919–1939* (1990).

Sidney Fine, *Sitdown: The General Motors Strike of 1936–1937* (1969).

Steve Fraser, *Labor Will Rule: Sidney Hillman and the Rise of American Labor* (1991).

Gary Gerstle, *Working-Class Americanism: The Politics of Labor in a Textile City, 1914–1960* (1989).

Colin Gordon, *New Deals: Business, Labor, and Politics in America, 1920–1935* (1994).

James A. Hodges, *New Deal Labor Policy and the Southern Cotton Textile Industry, 1933–1941* (1986).

Janet Irons, *Testing the New Deal: The General Textile Strike of 1934 in the American South* (2000).

August Meier and Elliott Rudwick, *Black Detroit and the Rise of the UAW* (1979).

David Milton, *The Politics of United States Labor: From the Great Depression to the New Deal* (1980).

Julie Novkov, *Constituting Workers, Protecting Women: Gender, Law, and Labor in the Progressive Era and New Deal Years* (2001).

Judith Sealander, *As Minority Becomes Majority: Federal Reaction to the Phenomenon of Women in the Work Force, 1920–1963* (1983).

Robert H. Zieger, *John L. Lewis: Labor Leader* (1988).

Neglected Americans

Rodolfo Acuna, *Occupied America: A History of Chicanos* (1988).

Christine Bolt, *American Indian Policy and American Reform* (1987).

Karen Ferguson, *Black Politics in New Deal Atlanta* (2002).

Donald L. Fixico, *The Invasion of Indian Country in the Twentieth Century: American Capitalism and Tribal Natural Resources* (1998).

Camille Guerin-Gonzales, *Mexican Workers and the American Dream: Immigration, Repatriation, and California Farm Labor, 1900–1939* (1994).

Robin D. G. Kelley, *Hammer and Hoe: Alabama Communists during the Great Depression* (1990).

John B. Kirby, *Black Americans in the Roosevelt Era: Liberalism and Race* (1980).

Doug McAdam, *Political Process and the Development of Black Insurgency, 1920–1970* (1982).

Harvard Sitkoff, *A New Deal for Blacks: The Emergence of Civil Rights as a National Issue,* vol. 1, *The Depression Decade* (1978).

Graham D. Taylor, *The New Deal and American Indian Tribalism: The Administration of the Indian Reorganization Act, 1935–1945* (1980).

Public Culture

E. Quita Craig, *Black Drama of the Federal Theatre Era: Beyond the Formal Horizons* (1980).

Jonathan Harris, *Federal Art and National Culture: The Politics of Identity in New Deal America* (1995).

Karal Ann Marling, *Wall-to-Wall America: A Cultural History of Post-Office Murals in the Great Depression* (1982).

Jane DeHart Matthews, *The Federal Theatre, 1935–1939: Plays, Relief, and Politics* (1967).

Richard McKinzie, *The New Deal for Artists* (1973).

GI WEB GEAR

Millions of American GIs strapped on web belts hooked with canteens, knives, and other military gear as they went into battle. Navy medical corpsman Leo H. Scheer wore this belt when Allied forces stormed the Normandy beaches on D Day, June 6, 1944. Scheer's landing craft sank as it approached Omaha Beach, and he swam ashore wearing this web gear. Once on land, he grabbed unused bandages from the belts of dead soldiers to bind the wounds of the living. The pockets of this belt are still stuffed with the bandages Scheer collected while Americans and their allies secured the beach and launched the great western offensive against Nazi Germany.

Jackson Hill / The National D-Day Museum.

25

The United States and the Second World War

1939–1945

O N A SUN-DRENCHED FLORIDA AFTERNOON in January 1927, Paul Tibbets took his first airplane ride. Twelve-year-old Tibbets cinched on a leather helmet, clambered into the front seat of the open cockpit of a cloth-covered red, white, and blue biplane, and sailed aloft over Miami. While the barn-storming pilot sitting behind him brought the plane in low over the Hialeah race track, Tibbets pitched Baby Ruth candy bars tethered to small paper parachutes to racing fans in the grandstands below. After two more candy bar drops over the race track, the pilot raced to the beach and swooped down to 200 feet as Tibbets tossed out the remaining candy bars and watched the bathers scramble for chocolate from heaven. After Tibbets and the pilot repeated their stunt for a week, sales of Baby Ruths soared for Tibbets's father's candy business, and Tibbets was hooked on flying.

Born in Quincy, Illinois, in 1915, Tibbets moved to Florida when he was nine, then migrated back and forth to the Midwest. He entered the University of Florida in 1933 and took flying lessons at the Gainesville airport. After transferring to the University of Cincinnati, he continued to fly in his spare time and in 1937 decided to join the Army Air Corps to become a military pilot.

Shortly after the Japanese attack on Pearl Harbor, Tibbets led a squadron of airplanes flying antisubmarine patrol against German U-boats lurking along the East Coast. When the heavily armored B-17 Flying Fortress bombers began to come off American assembly lines early in 1942, Tibbets took a squadron of the new planes from the United States to England. On August 17, 1942, Tibbets led the first American daytime bombing raid on German-occupied Europe, releasing 1,100 pounds of bombs from his B-17, nicknamed "Butcher Shop," on the railroad yards of Rouen in northern France—the first of some 700,000 tons of explosives dropped by over 330,000 American bombers during the air war in Europe.

After numerous raids over Europe, Tibbets was reassigned to the North African campaign, where his duties included ferrying the American commander, General Dwight D. Eisenhower, into the battle zone. Following eight months of combat missions, Tibbets returned to the United States and was ordered to test the new B-29 Super Fortress being built in Wichita, Kansas. The B-29 was much bigger than the B-17 and could fly higher and faster, making it ideal for the campaign against Japan. Tibbets's mastery of the B-29 caused him to be singled out in September 1944 to command a top-secret unit training for a special mission.

■ **Peacetime Dilemmas**
Roosevelt and Reluctant Isolation
The Good Neighbor Policy
The Price of Noninvolvement

■ **The Onset of War**
Nazi Aggression and War in Europe
From Neutrality to the Arsenal of Democracy
Japan Attacks America

■ **Mobilizing for War**
Home-Front Security
Building a Citizen Army
Conversion to a War Economy

■ **Fighting Back**
Turning the Tide in the Pacific
The Campaign in Europe

■ **The Wartime Home Front**
Women and Families, Guns and Butter
The Double V Campaign
Wartime Politics and the 1944 Election
Reaction to the Holocaust

■ **Toward Unconditional Surrender**
From Bombing Raids to Berlin
The Defeat of Japan
Atomic Warfare

■ **Conclusion: Allied Victory and America's Emergence as a Superpower**

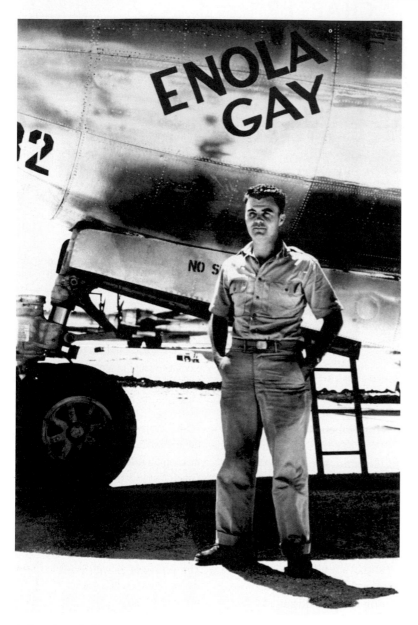

Colonel Paul Tibbets
Before taking off to drop the world's first atomic bomb on Hiroshima, Colonel Paul Tibbets posed on the tarmac next to his customized B-29 Super Fortress bomber, named *Enola Gay* in honor of his mother. A crew of eleven handpicked airmen accompanied Tibbets in the *Enola Gay* on their top-secret mission. After the war, President Harry S. Truman invited Tibbets to the White House and told him, "Don't you ever lose any sleep over the fact that you planned and carried out that mission. It was my decision. You had no choice."
© Bettmann/Corbis.

The mission, officials confided to Tibbets, was to be ready to drop on Japan a bomb that was so powerful it might bring the war to an end. Although no such bomb yet existed, American scientists and engineers were working around the clock to build one. Tibbets kept this secret from his men but took them and his B-29s to Utah to develop a way to drop such a powerful weapon without getting blown up by it. Tibbets trained his pilots to fly at 31,000 feet, then execute a dangerous, sharp, diving turn of 155 degrees that tested the limits of the aircraft but moved it beyond the range of the expected blast.

In May 1945, Tibbets took his B-29s and men to Tinian Island and trained for their secret mission by flying raids over Japanese cities and dropping ordinary bombs. The atomic bomb arrived on Tinian aboard the cruiser *Indianapolis* on July 26, just ten days after the successful test explosion in the New Mexico desert. Nicknamed "Little Boy," the bomb was twelve feet long and weighed 9,000 pounds. The explosive force of its nuclear core packed the equivalent of 40 million pounds of TNT or 200,000 of the 200-pound bombs Tibbets and other American airmen dropped on Europe.

At 2:30 A.M. on August 6, 1945, Tibbets and his crew of eleven and their atomic payload took off in the B-29 bomber *Enola Gay* and headed for Japan. Less than seven hours later, over the city of Hiroshima, Tibbets and his crew released Little Boy from the *Enola Gay*'s bomb bay. The plane bucked upward after dropping the 4.5-ton explosive, while Tibbets banked the plane sharply to the right and struggled to maintain control as the shock wave from the explosion blasted past and a purple cloud mushroomed nearly ten miles into the air. For an hour and a half as Tibbets and his crew flew back toward Tinian, they could see the mushroom cloud of the atomic destruction they had unleashed. Three days later, Tibbets's men dropped a second atomic bomb on Nagasaki, and in five days Japan surrendered.

Paul Tibbets's experiences traced an arc followed by millions of his fellow Americans during World War II, from the innocence of bombarding Miami with candy bars to the deadly nuclear firestorms that rained down on Japan. Like Tibbets, Americans joined their allies to fight the Axis powers in Europe and Asia. Like his *Enola Gay* crewmen—who hailed from New York, Texas, California, New Jersey, New Mexico, Maryland, North Carolina, Pennsylvania, Michigan, and Nevada—Americans from all regions united to defeat the **fascist** aggressors. American industries mobilized to produce advanced bombers—like the ones Tibbets piloted over Europe, North Africa, and Japan—along with enough other military equipment to supply the American armed forces and their allies. At enormous cost in human life and suffering, the war brought full employment and prosperity to Americans at home, ending the depression, providing new opportunities for women, and ushering the nation into the postwar world as a triumphant economic and—on the wings of Paul Tibbets's *Enola Gay*—atomic superpower.

Peacetime Dilemmas

The First World War left a dangerous and ultimately deadly legacy. The victors—especially Britain, France, and the United States—sought to avoid future wars at almost any cost. The defeated nations as well as those who felt humiliated by the Versailles peace settlement—particularly Germany, Italy, and Japan—aspired to reassert their power and avenge their losses by means of renewed warfare. Japan invaded the northern Chinese province of Manchuria in 1931 with ambitions to expand throughout Asia. Italy, led by the fascist Benito Mussolini since 1922, hungered for an empire in Africa. In Germany, National Socialist Adolf Hitler rose to power as chancellor in 1933 in a grandiose quest to dominate Europe and the world. These aggressive, militaristic, antidemocratic regimes seemed a smaller threat to most people in the United States during the 1930s than the economic crisis at home. Shielded from external threats by the Atlantic and Pacific oceans, Americans hoped to avoid entanglement in foreign woes and to concentrate on climbing out of the nation's economic abyss.

Roosevelt and Reluctant Isolation

Like most Americans during the 1930s, Franklin Roosevelt believed that the nation's highest priority was to attack the domestic causes and consequences of the depression. But unlike most Americans, Roosevelt had long advocated an active role for the United States in international affairs. As assistant secretary of the navy in Woodrow Wilson's administration, he championed the significance of naval strength in the global balance of power. After World War I, Roosevelt embraced Wilson's vision that the United States should take the lead in making the world "safe for democracy," and he continued to advocate American membership in the League of Nations during the **isolationist** 1920s. When he ran for governor of New York in 1928,

Roosevelt criticized Republican isolationists for undermining domestic prosperity by setting high tariffs and for subverting international peace by demanding that battered European nations pay off their wartime loans and reparations in full and on time.

The depression forced Roosevelt to retreat from his previous internationalism. He came to believe that energetic involvement in foreign affairs diverted resources and political support from domestic recovery. During his 1932 presidential campaign, he pulled back from his endorsement of the League of Nations and reversed his previous support for forgiving European war debts. Once in office, Roosevelt sought to combine domestic economic recovery with a low-profile foreign policy that encouraged free trade and disarmament. "Foreign markets must be regained if America's producers are to rebuild a full and enduring domestic prosperity," he explained in 1935. In turn, free trade required international peace, the goal of disarmament.

In pursuit of international amity, Roosevelt was constrained by economic circumstances and American popular opinion. After an opinion poll demonstrated popular support for recognizing the Soviet Union—an international pariah since the Bolshevik Revolution in 1917—Roosevelt established formal diplomatic relations in 1933. But when the League of Nations condemned Japanese and German aggression, Roosevelt did not enlist the nation in the League's attempts to keep the peace because he feared jeopardizing isolationists' support for **New Deal** measures in Congress. America watched from the sidelines when Japan withdrew from the League and ignored the limitations on its navy imposed after World War I. Likewise, the United States looked the other way when Hitler rearmed Germany and recalled its representative to the League in 1933, declaring that the peace-seeking body sought to thwart Germany's legitimate ambitions. Roosevelt worried that the League's inability to curb German and Japanese violations of League sanctions and the Versailles settlement threatened world peace. But he reassured Americans that the nation would not "use its armed forces for the settlement of any [international] dispute anywhere."

> Shielded from external threats by the Atlantic and Pacific oceans, Americans hoped to avoid entanglement in foreign woes and to concentrate on climbing out of the nation's economic abyss.

The Good Neighbor Policy

In his 1933 inaugural address, Franklin Roosevelt announced that the United States would pursue "the policy of the good neighbor" in international relations. A few weeks later, he emphasized that the good neighbor policy applied specifically to Latin America, where previous presidents had routinely sent U.S. military forces to intervene in local affairs. Now, Roosevelt said, the old policy of arrogant intervention would be replaced by a "helping hand" extended in a desire for friendly cooperation to create "more order in this hemisphere and less dislike." In December 1933 at the Inter-American Conference in Montevideo, Uruguay, Secretary of State Cordell Hull formalized the good-neighbor pledge that no nation had the right to intervene in the internal or external affairs of another.

This commitment to nonintervention did not indicate a U.S. retreat from empire in Latin America. Instead, the good neighbor policy declared that the United States would not depend on military force to exercise its influence in the region. When Mexico nationalized American oil holdings and revolution boiled over in Nicaragua, Guatemala, and Cuba during the 1930s, Roosevelt refrained from sending in the marines to defend the interests of American corporations. In 1934, Roosevelt even withdrew American marines from Haiti, which they had occupied since 1916. While nonintervention honored the principle of national self-determination, it also permitted the rise of dictators like Anastasio Somoza in Nicaragua and Fulgencio Batista in Cuba, who exploited and terrorized their nations with private support from U.S. businesses and the hands-off policy of Roosevelt's administration.

Military nonintervention also did not prevent the United States from exerting its economic influence in Latin America. In 1934, Congress passed the Reciprocal Trade Agreements Act, which gave the president power to reduce tariffs on goods imported into the United States from nations that agreed to lower their own tariffs on U.S. exports. By 1940, twenty-two nations had agreed to reciprocal tariff reductions, helping U.S. exports to Latin America double during Roosevelt's first two terms and contributing to the New Deal's goal of boosting the domestic economy through free trade. Although the economic power of the United States continued to overshadow that of its neighbors, the nonintervention policy planted seeds of friendship and hemispheric solidarity that grew in importance while events in Europe and Asia continued to erode international peace.

> The good neighbor policy declared that the United States would not depend on military force to exercise its influence in Latin America.

The Price of Noninvolvement

In Europe, fascist governments in Italy and Germany spouted belligerent rhetoric and threatened military aggression. Italian dictator Benito Mussolini proclaimed, "War is to the man what maternity is to the woman. . . . Peace [is] . . . depressing and a negation of all the fundamental virtues of man." In Germany, Hitler combined similar pronouncements with vigorous rebuilding of the nation's military strength. Although German rearmament openly defied the terms of the Versailles peace treaty, neither Britain nor France did more than register verbal protests. The overpowering desire to avoid conflict led Britain in 1935 to permit Germany to begin rebuilding its fleet of surface ships and submarines. Emboldened, Hitler plotted to avenge defeat in World War I by recapturing territories with German inhabitants, all the while accusing Jews of polluting the purity of the Aryan master race. The virulent anti-Semitism of Hitler and his Nazi Party unified non-Jewish Germans and attracted sympathizers among many other Europeans, even in France and Britain, thereby weakening support for opposing Hitler or defending Jews.

In Japan, a stridently militaristic government planned to follow the invasion of Manchuria in 1931 with conquests extending throughout Southeast Asia. The Manchurian invasion bogged down in a long and vicious war when Chinese Nationalists rallied around their leader Chiang Kai-shek to fight against the Japanese. Preparations for new conquests continued, however. Early in 1936, Japan openly violated naval limitation treaties it had agreed to and began to build a battle-ready fleet to achieve naval superiority in the Pacific.

In the United States, the hostilities in Asia and Europe reinforced isolationist sentiments. Popular disillusionment with the failure of Woodrow Wilson's idealistic goals caused many Americans to question the nation's participation in World War I. In 1933, Gerald Nye, a Republican from North Dakota, chaired a Senate committee that investigated why the United States had gone to war in 1917. The Nye committee concluded

The Quest for Disarmament
With startling swoops, a little white plane that evokes the dove of peace is covered by a blood-red hawk of a fighter plane, gun ablaze. The shouted cry "Disarm!" at the bottom of the poster expresses the view of peace advocates at the beginning of the 1930s that the way to make the world safe was to take weapons away from the strong, not to arm the weak. Soon after the poster appeared, the march of fascist aggression began to shift opinion toward the belief that nations could better attain collective security by using force to counter the enemies of peace.
Private Collection.

that greedy "merchants of death"—American weapons makers, bankers, and financiers—dragged the nation into the war to line their own pockets. The Nye committee persuaded many Americans that war profiteers might once again push the nation into a world war.

International tensions and the Nye committee report prompted Congress to pass a series of neutrality acts between 1935 and 1937, to avoid the circumstances that, they believed, had caused the nation to abandon its isolationism and become a combatant in World War I. The neutrality acts prohibited making loans and selling arms to

nations at war and authorized the president to warn Americans about traveling on ships belonging to belligerent countries.

By 1937, as the nation continued to struggle with the depression, intensifying conflicts overseas caused some Americans to call for a total embargo, not just on munitions but on all trade with warring countries. Roosevelt and Congress worried that such an embargo would hurt the nation's economy by limiting production and boosting unemployment. The Neutrality Act of 1937 sought to allow trade but prevent foreign entanglements by requiring warring nations to pay cash for nonmilitary goods and transport them in their own ships. This "cash-and-carry" policy seemed to reconcile the nation's desire for both peace and foreign trade. Although such trade benefited the domestic economy, it also helped foreign aggressors and thereby undermined peace. In short, by strenuously seeking to avoid war, American isolationism encouraged German and Japanese militarists, who concluded that the United States posed little threat to them.

The desire for peace in France, Britain, and the United States led Germany, Italy, and Japan to launch offensives on the assumption that the western democracies lacked the will to oppose them. In March 1936, Nazi troops marched into the industry-rich Rhineland on Germany's western border, in blatant violation of the Treaty of Versailles, which had ceded the region to France. One month later, Italian armies completed their conquest of Ethiopia, projecting fascist power into Africa. In December 1937, Japanese invaders captured Nanking and celebrated their triumph in a deadly rampage of murder, rape, and plunder that killed 200,000 Chinese civilians.

In Spain, a bitter civil war broke out in 1936 when fascist rebels led by General Francisco Franco attacked the democratically elected Republican government. Both Germany and Italy reinforced Franco with soldiers, weapons, and aircraft, while the Soviet Union provided much less aid to the Republican Loyalists. The Spanish civil war seemed to many observers a dress rehearsal for a coming worldwide conflict, but it did not cause European democracies or the U.S. government to help the Loyalists, despite sympathizing with their cause.

Spanish Civil War, 1936–1939

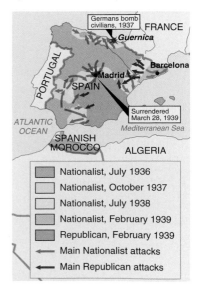

Germans bomb civilians, 1937
FRANCE
Guernica
PORTUGAL
Barcelona
Madrid
SPAIN
Surrendered March 28, 1939
ATLANTIC OCEAN
Mediterranean Sea
SPANISH MOROCCO
ALGERIA

	Nationalist, July 1936
	Nationalist, October 1937
	Nationalist, July 1938
	Nationalist, February 1939
	Republican, February 1939
←	Main Nationalist attacks
←	Main Republican attacks

More than 3,000 individual Americans enlisted in the Russian-sponsored Abraham Lincoln Brigade to fight for the Loyalists. But, abandoned by western nations, Loyalists and their allies were defeated in 1939 by the fascists. Germany and Italy welcomed Franco's victory, which created a fascist bulwark in southern and western Europe.

Hostilities in Europe, Africa, and Asia alarmed Roosevelt and other Americans. He sought to persuade most Americans to moderate their isolationism and find a way to support the victims of fascist aggression. Speaking in Chicago, the heartland of isolationism, in October 1937, Roosevelt declared that the "epidemic of world lawlessness is spreading" and warned that "mere isolation or neutrality" offered no remedy for the "contagion" of war. Instead, the president proposed that the United States "quarantine" aggressor nations and arrest the spread of war's contagion.

Roosevelt's speech ignited a storm of protest from isolationists. The *Chicago Tribune* accused the president of seeking to replace "Americanism" with "internationalism." Chastened by the popular outcry and by the failure of congressional leaders to echo his concerns, Roosevelt did not pursue the quarantine proposal. "It's a terrible thing," he remarked to an aide, "to look over your shoulder when you are trying to lead and find no one there." The strength of isolationist sentiment convinced Roosevelt that he needed to maneuver carefully if the United States were to help prevent fascist aggressors from conquering Europe and Asia, leaving the United States an isolated and imperiled island of **democracy**.

> Hostilities abroad alarmed Roosevelt and other Americans. He sought to persuade most Americans to moderate their isolationism and find a way to support the victims of fascist aggression.

The Onset of War

Between 1939 and 1941, fascist victories overseas eventually eroded American isolationism and engulfed the nation in a worldwide conflagration. But initially, fascist anti-Semitism, boastful saber-rattling, and military conquests in China, Ethiopia, and Spain failed to arouse many Americans. Trying to work their way out of the depression and refusing to be diverted by conflicts on the far shores of the Atlantic and Pacific, most Americans hoped to stay out of the seemingly endless conflicts that embroiled Europe and Asia. By 1939, however, continuing German and Japanese aggression caused more and more Americans to believe that it was time for the nation to take a stand. At first, taking a stand was limited to providing material support to the enemies of Germany and Japan, principally Britain, China, and the Soviet Union. But Japan's surprise attack on Pearl Harbor eliminated that restraint, and the nation began to mobilize for an all-out assault on foreign foes.

Nazi Aggression and War in Europe

Under the spell of isolationism, Americans passively watched Hitler's relentless campaign to dominate Europe. Under the ruse of uniting all German peoples regardless of the nation they happened to inhabit, Hitler bullied Austria in 1938 into accepting incorporation—*Anschluss*—into the Nazi Third Reich, expanding the territory under Germany's control. Having whetted his appetite for conquest, Hitler turned his attention to the German-speaking Sudetenland, granted to Czechoslovakia by the Versailles treaty. Although the Czechs were prepared to fight rather than surrender their territory, Britain and France hoped to avoid war by making a deal with Hitler. British prime minister Neville Chamberlain went to Munich, Germany, and offered Hitler terms of "appeasement," as he called it, that would give the Sudetenland to Germany if Hitler agreed to leave the rest of Czechoslovakia alone. On September 29, 1938, Hitler accepted Chamberlain's offer, solemnly promising that he would make no more territorial claims in Europe. Chamberlain returned to Britain proclaiming that his diplomacy had achieved "peace in our time." But since peace depended on Hitler keeping a promise he never intended to honor, Chamberlain's attempt at appeasement was doomed from the outset. In March 1939, Hitler boldly marched the German army into Czechoslovakia and conquered it without firing a shot (Map 25.1).

In April 1939, hardly pausing for breath, Hitler demanded that Poland return the German territory it had been awarded after World War I. Britain and France finally recognized that appeasement had failed and that Hitler would continue his aggression unless he was defeated by military might. Both Britain and France assured Poland that they would go to war with Germany if Hitler launched an eastward offensive across the Polish border. In turn, Hitler negotiated with

MAP 25.1   Axis Aggression through 1941
For different reasons, Hitler and Mussolini launched a series of surprise military strikes. Mussolini sought
to re-create the Roman Empire in the Mediterranean. Hitler struck to reclaim German territories occupied
by France after World War I and to annex Austria. When the German dictator began his campaign to rule
"inferior" peoples beyond Germany's border by attacking Poland, World War II broke out.

his bitter enemy, the Soviet premier Joseph
Stalin, offering him concessions in order to prevent the Soviet Union from joining Britain and
France in opposing a German attack on Poland.
Despite the enduring hatred between fascist
Germany and the **Communist** Soviet Union,
the two powers signed the Nazi-Soviet treaty of
nonaggression in August 1939, exposing Poland
to an onslaught by the German Wehrmacht
(army).

At dawn on September 1, 1939, Hitler unleashed the attack on Poland, exhorting his generals to "close your hearts to pity! Act brutally!"
in a *blitzkrieg* (literally, "lightning war") attack
led by tanks and airplanes that gave lethal mechanized support to the invading infantry. The attack triggered declarations of war from France
and Britain two days later, igniting a conflagration that raced around the globe, killing over 60
million people and maiming untold millions
more until it finally ended after Paul Tibbets's
historic flight in August 1945. But in September
1939, Germany seemed invincible as its armies
sped across Poland, causing many people to wonder if any nation could stop the Nazi war machine or if, sooner or later, all of Europe would

German Panzer

German Panzers, supported by well-coordinated aircraft of the German Luftwaffe, contributed speed, maneuverability, and firepower to blitzkrieg attacks. Hitler's mechanized army stunned foes with the lethal combination of tanks and airplanes racing west into France and east into Poland and the Soviet Union.

U.S. Army Ordnance Museum Foundation, Inc.

share Poland's fate: defeat, German occupation, and vicious authoritarian government enforced by merciless repression and unblinking terror.

After the Nazis overran Poland, Hitler paused for a few months before launching a westward blitzkrieg. In April 1940, German forces smashed through Denmark and Norway. In May, Germany invaded the Netherlands, Belgium, and Luxembourg, and then France. The French believed that their Maginot Line, a concrete fortification built after World War I and stretching from the Swiss border to the forested Ardennes region on the edge of Belgium, would halt the German attack (see Map 25.1). Designed to stop the plodding advance of foot soldiers in World War I–style trench warfare, the Maginot Line proved little more than a detour for Hitler's mechanized divisions, which wheeled around the fortification's northern end and raced south toward Paris.

The speed of the German attack trapped more than 300,000 British and French soldiers, who retreated to the port of Dunkirk, where an improvised armada of English vessels of every size and shape hurriedly ferried them to safety across the English Channel, leaving the Dunkirk beaches strewn with thousands of tons of military gear. By mid-June 1940, France had surrendered the largest army in the world, signed an armistice that gave Germany control of the entire French coastline and nearly two-thirds of the countryside, and installed a collaborationist government at Vichy in southern France headed by Philippe Pétain, and Hitler had strolled the

boulevards of Paris in triumph. With an empire that stretched across Europe from Poland to France, Hitler seemed poised to vault the English Channel and attack Britain.

The new British prime minister, Winston Churchill, vowed that Britain, unlike France, would never accept a humiliating surrender to Hitler. "We shall fight on the seas and oceans [and] . . . in the air," he proclaimed, "whatever the cost may be, we shall fight on the beaches, . . . on the landing grounds, . . . in the fields and in the streets . . . [and] we shall never surrender." Churchill's defiance stiffened British resolve for a last-ditch defense against Hitler's attack, which began in mid-June 1940 with wave after wave of German bombers targeting British military installations and cities, killing tens of thousands of civilians. The undermanned and outgunned Royal Air Force, fighting as doggedly as Churchill had predicted, finally won the Battle of Britain by November, clearing German bombers from British skies and handing Hitler his first frustrating defeat. Churchill lauded the valiant British pilots, proclaiming, "Never . . . was so much owed by so many to so few." Churchill left unspoken the pilots' advance knowledge of German plans made possible by British use of the new technology of radar and the ability to decipher Germany's top-secret military codes. But battered and exhausted, Britain could not hold out forever without American help, as Churchill repeatedly wrote Roosevelt in private.

From Neutrality to the Arsenal of Democracy

When the Nazi attack on Poland ignited the war in Europe, Roosevelt issued an official proclamation of American neutrality. Although most Americans strongly condemned German aggression and favored Britain and France, Roosevelt had to steer a political course that tacked between placating isolationists at home and helping the antifascist cause abroad. Roosevelt feared that if Congress did not repeal the arms embargo mandated by the Neutrality Act of 1937, France and Britain would soon succumb to the Nazi onslaught. The president's request for repeal of the arms embargo provoked isolationists to protest that the United States had no business interfering in a European conflict that did not threaten American shores. After heated debate, Congress voted in November 1939 to revise the neutrality legislation and allow belligerent nations to buy arms, as well as nonmilitary supplies, on a cash-and-carry basis.

In practice, the revised neutrality law permitted Britain and France to purchase American war materials and carry them across the Atlantic in their own ships. America could help the antifascist Allies at a distance, selling them war goods without exposing American ships to the German submarines lurking in the Atlantic. Such half-hearted efforts in support of the antifascist cause troubled Roosevelt. He wrote a friend, "What worries me is that public opinion . . . is patting itself on the back every morning and thanking God for the Atlantic Ocean (and the Pacific Ocean)," greatly underestimating "the serious implications" of the European war for "our own future."

Roosevelt knew that the serious implications for America included the possibility of British defeat and Nazi supremacy on the high seas, and he resolved to find some way to aid Britain short of entering a formal alliance or declaring war against Germany. Privately, Churchill pleaded for American destroyers, aircraft, and munitions but had no money to buy them under the prevailing cash-and-carry neutrality law. In May 1940, Roosevelt asked Congress for almost $1.3 billion in defense spending to expand the navy and multiply the

production of airplanes to 50,000 a year. By late summer, as the Battle of Britain raged in the skies over England, Roosevelt concocted a scheme to deliver fifty old destroyers to Britain in exchange for American access to British bases in the Western Hemisphere. Claiming the constitutional power to strengthen America's defenses by swapping destroyers for bases, Roosevelt took the first steps toward building a firm Anglo-American alliance against Hitler.

While Luftwaffe pilots bombed Britain, German officers lingered over leisurely meals in France, and Nazi officials administered their new territories in Poland, Austria, Czechoslovakia, and elsewhere, Roosevelt decided to run for an unprecedented third term as president in 1940. He hoped to woo voters away from their complacent isolationism to back the nation's international interests as well as New Deal reforms. But the presidential election, which Roosevelt won handily, provided no clear mandate for American involvement in the European war. The

The County of London Orchestra
The gallant resistance of the British to the bombing of their cities captured Americans' sympathy and helped to build support for U.S. entry into the war. Here in the Chelsea section of London in 1942, the County of London Orchestra and an audience of mostly children demonstrate how to carry on in the ruins with poise and a stiff upper lip.
Getty Images.

Republican candidate, Wendell Willkie, a former Democrat who generally favored New Deal measures and Roosevelt's foreign policy, attacked Roosevelt as a warmonger. Willkie's accusations caused the president to promise voters, "Your boys are not going to be sent into any foreign wars," a pledge counterbalanced by his repeated warnings about the threats to America posed by Nazi aggression.

> Empowered by the voters for another presidential term, Roosevelt maneuvered to support Britain in every way short of war.

Empowered by the voters for another presidential term, Roosevelt maneuvered to support Britain in every way short of war. In a fireside chat shortly after Christmas 1940, Roosevelt called Britain "the spearhead of resistance to [Nazi] world conquest" and proclaimed that it was incumbent on the United States to become "the great arsenal of democracy" and send "every ounce and every ton of munitions and supplies that we can possibly spare to help the defenders who are in the front lines." Events of the last year had proved, he said solemnly, "that no nation can appease the Nazis. . . . There can be no appeasement with ruthlessness."

In January 1941, Roosevelt proposed the Lend-Lease Act, which allowed the British to obtain arms from the United States without paying cash but with the promise to reimburse the United States when the war ended. The purpose of Lend-Lease, Roosevelt proclaimed, was to defend democracy and human rights throughout the world, specifically the Four Freedoms: "freedom of speech and expression . . . freedom of every person to worship God in his own way . . . freedom from want . . . [and] freedom from fear." Congress passed the Lend-Lease Act in March 1941, starting a flow of support to Britain that totaled more than $50 billion during the war, far more than all federal expenditures combined since Roosevelt had become president in 1933.

Lend-Lease placed the United States on a collision course with Germany. Nazi U-boats (submarines) prowled the Atlantic, preying on ships laden with supplies for Britain, making it only a matter of time before American citizens and American property would be attacked. While German U-boats sank British shipping at an alarming pace, Roosevelt provided naval escorts for Lend-Lease supplies and gave his commanders orders to "shoot on sight" any menacing German submarine they spotted, edging the nation ever closer to all-out combat.

Stymied in his plans for an invasion of England, Hitler turned his massive army eastward and on June 22, 1941, sprang a surprise attack on the Soviet Union, his erstwhile ally in the 1939 Nazi-Soviet nonaggression pact. Neither Roosevelt nor Churchill had any love for Joseph Stalin or communism, but they both welcomed the conversion of the Soviet Union to the anti-Nazi cause. Both western leaders understood that Hitler's attack on Russia would divert his divisions toward the eastern front and provide relief for the hard-pressed British. Roosevelt quickly persuaded Congress to extend Lend-Lease to the Soviet Union, beginning the shipment of millions of tons of trucks, jeeps, locomotives, and other equipment that, in all, supplied about 10 percent of Russian war materiel.

As Hitler's Wehrmacht raced across the Russian plains and Nazi U-boats tried to choke off supplies to Britain and the Soviet Union, Roosevelt met with Churchill aboard a ship near Newfoundland to cement the Anglo-American alliance. In August 1941, the two leaders issued the Atlantic Charter, pledging the two nations to freedom of the seas and free trade, as well as the right of national self-determination. Roosevelt told Churchill privately that the United States would continue to serve as the arsenal of democracy and that he would be on the lookout for some incident that might trigger public support for full-scale American entry into the war against Germany.

Japan Attacks America

Although the likelihood of war with Germany preoccupied Roosevelt, Hitler exercised a measure of restraint in directly provoking America, even though he boasted that "America is not dangerous to us." Japanese ambitions in Asia clashed more openly with American interests and commitments, especially in China and the Philippines. And unlike Hitler, the Japanese high command planned to attack the United States if necessary to pursue their aspirations to rule an Asian empire they termed the Greater East Asia Co-Prosperity Sphere. Appealing to widespread Asian bitterness toward white colonial powers like the British in India and Burma, the French in Indochina (now Vietnam), and the Dutch in the East Indies (now Indonesia), the Japanese campaigned to preserve "Asia for the Asians." Japan's invasion of China—which had lasted for ten years by 1941—proved that Japan's true goal was Asia for the Japanese (Map 25.2). Japan cov-

MAP 25.2   Japanese Aggression through 1941
Beginning with the invasion of Manchuria in 1931, Japan sought to force its imperialist control over most of East Asia. Japanese aggression was driven by the need for raw materials for the country's expanding industries and by the military government's devotion to martial honor.

eted China's raw materials and hoped to combine them with additional resources extracted from the nations forced into the Greater East Asia Co-Prosperity Sphere. Although the United States demanded that Japan pull out of China and retreat from its ambitions for a grand empire, the toothless rebukes did not deter the Japanese.

In 1940, Japan signaled a new phase of its imperial designs by entering a defensive alliance with Germany and Italy—the Tripartite Pact—and by receiving permission from the Vichy government in France to build airfields and station soldiers in northern Indochina. By 1941, U.S. naval intelligence cracked the Japanese secret code and learned that Tokyo also planned to invade the resource-rich Dutch East Indies. To thwart these plans, in July 1941 Roosevelt announced a trade embargo that denied Japan access to oil, scrap iron, and other goods essential for its war machines. Roosevelt hoped the embargo would strengthen factions within Japan who opposed the militarists and sought to restore relations with the United States.

The American embargo played into the hands of Japanese militarists headed by General Hideki Tojo, who seized control of the government in October 1941 and persuaded other leaders, including Emperor Hirohito, that swift destruction of American naval bases in the

Pearl Harbor Victims

Brothers Wesley and Edward Heidt from Los Angeles, California—shown here posing in their navy uniforms—were two of 34 pairs of brothers killed when Japanese warplanes attacked and sank the battleship *Arizona* in the surprise attack on Pearl Harbor on December 7, 1941. The life preserver and pennant from the *Arizona* were salvaged a few days after the attack. The official telegram informed the Heidt brothers' mother that her sons "lost their life in the service of their country," a tragic message received by hundreds of thousands of other American parents during the next four years.

U.S.S. *Arizona* Memorial, Hawaii, National Park Service/photos by Douglas Peebles.

Pacific would leave Japan free to follow its destiny. Decoded Japanese messages alerted American officials that an attack on U.S. forces was imminent somewhere in the Pacific, but exactly where and when, no American knew until it was too late. Early on the morning of December 7, 1941, 183 attack aircraft lifted off six Japanese carriers that had secretly steamed within striking range of the U.S. Pacific Fleet at Pearl Harbor on the Hawaiian island of Oahu. About 8 o'clock on this sleepy Sunday morning, the Japanese planes streaked from the sky, bombing and torpedoing the American fleet riding serenely at anchor in the harbor and destroying hundreds of aircraft parked in neat rows on the runways of Hickam Field. The devastating surprise attack sank or disabled 18 ships, including all of the fleet's battleships, killed more than 2,400 Americans, and wounded over 1,000, almost crippling U.S. war-making capacity in the Pacific. Luckily for the United States, Japanese pilots failed to destroy the vital machine shops and oil storage facilities at Pearl Harbor, and none of the nation's aircraft carriers was in port at the time of the attack.

The Japanese scored a stunning tactical success at Pearl Harbor, but in the long run the attack proved a colossal blunder. The victory infected many Japanese commanders with dangerous overconfidence about their military prowess. Worse for the Japanese, Americans instantly united in their desire to fight and avenge the attack, which Roosevelt termed "dastardly and unprovoked," vowing that "this form of treachery shall never endanger us again." On December 8, Congress unanimously endorsed the president's call for a declaration of war, except for pacifist Republican congresswoman Jeannette Rankin, of Montana, who had also opposed U.S. entry into World War I. Although neither Hitler nor Mussolini knew about the Japanese attack in advance, both Germany and Italy declared war against America on December 11, bringing the United States into all-out war with Axis powers in both Europe and Asia.

Bombing of Pearl Harbor, December 7, 1941

East Loch

Ford Island

U.S. Naval Air Station

Pearl Harbor

	Sunk
	Damaged
	Undamaged

Mobilizing for War

The time had come, Roosevelt announced, for the prescriptions of "Dr. New Deal" to be replaced by the stronger medicines of "Dr. Win-the-War." Military and civilian leaders rushed to secure the nation against possible attacks by its enemies, causing Americans of Japanese descent to be stigmatized and sent to internment camps. Roosevelt and his advisers lost no time enlisting millions of Americans in the armed forces to bring the isolationist-era military to fighting strength for a two-front war. The war emergency also required economic mobilization unparalleled in the nation's history. As Dr. Win-the-War, Roosevelt set aside New Deal goals of reform and plunged headlong into transforming the American economy into the world's greatest military machine, thereby achieving full employment and economic recovery, goals that had eluded the New Deal.

Home-Front Security

Shortly after declaring war against the United States, Hitler dispatched German submarines to hunt American ships along the Atlantic coast from Maine to Florida, where Paul Tibbets and other American pilots tried to destroy them. But the U-boats had devastating success for about eight months, sinking hundreds of U.S. ships and threatening to disrupt the Lend-Lease lifeline to Britain and the Soviet Union. The submarines benefited from the failure of port cities such as New York and Miami to observe the rules requiring blackouts, making it easier for the U-boats to spot vulnerable ships against the lighted horizon.

As hulks of destroyed vessels littered Atlantic beaches, blackouts became more rigorously enforced, and by mid-1942 the U.S. navy had chased German submarines away from the coast and into the mid-Atlantic, reducing the direct threat to the nation's homeland. Naval ships patrolled the nation's coasts, and fortifications were built to defend against seaborne assaults. While these and other security measures raised popular awareness of the possibility of an attack on the U.S. mainland, no such attack occurred. Within the continental United States, Americans remained sheltered by the Atlantic and Pacific oceans from the chaos and destruction the war brought to hundreds of millions in Europe and Asia.

The Road to War: The United States and World War II

1931	Japan invades Manchuria.
1933	Franklin D. Roosevelt becomes U.S. president.
	Adolf Hitler becomes German chancellor.
1935–1937	Congress passes series of Neutrality Acts to protect United States from involvement in world conflicts.
1936	**March.** Nazi troops invade Rhineland, violating Treaty of Versailles.
	July. Civil war breaks out in Spain.
	Mussolini's Fascist Italian regime conquers Ethiopia.
	November. Roosevelt reelected president.
1937	**December.** Japanese troops capture Nanking, China.
1938	Hitler annexes Austria.
	September 29. Hitler accepts offer of "appeasement" in Munich from British prime minister Neville Chamberlain.
1939	**March.** Hitler invades Czechoslovakia.
	August. Hitler and Stalin sign Nazi-Soviet nonaggression pact.
	September 1. Germany invades Poland, beginning World War II.
	United States and Britain conclude cash-and-carry agreement for arms sales.
1940	**Spring.** German blitzkrieg smashes through Denmark, Norway, Belgium, Holland, and into northern France.
	Japan signs Tripartite Pact with Germany and Italy.
	May–June. German armies flank the Maginot Line. France surrenders. British evacuation at Dunkirk.
	Summer/Fall. German bombing campaign against England.
	November. Roosevelt wins third term as president. Royal Air Force wins Battle of Britain.
1941	**March.** Congress approves Lend-Lease Act, making arms available to Britain.
	June 22. Hitler invades Soviet Union.
	August. Roosevelt and Churchill sign Atlantic Charter.
	October. Militarists led by Hideki Tojo take over Japan.
	December 7. Japanese bomb Pearl Harbor. United States declares war on Japan.
	December 11. Germany and Italy declare war on United States.

The government still worried constantly about espionage and internal subversion. Billboards and posters warned Americans that "Loose lips sink ships" and "Enemy agents are always near; if you don't talk, they won't hear." The campaign for patriotic vigilance focused on German and Japanese foes, but Americans of Japanese descent became targets of official and popular persecution.

About 320,000 people of Japanese descent lived in the United States in 1941, two-thirds of them in Hawaii, where they largely escaped wartime persecution because they were essential and valued members of society. On the mainland, in contrast, Japanese Americans were a tiny minority—even along the West Coast, where most of them worked on farms and in small businesses—subject to frenzied wartime suspicions and persecution. A prominent newspaper columnist echoed the widespread sentiment that "The Japanese . . . should be under armed guard to the last man and woman right now and to hell with habeas corpus until the danger is over." Although an official military survey concluded that Japanese Americans posed no danger, popular hostility fueled a campaign to round up all mainland Japanese Americans—two-thirds of them U.S. citizens. "A Jap's a Jap. . . . It makes no difference whether he is an American citizen or not," one official declared.

On February 19, 1942, Roosevelt issued Executive Order 9066, which authorized sending all Americans of Japanese descent to ten makeshift prison camps located in remote areas of the West, euphemistically termed "relocation centers" (Map 25.3). Allowed little time to secure or sell their properties, Japanese Americans lost homes and businesses worth about $400 million and lived out the war penned in by barbed wire and armed guards. (See "Documenting the American Promise," page 922.) Although several thousand Japanese Americans served with distinction in the U.S. armed forces and no case of subversion by Japanese Americans was ever uncovered, the Supreme Court, in its 1944 *Korematsu* decision, upheld Executive Order 9066's blatant violation of constitutional rights as justified by "military necessity."

Building a Citizen Army

In 1940, Roosevelt encouraged Congress to pass the Selective Service Act to register men of military age who would be subject to **draft** into the armed forces if the need arose. More than 6,000 local draft boards registered over 30 million men and, when war came, rapidly inducted them into military service. In all, more than 16 million men and women served in uniform during the war, two-thirds of them draftees, mostly young men between the ages of 18 and 26. Although only about one family in five had a family member in the military, nearly everybody had friends and neighbors who had gone off to war. Relatively few young, single men received exemptions. By the time the war ended, over 10 million had served in the army, nearly 4 million in the navy, 600,000 in the marines, and 240,000 in the coast guard. In addition, 350,000 women joined the Nurse's Corps and women's military units such as the Women's Army Corps, the navy's Women Accepted for Volunteer Emergency Service, and the Women's Marine Corps. Though barred from combat duty, these women worked at nearly every noncombatant assignment, eroding traditional barriers to women's military service.

The Selective Service Act prohibited discrimination "on account of race or color," and almost a million African American men and women donned uniforms, as did half a million Mexican Americans, 25,000 Native Americans, and 13,000 Chinese Americans. The racial insults and discrimination suffered by all people of color made some soldiers ask, as a Mexican American GI said on his way to the European

FBI Searching Japanese American Home
When President Roosevelt informed military commanders that they might "from time to time" remove persons deemed dangerous, he had reason to suspect that nearly all Japanese Americans would be affected. An army "expert" on Asian culture had already advised the War Department that "as you cannot . . . penetrate the Oriental thinking . . . the easiest course is to remove them all from the West Coast and place them . . . under guard." Intent on getting to the bottom of one Japanese American family's allegiance, an FBI agent in 1942 scrutinizes a picture album while family members whose home has been invaded look on helplessly.
Los Angeles Daily News Photographic Archive, Department of Special Collections, Charles E. Young Research Library, UCLA.

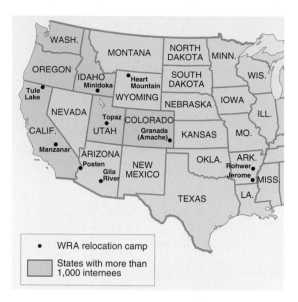

- • WRA relocation camp
- States with more than 1,000 internees

MAP 25.3 Western Relocation Authority Centers
Responding to prejudice and fear of sabotage, in 1942 President Roosevelt authorized the roundup and relocation of all Americans of Japanese descent. Taken from their homes in the cities and fertile farms of the far West, Japanese Americans were confined in desolate areas scattered as far east as the Mississippi River.

front, "Why fight for America when you have not been treated as an American?" Only black Americans were trained in segregated camps, confined in segregated barracks, and assigned to segregated units. The Red Cross even segregated the blood it supplied to treat battlefield casualties, thereby supposedly protecting wounded whites from being contaminated by black blood—needless to say, a practice without scientific merit. Secretary of War Henry Stimson opposed any change in the segregation of blacks, declaring that the military effort should not serve as a "sociological laboratory." Accordingly, most black Americans were consigned to manual labor positions, and relatively few served in combat until late in 1944, when the need for military manpower in Europe intensified. Then, as General George Patton told black soldiers in a tank unit in Normandy, "I don't care what color you are, so long as you go up there and kill those Kraut sonsabitches." Combat service slowly weakened the official military policy of racial segregation, and it was officially banned from the armed forces in 1948 by order of President Harry Truman, although genuine integration was delayed until the Korean War.

Homosexuals also served in the armed forces, although in much smaller numbers than black Americans. Secretary of War Stimson reminded commanding generals that they were expected to prosecute cases of sodomy, but in reality most officers, under pressure to field an army, followed the traditional policy of looking the other way. Lesbians volunteered for the newly formed women's branches of service. Allowed to serve, gay Americans, like other minorities, sought to demonstrate their worth under fire. "I was superpatriotic," a gay combat veteran recalled. Another gay GI remarked, "Who in the hell is going to worry about [homosexuality]" in the midst of the life-or-death realities of war?

Conversion to a War Economy

In 1940, the American economy remained mired in depression. Nearly one worker in seven was still without a job, factories operated far below their productive capacity, and the total federal budget was under $10 billion. Shortly after the attack on Pearl Harbor, Roosevelt announced the goal of converting the economy to produce "overwhelming . . . crushing superiority of equipment in any theater of the world war." In a rush to produce military supplies, factories were converted from producing passenger cars to assembling tanks and airplanes, and production of everything from bullets to shoes was ramped up to record levels. By the end of the war, there were more jobs than workers, plants were operating at full capacity, and the federal budget topped $100 billion.

To organize and oversee this tidal wave of military production, Roosevelt called upon business leaders to come to Washington and, for the token payment of a dollar a year, head new government agencies such as the War Production Board, which among other things, set production priorities and pushed for maximum output. Contracts flowed to large corporations such as General Electric, Ford, and U.S. Steel, often on a basis that guaranteed their profits. During the first half of 1942, the government issued contracts worth over $100 billion, a sum greater than the entire gross national product in 1941.

Booming wartime employment swelled union membership. To speed production, the government asked unions to pledge not to strike. Despite the relentless pace of work, union mem-

> By the end of the war, there were more jobs than workers, plants were operating at full capacity, and the federal budget topped $100 billion.

Japanese Internment

Determined that the bombing of Pearl Harbor would not be followed by more sneak attacks, military and political leaders on the West Coast targeted persons of Japanese descent—alien and citizen alike—as potential saboteurs.

DOCUMENT 1
Final Recommendations of the Commanding General, Western Defense Command and Fourth Army, Submitted to the Secretary of War

Early in 1942, General John DeWitt, commander of the Western Defense Command, persuaded President Franklin Roosevelt to issue an executive order authorizing the removal of the Japanese living in the United States. Subsequently, 110,000 Japanese Americans were confined to relocation camps for the duration of the war. DeWitt's recommendation expressed concern for military security by appealing to racist conceptions long used to curb Asian immigration. Japanese Americans and their supporters fought the internment order in the courts as a violation of fundamental constitutional rights, an argument rejected during the war by the U.S. Supreme Court. Long after the war ended, the U.S. government officially apologized for Japanese internment and issued modest monetary payments to survivors.

February 14, 1942
Memorandum for the Secretary of War.
Subject: Evacuation of Japanese and Other Subversive Persons from the Pacific Coast.

1. In presenting a recommendation for the evacuation of Japanese and other subversive persons from the Pacific Coast, the following facts have been considered:
   a. Mission of the Western Defense Command and Fourth Army.
     (1) Defense of the Pacific Coast of the Western Defense Command, as extended, against attacks by sea, land, or air;
     (2) Local protection of establishment and communications vital to the National Defense for which adequate defense cannot be provided by local civilian authorities.
   b. Brief Estimate of the Situation.
     (1) . . . The following are possible and probable enemy activities: . . .
       (a) Naval attack on shipping on coastal waters;
       (b) Naval attack on coastal cities and vital installations;
       (c) Air raids on vital installations, particularly within two hundred miles of the coast;
       (d) Sabotage of vital installations throughout the Western Defense Command.

Hostile Naval and air raids will be assisted by enemy agents signaling from the coastline and the vicinity thereof; and by supplying and otherwise assisting enemy vessels and by sabotage.

In the war in which we are now engaged racial affinities are severed by migration. The Japanese race is an enemy race and while many second and third generation Japanese born on United States soil, possessed of United States citizenship, have become "Americanized," the racial strains are undiluted. To conclude otherwise is to expect that children born of white parents on Japanese soil sever all racial affinity and become loyal Japanese subjects, ready to fight and, if necessary, to die for Japan in a war against the nation of their parents. . . .

It, therefore, follows that along the vital Pacific Coast over 112,000 potential enemies, of Japanese extraction, are at large today. There are indications that these are organized and ready for concerted action at a favorable opportunity. The very fact that no sabotage has taken place to date is a disturbing and confirming indication that such action will be taken.

SOURCE: *Final Recommendations,* report by General John Lesesne DeWitt to the United States Secretary of War, February 14, 1942.

DOCUMENT 2
An Oral History of Life in the Japanese American Detention Camps

Imprisoned in bleak surroundings far from home, Japanese internees sometimes succumbed to despair and bitterness. Looking back after forty years, Kazue Yamane recalled her confinement as a disturbing and baffling experience.

In April 1942, my husband and I and our two children left for camp, and my mother-in-law and father-in-law came about a month later. I wasn't afraid, but I kept asking in my mind, how could they? This is impossible. Even today I still think it was a nightmarish thing. I cannot reconcile myself to the fact that I had to go, that I was interned, that I was segregated, that I was taken away, even though it goes back forty years. . . .

I was separated from my husband; he went to the Santa Fe, New

Mexico, camp. All our letters were censored; all our letters were cut in parts and all that. So we were not too sure what messages was getting through and not getting through, but I do know that I informed him many times of his mother's condition. He should have been allowed to come back to see her, because I thought she wouldn't live too long, but they never did allow him to come back, even for her funeral. They did not allow that. I learned that a lot of the messages didn't get to him; they were crossed out. I now have those letters with me.

In 1944 I was left with his parents and our kids. But I had no time to think of what was going to happen because my child was always sick and I had been quite sick. . . .

My son knew what was going on, and he too had many times asked me why . . . you know, why? why? Of course, I had no explanation why this was happening to us.

SOURCE: Excerpt from *And Justice for All*, by John Tateishi. Copyright © 1999 by John Tateishi. Reprinted by permission of the University of Washington Press.

DOCUMENT 3
The Kikuchi Diary

Forcibly removed from his life as a student at the University of California at Berkeley, Charles Kikuchi sought in his prison camp diary to make sense of the internment and to judge where it would lead.

December 7, 1941, Berkeley, California
Pearl Harbor. We are at war! Jesus Christ, the Japs bombed Hawaii and the entire fleet has been sunk. I just can't believe it. I don't know what in the hell is going to happen to us, but we will all be called into the Army right away.

. . . The next five years will determine the future of the Nisei

[Japanese American citizens]. They are now at the crossroads. Will they be able to take it or will they go under? If we are ever going to prove our Americanism, this is the time. The Anti-Jap feeling is bound to rise to hysterical heights, and it is most likely that the Nisei will be included as Japs. I wanted to go to San Francisco tonight, but Pierre says I am crazy. He says it's best we stick on campus. In any event, we can't remain on the fence, and a positive approach must be taken if we are to have a place in fulfilling the Promise of America. I think the U.S. is in danger of going Fascist too, or maybe Socialist. . . .

I don't know what to think or do. Everybody is in a daze.

April 30, 1942, Berkeley
Today is the day that we are going to get kicked out of Berkeley. It certainly is degrading. . . .

I'm supposed to see my family at Tanforan as Jack told me to give the same family number. I wonder how it is going to be living with them as I haven't done this for years and years? I should have gone over to San Francisco and evacuated with them, but I had a last final to take. I understand that we are going to live in the horse stalls. I hope that the Army has the courtesy to remove the manure first. . . .

July 14, 1942
Marie, Ann, Mitch, Jimmy, Jack, and myself got into a long discussion about how much democracy meant to us as individuals. Mitch says that he would even go in the army and die for it, in spite of the fact that he knew he would be kept down. Marie said that although democracy was not perfect, it was the only system that offered any hope for a future, if we could fulfill its destinies. Jack was a little more skeptical. He even

suggested that we [could] be in such grave danger that we would then realize that we were losing something. Where this point was he could not say. I said that this was what happened in France and they lost all. Jimmy suggested that the colored races of the world had reason to feel despair and mistrust the white man because of the past experiences. . . .

In reviewing the four months here, the chief value I got out of this forced evacuation was the strengthening of the family bonds. I never knew my family before this and this was the first chance that I have had to really get acquainted.

SOURCE: Excerpts (pp. 43, 51, 183, 252) from *The Kikuchi Diary: Chronicle from an American Concentration Camp*, edited by John Modell. Copyright © 1973 by the Board of Trustees of the University of Illinois. Used with the permission of the University of Illinois Press and the author.

QUESTIONS FOR ANALYSIS AND DEBATE

1. What explains General DeWitt's insistence on evacuating the Japanese after he received the report of military investigators that no acts of sabotage had occurred?

2. How do the Kikuchi diary and the oral histories of life in the camps reveal the meaning of internment for the detainees?

3. Despite the internment of their families and friends in concentration camps, the Japanese American army unit in Italy earned a larger number of citations for combat heroism than any comparable army group. What hints in the documents here might help explain this combat record?

4. How did the internment camp experience influence the detainees' attitudes about their identity as Americans of Japanese descent?

Tank Production Line
The General Motors plant shown here assembled automobiles until Roosevelt called for American factories to covert to wartime production as rapidly as possible. This and other plants built tens of thousands of armored vehicles destined principally for American and Allied soldiers in the European theater, where they dueled with Hitler's Panzers.

General Motors Corp. Used with permission, GM Media Archives.

lions of shoes, socks, shirts, pants, and much more—in all more than double the combined production of Germany, Japan, and Italy. In the last 18 months of war, for example, every American in the Pacific theater could draw upon 8,000 pounds of military supplies, in stark contrast with each Japanese soldier's access to two pounds. Giving tangible meaning to the term "arsenal of democracy," this outpouring of military goods supplied not only U.S. forces but also sizable portions of the military needs of the Allies.

Fighting Back

The United States confronted a daunting military challenge in December 1941. The attack on Pearl Harbor destroyed much of its Pacific fleet, crippling the nation's ability to defend against Japan's massive offensive throughout the southern Pacific. In the Atlantic, Hitler's U-boats sank American ships, while German armies occupied most of western Europe and relentlessly advanced eastward into the Soviet Union. Roosevelt and his military advisers believed defeating Germany took top priority. To achieve that victory required preventing Hitler from defeating America's allies, Britain and the Soviet Union. If they fell, Hitler would command all the resources of Europe in a probable assault on the United States. To fight back effectively against Germany and Japan, the United States had to coordinate military and political strategy with its allies and muster all its human and economic assets. But in 1941, nobody knew if that would be enough.

Turning the Tide in the Pacific

In the Pacific theater, Japan's leading military strategist, Admiral Isoroku Yamamoto, ordered an all-out offensive throughout the southern Pacific. He believed that if his forces did not quickly conquer and secure the territories they targeted, Japan would eventually lose the war to America's far greater resources. Swiftly, the Japanese assaulted American airfields in the Philippines and captured U.S. outposts on Guam and Wake Island. Singapore, the great British naval base in Malaya, surrendered to the Japanese in February 1942, and most of Burma had fallen by March. All that stood in the way of Yamamoto's plan for Japan's domination of the

bers kept their no-strike pledge, with the important exception of the United Mine Workers, who walked out of the coal mines in 1943 behind their leader John L. Lewis, demanding a pay hike and earning the enmity of many Americans.

Overall, conversion to war production achieved Roosevelt's ambitious goal of "overwhelming . . . , crushing superiority" in military goods. At a total cost of $304 billion during the war, the nation produced an avalanche of military equipment, including 300,000 airplanes, 88,000 tanks, 7,000 ships, 3 million vehicles, as well as billions of bullets, not to mention mil-southern Pacific was the American stronghold in the Philippines.

The Japanese unleashed a withering assault against Philippine defenses in January 1942, causing the American commander General Douglas MacArthur to retreat to fortifications on the Bataan Peninsula across the harbor from Manila. Unsuccessful in repelling the Japanese attack, MacArthur slipped away to Australia in March, leaving General Jonathan Wainwright to hold out in the Corregidor fortress as long as possible. Wainwright finally surrendered in May 1942, and Japanese soldiers marched the weak and malnourished survivors sixty-five miles to a concentration camp. Hundreds of Americans and as many as 10,000 Filipinos died during the Bataan Death March, and 16,000 more perished within weeks from disease and brutality in the prison camp. By summer 1942, the Japanese war machine had swooped from its Philippine successes to conquer the oil-rich Dutch East Indies and was poised to strike Australia and New Zealand.

Reeling from Japanese assaults, Americans had learned that the soldiers of the Rising Sun were tough, fearless, and prepared to fight to the death for honor and their emperor. The Japanese had larger, faster, and more heavily armed ships than the United States, and their airplanes outperformed anything the Americans could send up against them. The unbroken series of Japanese victories caused Americans at home to worry about their own safety. A false report that Japanese fighter planes had been spotted near Los Angeles set off an antiaircraft barrage and inspired the commander of West Coast defenses to announce that "death and destruction [from enemy planes] are likely to come at any moment." But a daring raid on Tokyo in April 1942 by a squadron of carrier-based B-25 bombers led by Lieutenant Colonel James Doolittle boosted American morale and demonstrated that even the Japanese imperial capital lay within reach (barely) of American might.

In the spring of 1942, U.S. forces launched a major two-pronged counteroffensive that military officials hoped would reverse the Japanese advance. Forces led by General MacArthur moved north from Australia and attacked the Japanese in the Philippines. Far more decisively, Admiral Chester W. Nimitz sailed his battle fleet west from Hawaii to retake Japanese-held islands in the mid-Pacific. On May 7–8, 1942, in the Coral Sea just north of Australia, the American fleet and carrier-based warplanes de-

feated a Japanese armada that was sailing around the coast of New Guinea.

After victory in the Coral Sea, Nimitz learned from an intelligence intercept that the Japanese were massing an invasion force aimed at Midway Island, an outpost guarding the Hawaiian Islands. Nimitz maneuvered his carriers and cruisers into the Central Pacific to surprise the Japanese. In a furious battle that raged from June 3 to June 6, American naval ships and planes delivered a punishing blow, sinking a heavy cruiser, two destroyers, and four of Japan's six carriers, while the American armada lost only one carrier and a destroyer. The Battle of Midway reversed the balance of naval power in the Pacific and put the Japanese at a disadvantage for the rest of the war. Although Japan still wielded formidable naval firepower, it managed

Japanese Pilot's Flag

Japanese pilots often carried small flags covered with admonitions to fight hard and well. This flag belonged to a pilot named Imano, whose relatives sent him aloft with inscriptions that read "Let your divine plane soar in the sky. We who are left behind pray only for your certain success in sinking an enemy ship." Notably, the inscription emphasized harming Japan's enemies rather than returning home safe and sound.

U.S. Naval Academy Museum / photo by Richard D. Bond Jr.

to build only six more large carriers during the war while the U.S. fleet launched an additional seventeen large carriers and ninety-six smaller carriers, a disparity that proved the wisdom of Yamamoto's fear of America's vast human and material resources. The Battle of Midway turned the tide of Japanese advance in the Pacific but did little to dislodge Japan from the many places it had conquered and now stoutly defended.

The Campaign in Europe

In the dark months after Pearl Harbor, Hitler's eastern-front armies marched ever deeper into the Soviet Union while his western forces prepared to invade Britain. As in World War I, the Germans attempted to starve the British into submission by destroying their seaborne lifeline.

Radar Screen
The new technology of radar gave American military commanders unprecedented information about the location and power of their foes. The radar operator shown here aboard an American aircraft carrier in the Pacific is charting air strikes against Japan in 1945.
© Bettmann/Corbis.

Technological advances made German U-boats much more effective than they had been in World War I, and for month after month in 1941 and 1942 they sank Allied ships faster than new ones could be built. The fearsome toll of the U-boat campaign eventually reached more than 4,700 merchant ships, almost 200 warships, and 40,000 Allied seamen.

Until mid-1943, the outcome of the war in the Atlantic remained in perilous doubt. Then, newly invented radar detectors and production of sufficient destroyer escorts for merchant vessels allowed the Allies to convert the lurking U-boats from predators into vulnerable prey. After suffering a 75 percent casualty rate among U-boat crews, Hitler withdrew German submarines from the North Atlantic in late May 1943. In the next four months, more than 3,500 American supply ships crossed the Atlantic without a single loss. Winning the battle of the Atlantic allowed the United States to continue to supply its British and Soviet allies for the duration of the war and to reduce the imminent threat of a German invasion of Britain.

The most important strategic question confronting the United States and its allies was when and where to open a second front against the Nazis. Stalin demanded that America and Britain mount an immediate and massive assault across the English Channel into western France. A cross-channel invasion would force Hitler to divert his armies from the eastern front and relieve the pressure on the Soviet Union, which was fighting alone against the full strength of the German Wehrmacht. Churchill and Roosevelt were willing to delay opening a second front, allowing the Germans and the Soviets to slug it out, weakening both the Nazis and the Communists, and making an eventual Allied attack on western France more likely to succeed. Both Churchill and Roosevelt promised Stalin that they would open a second front, but they decided to strike first in southern Europe and the Mediterranean, which Churchill termed Europe's "soft under-belly." Roosevelt worried that this plan that would merely "peck on the periphery" of Nazi power and Stalin vehemently agreed, but Roosevelt ultimately backed Churchill's desire for an invasion of North Africa as a first step toward a second front.

The plan targeted a region of long-standing British influence in the eastern Mediterranean. In October 1942, British forces at El-Alamein in Egypt halted German general Erwin Rommel's drive to capture the Suez Canal, Britain's lifeline to the oil of the Middle East and to British colonies in India and South Asia. In November, an American army under General Dwight D. Eisenhower landed far to the west, in French Morocco. Propelled by American tank units commanded by General George Patton, the Allied armies caught the Germans in North Africa in a giant vise that finally squeezed shut in May 1943. The North African campaign killed and captured 350,000 Axis soldiers, pushed the Germans out of Africa, made the Mediterranean safe for Allied shipping, and opened the door for an Allied invasion of Italy.

In January 1943, while the North African campaign was still under way, Roosevelt traveled to the Moroccan city of Casablanca to confer with Churchill and other Allied leaders. Stalin, preoccupied with the Soviet army's last-ditch defense of Stalingrad against massive German assault, did not attend the meeting but urged his allies to keep their promise of opening a major second front in western Europe. Roosevelt and Churchill announced that they would accept nothing less than the "unconditional surrender" of the Axis powers, ruling out peace negotiations. But Churchill and Roosevelt concluded that they needed more time to amass sufficient forces for the cross-channel invasion of France that Stalin demanded. In the meantime, they planned to capitalize on their success in North Africa and strike against Italy, consigning the Soviet Union to bear the brunt of the Nazi war machine for another year.

On July 10, 1943, combined American and British amphibious forces landed 160,000 troops in Sicily. The badly equipped Italian defenders quickly withdrew to the mainland. Soon afterward, Mussolini was deposed in Italy, ending the reign of Italian fascism. Quickly, the Allies invaded the mainland, and the Italian government surrendered unconditionally. The Germans responded by rushing reinforcements to Italy and seizing control of Rome, turning the Allies' Italian campaign into a series of battles to liberate Italy from German occupation.

German troops dug into strong fortifications and fought to defend every inch of Italy's rugged terrain. Only after a long, deadly, and frustrating campaign up the Italian peninsula did the Allies finally liberate Rome in June 1944. Allied forces continued to push into northern Italy against stubborn German defenses for the remainder of the war, making the Italian campaign the war's deadliest for American infantrymen. One soldier wrote that his comrades died "like butchered swine" in attacks on German defenses that ended in death, not triumph.

While the Italian campaign occupied numerous German divisions that Hitler might otherwise have deployed on the Russian front, no German forces were in fact taken away from the ongoing attack on the Soviet Union. Stalin denounced the Allies' Italian campaign because it left "the Soviet Army, which is fighting not only for its country, but also for its Allies, to do the job alone, almost single-handed." The campaign exacted a high cost from the Americans and the British, consuming men and material that might have been reserved for a second front in France and bringing the Nazis no closer to unconditional surrender.

> The most important strategic question confronting the United States and its allies was when and where to open a second front against the Nazis.

The Wartime Home Front

The war effort mobilized Americans as never before. Factories strained to churn out ever more bombs, bullets, tanks, ships, and airplanes, which workers rushed to assemble, leaving farms and small towns to congregate in cities. Women took jobs with wrenches and welding torches, boosting the nation's workforce and fraying traditional notions that women's place was in the home rather than on the assembly line. Despite rationing and shortages, unprecedented government expenditures for war production brought prosperity to many Americans after years of depression-era poverty (Figure 25.1). While Americans in uniform risked their lives on battlefields in Europe and Asia, where millions of civilians suffered bombing, strafing, and all-out military assaults, Americans on the mainland enjoyed complete immunity from foreign attack—in sharp contrast to their Soviet and British allies. The wartime ideology of human rights provided justification for the many sacrifices Americans were required to make in support of the military effort, as well as establishing a standard of basic human equality that became a potent weapon in the campaign for equal rights at home.

> Despite rationing and shortages, unprecedented government expenditures for war production brought prosperity to many Americans after years of depression-era poverty.

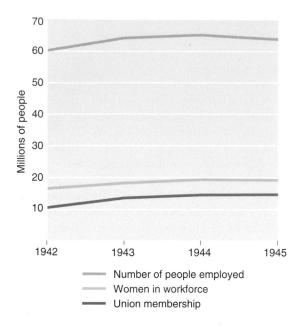

FIGURE 25.1   **World War II and the Economy, 1942–1945**
The end of the depression followed by war mobilization sent employment and union membership to high levels that continued into peacetime. Women lost many jobs in heavy industry after the war, but their increased numbers in the total workforce were sustained by the strong economy that followed.

"If you've sewed on buttons, or made button-holes, on a [sewing] machine, you can learn to do spot welding on airplane parts. If you've used an electric mixer in your kitchen, you can learn to run a drill press. If you've followed recipes exactly in making cakes, you can learn to load a shell." Millions of women responded, and by the end of the war, women working outside the home numbered eighteen million, 50 percent more than in 1939. Contributing to the war effort also paid off in wages that averaged $31 for a forty-eight-hour week, more than the typical steelworker earned in 1941. A Kentucky woman remembered her job at a munitions plant where she earned "the fabulous sum of $32 a week. To us it was an absolute miracle. Before that, we made nothing." Although men got paid an average of $54 for comparable wartime work, women accepted the pay differential and welcomed their chance to earn wages and help win the war at the same time. (See "American Places," page 929.)

Female Defense Worker

The war effort brought persons and activities together in unlikely ways, leading to unexpected outcomes. This photo appearing in the army magazine *Yank* sought to boost morale by presenting a defense worker as pinup girl. No one could know that the young propeller technician, nineteen-year-old Norma Jean Baker Dougherty, would later remake herself as the most glamorous of movie stars, Marilyn Monroe.

David Conover Images; © Norma Jean Enterprises, a division of 733548 Ontario Limited.

Women and Families, Guns and Butter

Wartime mobilization of the economy and the siphoning of millions of men into the armed forces left factories begging for women workers.

Millions of American women gladly left home toting a lunch pail and changed into overalls and work gloves to take their places on assembly lines in defense industries. At the start of the war, about a quarter of adult women worked outside the home, most as teachers, nurses, social workers, or domestic servants. Few women worked in factories, except for textile mills and sewing industries, because employers and male workers often discriminated against them. But wartime mobilization of the economy and the siphoning of millions of men into the armed forces left factories begging for women workers.

Government advertisements urged women to take industrial jobs by assuring them that their household chores had prepared them for work on the "Victory Line." One billboard proclaimed,

<hr />

AMERICAN PLACES

Rosie the Riveter/World War II Home Front National Historical Park, Richmond, California

On the eve of World War II, Richmond, California, on the San Francisco Bay, was a backwater town of some 20,000. By 1943, its population had skyrocketed to more than 100,000, and it had become the site of Kaiser Shipyards, the largest and most productive shipyards anywhere. Work never stopped during the war. Three shifts a day working seven days a week produced 747 cargo and troop-carrying Liberty and Victory ships.

With millions of men in uniform, tens of thousands of women were recruited to fill what were previously considered "men's jobs"—welders, riveters, ship fitters, heavy equipment operators. Any woman who worked in the defense industry was known as "Rosie the Riveter." Putting on coveralls, hard hats, and heavy gloves, women—including black, Hispanic, and Asian women—made up nearly one-third of Kaiser Shipyards' 90,000 workers at the height of the war. Women arrived from all parts of the country, but most came from the deep South and the Midwest, and most had never before held a job. One Richmond "Rosie" remembered, "We didn't care about the money. We all did what we could do for the war effort."

The park site sprawls over nearly five miles of shoreline and includes many historic buildings, most of them not yet open to the public. Already in place, however, is the Rosie the Riveter Memorial, an abstract rendition of a 441-foot-long Liberty ship. The Keel Walk leads visitors from the water's edge along a time line of facts about the home front during the war and past large panels holding photographs and quotations from "Rosies." One welder's memory is inscribed in granite: "It was hard to convince your lead man that you could do the work. When he assigned jobs, I used to follow him around and say, 'I could do that, I could do that.' He got sick of me and said, 'Okay, do it!' And of course, I could. I could do it." This is the only American memorial that honors women's labor during World War II.

The cargo ship S.S. *Red Oak Victory* is moored a short distance from the memorial. Built in Richmond and commissioned in December 1944, the ship saw service in the South Pacific. Barely saved from the scrap heap, *Red Oak Victory* is today a rusty hulk, but each day it welcomes dozens of dedicated volunteers who are laboring to preserve and restore the old ship.

FOR WEB LINKS RELATED TO THIS SITE AND OTHER AMERICAN PLACES, see "PlaceLinks" at bedfordstmartins.com/roark.

Rosie the Riveter Memorial
Rosie the Riveter/WWII Home Front National Historic Park/photo by Lew Watts.

Pitching in at Home
This poster adapts the standard children's book illustration style of the period to the war effort. White and middle class all, mother and children collect old golf clubs, cocktail shakers, and trophies—which dad, away at war, will never miss—so that these symbols of the American way of life can be recycled into armaments for defense.
Chicago Historical Society.

For more help analyzing this image, see the visual activity for this chapter in the Online Study Guide at bedfordstmartins.com/roark.

The majority of married women remained at home, occupied with domestic chores and child care. But they, too, pitched in to the war effort, planting Victory Gardens of home-grown vegetables, saving tin cans and newspapers for recycling into war materials, and hoarding pennies and nickels to buy war bonds. Many families scrimped to cope with the 30 percent inflation during the war. But families supported by men and women in manufacturing industries enjoyed wages that grew twice as fast as inflation.

The war influenced how all families spent their earnings. Buying a new washing machine or car was out of the question since factories that used to build them now made military goods. Many other consumer goods—such as tires, gasoline, shoes, and meat—were rationed at home to sustain military needs overseas. But most Americans had more money in their pockets than ever before, and they readily found things to spend it on, including movie tickets, cosmetics, recordings of music, and so much more that spending for personal consumption rose by 12 percent during the war.

The wartime prosperity and abundance enjoyed by most Americans contrasted with the experiences of their hard-pressed allies: Personal consumption fell by 22 percent in Britain; and in the Soviet Union food output plummeted to just one-third of prewar levels, creating widespread hunger and even starvation. Few went hungry in the United States, however. The government lifted the New Deal's restraints on agricultural production, and farm output grew by 25 percent every year during the war, providing an astonishing cornucopia that allowed surplus food to be exported to nourish the Allies.

The Double V Campaign

Fighting against Nazi Germany and its ideology of Aryan racial supremacy confronted Americans with the extensive racial prejudice in their own society. Roosevelt declared that black Americans were in the war "not only to defend America but . . . to establish a universal freedom under which a new basis of security and prosperity can be established for all—regardless of station, race, or creed." The *Pittsburgh Courier*, a leading black newspaper, seized upon such statements and asserted that the wartime emergency called for a "Double V" campaign seeking "victory over our enemies at home and victory over our enemies on the battlefields abroad." It was time, the *Courier* proclaimed, "to persuade, embarrass, compel and shame our government and our nation . . . into a more enlightened attitude."

In 1941, black organizations barraged Congress and the White House with petitions demanding that the federal government require companies receiving defense contracts to integrate their workforces. A. Philip Randolph, head of the Brotherhood of Sleeping Car Porters, promised that 100,000 African American marchers would descend on Washington if the president did not eliminate discrimination in defense industries. Roosevelt decided to risk offending his white allies in the South and in unions and issued Executive Order 8802 in mid-1941. It authorized a Committee on Fair Employment Practices to investigate and prevent race discrimination in employment. Civil rights champions hailed the act, and Randolph triumphantly called off the march.

Progress came slowly, however. In 1940, nine out of ten black Americans lived below the federal poverty line, and those who worked earned on average 39 percent of whites' wages. In search of better jobs and living conditions, five and a half million black Americans migrated from the South during the war to centers

A Plea for Inclusion

This illustration, drawn by black artist E. Simms Campbell for the cover of *Opportunity*, the journal of the National Urban League, advances a goal that was important to the League: the full inclusion of African Americans in the nation's economic life. To press home the extreme absurdity of restraining black potential in times of crisis, Campbell depicted a mob of puny bigots preventing John Henry, the fabled black laborer, from using his strength for liberation and service in the creation of weapons to defeat Nazism. John Henry was the perfect symbol of the war as a struggle for democracy against oppression and prejudice.
Yale University Library.

of industrial production in the North and West, making a majority of African Americans city dwellers for the first time in U.S. history. Many discovered that although laboring jobs were available, unions and employers often barred blacks from skilled jobs. At least eighteen major unions—including the machinists, ironworkers, shipbuilders, and railway workers—explicitly prohibited black members. Severe labor shortages and government fair employment pressures opened assembly-line jobs in defense plants to African American workers, causing black unemployment to drop by 80 percent during the war. But more jobs did not mean equal pay for black working people. Although the income of black families rose during the war, by the end of the conflict it still stood at half of white families' income.

Blacks' migration to defense jobs intensified racial antagonisms, which boiled over in the hot summer of 1943 when 242 race riots erupted in 47 cities. In Los Angeles, hundreds of white servicemen, claiming they were punishing draft dodgers, chased and beat young Chicano men who dressed in distinctive broad-shouldered, peg-legged zoot suits. The worst mayhem occurred in Detroit, where conflict between whites and blacks at a city park ignited a race war. Whites with clubs smashed through black neighborhoods, and blacks retaliated by destroying and looting white-owned businesses. In two days of violence, 25 blacks and 9 whites were killed, and scores more were injured.

Racial violence created impetus for the Double V campaign, officially supported by the National Association for the Advancement of Colored People (NAACP), which asserted black Americans' demands for the rights and privileges enjoyed by all other Americans—demands reinforced by the Allies' wartime ideology of freedom and democracy. While the NAACP focused on court challenges to segregation, other civil rights activists who wanted more direct confrontations founded a new organization in 1942, the Congress of Racial Equality (CORE), which organized picketing and sit-ins against **Jim Crow** restaurants and theaters. The Double V campaign greatly expanded membership in the NAACP, but achieved only limited success against racial discrimination at home during the war.

> The Double V campaign asserted black Americans' demands for the rights and privileges enjoyed by all other Americans—demands reinforced by the Allies' wartime ideology of freedom and democracy.

Wartime Politics and the 1944 Election

Americans rallied around the war effort in unprecedented unity. Despite the consensus on war aims, the strains and stresses of the nation's massive wartime mobilization made it difficult for Roosevelt to maintain his political coalition. Whites often resented blacks who migrated to northern cities, took jobs, and made themselves at home. Many Americans complained about government price controls and the rationing of scarce goods, while the war dragged on with no end in sight and casualties mounted. Magnifying the Democrats' problems, service overseas kept many Democratic voters from casting ballots in the 1942 congressional elections, and the low turnout helped Republicans gain congressional seats.

> In the 1944 presidential election, voters gave Roosevelt a 53.5 percent majority, his narrowest presidential victory, ensuring his continued leadership as Dr. Win-the-War.

Republicans seized the opportunity to roll back New Deal reforms. A **conservative** coalition of Republicans and southern Democrats succeeded in abolishing several New Deal agencies in 1942 and 1943, including the Work Projects Administration and the Civilian Conservation Corps. But the Democratic administration fought back. By persuading states to ease residency requirements and Congress to guarantee absentee ballots for servicemen, Democrats brought scattered members of the New Deal coalition back to the voting booth in 1944.

In June 1944, Congress unanimously approved the landmark GI Bill of Rights, promising to give veterans government funds for education, housing, and health care, and to provide loans to start businesses and buy homes when they returned from overseas. The GI Bill put the financial resources of the federal government behind the abstract goals of freedom and democracy for which veterans were fighting, and it empowered millions of GIs to better themselves and their families after the war.

After twelve turbulent years in the White House, Roosevelt was exhausted and gravely ill with heart disease. But he was determined to remain president until the war ended. "All that is within me cries out to go back to my home on the Hudson River," he declared. "But as a good soldier . . . I will accept and serve" if reelected president. Roosevelt's poor health made the selection of a vice presidential candidate unusually important. Convinced that many Americans had soured on **liberal** reform, Roosevelt dumped Vice President Henry Wallace, an outspoken **progressive**, and chose Senator Harry S. Truman of Missouri as his running mate. A reliable party man from a southern border state, Truman satisfied urban Democratic leaders while not worrying white southerners who were nervous about challenges to racial segregation.

The Republicans, confident of a strong conservative upsurge in the nation, nominated as their presidential candidate the governor of New York, Thomas E. Dewey, who had made his reputation as a tough crime fighter. In the 1944 presidential election, Roosevelt's failing health alarmed many observers, but his frailty was outweighed by Americans' unwillingness to change presidents in the midst of the war and by Dewey's failure to persuade most voters that the New Deal was a creeping **socialist** menace. The Germans and the Japanese seemed far greater menaces than four more years of President Roosevelt. Voters gave Roosevelt a 53.5 percent majority, his narrowest presidential victory, ensuring his continued leadership as Dr. Win-the-War.

Reaction to the Holocaust

The political cross-currents in the United States were tame in comparison with Hitler's vicious campaign to exterminate Jews. Since the 1930s, Nazis had persecuted Jews in Germany and every German-occupied territory, causing many Jews to seek asylum beyond Hitler's reach. (See "Beyond America's Borders," page 934.) Millions of Jews from southern and eastern Europe had arrived in the United States during the late nineteenth and early twentieth centuries. But after the immigration restriction laws of the 1920s, the open door slammed shut except for a small quota of immigrants from each nation. Some Americans sought to make exceptions to the quotas for Jews fleeing the Nazis' wrath, but many Americans resisted. Roosevelt sympathized with the refugees' pleas for help, but he did not want to jeopardize his foreign policy or offend American voters. After Hitler's Anschluss in 1938, thousands of Austrian Jews sought to immigrate to the United States, but 82 percent of Americans opposed admitting them, and they were turned away. Roosevelt tried to persuade countries in Latin America and Africa to accept refugees, but none complied. Friends of the refugees introduced legislation in Congress in 1939 that would have granted asylum to 20,000 German refugee children, most of them Jewish. The bill was defeated, in large measure because of American anti-Semitism; in 1940, refugee English children—few of whom were Jewish—were welcomed into the United States without delay.

In 1942, numerous reports filtered out of German-occupied Europe that Hitler was implementing a "final solution": Jews and other "undesirables"—such as Gypsies, religious and political dissenters, and homosexuals—were being sent to concentration camps. Old people, children, and others deemed too weak to work were systematically slaughtered and cremated while the able-bodied were put to work at slave labor until they died of starvation and abuse. Despite such reports, skeptical U.S. State Department officials refused to set aside quotas and grant asylum to refugees. The U.S. Office of War Information worried that charging the Germans with crimes against humanity might incite them to greater resistance and prolong the war. Most Americans, including top officials, believed the reports of the killing camps were exaggerated, and they clung to the conviction that such an inhumane nightmare could not be true. Only 152,000 of Europe's millions of Jews managed to gain refuge in the United States prior to America's entry into the war; thereafter, the number of refugees dropped steadily to a mere 2,400 in 1944. Those trapped in Europe could hope only for rescue by Allied armies.

The nightmare of the Holocaust was all too real. When Russian troops arrived at Auschwitz in Poland in February 1945, they found emaciated prisoners, many too weak to survive their liberation. Skeletal corpses, half burned, lay around them. Nearby were pits filled with the ashes of those who had been cremated. The Russians discovered sheds filled with loot the Nazis had stripped from the dead—clothing, gold fillings, false teeth, even cloth made from human hair. At last, the truth about the Nazis' Holocaust began to be known beyond the Germans who perpetrated and tolerated these atrocities and the men,

women, and children who succumbed to genocide. But by then it was too late for the nine million victims—mostly Jews—of the Nazis' crimes against humanity. (See "Historical Question," page 936.)

Toward Unconditional Surrender

By February 1943, Soviet defenders had finally defeated the massive German offensive against Stalingrad, turning the tide of the war in Europe. After gargantuan sacrifices in fighting that had lasted for eighteen months and killed more than 95 percent of the Russian soldiers and noncommissioned officers engaged at Stalingrad, the Red Army forced Hitler's Wehrmacht to turn back toward the west. Now the Soviets and their western allies faced the task of driving the Nazis out of eastern and western Europe and crushing them until they could fight no longer. It was long past time, Stalin proclaimed, for Britain and the United States to open a second front in France, but that offensive was postponed for more than a year after the Red Army's victory at Stalingrad. In the Pacific, the Allies had halted the expansion of the Japanese empire but now had the deadly task of dislodging Japanese defenders from the far-flung outposts they still occupied. Military planners in the United States maneuvered millions of soldiers, sailors, marines, and airmen in a strategy designed to annihilate Axis resistance by taking advantage of America's industrial superiority.

The Holocaust, 1933–1945

SWEDEN
DENMARK
LITH.
East Prussia
GERMANY
POLAND
CZECHOSLOVAKIA
SWITZ   AUSTRIA HUNGARY
ITALY
YUGOSLAVIA

• Principal German concentration and extermination camp

From Bombing Raids to Berlin

While the Allied campaigns in North Africa and Italy depended heavily on foot soldiers, tanks, and heavy artillery, British and American pilots flew bombing missions from England to the continent as an airborne substitute for the delayed second front on the ground. Because of the vulnerability of British bombers to the German Luftwaffe, British pilots flew raids at night; and because they could not hit

Nazi Anti-Semitism and the Atomic Bomb

During the 1930s, Jewish physicists fled Adolf Hitler's fanatical anti-Semitic persecutions and came to the United States, where they played a leading role in the research and development of the atomic bomb. In this way, Nazi anti-Semitism contributed to making the United States the first atomic power.

One of Germany's greatest scientists, Albert Einstein, won the Nobel Prize for physics in 1921. Among other things, Einstein's work demonstrated that the nuclei of atoms of physical matter stored almost inconceivable quantities of energy. A fellow scientist praised Einstein's discoveries as "the greatest achievements in the history of human thought."

Einstein was born in Germany in 1879, grew up in Munich, and by 1914 headed the Kaiser Wilhelm Institute for Physics in Berlin. But he was a Jew, and his ideas were ridiculed by German anti-Semites. A German physicist who had won the Nobel Prize in 1905 attacked Einstein for his "Jewish nonsense" that was "hostile to the German spirit." Einstein wrote to a friend, "Anti-Semitism is strong here [in Berlin] and political reaction is violent." In 1922, anti-Semitic extremists assassinated the German foreign minister, Walter Rathenau, a Jewish chemist and friend of Einstein. Einstein's associates warned him that he, too, was targeted for assassination.

By 1921, when Einstein won the Nobel Prize, Adolf Hitler, a former corporal in the German infantry, had already organized the Nazi Party and recruited a large private army to intimidate his opponents—Jews foremost among them. Jailed in 1923 for attempting to overthrow the German government, Hitler wrote his Nazi manifesto, *Mein Kampf*, which proclaimed that Jews and Communists had betrayed Germany in the First World War and needed to be eliminated. Jews, Hitler insisted, were "a foreign people," "inferior beings," the "personification of the devil," "a race of dialectical liars," "parasites," and "eternal blood-suckers" who had the "clear aim of ruining the . . . white race." Hitler's rantings attracted a huge audience in Germany, and his personal Nazi army, which numbered 400,000 by 1933, terrorized and murdered anyone who got in the way.

In January 1933, just weeks before Franklin Roosevelt's inauguration as president of the United States, Hitler became chancellor of Germany on a tidal wave of popular support for his Nazi Party. Within months, he abolished freedom of speech and assembly, outlawed all political opposition, and exercised absolute dictatorial power. On April 7, Hitler announced the Law for the Restoration of the Professional Civil Service, which stipulated that "civil servants of non-Aryan descent must retire." A non-Aryan was defined as any person "descended from non-Aryan, especially Jewish, parents or grandparents." The law meant that scientists of Jewish descent who worked for state institutions, including universities, no longer had jobs. About 1,600 intellectuals in Germany immediately lost their livelihood and their future in Hitler's Reich. Among them were about a quarter of the physicists in Germany, including Einstein and ten other Nobel Prize winners. The Nazis' anti-Semitism laws forced many leading scientists to leave Germany. Between 1933 and 1941, Einstein and about 100 other Jewish physicists joined hundreds of Jewish intellectuals in an exodus from Nazi Germany to the safety of the United States.

The refugee physicists scrambled to find positions in American universities and research institutes that would allow them to continue their studies. The accelerating pace of research in physics during the 1930s raised the possibility that a way might exist to release the phenomenal energy bottled up in atomic nuclei, perhaps even to create a superbomb. Einstein and other scientists considered that possibility remote. But many worried that if scientists loyal to Germany discovered a way to harness nuclear energy, then Hitler would have the power to spread Nazi terror throughout the globe.

The refugee physicists asked Einstein to write a letter to President Roosevelt explaining the military

specific targets, they bombed general areas, hoping to hit civilians, create terror, and undermine morale. Beginning with Paul Tibbets's flight in August 1942, American pilots flew heavily armored B-17s from English airfields in daytime raids on industrial targets vital for the German war machine, especially oil refineries and ball bearing factories.

German air defenses took a fearsome toll on Allied pilots and aircraft. In 1943, two-thirds of and political threats posed by the latest research in nuclear physics. In early October 1939, as Hitler's blitzkrieg swept through Poland, Roosevelt received Einstein's letter and immediately grasped the central point, exclaiming, "what you are after is to see that the Nazis don't blow us up." Roosevelt quickly convened a small group of distinguished American scientists, who convinced the president to authorize an all-out effort to learn whether an atomic bomb could be built and, if so, to build it. Only weeks before the

Japanese attack on Pearl Harbor, Roosevelt decided to launch the Manhattan Project, the top-secret atomic bomb program.

Leading scientists from the United States and Britain responded to the government's appeal: "No matter what you do with the rest of

your life, nothing will be as important to the future of the World as your work on this Project right now." Many of the most creative, productive, and irreplaceable scientists involved in the Manhattan Project were physicists who had fled Nazi Germany. Their efforts had brought the possibility of an atomic bomb to Roosevelt's attention. Having personally experienced Nazi anti-Semitism, they understood what was at stake—a world in which Hitler had the atomic bomb or his enemies did.

In the end, Hitler's scientists failed to develop an atomic bomb, and Germany surrendered before the American bomb was ready to go. But the Manhattan Project succeeded, as Paul Tibbets proved over Hiroshima, Japan, on August 6, 1945. After the war, Leo Szilard, a leader among the refugee physicists, remarked, "If Congress knew the true history of the atomic energy project . . . it would create a special medal to be given to meddling foreigners for distinguished services."

Einstein Becomes U.S. Citizen

Nazi laws that prohibited Jewish scientists from working in universities and research institutes also excluded Jews from public places such as shops, parks, and theaters—as proclaimed by signs like the one shown here. Nazi anti-Semitism caused Albert Einstein to renounce his German citizenship, emigrate to the United States, and—in the naturalization ceremony recorded in this photo—officially become an American citizen in 1940, along with his secretary Helen Dukas and his stepdaughter Margot Einstein.

Photo: Courtesy, American Institute of Physics Emilio Segré Visual Archives; sign: Arnold Kramer/United States Holocaust Memorial Museum.

BIBLIOGRAPHY

John Cornwell, *Hitler's Scientists: Science, War, and the Devil's Pact* (2003).
Daniel J. Kevles, *The Physicists: The History of a Scientific Community in Modern America* (1995).
Richard Rhodes, *The Making of the Atomic Bomb* (1986).
Paul Lawrence Rose, *Heisenberg and the Nazi Atomic Bomb Project* (1998).
S. S. Schweber, *In the Shadow of the Bomb: Bethe, Oppenheimer, and the Moral Responsibility of the Scientist* (2000).
Brian VanDeMark, *Pandora's Keepers: Nine Men and the Atomic Bomb* (2003).

American airmen did not survive to complete their 25-mission tour of duty. In all, 85,000 American airmen were killed in the skies over Europe. The arrival in February 1944 of America's durable and deadly P-51 Mustang fighter gave Allied bomber pilots superior protection and slowly began to sweep the Luftwaffe from the skies, allowing bombers to penetrate deep into Germany and pound civilian and military targets around the clock. In

Why Did the Allies Refuse to Bomb the Death Camps?

The Dead at Buchenwald
In this stark moment, all distance between official Washington and the Holocaust is breached. Soldiers and civilians pause somberly in the background as Senator Alben Barkley of Kentucky, stooped in sadness, tries to comprehend the incomprehensible.
Pentagon, U.S. Army Signal Corps.

Only a few days after the German blitzkrieg swept into Poland in September 1939, Adolf Hitler instructed military commanders to begin, as swiftly as possible, to make room for Germans in captured Polish territory by eliminating clergymen, aristocrats, intellectuals, and, above all, Jews. Soon Nazi soldiers began machine-gunning groups of unarmed, defenseless men, women, and children who stood in burial pits they had been forced to dig. Later, seeking more efficient means of annihilation, Nazi engineers devised airtight vans that roamed the countryside suffocating the condemned with carbon monoxide fumes.

To achieve the "final solution" to what Hitler and other Germans considered the Jewish menace to Aryan racial purity, the Nazis built death camps to slaughter millions in gas chambers and cremate their remains in gas ovens. Although the Nazis tried to keep the final solution a secret from the outside world, news that they were systematically killing millions of Jews at Auschwitz in Poland and in other locations leaked out in the summer of 1942. The World Jewish Congress appealed to the Allies to bomb the death camps and the railroad tracks leading to them in order to hamper the killing operation and block further shipments of victims.

The proposals to bomb the death camps got no farther than the desks of Assistant Secretary of War

April 1944, pilots began to target bridges and railroads in northwestern Europe in order to isolate German troops in northern France from reinforcements and prepare for the Allies' cross-channel invasion.

In November 1943, Churchill, Roosevelt, and Stalin met in Teheran, Iran, to plan the Allies' next step. Roosevelt conceded to Stalin that the Soviet Union would exercise de facto control of the eastern European countries that

John J. McCloy in Washington and British Foreign Secretary Anthony Eden in London. Both men were seasoned members of foreign service elites, which routinely discriminated against Jews. Intent on achieving military victory as soon as possible, they repeatedly turned aside bombing requests, arguing that the air forces could not spare resources from their military missions. There was an element of moral indifference as well. An eloquent plea from Jewish leader Chaim Weizmann elicited a rejection letter from Eden's Foreign Office that ended with tragic understatement: "I understand that this decision will be a disappointment to you, but be sure that the matter was considered exhaustively."

Tactically, however, the Allies had little reason to hesitate after 1943. The German air force could no longer muster much resistance. The Allies had sufficient planes to bomb the death camps without hindering the military campaign against Germany. And Allied refusal to commit heavy bombers to the mission because they would inevitably kill innocent people in the camps overlooked the reality that if nothing was done, all the inmates would die anyway. Auschwitz survivors recalled that they fervently prayed that Allied planes would bomb their hell into oblivion.

The U.S. Office of War Information avoided publicizing the death

Tragic Booty

In a shed not far from the bodies confounding Senator Barkley were these thousands of wedding rings. Nazis insisted that racial purity was their ideal goal. But the greed of jackals led them to strip these last marks of human affection from their victims.

National Archives.

camps, fearing that public accusations of genocide might inspire the Germans to prolong the war and cause more American casualties. Deprived of authoritative information to dispel widespread skepticism that death camps really existed, American newspapers relegated news of the Holocaust to the back pages. Even Supreme Court Justice Felix Frankfurter, a Jew and a veteran of fights against anti-Semitism, found the truth incomprehensible. After a member of the Polish underground gave him a detailed account of mass murder in Poland, Frankfurter denied the information as beyond the realm of possibility. "I did not say

this young man is lying," he explained. "I said I cannot believe him. There is a difference." At least once, though, the will to disbelieve wavered. Leon Kubowitski of the World Jewish Congress, after repeatedly being rebuffed by false arguments masquerading as "technical reasons" for not intervening, had a tense meeting with Assistant Secretary McCloy in December 1944. Kubowitski recalled that McCloy took him aside and asked anxiously, "Tell me the truth. Do you really believe that all those horrible things happened?"

By then it was too late. The death camps and their skeletal survivors were finally liberated by Allied armies in the spring of 1945. The Nazi captors fled after trying to hide their crimes against humanity by wrecking the gas chambers and crematoria. Before then, the only destruction of the camps' killing equipment had been carried out by the prisoners themselves. In the fall of 1944, four women prisoners smuggled dynamite from the munitions plant at Auschwitz to men assigned to remove ashes from the crematoria. The men managed to blow up one of the furnaces and kill several Nazi guards. Immediately, the Germans hanged the women and had the men shot. Their heroic acts were unknown to the Allied officials who chose not to send bombers to aid the doomed victims of Nazi mass murder.

the Red Army occupied as it rolled back the still-potent German Wehrmacht. Stalin agreed to enter the war against Japan once Germany finally surrendered, in effect promising to open a second front in the Pacific theater. Roosevelt and Churchill promised that they would at last launch a massive second-front assault in northern France. Code-named Overlord, the offensive was scheduled to begin in May 1944 with the combined manpower of four million Americans massed in England along with fourteen divisions from Britain, three from Canada, and one each from Poland and France.

General Eisenhower was assigned overall command of Allied forces, who assembled mountains of supplies that allowed each American GI to fight in Europe supported by 45 pounds of supplies a day, compared to 20 pounds per day for British soldiers and about 4 or 5 pounds for German combatants. German defenders, directed by General Erwin Rommel, fortified the cliffs and mined the beaches of northwestern France. But the huge deployment of Hitler's armies in the east trying to halt the Red Army's westward offensive left too few German troops to stop the millions of Allied soldiers waiting in

England. More decisive, years of Allied air raids had decimated the German Luftwaffe, which could send aloft only 300 fighter planes against 12,000 Allied aircraft.

Diversionary bombing and false radio messages about armies that in fact did not exist encouraged the Germans to expect an Allied invasion at the Pas de Calais area, where the English Channel is narrowest. The actual invasion site was 300 miles away on the beaches of Normandy (Map 25.4). After frustrating delays caused by stormy weather, Eisenhower launched the largest amphibious assault in world history on D Day, June 6, 1944. After paratroopers dropped behind German lines, Allied landing craft hit the Normandy beaches under cover of ferocious naval and air

D Day Invasion
"Taxi to Hell—and Back" is what Robert Sargent called his photograph of the D Day invasion of Normandy on June 6, 1944. Amid a dense fleet of landing craft, men lucky enough to have made it through rough seas and enemy fire struggle onto the beach to open a second front in Europe. The majority of soldiers in this first wave were cut down by enemy fire from the high cliffs beyond the beach.
Library of Congress.

MAP 25.4 The European Theater of World War II, 1942–1945
Russian reversal of the German offensive by breaking the sieges of Stalingrad and Leningrad, combined with Allied landings in North Africa and Normandy, placed Germany in a closing vise of armies from all sides.

READING THE MAP: By 1942, what nations or parts of nations in Europe were under Axis control? What nations had been absorbed before the war? What nations remained neutral, and what nations were members of the Allies?

CONNECTIONS: What were the three fronts in the European theater? When did the Allies initiate actions in each of them, and why did Churchill, Stalin, and Roosevelt disagree on the timing of the opening of these fronts?

FOR MORE HELP ANALYZING THIS MAP, see the map activity for this chapter in the Online Study Guide at bedfordstmartins.com/roark.

bombardment. Rough seas and deadly fire from German machine guns slowed the assault, but Allied paratroopers attacked German defenses from the rear, and rangers scaled the beachfront cliffs to knock out enemy gun emplacements and finally secure the beachhead.

Within a week, an avalanche of soldiers, tanks, and other military equipment rolled across the Normandy beaches and propelled Allied forces toward Germany. On August 25, the Allies liberated Paris from four years of Nazi occupation. Allied forces entered Germany on September 12, and in October they captured the city of Aachen. As the giant pincers of the Allied and Soviet armies closed on Germany in December 1944, Hitler ordered a counterattack to capture the Allies' essential supply port at Antwerp, Belgium. In the Battle of the Bulge (December 16, 1944–January 31, 1945), as the Allies termed it, German forces drove fifty-five miles into Allied lines before being stopped at Bastogne. More than 70,000 Allied soldiers were killed, including more Americans than in any other battle of the war. But the Nazis lost 100,000 men and hundreds of tanks, fatally depleting Hitler's reserves.

In February 1945, while Allied armies relentlessly pushed German forces backward, Churchill, Stalin, and Roosevelt met secretly at Yalta, a Russian resort town on the Black Sea, to discuss the plans for the postwar future. Seriously ill and noticeably frail, Roosevelt managed to secure Stalin's promise to permit votes of self-determination by people in the eastern European countries occupied by the Red Army. The Allies pledged to support Chiang Kai-shek as the leader of China. The Soviet Union obtained a role in the postwar government of Korea and Manchuria in exchange for entering the war against Japan after the defeat of Germany.

The "Big Three" also agreed on the creation of a new international peacekeeping organization, the United Nations (UN). All nations would have a place in the UN's General Assembly, but the Security Council would wield decisive power, and its permanent representatives from the Allied powers—China, France, Great Britain, the Soviet Union, and the

> Within a week of D Day, an avalanche of soldiers, tanks, and other military equipment rolled across the Normandy beaches and propelled Allied forces toward Germany.

United States—would possess a veto over UN actions. American response to the creation of the UN reflected the triumph of internationalism during the nation's mobilization for war. The Senate ratified the United Nations Charter in July 1945 by a vote of 89 to 2.

While Allied armies sped toward Berlin, Allied war planes bombed German roads, bridges, rail lines, war plants, and cities, dropping more bombs after D Day than in all previous European bombing raids combined. In February 1945, Allied bombers rained a firestorm of death and destruction on Berlin and Dresden, killing 60,000 civilians. By April 11, Allied armies sweeping in from the west reached the banks of the Elbe River, the agreed-upon rendezvous with the Red Army, and paused while the Soviets smashed into Berlin. In three weeks of vicious house-to-house fighting, the Red Army pulverized German defenses and captured Berlin on May 2. Hitler committed suicide on April 30, and on May 7 a provisional German government surrendered unconditionally. The war in Europe was finally over, for which 135,576 American soldiers, nearly 250,000 British troops, and 9 million Russian combatants had sacrificed their lives.

Roosevelt did not live to witness the end of the war. On April 12, while resting in Warm Springs, Georgia, the president suffered a fatal stroke. Americans grieved for the man who had led them through years of depression and world war, and they worried aloud about his successor, Vice President Harry Truman, who would have to steer the nation to victory over Japan and protect American interests in the postwar world.

The Defeat of Japan

At the outset of the war, Japan intended to use its navy to shield its economic empire in China and Southeast Asia. Instead, after the punishing defeats in the Coral Sea and at Midway, Japan had to quell renewed resistance on the Asian mainland and to fend off Allied naval and air attacks. In 1943 British and American forces, along with Indian and Chinese allies, launched an offensive against Japanese outposts in southern Asia, pushing through Burma and into China, where the armies of Chiang Kai-shek continued to resist conquest. In the Pacific, Americans and their allies attacked Japanese strongholds by sea, air, and land, moving island by island toward the Japanese homeland (Map 25.5).

> In the Pacific, Americans and their allies attacked Japanese strongholds by sea, air, and land, moving island by island toward the Japanese homeland.

Yalta Conference

In February 1945, President Roosevelt and British prime minister Winston Churchill met with Russian leader Joseph Stalin at the Black Sea resort of Yalta to plan the postwar reconstruction of Europe. Roosevelt, near the end of his life, and Churchill, soon to suffer reelection defeat, look weary next to the resolute "Man of Steel." Controversy would later arise over whether a stronger stand by the American and British leaders could have prevented the Soviet Union from imposing Communist rule on Eastern Europe.

U.S. Army.

The island-hopping campaign began in August 1942 when American marines landed on Guadalcanal in the southern Pacific, where the Japanese were constructing an airfield. For the next six months, a savage battle raged for control of the strategic area. Finally, during the night of February 7, 1943, Japanese forces withdrew. The terrible losses on both sides indicated to the marines how costly it would be to defeat Japan.

In mid-1943, American, Australian, and New Zealand forces launched offensives in New Guinea and the Solomon Islands that gradually secured the South Pacific. In the Central Pacific, amphibious forces conquered the Gilbert and Marshall Islands, which served as forward bases for decisive air assaults on the Japanese home islands. As the Allies attacked island after island, Japanese soldiers were ordered to refuse to surrender no matter how hopeless their plight. At Tarawa, a barren coral island of less than three square miles, three thousand Japanese defenders battled American marines for three days, killing

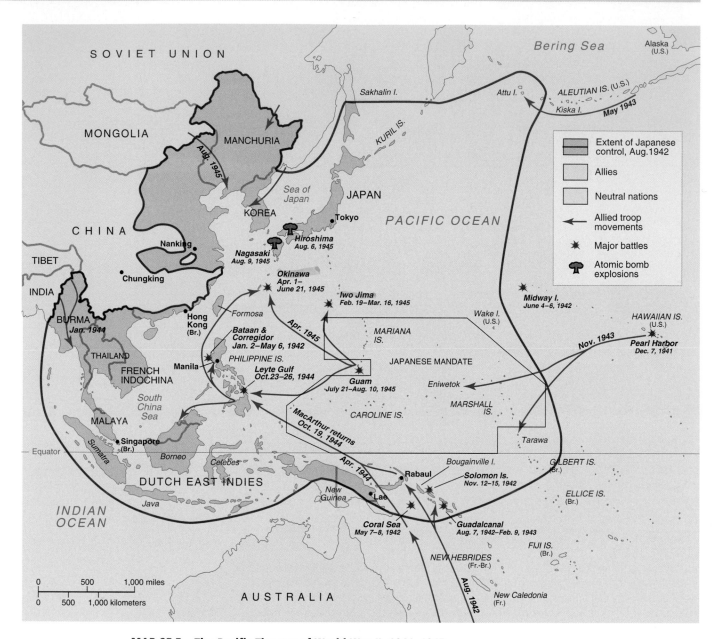

MAP 25.5   The Pacific Theater of World War II, 1941–1945
To drive the Japanese from their far-flung empire, the Allies launched two combined naval and military offensives—one to recapture the Philippines and then
attack Japanese forces in China, the other to hop from island to island in the
Central Pacific toward the Japanese mainland.

READING THE MAP: What was the extent of Japanese control up until August 1942?
Which nations in the Pacific theater sided with the Allies? Which nations remained
neutral?

CONNECTIONS: Describe the economic and military motivations behind the Japanese
domination of the region. How and when did they achieve this dominance? Judging from this map, what strategic and geographic concerns might immediately
have prompted Truman and his advisers to consider using the atomic bomb
against Japan?

FOR MORE HELP ANALYZING THIS MAP, see the map activity for this chapter in the
Online Study Guide at bedfordstmartins.com/roark.

a thousand marines and wounding two thousand until the seventeen Japanese survivors finally succumbed. Such fierce Japanese resistance spurred remorseless Allied attacks on Japanese-occupied islands, usually begun with air and naval bombardment, followed by amphibious landings by marines, and grinding, inch-by-inch combat to root Japanese fighters out of bunkers and caves with grenades, flamethrowers, and anything else at hand.

While the island-hopping campaign kept pressure on Japanese forces, the Allies invaded the Philippines in the fall of 1944. In the three-day Battle of Leyte Gulf, the greatest naval encounter in world history, the American fleet crushed the Japanese armada, clearing the way for Allied victory in the Philippines. While the Philippine campaign was under way, American forces captured two crucial islands from which they planned to launch an attack on the Japanese homeland—Iwo Jima, 750 miles from Japan, and Okinawa, only 370 miles from Tokyo. To defend Okinawa and prevent the American invaders from getting within close bombing range of their home islands, Japanese leaders ordered thousands of suicide pilots, known as *kamikaze*, to crash their bomb-laden planes into Allied ships. Like airborne torpedoes, kamikaze dived into American ships, causing fearsome destruction. But instead of destroying the American fleet, the

---

Marine Pinned Down on Saipan

Over 100,000 American GIs assaulted the Japanese garrison of 32,000 on Saipan in the Mariana Island chain in mid-June 1944. The Japanese fought to their deaths against overwhelming odds, prolonging the battle for nearly a month and inflicting 14,000 casualties on the American troops. The intensity of the fighting is visible on the face of the marine shown here. More than a thousand Japanese civilians, mostly women and children, rushed to the edge of a 200-foot cliff and committed suicide by leaping onto the rocks below to avoid surrendering. The suicidal defenses of the Japanese on Saipan persuaded American military planners that the final assault on the Japanese homeland would cause hundreds of thousands of American casualties.

Marine Corps Photo, National Archives.

Major Campaigns and Battles of World War II, 1939–1945

September 1, 1939	Germany attacks Poland.
September 3, 1939	Britain and France declare war on Germany.
April 1940	Germany attacks Denmark and Norway.
May 1940	Germany invades Netherlands, Belgium, Luxembourg, and France.
June 1940	Italy joins Germany in the war against the Allies.
June–November 1940	Battle of Britain.
June 22, 1941	Germany invades Soviet Union.
December 7, 1941	Japan attacks Pearl Harbor.
December 8, 1941	U.S. Congress declares war on Japan.
December 11, 1941	Germany and Italy declare war on the United States.
January 2–May 6, 1942	Battles of Bataan and Corregidor.
May 7–8, 1942	Battle of the Coral Sea.
June 3–6, 1942	Battle of Midway.
August 21, 1942–January 31, 1943	Battle of Stalingrad.
August 1942–February 1943	Battle for Guadalcanal.
October 1942	British halt Germans at Battle of El-Alamein.
November 1942–May 1943	Allies mount North African campaign.
July 10, 1943	Allies begin Italian invasion through Sicily.
June 1944	Allies liberate Rome from German occupation.
June 6, 1944	D Day—Allied forces invade Normandy.
August 25, 1944	Allies liberate Paris.
September 12, 1944	Allies enter Germany.
October 23–26, 1944	Battle for Leyte Gulf.
December 16, 1944–January 31, 1945	Battle of the Bulge.
February 19–March 16, 1945	Battle of Iwo Jima.
April 1–June 21, 1945	Battle of Okinawa.
May 2, 1945	Soviet forces capture Berlin.
August 6, 1945	United States drops atomic bomb on Hiroshima.
August 9, 1945	United States drops atomic bomb on Nagasaki.

kamikaze demolished the last vestige of the Japanese air force. By June 1945, the Japanese were nearly defenseless on sea and in the air. Still, their leaders prepared to fight to the death for their homeland.

Atomic Warfare

In mid-July 1945, as Allied forces were preparing for the final assault on Japan, American scientists tested a secret weapon at an isolated desert site near Los Alamos, New Mexico. In 1942, Roosevelt had authorized the top-secret Manhattan Project to find a way to convert nuclear energy into a superbomb before the Germans added such a weapon to their arsenal. More than 100,000 Americans, led by scientists, engineers, and military officers at Los Alamos, worked frantically at thirty-seven secret locations across the country to win the fateful race for an atomic bomb. Germany surrendered two and a half months before the first test on July 16, 1945, when scientists witnessed an awesome explosion equivalent to hundreds of tons of TNT that sent a mushroom cloud of debris eight miles into the atmosphere.

A delegation of scientists and officials, troubled by the bomb's destructive force, secretly proposed that the United States give a public demonstration of the bomb's cataclysmic power, hoping to persuade Japan's leaders to surrender. With the Japanese incapable of offensive action and blockaded by the Allied fleet, proponents of a demonstration were encouraged because Japanese emissaries were already putting out feelers about peace negotiations. But U.S. government officials quickly rejected such a demonstration: Americans had enough nuclear material for only three bombs, the demonstration bomb might fail to explode, and the Japanese might not surrender even if it did. Also, despite numerous defeats, Japan still had more than 6 million reserves at home fortified by over 5,000 kamikaze aircraft stockpiled for a last-ditch defense against the anticipated Allied assault, which U.S. military advisers estimated would cost the lives of at least 250,000 Americans.

President Truman heard about the successful bomb test at Los Alamos when he was in Potsdam, Germany, negotiating with Stalin about postwar issues. Truman vaguely mentioned to Stalin that the United States had a powerful new weapon, but, Truman wrote later, "The Russian premier showed no special interest. All he said was that he was glad to hear it and hoped we would make 'good use of it against the Japanese.'" Truman realized that the atomic bomb could hasten the end of the war with Japan, perhaps before the Russians could attack the Japanese in Korea and Manchuria, as Stalin pledged at Yalta to do. Within a few months after the defeat of Germany, Truman also recognized that the bomb gave the United States a devastating atomic **monopoly** that could be used to counter Soviet ambitions and advance American interests in the postwar world.

Truman, who had been a commander of combat troops on the ground in World War I, saw no reason not to use the atomic bomb against Japan if doing so would save American lives. But first he issued an ultimatum: Japan must surrender unconditionally or face utter ruin. When the Japanese failed to respond by the deadline, Truman ordered that a bomb be dropped on a Japanese city not already heavily damaged by American raids. On August 6, Colonel Paul Tibbets piloted the *Enola Gay* over Hiroshima and released an atomic bomb, leveling the city and incinerating 78,000 people. Three days later, after the Japanese government still refused to surrender, Tibbets-trained airmen dropped a second atomic bomb on Nagasaki, killing more than 100,000 civilians.

At last, a peace faction took control of the Japanese government, and with American assurance that the emperor could retain his throne

Hiroshima Bombing
This rare shot taken by a news photographer in Hiroshima immediately after the atomic bomb exploded on August 6, 1945, suggests the shock and incomprehension that survivors later described as their first reaction. On August 9, another atomic bomb created similar devastation in Nagasaki.
UN photo.

after the Allies took over, Japan surrendered on August 14. On a troop ship departing from Europe for what would have been the final assault on Japan, an American soldier spoke for millions of others when he heard the wonderful news that the killing was over: "We are going to grow to adulthood after all."

Conclusion: Allied Victory and America's Emergence as a Superpower

Shortly after Pearl Harbor, Hitler pronounced America "a decayed country" without "much future," a country "half Judaized, and the other half Negrified," a country "where everything is built on the dollar" and bound to fall apart. American mobilization for World War II disproved Hitler's arrogant prophecy, as Paul Tibbets's historic flight dramatized. At a cost of 405,399 American lives, the nation united with its allies to battle Axis aggressors in Europe and Asia and eventually to crush them into unconditional surrender. Almost all Americans believed they had won a "good war" against totalitarian evil. The Allies saved Asia and Europe from enslavement and finally halted the Nazis' genocidal campaign against Jews and others whom the Nazis considered inferior. To secure human rights and protect the world against future wars, the Roosevelt administration took the lead in creating the United Nations.

Wartime production lifted the nation out of the Great Depression. The gross national product soared to four times what it had been when Roosevelt became president in 1933. Jobs in defense industries eliminated chronic unemployment, provided wages for millions of women workers and African American migrants from southern farms, and boosted Americans' prosperity. Ahead stretched the challenge of maintaining that prosperity while reintegrating millions of uniformed men and women coming home from overseas.

By the end of the war, the United States had emerged as a global superpower. Wartime mobilization made the American economy the strongest in the world, buttressed by the military clout of the nation's nuclear monopoly. While the war left much of the world a smoldering wasteland, the American mainland enjoyed immunity from attack. The Japanese occupation of China left 50 million people without homes and millions more dead, maimed, and orphaned. The German offensive against the Soviet Union killed more than 26 million Russian soldiers and civilians. Germany and Japan lay in ruins, their economies as shattered as their military forces. The Allies killed more than 4 million Nazi soldiers and over 1.2 million Japanese combatants, as well as hundreds of thousands of civilians. But in the gruesome balance sheet of war, the Axis powers inflicted far more grief, misery, and destruction upon the global victims of their aggression than they suffered in return.

As the dominant western nation in the postwar world, the United States asserted leadership in the reconstruction of Europe while occupying Japan and overseeing its economic and political recovery. America soon confronted new challenges in the tense aftermath of the war, as Soviets seized political control of Eastern Europe, a Communist revolution swept China, and national liberation movements emerged in the colonial empires of Britain and France. The surrender of the Axis powers ended the battles of World War II, but the forces unleashed by the war shaped the United States and the rest of the world for decades to come.

FOR ADDITIONAL FIRSTHAND ACCOUNTS OF THIS PERIOD, see Chapter 25 in Michael Johnson, ed., *Reading the American Past*, Third Edition.

TO ASSESS YOUR MASTERY OF THE MATERIAL IN THIS CHAPTER, see the Online Study Guide at bedfordstmartins.com/roark.

FOR WEB LINKS RELATED TO TOPICS IN THIS CHAPTER, see "HistoryLinks," "DocLinks," and "PlaceLinks" at bedfordstmartins.com/roark.

CHRONOLOGY

1933
- Adolf Hitler becomes chancellor of Germany.
- United States formally recognizes Soviet Union.

1935–1937
- Congress seeks to shield America from world conflicts with neutrality acts.

1936
- Nazi Germany occupies Rhineland.
- Mussolini's fascist Italian regime conquers Ethiopia.
- Civil war breaks out in Spain.

1937
- Japanese troops capture Nanking.
- Roosevelt delivers speech urging U.S. "quarantine" against aggressor nations.

1938
- Hitler annexes Austria.
- British prime minister Neville Chamberlain meets with Hitler in Munich and agrees to German seizure of Sudetenland in Czechoslovakia.

1939
- German troops occupy remainder of Czechoslovakia without resistance.
- Nazi Germany and Soviet Union sign nonaggression pact.
- **September 1.** Germany's attack on Poland begins World War II.
- United States and Great Britain conclude cash-and-carry agreement for arms sales.

1940
- **May–June.** British troops evacuated at Dunkirk, France.
- **June.** German occupation of France begins.
- Roosevelt elected to a third term; defeats Wendell Willkie.

1941
- Lend-Lease Act enables Britain to obtain war materiel from United States on credit.
- **June.** Germany invades Soviet Union.
- **August.** Atlantic Charter devised by Roosevelt and Allies to guarantee human and international freedoms after war.

- **December 7.** Japanese launch surprise attack on Pearl Harbor; United States declares war on Japan.

1942
- Japan captures Philippines.
- Civil rights activists found Congress of Racial Equality (CORE).
- U.S. navy scores its first major victories in Battle of Coral Sea and at Midway.
- Roosevelt authorizes top-secret Manhattan Project.
- **November.** U.S. forces invade North Africa.
- Roosevelt authorizes internment of Japanese Americans.

1943
- Allied leaders agree that war will end only with unconditional surrender of Axis forces.
- "Zoot suit" riots occur in Los Angeles.
- U.S. forces invade Sicily.

1944
- **June 6.** Combined Allied army stages successful D Day landing at Normandy.
- Roosevelt elected to a fourth term; defeats Thomas E. Dewey.

1945
- Churchill, Roosevelt, and Stalin meet at Yalta to plan reconstruction of Europe after defeat of Germany.
- **April 12.** Roosevelt dies, and Vice President Harry Truman becomes president.
- **April 30.** Hitler commits suicide.
- **May 7.** Germany surrenders.
- **July.** U.S. Senate ratifies United Nations Charter, and U.S. tenure as a permanent member of the Security Council begins.
- **August 6.** United States drops atomic bomb on Hiroshima.

- **August 9.** United States drops atomic bomb on Nagasaki.
- **August 14.** Japan surrenders, ending World War II.

BIBLIOGRAPHY

General Works

Michael Beschloss, *The Conquerors: Roosevelt, Truman, and the Destruction of Hitler's Germany, 1941–1945* (2002).

Kenneth S. Davis, *FDR: Into the Storm, 1937–1940* (1993).

Kenneth S. Davis, *FDR: The War President, 1940–1943* (2000).

Thomas Fleming, *The New Dealers' War: Franklin D. Roosevelt and the War within World War II* (2001).

Martin Folly, *The U.S. and World War II: The Awakening Giant* (2002).

Paul Fussell, *Wartime* (1989).

Akira Iriye, *The Origins of the Second World War in Asia and the Pacific* (1987).

John Keegan, *The Second World War* (1989).

David M. Kennedy, *Freedom from Fear: The American People in Depression and War, 1929–1945* (1999).

Richard Ketchum, *The Borrowed Years, 1938–1941: America on the Way to War* (1989).

Eric Larrabee, *Commander in Chief: Franklin Delano Roosevelt, His Lieutenants, and Their War* (1987).

Jon Meacham, *Franklin and Winston: An Intimate Portrait of an Epic Friendship* (2003).

Michael S. Sherry, *In the Shadow of War: The United States since the 1930s* (1995).

Studs Terkel, *"The Good War": An Oral History of World War II* (1984).

Paul W. Tibbets Jr., *The Tibbets Story* (1978).

Gerhard Weinberg, *World at Arms: A Global History of World War II* (1994).

Foreign Policy

Tokomo Akami, *Internationalizing the Pacific: The U.S., Japan, and the Institute of Pacific Relations in War and Peace, 1919–1945* (2002).

Wayne S. Cole, *Roosevelt and the Isolationists, 1932–1945* (1983).

Thomas Connell, *America's Japanese Hostages: The World War II Plan for a Japanese-Free Latin America* (2002).

Robert Dallek, *Franklin D. Roosevelt and American Foreign Policy, 1932–1945* (1979).

Robert A. Divine, *The Illusion of Neutrality* (1982).

Max Paul Friedman, *Nazis and Good Neighbors: The U.S. Campaign against the Germans of Latin America in World War II* (2003).

Erwin F. Gellman, *Good Neighbor Diplomacy: United States Policies in Latin America, 1933–1945* (1979).

Waldo Heinrichs, *Threshold of War: Franklin D. Roosevelt and American Entry into World War II* (1988).

Robert Hilderbrand, *Dumbarton Oaks: The Origins of the United Nations and the Search for Postwar Security* (1990).

Akira Iriye, *The Globalizing of America, 1913–1945* (1995).

Walter LaFeber, *Inevitable Revolutions* (1983).

Robert Franklin Maddox, *The War within World War II: The U.S. and International Cartels* (2001).

Frederick W. Marks, *Wind over Sand: The Diplomacy of Franklin Roosevelt* (1988).

James McAllister, *No Exit: America and the German Problem, 1943–1954* (2002).

J. Robert Moskin, *Mr. Truman's War: The Final Victories of World War II and the Birth of the Postwar World* (2002).

David Reynolds, *From Munich to Pearl Harbor: Roosevelt's America and the Origins of the Second World War* (2001).

David F. Schmitz, *The United States and Fascist Italy, 1922–1944* (1988).

Gaddis Smith, *American Diplomacy during the Second World War, 1941–1945* (1985).

Geoffrey S. Smith, *To Save a Nation: American "Extremism," the New Deal, and the Coming of WW II* (1992).

Jonathan Utley, *Going to War with Japan, 1937–1942* (1985).

Andrew J. Whitfield, *Hong Kong, Empire, and the Anglo-American Alliance at War, 1941–1945* (2001).

Mobilization and the Home Front

Karen Anderson, *Wartime Women: Sex Roles, Family Relations, and the Status of Women during World War II* (1981).

D'Ann Campbell, *Women at War with America: Private Lives in a Patriotic Era* (1984).

Stephanie A. Carpenter, *On the Farm Front: The Women's Land Army in World War II* (2003).

Steven Casey, *Cautious Crusade: FDR, American Public Opinion and the War against Nazi Germany* (2001).

Michael Dobbs, *The Saboteurs: The Nazi Raid on America* (2004).

Daniel R. Ernst and Victor Jew, *Total War and the Law: The American Home Front in World War II* (2002).

Mark Jonathan Harris, Franklin D. Mitchell, and Steve J. Schechter, *The Home Front: America during World War II* (1985).

Susan Hartmann, *The Home Front and Beyond: American Women in the 1940s* (1982).

John Earl Haynes and Harvey Klehr, *Verona: Decoding Soviet Espionage in America* (1999).

John W. Jeffries, *Wartime America: The World War II Home Front* (1996).

Nelson Lichtenstein, *Labor's War at Home: The CIO in World War II* (1983).

Gerald D. Nash, *The American West Transformed: The Impact of the Second World War* (1985).

William L. O'Neill, *A Democracy at War: America's Fight at Home and Abroad in World War II* (1993).

Geoffrey Perret, *Days of Sadness, Years of Triumph: The American People, 1939–1945* (1985).

Ruth Sarles, *A Story of America First: The Men and Women Who Opposed U.S. Intervention in World War II* (2003).

William Tuttle, *Daddy's Gone to War: The Second World War in the Lives of America's Children* (1993).

Brian Waddell, *The War against the New Deal: World War II and American Democracy* (2001).

Military Organization and Campaigns

Gar Alperovitz, *The Decision to Use the Atomic Bomb and the Architecture of an American Myth* (1995).

Stephen E. Ambrose, *D-Day, June 6, 1944* (1994).

Anthony Beevor, *Stalingrad* (1998).

Anthony Beevor, *The Fall of Berlin, 1945* (2002).

Allan Berube, *Coming Out under Fire: The History of Gay Men and Women in World War Two* (1990).

Paul S. Boyer, *By the Bomb's Early Light: American Thought and Culture at the Dawn of the Atomic Age* (1985).

Richard Breitman, *Official Secrets: What the Nazis Planned, What the British and Americans Knew* (1998).

John Costello, *Virtue under Fire: How World War II Changed Our Social and Sexual Attitudes* (1986).

Gavan Daws, *Prisoners of the Japanese: POWs of World War II* (1992).

John Dower, *War without Mercy: Race and Power in the Pacific War* (1986).

Gordon A. Harrison, *Cross-Channel Attack* (2002).

D. Clayton James, *A Time for Giants: The Politics of the American High Command in World War II* (1987).

Dan Kurzman, *Day of the Bomb: Countdown to Hiroshima* (1986).

Robert Leckie, *Delivered from Evil: The Saga of World War II* (1987).

Gerald F. Linderman, *The World within War: America's Combat Experience in World War II* (1997).

Tim Maga, *America Attacks Japan: The Invasion That Never Was* (2002).

Evelyn M. Monahan and Rosemary Neidel-Greenlee, *And If I Perish: Frontline U.S. Army Nurses in World War II* (2003).

Michael Neufeld and Michael Berenbaum, *The Bombing of Auschwitz: Should the Allies Have Attempted It?* (2000).

Mark P. Parillo, *We Were in the Big One: Experiences of the World War II Generation* (2002).

Geoffrey Perret, *Winged Victory: The Army Air Forces in World War II* (1993).

Joseph Persico, *Roosevelt's Secret War: FDR and World War II Espionage* (2001).

Gordon W. Prange, *At Dawn We Slept* (1981).

Richard Rhodes, *The Making of the Atomic Bomb* (1986).

Ronald Schaffer, *Wings of Judgment: American Bombing in World War II* (1988).

Michael Schaller, *Douglas MacArthur: The Far Eastern General* (1989).

Peter Schrijvers, *The GI War against Japan: American Soldiers in Asia and the Pacific during World War II* (2002).

Michael S. Sherry, *The Rise of American Air Power: The Creation of Armageddon* (1987).

Ronald H. Spector, *Eagle against the Sun: The American War with Japan* (1985).

Murray Williamson and Allan R. Millett, *A War to Be Won: Fighting the Second World War, 1937–1945* (2000).

Thomas W. Zeiler, *Unconditional Defeat: Japan, America and the End of World War II* (2004).

Race and Minorities

Gerald Astor, *The Right to Fight: A History of African Americans in the Military* (1998).

Alison R. Bernstein, *American Indians and World War II: Toward a New Era in Indian Affairs* (1991).

Jeffrey F. Burton et al., *Confinement and Ethnicity: An Overview of World War II Japanese American Relocation Sites* (2002).

David P. Colley, *Blood for Dignity: The Story of the First Integrated Combat Unit in the U.S. Army* (2003).

Roger Daniels, *Concentration Camps: North American Japanese in the United States and Canada during World War II* (1971, 1989).

Jere Bishop Franco, *Crossing the Pond: The Native American Effort in World War II* (1999).

Peter H. Irons, *Justice at War: The Story of the Japanese American Internment Cases* (1983).

Daniel Kryder, *Divided Arsenal: Race and the American State during World War II* (2000).

Steven F. Lawson, *Running for Freedom: Civil Rights and Black Politics in America since 1941* (1991).

Brenda L. Moore, *Serving Our Country: Japanese American Women in the Military during World War II* (2003).

Bernard C. Nalty, *Strength for the Fight: A History of Black Americans in the Military* (1989).

Wendy Ng, *Japanese American Internment during World War II* (2002).

Page Smith, *Democracy on Trial: The Japanese American Evacuation and Relocation in World War II* (1995).

Ronald Takaki, *Strangers from a Different Shore: A History of Asian Americans* (1989).

Depicting the War

M. Joyce Baker, *Images of Women on Film: The War Years* (1981).

Thomas Doherty, *Projections of War: Hollywood, American Culture, and World War II* (1993).

Gerd Horten, *Radio Goes to War: The Cultural Politics of Propaganda during World War II* (2002).

Karal Ann Marling and John Wetenhall, *Iwo Jima: Monuments, Memories, and the American Hero* (1991).

Peter Maslowski, *Armed with Cameras: The American Military Photographers of World War II* (1993).

George H. Roeder Jr., *The Censored War: American Visual Experience during World War II* (1993).

Emily S. Rosenberg, *A Day Which Will Live: Pearl Harbor in American Memory* (2003).

Holly Cowan Shulman, *The Voice of America: Propaganda and Democracy, 1941–1945* (1991).

Michael S. Sweeney, *Secrets of Victory: The Office of Censorship and the American Press and Radio in World War II* (2001).

Frederick S. Voss, *Reporting the War: The Journalistic Coverage of World War II* (1994).

America and the Holocaust

Robert Abzug, *Inside the Vicious Heart: Americans and the Liberation of Nazi Concentration Camps* (1987).

Richard Breitman and Alan Kraut, *American Refugee Policy and European Jewry* (1987).

Lucy Dawidowicz, *The War against the Jews, 1933–1945* (1986).

Leonard Dinnerstein, *America and the Survivors of the Holocaust* (1982).

Deborah E. Lipstadt, *Beyond Belief: The American Press and the Coming of the Holocaust, 1933–1945* (1986).

Verne W. Newton, *FDR and the Holocaust* (1995).

Peter Novick, *The Holocaust in American Life* (1999).

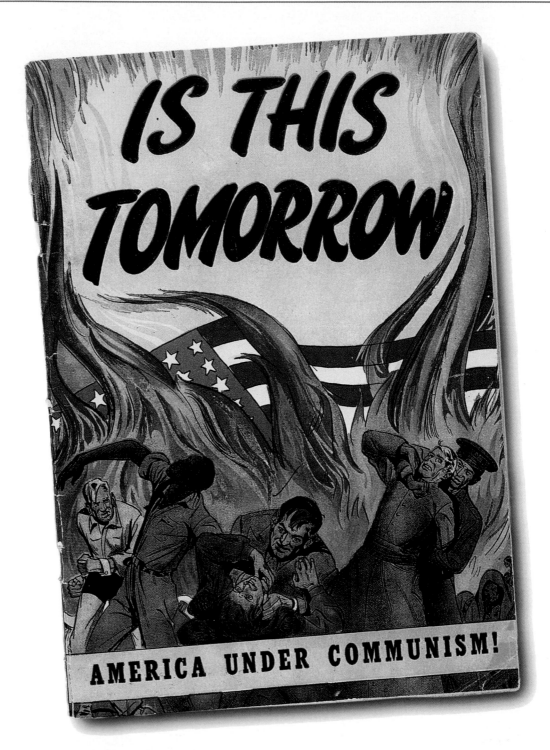

COLD WAR COMIC BOOK
Americans barely had time to celebrate the Allied victory in World War II when they perceived a new threat, posed by the Soviet Union. Fear of communism dominated much of postwar American life and politics, even invading popular culture. Four million copies of this comic book, published by a religious organization in 1947, painted a terrifying picture of what would happen to Americans if the Soviets took over the country. Such takeover stories appeared in movies, cartoons, and magazines as well as in other comic books.
Collection of Charles H. Christensen.

26

Cold War Politics in the Truman Years

1945–1953

O N NOVEMBER 5, 1946, President Harry S. Truman, his wife, and his daughter boarded the train back to Washington from Truman's hometown, Independence, Missouri, where they had gone to vote in the congressional elections. During the campaigns, Republicans had blasted Truman as incapable of dealing with economic problems and the threat of **communism**. Campaign slogans had jeered, "To Err is Truman," while the president's approval rating sank to a mere 32 percent. Many Democratic candidates had avoided mentioning his name and instead used recordings of the late Franklin Roosevelt's voice to stir voters. Playing poker with reporters on the train as the returns came in, Truman appeared unconcerned. But the results were devastating: The Republicans captured both the House and the Senate by substantial majorities, dominating Congress for the first time since 1932.

When Truman arrived in Washington at the lowest point of his presidency, only one member of his administration showed up to greet him, Undersecretary of State Dean Acheson. Acheson's gesture signaled a developing relationship of central importance to the two men and to postwar history. The fifty-three-year-old Acheson shared most of Truman's political principles, though their backgrounds differed sharply. Acheson had enjoyed an upper-class education at a private prep school, Yale University, and Harvard Law School. After clerking for Supreme Court Justice Louis Brandeis, he earned a comfortable living as a corporate lawyer. In contrast, Truman, the son of a Missouri farmer, had not attended college and had failed in a business venture before entering local politics in the 1920s.

Despite his wealth and privilege, Acheson supported much of the **New Deal** and staunchly defended organized labor. He spoke out against **isolationism** in the 1930s, and in 1941 he accepted President Roosevelt's offer of a job at the State Department. Shortly after Truman became president, the supremely confident Acheson wrote privately about shortcomings in Truman's "judgment and wisdom that the limitations of his experience produce," but he also found the fledgling president "straightforward, decisive, simple, entirely honest," a man who "will learn fast and will inspire confidence." In June 1947, Acheson left the State Department, but Truman lured him back in 1949 to be secretary of state during the president's second term. Acheson appreciated Truman's willingness to make tough decisions and admiringly noted that Truman's "ego never came between him and his job." Truman cherished Acheson's abiding loyalty, calling him "my good right hand."

■ **From the Grand Alliance to Containment**
The Cold War Begins
The Truman Doctrine and the Marshall Plan
Building a National Security State
Superpower Rivalry around the Globe

■ **Truman and the Fair Deal at Home**
Reconversion and the Postwar Economic Boom
Black and Mexican American Protest and the Politics of Civil Rights
The Fair Deal Flounders
The Domestic Chill: A Second Red Scare

■ **The Cold War Becomes Hot: Korea**
Korea and the Military Implementation of Containment
From Containment to Rollback to Containment
Korea, Communism, and the 1952 Election
An Armistice and the War's Costs

■ **Conclusion: The Cold War's Costs and Consequences**

Truman needed all the help he could get. The "accidental president" lacked the charisma, experience, and political skills with which Roosevelt had transformed both foreign and domestic policy, won four presidential elections, and forged a Democratic Party coalition that dominated national politics. Initially criticized and abandoned by many Roosevelt loyalists, Truman faced a resurgent Republican Party as well as revolts from within his own party. Besides addressing domestic problems that the New Deal had not solved—how to sustain economic growth and avoid another depression without the war to fuel the economy—Truman had to redefine the nation's foreign policy goals in a new international context.

Dean Acheson was instrumental in forging that foreign policy. As early as 1946, Acheson became convinced that the Soviet Union posed a major threat to U.S. security. With other officials, he helped to shape a policy designed to contain and thwart Soviet power wherever it threatened to spread. By 1947, a new term had been coined to describe the intense rivalry between the superpowers—**cold war**. The **containment** policy worked in Western Europe with the enunciation of the **Truman Doctrine**, implementation of the Marshall Plan, and creation of **NATO**; but communism spread in Asia, and at home a wave of anti-Communist hysteria erupted that harmed many Americans and stifled dissent and debate about U.S. policies.

As the preeminent foreign policy official, Acheson too reaped abuse from Republicans for being "soft on communism." At the height of the anti-Communist frenzy, Acheson received so much hate mail that guards were posted at his house. Yet he kept both his job and his sense of humor. When cab drivers asked him, "Aren't you Dean Acheson?" he would reply, "Yes. Do I have to get out?"

From the Grand Alliance to Containment

With victory over Japan in August 1945, Americans besieged the government for the return of their loved ones. Baby booties arrived at the White House with a note, "Please send my daddy home." Americans looked forward to the end of international crises and the dismantling of the large military establishment. They expected the Allies, led by the United States and working within the United Nations, to cooperate in the management of international peace. Postwar realities quickly dashed these expectations. A dangerous new threat seemed to arise as the wartime alliance forged by the United States, Great Britain, and the Soviet Union crumbled, and the United States began to develop the military and diplomatic means to contain the spread of Soviet power around the globe.

Dean Acheson
No individual had more to do with transforming America's role in the world after World War II than Dean Acheson, President Truman's closest foreign policy adviser. Acheson, shown here with Truman in 1945, criticized those who saw the cold war in black-and-white terms and communism as an evil that the United States could expel from the earth. Rather, he advocated that American leaders learn "to limit objectives, to get ourselves away from the search for the absolute, to find out what is within our powers."
Harry S. Truman Library.

The Cold War Begins

"The guys who came out of World War II were idealistic," reported Harold Russell, a young paratrooper who lost both hands in a training accident. "We felt the day had come when the wars were all over." Public opinion polls echoed the veterans' confidence in the promise of peace. But political leaders were less optimistic, especially Winston Churchill, who had always distrusted the Soviets. Once the Allies had overcome a common enemy, the prewar mistrust and antagonism between the Soviet Union and the West resurfaced over their very different visions of the postwar world.

The Western Allies' delay in opening a second front in Western Europe aroused Soviet suspicions during the war. The Soviet Union made supreme wartime sacrifices, losing more than twenty million citizens and vast portions of its agricultural and industrial capacity. At the war's end, Soviet leader Joseph Stalin wanted to make Germany pay for the rebuilding of the Soviet economy and to expand Soviet influence in the world. Above all, he wanted governments friendly to the Soviet Union on its borders in Eastern Europe, especially in Poland, through which Germany had attacked the Soviet Union twice within twenty-five years.

In contrast, enemy fire had never touched the mainland of the United States, and its 405,000 dead amounted to just 2 percent of the Soviet loss. With a vastly expanded productive capacity and a monopoly on atomic weapons, the United States emerged from the war the most powerful nation on the planet. That sheer power, along with U.S. economic interests, policymakers' understandings of how the recent war might have been avoided, and a sense that the United States had the best institutions and best intentions in the world, all affected how its leaders approached the Soviet Union in the aftermath of World War II.

Fearing a return of the depression, U.S. officials believed that a healthy economy depended on opportunities abroad. The United States needed access to raw materials, markets for its goods, and security for American investments overseas. These needs could be met best in countries with economic and political systems resembling its own, not in those where government controls interfered with the free flow of products and dollars. As Truman put it in 1947, "The American system can survive in America only if it becomes a world system."

Yet both leaders and citizens regarded their foreign policy not as a self-interested campaign to guarantee economic interests, but as the means to preserve national security and bring freedom, **democracy**, and capitalism to the rest of the world. Laura Briggs spoke for many Americans who believed "it was our destiny to prove that we were the children of God and that our way was right for the world."

Recent history also shaped postwar foreign policy. Americans believed that Britain, France, and the United States might have prevented World War II had they resisted rather than appeased Hitler's initial aggression. Secretary of the Navy James V. Forrestal, for example, argued against trying to "buy [the Soviets'] understanding and sympathy. We tried that once with Hitler." This "appeasement" analogy would be invoked time and again when the United States faced challenges to the international status quo.

> Once the Allies had overcome a common enemy, the prewar mistrust and antagonism between the Soviet Union and the West resurfaced over their very different visions of the postwar world.

The man with ultimate responsibility for U.S. policy was a keen student of history but came to the White House with little experience in international affairs. When Germany attacked the Soviet Union in 1941, then-senator Truman expressed his hope that the two would kill each other off. As president he envisioned Soviet-American cooperation, as long as the Soviet Union conformed with U.S. plans for the postwar world and restrained its expansionist impulses. Proud of his ability to make quick decisions, Truman was determined to be firm with the Soviets, knowing well that America's nuclear monopoly gave him the upper hand.

Soviet and American interests clashed first in Eastern Europe. Stalin insisted that the Allies' wartime agreements gave him a free hand in the countries defeated or liberated by the Red Army, just as the United States was unilaterally reconstructing governments in Italy and Japan. The Soviet dictator used harsh methods to install Communist governments in neighboring Poland and Bulgaria. Elsewhere, the Soviets initially tolerated non-Communist governments in Hungary and Czechoslovakia. And in the spring of 1946, Stalin responded to pressure from the West and removed troops from Iran on the Soviet Union's southwest border, allowing United States access to rich oil fields there.

Joseph Stalin: From Ally to Enemy
These two portrayals of the Soviet leader Joseph Stalin indicate how quickly
the World War II alliance disintegrated into the cold war. On the left in a
1944 issue of the popular magazine *Look,* Stalin is photographed with adoring schoolchildren.
The accompanying article depicts Stalin as an effective leader but also a sensitive man who
wrote poetry and loved literature. Only four years later, in 1948, *Look* published Stalin's life
story. The photo frames his face with communism's emblem, the hammer and sickle, which
symbolizes the alliance of workers and peasants. Whereas the 1944 piece had called Stalin a
"man of trenchant speech, indomitable will and extraordinary mental capacity [and] lover of
literature," the 1948 article emphasized his "rise to absolute power over millions of lives" and
depicted him as a "small man with drooping shoulders [who] tyrannizes one-fifth of the
world." What do these two items suggest about the role of the press in American society?
The Michael Barson Collection/Past Perfect; Collection of Janice L. and David J. Frent.

Stalin considered U.S. officials hypocritical in demanding democratic elections in Eastern Europe while supporting dictatorships friendly to U.S. interests in Cuba and other Latin American countries. The United States clung to its own sphere of influence while opposing Soviet efforts to create its own. But the Western Allies were unwilling to match tough words with military force; and their sharp protests failed to prevent the Soviet Union from establishing satellite countries in most of Eastern Europe.

In 1946, the wartime Allies contended over Germany's future. American policymakers wanted to strip the nation of its military capacity, but they also desired a rapid industrial revival in Germany to foster European economic recovery and thus America's own long-term prosperity. By contrast, the Soviet Union wanted Germany weak militarily and economically, and it sought heavy reparations that could be used to rebuild the devastated Soviet economy. Unable to settle their differences, the Allies divided Germany. The Soviet Union installed a puppet Communist govern-ment in the eastern section, and in December 1946, Britain, France, and the United States unified their occupation zones and began the process that established the Federal Republic of Germany—West Germany—in 1949 (Map 26.1).

The war of words escalated early in 1946. Boasting of the superiority of the Soviet system, Stalin told a Moscow audience in February that capitalist economies inevitably produced war. One month later, Truman traveled with Winston Churchill to Fulton, Missouri, where the former prime minister denounced Soviet suppression of the popular will in Eastern and central Europe. "From Stettin in the Baltic to Trieste in the Adriatic, an iron curtain has descended across the Continent," Churchill said. (See "Documenting the American Promise," page 956.) Although Truman did not officially endorse Churchill's **iron curtain** speech, his presence implied agreement with the idea of joint British-American strength to combat Soviet aggression. Stalin regarded the speech as "a call to war against the USSR."

In February 1946, career diplomat George F. Kennan, who had served in U.S. embassies in Eastern Europe and Moscow, wrote a comprehensive rationale for hard-line foreign policy. He downplayed the influence of Communist ideology in Soviet policy. Instead, Kennan stressed the Soviets' insecurity and their need to maintain authority at home, which prompted Stalin to exaggerate threats from abroad and to expand

Soviet power. All of these circumstances, Kennan argued, made it impossible to negotiate with Stalin, a conclusion shared by Secretary of State James F. Byrnes, Undersecretary Acheson, and other key Truman advisers.

Kennan predicted that the Soviet Union would retreat from efforts to expand its influence worldwide "in the face of superior force." Therefore, the United States should respond with "unalterable counterforce," making Russia "face frustration indefinitely," an approach that came to be called containment. Kennan expected that containment would eventually end in

MAP 26.1   The Division of Europe after World War II

The "iron curtain," a term coined by Winston Churchill to refer to the Soviet grip on Eastern and central Europe, divided Europe for nearly fifty years. Communist governments controlled the countries along the Soviet Union's western border. The only exception was Finland, which remained neutral.

READING THE MAP: Is the division of Europe between NATO, Communist, and neutral countries about equal? Why would the location of Berlin pose a problem for the Western allies?

CONNECTIONS: When was NATO founded, and what is its purpose? How did the postwar division of Europe compare with the wartime alliances?

FOR MORE HELP ANALYZING THIS MAP, see the map activity for this chapter in the Online Study Guide at bedfordstmartins.com/roark.

The Emerging Cold War

Although antagonism between the Soviet Union and the West stretched back to the Russian Revolution of 1917, the United States, the Soviet Union, Britain, and other powers had cooperated to win World War II and managed to reach compromises at the Yalta and Potsdam summits in 1945. Early in 1946, however, officials in both the Soviet Union and the West publicly expressed distrust and attributed hostile motivations to each other. Within the United States, disagreement developed about how to deal with the Soviet Union.

DOCUMENT 1
Joseph Stalin Addresses an Election Rally in Moscow, February 9, 1946

At an election rally in early 1946 ("election" in name only since there was just one Communist Party candidate for each position), Premier Joseph Stalin called on the Soviet people to support his program for economic development and postwar recovery. Although Stalin did not address cold war issues, leaders in the West viewed his comments about communism and capitalism, as well as his boasts about the strength of the Red Army, as a threat to peace.

It would be incorrect to think that the [Second World] war arose accidentally or as the result of the fault of some of the statesmen. Although these faults did exist, the war arose in reality as the inevitable result of the development of the world economic and political forces on the basis of monopoly capitalism.

Our Marxists declare that the capitalist system of world economy conceals elements of crisis and war, that the development of world capitalism does not follow a steady and even course forward, but proceeds through crises and catastrophes. The uneven development of the capitalist countries leads in time to sharp disturbances in their relations and the group of countries which consider themselves inadequately provided with raw materials and export markets try usually to change this situation and to change the position in their favor by means of armed force. As a result of these factors, the capitalist world is split into two hostile camps and war follows. . . .

Now victory [in World War II] means, first of all, that our Soviet social system has won, that the Soviet social system has successfully stood the test in the fire of war and has proved its complete vitality. . . .

The war has shown that the Soviet social system is a truly popular system, issued from the depths of the people and enjoying its mighty support. . . . The Soviet social system has proved to be more capable of life and more stable than a non-Soviet social system. . . .

Our victory implies that it was the Soviet armed forces that won. . . . The Red Army heroically withstood all the adversities of the war, routed completely the armies of our enemies and emerged victoriously from the war. This is recognized by everybody—friend and foe.

Now a few words on the plans for the work of the Communist Party in the near future. . . . The fundamental task of the new Five-Year Plan consists in restoring the areas of the country which have suffered, restoring the prewar level in industry and agriculture, and then exceeding this level.

Apart from the fact that in the very near future the rationing system will be abolished, special attention will be focused on expanding the production of goods for mass consumption, on raising the standard of life of the working people by consistent and systematic reduction of the costs of all goods, and on wide-scale construction of all kinds of scientific research institutes to enable science to develop its forces. I have no doubt that if we render the necessary assistance to our scientists they will be able not only to overtake but also in the very near future to surpass the achievements of science outside the boundaries of our country. [Stalin then announced goals for production of key materials.] Only under such conditions will our country be insured against any eventuality.

SOURCE: Excerpts from Joseph Stalin, *Vital Speeches of the Day*, February 9 (1946). Reprinted with permission.

DOCUMENT 2
Winston Churchill Delivers His "Iron Curtain" Speech at Westminster College, in Fulton, Missouri, March 5, 1946

Winston Churchill, former prime minister of Britain, stated that he spoke for himself alone, but President Harry Truman's presence on the platform at Westminster College suggested his approval of Churchill's assessment of Soviet actions. After reading Churchill's words, Stalin justified Soviet action in Eastern Europe as the means to "ensure its security," drew parallels between Hitler and Churchill, and called Churchill's words "a call to war with the Soviet Union."

The United States stands at this time at the pinnacle of world power. It is a solemn moment for the American democracy. With primacy in power is also joined an awe-inspiring accountability to the future. [Churchill then spoke of the need to support the United Nations.]

It would nevertheless be wrong and imprudent to intrust the secret knowledge or experience of the atomic bomb, which the United States, Great Britain and Canada now share, to the world organization [the United Nations], while it is still in its infancy. It would be criminal madness to cast it adrift in this still agitated and ununited world. No one in any country has slept less well . . . because this knowledge and the method and the raw materials to apply it are at present largely retained in American hands. I do not believe we should all have slept so soundly had the positions been reversed and some Communist or neo-Fascist state monopolized, for the time being, these dread agencies. The fear of them alone might easily have been used to enforce totalitarian systems upon the free democratic world. . . . God has willed that this shall not be, and we have at least a breathing space before this period has to be encountered, and even then, if no effort is spared, we should still possess so formidable superiority as to impose effective deterrents upon its employment or threat of employment by others. . . .

A shadow has fallen upon the scenes so lately lighted by the Allied victory. Nobody knows what Soviet Russia and its Communist international organization intends to do in the immediate future, or what are the limits, if any, to their expansive and proselytizing tendencies. I have a strong admiration and regard for the valiant Russian people and for my war-time comrade, Marshal Stalin. . . . We understand the Russians need to be secure on her western frontiers from all renewal of German aggression. . . . It is my duty, however, to place before you certain facts. . . .

From Stettin in the Baltic to Trieste in the Adriatic, an iron curtain has descended across the Continent. Behind that line lie all the capitals of the ancient states of central and eastern Europe. Warsaw, Berlin, Prague, Vienna, Budapest, Belgrade, Bucharest and Sofia, all these famous cities and the populations around them lie in the Soviet sphere and all are subject in one form or another, not only to Soviet influence but to a very high and increasing measure of control from Moscow. . . . The Communist parties, which were very small in all these eastern states of Europe, have been raised to pre-eminence and power far beyond their numbers and are seeking everywhere to obtain totalitarian control. Police governments are prevailing in nearly every case, and so far, except in Czechoslovakia, there is no true democracy. . . .

In front of the iron curtain which lies across Europe are other causes for anxiety. . . . In a great number of countries, far from the Russian frontiers and throughout the world, Communist fifth columns are established and work in complete unity and absolute obedience to the directions they receive from the Communist center.

I do not believe that Soviet Russia desires war. What they desire is the fruits of war and the indefinite expansion of their power and doctrines. . . . Our difficulties and dangers will not be removed by closing our eyes to them. They will not be removed by mere waiting to see what happens; nor will they be relieved by a policy of appeasement. . . .

From what I have seen of our Russian friends and allies during the war, I am convinced that there is nothing they admire so much as strength, and there is nothing for which they have less respect than for military weakness.

SOURCE: Excerpts from Winston Churchill, *Vital Speeches of the Day*, March 5 (1946). Reprinted with permission.

DOCUMENT 3
Henry A. Wallace Addresses an Election Rally at Madison Square Garden, New York, September 12, 1946

Throughout 1946, Henry A. Wallace, Franklin D. Roosevelt's vice president from 1941 to 1945, and Harry S. Truman's secretary of commerce, urged the president to take a more conciliatory approach toward the Soviet Union, a position reflected in a speech Wallace gave to a rally of leftist and other liberal groups in New York City. Compared with the more pro-Soviet speeches given that night, Wallace's speech was moderate and drew criticism from the U.S. Communist Party's newspaper. Nevertheless, Wallace's words in the context in which he delivered them seemed to the president to undermine his foreign policy. One week later, Truman asked for Wallace's resignation.

Tonight I want to talk about peace—and how to get peace. Never have the common people of all lands so longed for peace. Yet, never in a time of comparative peace have they feared war so much. . . .

During the past year or so, the significance of peace has been increased immeasurably by the atomic bomb, guided missiles and airplanes which soon will travel as fast as

(continued)

sound. . . . We cannot rest in the assurance that we invented the atom bomb—and therefore that this agent of destruction will work best for us. He who trusts in the atom bomb will sooner or later perish by the atom bomb—or something worse. . . .

To prevent war and insure our survival in a stable world, it is essential that we look abroad through our own American eyes and not through the eyes of either the British Foreign Office or a pro-British or anti-Russian press. . . . We must not let British balance-of-power manipulations determine whether and when the United States gets into war. . . .

To achieve lasting peace, we must study in detail just how the Russian character was formed—by invasions of Tartars, Mongols, Germans, Poles, Swedes, and French; by the czarist rule based on ignorance, fear and force; by the intervention of the British, French and Americans in Russian affairs from 1919 to 1921; by the geography of the huge Russian land mass situated strategically between Europe and Asia; and by the vitality derived from the rich Russian soil and the strenuous Russian climate. Add to all this the tremendous emotional power which Marxism and Leninism gives to the Russian leaders—and then we can realize that we are reckoning with a force which cannot be handled successfully by a "Get tough with Russia" policy. "Getting tough" never bought anything real and lasting—whether for schoolyard bullies or businessmen or world

powers. The tougher we get, the tougher the Russians will get. . . .

We most earnestly want peace with Russia—but we want to be met half way. We want cooperation. And I believe that we can get cooperation once Russia understands that our primary objective is neither saving the British Empire nor purchasing oil in the Near East with the lives of American soldiers. . . .

On our part we should recognize that we have no more business in the political affairs of Eastern Europe than Russia has in the political affairs of Latin America, Western Europe and the United States. . . . The Russians have no more business in stirring up native communists to political activity in Western Europe, Latin America and the United States than we have in interfering in the politics of Eastern Europe and Russia. We know what Russia is up to in Eastern Europe, for example, and Russia knows what we are up to. We cannot permit the door to be closed against our trade in Eastern Europe any more than we can in China. But at the same time we have to recognize that the Balkans are closer to Russia than to us—and that Russia cannot permit either England or the United States to dominate the politics of that area. . . .

Russian ideas of social-economic justice are going to govern nearly a third of the world. Our ideas of free enterprise democracy will govern much of the rest. The two ideas will endeavor to prove which can deliver the most satisfaction to the common

man in their respective areas of political dominance. . . . Under friendly peaceful competition the Russian world and the American world will gradually become more alike. The Russians will be forced to grant more and more of the personal freedoms; and we shall become more and more absorbed with the problems of social-economic justice.

SOURCE: Excerpts from Henry A. Wallace, *Vital Speeches of the Day*, September 12 (1946). Reprinted with permission.

QUESTIONS FOR ANALYSIS AND DEBATE

1. What lessons do these three leaders draw from World War II? What do they see as the most critical steps to preventing another war?

2. How do these three men describe the political and economic system of the Soviet Union? What differences do they see between the systems of the Soviet Union on the one hand and the United States and Western Europe on the other? How do their predictions about these systems differ?

3. What motives do these three men ascribe to Soviet actions? How do Churchill and Wallace differ in their proposals for the Western response to the Soviet Union?

4. Which leader do you think was most optimistic about the prospects for good relationships between Russia and the West? Which was most correct? Why?

"either the breakup or the gradual mellowing of Soviet power." This message reached a larger audience when, as "Mr. X," Kennan published an article in *Foreign Affairs* magazine in July 1947. Kennan later displayed dismay at the use of his ideas to justify what he considered an indiscriminate American response wherever communism seemed likely to succeed. But his analysis marked a critical turning point in the development of the cold war, providing a powerful rationale for using U.S. power throughout the world.

Not all public figures accepted the toughening line. In an election campaign speech in September 1946, Secretary of Commerce Henry A. Wallace, Truman's predecessor as vice president, urged greater understanding of the Soviets' concerns about their nation's security, insisting that "we have no more business in the political affairs of Eastern Europe than Russia has in the political affairs of Latin America." (See "Documenting the American Promise," page 956.) State Department officials were furious. When Wallace refused to be muzzled on foreign policy topics, Truman fired him.

The Truman Doctrine and the Marshall Plan

In 1947, the United States moved from tough words to action, implementing the doctrine of containment that would guide foreign policy for the next four decades. It was not an easy transition; despite public approval of a verbal hard line, Americans wanted to keep their soldiers and tax dollars at home. In addition to selling containment to the public, Truman had to gain the support of a Republican-controlled Congress, which included a forceful bloc, led by Ohio senator Robert A. Taft, opposed to a strong U.S. presence in Europe.

Crises in two Mediterranean countries triggered the implementation of containment. In February 1947, Britain informed the United States that its crippled economy could no longer sustain military assistance to Greece and Turkey. Turkey was trying to resist Soviet pressures, and Greece's government faced a challenge from internal leftists. Truman promptly sought congressional authority to send military and economic missions, along with $400 million in aid, to the two countries. At a meeting with congressional leaders, Undersecretary of State Acheson predicted that if Greece and Turkey fell, communism would soon consume three-fourths of the planet. After a stunned silence, Michigan senator Arthur Vandenberg, the Republican foreign policy leader and a recent convert from isolationism, warned that to get approval Truman would have to "scare hell out of the country."

Truman did just that. Outlining what would later be called the **domino theory**, he warned that if Greece fell to the rebels, "confusion and disorder might well spread throughout the entire Middle East . . . and would have a profound effect upon . . . Europe." Failure to step in, he said, "may endanger the peace of the world—and shall surely endanger the welfare of the nation." According to what came to be called the Truman Doctrine, the United

The Marshall Plan in Greece
Greece was one of sixteen European nations that participated in the European Recovery Program. In this photograph taken in December 1949, a parade through Athens marks the one-millionth ton of supplies sent to Greece as part of Marshall Plan aid. This truck carries wheat flour. Why would such a parade be staged? What effect might it have on the Greek people?
Library of Congress.

States must not just resist Soviet military power but must "support free peoples who are resisting attempted subjugation by armed minorities or by outside pressures." Congressional authorization of aid for Greece and Turkey did not entail formal acceptance of the Truman Doctrine. Yet the assumption that American security depended on rescuing any anti-Communist government from internal rebels or outside pressure became the cornerstone of U.S. foreign policy from 1947 until the end of the 1980s.

A much larger assistance program for Europe followed aid to Greece and Turkey. In May 1947, Dean Acheson described a war-ravaged Western Europe, with "factories destroyed, fields impoverished, transportation systems wrecked, populations scattered and on the borderline of starvation." American citizens were sending generous amounts of private aid, amounting to some $2 billion in the first six years

> In 1947, the United States moved from tough words to action, implementing the doctrine of containment that would guide foreign policy for the next four decades.

after the war, but Europe needed large-scale assistance. It was "a matter of national self-interest," Acheson argued, for the United States to provide aid. Only economic recovery could halt the growth of **socialist** and Communist parties in France and Italy and confine Soviet influence to Eastern Europe.

In March 1948, Congress approved the European Recovery Program—more commonly known as the Marshall Plan, after retired general George C. Marshall, then serving as secretary of state—and over the next five years the United States spent $13 billion to restore the economies of Western Europe. Marshall invited all European nations and the Soviet Union to cooperate in a request for aid, but as administration officials expected, the Soviets refused to meet the American terms of free trade and financial disclosure and ordered their East European satellites likewise to reject the offer. Sixteen nations became beneficiaries of Marshall Plan aid, which marked the first step toward the European Union. The assistance program was also good business for the United States, because the European nations spent most of the dollars to buy American products carried on American ships, and Europe's economic recovery expanded the realm of raw materials, markets, and investment opportunities available to American capitalists.

While Congress debated the Marshall Plan, in February 1948 the Soviets staged a brutal coup against the government of Czechoslovakia and installed a Communist regime. Next, Soviet leaders threatened Western access to Berlin. The former capital of Germany lay within Soviet-controlled East Germany, but all four Allies jointly occupied Berlin, dividing it into separate administrative units. As the Western Allies moved to organize West Germany as a separate nation, the Soviets retaliated by blocking roads and rail lines that connected West Germany to the Western-held sections of Berlin, cutting off food, fuel, and other essentials to two million inhabitants.

"We stay in Berlin, period," Truman insisted. Yet he wanted to avoid a confrontation with Soviet troops. So for nearly a year U.S. and British pilots airlifted 2.3 million tons of goods to sustain the West Berliners. Stalin hesitated to shoot down these cargo planes, and in 1949 he lifted the blockade. The city was then divided into East

Berlin Divided, 1948

The Berlin Airlift

These Germans living in West Berlin are greeting a U.S. plane carrying food, fuel, and other necessities to Berlin during the Soviet blockade that began in June 1948. Truman and his advisers were "prepared to use any means that may be necessary to stay in Berlin," and the president confided to his diary that "we are very close to war." To reduce that risk, Truman chose to supply the city with an airlift rather than sending ground convoys to shoot their way through Soviet lines. Apparently impressed with American resolve and resources, Stalin backed down and lifted the blockade in May 1949. The vulnerability of Germans like these helped to ease hostile feelings that other Europeans felt toward their former enemy.
© Bettmann/Corbis.

Berlin, under Soviet control, and West Berlin, which became part of West Germany. For many Americans, the Berlin airlift confirmed the wisdom of containment: When challenged, the Russians backed down, as Kennan had predicted.

Building a National Security State

The new policy of containment quickly acquired a military capacity to back it up. During the Truman years, the United States fashioned a five-pronged defense strategy: (1) development of atomic weapons, (2) strengthening traditional military power, (3) military alliances with other nations, (4) military and economic aid to friendly nations, and (5) an espionage network and secret means to subvert Communist expansion.

In September 1949, the United States lost its nuclear monopoly when officials confirmed that the Soviets had detonated an atomic bomb. Within months, Truman approved development of an even deadlier weapon, a hydrogen bomb based on a thermonuclear explosion equivalent to five hundred atomic bombs. By 1954, the United States had the capacity to deliver the "super bomb," but its advantage was brief. In November 1955, the Soviets exploded their own hydrogen bomb.

From the 1950s through the 1980s, **deterrence** formed the basis of American nuclear strategy. To deter the Soviet Union from attacking, the United States strove to maintain a more powerful nuclear force than the Soviets. Because the Russians pursued a similar policy, the superpowers became locked in an ever-escalating race for nuclear dominance. Albert Einstein, whose mathematical discoveries had laid the foundations for nuclear weapons, commented grimly on the enormous destructive force now possessed by the superpowers. The war that came after World War III, he said, would be fought with stones.

The United States also beefed up its conventional military power to deter Soviet threats that might not warrant nuclear retaliation. To streamline defense planning, Congress passed the National Security Act in 1947, uniting the military branches under a single secretary of defense and creating the National Security Council (NSC) to advise the president. As the Berlin crisis simmered in 1948, Congress stepped up military appropriations and enacted a peacetime **draft**. Congress also granted permanent status to the women's military branches, though it limited them to low numbers and rank and banned them from combat. With about 1.5 million men and women in uniform in 1950, the military strength of the United States had quadrupled since the 1930s, and defense expenditures claimed one-third of the federal budget.

Collective security, the third prong of postwar military strategy and the sharpest break from America's past, also developed during the Berlin showdown. In June 1948, the Senate approved the general principle of regional military alliances. One year later, the United States joined Canada and Western European nations in its first peacetime military alliance, the North Atlantic Treaty Organization (NATO), designed to counter a Soviet threat to Western Europe (see Map 26.1). For the first time in its history, the United States pledged to go to war if one of its allies were attacked.

The fourth element of defense strategy involved foreign assistance programs to strengthen friendly countries, such as aid to Greece and Turkey in 1947 and the Marshall Plan. In addition, in 1949 Congress approved $1 billion of military aid to its NATO allies and began economic assistance to nations in other parts of the world.

The fifth element of the national security state was development of the government's espionage capacities and the means to deter communism through covert activities. The National Security Act of 1947 created the Central Intelligence Agency (CIA) to gather information and to perform any "functions and duties related to intelligence affecting the national security" that the NSC might authorize. Eventually,

---

Cold War Spying

"Intelligence," the gathering of information to determine the capabilities and intentions of the enemy, was as old as human warfare, but it took on new importance with the onset of the cold war. Created by the National Security Act of 1947, the Central Intelligence Agency (CIA) became one of the most important tools for obtaining Soviet secrets, deceiving the enemy about U.S. plans, countering subversive activities on the part of Communists, and assisting local forces against leaders that the United States wanted to oust. While much of the CIA's intelligence function took place in Washington, where analysts combed through Communist newspapers, official reports, and leaders' speeches, agents behind the iron curtain perfomed the most dramatic work, gathering information with a variety of bugs and devices, such as this camera hidden inside a pack of cigarettes. Spying soon gained a prominent place in popular culture, most notably in more than a dozen movies featuring James Bond, British agent 007, created by former British naval intelligence agent Ian Fleming in 1952 and first appearing on screen in *Dr. No* in 1962. Jack Naylor Collection.

CIA agents conducted secret operations that toppled legitimate foreign governments and violated the rights of U.S. citizens. In many respects, the CIA was virtually unaccountable to Congress or the public.

By 1950, the United States had abandoned age-old tenets of foreign policy. Isolationism and neutrality had given way to a peacetime military alliance and economic and military efforts to control events far beyond U.S. borders. Short of war, the United States could not stop the descent of the iron curtain, but it aggressively and successfully promoted economic recovery and a military shield for the rest of Europe.

Superpower Rivalry around the Globe

Efforts to implement containment moved beyond Europe. In Africa, Asia, and the Middle East, World War II furthered a tide of national liberation movements against war-weakened **imperial** powers. Between 1945 and 1960, forty countries, with more than a quarter of the world's people, won their independence. These nations came to be referred to collectively, along with Latin America, as the **third world**, a term denoting countries outside the Western (first world) and Soviet (second world) orbits that had not yet developed industrial economies. Like Woodrow Wilson during World War I, Roosevelt and Truman promoted the ideal of self-determination: The United States granted independence to its own dominion, the Philippines, in 1946; applauded the British withdrawal from India; and encouraged France to relinquish its empire in Indochina. At the same time, both the United States and the Soviet Union cultivated governments in emerging nations that were friendly to their own interests.

Leaders of many liberation movements, impressed with the rapid economic growth of Russia, adopted socialist or Communist ideas, although few had formal ties with the Soviet Union. But American leaders insisted on viewing these movements as a threatening extension of Soviet power. Seeking to hold communism at bay by fostering economic development and political stability, in 1949 the Truman administration initiated the Point IV Program, providing technical aid to developing nations. Reflecting the Truman administration's cold war priorities, the modest amounts of such aid contrasted sharply with the huge sums provided to Europe.

In Asia, civil war raged in China, where the Communists, led by Mao Zedong (Mao Tsetung), fought the official Nationalist government under Chiang Kai-shek. While the Communists gained support among the peasants for their land reforms and valiant stand against the Japanese, Chiang's corrupt and incompetent government alienated much of the population. The so-called China bloc, a lobby that included Republican members of Congress and religious groups with missionary ties to China, pressured the Truman administration to save that nation from the Communists. Failing in its effort to promote negotiations between Chiang and Mao, the United States provided almost $3 billion in aid to the Nationalists during the civil war. Yet Truman and his advisers believed that to divert further resources from Europe to China would be futile, given the ineptness of Chiang's government.

In October 1949, Mao established the People's Republic of China (PRC), and the Nationalists fled to the island of Taiwan. The United States refused to recognize the existence of the PRC, blocked its admission to the United Nations, and sent aid to the Nationalist government in Taiwan. Nothing less than a massive U.S. military commitment could have stopped the Chinese Communists, but some Republicans cried that Truman and "the pro-Communists in the State Department" had "lost"

The Chinese Communist Movement
The leaders of the young Communist movement in China in 1937 exude confidence as they stand in a doorway to one of the cave dwellings where they lived and worked in Yan'an, in northwest China. Bo Gu (right) died in a plane crash in 1946. Zhou Enlai (left) and Mao Zedong (center) led the revolutionary forces to victory and the establishment of the People's Republic of China in 1949.
Peabody Museum, Harvard University.

China. Thus, China became a political albatross for the Democrats, who resolved never again to be vulnerable to charges of being soft on communism.

As it became clear that China would not be a stable capitalist ally in Asia, the administration reconsidered its plans for postwar Japan. Initially, the U.S. military occupation had aimed to reform the Japanese government, purge militarists from official positions, and decentralize the economy. But by 1948, U.S. policy had shifted to concentrate on economic recovery. The new goals were to help Japan rapidly reindustrialize and secure access to food, markets, and natural resources in Asia, and in a short time the Japanese economy was flourishing. American soldiers remained on military bases in Japan, but the official occupation ended when the two nations signed a peace treaty and a mutual security pact in September 1951. Like West Germany, Japan now sat squarely within the American orbit, ready to serve as an economic hub in a vital area.

The one area where cold war considerations did not control American policy was Palestine. In 1943, then-Senator Harry Truman spoke passionately about Nazi Germany's systematic extermination of Jews, asserting, "This is not a Jewish problem, it is an American problem—and we

Israel, 1948

Jewish state
Palestinian territories

must . . . face it squarely and honorably." As president, he had the opportunity to make good on his words. Jews had been migrating to Palestine, their biblical homeland, since the nineteenth century, resulting in tension and hostilities between Palestinian Arabs and Jews. After World War II, as hundreds of thousands of European Jews sought refuge and creation of a national homeland in Palestine, fighting devolved into brutal terrorism on both sides.

Truman's foreign policy experts saw American-Arab friendship as a critical barrier against Soviet influence in the Middle East and as a means to secure access to Arabian oil. Uncharacteristically defying his advisers, the president responded instead to pressure from Jewish organizations, his moral commitment to Holocaust survivors, and his interest in the American Jewish vote for the 1948 elections. When Jews in Palestine declared the state of Israel in May 1948, Truman quickly recognized the new country and made its defense the cornerstone of U.S. policy in the Middle East.

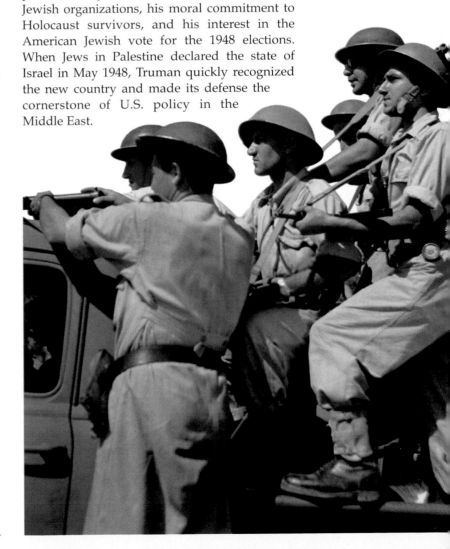

Haganah Troops Mobilize in Palestine
The Haganah originated in the 1910s as a paramilitary group to defend Jewish settlers in Palestine as they struggled with Arabs hostile to the growing presence of Zionists committed to building a Jewish state there. Because Palestine was governed by the British under a League of Nations mandate, Haganah was an illegal, underground organization, yet it gathered substantial numbers and weapons by the end of World War II. After Israel declared itself a nation in 1948, Haganah became the core of the Israel Defense Forces, Israel's main military organization. In this photo, Haganah troops are mobilizing in July 1948 to defend the new state from the armies of the surrounding nations of Syria, Jordan, Egypt, Lebanon, and Iraq. The Israelis won the war, but the consolidation of the state of Israel created 700,000 Arab refugees and an issue that would fuel turmoil in the area for decades to come.
© Bettmann/Corbis.

Truman and the Fair Deal at Home

Referring to the Civil War general who coined the phrase "War is hell," Truman said in December 1945, "Sherman was wrong. I'm telling you I find peace is hell." Challenged by crises abroad, Truman also faced shortages, strikes, inflation, and other problems attending the reconversion of the economy to peacetime production. At the same time, he tried to expand New Deal reform, with his own "Fair Deal" agenda, which proposed initiatives in civil rights, housing, education, and health care. In sharp contrast to his success with Congress in foreign policy, however, Truman achieved but a modest slice of his domestic agenda.

Reconversion and the Postwar Economic Boom

Despite deprivations during World War II, most Americans had enjoyed a higher standard of living than ever before. Economic experts as well as ordinary citizens worried about both sustaining that standard and providing jobs for millions of returning soldiers. Truman wasted no time

unveiling his plan, asking Congress to enact a twenty-one-point program of social and economic reforms. "Not even President Roosevelt ever asked for as much at one sitting," exploded Republican leader Joseph W. Martin Jr.

Congress approved only one of Truman's key proposals—full-employment legislation—and even that was watered down. The Employment Act of 1946 invested the federal government with responsibility "to promote maximum employment, production, and purchasing power," thereby formalizing what had been implicit in Roosevelt's actions to counter the depression—government's responsibility for maintaining a healthy economy. The law created a Council of Economic Advisors to assist the president, but it authorized no new powers to translate the government's obligation into effective action.

Inflation, not unemployment, turned out to be the most severe problem in the early postwar years. Unable to buy civilian goods during the war, in 1945 consumers had $30 billion of savings that they now itched to spend. But shortages of meat, automobiles, housing, and a host of other items persisted. Six million people wanted new cars in 1946, twice as many as the industry managed to produce. Housing was so scarce that returning veterans lived in basements and garages. Until industry could convert fully to civilian production and make more goods available, consumer demand would continue to drive up prices.

Labor relations were another thorn in Truman's side. Organized labor survived the war stronger than ever, its 14.5 million members making up 35 percent of the civilian workforce. "The workers felt they were in a good bargaining position," recalled Henry Fiering, an organizer for the United Electrical Workers, "so they went after some more things." Union members feared erosion of wartime gains. With wages frozen during the war, the rising incomes enjoyed by working-class families had come largely from the availability of higher-paying jobs and the chance to work longer hours than before. The end of overtime meant a 30 percent cut in take-home pay for most workers.

Women who had flocked into wartime jobs also saw their earnings decline. Some were ready to return to their homes, but polls indicated that as many as 68 to 85 percent wanted to keep their jobs. Most who remained in the workforce had to settle for relatively low-paying jobs in light industry or the service sector (Figure 26.1). Displaced from her shipyard work, Marie

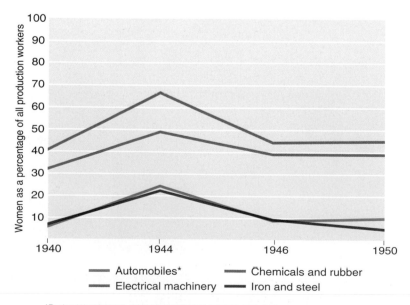

FIGURE 26.1 Women Workers in Selected Industries, 1940–1950
Women demolished the idea that some jobs were "men's work" during World War II, but they failed to maintain their gains in the manufacturing sector after the war.

Women as a percentage of all production workers

Automobiles*
Electrical machinery
Chemicals and rubber
Iron and steel

*During World War II, this industry did not produce cars, but rather military transportation such as jeeps, tanks, aircraft, etc.

Schreiber found work as a cashier. "You were back to women's wages, you know . . . practically in half," she recalled. (See "Historical Question," page 966.)

Paying scant attention to the problems of women workers, unions sought to preserve wartime gains with the weapon they had relinquished during the war. More strikes took place in 1946 than at any other time in U.S. history, with five million workers disrupting production in nearly every major industry. Workers saw corporate executives profiting at their expense. Shortly before his union voted to strike, a former marine and the men he carpooled with calculated that a lavish party given by a company executive had cost more than they earned for a whole year's work in the steel mill. "That sort of stuff made us realize, hell we *had* to bite the bullet . . . the bosses sure didn't give a damn for us."

Veterans Go to College

So many World War II veterans wanted to use their GI benefits for higher education that colleges were overwhelmed; many had to turn away students. These veterans, sprinting out of the building where they just registered, express their joy at having been admitted to Indiana University in 1947.

Indiana University.

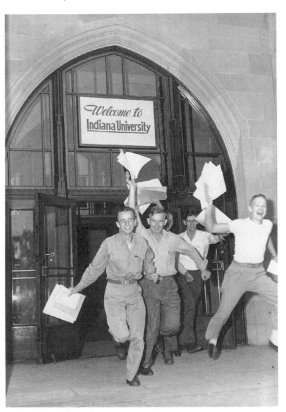

Although most Americans approved of unions in principle, they became fed up with labor stoppages, blamed unions for rising prices and shortages of consumer goods, and called for more government restrictions on organized labor. Truman shared the public's exasperation and expressed dismay that the wartime unity and sense of sacrifice had given way to greed and selfishness. In a letter to his mother in October 1945, he spread the blame around: "The Congress [is] balking, labor has gone crazy, and management isn't far from insane in selfishness." In May 1946, after coal miners rejected government recommendations for a settlement, Truman placed the mines under federal control. When the massive wave of strikes subsided at the end of 1946, workers had won wage increases of about 20 percent, but the loss of overtime along with rising prices left their purchasing power only slightly higher than in 1942.

"The conversion period was not as traumatic as everybody was afraid it was going to be," Henry Fiering remembered. By 1947, the nation had survived the strains of reconversion and avoided a postwar depression. Wartime profits enabled businesses to invest in new plants and equipment. Consumers used their wartime savings to buy the houses, cars, and appliances that had lain beyond their reach during the depression and war. Both defense spending and the $38 billion in grants and loans that enabled war-stricken countries to purchase American products also stimulated the economy. A soaring birthrate, 25 percent higher in 1949 than in 1940, further sustained consumer demand. The United States entered into a remarkable economic boom that lasted through the 1960s and flooded the American people with new consumer goods. (See chapter 27.)

The nation's gratitude to its returning warriors provided yet another economic boost, resulting in the only large welfare measure passed after the New Deal. The Servicemen's Readjustment Act (the GI Bill), enacted in 1944, offered 16 million veterans job training and education; unemployment compensation while they looked for jobs; and low-interest loans to purchase homes, farms, and small businesses. By 1948, some 1.3 million veterans had bought houses with government loans, and by 1956 veterans had used $14.5

> Paying scant attention to the problems of women workers, unions sought to preserve wartime gains with the weapon they had relinquished during the war. More strikes took place in 1946 than at any other time in U.S. history.

What Happened to Rosie the Riveter?

Although studies have been made of the postwar lives of World War II soldiers, we know much less about another group of veterans—the women who helped fight the war on the domestic front and who were recognized in the popular song "Rosie the Riveter." Statistics show that women's employment fell by more than 2 million between 1945 and 1947. But gross statistics do not reveal which women left the labor force and why, and they obscure the experiences of women who continued to work but in different jobs.

We do know what public officials and business and labor leaders expected of women who had taken up men's work during the war. With the shadow of the depression still hovering, Americans doubted that the economy could accommodate the 6 million new women workers along with millions of returning veterans once wartime production had ceased. A nearly universal response to anxieties about unemployment pushed a big part of the responsibility onto women: Their wartime duty to produce the goods needed for victory was replaced with their postwar obligation to withdraw from the labor force.

The message that they should quit their jobs "for the sake of their homes as well as the labor situation" overwhelmed women. The company newspaper at Kaiser shipyards in the Pacific Northwest proclaimed in May 1945, "The Kitchen—Women's Big Post-War Goal." Putting words into the mouths of Kaiser's female employees, the article asserted, "Brothers,

the tin hat and welder's torch will be yours! . . . The thing we want to do is take off these unfeminine garments and button ourselves into something starched and pretty." A General Electric ad predicted that women would welcome a return to "their old housekeeping routine" because GE intended to transform housework with new appliances. Some experts connected married women's employment to their obligations to help their husbands readjust to civilian life. A psychiatrist warned that women's economic independence might "raise problems in the future," urging women to realize that "reunion means relin-

Sisters under the apron—Yesterday's war worker becomes today's housewife.

What's Become of Rosie the Riveter?

Women's Postwar Future
This photograph headed a *New York Times Magazine* article in June 1946. Written by the director of the Women's Division of the Department of Labor, the article discussed the needs of women workers, stressing their right to work and to equal pay, but also assumed that women would all but vanish from heavy manufacturing.
Ellen Kaiper Collection, Oakland.

quishing [independence]—to some extent at any rate."

Other evidence suggests that many women did not have to be told to give up their wartime jobs. Skyrocketing marriage rates and birthrates from that period reveal the attraction of home and family life to people compelled to postpone marriage and childbearing. Thanks to the accumulation of wartime savings, veterans' benefits, and favorable opportunities for men in the postwar economy, many families found it possible to rely on a single earner.

The double burdens placed on married women who took wartime jobs suggest another reason for women's voluntary withdrawal from the workforce. The wartime scarcity of goods had made housekeeping much more difficult, especially for women who typically worked forty-eight hours a week with one day off. Shopping became a problem: Stores often sold out of goods early in the day, and few shops kept evening or Sunday hours. Washing machines, refrigerators, vacuum cleaners, and other labor-saving appliances were not produced at all during the war. Child care centers accommodated only about 10 percent of the children of employed mothers. Employed women with families to care for were simply worn out.

Yet surveys reported that 75 percent of women in wartime jobs wanted—and usually needed—to keep working. As two women employed at a Ford plant in Memphis put it, "Women didn't stop eating when the war stopped." Those who struggled to remain in the workforce experienced the most wrenching changes. The vast majority were able to find jobs; in fact, women's workforce participation began growing again in 1947 and equaled the wartime peak by 1950. But women lost the traditionally male, higher-paying jobs in durable goods industries (such as iron and steel, automobile, and machinery production) and were pushed back into the lower-paying light manufacturing and service industries that had customarily welcomed them. In the words of one historian, "Rosie the Riveter had become a file clerk."

Statistics tell part of the story of this displacement. Women virtually disappeared from shipbuilding, and their share of jobs in the auto industry fell from 25 percent in 1944 to 10 percent in 1950. In the burgeoning Los Angeles aircraft industry, the proportion of women plunged from 40 percent at its wartime height to 12 percent in 1948, rising to just 25 percent in the 1950s. Even in light manufacturing, such as the electrical goods industry, where women had claimed one-third of the prewar jobs, women maintained their numbers but were bumped down to lower-paying work. During the war, women had narrowed the wage gap between men and women, but in 1950, women earned only 53 percent of what men did.

How women reacted to their displacement can be pieced together to some extent from what they were willing to say to reporters and oral history interviewers and what they wrote to government agencies and labor unions. "Women do not expect or want to hold jobs at the expense of returning soldiers," proclaimed a resolution passed by the Women's Trade Union League, expressing its members' overwhelming support for veterans' claims to jobs based on seniority awarded for the years of their wartime service. Tina Hill, a black worker at North American Aircraft in Los Angeles, said, "[Being laid off] didn't bother me much. I was just glad that the war was over . . . [and] my husband had a job." Nonetheless, after doing domestic work, she accepted readily when North American called her back: "Was I a happy soul!"

When management violated women's seniority rights by hiring nonveterans, some women protested bitterly. According to one automobile worker, "We have women laid off with seniority . . . and every day they hire in new men off the street. They hire men, they say, to do the heavy work. . . . During the war they didn't care what kind of work we did." When Ford laid off women with as much as twenty-seven years' seniority, 150 women picketed with signs that read, "The Hand That Rocks the Cradle Can Build Tractors, Too." A worker infuriated by her union's failure to protect women's seniority rights told a reporter, "We are making the bullets now, and we will give the [union executive] board members a blast that will blow them out of their shoes."

Protests from a minority of women workers could not save the jobs that the "Rosies" had held during the war. Despite women's often exemplary performance, most employers still saw women and men as different species fit for different roles and deserving of different rewards. Most labor unions paid lip service to representing all their members, but even the most progressive unions gave low priority to protecting women's seniority rights. In the absence of a feminist movement that could have given both visibility and credibility to their claims for equal treatment, most Rosie the Riveters resigned themselves to "women's work."

million in education benefits. Helping 2.2 million ex-soldiers attend college, the subsidies sparked a boom in higher education. A drugstore clerk before his military service, Don Condren was able to get an engineering degree and to buy his first house. "I think the GI Bill gave the whole country an upward boost economically," he said.

Yet prosperity was not universal. The real gains came during the war, and while wages and salaries increased by 23 percent from 1945 to 1950, prices went up by 36.2 percent. A recession in 1949 threw 7 percent of the labor force out of work, abating only when the Korean War sparked economic recovery. Moreover, despite the return to peacetime production, one-third of all Americans still lived in poverty.

Black and Mexican American Protest and the Politics of Civil Rights

"I spent four years in the army to free a bunch of Frenchmen and Dutchmen," an African American corporal declared, "and I'm hanged if I'm going to let the Alabama version of the Germans kick me around when I get home." Black men and women filled 16 percent of military positions in World War II; they as well as civilians resolved that the return to peace would not be a return to the racial injustices of prewar America. Their political clout had grown with the migration of two million African Americans to northern and western cities, where they could vote and their ballots could make a difference. Even in the South, the proportion of blacks who were allowed to vote inched up from 2 percent to 12 percent in the 1940s. Pursuing civil rights through the courts and Congress, the National Association for the Advancement of Colored People (NAACP) counted half a million members.

In the postwar years, individual African Americans broke through the color barrier, achieving several "firsts." Jackie Robinson integrated major league baseball when he started at first base for the Brooklyn Dodgers in 1947, braving abuse from fans and players to win the Rookie of the Year Award. In 1950, Ralph J. Bunche received the Nobel Peace Prize for his contributions to the United Nations, and Gwendolyn Brooks was awarded the Pulitzer Prize for poetry.

> Black men and women filled 16 percent of military positions in World War II; they as well as civilians resolved that the return to peace would not be a return to the racial injustices of prewar America.

Still, in most respects little had changed, especially in the South, where violence greeted African Americans' attempts to assert their rights. Armed white men turned back Medgar Evers (who would become a key civil rights leader in the 1960s) and four other veterans trying to vote in Mississippi. A mob lynched Isaac Nixon for voting in Georgia, and an all-white jury acquitted the men accused of his murder. In the South, governors, U.S. senators, and other politicians routinely intimidated potential black voters with threats of economic retaliation and violence.

The cold war heightened American leaders' sensitivity to racial issues, as the United States and Soviet Union competed for the allegiance of

Jackie Robinson

John Roosevelt Robinson slides into home plate in a game against the Philadelphia Phillies in 1952. Before becoming the first African American to play modern major league baseball in 1947, Robinson had excelled in track and football as well as baseball at UCLA and had been an army officer in World War II. Even his brilliant play for the Brooklyn Dodgers did not save him from fans' and players' racist taunts or exclusion from restaurants and hotels that catered to his white teammates. Having paved the way for other black players, Robinson competed until 1956. *The Michael Barson Collection/Past Perfect.*

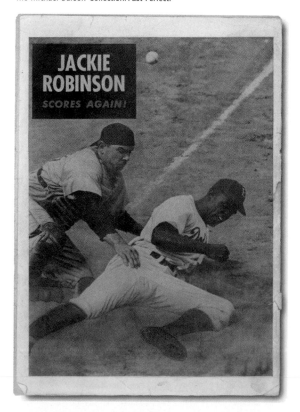

new nations with nonwhite populations emerging in Asia and Africa. How could the United States counter Soviet propaganda about its treatment of blacks when that propaganda reflected reality and African Americans themselves were petitioning the United Nations to pressure the government on their behalf? Even Dean Acheson, far from a champion of racial equality, recognized the costs of discrimination and segregation to national interests abroad, noting that "hostile reaction [to such practices] among normally friendly peoples . . . is growing in alarming proportions," endangering "our moral leadership of the free and democratic nations of the world."

"My very stomach turned over when I learned that Negro soldiers just back from overseas were being dumped out of army trucks in Mississippi and beaten," wrote Truman, shaken by the violence and under pressure to act by civil rights leaders and **liberals**. Wrestling with the Democrats' need for northern black and liberal votes as well as white southern votes, Truman acted more boldly on civil rights than had any previous president. In 1946, he created a Committee on Civil Rights, and in February 1948 he asked Congress to enact the committee's recommendations. The first president to address the NAACP, in June 1947, Truman asserted that all Americans should have equal rights to housing, education, employment, and the ballot.

As with much of his domestic program, the president failed to follow up aggressively on his bold words. In the throes of the 1948 election campaign and pressured by civil rights activists, Truman did issue an executive order to desegregate the armed services, but it lay unimplemented until the Korean War. A large gap loomed between what Truman said about civil rights and what his government accomplished, yet desegregation of the military and the administration's support of civil rights cases in the Supreme Court contributed to far-reaching changes, while his Civil Rights Committee set an agenda for years to come. Breaking sharply with the past, Truman used his office to set a moral agenda for the nation's longest unfulfilled promise.

Although discussion of race and civil rights initiatives were usually linked to African Americans, Mexican Americans endured similar injustices, and they too raised their voices after

Segregation
Signs like this one in Mobile, Alabama, were a normal feature of life in the South from the late nineteenth century until the 1960s. State and local laws mandated segregation in every aspect of life, literally from the cradle to the grave. African Americans could not use white hospitals, cemeteries, schools, libraries, swimming pools, playgrounds, restrooms, or drinking fountains. They were relegated to balconies in movie theaters and kept apart from whites in all public meetings. This scene was captured by the self-trained Gordon Parks, an African American who was one of the most notable photographers of the twentieth century as well as a filmmaker, composer, and author.
© Gordon Parks.

World War II. In 1929, Mexican Americans had formed the League of United Latin-American Citizens (LULAC) to combat discrimination and segregation in the Southwest. Like black soldiers, Mexican American veterans believed, as one of them insisted, "We had earned our credentials as American citizens. We had paid our dues. . . . We were not about to take any crap." Responding to difficulties Mexican Americans encountered in trying to obtain veterans' benefits, in 1948 a group in Corpus Christi, Texas, led by Dr. Héctor Peréz García, a combat surgeon decorated with the Bronze Star, formed the American GI Forum. The organization took off when the wife of Felix Longoria, who had given his life in the Philippines, was refused the use of a funeral chapel in Three Rivers, Texas, "because the whites wouldn't like it" and was told that her husband would be buried in the Mexican section of the cemetery. With the help of Senator Lyndon Johnson, they arranged to lay him to rest in Arlington National Cemetery, and the GI Forum went on to become a key national organization battling discrimination and electing sympathetic officials.

The routine segregation of children in the public schools also energized Mexican Americans.

Truman's Whistle-Stop Campaign
Harry Truman rallies a crowd from his campaign train at a stop in Bridgeport, Pennsylvania, in October 1948. His campaign theme song, "I'm Just Wild about Harry," was borrowed, with the words slightly changed, from the 1921 musical *Shuffle Along*. This was the last presidential election in which the pollsters predicted the wrong winner. They stopped taking polls in mid-October, after which many voters apparently changed their minds. One commentator praised the American citizenry, who "couldn't be ticketed by the polls, knew its own mind and had picked the rather unlikely but courageous figure of Truman to carry on its banner." In what ways have presidential campaigns changed since Harry Truman's time?
Photo: Truman Library; Sheet music: Collection of Janice L. and David J. Frent.

For more help analyzing this image, see the visual activity for this chapter in the Online Study Guide at bedfordstmartins.com/roark.

Parents filed a class action suit in Orange County, California, winning a federal circuit court decision in 1947 that outlawed the practice of separating Mexican American and white children in the schools. In 1948, LULAC and the GI Forum cooperated in a suit producing a federal court verdict that prohibited any Texas school district from segregating Mexican American students in separate schools or classes. Such projects, which paralleled the efforts of the NAACP on behalf of African Americans that would culminate in the *Brown* decision in 1954 (see chapter 27), along with challenges to discrimination in employment and other areas and efforts for political representation, demonstrated a growing mobilization of Mexican Americans in the Southwest.

The Fair Deal Flounders

Republicans capitalized on public frustrations with economic reconversion in the 1946 congressional elections, accusing the administration of "confusion, corruption, and communism."

Capturing Congress for the first time in fourteen years, Republicans looked eagerly to the 1948 presidential campaign. Many Republicans campaigned against New Deal "bureaucracy" and "radicalism" in 1946, and the Eightieth Congress weakened some reform programs and enacted tax cuts favoring higher-income groups over Truman's veto.

Organized labor took the most severe attack, when Congress passed the Taft-Hartley Act over Truman's veto in 1947. Called a "slave labor" law and "Tuff-Heartless" by unions, the law reduced the power of organized labor and made it more difficult to organize workers. For example, states could now pass "right-to-work" laws, which banned the practice of requiring all workers to join a union once a majority had voted for it. Many states, especially in the South and West, rushed to enact such laws, encouraging the relocation of industry there. Taft-Hartley also compelled union leaders to swear that they were not Communists and to make public annual financial reports. It maintained the New Deal principle of government protection for **collective bargaining**, but it put the government more squarely between labor and management and between unions and individual workers.

As the 1948 elections approached, Truman faced not only a resurgent Republican Party headed by its nominee Thomas E. Dewey, but also two revolts within his own party. On the left, Henry A. Wallace, whose foreign policy views had cost him his cabinet seat, led a new Progressive Party. On the right, South Carolina governor J. Strom Thurmond headed the States' Rights Party—the Dixiecrats—formed by southern Democrats who had walked out of the 1948 Democratic Party convention when it passed a liberal civil rights plank.

Almost alone in believing he could win, Truman crisscrossed the country by train, answering supporters' cries of "Give 'em hell, Harry." So bleak were Truman's prospects that the confident Dewey ran a low-key campaign and, on election night, the *Chicago Daily Tribune* printed its next day's issue with the headline DEWEY DEFEATS TRUMAN. But Truman took 303 electoral votes to Dewey's 189, as his party regained control of Congress (Map 26.2). His unexpected victory attested to his skills as a campaigner, broad support for his foreign policy, the enduring popularity of New Deal reform, and the booming economy. Yet Thurmond's capture of 39 electoral votes signaled a break in the traditionally solid Democratic South, foreshad-

owing the political realignment that would result in a two-party region in the 1970s.

Truman failed to turn his victory into success for his Fair Deal agenda. Congress made modest improvements in Social Security and raised the minimum wage, but it passed only one significant reform measure. The Housing Act of 1949 authorized 350,000 units of government-constructed housing over the next fifteen years. Although it fell far short of actual need, the legislation represented a landmark commitment by the government to address the housing needs of the poor.

With southern Democrats often joining the Republicans, Congress rejected Truman's civil rights measures and proposals for a federal health care program, federal aid to education, and a new agriculture program to benefit small farmers and consumers. His efforts to revise immigration policy produced the McCarran-Walter Act of 1952, ending the outright ban on immigration and citizenship for Japanese and other Asians. But the law also authorized the government to bar immigration of suspected Communists and homosexuals and maintained the discriminatory quota system established in the 1920s. Truman denounced that provision as "unworthy of our traditions and our ideals . . . and a slur on the patriotism, the capacity, and the decency of a such a large part of our citizenry," but Congress passed the bill over his veto.

MAP 26.2   The Election of 1948

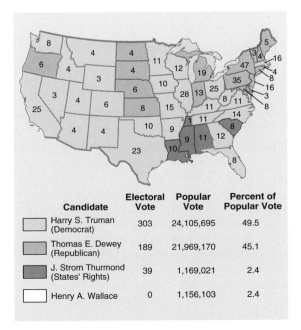

Candidate	Electoral Vote	Popular Vote	Percent of Popular Vote
Harry S. Truman (Democrat)	303	24,105,695	49.5
Thomas E. Dewey (Republican)	189	21,969,170	45.1
J. Strom Thurmond (States' Rights)	39	1,169,021	2.4
Henry A. Wallace	0	1,156,103	2.4

The Red Scare
This map, titled "The Bear Grows and Grows," appeared in the Sunday magazine section of the *New York News* in November 1947. What impact might such an image have on newspaper readers?
The Michael Barson Collection/Past Perfect.

Although he blamed political opponents for defeating his Fair Deal, in fact Truman chose to devote much more energy to foreign policy than to his domestic proposals. Moreover, by late 1950, the Korean War embroiled Truman in controversy, diverted his attention from domestic affairs, and depleted his power as a legislative leader.

The Domestic Chill: A Second Red Scare

Truman's domestic program also suffered from a wave of anti-Communist hysteria that weakened left and liberal forces. Both "Red-baiting" (attempts to discredit individuals or ideas by associating them with Communists) and official retaliation against leftist critics of the government had flourished during the Red scare at the

end of World War I. A second Red scare convulsed the nation after World War II, born of partisan political maneuvering, collapse of the Soviet-American alliance, setbacks in U.S. foreign policy, and disclosures of Soviet espionage.

Warnings about subversion and attacks on Communists and other radicals went back to the 1920s, but the cold war greatly intensified them. Republicans jumped on cold war setbacks, such as the Communist triumph in China, to accuse Democrats of fostering internal subversion. Wisconsin senator Joseph R. McCarthy, the leading crusader, avowed that "the Communists within our borders have been more responsible for the success of Communism abroad than Soviet Russia." Revelations of Soviet espionage furnished some credibility to such charges. For example, a number of ex-Communists, including

Whittaker Chambers and Elizabeth Bentley, testified that they and others had provided secret documents to the Soviets. In 1950, a British physicist working on the atomic bomb project confessed that he was a spy and implicated several Americans, including a couple, Ethel and Julius Rosenberg. The Rosenbergs pleaded innocent but were convicted of conspiracy to commit espionage and electrocuted in 1953.

Records opened in the 1990s showed that the Soviet Union did receive secret documents from Americans, such as Alger Hiss and Julius Rosenberg, but at most such information may have marginally hastened Soviet development of nuclear weapons. At the peak of the hysteria, the

Senator Joseph R. McCarthy

Although the Wisconsin senator made his reputation from anticommunism, he seized that issue more from the need to have a platform for his 1950 reelection campaign than from genuine concern grounded in real evidence. McCarthy had loved politics from his high school days in Appleton, Wisconsin, and easily distorted the truth to promote his political ambitions. The 1946 campaign poster in this photograph highlights his World War II career, which he presented as one involving dangerous combat missions as a tail-gunner. In fact, he spent his time as an intelligence officer debriefing combat pilots; his only missions were flights over islands already evacuated by the Japanese.

© Bettmann/Corbis.

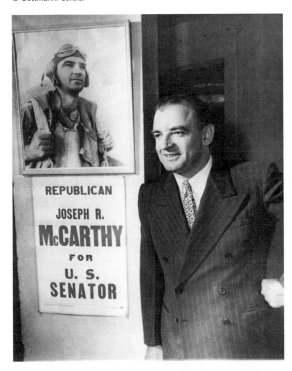

U.S. Communist Party counted only about 20,000 members, some of them undercover FBI agents. The vast majority of individuals prosecuted in the Red scare were guilty of nothing more than having joined the Communist Party, associated with Communists, or supported radical causes. And most of the charges involved activities that took place long before the cold war had made the Soviet Union an enemy. Red-hunters cared little for such distinctions, however. For more than ten years following World War II, congressional committees and a host of other official bodies ordered citizens to testify about their past and present political associations. If they refused, anti-Communists charged that silence was tantamount to confession, and these "unfriendly witnesses" lost their jobs and suffered public ostracism.

Senator McCarthy's influence was so great that **McCarthyism** became a term synonymous with the anti-Communist crusade. Attacking individuals recklessly, in 1950 McCarthy claimed to have a list of 205 "known Communists" employed in the State Department. Dean Acheson, "a pompous diplomat in striped pants, with a phony British accent," he charged, said that Jesus Christ "endorsed communism, high treason, and betrayal of a sacred trust." Even though most of his charges were absurd—such as the allegation that retired general George C. Marshall belonged to a Communist conspiracy—the press covered McCarthy avidly.

Not all Republicans joined McCarthy, nor did the party have a monopoly on the politics of anticommunism. Shortly after being stung with charges of communism in the 1946 midterm elections, in March 1947, President Truman issued Executive Order 9835 requiring investigation of every federal employee. In effect, Truman's "loyalty program" violated the principles of American justice by allowing anonymous informers to make charges and placing the burden of proof on the accused. More than two thousand civil service employees lost their jobs, and another ten thousand resigned while the program continued into the mid-1950s. "A nightmare from which there [was] no awakening" was how State Department employee Esther Brunauer described it when she and her husband, a chemist in the navy, both lost their jobs. Years later, Truman admitted that the loyalty program had been a mistake.

> Senator McCarthy's influence was so great that "McCarthyism" became a term synonymous with the anti-Communist crusade.

The administration also went directly after the Communist Party, prosecuting its leaders under the Smith Act, passed in 1940, which made it a crime to "advocate the overthrow and destruction of the Government of the United States by force and violence." Although civil libertarians argued that the guilty verdicts violated First Amendment rights to freedom of speech, press, and association, the Supreme Court ruled in 1951 (*Dennis v. United States*) that the Communist threat overrode constitutional guarantees.

The domestic cold war spread beyond the nation's capital. State and local governments undertook investigations, demanded loyalty oaths, fired individuals suspected of disloyalty, banned books from public libraries, and more. In addition, a 1950 Senate report claimed that "moral turpitude" and susceptibility to blackmail made homosexuals unfit for government jobs. A 1950s tabloid attempted to shock readers with the news that "more than ninety twisted twerps had been swished out of the State department" and "at least 6,000 homosexuals [were still] on the government payroll." Fired from civil service jobs and drummed out of the military, gay men and women also underwent surveillance and harassment at the hands of the FBI and local police forces. Rutgers, Harvard, Michigan, and other universities dismissed professors, and public school teachers lost their jobs in New York, Philadelphia, Los Angeles, and elsewhere. The House Un-American Activities Committee (HUAC) took on the movie industry in 1947. When ten writers and directors refused to testify, they went to prison and later were blacklisted from Hollywood jobs. Because the Communist Party had helped organize unions and championed racial justice, labor and civil rights activists, too, fell prey to McCarthyism. As African American activist Jack O'Dell remembered, "The segregationists defended segregation by saying they weren't against . . . equal rights for blacks—they were against communism. But their interpretation of Communist was anybody who supported the right of blacks to have civil rights."

McCarthyism caused untold economic and psychological harm to individuals innocent of breaking any law. Thousands of people found themselves humiliated and discredited, hounded from their jobs, even in some cases imprisoned. The anti-Communist crusade violated fundamental constitutional rights of freedom of speech and association, stifled expression of dissenting ideas, and removed unpopular causes from public contemplation.

The Cold War Becomes Hot: Korea

The cold war erupted into a shooting war in June 1950, when troops from Communist North Korea invaded South Korea. For the first time, Americans went into battle to implement containment. Confirming the global reach of the Truman Doctrine, U.S. involvement in Korea also marked the militarization of American foreign policy. The United States, in concert with the United Nations, ultimately held the line in Korea, but at a great cost in lives, dollars, and domestic unity.

Korea and the Military Implementation of Containment

The war grew out of the artificial division of Korea after World War II. Having expelled the Japanese, who had controlled Korea since 1904, the United States and the Soviet Union divided Korea at the thirty-eighth parallel into two occupation zones (Map 26.3). The Soviets supported the Korean Communist Party in the north, while the United States backed the Korean Democratic Party in the south. With Moscow and Washington unable to agree on a unification plan, in July 1948 the United Nations sponsored elections in South Korea. The American-favored candidate, Korean nationalist Syngman Rhee, was elected president, and the United States withdrew most of its troops. In the fall of 1948, the Soviets established the People's Republic of North Korea under Kim Il-sung and also withdrew. U.S. Defense and State Department officials did not consider Korea to be of vital strategic interest, and many doubted that Rhee's repressive government could sustain popular support. But because Rhee was staunchly anti-Communist, Truman authorized a small amount of economic and military aid to South Korea.

Skirmishes between North and South Korean troops had occurred since 1948, with both sides crossing the thirty-eighth parallel. In June 1950, however, 90,000 North Koreans swept into South Korea. Truman's advisers immediately assumed that the Soviet Union, China, or both had instigated the attack. Revelations decades later indicated that both the Russians and the Chinese had acquiesced, but with little enthusiasm, in North Korean plans. Kim wanted to bolster his position by championing Korean

MAP 26.3 The Korean War, 1950–1953
After each side had plunged deep into its enemy's territory, the Korean War ended in 1953 with the dividing line between North and South Korea being nearly the same as it had been before the war.

READING THE MAP: How far south did the North Korean forces progress at the height of their invasion? How far north did the UN forces get? What countries border Korea?
CONNECTIONS: What dangers did the forays of MacArthur's forces to within forty miles of the Korean-Chinese border pose? Why did Truman forbid MacArthur to approach that border? What political considerations on the home front influenced Truman's policy and military strategy regarding Korea?

FOR MORE HELP ANALYZING THIS MAP, see the map activity for this chapter in the Online Study Guide at bedfordstmartins.com/roark.

unification, and the substantial opposition to the Rhee government, including a guerrilla insurgency, suggested that many South Koreans would support the North Korean army.

On June 30, six days after learning of the attack, Truman decided to commit ground troops, believing that Korea was "the Greece of the

Far East" and that the United States must "put up a fight [against communism] right now." Moreover, a non-Communist South Korea was a key element in U.S. plans to revive Japan economically and to make that nation the core of its defense strategy in Asia. Because the Soviet Union was boycotting the UN Security Council for its refusal to seat a delegate from the People's Republic of China, the U.S. representative was able to obtain UN sponsorship of a collective effort to repel the attack. Authorized to appoint a commander for the UN force, Truman named General Douglas MacArthur, hero of the American World War II victory in the Pacific and head of the postwar occupation of Japan.

> Truman decided to commit ground troops, believing that Korea was "the Greece of the Far East."

Sixteen nations, including many NATO allies, sent troops to Korea, but the United States furnished most of the personnel and weapons, deploying almost 1.8 million troops and essentially dictating military strategy. By failing to ask Congress for a declaration of war, Truman violated at least the spirit if not the letter of the Constitution. Moreover, although Congress authorized the mobilization of troops and appropriated funds to fight the war, the president's political opponents called it "Truman's war" when the military situation worsened.

The first American soldiers rushed to Korea unprepared and ill equipped. The North Koreans took the capital of Seoul and drove deep into the south between June and September, forcing UN troops to retreat south to Pusan. Then, in September, General MacArthur launched a bold counteroffensive at Inchon, 180 miles behind North Korean lines. By mid-October, UN forces had pushed the North Koreans back to the thirty-eighth parallel. Now came the momentous decision of whether to invade North Korea and seek to unify Korea under UN supervision.

From Containment to Rollback to Containment

"Troops could not be expected . . . to march up to a surveyor's line and stop," remarked Dean Acheson, now secretary of state, reflecting sentiment among the public and most government officials to transform the military objective from containment to elimination of the enemy and unification of Korea. Pennsylvania congressman Hugh D. Scott and other Republicans in fact insisted that stopping at the thirty-eighth parallel would be "to subvert our military victory." Thus, for the only time during the cold war, the United States tried to roll back communism. With UN approval, on September 27, 1950, Truman ordered MacArthur to move beyond the thirty-eighth parallel if necessary to destroy North Korean forces. Concerned about possible intervention by China and the Soviet Union, Truman directed the general to keep UN troops away from the Korean-Chinese border. Yet MacArthur sent UN forces to within forty miles of China, whereupon more than 150,000 Chinese troops crossed the Yalu River into Korea. With Chinese help, by December 1950, the North Koreans had recaptured Seoul.

Then, under the leadership of General Matthew B. Ridgway, the Eighth Army turned the tide again. After three months of grueling battle, UN forces worked their way back to the thirty-eighth parallel. At that point, Truman decided to seek a negotiated settlement. When the goal of the war reverted to containment, MacArthur was furious. To him, a holding action against communism represented defeat. Truman and his advisers, however, adamantly opposed a wider war in Asia. According to General Omar Bradley, chairman of the Joint Chiefs of Staff, MacArthur wanted to wage "the wrong war, at the wrong place, at the wrong time, with the wrong enemy."

MacArthur took his case public, in effect challenging the president's authority to make foreign policy and violating the principle of civilian control over the military. Fed up with MacArthur's insubordination, Truman fired him in April 1951. Many Americans, however, sided with MacArthur and castigated Truman. "Quite an explosion. . . . Letters of abuse by the dozens," Truman recorded in his diary. The general came

POWs in Korea

These demoralized U.S. soldiers reflect the grim situation for U.S. forces during the early months of the Korean War. Their North Korean captors forced them to march through Seoul in July 1950, carrying a banner proclaiming the righteousness of the Communist cause and attacking U.S. intervention.

Wide World Photos, Inc.

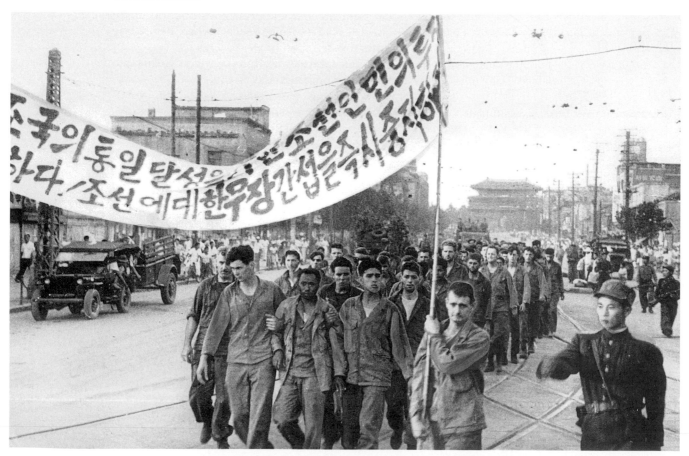

AMERICAN PLACES

The Harry S. Truman Library, Independence, Missouri

Entrance to the Harry S. Truman Library and Museum
Harry S. Truman Library.

When he left office in 1953, Truman said that the two things he most wanted were to become a grandfather (which he did) and to have a library established to document the history of his presidency. His was not the first presidential library. Franklin Roosevelt had donated his personal and official papers to the federal government; he also bestowed part of his estate at Hyde Park, New York, for a library and a museum. Truman's friends and associates helped him raise money, and in 1957 the Truman Library was dedicated on a site in Independence, Missouri, down the street from the house where Truman and his wife Bess had lived since their wedding.

From childhood, Truman avidly read history, believing passionately that effective public action depended on knowledge of the past. "There is nothing new in the world except the history you do not know," he said. His desire for a place to house the raw materials that scholars would used to reconstruct the history of his own life and administration helped to ensure that Roosevelt's initiative would not be a singular phenomenon; every president thereafter has followed suit. The federal government administers the presidential libraries through the National Archives and Records Administration.

In addition to letters, memos, reports, films, correspondence from the public, and other documents that Truman donated, he also encouraged family members, friends, and officials in his administration, such as Dean Acheson, to deposit their own papers. Scholars from all over the world visit the library in Independence to conduct research on the history of the Truman period. Some of the most important of these documents, including Truman's thoughts on dropping the atomic bomb and his decision to go to war in Korea, are available on the library's Web site.

The Truman Library also houses a museum containing thousands of objects, such as the footlocker Truman used as a soldier in France during World War I; political cartoons; gifts from foreign dignitaries and ordinary Americans; the cabinet chairs Truman and Acheson used; campaign paraphernalia; and gowns worn by the First Lady. A permanent interactive exhibit provides a close-up view of key events and decisions, such as the use of the atomic bomb, the recognition of Israel, the cold war, and the election of 1948. Visitors can walk through a replica of the Oval Office in the museum, and from time to time special exhibits have featured Truman's letters to Bess, NATO at 50, and desegregation of the armed services. Several of these exhibits are available online at the library's Web site, along with pages from Truman's diary and other key documents, photographs, and audio clips of Truman speaking on such topics as the United Nations, NATO, and Korea.

Harry and Bess Truman are buried in the library's courtyard, their gravestones displaying epitaphs that Truman wrote. His own simply provides the dates of his birth and death, notes the birth of their daughter, and lists the public offices that he held, reflecting his characteristic unpretentiousness. Truman's down-to-earth nature and his small-town, Midwest roots come to life in many of the displays and documents throughout the library; at the same time visitors are struck by how this ordinary man led the nation through extraordinary times and made extraordinary decisions.

FOR WEB LINKS RELATED TO THIS SITE AND OTHER AMERICAN PLACES, see "PlaceLinks" at bedfordstmartins.com/roark.

home to a hero's welcome, while baseball fans booed Truman when he appeared at Griffith Stadium on opening day.

Siding with MacArthur enabled Americans to hold on to their belief that the United States was all-powerful and to pin the Korean stalemate on the government's ineptitude or willingness to shelter subversives.

The adulation of MacArthur reflected American frustrations with containment. Why should Americans die simply to preserve the status quo rather than destroy the enemy once and for all? Siding with MacArthur enabled Americans to hold on to their belief that the United States was all-powerful and to pin the Korean stalemate on the government's ineptitude or willingness to shelter subversives. Moreover, Truman's earlier success in "scaring the hell" out of the American people over the threat of communism in the Mediterranean came back to haunt him. If communism was so evil, why not stamp it out as MacArthur wanted? When Congress investigated MacArthur's firing, all of the top military leaders supported the president, yet Truman never recovered from the political fallout. Nor was he able to end the war in Korea. Cease-fire negotiations began in July 1951, but peace talks dragged on for two more years, while twelve thousand more U.S. soldiers died.

Korea, Communism, and the 1952 Election

Popular discontent with Truman's war gave the Republicans a decided edge in the election battles of 1952. Their presidential candidate, General Dwight D. Eisenhower, enjoyed immense stature for his role in World War II. Reared in modest circumstances in Abilene, Kansas, Eisenhower attended West Point and rose steadily through the army ranks. As supreme commander in Europe, he won widespread acclaim for leading the Allied armies to victory over Germany. After the war, he served as army chief of staff and then as president of Columbia University. In 1950, Truman appointed Eisenhower the first supreme commander of NATO forces.

Both Republicans and Democrats had courted Eisenhower for the presidency in 1948. Although he believed that civilian control over the military worked best when professional soldiers kept out of politics, he found compelling reasons to run in 1952. Eisenhower agreed with the broad scope of Democratic foreign policy, but he deplored the Democrats' efforts to solve domestic problems with costly new federal programs. He equally disliked the foreign policy views of the leading Republican presidential contender, Senator Robert A. Taft, who attacked containment and sought to cut defense spending. Eisenhower decided to run as much to stop Taft and the **conservative** wing of the party as to turn the Democrats out of the White House.

Eisenhower defeated Taft for the nomination, but the old guard prevailed on the party platform. It excoriated containment as "negative, futile, and immoral" and charged the Truman administration with shielding "traitors to the Nation in high places." Eisenhower's choice of thirty-nine-year-old Senator Richard M. Nixon for his running mate helped to appease the Republican right wing and ensured that anticommunism would be a major theme of the campaign.

Richard Milhous Nixon grew up in southern California, raised by a Quaker mother and father who operated a grocery store. After working his way through college and law school, he served in the navy and briefly practiced law. In 1946, he entered politics, helping the Republicans recapture Congress by defeating a liberal incumbent for a seat in the House of Representatives. Nixon quickly made a name for himself as a member of HUAC and a key anti-Communist. In his 1950 bid for the Senate, he ran an effective smear campaign against the liberal congresswoman Helen Gahagan Douglas, charging her with being "pink [Communist] right down to her underwear."

Having decided not to run for another term, Truman persuaded Adlai E. Stevenson, governor of Illinois, to seek the Democratic nomination. A popular governor and acceptable to both liberals and southern Democrats, Stevenson easily won the nomination. He could not escape the domestic fallout from the Korean War, however, nor could he match the popular appeal of Eisenhower, the World War II hero.

The Republican campaign stumbled just once, over the last item of its "Korea, Communism, and Corruption" campaign. A newspaper reported that Nixon had accepted $18,000 from supporters in California. Although such gifts were then common in politics, Democrats leaped to attack Nixon. As newspaper editorials called for Nixon to withdraw from the ticket, most of Eisenhower's advisers urged him to dump his running mate.

Nixon saved himself by exploiting the new medium of television. In an emotional nationwide appeal, he disclosed his finances and documented his modest standard of living.

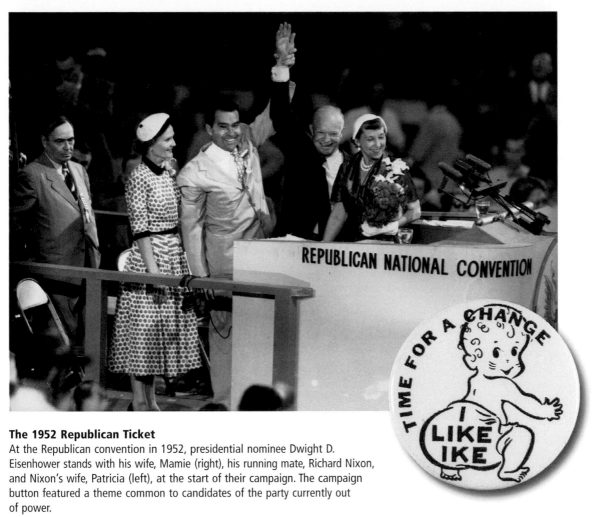

The 1952 Republican Ticket
At the Republican convention in 1952, presidential nominee Dwight D. Eisenhower stands with his wife, Mamie (right), his running mate, Richard Nixon, and Nixon's wife, Patricia (left), at the start of their campaign. The campaign button featured a theme common to candidates of the party currently out of power.
© Bettmann/Corbis; Collection of Janice L. and David J. Frent.

Conceding that the family pet, Checkers, could be considered an illegal gift, he vowed that he would not break his daughters' hearts by returning the cocker spaniel. The overwhelming popular response to the "Checkers speech" turned the tide for Nixon and convinced Eisenhower to keep him on the ticket.

With the issue of corruption neutralized, the Republicans harped on communism at home and failure to achieve victory in Korea. Less than two weeks before the election, Eisenhower announced dramatically, "I shall go to Korea," and voters registered their confidence in his ability to end the war. Cutting sharply into traditional Democratic territory, Eisenhower won several southern states and, overall, 55 percent of the popular vote. His coattails carried a narrow Republican majority to Congress.

An Armistice and the War's Costs

Eisenhower made good on his pledge to end the Korean War. In July 1953, the two sides reached an armistice that left Korea divided just as it had been three years earlier (see Map 26.3). The war took the lives of 36,000 Americans and wounded more than 100,000. Nick Tosques, among thousands of U.S. soldiers who were taken prisoners of war, spent two and a half years in a POW camp. "They interrogated us every day, and also at night," he recalled. "You never knew when they were coming for you. . . . Pretty soon I was telling them anything, just to keep from getting hit. . . . There were times when I did lose hope of ever getting back." South Korea lost more than 1 million people to war-related causes, and more than 1.8 million North Koreans and Chinese were killed or wounded.

The nature of the war and the unpopularity of the Rhee government made it difficult for soldiers to distinguish between friends and enemies, since civilian populations sometimes harbored North Korean agents. Consequently, as one journalist reported, the situation "forced upon our men in the field, acts and attitudes of the utmost savagery . . . the blotting out of villages where the enemy might be hiding, the shooting and shelling of refugees who may be North Koreans."

The Truman administration judged the war a success for its containment policy, since the United States had supported its promise to help nations that were resisting communism. Both Truman and Eisenhower managed to contain what amounted to a world war—involving twenty nations altogether—within a single country. Moreover, despite the presidents' threats to use nuclear bombs, they limited the Korean War to a conflict fought with conventional weapons.

The war had an enormous effect on defense policy and spending. In April 1950, two months before the Korean War began, the National Security Council completed a top-secret report on the nation's military strength. NSC 68, as the document was called, warned that the survival of the nation required a massive military buildup. Truman took no immediate action on its recommendations to triple the defense budget. Nonetheless, the Korean War brought about nearly all of the military buildup called for in NSC 68, vastly increasing U.S. capacity to act as a global power. Using the Korean crisis to expand American might elsewhere, Truman persuaded Congress to approve the rearming of West Germany and the commitment of troops to NATO. Military spending shot up from $14 billion in 1950 to $50 billion in 1953 and remained above $40 billion thereafter. By 1953, defense spending claimed 60 percent of the federal budget, and the size of the armed forces had tripled.

To General Matthew Ridgway, who succeeded MacArthur as commander of the UN forces, Korea taught the lesson that U.S. forces should never again fight a land war in Asia. Eisenhower concurred. Nevertheless, the Korean War induced the Truman administration to expand its role in Asia by increasing aid to the French, who were fighting to hang on to their colonial empire in Indochina. As U.S. marines retreated from a battle against Chinese soldiers in 1950, they sang, prophetically, "We're Harry's police force on call,/So put back your pack on,/The next step is Saigon,/Cheer up, me lads, bless 'em all."

Conclusion: The Cold War's Costs and Consequences

Dean Acheson titled his memoir about the Truman years *Present at the Creation*, aptly capturing the magnitude of change that marked the aftermath of World War II. More than any development in the postwar world, the cold war defined American politics and society for decades to come. Truman's decision to oppose communism throughout the world marked the most momentous foreign policy initiative in the nation's history. It transformed the federal government, shifting its priorities from domestic to external affairs, greatly expanding its budget, and substantially increasing the power of the president. Military spending helped transform the nation itself, as defense contracts encouraged economic and population booms in the West and Southwest. The nuclear arms race attending the cold war put the people of the world at risk, consumed resources that might have been used to improve living standards, and skewed the economy toward dependence on military projects. While debate about who was responsible for the cold war and whether it could have been avoided persisted, no one could doubt its impact on American society or the world.

In sharp contrast to foreign policy, the domestic policies of the postwar years reflected continuity with the past. Preoccupied with foreign policy, Truman failed to mobilize support for his ambition to assist the disadvantaged with new initiatives in education, health, agriculture, and civil rights, but he successfully defended most New Deal reforms. Although the poor and minorities suffered from the inattention to domestic problems, the boost to industry from cold war spending and the reconstruction of Western Europe and Japan contributed to an economic boom that lifted the standard of living for a majority of Americans.

Many Americans had difficulty accepting the terms of the cold war, not accustomed to paying sustained attention to the rest of the world or to fighting wars without total defeat of the enemy. Consequently, another high cost of the cold war was the anti-Communist hysteria, which silenced the left, stifled debate, and narrowed the range of ideas acceptable for political discussion. Partisan politics and the Truman administration's constant rhetoric about the Communist menace fueled McCarthyism, but the obsession with subversion also fed on popular frustrations over the failure of containment to produce clear-cut victories. Convulsing the nation in bitter disunity, McCarthyism reflected a loss of confidence in American power. It would be a major challenge of the next administration to restore that unity and confidence.

FOR ADDITIONAL FIRSTHAND ACCOUNTS OF THIS PERIOD, see Chapter 26 in Michael Johnson, ed., *Reading the American Past,* Third Edition.

TO ASSESS YOUR MASTERY OF THE MATERIAL IN THIS CHAPTER, see the Online Study Guide at bedfordstmartins.com/ roark.

FOR WEB LINKS RELATED TO TOPICS IN THIS CHAPTER, see "HistoryLinks," "DocLinks," and "PlaceLinks" at bedfordstmartins.com/roark.

CHRONOLOGY

1945 • Harry S. Truman becomes president of United States upon death of Franklin D. Roosevelt.

1946 • Postwar labor unrest erupts throughout United States.

• Truman creates Committee on Civil Rights.

• United States grants independence to Philippines.

• Congress passes Employment Act, signifying government's responsibility for healthy economy.

• Congressional elections result in Republican control of 80th Congress.

1947 • George F. Kennan's article on policy of containment appears in *Foreign Affairs.*

• National Security Act unifies military services under secretary of defense and creates National Security Council (NSC) and Central Intelligence Agency (CIA).

• Truman asks Congress for aid to Greece and Turkey to counter communism and announces Truman Doctrine.

• Truman establishes by executive order a loyalty and security program designed to eliminate Communists and their sympathizers from the federal government.

1948 • Congress approves Marshall Plan, providing massive aid to stimulate European recovery.

• Congress makes women permanent part of armed services.

• Truman issues executive order to desegregate armed services.

• Mexican American veterans found the American GI Forum to fight discrimination.

• United States recognizes state of Israel.

• Truman defeats Thomas E. Dewey to win full term as president.

1948–1949
• Soviets block access to West Berlin, setting off Berlin crisis and eleven-month Western airlift.

1949 • Communists under Mao Zedong win Chinese civil war and take over mainland China; Nationalists under Chiang Kai-shek retreat to Taiwan.

• North Atlantic Treaty Organization (NATO) forms to counter Soviet threat to Western Europe.

• Truman administration initiates Point IV technical aid program to assist third world nations.

• Soviet Union explodes atomic bomb.

1950 • Senator Joseph McCarthy begins campaign against alleged Communists in United States, ushering in the period of anti-Communist hysteria known as McCarthyism.

• Truman approves development of hydrogen bomb.

• United States sends troops to South Korea to repel North Korean assault.

1951 • Truman relieves General Douglas MacArthur of command in Korea for insubordination.

• United States ends postwar occupation of Japan; the two nations sign peace treaty and mutual security pact.

1952 • Republican Dwight D. Eisenhower elected president.

1953 • Armistice halts Korean War.

BIBLIOGRAPHY

General Works

John Patrick Diggins, *The Proud Decades: America in War and Peace, 1941–1960* (1988).

Alonzo L. Hamby, *Man of the People: A Life of Harry S. Truman* (1995).

Melvyn Leffler, *A Preponderance of Power: National Security, the Truman Administration, and the Cold War* (1992).

David McCullough, *Truman* (1992).

Steve Neal, *Harry and Ike: The Partnership That Remade the Postwar World* (2001).

William L. O'Neill, *American High: The Years of Confidence, 1945–1960* (1986).

James T. Patterson, *Grand Expectations: The United States, 1945–1974* (1996).

William E. Pemberton, *Harry S. Truman: Fair Dealer and Cold Warrior* (1989).

Lisle A. Rose, *The Cold War Comes to Main Street: America in 1950* (1999).

Michael S. Sherry, *In the Shadow of War* (1995).

Stephen Whitfield, *The Culture of the Cold War* (1990).

Domestic Politics and Policies

Kevin Boyle, *The UAW and the Heyday of American Liberalism, 1945–1968* (1995).

John C. Culver and John Hyde, *American Dreamer: The Life and Times of Henry A. Wallace* (2000).

Richard M. Dalfiume, *Desegregation of the U.S. Armed Forces: Fighting on Two Fronts* (1969).

Richard O. Davies, *Housing Reform during the Truman Administration* (1966).

Gary A. Donaldson, *Truman Defeats Dewey* (1998).

John Egerton, *Speak Now against the Day: The Generation before the Civil Rights Movement in the South* (1994).

Kari Frederickson, *The Dixiecrat Revolt and the End of the Solid South, 1932–1968* (2001).

Michael R. Gardner, *Harry Truman and Civil Rights: Moral Courage and Political Risks* (2002).

Susan M. Hartmann, *Truman and the 80th Congress* (1971).

Zachary Karabell, *The Last Campaign: How Harry Truman Won the 1948 Election* (2000).

R. Alton Lee, *Truman and Taft-Hartley* (1966).

Nelson Lichtenstein, *The Most Dangerous Man in Detroit: Walter Reuther and the Fate of American Labor* (1996).

Norman D. Markowitz, *The Rise and Fall of the People's Century: Henry A. Wallace and American Liberalism, 1941–1948* (1973).

Allen J. Matusow, *Farm Policies and Politics in the Truman Years* (1967).

Keith W. Olson, *The G.I. Bill, the Veterans, and the Colleges* (1974).

James Patterson, *Mr. Republican: A Biography of Robert A. Taft* (1974).

William B. Pickett, *Eisenhower Decides to Run: Presidential Politics and Cold War Strategy* (2000).

Monte M. Poen, *Harry S. Truman versus the Medical Lobby: The Genesis of Medicare* (1979).

Jules Tygiel, *Baseball's Great Experiment: Jackie Robinson and His Legacy* (1997).

Robert Zieger, *The CIO, 1935–1955* (1995).

Origins of the Cold War

Gar Alperovitz, *Atomic Diplomacy* (rev. ed., 1994).

Carolyn Eisenberg, *Drawing the Line: The American Decision to Divide Germany, 1944–1949* (1996).

John Fousek, *To Lead the Free World: American Nationalism and the Cultural Roots of the Cold War* (2000).

John L. Gaddis, *The United States and the Origins of the Cold War* (rev. ed., 2000).

James L. Gormly, *The Collapse of the Grand Alliance, 1945–1948* (1987).

Fraser J. Harbut, *The Iron Curtain: Churchill, America, and the Origins of the Cold War* (1986).

Michael Hogan, *A Cross of Iron: Harry S. Truman and the Origins of the National Security State* (1998).

Bruce R. Kuniholm, *The Origins of the Cold War in the Near East* (1980).

Ernest R. May, ed., *American Cold War Strategy: Interpreting NSC 68* (1993).

Wilson D. Miscamble, *George F. Kennan and the Making of Foreign Policy, 1947–1950* (1992).

Arnold A. Offner, *Another Such Victory: President Truman and the Cold War, 1945–1953* (2002).

Chester J. Pach Jr., *Arming the Free World: The Origins of the United States Military Assistance Program, 1945–1950* (1990).

Robert A. Pollard, *Economic Security and the Origins of the Cold War* (1985).

Michael Schaller, *The American Occupation of Japan: The Origins of the Cold War in Asia* (1985).

Randall B. Woods and Howard Jones, *Dawning of the Cold War: The United States' Quest for Order* (1994).

Daniel Yergin, *Shattered Peace: The Origins of the Cold War and the National Security State* (1977).

Foreign Policy

Dean Acheson, *Present at the Creation* (1969).

Carol Anderson, *Eyes Off the Prize: The United Nations and the African American Struggle for Human Rights, 1944–1955* (2003).

William S. Borden, *The Pacific Alliance: United States Foreign Economic Policy and Japanese Trade Recovery, 1947–1955* (1984).

James Chace, *Acheson: The Secretary of State Who Created the American World* (1998).

Gordon H. Chang, *Friends and Enemies: The United States, China, and the Soviet Union, 1948–1972* (1990).

Michael J. Cohen, *Truman and Israel* (1990).

Peter L. Hahn, *The United States, Great Britain, and Egypt: Strategy and Diplomacy in the Early Cold War* (1991).

Gary R. Hess, *The United States' Emergence as a Southeast Asian Power, 1940–1950* (1987).

Walter L. Hixon, *George F. Kennan: Cold War Iconoclast* (1989).

Michael J. Hogan, *The Marshall Plan: America, Britain, and the Reconstruction of Western Europe, 1947–1952* (1987).

Walter Isaacson and Evan Thomas, *The Wise Men: Six Friends and the World They Made: Acheson, Bohlen, Harriman, Kennan, Lovett, McCloy* (1986).

Lawrence S. Kaplan, *The United States and NATO: The Formative Years* (1984).

Stuart W. Leslie, *The Cold War and American Science* (1993).

Thomas J. McCormick, *America's Half-Century: United States Foreign Policy in the Cold War* (1989).

Brenda Gayle Plummer, *Rising Wind: Black Americans and U.S. Foreign Affairs, 1935–1960* (1996).

Richard Rhodes, *Dark Sun: The Making of the Hydrogen Bomb* (1995).

David Rudgers, *Creating the Secret State: The Origins of the Central Intelligence Agency, 1943–1947* (2000).

Michael Schaller, *Altered States: The United States and Japan since the Occupation* (1997).

Nancy B. Tucker, *Patterns in the Dust: Chinese-American Relations and the Recognition Controversy, 1949–1950* (1983).

Evan M. Wilson, *Decision on Palestine: How the U.S. Came to Recognize Israel* (1979).

Lawrence S. Wittner, *American Intervention in Greece, 1943–1949* (1982).

McCarthyism

Michael R. Belknap, *Cold War Political Justice: The Smith Act, the Communist Party, and American Civil Liberties* (1977).

Larry Ceplair and Steven Englund, *The Inquisition in Hollywood: Politics in the Film Community* (1980).

Richard M. Freeland, *The Truman Doctrine and the Origins of McCarthyism: Foreign Policy, Domestic Politics, and International Security, 1946–1948* (1972).

Richard M. Fried, *Nightmare in Red: The McCarthy Era in Perspective* (1990).

John Earl Haynes, *Red Scare or Red Menace: American Communism and Anticommunism in the Cold War Era* (1990).

John Earl Haynes and Harvey Klehr, *Venona: Decoding Soviet Espionage in America* (1999).

Stanley I. Kutler, *The American Inquisition* (1982).

David Oshinsky, *A Conspiracy So Immense: The World of Joe McCarthy* (1983).

Richard Gid Powers, *Not without Honor: The History of American Anticommunism* (1995).

Ronald Radosh and Joyce Milton, *The Rosenberg File: A Search for the Truth* (1983).

Ellen W. Schrecker, *No Ivory Tower: McCarthyism and the Universities* (1986).

Ellen W. Schrecker, *Many Are the Crimes: McCarthyism in America* (1998).

Peter L. Steinberg, *The Great "Red" Menace: United States Persecution of American Communists, 1947–1952* (1984).

Sam Tannenhaus, *Whittaker Chambers* (1997).

Allen Weinstein, *Perjury: The Hiss-Chambers Case* (1978).

Allen Weinstein and Alexander Vassiliev, *The Haunted Wood: Soviet Espionage in America* (1999).

Korea

Jian Chen, *China's Road to the Korean War* (1996).

Bruce Cumings, *The Origins of the Korean War*, 2 vols. (1981, 1990).

Rosemary Foot, *The Wrong War: American Policy and the Dimensions of the Korean Conflict, 1950–1953* (1984).

Burton I. Kaufman, *The Korean War: Challenges in Crisis, Credibility, and Command* (1986).

Paul J. Pierpaoli Jr., *Truman and Korea: The Political Culture of the Early Cold War* (1999).

Stanley Sandler, *The Korean War: No Victors, No Vanquished* (1999).

William Stueck, *The Korean War: An International History* (1995).

William Stueck, *Rethinking the Korean War: A New Diplomatic and Strategic History* (2002).

Richard C. Thornton, *Odd Man Out: Truman, Stalin, Mao and the Origins of the Korean War* (2000).

John Toland, *In Mortal Combat: Korea, 1950–1953* (1992).

Stanley Weintraub, *MacArthur's War: Korea and the Undoing of an American Hero* (2000).

Richard Whelan, *Drawing the Line: The Korean War, 1950–1953* (1990).

1956 CADILLAC CONVERTIBLE

The automobile reflected both corporate and family prosperity in the 1950s. This car was manufactured by General Motors, the biggest and richest corporation in the world and the first to sell a billion dollars' worth of products. Costing about $5,000, the Cadillac was GM's top-of-the-line car, one of the first purchases the McDonald brothers made when they struck it rich with their hamburger stand in California. Even the cheaper models that average Americans could afford featured the gas-guzzling size and space-age style of this Cadillac. A massive interstate highway system begun in 1956 boosted automobile travel, and widespread car ownership went hand in hand with Americans' move to the suburbs.

Ron Kimball Photography.

27

The Politics and Culture of Abundance

1952–1960

TRAILED BY REPORTERS, U.S. vice president Richard M. Nixon led Soviet premier Nikita Khrushchev through the American National Exhibition in Moscow in July 1959. The display of American consumer goods followed an exhibition of Soviet products in New York, part of a cultural exchange between the two superpowers that reflected a slight thaw in the **cold war**. Both Khrushchev and Nixon seized on the propaganda potential of the moment. As they made their way through the display, their verbal sparring turned into a slugfest of words and gestures that reporters dubbed "the kitchen debate."

Showing off a new color television set, Nixon told Khrushchev that the Soviet Union "may be ahead of us . . . in the thrust of your rockets for . . . outer space," but the United States outstripped the Soviets in consumer goods. "Any steelworker could buy this house," Nixon boasted, as they walked through a six-room ranch-style model. Khrushchev retorted that in the Soviet Union, "you are entitled to housing," whereas in the United States the poor were reduced to sleeping on the pavement.

While the two men inspected appliances in the model kitchen, Nixon declared, "These are designed to make things easier for our women." Khrushchev responded that his country did not have "the capitalist attitude toward women" and appreciated women's contributions to the economy, not their domesticity. The Soviet leader found many of the items on display interesting, he said, but he added that "they are not needed in life. . . . They are merely gadgets." In reply, Nixon insisted, "Isn't it far better to be talking about washing machines than machines of war?" Khrushchev agreed, yet he affirmed the persistence of cold war tensions when he later blustered, "We too are giants. You want to threaten—we will answer threats with threats."

The Eisenhower administration in fact had begun with threats to the Soviet Union. Republican campaigners vowed to roll back **communism** and liberate "enslaved" peoples under Soviet rule. In practice, however, Eisenhower settled for a **containment** policy much like that of his predecessor, Harry S. Truman, though Eisenhower relied more on nuclear weapons and on secret actions by the Central Intelligence Agency (CIA). Yet, as Nixon's visit to Moscow demonstrated, Eisenhower took advantage of political changes in the Soviet Union to reduce tensions in Soviet-American relations.

Continuity with the Truman administration also characterized domestic policy. Although Eisenhower favored the business community with tax cuts and opposed strong federal efforts in health care, education, and race relations, he did not propose to roll back **New Deal** programs. A majority of

- **Eisenhower and the Politics of the "Middle Way"**
  The President and McCarthy
  Modern Republicanism
  Termination and Relocation of Native Americans
  The 1956 Election and the Second Term

- **Liberation Rhetoric and the Practice of Containment**
  The "New Look" in Foreign Policy
  Applying Containment to Vietnam
  Interventions in Latin America and the Middle East
  The Nuclear Arms Race

- **New Work and Living Patterns in an Economy of Abundance**
  Technology Transforms Agriculture and Industry
  Burgeoning Suburbs and Declining Cities
  The Rise of the Sun Belt
  The Democratization of Higher Education

- **The Culture of Abundance**
  A Consumer Culture
  The Revival of Domesticity and Religion
  Television Transforms Culture and Politics
  Countercurrents

- **Emergence of a Civil Rights Movement**
  African Americans Challenge the Supreme Court and the President
  Montgomery and Mass Protest

- **Conclusion: Peace and Prosperity Mask Unmet Challenges**

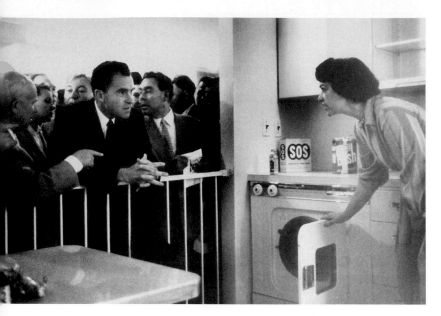

The Kitchen Debate
Soviet premier Nikita Khrushchev (left) and Vice President Richard M. Nixon (center) debate the relative merits of their nations' economies at the American National Exhibition held in Moscow in 1959.
Howard Sochurek/TimePix/Getty.

Eisenhower and the Politics of the "Middle Way"

Moderation was the guiding principle of Eisenhower's domestic agenda and leadership style. Favoring in 1953 a "middle way between untrammeled freedom of the individual and the demands for the welfare of the whole Nation," he pledged that his administration would "avoid government by bureaucracy as carefully as it avoids neglect of the helpless." Claiming that Democrats appealed to divisive class interests, Eisenhower presented himself as a leader above partisan politics and interest groups who would govern by compromise and consensus. Nicknamed "Ike" by his friends and the public, the confident war hero remained popular throughout his presidency.

The President and McCarthy

The new president attempted to distance himself from the anti-Communist fervor that had plagued the Truman administration. Eisenhower shared Senator Joseph McCarthy's goal of eliminating communism from American life, and though he deplored McCarthy's methods, he made little effort to silence him, privately explaining that he would not demean the presidency by getting into "a pissing contest with that skunk." Eisenhower feared that denouncing McCarthy would alienate powerful **conservative** Republicans in Congress, and many Republicans realized the benefits from McCarthy's attacks on Democrats. While one senator called McCarthy an "SOB," he shrewdly observed that "sometimes it's useful to have SOB's around to do the dirty work." Even under a Republican administration, McCarthy continued his allegations of Communists in the government, and thousands of federal employees lost their jobs.

Eisenhower correctly predicted that McCarthy would ultimately destroy himself. With the end of the Korean War, popular frustrations over containment abated, and the anti-Communist hysteria subsided. In 1954, McCarthy tightened his own noose when he went after the army. As he hurled reckless charges of communism against military personnel during weeks of televised hearings, public opinion turned against him. "Have you left no sense of decency?" demanded the army's lawyer. A Senate vote to condemn him in December 1954 marked the end of his influence, but Eisenhower's inaction had

Americans enjoyed astounding material gains under the immensely popular president and seemed content with his "moderate Republicanism."

Cold war weapons production spurred the economy, whose vitality stimulated suburban development, contributed to the burgeoning populations and enterprise in the West and Southwest, and enabled millions of Americans to buy the products on display in Moscow. As new homes, television sets, and household appliances transformed their patterns of living, Americans took part in a dominant **consumer culture** that also celebrated marriage, family, and traditional gender roles, even as more and more married women took jobs outside their homes.

The cold war and the economic boom helped African Americans mount a strong challenge to tradition in the 1950s. Large numbers of African Americans took direct action against segregation and disfranchisement, developing the institutions, leadership, and strategies to mount a civil rights movement of unprecedented size and power.

> Although Eisenhower deplored McCarthy's methods, he made little effort to silence him.

allowed the senator to spread his poison longer than he might otherwise have done.

Modern Republicanism

In contrast to the Old Guard conservatives in his party who wanted to repeal much of the New Deal and preferred a unilateral approach to foreign policy, Eisenhower preached "modern Republicanism." This meant resisting additional federal intervention in economic and social life, but it did not mean turning the clock back to the 1920s. Democratic control of Congress after the elections of 1954 further contributed to the moderate approach of the Eisenhower administration (1953–1961), whose record overall maintained the course charted by the New Deal and Fair Deal.

Despite his claim to be above interest-group politics, Eisenhower turned for advice almost exclusively to business leaders and chose wealthy executives and attorneys for his cabinet. When he appointed Martin Durkin, president of the plumbers union, as secretary of labor, a liberal journal quipped that Eisenhower had "picked a cabinet of eight millionaires and one plumber." Eisenhower also sought advice from his "gang," a group of wealthy businessmen with whom he socialized.

Eisenhower sometimes echoed the conservative old-guard Republicans' conviction that government was best left to the states and economic decisions to private business. "If all Americans want is security, they can go to prison," Eisenhower commented about social welfare in 1949. Yet, although **liberals** scorned the president's conservatism by calling him "Eisenhoover," the **welfare state** actually grew during his administration, and the federal government took on new projects. The "middle way" applied the brakes, but it did not reduce federal responsibility for economic development and for assistance to poor Americans.

In 1954, Eisenhower signed laws expanding Social Security and continuing the federal government's modest role in financing public housing. He enlarged the government by obtaining congressional approval for a Department of Health, Education, and Welfare, naming former Women's Army Corps commander and Texas publisher Oveta Culp Hobby to head it, the second female appointed to a cabinet post. And

Polio Vaccine Distribution in the South
In 1954, American children lined up to be inoculated with the new vaccine to prevent polio. But as this scene from Blytheville, Arkansas, shows, children waiting to receive the vaccine stood in strictly segregated lines.
Charles Bell, *Memphis Commercial Appeal.*

when the spread of polio neared epidemic proportions in the 1950s, Eisenhower obtained funds from Congress to distribute a vaccine, even though conservatives preferred that states assume that responsibility.

Eisenhower's greatest domestic initiative was the Interstate Highway and Defense System Act of 1956. Promoted as essential to the nation's cold war defense strategy and an impetus to economic growth, the act authorized construction of a national highway system, with the federal government paying most of the costs through increased fuel and vehicle taxes. Millions of Americans benefited from the greater ease of travel and improved transportation of goods, and the new highways also spurred growth in the fast-food and motel industries as well as the development of shopping malls. The most substantial gains went to the trucking, construction, and automobile industries, which had lobbied hard for the law. The monumental highway project eventually exacted severe costs, unforeseen at the time, in the form of air pollution, energy consumption, declining railroads and other forms of mass transportation, and decay in central cities (Map 27.1).

> Eisenhower's "middle way" applied the brakes, but it did not reverse federal responsibility for economic development and for assistance to poor Americans.

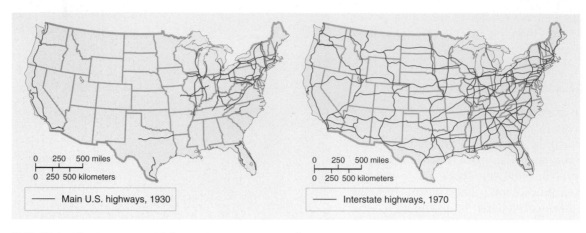

MAP 27.1   The Interstate Highway System, 1930 and 1970
Built with federal funds authorized in the Interstate Highway Act of 1956, superhighways soon crisscrossed the nation. Trucking, construction, gasoline, and travel were among the industries that prospered, but railroads suffered from the subsidized competition.

READING THE MAP: What regions of the United States had main highways in 1930? What regions did not? How had the situation changed by 1970?
CONNECTIONS: What impact did the growth of the interstate highway system have on migration patterns in the United States? What benefits did the new interstate highways bring to Americans and at what costs?

FOR MORE HELP ANALYZING THIS MAP, see the map activity for this chapter in the Online Study Guide at bedfordstmartins.com/roark.

> Most urban Indians remained in or near poverty, and even many who had welcomed relocation eventually determined that they needed to resist "assimilation to the degree that we would . . . lose our culture and our [way] of living."

In other areas, Eisenhower restrained federal activity in favor of state governments and private enterprise. His large tax cuts, for example, directed most benefits to business and the wealthy, and he stubbornly resisted a larger federal role in health care, education, and civil rights. Moreover, whereas Democrats sought to keep nuclear power in government hands, Eisenhower signed legislation authorizing the private manufacture and sale of nuclear power. Workers broke ground at Shippingport, Pennsylvania, for the first commercial nuclear power plant in 1954.

Termination and Relocation of Native Americans

The Eisenhower administration's efforts to restrict federal activity also helped shape a new direction in Indian policy, reversing the emphasis on strengthening tribal governments and preserving Indian culture established in the Indian Reorganization Act of 1934 (see chapter 24). After World War II, when some 25,000 Indians had left their homes for military service and another 40,000 for work in defense industries, policymakers began to push harder for assimilating Native Americans and ending their special relationships with government. To some officials, who reflected the cold war emphasis on conformity and national unity, the communal practices of Indians resembled socialism and stifled individual initiative. Commissioner of Indian Affairs Glenn Emmons expressed the pragmatic view that tribal lands could not produce sufficient income to lift Indians from poverty, but he also revealed the ethnocentrism of policymakers when he insisted that Indians wanted to "work and live like Americans."

By the 1950s, the government had implemented a three-part program of compensation, termination, and relocation. In 1946, Congress established a commission to discharge once and for all any claims by Native Americans for lands taken from them by the government. When it closed in 1978, the Indian Claims Commission had settled 285 cases with compensation

Indian Relocation

As part of its new emphasis on assimilation in the late 1940s and 1950s, the Bureau of Indian Affairs distributed this leaflet to entice Native Americans to move from their reservations to cities. Either with government assistance or on their own, thousands of Indians relocated in the years after World War II. In 1950, just 13.4 percent of Indians lived in urban areas; by 1970, 44 percent did so, and by 1990 the figure had reached 63 percent. Which of the features on this leaflet do you think would be most appealing to Native Americans living on reservations? Which might evoke little interest?

National Archives.

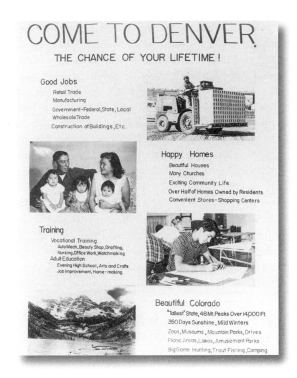

exceeding $800 million. The second policy—termination—began during the Truman administration under Dillon S. Myer, who had managed the internment of Japanese Americans during World War II and who became commissioner of Indian affairs in 1950. Believing that the Bureau of Indian Affairs should "not do anything which others can do as well or better" and "nothing for Indians which Indians can do for themselves," Myer proposed to end the special relationship between Indians and the federal government and to eliminate health and educational services to Indian tribes, initiatives that were carried out under his successor.

Beginning in 1953, Eisenhower signed bills transferring jurisdiction over tribal lands in several states to state and local governments. The loss of federal hospitals, schools, and other special arrangements devastated some tribes. As had happened after passage of the Dawes Act in 1887 (see chapter 18), some corporate interests and individuals took advantage of the opportunity to purchase Indian lands cheaply. According to one Indian leader, some of his people saw termination as "severing of ties already loose and ineffective," but to the great majority it was "like the strike of doom." Decades later the Menominees and the Klamaths secured restoration of their tribal status, and the government abandoned termination in the 1960s.

Relocation, the third piece of Native American policy, began with a pilot program in

Selected Indian Relocations, 1950–1970

1948 and grew to involve more than 100,000 Native Americans by 1973, although even more moved without federal assistance. The government encouraged Indians to move to cities, providing one-way bus tickets and, at their destinations, relocation centers to help with housing, job training, and medical care. To make it difficult to return home, officials sent them to cities far away from their reservations—South Dakota Sioux to California, for example, and Alaskan Natives to Chicago. Yet about one-third of those relocated went back to the reservation, and most of those who stayed faced great difficulties: racism, lack of adequately paying jobs for which they had skills, poor housing in what became Indian ghettos, and above all the loss of their traditional culture. "I wish we had never left home," sighed one woman. "It's dirty and noisy, and people all around, crowded. . . . It seems like I never see the sky or trees." Her sons were headed for reform school, and her husband was out of work and drinking.

Some who overcame these obstacles applauded the program. One man did not mind that his grandchildren did not consider themselves Indians; he contrasted the urban job and educational opportunities with the reservation where "I see no jobs, nothing to do, everyone just drinks." But most urban Indians remained in or near poverty, and even many who had welcomed relocation eventually determined that they needed to resist "assimilation to the degree that we would lose our identity as Indian people, lose our culture and our [way] of living." Within two decades, when a national pan-Indian movement emerged to do just that and demand much more for Indians, that new militancy was very much the product of the urbanization of Native Americans (see chapter 28).

The 1956 Election and the Second Term

While not all people in the United States were living the American dream, with the nation at peace and the economy booming, Eisenhower easily defeated Adlai Stevenson in 1956, losing only seven states. But two years later, the Democrats all but wiped out the Republican Party, gaining a 64–34 majority in the Senate and a 282–135 advantage in the House. Though Ike captured voters' hearts, a majority of voters remained wedded to the programs and policies of the Democrats.

In part because of the Democratic resurgence, Eisenhower faced more serious leadership challenges in his second term. The economy plunged into a recession, and unemployment rose to 7 percent. Eisenhower fought with Congress over the budget and vetoed bills providing for expanded public works projects, a high level of price supports for farmers, and housing and urban development. The president and Congress did reach agreement in two key areas: enacting the first, though largely symbolic, civil rights legislation in a century and establishing a new role for the government in education.

In the end, the first Republican administration after the New Deal left the size and functions of the federal government intact, though it tipped policy somewhat more in favor of corporate interests. Unparalleled prosperity graced the Eisenhower years, and inflation was kept low. The late-1957 recession was one of two in the 1950s, but the economy recovered without putting to a test the president's aversion to substantial federal intervention.

Liberation Rhetoric and the Practice of Containment

At his 1953 inauguration, Eisenhower warned that "forces of good and evil are massed and armed and opposed as rarely before in history." Like Truman, he saw communism as a threat to the nation's security and economic interests. Eisenhower's foreign policy differed from Truman's, though, in three areas: its rhetoric, its means, and—after Stalin's death in 1953—its movement toward accommodation with the Soviet Union.

Republican rhetoric—voiced most prominently by Secretary of State John Foster Dulles—deplored containment as "negative, futile, and immoral" because it accepted the existing Soviet sphere of control. Yet, despite promises to roll back Soviet power, the Eisenhower administration continued the containment policy, actively intervening at the margins of Communist power in Asia, the Middle East, and Latin America, but not at its core in Europe.

The "New Look" in Foreign Policy

To meet his goals of balancing the federal budget and cutting taxes, Eisenhower determined to control military expenditures. Moreover, he feared that massive defense spending would threaten the economic strength of the nation. A state based on warfare could destroy the very society it was intended to protect. As he declared in 1953, "Every gun that is made, every warship launched, every rocket fired signifies, in the final sense, a theft from those who hunger and are not fed, those who are cold and not clothed."

Reflecting Americans' confidence in technology and opposition to a large peacetime army, Eisenhower's defense strategy concentrated U.S. military strength in nuclear weapons along with planes and missiles to deliver them. By 1955, one U.S. bomber carried more force than all the explosives ever detonated in the history of humankind. Instead of spending huge amounts for large ground forces of its own, the United States would give friendly nations American weapons and back them up with an ominous nuclear arsenal.

This was Eisenhower's "New Look" in foreign policy. Airpower and nuclear weapons provided, in Secretary of State Dulles's words, a "maximum deterrent at bearable cost" or, as Defense Secretary Charles Wilson put it, a

The Nuclear Arms Race
This *Newsweek* cover of Soviet leader Nikita Khrushchev and President Dwight D. Eisenhower balanced on the head of a nuclear missile suggests the precarious world created by the nuclear arms race. The table on which the two men sit refers to the arms limitation negotiations under way when the magazine came off the press in 1959.

"bigger bang for the buck." Dulles believed that America's willingness to "go to the brink" of war with its intimidating nuclear superiority—a strategy called **brinksmanship**—would block any Soviet efforts to expand.

Nuclear weapons could not stop a Soviet nuclear attack, but, in response to one, they could inflict enormous destruction on the USSR. The certainty of "massive retaliation" was meant to deter the Soviets from launching an attack. Because the Soviet Union could respond similarly to an American first strike, this nuclear standoff became known as mutually assured destruction, or MAD. Winston Churchill called it a "mutual balance of terror." Yet leaders of each nation sought not just balance, but nuclear superiority, and pursued an ever-escalating arms race.

Nuclear weapons were useless, however, in rolling back the **iron curtain**, because they would destroy the very peoples whom the United States promised to liberate. When a re-

volt against the Soviet-controlled government began in Hungary in 1956, Dulles's liberation rhetoric proved to be empty. A radio plea from the Hungarian Freedom Fighters cried, "SOS! They just brought us a rumor that the American troops will be here within one or two hours." But help did not come. Eisenhower was unwilling to risk U.S. soldiers and possible nuclear war, and Soviet troops soon suppressed the insurrection, killing thirty thousand Hungarians.

Applying Containment to Vietnam

A major challenge to the containment policy came in Southeast Asia, where in 1945 a nationalist coalition called the Vietminh, led by Ho Chi Minh, had proclaimed Vietnam's independence from France. When France fought to maintain its colony, Ho fought back, and the area plunged into war (see Map 29.2 in chapter 29). Because Ho declared himself a Communist, the Truman administration quietly began to provide aid to the French.

Eisenhower viewed communism in Vietnam much as Truman had regarded it in Greece and Turkey, a view that became known as the **domino theory**. "You have a row of dominoes," Eisenhower explained, and "you knock over the first one, and what will happen to the last one is the certainty that it will go over very quickly." A Communist victory in Southeast Asia, he warned, could trigger the fall of Japan, Taiwan, and the Philippines. By 1954, the United States was contributing 75 percent of the cost of France's war, but Eisenhower resisted a larger role. When the French asked for troops and airplanes from the United States in order to avert almost certain defeat at Dien Bien Phu, Eisenhower firmly said no. Conscious of U.S. losses in the Korean War, he would not commit troops to another ground war in Asia.

Dien Bien Phu fell in May 1954 and with it the French colony of Vietnam. Two months later in Geneva, France signed a truce. The Geneva accords temporarily partitioned Vietnam at the seventeenth parallel, separating the Vietminh in the north from the puppet government established

Geneva Accords of 1954

by the French in the south and prohibiting both from joining a military alliance or permitting foreign bases on their soil. Within two years, the Vietnamese people were to vote in elections for a unified government. The United States promised to support free elections but did not sign the accords.

Some officials warned against U.S. involvement in Vietnam. An intelligence study, for example, predicted that even with American assistance, the chances of securing a viable government in the South were "poor." Defense Secretary Wilson could "see nothing but grief in store for us if we remained in that area." Eisenhower and Dulles, however, believed that a Communist Vietnam would threaten all of Asia and moved to prop up the dominoes with a new alliance. In September 1954, the United States joined with Britain, France, Australia, New Zealand, Thailand, Pakistan, and the Philippines in the Southeast Asia Treaty Organization (SEATO), committed to the defense of Cambodia, Laos, and South Vietnam. The ink was barely dry on the treaty when the United States began to send weapons and military advisers to South Vietnam and put the CIA to work infiltrating and destabilizing North Vietnam. Fearing that the popular vote mandated by the Geneva accords would result in a Communist victory, the United States supported South Vietnamese prime minister Ngo Dinh Diem's refusal to hold the election.

Between 1955 and 1961, the United States provided $800 million to the South Vietnamese army (ARVN). Yet even with U.S. dollars, the ARVN was grossly unprepared for the **guerrilla warfare** that began in the late 1950s. In 1959, Ho Chi Minh's government in Hanoi began sending military assistance to Vietminh rebels in the south, who stepped up their guerrilla attacks on the Diem government. The insurgents gained control over villages not only through sheer military power but also because the largely rural and Buddhist peasants were alienated from the Catholic, Westernized, French-speaking Diem and outraged by his repressive regime. Unwilling to abandon containment, Eisenhower handed over the deteriorating situation—along with a firm commitment to defend South Vietnam against communism—to his successor.

Fidel Castro Triumphs in Cuba

Fidel Castro came from a privileged family and earned a law degree at the University of Havana, but he spent his youth working for the overthrow of Cuban dictator Fulgencio Batista. After leading an assault on Batista's soldiers in 1953, he spent two years in prison and then slowly built up an army of guerrilla fighters. "I began revolution with 82 men," he said. "If I had [to] do it again, I do it with 10 or 15 and absolute faith. It does not matter how small you are if you have faith and plan of action." He is shown at the city hall of Santa Clara just before his triumphal march to Havana in January 1959.

Andrew St. George/Magnum Photos, Inc.

Interventions in Latin America and the Middle East

While buttressing friendly governments in Asia, the Eisenhower administration also worked to topple unfriendly ones in Latin America and the Middle East. The CIA became an important arm of foreign policy in the 1950s, as Eisenhower relied on behind-the-scenes efforts and covert activities against governments that appeared too leftist and threatened U.S. economic interests. Increasingly, the administration conducted foreign policy behind the back of Congress.

The Eisenhower administration employed clandestine activities in Guatemala, where the government was not Communist or Soviet controlled but accepted support from the local Communist Party (see Map 29.1 in chapter 29).

In 1954, when the reformist president Jacobo Arbenz sought to nationalize land owned but not used by a U.S. corporation, the United Fruit Company, Eisenhower authorized the CIA to carry out covert operations destabilizing Guatemala's economy and assisting a coup. A military dictatorship friendly to United Fruit replaced Arbenz's popularly elected government.

"We're going to take care of Castro just like we took care of Arbenz," promised a CIA agent when Cubans' desire for political and economic autonomy erupted in 1959. American companies had long controlled major Cuban resources—especially sugar, tobacco, and mines—and decisions made in Washington directly influenced the lives and livelihoods of the Cuban people. An uprising in 1959 led by Fidel Castro drove out the U.S.-supported dictator Fulgencio Batista and led the CIA to warn Eisenhower that "Communists and other extreme radicals appear to have penetrated the Castro movement." When the United States denied Castro's requests for loans, he turned for help to the Soviet Union. And when U.S. companies refused Castro's offer to purchase them at their assessed value, he began to nationalize their property. Many anti-Castro Cubans fled to the United States and reported his atrocities, including the execution of hundreds of Batista's supporters. Before leaving office, Eisenhower broke off diplomatic relations with Cuba and authorized the CIA to train Cuban exiles for an invasion.

In the Middle East, as in Guatemala, the CIA intervened to support an unpopular dictatorship and help American corporations (see Map 31.2 in chapter 31). In 1951, the left-leaning prime minister of Iran, Mohammed Mossadegh, had nationalized oil fields and refineries, thereby threatening Western oil interests. While accepting support from the Iranian Communist Party, Mossadegh also challenged the power of the shah, Mohammad Reza Pahlavi, Iran's hereditary leader, who favored foreign oil interests and the Iranian wealthy classes.

For all of these reasons, Eisenhower authorized CIA agents to instigate a coup against Mossadegh by bribing army officers and paying

Iranians to demonstrate against the government. In August 1953, army officers took Mossadegh prisoner and reestablished the shah's power, whereupon Iran renegotiated oil concessions, giving U.S. companies a 40 percent share. Although the intervention worked in the short run, Americans in the 1970s and 1980s would feel the full fury of Iranian opposition to the repressive government that the United States had helped to reinstall.

Elsewhere in the Middle East, the Eisenhower administration shifted from Truman's all-out support for Israel to fostering friendships with Arab nations. Hindering such efforts, however, were U.S. demands that smaller nations take the American side in the cold war, even when those nations preferred neutrality and the opportunity for assistance from both Western and Communist nations. In 1955, Secretary of State Dulles began talks with Egypt about American support to build the Aswan Dam on the Nile River. But in 1956, Egypt's leader, Gamal Abdel Nasser, sought arms from Communist Czechoslovakia, formed a military alliance with other Arab nations, and recognized the People's Republic of China.

Unwilling to tolerate such independence, Dulles called off the deal for the dam. On July 26, 1956, Nasser responded by seizing the Suez Canal, then owned by Britain and France. Taking the canal advanced Nasser's prestige and power in the region, because it coincided with **nationalist** aspirations in the Arab world, and revenue from the canal could provide capital for constructing the dam. In response to the seizure, Israel, whose forces had been skirmishing with Egyptian troops along their common border since 1948, attacked Egypt, with military help from Britain and France.

Eisenhower opposed the intervention, recognizing that the Egyptians had claimed their own territory and recognizing that Nasser "embodie[d] the emotional demands of the people . . . for independence." He put economic pressure on

> While buttressing friendly governments in Asia, the Eisenhower administration also worked to topple unfriendly ones in Latin America and the Middle East.

The Suez Crisis, 1956

The Suez Crisis, 1956
Oct. 29th–Nov. 5th

⟵ Israeli troop movements

0   25   50 miles
0   50 kilometers

994 CHAPTER 27 • THE POLITICS AND CULTURE OF ABUNDANCE

Britain and France while calling on the United Nations to arrange a truce. Lacking U.S. support, the French and British soon pulled back, forcing Israel to retreat from territory it had captured in the Sinai peninsula of Egypt.

Although staying out of the Suez crisis, Eisenhower made clear that the United States would actively combat communism in the Middle East. In March 1957, Congress passed a joint resolution approving economic and military aid to any Middle Eastern nation "requesting assistance against armed aggression from any country controlled by international communism." The president invoked this "Eisenhower Doctrine" to send aid to Jordan in 1957 and troops to Lebanon in 1958 to counter anti-Western pressures on those governments.

The Nuclear Arms Race

While Eisenhower's foreign policy centered on countering perceived Communist inroads abroad, a number of events encouraged the president to seek reduction of superpower tensions and accommodation with the Soviet Union. After Stalin's death in 1953, a more moderate leadership under Nikita Khrushchev emerged. The Soviet Union signed a peace treaty with Austria guaranteeing Austrian neutrality and removed its troops. Like Eisenhower, who remarked privately that the arms race would lead "at worst to atomic warfare, at best to robbing every people and nation on earth of the fruits of their own toil," Khrushchev worried about the domestic costs of the cold war and wanted to reduce defense spending and the threat of nuclear devastation.

> American nuclear superiority did not guarantee security, because the Soviet Union possessed sufficient nuclear weapons to devastate the United States.

Eisenhower and Khrushchev met in Geneva in 1955 at the first summit conference since the end of World War II. Though it produced no significant agreements, the meeting symbolized a lessening of tensions—in Eisenhower's words, "a new spirit of conciliation and cooperation." In 1959, Khrushchev visited the United States, and Nixon went to the Soviet Union, where he engaged in the famous kitchen debate. By 1960, the two sides were within reach of a ban on nuclear testing, and Khrushchev and Eisenhower agreed to meet again in Paris in May.

To avoid jeopardizing the summit, Eisenhower decided to cancel espionage flights over the Soviet Union, but his order came one day too late. On May 1, 1960, a Soviet missile shot down a U-2 spy plane over Soviet territory. The State Department first denied that U.S. planes had been violating Soviet air space, but then the Soviets produced the pilot and the photos taken on his flight. Eisenhower met with Khrushchev briefly in Paris, but the U-2 incident dashed all prospects for a nuclear arms agreement.

Eisenhower's "more bang for the buck" defense budget enormously increased the U.S. nuclear capacity, more than quadrupling the stockpile of nuclear weapons. By the time he left office in 1961, the United States had installed seventy-two intercontinental ballistic missiles (ICBMs) in the United States and Britain and was prepared to deploy more in Italy and Turkey. The first Polaris submarine carrying nuclear missiles was launched in November 1960.

In August 1957, the Soviets test-fired their first ICBM and two months later beat the United States into space by launching *Sputnik*, the first artificial satellite to circle the earth. Senate majority leader Lyndon Johnson called the Soviet success a scientific Pearl Harbor, and other leaders warned that the United States lagged behind not only in missile development and space exploration but also in science and education. When the United States tried to launch a response to *Sputnik*, its satellite exploded, prompting news headlines calling it a "Stayputnik" and a "Flopnik." A successful satellite launch came finally in January 1958.

Eisenhower insisted that the United States possessed nuclear superiority, but in 1957 he could not reveal the evidence for his confidence, the top-secret U-2 surveillance of the Soviet Union. He tried to diminish public panic, establishing the National Aeronautics and Space Administration (NASA) in July 1958 and approving a gigantic budget increase for space research and development. In addition, he signed the National Defense Education Act, providing loans and scholarships for students in math, foreign languages, and science.

American nuclear superiority did not guarantee security because the Soviet Union possessed sufficient nuclear weapons to devastate the United States. Instructed to "duck and cover," American schoolchildren dove under their desks or crouched on the floor during regular drills to prepare for a nuclear attack. Most Americans did not follow Civil Defense Administration recommendations to construct home bomb shelters, and few could respond to real estate ads that offered "good bomb immunity," but

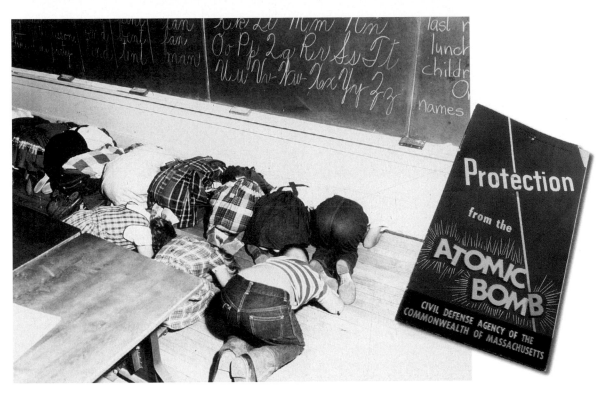

The Age of Nuclear Anxiety
Within just five years after World War II, governments throughout the United States were educating the public about the nuclear threat and urging them to prepare. As schools routinely held drills to prepare for possible Soviet attacks, children directly experienced the anxiety and insecurity of the 1950s nuclear arms race. This pamphlet about how to survive an atomic attack was published by the federal government and distributed to the general public. How effective do you think the strategy pictured here would have been in the event of a nuclear attack?
Archive Photos; Lynn Historical Society.

FOR MORE HELP ANALYZING THIS IMAGE, see the visual activity for this chapter in the Online Study Guide at bedfordstmartins.com/roark.

they did realize how precarious nuclear weapons had made their lives. "Facing a Danger Unlike Any Danger That Has Ever Existed," headlined an ad placed by the Committee for a Sane Nuclear Policy, an organization founded to oppose the nuclear arms race, with 130 chapters by 1958.

As he left office, Eisenhower warned about the growing influence of the **military-industrial complex** in American government and life. To contain the defense budget, Eisenhower had struggled against persistent pressures from defense contractors who, in tandem with the military, sought more dollars for newer, more powerful weapons systems. In his farewell address, he warned that the "conjunction of an immense military establishment and a large arms industry . . . exercised a total influence . . . in every city, every state house, every office of the

federal government." The cold war had created a warfare state.

New Work and Living Patterns in an Economy of Abundance

American military spending helped stimulate domestic prosperity. Economic productivity increased enormously in the 1950s (Figure 27.1), a multitude of new items came on the market, consumption became the order of the day, and millions of Americans enjoyed new homes in the suburbs. Prosperity enabled young people to stay in school longer, as higher education became the norm for the middle class. Although every section of the nation enjoyed the new abundance,

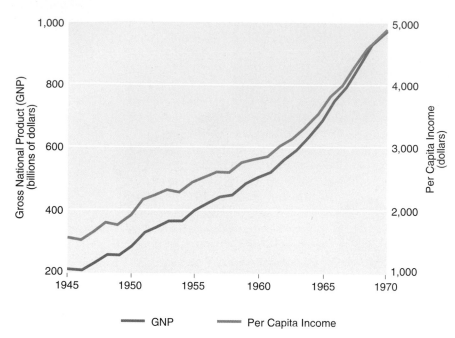

FIGURE 27.1 The Postwar Economic Boom: GNP and Per Capita Income, 1945–1970
American dominance of the worldwide market, innovative technologies that led to new industries such as computers and plastics, population growth, and increases in worker productivity all contributed to the enormous economic growth of the United States after World War II.

the West and Southwest especially boomed in production, commerce, and population.

Work itself changed: Fewer people labored on farms; service sector employment overtook manufacturing jobs; and women's employment grew. These economic shifts disadvantaged some Americans, and some forty million people—20 percent of the population—lived in poverty. Most Americans, however, enjoyed a higher standard of living, leading the economist John Kenneth Galbraith to call the United States "the affluent society."

Technology Transforms Agriculture and Industry

Between 1940 and 1960, the output of American farms mushroomed, while the number of farmworkers declined by nearly one-third. Farmers achieved nearly miraculous productivity through greater crop specialization, more intensive use of fertilizers, and, above all, mechanization. Tractors, mechanical pickers, and other machines increasingly substituted for human and animal power. A single mechanical cotton picker replaced fifty people and cut the cost of harvesting a bale of cotton from $40 to $5.

The decline of family farms and the growth of large commercial farming, or **agribusiness**, were both causes and consequences of mechanization. Larger farmers benefited handsomely from federal price supports begun in the New Deal, and they could afford technological improvements, whereas smaller producers lacked capital to invest in the machinery necessary to compete. Consequently, average farm size more than doubled between 1940 and 1964, while the farm population sank from thirty million to thirteen million, and the number of farms fell by more than 40 percent.

Many small farmers who hung on constituted a core of rural poverty often overlooked in the celebration of affluence. Southern landowners replaced sharecroppers with machines, forcing them off the land. Hundreds of thousands of African Americans joined an exodus to cities, where racial discrimination and a lack of jobs for which they could qualify mired many in urban poverty. A Mississippi woman whose family had worked on a plantation since slavery reported that most of her relatives headed for Chicago when they heard that "it was going to be machines now that harvest the crops." Worrying that "it might be worse up there," she agonized, "I'm afraid to leave and I'm afraid to stay, and whichever I do, I think it might be real bad for my boys and girls."

As in agriculture, new technology increased industrial production. Between 1945 and 1960, for example, the automobile industry cut in half the number of labor-hours needed to manufacture a car. Technology also transformed such industries as electronics, chemicals, and air transportation and promoted the growth of television, plastics, computers, and other newer industries. American businesses enjoyed access to cheap oil, and the nation's dominance in the international economy guaranteed ample markets abroad and little foreign competition. Moreover, even with Eisenhower's conservative fiscal policies, government spending reached $80 billion annually and created new jobs.

Labor unions enjoyed their greatest success during the 1950s, and real earnings for production workers shot up 40 percent. The merger in 1955 of the American Federation of Labor (AFL) and the Congress of Industrial Organizations (CIO) lessened internal conflicts and improved labor's bargaining position. As one worker put it, "We saw continual improvement in wages, fringe benefits like holidays, vacation, medical plans . . . all sorts of things that provided more security for people." Such benefits became a staple of most union contracts, though workers in heavy industries such as steel and automobiles did much better than those in food processing, garment making, and other light manufacturing. Unlike most industrial nations, where government provided most of the benefits, the United States developed a mixed system in which company-funded programs won by unions through **collective bargaining** played a larger role. This system resulted in wide disparities among workers, severely disadvantaging those not represented by unions.

While the absolute number of organized workers continued to increase, union membership peaked at 27.1 percent of the labor force in 1957. Technological advances chipped away at

jobs in heavy industry, reducing the number of workers in the steel, copper, and aluminum industries by 17 percent. "You are going to have trouble collecting union dues from all of these machines," commented a Ford manager at a newly automated engine plant to union leader Walter Reuther. Moreover, the economy as a whole was shifting from production to service. Instead of making products, more and more workers distributed goods, performed services, kept records, provided education, or carried out government work. Unions made some headway in these fields—union membership among local, state, and federal government employees became especially strong in the next few decades—but most service industries resisted unionization, and many of the workers—such as janitors, food servers, and domestics—performed hard manual labor for low wages.

The growing clerical and service occupations swelled the demand for female workers. By

Poverty in an Era of Abundance
The Whiteheads, a coal-mining family in Kentucky, represented the hidden side of the affluent postwar era. Mrs. John Whitehead, shown here, lived with her husband, their six children, and their six grandchildren in this three-room house. It had neither running water nor electricity, and the only access to the house was over a mountain trail.
National Archives.

Technology Transforms Agriculture
A mechanical cotton picker was patented as early as 1850, but the abundant supply of slave labor and then sharecroppers delayed its widespread use until after World War II. In 1950, machines harvested just 5 percent of cotton in the South, but ten years later mechanization accounted for 50 percent of the crop. This kind of technological advance was both cause and effect of the movement of African Americans out of the rural South. In this photo, cotton harvesters munch their way through a North Carolina cotton field in the 1950s.
United States Department of Agriculture.

the end of the 1950s, 35 percent of all women over age sixteen worked outside the home—twice as many as in 1940—and women held more than one-third of all jobs. Women entered a sharply segregated workplace. The vast majority worked in clerical jobs, light manufacturing, domestic service, teaching, and nursing, and because these were female occupations, wages were relatively low. In 1960, the average full-time female worker earned just 60 percent of the average male worker's wages. At the bottom of the employment ladder, black women took home only 42 percent of what white men earned.

Burgeoning Suburbs and Declining Cities

Although suburbs had existed since the nineteenth century, nothing symbolized the affluent society more than their tremendous expansion in the 1950s: Eleven million of the thirteen million new homes were built in the suburbs, and by 1960, one in four Americans lived there. As Vice President Nixon boasted to Khrushchev during the kitchen debate, the suburbs were accessible to families with modest incomes. Builder William J. Levitt modified the factory assembly-line process, planning nearly identical units so that individual construction work-

> Nothing symbolized the affluent society more than the tremendous expansion of suburbs.

ers could move from house to house and perform the same single operation in each, such as caulking windows or installing bathtubs. In 1949, families could purchase these mass-produced houses in his 17,000-home development called Levittown, on Long Island, New York, for just under $8,000. Developments similar to Levittown, as well as more luxurious ones, quickly went up throughout the country.

While private industry built the suburbs, the government subsidized home ownership with low-interest mortgage guarantees through the Federal Housing Administration and the Veterans Administration and by making interest on mortgages tax deductible. A veteran could buy a house in Levittown with payments of just $58 per month for twenty-five years. Moreover, thousands of interstate highway miles ran through urban areas, indirectly subsidizing suburban development. Without the automobile and the freeway, the suburban explosion could not have occurred.

Suburban culture was not without detractors. Social critic Lewis Mumford blasted the suburbs as "a multitude of uniform, unidentifiable houses, lined up inflexibly, at uniform distances, on uniform roads, in a treeless communal wasteland, inhabited by people of the same class, the same income, the same age group." By the 1960s, suburbs came under attack for bulldozing the natural environment, leveling hills and trees, creating groundwater contamination, and disrupting wildlife patterns. Moreover, the growing suburbs contributed to a more polarized society, especially along racial lines. Each Levittown homeowner signed a contract pledging that "no dwelling shall be used or occupied by members of other than the Caucasian race." Although the Supreme Court declared such covenants unenforceable in 1948, suburban America remained dramatically segregated.

As white residents joined the suburban migration, blacks moved to cities in search of economic opportunity, increasing their numbers in most cities by 50 percent during the 1950s. Black migrants to the North and East, however, came to cities that were already in decline, losing not only population but also commerce and industry to the suburbs or to southern and western states. "Detroit is in the doldrums," commented social welfare worker Mary Jorgensen in 1952; indeed, the city lost more than 100,000 manufacturing jobs in the 1950s. New business facilities began to ring central cities, and shoppers gradually chose suburban malls over downtown department stores. Many of the new jobs lay beyond the reach of the recent black arrivals to the inner cities.

The Rise of the Sun Belt

Americans were on the move westward as well as to the suburbs. Architect Frank Lloyd Wright quipped that the nation itself seemed to tip westward: Everything not bolted down was sliding toward California. No regions experienced the postwar economic and population booms more intensely than the West and Southwest. Americans had been moving westward, of course, since the nineteenth century, and the depression and Dust Bowl had sent more. After World War II, California's inhabitants more than doubled, and it overtook New York as the most populous state. Sports franchises followed fans: In 1958, the Brooklyn Dodgers moved to Los Angeles, joined by the Minneapolis Lakers three years later.

A warm climate and a pleasant natural environment drew new residents to the West and Southwest, but no magnet proved stronger than the promise of economic opportunity (Map 27.2). As

railroads had fueled western growth in the nineteenth century, the automobile and airplane spurred the post– World War II surge, providing efficient transportation for people and products. The technology of air-conditioning made possible industrial development in the so-called **Sun Belt**, which stretched from Florida to California. Crucial to the region's population explosion, air-conditioning cooled nearly eight million Sun Belt homes by 1960. (See "The Promise of Technology," page 1001.)

So important was the cold war defense industry to the South and West that it was later referred to as the "Gun Belt." The aerospace industry boomed in Seattle–Tacoma, Los Angeles, Tucson, and Dallas–Fort Worth, and military bases helped underwrite prosperity in such cities as San Diego and San Antonio (Table 27.1).

> A warm climate and a pleasant natural environment drew new residents to the West and Southwest, but no magnet proved stronger than the promise of economic opportunity.

An African American Suburb

The pioneer of mass-produced suburban housing, William J. Levitt, reflected the racism that kept blacks out of suburbia when he said, "We can solve a housing problem, or we can try and solve a racial problem, but we cannot combine the two." These African Americans developed their own suburb, a planned community for middle-class blacks in Richmond, California, which welcomed the first families in 1950. Richmond Public Library.

Although defense dollars benefited other regions, the Sun Belt captured the lion's share of cold war spending for research and production of bombers and missiles, other weapons, and satellites. In California alone, the federal government spent more than $100 billion for defense between 1945 and 1965. By the 1960s, nearly one of every three California workers held a defense-related job.

The surging populations and industries brought with them needs that soon raised environmental concerns. Providing sufficient water and power to cities and to agribusiness meant replacing free-flowing rivers in the West with a series of dams and reservoirs. Five dams along the Missouri inundated Indian tribal lands in violation of treaty rights. Sprawling urban and suburban settlement without efficient public transportation contributed to blankets of smog over cities like Los Angeles. Development began to degrade the very environment that people came to enjoy, and inhabitants became less hospitable to newcomers. "Come and visit again and again," Oregon's governor told conventioneers in 1971, "but for heaven's sake, don't come here to live."

The high-technology basis of postwar economic development drew well-educated, highly skilled workers to the West. But the economic promise also attracted the poor. "We see opportunity all around us here. . . . We smell freedom here, and maybe soon we can taste it," commented a black mother in California. Between 1945 and 1960, more than one-third of the African Americans who left the South moved west, and more blacks moved to California than to any other state.

MAP 27.2   The Rise of the Sun Belt, 1940–1980

The growth of defense industries, a nonunionized labor force, and the spread of air-conditioning all helped spur economic development and population growth, which made the Sun Belt the fastest-growing region of the nation between 1940 and 1980.

READING THE MAP: What states experienced an over 20 percent growth in population? What states experienced the largest population growth?

CONNECTIONS: What stimulated the population boom in the Southwest? What role did the cold war play in this boom? What role did African Americans play in the western population boom?

FOR MORE HELP ANALYZING THIS MAP, see the map activity for this chapter in the Online Study Guide at bedfordstmartins.com/roark.

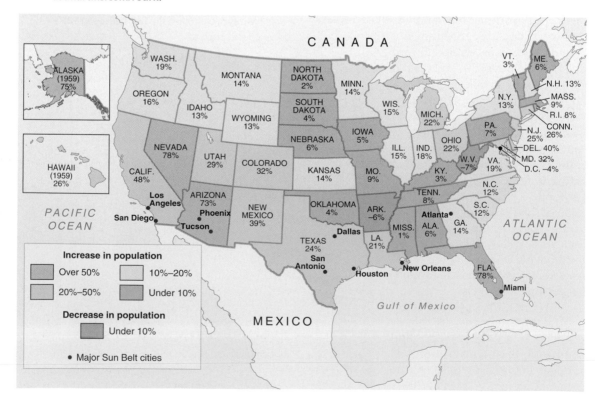

Air-Conditioning

Combining two technological advances of the late nineteenth century, refrigeration and electricity, air-conditioning developed primarily in response to the needs of industry. In 1902, Willis Haviland Carrier, a twenty-six-year-old American engineer who formulated basic theories of air-conditioning, designed the first system to control temperature and humidity and installed it in a Brooklyn printing plant. In 1915, he founded the Carrier Corporation to manufacture air-conditioning equipment.

Because fibers are sensitive to moisture, the textile industry provided an early and important market for air-conditioning. The process also helped to popularize movie theaters by making them a cool as well as an entertaining retreat during hot summer months. Room air conditioners began to appear in the 1930s. This 1950 Carrier ad promoted the clean air in homes and offices that would come with purchase of a room air conditioner. Fewer than a million homes had room air conditioners in 1950, but nearly eight million did in

1960, and more than half of all homes had some form of air-conditioning by 1975, as its status changed from a luxury to a necessity. By the end of the twentieth century, more than 80 percent of

EXCUSE MY DUST

Carrier   AIR CONDITIONING · REFRIGERATION

"That's Modern Air Control!"
Ads like this one for the Carrier room air conditioner promised consumers that homes could be cool as well as clean.
Courtesy Carrier Corporation.

households had air-conditioning, and it had become standard equipment on automobiles.

Air-conditioning was a mixed blessing. On the one hand, companies no longer had to shut down and send workers home when heat and humidity became unbearable, and air quality inside businesses, homes, and cars improved. On the other hand, air conditioners consumed large amounts of energy and contributed to outdoor air pollution. Like other technologies such as television and, more recently, the Internet, air-conditioning had an isolating effect as people deserted front porches and backyards for closed-up houses and thus curtailed their interactions with neighbors. Perhaps its greatest impact on the nation was to make possible the population explosion in the Sun Belt. By facilitating the movement of commerce, industry, and tourism to the South and Southwest, air-conditioning made that region more like the rest of the nation. One historian of the South, referring disparagingly to the transformation worked by air-conditioning on that region, proclaimed that "[General Electric] has proved a more devastating invader than even General Sherman."

The Mexican American population also grew, especially in California and Texas. To supply California's vast agribusiness industry, the government continued the *bracero* program begun during World War II (see chapter 25). Until the program ended in 1964, more than 100,000 Mexicans entered the United States each year to labor in the fields—and many of them stayed, legally or illegally. But while the government encouraged the use of Mexican labor, it reflected white Americans' opposition to permanent Mexican immigration, launching a series of raids in 1954 called "Operation Wetback." Designed to ferret out and deport illegal

TABLE 27.1	THE GROWING SUN BELT CITIES, 1920–1980			
	1920	*1940*	*1960*	*1980*
Los Angeles	879	2,916	6,039	7,478
Houston	168	529	1,418	2,905
Dallas	185	527	1,084	2,430
Atlanta	249	559	1,017	2,030
San Diego	74	289	1,033	1,862
Miami	30	268	935	1,626
Phoenix	29	186	664	1,509
New Orleans	398	552	907	1,256
San Antonio	191	338	716	1,072
Tucson	20	37	266	531

Population in thousands.

immigrants, the operation made U.S. citizens of Mexican descent feel unwelcome and threatened them with incidents of mistaken identity.

At the same time, Mexican American citizens gained a small victory in their ongoing struggle for civil rights in *Hernandez v. Texas.* When a Texas jury convicted Pete Hernandez of murder, lawyers

Rounding Up Undocumented Migrants
Not all Mexican Americans who wanted to work in the United States were accommodated by the bracero program. In 1953, Los Angeles police arrested these men who did not have legal documents and were hiding in a freight train. Americans used the crude term "wetback" to refer to illegal immigrants because many of them swam across the Rio Grande, at the border between the United States and Mexico. © Bettmann/Corbis.

from the American GI Forum and the League of United Latin-American Citizens (see chapter 26) appealed on the grounds that persons of Mexican origin had been systematically excluded from jury service for decades. In the first Mexican American civil rights case of the post–World War II era, the Supreme Court ruled unanimously that Hispanics represented a distinct group and that their systematic exclusion from juries violated the constitutional guarantee of equal protection.

Free of the discrimination faced by minorities, white Americans reaped the fullest fruits of prosperity in the West. In April 1950, California developers advertised the opening of Lakewood, a large housing development in Los Angeles County. On the first day of sales, 30,000 people lined up to purchase tract houses for $8,000 to $10,000. Many of the new homeowners were veterans, blue-collar and lower-level white-collar workers whose defense-based jobs at McDonnell Douglas and other aerospace corporations or at the Long Beach naval base enabled them to fulfill the American dream of the 1950s. A huge shopping mall, Lakewood Center, offered myriad products of the consumer culture. And California implemented a tremendous expansion of higher education. Their children had access to community colleges, four campuses of California State University, and two campuses of the University of California system— all within easy reach of Lakewood.

The Democratization of Higher Education

California's system was only the largest element in a spectacular transformation of higher education. Between 1940 and 1960, enrollments leaped from 1.5 million to 3.6 million; and more than

Moving into the Suburbs

In 1953, Leo Ferguson responded to an ad in a St. Louis newspaper calling for engineers to work at North American Aviation and moved his family from Alton, Illinois, to Lakewood, California. Using cash and installment payments, the Fergusons purchased their $10,290 house and $6,800 worth of additional products. What does the photograph tell us about the kinds of items that fueled the consumer economy?

J. B. Eyerman/TimePix/Getty.

40 percent of young Americans attended college by the mid-1960s, in contrast to 15 percent in the 1940s. More families could afford to keep their children in school longer, and the federal government subsidized the education of more than two million World War II and Korean War veterans. The cold war also sent millions of federal dollars to universities for defense-related research. Total tax dollars spent for higher education more than doubled from 1950 to 1960, as state governments vastly expanded the number of four-year colleges and universities, and municipalities began to build two-year junior or community colleges.

The GI Bill made college possible for thousands of African Americans, the majority of whom attended black institutions. College enrollments of blacks surged from 37,000 in 1941 to 90,000 in 1961. Yet African Americans constituted only about 5 percent of all college students,

less than half their percentage in the general population. Unlike their white counterparts, among whom women received just 33 percent of college degrees in 1960, black men and women attended college in nearly equal numbers.

For a time, the democratization of higher education increased the educational gap between white men and women. The numbers of college women grew, but they did not keep pace relative to those of men. In 1940, women earned 40 percent of undergraduate degrees, but as veterans flocked to college campuses, women's proportion fell to 25 percent in 1950. Even by 1960, women constituted just 33 percent of college graduating classes.

The large veteran enrollments also introduced a new feature of college life—the married student. Colleges that had previously forbidden students to marry relaxed the rule to accommodate the mature, war-tempered population.

Unlike men, however, women dropped out of college upon marriage, taking jobs to enable their husbands to stay in school and earning their own "Ph.T's" by "putting hubby through." Reflecting gender-role norms of the 1950s, most college women responding to a survey agreed that "it is natural for a woman to be satisfied with her husband's success and not crave personal achievement." Yet just a decade later, many of these same women would express resentment at their second-class status by joining the **feminist** movement.

Some observers in the 1950s termed college students a "silent generation," pointing to their apparent passivity, caution, and conformity. Students seemed too eager to suspend independent, critical thinking in favor of pleasing their professors and getting good grades to launch them on profitable careers. Those who remembered favorably the student generation of the 1930s found students in the 1950s apolitical or safely conservative.

The Culture of Abundance

With increased prosperity in the 1950s, more people married and the birthrate soared. Religious observance expanded even as Americans sought satisfaction in material possessions. Television entered the homes of most Americans, helping to promote a consumer culture. Dominant values favored family life and traditional gender roles, consumption, and conformity. Undercurrents of rebellion, especially among youth, defied some of the dominant norms but did not greatly disrupt the complacency of the 1950s.

A Consumer Culture

"If you grew up in the 1950s," journalist Robert Samuelson remembered, "you were a daily witness to the marvels of affluence . . . [to] a seemingly endless array of new gadgets and machines." Scorned by Khrushchev during the kitchen debate as worthless gadgets, consumer items flooded American society in the 1950s. Although the purchase and display of consumer goods had always been part of American life (see chapter 23), by the 1950s consumption had become a reigning value, vital for economic prosperity and essential to individuals' identity and status. While not altogether disappearing, the work ethic competed with a newer norm that stressed satisfaction and joy through the purchase and use of new products. The man who designed Ford automobiles captured this emphasis on happiness and also the corporate strategy of obsolescence when he remarked, "We design a car to make a man unhappy with his 1957 Ford 'long about the end of 1958."

The consumer culture rested on a firm material base. Between 1950 and 1960, the gross national product (the value of all goods and services produced during a year) as well as median family income grew by 25 percent in constant dollars. Alongside a 20 percent poverty rate, economists claimed that 60 percent of Americans enjoyed middle-class incomes in 1960. By the late 1950s, four of every five families owned television sets and washing machines, nearly all had refrigerators, and the majority owned at least one car.

Several forces spurred this unparalleled abundance. A population surge—from 152 million in 1950 to 180 million in 1960—expanded demand for products and boosted industries ranging from housing to baby goods to music. Consumer borrowing also fueled the economic boom, as people increasingly bought houses, cars, and appliances on installment plans. Diner's Club issued the first credit card in 1951, and American Express followed in 1958. Private debt, which more than doubled during the decade to reach $263 billion by 1960, was a key element of the consumer culture. Shopping itself changed as the number of shopping centers quadrupled between 1957 and 1963. Instead of taking a bus or streetcar downtown to the city center, suburbanites could drive to malls now accessible along new highways.

To encourage more and more consumption, corporate executives tripled the dollars they spent on advertising between World War II and 1959. By then, large advertising companies earned more than half their revenues from TV, which soon began to target specific markets. "For toys and games we go right to children audiences. For a household product to women," reported a media advertising director. Nor did television's support of consumption stop with commercials. Its programs also tantalized viewers with things to buy, especially the quiz shows. For example, women with the most pitiful personal stories won fur coats, vacuum cleaners, and other merchandise on *Queen for a Day*. To win on another popular show, *The Price Is Right*, required consumer skills, as contestants had to guess the retail prices of such items as cameras, appliances, furniture, and vacations.

Although the sheer need to support themselves and their families accounted for most of women's presence in the labor force, a desire to secure some of the new abundance for their families pulled increasing numbers of women out of the home. Married women working part-time filled many of the sales positions in the new shopping malls. In fact, married women experienced the largest increases in employment in the 1950s. As one woman remarked, "My Joe can't put five kids through college . . . and the washer had to be replaced, and Ann was ashamed to bring friends home because the living room furniture was such a mess, so I went to work." Increasingly families needed a second income to meet the standards for happiness imposed by the consumer culture.

The Revival of Domesticity and Religion

Even though married women took jobs in unprecedented numbers, a dominant ideology celebrated traditional family life and conventional gender roles. Despite the fact that more than one-third of mothers with school-age children left the home for work, the family ideal defined by popular culture and public figures persisted: a male breadwinner, a full-time homemaker, and three or four children in a new suburban home.

The emphasis on home and family life reflected to some extent anxieties about the cold war and nuclear menace. Not unlike Nixon in the kitchen debate, one government official saw women's role in cold war terms, charging that the Soviet Union viewed women "first as a source of manpower, second as a mother," and insisting that "the highest calling of a woman's sex is the home." *Life* magazine echoed the sentiment: "Of all the accomplishments of the American woman, the one she brings off with the most spectacular success is having babies."

Writer and feminist Betty Friedan gave a name to the idealization of women's domestic roles in her book *The Feminine Mystique*, published in 1963. Friedan criticized advertisers, social scientists, educators, women's magazines, and public officials for pressuring women to seek fulfillment in serving others. According to the feminine mystique that they promulgated, biological differences fitted men and women for entirely different roles in life. The ideal woman kept a spotless house, raised perfect children, served her husband's career, and provided him emotional and sexual satisfaction. The feminine mystique reinforced the notion that strong men and subservient women were as important to the survival of the nuclear family as virile political leadership was to the survival of the nation. Not many women then directly challenged the feminine mystique, but Edith Stern, a college-educated writer, maintained that "many arguments about the joys of housewifery have been advanced, largely by those who have never had to work at it," while she deplored the "incalculable skilled services" that were "buried in the homemade cakes the family loves and sunk in the suds of the week's wash."

Although the glorification of domesticity clashed with married women's increasing participation in the labor force, the lives of many Americans did embody the family ideal. Postwar prosperity enabled people to marry earlier and to have more children. Whereas its general trend over the twentieth century was downward, the American birthrate soared during the period 1945 to 1965, reaching a peak in 1957 with 4.3 million births and producing the "baby boom" generation (see appendix, page A-49). The norms for child rearing were more demanding than ever before. Dr. Benjamin Spock's best-selling *Common Sense Book of Baby and Child Care* (1946) advocated a permissive approach requiring mothers' full-time involvement instead of the traditional emphasis on strictness and rigid schedules. Experts also urged fathers to cultivate family "togetherness" and spend more time with their children.

Along with a renewed emphasis on family life, the 1950s witnessed a surge of interest in religion. By 1960, about 63 percent of Americans belonged to churches and synagogues, up from 50 percent in 1940. Polls reported that 95 percent of all Americans believed in God. Evangelism took on new life, most notably in the nationwide crusades of Baptist minister Billy Graham, whose powerful oratory moved mass audiences to accept Christ. Congress linked religion more closely to the state by adding "under God" to the pledge of allegiance in 1954 and by requiring in 1955 that "In God We Trust" be printed on all currency.

> Even though married women took jobs in unprecedented numbers, a dominant ideology celebrated traditional family life and conventional gender roles.

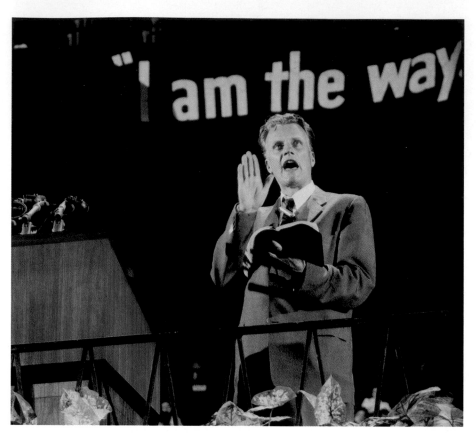

Evangelist Billy Graham

A young Baptist minister from North Carolina, Billy Graham electrified mass audiences across the country, entreating them to find salvation in Jesus Christ and to uphold Christian moral standards. Perhaps reflecting their ambivalence about their avid participation in a consumer society, Americans flocked to hear him even as he condemned their sinfulness in being "materialistic, worldly, secular, greedy, and covetous." So large were his audiences that Graham extended his 1957 New York crusade from eight to sixteen weeks. Here he preaches in Madison Square Garden.

Gjon Mili/TimePix/Getty.

and a need for social outlets. One commentator, for example, noted that 53 percent of Americans could not name any book of the New Testament.

Television Transforms Culture and Politics

Just as family life and religion offered a respite from cold war anxieties, so too did the new medium of television. In 1950, fewer than 10 percent of American homes boasted a television set, but by 1960 about 87 percent of all households owned one. On average, Americans spent more than five hours each day in front of the screen.

Television kept people at home more but did not necessarily enhance family relationships, since parents and children focused their attention on the screen, not each other. The new medium altered eating habits; in 1954, the frozen dinner appeared, a complete meal in a portable tray that enabled families to spend the dinner hour in front of the TV. Noticing that the heaviest water consumption took place on the hour and half hour, civil engineers in Toledo, Ohio, realized that television regulated even trips to the bathroom.

Viewers especially tuned in to situation comedies, which projected the family ideal and the feminine mystique into millions of homes. On TV, married women did not work outside the home and deferred to their husbands, though they often got the upper hand through subtle manipulation. In the most popular television show of the early 1950s, *I Love Lucy*, the husband-and-wife team of Lucille Ball and Desi Arnaz played the couple Lucy and Ricky Ricardo. In step with the trends, they moved from an apartment in the city to a house in suburbia. Ricky would not let Lucy get a job, and many plots depicted her zany attempts to thwart his objections.

Television began to affect politics in the 1950s. Richard Nixon's "Checkers speech" reached a nationwide audience and kept him on the Republican ticket in 1952. Senator McCarthy's reckless attacks on army members televised nationwide contributed to his downfall. Eisenhower's 1952 presidential campaign used TV ads for the first time, and by 1960, television played a key role in election campaigns. Reflecting on his

Eisenhower's pastor attributed the renewed interest in religion to the prosperous economy that "provided the leisure, the energy, and the means for a level of human and spiritual values never before reached." Religion also offered reassurance and peace of mind in the nuclear age, while ministers like Graham turned the cold war into a holy war, labeling communism "a great sinister anti-Christian movement masterminded by Satan." Some critics questioned the depth of the religious revival, attributing the growth in church membership to a desire for conformity narrow victory in 1960, president-elect John F. Kennedy remarked, "We wouldn't have had a prayer without that gadget."

Television transformed politics in other ways. Money played a much larger role in elections because candidates needed to raise huge sums for expensive TV spots. The ability to appeal directly to voters in their living rooms put a premium on personal attractiveness and encouraged candidates to build their own campaign organizations, relying less on political parties. The declining strength of parties and the growing power of money in elections were not new trends, but television did much to accelerate them.

Unlike government-financed television in Europe, American TV was paid for by private enterprise. What NBC called a "selling machine in every living room" became the major vehicle for hawking the products of the affluent society and creating a consumer culture. In the mid-1950s, advertisers spent $10 billion to push their goods on TV, and the soap manufacturer Procter & Gamble spent more than 90 percent of its advertising budget on the new medium. Advertisers did not hesitate to interfere with shows that might jeopardize the sale of their products. The cigarette company that sponsored the *Camel News Caravan*, for example, banned any news film clips showing "No Smoking" signs.

In 1961, Newton Minow, chairman of the Federal Communications Commission, called television a "vast wasteland." While acknowledging some of TV's great achievements, particularly documentaries and drama, Minow depicted it as "a procession of game shows, . . . formula comedies about totally unbelievable families, blood and thunder, mayhem, violence, sadism, murder . . . and cartoons." But viewers kept tuning in. In little more than a decade, television came to dominate Americans' leisure time, influence their consumption patterns, and shape their perceptions of the nation's leadership.

Countercurrents

Pockets of dissent underlay the complacency of the 1950s. Some intellectuals took exception to the politics of consensus and to the materialism and conformity celebrated in popular culture. In *The Lonely Crowd* (1950), sociologist David Riesman lamented a shift from the "inner-directed" to the "other-directed" individual. In contrast to the independent thinking that had characterized earlier Americans, Riesman found a regrettable eagerness to adapt to external standards of behavior and belief. Sharing that distaste for the importance of "belonging," William H. Whyte Jr., in his popular book *The Organization Man* (1956), blamed the modern corporation. When employees had to tailor their behavior and ideas to those of the group, these "organization men" sacrificed risk taking and independence to dull conformity. And Vance Packard's 1959 best seller, *The Status Seekers*, decried "the vigorous merchandising of goods as status-symbols," while arguing that in this era of abundance "class lines in several areas of our national life appear to be hardening."

Less direct challenges to mainstream standards appeared in the everyday behavior of large numbers of Americans, especially youth. "Roll over Beethoven and tell Tchaikovsky the news!" belted out Chuck Berry in his 1956 hit record celebrating a new form of music. White teenagers lionized Elvis Presley, who shocked their parents with his tight pants, hip-rolling gestures, and sensuous

> In little more than a decade, television came to dominate Americans' leisure time, influence their consumption patterns, and shape their perceptions of the nation's leadership.

The Made-for-TV Family
This scene is from the popular television sitcom *Father Knows Best*, which ran from 1954 to 1963. Along with shows such as *Ozzie and Harriet* and *Leave It to Beaver*, it idealized white family life. In these shows, no one got divorced or became gravely ill, no one took drugs or seriously misbehaved, fathers held white-collar jobs, mothers did not work outside the home, and husbands and wives slept in twin beds. In what ways do today's sitcoms differ from those of the 1950s?

Culver Pictures/Picture Research Consultants.

music, a blend of country and western and black rhythm and blues. "Before there was Elvis . . . I started going crazy for 'race music,'" recalled a white man of his teenage years. "It had a beat. I loved it. . . . That got me into trouble with my parents and the schools." His experience illustrated African Americans' contributions to rock and roll as well as the rebellion expressed by white youths' attraction to black music.

Just as rock and roll's sexual suggestiveness violated norms of middle-class respectability, Americans' sexual behavior often departed from the family ideal of the postwar era. Two books published by Alfred Kinsey and other researchers at Indiana University, *Sexual Behavior in the Human Male* (1948) and *Sexual Behavior in the Human Female* (1953), uncovered a surprising range of sexual conduct. Surveying more than 16,000 individuals, Kinsey found that 85 percent of the men and 50 percent of the women had had sex before marriage; half of the husbands and a quarter of the wives had engaged in adultery; and one-third of the men and one-seventh of the women reported homosexual experiences.

Although Kinsey's sampling procedures later cast doubt on his ability to generalize across the population, the books became best sellers. They also drew a firestorm of outrage, especially because Kinsey refused to make moral judgments. Evangelist Billy Graham protested "the damage this book will do to the already deteriorating morals of America," and the Rockefeller Foundation stopped funding Kinsey's work.

The most blatant revolt against conventionality came from the self-proclaimed Beat generation, a small group of literary figures based in

Elvis Presley
Young people seeking escape from white middle-class conformity thrilled to Elvis Presley's pulsating music, long sideburns and ducktail haircut, colorful clothing, and suggestive movements. His gyrating hips, illustrated in these 1957 photographs, led to the appellation "Elvis the Pelvis." Adult viewers complained about his "grunt and groin antics" and "unnecessary bump and grind routine."
© Bettmann/Corbis.

New York City's Greenwich Village and in San Francisco. Rejecting nearly everything in mainstream culture—patriotism, consumerism, technology, conventional family life, discipline—the Beats celebrated spontaneity and absolute personal freedom, including drug consumption and freewheeling sex. In his landmark poem *Howl* (1956), Allen Ginsberg inveighed against "Robot apartments! invisible suburbs! skeleton treasuries! blind capitals! demonic industries! . . . monstrous bombs!" and denounced the social forces that "frightened me out of my natural ecstasy!" In 1957, Jack Kerouac, who gave the Beat generation its name, published the best-selling novel *On the Road* (1957), whose energetic, bebop-style prose narrated the restless and impetuous cross-country traveling of two young men. The Beats' rebelliousness would provide a model for a much larger movement of youthful dissidents in the 1960s.

Bold new styles in the visual arts also showed the 1950s to be more than a decade of bland conventionality. An artistic revolution that flowered in New York City, known as "action painting," "abstract expressionism," or the "New York school," rejected the idea that painting should represent recognizable forms. Jackson Pollock and other abstract expressionists, emphasizing energy and spontaneity, poured, dripped, and threw paint on canvases or substituted sticks and other implements for brushes. Reflecting the sweep of anticommunism in the 1950s, one conservative congressman condemned abstract art as part of "a sinister conspiracy conceived in the black heart of Russia." Yet the new form of painting so captivated and redirected the Western art world that New York replaced Paris as its center.

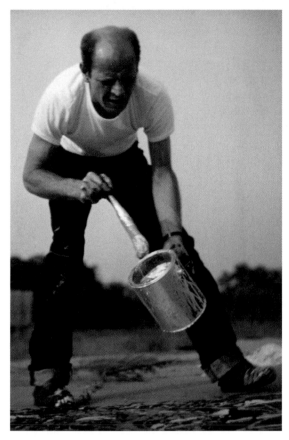

Jackson Pollock
The leading artist in the post–World War II revolution in painting, Jackson Pollock, illustrates his technique of pouring and splattering paint onto the canvas. He worked with the canvas on the floor because, he said, "I feel nearer, more a part of the painting. . . . I can walk around it, work from the four sides and be literally 'in' the painting."
Hans Namuth ©1990 Hans Namuth Estate. Courtesy Center for Creative Photography, the University of Arizona.

Emergence of a Civil Rights Movement

African Americans conducted the most dramatic challenge to the status quo of the 1950s as they sought to break the chains that had replaced the literal bonds of slavery. Every southern state mandated rigid segregation in public settings from hospitals and schools to drinking fountains and restrooms. Southern voting laws and practices disfranchised the vast majority of African Americans; employment discrimination kept them at the bottom of the economic ladder.

Although black protest was as old as American racism, in the 1950s a grassroots movement arose that attracted national attention and the support of white liberals. The Supreme Court delivered significant institutional reforms, but blacks themselves directed the most important changes. Ordinary African Americans in substantial numbers sought their own liberation, building a movement that would transform race relations in the United States.

African Americans Challenge the Supreme Court and the President

A number of factors spurred black protest in the 1950s. Between 1940 and 1960, more than three million African Americans moved from the South into areas where they could vote and exert pressure on politicians. The cold war raised white leaders' concern that its poor treatment of minorities handicapped the United States in competing with the Soviet Union. In the South, the system of segregation itself meant that African Americans controlled certain resources essential to a movement, such as churches and colleges, where leadership skills could be honed and a mass base and organizational network developed.

The legal strategy of the major civil rights organization, the National Association for the Advancement of Colored People (NAACP), reached its crowning achievement with the Supreme Court decision in *Brown v. Board of Education* in 1954. *Brown* was actually a consolidation of five separate suits that reflected the growing determination of black Americans to fight for their rights. Oliver Brown, a welder in Topeka, Kansas, filed suit because his eight-year-old daughter had to pass by a white school just seven blocks from their home to attend a black school more than a mile away. In Virginia, sixteen-year-old Barbara Johns, angered at the wretched conditions in her black high school, came home from school one day and declared, "I walked out of school this morning and carried 450 students with me." "Took my breath away," her grandmother recalled. That strike resulted in another of the suits joined together in *Brown*. The lead lawyer for the NAACP, future Supreme Court justice Thurgood Marshall, urged the Court to overturn the precedent established in *Plessy v. Ferguson* (1896), which had made "separate but equal" the law of the land (see chapter 17). A unanimous Court, headed by Chief Justice Earl Warren, declared, "Separate educational facilities are inherently unequal" and thus violated the Fourteenth Amendment.

It was one thing to issue a decision, another matter entirely to see it enforced. The Court called for desegregation "with all deliberate speed" but established no deadlines or guidelines. Ultimate responsibility for enforcement lay with President Eisenhower, but he refused to endorse *Brown*, just as he kept silent in 1955 when whites lynched Emmett Till, a fourteen-

> Ordinary African Americans in substantial numbers sought their own liberation, building a movement that would transform race relations in the United States.

year-old black boy who had allegedly whistled at a white woman in Mississippi. Reflecting his own racial prejudice, preference for a limited federal government, and a leadership style that favored consensus and gradual progress, Eisenhower would not urge the South to comply with desegregation. Such inaction fortified southern resistance to school desegregation and contributed to the gravest constitutional crisis since the Civil War.

The crisis came in Little Rock, Arkansas, in September 1957. Local officials dutifully prepared for the integration of Central High School, but Governor Orval Faubus sent Arkansas National Guard troops to block the enrollment of nine black students, claiming that their presence would cause public disorder. Later, Faubus agreed to allow the black students to enter, but he withdrew the National Guard, leaving the students to face an angry mob of whites. "During those years when we desperately needed approval from our peers," Melba Patillo Beals remembered, "we were victims of the most harsh rejection imaginable." As television cameras transmitted the ugly scene across the nation, Eisenhower was forced to send regular army troops to take federal control of the Arkansas National Guard, the first federal military intervention in the South since Reconstruction.

Escorted by paratroopers, the black students stayed in school, and Eisenhower withdrew the army in November. Other southern cities avoided integration by closing public schools and using tax dollars to support private, white-only schools. In 1961—nearly seven years after *Brown*—only 6.4 percent of southern black students attended integrated schools. (See "Documenting the American Promise," page 1012.)

Eisenhower did order the integration of public facilities in Washington, D.C., and on military bases, and he supported the first federal civil rights legislation since Reconstruction. Yet the Civil Rights Acts of 1957 and 1960 lacked effective enforcement mechanisms, leaving southern blacks still unprotected in the exercise of basic rights. Baseball star Jackie Robinson spoke for many African Americans when he wired Eisenhower, "We disagree that half a loaf is better than none. Have waited this long for bill with meaning—can wait a little longer." Eisenhower did appoint the first black professional to the White House staff, but E. Frederick Morrow confided to his diary, "I feel ridiculous . . . trying to defend the administration's record on civil rights."

Montgomery and Mass Protest

From slave revolts and individual acts of defiance through the legal and lobbying efforts of the NAACP, black protest had a long tradition in American society. What set the civil rights movement of the 1950s and 1960s apart were the masses of people involved, their willingness to confront white institutions directly, and the use of nonviolence and passive resistance to bring about change. The Congress of Racial Equality (CORE) and other groups had experimented with these tactics in the 1940s, and African Americans had boycotted the segregated bus system in Baton Rouge, Louisiana, in 1953, but the first sustained protest to claim national attention began in Montgomery, Alabama, on December 1, 1955.

On that day, police arrested a black woman, Rosa Parks, for violating a local segregation ordinance. Riding a crowded bus home from her job as a seamstress in a department store, she re-fused to give up her seat so that a white man could sit down. "People always say that I didn't give up my seat because I was tired, but that isn't true," Parks recalled. "I was not tired physically . . . I was not old . . . I was forty-two. No, the only tired I was, was tired of giving in." The bus driver called the police, who promptly arrested her.

Parks had long been active in the local NAACP, headed by E. D. Nixon, who was also president of the local Brotherhood of Sleeping Car Porters. They and others had already talked about challenging bus segregation. A possible boycott had engaged another group, the Women's Political Council (WPC), composed of black professional women and led by Jo Ann Robinson, an English professor at Alabama State College who had been humiliated by a bus driver when she had inadvertently sat in the white section. Such local individuals and organizations, long committed to improving conditions for African Americans, laid critical foundations for the black freedom struggle throughout the South.

School Integration in Little Rock, Arkansas

The nine African American teenagers who integrated Central High School in Little Rock, Arkansas, endured nearly three weeks of threats and hateful taunts before they even got through the doors. Here Elizabeth Eckford tries to ignore the angry students and adults as she approaches the entrance to the school only to be blocked by the Arkansas National Guard troops. Even after Eisenhower intervened to enable the "Little Rock Nine" to attend school, they were called names, tripped, spat upon, and otherwise harassed by some white students. When Minnijean Brown, one of the black students, could take no more, she dumped a bowl of chili on a white boy who had taunted her. After she was expelled for that, cards circulated among white students reading, "One Down . . . Eight to Go." Francis Miller/TimePix/Getty.

The *Brown* Decision

Brown v. Board of Education of Topeka *was the principal Supreme Court decision in the transformation of African Americans' legal and political status during the 1950s and 1960s. Responding to lawsuits argued by NAACP lawyers, the* Brown *ruling was the culmination of a series of Supreme Court rulings between 1938 and 1950 that chipped away at an earlier Court's decision in* Plessy v. Ferguson *(1896) permitting "separate but equal" public facilities.*

DOCUMENT 1
Brown v. Board of Education of Topeka, May 1954

In 1954, Chief Justice Earl Warren delivered the unanimous opinion of the Supreme Court in Brown v. Board of Education of Topeka, *declaring racial segregation in public education unconstitutional and explaining why.*

In these days, it is doubtful that any child may reasonably be expected to succeed in life if he is denied the opportunity of an education. Such an opportunity, if the state has undertaken to provide it, is a right that must be made available to all on equal terms. . . .

We come then to the question presented: Does segregation of children in public schools solely on the basis of race, even though the physical facilities and other "tangible" factors may be equal, deprive the children of the minority group of equal educational opportunities? We believe that it does. . . .

In *McLaurin* [a 1950 case], the Court, in requiring that a Negro ad-

mitted to a white graduate school be treated like all other students, again resorted to intangible considerations: ". . . his ability to study, to engage in discussions and exchange views with other students, and, in general, to learn his profession." Such considerations apply with added force to children in grade and high schools. To separate them from others of similar age and qualifications solely because of their race generates a feeling of inferiority as to their status in the community that may affect their hearts and minds in a way unlikely ever to be undone.

We conclude that in the field of public education the doctrine of "separate but equal" has no place. Separate educational facilities are inherently unequal.

Source: *Brown,* 347 U.S. 483 (1954).

DOCUMENT 2
Southern Manifesto on Integration, March 1956

The Brown *decision, along with a second Supreme Court ruling in 1955 about implementing desegregation, outraged many southern whites. In 1956, more than one hundred members of Congress signed a manifesto pledging resistance to the rulings.*

We regard the decision of the Supreme Court in the school cases as a clear abuse of judicial power. It climaxes a trend in the Federal judiciary undertaking to legislate . . . and to encroach upon the reserved rights of the states and the people.

The original Constitution does not mention education. Neither does

the Fourteenth Amendment nor any amendment. . . . The Supreme Court of the United States, with no legal basis for such action, undertook to exercise their naked judicial power and substituted their personal political and social ideas for the established law of the land.

This unwarranted exercise of power by the court, contrary to the Constitution, is creating chaos and confusion in the states principally affected. It is destroying the amicable relations between the white and negro races that have been created through ninety years of patient effort by the good people of both races. It has planted hatred and suspicion where there has been heretofore friendship and understanding. . . .

We pledge ourselves to use all lawful means to bring about a reversal of this decision which is contrary to the Constitution and to prevent the use of force in its implementation.

Source: "Southern Manifesto on Integration" (1956).

In the face of white hostility, black children carried the burden of implementing the Brown *decision. The following accounts by black students reflect varied experiences, but even those who entered white schools fairly easily found obstacles to their full participation in school activities. Nonetheless, they cherished the new opportunities, favoring integration for reasons different from those given by the Supreme Court.*

DOCUMENT 3
A High School Boy in Oak Ridge, Tennessee, 1957

I like it a whole lot better than the colored school. You have a chance to learn more and you have more sports. I play forward or guard on the basketball team, only I don't get to participate in all games. Some teams don't mind my playing. Some teams object not because of the fellows on the team, but because of the people in their community. Mostly it's the fans or the board of education that decides against me. . . . The same situation occurs in baseball. I'm catcher, but the first game I didn't get to participate in. A farm club of the major league wrote the coach that they were interested in seeing me play so maybe I'll get to play the next time.

SOURCE: Dorothy Sterling, *Tender Warriors* (New York: Hill and Wang, 1958), 83. Copyright © 1958 by Dorothy Sterling. Reprinted with permission.

DOCUMENT 4
A High School Girl in Louisville, Kentucky, 1957

I'm accepted now as an individual rather than as a person belonging to the Negro race. People say to me, "I'm glad I met you because if I met someone else I might not have liked them." I don't think it's fair, this individual acceptance. I feel like I was some ambassador from some foreign country.

I couldn't go out for any extracurricular activities. Cheerleading, band, drum majorettes, the people who are members of these organizations, they go to camps in the summer which are segregated. Well, what can you do? It just leaves me out. It's not the school, it's the community.

SOURCE: Dorothy Sterling, *Tender Warriors* (New York: Hill and Wang, 1958), 83. Copyright © 1958 by Dorothy Sterling. Reprinted with permission.

DOCUMENT 5
A High School Girl in the Deep South, May 1966

The first day a news reporter rode the bus with us. All around us were state troopers. In front of them were federal marshals. When we got to town there were lines of people and cars all along the road. A man without a badge or anything got on the bus and started beating up the newspaper reporter. . . . He was crying and bleeding. When we got to the school the students were all around looking through the windows. The mayor said we couldn't come there because the school was already filled to capacity [and] if six of us came in it would be a fire hazard. He told us to turn around and go back. We turned around and the students started yelling and clapping. When we went back [after obtaining a court order] there were no students there at all. There were only two teachers left so they had to bring a couple of teachers from other places. [The white students did not return, so the six black students finished the year by themselves.] The shocking thing was during the graduation ceremonies. All six of the students got together to make a speech. After we finished, I looked around and saw three teachers crying. The principal had tears in his eyes and he got up to make a little speech about us. He said at first he didn't think he would enjoy being around us. You could see in his face that he was really touched. We said something like we really enjoyed school together and that we were glad they stuck it out and all that kind of stuff.

SOURCE: *In Their Own Words: A Student Appraisal of What Happened after School Desegregation* (Washington, D.C.: Department of Health, Education, and Welfare, Office of Education, 1966), 17–18.

DOCUMENT 6
A High School Girl in the Deep South, May 1966

I chose to go because I felt that I could get a better education here. I knew that the [black] school that I was then attending wasn't giving me exactly what I should have had. As far as the Science Department was concerned, it just didn't have the chemicals we needed and I just decided to change. When I went over the students there weren't very friendly and when I graduated they still weren't. They didn't want us there and they made that plain, but we went there anyway and we stuck it out. The lessons there were harder, lots harder, but I studied and I managed to pass all my subjects.

SOURCE: *In Their Own Words: A Student Appraisal of What Happened after School Desegregation* (Washington, D.C.: Department of Health, Education, and Welfare, Office of Education, 1966), 44.

QUESTIONS FOR ANALYSIS AND DEBATE

1. What reasons did the Supreme Court give in favor of desegregation? What reasons did black students give for wanting to attend integrated schools? How did these reasons differ?

2. What arguments did the southern legislators make against the Supreme Court decision? Did they question its power to make the decision or the content of the decision itself?

3. What obstacles remained for African American students to confront once they had been admitted to integrated schools?

4. What conditions do you feel would be worth enduring to obtain a better education?

1014   CHAPTER 27 • THE POLITICS AND CULTURE OF ABUNDANCE

1952–1960

When word came of Parks's arrest and her decision to fight the case, WPC leaders immediately mobilized teachers and students to distribute flyers calling for Montgomery blacks to stay off the buses. E. D. Nixon called a mass meeting for December 5 at the Holt Street Baptist Church, where so many gathered that a crowd of people stretched for blocks outside. Those assembled founded the Montgomery Improvement Association (MIA) to organize a bus boycott among the African American community. The MIA ran a system of volunteer car pools and marshaled more than 90 percent of the black community to sustain the year-long boycott. It held mass meetings to keep up the spirits of those who had to depend on the car pool to get to work and back, brave bad weather on foot to keep a job or get to the grocery store, or face harassment from policemen. Jo Ann Robinson, though a cautious

> Montgomery demonstrated that blacks could sustain a lengthy protest and would not be intimidated.

driver, got seventeen traffic tickets in the space of two months.

Elected to head the MIA was Martin Luther King Jr., a newcomer to Montgomery and pastor at the Dexter Avenue Baptist Church. At only twenty-six, King had a doctorate in theology from Boston University. A captivating speaker before blacks who gathered regularly at churches throughout the boycott, King inspired their courage and commitment by linking racial justice to the redeeming power of Christian love. He promised, "If you will protest courageously and yet with dignity and Christian love . . . historians will have to pause and say, 'There lived a great people—a black people—who injected a new meaning and dignity into the veins of civilization.' This is our challenge and our overwhelming responsibility." (See "American Places," page 1015.)

Montgomery blacks summoned their courage and determination in abundance. They walked miles to get to work, contributed their meager financial resources, and stood up with dignity to

Montgomery Civil Rights Leaders
During the Montgomery bus boycott, local white officials sought to intimidate African Americans with arrests and lawsuits. Here Rosa Parks, one of ninety-two defendants, ascends the steps of the Montgomery County courthouse in March 1956, accompanied by longtime civil rights leader E. D. Nixon. He felt that Parks would be a perfect plaintiff in a suit against segregation, and Parks agreed. "The white people couldn't say that there was anything I had done to deserve such treatment except to be born black."
Wide World Photos.

AMERICAN PLACES

Martin Luther King Jr. National Historic Site, Atlanta, Georgia

On January 15, 1929, Martin Luther King Jr. was born in his parents' bedroom on the second floor of a house on 501 Auburn Street in Atlanta, Georgia. King's maternal grandfather, the Reverend A. D. Williams, had bought the Queen Anne–style house in 1909, and King lived there with his parents, grandparents, older sister, and younger brother until he was twelve years old. Just two blocks away stood Ebenezer Baptist Church, a three-story red brick and stucco Gothic revival–style building, where King's father, his grandfather, and eventually King himself all served as pastors.

The house and church were part of the larger Sweet Auburn district, just east of downtown Atlanta and the center of a vibrant and achieving African American community during King's youth. At the age of thirteen, he took a segregated bus to the west side of the city to attend the only black public high school in Atlanta. Segregation restricted black Atlantans, but—as in most cities—at the same time it made possible flourishing black-owned businesses in the Auburn neighborhood, including banks, insurance companies, barber shops, laundries, drugstores, and restaurants. King remembered his neighborhood as a "wholesome community," though none of the residents were of the "upper upper

Martin Luther King Jr. Birthplace
Martin Luther King Jr. National Historic Site.

class." Yet he grew up in an environment with substantial class and occupational diversity. Black teachers, doctors, ministers, and business owners called the Auburn district home, as did domestic workers, laundry workers, and laborers. Solid Victorian houses, like the one where King was born, were interspersed with small cottages, boardinghouses, and businesses. African Americans in such neighborhoods as Auburn Street developed close community ties and a sense of collective identity that nourished the civil rights struggle.

Today visitors can walk through King's birth home, Ebenezer Baptist

Church, and the Auburn neighborhood, which have been preserved and restored as part of the Martin Luther King Jr. National Historic Site, an urban park of about thirty-eight acres established in 1980. Sweet Auburn continues as a "real" neighborhood, but along with King's house and church, several buildings have been restored to their 1930s appearance. The historic site also includes the Martin Luther King Jr. Center for Nonviolent Social Change, Inc., established in 1968 by Coretta Scott King to preserve and advance her husband's work in civil rights and human rights. Completed in 1981, the King Center complex includes a museum with artifacts from King's life, a library and archives that house his papers, and a conference center as well as King's tomb.

A visit to the Web site offers a virtual tour through the rooms of the King house and photographs and information about Ebenezer Church and the neighborhood. The Web site also contains many of King's writings, including a speech he wrote as a high school junior, "The Negro and the Constitution," which won first place in an oratorical contest sponsored by the black Elks. Exploring such documents and the streets of Sweet Auburn provides an understanding of the solid, middle-class, church-oriented community that produced Martin Luther King Jr. and fired his lifelong sense of injustice and the possibility of redemption.

FOR WEB LINKS RELATED TO THIS SITE AND OTHER AMERICAN PLACES, see "PlaceLinks" at bedfordstmartins.com/roark.

legal, economic, and physical intimidation. One older woman insisted, "I'm not walking for myself, I'm walking for my children and my grandchildren." Authorities arrested several leaders, and whites firebombed King's house. Yet the

movement persisted, and in November 1956, the Supreme Court finally declared unconstitutional Alabama's laws requiring bus segregation. Although the Montgomery movement's victory came from Washington rather than the local power structure, it had demonstrated that blacks could sustain a lengthy protest and would not be intimidated.

In January 1957, black clergy from across the South met to coordinate local protests against segregation and to secure the ballot for blacks. They founded the Southern Christian Leadership Conference (SCLC) and chose King to head it. Although dominated by ministers, the SCLC owed much of its success to Ella Baker, a seasoned activist who came from New York to set up and run its office.

King's face on the cover of *Time* magazine in February 1957 marked his rapid rise to national and international fame. He crisscrossed the nation and the world, speaking to large audiences, raising funds, and meeting with other activists. In June 1958, Eisenhower extended his first invitation to black leaders, and King and three others met with the president. Meanwhile, in the late 1950s, the SCLC, NAACP, and CORE developed centers in several southern cities, paving the way for a mass movement that would revolutionize the racial system of the South.

Martin Luther King Jr. in Montgomery

Martin Luther King Jr. preaches at the First Baptist Church during the Montgomery bus boycott. First Baptist was the congregation of Ralph D. Abernathy, the man who would become King's close associate in the crusades to come. The importance of churches as inspiration for and organizing centers in the black freedom struggle was not lost on white racists, who bombed First Baptist and three other black churches in Montgomery during the boycott.

Dan Weiner, courtesy Sandra Weiner.

Conclusion: Peace and Prosperity Mask Unmet Challenges

At the American National Exhibition in Moscow in 1959, the consumer goods that Nixon proudly displayed to Khrushchev and the cold war competition that crackled through their dialogue reflected two dominant themes of the 1950s: the prosperity of the U.S. economy and the superpowers' success in keeping cold war competition within the bounds of peace. The tremendous economic growth of the 1950s, which raised the standard of living for most Americans, resulted in part from the cold war: One of every ten American jobs depended directly on defense spending.

Affluence helped to change the very landscape of the United States. Suburban housing developments sprang up, interstate highways began to divide cities and connect the country, farms declined in number but grew in size, and population and industry moved south and west. Daily habits and even values of ordinary people changed as the economy became more service oriented and the opportunity to buy a host of new products intensified the growth of a culture based on consumption.

The general prosperity and seeming conformity, however, masked a number of developments and problems that Americans would face head-on in later years: rising resistance to an unjust racial system, a 20 percent poverty rate, the movement of married women into the labor force, and the emergence of a self-conscious youth generation. Although the federal government's defense spending and housing, highway, and education subsidies played a large role in the economic boom, in general Eisenhower tried to curb domestic programs and let private enterprise have its way. His administration maintained the welfare state inherited from the Democrats but opposed further reforms.

In global affairs, Eisenhower exercised restraint on large issues, recognizing the limits of U.S. power. In the name of **deterrence**, he promoted development of more destructive atomic weapons, but he resisted pressures for even larger defense budgets. Still, Eisenhower took from Truman the assumption that the United

States must fight communism everywhere, and when movements in Iran, Guatemala, Cuba, and Vietnam seemed too radical, too friendly to communism, or too inimical to American economic interests, he tried to undermine them, often with secret operations.

Thus, although Eisenhower presided over eight years of peace and prosperity, his foreign policy inspired anti-Americanism, established dangerous precedents for the expansion of executive power, and forged commitments that future generations would deem unwise. As Eisenhower's successors took on the struggle against communism and grappled with the domestic challenges of race, poverty, and urban decay that he had avoided, the tranquillity and consensus of the 1950s would give way to the turbulence and conflict of the 1960s.

FOR ADDITIONAL FIRSTHAND ACCOUNTS OF THIS PERIOD, see Chapter 27 in Michael Johnson, ed., *Reading the American Past*, Third Edition.

TO ASSESS YOUR MASTERY OF THE MATERIAL IN THIS CHAPTER, see the Online Study Guide at bedfordstmartins.com/ roark.

FOR WEB LINKS RELATED TO TOPICS IN THIS CHAPTER, see "HistoryLinks," "DocLinks," and "PlaceLinks" at bedfordstmartins.com/roark.

CHRONOLOGY

1952
- Dwight D. Eisenhower elected president of United States.
- *I Love Lucy* becomes number-one television show.

1953
- Government implements policy of termination of special status of American Indians and relocates thousands off reservations.
- CIA engineers coup against government of Mohammed Mossadegh in Iran.

1954
- CIA stages coup against government of Jacobo Arbenz in Guatemala.
- France signs Geneva accords, withdrawing from Vietnam.
- United States organizes Southeast Asia Treaty Organization (SEATO) in wake of French defeat in Vietnam; Eisenhower administration begins aid program to government of South Vietnam.
- Government launches Operation Wetback, a series of raids designed to seek out and deport illegal immigrants from Mexico.
- Ground broken in Pennsylvania for first commercial nuclear power plant.
- In *Hernandez v. Texas*, U.S. Supreme Court declares exclusion of Mexican Americans from jury service a violation of constitutional rights.
- In *Brown v. Board of Education*, U.S. Supreme Court declares segregation in public schools unconstitutional.
- Senate condemns Senator Joseph McCarthy, effectively ending his four-year campaign of Red-baiting.

1955
- Eisenhower and Khrushchev meet in Geneva for first superpower summit since end of World War II.

1955–1956
- Montgomery, Alabama, bus boycott by African Americans focuses national attention on civil rights.

1956
- Interstate Highway and Defense System Act provides federal funds for road-building activities previously done by state and local governments.
- Eisenhower reelected by landslide to second term.
- Allen Ginsberg publishes poem *Howl*, expressing rebelliousness of Beat generation.

1957
- Martin Luther King Jr. and others found Southern Christian Leadership Conference (SCLC) to organize protests against segregation.
- Soviets launch *Sputnik*, first satellite to orbit Earth.
- Labor union membership peaks at 27.1 percent of labor force.
- Jack Kerouac publishes *On the Road*, best-selling novel of the Beat generation.

1958
- Eisenhower establishes the National Aeronautics and Space Administration (NASA).

1959
- American National Exhibition in Moscow is scene of "kitchen debate" between Nixon and Khrushchev.

1960
- Soviets shoot down U.S. U-2 spy plane, causing rift in U.S.-Soviet relations.
- Women represent one-third of labor force; 35 percent of women work outside the home.
- One-quarter of Americans live in suburbs.

BIBLIOGRAPHY

General Works

William Chafe, *The Unfinished Journey: America since World War II* (1986).

John Patrick Diggins, *The Proud Decades: America in War and Peace, 1941–1960* (1988).

Alan Ehrenhalt, *The Lost City: Discovering the Forgotten Virtues of Community in the Chicago of the 1950s* (1995).

David Halberstam, *The Fifties* (1993).

Douglas T. Miller and Marion Nowak, *The Fifties: The Way We Really Were* (1977).

J. Ronald Oakley, *God's Country: America in the Fifties* (1986).

William L. O'Neill, *American High: The Years of Confidence, 1945–1960* (1986).

James T. Patterson, *Grand Expectations: The United States, 1945–1974* (1996).

Michael S. Sherry, *In the Shadow of War: The United States since the 1930s* (1995).

Domestic Politics and Policies

Charles C. Alexander, *Holding the Line: The Eisenhower Era, 1952–1961* (1975).

Craig Allen, *Eisenhower and the Mass Media: Peace, Prosperity, and Prime-Time TV* (1993).

Stephen E. Ambrose, *Eisenhower*, vol. 2, *The President* (1984).

Jeff Broadwater, *Eisenhower and the Anti-Communist Crusade* (1992).

Robert F. Burk, *Dwight D. Eisenhower: Hero and Politician* (1986).

Fred I. Greenstein, *The Hidden-Hand Presidency: Eisenhower as Leader* (1982).

Chester J. Pach Jr. and Elmo Richardson, *The Presidency of Dwight D. Eisenhower* (rev. ed., 1991).

Geoffrey Perret, *Eisenhower* (1999).

Gary W. Reichard, *The Reaffirmation of Republicanism* (1975).

Foreign Policy

Stephen E. Ambrose, *Ike's Spies: Eisenhower and the Espionage Establishment* (1981).

Michael R. Beschloss, *Mayday: Eisenhower, Khrushchev, and the U-2 Affair* (1986).

Gunter Bischof and Saki Dockrill, eds., *Cold War Respite: The Geneva Summit of 1955* (2000).

Blanche Wiesen Cook, *The Declassified Eisenhower: A Divided Legacy of Peace and Political Warfare* (1981).

Robert A. Divine, *The Sputnik Challenge* (1993).

Michael S. Foley, *American Orientalism: The United States and the Middle East since 1945* (2002).

Steven Z. Freiberger, *Dawn over Suez: The Rise of American Power in the Middle East, 1953–1957* (1992).

George C. Herring, *America's Longest War: The United States and Vietnam, 1950–1975* (2nd rev. ed., 1986).

Richard H. Immerman, *The CIA in Guatemala* (1982).

Richard H. Immerman, *John Foster Dulles and the Diplomacy of the Cold War* (1990).

Stanley Karnow, *Vietnam: A History* (rev. ed., 1991).

Stephen Kinzer, *All the Shah's Men: An American Coup and the Roots of Middle East Terror* (2003).

Walter LaFeber, *Inevitable Revolutions: The United States in Central America* (1983).

Donald Neff, *Warriors at Suez: Eisenhower Takes America into the Middle East* (1981).

Stephen G. Rabe, *Eisenhower and Latin America: The Foreign Policy of Anticommunism* (1988).

Andrew J. Rotter, *The Path to Vietnam: Origins of the American Commitment to Southeast Asia* (1987).

David L. Snead, *The Gaither Committee, Eisenhower, and the Cold War* (1999).

Philip Taubman, *Secret Empire: Eisenhower, the C.I.A., and the Hidden Story of America's Space Espionage* (2003).

Lawrence S. Wittner, *The Struggle against the Bomb*, 2 vols. (1993, 1997).

Women, Gender Roles, and the Family

Wini Breines, *Young, White, and Miserable: Growing Up Female in the Fifties* (1992).

Stephanie Coontz, *The Way We Never Were: American Families and the Nostalgia Trip* (1992).

Barbara Ehrenreich, *The Hearts of Men: American Dreams and the Flight from Commitment* (1983).

Betty Friedan, *The Feminine Mystique* (1963).

James Howard Jones, *Alfred C. Kinsey: A Public/Private Life* (1998).

Elaine Tyler May, *Homeward Bound: American Families in the Cold War Era* (1988).

Joanne Meyerowitz, ed., *Not June Cleaver: Women and Gender in Postwar America, 1945–1960* (1994).

Steven Mintz and Susan Kellogg, *Domestic Revolutions: A Social History of American Family Life* (1988).

Arlene Skolnick, *Embattled Paradise: The American Family in an Age of Uncertainty* (1991).

Rickie Solinger, *Wake Up Little Susie: Single Pregnancy and Race before Roe v. Wade* (1992).

Economic and Social Developments

Rosalyn Baxandall and Elizabeth Ewen, *Picture Windows: How the Suburbs Happened* (2000).

Lizabeth Cohen, *A Consumers' Republic: The Politics of Mass Consumption in Postwar America* (2003).

Gail Cooper, *Air-Conditioning America: Engineers and the Controlled Environment, 1900–1960* (1998).

Ruth Schwartz Cowan, *A Social History of American Technology* (1997).

Richard O. Davies, *The Age of Asphalt: The Automobile, the Freeway, and the Condition of Metropolitan America* (1975).

Herbert Gans, *The Levittowners: Ways of Life and Politics in a New Suburban Community* (2nd ed., 1982).

Kenneth T. Jackson, *Crabgrass Frontier: The Suburbanization of the United States* (1985).

Barbara Kelly, *Expanding the American Dream: Building and Rebuilding Levittown* (1993).

Tom Lewis, *Divided Highways: Building the Interstate Highways, Transforming American Life* (1999).

Michael P. Malone and Richard W. Etulain, *The American West: A Twentieth-Century History* (1989).

Raymond A. Mohl, *Searching for the Sunbelt: Historical Perspectives on a Region* (1993).

Gerald D. Nash, *The American West in the Twentieth Century* (1973).

Adam Rome, *The Bulldozer in the Countryside: Suburban Sprawl and the Rise of American Environmentalism* (2001).

Mark H. Rose, *Interstate: Express Highway Politics, 1941–1956* (1979).

Bruce J. Schulman, *From Cotton Belt to Sunbelt: Federal Policy, Economic Development, and the Transformation of the South, 1938–1980* (1994).

Jon C. Teaford, *The Twentieth-Century American City* (1993).

Religion and Culture

Erik Barnouw, *Tube of Plenty: The Evolution of American Television* (rev. ed., 1982).

James L. Baughman, *The Republic of Mass Culture: Journalism, Film-making, and Broadcasting in America since 1941* (1997).

William Boddy, *Fifties Television: The Industry and Its Critics* (1994).

Paul Boyer, *By the Dawn's Early Light: American Thought and Culture at the Dawn of the Atomic Age* (1985).

James Campbell, *This Is the Beat Generation: New York–San Francisco–Paris* (2001).

Robert Ellwood, *The Fifties Spiritual Marketplace: American Religion in a Decade of Conflict* (1997).

Simon Frith, *Sound Effects: Youth, Leisure, and the Politics of Rock and Roll* (1981).

Serge Guilbaut, *How New York Stole the Idea of Modern Art: Abstract Expressionism, Freedom, and the Cold War* (1983).

Peter Guralnick, *Last Train to Memphis: The Rise of Elvis Presley* (1994).

Peter Guralnick, *Careless Love: The Unmaking of Elvis Presley* (1999).

James Hudnut-Beumler, *Looking for God in the Suburbs: The Religion of the American Dream and Its Critics, 1945–1965* (1994).

David Mark, *Democratic Vistas: Television in American Culture* (1984).

Karal Ann Marling, *As Seen on TV: The Visual Culture of Everyday Life in the 1950s* (1994).

Lary May, ed., *Recasting America: Culture and Politics in the Age of the Cold War* (1989).

James Miller, *Flowers in the Dustbin: The Rise of Rock and Roll, 1947–1977* (1999).

Lynn Spigel, *Make Room for TV: Television and the Family Ideal in Postwar America* (1992).

Cecelia Tichi, *Electronic Hearth: Creating an American Television Culture* (1991).

Steven Watson, *The Birth of the Beat Generation: Visionaries, Rebels, and Hipsters, 1944–1960* (1995).

Stephen J. Whitfield, *The Culture of the Cold War* (1991).

Robert Wuthnow, *The Restructuring of American Religion: Society and Faith since World War II* (1988).

Minorities and Civil Rights

Melba Patillo Beals, *Warriors Don't Cry: A Searing Memoir of the Battle to Integrate Little Rock's Central High* (1994).

Thomas Borstelmann, *The Cold War and the Color Line: American Race Relations in the Global Arena* (2001).

Taylor Branch, *Parting the Waters: America in the King Years, 1954–1963* (1988).

Robert Fredrick Burk, *The Eisenhower Administration and Black Civil Rights* (1984).

Mary L. Dudziak, *Cold War Civil Rights: Race and the Image of American Democracy* (2000).

John Egerton, *Speak Now against the Day: The Generation before the Civil Rights Movement in the South* (1994).

Adam Fairclough, *To Redeem the Soul of America: The Southern Christian Leadership Conference and Martin Luther King Jr.* (1987).

Donald L. Fixico, *Termination and Relocation: Federal Indian Policy, 1945–1960* (1986).

David J. Garrow, *Bearing the Cross: Martin Luther King Jr. and the Southern Christian Leadership Conference* (1986).

David J. Garrow, ed., *The Montgomery Boycott and the Women Who Started It: The Memoir of Jo Ann Gibson Robinson* (1987).

Arnold R. Hirsch, *Making the Second Ghetto: Race and Housing in Chicago, 1940–1960* (1998).

Richard Kluger, *Simple Justice: The History of* Brown v. Board of Education *and Black America's Struggle for Equality* (1976).

Doug McAdam, *Political Process and the Development of Black Insurgency, 1930–1970* (1982).

R. Warren Metcalf, *Termination's Legacy: The Discarded Indians of Utah* (2002).

Aldon D. Morris, *The Origins of the Civil Rights Movement: Black Communities Organizing for Change* (1984).

E. Frederick Morrow, *Black Man in the White House* (1963).

James T. Patterson, Brown v. Board of Education: *A Civil Rights Milestone and Its Troubled Legacy* (2001).

Barbara Ransby, *Ella Baker and the Black Freedom Movement* (2003).

Thomas J. Sugrue, *The Origins of the Urban Crisis: Race and Inequality in Postwar Detroit* (1996).

Mark V. Tushnet, *Making Civil Rights Law: Thurgood Marshall and the Supreme Court, 1936–1961* (1995).

Juan Williams, *Thurgood Marshall: American Revolutionary* (1998).

"COUNTRY JOE" McDONALD'S GUITAR
Music was an omnipresent element of protest movements in the 1960s. Civil rights demonstrators sang "We Shall Overcome," antiwar rallies featured folk singers, and hippies turned on to acid rock. The guitar was the central musical instrument for each kind of music: traditional African American, folk, and rock. This wooden acoustic guitar, adorned with a peace symbol, belonged to "Country Joe" McDonald, who started his band, Country Joe and the Fish, at a draft protest in Oakland, California, in 1965. The band was one of many that originated in the San Francisco Bay area, but its popularity soon spread across the country.
The Oakland Museum of California.

28

Reform, Rebellion, and Reaction

1960–1974

O N AUGUST 31, 1962, Fannie Lou Hamer boarded a bus carrying eighteen African Americans from Ruleville, Mississippi, to the county seat in Indianola, where they intended to register to vote. Blacks made up more than 60 percent of Sunflower County's population but only 1.2 percent of registered voters. Before young civil rights activists arrived in Ruleville to start a voter registration drive, Hamer recalled, "I didn't know that a Negro could register and vote." Her forty-five years of poverty, exploitation, and political disfranchisement typified the lives of most blacks in the rural South. The daughter of sharecroppers, Hamer began work in the cotton fields at age six, attending school in a one-room shack from December to March and only until she was twelve. In her late twenties, she married Perry Hamer and moved onto the plantation where he sharecropped. She worked in the fields, did domestic work for the plantation owner, and recorded the cotton sharecroppers brought in to be weighed.

At Indianola, Hamer and her companions defied a hostile, white, gun-carrying crowd to enter the county courthouse. Using a common practice to keep blacks from the voting booth, the registrar tested Hamer on an obscure section of the state constitution. Since her schooling had not included Mississippi's constitution, she, predictably, failed the test but resolved to try again. When she arrived home, her plantation-owner boss ordered her to withdraw her registration application or get off his land. Refusing to back down, Hamer left the plantation. Ten days later, sixteen bullets flew into the home of friends who had taken her in. Refusing to be intimidated, she tried again to register (and succeeded on the third attempt), attended a civil rights leadership training conference, and began to mobilize others to vote. In 1963, she and other activists were arrested in Winona, Mississippi, and beaten so brutally that Hamer went from the jail to the hospital, refusing to see her family, except for one sister, who could not recognize her battered face.

Fannie Lou Hamer's courage and determination made her a prominent figure in a movement that shook the nation's conscience, raised hopes for change, provided a model of protest for other groups, and transformed national policy. Although the federal government often tried to curb civil rights activists, the two Democratic presidents of the 1960s favored a **progressive** government and—helped by a prosperous economy—put solving social and economic problems high on the national agenda. After John F. Kennedy was assassinated in November 1963, Lyndon B. Johnson launched the **Great Society**—a multitude of efforts to promote racial justice, education, medical

- **Liberalism at High Tide**
  The Promise and Substance of Kennedy's New Frontier
  Assassination of a President
  Johnson Fulfills the Kennedy Promise
  Completing the Great Society Agenda
  Assessing the War on Poverty
  The Judicial Revolution

- **The Second Reconstruction**
  The Flowering of the Black Freedom Struggle
  The Response in Washington
  Black Nationalism

- **A Multitude of Movements**
  Native American Protest
  Latino Struggles for Justice
  Student Rebellion, the New Left, and the Counterculture
  A New Movement to Save the Environment

- **The New Wave of Feminism**
  A Movement Emerges
  The Many Facets and Achievements of Feminism
  A Counter Movement Arises

- **The Persistence of Liberal Reform in the Nixon Administration**
  Extending the Welfare State and Regulating the Economy
  Responding to Demands for Social Justice

- **Conclusion: Achievements and Limitations of Liberalism**

Mississippi Freedom Democratic Party Rally
Fannie Lou Hamer (left foreground) and other activists sing at a rally outside the Democratic National Convention hall in 1964, supporting the Mississippi Freedom Democratic Party (MFDP) in its challenge to the all-white delegation sent by the regular Mississippi Democratic Party. Next to Hamer is Eleanor Holmes Norton, a civil rights lawyer, and Ella Baker (far right), who helped organize the Southern Christian Leadership Conference and later managed MFDP headquarters in Washington, D.C.
Matt Herron/Take Stock.

care, urban development, and environmental and economic health. Those who struggled for racial justice lost property, personal safety, and sometimes their lives, but by the end of the decade, law had caught up with the American ideal of equality.

Yet legal change did not go far enough. Strong civil rights legislation and pathbreaking Supreme Court decisions affected little the deplorable economic conditions of African Americans, on which Hamer and others increasingly focused after 1965. Nor was the political establishment a consistently reliable ally, as Hamer found out in 1964 when President Johnson and his allies rebuffed black Mississippi Democrats' efforts to be represented at the Democratic National Convention. "We followed all the laws that the white people themselves made," she said, only to find that "the white man is not going to give up his power to us. . . . We have to take for ourselves." By 1966, a minority of African American activists were demanding black power; the movement soon splintered, and white support sharply declined. A growing number of **conservatives** protested that the Great Society went too far and condemned the challenge to American values and institutions mounted by blacks, students, and others.

Although disillusioned and often frustrated, Fannie Lou Hamer remained an activist until her death in 1977, mingling with new social movements stimulated by the black freedom struggle. In 1969, she supported Mississippi Valley State College students' demands for black studies courses and a greater voice in campus decisions. In 1972, she attended the founding conference of the National Women's Political Caucus, established to achieve greater representation for women in government. The caucus was part of a much broader feminist movement emerging during the period, one that promoted a revolution in women's legal status as well as important changes in the everyday relationships between women and men.

Feminists and other groups, including ethnic minorities, environmentalists, and gays and lesbians, benefited and borrowed from the ideas, tactics, and policy precedents of the civil rights movement. These movements helped to carry the tide of reform into the 1970s and to push the Republican administration of Richard M. Nixon to sustain the **liberalism** of the 1960s with its emphasis on a strong government role in regulating the economy and guaranteeing the welfare and rights of all individuals. Despite its conservative rhetoric designed to ride a backlash against increasing the authority of government to solve social problems, the Nixon administration would implement school desegregation and **affirmative action** and adopt pathbreaking measures in such areas as environmental regulation, equality for women, and justice for Native Americans. The years between 1960 and 1974 contained the greatest efforts to reconcile America's promise with reality since the New Deal.

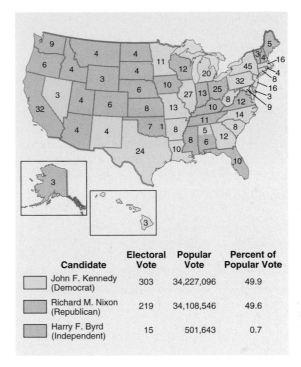

Candidate	Electoral Vote	Popular Vote	Percent of Popular Vote
John F. Kennedy (Democrat)	303	34,227,096	49.9
Richard M. Nixon (Republican)	219	34,108,546	49.6
Harry F. Byrd (Independent)	15	501,643	0.7

MAP 28.1   The Election of 1960

Liberalism at High Tide

At the Democratic National Convention in 1960, John F. Kennedy announced that the United States faced "a New Frontier . . . of unfulfilled hopes and threats," and he promised to confront "unsolved problems of peace and war, unconquered pockets of ignorance and prejudice, unanswered questions of poverty and surplus." Four years later, Lyndon B. Johnson invoked the ideal of a "Great Society, [which] rests on abundance and liberty for all [and] demands an end to poverty and racial injustice." Acting under the liberal faith that government could and should use its power to solve social and economic problems, end injustice, and promote the welfare of all citizens, the Democratic administrations of the 1960s won legislation on civil rights, poverty, education, medical care, housing, consumer protection, and environmental protection.

The Promise and Substance of Kennedy's New Frontier

John F. Kennedy grew up in privilege, the child of an Irish Catholic businessman who served in Franklin D. Roosevelt's administration and nourished political ambitions for his sons. Helped by

a distinguished World War II navy record, Kennedy won election to the House of Representatives in 1946 and the Senate in 1952. His record in Congress was unremarkable, but with a powerful political machine, his family's fortunes, and a handsome and dynamic appearance, Kennedy won the Democratic presidential nomination in 1960. He stunned many Democrats by choosing as his running mate Lyndon B. Johnson of Texas, who had bid for the presidency himself and was detested by liberals who viewed him as a typical southern conservative.

Kennedy defeated his Republican opponent, Vice President Richard M. Nixon, in an excruciatingly close election (Map 28.1). African American voters contributed to his victory, helping to offset the 52 percent of the white vote cast for Nixon and contributing to his 120,000-vote margin overall and to close victories in such key states as Illinois and Michigan. Lyndon Johnson helped the ticket carry most of the South, and a rise in unemployment in 1960 also favored the Democrats. Finally, Kennedy benefited from the nation's first televised presidential debates, appearing cool, confident, and in command of the issues, beside a nervous, sweaty, and pale Nixon.

The Kennedy administration projected energy, idealism, and glamour, though in fact Kennedy was a cautious, pragmatic politician.

The first president to hold live televised press conferences, Kennedy charmed the press corps and the people with his grace, vigor, and self-mocking wit. He kept hidden from the public serious health problems as well as affairs with several women, recklessly making himself vulnerable to blackmail and risking the dignity of his office. Journalists turned a blind eye, instead projecting warm images of an energetic, youthful president with his chic and cultured wife, Jacqueline.

At his inauguration, the forty-three-year-old Kennedy declared that a "new generation" was assuming leadership and called on Americans to cast off complacency and self-indulgence and serve the common good. "Ask not what your country can do for you," he implored, "ask what you can do for your country." Though Kennedy's idealism inspired many, especially the young, to replace self-interest with service to a larger cause, he failed to redeem campaign promises to expand the **welfare state**. Nor did he assume leadership on behalf of racial justice until late in his term, when civil rights activists gave him no choice. Referring to a book by Kennedy, *Profiles in Courage* (1956), liberals jokingly disparaged his leadership by suggesting that he show "less profile and more courage."

Kennedy did win support for a $2 billion slum clearance and urban renewal program; for the Area Redevelopment Act of 1961, offering incentives to businesses to locate in depressed areas; and for the Manpower Development and Training Act of 1962, which provided training for the unemployed. But two important items on the Democratic agenda since the Truman administration, federal aid to education and health care for the elderly, got nowhere.

Kennedy had promised to "get this country moving again," making economic growth a key objective. "A rising tide lifts all boats" expressed Kennedy's belief that economic growth could eradicate poverty and solve most social problems. He also focused on growth to make the nation more competitive with the Soviet Union. Economic advisers argued that infusing money into the economy by reducing taxes would increase demand, boost production, and decrease unemployment. To that end, Kennedy asked Congress to pass an enormous tax cut in 1963. This use of fiscal policy to stimulate the economy even when there was no recession gained the name "the new economics."

> Though Kennedy's idealism inspired many to replace self-interest with service to a larger cause, he failed to redeem campaign promises to expand the welfare state. Nor did he assume leadership on behalf of racial justice until late in his term.

The Kennedy Appeal
The youth and glamour of the Kennedy administration are apparent in this photo of the president and his wife attired for his inauguration gala. The gown that Jacqueline Kennedy had designed by Oleg Cassini for the occasion bore a cockade at the waist, indicating her French ancestry and keen interest in history and culture, which were reflected in White House social events that elevated Washington's cultural scene by featuring artists, writers, scholars, and musicians throughout the Kennedy presidency. The president was well aware of his wife's appeal to the public, asking the driver of their limousine to "turn on the lights so they can see Jackie."
© Bettmann/Corbis.

John F. Kennedy's Funeral
For a few days following November 22, 1963, normal life stopped in the United States. Schools and businesses were closed, and tens of thousands of Americans traveled to Washington, D.C., to file past Kennedy's coffin in the rotunda of the Capitol. The relatively new medium of television unified the nation, as it allowed millions of viewers to experience every moment of that long, terrible weekend, culminating in the funeral procession, shown here. The president's widow, Jacqueline Kennedy, is escorted in the procession by the president's brothers Robert (left) and Edward (right).
© Henri Dauman, 1963, NYC.

Kennedy did not live to see approval of his bill. Passed in February 1964, the law contributed to the greatest economic boom since World War II. Unemployment dropped to 4.1 percent, and the gross national product shot up by 7 to 9 percent annually between 1964 and 1966. Some liberal critics of the tax cut, however, maintained that economic growth alone would not eliminate poverty, arguing instead for increased spending on social programs.

Poverty had gained Kennedy's attention in 1960, when he campaigned in Appalachia for the votes of the rural poor. In 1962, he read *The Other America*, in which the political activist Michael Harrington described the poverty of more than one in every five Americans "maimed in body and spirit, existing at levels beneath those necessary for human decency." During the summer of 1963, Kennedy asked aides to plan an attack on poverty, and he also issued a dramatic call for a comprehensive civil rights bill, marking a turning point in his attitude toward domestic problems. Whether he could have achieved these breakthroughs was left unanswered by his assassination on November 22, 1963.

Assassination of a President

The murder of the president touched Americans as had no other event since the end of World War II. Within minutes of the shooting—which occurred as the Kennedy motorcade passed through Dallas, Texas, on November 22, 1963—radio and television broadcast the unfolding horror to the nation. Millions watched the return of *Air Force One* to Washington bearing the president's coffin, his widow in her bloodstained suit, and the new president, Lyndon Baines Johnson.

Stunned Americans struggled with what had happened and why. Soon after the assassination, police arrested Lee Harvey Oswald and concluded that he had fired the shots from a nearby building. Two days later, as a television audience watched Oswald being transferred from one jail to another, a local nightclub operator, Jack Ruby, killed him. Suspicions arose that Ruby murdered Oswald to cover up a conspiracy by ultraconservative Texans who hated Kennedy, or by Communists who supported Castro's Cuba. To get at the truth, President

Johnson appointed a commission headed by Chief Justice Earl Warren, which concluded in September 1964 that both Oswald and Ruby had acted alone. Although several experts pointed to errors and omissions in the report, and some contested the lone-killer explanation, most scholars agreed that no conspiracy had existed.

Debate continued over how to assess Kennedy's domestic record. It had been unremarkable in his first two years, but his initiatives on taxes, civil rights, and poverty in 1963 suggested an important shift. Whether Kennedy could have persuaded Congress to enact his proposals cannot be known. In the words of journalist James Reston, "What was killed was not only the president but the promise. . . . He never reached his meridian: We saw him only as a rising sun."

Johnson Fulfills the Kennedy Promise

Lyndon Johnson assumed the presidency with a wealth of political experience. A self-made man from the Texas hill country, he had won election to the House of Representatives in 1937 and to the Senate in 1948. By 1955, he had secured the top post of Senate majority leader, which he used brilliantly to forge a Democratic consensus on the Civil Rights Acts of 1957 and 1960 and other programs.

Johnson's coarse wit, extreme vanity, and Texas accent repulsed those who preferred the sophisticated Kennedy style. Lacking his predecessor's eloquence, Johnson excelled behind the scenes, where he could entice or threaten legislators into support of his objectives. The famous "Johnson treatment" became legendary (see photograph to the right). In his ability to

achieve consensus around his goals—and in the means to which he was willing to resort—he had few peers in American history.

"I had to take the dead man's program and turn it into a martyr's cause," Johnson declared, entreating Congress to act so that "John Fitzgerald Kennedy did not live or die in vain." By trimming the federal budget and promising government frugality, he won over fiscal conservatives and signed Kennedy's tax cut bill in February 1964. Still more revolutionary was the Civil Rights Act of July 1964, the strongest such measure since Reconstruction, and one requiring every ounce of Johnson's political skills to pry sufficient votes from Republicans to balance the "nays" of southern Democrats.

Fast on the heels of the Civil Rights Act came a response to Johnson's call for "an unconditional war on poverty." The Economic Opportunity Act of 1964 authorized ten programs under a newly created Office of Economic Opportunity, allocating $800 million for the first year (about 1 percent of the federal budget). Many provisions targeted impoverished youth—from Head Start, a preschool program, to work-study grants for college students and a Job Corps providing job training. There were also loans to businesses willing to hire the long-term unemployed; aid to small farmers; and the Volunteers in Service to America (VISTA) program, which paid modest wages to volunteers working with the disadvantaged. A legal services program provided lawyers for the poor, leading to lawsuits that enforced their rights to welfare programs.

The most novel and controversial part of the law, the Community Action Program (CAP), required "maximum feasible participation" of the poor themselves in antipoverty programs, thus challenging the system itself. Poor people began to organize community action programs to take control of their neighborhoods and to make welfare agencies, school boards, police departments, and housing authorities more accountable to the people they served. When mayors complained that activists were challenging local

The "Johnson Treatment"

Abe Fortas, a distinguished lawyer who had argued a major criminal rights case, *Gideon v. Wainwright* (1963), before the Supreme Court, was a close friend and adviser to President Lyndon Johnson. This photograph of the president and Fortas taken in July 1965 illustrates how Johnson used his body as well as his voice to bend people to his will.
Yoichi R. Okamoto/LBJ Library Collection.

governments and "fostering class struggle," Johnson backed off from pushing genuine representation for the poor. Nonetheless, CAP gave people usually excluded from government an opportunity to act on their own behalf and to develop leadership skills. To a Mississippi sharecropper who left school to work before he learned to read and write, a local CAP literacy program provided basic skills and self-respect. It "has meant more to me than I can express," he said. "I can now write my name and I will be able to help my younger children when they start school."

Completing the Great Society Agenda

Having steered the nation through the assassination trauma and established his capacity for national leadership, Johnson projected stability and security in the midst of a booming economy. Few voters wanted to risk the dramatic change promised by his Republican opponent in the 1964 election, Arizona senator Barry M. Goldwater, who attacked the welfare state and suggested using nuclear weapons if necessary to crush **communism** in Vietnam. Although Goldwater captured five southern states, Johnson achieved a record-breaking landslide of 61 percent of the popular vote, and Democrats won resounding majorities in the House (295–140) and Senate (68–32). Yet, as we shall see in chapter 30, Goldwater's campaign aroused considerable grassroots support, contributing to the growth and ultimate ascendancy of conservatism in national politics.

"I want to see a whole bunch of coonskins on the wall," Johnson told his aides, using a hunting analogy to stress his ambitious legislative goals that would usher in what he called the "Great Society." In the sheer amount and breadth of new laws, Johnson succeeded mightily, persuading Congress to act on discrimination, poverty, education, medical care, housing, consumer and environmental protections, and more. Public opinion polls gave unusually high marks to both the president and Congress. Reporters called the legislation of the Eighty-ninth Congress (1965–1966) "a political miracle."

The Economic Opportunity Act of 1964 was the opening shot in the war on poverty. Congress doubled the program's funding in 1965 and passed two new initiatives—the Appalachian Regional Development Act and the Public Works and Economic Development Act. Targeting de-

pressed regions that the general economic boom had bypassed, these measures—like the tax cut of 1964—sought to help the poor indirectly by stimulating economic growth and providing jobs through road building and other public works projects.

A second approach endeavored to equip the poor with the skills necessary to find jobs. The largest assault on poverty through education was the Elementary and Secondary Education Act of 1965, which for the first time authorized federal funds to aid school districts. The law allocated dollars based on the number of poor children whom districts educated, and it provided equipment and supplies to private and parochial schools to be used for poor children. That same year, Congress passed the Higher Education Act, vastly expanding federal assistance to colleges and universities for buildings, programs, scholarships, and low-interest student loans.

Other antipoverty efforts provided direct aid, like a new food stamp program that largely replaced surplus food distribution, giving poor people greater choice in obtaining food. Rent supplements also allowed some poor families more options, enabling them to avoid public housing projects. In addition, with the Model Cities Act, Congress authorized more than $1 billion to improve conditions in the nation's slums.

The federal government's responsibility for health care grew even more. Trimming Truman's proposed plan for government-sponsored universal care, Johnson focused on the elderly, who constituted a large portion of the nation's poor. Congress responded with the Medicare program, providing the elderly with universal compulsory medical insurance financed largely through Social Security taxes. A separate program, Medicaid, authorized federal grants to supplement state-paid medical care for poor people under sixty-five.

A Tribute to Johnson for Medicare
George Niedermeyer, who lived in Hollywood, Florida, and received a Social Security pension, painted wood pieces and glued them together to create this thank-you to President Johnson for establishing Medicare. He entrusted his congressional representative, Claude Pepper, known for his support for the interests of the elderly, to deliver the four-foot tall tribute to Johnson in 1967.
LBJ Library, photo by Henry Groskinsky.

The assumption of national responsibility for social justice also underlay key civil rights legislation. Pressured by the black freedom struggle, Johnson got Congress to pass the Voting Rights Act of 1965, which banned literacy tests like the one that stymied Fannie Lou Hamer, and authorized federal intervention to ensure access to the voting booth. Another form of discrimination fell with the Immigration and Nationality Act of 1965, which abolished fifty-year-old quotas based on national origins that were biased against immigrants from areas outside northern and western Europe. It maintained caps on the number of immigrants and for the first time limited those from the Western Hemisphere; yet the law made possible a tremendous—and unanticipated—surge of immigration near the end of the century (see chapter 31).

> Measured by statistics, the reduction in poverty in the 1960s was considerable.

Great Society benefits reached well beyond the poverty-stricken and victims of discrimination. Medicare covered the elderly, regardless of income. In 1965, liberal activist and future Green Party presidential candidate Ralph Nader published *Unsafe at Any Speed*, an exposé and indictment of the automobile industry; he and others led a growing consumer movement that won legislation to make automobiles safer and to raise standards for the food, drug, and cosmetics industries. In 1965, Johnson became the first president to send Congress a special message on the environment, obtaining measures to control water and air pollution and to preserve the natural beauty of the American landscape. The National Arts and Humanities Act of 1965 funded artists, musicians, writers, and scholars and brought their work to public audiences.

The flood of reform legislation dwindled to a trickle after 1966, when midterm elections trimmed the Democrats' majorities in Congress and a backlash against government programs arose. Even though most poor people were white, whites tended to associate antipoverty programs with African Americans and expressed their opposition with buttons reading "I fight poverty—I work." The Vietnam War dealt the largest blow to Johnson's ambitions, diverting his attention from domestic affairs, spawning an antiwar movement that crippled his leadership, devouring tax dollars, increasing the **federal deficit**, and fueling inflation.

Against these odds, in 1968 Johnson pried out of Congress one more civil rights law, which banned discrimination in housing and jury service. He also signed the National Housing Act of 1968, which authorized an enormous increase in construction of low-income housing—1.7 million units over three years—and by leaving construction and ownership in private hands, a new way of providing it. Government-guaranteed low-interest loans spurred developers to build housing for the needy and enabled poor people to purchase those houses.

Assessing the War on Poverty

Measured by statistics, the reduction in poverty in the 1960s was considerable. The number of impoverished Americans fell from forty million in 1959 to twenty-five million in 1968, from over 20 percent of the population to around 13 percent (Figure 28.1). Especially through the community action programs, those whom Johnson had said "lived on the outskirts of hope" gained more control of their circumstances and a sense of their right to a fairer share of America's bounty. One observer remarked on a new "mood of applicants in welfare waiting rooms. . . . They were no longer as humble, as self-effacing, as pleading." Rosemary Bray described another new attitude, writing about her family that "five people on welfare for eighteen years had become five working, taxpaying adults" by 1980. Attributing that achievement to a number of factors, including her mother's sheer will and ability to stretch a handful of coins into an adequate meal, she concluded, "What fueled our dreams and fired our belief that our lives could change for the better was the promise of the civil rights movement and the war on poverty."

Certain groups fared much better than others, however. Large numbers of the aged and members of male-headed families rose out of poverty, while the plight of female-headed families actually worsened. Although African American family income grew from 54 percent of white family income to 61 percent, whites escaped poverty at a faster rate than blacks, who constituted one-third of the poor population in the 1970s. Moreover, as Johnson had intended, no significant redistribution of income resulted, despite large increases in subsidies for food stamps, housing, medical care, and the **New Deal** program Aid to Families with Dependent Children (AFDC). The poorest 20 percent of the population received 5.1 percent of total national income in 1964 and 5.4 percent in 1974.

Conservatives charged that Great Society programs discouraged initiative by giving the poor "handouts." George Gilder, for example, insisted, "The only dependable route from poverty is always work, family, and faith." Critics on the left claimed that the emphasis on training and education placed the responsibility for poverty on the poor themselves rather than on an economic system that could not provide enough adequately paying jobs. Most training programs prepared graduates for low-level jobs and could not guarantee employment. Surveys in 1966 and 1967, for example, found 28 percent of Job Corps graduates unemployed six months after finishing their training.

Who reaped the greatest benefits from Great Society programs? Most of the funds for economically depressed areas built highways and thus helped the construction industry. Real estate developers, investors, and moderate-income families benefited most from the National Housing Act of 1968. As commercial development and high-income housing often displaced the poor in slum clearance programs, blacks called urban renewal "Negro removal." Physicians' fees and hospital costs soared after enactment of Medicare and Medicaid.

Some critics argued that ending poverty required a redistribution of income—raising taxes and using those funds to create jobs, overhaul social welfare systems, and rebuild slums. Great Society programs did invest more heavily in the public sector, but Johnson's antipoverty efforts relied on economic growth rather than new taxes on the rich or middle class to increase revenues. Determined to avoid conflict, Johnson would not take from the advantaged to provide for the poor. Economic prosperity allowed spending for the poor to rise and significantly improved the lives of millions, but that spending never approached the amounts necessary to claim victory in the War on Poverty. Johnson himself conceded as much, but he insisted, "no one would ever again be able to ignore the poverty in our midst."

The Judicial Revolution

A key element of liberalism's ascendancy during the Kennedy and Johnson years emerged in the

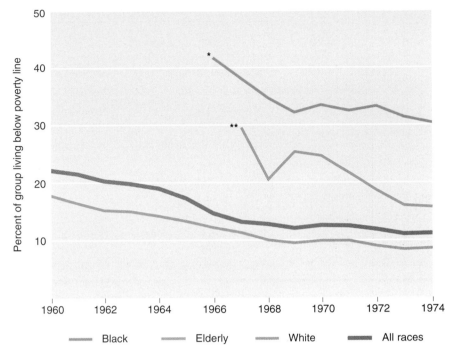

*Statistics on blacks for years 1960–1965 not available.
**Statistics on the elderly for years 1960–1966 not available.

FIGURE 28.1 Poverty in the United States, 1960–1974
The short-term effects of economic growth and the Great Society's attack on poverty are seen here. Which groups experienced the sharpest decline in poverty, and what might account for the differences?

Supreme Court under Chief Justice Earl Warren, who presided from 1953 to 1969. Expanding the Constitution's promise of equality and individual rights, the Court's decisions supported an activist government to prevent injustice and discrimination and provided new protections to disadvantaged groups and accused criminals. Following the path-breaking *Brown* school desegregation decision of 1954 (see chapter 27), the Court ruled against all-white public facilities and struck down educational plans devised by southern states to avoid integration. The Court also upheld the rights of freedom of assembly and speech, thereby enabling the black freedom struggle to continue sit-ins, mass marches, and other tactics critical to its success.

Chief Justice Warren considered *Baker v. Carr* (1963) his most important decision. The case grew out of a complaint that Tennessee electoral districts were so inequitably drawn that sparsely

> The Court's decisions supported an activist government to prevent injustice and discrimination and provided new protections to disadvantaged groups and accused criminals.

Reforms of the Great Society, 1964–1968

1964

Twenty-fourth Amendment	Abolishes poll tax as prerequisite for voting.
Tax Reduction Act	Provides $10 billion in tax cuts over 1964–1965.
Civil Rights Act	Bans discrimination in public accommodations, public education, and employment and extends protections to Indians on reservations.
Economic Opportunity Act	Creates programs for the disadvantaged, including Head Start, VISTA, Job Corps, and CAP.
Wilderness Preservation Act	Sets aside 9.1 million acres of national forest for protection.

1965

Elementary and Secondary Education Act	Provides $1.3 billion in aid to elementary and secondary schools.
Medical Care Act	Provides health insurance (Medicare) for all citizens age 65 and over. Extends federal health benefits to welfare recipients (Medicaid).
Voting Rights Act	Bans literacy tests and other voting tests and authorizes the federal government to act directly to enable African Americans to register and vote.
Executive Order 11246	Bans discrimination on the basis of race, religion, and national origin by employers awarded government contracts and requires them to "take affirmative action to ensure equal opportunity."
Department of Housing and Urban Development (HUD)	New government department created to provide programs to address housing and community issues.
National Arts and Humanities Act	Creates National Endowment for the Humanities (NEH) and National Endowment for the Arts (NEA) to support the work of artists, musicians, writers, and scholars.
Water Quality Act	Requires states to set and enforce water quality standards.
Immigration and Nationality Act	Abolishes fifty-year-old quotas based on national origins, increasing the number of non-Western and southern and eastern European immigrants.
Air Quality Act	Imposes air pollution standards for motor vehicles.
Higher Education Act	Expands federal assistance to colleges and universities.

1966

National Traffic and Motor Vehicle Safety Act	Establishes federal safety standards.
Highway Safety Act	Requires federally approved safety programs at the state level.
Department of Transportation	New government department created to administer transportation programs and policies.
Model Cities Act	Authorizes more than $1 billion to ameliorate nation's slums.

1967

Executive Order 11375	Extends earlier executive order banning discrimination and requiring affirmative action by federal contractors to cover women.

1968

Civil Rights Act of 1968	Bans discrimination in housing and in jury service.
National Housing Act	Subsidizes the private construction of 1.7 million units of low-income housing.

populated rural districts had far more representatives than densely populated urban areas. Using the Fourteenth Amendment guarantee of "equal protection of the laws," the Court in *Baker* and companion cases established the principle of "one person, one vote" both for state legislatures and for the House of Representatives. President Kennedy publicly endorsed the decision, claiming that "the right to have each vote count equally is basic to the successful operation of a democracy." Most states were required to redraw electoral districts, helping to make state legislatures more responsive to metropolitan interests.

The egalitarian thrust of the Warren Court also touched the criminal justice system as it overturned a series of convictions on the grounds that the accused had been deprived of "life, liberty, or property, without due process of law," a denial of their Fourteenth Amendment rights. Furthermore, the Court decided that states as well as the federal government were subject to the Bill of Rights, with rulings that transformed law enforcement practices and the treatment of individuals accused of crime. In *Gideon v. Wainwright* (1963) (see appendix, page A-43), the Court ruled that when accused criminals could not afford to hire lawyers, states must provide them without charge. In *Escobedo v. Illinois* (1964), the justices extended the right to counsel to the period when suspects are being questioned by police officers. Two years later, in *Miranda v. Arizona* (see appendix, page A-43), the Court ruled that officers must inform suspects of their rights upon arrest; and it overturned convictions based on evidence obtained by unlawful arrest, by electronic surveillance, or without a search warrant.

As Supreme Court decisions overturned judicial precedents and often moved ahead of public opinion, critics accused the justices of obstructing law enforcement and letting criminals go free. Sam Yorty, the mayor of Los Angeles, for example, equated *Miranda* with "handcuffing the police." Liberals, however, argued that these rulings promoted equal treatment in the criminal justice system: The wealthy always had access to legal counsel, and practiced criminals were well aware of their right to remain silent. The beneficiaries of the decisions were the poor and the ignorant, as well as the general population, whose right to privacy was strengthened by the Court's stricter guidelines for admissible evidence.

The Warren Court also fortified protections for people suspected of being Communists or subversives, setting limits, for example, on government officials who investigated and prosecuted them. Like the criminal justice cases, these rulings guaranteed the rights of people on the margins of American society and aroused opposition.

The Court's decisions on prayer and Bible reading in public schools provoked even greater outrage. In *Abington School District v. Schempp* (1963), it overturned a Pennsylvania law requiring Bible reading and prayer in the schools as a violation of the First Amendment principle of separation of church and state. The evangelist Billy Graham charged that the Court was "taking God and moral teaching from the schools." Later decisions ruled out official prayer in public schools even if students were not required to participate. Even though these decisions left students free to pray on their own, an infuriated Alabama legislator cried, "They put Negroes in the schools and now they've driven God out." The Court's supporters, however, declared that the religion cases protected the rights of non-Christians and atheists.

Two or three justices who believed that the Court was overstepping its authority often issued sharp dissents. Outside the Court, opponents worked to pass laws or constitutional amendments that would upset despised decisions, and billboards demanded, "Impeach Earl Warren." Nonetheless, the Court's major decisions withstood Warren's retirement in 1969 and the test of time.

The Second Reconstruction

Before the Great Society reforms of the mid-1960s—and, in fact, contributing to them—African Americans had already mobilized a movement that struck down legal separation and discrimination in the South. While the first Reconstruction in the aftermath of the Civil War reflected the power of northern Republicans, the second Reconstruction depended heavily on the courage and determination of black people themselves. In the words of Sheyann Webb, one of thousands of marchers in the 1965 Selma, Alabama, campaign for voting rights, "We were just people, ordinary people, and we did it."

The early black freedom struggle, focused on legal rights in the South, won widespread acceptance. But when African Americans began to attack racial injustice in the rest of the country as well as the deplorable economic conditions that equal rights left untouched, a strong backlash developed as the movement itself lost cohesion.

The Flowering of the Black Freedom Struggle

The Montgomery bus boycott of 1955–1956 gave racial issues national visibility, produced a leader in Martin Luther King Jr., and demonstrated the effectiveness of mass organization. In the 1960s, protest expanded dramatically, mobilizing blacks into direct and personal confrontation with the people and institutions that segregated and discriminated against them: lunch counters, department stores, public parks and libraries, buses and depots, voting registrars, and police forces.

Massive direct action began in February 1960, when four African American students at North Carolina A&T College in Greensboro requested service at the whites-only Woolworth's lunch counter. Within days, hundreds of young people joined their demonstration, and others launched sit-ins in thirty-one cities in eight southern states. In April, Ella Baker, executive secretary of the Southern Christian Leadership Conference (SCLC), called activists together from campuses across the South. Choosing independence from the older civil rights organizations, they founded the Student Nonviolent Coordinating Committee (SNCC, pronounced "snick"), creating a decentralized, nonhierarchical structure that encouraged leadership and decision making at the grassroots level.

Lunch Counter Sit-in

John Salter Jr., a professor at Tougaloo College, and students Joan Trumpauer and Anne Moody take part in a 1963 sit-in at the Woolworth's lunch counter in Jackson, Mississippi. Shortly before this photograph was taken, whites had thrown two students to the floor, and police had arrested one student. Salter was spattered with mustard and ketchup. Moody would publish a popular book in 1968 about her experiences in the black freedom struggle, *Coming of Age in Mississippi*.

State Historical Society of Wisconsin.

For more help analyzing this image, see the visual activity for this chapter in the Online Study Guide at bedfordstmartins.com/roark.

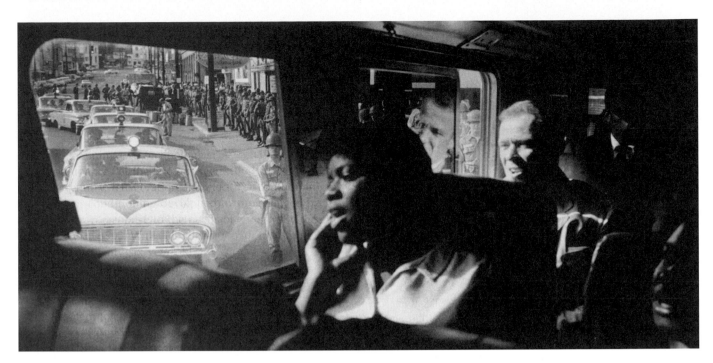

Freedom Riders

In 1961, black and white activists embarked on Freedom Rides into the South in an effort to implement the Supreme Court decision that declared segregation in interstate travel unconstitutional. When angry whites in Alabama attacked them with clubs, iron bars, and smoke bombs, the Kennedy administration sent agents to investigate and pressed state officials to protect the riders, while at the same time urging activists to stop the rides for a while. In this photo, the Freedom Riders sing while Alabama state police and national guardsmen escort their bus. Protection was sporadic, however. After a bus carrying SNCC activists arrived in Montgomery, the escort disappeared, and a white mob set upon the riders. The riders persisted, nonetheless. Several hundred reached Jackson, Mississippi, where they were arrested; 300 served time in Mississippi jails.

Bruce Davidson/Magnum Photos, Inc.

SNCC initially embraced civil disobedience and the nonviolence principles of Martin Luther King Jr. Students would directly confront their oppressors and stand up for their rights, but they would not respond if attacked. At SNCC's founding conference, James Lawson explained how that strategy could change the hearts of racists: "We affirm . . . nonviolence as a foundation of our purpose, the presupposition of our faith, and the manner of our action." With its appeal to human conscience, "nonviolence nurtures the atmosphere in which reconciliation and justice become actual possibilities."

The activists' optimism and commitment to nonviolence soon underwent severe testing. Although some cities quietly met student demands, more typically the students encountered violence. Hostile whites poured food over demonstrators, burned them with cigarettes, called them "niggers," and pelted them with rocks. Local police went after protesters with dogs, clubs, fire hoses, and tear gas; they arrested more than 3,600 civil rights demonstrators in the year following the Greensboro sit-in.

In May 1961, the Congress of Racial Equality (CORE) organized Freedom Rides to integrate interstate transportation in the South. Six whites and seven blacks boarded two buses in Washington, D.C., bound for New Orleans. When they got to Alabama, white hoodlums bombed a bus and beat the riders with baseball bats. After a huge mob attacked the activists in Montgomery, Attorney General Robert Kennedy dispatched federal marshals to restore order. But when the buses reached Jackson, Mississippi, the Freedom Riders

Civil Rights Freedom Rides, May 1961

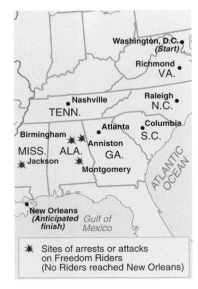

were promptly arrested, and several hundred spent part of the summer in Mississippi jails.

Encouraged by Kennedy administration officials who viewed voter registration as less controversial than civil disobedience (and more likely to benefit the Democratic Party), SNCC and other groups began a Voter Education Project in the summer of 1961. Seeking to register black voters in the Deep South, they too met violence. Whites bombed black churches, threw tenant farmers out of their homes, and beat and jailed activists like Fannie Lou Hamer. In June 1963, a white man gunned down Mississippi NAACP leader Medgar Evers in front of his house in Jackson; the murderer eluded conviction until the 1990s.

Television revealed to the world the brutality of southern resistance to racial equality in April 1963, when Martin Luther King Jr. launched a campaign in Birmingham, Alabama, to integrate public facilities and open jobs to African Americans. The city's police chief, Eugene "Bull" Connor, responded with police dogs, electric cattle prods, and high-pressure hoses. Hundreds of demonstrators, including children, went to jail, and firebombs exploded at King's motel and his brother's house. Four months later, a bomb killed four black girls attending Sunday school in Birmingham.

The largest demonstration drew 250,000 blacks and whites to the nation's capital in August 1963, where King put his indelible stamp on the day. Speaking from the Lincoln Memorial and invoking the Bible, Negro spirituals, and the nation's patriotic anthems, King drew on all the passion and skills that made him the greatest orator of his day. "I have a dream," he repeated again and again, that "the sons of former slaves and the sons of former slave owners will be

> The largest civil rights demonstration drew 250,000 blacks and whites to the nation's capital in August 1963, where King put his indelible stamp on the day.

The March on Washington

More than a quarter of a million Americans, including 50,000 whites, gathered on the Mall in the nation's capital on August 28, 1963, to pressure the government to support African Americans' civil rights. Here, Martin Luther King Jr. is about to mesmerize the crowd with his "I have a dream" speech. Afterward, Malcom X said to march organizer Bayard Rustin, "You know this dream of King's is going to be a nightmare before it's over." Francis Miller/TimePix/Getty.

The Selma March for Voting Rights
In 1963, the Student Nonviolent Coordinating Committee (SNCC) began a campaign for voting rights in Selma, Alabama, where white officials had registered only 335 of the 15,000 African Americans of voting age. As often happened, after younger activists had gotten things started, Martin Luther King Jr. came to Selma in January 1965. He planned a fifty-four-mile march from Selma to Montgomery, the state capital, to insist that blacks be registered, but, warned of a serious threat on his life, he did not lead the march. In this photo, young African Americans carrying the flag march with nuns, priests, and other supporters. During the march, Juanita Williams wore out her shoes (shown here), which are now displayed at the National Museum of History in Washington, D.C. What do you think motivated the marchers to carry the American flag?
Steve Shapiro/TimePix/Getty; Smithsonian Institution, Washington, D.C.

able to sit down together at the table of brotherhood." With the crowd roaring in support, he imagined the day "when all of God's children . . . will be able to join hands and sing . . . 'Free at last, free at last; thank God Almighty, we are free at last.'"

Yet the euphoria of the March on Washington quickly faded as activists returned to continued violence in the South. In 1964, the Mississippi Freedom Summer Project mobilized more than a thousand northern black and white college students to conduct a voter education registration drive. Resistance was fierce. By the end of the summer, only twelve hundred new voters had been allowed to register; whites had killed several activists, beaten eighty, arrested more than a thousand, and burned thirty-five black churches. Less apparent resistance came from the federal government itself, as the FBI spied on King and other leaders and expanded its activities to "expose, disrupt, misdirect, discredit, or otherwise neutralize" black protest.

Still the movement persisted. In March 1965, Alabama troopers used such fierce force to turn back a fifty-four-mile march from Selma to the state capitol in Montgomery that the incident earned the name "Bloody Sunday." After several days, President Johnson called up the Alabama National Guard to protect the marchers. Before the Selma campaign was over, whites had killed three demonstrators. Battered and hospitalized on Bloody Sunday, John Lewis, chairman of SNCC (and later a congressman), managed to make the final march to the capitol, which he counted as one of the most meaningful events in his life: "In October of that year the Voting Rights bill was passed and we all felt we'd had a part in it."

The Response in Washington

Civil rights leaders would have to wear sneakers, Lyndon Johnson said, if they were going to keep up with him. But both Kennedy and

Johnson acted more in response to the black freedom struggle than on their own initiative, moving only when events gave them little choice. Kennedy sent federal marshals to Montgomery to protect the Freedom Riders, dispatched troops to enable air force veteran James H. Meredith to enroll in the all-white University of Mississippi in 1962, and called up the Alabama National Guard during the Birmingham demonstrations in May 1963. But, well aware of the political costs of deploying federal force, he told activists pleading for more federal protection that law enforcement was a local matter.

In June 1963, Kennedy finally made good on his promise to seek strong antidiscrimination legislation. Pointing to the injustice suffered by blacks, Kennedy asked white Americans, "Who among us would then be content with the counsels of patience and delay?" Johnson took up Kennedy's commitment with passion, assisted by a number of factors. Scenes of violence against peaceful demonstrators appalled many television viewers across the nation. The resulting public support, the "Johnson treatment," and the president's ability to turn the measure into a memorial to the martyred Kennedy all produced the most important civil rights law since Reconstruction.

> Public support, the "Johnson treatment," and the president's ability to turn the measure into a memorial to the martyred Kennedy all produced the most important civil rights law since Reconstruction.

The Civil Rights Act of 1964 guaranteed access for all Americans to public accommodations, public education, employment, and voting, thus sounding the death knell for the South's system of segregation and discrimination. The law also extended constitutional protections to Indians on reservations. Title VII of the measure, banning discrimination in employment, not only attacked racial inequality outside the South but also outlawed job discrimination against women. Introduced by a conservative southerner in hopes of defeating the entire bill, the sex provision was pushed by a small group of women's rights advocates. Because Title VII applied not just to wages but to every aspect of employment, including hiring and promotion, it represented a giant step toward equal employment opportunity for white women as well as racial minorities.

Responding to black voter registration drives in the South, Johnson soon demanded a law that would remove "every remaining obstacle to the right and the opportunity to vote." In August 1965, he signed the Voting Rights Act, which empowered the federal government to intervene directly to enable African Americans to register and vote. A major transformation began in southern politics. (See Map 28.2 and "Historical Question," page 1038.)

Two more measures completed Johnson's civil rights record. The Civil Rights Act of 1968 banned racial discrimination in housing and jury selection and authorized federal intervention when states failed to protect civil rights workers from violence. In addition, Johnson used his presidential authority in September 1965 to issue Executive Order 11246, banning discrimination by employers holding government contracts (affecting about one-third of the labor force) and also obligating them to take affirmative action to ensure equal opportunity. Extended to cover women in 1967, the controversial affirmative action program was called "reverse discrimination" by many people who incorrectly thought that affirmative action required rigid quotas and hiring unqualified candidates. In fact, it required employers to counter the effects of centuries of oppression by acting forcefully to align their labor force with the available pool of qualified candidates. Most large businesses came to see affirmative action as a good employment practice.

Black Nationalism

By 1966, civil rights activism had undergone dramatic changes. Black protest extended from the South to the entire nation, demanded not just legal equality but also economic justice, and no longer held nonviolence as its basic principle. None of these developments was entirely new. For example, some African Americans had armed themselves in self-defense since Reconstruction, and even in the 1950s and early 1960s many activists doubted that demonstrators' passive suffering in the face of violence would change the hearts of racists. Still, the black freedom struggle began to show a different face, one more threatening to the white majority.

In part the new emphases resulted from earlier successes, as legal oppression receded only to reveal other injustices more subtle but no less pervasive. Integration and legal equality did little to improve the material conditions of blacks; and black rage at oppressive conditions erupted in waves of urban riots from 1964 to 1968. The Watts district of Los Angeles in August 1965, Newark and Detroit in July 1967, and the nation's capital in April 1968 saw the most destruction, but

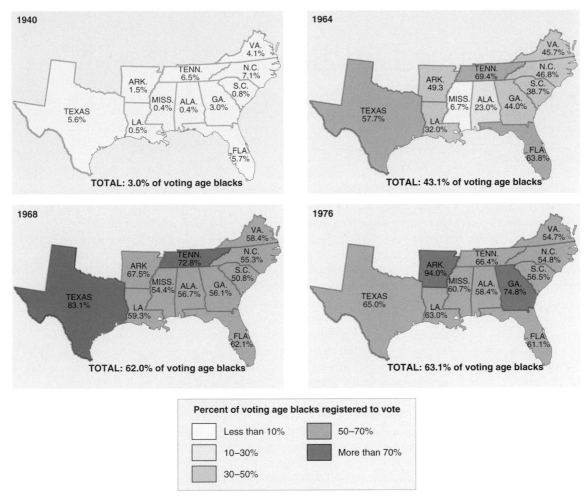

1940

VA. 4.1%
TENN. 6.5%
N.C. 7.1%
ARK. 1.5%
S.C. 0.8%
MISS. 0.4%
ALA. 0.4%
GA. 3.0%
TEXAS 5.6%
LA. 0.5%
FLA. 5.7%

TOTAL: 3.0% of voting age blacks

1964

VA. 45.7%
TENN. 69.4%
N.C. 46.8%
ARK. 49.3
S.C. 38.7%
MISS. 6.7%
ALA. 23.0%
GA. 44.0%
TEXAS 57.7%
LA. 32.0%
FLA. 63.8%

TOTAL: 43.1% of voting age blacks

1968

VA. 58.4%
TENN. 72.8%
N.C. 55.3%
ARK 67.5%
S.C. 50.8%
MISS. 54.4%
ALA. 56.7%
GA. 56.1%
TEXAS 83.1%
LA. 59.3%
FLA. 62.1%

TOTAL: 62.0% of voting age blacks

1976

VA. 54.7%
TENN. 66.4%
N.C. 54.8%
ARK. 94.0%
S.C. 56.5%
MISS. 60.7%
ALA. 58.4%
GA. 74.8%
TEXAS 65.0%
LA. 63.0%
FLA. 61.1%

TOTAL: 63.1% of voting age blacks

Percent of voting age blacks registered to vote

- [ ] Less than 10%
- [ ] 10–30%
- [ ] 30–50%
- [ ] 50–70%
- [ ] More than 70%

MAP 28.2 The Rise of the African American Vote, 1940–1976
Voting rates of southern blacks increased gradually in the 1940s and 1950s but shot up dramatically in the deep South after the Voting Rights Act of 1965 provided for federal agents to enforce African Americans' right to vote.

READING THE MAP: When did the biggest change in African American voter registration occur in the South? Which states had the highest and which had the lowest voter registration rates in 1968?
CONNECTIONS: What role did African American voters play in the 1960 election? What were the targets of three major voting drives in the 1960s?

FOR MORE HELP ANALYZING THIS MAP, see the map activity for this chapter in the Online Study Guide at bedfordstmartins.com/roark.

violence visited hundreds of cities, usually after an incident between white police and local blacks. Rioting in Detroit brought 43 deaths (30 at the hands of law enforcement personnel and most of them black), 7,000 arrests, 1,300 destroyed buildings, and 2,700 looted shops. "Our nation is moving toward two societies, one black, one white—separate and unequal," warned the Kerner Commission, appointed by Johnson to investigate the turmoil, but little was done about the basic conditions from which riots sprang.

In the North, a powerful new challenge to the ethos of nonviolence arose. Malcolm Little grew up in poverty and went to prison at the age of twenty-one for attempted burglary. There he educated himself, joined the Nation of Islam, whose adherents called themselves Black Muslims, and changed his name to Malcolm X, to symbolize the African identity stripped from his ancestors. Released from jail in 1952, he went to work for the Nation of Islam, which drew on the long tradition of **black nationalism** and its emphasis on racial

What Difference Did Black Voting Rights Make?

Born to poor black sharecroppers in the Mississippi Delta, Unita Blackwell hearkened in church one Sunday in 1964 when a SNCC worker talked about voter registration. The very next day she went to the courthouse where, as had happened to Fannie Lou Hamer and hundreds of other African Americans, officials refused her application. Undeterred, she succeeded on the third try, threw herself into activism as a SNCC organizer, and saw her share of jail cells. In fact, she and her husband planned their protest activities so that only one would risk arrest and the other would remain free to care for their child. A founder of the Mississippi Freedom Democratic Party, established to challenge the all-white state organization, Blackwell saw the challenge fall to compromise at the 1964 Democratic National Convention. But four years later, she participated in the national convention with Mississippi's reconfigured biracial delegation. Subsequently, she served as vice chair of the state Democratic Party and on the Democratic National Committee. When her small town of Mayersville incorporated in 1976, Blackwell won election as its first mayor and the first black female mayor in Mississippi.

Blackwell's career is but one measure of the transformations generated by African Americans' struggle for the most basic right of citizenship. Their determination to register to vote and the resulting resistance and violence of southern whites created a crisis that the federal government could not ignore. Its response—the Voting Rights Act of 1965 and subsequent extensions—suspended the literacy tests that had been used to disqualify blacks but not whites, and it brought electoral operations in most southern states under federal supervision. The law required the Justice Department to approve in advance any changes in state procedures that might disadvantage black voters, and it empowered the attorney general to send federal agents to observe registration and election processes and even to register voters in areas of continued white resistance.

"Legislation is not self-implementing," warned NAACP leader Roy Wilkins. "There is work to be done." As was the case with its passage, implementation of the Voting Rights Act depended on the efforts of African Americans themselves. More than two hundred voter registration drives between 1966 and 1968 paid off in dramatic increases in the numbers of blacks registered. Throughout the South, the proportion of African Americans on voter rolls jumped from 43 percent in 1964 to 62 percent in 1968. In Mississippi, the total leaped from just 6.7 percent in 1964 to 68 percent in 1968. African Americans also gained political offices in unprecedented numbers. Fewer than two dozen blacks held elective office in the South in 1964. In 1970, they claimed almost 500 elected government posts, and two years later the number reached nearly 1,200. Just seven years after whites bludgeoned civil rights activists during the Selma voting drive, black candidates won half of the ten seats on Selma's city council. With the victories of Barbara Jordan from Houston, Texas, and Andrew Young from Atlanta, Georgia, in 1972, the former Confederacy sent its first African Americans to the House of Representatives since the late nineteenth century.

Black electoral success was not limited to the South. Across the nation, African Americans held 1,500 elected positions in 1970, and by 1990 that number exceeded 7,000. The greatest progress came at the local level. The number of black city council members vaulted from 552 in 1970 to nearly 3,000 in 1989, and the number of black mayors grew sixfold, to more than 300, in the 1990s. The total of black representatives in Congress inched up from 10 in 1970 to 25 in 1990 and to 37 in the 1996 elections. Electoral success translated into tangible benefits. When black officials took office, their constituents saw improvements in public facilities,

pride, black autonomy and enterprise, and separation from the dominant white culture and institutions. Malcolm X attracted a large following, especially in urban ghettos, calling for black pride and autonomy, separation from the "corrupt [white] society," and self-defense against white violence. In 1964, he left the Nation, began to cultivate a wider constituency, and expressed an openness to working with whites. At a Harlem rally in February 1965, three Black Muslims shot and killed him.

The ideas espoused by Malcolm X resonated with younger activists. At a June 1966 rally in Greenwood, Mississippi, SNCC chairman Stokely police protection, roads, trash collection, and other basic services. Referring to Unita Blackwell's accomplishments as mayor, a Mayersville resident noted, "She brought in the water tower. Mostly it was pumps then. . . . Sewage, too. There wasn't nothing but those little old outdoor houses." Another constituent pointed to "old folks' houses. And paved streets. I grew up here when they wasn't paved." Black local officials also awarded more government jobs to African Americans and contracts to minority businesses. Elected mayor of Atlanta in 1973, Maynard Jackson appointed a black police chief and increased blacks' share of city jobs from 42 to 51 percent.

Most black officials had far less power than Jackson, but even when they were outnumbered by whites, they could at least introduce issues of concern to blacks that whites had ignored, and they gained access to information about behind-the-scenes government. An African American serving on a city council in Florida pointed out that "no matter what happened, [my white colleagues] knew I was listening to everything that went on." Activist Fannie Lou Hamer noted the psychological benefits of electoral progress. When blacks had no political voice, she recalled, "some white folks would drive past your house in a pickup truck with guns hanging up on the back and give you hate stares. . . . Those same people now call me Mrs. Hamer."

Yet increased political power did not guarantee African

Registering to Vote

Two civil rights volunteers during the 1964 Mississippi Freedom Summer campaign help a couple fill out voter registration forms. The form included a question asking the applicant to interpret a portion of the state's constitution, one of the ways white officials kept African Americans from voting in southern states before passage of the Voting Rights Act in 1965.

Charles Moore/Black Star/Stockphoto.com.

Americans economic equality or even material security. Their minority status in the population and their residential dispersion, combined with many whites' disinclination to vote for blacks, meant that even by 1990 African Americans occupied fewer than 2 percent of all elected positions in the nation. As African Americans looked to increase their political force and shape policy to meet their needs, they sought to revive grassroots activism and form coalitions with other racial and ethnic groups. In addition, they considered a number of electoral strategies to solidify black and minority strength in a majoritarian system: reducing the number of at-large elections, which dilute minorities' power, and increasing the number of single-member district systems; monitoring electoral redistricting to ensure as many black-majority districts as possible; and supporting proportionate or cumulative voting.

Despite the limited reach of black enfranchisement, most experts nonetheless view the voting rights revolution as the most successful of all civil rights initiatives. As Unita Blackwell put it, "We didn't have nothing, and we changed the whole world with nothing. We changed a whole outlook."

Carmichael gave those principles a new name when he shouted, "We want black power." "Black power" quickly became the rallying cry in SNCC and CORE, and the black power movement riveted national attention in the late 1960s. A young autoworker in Detroit enthused, "I dig what Stokely Carmichael said . . . whites appear to be friendly by passing a few laws, but my basic situation gets worse and worse."

Carmichael called integration "a subterfuge for the maintenance of white supremacy" and rejected assimilation because it implied the superiority of white institutions and values. African Americans were encouraged to develop

Malcolm X in Egypt
Malcolm X stands in front of the pyramids in Egypt during a trip to Africa and the Middle East in 1964. Partly as a result of meeting Muslims of all colors as well as whites who were committed to ending racism, he no longer equated whites with the devil. "The white man is not inherently evil," he concluded, "but America's racist society influences him to act evilly."
John Launois/Black Star/Stockphoto.com.

Afro Rake
In a movement that paralleled the white counterculture in the 1960s and 1970s, young African Americans began to reject middle-class blacks' tendency to fashion their appearance after that of whites. They adopted African styles of dress and let their hair grow into a natural Afro style. In her poem "Homage to My Hair," Lucille Clifton celebrated the expression of authentic black identity: "when I feel her jump up and dance i hear the music! my God i'm talking about my nappy hair!" African Americans used combs like this Afro rake or pik, which makes further political statements with its clenched fist and peace symbol.
Salamandu, courtesy National Afro-American Museum and Cultural Center; Courtesy Antonio's Manufacturing Inc., Cresson, PA.

independent businesses, control their own schools and communities, and form all-black political organizations. The phrase "Black is beautiful" emphasized pride in African American culture and connections to blacks around the world. Referring to revolutionary movements in Africa and elsewhere, Carmichael declared, "We see that our freedom, our liberation, depends on these people and vice versa, their liberation depends on us, so we must wage the same struggle."

According to black power advocates, nonviolence brought only more beatings and killings. Malcolm X had once said, "If someone puts a hand on you, send him to the cemetery." Carmichael agreed: "Black people should and must fight back." After police killed an unarmed black teenager in San Francisco in 1966, Huey Newton and Bobby Seale organized the Black Panther Party for Self-Defense in 1966 and armed its members for self-defense against police brutality. The press paid an inordinate amount of attention to black radicals, and the black power movement encountered a severe white backlash. Although the urban riots of the mid-1960s erupted spontaneously, triggered by specific incidents usually involving abusive treatment of blacks by police, horrified whites blamed the riots on black power militants. By 1966, a full 85 percent of the white population thought that African Americans were pressing for too much too quickly, up from 34 percent two years earlier. A woman from Orange County, California, asserted her belief that "integration depends considerably on the Negro himself. If he will straighten up and live right he'll naturally be accepted." White autoworkers in St. Louis displayed anxiety about African American competition for their jobs when they set up a can of shoe polish by a sign stating, "Paint your face black and you can get anything."

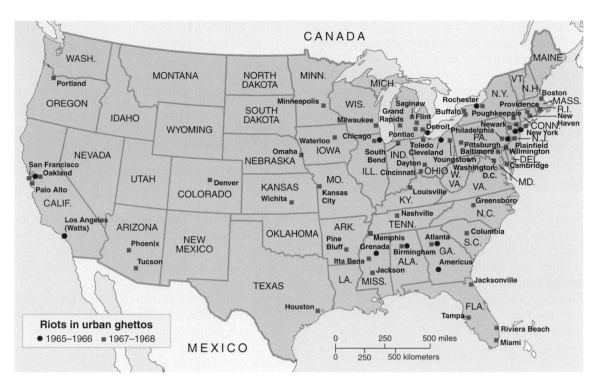

MAP 28.3   Urban Riots, 1965–1968

As black residents of the Watts district of Los Angeles watched a white police officer strike a twenty-one-year-old African American, whom he had just pulled over for driving drunk, one of the onlookers shouted, "We've got no rights at all—it's just like Selma." The altercation escalated into a full-scale five-day riot, during which young blacks set fires, looted, and attacked police and firefighters. When thousands of national guardsmen and police finally quelled the riot, 34 people were dead, 900 blacks had been injured and 4,000 arrested, hundreds of families had lost their homes, and scores of businesses had been wiped out. Although usually not on so large a scale, similar violence erupted in dozens of cities across the nation during the next three summers, as this map indicates. The urban violence provoked an intense backlash among whites against black aspirations, yet rioting and looting seemed to many young blacks the only means available to protest the poverty, lack of opportunity, and official insensitivity that they experienced daily in the ghettos. As one government worker commented when parts of Washington, D.C., went up in flames after Martin Luther King's death in 1968, "The black people in this city were really happy for three days. They have been kicked so long, and this is the one high spot in their life."

READING THE MAP: In what regions and cities of the United States were the 1960s riots concentrated? What years saw the greatest unrest?

CONNECTIONS: What were some of the causes of racial unrest in America's cities during this period? Whom did whites generally hold responsible for the riots and why?

FOR MORE HELP ANALYZING THIS IMAGE, see the map activity for this chapter in the Online Study Guide at bedfordstmartins.com/roark.

Martin Luther King Jr. agreed with black power advocates on the need for "a radical reconstruction of society." He himself expanded the scope of the struggle, mounting in 1965 a drive for better jobs, schools, and housing in Chicago and planning a Poor People's March to Washington in 1968 to seek greater antipoverty efforts. Yet he clung to nonviolence and integration as the means to this end. In 1968, the thirty-nine-year-old leader went to Memphis to support striking municipal garbage workers. There, on April 4, King was shot and killed by an escaped white convict.

Although they made the headlines, black power organizations failed to capture the massive support that African Americans gave King and other earlier leaders. Black militants were harassed by the FBI and jailed; some encounters with law officers left both black militants and police dead. Black nationalism's emphasis on racial pride and culture and its critique of American institutions, however, resonated broadly and helped to shape the protest of other groups.

A Multitude of Movements

The civil rights movement's undeniable moral claims helped to make protest respectable, while its impact on public opinion and government policy encouraged other groups with grievances. Native Americans, Latinos, college students, women, and others drew on the black freedom struggle for inspiration and models of activism. These groups engaged in direct-action protests, expressed their own cultural nationalism, and challenged dominant institutions and values.

Native American Protest

Protest was not new to the group of Americans with the oldest grievances, but Native American activism took on fresh militancy and goals in the 1960s. Contrary to the intention of Indian policy established in the 1940s and 1950s to assimilate Native Americans, the termination policy stirred Indian resistance, and the relocation programs stimulated a sense of Indian identity across tribal lines and a desire to preserve traditional culture among those who moved to cities. In 1961, a new, more militant generation of Native Americans expressed growing discontent with the government and with the older Indian leadership by forming the National Indian Youth Council (NIYC). Johnson's War on Poverty encouraged Native Americans to expect funds for and control over projects to ameliorate desperate living conditions in the cities and on reservations. The cry "red power" reflected the influence of black radicalism on Native Americans who rejected the goal of assimilation and sought the freedom to control their own circumstances. As NIYC founding member Clyde Warrior put it, "For the sake of the spiritual and material well-being of our total community, we must be able to demonstrate competence to ourselves. . . . We must make decisions about our own destinies."

Native Americans demonstrated and occupied land and public buildings, claiming rights to natural resources and territory that they had owned collectively before European settlement. For example, beginning in 1963 Northwest Indians mounted "fish-ins" to enforce century-old treaty rights. Native American militancy captured world attention in 1969, when several dozen seized Alcatraz Island, an abandoned federal penitentiary in San Francisco Bay, claiming their right to this "surplus" land under the Fort Laramie Treaty of 1868. They held on to the island for nineteen months, using the occupation to publicize the injustices Indians had suffered, promote pan-Indian cooperation, celebrate traditional cultures, and inspire other activists. (See "American Places," page 1043.) One of the organizers of the occupation, Dr. LaNada Boyer, a Shosone-Bannock and the first Native American to attend the University of California, Berkeley, said of Alcatraz, "We were able to raise, not only the consciousness of other American people, but our own people as well, to reestablish our identity as Indian people, as a culture, as political entities."

In Minneapolis in 1968, two Chippewas, Dennis Banks and George Mitchell, founded the American Indian Movement (AIM) to attack problems in cities, where about 300,000 Indians lived. AIM sought to protect Indians from police harassment, secure antipoverty funds, and establish "survival schools" to teach Indian history and values. The new movement's appeal quickly spread beyond urban areas and seized many Indians, especially young people, with a sense of purpose. AIM members did not have "that hangdog reservation look I was used to," Lakota activist and author Mary Crow Dog wrote, and their visit to her South Dakota reservation "loosened a sort of earthquake inside me." Recalling that her early life had been "just one endless vicious cycle of drinking and fighting, drinking and fighting," Crow Dog was able to break out of that cycle with her commitment to AIM.

AIM leaders helped organize the "Trail of Broken Treaties" caravan to the nation's capitol in 1972, when some of the activists took over the Bureau of Indian Affairs. The occupiers expressed their outrage at the bureau's paternalism, policies, and bureaucratic interference in Indians' lives by destroying the offices when the government announced its intention to remove the protesters. A much longer siege occurred on the Lakota Sioux reservation in South Dakota, where conflicts between AIM militants and older

AMERICAN PLACES

Alcatraz Island, San Francisco, California

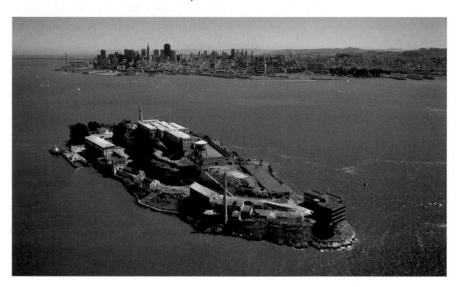

Alcatraz Island and San Francisco Bay
© Gerald French/Corbis.

In 1854, the U.S. army installed the first fortifications on the seventeen-acre Alcatraz Island in San Francisco Bay, and within a few years it also began to house military prisoners there. From time to time, other groups were incarcerated there, including Southern loyalists during the Civil War, conscientious objectors during World War I, and Native Americans. In 1895, seventeen Hopis were imprisoned when they refused government efforts to turn them into farmers (traditionally the work of Hopi women) and resisted the educating of Indian children in government boarding schools. After 1907, Alcatraz was used exclusively as a military prison. Recognizing how the turbulent waters surrounding the island made it nearly escape-proof, in 1934 the government converted it into a maximum security prison to house what it considered the most hard-ened criminals, including the Chicago gangster Al Capone.

After the government closed the prison in 1963, local Indian activists began to view the island as surplus federal property and subject to treaties promising such land to Native Americans. On November 20, 1969, seventy-eight Indians, mostly college students, braved harsh winds and waves in several boats to make a successful landing on the island. John Trudell, a Sioux, expressed the excitement of the occupiers: "When I got . . . on that island, here's all these Native people. I didn't know any of them, but yet I did. It was like going home." The group was led by Richard Oakes, a Mohawk and former ironworker, now a student at San Francisco State College in its brand-new Native American studies program. Members of many tribes, the occupiers called themselves "Indians of All Tribes" and issued a proclamation declaring that "we reclaim the land . . . in the name of all American Indians by right of discovery." Referring mockingly to the Dutch colonists who had paid Indians for Manhattan Island in 1626, the proclamation declared, "We will purchase said Alcatraz Island for twenty-four dollars in glass beads and red cloth."

Although severely challenged by internal dissension and the difficulty of obtaining supplies, protesters managed to hold the island for nineteen months, gaining enormous publicity for their cause. For a time the Nixon administration took a hands-off approach, hoping that the occupiers would give up their demands for title to the island and creation of a university and cultural center. Eventually the government removed a barge that had supplied fresh water to the island and shut down electric power. On June 10, 1971, government agents landed on Alcatraz and removed the fifteen Native Americans who were left. While the occupiers failed in their ultimate goals, they energized Native American protest. "Alcatraz encouraged young people to become themselves, as opposed to hiding their Indianness," said Blackfoot longshoreman Joseph Myers. Even a government memo acknowledged that Alcatraz was a "symbol of the lack of attention to [their] unmet needs."

Today visitors can experience the history of Alcatraz Island as military fort, penitentiary, and site of the Indian occupation in person or on the Web. Both sites are operated by the National Park Service. A stroll or scroll through provides a detailed history of the occupation, natural features of the island, dramatic photographs, and passionate expressions of the people who defied the government to reclaim their heritage and rights as American citizens.

FOR WEB LINKS RELATED TO THIS SITE AND OTHER AMERICAN PLACES, see "PlaceLinks" at bedfordstmartins.com/roark.

Occupation of the Bureau of Indian Affairs
Native American activists despised the Bureau of Indian Affairs (BIA), an agency of the Department of the Interior that supervised and provided services to recognized tribes. The bureau was a
symbol of all the injustices they endured. Although President Nixon nearly tripled the BIA's budget,
his administration spent little on off-reservation Indians. Representing these urban Indians, the
American Indian Movement organized the "Trail of Broken Treaties" caravan to Washington, D.C.,
and on November 2, hundreds of Indians occupied the BIA. Pressured by the Nixon administration
and fearful that riot police would attack them, the occupiers agreed to leave after six days, with
promises that the government would create a task force to study their grievances, that it would
not prosecute them, and that it would finance their travels home. Like the much longer seizure of
Alcatraz (see "American Places," page 1043), the demonstrators failed to win their demands but
gained attention for their cause. What is the significance of the flag in this photo?
© Bettmann/Corbis.

tribal leaders led AIM to take over—for seventy-
two days—the village of Wounded Knee, where
U.S. troops had massacred more than 100 Sioux
in 1890.

Although these dramatic occupations failed
to achieve their specific goals, the wave of Indian
protest produced the end of relocation and termination policies; greater tribal sovereignty and
control over community services; enhanced
health, education, and other services; and protection of Indian religious practices. A number of
laws and court decisions restored rights to
ancestral lands or compensated Indian tribes
for land seized in violation of treaties. Native
Americans recovered a measure of identity and
pride, greater respect for and protection of their
culture, and, in the words of President Johnson's

special message on the "Forgotten American" in
1968, recognition of "the right of the First
Americans to remain Indians while exercising
their rights as Americans."

Latino Struggles for Justice

The fastest-growing minority group in the 1960s
was Latinos, or Hispanic Americans, an extraordinarily varied population encompassing people
of Mexican, Puerto Rican, Caribbean, and other
Latin American origins. (The term *Latino* stresses
their common bonds as a minority group in the
United States; the less political term *Hispanic* also
includes those with origins in Spain.) People of
Puerto Rican and Caribbean descent tended to
live in East Coast cities, but more than half of the

Latino population of the United States—some six million Mexican Americans—lived in California, Texas, Arizona, New Mexico, and Colorado. In addition, thousands illegally crossed the two-thousand-mile border between Mexico and the United States in search of economic opportunity.

Mexican Americans had always organized to push for political power and economic rights. As we saw in chapter 26, middle-class Mexican Americans had formed the League of United Latin-American Citizens (LULAC) in 1929, which provided aid to newer immigrants and, like the NAACP, fought segregation and discrimination through litigation. In the 1960s, however, young Mexican Americans, like African Americans and Native Americans, increasingly rejected traditional politics in favor of direct action. One symbol of this generational challenge was young activists' adoption of the term *Chicano* (from *mejicano*, the Spanish word for "Mexican").

Chicano protest drew national attention to California, where Cesar Chavez and Dolores Huerta organized a movement to improve the wretched conditions of migrant agricultural workers. As a child moving from farm to farm with his family, often crowded into soggy tents or tarpaper cabins, exploited by labor contractors, Chavez had to change schools frequently and stopped after the eighth grade. He encountered indifference and discrimination in the educational system, where speaking Spanish was forbidden. One teacher, he recalled, "hung a sign on me that said, 'I am a clown, I speak Spanish.'" After serving in the navy during World War II and starting a family, Chavez began to organize voter registration drives among Mexican Americans and to study labor history and the ideas of Catholic reformers and Mahatma Gandhi.

In contrast to Chavez, Dolores Huerta grew up in an integrated urban neighborhood and avoided the farmworkers' grinding poverty and exploitation, but she witnessed subtle forms of discrimination. Once, for example, a high school teacher challenged her authorship of an essay because it was so well written. After completing community college and starting a family, at the age of twenty-five she met Chavez; determined that a union was the key to improving the lives of farmworkers, they founded the United Farm Workers (UFW) in 1962. Although Chavez headed the union until his death in 1993, Huerta was indispensable to its vitality. According to Luis Valdez, who headed the Farm Workers Theater, "Dolores was a thirty-five-year-old firebrand in 1965, and she was commanding crusty

Cesar Chavez in the Vineyards
Cesar Chavez, whose grandfather had migrated to the United States in the nineteenth century, experienced the plight of farmworkers when his family lost its business and farm in Arizona during the depression. Here he meets with grape pickers in California during the national grape boycott of 1965. The boycott's proclamation listed these aims: "just wages, humane working conditions, protection from the misuse of pesticides, and the fundamental right of collective bargaining."
Arthur Schatz / TimePix / Getty.

macho *campesinos* twenty years her senior." UFW marches and strikes gained widespread support, and a national boycott of California grapes helped the union win a wage increase for the workers in 1970. Although the UFW struggled and lost membership, it helped politicize Mexican Americans and improved the lives of thousands of farmworkers. In 1999, California made Chavez's birthday a state holiday.

Chicanos mobilized elsewhere to end discrimination in employment and education, gain political power, and combat police brutality. In southwestern cities in 1968, high school students launched a wave of strikes, called "Blow Outs," to protest racism in the public schools. "Teachers, Sí, Bigots, No!" their signs declared. In Denver, Colorado, Rodolfo "Corky"

> Chicanos mobilized to end discrimination in employment and education, gain political power, and combat police brutality.

Gonzales set up "freedom schools," where Chicano children studied Spanish and Mexican American history and chanted, "Chicano power." The nationalist strains of Chicano protest were evident in La Raza Unida (the United Race), a political party founded by José Angel Gutierrez in Texas and based on cultural pride and brotherhood. With blacks and Native Americans, Chicanos continued to be overrepresented among the poor but gradually won more political offices, more effective enforcement of antidiscrimination legislation, and greater respect for their culture.

Student Rebellion, the New Left, and the Counterculture

Although materially and legally more secure than their African American, Indian, and Latino counterparts, white youth joined them in expressing dissent, supporting the black freedom struggle, and launching student protests, the antiwar movement, and the new **feminist** movement. Challenging establishment institutions and traditional values, these movements, along with those of racial and ethnic minorities, formed part of a reinvigorated political left and helped change higher education, the family, the national government, and other key institutions.

> Although materially and legally more secure than their African American, Indian, and Latino counterparts, white youth joined them in expressing dissent, supporting the black freedom struggle, and launching student protests, the antiwar movement, and the new feminist movement.

The central organization of white student protest was Students for a Democratic Society (SDS), formed in 1960 by a remnant of an older **socialist**-oriented student organization. In 1962, some sixty members met in Port Huron, Michigan, to draft a statement of purpose. "We are people of this generation, bred in at least modest comfort, housed now in universities, looking uncomfortably at the world we inherit," the statement began. The idealistic students criticized the complacency of their elders, the remoteness of decision makers from the people, and the powerlessness and alienation generated in a society run by impersonal bureaucratic institutions. SDS aimed to mobilize a "New Left," around the goals of civil rights, peace, and universal economic security. It remained small until 1965, but other forms of student activism soon followed.

A free speech movement, the first large-scale white student protest, arose at the University of California, Berkeley, in 1964, when university officials banned student organizations from setting up tables to recruit support for various causes. Led by whites back from civil rights work in the South, the students claimed the right to freedom of expression and political action. Jack Weinberg, one of the leaders, recalled the students' reaction to the university ban: "They may prohibit it, but we're not going to stop doing it." They occupied the administration building, and more than seven hundred were arrested before the California Board of Regents overturned the new restrictions.

Hundreds of student rebellions followed on campuses across the country. Opposition to the Vietnam War activated the largest number of students, who held rallies and took over buildings to protest universities' links to the war. But they also demanded curricular reforms, more financial aid for minority and poor students, independence from paternalistic rules, and a larger voice in campus decision making. (See "Documenting the American Promise," page 1048.) Protesting a variety of restrictions on student behavior, radicals at the University of Florida equated their campus to a ghetto. "Like all ghettos, it has its managers (the administration), its Uncle Toms (the intimidated, status-berserk faculty), its raw natural resources processed for outside exploitation and consumptions (the students)," their underground paper declared.

Growing up alongside and often overlapping the New Left and student movements was the counterculture, a rebellion that drew on the ideas of the Beats of the 1950s. Cultural radicals, or "hippies," as they were called, rejected many mainstream values, such as the work ethic, materialism, rationality, order, and sexual control. Seeking personal rather than political change, they advocated "Do your own thing" and drew attention with their long hair and wildly colorful clothing. The Haight-Ashbury district of San Francisco harbored the most famous hippie community, but thousands of radicals established communes in cities or on farms, where they renounced private property and shared everything, often including sex partners. They sought to discard inhibitions and elevate their senses with illegal drugs such as marijuana and LSD. As counterculture guru Timothy Leary advised, "Turn on, tune in, drop out."

Rock and folk music defined both the counterculture and the political left. English groups

Woodstock
The Woodstock Music Festival, held on a farm near Bethel, New York, in August 1969, featured the greatest rock and folk musicians of the era and epitomized the values and hopes of the counterculture. Despite terrible conditions created by bad weather and the failure of festival organizers to plan for so many people, the youthful crowd of 400,000 created a loving, peaceful community for three days filled with music, sex, and drugs. What symbols of the counterculture can you pick out in this photo?
John Dominis/Image Works.

such as the Beatles and the Rolling Stones and homegrown products such as Bob Dylan, Janis Joplin, the Jefferson Airplane, and Jerry Garcia's Grateful Dead took American youth by storm. Music during the 1960s often carried insurgent political and social messages. Despairing of the violence around the world and the threat of nuclear annihilation, "Eve of Destruction," a top hit of 1965, reminded young men, "You're old enough to kill but not for votin'." Other popular songs derided authority, touted drug use and sexual freedom, and called for peace, love, and revolution.

The hippies faded away in the 1970s, but many elements of the counterculture—from rock music to jeans and long hair—filtered into the mainstream. Sex outside marriage and tolerant attitudes about sexual morality spawned what came to be called a "sexual revolution," with help

from the birth-control pill newly available in the 1960s. Self-fulfillment became a dominant concern of many Americans, and questioning of authority became much more widespread.

A New Movement to Save the Environment

Although it differed from the identity-based politics of racial, ethnic, and youth-oriented groups, environmentalism likewise contributed to a redefinition of liberalism in the 1960s and beyond. One aspect of the new environmental movement resembled the conservation movement born in the Progressive era and championed by Theodore Roosevelt to preserve portions of the natural world for recreational and aesthetic purposes (see chapter 21). Such efforts seemed all the more necessary with the post–World War II explosion

Student Protest

SOURCE: Edward Schwartz, "He Who Must Obey the Rule Should Make It," in Immanuel Wallerstein and Paul Starr, eds., *The University Crisis Reader*, vol. 1, *The Liberal University under Attack* (New York: Random House, 1971), 482–84. Copyright © 1971 by Random House, Inc. Reprinted with permission.

The waves of student protest that rolled across college campuses in the 1960s were all the more surprising because observers had found the "silent generation" of the 1950s so complacent and conformist. Although the majority of college students did not participate in the rebellions, a sizable number at all kinds of colleges and universities challenged traditional authorities, criticized established institutions, and demanded a voice for themselves in the decisions that affected their lives.

DOCUMENT 1
Edward Schwartz on Student Power, October 1967

This statement was written by student activist Edward Schwartz to represent the views of the National Student Association, the largest college-student organization in the 1960s. It was ironic that this association, which contributed to the student upheaval in the 1960s, had been founded a decade earlier, with secret funding from the CIA, as a liberal group to counter communism.

The educational premise behind demands for student power reflects the notion that people learn through living, through the process of integrating their thoughts with their actions, through testing their values against those of a community, through a capacity to act. College presidents who invoke legal authority to prove educational theory assume that growth is the ability to accept what the past has created. Student power is a medium through which people integrate their own experience with a slice of the past which seems appropriate, with their efforts to intensify the relationships between the community within the university.

Let this principle apply—he who must obey the rule should make it.

Students should make the rules governing dormitory hours, boy-girl visitation, student unions, student fees, clubs, newspapers, and the like. Faculty and administrators should advise—attempt to persuade, even. Yet the student should bear the burden of choice.

Students and faculty should co-decide curricular policy.

Students, faculty, and administration should co-decide admissions policy, overall college policy affecting the community, even areas like university investment. . . . Student power should not be argued on legal grounds. It is not a legal principle. It is an educational principle.

Student power is threatening to those who wield power now, but this is understandable. A student should threaten his administrators outside of class, just as bright students threaten professors inside of class. Student power ultimately challenges everyone in the university—the students who must decide; the faculty and administrators who must rethink their own view of community relations in order to persuade.

People who say that student power means anarchy imply really that students are rabble who have no ability to form community and to adhere to decisions made by community. Student power is not the negation of rules—it is the creation of a new process for the enactment of rules. Student power is not the elimination of authority, it is the development of a democratic standard of authority.

DOCUMENT 2
Demands of Howard University Students, February 1968

African American students launched campus protests even at universities where most faculty and administrators were black, like Howard University in Washington, D.C. Following are demands of black students at Howard, printed in the campus newspaper, The Spear and Shield.

1. We demand the immediate resignation of the following Howard administrators on the grounds of their incompetence and obvious unwillingness to work toward a black Howard University. [There followed names of the president, vice president, and liberal arts dean.]
2. We demand the institution of the following curriculum changes by next semester:

   a. We demand that Howard should be the center of Afro-American thought. We demand that the economics, government, literature, and social science departments begin to place more emphasis on how these disciplines may be used to effect the liberation of black people in this country.
   b. We demand the institution of non-prerequisite courses in Negro History.
   c. We demand the immediate abolishment of Freshman Assembly. Black students are not culturally deprived.

3. We demand the immediate reinstatement of all Howard instructors who have been unjustifiably dismissed for their political activism.

4. We demand a Black Awareness Research Institute at Howard University.

5. Students are trained to be leaders only by learning to accept responsibility. We demand therefore . . . student control in matters that concern only students.

    a. The student judiciary and codification of rules presently submitted to the Faculty Senate Steering Committee should be immediately instituted.

    b. That students must be authorized to control the budgeting and expenditure of the student activity fee.

6. Howard must be made relevant to the black community. The University campus must be made more available to all black people and programs must be instituted to aid the black community in the struggle against oppression.

7. We demand that Howard personnel begin to treat students like black people should treat black people, with respect and courtesy.

SOURCE: Howard University: February 1968, "The Spear and Shield," in Immanuel Wallerstein and Paul Starr, eds., *The University Crisis Reader*, vol. 2, *Confrontation and Counterattack* (New York: Random House, 1971), 485–86. Copyright © 1971 by Random House, Inc. Reprinted with permission.

DOCUMENT 3
SDS Explanation of
the Columbia Strike,
September 1968

One of the longest and most violent student protests occurred in New York City at Columbia University in April and May 1968, when white and black students occupied five buildings for a week; a subsequent student strike closed the university for the rest of the academic year. One of the key issues arose from the university's practice of expanding by buying up land in neighboring Harlem and evicting black tenants. The members of the Columbia SDS chapter, one of various factions among the protesters, rationalized their actions in the following statement.

When we seized five buildings at Columbia University, we engaged the force of wealth, privilege, property—and the force of state violence that always accompanies them—with little more than our own ideals, our fears, and a vague sense of outrage at the injustices of our society. Martin Luther King had just been shot, his name demeaned by Columbia officials who refused to grant a decent wage to Puerto Rican workers, and who had recently grabbed part of Harlem for a student gym. . . .

For years Columbia Trustees had evicted tenants from their homes, taken land through city deals, and fired workers for trying to form a union. For years they had trained officers for Vietnam who, as ROTC literature indicates, killed Vietnamese peasants in their own country. In secret work for the IDA [Institute for Defense Analysis] and the CIA, in chemical-biological war research for the Department of War, the Trustees implicated their own University in genocide. They had consistently . . . lied to their own constituents and published CIA books under the guise of independent scholarship. . . . We lived in an institution that channeled us, marked us, ranked us, failed us, used us, and treated masses of humanity with class contempt. . . .

The collegiate wing of privilege could not shield us from the decay and violence in our society. The University was not, as we first believed, a sanctuary from the world; it was, in fact, a proponent of the most violent system the centuries have created—the system of capital. . . .

Columbia, standing at the top of a hill, looked down on Harlem. . . . People who survived in Harlem had been evicted by the Trustees from Morningside or still paid rent to Columbia. . . . We walked to our classrooms across land that had been privatized; we studied in buildings that had once been homes in a city that is underhoused; and we listened to the apologies for Cold War and capital in our classes.

Columbia professors often claim that the University is a neutral institution. . . . Many professors pursue all sides of a question as an end in itself. They find a certain refuge in the difficulty of defining good and evil. The result is a clogging of their moral sense, their capacity for collective justice. . . . What liberals call neutrality is really one of the ways by which the faculty protects its special status in society.

A University could not, even if it wanted, choose to be really value-free. It can choose good values; it can choose bad values; or it can remain ignorant of the values on which it acts. . . . A social institution should at least articulate its own perspective, so that its own values may be consciously applied or modified. It is a typical fallacy of American teaching, that to remain silent on crucial issues is to be objective with your own constituents. Actually a "neutral" institution is far more manipulative than a University committed to avowed goals and tasks.

(continued)

DOCUMENT 4
Chicago Women's Liberation on Sexism in Higher Education, February 1969

In January 1969, the University of Chicago refused to reappoint Dr. Marlene Dixon, an assistant professor of sociology who had incorporated the study of women into her teaching. While officials insisted that Dixon did not meet the university's academic standards, her supporters believed that she was fired for her radical beliefs and because she was female. SDS and other factions of radical students protested for two weeks but failed to save Dixon's job. Chicago Women's Liberation, one of the radical groups that grew out of women's activism in the New Left, issued this statement addressing broader issues.

What does women's freedom mean? . . . It means the freedom to be one's own person in an integrated life of work, love, play, motherhood: the freedoms, rights and privileges of first class citizenship, of equality in relationships of love and work: the right to choose to make decisions or not to: the right to full self-realization and to full participation in the life of the world. . . . To achieve these rights we must struggle as all other oppressed groups must struggle: one only has the rights one fights for. . . .

At the U of C we see the first large action, the first important struggle of women's liberation. This university—all universities—discriminate against women, impede their full intellectual development, deny them places on the faculty, exploit talented women and mistreat women students.

DOCUMENT 5
Counterthrust on Student Power, Spring 1967

While the majority of students simply avoided involvement in campus rebellions, some students actively criticized the protesters. The largest conservative student organization was Young Americans for Freedom, which more than doubled in size during the 1960s. The following selection, from a leaflet entitled "Student Power Is a Farce," reflected the views of Counterthrust, a conservative group at Wayne State University in Michigan.

Our University is being treated to the insanity of Left-Wing students demanding the run of the University. . . . Wayne students are told by the Left that "student power" merely means more democracy on campus. This is an outright lie! Student power is a Left-Wing catchword symbolizing campus militancy and radicalism. In actuality, the Left-Wing, spearheaded by the SDS [Students for a Democratic Society] want to radically alter the university community. . . .

The Leftists charge a sinister plot by private enterprise to train students for jobs at taxpayers' expense. Evidently it never occurred to the SDS that private enterprise is also the biggest single taxpayer for schools. But, of course, that would require a little thought on the part of the SDS which they have already demonstrated they are incapable of. . . .

The byword of student power-union advocates is Radicalism. . . . Fraternities and student Governments will have no place in student power-unions since both are considered allies of the status quo and thus useless. . . . As responsible Wayne students, we cannot allow our University to be used by Leftists for their narrow purposes. We were invited to this campus by the Michigan Taxpayer to receive an education. Let us honor that invitation.

of economic growth. In the West especially, the expanding economy and mushrooming population necessitated greater supplies of water and power, and environmental groups mobilized to stop construction of dams that would disrupt national parks and wilderness areas.

The new environmentalists, however, dramatically broadened the agenda of the conservationists; now the focus turned to the ravaging effects of industrial development on human life and health. The polluted air and water and spread of deadly chemicals attending economic growth threatened wildlife, plants, and the delicate ecological balance that sustained human life. To the leaders of a new organization, Friends of the Earth, unlimited economic growth was "no longer healthy, but a

DOCUMENT 6
George F. Kennan's Speech on Student Protest, December 1967

*George F. Kennan, the foreign policy expert who had articulated the **containment** policy in 1947, reflected the views of many critics of student protest when he gave this speech at Swarthmore College in Pennsylvania.*

There is an ideal that has long been basic to the learning process, one that stands at the very center of our modern institutions of higher education. It is the ideal of the association of the process of learning with a certain remoteness from the contemporary scene—a certain detachment and seclusion, a certain voluntary withdrawal and renunciation of participation in contemporary life in the interests of the achievement of a better perspective on that life when the period of withdrawal is over. It is an ideal that does not predicate any total conflict between thought and action, but recognizes that there is a time for each. . . .

What strikes one first about the angry militancy [among current students] is the extraordinary degree of certainty by which it is inspired: certainty of one's own rectitude, certainty of the correctness of one's own answers, certainty of the accuracy and profundity of one's own analysis of the problems of contemporary society, certainty

as to the iniquity of those who disagree. . . . One is struck to see such massive certainties already present in the minds of people who not only have not studied very much but presumably are not studying a great deal, because it is hard to imagine that the activities to which this aroused portion of our student population gives itself are ones readily compatible with quiet and successful study. . . .

I am not saying that students should not be concerned, should not have views, should not question what goes on in the field of national policy. . . . Some of us, who are older, share many of their misgivings, many of their impulses. . . .

I have seen more harm done in this world by those who tried to storm the bastions of society in the name of utopian beliefs, who were determined to achieve the elimination of all evil . . . than by all the humble efforts of those who have tried to create a little order and civility and affection within their own intimate entourage, even at the cost of tolerating a great deal of evil in the public domain. Behind this modesty, after all, there has been the recognition of a vitally important truth—a truth that the Marxists, among others, have never brought themselves to recognize; namely that the decisive seat of evil in this world is not in social and political institutions, and not even, as a rule, in the ill will or iniquities of statesmen, but simply in the weak-

ness and imperfection of the human soul itself.

SOURCE: George F. Kennan, "Rebels without a Program," *The University Crisis Reader*, vol. 1, *The Liberal University under Attack* (New York: Random House, 1971), 12–23. Copyright © 1971 by Random House, Inc. Reprinted with permission.

QUESTIONS FOR ANALYSIS AND DEBATE

1. What different ideas about the nature and purposes of the university do these writers present? How do they differ in their view of students' capabilities and rights?

2. Do you agree or disagree with George Kennan's insistence that universities should maintain "a certain remoteness from the contemporary scene" in order to achieve "a better perspective" on current issues? Why or why not?

3. Consider the different backgrounds and circumstances of the authors of these writings. Are factors such as age, race, gender, and economic class important to the viewpoints expressed? Why or why not?

4. To what extent do your own campus policies and practices suggest that student protest made a difference? What changes that the protesters demanded do not appear at your college? Should they?

---

cancer." An oil spill from a drilling operation off the coast of Santa Barbara, California, blackened hundreds of square miles of ocean and thirty miles of beaches in January 1969 and provided a dramatic image of pollution. President Nixon's adviser on the environment considered it "comparable to tossing a match into a gasoline tank: it exploded into the environmental revolution."

Biologist Rachel Carson had already drawn national attention to environmental concerns in 1962 with her best seller *Silent Spring*, which described the harmful effects of toxic chemicals, particularly dioxin and the pesticide DDT. Older conservation organizations such as the Sierra Club and the Wilderness Society expanded their agendas, and a host of new organizations arose.

Millions of Americans expressed environmental concerns on the first observation of Earth Day in April 1970. In Wisconsin, students distributed fliers encouraging recycling, and a group of Detroit women picketed a steel plant that polluted a river with industrial waste. Girl Scouts cleaned garbage from the Potomac River, African Americans in St. Louis dramatized the effects of poisons in lead paint, students in Michigan smashed a Ford to protest auto emissions, and people all over the country planted trees. Harvard law student Denis Hayes, who organized a teach-in on Earth Day, reported that environmentalists were prepared to do "whatever it takes. This may be our last chance."

Responding to these concerns, the federal government staked out a broad role in environmental regulation in the 1960s and 1970s. Lyndon Johnson became the first president to send Congress a special message on the environment, obtaining measures to control air and water pollution and to preserve the American landscape. In 1970, President Richard Nixon's State of the Union message called "clean air, clean water, open spaces . . . the birthright of every American," and he created the Environmental Protection Agency (EPA) to enforce clean air and water policies and regulate pesticides. That same year, Congress passed the Occupational Safety and Health Act (OSHA), protecting workers against workplace accidents and disease. The Clean Air Act of 1970 set national standards for air quality and restricted factory and automobile emissions of carbon dioxide and other pollutants. Despite challenges from industry and lenient enforcement, and even in the face of population and economic growth, by 1990 air pollutants had decreased by one-third in major cities.

Environmentalism challenged the dominant values of consumption and growth that characterized the post–World War II era. But, especially by the late 1970s, when antigovernment sentiment rose and the economy slumped, it was not unusual for the imperative of economic growth to trump environmental concerns. Corporations seeking to expand, apply new technologies, or exploit natural resources resisted restrictions. "If you're hungry and out of work, eat an environmentalist," read a union bumper sticker reflecting fears that regulations threatened jobs. Many Americans who expressed support for protecting the environment at the same time valued economic expansion, personal acquisition, and convenience. Yet, despite these struggles and contradictions, the environmental movement achieved cleaner air and water, a reduction in toxic wastes, and some preservation of endangered species and wilderness. And Americans now recognized that human ingenuity had developed the power to destroy life on earth.

The New Wave of Feminism

On August 26, 1970, fifty years after women won the right to vote, tens of thousands of women across the country took to the streets. Participants included radical women in jeans and conservatively dressed suburbanites, peace activists and politicians, and a sprinkling of women of color. They carried signs reading "Sisterhood Is Powerful" and "Don't Cook Dinner—Starve a Rat Today." Some of the banners opposed the war in Vietnam, and others demanded racial justice, but women's own liberation stood at the forefront.

Beginning in the 1960s, the women's movement reached high tide in the 1970s and persisted in various forms into the twenty-first century. By that time women had experienced tremendous transformations in their legal status, public opportunities, and personal and sexual relationships; and popular expectations about appropriate gender roles had shifted dramatically.

A Movement Emerges

After women won the right to vote in 1920, feminism receded from national attention, but small groups of women continued to work for women's rights and opportunities in such areas as employment, jury service, and electoral politics. Beginning in the 1940s, large demographic changes laid the preconditions for a resurgence of feminism. Women did not abandon the workplace after World War II, as more and more women, especially wives and mothers, took jobs. Consequently, the importance of their paid work to the economy and to their families belied the idea of women as dependent, domestic beings and awakened their recognition of the inferior conditions of their employment. Moreover, the democratization of higher education brought more and more women to college campuses,

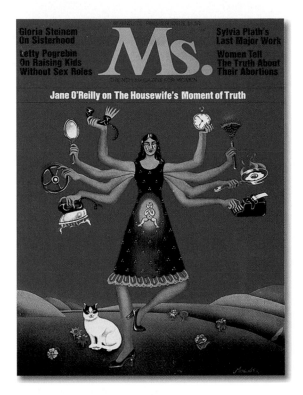

Gloria Steinem On Sisterhood

Letty Pogrebin On Raising Kids Without Sex Roles

Sylvia Plath's Last Major Work

Women Tell The Truth About Their Abortions

Jane O'Reilly on The Housewife's Moment of Truth

First Issue of *Ms.* Magazine

In 1972, Gloria Steinem and other journalists and writers published the premier issue of the first mass-circulation magazine for and controlled by women. *Ms.: The New Magazine for Women* ignored the recipes and fashion tips of typical women's magazines. It featured literature by women writers and articles on a broad range of feminist issues. A scholar later wrote that it was "mind-blowing. Here was, written down, what [women] had not yet admitted they felt, had always feared to say out loud, and could not believe was now before their eyes, in public, for all to read."

What concerns are suggested by this cover of the first issue? What is the significance of the woman's multiple arms?

Courtesy, Lang Communications.

where their aspirations expanded beyond the confines of domesticity and of routine, subordinate work.

Policy initiatives in the early 1960s reflected both these larger transformations and the specific efforts of small bands of women's rights activists in the 1940s and 1950s, and sparked new activism. In 1961, Assistant Secretary of Labor Esther Peterson persuaded Kennedy to strengthen his support among women by appointing a President's Commission on the Status of Women (PCSW). Chaired by Eleanor Roosevelt, the commission reported its findings in October 1963, eight months after Betty Friedan

attacked sex discrimination in *The Feminine Mystique* (see chapter 27). Although not challenging women's traditional roles, the commission reported widespread discrimination against women and recommended remedies. Spawning counterparts in all the states, the PCSW created networks of motivated women eager for action who would launch a grassroots women's movement a few years later.

The PCSW highlighted a practice that women's organizations and labor unions had sought to eliminate for two decades: the age-old custom of paying women less than men for the same work. They achieved that goal when Kennedy signed the Equal Pay Act in June 1963, making wage disparities based solely on gender illegal. Within a few years, women began to win pay increases and back pay worth millions of dollars, although forty years later, women still had not closed the income gap.

Just as it inspired other protests, the black freedom struggle also gave an immense boost to the rise of a new women's movement, by creating a moral climate sensitive to injustice and providing precedents and strategies that feminists followed. For example, by piggybacking onto civil rights measures, feminists gained the ban against sex discrimination in Title VII of the Civil Rights Act of 1964 and the extension of affirmative action to women. Their expectations raised by these new policies, feminists grew impatient when the government failed to take them seriously and moved slowly to enforce them. The head of the Equal Employment Opportunity Commission (EEOC), enforcement agency for Title VII, called the provision "a fluke . . . conceived out of wedlock" and told reporters that men were entitled to have female secretaries. Outraged by such attitudes and deciding that they needed a "civil rights organization for women," in 1966 Betty Friedan and others founded the National Organization for Women (NOW) "to bring women into full participation in the mainstream of American society now, exercising all the privileges and responsibilities thereof in truly equal partnership with men."

Simultaneously, a more radical feminism grew among women in the black freedom struggle and the New Left. In 1964, two white women in SNCC, Mary King and Casey Hayden, recognized the contradiction between the ideal of equality and women's actual status in the movement, and in 1965 they began circulating their ideas to other New Left women. King and Hayden argued that, like blacks, women were subject to a "caste system . . . forcing them to work around or outside hierarchical structures of power which may exclude them" and were also subordinated in personal relations. When most male radicals reacted with indifference or ridicule to such ideas, women began to walk out of male-dominated political meetings, and by 1967 they had created an independent women's liberation movement composed of small groups across the nation.

Women's liberation demonstrations began to gain public attention, especially when dozens of women picketed the Miss America beauty pageant in 1968, protesting against being forced "to compete for male approval [and] enslaved by ludicrous 'beauty' standards." They crowned a sheep Miss America and set up a "freedom trash can," inviting women to throw away their "bras, girdles, curlers, false eyelashes, wigs, and *Cosmopolitan*," which they called "objects of female torture." The range of feminist activism ran the gamut from lobbying Congress and state legislatures to direct action. Women began to speak publicly about personal experiences that had always been shrouded in secrecy, such as rape and abortion. They marched by the tens of thousands for a variety of causes, and a handful of women illegally occupied state capital buildings and went on hunger strikes. Throughout the country, women joined consciousness-raising groups where they discovered that what they had considered "personal" problems reflected an entrenched system of discrimination against and devaluation of women.

The Many Facets and Achievements of Feminism

Radical feminists, who called their movement "women's liberation," differed from feminists in NOW and other more mainstream groups in several ways, particularly in the early years of feminism's resurgence. NOW focused on achieving equal treatment for women in the public sphere, while women's liberation emphasized women's subordination in the family and other personal relationships. Groups like NOW wanted to integrate women into existing institutions, while radical groups, ranging from New York City's Radical Feminists to Dayton, Ohio's Women's Liberation, insisted that women would never achieve justice until economic, political, and social institutions were totally transformed. On the national level, NOW existed as a typical hierar-

chical organization, while radical women met throughout the country in small groups where decision by consensus prevailed. Differences between these two strands of feminism blurred in the 1970s, as NOW and other mainstream groups embraced many of the issues raised by radicals.

A protest that occurred simultaneously with the Miss America contest, the NAACP-sponsored Miss Black America contest, indicated the complicated relationships between black women and feminism that arose from their interlocking racial and gender identities. On the one hand, by opposing the exclusion of African Americans from the mainstream contest, the Miss Black America contest seemed to support conventional gender norms that valued women in terms of their appearance. Yet the alternative pageant also expressed racial pride, as Saundra Williams, the winner, wore her hair in a natural Afro style, performed an African dance, and discussed her participation in civil rights demonstrations. Because the gender of black women was shaped by race, and because some African American men saw feminism as "an attempt by the power structure to divide black men and women," black women could not easily identify with feminist aims that were defined by white women.

Although NOW elected a black president, Aileen Hernandez, in 1970, white middle-class women predominated in the new feminism's national leadership and much of its constituency. Women of color criticized white women's organizations for their frequent indifference to the concerns of women unlike themselves, such as the disproportionate poverty experienced by minority women, their greater risk of being sterilized without their consent, and their vulnerability to additional layers of discrimination based on race or ethnicity. Cellestine Ware, an African American writer and a founder of New York Radical Feminists, insisted that black and white women could work together "only if the movement changes its priorities to work on issues that affect the lives of minority group women."

Yet support for feminism was exceedingly multifaceted. Most African American women worked through their own groups such as the older National Council of Negro Women and the National Black Feminist Organization, founded in 1973. Similarly, in the early 1970s American Indian women and Mexican American women founded national organizations, and Asian American women formed their own local movements. Blue-collar women organized the National

Coalition of Labor Union Women in 1974. Lesbians established collectives throughout the country as well as their own caucuses in organizations such as NOW. Women founded a host of other groups that focused on single issues such as health, abortion rights, education, and violence against women. Finally, U.S. feminists interacted with and learned from their sisters abroad, joining a movement that crossed national borders. (See "Beyond America's Borders," page 1056.)

Common threads underlay the great diversity of organizations, issues, and activities. Above all, feminism represented the belief that women were barred from, unequally treated in, or poorly served by the male-dominated public arena, encompassing politics, medicine, law, education, and religion. Feminists also sought equality in the private sphere, challenging traditional norms that identified women primarily as wives and mothers or sex objects, subservient to men.

Although more an effect than a cause of women's rising employment, feminism lifted female aspirations and helped lower barriers to jobs and offices monopolized by men. Women made some inroads into skilled crafts and management positions. Between 1970 and 2000, their share of law degrees shot up from 5 percent to nearly 50 percent, and their proportion of medical degrees from less than 10 percent to more than 35 percent. Women gained political offices very slowly; yet by 2000, they constituted more than 10 percent of Congress and more than 20 percent of all state executives and legislators.

Feminist activism produced the most sweeping changes in laws and policies concerning women since they had won the right to vote in 1920. In 1972, Congress passed an Equal Rights Amendment to the Constitution (ERA) that would outlaw differential treatment of men and women under all state and federal laws. Title IX of the Education Amendments Act of 1972 banned sex discrimination in all aspects of education, such as admissions, athletics, and faculty hiring. Congress also outlawed sex discrimination in the granting of loans in 1974, opened U.S. military academies to women in 1976, and prohibited discrimination against pregnant workers in 1978. Moreover, the Supreme Court struck down laws that treated men and women differently in Social Security, welfare and military benefits, and workers' compensation.

At the state and local levels, radical feminists won laws forcing police departments and the legal system to treat rape victims more justly and humanely. Activists set up shelters for battered women and their children, and they won state laws ensuring greater protection for victims of domestic violence and more effective prosecution of offenders. Feminists pressured state legislatures to end restrictions on abortion, and many testified publicly about their own illegal abortions. "Without the full capacity to limit her own reproduction," abortion rights activist Lucinda Cisler insisted, "a woman's other 'freedoms' are tantalizing mockeries that cannot be exercised." In 1973, the Supreme Court issued the landmark *Roe v. Wade* (see appendix, page A-44) decision, ruling that the Constitution protects the right to abortion, which states cannot prohibit in the early stages of pregnancy. However, later decisions allowed state governments to impose restrictions on that right, such as denying coverage under Medicaid and other government-financed health programs, thereby making it harder for poor women to obtain abortions.

A Counter Movement Arises

Public opinion polls registered majority support for most feminist goals, yet by the mid-1970s feminism faced a strong counter movement focused on preventing ratification of the ERA. Most states rushed to ratify the amendment, yet by 1973 a powerful opposition developed, led by Phyllis Schlafly, a conservative activist in the Republican Party and a Goldwater supporter in 1964. Schlafly mobilized a highly effective host of women at the grassroots level who believed that traditional gender roles were God-given and feared that feminism would devalue their own roles as wives and mothers. These women, marching on state capitols, persuaded some male legislators to block ratification. When the time limit ran out in 1982, only thirty-five states had ratified the amendment, three short of the necessary three-fourths majority. (See "Historical Question" in chapter 30, page 1118, and Map 30.3.)

Opposition to the right to abortion was even more intense. Many Americans believed that human life begins with conception, equating abortion with murder. The Catholic Church and other

> Feminist activism produced the most sweeping changes in laws and policies concerning women since they had won the right to vote in 1920.

Transnational Feminisms

When large numbers of American women began to protest sex discrimination in the 1960s, most were unaware that they belonged to a movement stretching more than one hundred years back in history and across oceans. In 1850, Ernestine Rose, who had been born in Poland and lived in Berlin, Paris, and London, told a women's rights convention in Massachusetts, "We are not contending here for the rights of the women of New England, or of old England, but of the world." Her statement affirmed the connections among women from France, Germany, England, Hungary, Finland, Belgium, and the United States, who wrote and visited each other and exchanged ideas and inspiration in the first international women's movement.

By the early twentieth century, women had formalized such connections. For example, the International Alliance of Women, founded in 1904 initially to promote global woman **suffrage**, expanded its agenda to include equal pay and employment, prostitution, peace, married women's citizenship, and more. By 1929, the Alliance claimed national organizations in fifty-one countries, including the United States and most of Europe, China, Egypt, India, Japan, Palestine, and several Latin American nations.

The search for a "universal sisterhood" revealed deep cleavages among the women who represented the nations of the Alliance. At its 1935 conference in Istanbul, Shareefeh Hamid Ali, representing India, warned that "any arrogant assumption of superiority or of patronage on the part of Europe or America . . . will alienate . . . the womanhood of Asia and Africa." White, Christian women from the United States and Europe dominated the organization and all too readily assumed that they could speak for all women. But oppression and discrimination looked quite different to women in other parts of the world. For example, in **colonized** countries such as India and Egypt, feminism arose alongside movements for independence from the very **imperial** nations that were home to most Alliance leaders. Egyptian feminist and nationalist Huda Sha'arawi was the only Muslim among the international leadership. She worked closely with the Alliance on many issues, but she realized the need to address the particular interests of Arab women overlooked or opposed by Euro-American feminists, and she established an Arab Feminist Union in 1945.

Temporarily disrupted by World War II, global connections among women increased dramatically with the creation of the United Nations. In a pathbreaking move, nations signing the UN Charter in 1945 affirmed "the equal rights of men and women" and "fundamental freedoms for all without distinction as to race, sex, language, or religion." Two years later, the UN established a Commission on the Status of Women, creating a forum for women from around the globe to meet and be heard; and in 1948 it adopted a Universal Declaration of Human Rights, which enumerated an extensive set of rights and explicitly rejected sex discrimination. Women pressed hard for such guarantees— including Eleanor Roosevelt, U.S. delegate to the UN who chaired the commission that drafted the declaration; Hansa Mehta, legislator and women's rights advocate from India; and Minerva Bernardino of the Dominican Republic.

These and other international commitments to justice for women went far beyond any rights guaranteed to women by the American legal system or those of most other nations, thereby setting standards and raising expectations. The UN, for example, asserted women's right to equal pay in 1951, twelve years before the U.S. Congress passed the Equal Pay Act of 1963, and the international body attacked discrimination in education a decade before Congress passed Title IX. While the dominant nations in the UN concentrated on security concerns, not women's issues, women around the world used these bold UN commitments to equality to advocate for rights in their own countries.

The UN helped launch a global feminist movement of unparalleled size and diversity when it declared 1975 International Women's Year and sponsored a conference in Mexico City. The unprecedented decision reflected a number of factors: growing concern about a rapidly increasing world population; rising interest in women's roles in economic development; the surge of feminism in member nations; and pressures from delegates to the UN's Commission on the Status of Women. Six thousand women came to Mexico City on their own, while official delegates from 125 nations approved a World Plan of Action for Women and prompted the UN to declare the UN Decade for Women (1976–1985).

International Women's Year Tribune

A majority of delegates at the UN International Women's Year Conference in Mexico City in July 1975 were women, but men provided the leadership and most of the speeches, and delegates frequently took positions mandated by their government but not necessarily representing the interests of women. In contrast, nongovernmental organizations associated with the UN sponsored a Tribune on the other side of the city, where 6,000 women, most of whom came to the conference on their own, attended workshops that they or their organizations designed. The Tribune was chaotic and confrontational, reflecting differences between Western women promoting equal rights and women from developing countries demading attention to poverty, and disagreements over whether such issues as apartheid in South Africa or the lack of self-government for Palestinians were women's issues. Yet most women were enlightened and energized by the gathering. A woman from Nigeria emphasized the "sharing and participation. You have pain for so many years, and now I know that women all over the world have this same pain. If this is all I get out of the Tribune, then that's enough."
© Bettye Lane.

In response to the Mexico City meeting's call for action in individual countries, the U.S. government sponsored a National Women's Conference in Houston, Texas, in 1977. More than 2,000 state delegates, representing a cross section of American womanhood, attended. They adopted a National Plan of Action, not only supporting such typical feminist goals as ratification of the ERA and reproductive freedom, but also addressing the needs of specific groups of women, including the elderly, lesbians, racial minorities, rural women, and homemakers. For the first time, the U.S. women's movement had a comprehensive national agenda setting goals for decades to come.

The three themes established for the UN Decade for Women—equality, development, peace—reflected an effort to address the enormously diverse needs of women throughout the world. Feminists from the United States and Europe who focused on equal rights met criticism from women representing impoverished **third world** countries—home to two-thirds of the world's women—who often took the position that "to talk feminism to a woman who has no water, no food, and no home is to talk nonsense." Ever larger UN-sponsored meetings followed Mexico City—Copenhagen in 1980, Nairobi in 1985, and Beijing in 1995, where 20,000 convened in an unofficial forum. From these global exchanges American feminists learned that they would have to revise their Western-centered perspective on women's needs if they hoped to participate in a truly international movement.

The UN Convention on the Elimination of All Forms of Discrimination against Women

(continued)

(CEDAW), passed by the General Assembly in 1979, reflected the broadening definition of feminism and a new understanding of what constituted "women's issues." The most sweeping declaration of women's rights by any official body, CEDAW proclaimed not only women's right to work, education, and political participation, but also the obligation to safeguard women's interests in economic development programs and to eliminate all forms of colonialism. By 2002, more than 165 nations had ratified the treaty. Among the major nations, the only country not to approve was the United States, where conservatives charged that it would promote abortion and weaken the family.

American feminists also learned that the United States was not always the most advanced nation when it came to women's welfare and status. For example, employed women in most other industrialized countries were entitled to paid maternity leave, and their children had access to public child care. By 2000, women had headed governments in more than 30 other countries, including Indira Gandhi in India, Golda Meir in Israel, and Margaret Thatcher in England. Many other nations, such as Argentina, Egypt, France, India, and the European Union, had some form of affirmative action to increase the numbers of women in government. And while American women held 13.8 percent of the seats in the House of Representatives, women constituted 20 percent of the lower house in South Korea, 25 percent in Mozambique, 30 percent in Germany, and more than 35 percent in Norway, Denmark, and Sweden. Yet, despite enormous differences among women around the world, internationally minded feminists were determined to find common ground. For, as Gertrude Mongella, secretary general of the Beijing conference, insisted in 1995, "A revolution has begun and there is no going back. . . . This revolution is too just, too important, and too long overdue."

BIBLIOGRAPHY

Bonnie Anderson, *"Joyous Greetings": The First International Women's Movement, 1830–1860* (2000).

Arvonne S. Fraser, *The U.N. Decade for Women* (1987).

Estelle B. Freedman, *No Turning Back: The History of Feminism and the Future of Women* (2002).

Angela Miles, *Integrative Feminisms: Building Global Visions, 1960s–1990s* (1996).

Hilkka Pietilä and Jeanne Vickers, *Making Women Matter: The Role of the United Nations* (1994).

Leila J. Rupp, *Worlds of Women: The Making of an International Women's Movement* (1997).

Deborah Stienstra, *Women's Movements and International Organizations* (1994).

religious organizations provided institutional support for their protest; conservative politicians and their supporters constituted another segment of the right-to-life movement. Like ERA opponents with whom they often overlapped, the right-to-life movement mobilized thousands of women who believed that abortion disparaged motherhood and who saw feminism as a threat to their traditional roles.

Feminists faced a host of other challenges. Despite some inroads into male-dominated occupations, most women still worked in low-paying, traditionally female jobs. Employed women continued to bear primary responsibility for their homes and families, thereby working a "double day." Congress's effort to ease this burden with a comprehensive child care bill fell to President Nixon's veto in 1971. As the number of female-headed families doubled from 10 percent to 20 percent of all American families by the end of the century, the situation of working mothers became even more critical.

The Persistence of Liberal Reform in the Nixon Administration

Feminism was not the only movement to arouse strong antagonism. Opposition to civil rights measures, Great Society reforms, protest groups, and changing gender roles and sexual mores—along with frustrations surrounding the war in Vietnam (see chapter 29)—spawned a third-party challenge in 1968 and delivered the White House to Republican Richard M. Nixon. As presidential candidate, Nixon attacked the Great Society for "pouring billions of dollars into programs that have failed," and he promised to represent the "forgotten Americans, the non-shouters, the non-demonstrators."

Yet, despite Nixon's desire to attract southern whites and other Democrats disaffected by Johnson's reforms and by Democrat support for

Nixon's 1968 Campaign
Seeking the presidency in the turbulent year of protests, riots, and assassinations, Richard Nixon tried to appeal to a broad constituency of voters, reflected in this campaign poster. Prominent Republicans of all stripes appear, including the liberal Nelson Rockefeller and conservative Barry Goldwater. While the sign "Champion of Forgotten America" spoke to white Americans alienated by the Great Society's programs for minorities and the poor, the appearance of the black Republican senator Edward Brooke and Wilt Chamberlain of the Los Angeles Lakers nodded to African Americans. Nixon also appealed to youth by supporting the vote for eighteen-year-olds and promising to end the draft.
Collection of Janice L. and David J. Frent.

minority group causes, liberal policies persisted during his tenure as president. The Nixon administration either promoted or at least accepted substantially greater federal assistance to the poor, new protections for African Americans, Native Americans, women, and other groups, major environmental regulations, and financial policies deviating sharply from traditional Republican economics. As we shall see in chapter 30, Nixon's rhetoric and some of his policies played to a growing conservatism in American politics; yet the liberalism of the 1960s persisted into the early 1970s.

Extending the Welfare State and Regulating the Economy

The liberal policies of the Nixon administration reflected a number of forces. Not only did the Democrats retain control of Congress, but Nixon wanted to preserve support from moderates in his party and achieve Republican ascendancy by attracting some traditional Democrats. He could not entirely ignore grassroots movements, and his body of advisers included several who were sympathetic to environmentalism, Indian rights, and other reforms. Serious economic problems also compelled new approaches, and although Nixon's real passion lay in foreign rather than domestic policy, he knew that history's approving gaze would depend in part on how he handled problems at home.

Under Nixon, government assistance programs actually grew. Congress resisted many of his attacks on antipoverty programs, refusing, for example, to eliminate the Office of Economic Opportunity. Key programs such as Medicare and Medicaid, Head Start, Legal Services, and job training remained intact. Indeed, the federal budget for social services exceeded defense spending for the first time since World War II. Social Security benefits—now required to rise with the cost of living—increased; subsidies for low-income housing tripled; and a new billion-dollar program provided Pell grants (named for the bill's sponsor) for low-income students to attend college. In response to growing public concern about undernourishment, Nixon supported a huge expansion of the food stamp program, which benefited 12.5 million recipients. Noting the disparity between Nixon's political speeches designed to gain votes and his actual practice as president, his disgruntled speechwriter, the archconservative Pat Buchanan, grumbled, "Vigorously did we inveigh against the Great Society, enthusiastically did we fund it."

Nixon also acted contrary to his rhetoric against a growing federal bureaucracy by expanding controls over the economy when economic crises and energy shortages induced him to increase the federal government's power in the marketplace. Throughout the post–World War II economic boom, the nation's abundant oil deposits and access to cheap Middle Eastern oil had encouraged the building of large cars and glass-enclosed skyscrapers with no concern for fuel efficiency. The traditional American assumption that energy resources were boundless and the resulting wasteful practices meant that by the 1970s the United States, with just 6 percent of the world's population, consumed one-third of its fuel resources.

In the fall of 1973, the United States faced its first energy crisis when Arab nations, furious at the nation's support of Israel during the Yom Kippur War (see chapter 29), cut off oil shipments to the United States. As oil supplies fell in the winter of 1973–74, long lines formed at gas stations, where prices had nearly doubled, many homes were cold, and some schools closed. In response, Nixon authorized temporary emergency measures allocating petroleum and establishing a national 55-mile-per-hour speed limit to save gasoline. By the spring of 1974, the crisis had eased, but the United States had yet to come to grips with its seemingly unquenchable demand for fuel and dependence on foreign oil.

> Nixon expanded the government's regulatory role with a host of environmental protection measures.

Soaring energy prices contributed to severe economic problems. Fueled by the Vietnam War, by 1969 inflation had risen to 7 percent, an enormous increase for Americans used to rates of about 2 percent. In 1970, unemployment hit the economy hard. This unprecedented combination of a stagnant economy and inflation was dubbed "stagflation." Domestic troubles were compounded by the decline of American dominance in the international economy. Having fully recovered from World War II, the economies of Japan and Western Europe grew faster than that of the United States in the 1970s. Foreign cars, electronic equipment, and other products competed favorably with American goods throughout the world. In 1971, for the first time in decades, the United States imported more than it exported. Because the amount of dollars in foreign hands exceeded U.S. gold reserves, the nation could no longer back up its currency with gold.

The president's response to these economic problems diverged from conventional Republican doctrine. With an eye to the 1972 election, Nixon announced a "New Economic Policy" in August 1971. He abandoned the convertibility of dollars into gold, devalued the dollar to make American goods cheaper in foreign markets and thus increase exports, and imposed a 10 percent surcharge on most imports. Nixon also froze wages and prices, thus enabling the government to stimulate the economy without fueling more inflation. In the short run, these

policies worked. Exports surged ahead of imports, inflation subsided, unemployment fell below 5 percent, and Nixon was resoundingly reelected in 1972. Yet the New Economic Policy treated the economy only superficially. The lifting of price and wage controls in 1973, the Arab oil embargo, and rising food prices sent the consumer price index soaring by 11 percent by 1974. Unemployment also crept back up, and Nixon's successor inherited the most severe economic crisis since the depression of the 1930s.

More successfully, Nixon expanded the government's regulatory role with a host of environmental protection measures. Influenced especially by his domestic policy chief, John Ehrlichman, Nixon responded to growing public concern for the environment, proclaiming in 1970 that the nation must make "reparations for the damage we have done to our air, to our land and to our water." In addition to establishing the Environmental Protection Agency, Nixon signed strong clean-air legislation and measures to regulate noise pollution, oil spill cleanup, and the dumping of pesticides into the oceans. Although environmentalists claimed that Nixon failed to do enough, pointing particularly to his veto—for budgetary reasons—of the Clean Water Act of 1972, which Congress overrode, no previous administration had matched the initiatives undertaken under Nixon.

Responding to Demands for Social Justice

Nixon's 1968 campaign had exploited antipathy to black protest and new civil rights policies in order to woo white southerners and northern workers away from the Democratic Party, yet his administration had to answer to the courts and Congress. In 1968, fourteen years after the *Brown* decision, school desegregation had barely touched the South: Two-thirds of African American children did not have a single white schoolmate. Like Eisenhower, Nixon was reluctant to use federal power to compel integration, but the Supreme Court overruled efforts by the Justice Department to delay court-ordered desegregation and compelled the administration to enforce the law. By the time Nixon left office, fewer than one in ten southern black children attended totally segregated schools.

The Nixon administration also began to implement affirmative action, requiring contractors and unions to employ more minority workers on federally funded construction projects and awarding more government contracts and loans to minority businesses. Congress took the initiative in other areas. In 1970, it extended the Voting Rights Act of 1965 by five years; and in 1972, Congress strengthened the Civil Rights Act of 1964 by enlarging the enforcement powers of the EEOC and authorizing it to initiate lawsuits against employers suspected of discrimination.

While women as well as minority groups benefited from the implementation of affirmative action and the strengthened EEOC, several measures of the Nixon administration specifically attacked sex discrimination. The president had quite conventional—and patronizing—attitudes about women's capabilities and appropriate roles, responding to criticism that he had not appointed many women to federal jobs as "Much ado about *nothing!*" Yet again he confronted a growing popular movement and listened to more open-minded advisers and Republican feminists. Nixon vetoed a child care bill and publicly opposed abortion, but he signed the pathbreaking Title IX, banning sex discrimination in education, and a measure providing women equal access to credit.

President Nixon gave more public support for justice to Native Americans than to any other protest group. While not giving in to radical demands, the administration dealt cautiously with extreme protests, such as the occupations of Alcatraz Island, the Bureau of Indian Affairs, and Wounded Knee. Nixon denounced termination and forced assimilation, calling for "self-determination among the Indian people." He signed measures recognizing claims of Alaskan and New Mexican Indians and restoring tribal status to the Menominee, whose status had been terminated in 1961, and he set in motion legislation restoring additional tribal lands and granting Indians more control over their schools and other service institutions.

Conclusion: Achievements and Limitations of Liberalism

Senate majority leader Mike Mansfield was not alone in concluding that Lyndon Johnson "has done more than FDR ever did, or ever thought of doing." Yet opposition to his leadership grew so strong by 1968 that Johnson abandoned hopes for reelection. As his liberal vision lay in ruins,

he asked, "How was it possible that all these people could be so ungrateful to me after I have given them so much?"

Fannie Lou Hamer could have provided a number of reasons. Support from the federal government was minimal when local officials arrested and beat her and others who were organizing Mississippi blacks to obtain their rights. "We learned the hard way that even though we had all the law and all the righteousness on our side—that white man is not going to give up his power to us," Hamer concluded. Moreover, her efforts to use Johnson's antipoverty programs to help poor blacks in Mississippi eventually ended in failure. Internal problems hampered her projects, but they also reflected some of the more general shortcomings of the War on Poverty. Inadequately planned and funded, many antipoverty programs ended up benefiting industry and the nonpoor as much as or more than the impoverished. Because Johnson refused to ask for sacrifices from prosperous Americans, the Great Society never approached the redistribution of wealth and resources that would have been necessary for the elimination of poverty.

Black aspirations exceeded white Americans' commitment to genuine equality. It was easy for northerners to be sympathetic when the civil rights movement focused on crude and blatant forms of racism in the South. But when it attacked the subtler racism that existed throughout the nation and sought equality in fact as well as in rights, the black freedom struggle confronted a powerful backlash. By the end of the 1960s, the revolution in the legal status of African Americans was complete, but the black freedom struggle had lost much of its momentum, and African Americans remained, with Native Americans and Chicanos, at the bottom of the economic ladder.

Critics of Johnson's Great Society on the left as well as on the expanding right overlooked its more successful and lasting elements. Medicare and Medicaid provided access to health care for the elderly and the poor and contributed to a sharp decline in poverty among aged Americans. Programs of federal aid for education and housing became permanent elements of national policy. Moreover, even though swept into the White House on a backlash against the liberalism of the 1960s, Richard Nixon's administration implemented school desegregation in the South and affirmative action, expanded government assistance to the disadvantaged, initiated substantial environmental regulations, and secured new rights for Native Americans and women. Although the material status of minorities remained below that of white Americans, new policies provided greater opportunities for those able to take advantage of them. Women especially benefited from the decline of discrimination, and significant numbers of African Americans and other minority groups began to enter the middle class.

Yet the perceived shortcomings of government programs contributed to social turmoil and fueled the resurgence of conservative politics. Young radicals launched direct confrontations with the government and universities that, together with racial conflict, escalated into political discord and social disorder not seen since the union wars of the 1930s. The war in Vietnam polarized American society as much as did racial

issues or the behavior of young people, and Johnson's and Nixon's conduct of the war undermined faith in presidential leadership. The war starved the Great Society, devouring revenues that might have been used for social reform and eclipsing the substantial progress that had actually been achieved.

FOR ADDITIONAL FIRSTHAND ACCOUNTS OF THIS PERIOD, see Chapter 28 in Michael Johnson, ed., *Reading the American Past*, Third Edition.

TO ASSESS YOUR MASTERY OF THE MATERIAL IN THIS CHAPTER, see the Online Study Guide at bedfordstmartins.com/roark.

FOR WEB LINKS RELATED TO THE TOPICS IN THIS CHAPTER, see "HistoryLinks," "DocLinks," and "PlaceLinks" at bedfordstmartins.com/roark.

CHRONOLOGY

1960
- African American college students in Greensboro, North Carolina, stage sit-in at whites-only lunch counter.
- Democrat John F. Kennedy elected president.
- Student Nonviolent Coordinating Committee (SNCC) established to mobilize young people for direct action for civil rights.
- Students for a Democratic Society (SDS) founded to promote participatory democracy, economic justice, and peace.

1961
- Congress of Racial Equality (CORE) sponsors Freedom Rides to desegregate interstate transportation in South.

1962
- Michael Harrington's *The Other America* published, exposing widespread poverty in the United States.
- Cesar Chavez and Dolores Huerta found United Farm Workers (UFW) to better conditions for Chicano migrant laborers.

- Rachel Carson's *Silent Spring* published, exposing the dangers of dioxin, DDT, and other poisons to the environment.

1963
- Betty Friedan's best-selling book *The Feminine Mystique* published.

- President's Commission on the Status of Women issues report documenting widespread sex discrimination.
- Equal Pay Act makes wage disparities based solely on gender illegal.
- *Baker v. Carr* mandates electoral redistricting to enforce "one person, one vote" principle.
- *Abington School District v. Schempp* outlaws prayer in public schools.
- Mississippi NAACP leader Medgar Evers assassinated in Jackson.
- March on Washington becomes largest civil rights demonstration in U.S. history.
- President Kennedy assassinated in Dallas, Texas; Vice President Lyndon B. Johnson becomes president.

1964
- Congress enacts Civil Rights Act, the strongest such measure since Reconstruction.
- Economic Opportunity Act launches Lyndon Johnson's War on Poverty.

- Free speech movement, first large-scale white student protest of 1960s, organized at University of California, Berkeley.
- Malcolm X breaks from Nation of Islam and attracts wide following.

- President Johnson elected to full term in landslide over Republican senator Barry Goldwater.
- Tax cut bill proposed by Kennedy administration passes.

1965
- Malcolm X assassinated in New York City.
- Selma-to-Montgomery march for voting rights; Johnson orders federal protection for marchers after they are attacked.
- Congress passes Voting Rights Act, establishing protections for minorities' access to the ballot.
- **August**. The Watts district of Los Angeles erupts in riots protesting police brutality.

1965–1966

- 89th Congress passes most of Johnson's Great Society domestic programs, including antipoverty measures, public works acts, aid to education, and Medicare/Medicaid.

1966
- Black Panther Party founded, advocating African American economic and political autonomy.
- In *Miranda v. Arizona*, Supreme Court requires police to inform suspects of their rights.
- National Organization for Women (NOW) founded.

1967
- **July**. Riots break out in Detroit.

1968
- Martin Luther King Jr. assassinated in Memphis, Tennessee; riots erupt in Washington, D.C., and elsewhere.
- American Indian Movement (AIM) founded.
- Republican Richard M. Nixon elected president.

1969
- Native Americans occupy Alcatraz Island.

1970
- Earth Day demonstrations held to support environmental goals.
- Congress passes Occupational Safety and Health Act to improve workplace conditions.
- Environmental Protection Agency established by Nixon.
- Clean Air Act sets standards, imposes restrictions on emissions of pollutants.
- Native American Women's Association founded.
- Women Strike for Peace and Equality demonstrations take place nationwide.

1971
- First national Mexican American women's conference held.
- Nixon's New Economic Policy abandons gold standard, imposes price and wage controls.

1972
- Title IX of Education Amendments bans sex discrimination in education.
- Congress passes Equal Rights Amendment, sends it to states for ratification.
- American Indians' "Trail of Broken Treaties" caravan to Washington, D.C., and seizure of the Bureau of Indian Affairs.

1973
- AIM members occupy Wounded Knee to press Indian claims against the U.S. government.
- National Black Feminist Organization founded.
- In *Roe v. Wade*, Supreme Court rules that abortion is constitutionally protected.

BIBLIOGRAPHY

General Works

John Morton Blum, *Years of Discord: American Politics and Society, 1961–1974* (1991).

David Burner, *Making Peace with the 60s* (1996).

David Farber, *The Age of Great Dreams: America in the 1960s* (1994).

Hugh Davis Graham, *The Civil Rights Era: Origins and Development of National Policy, 1960–1972* (1990).

Maurice Isserman and Michael Kazin, *America Divided: The Civil War of the 1960s* (2000).

Allen J. Matusow, *The Unraveling of America: A History of Liberalism in the 1960s* (1984).

Douglas T. Miller, *On Our Own: Americans in the Sixties* (1996).

Edward P. Morgan, *The Sixties Experience: Hard Lessons about Modern America* (1991).

William L. O'Neill, *Coming Apart: An Informal History of America in the 1960s* (1971).

Barbara L. Tischler, ed., *Sights on the Sixties* (1992).

The Black Freedom Struggle

Peter J. Albert and Ronald Hoffman, eds., *We Shall Overcome: Martin Luther King Jr. and the Black Freedom Struggle* (1990).

Jervis Anderson, *Bayard Rustin: Troubles I've Seen* (1997).

Taylor Branch, *Parting the Waters: America in the King Years, 1954–63* (1988).

Taylor Branch, *Pillar of Fire: America in the King Years, 1963–65* (1998).

James W. Button, *Black Violence: Political Impact of the 1960s Riots* (1978).

Clayborne Carson, *In Struggle: SNCC and the Black Awakening of the 1960s* (1981).

David L. Chappell, *Inside Agitators: White Southerners in the Civil Rights Movement* (1994).

John Dittmer, *Local People: The Struggle for Civil Rights in Mississippi* (1994).

Michael Eric Dyson, *Making Malcolm: The Myth and Meaning of Malcolm X* (1995).

David J. Garrow, *Protest at Selma: Martin Luther King Jr. and the Voting Rights Act of 1965* (1978).

David J. Garrow, *Bearing the Cross: Martin Luther King Jr. and the Southern Christian Leadership Conference* (1986).

Peter L. Goldman, *The Death and Life of Malcolm X* (1979).

Ralph G. Gomes and Linda Faye Williams, eds., *From Exclusion to Inclusion: The Long Struggle for African American Political Power* (1992).

Steven F. Lawson, *Running for Freedom: Civil Rights and Black Politics in America since 1941* (1991).

Chana Kai Lee, *For Freedom's Sake: The Life of Fannie Lou Hamer* (1999).

John Lewis with Michael D'Orso, *Walking with the Wind: A Memoir of the Movement* (1998).

Doug McAdam, *Freedom Summer* (1989).

August Meier and Elliott M. Rudwick, *CORE: A Study in the Civil Rights Movement, 1942–1968* (1973).

Stephen B. Oates, *Let the Trumpet Sound: The Life of Martin Luther King Jr.* (1982).

Kenneth O'Reilly, *"Racial Matters": The FBI's Secret File on Black America, 1960–1972* (1989).

Frank R. Parker, *Black Votes Count: Political Empowerment in Mississippi after 1965* (1990).

Charles Payne, *I've Got the Light of Freedom: The Organizing Tradition and the Mississippi Freedom Struggle* (1995).

Bruce Perry, *Malcolm: The Life of a Man Who Changed Black America* (1991).

James R. Ralph Jr., *Northern Protest: Martin Luther King Jr., Chicago, and the Civil Rights Movement* (1993).

Barbara Ransby, *Ella Baker and the Black Freedom Movement: A Radical Democratic Vision* (2003).

Belinda Robnett, *How Long? How Long? African-American Women in the Struggle for Civil Rights* (1997).

Timothy Tyson, *Radio Free Dixie: Robert F. Williams and the Roots of Black Power* (1999).

Frederick M. Wirt, *"We Ain't What We Was": Civil Rights in the New South* (1997).

Politics and Policies

David Burner, *John F. Kennedy and a New Generation* (1988).

Robert Caro, *The Years of Lyndon Johnson*, vols. 1, 2, and 3 (1982, 1990, and 2002).

Paul K. Conkin, *Big Daddy from the Pedernales: Lyndon Baines Johnson* (1986).

Robert Dallek, *Flawed Giant: Lyndon B. Johnson, 1960–1973* (1998).

Robert Dallek, *An Unfinished Life: John F. Kennedy, 1917–1963* (2003).

James N. Giglio, *The Presidency of John F. Kennedy* (1992).

Robert Alan Goldberg, *Barry Goldwater* (1995).

Joan Hoff, *Nixon Reconsidered* (1994).

Michael B. Katz, *The Undeserving Poor: From the War on Poverty to the War on Welfare* (1989).

Doris Kearns, *Lyndon Johnson and the American Dream* (1976).

Robert Mann, *The Walls of Jericho: Lyndon Johnson, Hubert Humphrey, Richard Russell, and the Struggle for Civil Rights* (1996).

Rick Perlstein, *Before the Storm: Barry Goldwater and the Unmaking of the American Consensus* (2001).

Gerald Posner, *Case Closed: Lee Harvey Oswald and the Assassination of JFK* (1993).

Jill Quadagno, *The Color of Welfare: How Racism Undermined the War on Poverty* (1994).

Richard Reeves, *President Kennedy: Profile of Power* (1993).

Mark Stern, *Calculating Visions: Kennedy, Johnson, and Civil Rights* (1992).

Irwin Unger, *The Best of Intentions: The Triumph and Failure of the Great Society* (1996).

Tom Wicker, *One of Us: Richard Nixon and the American Dream* (1991).

Protest Movements

Terry H. Anderson, *The Movement and the Sixties* (1995).

Stewart Burns, *Social Movements of the 1960s: Searching for Democracy* (1990).

David Chalmers, *And the Crooked Places Made Straight: The Struggle for Social Change in the 1960s* (1991).

Martha F. Davis, *Brutal Need: Lawyers and the Welfare Rights Movement, 1960–1973* (1993).

Vine Deloria Jr., *Behind the Trail of Broken Treaties* (1974).

Ignacio M. Garcia, *United We Win: The Rise and Fall of La Raza Unida Party* (1989).

Todd Gitlin, *The Sixties: Years of Hope, Days of Rage* (1987).

Juan Gómez-Quiñones, *Chicano Politics: Reality and Promise, 1940–1990* (1990).

Manuel G. Gonzales, *Mexicanos: A History of Mexicans in the United States* (1999).

Richard Griswold del Castillo and Richard A. Garcia, *Cesar Chavez: A Triumph of Spirit* (1995).

Laurence M. Hauptman, *The Iroquois Struggle for Survival: World War II to Red Power* (1986).

Maurice Isserman, *If I Had a Hammer . . . : The Death of the Old Left and the Birth of the New Left* (1987).

George Katsiaficas, *The Imagination of the New Left: A Global Analysis of 1968* (1987).

Cyril Levitt, *Children of Privilege: Student Revolt in the Sixties* (1984).

Peter B. Levy, *The New Left and Labor in the 1960s* (1994).

Peter Matthiessen, *In the Spirit of Crazy Horse* (1983).

James Miller, *"Democracy Is in the Streets": From Port Huron to the Siege of Chicago* (1987).

Joan Moore and Harry Pachon, *Hispanics in the United States* (1985).

Donald L. Parman, *Indians and the American West in the Twentieth Century* (1994).

Doug Rossinow, *The Politics of Authenticity: Liberalism, Christianity, and the New Left in America* (1998).

John D. Skrentny, *The Minority Rights Revolution* (2002).

William Wei, *The Asian American Movement* (1993).

Cultural Change, Sexual Revolution, and Feminism

David Allyn, *Make Love, Not War: The Sexual Revolution, an Unfettered History* (2000).

Beth Bailey, *Sex in the Heartland* (1999).

Maxine Leeds Craig, *Ain't I a Beauty Queen? Black Women, Beauty, and the Politics of Race* (2002).

Flora Davis, *Moving the Mountain: The Women's Movement since 1960* (1991).

Alice Echols, *Daring to Be Bad: Radical Feminism in America, 1967–1975* (1989).

Sara Evans, *Personal Liberation: The Roots of Women's Liberation in the Civil Rights Movement and the New Left* (1978).

Sara Evans, *Tidal Wave: How Women Changed America at Century's End* (2003).

Judith Ezekiel, *Feminism in the Heartland* (2002).

Jo Freeman, *The Politics of Liberation* (1975).

David Garrow, *Liberty and Sexuality: The Right to Privacy and the Making of* Roe v. Wade (1994).

Cynthia Harrison, *On Account of Sex: The Politics of Women's Issues, 1945–1968* (1988).

Susan M. Hartmann, *The Other Feminists: Activists in the Liberal Establishment* (1998).

Daniel Horowitz, *Betty Friedan and the Making of* The Feminine Mystique (1998).

James Miller, *Flowers in the Dustbin: The Rise of Rock and Roll, 1947–1977* (1999).

Ruth Rosen, *The World Split Open: How the Modern Women's Movement Changed America* (2000).

William L. Van Deburg, *New Days in Babylon: The Black Power Movement and American Culture, 1965–1975* (1993).

The Supreme Court

Archibald Cox, *The Warren Court: Constitutional Decision as an Instrument of Reform* (1968).

Richard Y. Funston, *Constitutional Counterrevolution? The Warren Court and the Burger Court: Judicial Policy Making in Modern America* (1977).

Philip B. Kurland, *Politics and the Warren Court* (1970).

Paul L. Murphy, *The Constitution in Crisis Times, 1918–1969* (1972).

Lucas A. Powe Jr., *The Warren Court and American Politics* (2000).

Bernard Schwartz, *Super Chief: Earl Warren and His Supreme Court, a Judicial Biography* (1983).

Bernard Schwartz, ed., *The Warren Court: A Retrospective* (1996).

Melvin I. Urofsky, *The Continuity of Change: The Supreme Court and Individual Liberties, 1953–1986* (1991).

FATIGUE HAT WITH BUTTONS

The button on this fatigue hat belonging
to a veteran who served two tours of duty
demonstrates veterans' response to the many Americans who just wanted to forget the war that the United States
failed to win. Because their war was so different from other American wars, Viet-
nam veterans often returned home to hostility or indifference. The POW-MIA pin refers to prisoners of war and those
missing in action. This man was unusual in serving two tours of duty in Vietnam; most soldiers served only one year.
Why might he have gone back for a second tour? How might his experiences have differed in the two periods separated by five years?

Nancy Gewitz / Antique Textile Resource / Picture Research Consultants & Archives.

29

Vietnam and the Limits of Power

1961–1975

A S CHARLES ANDERSON'S PLANE prepared to land, the pilot announced, "Gentlemen, we'll be touching down in Da Nang, Vietnam, in about ten minutes. . . . Fasten your seat belts, please. On behalf of the entire crew and staff, I'd like to say we've enjoyed having you with us . . . and we hope to see all of you again next year on your way home. Goodbye and good luck." Like most soldiers after 1966, Charles Anderson went to war on a commercial jetliner, complete with stewardesses (as they were called then) in miniskirts.

Military personnel traveling to battle like business executives or tourists only hints at how different the Vietnam War was from America's previous wars. Marine infantry officer Philip Caputo landed at Da Nang in March 1965 confident that the enemy "would be quickly beaten and that we were doing something altogether noble and good." But in just a few months, "what had begun as an adventurous expedition had turned into an exhausting, indecisive war of attrition in which we fought for no other cause than our own survival."

Another soldier discovered even more quickly that "something was wrong." Wondering why the bus taking him from the air base to the compound had wire mesh over the windows, he was told, "The gooks will throw grenades through the windows." Soldiers in Vietnam initially used the racist word *gook* to refer to the enemy—the North Vietnamese or their supporters in the south—but it quickly became a term used for any Vietnamese. "From one day to the next, you could see for yourself changes coming over guys on our side—decent fellows, who wouldn't dream of calling an Oriental a 'gook' back home," reported one American. The problem was that "they couldn't tell who was their friend and who wasn't. Day after day, out on patrol we'd come to . . . a shabby village, and the elders would welcome us and the children come running with smiles on their faces, waiting for the candy we'd give them. But . . . just as we were leaving the village behind, the enemy would open up on us, and there was bitterness among us that the villagers hadn't given us warning."

Americans' horrifying and bewildering experiences in Vietnam grew out of **cold war** commitments made in the 1940s and 1950s by Presidents Harry S. Truman and Dwight D. Eisenhower. John F. Kennedy wholeheartedly took on those commitments, promising more flexible and vigorous efforts to thwart **communism**. In the most memorable words of his 1961 inauguration, he declared, "Let every nation know, whether it wishes us well or ill, that we shall pay any price, bear any burden, meet any hardship, support any friend, oppose any foe to assure the survival and the success of liberty."

■ **New Frontiers in Foreign Policy**
Meeting the "Hour of Maximum Danger"
New Approaches to the Third World
The Arms Race and the Nuclear Brink
Venturing into a Quagmire in Vietnam

■ **Lyndon Johnson's War against Communism**
Toward an All-Out Commitment in Vietnam
Preventing Another Castro in Latin America
The Americanized War

■ **A Nation Polarized**
The Widening War at Home
1968: Year of Upheaval

■ **New Opportunities and Dangers in a Multipolar World**
Moving toward Détente with the Soviet Union and China
Shoring Up Anticommunism in the Third World

■ **Nixon's Search for Peace with Honor in Vietnam**
Vietnamization and Negotiations
Nixon's War
The Peace Accords and the Fall of Saigon
The Legacy of Defeat

■ **Conclusion: An Unwinnable War**

Fighting the Climate and Geography
Steamy tropical conditions and inhospitable terrain were among the nonhuman enemies U.S. troops faced in Vietnam. Soldiers like this one making his way under fire through a rice paddy in 1966 were soaked for weeks on end. Veteran Philip Caputo wrote about "being pounded numb by ceaseless rain" during the monsoon; "at night we squatted in muddy holes, picked off the leeches that sucked on our veins."

Henri Gilles Huet/World Wide Photos, Inc.

Vietnam became the foremost test of Kennedy's pledge. He sent increasing amounts of American arms and personnel to sustain the South Vietnamese government, and Lyndon B. Johnson dramatically escalated that commitment. By 1965, the civil war in Vietnam had become America's war, with 543,000 military personnel serving there at peak strength in 1968 and more than 3 million total throughout the war's duration. Yet this massive intervention not only failed to defeat North Vietnam but also added a new burden to the costs of fighting the cold war—intense discord at home. The Vietnam War cost President Johnson another term in office and contributed to the political demise of his Republican successor, Richard M. Nixon. Some Americans lauded the U.S. goal in Vietnam and decried only the nation's unwillingness to pursue it effectively. Others believed that preserving a non-Communist South Vietnam was neither in the best interests of the United States nor within its capacity or moral right to achieve.

But none could deny the war's enormous costs. "The promises of the Great Society have been shot down on the battlefield of Vietnam," said Martin Luther King Jr. In addition to derailing domestic reform, the war exacted a heavy toll in American lives and dollars, kindled internal conflict, and led to the violation of the rights of antiwar protesters. Like the African American freedom struggle, Vietnam had a deep and lasting effect on the nation.

Even as the United States incurred tremendous costs in fighting communism in Vietnam (and intervened on a much smaller scale in other **third world** countries), its leaders moved to ease cold war tensions with the major Communist powers—the Soviet Union and China. The United States and Russia cooperated during the 1960s to limit nuclear testing and the spread of nuclear weapons; in 1972, they agreed to the first restrictions on the development of new weapons since the beginning of the nuclear age. In addition, Nixon's historic visit to China in 1972 marked abandonment of the policy of isolating China and paved the way for normal diplomatic relations by the end of the 1970s.

New Frontiers in Foreign Policy

John F. Kennedy moved quickly to fulfill his promise to pursue **containment** with a more aggressive yet more flexible foreign policy, expanding the nation's ability to wage nuclear, conventional, or **guerrilla warfare**. His secretary of defense, Robert S. McNamara, and several other advisers shared the president's youth, Ivy League education, and competitiveness. Exuding confidence and eager to apply technology to problem solving, they welcomed danger and risk—characteristics that sometimes contributed to foreign policy crises under both Kennedy and Johnson.

In order to ensure U.S. superiority over the Soviet Union in every domain, Kennedy accelerated the nation's space exploration program and increased attention to the third world. In his unflinching determination to halt communism, Kennedy took the United States to the brink of nuclear war during the 1962 Cuban missile crisis. Less dramatically but no less tenaciously, Kennedy stepped up American arms and personnel to save the government of South Vietnam from Communist insurgents.

Meeting the "Hour of Maximum Danger"

Kennedy and other Democrats criticized the Eisenhower administration for relying too heavily on nuclear weapons. They wanted to build up conventional ground forces as well, to provide the nation a **flexible response** to Communist expansion. They also charged that limits on defense spending had allowed the United States to fall behind even in nuclear capability. In January 1961, Kennedy warned that the nation faced a grave peril: "Each day the crises multiply. . . . Each day we draw nearer the hour of maximum danger."

Although the president exaggerated the actual threat to national security, several developments in 1961 heightened the sense of crisis and provided rationalization for a military buildup. In a speech made shortly before Kennedy's inauguration, Soviet premier Nikita Khrushchev had encouraged "wars of national liberation," thereby aligning the Soviet Union with independence movements (usually anti-Western) in the third world. Khrushchev wanted to bolster Soviet leadership of the Communist world against challenges by the People's Republic of China, and to shore up his political position at home by projecting forcefulness abroad. U.S. officials, however, saw in his words a threat to the status quo of containment.

Nowhere was the perceived threat closer to home than in Cuba, just ninety miles from the United States. Fidel Castro's revolution had already moved Cuba into the Soviet orbit; and under Eisenhower, the CIA had been planning an invasion by anti-Castro exiles. Kennedy ordered the invasion to proceed even though his military advisers gave it only a fair chance of success. To do otherwise, the president believed, would create an appearance of weakness.

MAP 29.1   U.S. Involvement in Latin America and the Caribbean, 1954–1994
During the cold war, the United States frequently intervened in Central American and Caribbean countries to suppress Communist or leftist movements.

READING THE MAP: How many and which Latin American countries did the United States directly invade? What was the extent of U.S. indirect involvement in other upheavals in the region?
CONNECTIONS: What role did geographic proximity play in U.S. policy toward the region? What was the significance of the Cuban missile crisis for U.S. foreign policy? Did the political party of the intervening administration make a difference? Why or why not?

FOR MORE HELP ANALYZING THIS MAP, see the map activity for this chapter in the Online Study Guide at bedfordstmartins.com/roark.

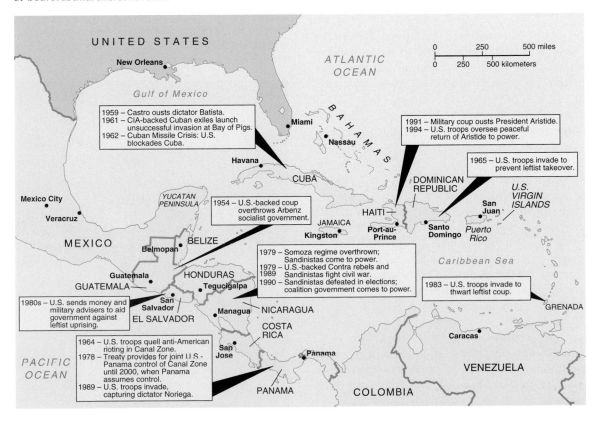

On April 17, 1961, about 1,300 anti-Castro exiles who had been trained and armed by the CIA landed at the Bay of Pigs on the south shore of Cuba (Map 29.1). Contrary to expectations, no popular uprising materialized to support the anti-Castro brigade. Kennedy refused to supply direct military support, and the invaders quickly fell to Castro's forces, who through intelligence leaks knew about the invasion and were prepared. The disaster was humiliating for Kennedy and the United States, posing a stark contrast to Kennedy's inaugural promise of a new, more effective foreign policy. The attempted armed interference in another nation compromised the moral authority of the United States, evoked memories of **Yankee imperialism** among Latin American countries, aligned Cuba even more closely with the Soviet Union, and helped Castro consolidate his power.

> The attempted armed interference in another nation compromised the moral authority of the United States, evoked memories of Yankee imperialism, aligned Cuba even more closely with the Soviet Union, and helped Castro consolidate his power.

Shortly before the Bay of Pigs invasion, the United States had suffered a psychological blow when a Soviet astronaut became the first human to orbit the earth. In May 1961, Kennedy called for a huge new commitment to the space race. "If we are to win the battle that is now going on around the world between freedom and tyranny," the United States must "take a clearly leading role in space achievement." His goal: an American on the moon within six to eight years. Congress authorized the Apollo program and boosted appropriations for space exploration. In 1962, John H. Glenn orbited the earth. Then in 1969, the United States surpassed the Soviet Union when Neil A. Armstrong and Edwin E. "Buzz" Aldrin Jr. became the first humans to set foot on the moon.

Early in his presidency, Kennedy sought a meeting with Khrushchev "to show him that we can be as tough as he is." The two met in June 1961, in Vienna, Austria, but contrary to Kennedy's expectations, Khrushchev was belligerent and threatening and shook the president's confidence. The stunned president reported to a journalist, "He just beat [the] hell out of me. . . . If he thinks I'm inexperienced and have no guts . . . we won't get anywhere with him." Khrushchev demanded an agreement recognizing the existence of two Germanys; otherwise, he warned, the Soviets would sign a separate treaty with East Germany, a move that would threaten America's occupation rights in West Berlin and its access to the city, which lay some one hundred miles within East Germany. Kennedy responded by substantially increasing U.S. military forces in Europe.

The massive exodus of East Germans into West Berlin, which had begun shortly after Berlin was partitioned following World War II, caused the Communists major embarrassment. To stop this flow of escapees from behind the **iron curtain**, on August 13, 1961, East Germany erected a wall between East and West Berlin, shocking the world. With the Berlin Wall stemming the tide of migration, Khrushchev backed off from his threats. But not until 1972 did the superpowers recognize East and West Germany as separate nations and guarantee Western access to West Berlin.

Humans Reach the Moon

In July 1969, less than a decade after President John F. Kennedy announced the goal of "landing a man on the moon and returning him safely to earth," the space capsule *Apollo 11* carried astronauts Edwin E. ("Buzz") Aldrin Jr. and Neil A. Armstrong to the moon. As millions of people watched on television, Armstrong became the first human to step on the moon's surface, saying, "That's one small step for a man, one giant leap for mankind." Armstrong and Aldrin collected rock samples and conducted scientific experiments. In this photo, Aldrin appears with a flag that had to be stretched on supports because the moon is windless.

NASA/Johnson Space Center.

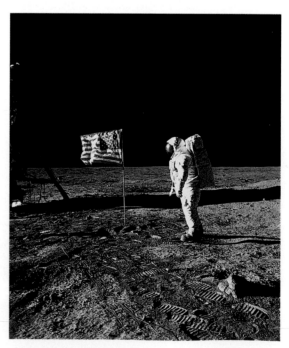

Kennedy used the Berlin crisis to add $3.2 billion to the defense budget and to expand the military by 300,000 troops. This buildup of conventional forces met Kennedy's demand for "a wider choice than humiliation or all-out nuclear action" by providing a "flexible reponse" strategy. When the Soviet Union terminated its three-year moratorium on nuclear testing, the United States followed suit and vigorously developed new weapons and delivery systems.

New Approaches to the Third World

The Kennedy administration sought to complement its hard-line policy toward the Soviet Union with fresh approaches to the independence movements that had convulsed the world since the end of World War II. In 1960 alone, seventeen African nations gained their independence. Much more than his predecessors, the president publicly supported third world **democratic** and **nationalist** aspirations, believing that the United States could win over developing nations by helping to fulfill hopes for independence and democracy. To that end, Kennedy created the Alliance for Progress, promising $20 billion in aid for Latin America over the next decade. Like the Marshall Plan, the Alliance for Progress was designed to thwart communism and hold nations within the American sphere by fostering economic development. Likewise, the new Agency for International Development (AID) emphasized economic aid over military aid in foreign assistance programs.

In 1961, Kennedy launched his most dramatic third world initiative: the Peace Corps. Exemplifying the personal sacrifice summoned by Kennedy in his inaugural address, the program attracted idealistic volunteers, such as one who expressed his discomfort at having been "born between clean sheets when others were issued into the dust with a birthright of hunger." After studying a country's language and culture, Peace Corps volunteers went to work directly with its people, opening schools, providing basic health care, and assisting with agriculture, nutrition, and small economic enterprises. By the mid-1970s, more than 60,000 volunteers had fanned out around the globe, serving two-year stints in Latin America, Africa, and Asia.

Nevertheless, Kennedy's foreign aid initiatives fell far short of their objectives. Though generally welcomed, Peace Corps projects numbered too few to make a dent in the poverty and suffering in third world countries. By 1969, the

Peace Corps Volunteers in Bolivia
The majority of Peace Corps volunteers worked on educational projects in developing countries. Others helped increase food production, build public works, and curb diseases, as did these volunteers, Rita Helmkamp and Ed Dennison, vaccinating a young Bolivian girl. President John F. Kennedy saw the Peace Corps volunteers, with their dedication to freedom, "overcoming the efforts of Mr. Khrushchev's missionaries who are dedicated to undermining that freedom." In the course of their missions, however, some volunteers came to question the single-minded focus of U.S. policy on anticommunism.
David S. Boyer © National Geographic Society.

United States had provided only half of the $20 billion promised to the Alliance for Progress, and much of that funded military projects or was skimmed off by corrupt ruling elites. In addition, a soaring birthrate in Latin America counteracted economic gains, and these nations increasingly bore heavy foreign debt.

Kennedy also reverted to direct military means to bring political stability to the third world. Although he supported popular movements' efforts to gain independence and better living conditions, he drew the line at uprisings that appeared to have Communist connections or goals. Even though a growing split between the Soviet Union and Communist China suggested otherwise, Kennedy clung to the basic cold war tenet: Communism was a monolithic force and had to be contained, no matter what form it took.

To that end, he promoted counterinsurgency forces to put down insurrections that smacked of communism. The showcase of the administration's counterinsurgency strategy was an elite military corps trained to wage guerrilla warfare. Called "special forces," the corps had been established under Eisenhower to aid groups sympathetic to the United States and opposed to Communist-leaning national liberation movements. Kennedy rapidly expanded the special forces, called them the Green Berets (after their official headgear), and equipped them with the latest technology.

The Arms Race and the Nuclear Brink

The final piece of Kennedy's defense strategy was to strengthen American nuclear superiority over the Soviet Union. This drive for nuclear dominance increased the number of U.S. nuclear weapons based in Europe from 2,500 to 7,200 and multiplied fivefold the supply of intercontinental ballistic missiles (ICBMs). Concerned that this buildup would enable the United States to launch a first strike and wipe out Soviet missile sites before the Soviets could respond, the Kremlin stepped up its own ICBM program. Thus began the most intense arms race in history.

The superpowers came perilously close to using their weapons of terror in 1962, when Khrushchev decided to install nuclear missiles in Cuba, probably intending to get the United States to withdraw from Berlin in exchange for the Soviets withdrawing the missiles from Cuba. On October 16, the CIA showed Kennedy aerial photographs of launching sites under construction in Cuba for missiles with ranges of 1,000 and 2,200 miles. Considering this an intolerable threat to the United States, the president met daily in secret with a small group of advisers to manage the ensuing thirteen-day Cuban missile crisis. On October 22, he told a television audience that he had placed the military on full alert and was imposing a "strict quarantine on all offensive military equipment" headed from the Soviet Union to Cuba. The U.S. navy would turn back any Soviet vessel suspected of carrying offensive missiles to Cuba. (Only later did the United States find out that offensive missiles were already there.) Kennedy warned Khrushchev that any attack launched from Cuba would trigger a full nuclear assault against the Soviet Union. The number of bomb shelters Americans built leaped during those tense days.

Projecting the appearance of toughness was paramount to Kennedy, who called the missiles an "unjustified change in the status quo which cannot be accepted . . . if our courage and our commitments are ever to be trusted again by either friend or foe." According to his speechwriter, Theodore Sorensen, although the missiles did not "alter the strategic balance in fact . . . that balance would have been substantially altered in appearance; and in matters of national will and world leadership such appearances contribute to reality." But if Kennedy was willing to risk nuclear war for appearances, he also exercised caution. He refused advice from the military to bomb the missile sites and instead ordered the quarantine to allow time for negotiations. On October 24, some of the Russian ships carrying nuclear warheads toward Cuba suddenly turned back. Kennedy matched Khrushchev's restraint. When one ship crossed the blockade line, he ordered the navy to follow it rather than attempt to stop it. "We don't want to push him [Khrushchev] to a precipitous action," he said.

While Americans experienced the cold war's most fearful days, Kennedy and Khrushchev exchanged offers and counteroffers. Finally, the Soviets removed the missiles and pledged not to

Cuban Missile Crisis, 1962

- U.S. blockade zone
- Range of Soviet missiles
- Soviet missile and jet bomber bases

Preparing for the Worst during the Cuban Missile Crisis

Waiting out the tense days after President Kennedy issued the ultimatum to the Soviet Union to halt shipments of missile materials to Cuba, many Americans tried to prepare for the worst possible outcome. Owners of Chalet Suzanne, a hotel in Lake Wales, Florida, canned several thousand cases of well water, labeled NASK for Nuclear Attack Survival Kit. Courtesy Chalet Suzanne Foods, Inc., Lake Wales, Florida. Photo by David Woods.

introduce new offensive weapons into Cuba. The United States promised not to invade the island. Secretly, Kennedy also agreed to remove U.S. missiles based in Turkey and aimed at the Soviet Union.

In miscalculating Kennedy's resolution, the Soviets lost ground in their contest with China for the allegiance of third world countries, and the missile crisis contributed to Khrushchev's fall from power two years later. Kennedy emerged triumphant. The image of an inexperienced president fumbling the Bay of Pigs invasion and being bullied by Khrushchev in Vienna gave way to that of a brilliant leader combining firmness with restraint, bearing the United States through its "hour of maximum danger."

Having proved his toughness, Kennedy could afford to be conciliatory. After the Cuban missile crisis, Kennedy acted to prevent future confrontations. He and Khrushchev installed a special telephone "hot line" to speed top-level communication at critical moments. In a major speech at American University in June 1963, Kennedy called for a reexamination of cold war assumptions, asking Americans "not to see conflict as inevitable." Acknowledging the superpowers' immense differences, Kennedy stressed what they had in common: "We all inhabit this small planet. We all breathe the same air. We all cherish our children's future and we are all mortal."

Responding to pressures from scientists and other Americans alarmed by the dangers of nuclear weapons, Kennedy also called for an end to "a vicious cycle" in which "new weapons beget counterweapons." In August 1963, the United States, the Soviet Union, and Great Britain signed a limited test ban treaty. Because France and China refused to sign, the agreement failed to stop the proliferation of nuclear weapons. Nonetheless, it reduced the threat of radioactive fallout from nuclear testing and raised hopes for superpower accord on other issues.

Venturing into a Quagmire in Vietnam

The new approach that Kennedy outlined at American University did not mean abandoning South Vietnam to communism. He had criticized the idea of "a Pax Americana enforced on the world by American weapons of war," but he increased the flow of those weapons into South Vietnam. His early foreign policy setbacks suggested the need to make a strong stand somewhere, and he also remembered the political

blows to the Democratic Party when China was "lost" in 1949.

Kennedy's strong anticommunism, his interpretation of the lessons of history, and his commitment to an activist foreign policy prepared him to take a stand in Vietnam. The new counterinsurgency program provided the means. Kennedy's key military adviser, General Maxwell

U.S. Involvement in Vietnam

1954	**May** French colonial presence ends with Vietnamese victory at Dien Bien Phu.
	July Geneva accords establish temporary division of North and South Vietnam at the seventeenth parallel and provide for free elections.
	September United States joins with European, East Asian, and other nations to form the Southeast Asia Treaty Organization (SEATO).
	Eisenhower administration begins to send weapons and military advisers to South Vietnam to bolster Diem government.
1955–1961	United States sends $8 million in aid to South Vietnamese army (ARVN) to support its struggle with North Vietnamese government.
1961–1963	Under Kennedy administration, military aid to South Vietnam doubles, and number of military advisers reaches 9,000.
1963	South Vietnamese military overthrows Diem's government.
1964	President Johnson uses Gulf of Tonkin incident to escalate the war.
1965	Johnson administration initiates Operation Rolling Thunder, intensifies bombing of North Vietnam.
1965–1967	Number of U.S. troops in Vietnam increases, reaching 543,000 in 1968, but U.S. and ARVN forces make only limited progress against the guerrilla forces, resulting in a stalemate.
1968	**January 30** Tet Offensive causes widespread destruction and heavy casualties.
	March 31 Johnson announces reduction in bombing of North Vietnam, plans for peace talks, and his decision not to run for another presidential term.
1969	Nixon administration initiates secret bombing of Cambodia, increases bombing of the North while reducing U.S. troops in the South, and pursues peace talks.
1970	Nixon orders joint U.S.- ARVN invasion of Cambodia.
1970–1971	U.S. troops in Vietnam decrease from 334,600 to 140,000.
1972	With peace talks stalled in December, Nixon administration orders the most devastating bombing of North Vietnam that would occur throughout the conflict.
1973	On January 27, the United States, North Vietnam, and South Vietnam sign formal accord in Paris marking end of U.S. involvement.
1975	North Vietnam launches a new offensive in South Vietnam, defeating ARVN. Vietcong troops occupy Saigon and rename it Ho Chi Minh City.

Taylor, thought that Vietnam would be a good testing ground for the Green Berets. Holding firm in Vietnam would show the Soviets that sponsoring wars of national liberation would be "costly, dangerous, and doomed to failure."

Two major problems, however, undercut Taylor's analysis. First, the South Vietnamese insurgents—called Vietcong, short for *Vietnam Cong-san* ("Vietnamese Communists"), by the Americans—were an indigenous force whose initiative came from within, not from the Soviet Union or China. Even Ho Chi Minh's Communist government in North Vietnam did not supply weapons or soldiers to the rebels in the south until 1959, after those rebels had initiated guerrilla activities against the South Vietnamese government on their own. Because the Saigon government refused to hold the elections promised in the Geneva accords and was determined to exterminate its opponents, the rebels saw no choice but to take up arms.

The second problem lay in the South Vietnamese government and army (the Army of the Republic of Vietnam, or ARVN), which proved to be ineffective at containing communism. Ngo Dinh Diem, South Vietnamese premier from 1954 to 1963, chose self-serving military leaders merely for their personal loyalty. The government's corruption and repression of opponents alienated many South Vietnamese, not just the Communists.

Intervention by North Vietnam made matters worse. In 1960, the Hanoi government established the National Liberation Front (NLF), composed of South Vietnamese rebels but directed by the northern army. In addition, Hanoi constructed a network of infiltration routes (called the "Ho Chi Minh Trail") in neighboring Laos and Cambodia, through which it sent people and supplies to help liberate the south (Map 29.2). Violence escalated between 1960 and 1963, bringing the Saigon government close to collapse.

When Kennedy took office, more than $1 billion of aid and seven hundred U.S. military advisers had failed to stabilize South Vietnam. He resisted pressure from some advisers for an all-out effort, but he began to escalate the American

MAP 29.2   The Vietnam War, 1964–1975

The United States sent more than two million soldiers to Vietnam and spent more than $150 billion on the longest war in American history, but it was unable to prevent the unification of Vietnam under a Communist government.

READING THE MAP: What accord divided Vietnam into two nations? When was it signed, and where was the line of division drawn? Through what countries did the Ho Chi Minh Trail go?

CONNECTIONS: What was the Gulf of Tonkin incident, and how did the United States respond? What was the Tet Offensive, and how did it affect the war?

FOR MORE HELP ANALYZING THIS MAP, see the map activity for this chapter in the Online Study Guide at bedfordstmartins.com/roark.

commitment. At the same time he worried that each step was "like taking a drink. . . . The effect wears off, and you have to take another." By spring 1963, military aid doubled, and the nine thousand Americans who were serving in Vietnam as military advisers occasionally participated in actual combat. Although the United States extracted new promises of reform from Diem, the South Vietnamese government never made good on them.

American officials assumed that the military's superior technology and sheer power could stem the Communist tide in South Vietnam. Yet advanced weapons were ill suited to the guerrilla warfare practiced by the enemy, who launched on U.S. and ARVN forces sporadic surprise attacks that were designed to weaken support for the South Vietnamese government rather than to gain territory. In addition, U.S. weapons and strategy harmed the very people they were intended to save. Thousands of peasants were uprooted and resettled in "strategic hamlets" supposedly secure from the Communists. Those left in the countryside fell victim to bombs—containing the highly flammable substance napalm—dropped by the U.S.-backed ARVN in an effort to quell the Vietcong. In January 1962, U.S. planes began to spray herbicides to destroy the Vietcong's jungle hideouts and food supply.

South Vietnamese military leaders effected a coup on November 2, 1963, brutally executing Premier Diem and his brother who headed the secret police. Although shocked by the killings, Kennedy indicated no change in policy. In a speech to be given on the day he was assassinated, Kennedy called Americans to their responsibilities as "the watchmen on the walls of world freedom." Referring specifically to Southeast Asia, his undelivered speech warned, "We dare not weary of the task." At his death, 16,000 Americans had served in Vietnam and 100 had died there.

Lyndon Johnson's War against Communism

The cold war assumptions that shaped Kennedy's foreign policy underlay the new president's approach to Southeast Asia and Latin America as well. Retaining Kennedy's key advisers, Lyndon Johnson continued his massive buildup of nuclear weapons and conventional and counter-

insurgency forces. In 1965, when the South Vietnamese government approached collapse, Johnson made the fateful decisions to order U.S. troops into combat and initiate sustained bombing of the north. That same year, Johnson sent U.S. marines to the Dominican Republic to crush a leftist rebellion.

Toward an All-Out Commitment in Vietnam

Having sent more military advisers, weapons, and economic aid to South Vietnam during his first year as president, in August 1964 Lyndon Johnson seized an opportunity to increase the pressure on North Vietnam. American ships routinely engaged in espionage in the Gulf of Tonkin off the coast of North Vietnam, and two U.S. destroyers reported that North Vietnamese gunboats had fired on them on August 2 and 4 (see Map 29.2). Johnson quickly ordered air strikes on North Vietnamese torpedo bases and oil storage facilities, and he sought authority from Congress to take "all necessary measures to repel any armed attacks against the forces of the United States and to prevent further aggression." His portrayal of the situation was at best misleading, revealing neither the uncertainty about whether the second attack had even occurred nor the provocative U.S. actions (staging covert raids and operating close to the North Vietnamese coast). Congress supported Johnson's plan by passing the Gulf of Tonkin Resolution on August 7, 1964, with just two senators voting no.

> In 1965, when the South Vietnamese government approached collapse, Johnson made the fateful decisions to order U.S. troops into combat and initiate sustained bombing of the north.

Johnson's tough stance only two months before the 1964 elections helped counter the charges made by his opponent, Arizona's Senator Barry Goldwater, that he was "soft on communism." Yet the president also presented himself as the peace candidate. When Goldwater proposed massive bombing of North Vietnam, Johnson assured Americans that "we are not going to send American boys nine or ten thousand miles away from home to do what Asian boys ought to be doing for themselves."

Soon after winning reelection, however, Johnson did widen the war. He rejected peace overtures from North Vietnam, which insisted on American withdrawal and a coalition government in South Vietnam as steps toward ultimate

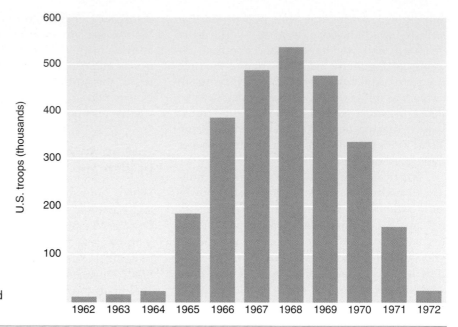

FIGURE 29.1 U.S. Troops in Vietnam, 1962–1972
The steepest increases in the American military presence in Vietnam came in 1965 and 1966. Although troop levels declined in 1971 and 1972, the United States continued massive bombing attacks.

unification of the country. Instead he accepted the advice of Secretary of Defense Robert S. McNamara and other officials to begin a bombing campaign against the North. Operation Rolling Thunder, a strategy of gradually intensified bombing of North Vietnam, began in February 1965. Less than a month later, the first U.S. combat troops landed near Da Nang, South Vietnam. In July, Johnson shifted U.S. troops from defensive to offensive operations and authorized the dispatch of 50,000 more soldiers (Figure 29.1). Those decisions, whose import was downplayed for Congress and the public, marked a critical turning point. Now it was genuinely America's war.

Preventing Another Castro in Latin America

Closer to home, Johnson faced perpetual problems in Latin America despite the efforts of the Alliance for Progress. Thirteen times during the 1960s, military coups toppled Latin American governments, and local insurgencies grew apace. The administration's response to such turmoil varied from case to case but centered on the determination to prevent any more Castro-type revolutions.

In 1964, riots erupted in the Panama Canal Zone, which the United States had seized and made a U.S. territory early in the century.

> Johnson's Latin American policy generated new cries of "Yankee imperialism."

Instigated by Panamanian nationalists who viewed the United States as a colonial power, the riots left four U.S. soldiers and more than twenty Panamanians dead. Johnson sent troops to quell the disturbance, but he also initiated negotiations that eventually led to Panamanian authority over the canal in 2000.

Meanwhile, Johnson's Latin American policy generated new cries of "Yankee imperialism," an ongoing complaint about U.S. interference in the region. In 1961, voters in the Dominican Republic ousted a longstanding dictator and elected a constitutional government headed by Juan Bosch, who was overthrown by a military coup two years later. In 1965, when Bosch supporters rallied in an uprising against the military government, Johnson sent more than 20,000 soldiers to take control of the island. After a truce was arranged, Dominicans voted in a constitutional government under a moderate rightist in 1966.

This first outright show of Yankee force in Latin America in forty years damaged the administration at home and abroad. Although the administration had justified intervention on the grounds that Communists were among the rebels, it quickly became clear that they had played no significant role, and U.S. intervention kept the reform-oriented Boschists from returning to power. Moreover, the president had not consulted the Dominicans or the Organization of American States (OAS), to which the United States had pledged to respect national sovereignty in Latin America. Once the troops had landed in the Dominican Republic, Johnson asked for approval from the OAS, but Mexico, Chile, Venezuela, and other nations refused to grant it.

The Americanized War

The apparent success in the Dominican Republic no doubt encouraged the president to press on in Vietnam. From Operation Rolling Thunder in 1965 to early 1968, the United States gradually escalated attacks against the North Vietnamese and their Vietcong allies, endeavoring to break their will while avoiding provoking intervention by the Chinese, as they had done in Korea. Johnson himself scrutinized military plans, boasting, "They can't even bomb an outhouse without my approval."

Over the course of the war, U.S. pilots dropped 3.2 million tons of explosives, more than the United States had launched in all of World War II. Claiming monthly death tolls of more than 2,000 North Vietnamese, the intensive bombing nonetheless failed to dampen the Hanoi government's commitment. (See "Historical Question," page 1078.) In the South, the United States rained down more than twice the tonnage of bombs dropped on North Vietnam.

Because there was no battlefront as in previous wars, General William Westmoreland's strategy of attrition was designed to search out and kill the Vietcong and North Vietnamese regular army. The military used helicopters extensively to conduct offensives all over South Vietnam. (See "The Promise of Technology," page 1082.) Officials calculated progress not in territory seized but in "body counts" and "kill ratios" — the number of enemies killed relative to the cost in American and ARVN lives. According to U.S. army officer Colin Powell, who served in Vietnam in 1962 and again in 1968–69, "The Army desperately needed something to measure. What military objectives could we claim in this week's report? A hill? A valley? A hamlet? Rarely. Consequently, bodies became the measure." In this situation, American soldiers did not always distinguish between military combatants and civilians; according to Lieutenant Philip Caputo, the operating rule was "if it's dead and Vietnamese, it's VC [Vietcong]." A helicopter pilot summed up the attrition strategy when, after a brutal battle, his comrade asked, "What did we win? We don't have any more real estate, no new villages are under American control, and

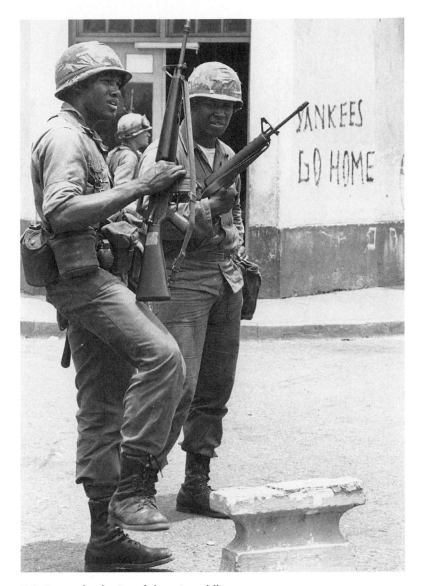

U.S. Troops in the Dominican Republic
These U.S. paratroopers were among the 20,000 troops sent to the Dominican Republic in April and May 1965. The American invasion helped restore peace but kept the popularly elected government of Juan Bosch from regaining office. Dominicans expressed their outrage in anti-American slogans that greeted troops throughout the capital, Santo Domingo. Bosch himself said, "This was a democratic revolution smashed by the leading democracy in the world."
© Bettmann/Corbis.

it took everything we had to stop them." The pilot responded, "More of them got killed than us. It's that simple."

In contrast to World War II, when the average soldier was twenty-six years old, teenagers fought the Vietnam War. Until the Twenty-sixth Amendment reduced the voting age from twenty-one to eighteen in 1971, most soldiers, whose average age was nineteen, could not even

Why Couldn't the United States Bomb Its Way to Victory in Vietnam?

World War II demonstrated the critical importance of airpower in modern war. According to the official U.S. study of strategic bombing during World War II, "No nation can long survive the free exploitation of air weapons over its homeland." In the Vietnam War, U.S. planes delivered even more explosives than they had in World War II. Why, then, did strategic bombing not bring victory in Vietnam?

"Our airpower did not fail us; it was the decision makers," asserted Admiral U. S. Grant Sharp, World War II veteran and commander in chief of the Pacific Command during the Vietnam War. Military officials welcomed President Johnson's order to begin bombing North Vietnam in February 1965 as a means to destroy the North's capacity and will to support the Communist insurgents in South Vietnam. But they chafed at Johnson's strategy of gradual escalation and the restrictions he imposed on Operation Rolling Thunder, the three-and-a-half-year bombing campaign. Military officials believed that the United States should have begun Operation Rolling Thunder with all-out massive bombing and continued until the devastation brought North Vietnam to its knees. Instead, they charged, civilian decision makers compelled the military to fight with

one hand tied behind its back. Their arguments echoed General Douglas MacArthur's criticism of Truman's policy during the Korean War—though these officials did not repeat MacArthur's insubordination.

Unlike military officials, who could single-mindedly focus on defeating the enemy, the president needed to balance military objectives against political considerations and found compelling reasons to limit the application of airpower. Recalling the Korean War, Johnson noted that "China is there on the [North Vietnamese] border with 700 million men," and he studiously avoided action that might provoke intervention by the Chinese, who now possessed nuclear weapons. Johnson's strategy also aimed to keep the Soviet Union out of the war, to avoid inflaming antiwar sentiment at home, and to avert international criticism of the United States.

Consequently, the president would not permit bombing of areas where high civilian casualties might result and areas near the Chinese border. He banned strikes on airfields and missile sites that were under construction and thus likely to contain Chinese or Soviet advisers, and he refused to mine North Vietnam's harbors, through which Soviet ships imported goods to North Vietnam. But Johnson did es-

calate the pressure, increasing the intensity of the bombing fourfold by 1968. In all, Operation Rolling Thunder rained 643,000 tons of bombs on North Vietnam between 1965 and 1968.

Military leaders agreed with Johnson's desire to spare civilians. The Joint Chiefs of Staff never proposed, for example, strikes against a system of dikes and dams that could have disrupted food production and flooded Hanoi under twenty feet of water. Rather, they focused on destroying North Vietnam's industry and transportation system. Noncombatant casualties in North Vietnam contrasted sharply with those in World War II, when Anglo-American bombing of Dresden, Germany, alone took more than 35,000 civilian lives and the fire-bombing of Japan caused 330,000 civilian deaths. In three and a half years, Operation Rolling Thunder's bombing claimed an estimated 52,000 civilian lives.

The relatively low level of economic development in North Vietnam and the North Vietnamese government's ability to mobilize its citizens counteracted the military superiority of the United States. Sheer man-, woman-, and child-power compensated for the demolition of transportation sources, industry sites, and electric power plants. When bombs struck a rail line, civilians rushed with bicycles to unload a train's cargo, carry it beyond the break, and load it onto a second train. Three hundred thousand full-time workers and 200,000 farmers labored in their spare time to keep the Ho Chi Minh Trail usable in spite of heavy bombing. When bridges were destroyed, the North Vietnamese resorted to ferries and pontoons made from bamboo, and they rebuilt bridges slightly

The B-52 Bomber

After 1965, B-52 bombers constantly filled the skies over Vietnam, and at times over Laos and Cambodia. Designed originally to deliver nuclear bombs, a single B-52 carried thirty tons of explosives. A mission of six planes could destroy an area one-half mile wide by three miles long. The B-52 flew too high to be heard on the ground, but its bombs hit with such force that they could kill people in underground shelters.

Co Rentmeester, *Life* magazine / TimePix / Getty.

substantially curtailed the effect of Operation Rolling Thunder, and the Soviet-installed modern defense systems made the bombing more difficult and dangerous for U.S. pilots.

In July 1969, Seventh Air Force commander General William W. Momyer commented on Operation Rolling Thunder to the retiring air force chief of staff: "We had the force, skill, and intelligence, but our civilian betters wouldn't turn us loose." Johnson refused to turn the military loose because in addition to the goal he shared with the military—breaking Hanoi's ability to support insurgency in the South—he also wanted to keep China and the Soviet Union (and nuclear weapons) out of the war and to contain domestic and international criticism of U.S. policy. Whether a more devastating air war would have provoked Chinese or Soviet intervention can never be known.

Nor can we know whether all-out bombing of the North could have guaranteed an independent non-Communist government in the South. We do know that Johnson's military advisers imposed their own restraints, never recommending the wholesale attacks on civilians that took place in World War II. Short of decimating the civilian population, it is questionable whether more intense bombing could have completely halted North Vietnamese support for the Vietcong, given the nature of the North Vietnamese economy, the determination and ingenuity of its people, and the plentiful assistance from China and the Soviet Union. Whether the strategic bombing that worked so well in a world war against major industrial powers could be effective in a third world guerrilla war remained in doubt after the Vietnam War.

underwater to make them harder to detect from the air. They dispersed oil storage facilities and production centers throughout the countryside, and when bombs knocked out electric power plants, the Vietnamese turned to more than two thousand portable generators and used oil lamps and candles in their homes.

North Vietnam's military needs were relatively small, and officials found ample means to meet them. In 1967, North Vietnam had only about 55,000 soldiers in South Vietnam, and because they waged a guerrilla war with only sporadic fighting, the insurgents in the South did not require huge amounts of supplies.

Even after Communist forces in the South increased, the total nonfood needs of these soldiers were estimated at just one-fifth of what a single U.S. division required. What U.S. bombs destroyed, the North Vietnamese replaced with Chinese and Soviet imports. China provided 600,000 tons of rice in 1967 alone, and it supplied small arms and ammunition, vehicles, and other goods throughout the war. Competing with China for influence in North Vietnam and favor in the third world, the Soviets contributed tanks, fighter planes, surface-to-air missiles, and other sophisticated weapons. An estimated $2 billion of foreign aid vote for the officials who sent them to war. Men of all classes had fought World War II, but Vietnam was the war of the poor and working class, who constituted about 80 percent of the troops. More privileged youth found ways to avoid the **draft**, usually through college deferments or by using family connections to get into the National Guard. Sent from Plainville, Kansas, to Vietnam in 1965, Mike Clodfelter could not recall "a single middle-class son of the town's businessmen, lawyers, doctors, or ranchers from my high school graduating class who experienced the Armageddon of our generation."

> Men of all classes had fought World War II, but Vietnam was the war of the poor and working class, who constituted about 80 percent of the troops.

Much more than World War II, the Vietnam War was a men's war; women's share of all military personnel during the Vietnam era was just half what it was during World War II. The United States did not undergo full mobilization for the war in Vietnam; consequently, officials did not seek women's sacrifices for the war effort. In response to a journalist who said that some military women were distressed because they had not been called to serve in Vietnam, President Johnson joked, "Well there is always a chance of anything taking place when our women are sufficiently distressed," and the reporters guffawed. Still, estimates of 7,500 to 10,000 women served in Vietnam, the vast majority of them nurses. Although women were not allowed to carry weapons, they did come under enemy fire, and eight lost their lives. Most difficult for most of the women was their helplessness in the face of the dead and maimed bodies they tended. "When you finally saved a life," said Peggy DuVall, "you wondered what kind of life you had saved."

Early in the war, African Americans constituted 31 percent of combat troops, often choosing the military over the meager opportunities in the civilian economy. Special forces ranger Arthur E. Woodley Jr. believed, "I was just what my country needed. A black patriot. . . . The only way I could possibly make it out of the ghetto was to be the best soldier I possibly could." Death rates among black soldiers were disproportionately high until 1966, when the military adjusted personnel assignments to produce a more racially balanced distribution of sacrifice.

The young American troops faced extremely difficult conditions. Soldiers fought in thick jungles and swamps filled with leeches, in oppressive heat, rain, and humidity. Lieutenant Caputo remembered "weeks of expectant waiting and, at random intervals, conducting vicious manhunts through jungles and swamps where snipers harassed us constantly and booby traps cut us down one by one." Soldiers in previous wars had served "for the duration," but Vietnam warriors had one-year tours of duty; a commander called it "the worst personnel policy in history," because men had less incentive

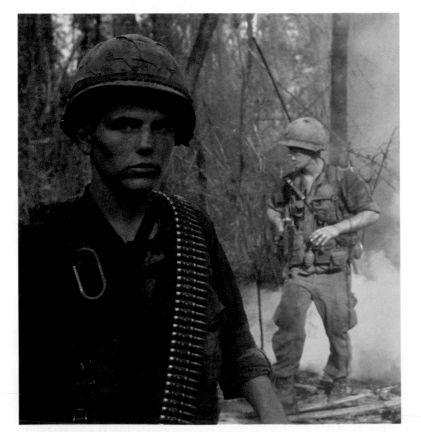

Vietnam: The War of the Young
The faces of these soldiers in the jungle near Hue in 1968 reflect the youth of the soldiers who fought the Vietnam War, in which the average age was nineteen. When one young marine received his supplies, he wondered "What did I need with shaving equipment? I was only seventeen. I didn't have hair under my *arms*, let alone my face." The youth of the soldiers intensified the emotional trauma felt by the military nurses who cared for them. One nurse remembered a dying soldier "in so much pain and so scared, asking for his mom." Another sobbed over a snapshot that fell out of a dying soldier's pocket: "It is a picture of the soldier and his girl—dressed for a prom." Kyoichi Savada/Corbis.

to fight near the end of their tour, wanting merely to stay alive and whole. The U.S. military inflicted great losses on the enemy, estimated at more than 200,000 by the end of 1967. Yet it could claim no more than a stalemate. In the words of infantryman Tim O'Brien, who later became an award-winning author, "We slay one of them, hit a mine, kill another, hit another mine. . . . And each piece of ground left behind is his [the enemy's] from the moment we are gone on our next hunt."

The South Vietnamese government itself was an obstacle to victory. After a series of coups and short-lived regimes, in 1965 the government settled into a period of stability led by Air Marshal Nguyen Cao Ky and General Nguyen Van Thieu. But graft and corruption continued to flourish, and Ky and Thieu failed to rally popular support. In the intensified fighting and inability to distinguish friend from foe, thousands of South Vietnamese civilians were killed and wounded, their farms and villages bombed and burned. By 1968, five million people, nearly 30 percent of the population, had become refugees. Huge infusions of American dollars and goods produced rampant inflation, hurt local industries, and increased dependence on foreign aid.

Johnson's decisions that Americanized the war flowed logically from the commitments of three presidents before him. All the same, 1965 marked a critical turning point: The rationale for involvement in the war shifted from the need to contain communism in Southeast Asia to the need to prove to the world the ability of the United States to make good on its commitments.

A Nation Polarized

Soon President Johnson was fighting a war on two fronts. Domestic opposition to the war grew significantly after 1965, and the United States experienced internal conflict unparalleled since the Civil War. Television brought the carnage of Vietnam into American homes day after day, making it the first "living-room war." Torn between his domestic critics and the military's clamor for more troops, in March 1968 Johnson announced restrictions on the bombing, a new

effort at negotiations, and his decision not to pursue reelection. Throughout 1968, demonstrations, violence, and assassinations convulsed the nation. Vietnam took center stage in the election, and voters narrowly favored the Republican candidate, former vice president Richard Nixon, who promised to "bring Americans together again" and to achieve "peace with honor."

The Widening War at Home

Before 1965, American actions in Vietnam evoked little domestic criticism. But Johnson's authorization of Operation Rolling Thunder sparked a mass movement against the war. In April 1965, Students for a Democratic Society (SDS) recruited 20,000 people for the first major protest, a rally in Washington, D.C., and SDS chapters sprang up on more than 300 college campuses across the country. Thousands of young people joined campus protests against Reserve Officers Training Corps (ROTC) programs, CIA recruiters, manufacturers of war materials, and university departments that conducted research for the Department of Defense. In 1967, Martin Luther King Jr. rebuked his government as "the greatest purveyor of violence in the world today," calling opposition to the war "the privilege and burden of all of us who deem ourselves bound by allegiances and loyalties which are broader and deeper than nationalism." Environmentalists attacked the use of chemical weapons, such as the deadly dioxin-product Agent Orange that the military was raining on Vietnam to destroy foliage where the enemy might hide. A new draft policy in 1967 ended deferments for postgraduate education and upped male students' stake in ending the war. In the spring of 1968, as many as one million college and high school students participated in a nationwide strike.

Antiwar sentiment also entered society's mainstream. The *New York Times* began questioning administration policy in 1965, and by 1968 media critics included the *Wall Street Journal, Life* magazine, and popular TV journalist Walter Cronkite. Clergy, businesspeople, scientists, and physicians formed their own groups to pressure Johnson to stop the bombing and start negotiations. Though most of organized labor supported the president, some union members joined the peace movement.

> Domestic opposition to the war grew significantly after 1965, and the United States experienced internal conflict unparalleled since the Civil War.

The Military Helicopter

Reflecting on how the Vietnam War would have been fought without helicopters, General William C. Westmoreland concluded, "We would have been fighting a different war, for a smaller area, at a greater cost, with less effectiveness." Waging war in Vietnam without helicopters, he maintained, would have been like fighting Hitler's army in Europe without tanks.

It took more than three decades after the first successful airplane flight for engineers to develop an aircraft that could take off and land vertically, move in any direction, and remain stationary in the air. The man frequently identified as the inventor of the helicopter in the United States, Russian engineer Igor Sikorsky, developed two helicopters in 1909 and 1910, but neither succeeded. After the Russian Revolution of 1917, Sikorsky emigrated to the United States and organized a company that produced airplanes while he continued to work on the helicopter. German engineers produced the first practical helicopter in 1936, but the United States was not far behind.

As was true of much new technology in the twentieth century, federal dollars supported research and development. In 1938, Congress first appropriated funds to develop the helicopter, and Sikorsky and his associates produced the first helicopter for the Army Air Corps in 1942. During World War II, the United States used helicopters for some rescue operations in the Pacific theater, and Germany used them for artillery spotting and reconnaissance. The American military employed helicopters for medical evacuations in Korea, but not until manufacturers replaced piston engines with smaller, lighter gas-turbine engines did helicopters play a central role in military operations.

Although the army developed its plans for the use of helicopters in the 1950s within the context of nuclear warfare, once the United States began to assist with military operations of the South Vietnamese, the helicopter became a central feature of the war. The particular nature of the conflict in Vietnam—the guerrilla tactics of the enemy, the conduct of fighting all over South Vietnam rather than across a fixed battlefront, and the mountains and dense jungles, with limited landing areas—put a premium on the helicopter's mobility and maneuverability. Already in December 1961, long before U.S. troops actually saw combat in Vietnam, the army employed thirty-two of its helicopters to transfer some one thousand South Vietnamese paratroopers for an attack on suspected Vietcong headquarters. To U.S. army captain Colin Powell serving as an adviser to a South Vietnamese army battalion in a remote spot near the Laotian border in 1962, the helicopter "became my closest link to the world I had left." One piloted by a U.S. marine came every two weeks, and at those times, Powell remembered, "my anticipation was almost sexual. This flier brought my latest batch of paperbacks, my carton of Salems, and my mail."

The UH-1 Iroquois (known as "Huey") was the most widely used helicopter; thousands of them carried infantry units all over South Vietnam. One marine commented that "we commuted to and from the war," though it was hardly an ordinary commute when helicopters had to land in the midst of enemy fire. Choppers also transported artillery and ammunition, performed reconnaissance, picked up downed pilots, and evacuated the dead and wounded. Mounted with machine guns and grenade launchers, helicopters served as attack vehicles. The largest, the CH-47 ("Chinook"), could carry thirty-three soldiers or considerable amounts of cargo and even rescue smaller downed aircraft. Chinooks also dropped two and a

Increasing numbers of prominent Democratic senators, including J. William Fulbright, George McGovern, and majority leader Mike Mansfield, urged Johnson to substitute negotiation for force. Fulbright's book, *The Arrogance of Power*, warned against "the tendency of great nations to equate power with virtue" and urged American leaders not to think of the country as "God's chosen saviour of mankind."

Opposition to the war took diverse forms: letter-writing campaigns to officials, teach-ins on college campuses, mass marches, student strikes, withholding of federal taxes, draft card burnings, civil disobedience against military centers and producers of war materials, and attempts to stop trains carrying troops. Although the peace movement never claimed a majority of the population, it focused media attention on the war

Helicopters in Vietnam

This helicopter brings ammunition in 1968 to U.S. soldiers in Khe Sanh, in the far northwest region of South Vietnam. Before and during the Tet Offensive, thousands of North Vietnamese forces surrounded and shelled the garrison of six thousand marines, making the ability to supply Khe Sanh from helicopters essential. This photo was taken by Larry Burrows, who died three years later during the invasion of Laos. The helicopter in which he and three other well-known combat photographers were traveling exploded after being hit by a North Vietnamese antiaircraft gun.

Photograph by Larry Burrows, LIFE © Time, Inc., 1968.

dead to 6:1, in contrast to a World War II ratio of 2.6:1. So central were helicopters to a soldier's experience that, one man noted, "When the helicopters flew off, a feeling of abandonment came over us."

Journalists hitched rides on helicopters "like taxis" to see the war firsthand. Michael Herr, who wrote for *Esquire* and other magazines, flew on hundreds of them, remembering "choppers rising straight out of small cleared jungle spaces, wobbling down onto city rooftops, cartons of rations and ammunition thrown off, dead and wounded loaded on. Sometimes they were so plentiful and loose that you could touch down at five or six places a day."

The massive use of helicopters, of course, failed to defeat the enemy in Vietnam. Although air mobility played a key role in the successes that the United States and South Vietnamese armies did achieve, it could not win the war alone. In the words of one military adviser, "After all, when you come to think of it, the use of helicopters is a tacit admission that we don't control the ground. And in the long run, it's control of the ground that wins or loses the war." Helicopters remained important to the very end of the U.S. presence in Vietnam. As Saigon fell to the Communists in 1975, choppers carried the last Americans out of danger.

half tons of napalm on the enemy in just one delivery.

Helicopters enabled military personnel to receive unprecedented support. In Vietnam it was not unusual for American soldiers in the field to be provided with hot meals rather than cold C rations. More important was the medical evacuation helicopter, called the "Dust-off," which

could hoist to safety injured soldiers without touching land. Most of those wounded in Vietnam were promptly evacuated to hospitals, and those with grave injuries were sped to base facilities in the Pacific region or the United States. The improvements in medical evacuation, combined with advances in medicine, helped to raise the ratio of surviving wounded to

and severely limited the administration's options. The twenty-year-old consensus about cold war foreign policy had broken down.

Many would not fight in the war. The World Boxing Association stripped Muhammad Ali of his world heavyweight title when he refused to serve in what he called a "white man's war." More than 170,000 men who opposed the war on moral or religious grounds gained conscientious

objector status and performed nonmilitary duties at home or in Vietnam. About 60,000 fled the country to escape the draft, and more than 200,000 were accused of failing to register or committing other draft offenses.

When he got his induction notice in 1968, Tim O'Brien agonized over what to do. He opposed the war, yet to avoid the draft would bring criticism and embarrassment to his family in his

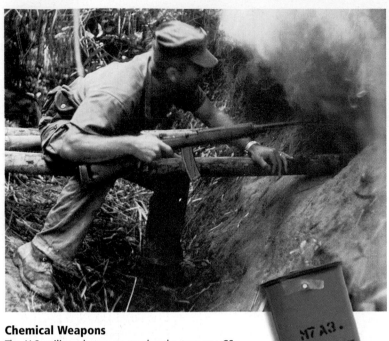

Chemical Weapons
The U.S. military began to employ the tear gas CS (o-chlorobenzylidenemalononitrile) in grenades in Vietnam in 1964 and was discharging more than two million pounds of CS a year by 1969. It was used in operations such as the one shown here. The marine has just thrown a CS gas grenade into a tunnel to flush out the enemy and make the tunnel unusable for several months. Military planes also dropped or sprayed CS from the air to rid large areas of land of enemy forces. CS is usually not lethal but has incapacitating effects. Nonetheless, its use evoked criticism at home and from abroad. The *New York Times* noted that "no other country has employed such a weapon in recent warfare." The Political Committee of the UN General Assembly maintained that generally recognized rules of warfare prohibited the use of any chemical agents.
James H. Pickerell / Stock Connection; Ordinance Museum / Aberdeen Proving Grounds.

small-town Minnesota community, whose leaders expected young men to serve their country. In addition, he said, "I owed the prairie something. For twenty-one years I'd lived under its laws, accepted its education . . . wallowed in its luxuries, played on its Little League teams." In the end, he could not bring himself to desert the country that he had never before thought of leaving. Though he held to his belief that "the war was wrong," O'Brien served in the army.

Opponents of the war held far from unanimous views. Some condemned the war on moral grounds, insisting that their country had no right to interfere in another country and stressing the suffering of the Vietnamese people. Their goal was total withdrawal. As American intervention esca-

lated with no tangible results, a larger segment of antiwar sentiment reflected practical considerations—that the war could not be won or that the cost would be too great to bear. Not demanding withdrawal, those activists wanted Johnson to stop bombing North Vietnam and seek negotiations.

The antiwar movement outraged millions of Americans who supported the war. Some members of the generation who had fought against Hitler could not understand younger men's refusal to support the government. Working-class people were no more pro-war than other groups, but they were especially conscious of the class dimensions of the war and the public opposition to it. A firefighter whose son had died in Vietnam said bitterly, "It's people like us who give up our sons for the country. The businesspeople, they run the country and make money from it. The college types . . . go to Washington and tell the government what to do. . . . But their sons don't end up in the swamps over there, in Vietnam."

President Johnson tried a number of means to silence critics. To avoid focusing attention on the war's burdens, he eschewed price and wage controls, imposed in other wars to control inflation, and delayed asking for a tax increase to pay for the war. Congress passed a 10 percent surcharge on federal income taxes in June 1968, after Johnson promised to cut domestic spending. The Great Society programs suffered, but the surcharge failed to reverse the inflationary surge.

The president agonized over casualty reports and felt personally wounded when protesters chanted outside the White House, "Hey, hey, LBJ, how many kids have you killed today?" Reacting harshly to antiwar sentiment, he misled the public about the war's progress, tried to discredit opponents by labeling them "nervous Nellies" or Communists, and ordered the CIA to spy on peace advocates. Without the president's specific authorization, the FBI infiltrated the peace movement, disrupted its work, and spread false information about activists. However, even the resort to illegal measures failed to subdue the opposition.

1968: Year of Upheaval

By late 1967—two years after the Americanization of the war—public impatience and frustration had intensified. On one side were the so-called **hawks**, who charged that the United States was fighting with one hand tied behind its

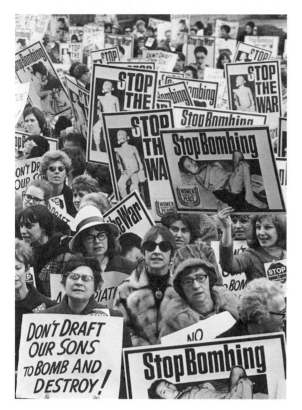

Mothers against the War
Women played an active role in the opposition to the
Vietnam War —and not just college students or radicals.
In 1961, years before Vietnam became an issue, Women
Strike for Peace (WSP) was founded to work for nuclear
disarmament. Identifying themselves as "concerned
housewives" and mothers, an estimated 50,000 women
throughout the country staged a one-day protest, calling
on President Kennedy to "End the Arms Race—Not the
Human Race." As early as 1963, WSP began to "alert the
public to the dangers and horrors of the war in Vietnam,"
and throughout the war it played a vigorous role in the
antiwar movement, mobilizing around the slogan "Not
Our Sons, Not Your Sons, Not Their Sons." In February
1967, WSP became the first group to take the antiwar
protest to the Pentagon. The women in this photograph
were among more than 2,000 women who gathered at
the Pentagon, using their shoes to bang against the
doors that were locked as they approached. Newspaper
readers in the United States and around the world saw
dramatic images of these women outraged at the refusal
of officials to meet with them.
© Bettmann/Corbis.

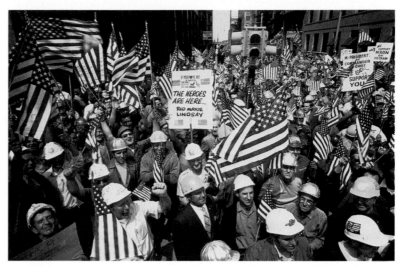

Pro-War Demonstrators
Advocates as well as opponents of the war in Vietnam took to the streets, as
these New Yorkers did in support of the U.S. invasion of Cambodia in May 1970.
Construction workers—called "hard hats"—and other union members marched
with American flags and posters championing President Nixon's policies and blast-
ing New York Mayor John Lindsay for his antiwar position. Following the demonstration, sympathetic union leaders presented Nixon with an honorary hard hat.
Paul Fusco/Magnum Photos, Inc.

For more help analyzing this image, see the visual activity for this chapter in the
Online Study Guide at bedfordstmartins.com/roark.

back and called for the government to apply
more power against North Vietnam. The **doves**
wanted de-escalation or withdrawal. Most people were torn between weariness with the war
and worry about abandoning the American commitment. As one woman said to a pollster, "I
want to get out but I don't want to give up."

Grave doubts about the war penetrated
the administration itself in 1967. Secretary of
Defense Robert McNamara, a principal architect
of U.S. involvement, now believed that the
North Vietnamese "won't quit no matter how
much bombing we do." And he feared for the
image of the United States, "the world's greatest
superpower killing or seriously injuring 1,000
noncombatants a week, while trying to pound a
tiny, backward nation into submission on an
issue whose merits are hotly disputed."
McNamara kept those views to himself until
thirty years later, but in early 1968 he left the administration.

The critical turning point came with the Tet
Offensive, which began on January 30, 1968. Just
a few weeks after General Westmoreland had reported that "the enemy has been driven away
from the population centers [and] has been compelled to disperse," the North Vietnamese and
Vietcong attacked key cities and every major
American base in South Vietnam. This was the
biggest surprise of the war, and not simply because both sides had customarily observed a
truce during the Vietnamese New Year holiday

The Tet Offensive underscored the credibility gap between official statements and the war's actual progress.

(called Tet). The offensive displayed the Communists' vitality and refusal to be intimidated by the presence of half a million American soldiers. Militarily, the enemy suffered a defeat, losing more than 30,000 men, ten times as many as ARVN and U.S. forces. Psychologically, however, Tet was devastating to the United States.

The Tet Offensive underscored the credibility gap between official statements and the war's actual progress. TV anchorman Walter Cronkite wondered, "What the hell is going on? I thought we were winning the war." The attacks created a million more South Vietnamese refugees as well as widespread destruction, especially in the ancient city of Hue, whose **archaeological** treasures were reduced to rubble. Explaining how he had defended a village, a U.S. army official said, "We had to destroy the town to save it." The statement epitomized for more and more Americans the brutality and senselessness of the war.

In the aftermath of Tet, Johnson considered a request from Westmoreland for 200,000 more troops. He conferred with advisers in the Defense Department and an unofficial group of foreign policy experts, dubbed the "Wise Men," who had been key architects of cold war policies since World War II. Dean Acheson, secretary of state under Truman, summarized their conclusion: "We can no longer do the job we set out to do in the time we have left and we must begin to take steps to disengage."

On March 31, 1968, Lyndon Johnson announced in a televised speech that the United States would reduce its bombing of North Vietnam and that he was prepared to begin peace talks with its leaders. Then he stunned his audience by declaring that he would not run for reelection. The announcement marked the end of the gradual escalation that had begun in 1965. What followed was a shift from "Americanization" to "Vietnamization" of the war, but it was a shift in strategy, not in policy. The United States maintained its goal of a non-Communist South Vietnam; it simply aimed to reach that goal by relying more heavily on the South Vietnamese.

Negotiations began in Paris in May 1968. But the United States would not agree to recognition of the Hanoi government's National Liberation Front, to a coalition government, or to American withdrawal. The North Vietnamese would agree to nothing less. Although the talks continued, so did the fighting.

Meanwhile, violence escalated at home. In June, two months after the murder of Martin Luther King Jr. and the ensuing riots, another assassination shook the nation. Running for the Democratic presidential nomination, Senator Robert F. Kennedy, the late president's brother, had just celebrated his triumph in the California primary when he was shot by a Palestinian Arab refugee, Sirhan B. Sirhan, who was outraged by Kennedy's support for Israel.

Spring 1968 also saw campus demonstrations intensify around the world as well as in the United States, where some two hundred protests occurred before summer. In the bloodiest action, students took over buildings at Columbia University in New York City, demanding that the university stop uprooting African Americans

The Tet Offensive

Launched by the North Vietnamese in January 1968, the Tet Offensive took the war to major cities for the first time. NLF troops quickly occupied Hue, the ancient imperial city, and held it for nearly a month. Supported by aerial bombing, U.S. marines finally took back the city, street by street. A journalist who had also covered the Korean War reported, "Nothing I saw . . . has been as terrible, in terms of destruction and despair, as what I saw in Hue." More than half of its 17,000 houses were leveled. Here, marines fight from rubble that was once part of the Citadel of Hue.

John Olson, U.S. Army/National Archives.

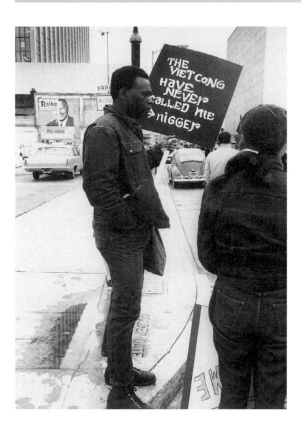

African American Antiwar Protest

The first expression of African American opposition to the war in Vietnam occurred in Mississippi in July 1965 when a group of civil rights workers called for draft resistance. Blacks should not fight for freedom in Vietnam "until all the Negro People are free in Mississippi," and they should not "risk our lives and kill other Colored People in Santo Domingo and Viet Nam." This protester on the West Coast in April 1967 expresses similar sentiments.

Joe Flowers / Black Star / Stockphoto.com.

International Party (Yippies), a splinter group of SDS. Its leaders, Abbie Hoffman and Jerry Rubin, urged students to demonstrate their hatred of the establishment by provoking the police to violence and creating chaos in the backyard of the Democratic convention. The Yippies brought a live pig to Chicago as their candidate. "Our concept of revolution," Hoffman declared, "is that it's fun."

Chicago's leading Democrat, Mayor Richard J. Daley, issued a ban on rallies and marches, ordered a curfew, and mobilized thousands of police. On August 25, demonstrators responded to police orders to disperse with insults and jeers, whereupon police attacked protesters with tear gas and clubs. Street battles continued for three days, culminating in what an official commission later termed a "police riot" on the night of August 28. Taunted by the crowd, the police

Protest in Chicago

The worst violence surrounding the 1968 Democratic National Convention in Chicago came on August 28 when protesters decided to assemble in Grant Park and march to the convention site. Mayor Daley refused them a parade permit and dispatched the police and the Illinois National Guard to the park to keep them from marching. As protesters listened to speeches in the park, a group of young men tore down the American flag and replaced it with a red T-shirt, prompting the police to go after the demonstrators with their clubs. Later that night when activists tried to march to the convention, the police struck out widely and wildly, bloodying and teargassing many people who were not connected to the radicals.

Jeffrey Blankfort / Jeroboam.

in the neighboring community, do more to meet black students' needs, stop research for the Department of Defense, and grant amnesty to student demonstrators. When negotiations failed, university officials called in the city police, who cleared the buildings, injuring more than one hundred demonstrators and arresting more than seven hundred others. An ensuing student strike prematurely ended the academic year. (See "Documenting the American Promise," chapter 28, page 1048.)

In August, protesters battled the police in Chicago, where the Democratic Party had convened to nominate its presidential ticket. Several thousand demonstrators came to the city, some to support the peace candidate Senator Eugene McCarthy, others to act more aggressively. Many of the latter had been mobilized by the Youth

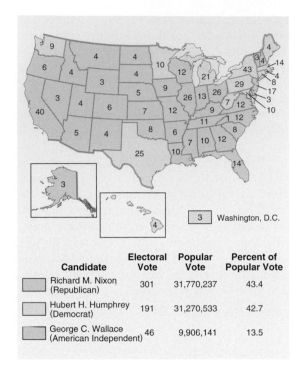

Candidate	Electoral Vote	Popular Vote	Percent of Popular Vote
Richard M. Nixon (Republican)	301	31,770,237	43.4
Hubert H. Humphrey (Democrat)	191	31,270,533	42.7
George C. Wallace (American Independent)	46	9,906,141	13.5

MAP 29.3   The Election of 1968

> The 1968 elections revealed deep cracks in the coalition that had, except during the Eisenhower years, kept the Democrats in power for thirty years.

used mace and nightsticks, clubbing not only those who had come to provoke violence but also reporters, peaceful demonstrators, and convention delegates.

The bloodshed in Chicago and upheaval across the country had little effect on the outcome of either major party's convention. Peace Democrats lost the presidential nomination, as Vice President Hubert H. Humphrey trounced Eugene McCarthy by nearly three to one. McCarthy's refusal to share the podium with Humphrey as the convention ended underscored the bitter split within the party. In contrast, the Republican convention peacefully nominated former vice president Richard Nixon on the first ballot. For his running mate, Nixon chose Maryland governor Spiro T. Agnew, hoping to gather southern support while not alienating northern and western voters.

For the first time in nearly fifty years, a strong third party entered the electoral scene. Staunch segregationist former Alabama governor George C. Wallace ran on the ticket of the American Independent Party. Wallace appealed to Americans nationwide who believed that civil rights and antipoverty programs benefited the undeserving at their expense and who were outraged by assaults on traditional values by students and others. Nixon guardedly played on resentments that fueled the Wallace campaign, appealing to "the forgotten Americans, the non-shouters, the non-demonstrators."

Few differences separated the two major-party candidates on the central issue of Vietnam. Nixon promised to "bring an honorable end" to the war but did not indicate how he would do it. Humphrey had strong reservations about U.S. policy in Vietnam, yet as vice president he wanted to avoid a break with Johnson. Finally Johnson boosted Humphrey's campaign when he announced a halt to the bombing of North Vietnam. By election eve, Nixon and Humphrey were neck-and-neck.

With nearly ten million votes (13 percent of the total), the American Independent Party produced the strongest third-party finish since 1924. Nixon edged out Humphrey by just half a million popular votes, prevailing more strongly in the electoral college, with 301 votes to Humphrey's 191 and Wallace's 46. The Democrats lost a few seats in Congress but kept control of both the House and the Senate (Map 29.3).

The 1968 elections revealed deep cracks in the coalition that had, except during the Eisenhower years, kept the Democrats in power for thirty years. The Democrats' policies on race moved most of the former "solid South" behind Nixon or Wallace, shattering a century of Democratic Party dominance in that region. Large numbers of blue-collar workers broke union ranks to vote for Wallace or Nixon, along with other groups associating the Democrats with racial turmoil, inflation, antiwar protesters, changing sexual mores, urban riots, and America's impotence in Vietnam. These resentments continued to simmer, soon to be mobilized into a resurging right in American politics (see chapter 30).

New Opportunities and Dangers in a Multipolar World

Vietnam may have dominated the 1968 election campaigns, but Richard Nixon's ambitious foreign policy goals extended far beyond ending that war. The challenges of foreign policy captured Nixon's greatest enthusiasm, and he hoped to make his mark on history by applying his broad understanding of international relations to a changing world. Nixon believed that the "rigid and bipolar world of the 1940s and 1950s" was giving way to "the fluidity of a new era of multi-lateral diplomacy." Diverging from Republican orthodoxy, his dramatic overtures to the Soviet Union and China reduced decades-old hostilities.

Yet, as reflected in Nixon's aggressive pursuit of the war in Vietnam, anticommunism remained central to American policy. In Latin America, Africa, and the Middle East, the administration threw its support behind repressive regimes when the alternative appeared too close to communism.

Moving toward Détente with the Soviet Union and China

Even while fighting against communism in Vietnam, the United States reached some accord with the major Communist nations. In 1968, building on negotiations that began under Eisenhower and included Kennedy's 1963 nuclear test ban treaty, the United States, the Soviet Union, and sixty other nations agreed to a Nuclear Non-Proliferation Treaty. American ratification of the treaty was delayed when the Soviets invaded Czechoslovakia in 1968 to put down an opposition movement; but in 1969, Nixon asked the Senate for approval, and the treaty became effective in 1970. Designed to prevent the spread of nuclear weapons, the treaty lacked adherence from such key nations as China, France (both of whom eventually signed), India, Israel, and Pakistan. The nuclear superpowers, on the one hand, gave up little by agreeing not to help other nations acquire nuclear bombs; non-nuclear signatories, on the other hand, committed themselves to retaining that status.

While the nonproliferation treaty was largely the work of his predecessors, Nixon took the initiative in a dramatic move toward China. The president's most important adviser was national security assistant Henry A. Kissinger, a German-born refugee from Hitler's Holocaust and a Harvard professor of international relations. Both men saw opportunity in the growing Soviet-Chinese discord. If these two nations checked each other's power, their threat to the United States would lessen; thus, according to Nixon, Soviet-Chinese hostility "served our purpose best if we maintained closer relations with

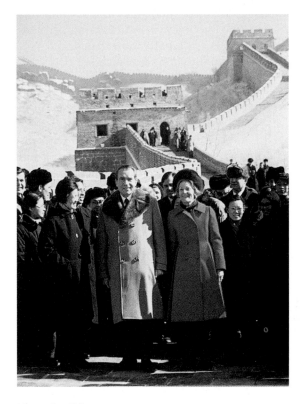

Nixon in China

"This was the week that changed the world," proclaimed President Richard M. Nixon in February 1972, emphasizing the stunning turnaround in relations with America's former enemy, the People's Republic of China. Nixon's trip was meticulously planned to dramatize the event on television and, aside from criticism from some conservatives, won overwhelming support from Americans. The Great Wall of China forms the setting for this photograph of Nixon and his wife Pat.

Nixon Presidential Materials Project, National Archives and Record Administration.

each side than they did with each other." Working with Kissinger and often in secret, Nixon exploited the deterioration in Soviet-Chinese relations that had begun in the early 1960s.

Following two years of secret negotiations, in February 1972, Nixon became the nation's first president to set foot on Chinese soil—an astonishing act by a man who had climbed the political ladder as a fervent anti-Communist. Recognizing that his anti-Communist credentials were what enabled him to conduct this shift in U.S.-Chinese relations with no significant objections at home, Nixon remarked to Chinese leader Mao Zedong, "Those on the right can do what those on the left only talk about." Although the act was largely symbolic, cultural and scientific exchanges followed, and American manufacturers began to find markets in China—small steps in the process of **globalization** that would take giant strides in the 1990s (see chapter 31).

As Nixon and Kissinger hoped, the warming of U.S.-Chinese relations increased Soviet responsiveness to their strategy of **détente**, their term for easing conflict with the Soviet Union. Détente did not mean abandoning containment but instead focusing on issues of common concern, such as arms control and trade. Containment would be achieved not only by military threat but also by ensuring that Russian and Chinese stakes in a stable international order would restrain Russia and China from precipitating crises. Nixon's goal was "a stronger healthy United States, Europe, Soviet Union, China, Japan, each balancing the other."

In May 1972, three months after his trip to China, Nixon visited Moscow, signing several agreements on trade and cooperation in science and space. Most significantly, Soviet and U.S. leaders concluded arms limitation treaties that had grown out of the Strategic Arms Limitation Talks (SALT) begun in 1969. Both sides agreed to limit antiballistic missile systems (ABMs) to two each. Giving up pursuit of a defense against nuclear weapons was a move of crucial importance, because it prevented either nation from building so secure an ABM defense against a nuclear attack that it would risk a first strike.

Gerald Ford, who became president when Nixon resigned in 1974 (see chapter 30), failed to sustain widespread support of détente. The secrecy of the Nixon-Kissinger initiatives had alienated legislators, and some Democrats charged that détente ignored Soviet violations of human rights. Members of both parties worried that Soviet strength was overtaking that of the United States. In response,

> Even while applying practical politics rather than ideology to U.S. relations with China and the Soviet Union, in Vietnam and elsewhere Nixon and Kissinger actively resisted social revolutions that might lead to communism.

Congress derailed trade agreements with the Soviet Union, refusing economic favors unless the Soviets stopped their harsh treatment of internal dissidents and Jews.

Further negotiations on limiting strategic arms went nowhere, but U.S., Soviet, and European leaders signed a historic agreement in 1975 in Helsinki, Finland, formally recognizing the existing post–World War II boundaries in Europe and also committing the signers to respect the human rights of their citizens. The agreement outraged **conservatives** at home because it meant U.S. acceptance of the Soviets' domination over their satellite countries in Eastern Europe—a condition to which American leaders had objected so bitterly thirty years earlier as the cold war began.

Shoring Up Anticommunism in the Third World

Nixon promised in 1973, "The time has passed when America will make every other nation's conflict our own . . . or presume to tell the people of other nations how to manage their own affairs." Yet even while applying practical politics rather than ideology to U.S. relations with China and the Soviet Union, in Vietnam and elsewhere Nixon and Kissinger continued to equate Marxism with a threat to U.S. interests and actively resisted social revolutions that might lead to communism.

The Nixon administration found such a threat in Salvador Allende, a self-proclaimed Marxist who was elected president of Chile in 1970. Since 1964, the Central Intelligence Agency (CIA) and U.S. corporations concerned about nationalization of their Chilean properties had assisted Allende's opponents. When Allende won the election, Nixon ordered the CIA director to make the Chilean economy "scream" and thus destabilize his government. In 1973, with the help of the CIA, the Chilean military engineered a coup, killed Allende, and established a brutal dictatorship under General Augusto Pinochet, who twenty-five years later was

Chile

found guilty of torture, murder, and terrorism by an international court.

In other parts of the world, too, the Nixon administration stood by repressive governments. It eased pressures on white minority governments that tyrannized blacks in southern Africa, believing that, as a National Security Council (NSC) memorandum put it, the "whites are here to stay. . . . There is no hope for the blacks to gain the political rights they seek through violence, which will lead only to chaos and increased opportunities for Communists." In the Middle East, the United States supported the harsh regime of the shah of Iran—whom the CIA had helped regain power in 1953—because it considered Iran a stable anti-Communist ally with enormous petroleum reserves. Nixon secretly began massive arms shipments to the shah in 1972, cementing a relationship that would ignite a new crisis when the shah was overthrown in 1979 (see chapter 30).

Like his predecessors, Nixon pursued a delicate balance between defending Israel's security and seeking the goodwill of Arab nations strategically and economically important to the United States. Conflict between Israel and the Arab nations had escalated into the all-out Six-Day War in 1967, when Egypt massed troops on Israel's border and Israel launched a preemptive strike. Although Syria and Jordan joined the war on Egypt's side, Israel won a stunning victory, seizing territory that amounted to twice its original size. Israeli forces took control of the Sinai Peninsula and Gaza Strip from Egypt, the Golan Heights from Syria, and the West Bank from Jordan, which included the Arab sector of Jerusalem, a city sacred to Jews, Christians, and Muslims alike.

That decisive victory did not quell Middle Eastern turmoil. In October 1973, on the Jewish holiday Yom Kippur, Egypt and Syria surprised Israel with a full-scale attack. When the Nixon administration sided with Israel, the Arab nations retaliated with an oil embargo that created severe shortages in the United States and height-

Israeli Territorial Gains in the Six-Day War, 1967

ened environmentalists' concerns about the nation's wasteful use of energy. After Israel repulsed the attack, Kissinger attempted to mediate between Israel and Arab nations, efforts that continued for the next three decades with only limited success. The Arab countries refused to recognize Israel's right to exist; Israel would not withdraw from the territories occupied during the Six-Day War and began to settle Israelis there; and no solution could be found for the Palestinian refugees who had been displaced by the creation of Israel in the late 1940s. The simmering conflict contributed to anti-American sentiment among Arabs who viewed the United States as Israel's supporter.

Nixon's Search for Peace with Honor in Vietnam

"I'm not going to end up like LBJ, holed up in the White House afraid to show my face on the street," the new president asserted. "I'm going to stop that war. Fast." Although he began a gradual withdrawal of U.S. ground troops, Nixon was no more willing than Johnson to allow South Vietnam to fall to the Communists. Neither was he more able to prevent it, despite expanding military operations into Cambodia and Laos and sporadically but ferociously bombing North Vietnam. In January 1973, the administration concluded a truce that ended the direct involvement of the United States and led to total victory for the North Vietnamese in April 1975.

Vietnamization and Negotiations

Nixon and Kissinger embraced the overriding goal of the three preceding administrations: a non-Communist South Vietnam. By 1969, however, that goal had become almost incidental to the larger objective of maintaining American credibility. Regardless of the wisdom of the initial intervention, Kissinger asserted, "the commitment of 500,000 Americans has settled the importance of Vietnam. For what is involved now is confidence in American promises."

From 1969 to 1972, Nixon and Kissinger pursued a four-pronged approach. First, they tried to strengthen the South Vietnamese military and government. Second, to disarm the antiwar movement at home, Nixon gradually replaced U.S. forces with South Vietnamese soldiers and American technology and bombs. Third, Nixon and Kissinger negotiated with both North Vietnam and the Soviet Union. Fourth, the military applied enormous firepower to persuade Hanoi to accept American terms at the bargaining table.

As part of the Vietnamization of the war, ARVN forces grew to over one million, supported with the latest American equipment and training. The South Vietnamese air force became the fourth largest in the world. U.S. advisers and funds also promoted land reform, village elections, and the building of schools, hospitals, and transportation facilities.

The other side of Vietnamization was the withdrawal of U.S. forces. The number of GIs decreased from 543,000 in 1968 to 140,000 by the end of 1971. Tim O'Brien boarded the plane back home in March 1971 wondering, "What kind of war is it that begins and ends this way, with a pretty girl [the stewardess], cushioned seats, and magazines." Despite reduced draft calls and casualties (from nearly 800 deaths a month in 1969 to 352 in 1970), more than 20,000 Americans perished in Vietnam during the last four years of the war. Having been exposed to the antiwar movement at home, many of the remaining soldiers had less faith in the war than their predecessors had. In addition to mounting racial tensions among soldiers, hundreds of incidents of "fragging" (attacks on officers by enlisted men) occurred, more than in any previous wars, and many soldiers sought escape in illegal drugs. In a 1971 report, "The Collapse of the Armed Forces," a retired Marine Corps colonel described the lack of discipline: "Our army that now remains in Vietnam [is] near mutinous."

Nixon and Kissinger also endeavored to link Soviet interest in expanded trade and arms reductions with U.S. goals in Vietnam. However, their breakthroughs in summit diplomacy with the Soviet Union and China failed to change the course of the war. Nor did intensification of bombing achieve its objective. Echoing Johnson, Kissinger believed that a "fourth-rate power like North Vietnam" had to have a "breaking point," but the hundreds of thousands of tons of bombs delivered by U.S. pilots failed to find it. Fierce application of American power bought time, but little else. (See "Historical Question," page 1078.)

Nixon's War

In the spring of 1969, Nixon began a ferocious air war in Cambodia, carefully hiding it from Congress and the public for more than a year. Seeking to knock out North Vietnamese sanctuaries in Cambodia, the campaign dropped more than 100,000 tons of bombs but succeeded only in sending the North Vietnamese to other hiding places. To support a new, pro-Western Cambodian government installed through a military coup in 1970 and "to show the enemy that we were still serious about our commitment in Vietnam," in April 1970 Nixon ordered a joint U.S.-ARVN invasion of Cambodia.

That order made Vietnam "Nixon's war" and provoked outrage at home. Nixon made a belligerent speech defending his move and emphasizing the importance of U.S. credibility: "If when the chips are down, the world's most powerful nation acts like a pitiful helpless giant, the forces of totalitarianism and anarchy will threaten free nations" everywhere. Upon reading Nixon's speech, a cabinet member predicted, "This will make the students puke." They did more. More than 100,000 people protested in Washington, and students demonstrated and boycotted classes on hundreds of campuses. At Kent State University in Ohio, National Guard troops were dispatched after protesting students burned an old ROTC building. Then, at a peaceful rally on May 4, 1970, nervous troops being pelted by rocks fired at students, killing four and wound-

U.S. Invasion of Cambodia, 1970

THAILAND

LAOS

CAMBODIA

Phnom Penh

SOUTH VIETNAM

Saigon

← U.S. invasion of Cambodia

NIXON'S SEARCH FOR PEACE WITH HONOR IN VIETNAM

ing ten others. "They're starting to treat their own children like they treat us," commented a black woman in Harlem. In a confrontation at Jackson State College in Mississippi on May 14, police shot into a dormitory, killing two black students. In August, police used tear gas and clubs against protesters at a Chicano antiwar rally in Los Angeles.

Upon learning of the bombing and invasion of Cambodia, furious legislators attempted to curb the president. The Senate voted to terminate the Gulf of Tonkin Resolution, which had given the president virtually a blank check in Vietnam, and to cut off funds for the Cambodian operation. The House of Representatives refused to go along, but Congress was clearly becoming an obstacle to the Nixon administration's plans. By the end of June, Nixon pulled out all U.S. soldiers from Cambodia.

My Lai Massacre
When U.S. forces attacked My Lai in March 1968, they believed that the village was a Vietcong stronghold and expected a fierce fight. Even though they encountered no enemy forces, the men of Charlie Company systematically killed every inhabitant, nearly all of whom were old men, women, and children. Estimates put the death toll at more than 400 villagers. Twelve officers and enlisted men were charged with murder or assault to commit murder, but only one, First Lieutenant William Calley, was convicted. Though convicted of premeditated murder, Calley was paroled after serving less than four years in prison. This photograph of murdered villagers was taken by an army photographer.
Ron Haeberle/TimePix/Getty.

The invasion of Cambodia failed to break the will of the North Vietnamese, but it set in motion a terrible tragedy for the Cambodian people. The North Vietnamese moved further into Cambodia and increased their support of the Khmer Rouge, an organization of Communist insurgents attempting to overthrow the U.S.-supported government of Lon Nol. A brutal civil war raged until 1975, when the Khmer Rouge triumphed and imposed a savage rule, slaughtering millions of Cambodians and giving the name "killing fields" to the land of this historically peaceful people.

In 1971, Vietnam veterans themselves became a visible part of the peace movement, the first men in U.S. history to organize against a war in which they had fought. Veterans held a public investigation of "war crimes" in Vietnam, rallied in front of the Capitol, and cast away their war medals. In May 1971, veterans numbered among the 40,000 protesters who engaged in civil disobedience in an effort to shut down Washington. Officials made more than 12,000 arrests, which courts later ruled violations of protesters' rights.

After the spring of 1971, there were fewer massive antiwar demonstrations, but protest continued. Public attention focused on the court-martial of Lieutenant William Calley, which began in November 1970 and resulted in his conviction. During the trial, Americans learned that Calley's company had massacred more than 400 civilians in the hamlet of My Lai in March 1968. Among those murdered were children and women, an atrocity that the military had covered up for more than a year.

Administration policy suffered another blow in June 1971 with publication of the *Pentagon Papers*, a secret government study critical of U.S. policy in Vietnam. Daniel Ellsberg, once a civilian adviser in Vietnam and an aide to Henry Kissinger, had worked on the study. Frustrated in his attempts to persuade officials of the war's futility, Ellsberg copied the papers and gave them to the *New York Times*. Administration efforts to prevent their publication were defeated

> In 1971, Vietnam veterans themselves became a visible part of the peace movement, the first men in U.S. history to organize against a war in which they had fought.

by the Supreme Court as a violation of freedom of the press. The *Pentagon Papers* heightened disillusionment with the war by casting doubts on the government's credibility. More than 60 percent of respondents to a public opinion poll in 1971 considered it a mistake to have sent American troops to Vietnam; 58 percent believed the war to be immoral (Figure 29.2).

The Peace Accords and the Fall of Saigon

Nixon and Kissinger continued to combine military force and negotiation. In March 1972, responding to a strong North Vietnamese offensive, the United States resumed sustained bombing of the North, mined Haiphong and other harbors for the first time, and announced a naval blockade. With peace talks stalled, in December Nixon ordered the most devastating bombing of North Vietnam yet: In twelve days, U.S. planes dropped more bombs than they had in all of 1969–1971.

The ferocious bombing, called "jugular diplomacy" by Kissinger, was costly to both sides, and resumed talks brought agreement.

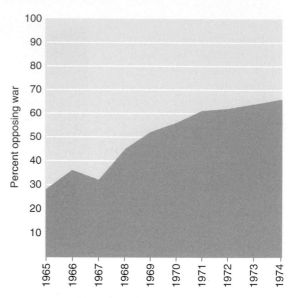

FIGURE 29.2 Public Opinion about the Vietnam War, 1965–1974
This chart reflects the percentage of people answering "yes" to a Gallup poll question: "In view of the developments since we entered the fighting in Vietnam, do you think the United States made a mistake in sending troops to fight in Vietnam?"

On January 27, 1973, representatives of the United States, North Vietnam, the South Vietnamese government, and the Vietcong (now called the People's Revolutionary Government) signed a formal accord in Paris. The agreement required removal of all U.S. troops and military advisers but allowed North Vietnamese forces to remain. Both sides agreed to return prisoners of war. Nixon announced that the agreement brought "peace with honor," but it actually

Evacuating South Vietnam
As Communist troops rolled south toward Saigon in the spring of 1975, desperate South Vietnamese attempted to flee along with the departing Americans. Here a CIA employee helps Vietnamese board a helicopter from the top of a building a half mile from the U.S. embassy. Thousands of Vietnamese who wanted to be evacuated were left behind. But even though space for evacuees was desperately limited, South Vietnamese president Nguyen Van Thieu fled with fifteen tons of baggage on a U.S. plane to Taiwan.
© Bettmann/Corbis.

allowed only a face-saving withdrawal for the United States. The South Vietnamese government remained in power for just a little more than two years.

Fighting resumed immediately among the Vietnamese. Nixon's efforts to support the South Vietnamese government, and indeed his ability to govern at all, were increasingly eroded by what came to be known as the Watergate scandals (discussed in chapter 30). In 1975, North Vietnam launched a new offensive in South Vietnam and on May 1 occupied Saigon and renamed it Ho Chi Minh City to honor the Communist leader.

Confusion, humiliation, and tragedy marked the hasty evacuation of Americans and their South Vietnamese allies. The United States got its own citizens out, along with 150,000 South Vietnamese, but it lacked sufficient transport and time to evacuate all those who wanted to leave. U.S. marines beat back desperate Vietnamese trying to escape through the U.S. Embassy. Some South Vietnamese troops, frightened and angry at being left behind, fired on departing Americans.

The Legacy of Defeat

It took Nixon four years to end the war. During that time, the conflict expanded into Cambodia and Laos, Southeast Asia endured massive bombing campaigns, and with a Republican president now conducting it, the Vietnam War became genuinely bipartisan. Although increasing numbers of legislators criticized the war, Congress never denied the funds to fight it.

Only after the peace accords did the legislative branch stiffen its constitutional authority over the making of war. In November 1973, Congress passed the War Powers Act requiring the president to report to Congress within forty-eight hours of deploying military forces abroad. If Congress failed to endorse the president's action within sixty days, the troops would have to be withdrawn.

The dire predictions of three presidents that a Communist victory in South Vietnam would set the dominoes cascading did not materialize. Although Vietnam, Laos, and Cambodia all fell within the Communist camp in the spring of 1975, Thailand, Burma, Malaysia, and the rest of Southeast Asia did not. When China and Vietnam reverted to their historically hostile relationship, the myth of a monolithic Communist power overrunning Asia evaporated.

TABLE 29.1	VIETNAM WAR CASUALTIES
United States	
Killed in action	47,382
Wounded	153,303
Died, noncombat	1,811
Missing, captured	10,753
South Vietnam	
Killed in action	110,357
Military wounded	499,026
Civilians killed	415,000
Civilians wounded	913,000
Communist Regulars and Guerrillas	
Killed in action	666,000

Source: U.S. Department of Defense.

While most Americans wanted simply to forget defeat in Vietnam, veterans and those who lost loved ones could not so easily put the war behind them. The nation had always honored its soldiers' sacrifices, but three unique elements of the Vietnam War denied veterans the traditional homecoming: its lack of strong support at home, its character as a guerrilla war, and its ultimate failure. As one veteran remarked, "The left hated us for killing, and the right hated us for not killing enough."

Because the Vietnam War was in large part a civil, guerrilla war, combat was especially brutal (Table 29.1). The terrors of conventional warfare were multiplied, and so were the opportunities and motivations to commit atrocities. The massacre at My Lai was only the most publicized war crime. To demonstrate the immorality of the war, peace advocates stressed the atrocities, contributing to an image of the Vietnam War veteran as dehumanized and violent and thus deserving of public hostility or indifference.

> Three unique elements of the Vietnam War denied veterans the traditional homecoming: its lack of strong support at home, its character as a guerrilla war, and its ultimate failure.

Veterans largely expressed two kinds of reactions to the defeat. Many regarded the commitment as an honorable one and felt betrayed by the government for not letting them and their now-dead comrades win the war. Others blamed the government for sacrificing the nation's youth in an immoral or useless war. These soldiers best expressed their sense of the war's futility in

AMERICAN PLACES

The Vietnam Veterans Memorial, Washington, D.C.

Deciding how to memorialize the men and women who served in Vietnam was nearly as controversial as the war itself. In 1979, a group of Vietnam veterans, led by Jan C. Scruggs, who had been wounded and decorated as an infantry corporal, formed the Vietnam Veterans Memorial Fund (VVMF). The Memorial Fund received authorization from Congress in 1980 to raise money to erect a memorial on national park land in commemoration of the men and women who served with the U.S. Armed Forces during the Vietnam War. Well aware that "so many veterans met with ridicule and contempt upon returning home," VVWF intended the memorial to "be a place where that injustice could at long last be rectified."

The Memorial Fund conducted a national competition for design of the monument. Eight experts judged nearly fifteen hundred designs, unanimously selecting the one by Maya Ying Lin of Athens, Ohio, whose parents had fled China in 1948. The twenty-one-year-old architecture major at Yale University imagined a 500-foot sloping, V-shaped wall of polished black granite, ten feet high at the vertex and inscribed with the names of every serviceman and servicewoman who perished in Vietnam, in the order of their deaths. The chronological order gives each one a place in history; and, as Lin explained in her design entry, "these names, seemingly infinite in number, convey the sense of overwhelming numbers, while unifying these individuals into a whole."

The VVMF had wanted to separate "the issue of the service of the individual men and women from the issue of U.S. policy in Vietnam [and thus] to begin a process of national reconciliation." But there were immediate objections to Lin's design. Marine lieutenant James Webb, who was wounded three times and had won many decorations, hated the design; he found it negative, unpatriotic, symbolic of failure, a "black ditch," "a black gash of shame." To appease critics who wanted a more positive, heroic, lifelike monument, a traditional sculpture of three servicemen was added to the site. In 1993, the memorial received another statue, this one showing three uniformed women tending a fallen soldier, to honor all of the women who served.

A number of Web sites allow visitors to get a close view of the wall and a feel for the emotions that continue to surround the memorial and the war. There is a "virtual wall" site, where you can focus in on particular sections to read the names etched into the granite. Other sites feature pictures, recollections, poems, and a message board where veterans and their families and friends write in to locate com-

the slang term they used for a comrade's death: He was "wasted." Often identifying with the Vietnamese more than with their white comrades, veterans belonging to minority groups had more reason to doubt the nobility of their purpose. A Native American soldier assigned to resettle Vietnamese civilians found it to be "just like when they moved us to the rez [reservation]. We shouldn't have done that."

"We would not return to cheering crowds, parades, and the pealing of great cathedral bells," wrote Philip Caputo. Most veterans came home to public neglect, while some faced harassment from antiwar activists who did not distinguish the war from the warriors. A veteran remembered the "feelings of rejection and scorn that a bunch of depressed and confused young men experienced when they returned home

from doing what their country told them to do." Government benefits were less generous to Vietnam War veterans than they had been to World War II and Korean War soldiers. The women who had served felt even more isolated and ignored by the government, the public, and veterans' groups. Yet two-thirds of Vietnam veterans said that they would serve again, and most veterans readjusted well to civilian life under difficult circumstances.

Nonetheless, the Veterans Administration (VA) estimated that nearly one-sixth of the three million veterans suffered from post-traumatic stress disorder, with its symptoms of fear, recurring nightmares, feelings of guilt and shame, violence, drug and alcohol abuse, and suicidal tendencies. Thirty years after doing army intelligence work in Saigon, Doris Allen "still hit the

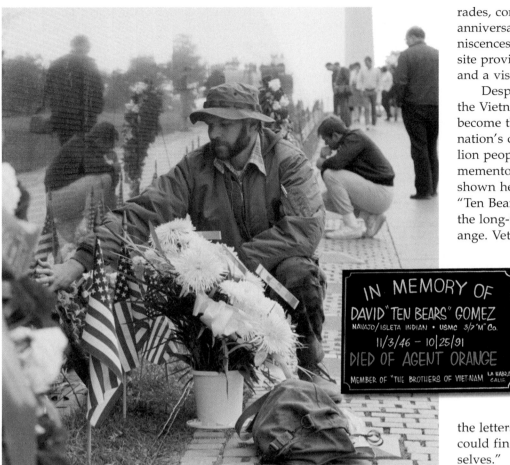

rades, commemorate birthdays or anniversaries, and exchange reminiscences. The memorial's official site provides a history of its creation and a visitor's guide.

Despite the initial controversy, the Vietnam Veterans Memorial has become the most popular site in the nation's capital, visited by 4.4 million people each year. Many leave mementos, such as the small plaque shown here memorializing David "Ten Bears" Gomez, who died from the long-term effects of Agent Orange. Veterans especially appreciate the opportunity to connect in a tangible way with their lost comrades and to heal themselves. As one explained at the memorial's dedication in 1982, they came "to find the names of those we lost in the war, as if by tracing the letters cut into the granite we could find what was left of ourselves."

The Vietnam Veterans Memorial
© Bettmann/Corbis; National Archives.

FOR WEB LINKS RELATED TO THIS SITE AND OTHER AMERICAN PLACES, see "PlaceLinks" at bedfordstmartins.com/roark.

floor sometimes when I hear loud bangs." In the late 1970s, many of those who had served in Vietnam began to display a different set of symptoms: They produced deformed children and fell ill themselves with cancer, severe skin disorders, and other ailments. Veterans claimed a link between these illnesses and Agent Orange, an herbicide that contained the deadly poison dioxin, which the military had sprayed by the millions of gallons over Vietnam. Scientists disagreed about the chemical's effects, and not until 1991 did Congress provide assistance to veterans with diseases linked to the poison.

The government's new position on Agent Orange coincided with a shift in the climate surrounding Vietnam War veterans. "It wasn't until the early 1980s," one veteran observed, "that it became 'all right' to be a combat veteran." The Vietnam War began to enter the realm of popular culture with novels, TV shows, and hit movies depicting a broad range of military experience—from soldiers reduced to brutality to men and women serving with courage and integrity.

The incorporation of the Vietnam War into the collective experience was symbolized most dramatically in the Vietnam Veterans Memorial unveiled in Washington, D.C., in November 1982. Designed by Yale architect student Maya Lin, the black, V-shaped wall inscribed with the names of 58,000 men and women lost to the war became the second most visited site in the capital. In an article describing the memorial's dedication, a Vietnam combat veteran spoke to and for his former comrades: "Welcome home. The war is over." (See "American Places," above.)

Conclusion: An Unwinnable War

Vietnam was America's longest war. The United States spent $150 billion and sent 2.6 million of its young men and women to Vietnam. Of those, 58,000 never returned, and 150,000 suffered serious injury. The war shattered consensus at home and contributed to the most severe internal disorder in a century. It increased presidential power at the expense of congressional authority and public accountability and led to the downfall of two presidents.

The Vietnam War was a logical extension of the nation's post–World War II commitment to containment everywhere on the planet. Yet even as Nixon and Kissinger took steps to ease cold war tensions with the major Communist powers, the Soviet Union and China (who were also the main suppliers of the North Vietnamese), they relentlessly pursued a war to keep South Vietnam from falling to communism. To do otherwise, they believed, would threaten the credibility of American policy and make the United States appear weak. Defeat in Vietnam did not make the United States the "pitiful helpless giant" predicted by Nixon, but it did suggest the relative decline of U.S. power and the impossibility of containment on a global scale.

One of the constraints on U.S. power was the tenacity of revolutionary movements that were determined to achieve national independence. Marine lieutenant Philip Caputo recalled the surprise at discovering "that the men we had scorned as peasant guerrillas were, in fact, a lethal, determined enemy." U.S. officials badly underestimated the sacrifices that the enemy was willing to make to achieve national liberation. Policymakers overestimated the effectiveness of American technological superiority, and they failed to realize how easily the United States could be perceived as a colonial intruder, no more welcome than the French had been.

A second constraint on Eisenhower, Kennedy, Johnson, and Nixon was their resolve to avoid a major confrontation with the Soviet Union or China. For Johnson, who conducted the largest escalation of the war, caution was especially critical so as not to provoke direct intervention by the Communist superpowers. After China exploded its first atomic bomb in 1964, the potential heightened for the Vietnam conflict to escalate into worldwide disaster.

Third, in Vietnam the United States faced the problem of containment by means of an extremely weak ally. The South Vietnamese government never won the support of its people, and the intense devastation and suffering the war brought to civilians only made things worse. Short of taking over the South Vietnamese government and military, the United States could do little to strengthen South Vietnam's ability to resist communism.

Finally, domestic opposition to the war constrained the options of Johnson and Nixon. From its origin in 1965, the antiwar movement grew to include significant portions of mainstream America by 1968. As the war dragged on, with increasing American casualties and growing evidence of the damage being inflicted on innocent Vietnamese, more and more civilians wearied of the conflict. Even some who had fought the war joined the movement, including Philip Caputo, who sent his campaign ribbons and a bitter letter of protest to the White House. By 1968, distinguished experts who had fashioned and implemented the containment policy recognized that erosion of support for the war made its continuation untenable. Five years later, Nixon and Kissinger bowed to the resolution of the enemy and the limitations of U.S. power. As the war wound down, passions surrounding it contributed to a rising conservative movement that would substantially alter the post–World War II political order.

FOR ADDITIONAL FIRSTHAND ACCOUNTS OF THIS PERIOD, see Chapter 29 in Michael Johnson, ed., *Reading the American Past*, Third Edition.

TO ASSESS YOUR MASTERY OF THE MATERIAL IN THIS CHAPTER, see the Online Study Guide at bedfordstmartins.com/roark.

FOR WEB LINKS RELATED TO THE TOPICS IN THIS CHAPTER, see "HistoryLinks," "DocLinks," and "PlaceLinks" at bedfordstmartins.com/roark.

CHRONOLOGY

1961
- CIA-backed Cuban exiles launch unsuccessful invasion of Cuba at Bay of Pigs.
- Berlin Wall erected, dividing East and West Berlin.
- Kennedy administration increases military aid and military advisers in South Vietnam.
- Kennedy administration creates Alliance for Progress and Peace Corps.

1962
- Cuban missile crisis results in Soviet removal of missiles in Cuba.

1963
- Limited nuclear test ban treaty signed by United States and Soviet Union.
- South Vietnamese military overthrows President Ngo Dinh Diem.

1964
- U.S. troops quell anti-American rioting in Panama Canal Zone.
- President Johnson uses Gulf of Tonkin incident to get congressional resolution of support for escalating the war in Vietnam.

1965
- First major protest demonstration in Washington, D.C., against Vietnam War attracts 20,000 people.
- Johnson administration initiates Operation Rolling Thunder, intensifies bombing of North Vietnam.
- Johnson orders increase in number of U.S. troops in Vietnam; peak is 543,000 in 1968.
- U.S. troops invade Dominican Republic to prevent leftist government from taking power.

1968
- Hundreds of thousands of Americans demonstrate against Vietnam War.
- Vietnamese Communists' Tet Offensive leads Johnson administration to reverse its policy in Vietnam and seek negotiated settlement.
- In wake of Tet Offensive, Johnson decides not to seek second term.
- Republican Richard Nixon elected president.

1969
- Neil Armstrong and "Buzz" Aldrin become first humans to land on the moon.
- Nixon orders secret bombing of Cambodia to eliminate enemy sanctuaries and supply lines.

1970
- Nixon orders joint U.S.–South Vietnamese invasion of Cambodia.
- Students killed by national guardsmen and police during campus protests at Kent State and Jackson State.
- Nuclear Non-Proliferation Treaty signed by United States, Soviet Union, and 60 other nations goes into effect.

1971
- *New York Times* publishes *Pentagon Papers*, a secret government study critical of U.S. policy in Vietnam.

1972
- Nixon becomes first U.S. president to visit China.
- Nixon visits Moscow to sign arms limitation treaties with Soviets.

1973
- Paris accords between the United States, North and South Vietnam, and Vietcong bring formal end to U.S. role in Vietnam.
- Congress enacts War Powers Act, limiting president's ability to send Americans to war without congressional consent.
- CIA-backed military coup in Chile topples leftist president Salvador Allende, bringing military dictatorship of Augusto Pinochet to power.
- Arab oil embargo in retaliation for U.S. support of Israel in the Yom Kippur War.

1975
- North Vietnam launches final offensive and takes over all of South Vietnam, ending war in Vietnam.
- Helsinki accords signed by United States, Soviet Union, and European nations recognize post–World War II boundaries of Europe and promise human rights to their citizens.

BIBLIOGRAPHY

General Works

David Halberstam, *The Best and the Brightest* (1972).
George C. Herring, *America's Longest War: The United States and Vietnam, 1950–1975* (1986).
Walter A. McDougall, *The Heavens and the Earth: A Political History of the Space Age* (1985).
Kim McQuaid, *The Anxious Years: America in the Vietnam and Watergate Era* (1989).
Charles Murray and Catherine Bly Cox, *Apollo: The Race to the Moon* (1989).
James S. Olson and Randy Roberts, *Where the Domino Fell: America and Vietnam, 1945–1990* (1996).
Irwin Unger and Debi Unger, *Turning Point: 1968* (1988).
Marilyn B. Young, *The Vietnam Wars, 1945–1990* (1991).

Foreign Policy in the 1960s

Warren Bass, *Support Any Friend: Kennedy's Middle East and the Making of the U.S.-Israel Alliance* (2003).
William Bundy, *A Tangled Web: The Making of Foreign Policy in the Nixon Presidency* (1998).
Elizabeth Cobbs Hoffman, *All You Need Is Love: The Peace Corps and the Spirit of the 1960s* (1998).
Walter Isaacson, *Kissinger: A Biography* (1992).
Keith L. Nelson, *The Making of Détente: Soviet-American Relations in the Shadow of Vietnam* (1995).
Thomas G. Paterson, ed., *Kennedy's Quest for Victory: American Foreign Policy, 1962–1963* (1989).
Gerald T. Rice, *The Bold Experiment: JFK's Peace Corps* (1986).
Robert D. Schulzinger, *Henry Kissinger: Doctor of Diplomacy* (1989).
Thomas Alan Schwartz, *Lyndon Johnson and Europe: In the Shadow of Vietnam* (2003).
D. Michael Shafe, *Deadly Paradigms: The Failure of the U.S. Counterinsurgency Policy* (1988).
Deborah Shapley, *Promise and Power: The Life and Times of Robert McNamara* (1993).

The United States and Latin America

Graham T. Allison and Philip Zelikow, *Essence of Decision: Explaining the Cuban Crisis* (2nd ed., 1999).
James G. Blight and Philip Brenner, *Sad and Luminous Days: Cuba's Struggle with the Superpowers after the Missile Crisis* (2002).
Aleksandr Fursenko and Timothy J. Naftali, *One Hell of a Gamble: The Secret History of the Cuban Missile Crisis* (1998).
Trumball Higgins, *The Perfect Failure: Kennedy, Eisenhower, and the CIA at the Bay of Pigs* (1987).
Lester D. Langley, *America and the Americans: The United States in the Western Hemisphere* (1989).
Jerome Levinson and Juan de Onis, *The Alliance That Lost Its Way* (1970).
Abraham Lowenthal, *The Dominican Intervention* (1972).
James A. Nathan, ed., *The Cuban Missile Crisis Revisited* (1992).
Thomas G. Paterson, *Contesting Castro: The United States and the Triumph of the Cuban Revolution* (1994).
Stephen G. Rabe, *The Most Dangerous Area in the World: John F. Kennedy Confronts Communist Revolution in Latin America* (1999).

Robert Smith Thompson, *The Missiles of October: The Declassified Story of John F. Kennedy and the Cuban Missile Crisis* (1992).
Robert Weisbrot, *Maximum Danger: Kennedy, the Missiles, and the Crisis of American Confidence* (2001).
Mark J. White, *Missiles in Cuba: Kennedy, Khrushchev, Castro, and the 1962 Crisis* (1997).

The War in Vietnam

David L. Anderson, *Shadow on the White House: Presidents and the Vietnam War* (1993).
Loren Baritz, *Backfire: A History of How American Culture Led Us into Vietnam and Made Us Fight the Way We Did* (1985).
Larry Berman, *Lyndon Johnson's War: The Road to Stalemate in Vietnam* (1989).
Robert Buzzanco, *Masters of War: Military Dissent and Politics in the Vietnam Era* (1996).
Mark Clodfelter, *The Limits of Air Power: The American Bombing of North Vietnam* (1989).
Bernard Fall, *The Two Vietnams: A Political and Military Analysis* (1967).
Frances FitzGerald, *Fire in the Lake: The Vietnamese and the Americans in Vietnam* (1972).
Lloyd C. Gardner, *Pay Any Price: Lyndon Johnson and the Wars for Vietnam* (1995).
James William Gibson, *The Perfect War: Technowar in Vietnam* (1986).
Allan E. Goodman, *The Lost Peace: America's Search for a Negotiated Settlement of the Vietnam War* (1978).
Ellen J. Hammer, *A Death in November: America in Vietnam, 1973* (1987).
Michael H. Hunt, *Lyndon Johnson's War: America's Cold War Crusade in Vietnam* (1996).
Arnold R. Isaacs, *Without Honor: Defeat in Vietnam and Cambodia* (1983).
Arnold R. Isaacs, *Vietnam Shadows: The War, Its Ghosts, and Its Legacy* (1997).
David Kaiser, *American Tragedy: Kennedy, Johnson, and the Origins of the Vietnam War* (2000).
Stanley Karnow, *Vietnam: A History* (rev. ed., 1991).
Jeffrey P. Kimball, *Nixon's Vietnam War* (1998).
Gabriel Kolko, *Anatomy of a War: Vietnam, the United States, and the Modern Historical Experience* (1985).
A. J. Langguth, *Our Vietnam/Nuoc Viet Ta: A History of the War, 1954–1975* (2000).
Michael Lind, *Vietnam, the Necessary War: A Reinterpretation of America's Most Disastrous Military Conflict* (1999).
Fredrik Logevall, *Choosing War: The Lost Chance for Peace and the Escalation of the War in Vietnam* (1999).
Robert S. McNamara, *In Retrospect: The Tragedy and Lessons of Vietnam* (1995).
Robert S. McNamara, et al., *Argument without End: In Search of Answers to the Vietnam Tragedy* (1999).
Edwin E. Moïse, *Tonkin Gulf and the Escalation of the Vietnam War* (1996).
John M. Newman, *JFK and Vietnam: Deception, Intrigue, and the Struggle for Power* (1992).
John Prados, *The Hidden History of the Vietnam War* (1995).
Jeffrey Record, *The Wrong Way: Why We Lost in Vietnam* (1998).

Ronald H. Spector, *After Tet: The Bloodiest Year in Vietnam* (1993).
Roger Warner, *Shooting at the Moon: The Story of America's Clandestine War in Laos* (1997).

Those Who Served

Christian G. Appy, *Working-Class War: American Combat Soldiers in Vietnam* (1993).
Lawrence M. Baskir and William A. Strauss, *Chance and Circumstance: The Draft, the War, and the Vietnam Generation* (1978).
Alfred S. Bradford, *Some Even Volunteered: The First Wolfhounds Pacify Vietnam* (1994).
Philip Caputo, *A Rumor of War* (1977).
David Donovan, *Once a Warrior King: Memories of an Officer in Vietnam* (1985).
Bernard Edelman, ed., *Dear America: Letters Home from Vietnam* (1985).
Peter Goldman, *Charlie Company: What Vietnam Did to Us* (1983).
Bob Greene, *Homecoming: When the Soldiers Returned from Vietnam* (1989).
Ron Kovic, *Born on the Fourth of July* (1976).
Myra MacPherson, *Long Time Passing: Vietnam and the Haunted Generation* (1984).
Kathryn Marshall, *In the Combat Zone: Vivid Personal Recollections of the Vietnam War from the Women Who Served There* (1987).
Harry Maurer, *Strange Ground: Americans in Vietnam, 1945–1975, an Oral History* (1998).
Harold G. Moore, *We Were Soldiers Once—and Young: Ia Drang, the Battle That Changed the War in Vietnam* (1992).
Stewart O'Nan, ed., *The Vietnam Reader* (1998).
Al Santoli, *Everything We Had: An Oral History of the Vietnam War* (1981).
Neil Sheehan, *A Bright Shining Lie: John Paul Vann and America in Vietnam* (1988).
James E. Westheider, *Fighting on Two Fronts: African Americans and the Vietnam War* (1997).
John Wheeler, *Touched with Fire: The Future of the Vietnam Generation* (1984).

The Antiwar Movement

Charles DeBenedetti, with Charles Chatfield, *An American Ordeal: The Antiwar Movement in the Vietnam Era* (1990).
Michael S. Foley, *Confronting the War Machine: Draft Resistance during the Vietnam War* (2003).
Adam Garfinkle, *Telltale Hearts: The Origins and Impact of the Vietnam Antiwar Movement* (1995).
Todd Gitlin, *The Whole World Is Watching* (1980).
Andrew E. Hunt, *The Turning: A History of Vietnam Veterans against the War* (1999).
Rhodri Jeffreys-Jones, *Peace Now! American Society and the Ending of the Vietnam War* (1999).
Thomas Powers, *Vietnam: The War at Home* (1973).
Melvin Small, *Johnson, Nixon, and the Doves* (1988).
Melvin Small and William D. Hoover, eds., *Give Peace a Chance: Exploring the Vietnam Antiwar Movement* (1992).
Amy Swerdlow, *Women Strike for Peace: Traditional Motherhood and Radical Politics in the 1960s* (1993).
Michael Useem, *Conscription, Protest, and Social Conflict: The Life and Death of a Draft Resistance Movement* (1983).
Nancy Zaroulis and Gerald Sullivan, *Who Spoke Up? American Protests against the War in Vietnam* (1984).

Domestic Politics

Dan T. Carter, *The Politics of Race: George Wallace, the Origins of the New Conservatism, and the Transformation of American Politics* (1995).
Stephan Lesher, *George Wallace: American Populist* (1994).
David Rudenstine, *The Day the Presses Stopped: A History of the Pentagon Papers Case* (1996).
Jonathan Schell, *The Time of Illusion* (1976).
Theodore H. White, *The Making of the President, 1968* (1970).
Jules Witcover, *Eighty-Five Days: The Last Campaign of Robert Kennedy* (1969).

MAKING AMERICA "REAGAN COUNTRY"

This delegate badge from the 1980 Republican National Convention
played on themes that would characterize Ronald Reagan's presidential campaigns and the
politics and policies of the 1980s. Just as the badge appealed to patriotic sentiments with the flag, the
Statue of Liberty, and the space program, Reagan encouraged Americans to take pride in their nation and
celebrate its achievements rather than to focus on its shortcomings. His image as a cowboy brought to
mind some of the movies he had acted in and his favorite recreation—working on the ranch he owned in
California—as well as the independence and rugged individualism in the West, where he had made his
home since the 1940s. The West produced a key element in the surge of conservatism that ensured Reagan's victory in 1980, shaped his administration's antigovernment, anti-Communist agenda, and reversed
the liberal direction that national politics had taken in the 1960s.

National Museum of American History, Smithsonian Institution, Behring Center.

America Moves to the Right

1969–1989

W HEN CONSERVATIVE REPUBLICAN BARRY GOLDWATER spoke to the National Federation of Republican Women in 1963, Phyllis Schlafly, who had invited him, experienced "one of the most exciting days of my life." Like Goldwater, she opposed the moderate Republicanism that had guided the Eisenhower administration and still captured the party leadership. Both Schlafly and Goldwater called for the United States to go beyond simply containing **communism** and to eliminate that evil threat entirely. And both wanted to cut back the government in Washington, especially its role in providing social welfare and enforcing civil rights. Disappointed by Goldwater's loss to Lyndon Johnson in the presidential race of 1964, Schlafly nevertheless took heart in the ability of the **conservatives** to engineer his nomination and continued her efforts to move the Republican Party to the right. Capitalizing on opposition to the policy innovations and turmoil of the 1960s, she added new issues to the conservative agenda and helped to build a grassroots movement on the right that would redefine not only the Republican Party, but American politics and policy into the twenty-first century.

Phyllis Stewart was born in St. Louis in 1924, attended Catholic schools and Washington University, and earned an M.A. in government from Radcliffe College in 1945. Four years later she married Fred Schlafly, an Alton, Illinois, attorney whose anticommunism and antigovernment passions equaled hers. The mother of six children, Schlafly claimed, "I don't think there's anything as much fun as taking care of a baby," and she asserted, "I'd rather scrub bathroom floors than write the newsletter." Yet while she insisted that caring for home and family was women's most important career, Schlafly spent much of her time in politics—writing, speaking, testifying before legislative committees, and losing two bids for Congress in her heavily Democratic district, in 1952, when she was already a mother, and in 1970. Her book, *A Choice Not an Echo*, which she self-published in 1964, excoriated the control of the Republican Party by a **liberal** elite eastern establishment, pushed Barry Goldwater as "the obvious choice" for president, and sold over a million copies. Beginning in 1967, she also published *The Phyllis Schlafly Report*, a monthly newsletter dealing with current political issues. Throughout the 1950s and 1960s, Schlafly focused on the need for stronger efforts against communism at home and abroad, a more powerful military, and a less active government in domestic affairs—all traditional conservative goals.

In the 1970s, however, Schlafly began to pay attention to a host of new issues, including **feminism** and the Equal Rights Amendment, abortion, gay

- **Nixon and the Rise of Postwar Conservatism**
  The Emergence of a Grassroots Conservative Movement
  Nixon Courts the Right

- **Constitutional Crisis and Restoration**
  The Election of 1972
  Watergate
  The Ford Presidency and the Election of 1976

- **The "Outsider" Presidency of Jimmy Carter**
  Retreat from Liberalism
  Carter Promotes Human Rights
  The Cold War Intensifies

- **Ronald Reagan and the Conservative Ascendancy**
  Appealing to the New Right and Beyond
  Unleashing Free Enterprise
  Winners and Losers in a Flourishing Economy

- **Continuing Struggles over Rights and the Environment**
  The Conservative Shift in the Federal Courts
  Feminism on the Defensive
  The Gay and Lesbian Rights Movement
  Conflicts over Environmental Protections

- **Ronald Reagan Confronts an "Evil Empire"**
  Militarization and Interventions Abroad
  The Iran-Contra Scandal
  A Thaw in Soviet-American Relations

- **Conclusion: Reversing the Course of Government**

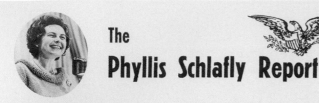

VOL. 5, NO. 10, SECTION 2   Box 618, ALTON, ILLINOIS 62002   **MAY, 1972**

The Fraud Called The Equal Rights Amendment

If there ever was an example of how a tiny minority can cram its views down the throats of the majority, it is the Equal Rights Amendment, called ERA. A noisy claque of women's lib agitators rammed ERA through Congress, intimidating the men into voting for it so they would not be labeled "anti-woman."

The ERA passed Congress with big majorities on March 22, 1972 and was sent to the states for ratification. When it is ratified by 38 states, it will become the law of the land. Within two hours of Senate passage, Hawaii ratified it. New Hampshire and Nebraska, both anxious to be second, rushed their approval the next day. Then in steady succession came Iowa, Idaho, Delaware, Kansas, Texas, Maryland, Tennessee, Alaska, Rhode Island, and New Jersey. As this goes to press, 13 states have ratified it and others are on the verge of doing so.

Three states have rejected it: Oklahoma, Vermont and Connecticut.

What is ERA? The Amendment reads: "Equality of rights under the law shall not be denied or abridged by the United States or by any state on account of sex."

Does that sound good? Don't kid yourself. This innocuous-sounding amendment will take away far more important rights than it will ever give. This was made abundantly clear by the debate in Congress. Senator Sam Ervin (D., N.C.) called it "the most drastic measure in Senate history." He proved this by putting into the *Congressional Record* an article from the *Yale Law Journal* of April 1971.

The importance of this *Yale Law Journal* article is that both the proponents and the opponents of ERA agree that it is an accurate analysis of the consequences of ERA. Congresswoman Martha Griffiths, a leading proponent of ERA, sent a copy of this article to every member of Congress, stating that "It... understand the purposes and effect... Rights Amendment... The artic... ERA will work in m...

An... Ba...

the most important of all women's rights.

"In all states husbands are primarily liable for the support of their wives and children.... The child support sections of the criminal nonsupport laws ... could not be sustained where only the male is liable for support." (YLJ, pp. 944-945)

"The Equal Rights Amendment would bar a state from imposing greater liability for support on a husband than on a wife merely because of his sex." (YLJ, p. 945)

"Like the duty of support during marriage and the obligation to pay alimony in the case of separation or divorce, nonsupport would have to be eliminated as a ground for divorce against husbands only... " (YLJ, p. 951)

"The Equal Rights Amendment would not require that alimony be abolished but only that it be available equally to husbands and wives." (YLJ, p. 952)

2. ERA will wipe out the laws which protect only women against sex crimes such as rape.

"Courts faced with criminal laws which do not apply equally to men and women would be likely to invalidate the laws rather than extending or rewriting them to apply to women and men alike." (YLJ, p. 966)

"Seduction laws, statutory rape laws, laws prohibiting obscene language in the presence of women, prostitution and 'manifest danger' laws ... The Equal Rights Amendment would not permit such laws, which base their sex discriminatory classification on social stereotypes." (YLJ, p. 954)

"The statutory rape laws, which punish men for having sexual intercourse with any wom... under an age specified by law ... suffer from s... fect under the E...ual Rights Amendme...

"To ...

The Phyllis Schlafly Report

Phyllis Schlafly's monthly newsletter to members of her conservative Eagle Forum began in 1967 with articles attacking federal social programs and calling for stronger measures and weapons to fight the cold war against communism. When Congress passed the Equal Rights Amendment in 1972, the *Report* began to add antifeminism and other concerns of the New Right to its agenda, including opposition to abortion rights, sex education in the schools, and protections for gays and lesbians. Schlafly's attacks on feminism appealed to many people; subscribers to her newsletter numbered more than 35,000 in the mid-1970s. The feminist leader Betty Friedan told Schlafly, "I consider you a traitor to your sex. I consider you an Aunt Tom."

Courtesy of Phyllis Schlafly.

---

rights, busing for racial integration, and religion in the schools. Her positions resonated with many Americans who were fed up with the protest movements, the expansion of government, and the challenges to authority and tradition that seemed to define the 1960s. Moreover, the votes of those Americans began to reshape American politics—in Richard Nixon's victories in the presidential elections of 1968 and 1972; in the presidency of Jimmy Carter, whose policies stood substantially to the right of the Democratic administrations of the 1960s; and in conservative Ronald Reagan's capture of the Republican Party, the presidency, and the political agenda in 1980.

Although Richard Nixon did not embrace the entire conservative agenda, he sought to make the Republicans the dominant party by appealing to disaffected blue-collar and southern white Democrats. Nixon resigned the presidency in disgrace in 1974, and his Republican successor, Gerald Ford, occupied the Oval Office for little more than two years; but the shift of the political spectrum to the right continued even when the Democrats captured the White House in 1976. Antigovernment sentiment grew out of the deceptions of the Johnson administration, Nixon's abuse of presidential powers, and the inability of Presidents Ford and Carter to resolve domestic and foreign crises. As Americans saw their incomes decline because of surging unemployment and inflation, many lost confidence in government and became convinced that their taxes were too high.

In 1980, Phyllis Schlafly saw her call for "a choice, not an echo" realized when Ronald Reagan won the presidency. Cutting taxes and government regulations, attacking social programs, expanding the nation's military capacity, and putting pressure on the Soviet Union and communism in the **third world**, Reagan addressed the hopes of traditional conservatives. Like Schlafly, he also championed the concerns of the **New Right**, opposing abortion and sexual permissiveness and supporting a larger role for religion in public life. Reagan's goals encountered resistance from feminists, civil rights groups, environmentalists, and others who fought to keep what they had won in the 1960s. Although his administration failed to enact the entire conservative agenda, left the government with an enormous national debt, and engaged in illegal activities to thwart communism in Latin America, Reagan's popularity helped send another Republican, his vice president, George H. Bush, to the White House at the end of his second term. And Reagan's determined optimism and spirited leadership contributed to a revival in national pride and confidence.

Nixon and the Rise of Postwar Conservatism

Although, as we have seen in chapter 28, Nixon acquiesced in the continuation of most **Great Society** programs and even approved pathbreaking new measures in such areas as the environment, Native American rights, and women's rights, his public rhetoric and certain of his actions as president signified the country's rightward move in both politics and sentiment. During Nixon's years in office, a new strand of conservatism began to join the older movement that focused on anticommunism, a strong national defense, and a limited role for the federal government in domestic affairs. The new conservatism, which Phyllis Schlafly helped promote, condemned much of the Great Society and other developments of the 1960s, including antiwar protests, civil rights demonstrations, liberal Supreme Court decisions, the sexual revolution, and feminism.

The Emergence of a Grassroots Conservative Movement

Although Lyndon Johnson's landslide victory over Barry Goldwater in 1964 appeared to signify liberalism triumphant, those election results actually concealed a rising conservative movement. Defining his purpose as "enlarging freedom at home and safeguarding it from the forces of tyranny abroad," Goldwater echoed the ideas of conservative intellectuals who argued that government intrusion into economic life hindered prosperity, stifled personal responsibility, and interfered with individuals' rights to determine their own values. While they assailed big government in domestic affairs, they demanded a strong military to eradicate "Godless communism."

A growing grassroots movement, vigorous especially in the South and West and including middle-class suburban women and men, members of the rabidly anti-Communist John Birch Society, and college students in the new Young Americans for Freedom had enabled Goldwater, an Arizona senator, to win the nomination. They did not give up when he lost the election. Margaret Minek, who had organized for Goldwater in her community, insisted, "We have a . . . flame . . . burning and the energy it gives off needs to be utilized." Newly energized conservatives like Minek in California contributed to Ronald

Reagan's defeat of the incumbent liberal governor, Edmund Brown, in 1966, another sign of the rising strength of the right. Linking his opponent with the student disruptions at the University of California at Berkeley (Reagan called them "the filthy speech movement") and the Watts riot, Reagan capitalized on popular fears about rising taxes, student challenges to authority, and black demands for justice. He claimed in one campaign speech that "if an individual wants to discriminate against Negroes or others in selling or renting his house he has a right to do so."

Although the rise of grassroots conservatism was not limited to the West and South, a number of elements in the **Sun Belt** were conducive to its growth in areas such as Orange County, California; Dallas, Texas; Scottsdale, Arizona; and Jefferson Parish, Louisiana. Areas that hosted strong conservative movements contained relatively homogeneous, skilled, and affluent populations, and their economies depended heavily on military bases and defense production. The West harbored a long-standing tradition of **Protestant** morality, individualism, and opposition to interference by a remote federal government. That tradition continued with the emergence of the New Right, even though it was hardly consistent with the western states' economic dependence on military and defense spending.

> Although the rise of grassroots conservatism was not limited to the West and South, a number of elements in the Sun Belt were conducive to its growth there.

The South shared the West's antipathy to the federal government, but there hostility to racial change was much more central to the new conservatism. After signing the Civil Rights Act of 1964, President Lyndon Johnson remarked to a friend, "I think we just delivered the South to the Republican Party." Indeed, Barry Goldwater won a majority in five southern states in 1964.

Grassroots movements emerged around a number of issues that conservatives believed marked the "moral decline" of their nation. For example, in 1968, Eleanor Howe mobilized her community to eliminate sex education from the schools in Anaheim, California, when she examined the curriculum and found that "nothing depicted my values. . . . It wasn't so much the information. It was the shift in values." In 1970, Alice Moore launched a campaign in Charleston, West Virginia, against a sex education curriculum that she found anti-American and anti-Christian and based on an "atheistic and relativistic view of morality." Decisions by the Warren Court on such issues as school prayer, obscenity, and birth control also galvanized conservatives to restore "traditional values" to the nation.

Nixon Courts the Right

In the 1968 campaign, Nixon's "southern strategy" had exploited antipathy to black protest and new civil rights policies, wooing white southerners away from the Democratic Party as well as considerable numbers of northern voters. Republicans hoped to use the "southern strategy" to make further inroads into traditional Democratic strongholds in the 1972 election.

The Nixon administration reluctantly enforced court orders to achieve high degrees of integration in southern schools, but it stymied efforts to deal with segregation outside the South. School segregation was widespread in northern and western cities, where residential patterns left half of all African American children attending virtually all-black schools. After courts began to order the transfer of students between schools in white and black neighborhoods to achieve desegregation, and the Supreme Court assented in *Swann v. Charlotte-Mecklenburg Board of Education* in 1971, busing became "political dynamite," according to a Gallup poll. Phyllis Schlafly spoke for many busing opponents when she wrote in 1972, "We've had all we can take of judicial interference with local schools."

Although children had been riding buses to school for decades, especially in rural areas, busing for racial integration provoked outrage. Such fury erupted in Boston in 1974 when black students began to attend the formerly all-white South Boston High School. Nearly all the white students boycotted classes, and angry white crowds threw rocks at black students disembarking from buses. The whites most affected came from working-class families, who remained in cities abandoned by the more affluent and whose children were usually the ones riding buses to predom-

> School segregation was widespread in northern and western cities, where residential patterns left half of all African American children attending virtually all-black schools.

inantly black schools where overcrowding and deficient facilities often meant inferior education. Clarence McDonough fingered the liberal officials who bused his "kid half way around Boston so that a bunch of politicians can end up their careers with a clear conscience." Phyllis Schlafly echoed the sentiment, pointing out, "None of the justices who ordered busing ever sent their children to inner-city schools or allowed them to be the victims of forced busing." African Americans themselves were conflicted about the benefits of sending their children on long rides to schools where teachers might not welcome or respect them. Nixon failed to persuade Congress to end court-ordered busing, but after he had appointed four new justices, the Supreme Court moved in the president's direction in 1974. In a five-to-four decision concerning the Detroit public schools (*Milliken v. Bradley*), the Court imposed strict limits on the use of busing to achieve racial balance.

Nixon also sought to implement the southern strategy and ride the backlash against liberalism through his judicial appointments. He believed that the Supreme Court under Chief Justice Earl Warren had been "unprecedentedly politically active . . . too often using their interpretation of the law to remake American society according to their own social, political, and ideological precepts." Appealing to Americans outraged by the Warren Court's liberal decisions, Nixon planned to reverse the Court's direction. When Warren resigned in June 1969, Nixon replaced him with Warren E. Burger, a federal appeals court judge who was seen as a **strict constructionist**—someone inclined to interpret the Constitution narrowly and to limit government intervention to protect individual rights.

Unions and civil rights groups, however, mounted strong campaigns against Nixon's next two nominees, conservative southern judges, and the Senate forced him to settle on more moderate candidates. The Burger Court proved more sympathetic than the Warren Court to the president's agenda, restricting somewhat the protections of individual rights established by the previous Court. For example, the Court limited the range of **affirmative action** in *Regents of the University of California v. Bakke* (1978) (see "Significant Supreme Court Cases," page A-44). Yet that decision did allow affirmative action programs to attack the results of past discrimination as long as strict quotas or racial classifications were not involved. (The Court reaffirmed this position in 2003.) In *Bakke* and other cases,

Integration of Public Schools, 1968

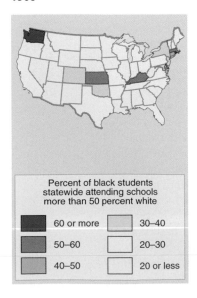

Percent of black students statewide attending schools more than 50 percent white

60 or more	30–40
50–60	20–30
40–50	20 or less

School Busing
Controversy over busing as a means to integrate public schools erupted in Boston when the school year started in autumn 1974. Opposition was especially high in white ethnic neighborhoods like South Boston. Residents there resented liberal judges from the suburbs assigning them the burden of integration. Clashes between blacks and whites in South Boston, such as this one in February 1975 outside Boston's Hyde Park High School, prompted authorities to dispatch police to protect black students.
AP / Wide World.

the Burger Court continued to uphold liberal programs of the 1960s.

Nixon's southern strategy and the backlash against the civil rights revolution of the 1960s ended the Democratic hold on the "solid South." In 1964, Senator Strom Thurmond of South Carolina, who had headed the Dixiecrat challenge to Truman in 1948, changed his party affiliation to Republican. North Carolina senator Jesse Helms followed suit in 1971, and aspirants for office throughout the South began to realize that Democratic candidates had a dim future in that region. Although Republicans never realized the dominance held by the Democrats in 1950, when only two southern Republican representatives sat in Congress, by 2002 Republicans held the majority of southern seats in the House and Senate and four of the seven governorships in the South.

In addition to courting the votes of Americans uncomfortable with the pace of racial change, Nixon aligned himself with those fearful about women's changing roles and new demands. In 1971, he vetoed a bill providing federal funds for day care centers with a message that combined the old and new conservatism. Parents should purchase child care services "in the private, open market," he insisted, not through a fiscally irresponsible program requiring "a new army of bureaucrats." At the same time, he played to concerns of social conservatives by warning about the "family-weakening

implications" of the measure that would replace "the family-centered approach [with] communal approaches to child rearing." And, in response to the movement to liberalize abortion laws, Nixon took the side of the "defenders of the right to life of the unborn." He did not comment publicly on *Roe v. Wade* (1973), but his earlier stance against abortion anticipated the Republican Party's eventual embrace of an issue that Phyllis Schlafly and others would use to mobilize forces on the right.

Constitutional Crisis and Restoration

Nixon's ability to attract Democrats resulted in a resounding landslide victory in the 1972 election. Two years later, however, the so-called Watergate scandals caused him to abandon his office. Nixon's abuse of power and efforts to cover up crimes committed by subordinates betrayed the public trust and forced the first presidential resignation in history. His hand-picked successor, Gerald Ford, helped to restore confidence in the presidency, but the aftermath of Watergate and severe economic

> Nixon's abuse of power and efforts to cover up crimes committed by subordinates betrayed the public trust and forced the first presidential resignation in history.

problems returned the White House to the Democrats in 1976. Nonetheless, so robust was the conservative tide that it not only survived the temporary setback when Nixon resigned the presidency, it quickly challenged the Democratic administration that followed.

The Election of 1972

Nixon's most spectacular foreign policy initiatives, **détente** with the Soviet Union and the opening of relations with China (see chapter 29), heightened his prospects for reelection in 1972. Although the war in Vietnam continued, antiwar protests diminished with the decrease in American ground forces and casualties. Nixon's New Economic Policy had temporarily checked inflation and unemployment, and his attacks on busing and antiwar protesters had appealed to the right, positioning him favorably for the 1972 election.

A large field of contenders vied for the Democratic nomination, including New York representative Shirley Chisholm, the first African American politician to make a serious bid for the presidency, who won 151 delegate votes. On the right, Governor George Wallace of Alabama captured a series of southern primaries as well as those in Michigan and Maryland, but his campaign was cut short when a deranged man shot him, leaving Wallace paralyzed below the waist. Democratic senator George S. McGovern of South Dakota, who had defeated a large field of contenders, came to the Democratic convention as the clear leader, and the composition of the convention delegates made his position even stronger.

After the bitter 1968 convention, the Democrats had initiated key reforms, requiring delegations to represent the relative proportions of minorities, women, and youth in their states. These newcomers displaced many regular Democrats—officeholders, labor leaders, and representatives of traditional ethnic groups. One party regular thought that "the Democratic Party was taken over by the kooks," and another, referring to the considerable numbers of young people and women, remarked that there was "too much hair, and not enough cigars at this convention." Though easily nominated, McGovern struggled against Nixon from the outset. Republicans portrayed him as a left extremist; and his support for busing, his call for immediate withdrawal from Vietnam, and his pledge to cut $30 billion from the Pentagon's budget alienated conservative Democrats.

Nixon gained 60.7 percent of the popular vote, carrying every state except Massachusetts in a landslide victory second only to Johnson's in 1964. Although the Democrats maintained control of Congress, Nixon won a majority of votes among southerners, Catholics, urbanites, and blue-collar workers, all traditionally strong supporters of the Democratic Party. The president had little time to savor his triumph, however, as revelations began to emerge about crimes and misdemeanors that had been committed to ensure the victory.

Watergate

During the early morning hours of June 17, 1972, five men working for Nixon's reelection campaign crept into Democratic Party headquarters in the Watergate complex in Washington. Intending to repair a bugging device installed in an earlier break-in, they were discovered and arrested on the scene. In trying to

Shirley Chisholm Runs for President

From an active political career in the Democratic Party, grassroots community groups, the League of Women Voters, and the New York State Assembly, Shirley Chisholm became the first African American woman elected to the House of Representatives in 1968. She won that election against James Farmer, a founder of CORE, whose campaign stressed the need for "a strong male image" and a "man's voice in Washington." Chisholm entered the race for the Democratic presidential nomination in 1972 knowing that her chances were slim but asserting that minority women were "used to taking up seemingly impossible challenges . . . and in the process increas[ing] the chance that success would come, someday." Here she announces her candidacy at the Concord Baptist Church in Brooklyn in January 1972.

Dan Hogan Charles/New York Times/Getty Images.

The Gap in the Watergate Tapes

Franklin Roosevelt installed the first recording apparatus in the White House under his desk in 1940, but neither he, Truman, nor Eisenhower recorded conversations extensively. John F. Kennedy was the first president to put in a complete taping network; and Richard Nixon was the first to use a voice-activated system, which taped about 2,800 hours of conversations in which most participants did not know they were being recorded. When Nixon was compelled to turn over the tapes during the Watergate investigation, an 18½-minute gap was discovered in a conversation between Nixon and his chief of staff, H. R. Haldeman, just three days after the Watergate break-in. Nixon's secretary Rose Mary Woods said that her foot must have slipped while she was transcribing the tape, using the transcription machine pictured above; but others, noting that the 18 minutes contained several separate erasings, suggested that the clumsiness of the deed linked it to Nixon.

Nixon Presidential Materials Project, National Archives and Records Administration.

cover up the connection between those arrested and administration officials, Nixon and his aides set in motion the most serious constitutional crisis since the Civil War. Reporters dubbed it "Watergate."

Over the next two years, Americans learned that Nixon and his associates had engaged in other abuses, such as accepting illegal campaign contributions, using so-called dirty tricks to sabotage Democratic candidates, and unlawfully attempting to silence critics of the Vietnam War. Nixon was not the first president to lie to the public or to misuse power. Every president since Franklin D. Roosevelt had enlarged the powers of the presidency, justifying his actions as necessary to protect national security. This expansion of executive powers, often called the "imperial presidency," weakened some of the traditional **checks and balances** on the executive branch and opened the door to abuses.

Watergate began when White House adviser Charles Colson established a secret unit nicknamed the "plumbers" to stop the kinds of "leaks" that had led to publication of the *Pentagon Papers* in 1971. These men soon turned to projects to disrupt the Democratic presidential nomination process and discredit potential candidates, and in 1972 they staged the Watergate break-in to bug the Democratic Party's phones. After the arrest of the Watergate burglars, Nixon secretly plotted to conceal links between the burglars and the White House, while publicly denying any connection to the break-in. When investigations by a grand jury and the Senate suggested that White House aides had been involved, Nixon decided that it was time to act.

In April 1973, the president accepted official responsibility for Watergate but denied any personal knowledge of the break-in or of a cover-up. He also announced the resignations of three White House aides and Attorney General Richard Kleindienst. In May, he authorized the appointment of an independent special prosecutor, Archibald Cox, to conduct an investigation. Meanwhile, sensational revelations exploded in the Senate investigating committee, headed by Democrat Samuel J. Ervin of North Carolina. Counsel to the President John Dean described projects to harass "enemies" through tax audits and other illegal means and asserted that the president had long known of efforts to cover up the Watergate burglary. The most damaging blow struck when a White House aide disclosed that all conversations in the Oval Office were taped. Both Cox and the Ervin committee immediately asked for tapes related to Watergate. When Nixon refused, citing executive privilege and separation of powers, Cox and Ervin took their case to federal district court.

At the same time, more disclosures revealed Nixon's misuse of federal funds and tax evasion. In August 1973, Vice President Spiro Agnew was compelled to resign after an investigation revealed that he had taken bribes while governor of Maryland. Although Nixon's choice of House minority leader Gerald Ford of Michigan to succeed Agnew won widespread approval, the vice president's resignation further tarnished the administration.

On October 19, 1973, Nixon ordered special prosecutor Cox to cease his efforts to obtain the Oval Office tapes. When Cox refused, Nixon ordered Attorney General Elliot Richardson to fire Cox. Richardson instead resigned, as did the next man in line at the Justice Department. Finally, the solicitor general, Robert Bork, agreed to carry out the president's order. The press called the series of dismissals and resignations the "Saturday night massacre," 250,000 telegrams

Nixon's Farewell

The first president in Amercian history to resign the presidency, Nixon did not admit guilt, even though tapes of his conversations indicated that he had obstructed justice, abused his power, and lied. In the decades after his resignation, he gradually rehabilitated his reputation and became an elder statesman and foreign-policy adviser. All the living presidents attended his funeral in 1994. In this photo, he and his family say goodbye to his successor, Gerald Ford, and Betty Ford, and prepare to board the helicopter that would take them away from the White House for the last time.

Nixon Presidential Materials Project, National Archives and Records Administration (E3398-09).

condemning Nixon's action flooded the White House, and his popular support plummeted to 27 percent.

In February 1974, the House of Representatives voted to begin an **impeachment** investigation. In April, Nixon began to release edited transcripts of the tapes. As the public read passages sprinkled with "expletive deleted," the House Republican leader Hugh Scott of Penn-

sylvania abandoned his support of the president, calling the transcripts a "deplorable, shabby, disgusting, and immoral performance by all." The transcripts included Nixon's orders to John Mitchell, his former attorney general and head of his reelection committee, and Dean in March 1973: "I don't give a shit what happens. I want you all to stonewall it, let them plead the Fifth Amendment, cover up or anything else, if it'll save it—save the plan."

In July 1974, the House Judiciary Committee began debate over specific charges for impeachment: (1) obstruction of justice, (2) abuse of power, (3) contempt of Congress, (4) unconstitutional waging of war by the secret bombing of Cambodia, and (5) tax evasion and the selling of political favors. While the last two counts failed to get a majority, the committee voted to take the first three charges to the House, where a vote of impeachment seemed certain. On July 24, a unanimous Supreme Court ordered the president to hand over the remaining tapes. Transcripts of tapes released August 5 revealed that just six days after the break-in, Nixon and aides had discussed manipulating the CIA to hinder the FBI's investigation of the burglary. This was sufficient evidence to seal his fate.

Nixon announced his resignation to a national television audience on August 8, 1974. Acknowledging some incorrect judgments, he insisted that he had always tried to do what was best for the nation. The next morning, Nixon ended a rambling, emotional farewell to his staff with some advice: "Always give your best, never get discouraged, never get petty; always remember, others may hate you, but those who hate you don't win unless you hate them, and then you destroy yourself." Had he practiced that advice, he might have saved his presidency.

The Ford Presidency and the Election of 1976

Gerald R. Ford, who had represented Michigan in the House of Representatives since 1948, had built a reputation as a conservative party loyalist who treated opponents with respect. Not a brilliant thinker, Ford was known for his integrity, humility, and dedication to public office. "I'm a Ford, not a Lincoln," he acknowledged. Most of official Washington and the American public looked favorably on his succession as president.

Upon taking office, Ford announced, "Our long nightmare is over," but he shocked many Americans when he ended the particular nightmare of the former president. On September 8, 1974, Ford granted Nixon a pardon "for all offenses against the United States which he . . . has committed or may have committed or taken part in" during his presidency. It was the most generous presidential pardon ever issued, saving Nixon from nearly certain indictment and trial. Thirty of his associates ultimately were convicted or pleaded guilty. The pardon provoked a tremendous outcry from Congress and the public. Capitalizing on revulsion over Watergate and the pardon, Democrats made impressive gains in the November congressional elections.

With the Democrats in control, Congress sought to guard against the types of abuses revealed in the Watergate investigations. The Federal Election Campaign Act of 1974, for example, established public financing of presidential campaigns, though it failed to stop the ever-larger campaign donations that candidates found ways to solicit from interest groups, corporations, labor unions, and wealthy individuals. In 1978, Congress passed an independent counsel law establishing a nonpartisan procedure for the appointment of special prosecutors who could not be fired. The law was used to investigate possibly criminal actions by Presidents Reagan and Clinton (see chapter 31) as well as more than a dozen lesser officials before it expired in 1998.

Special investigating committees in Congress discovered a host of illegal FBI and CIA activities stretching back to the 1950s. Both agencies had harassed political dissenters, and the CIA had made plans to assassinate Fidel Castro and other foreign leaders. In response to these revelations, President Ford established new controls on covert operations, and Congress created permanent committees to oversee the intelligence agencies. Yet these measures did little to diminish the public cynicism and lack of trust in government that had been developing since the Johnson years.

Ford carried a number of burdens into the 1976 presidential race. Underlying weaknesses in the U.S. economy remained: a low growth rate, high unemployment, a foreign trade deficit, and high energy prices tied to dependence on oil from abroad. Ford also faced a major challenge from the Republican right, as California governor Ronald Reagan came close to capturing the nomination.

The Democrats nominated James Earl "Jimmy" Carter Jr., former state senator and governor of Georgia. A graduate of the U.S. Naval Academy, Carter spent seven years in the navy before his father's death called him back to Plains, Georgia, to run the family peanut farming business. Highly intelligent and well prepared on the issues, the soft-spoken Carter stressed his small-town roots, deep religious commitment, and distance from the suspect national government. Although Carter selected liberal senator Walter F. Mondale of Minnesota as his running mate and accepted a platform compatible with traditional Democratic principles, his nomination nonetheless represented a decided rightward turn in the party.

After the revelations of corruption in the Nixon administration, the candidate who carried his own bags, lived modestly, and went home from the campaign trail almost every week to teach a Bible class at his Baptist church had considerable appeal. Carter also benefited from the country's economic problems and from his ability to attract votes from the traditional Democratic coalition of blacks, southerners, organized labor, and ethnic groups. Yet, although Democrats retained substantial margins in Congress, Carter received just 49.9 percent of the popular vote to Ford's 47.9 percent (Map 30.1).

MAP 30.1 The Election of 1976

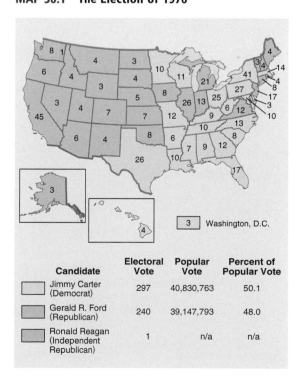

Candidate	Electoral Vote	Popular Vote	Percent of Popular Vote
Jimmy Carter (Democrat)	297	40,830,763	50.1
Gerald R. Ford (Republican)	240	39,147,793	48.0
Ronald Reagan (Independent Republican)	1	n/a	n/a

The "Outsider" Presidency of Jimmy Carter

Carter promised that he would lead a government that was "competent," as well as "honest, decent, open, fair, and compassionate." He also warned Americans that "we can neither answer all questions nor solve all problems." His personal honesty and decency helped to revive trust in the presidency but did not inspire confidence in his own ability to lead the nation through domestic and foreign crises. He faced at more intense levels the energy shortages and stagflation (see chapter 28) that had confounded his predecessors, and he presided over deteriorating Soviet-American relations and renewed instability in the Middle East.

> Carter faced at more intense levels the energy shortages and stagflation that had confounded his predecessors, and he presided over deteriorating Soviet-American relations and renewed instability in the Middle East.

Retreat from Liberalism

Jimmy Carter vowed "to help the poor and aged, to improve education, and to provide jobs" but at the same time "not to waste money." He wanted a government that would help those in need, but one that also was efficient and prudent in its spending. When these aims conflicted, especially when inflation threatened economic stability, Carter's commitment to reform took second place. Americans seeing their material status eroded by stagflation became less willing to see their tax dollars used to benefit the disadvantaged, though their opposition to government programs did not extend to those such as Social Security and Medicare that helped the middle class. As Carter leaned in the direction of fiscal stringency, liberal Democrats accused him of deserting the Democratic reform tradition that stretched back to Franklin D. Roosevelt.

Although Carter's outsider status helped him win the presidency, it left him without strong ties to party insiders or prominent legislators.

Jimmy Carter's Inauguration
After his inauguration in January 1977, Jimmy Carter eschewed the customary presidential limousine and instead walked with his wife, daughter, and two sons and their wives down Pennsylvania Avenue from the Capitol to the White House. He wanted to emphasize his opposition to some of the trappings of office that separated government from the people. Ordering cabinet heads to drive their own cars, he said, "Government officials can't be sensitive to your problems if we are living like royalty here."
Jimmy Carter Presidential Library.

Moreover, his comprehensive proposals went against the congressional tendency to tackle problems with a piecemeal, incremental approach. Legislators complained of inadequate consultation and Carter's tendency to flood them with a mass of unprioritized proposals.

Even a president without those liabilities might not have done much better than Carter, as Congress itself diminished the ability of party leaders to deliver a united front. While it flexed its muscles in response to Watergate and abuses of presidential power, Congress reduced the power of committee chairs, weakened party control over legislators, and decentralized the decision-making process. In addition, because primary elections rather than party conventions now controlled the nominating process, candidates depended less on party support and more on campaign funds from interest groups, which they used to appeal directly to voters through television.

The Carter administration did little better with the formidable problems that had plagued the Nixon and Ford administrations—unemployment, inflation, and slow economic growth. With new tax cuts and increased federal spending on public works and public service jobs programs, unemployment receded for a time. But in 1978, rising inflation impelled Carter to curtail federal spending and the Federal Reserve Board to increase interest rates and tighten the money supply. These policies not only failed to halt inflation, which surpassed 13 percent in 1980, but also contributed to rising unemployment, reversing gains made in Carter's first two years.

Nor did Carter achieve much progress on traditional Democratic issues. His commitment to holding down the federal budget frustrated Democrats pushing for comprehensive welfare reform and a national health insurance program. To ensure solvency in Social Security, Carter and Congress agreed to raise employer and employee contributions, but this also increased the tax burden of lower- and middle-income Americans.

In contrast, corporations and wealthy individuals gained from new legislation. A sharp cut in the capital gains tax benefited high-income individuals. When the Chrysler Corporation approached bankruptcy in 1979, Congress provided $1.5 billion worth of loan guarantees to ensure the survival of the tenth largest corporation in the country. Pleasing to conservatives were Carter's proposals to give greater rein to free enterprise. Congress complied, deregulating airlines in 1978 and the banking, trucking, and railroad industries in 1980.

"We are struggling with a profound transition from a time of abundance to a time of growing scarcity in energy," Carter insisted in 1979, pointing to the nation's enormous consumption of energy and its dependence on oil from the unstable Middle East. The president fought for a comprehensive program and gave that issue cabinet status by creating a Department of Energy. Although the United States was even more dependent on foreign oil than it had been during the energy crisis linked to the Yom Kippur War of 1973, Carter's efforts fell victim to his poor relationship with Congress and to competing demands among energy producers and consumers. Congress did pass legislation to penalize gas-guzzling automobiles and provide other incentives to conserve energy. And in 1979, when another Middle Eastern crisis created the most severe energy shortage yet, Congress authorized more measures to limit consumption and decrease the need for foreign oil. Still, they fell short of Carter's comprehensive proposal, and American industry and individuals continued to devour energy. At the end of the century, the United States, with only about 6 percent of the world's population, consumed more than 25 percent of global oil production.

Carter Promotes Human Rights

Campaigning for president in 1976, Jimmy Carter charged his predecessors' foreign policy with violating the nation's principles of freedom and human dignity. "We've seen a loss of morality . . . and we're ashamed of what our government is as we deal with other nations around the world," he said. The cynical support of dictators, the secret diplomacy, the interference in the internal affairs of other countries, and the excessive reliance on military solutions—Carter promised to reverse them all.

Human rights formed the cornerstone of his approach. Administration officials chastised governments that denied their citizens basic political and civil rights. They also applied economic pressure, denying aid or trading privileges to such nations as Argentina, Chile, and El Salvador, and to the white minority governments of Rhodesia and South Africa, which blatantly violated the rights of their black majorities. Yet glaring inconsistencies appeared in the human rights policy. Concluding the process that Nixon and Kissinger had begun, Carter established formal

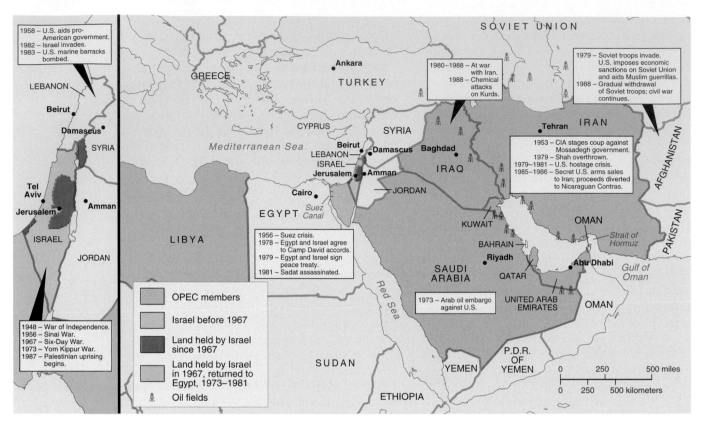

MAP 30.2 The Middle East, 1948–1989

Determination to preserve access to the rich oil reserves of the Middle East and commitment to the security of Israel were the fundamental—and often conflicting—principles of U.S. foreign policy in that region.

READING THE MAP: Where did the United States become involved diplomatically or militarily in the Middle East between 1948 and 1989? Which countries are members of OPEC?

CONNECTIONS: What role did U.S. foreign policy regarding the Middle East and events in Israel play in provoking the 1973 Arab oil embargo against the United States? What precipitated the taking of U.S. hostages in Iran in 1979? Was U.S. intervention in the country a factor? If so, why?

FOR MORE HELP ANALYZING THIS MAP, see the map activity for this chapter in the Online Study Guide at bedfordstmartins.com/roark.

---

diplomatic relations with the People's Republic of China in 1979, even though the Chinese government blatantly refused to grant **democratic** rights to its people. Moreover, the administration invoked no sanctions against repressive governments in Iran, South Korea, and the Philippines, thus sacrificing human rights ideals to strategic and security considerations.

Cold war considerations vied with human rights concerns in Carter's approach to Nicaragua, which had been ruled since 1936 by the corrupt and viciously oppressive Somoza regime. U.S. officials complained about the dictatorship's excesses and invoked some economic sanctions, but when a rebellion erupted, their greatest concern was to contain Communist influence in the anti-Somoza movement. Officials were particularly uneasy about the Sandinistas, a leading element in the opposition with ties to Cuba. Nonetheless, when the Somoza regime fell in 1979 and Sandinista leader Daniel Ortega assumed power, Carter extended recognition and economic aid to the new government. Critics attacked Carter for pressuring the Somoza regime on human rights and recognizing the Ortega government, demanding instead the more typical test for U.S. support during the cold war years—whether a country was anti-Communist and friendly to American interests, not how it treated its citizens.

Applying moral principles to relations with Panama, Carter sped up negotiations over control of the Panama Canal—the most conspicuous symbol of **Yankee imperialism**. In 1977, the United States and Panama signed treaties providing for joint control of the canal until 2000, when Panama would take over. Treaty supporters viewed the agreement as recompense for the blatant use of U.S. power to obtain the canal in 1903. Angry opponents insisted on retaining the vital waterway. "We bought it, we paid for it, it's ours," claimed Ronald Reagan during the presidential primaries of 1976. Only after the Carter administration undertook a massive campaign to rally support did the Senate ratify the treaties by the narrowest margins.

Seeking to apply his moral authority toward peace in the Middle East, Carter seized on the courage of Egyptian president Anwar Sadat, the first Arab leader to risk his political career by talking directly with Israeli officials. When initial discussions between Sadat and Israeli prime minister Menachem Begin faltered, Carter invited them to the presidential retreat at Camp David, Maryland, and spent thirteen days there mediating between the two. The Camp David accords led to an agreement that Begin and Sadat signed at the White House in March 1979: Egypt became the first Arab state to recognize Israel, and Israel agreed to gradual withdrawal from the Sinai Peninsula, territory that it had seized in the 1967 war (Map 30.2). Although the issues of Palestinian self-determination in other Israeli-occupied territories—the West Bank and Gaza—and the plight of Palestinian refugees remained unresolved, the first meaningful steps toward peace in the Middle East had been taken.

The Cold War Intensifies

Elsewhere, Carter was unable to duplicate his success with the Panama treaties and the Egypt-Israel accord. Preferring to pursue national security through nonmilitary means, Carter initially sought accommodation with the Soviet Union. But in 1979, he abandoned efforts to obtain Senate ratification of a new strategic arms limitation treaty and began development of intermediate-range missiles to be deployed in Western Europe and an enormous new missile system for the United States.

Carter's decision for the military buildup, which conservatives like Phyllis Schlafly had been pushing for years, came in 1979 when the Soviet Union invaded its neighbor Afghanistan, whose recently installed Communist government was threatened by Muslim opposition (see Map 30.2). Insisting that the Soviet aggression "could pose the greatest threat to peace since the Second World War," Carter also imposed economic sanctions on the Soviet Union, barred U.S. participation in the 1980 Olympic Games in Moscow, and obtained legislation requiring all nineteen-year-old men to register for the **draft**.

The president claimed that Soviet actions jeopardized oil supplies from the Middle East and announced his own "Carter Doctrine," threatening the use of any means necessary to prevent an outside force from gaining control of the Persian Gulf. His human rights policy fell by the wayside as the United States stepped up aid to Afghanistan's neighbor, Pakistan, then under a military dictatorship. Finally, Carter called for hefty increases in defense spending over the next five years.

Events in Iran encouraged this reversion to a hard-line, militaristic approach. All the U.S. arms and aid had not enabled the shah to quash Iranian dissidents who still resented the CIA's role in the overthrow of the Mossadegh government in 1953 (see chapter 27), condemned the shah's savage attempts to silence opposition, and detested his adoption of Western culture and values. In 1979, a revolution forced the shah out of Iran and gave Ayatollah Ruholla Khomeini and other Shiite Islamic **fundamentalists** control of the government. These forces were intensely hostile to the United States, which they blamed for supporting the shah's brutalities and undermining the religious foundations of their country.

When Carter permitted the shah to enter the United States for medical treatment, anti-American demonstrations escalated in Teheran. On November 4, 1979, a crowd broke into the U.S. Embassy and seized more than 60 Americans, demanding that the shah be returned for trial. When Khomeini supported the captors, Carter froze Iranian assets in U.S. banks and placed an embargo on Iranian oil. He sent a small military operation into Iran in April 1980, but the rescue mission failed and the hostages remained prisoners until January 1981.

The aborted mission fed Americans' feelings of impotence, simmering since the nation's defeat in Vietnam. Those frustrations in turn produced support for a more militaristic foreign policy. Opposition to Soviet-American détente, combined with the Soviet invasion of

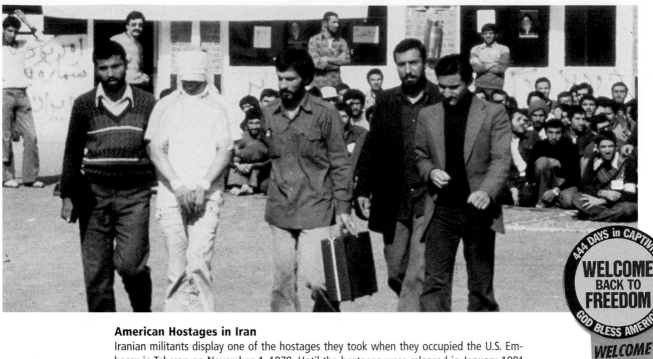

American Hostages in Iran
Iranian militants display one of the hostages they took when they occupied the U.S. Embassy in Teheran on November 4, 1979. Until the hostages were released in January 1981, Americans regularly watched TV images of the captives being paraded before angry Iranian crowds. Many Americans tied yellow ribbons around trees and car antennas or wore them to demonstrate their concern for the hostages and hopes for their safe return. Because the hostages served as humiliating symbols of the limitations of American power, a surge of celebration accompanied their release. "I am overjoyed. I feel proud again," said a New Hampshire police officer.

Ph. Ledru/Sygma; Collection of Janice L. and David J. Frent.

Afghanistan, nullified the thaw in relations that Nixon and Kissinger had begun. The American hostages in Iran filled the news during the 1980 presidential campaign and contributed to Carter's defeat. Iran released the hostages on the day he left office, but relations with the United States remained tense.

Ronald Reagan and the Conservative Ascendancy

Ronald Reagan's victory in 1980 marked the most important turning point in politics since Franklin D. Roosevelt won the presidency in 1932. Eisenhower and Nixon had campaigned as middle-of-the-road Republicans, but Reagan's success established conservatism's dominance in the Republican Party. Since the 1930s, the Democratic Party had defined the major issues; in the 1980s, the Republicans assumed that ini-

tiative, while the Democrats moved toward the right in their search for voter support. On the domestic front, the Reagan administration left its most important mark on the economy: victory over inflation, deregulation of industry, a moratorium on social spending, enormous tax cuts, and a staggering budget deficit. Economic expansion brought great wealth to some, but the percentage of Americans in poverty increased, and income distribution became more unequal.

Appealing to the New Right and Beyond

The oldest candidate ever nominated for the presidency, Ronald Reagan was born in Tampico, Illinois, in 1911. After attending Eureka, a small religious college, he worked as a sportscaster before becoming a movie actor and, later, president of the Screen Actors Guild. He initially shared the politics of his staunchly Democratic father but moved to the right in the 1940s and

1950s and campaigned for Goldwater in 1964. Reagan's political career took off when he was elected governor of California in 1966. Although he ran as a conservative, in office he displayed considerable flexibility, approving a major tax increase, a strong water pollution bill, and a liberal abortion law. Displaying similar agility in his 1980 presidential campaign, he softened earlier attacks on issues such as Social Security and chose the moderate Republican George H. Bush as his running mate.

Despite this move to the center, some Republicans balked at his nomination and at the party platform, which reflected the domination of the party's right wing. For example, Phyllis Schlafly persuaded the party to reverse its forty-year support for the Equal Rights Amendment, sparking moderate and liberal Republican women to march in protest outside the convention hall. (See "Historical Question," page 1118). Some of them, along with other anti-Reagan Republicans, found a more acceptable candidate in John B. Anderson, congressman from Illinois, who deserted his party to run as an independent.

The economic recession and the country's declining international stature—symbolized by the dozens of Americans held hostage in Iran—provided ample weapons for Reagan's campaign. Repeatedly Reagan reminded voters of the "misery index"—the combined rates of unemployment and inflation—asking, "Are you better off now than you were four years ago?" He promised to "take government off the backs of the people" and to restore Americans' morale and other nations' respect. A narrow majority of voters, 51 percent, responded to Reagan's upbeat message. Carter won 41 percent of the vote, and 7 percent went to Anderson. The Republicans picked up thirty-three new seats in the House and won control of the Senate for the first time since the 1950s.

While the economy and Iran sealed Reagan's victory, he also benefited from the burgeoning grassroots conservatism. An extraordinarily adept politician, Reagan appealed to a wide spectrum of groups and sentiments: free-market advocates, militant anti-Communists, fundamentalist Christians, southerners, and white working-class Democrats disenchanted with the Great Society and suffering from the high inflation and unemployment rates of the last years of the Carter administration.

A critical portion of Reagan's support came from religious conservatives, who constituted a relatively new phenomenon in politics, known

Ronald Reagan Nominated for President
Nancy and Ronald Reagan respond to cheers at the Republican National Convention where he was nominated for president in the summer of 1980. Reagan became one of the most popular presidents of the twentieth century, though his wife did not always share his high ratings from the American people.
Lester Sloan / Woodfin Camp & Associates.

as the New Right or New Christian Right. During the 1970s, **evangelical** and fundamentalist Christianity claimed thousands of new adherents and made adept use of sophisticated mass-mailing techniques and the "electronic ministry." Evangelical ministers such as Jim Bakker and Pat Robertson preached to huge television audiences, attacking feminism, abortion, homosexuality, and pornography and calling for restoration of old-fashioned "family values." They wanted prayer back in, and sex education out of, the schools. Robertson, for example, believed that "non-Christian people and atheistic people" were using the Constitution "to destroy the very

> Reagan reminded voters of the "misery index"—the combined rates of unemployment and inflation—asking, "Are you better off now than you were four years ago?"

Why Did the ERA Fail?

The proposed Equal Rights Amendment to the U.S. Constitution guaranteed briefly and simply that women and men would be treated equally under the law: "Equality of rights under the law shall not be denied or abridged by the United States or by any State on account of sex." Two more short sections provided that Congress would have enforcement powers and that the ERA would take effect two years after ratification. By the 1970s it had become the symbol of the late-twentieth-century women's movement.

Members of a small militant feminist organization, the National Woman's Party, first proposed an equal rights amendment to the Constitution in 1923, but it won little support either in Congress or among the public before the resurgence of feminism in the mid-1960s. In 1968, the National Organization for Women made it a key objective and, armed with support from traditional women's organizations and liberal groups, began to pressure Congress. The pressure took many forms, including civil disobedience. In early 1970, for example, NOW members disrupted a Senate subcommittee hearing on extending the vote to eighteen-year-olds, demanding that the Senate schedule hearings on the ERA. Initially fearing arrest, according to Wilma Scott Heide, who would become NOW president in 1971, the women soon learned that "we could do almost anything and get away with it . . . they didn't want to make martyrs out of us." Feminists and their allies lobbied Congress, and women in both political parties mobilized a letter-writing campaign, flooding some congressional offices with 1,500 letters a month.

Despite opposition in committee hearings, both houses of Congress passed the amendment by overwhelming margins, 354 to 23 in the House and 84 to 8 in the Senate. Within three hours of Senate passage in March 1972, Hawaii rushed to become the first state to ratify. By the end of 1972, 23 states had done so. Public opinion heavily favored ratification, peaking at 74 percent in favor in 1974 and never falling below 52 percent, while the opposition never surpassed 31 percent. Yet even after Congress extended the time period for ratification until 1982, the ERA failed. The Constitution requires approval of amendments by three-fourths of the states, and only 35 states ratified, three short of the minimum needed (see Map 30.3). Why did a measure with so much congressional and popular support fail?

The ERA encountered well-organized and passionate opposition linked to the growing conservative forces in the 1970s. Opponents ranged from religious organizations, such as the National Council of Catholic Women, to local groups such as HOTDOGS (Humanitarians Opposed to the Degradation of Our Girls), sponsored by the John Birch Society in Utah. Leading the resistance was Phyllis Schlafly.

Conservatives' opposition to the ERA reflected in part their traditional distaste for big government and their demand for a strong defense system to counter communism. Schlafly predicted that the amendment would transfer power from state legislatures and even from families to the federal government. Putting women in foxholes alongside men, she warned, would surely result from ratification of the ERA and that in turn would weaken the military and make the United States more vulnerable to communism. To a large extent, it was this linking of antifeminist goals with issues of long-standing concern to conservatives that made the New Right "new" as it developed a "pro-family" focus in the late 1970s.

The strategy of ERA opponents was to raise fears about the effects of the amendment. They could make extravagant arguments because its brevity and simplicity precluded anyone from saying with absolute certainty how courts would interpret it. Senator Samuel J. Ervin Jr., nationally known and highly respected for his chairing of the Watergate hearings, claimed that the ERA would eliminate laws against rape, require male and female prisoners to be housed together, and deprive women of alimony and child support. Others claimed that it would legalize homosexual marriage. Overall, the anti-ERA forces emphasized sex differences. By destroying the distinct sex roles on which the family was based, Erwin claimed, ERA would destroy the family and produce "increased rates of alcoholism, suicide, and possible sexual deviation."

Anti-ERA leaders were adept at framing arguments that spoke to many women's religious beliefs and their definitions of their own self-interest. In contrast to feminists who viewed traditional sex roles as constructed by society, anti-ERA men and women believed that they were God given. Evangelical minister and politician Jerry Falwell declared the ERA "a definite violation of holy Scripture [and its] mandate that 'the

Marching for Ratification of the ERA
About three thousand marchers parade down Pennsylvania Avenue in Washington, D.C., on August 26, 1977. On the fifty-seventh anniversary of ratification of the Nineteenth Amendment, which extended the right to vote to women, these advocates expressed their demand for ratification of the Equal Rights Amendment, carrying its words on their banner.
© Bettye Lane © Photo Researchers.

Phyllis Schlafly
The most prominent antifeminist, Phyllis Schlafly, is shown in her home in Alton, Illinois, in 1987. Despite time-consuming and energetic political activities that involved traveling and speaking all over the country, she insisted on calling herself a housewife. She poses with a pillow that signals her domesticity and political aim.
© Bettmann/Corbis.

husband is the head of the wife.'" Many ERA opponents were full-time housewives who had no stake in equal treatment in the marketplace and who feared that the amendment would eliminate the duty of men to support their families. They had entered traditional marriages where, in exchange for raising children and caring for home and husbands, they expected economic support. Schlafly stressed the unfairness of changing the rules in the middle of the game, noting that "ERA does not even include a 'grandmother' clause." Women in both camps recognized the precariousness of economic security; but while feminists wanted to render women self-sustaining, antifeminists wanted men to bear responsibility for their support.

Phyllis Schlafly and other conservative leaders skillfully mobilized women who saw their traditional roles threatened. In October 1972, she established a national movement, STOP (Stop Taking Our Privileges) ERA, so carefully organized that it could respond immediately when action was necessary. Thus when a state legislature began to consider ratification, STOP ERA women deluged legislators with letters and lobbied them personally in state capitals. In Illinois, for example, they gave lawmakers apple pies with notes attached that read: "My heart and my hand went into this dough/For the sake of the family please vote 'no.'" Opponents also brought baby girls to the legislature wearing signs that pleaded, "Please don't draft me." Another opposition group, Happiness of Womanhood (HOW), presented California legislators with mice bearing the message, "Do you want to be a man or a mouse?" And housewives in North Carolina took home-baked bread to members of the state legislature with notes reading, "To the breadwinners from the breadbakers."

ERA opponents had an easier task than supporters, for all they had to do was to convince a minority of legislators in a minority of states to preserve the status quo. The framers of the Constitution had stacked the odds against revision. Supporters, by contrast, had to persuade a majority of lawmakers in three-quarters of the states that the need to guarantee

(continued)

women equal rights was urgent and that it could not be accomplished without a constitutional amendment. In addition, in contrast to the suffrage movement, which for decades gradually built up support through local and state campaigns, the ERA forces concentrated on winning Congress and did so in less than ten years. Amendment supporters were not prepared for the state campaigns, and the intensity of the opposition took them by surprise. By the time ERA proponents got organized on the state level, the momentum for ratification had already stalled.

Feminists still had to overcome the tendency of men to trivialize women's issues or to take them less seriously than other concerns. For example, when the House initially passed the ERA in 1970, the *New York Times* printed an editorial criticizing it under the title "The Henpecked House." The conservative syndicated columnist James J. Kilpatrick said

that the ERA was "the contrivance of a gang of professional harpies" and that congressmen had voted for it simply to "get these furies off their backs." The very gains feminists made in the 1960s and 1970s also worked against approval of the ERA. Congress had already banned sex discrimination in employment, education, credit, and other areas; and the Supreme Court used the equal protection clause of the Fourteenth Amendment to strike down several state and federal laws that treated men and women differently. Even though the Court did not ban all distinctions based on sex, its decisions made it harder for ERA advocates to demonstrate the urgency of constitutional revision.

So why did the ERA fail? It failed because a handful of men in a handful of state legislatures voted against it. The shift of only a few votes in states such as Illinois and North Carolina would have meant

ratification. Phyllis Schlafly's forces played a key role in the defeat, because men could vote "no" and take cover behind the many women who opposed it. And those women proved willing to commit time, energy, and money to block ratification because conservative leaders convinced them that the ERA threatened their very way of life.

Feminists did not leave the ERA battle empty-handed, however. The National Organization for Women grew enormously during the struggle for ratification. Thousands of women were mobilized across the political spectrum and participated in the political arena for the first time. Fourteen states passed their own equal rights amendments after 1970. And feminists continued to struggle in the legislative and judicial arenas for the expansion of women's rights, struggles that continue to bear fruit in the twenty first century.

foundation of our society." Although the Christian Right was predominately Protestant, some Catholics, like Phyllis Schlafly, shared the fundamentalists' goal of a return to their version of "Christian values."

Conservatives created a raft of political organizations, such as the Moral Majority, founded by minister Jerry Falwell in 1979 with the goals of fighting "left-wing, social-welfare bills . . . pornography, homosexuality, the advocacy of immorality in school textbooks," and pushing for a "Family Protection Agency." The Christian Coalition, which Pat Robertson formed in 1989, claimed 1.6 million members and control of the Republican Party in more than a dozen states within a few years. The instruments of more traditional conservatives— those who advocated limited government at home and militant anticommunism abroad— likewise flourished. These included publications such as the *National Review*, edited by William F. Buckley Jr., and think tanks such as the

American Enterprise Institute and the Heritage Foundation, which supported experts who developed new policy approaches. The monthly *Phyllis Schlafly Report* (see photo on page 1104) continued to merge the sentiments of the old and new right, which were also manifest in its publisher's organization, Eagle Forum.

Reagan embraced the full spectrum of conservatism, ignoring certain inconsistencies. For example, the New Right's demand for the government to intervene in private matters by outlawing abortion and homosexuality conflicted with the traditional conservative attachment to **laissez-faire**. Reagan avowed agreement on abortion, school prayer, and other New Right issues, yet he was careful not to alienate the more traditional conservatives by pushing hard on socalled moral or social issues. Rather, his major achievements lay in areas most important to the older right—strengthening the nation's antiCommunist posture and reducing taxes and government restraints on free enterprise. "In the present crisis," Reagan argued, "government is not the solution to our problem, government is the problem."

Reagan's admirers, however, stretched far beyond conservatives. The extraordinarily popular president was liked even by Americans who opposed his policies and even when he made glaring mistakes. At one meeting, he failed to recognize his own secretary of housing and urban development, calling him "Mr. Mayor." On another occasion, he proclaimed that vegetation caused 90 percent of all air pollution. He made so many misstatements that aides tried to keep him away from reporters, and they carefully scripted the former actor's public appearances.

Democratic representative Patricia Schroeder tagged Reagan the "Teflon President" because none of his administration's mistakes, even his own errors and falsehoods, seemed to stick to him. His confidence and easygoing humor were a large part of his appeal. Ignoring darker aspects of the nation's past, he presented a version of history that Americans could feel good about. Listeners understood Reagan's declaration that it was "morning in America" as a promise that the best was yet to come for the nation. He also gained public sympathy after being shot by a would-be assassin in March 1981. Just before surgery for removal of the bullet, Reagan joked to physicians, "I hope you're Republicans." So great was Reagan's appeal that his popularity withstood serious charges of executive branch misconduct in foreign policy in his second term.

Unleashing Free Enterprise

Reagan's first domestic objective was a massive tax cut. Although tax reduction, especially in the face of a large budget deficit, contradicted traditional Republican economic doctrine, Reagan relied on a new theory called **supply-side economics**, which held that cutting taxes would actually increase revenue. Supply-siders insisted that lower taxes would enable businesses to expand, that individuals would work harder because they could keep more of their earnings, and that tax reduction would increase the production of goods and services—the supply— which in turn would boost demand. To allay worries about the budget deficit, Reagan promised to cut federal expenditures, a position fully compatible with his antigovernment views.

In the summer of 1981, Congress passed the Economic Recovery Tax Act, resulting in the largest tax reduction in U.S. history. The legislation cut the tax rate of individuals with the lowest incomes from 14 to 11 percent and lowered the rate of individuals with the highest incomes from 70 to 50 percent. Corporations also received tax breaks, and taxes on capital gains, gifts, and inheritances fell. A second measure, the Tax Reform Act of 1986, reduced tax rates even more, lowering the maximum rate on individual income to 28 percent and on business income to 35 percent. The entire tax structure became more regressive—that is, affluent Americans saved far more on their tax bills than did average taxpayers, and the distribution of wealth was further skewed in favor of the rich.

"Hack, chop, crunch!" were *Time* magazine's words for the administration's efforts to free private enterprise from government restraints. Carter had confined deregulation to particular industries, such as air transportation and banking, while increasing regulation in health, safety, and environmental protection. The Reagan administration, by contrast, pursued across-the-board deregulation. It declined to enforce the Sherman Antitrust Act—the 1890 law designed to reduce **monopoly** and promote competition (see chapter 17)—against an unprecedented number of business mergers and takeovers. Reagan also loosened restraints on business imposed by employee health and safety measures, and he weakened organized labor. When thirteen thousand members of the Professional Air Traffic Controllers Organization (PATCO) struck in 1981, Reagan fired them, destroying their union. Blaming environmental laws for the nation's sluggish economic growth, Reagan targeted them too for deregulation, but popular support for environmental protection blocked the complete realization of Reagan's goals.

Deregulation of the banking industry, begun under Carter and supported by Democrats and Republicans alike, created a crisis in the savings and loan industry. Some of the newly deregulated savings and loan institutions (S&Ls) extended enormous loans to real estate developers and invested in other high-yield but risky ventures. S&L owners reaped lavish profits, and their depositors enjoyed high interest rates. But then real estate values began to plunge, and hundreds of S&Ls went bankrupt. After Congress voted to bail out the S&L industry in 1989, the burden of the largest financial scandal in U.S. history fell on American taxpayers.

> Deregulation of the banking industry, begun under Carter and supported by Democrats and Republicans alike, created a crisis in the savings and loan industry.

The S&L crisis deepened the **federal deficit**, which soared during the 1980s despite Reagan's pledge to pare federal spending. When the administration cut funds for food stamps, job training, aid to low-income students, health services, and other welfare programs, hundreds of thousands of people lost benefits, and those with incomes just around the poverty line were hardest hit. Increases in defense spending, however, far exceeded the budget cuts, and the deficit continued to climb: from $74 billion when Carter left office in 1981 to a high of $220 billion in 1986. Under Reagan, the nation's debt grew from $834 billion to $2.3 trillion, and interest on the debt consumed one-seventh of all federal expenditures.

It took the severest recession since the 1930s to squeeze inflation out of the U.S. economy. Beginning in 1981, unemployment rose sharply, approaching 11 percent late in 1982. Record numbers of banks and businesses closed, and 12 million workers could not find jobs. The threat of unemployment further undermined organized labor, forcing unions to make concessions that management insisted were necessary for industry's survival. The economy recovered in 1983 and entered an unprecedented period of growth, yet unemployment never fell below 5 percent during the decade.

The economic upswing and Reagan's own popularity posed a formidable challenge for the Democrats in the 1984 election. Walter F. Mondale, vice president under Carter, won the Democratic nomination. Although he electrified the Democratic National Convention by choosing as his running mate New York representative Geraldine A. Ferraro, the first woman on a major party ticket, it failed to save the Democrats from a humiliating defeat. Reagan charged his opponents with concentrating on America's failures, while he emphasized success and possibility. Democrats, he claimed, "see an America where every day is April 15th [the due date for income tax returns] . . . we see an America where every day is the Fourth of July."

Voters responded to the president's sunny vision and to the economic comeback, giving him a landslide 59 percent of the vote. Winning only the state of Minnesota, the Democrats pondered how to stem the exodus of longtime loyalists—particularly southern white males—to the Republican Party. Stung by Republican charges that the Democratic Party was captive to "special interests" such as labor, women, and minorities, some Democratic leaders urged that the party shift more toward the right.

Winners and Losers in a Flourishing Economy

After the recession of 1981–82, the economy took off, bringing great fortunes to some as popular culture celebrated making money and displaying wealth. Books by business wizards topped bestseller lists, the press described lavish parties costing millions of dollars, and popular magazines featured articles such as "They're like Us, except They're Rich." College students told poll takers that their primary ambition was to make money.

Participating conspicuously in the affluence of the 1980s were members of the baby boom generation known popularly as "yuppies," short for "young urban professionals." These mostly white, well-educated young men and women tended to live in urban condominiums and to pursue fast-track careers; in their leisure time, they consumed lavishly—fancy cars, gourmet food, expensive vacations, and electronic gadgets. Though definitely a minority, they established consumption standards that many tried to emulate.

Many of the newly wealthy achieved success from moving assets around rather than from producing goods. Notable exceptions included Steven Jobs, who invented the Apple computer in his garage, and Liz Claiborne, who in thirteen years turned a $250,000 investment into a billion-dollar fashion enterprise. But many others got rich—or richer—by manipulating debt and restructuring corporations through mergers and takeovers. "To say these guys are entrepreneurs is like saying Jesse James was an entrepreneur," opined Texas businessman Ross Perot, who defined entrepreneurship as making things, not money. Most financial wizards operated within the law, but occasionally greed led to criminal convictions. Michael Milken pioneered in issuing junk bonds, so called because they offered high risk and high yield. He took home well over $50 million a year, but he and others landed in jail for using insider information to maximize their financial manipulations.

Other problems remained, even in an abundant economy. The steel, automobile, and electronics industries were surpassed by those of Germany and Japan; Americans bought more Volkswagens and Hondas and fewer Fords and

Chevrolets. With Americans purchasing more foreign-made goods than domestic producers were able to sell abroad, the nation's trade deficit (the difference between imports and exports) soared to $126 billion by 1988.

International competition forced the collapse of some older companies, while others moved factories and jobs abroad to be closer to foreign markets or to benefit from the low wage standards of such countries as Mexico and Korea. Service industries expanded during this process of **de-industrialization** and created new jobs at home, but former blue-collar workers forced to take those jobs found their wages substantially lower. When David Ramos was laid off in 1982 from his $12.75-an-hour job in a steel plant, his wages fell to $5 an hour as a security guard, forcing his family to rely on food stamps. Overall, the number of full-time workers earning wages below the poverty level ($12,195 for a family of four in 1990) rose sharply from 12 to 18 percent of all workers in the 1980s.

The weakening of organized labor combined with the decline in manufacturing to erode the position of blue-collar workers like David Ramos and Chicago steelworker Ike Mazo. "They're telling you you're not a good citizen if you're not willing to accept less," Mazo fumed, contemplating the $6-an-hour jobs available to him. "It's an attack on the living standards of workers." Increasingly, a second income was needed to stave off economic decline. By 1990, nearly 60 percent of married women with young children worked outside the home. Yet even with two incomes, fewer young families could purchase their first home or provide a good life for their children. "I worry about their future every day," Mazo's wife confessed. "Will we be able to put them through college? . . . Will they be out in the workforce working for four dollars an hour?" The average $10,000 disparity between male and female annual earnings made things even harder for the nearly 20 percent of female-headed families. One mother of two, divorced from an abusive husband, supplemented her paycheck by selling her blood and accepting help from her church. Mark Burke, who had worked at a rubber plant in Barberton, Ohio, lost his job in 1980 when the plant closed. Among the 80 percent of workers displaced from the rubber industry and unable to find jobs that paid as well, he lamented, "There's a big difference between what I could be and what I am."

In keeping with conservative philosophy, Reagan avoided substantial government efforts

FIGURE 30.1 The Growth of Inequality: Changes in Family Income, 1969–1998
For three decades after World War II, income increased for all groups on the economic ladder. After 1979, the income of the poorest families declined, while the income of the richest 20 percent of the population grew substantially.

to reverse this growing income inequality (which his tax policies encouraged), insisting that a booming economy would benefit everyone. Average personal income did rise during his tenure, but the trend toward greater economic inequality that had begun in the 1970s intensified in the 1980s, in part because of the new tax policies. The rich got richer, a portion of the middle class did well, and the poor got poorer. Personal income shot up sharply for the wealthiest 20 percent of Americans while it fell for the poorest by 9.8 percent between 1979 and 1987. No longer could all Americans expect, as they had in the two decades following World War II, that their children would do better than they had done (Figure 30.1).

Poverty statistics, too, revealed a reversal of the trend toward greater equality. Between 1980 and 1988, poor people increased from 11.7 to 13.5 percent of total U.S. population—the highest poverty rate in the industrialized world. A relatively low poverty rate among the elderly testified to the lasting success of Social Security and Medicare. Less fortunate were large segments of other groups that the economic boom had bypassed: racial minorities, female-headed families, and children. One child in every five lived in poverty.

Even before the 1990 recession, affluent urbanites walked past numerous men and women sleeping in subway stations, on grates over steam vents, and on park benches. Experts debated the total number of homeless Americans—

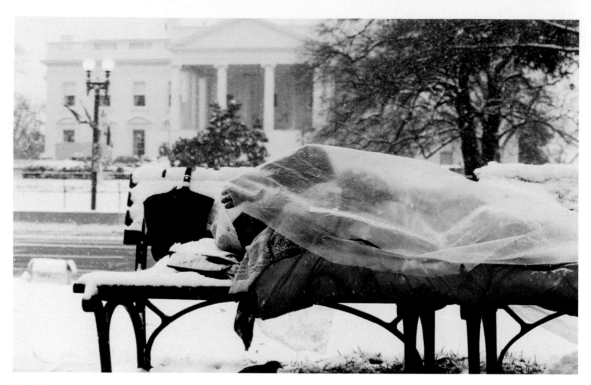

Homelessness
The increased presence of homeless people in cities across the nation challenged the view of the 1980s as a decade of prosperity. Hundreds of homeless people could be found on the sidewalks of the nation's capital every night. In November 1987, during the first snowfall of the season, a homeless man sleeps in Lafayette Square across from the White House. What might the location of this homeless man suggest to viewers of the photograph?
© Bettmann/Corbis.

estimates ranged from 350,000 upward—but no one doubted that homelessness had increased. Women and children constituted the fastest-growing population without shelter. Those without homes included the victims of long-term unemployment, erosion of welfare benefits, and slum clearance as well as individuals suffering from mental illness, drug abuse, and alcoholism.

Continuing Struggles over Rights and the Environment

The dominance of conservatism and the laissez-faire inclination of the Reagan administration threw social movements on the defensive. As the Reagan administration, often supported by the increasingly conservative federal courts, moved away from the national commitment to equal opportunity undertaken in the 1960s, feminists and minority groups fought to defend protections they had won in the 1960s and 1970s. They

achieved some limited gains. A newer movement advocating rights for gay men and lesbians gained visibility and helped to edge attitudes toward greater tolerance for homosexuality. Environmentalists, too, clashed with the Reagan administration, as they sought to maintain regulations enacted in the 1970s and as the world faced new threats to human life and health.

The Conservative Shift in the Federal Courts

Since the 1950s, liberals had grown accustomed to counting on the federal judiciary as a powerful ally in their struggles for civil rights and social justice. But in the 1980s, they saw their allies slipping away as more and more conservative justices populated the Supreme Court and lower federal courts. Given the opportunity to appoint half of the 761 federal court judges and three new Supreme Court justices, President Reagan carefully selected candidates who had strongly conservative views. With these appointments, the tide began to turn in favor of strict construction—the literal application of the original aims of the Constitution's authors that limits judicial power to protect individual rights.

The Supreme Court did not execute an abrupt about-face: It upheld important affirmative action and antidiscrimination policies and ruled that sexual harassment in the workplace constituted sex discrimination. And, in one key case, Congress stepped in to defend antidiscrimination policy. In 1984, the Justice Department persuaded the Supreme Court to severely weaken Title IX of the Education Amendments Act of 1972, a crucial law promoting equal opportunity in education. *Grove City v. Bell* (1984) allowed the Justice Department to abandon dozens of civil rights cases against schools and colleges, but it also galvanized a coalition of civil rights organizations and groups representing women, the aged and disabled, and their allies. In 1988, Congress passed the Civil Rights Restoration Act, which reversed the administration's victory in *Grove City* and—going further—banned any organization that practiced discrimination on the basis of race, color, national origin, sex, disability, or age from receiving government funds.

Nonetheless, Reagan's Supreme Court appointees tipped the balance to the right. Sandra Day O'Connor was a moderate conservative, but the appointments of Antonin Scalia and Anthony M. Kennedy gave strict constructionists a slim majority. The full impact of these appointments continued after Reagan left office. The Court allowed states to impose restrictions that limited access to abortion for poor and uneducated women and those living in rural areas. Other rulings weakened protections against employment discrimination and whittled away at legal safeguards against the death penalty.

Feminism on the Defensive

One of the signal achievements of the New Right was capturing the Republican Party's position on women's rights. For the first time in its history, the Republican Party took an explicitly antifeminist tone, opposing both the Equal Rights Amendment and a woman's right to abortion, key goals of women's rights activists. When the time limit for ratification of the ERA ran out in 1982 (Map 30.3), Phyllis Schlafly could claim victory on the issue that first galvanized her antifeminist campaign. (See chapter 28 and "Historical Question," page 1118.)

Cast on the defensive, feminists began to focus more on women's economic and family problems; and they found some common ground with the Reagan administration in two measures that addressed women's economic distress. The Child Support Enforcement Amendments Act helped single and divorced mothers to collect court-ordered child support payments from absent parents. The Retirement Equity Act of 1984 benefited divorced and older women by strengthening their claims to their husbands' pensions and enabling women to qualify more easily for private retirement pensions.

The Reagan administration had its own concerns about women, specifically about the **gender gap**—women's tendency to vote for liberal and Democratic candidates in larger numbers

> With Reagan's judicial appointees, the tide began to turn in favor of strict construction—the literal application of the original aims of the Constitution's authors that limits judicial power to protect individual rights.

Confrontations over Abortion

Failing to win a constitutional amendment banning abortion, in the late 1970s and 1980s some groups in the right-to-life movement adopted more militant tactics, picketing abortion clinics, yelling at patients and employees, and trying to block entrance into clinics. The pro-choice activists shown here defend clinic access and the right to abortion.

Paul S. Howell/Gamma Liaison.

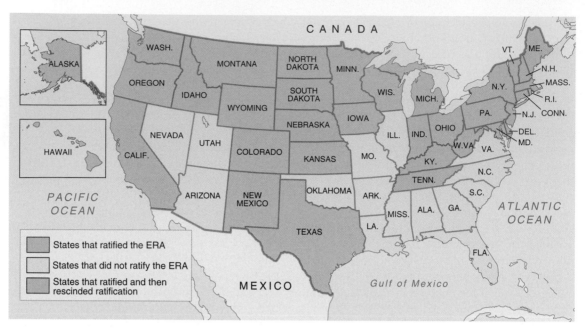

MAP 30.3   The Fight for the Equal Rights Amendment
Many states that failed to ratify the Equal Rights Amendment had previously refused to ratify the woman suffrage amendment (or ratified it decades later, as did North Carolina in 1971).

READING THE MAP: How many states ratified the amendment, and how many did not? Did any regions overwhelmingly support or oppose the ERA?
CONNECTIONS: What was the goal of the ERA? Who were its opponents, and what were their main points of opposition?

FOR MORE HELP ANALYZING THIS MAP, see the map activity for this chapter in the Online Study Guide at bedfordstmartins.com/roark.

than men did. (Party leaders welcomed the opposite element of that trend: white men's movement into Republican ranks.) Reagan appointed three women to cabinet posts and, in 1981, selected the first woman, Sandra Day O'Connor, for the Supreme Court. But these actions accompanied a general decline in the number of women and minorities in high-level positions. And with higher poverty rates than men, women suffered most from Reagan's budget cuts in social programs.

Although court decisions placed restrictions on women's ability to obtain abortions, feminists successfully fought to retain the basic principles of *Roe v. Wade*. The women's movement, however, hit a stone wall in efforts to improve day care services and promote pay equity—equal pay for traditionally female jobs that were comparable in worth to jobs performed primarily by men. Like other pressure groups, the women's movement pursued locally what it failed to achieve at the federal level. The pay equity movement took hold in several states, and many states strengthened their laws against rape.

States also increased funding for domestic violence programs and stepped up efforts to protect victims and prosecute abusers.

The Gay and Lesbian Rights Movement

Influenced by minority struggles, the New Left, the counterculture, and feminism, gay men and lesbians began to claim equal rights and to express pride in their sexual identities. Although an organization for homosexual rights had existed as early as 1924, and small groups like the Mattachine Society and the Daughters of Bilitis mobilized in the 1950s, not until the 1980s did a national mass movement emerge. It grew out of the social upheaval of the 1960s and was sparked by the Stonewall riot of 1969, when gay men and lesbians fought back against a police raid on the Stonewall Inn, a gay bar in New York City's Greenwich Village. Linking their cause with that of other minorities, they asserted, "A common struggle will bring common triumph."

Lesbians and gay men began to organize across the nation in the 1970s, demonstrating and lobbying for an end to discrimination and affirmation of their own decisions about whom to love. One result of their efforts came in 1973 when the American Psychiatric Association ended its categorization of homosexuality as a mental disease. Although the Supreme Court upheld the right of states to enforce laws against sodomy until 2003, most states had taken such laws off the books by the 1980s.

The acquired immune deficiency syndrome (AIDS) epidemic, which researchers identified in 1981, further mobilized the gay and lesbian rights movement in the 1980s, because initially male homosexuals were disproportionately afflicted. As the disease swept through communities of gay men in New York, San Francisco, and elsewhere, gay men and lesbians organized to promote public funding for AIDS education, prevention, and treatment.

The gay and lesbian rights movement helped thousands of closeted homosexuals experience the relief of "coming out." Their visibility helped to increase awareness (if not always acceptance) of homosexuality among the larger population. Activists organized gay rights and gay pride marches throughout the country and began to win local victories, gaining some protections against discrimination. (See "Documenting the American Promise," page 1128.) Beginning with the election of Elaine Noble to the Massachusetts legislature in 1974, several openly gay politicians won offices from mayor to member of Congress; and the Democrats began to include gay rights in their party platforms.

Popular attitudes about homosexuality moved toward greater tolerance but remained complex. For example, by the end of the century 84 percent of respondents to public opinion polls supported equal job opportunities for gays and lesbians, but 59 percent thought homosexuality was morally wrong. These diverse attitudes were reflected in uneven changes in policies. In some states and cities, lesbians and gay men won protections that were enjoyed by heterosexual citizens. Dozens of cities banned job discrimination against homosexuals, and beginning with Wisconsin in 1982, eleven states made sexual orientation a protected category under civil rights laws. Nearly one hundred cities and many large corporations began to offer health insurance and other benefits to domestic partners. After the Vermont Supreme Court ruled that gay couples were unconstitutionally discriminated against in 1999, the Vermont legislature created for same-sex couples a category called "civil unions," which entitled them to rights available to married couples in areas such as inheritance, taxes, and medical decisions.

Even as popular TV shows and movies increasingly featured gay men and lesbians, most

> Influenced by minority struggles, the New Left, the counterculture, and feminism, gay men and lesbians began to claim equal rights and to express pride in their sexual identities.

Gay Pride Parades

In June 1970, gays and lesbians marched in New York City to commemorate the first anniversary of the Stonewall riot. Since then, gay pride parades have taken place throughout the United States and in other countries every year in June. A history professor, Robert Dawidoff, pointed out that the parades were not about "flaunting private things in public," as some people charged, but a way for gay men and lesbians to express "pride in our history . . . in having survived the thousand petty harassments and reminders of a special status we neither seek nor merit." Increasingly, friends, supporters, and families of homosexuals participate in the parades, as these family members do in a Los Angeles parade.

© Bettmann/Corbis.

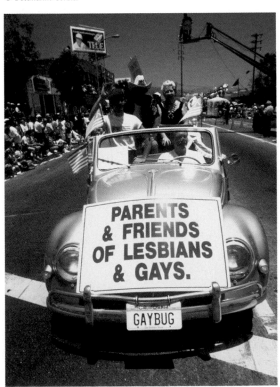

Antidiscrimination Laws for Gays and Lesbians, 2000

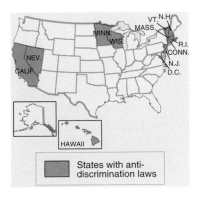

States with antidiscrimination laws

Protecting Gay and Lesbian Rights

Since the 1970s, the gay and lesbian rights movement has worked for passage of laws and ordinances to protect homosexuals from discrimination. In 1982, Wisconsin became the first state to ban discrimination on the basis of sexual orientation, following the lead of several cities throughout the United States that passed gay rights ordinances in the 1970s. By the mid-1990s, nine states and more than eighty cities had such legislation on the books. These measures ignited controversy that surrounded the issue into the twenty-first century.

DOCUMENT 1
Ordinance of the City of Minneapolis, 1974

In 1974, the city council of Minneapolis amended its civil rights ordinance to cover discrimination based on sexual preference. The law provided a rationale for banning discrimination and, unlike some laws focusing exclusively on employment, encompassed a broad range of activities.

It is determined that discriminatory practices based on race, color, creed, religion, national origin, sex, or affectional or sexual preference, with respect to employment, labor union membership, housing accommodations, property rights, education, public accommodations, and public services, or any of them, tend to create and intensify conditions of poverty, ill health, unrest, civil disobedience, lawlessness, and vice and adversely affect the public health, safety, order, convenience, and gen-

eral welfare; such discriminatory practices threaten the rights, privileges, and opportunities of all inhabitants of the city and such rights, privileges, and opportunities are hereby to be declared civil rights, and the adoption of this Chapter is deemed to be an exercise of the policy power of the City to protect such rights.

SOURCE: Norman Dorsen and Aryeh Neier, eds., *The Rights of Gay People: The Basic ACLU Guide to a Gay Person's Rights* (New York: Dutton, 1992), 251.

DOCUMENT 2
Letter to the Editor of the *New York Times* from Paul Moore, November 23, 1981

Paul Moore, Episcopal bishop of New York, made a religious argument for gay rights in his letter to the editor of the New York Times.

I quote our diocesan resolution: "Whereas this Convention, without making any judgment on the morality of homosexuality, agrees that homosexuals are entitled to full civil rights. Now therefore be it resolved this Convention supports laws guaranteeing homosexuals all civil rights guaranteed to other citizens."

The Bible stands for justice and compassion for all of God's children. To deny civil rights to anyone for something he or she cannot help is against the clear commandment of

justice and love, which is the message of the word of God.

As a New Yorker I find it incredible that this great city, populated by more gay persons than any other city in the world, still denies them basic human rights. They make an enormous contribution to the commercial, artistic, and religious life of our city.

SOURCE: Paul Moore, letter to the editor, *New York Times*, December 8, 1981.

DOCUMENT 3
Vatican Congregation for the Doctrine of the Faith, August 6, 1992

The following statement from the Roman Catholic Church reflects the views of many religious groups that take positions against gay rights.

"Sexual orientation" does not constitute a quality comparable to race, ethnic background, etc., in respect to nondiscrimination. Unlike these, homosexual orientation is an objective disorder and evokes moral concern.

There are areas in which it is not unjust discrimination to take sexual orientation into account, for example, in the placement of children for adoption or foster care, in employment of teachers or athletic coaches, and in military recruitment.

SOURCE: Vatican Congregation for the Doctrine of the Faith, *Origins*, August 6, 1992.

DOCUMENT 4
Testimony of Charles Cochrane Jr. before the House Subcommittee on Employment Opportunities of the Committee on Education and Labor, January 27, 1982

Although the U.S. Congress has never enacted legislation banning discrimination on the basis of sexual orientation, it has considered a number of bills for that purpose. Charles Cochrane Jr., an army veteran and police sergeant, testified on behalf of such a bill in 1982.

I am very proud of being a New York City policeman. And I am equally proud of being gay. I have always been gay.

I have been out of the closet for 4 years. November 6 was my anniversary. It took me 34 years to muster enough courage to declare myself openly.

We gays are loathed by some, pitied by others, and misunderstood by most. We are not cruel, wicked, cursed, sick, or possessed by demons. We are artists, business people, police officers, and clergymen. We are scientists, truck drivers, politicians; we work in every field. We are loving human beings who are in some ways different. . . .

During the early years of my association with the New York City Police Department a great deal of energy did go into guarding and concealing my innermost feelings. I believed that I would be subjected to ridicule and harassment were my colleagues to learn of my sexual orientation. Happily, when I actually began to integrate the various aspects of my total self, those who knew me did not reject me.

Then what need is there for such legislation as H.R. 1454? The crying need of others, still trapped in their closets, who must be protected, who must be reassured that honesty about themselves and their lives will not cost them their homes or their jobs. . . .

The bill before you will not act as a proselytizing agent in matters of sexual orientation or preference. It will not include affirmative action provisions. Passage of this bill will protect the inherent human rights of all people of the United States, while in no way diminishing the rights of those who do not see the need for such legislation. Finally, it will signify, quite clearly, recognition and compassion for a group which is often maligned without justification.

SOURCE: U.S. House Subcommittee on Employment Opportunities of the Committee on Education and Labor, *Hearing on H.R. 1454,* 97th Cong., 2nd sess., 1982, 54–56.

DOCUMENT 5
Carl F. Horowitz, "Homosexuality's Legal Revolution," May 1991

Carl Horowitz, a policy analyst at a conservative think tank, the Heritage Foundation, expresses arguments of those opposed to government protection of homosexual rights.

Homosexual activists have all but completed their campaign to persuade the nation's educational establishment that homosexuality is normal "alternative" behavior, and thus any adverse reaction to it is akin to a phobia, such as fear of heights, or an ethnic prejudice, such as anti-Semitism.

The movement now stands on the verge of fully realizing its use of law to . . . intimidate heterosexuals uncomfortable about coming into contact with it. . . .

The movement seeks to win sinecures through the state, and over any objections by "homophobic" opposition. With a cloud of a heavy fine or even a jail sentence hanging over a mortgage lender, a rental agent, or a job interviewer who might be discomforted by them, homosexuals under these laws can win employment, credit, housing, and other economic entitlements. Heterosexuals would have no right to discriminate against homosexuals, but apparently, not vice versa. . . .

These laws will create market bottlenecks. Heterosexuals and even "closeted" homosexuals will be at a competitive disadvantage for jobs and housing. . . .

The new legalism will increase heterosexual anger—and even violence—toward homosexuals.

SOURCE: Carl F. Horowitz, "Homosexuality's Legal Revolution," *Freeman,* May 1991.

QUESTIONS FOR ANALYSIS AND DEBATE

---

1. According to these documents, how would heterosexuals be affected by laws protecting gay and lesbian rights?
2. Which of these documents suggest that the civil rights movement influenced the authors' views on homosexual rights?
3. What do you think is the strongest argument for government protection of homosexual rights? What do you think is the strongest argument against government protection?

remained vulnerable to intolerance and some-times violence. The Christian Right targeted gays and lesbians as symbols of national im-morality and succeeded in overturning some ho-mosexual rights measures, which in any case lagged far behind the civil rights guarantees that racial minorities and women had achieved.

Conflicts over Environmental Protections

While feminists and the gay and lesbian rights movement battled the "family values" wing of conservatism, environmentalists struggled against conservatives hostile to federal regulations on free enterprise. In the late 1970s, environmen-talists won new protections, aided by crises and disasters that brought national attention to the costs of unregulated economic develop-ment. Residents at Love Canal in Niagara Falls, New York, for exam-ple, discovered that their houses and school sat atop highly toxic waste products from a nearby chemical company and fought to get officials to recognize the dan-ger. The state finally agreed to help the families relocate in 1978. Lois Gibbs, a Love Canal resident who eventually headed a national move-ment against toxic wastes, ex-plained how she and many other women became environmentalists: "I never thought of myself as an activist or an organizer. I was a housewife, a mother, but all of a sudden it was my family, my children, and my neighbors."

> While feminists and the gay and lesbian rights movement battled the "family values" wing of conservatism, environmen-talists struggled against conservatives hostile to federal regulations on free enterprise.

Warning of radiation leakage, potential acci-dents, and the hazards of nuclear wastes, envi-ronmentalists also targeted nuclear power plants, which by 1977 produced about 11 percent of the country's electricity. French and German citizens demonstrated against nuclear plants in 1971, and Americans followed suit. In 1976, hun-dreds of members of the Clamshell Alliance went to jail for attempting to block construction of a nuclear plant in Seabrook, New Hampshire. Groups such as Abalone Alliance in California, Citizen Alert in Nevada, and SHAD (Sound and Hudson Against Atomic Development) on Long Island, New York, sprung up across the United States to demand an environment safe from nu-clear radiation and waste.

The perils of nuclear energy came into dra-matic focus in March 1979, when an accident occurred at the Three Mile Island nuclear facility near Harrisburg, Pennsylvania, and technicians worked for days to prevent a meltdown of the reactor core. Popular opposition and the great expense of building nuclear power plants stalled further development of the industry; but antinu-clear activism endured as part of the environ-mental movement, especially after the explosion of a nuclear reactor and the spread of deadly ra-diation in Chernobyl, Ukraine, in 1986.

The Carter administration responded to the Love Canal disaster by sponsoring legislation in 1980 to create the so-called Superfund, $1.6 bil-lion for cleanup of hazardous wastes left by the

Controversy over the Environment

Secretary of the Interior James Watt joined the Reagan cabinet committed to dismantling much of the environ-mental regulation of the previous two decades. His efforts drew considerable opposition, and he failed to turn back the clock substantially. In 1983, President Reagan ap-pointed a more moderate replacement. What exactly does this *Newsweek* cover suggest that Watt wants to do to the environment?

FOR MORE HELP ANALYZING THIS IMAGE, see the visual activity for this chapter in the Online Study Guide at bedfordstmartins.com/roark.

Illustration by Wilson McLean. Reprinted with permission of the artist and *Newsweek* magazine.

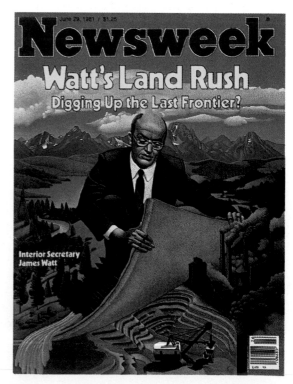

chemical industry. Carter also signed laws to improve clean air and water programs; to preserve vast areas of Alaska from commercial exploitation; and to control strip mining, which left ugly scars on the land. During the gasoline shortage brought on by the Iranian revolution in 1979, Carter attempted to balance the development of domestic fuel sources with environmental concerns; acknowledging that "some of the new technologies we will need to develop pose environmental risks," he angered some in the environmental movement. But he also won legislation to conserve energy and to provide incentives for the development of environmentally friendly alternative fuels, such as solar energy. (See "The Promise of Technology," page 1132.)

Although Ronald Reagan loved the outdoors and relished his retreats to his isolated ranch in the mountains of southern California during his presidency, in contrast to Carter he blamed environmental laws for the nation's sluggish economic growth and targeted them for deregulation. His first secretary of the interior, James Watt, declared, "We will mine more, drill more, cut more timber," and released federal lands to private exploitation, while the head of the Environmental Protection Agency eased enforcement of air and water pollution measures. The popular outcry that resulted led to the resignation of several environmental officials and the failure of other deregulatory goals, and it indicated that the concerns and values of the environmental movement had to some extent become part of the public consciousness.

Ronald Reagan Confronts an "Evil Empire"

Running for president in 1980, Ronald Reagan had capitalized on the Soviet invasion of Afghanistan and the Iranian hostage crisis, accusing Carter of weakening the military and losing the confidence of the nation's allies and its enemies' respect. As president, he accelerated the arms buildup begun by Carter and harshly censured the Soviet Union, calling it "an evil empire." Yet despite the new aggressiveness—or, as some argued, because of it—Reagan presided over the most impressive thaw in superpower conflict since the shattering of the World War II alliance. On the periphery of the cold war, however, Reagan practiced militant anticommunism, authorizing aid to antileftist movements in Asia,

Africa, and Central America and dispatching troops to both the Middle East and the Caribbean. When Congress blocked Reagan's efforts to assist opponents of the leftist Sandinista government in Nicaragua, administration officials resorted to secret and illegal means to effect their agenda.

Militarization and Interventions Abroad

Reagan sought to expand the military with new bombers and missiles, an enhanced nuclear force in Europe, a larger navy, and a rapid-deployment force. Despite the growing budget deficit, Congress approved most of these programs, and military expenditures shot up by one-third in the first half of the 1980s. Throughout Reagan's presidency, defense spending averaged $216 billion a year, up from $158 billion in the Carter years and higher even than in the Vietnam era.

Justifying the military buildup as a means to negotiate with the Soviets from a position of strength, Reagan provoked an outburst of pleas to halt the arms race. A rally demanding a freeze on additional nuclear weapons drew 700,000 people in New York City in 1982. Hundreds of thousands demonstrated across Europe, stimulated by fears of new U.S. missiles scheduled for deployment in **North Atlantic Treaty Organization (NATO)** countries in 1983.

Reagan startled many of his own advisers in March 1983 by announcing plans for research on the Strategic Defense Initiative (SDI). Immediately dubbed "Star Wars" by critics who doubted its feasibility, the project would deploy lasers in space to destroy enemy missiles before they could reach their targets. Reagan conceded that SDI could appear as "an aggressive policy" allowing the United States to strike first and not fear retaliation. The Soviets reacted angrily because SDI development violated the 1972 ABM treaty and would require the Soviets to invest huge sums in their own Star Wars technology. SDI research continued under future administrations, but with no workable results despite more than $60 billion in funding.

The U.S. military buildup placed the Soviets on the defensive but did not guarantee American

> On the periphery of the cold war, Reagan practiced militant anticommunism, authorizing aid to antileftist movements in Asia, Africa, and Central America and dispatching troops to both the Middle East and the Caribbean.

Solar Energy

"We want to inherit a clean earth," read a child's appeal to a conference on energy and the environment in Norway in 1990. "Why shouldn't we be allowed to live as you did when you were little? Play in fresh forests, fish in any water, drink clean water from the river. . . . We must find energy that does not pollute." The oil crises of the 1970s and growing concerns about the environmental effects of energy generated by coal, oil, and nuclear reactions had already sparked American interest in renewable energy, especially solar energy, an endless and environmentally clean source of fuel for homes and businesses.

Solar rays can be used directly for heating and lighting buildings by means of solar-thermal technologies, which concentrate the sun's rays to heat a liquid. That fluid is then used to warm buildings or create steam to turn a generator and create electricity. A Swiss scientist built the world's first solar collector in 1767, and in 1891 the Baltimore inventor Clarence Kemp patented the first commercial solar water heater. By the end of the twentieth century, more than 1.2 million buildings in the United States had solar water heating systems, and more than 250,000 swimming pools were warmed by the sun's rays. President Jimmy Carter put solar water heating panels on the White House to symbolize the importance of energy in his domestic program.

The other most common way to transfer sunlight into power is through photovoltaic systems (PVs), a process observed by a French physicist in 1839. Bell Telephone Laboratories developed a silicon PV cell in 1954; and in 1958, the American space program began to pioneer in the development of PVs when it used solar energy to power the *Vanguard* space satellite's radio. When sunlight hits the panels that make up photovoltaic systems, a chemical reaction occurs, releasing electricity. During the energy crises of the 1970s, the Federal Photovoltaic Utilization Program tested more than 3,000 PV systems.

Environmental advocates predicted that the sun could provide nearly one-fifth of the country's electricity by 2000; and the price of individual solar cells fell rapidly. Yet solar power has not reached its fullest potential. As the energy crises of the 1970s passed, opposition to government spending for research and subsidies increased, especially from corporations producing energy from fossil fuels. President Bill Clinton initiated a program in 1997 aimed at adding one million residential solar power systems by 2010, but the program was dependent on state subsidies, and the responses of most states were lukewarm. California was an exception. A program called PV Pioneers in Sacramento, for example, recruited a waiting list of more than 700 volunteers who agreed to pay a small surcharge on their electric bill to install solar panels on their roofs.

The greatest use of solar energy occurred in private homes. Although

---

security. Although Iran released the American hostages, terrorism continued to threaten the United States. In October 1983, an Islamic extremist drove a bomb-filled truck into a U.S. marine barracks in Lebanon, killing 241 Americans (see Map 30.2). The attack caused Reagan to pull out U.S. troops sent to Lebanon as part of a peacekeeping mission to monitor the withdrawal of Israeli and Palestinian Liberation Organization forces. Faced with other incidents of murder, kidnapping, and hijacking by various Middle Eastern extremist groups, Reagan refused to negotiate, insisting that to bargain with terrorists would only encourage more assaults.

The Reagan administration sought to contain leftist movements close to home and across the globe. In October 1983, U.S. troops invaded Grenada, a small island nation in the Caribbean that had succumbed to a left-wing, Marxist coup. In Asia, the United States moved more quietly, aiding the Afghan rebels' war against Afghanistan's Soviet-backed government. In the African nation of Angola, the United States armed rebel forces against the Soviet- and Cuban-backed government. Reagan also sided with the South African government that was brutally suppressing black protest against apartheid. In 1985, Congress had to override Reagan's veto such housing cost more to build and construction was not compatible with mass-production methods used in many housing developments, demand for "green" houses grew gradually. A retired couple in Maine, Debbi and Bill Lord, paid about 15 percent more to build their house with solar panels and other energy-smart features. Their designer Steven Strong had gone into the solar energy business after working as a consultant on the Alaska pipeline, which prompted him to shift his career to finding better ways than "going to the ends of the Earth to extract the last drop of fossil fuel." Although the Lords paid only $7.55 a month to the electric company, they didn't expect to make up for the extra cost of their house. Still, Bill Lord favored solar power because it was "practical," and "I like the idea of minimally impacting the environment." His wife agreed: "I think you walk softly on the Earth when you do this."

As Americans turned slowly to solar energy, by 2003 Japan had replaced the United States as the leading producer of solar panels. Having almost no domestic sources of fuel and depending on imported and expensive energy, Japan generated half of the world's solar power; the government subsidized about one-third of the cost of the solar panels. By the twenty-first century, the United States was drawing about 11 percent of its electricity from renewable sources such as solar power, but its future depended on the reliability and cost of more traditional forms of energy and on Americans' willingness to trade off short-term costs for energy independence and a healthier and cleaner environment.

Solar Home
The house of Bill and Debbi Lord in Kennebunkport, Maine, employs both of solar energy's key technologies. On one side of the south-facing roof shown here, photovoltaic panels collect the sun's rays, which are converted to electricity for the house. On the other side of the roof are solar thermal collector panels, which heat water for direct use and for warming the house through radiant tubing in the floors. The Lords also practice "green" transportation. Instead of using gasoline or petrodiesel, their Volkswagen runs on biodiesel, a soybean product.
Maine Solar House/www.solarhouse.com.

in order to impose economic sanctions against South Africa.

Administration officials were most fearful of left-wing movements in Central America that, according to Reagan, threatened to "destabilize the entire region from the Panama Canal to Mexico." When a leftist uprising occurred in 1981 in El Salvador, the United States sent money and military advisers to prop up the government even though it had committed murderous human rights violations and opposed social reform.

In neighboring Nicaragua, where Reagan aimed to unseat the left-wing Sandinistas, the administration aided the Contras (literally, "opposers"), a coalition of armed opposition to the Sandinistas that included many individuals from the ousted Somoza regime. Fearing another Vietnam, many Americans opposed aligning the United States with reactionary forces not supported by the majority of Nicaraguans; and Congress repeatedly instructed the president to stop aid to the Contras or limit it to nonmilitary purposes.

Deliberately violating congressional will, the administration secretly provided weapons and training to the Contras. The CIA directed assaults on economic targets and helped to mine Nicaraguan harbors in 1984. Through legal and

Terrorist Bombing of Marines in Beirut
In 1982, President Reagan sent U.S. troops to join a multinational force to quell fighting between Israelis and Palestinians in Lebanon. On October 23, 1983, members of Islamic Jihad, a group of anti-American fanatics sponsored by Iran, demonstrated their hostility to an American presence in the Middle East by exploding a car bomb outside the U.S. marine compound near the Beirut airport and killing 241 Americans. Secretary of Defense Caspar Weinberger then moved to withdraw the marines, supported by his assistant, army colonel Colin Powell, who believed that "America [was] sticking its hand into a thousand-year-old hornet's nest" in the Middle East. The question of whether and when to risk American lives abroad for peacekeeping or humanitarian purposes would be one of the most difficult problems facing policymakers in the ensuing decades.
Bill Pierce © Bettmann/Corbis/Sygma.

El Salvador and Nicaragua

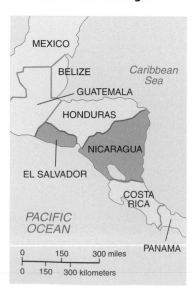

NSC aide marine lieutenant colonel Oliver North, and CIA director William Casey arranged to sell arms to Iran, then at war with neighboring Iraq. In exchange, Iranians were to pressure Muslim terrorists to release seven American hostages being held in Lebanon (see Map 30.1). Funds from the arms sales were then channeled through Swiss bank accounts to aid the Nicaraguan Contras. Over the objections of Secretary of State George Shultz and Defense Secretary Caspar Weinberger, Reagan approved the arms sales, but the three subsequently denied knowing that the proceeds were diverted to the Contras.

When news of the affair surfaced in November 1986, the Reagan administration faced serious charges. The president who had pledged never to bargain with terrorists had allowed his aides to do so, violating U.S. neutrality in the Iran-Iraq War. Even worse, the administration had defied Congress's express ban on military aid for the Contras. Although North and others destroyed incriminating documents, enough remained to demonstrate the culpability of seven individuals. Brought to trial by an independent prosecutor appointed by Reagan, all pleaded guilty or were convicted of lying to Congress and destroying evidence. North's felony conviction was later overturned on a technicality, and President George H. Bush pardoned the other six officials in December 1992. The independent prosecutor's final report, issued in 1994, found no evidence that Reagan had broken the law; but it concluded that both Reagan and Vice President Bush had known about the diversion of funds to the Contras and that Reagan had "knowingly participated or at least acquiesced" in covering up the scandal—the most serious case of executive branch misconduct since Watergate.

A Thaw in Soviet-American Relations

Reagan weathered Iran-Contra in part because Americans applauded a momentous thaw in the cold war. The new Soviet-American accord depended on Reagan's flexibility and an innovative Soviet head of state who recognized that his country's domestic problems demanded a relaxation of cold war antagonism. Mikhail Gorbachev assumed power in 1985 determined to revitalize an inefficient Soviet economy incapable of delivering basic consumer goods. Hoping to stimulate production and streamline distribution, Gorbachev

illegal means, the Reagan administration sustained the Contras and helped wreck the Nicaraguan economy, thereby undermining support for the Sandinista government. After nine years of civil war, Nicaragua's president, Daniel Ortega, agreed to a political settlement, and when he was defeated by a coalition of all the opposition groups, he stepped aside.

The Iran-Contra Scandal

Secret aid to the Contras was part of a larger project that came to be known as the Iran-Contra scandal. It began in 1985, when heads of the National Security Council, introduced some elements of free enterprise and proclaimed a new era of *glasnost* (greater freedom of expression), eventually allowing new political parties, contested elections, and challenges to Communist rule.

Concerns about immense defense budgets moved both Reagan and Gorbachev to the negotiating table. Enormous military expenditures stood between the Soviet premier and his goal of economic revival. With Congress increasingly criticizing the arms race and growing popular support for arms reductions, Reagan made disarmament a major goal in his last years in office and readily responded when Gorbachev took the initiative.

A positive personal chemistry developed between Reagan and Gorbachev, who met four times between 1985 and 1988. By December 1987, the superpowers had completed an intermediate-range nuclear forces (INF) agreement, eliminating all short- and medium-range missiles from Europe and providing for on-site inspection for

the first time. George H. Bush, Reagan's successor, achieved another breakthrough in June 1990, with a strategic arms reduction treaty (START) that cut about 30 percent of each superpower's nuclear arsenal.

In 1988, Gorbachev further reduced tensions by announcing a gradual withdrawal from Afghanistan, which had become the Soviet equivalent of America's Vietnam. In Africa, the Soviet Union, the United States, and Cuba agreed on a political settlement for the civil war in Angola. And in the Middle East, both superpowers supported a cease-fire and peace talks in the eight-year war between Iran and Iraq.

> The new Soviet-American accord depended on Reagan's flexibility and an innovative Soviet head of state who recognized that his country's domestic problems demanded a relaxation of cold war antagonism.

Nuclear Freeze Campaign

Sixteen-year-old Justin Martino made this mask to wear in a march on the Pentagon in 1985 supporting disarmament and world peace. Martino wanted to symbolize his belief that "the arms race has no end except the end of life," and he later contributed the mask to the Smithsonian Museum of American History. The worldwide demonstrations for nuclear disarmament achieved limited success when the United States and Soviet Union signed arms limitation agreements in 1987.

Smithsonian Institution, Washington, D.C.

Conclusion: Reversing the Course of Government

"Ours was the first revolution in the history of mankind that truly reversed the course of government," boasted Ronald Reagan in his farewell address in 1989. The word *revolution* exaggerated the change, but his administration did mark the slowdown or reversal of expanding federal budgets, programs, and regulations that had taken off in the 1930s. Although he did not deliver on the social or moral issues dear to the heart of the New Right, to Phyllis Schlafly, Reagan represented the "choice not an echo" that she had called for in 1964, as he used his skills as "the Great Communicator" to cultivate antigovernment sentiment and undo the liberal assumptions of the **New Deal**.

Hostility toward and distrust of the federal government grew along with the backlash against the reforms of the 1960s and the conduct of the Vietnam War. Watergate and other misdeeds of the Nixon administration further disillusioned Americans. Presidents Ford and Carter restored morality to the White House, but neither could solve the gravest economic problems since the Great Depression—a low rate of economic growth, stagflation, and an increasing trade deficit. Even the Democrat Carter gave higher priority to fiscal austerity than to social reform, and he began the government's retreat from regulation of key industries.

The Cold War Thaws
U.S. president Ronald Reagan and Soviet premier Mikhail Gorbachev shake hands as they meet at a five-day summit in June 1988 for a round of Strategic Arms Reduction Talks (START). Moving beyond the Strategic Arms Limitation Talks (SALT) agreements of the 1970s, these negotiations aimed to reduce rather than limit nuclear warheads and the bombers that carried them. The talks culminated with a comprehensive treaty signed by Reagan's successor George H. Bush and Gorbachev in July 1991.
David Burnett / Contact Press Images.

During the Reagan years, as a new conservative movement flourished, the United States turned explicitly away from the assumptions that had shaped domestic policy since the New Deal. Republican presidents Eisenhower and Nixon had attempted to curb the role of the federal government, but no president before Ronald Reagan had so castigated its activities. His tax cuts, combined with hefty increases in defense spending, created a federal deficit crisis that justified cuts in social welfare spending and made new federal initiatives unthinkable. Many Americans continued to approve of specific federal programs at the end of the Reagan years, but public sentiment about the government in general had undergone a U-turn from the Roosevelt era. Instead of seeing the government as a helpful and problem-solving institution, they believed it was not only ineffective at solving national problems but often made things worse. As Reagan appointed new Supreme Court justices, that body also retreated from its earlier liberalism, in which it had upheld the government's authority to protect individual rights and regulate the economy.

With his optimistic rhetoric, Ronald Reagan also lifted the confidence of Americans about their nation and its promise, confidence that had eroded with the economic and foreign-policy blows of the 1970s. Beginning his presidency with harsh rhetoric against the Soviet Union and a huge military buildup, Reagan left office having helped move the two superpowers to the highest level of cooperation since the cold war began. Although that accord was not welcome to strong anti-Communist conservatives like Phyllis Schlafly, it signaled developments that would transform American-Soviet relations—and the world—in the next decade.

FOR ADDITIONAL FIRSTHAND ACCOUNTS OF THIS PERIOD, see Chapter 30 in Michael Johnson, ed., *Reading the American Past,* Third Edition.

TO ASSESS YOUR MASTERY OF THE MATERIAL IN THIS CHAPTER, see the Online Study Guide at bedfordstmartins.com/roark.

FOR WEB LINKS RELATED TO TOPICS IN THIS CHAPTER, see "HistoryLinks," "DocLinks," and "PlaceLinks" at bedfordstmartins.com/roark.

CHRONOLOGY

1964
- Conservatives capture Republican presidential nomination for Barry Goldwater.

1966
- Ronald Reagan wins election to California governorship as a conservative.

1968
- Richard Nixon elected president.

1969
- Nixon appoints Warren E. Burger chief justice of U.S. Supreme Court.
- Stonewall riot in New York City helps spark gay and lesbian rights movement.

1971
- Nixon vetoes comprehensive child care bill.
- In *Swann v. Charlotte-Mecklenburg Board of Education*, U.S. Supreme Court affirms transfer of students between schools in white and black neighborhoods to achieve desegregation.

1972
- Nixon campaign aides apprehended breaking into Democratic Party headquarters in Watergate complex.
- Nixon reelected by landslide to a second term.

1974
- Nixon resigns as president in face of certain impeachment by House of Representatives over his role in Watergate affair; Gerald Ford becomes president.
- Ford pardons Nixon of any crimes he may have committed while president.
- In *Milliken v. Bradley*, U.S. Supreme Court imposes some limitations on use of busing to achieve racial integration in schools.

1976
- Jimmy Carter elected president.

1977
- United States signs treaties providing for return of Panama Canal to Panama in 2000.

1978
- Carter helps negotiate peace agreement between Egypt and Israel (Camp David accords).
- In *Bakke case*, U.S. Supreme Court rules against racial quotas but upholds use of affirmative action to remedy effects of past discrimination.
- Discovery of toxic wastes in the Love Canal neighborhood of Niagara Falls, New York, brings national attention to environmental effects of industrial dumping.

1978–1980
- Congress passes bills deregulating airlines, banking, trucking, and railroad industries.

1979
- Carter establishes formal diplomatic relations with the People's Republic of China.

- Soviet Union invades Afghanistan; United States imposes economic sanctions.
- Hostage crisis in Iran begins.
- Rev. Jerry Falwell founds Moral Majority to involve evangelical Christians in politics.

1979–1980
- Congress enacts measures to conserve energy and increase its production.

1980
- Congress passes Superfund legislation to clean up toxic wastes.
- Ronald Reagan elected president, defeating incumbent Jimmy Carter.

1981
- Researchers identify a virus as the cause of AIDS epidemic.
- Congress passes Economic Recovery Tax Act, resulting in the largest tax cut in U.S. history.
- Reagan appoints first female justice to U.S. Supreme Court: Sandra Day O'Connor.

1981–1982
- Economic recession pushes unemployment rate above 10 percent.

1982
- Large peace marches held in the United States and Europe to limit nuclear weapons.

1983
- United States invades Grenada and topples its Marxist government.
- United States terminates peacekeeping mission in Lebanon after a terrorist bombs U.S. marine barracks and kills 241 Americans.
- Reagan announces plans for Strategic Defense Initiative ("Star Wars"), a space-based missile defense system.

1984
- Reagan reelected to a second term.

1986
- Iran-Contra scandal shakes Reagan administration.
- Federal budget deficit reaches all-time high of $220 billion.

1987
- Soviet premier Mikhail Gorbachev and President Reagan sign INF agreement, eliminating all short- and medium-range missiles from Europe.

1988
- Congress passes Civil Rights Restoration Act, strengthening safeguards against discrimination on the basis of race, color, national origin, sex, disability, or age.

BIBLIOGRAPHY

Foreign Policy

Zbigniew Brzezinski, *Power and Principle: Memoirs of the National Security Adviser, 1977–1981* (1983).

Beth A. Fischer, *The Reagan Reversal: Foreign Policy and the End of the Cold War* (1997).

Frances FitzGerald, *Way Out There in the Blue: Reagan, Star Wars, and the End of the Cold War* (2000).

Raymond I. Garthoff, *Détente and Confrontation: American-Soviet Relations from Nixon to Reagan* (rev. ed., 1994).

David Kyvig, ed., *Reagan and the World* (1990).

Sanford Lakoff and Herbert F. York, *A Shield in Space?* (1989).

Peter Schweizer, *Victory: The Reagan Administration's Secret Strategy That Hastened the Collapse of the Soviet Union* (1995).

George P. Shultz, *Turmoil and Triumph: My Years as Secretary of State* (1993).

Gaddis Smith, *Morality, Reason, and Power: American Diplomacy in the Carter Years* (1986).

Strobe Talbott, *The Master of the Game: Paul Nitze and the Nuclear Peace* (1988).

Cyrus Vance, *Hard Choices: Critical Years in America's Foreign Policy* (1983).

Daniel Wirls, *Buildup: The Politics of Defense in the Reagan Era* (1992).

The United States and the Middle East

James A. Bill, *The Eagle and the Lion: The Tragedy of American-Iranian Relations* (1988).

Theodore Draper, *A Very Thin Line: The Iran-Contra Affair* (1991).

Mark J. Gasiorowski, *U.S. Foreign Policy and the Shah: Building a Client State in Iran* (1991).

Douglas Little, *American Orientalism: The United States and the Middle East since 1945* (2002).

Benny Morris, *Righteous Victims: A History of the Zionist-Arab Conflict, 1881–1999* (1999).

The United States and Latin America

Cynthia J. Arnson, *Crossroads: Congress, the Reagan Administration, and Central America* (1989).

Thomas Carothers, *In the Name of Democracy: U.S. Policy toward Latin America in the Reagan Years* (1991).

J. Michael Hogan, *The Panama Canal in American Politics* (1986).

Robert Kagan, *A Twilight Struggle: American Power and Nicaragua, 1977–1990* (1996).

William M. LeoGrande, *Our Own Backyard: The United States in Central America, 1977–1992* (1998).

Energy and the Environment

Thomas R. Dunlap, *DDT: Scientists, Citizens, and Public Policy* (1981).

J. Brooks Flippen, *Nixon and the Environment* (2000).

Samuel P. Hays, *A History of Environmental Politics since 1945* (2000).

Martin V. Melosi, *Coping with Abundance: Energy and Environment in Industrial America* (1985).

Roderick Frazier Nash, *American Environmentalism: Readings in Conservation History* (1990).

Hal K. Rothman, *The Greening of a Nation? Environmentalism in the United States since 1945* (1998).

Philip Shabecoff, *A Fierce Green Fire: The American Environmental Movement* (1993).

Daniel Yergin, *The Prize: The Epic Quest for Oil, Money, and Power* (1990).

Conservatism and Right-Wing Movements

John A. Andrew, *The Other Side of the Sixties: Young Americans for Freedom and the Rise of Conservative Politics* (1997).

William C. Berman, *America's Right Turn: From Nixon to Clinton* (1998).

Earl Black and Merle Black, *The Rise of Southern Republicans* (2002).

Matthew Dallek, *The Right Moment: Ronald Reagan's First Victory and the Decisive Turning Point in American Politics* (2000).

Thomas Byrd Edsall with Mary D. Edsall, *Chain Reaction: The Impact of Race, Rights, and Taxes on American Politics* (1992).

Lee Edwards, *The Conservative Revolution: The Movement That Remade America* (1999).

Carol Felsenthal, *Sweetheart of the Silent Majority* (1981).

Thomas Ferguson and Joel Rogers, *Right Turn: The Decline of the Democrats and the Future of American Politics* (1986).

Godfrey Hodgson, *The World Turned Right Side Up: A History of the Conservative Ascendancy in America* (1996).

William Martin, *With God on Our Side: The Rise of the Religious Right in America* (1996).

Lisa McGirr, *Suburban Warriors: The Origins of the New American Right* (2001).

Jonathan M. Schoenwald, *A Time for Choosing: The Rise of Modern Conservatism* (2001).

Social Movements, Rights, and the Supreme Court

Barry D. Adam, *The Rise of a Gay and Lesbian Movement* (rev. ed., 1995).

Norman C. Amaker, *Civil Rights and the Reagan Administration* (1988).

John D'Emilio, Urvashi Vaid, and William B. Turner, *Creating Change: Sexuality, Public Policy, and Civil Rights* (2000).

Susan M. Hartmann, *The Other Feminists: Activists in the Liberal Establishment* (1998).

Lisa Keen and Suzanne B. Goldberg, *Strangers to the Law: Gay People on Trial* (1998).

Dean J. Kotlowski, *Nixon's Civil Rights: Politics, Principle, and Policy* (2001).

Jane J. Mansbridge, *Why We Lost the ERA* (1986).

Donald G. Mathews and Jane Sherron De Hart, *Sex, Gender, and the Politics of the ERA* (1990).

Herman Schwartz, *Packing the Courts: The Conservative Campaign to Rewrite the Constitution* (1988).

Randy Shilts, *And the Band Played On: Politics, People, and the AIDS Epidemic* (1987).

James F. Simon, *The Center Holds: The Power Struggle inside the Rehnquist Court* (1995).

Melvin Urofsky, *A Conflict of Rights: The Supreme Court and Affirmative Action* (1991).

The Economy and Its Casualties

Michael Bernstein, David E. Adler, and Robert Heilbroner, *Understanding American Economic Decline* (1994).

W. Carl Biven, *Jimmy Carter's Economy: Policy in an Age of Limits* (2003).

Jefferson Cowie, *Capital Moves: RCAs Seventy-year Quest for Cheap Labor* (1999).

Kathleen Day, *S&L Hell: The People and the Politics behind the $1 Trillion Savings and Loan Scandal* (1993).

Kathryn Marie Dudley, *The End of the Line: Lost Jobs, New Lives in Postindustrial America* (1994).

Bennett Harrison and Barry Bluestone, *The Great U-Turn: Corporate Restructuring and the Polarizing of America* (1988).

Jennifer L. Hochschild, *Facing Up to the American Dream: Race, Class, and the Soul of the Nation* (1995).

Christopher Jencks, *The Homeless* (1994).

Kevin Phillips, *The Politics of Rich and Poor: Wealth and the American Electorate in the Reagan Aftermath* (1990).

Robert J. Samuelson, *The American Dream in the Age of Entitlement, 1945–1995* (1996).

John E. Schwartz and Thomas J. Volgy, *The Forgotten Americans* (1993).

John W. Sloan, *The Reagan Effect: Economics and Presidential Leadership* (1999).

Adam Smith, *The Roaring '80s* (1988).

Watergate

Carl Bernstein and Bob Woodward, *All the President's Men* (1974).

Stanley I. Kutler, *The Wars of Watergate: The Last Crisis of Richard Nixon* (1990).

Stanley I. Kutler, ed., *Abuse of Power: The New Nixon Tapes* (1997).

Kathryn S. Olmstead, *Challenging the Secret Government: The Post-Watergate Investigations of the CIA and FBI* (1996).

Keith W. Olson, *Watergate: The Presidential Scandal That Shook America* (2003).

Presidents and Politics

Lou Cannon, *President Reagan: The Role of a Lifetime* (1991).

Gary M. Fink and Hugh Davis Graham, eds., *The Carter Presidency: Policy Choices in the Post–New Deal Era* (1998).

Haynes Johnson, *Sleepwalking through History: America in the Reagan Years* (1992).

Burton I. Kaufmann, *The Presidency of James Earl Carter* (1993).

Michael Schaller, *Reckoning with Reagan: America and Its President of the 1980s* (1992).

Melvin Small, *The Presidency of Richard Nixon* (1999).

Tom Wicker, *One of Us: Richard Nixon and the American Dream* (1991).

A SHRINKING WORLD

The cellular telephone is one of the new technologies contributing to the process of globalization that intensified with the end of the cold war in 1990. Connecting users to conventional telephone networks through microwave radio frequencies, wireless phones began to be used in Tokyo in 1979, and the first American system began in 1983. By the end of the century, hundreds of millions of people used cell phones around the world, not only to call friends and business associates but also to connect to the Internet and send and receive e-mail. Cellular systems have improved communication for people in countries that lack a good wire-based telephone system, facilitating commerce as well as connecting far-flung family members and other individuals. By 2003, cell phones comprised 43 percent of all phones in the United States; in European and other countries, cell phones outnumbered traditional phones. Terrorists who struck the World Trade Center towers and the Pentagon on September 11, 2001, used mobile devices to coordinate the attacks, and many victims of the terror spoke their last words to loved ones over cell phones. Wireless phones decorated with the American flag became popular expressions of patriotism in the aftermath of the attacks.

Kit Hinricks/Pentagon Design.

31

The End of the Cold War and the Challenges of Globalization

Since 1989

O N APRIL 22, 1988, Ronald Reagan's national security adviser, army general Colin L. Powell, returned to his Moscow hotel from the Kremlin, where he had heard Premier Mikhail Gorbachev announce plans that would dramatically alter the government and economy of the Soviet Union. "Lying there in bed," Powell recalled, "I realized that one phase of my life had ended, and another was about to begin. Up until now, as a soldier, my mission had been to confront, contain, and if necessary, combat communism. Now I had to think about a world without a Cold War." For the next sixteen years, Powell would be a key figure helping to define his country's new role in a world transformed.

Colin Powell was born in New York City's Harlem in 1937 and grew up in the Bronx, the son of parents who had immigrated from Jamaica in 1920. His father had begun as a gardener and ultimately became head of the shipping department of a garment manufacturer, where his mother worked as a seamstress. Powell attended public schools and then City College of New York, where he joined the army's Reserve Officers Training Corps program (ROTC), which became the center of his collegiate experience. "The discipline, the structure, the camaraderie, the sense of belonging," he said, "were what I craved." Commissioned as a lieutenant when he graduated in 1958, Powell began a lifelong career in military and public service, rising to the highest rank of four-star general. He chose to stay in the army after fulfilling his ROTC obligation primarily because "I loved what I was doing." But he also recognized that "for a black, no other avenue in American society offered so much opportunity."

The two tours of duty that he served in Vietnam were defining experiences for Powell, just as the war was for many Americans. Powell learned from Vietnam that "you do not squander courage and lives without clear purpose, without the country's backing, and without full commitment." In his subsequent capacities as national security adviser to Ronald Reagan, as chairman of the Joint Chiefs of Staff in the George H. W. Bush and William Jefferson Clinton administrations, and as secretary of state under George W. Bush, Powell endeavored to ensure that his country did not engage in "half-hearted warfare for half-baked reasons that the American people could not understand or support."

- **Domestic Stalemate and Global Upheaval: The Presidency of George H. W. Bush**
  Gridlock in Government
  The End of the Cold War
  Going to War in Central America and the Persian Gulf
  The 1992 Election

- **The Clinton Administration's Search for the Middle Ground**
  Clinton's Promise of Change
  Changing the Face of Government
  The Clinton Administration Moves Right
  Impeaching the President
  The Booming Economy of the 1990s

- **The United States in a Globalizing World**
  Defining America's Place in a New World Order
  Debates over Globalization
  Liberalizing Foreign Trade
  The Internationalization of the United States

- **President George W. Bush: Conservatism at Home and Radical Initiatives Abroad**
  The Disputed Election of 2000
  The Domestic Policies of a "Compassionate Conservative"
  The Globalization of Terrorism
  Unilateralism, Preemption, and the Iraq War

- **Conclusion: Defining the Government's Role at Home and Abroad**

Secretary of State Colin Powell
Among the many characteristics that helped Colin Powell rise through the ranks of the army and serve in four presidential administrations were his loyalty and discretion. The decision by George W. Bush to invade Iraq in March 2003 ran counter to his secretary of state's commitment to acting through the international community and sacrificing American lives only when a vital interest was at stake and a plan for ending the intervention had been established. Although Powell's position lost out to the more hawkish Vice President Dick Cheney and Secretary of Defense Donald Rumsfeld, Powell stayed in his job and defended administration policy. In this photo taken in the White House in February 2003, he listens to Rumsfeld; National Security Adviser Condoleezza Rice stands behind them.
Charles Ommanney/Contact Press Images for Newsweek.

Powell's sense that Gorbachev's reforms would bring about the end of the **cold war** became reality more quickly than anyone anticipated. Eastern Europe broke free from **Communist** control in 1989, and the Soviet Union disintegrated in 1991. As the lone superpower, throughout the 1990s the United States deployed both military and diplomatic power during episodes of instability in Latin America, the Middle East, Eastern Europe, and Asia, almost always in concert with the major nations of Europe and Asia. In 1991, in its first full-fledged war since Vietnam, it led a United Nations–authorized force of twenty-eight nations to repel Iraq's invasion of Kuwait.

In the mid-1990s during a temporary retirement from public service, Powell remarked that "neither of the two major parties fits me comfortably." Many Americans seemed to agree: They turned Republican George H. W. Bush out of office in 1992 but elected Republican Congresses during Democrat Bill Clinton's administration; when Republican George W. Bush entered the White House in 2001, he faced a nearly evenly divided Congress. Between 1989 and 2000, domestic policies reflected a slight retreat from the **conservatism** of the Reagan years: The Bush administration saw tighter environmental protections and new rights for people with disabilities, and Clinton signed measures strengthening gun control and aiding low wage earners. But the pendulum swung back in the early years of the second Bush presidency.

All three presidents shared a commitment to economic growth and to hastening the globalizing processes that were linking nations together in an increasingly connected economy. As capital, products, and people crossed national boundaries at greater speed, the United States itself became more diverse with a surge of immigration rivaling that of a century earlier, which had brought Powell's parents to the United States. Powell cheered **globalization**, predicting in the 1990s that the world would become "defined by trade relations, by the flow of information, capital, technology, and goods, rather than by armies glaring at each other across borders."

Powell was not so naive as to anticipate a world "without war or conflict," and he pointed to challenges such as nuclear proliferation, **nationalist** passions in areas of former Soviet dominance, civil wars in Africa, and Islamic **fundamentalism.** But he was as shocked as other Americans when in September 2001 deadly terrorist attacks on New York City, the nation's economic center, and Washington, D.C., its political and military core, exposed American vulnerability to new and horrifying international threats. The administration's response to terrorism overwhelmed Secretary of State Powell's commitments to internationalism, multilateralism, and military restraint, as George W. Bush began a second war against Iraq, implementing a radical shift in U.S. foreign policy based on preemptive attacks against presumed threats and going it alone if necessary.

Domestic Stalemate and Global Upheaval: The Presidency of George H. W. Bush

When Vice President George H. W. Bush announced his candidacy for the presidency in 1987, he declared, "We don't need radical new directions." Generally satisfied with the agenda set by Ronald Reagan and facing a Democratic-controlled Congress, Bush proposed few domestic initiatives. His dispatch of troops to oust the corrupt dictator of Panama represented a much longer continuity, following a century of American intervention in Latin America. Yet, as the most dramatic changes since the 1940s swept through the world, his government confronted situations that did not fit the simpler free-world versus communism framework that had guided foreign policy since World War II. Most Americans approved of Bush's handling of two challenges to American foreign policy and military capacity: disintegration of the Soviet Union and its hold over Eastern Europe and Iraq's invasion of neighboring Kuwait. But voters' concern over a sluggish economy and other domestic problems limited Bush to one term in the White House.

Gridlock in Government

The son of a wealthy New England senator, George Herbert Walker Bush grew up in a privileged milieu that put a premium on public service. He fought in World War II, earned a Yale degree, and then settled in Texas to make his own way in the oil industry and politics. He served in Congress during the 1960s and headed the CIA during the Nixon-Ford years. When Ronald Reagan achieved a commanding lead in the 1980 primaries, Bush put his own presidential ambitions on hold, adjusted his more moderate policy positions to fit Reagan's conservative agenda, and accepted second place on the Republican ticket.

Michael Dukakis, governor of Massachusetts, won the Democratic Party nomination, defeating several candidates. An important contender was the Reverend Jesse Jackson, who had fought civil rights battles with Martin Luther King Jr, and whose Rainbow Coalition campaign centered on the needs of minorities, women, working-class families, and the poor. He won several primaries, gathering 7 million votes, but his race, lack of government experience, and position on the left of the party proved to be insuperable obstacles. On election day, half the eligible voters stayed home, indicating the electorate's general disgust with the negative campaigning or their satisfaction with the Republican record on peace and prosperity. Divided government would remain, however: 54 percent of the voters chose Bush, but the Democrats gained seats in the House and Senate.

Although President Bush saw himself primarily as guardian and beneficiary of the Reagan legacy, he promised "a kinder, gentler nation" and was more inclined than Reagan to approve government activity in the private sphere. For example, he signed the Clean Air Act of 1990, the strongest, most comprehensive environmental law in history; it required power plants to cut sulfur dioxide emissions by more than half by the year 2000 and oil companies to develop cleaner-burning gasoline. Some 40 million Americans reaped the benefits of another regulatory measure, the 1991 Americans with Disabilities Act, which banned job discrimination against the disabled and required that private businesses, public accommodations, and transportation be made handicapped-accessible. Cynthia Jones, publisher of *Mainstream Magazine*, which reported on disability politics, attended the bill's signing on the White House lawn. When a breeze stirred the crowd, she remembered with jubilation, "It was kind of like a new breath of air was sweeping across America. . . . People knew they had rights. That was wonderful."

Yet Bush needed to satisfy party conservatives. His most famous campaign pledge was "Read my lips: No new taxes," and he opposed most proposals requiring additional federal funds. "If you're looking for George Bush's domestic program, and many people are, this is

> Most Americans approved of George H. W. Bush's handling of two challenges to American foreign policy and military capacity. But voters' concern over a sluggish economy and other domestic problems limited Bush to one term.

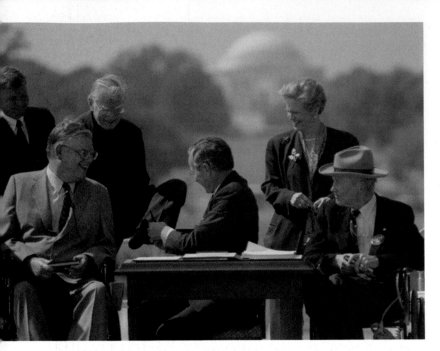

President George H. W. Bush Signs the Americans with Disabilities Act
After signing the landmark measure guaranteeing civil rights for people with disabilities on July 26, 1990, President Bush presented a pen to the Reverend Dr. Harold Wilke. A minister, professor, and disability rights leader, Wilke accepted the pen with his foot because he was born without arms. On the left, Vice President Daniel Quayle watches.
© Bettmann/Corbis.

from cities to pay wages well above the federal minimum wage. And in 1999, California passed a gun control bill with much tougher restrictions on assault weapons than reformers had been able to get through Congress.

A huge **federal budget deficit** inherited from the Reagan administration impelled the president and Congress to break their deadlock. In 1990, Bush reluctantly abandoned his "no new taxes" pledge and agreed to modest tax increases for high-income Americans and higher levies on gasoline, cigarettes, alcohol, and luxury items. Although the budget agreement brought in new revenues and Congress limited spending, three years later the deficit soared even higher, boosted by rising costs in entitlement programs such as Social Security and Medicare-Medicaid as well as by spending on unforeseen emergencies of war and natural disasters. The new taxes affected only slightly the massive tax reductions of the early 1980s, leaving intact a key element of Reagan's legacy.

Bush also continued Reagan's efforts to create a more conservative Supreme Court. His first nominee, federal appeals judge David Souter, won easy confirmation by the Senate. But in 1991, when the only African American on the Court, Justice Thurgood Marshall, retired, Bush set off a national controversy by nominating Clarence Thomas, a conservative black appeals judge, who had opposed **affirmative action** as head of the Equal Employment Opportunity Commission (EEOC) under Reagan. Charging that Thomas would not protect minority rights, the National Association for the Advancement of Colored People (NAACP) and other **liberal** organizations fought the nomination. Then Anita Hill, a law professor and former EEOC employee, stunned the nation by accusing Thomas of sexual harassment.

The Senate Judiciary Committee investigated the charges during three days of nationally televised hearings. Thomas angrily denied the alleged incidents, and Hill's testimony failed to sway the Senate, which voted narrowly to confirm him. The hearings did sensitize the public to sexual harassment, and they angered many women, including a dozen House members, who expressed outrage at the shabby treatment that Hill received from senators seeking to discredit her. **Feminists** complained that men "still don't get it" and redoubled their efforts to get more women into office. But Thomas's confirmation solidified the Supreme Court's shift to the right.

it: the veto pen," charged Democratic House majority leader Richard Gephardt in 1991. Bush blocked Congress thirty-six times, vetoing bills that would have lifted abortion restrictions, extended unemployment benefits, raised taxes, mandated family and medical leave for workers, and reformed campaign financing. By the end of his term, press reports were filled with the words *stalemate, gridlock,* and *divided government.*

Continuing a trend begun during the Reagan administration, states tried to compensate for this paralysis, becoming more innovative than Washington. "Our federal politics are gridlocked, and governors have become the ones who have to have the courage to put their necks out," said a spokesperson for governors. States passed bills to block corporate takeovers, establish parental leave policies, require equal pay for jobs of equal worth, improve food labeling, and protect the environment. Beginning in the 1980s, a few states began to pass measures guaranteeing gay and lesbian rights. (See "Documenting the American Promise," page 1128.) In the 1990s, dozens of cities passed ordinances requiring businesses with tax abatements or other benefits

The End of the Cold War

The forces of change that Gorbachev had encouraged in the Communist world (see chapter 30) swept through Eastern Europe in 1989, where popular uprisings demanded an end to state repression, official corruption, and economic bureaucracies unable to deliver an acceptable standard of living. Communist governments toppled like dominoes (Map 31.1). East Germany opened its border with West Germany, and in November 1989, ecstatic Germans danced on the Berlin Wall, which had separated East and West since 1961, using whatever was at hand to demolish that dominant symbol of the cold war. An amazed East Berliner crossed over the line exclaiming, "They just let us go. I can't believe it."

Unification of East and West Germany into one nation sped to completion in 1990. The Warsaw Pact dissolved, and by 2000 three former **iron curtain** countries—the Czech Republic, Hungary, and Poland—had joined **NATO**, and more were in line to become members. Although U.S. military forces remained in Europe as part of NATO, the commanding role of the United States had been eclipsed. The same was true of its economic clout: Western Europe, including unified Germany, formed a common economic market in 1992. The destiny of Europe, to which the United States and the Soviet Union had held the key for forty-five years, now lay in European hands.

By the end of 1991, Gorbachev's initiatives had brought his own downfall. Inspired by the liberation of Eastern Europe, republics within the Soviet Union sought their own independence, while Moscow's efforts at economic change brought widespread destitution. According to one Muscovite, "Gorbachev knew how to bring us freedom but he did not know how to make sausage." In December, Boris Yeltsin, president

> On November 12, 1989, ecstatic Germans danced on the Berlin Wall, using whatever was at hand to demolish that dominant symbol of the cold war.

Fall of the Berlin Wall

After 1961, the Berlin Wall stood as the prime symbol of the cold war and the iron grip of communism over Eastern Europe and the Soviet Union. More than four hundred easterners were killed trying to flee. After Communist authorities opened the wall on November 9, 1989, permitting free travel between East and West Germany, Berliners from both sides gathered at the wall to celebrate.
Eric Bouvet/Gamma Press Images.

FOR MORE HELP ANALYZING THIS IMAGE, see the visual activity for this chapter in the Online Study Guide at bedfordstmartins.com/roark.

MAP 31.1   Events in Eastern Europe, 1989–2002
The overthrow of Communist governments throughout eastern and central Europe and the splintering of the Soviet Union into more than a dozen separate nations were the most momentous changes in world history since World War II.

READING THE MAP: Which country was the first to overthrow its Communist government? Which was the last? In which nations did elections usher in change in government?
CONNECTIONS: What problems did Mikhail Gorbachev try to solve, and how did he try to solve them? What policy launched by Ronald Reagan contributed to Soviet dilemmas? Did it create any problems in the United States?

FOR MORE HELP ANALYZING THIS MAP, see the map activity for this chapter in the Online Study Guide at **bedfordstmartins.com/roark**.

of the Russian Republic, announced that Russia and eleven other republics had formed a new entity, the Commonwealth of Independent States (CIS), and other former Soviet states declared independence. With nothing left to govern, Gorbachev resigned.

China and North Korea resisted the liberalizing tides sweeping the world. In 1989, the Chinese military killed hundreds of pro-democracy demonstrators in Tiananmen Square in Beijing, and the Communist government arrested some 10,000 citizens as it cracked down on advocates of reform. North Korea remained under a Communist dictatorship that threatened

to develop nuclear weapons and to deliver materials that could help other nations achieve a nuclear capacity.

"The post–cold war world is decidedly not postnuclear," declared one U.S. official. In 1996, the world took a small step back from the nuclear brink when the UN General Assembly overwhelmingly approved a total nuclear test ban treaty. Yet India and Pakistan, hostile neighbors, refused to sign and both exploded atomic devices in 1998, increasing the nuclear risk in South Asia. Moreover, in a highly partisan vote, the Republican-controlled Senate defeated U.S. ratification of the treaty in October 1999, halting a decade of progress on nuclear weapons control.

Going to War in Central America and the Persian Gulf

Despite the diminishing threat of the Soviet Union during his four years in office, President Bush twice sent U.S. soldiers into battle. Nearly every cold war president before him had dispatched aid or troops to Central America and the Caribbean in the name of suppressing communism; but Bush intervened in Panama in 1989 for different reasons. The United States had tolerated the repressive regime of Panamanian dictator Manuel Noriega when he served as a CIA informer about Communist activities in the 1980s. But in 1989, after Noriega was indicted for drug trafficking by a grand jury in Miami, Florida, and after his troops killed an American marine, President Bush ordered 25,000 military personnel into Panama to capture the dictator. In an invasion labeled "Operation Just Cause," U.S. forces quickly overcame Noriega's troops, at the cost of 23 Americans and hundreds of Panamanians, many of them civilians. Chairman of the Joint Chiefs of Staff Colin Powell noted that "our euphoria over our victory in Just Cause was not universal": Both the United Nations and the Organization of American States censured the unilateral action by the United States.

If the resort to military intervention in Panama fit within the century-old tradition of **Yankee imperialism**, Bush's second military engagement represented a decided break with the past, demonstrating how much the cold war's end had changed the world. Former cold war enemies worked together when, in August 1990, Iraq occupied the small, oil-rich country of Kuwait to its south (Map 31.2). Struggling with an enormous debt from ten years of war against Iran, Iraqi dictator Saddam Hussein desperately needed revenues and sought control of Kuwait. Within days of invading Kuwait, Iraqi troops moved toward the Saudi Arabian border, threatening the world's largest oil reserves.

President Bush reacted quickly. He invoked principles of national self-determination and international law, but the need to maintain access to oil drove the U.S. response. As the largest importer of oil, the United States consumed one-fourth of the world supply. With the consent of Saudi Arabia, Bush ordered a massive mobilization of land, air, and naval forces and assembled more than thirty nations in an international

coalition to stand up to Iraq. "The community of nations has resolutely gathered to condemn and repel lawless aggression," Bush announced. "With few exceptions, the world now stands as one."

Reflecting the end of superpower conflict in the Middle East, the Soviet Union joined the United States in condemning Hussein and cut off arms shipments to Iraq. The UN declared an embargo on Iraqi oil and authorized the use of force if Iraq did not withdraw from Kuwait by January 15, 1991. By early January, the United States had deployed 400,000 soldiers to Saudi Arabia, joined by 265,000 troops from some two dozen nations, including Egypt, Syria, and several other Arab states.

When Bush asked Congress to approve war in January 1991, considerable public and legislative

> By early January 1991, the United States had deployed 400,000 soldiers to Saudi Arabia, joined by 265,000 troops from some two dozen nations, including Egypt, Syria, and several other Arab states.

The Gulf War

These soldiers from the Twenty-fourth Infantry arrived in Saudi Arabia in August 1990 as part of the U.S.-led effort to drive Iraq out of Kuwait. For the first time, women served in combat-support positions: More than 33,000 were stationed throughout the Gulf; 11 died, and 2 were held as prisoners of war. Among their duties were piloting planes and helicopters, directing artillery, and fighting fires. Reuters Newmedia/Corbis.

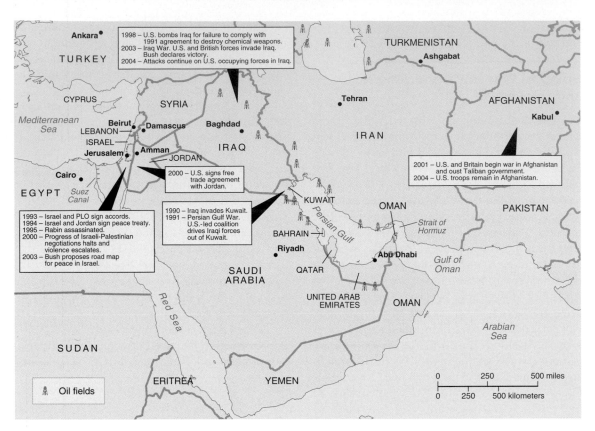

MAP 31.2 Events in the Middle East, 1989–2004

During the Persian Gulf War of 1991, Egypt, Syria, and other Middle Eastern nations joined the coalition against Iraq, and the 22-member Arab League supported the war as a means to liberate Kuwait. After September 11, 2001, the Arab League approved of U.S. military operations in Afghanistan because the attacks "were an attack on the common values of the world, not just on the United States." Yet, except for the countries where the United States had military bases—Bahrain, Kuwait, Qatar, and Saudi Arabia—no Arab country supported the American invasion and occupation of Iraq in 2003. Arab hostility to the United States also reflected the deterioration of Israeli-Palestinian relations from 2000 to 2004, as Arabs charged that the United States allowed Israel to deny Palestinians land and liberty.

sentiment favored waiting to see whether the embargo would force Hussein to back down. Within the administration, Colin Powell quietly urged such restraint. In Congress, Democratic senator George J. Mitchell agreed on the need to free Kuwait but asked, "Should we start with war, before other means have been fully exhausted?" Linking the crisis to the failure of U.S. energy conservation, Democratic senator Edward M. Kennedy insisted, "Not a single American life should be sacrificed in a war for the price of oil." Congress debated for three days and then authorized war by margins of five votes in the Senate and sixty-seven in the House. On January 17, 1991, the U.S.-led coalition launched Operation Desert Storm, a forty-day air war against Iraq, bombing military targets,

power plants, oil refineries, and transportation networks. Having severely crippled Iraq, the coalition stormed into Kuwait with massive ground forces on February 23, and within one hundred hours Hussein announced that he would withdraw from Kuwait (see Map 31.2).

"By God, we've kicked the Vietnam syndrome once and for all," President Bush exulted on March 1. Most Americans found no moral ambiguity in the Persian Gulf War and took pride in the display of military competence. In contrast to the loss of 50,000 American lives in Vietnam, 270 U.S. servicemen and women perished in Desert Storm. The United States stood at the apex of global leadership, steering a coalition in which Arab nations fought beside their former colonial rulers.

Yet victory did not bring stability to the Middle East. Israel, which had endured Iraqi missile attacks, was more secure, but the Israeli-Palestinian conflict remained intractable. Despite military losses, Saddam Hussein remained in power and turned his war machine on Iraqi Kurds and Shiite Muslims whom the United States had encouraged to rebel. Hussein continued to develop chemical, biological, and nuclear weapons, while Iraqi citizens suffered malnutrition, disease, and death caused by the continuing embargo and the destruction of the nation's fuel, communications, and transportation systems.

The 1992 Election

Despite ongoing instability in the Middle East, in March 1991 Bush's chances for reelection in 1992 looked golden. The Gulf War victory catapulted his approval rating to 88 percent, causing the most prominent Democrats to opt out of the presidential race. But that did not deter William Jefferson "Bill" Clinton, who at age forty-five had served as governor of Arkansas for twelve years. Like Jimmy Carter in 1976 and Michael Dukakis in 1988, Clinton and his running mate, Tennessee senator Albert Gore Jr., presented themselves as "New Democrats." Both belonged to the Democratic Leadership Council, which Clinton had helped found in 1985 to rid the party of its liberal image.

In an approach reminiscent of Richard Nixon's appeal to the "silent majority" in 1968, Clinton promised to work for the "forgotten middle class," who "do the work, pay the taxes, raise the kids, and play by the rules." Clinton deliberately distanced himself from Jesse Jackson and his Rainbow Coalition and appealed to voters who believed that some Americans were getting a free ride at their expense. "We're going to put an end to welfare as we know it," Clinton claimed. Disavowing the "tax and spend" label that Republicans pinned on his party, he promised a tax cut for the middle class and pledged to reinvigorate government and the economy.

With no new crises to display his talents in foreign policy, Bush was vulnerable to voters' concerns about the economy. As foreign competition drove businesses to trim budgets, victims of corporate downsizing worried about finding new jobs while other workers worried about keeping theirs. Unemployment edged over 7 percent in 1992. A sign at Clinton headquarters

insisting "It's the economy, stupid" reflected the campaign's focus on bread-and-butter issues.

The popularity of a third candidate revealed Americans' frustrations with government and the major parties. In announcing his candidacy on the popular TV talk show *Larry King Live*, self-made Texas billionaire H. Ross Perot set the tone of his unconventional campaign. Although he gave no press conferences, he had plenty of money, used television extensively, and attracted a sizable grassroots movement with his down-to-earth personality and appeals to voters' disgust with Washington. Perot's candidacy hurt the president more than it hurt Clinton, and it established the federal budget deficit as a key campaign issue.

Fifty-five percent of those eligible showed up at the polls, just barely reversing the thirty-year decline in voter turnout. Americans gave Clinton 43 percent of their votes, Bush 38 percent, and Perot 19 percent—the strongest third-party finish since Theodore Roosevelt's Progressive Party candidacy in 1912. Although casting two-thirds of their votes against Bush

---

Clinton and Gore on Tour

The gregarious Bill Clinton excelled at political campaigning, and the youth of the first baby-boomer candidates appealed to many. During the 1992 presidential election campaign, Clinton and his wife, Hillary—accompanied by running mate Al Gore and his wife, Tipper—went out on several bus tours as a way of demonstrating the Democrats' connection to ordinary people. Not far from this campaign stop in Sylvester, Georgia, the bus caravan passed by a handmade sign that read "Bubbas for Clinton/Gore."

© Ira Wyman/Sygma/Corbis.

demonstrated a mandate for change, voters formed no majority around a particular direction that change should take.

The Clinton Administration's Search for the Middle Ground

The president who asserted "The era of big government is over" was not Ronald Reagan but Bill Clinton, reflecting the Democratic Party's move to the right that had begun with Jimmy Carter in the 1970s. Clinton did not completely abandon the principles that had guided the party in the 1960s. He signed important measures benefiting the working poor, delivered incremental reforms to feminists, environmentalists, and other groups, and spoke out in favor of affirmative action and gay rights. Yet his administration attended more to the concerns of middle-class Americans than to the needs of the poor and restrained federal programs and appropriations for the disadvantaged.

The Clinton administration ended its eight years with a surplus in the federal budget and the longest economic boom in history. Although various factors generated the prosperity, many Americans identified Clinton with the buoyant economy, returned him to office for a second term, and continued to support him even when his reckless sexual behavior resulted in **impeachment**. Although the Senate did not find sufficient cause to remove him from office, the scandal crippled Clinton's leadership in his last years in office.

> The Clinton administration attended more to the concerns of middle-class Americans than to the needs of the poor and restrained federal programs and appropriations for the disadvantaged.

Clinton's Promise of Change

Clinton wanted to restore confidence in government as a force for good but avoid alienating antigovernment voters by proposing new large federal programs, and in any case, the budget deficit—$4.4 trillion in 1993—precluded such spending. Just as Clinton was short on cash for using government in positive ways, he also lacked political capital, for the Republicans controlled Congress for all but his first two years in office. Moreover, the end of the cold war de-

prived the president of a national agenda around which to unite Americans and eliminated the rationale that domestic reform was necessary to combat communism abroad.

The popular mandate for change, nonetheless, allowed the New Democrat president to exert some federal authority to solve national problems. Using his executive powers to reverse Reagan and Bush policies, Clinton eased restrictions on abortion and signed several bills that Republicans had previously blocked. In 1993, Congress enacted gun control legislation; a $30 billion anticrime program; and the Family and Medical Leave Act, which enabled workers in larger companies to take time off for childbirth, adoption, and family medical emergencies. The Violence against Women Act of 1994 authorized $1.6 billion and new remedies for combating sexual assault and domestic violence. Clinton vetoed measures that would have weakened environmental standards, and he achieved stricter air pollution controls and protection for wilderness areas, national forests, and national parks. Other liberal measures of the Clinton administration included an increase of the minimum wage, expansion of aid to low- and moderate-income college students, and creation of AmeriCorps, a program enabling students to pay for their education with community service. "I know that I have made a difference in my community and the individuals that live in it," Maria Moore reported proudly after working on a neighborhood development project in Mesa, Arizona. Others helped to meet needs in education, housing, health, and the environment; and when fires raged through southern California in October 2003, dozens of AmeriCorps members helped feed firefighters and set up shelters for people driven from their homes.

Most significantly, to fulfill his campaign promise that no full-time worker should live in poverty, Clinton pushed through a substantial increase in the Earned Income Tax Credit (EITC) for low wage earners, a program begun in 1975. EITC gave tax reductions to people who worked full-time at meager wages or, if they paid no taxes, a government subsidy to lift their family income above the poverty line. By 2000, 15 million low-income families were benefiting from EITC, almost one-half of them minorities. One expert called it "the largest antipoverty program since the Great Society."

Even before Clinton took office, the economy had begun to rebound, and the boom that followed helped boost his popularity through the 1990s. Economic expansion, along with budget cuts, tax increases, and declining unemployment, reduced the federal budget deficit by about half between 1992 and 1996 and in 1998 produced the first surplus since 1969. Despite the biggest tax cut since 1981—a 1997 law reducing levies on estates and capital gains and providing tax credits for families with children and for higher education—the surplus grew. The seemingly inexorable growth of government debt had turned around.

Clinton stumbled badly, however, over an ambitious health care reform plan to provide universal coverage that would have included the 39 million Americans without health insurance and to curb steeply rising medical costs. Under the direction of First Lady Hillary Rodham Clinton, the administration presented a complex bill that much of the health care industry charged would mean higher taxes and government interference in health care decisions. Although the bill failed, Congress did enact piecemeal reform by enabling workers who changed jobs to retain health insurance and by passing a new health care program for 5 million uninsured children. Yet the number of uninsured Americans surpassed 40 million, about 15 percent of the population, in 2004; and health care became an even more critical issue in the twenty-first century.

Changing the Face of Government

Along with promoting a more active federal government, Clinton wanted to choose his appointments to create a government that "looked like America." In so doing, he built on the gradual progress made by women and minorities during the previous decades. By 1990, more than 7,000 African Americans held public office, an increase of nearly 50 percent from 1980. Cities registered the most impressive gains. Black mayors presided over Atlanta, Chicago, Los Angeles, Philadelphia, and other large cities. David Dinkins's election as mayor of New York City in 1989 epitomized the rise of black leaders even among predominantly white electorates. The presidential campaigns of Jesse Jackson in 1984 and 1988 inspired African Americans and demonstrated white willingness to support a minority candidate. In 1989, Democrat L. Douglas Wilder of Virginia became the first black governor since Reconstruction, joining the only Hispanic governor, Republican Bob Martinez of Florida. Women similarly had been edging slowly into the corri-

dors of political power. By the end of the 1980s, they had made their marks as governors of Kentucky, Vermont, and Nebraska; and several large cities boasted women mayors, including Jane Byrne of Chicago and Dianne Feinstein of San Francisco, who later became one of California's two female senators.

In the executive branch, Clinton appointed the most diverse group of department heads ever assembled. Of twenty-three key appointments, six were women, three African American, and two Latino; as Secretary of Commerce he chose the first Asian American to serve in the cabinet, Norman Y. Mineta, who had spent part of his childhood in a Japanese American internment camp. Janet Reno became the first female attorney general, and Madeleine K. Albright the first female secretary of state. Clinton's judicial appointments had a similar cast. Of his first 129 appointments to federal courts, nearly one-third were women, 31 were black, and 11 were Hispanic. In June 1993, he appointed the second woman to the Supreme Court, Ruth Bader Ginsburg, a self-identified feminist who had planned legal strategy and won key women's rights rulings from the Supreme Court before she became an appeals court judge in 1980.

The appointments of Clinton's successor, George W. Bush, would continue to reflect diversity in the highest levels of the executive branch. He chose Colin Powell for secretary of state and appointed African American Condoleezza Rice as his national security adviser. Five of his top-level appointees were women, including Secretary of Labor Elaine L. Chao, the first Asian American woman to serve in the cabinet; and Housing and Urban Development secretary Mel Martinez was a Latino. Gains for women and minorities came more slowly in Congress. When the 107th Congress convened in January 2001, two Asian Americans and one American Indian were the only ethnic minorities in the Senate. Thirty-six African Americans served in the 435-member House of Representatives, along with nineteen Hispanics and four Asian Americans. Women held seventy-two seats in Congress, 13.5 percent of the total, and less than in nearly every European assembly. One of these was Hillary Rodham Clinton, the new senator from New York and the first First Lady to run for political office.

> The number of uninsured Americans surpassed 40 million, about 15 percent of the population, in 2000; and health care became an even more critical issue in the twenty-first century.

The Clinton Administration Moves Right

While parts of Clinton's agenda sustained the traditional Democratic turn to government to help the disadvantaged, his presidency in general moved the party to the right. The 1994 elections swept away the Democratic majorities in both houses of Congress and contributed to Clinton's embrace of Republican issues such as reforming welfare and downsizing government. Led by Representative Newt Gingrich of Georgia, Republicans considered the 1994 elections a mandate for their "contract with America," a conservative platform that included drastic contraction of the federal government, deep tax cuts, and a constitutional amendment to ban abortions. Opposition from Democrats and more moderate Republicans stymied most of the contract pledges, but Gingrich succeeded in moving the debate to the right.

Far from Washington, a more extreme antigovernment movement emerged in the form of grassroots armed militias claiming the need to defend themselves from government tyranny. Anticipating government repression, they stockpiled, according to one militia leader, "the four Bs: Bibles, bullets, beans, and bandages," and they embraced a variety of sentiments including opposition to taxes, to gun control, and to the United Nations, and a defense of white Christian supremacy. Their ranks grew with passage of gun control legislation and after government agents stormed the headquarters of an armed religious cult in Waco, Texas, in April 1993, resulting in more than 80 deaths. On the second anniversary of that event, in the worst terrorist attack in the nation's history up to then, a bomb leveled a federal building in Oklahoma City, taking 169 lives. Authorities quickly arrested two militia members, who were tried and convicted in 1997.

Clinton bowed to conservative views on issues relating to homosexual rights. In 1993, opposition from military leaders, including his chairman of the Joint Chiefs of Staff, Colin Powell, enlisted men, and key legislators, caused him to back away from a campaign promise to lift the ban on homosexuals in the military. Instead, he announced the "don't ask, don't tell" policy, forbidding officials from asking military personnel about their sexuality but allowing dismissal of men and women who admitted they were gay or engaged in homosexual behavior. According to Cathleen Glover, who was discharged for being a lesbian, "The military preaches integrity, integrity, integrity but asks you to lie to everyone around you." What began as an effort to promote tolerance ended in a 67 percent jump in discharges of gay men and lesbians. In 1996, Clinton also signed the Defense of Marriage Act, prohibiting the federal government from recognizing state-licensed marriages between same-sex couples.

Clinton's determination to cast himself as a centrist was nowhere more apparent than in his handling of welfare reform. Since Lyndon Johnson's War on Poverty in the 1960s (see chapter 28), public sentiment had shifted. Instead of blaming poverty on a shortage of adequate jobs, poor education, and other external circumstances, more people were inclined to place responsibility on the poor themselves and on government welfare programs, which they charged kept people in cycles of dependency. Nearly everyone considered work better than welfare but disagreed about whether the economy could provide sufficient jobs at decent wages and how much government assistance poor people needed in the transition from welfare to work. Most estimates showed that it cost less to support a family on welfare than to provide job training, child care, and other supports necessary for that transition.

Clinton vetoed two measures on welfare reform, thereby forcing a less punitive bill, which he signed as the 1996 election approached. The Personal Responsibility and Work Opportunity Reconciliation Act abolished Aid to Families with Dependent Children (AFDC) and with it the nation's pledge to provide a minimum level of subsistence for all its children. In place of AFDC, the law authorized grants to the states along with two-year limits on welfare payments whether or not the recipient could find a job. The law set a lifetime limit of aid at five years, barred legal immigrants who had not become citizens from obtaining food stamps and other benefits, and allowed states to stop Medicaid to legal immigrants.

A "moment of shame," cried Marian Wright Edelman, president of the Children's Defense Fund, when Clinton signed the bill. State and local officials across the country scrambled to understand the law and how to implement it. "We certainly endorse the overall direction toward work," a Minnesota official said, while ex-

> Clinton's determination to cast himself as a centrist was nowhere more apparent than in his handling of welfare reform.

pressing grave concern about how the law would operate. "A child could very well have to go to foster care," predicted a Louisiana social worker. Critics proved wrong in their most severe predictions. By 2000, welfare rolls had been cut nearly in half, and because of the strong economy the poverty rate fell to 11.4 percent, its lowest in more than two decades. That did not mean, however, that all former welfare recipients were now self-supporting. Forty percent of former welfare mothers were not working regularly after being cut from the rolls, and those with jobs earned on average only about $12,000 a year.

Clinton's signature on the new law denied the Republicans a partisan issue. In the 1996 election campaign, the president ran as a moderate who would save the country from extremist Republicans. In fact, the Republican Party also moved to the center, passing over a field of conservatives to nominate Kansan Robert Dole, a World War II hero and former Senate majority leader who had served in Washington for more than two decades.

Whether out of satisfaction with a favorable economy or boredom with the candidates, about half of the electorate stayed home. Fifty percent of voters chose Clinton, while 41 percent favored Dole, and 9 percent Perot, who ran again as a third-party candidate. The largest **gender gap** to date appeared in the election: Women gave 54 percent of their votes to Clinton and 38 percent to Dole, while men split their votes nearly evenly. Although Clinton won reelection with room to spare, voters sent a Republican majority back to Congress.

Impeaching the President

Clinton's ability to capture the middle ground of the electorate, along with the nation's economic resurgence, enabled the self-proclaimed "comeback kid" to survive scandals and an impeachment trial in 1998. Early in the first Clinton administration, charges of illegalities related to firings of White House staff, political use of FBI records, and the Clintons' involvement in a real estate deal in Arkansas nicknamed "Whitewater" led to an official investigation by an independent prosecutor. Clinton also faced a sexual harassment lawsuit filed in 1994 by a state employee, who asserted that in 1991 the Arkansas governor had made unwanted sexual advances. A federal court threw out her suit in April 1998, but Clinton's sexual recklessness continued to threaten his presidency.

Clinton's Impeachment
This cartoon expresses the consternation of Republicans when President Clinton's approval ratings remained high despite the revelation of his affair with Monica Lewinsky and his subsequent impeachment. Many Americans, though not condoning the president's behavior, separated what they considered his private actions from his public duties and criticized prosecutor Kenneth Starr and the Republicans for not doing the same.

In January 1998, independent prosecutor Kenneth Starr, who had taken over the Whitewater probe in 1994, began to investigate the most inflammatory charge—that Clinton had had sexual relations with a twenty-one-year-old White House intern, Monica Lewinsky, and then lied about it to a federal grand jury. Clinton first vehemently denied the charge but subsequently bowed to the mounting evidence against him. Starr took his case for impeachment to the House of Representatives, which in December 1998 voted, mostly along party lines, to impeach the president on two counts: perjury and obstruction of justice. Clinton became the second president—after Andrew Johnson, in 1868—to be impeached by the House and tried by the Senate.

Most Americans believed that the president had acted inappropriately with Lewinsky, yet they continued to approve his presidency and to oppose impeachment. Some saw Starr as a fanatic invading individuals' privacy; most people separated what they considered the president's private actions from his public duties. One man said, "Let him get a divorce from his wife. Don't take him out of office and disrupt the country." Those favoring impeachment insisted that the president was not above the law, that he must set a high moral standard for the nation, and that lying to a grand jury, even over a private matter, was a serious offense.

The Senate conducted the impeachment trial with much less partisanship than that displayed in the House. A number of senators believed that Clinton had committed perjury and obstruction of justice but did not find those actions to constitute the high crimes and misdemeanors required by the Constitution for his removal. With a two-thirds majority needed for that result, the Senate voted 45 to 55 on the perjury count and 50 to 50 on the obstruction of justice count. A majority of senators, including some Republicans, seemed to agree with a Clinton advocate that the president's behavior, while "indefensible, outrageous, unforgivable, shameless," was insufficient to warrant his removal from office.

The investigation that triggered events leading up to impeachment culminated in 2000 with the independent counsel's finding of insufficient evidence that the Clintons disobeyed the law in the Whitewater land deals. The investigation had lasted six years and cost almost $60 million of federal funds. In the face of widespread dissatisfaction with Whitewater and other investigations by special prosecutors, Congress let the independent counsel act expire in 1998.

The Booming Economy of the 1990s

Clinton's ability to weather the impeachment crisis drew incalculable help from the prosperous economy, which took off in 1991 and began the longest period of economic growth in U.S. history. During the 1990s, the gross domestic product grew by more than one-third, thirteen million new jobs were created, unemployment reached its lowest point in twenty-five years, inflation remained in check, and the stock market soared.

Clinton eagerly took credit for the thriving economy, and his policies did contribute to the boom. He made deficit reduction a priority, and in exchange the Federal Reserve Board and bond market traders lowered interest rates, which in turn encouraged economic expansion by making money easier to borrow. Businesses also prospered because they had squeezed down their costs through restructuring

> Clinton's ability to weather the impeachment crisis drew incalculable help from the prosperous economy, which took off in 1991 and began the longest period of economic growth in U.S. history.

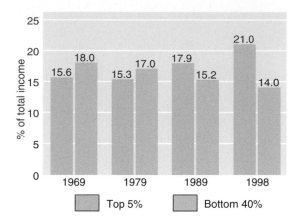

FIGURE 31.1 The Growth of Inequality: Changes in Family Income, 1969–1998
For most of the post–World War II period, income increased for all groups on the economic ladder. But after 1979, the income of the poorest families actually declined, while the income of the richest 20 percent of the population grew substantially.

Copyright © 1989 by the New York Times Co. Reprinted by permission.

and laying off workers. Economic problems in Europe and Asia helped American firms become more competitive in the international market. Above all, the computer revolution and the application of information technology to the production and distribution of goods and services tremendously boosted productivity. By the end of the century, half the workforce used computers on the job.

People at all income levels benefited from the economic boom, but it had uneven effects. In contrast to the economic expansion of the 1950s and 1960s, gaps between rich and poor and between the rich and the middle class that had been growing since the 1970s failed to narrow (Figure 31.1). This persistence of inequality in a rising economy was linked in part to what fueled the boom—the growing use of information technology, which increased demand for highly skilled workers while the movement of manufacturing jobs abroad lessened opportunities and wages for those not trained in the requisite skills. In addition, deregulation, globalization, and the continuing decline of unions hurt lower-skilled workers, and the national minimum wage failed to keep up with inflation.

Although more minorities than ever attained middle-class status, in general people of color remained lowest on the economic ladder. Reflecting Colin Powell's observation that "race still casts a shadow over our society," when the median income for white families surpassed

$44,000 in 2001, it stood at just $29,500 and $33,565 for African American and Hispanic American households, respectively. Overall, median family income for Asian Americans surpassed that of whites, but only because Asian families had more wage earners. In 2001, poverty afflicted about 23 percent of blacks and Latinos and 25 percent of American Indians, more than double the white rate of 10 percent.

The United States in a Globalizing World

America's economic success in the 1990s was linked to its dominance in the world economy. From that position, President Clinton tried to shape the tremendous economic transformations occurring in a process that came to be called globalization, the growing integration and interdependence of national citizens and economies. His administration lowered a number of barriers that impeded trade across national borders, but it also faced stiff opposition from those who pointed out the economic deprivation and environmental devastation that often resulted from the liberalization of international trade.

In contrast to his clear vision about the U.S. role in the global economy, Clinton and his advisers seemed less certain about the use of military and diplomatic power. Clinton took military action in Somalia, Haiti, the Middle East, and eastern Europe, and he pushed hard to ease the conflict between Israel and the Palestinians. Yet no new global strategy emerged to replace **containment** of communism as the decisive factor in the exercise of American power abroad.

Defining America's Place in a New World Order

In 1991, President George H. W. Bush had declared a "new world order" emerging from the ashes of the cold war. As the sole superpower, the United States was determined to lead the nations of the world and serve as its model of freedom and **democracy**. Without the overarching goal of containing communism, however, policymakers struggled to define a guiding principle that would determine where and how the nation would use its military and diplomatic power in a post–cold war world of some 190 nations. Acting in the face of Saddam Hussein's naked aggres-

sion and threat to vital oil reserves seemed the obvious course to Bush and his advisers in 1991. Determining the appropriate action in other areas of instability, however, proved much more difficult, and the United States under both Bush and Clinton applied its force inconsistently throughout the 1990s.

Africa was a case in point, where civil wars, famine, and extreme human suffering rarely evoked a strong American response. Bush had ended economic sanctions against South Africa in 1991, as it began to recognize the rights of its black majority. In 1994, that nation elected its first black president, Nelson Mandela, who had spent twenty-seven years in prison for fighting apartheid. Guided largely by humanitarian concern, in 1992 President Bush had attached U.S. forces to a U.N. operation in the small northern African country of Somalia, where famine and civil war raged. In 1993, when President Clinton allowed the humanitarian mission to turn into "nation building"—an effort to establish a stable government—eighteen U.S. soldiers were killed. The outcry at home suggested that most Americans were unwilling to sacrifice lives when no vital economic or political interest seemed threatened. Indeed, both the United States and the United Nations stood by in 1994 when more than a half million people were massacred in a brutal civil war in the central African nation of Rwanda.

As always, the United States was more inclined to use force nearer its borders, but it did so in the case of Haiti as part of an international effort. When a military coup overthrew their democratically elected president, Jean-Bertrand Aristide, thousands of Haitians tried to escape political violence and poverty, many on flimsy boats heading for Florida. With anti-immigrant sentiment already high in the nation, President Clinton was pressed hard to stop the refugee flow. (See "Historical Question," page 1156.) He got the United Nations to impose economic sanctions on Haiti, and when that failed, Clinton threatened the military regime with a UN-authorized intervention of U.S. troops. In September 1994, hours before 20,000 troops were to invade Haiti, the military leaders promised to step down. U.S. forces peacefully landed and began disarming Haitian troops, and Aristide was

> Without the overarching goal of containing communism, policymakers struggled to define a guiding principle that would determine where and how the nation would use its military and diplomatic power in a post–cold war world of some 190 nations.

Still a Promised Land?

"The United States is our land. . . . We intend to maintain it so. The day of unalloyed welcome to all peoples, the day of indiscriminate acceptance of all races, has definitely ended." So spoke Washington senator Albert Johnson in 1924, just after Congress severely limited immigration with passage of the National Origins Act, which Johnson had sponsored. Thereafter, immigration, which had forcefully shaped American society since its beginning, ebbed for several decades as the restrictive law combined with the Great Depression and World War II to discourage potential newcomers. In fact, during the worst years of the depression, more people abandoned the United States than chose to migrate there. Yet the immigration question had not been finally settled. By the 1980s, large numbers of immigrants once more were entering the United States, reigniting old debates about whether Americans should share their promise of political freedom and economic opportunity with people from other lands.

What reopened the door to immigration after World War II? Economic considerations always loomed large in prompting migration to the United States and in determining how welcome immigrants would be: The twenty-five-year economic boom that followed World War II exerted a positive force on both ends. In fact, until 1964 the U.S. government actively encouraged the temporary migration of Mexicans by continuing the so-called *bracero program* begun during World War II to fill a shortage of agricultural workers. Hundreds of thousands of Mexicans established social networks in the United States and grew accustomed to crossing the border for jobs, even when the jobs were back-breaking and low paying by U.S. standards. When the *bracero* program ended, many Mexicans continued to come north for work, with or without legal authorization.

In addition to a prosperous economy, a growing tolerance toward people of different races and ethnic groups in the decades following World War II contributed to the increase in immigration. Like the key civil rights laws passed around the same time, the Immigration Act of 1965 reflected a belief that people should be treated as individuals rather than as members of a particular group. The new immigration law ended the national quotas that were so insulting to non–Western European groups, although it for the first time placed limits on newcomers from the Western Hemisphere. It made possible a tremendous rise in the volume of immigration and facilitated a huge increase in migrants from Asia and Latin America, a result that the law's sponsors did not anticipate.

The 1965 law set an annual ceiling of 270,000, but the actual volume was much higher. Besides those who came illegally, hundreds of thousands fell into special categories that gained them legal admission above and beyond the limit. In 1986, for example, the United States admitted 335,000 immigrants over the ceiling; about two-thirds of these were children, spouses, or parents of U.S. citizens, and the rest were political refugees and asylum seekers. Migration chains were thus estab-lished by which, once newcomers became citizens, their sisters, brothers, and adult children received special preference, while even closer relatives gained entry without regard to the limit.

The new waves of immigration also grew directly from foreign policy after World War II. The cold war spread U.S. military and other personnel throughout the world, enabling foreigners to learn about the United States and make personal contacts with Americans. Once the cold war identified communism as an unmitigated evil, the United States could hardly refuse asylum to its enemy's victims. In the twenty-five years following Fidel Castro's revolution in 1959, for example, more than 800,000 Cubans fled to the United States. The Vietnam War and its aftermath brought more than 600,000 Vietnamese, Laotians, and Cambodians in the decade following 1974.

Not all refugees entered the United States so easily, for refugee policy bore a distinct anti-Communist bias. Haitians, Salvadorans, and others fleeing right-wing dictatorships were frequently turned back or, having reached the United States, were denied asylum and deported. "Why let Poles stay but not Salvadorans?" demanded one advocate for these refugees, pointing out the more favorable treatment given to immigrants from Communist countries.

Even though U.S. policy failed to accommodate all who wanted to immigrate, by the 1980s immigration was once more a major force in American society. During that decade, the 6 million legal and estimated 2 million undocumented immigrants accounted for more than one-third of total population growth. Seventy-five percent of the immigrants settled in just seven states,

Cuban Refugees
These Cubans are being towed by the U.S. Coast Guard into port at Miami, Florida. Their desire for the expected economic opportunity and political freedom of the United States is evinced in their willingness to flee Cuba on a crowded, makeshift vessel. Some "boat people" drowned in these risky ventures.
Jon Kral/Miami Herald.

with California, New York, Texas, and Florida receiving the most. After the 1990 census, California won five additional seats in the House of Representatives solely on the basis of immigrant additions to the population. A 1983 *Time* magazine article called Los Angeles "the new Ellis Island" because of its large Asian and Hispanic populations.

The higher volume of immigration, its **third world** sources, and the economy's recession combined to reactivate nativist sentiment in the 1980s. Increasingly, Americans saw immigrants as taking jobs from the native-born and acting as a drain on schools, health care, police, and other services; and Congress sought to reduce illegal immigration with the Immigration Reform and Control Act of 1986. In the 1990s, anti-immigrant sentiment grew especially strong in California, then reeling from an economic slump owing to the downsiz-

ing of defense production. That state took in more than one-third of the nation's immigrants in the 1980s and an estimated one-half of the undocumented ones. Congress reflected national anti-immigrant feelings by restricting health care, food stamps, and other benefits to immigrants in the welfare reform legislation of 1996.

Greatest hostility focused on people who entered without legal documentation, a phenomenon that the 1986 law penalizing employers of such people had not significantly curtailed. Some states, including California, Florida, and New Jersey, filed lawsuits charging the federal government with failure to stop the flow of illegal immigration and suing for the costs it added to state budgets. In 1994, California voters passed a referendum that barred the children of illegal immigrants from attending public schools, although the courts later ruled it unconstitutional.

Economic and political crises elsewhere and the continuing appeal of the United States meant that high levels of immigration—legal and illegal—persisted into the twenty-first century. Anti-immigrant sentiment diminished somewhat as jobs became plentiful during the spectacular economic boom at the end of the twentieth century. The chief executive of a semiconductor firm who filled more than one-third of his administrative and engineering positions with immigrants, lashed out at restrictionist legislators: "They want to send back the first-round draft choices of the intellectual world so that they can compete against us in their homelands."

The terrorist attacks in 2001, by contrast, made things more difficult for immigrants, especially Muslims or those who looked as though they might be Muslims. Seeking to deter terrorists, the Immigration and Naturalization Service increased border surveillance and required documentation that complicated the application process for visas, for example, increasing the obstacles to foreign students who wanted to attend American colleges. Moreover, the pendulum of anti-immigrant sentiment swung back again with the recession that began in 2001 and saw the loss of 2.6 million jobs. Still, there seemed no end to the desires of people around the world to enjoy the economic opportunity and freedoms of the United States. America entered the twenty-first century as it had the twentieth, with a rapidly diversifying society, continuing to make itself, as sociologist Nathan Glazer put it, a "permanently unfinished country."

restored to power. Initially a huge success, U.S. policy would continue to be tested as Haiti faced grave economic and political challenges and a new rebellion in 2004.

In eastern Europe, the collapse of communism ignited the most severe crisis on the continent since the 1940s. During the cold war, the Communist government of Yugoslavia, a federation of six republics, had held ethnic tensions in check, and many Muslims, Croats, and Serbs had grown accustomed to living and working together. After the Communists were swept out in 1989, Yugoslavia splintered into separate states and fell into civil war as ruthless leaders exploited ethnic differences to bolster their power. The Serbs' aggression against the Bosnian Muslims in particular horrified much of the world.

As reports of terror, rape, and torture in Bosnia increased, American leaders worried about the image of the world's strongest nation unwilling to use its power to stop the violence. In November 1995, the United States brought the leaders of Serbia, Croatia, and Bosnia to Dayton, Ohio, where they hammered out a peace treaty. President Clinton then agreed to send 20,000 American troops to Bosnia as part of a NATO peacekeeping mission.

In 1998, new fighting broke out in the southern Serbian province of Kosovo, where ethnic Albanians, who constituted 90 percent of the population, were making a bid for independence. The Serbian army brutally retaliated, driving out one-third of Kosovo's 1.8 million Albanian Muslims. When Serbian president Slobodan Milosevic refused to agree to a peace settlement in 1999, NATO launched a U.S.-led bombing attack on Serbian military and government targets. Three months of bombing forced Serbia to agree to a settlement. Serbians voted Milosevic out of office in October 2000, and he was brought before an international tribunal in 2002 for genocide.

Breakup of Yugoslavia

President Clinton was less hesitant to deploy American power when he could send missiles rather than men and women, and he also proved willing to act without international support or UN sanction. In August 1998, bombs exploded in U.S. embassies in Kenya and Tanzania, killing 12 Americans and more than 250 Africans. In response, Clinton ordered missile attacks on terrorist training camps in Afghanistan and facilities in Sudan controlled by Osama bin Laden, a Saudi-born millionaire who financed an Islamic-extremist terrorist network and had directed the embassy bombings.

A few months later, in December 1998, Clinton launched air strikes against Iraqi military installations. At the end of the Gulf War in 1991, Saddam Hussein had agreed to eliminate Iraq's chemical, germ, and nuclear weapons and to allow UN inspections. But he resisted full compliance with the agreement and tried to block inspection officials, prompting the U.S. attacks. Whereas Bush had acted in the Gulf War with the support of an international force that included Arab states, Clinton acted unilaterally and in the face of Arab opposition.

Elsewhere in the Middle East, Clinton used diplomatic rather than military power, continuing the decades-long efforts to ameliorate the Israeli-Palestinian conflict. In 1993, Yasir Arafat, head of the Palestine Liberation Organization (PLO), and Yitzhak Rabin, Israeli prime minister, for the first time recognized the existence of the other's state and agreed to Israeli withdrawal from and Palestinian self-government in the Gaza Strip and Jericho. Less than a year later, in July 1994, Clinton presided over another turning point as Rabin and King Hussein of Jordan signed a declaration of peace. Yet obdurate issues remained to be settled: control of Jerusalem, with sites sacred to Christians, Jews, and Muslims alike; the fate of Palestinian refugees; and the more than 200,000 Israeli settlers living in the West

Events in Israel since 1989

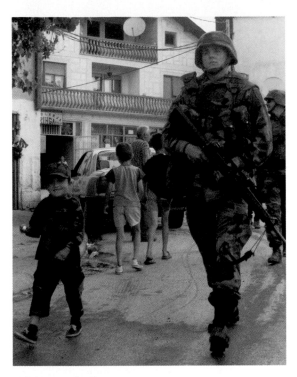

U.S. Troops in Kosovo

In 1999, American troops joined a NATO peacekeeping unit in the former Yugoslav province of Kosovo after a U.S.-led NATO bombing campaign forced the Serbian army to withdraw. The NATO soldiers were dispatched to monitor the departure of Serbian troops, assist the return of ethnic Albanians who had fled the Serb army, and reestablish civil governments. Here, an ethnic Albanian boy walks beside Specialist Brent Baldwin from Jonesville, Michigan, as he patrols the town of Gnjilane in southeast Kosovo in May 2000.

Wide World Photos, Inc.

Bank, the land seized by Israel in 1967, where 3 million Palestinians were determined to establish their own state. Negotiations between the two parties broke down in 2000, and violence between Israelis and Palestinians consumed the area. A year after the George W. Bush administration proposed a "roadmap" to peace in April 2003, casualties continued to mount on both sides.

Debates over Globalization

Although the Clinton administration sometimes seemed uncertain about the use of military force, it moved energetically on the economic side to speed up the growth of a "global marketplace." The process of globalization had begun in the fifteenth century, when Europeans began to trade with and populate other parts of the world.

Between the U.S. Civil War and World War I, the flow of products, capital, and labor crossed national boundaries in ever larger numbers. In that era, globalization was based on **imperialism**, as Western nations took direct control of foreign territories, extracted their natural resources, and restricted manufacturing.

In contrast, late-twentieth-century globalization advanced among sovereign nations and involved the industrialization of less developed areas, such as Korea and China. Other distinguishing marks of the more recent globalization were its scope and intensity: The Internet, cell phones, and other new communications technology connected nations, corporations, and individuals—nearly the entire planet—at much greater speed and much less cost than at any previous time (see "The Promise of Technology," page 1160).

As Clinton worked to diminish impediments to the free flow of products and capital across national borders, debates over globalization in the United States and elsewhere raged over which trade barriers to eliminate and under what conditions. In a world economy characterized by **laissez-faire** capitalism, who would protect workers' health and security, human rights, and the environment?

Tens of thousands of activists dramatized the debate when they assembled in Seattle, Washington, in November 1999 to protest at a meeting of the World Trade Organization (WTO), an international economic body established in 1994 to liberalize trading policies and practices and mediate economic disputes between some 135 member nations. Most of the demonstrators marched peacefully, but police used tear gas and arrested hundreds who practiced civil disobedience and blocked traffic. Activists charged the WTO with promoting a global economy that undercut standards and wages for workers, destroyed the environment, and devastated poorer, developing nations. These protesters reflected new alliances: Referring to some environmentalists dressed as sea turtles, an endangered species, one sign read, "Teamsters and Turtles—Together at Last." Gauging the profound impact of the demonstrations, California state senator Tom Hayden, the former student radical from the 1960s, proclaimed, "These protests have made WTO a household word."

Tico Almeida, a new college graduate, was thrilled in Seattle to hear "workers and unions from rich and poor countries alike stand together

The Internet

The network that links millions of computers throughout the world began to alter the lives of millions of Americans in the 1990s. Just 313,000 computers were linked to the Internet in 1990; six years later, 10 million were connected. By the year 2000, a majority of Americans logged on to the Internet at home or at work to e-mail coworkers, friends, and relatives, shop, chat with strangers around the world, listen to music, play games, buy and sell stocks, do homework assignments, and more.

Like many technological innovations of the post–World War II era, the Internet was a product of government funding inspired by the cold war. Shortly after the Soviets launched *Sputnik*, in 1958 President Eisenhower created the Advanced Research Projects Agency (ARPA) to push research on technology. In 1969, the U.S. Department of Defense established ARPANET, which developed a system called packet switching, a technology first invented by MIT graduate student Leonard Kleinrock to route digitized messages between computers. Not only would such a system be able to handle vast amounts of information—allowing many users to share computers and communications lines—but it would provide security for military secrets and enable communication to continue even if some computers were damaged by an enemy attack. By 1971, ARPANET linked twenty-three computers, most of them at research universities.

Universities and research centers rushed to join ARPANET, but some were turned down because the military restricted access for security reasons. New networks soon developed, and the military created its own separate network in 1982. Meanwhile, the National Science Foundation (NSF) took over much of the technology and sponsored development of a civilian "backbone network" called NSFNET. With technology developed under ARPA, disparate networks could now connect with one another through Transmission Control Protocol/Internet Protocol (TCP/IP), or sets of instructions that translated each network's system for other networks' systems. In 1980, fewer than 200 networks were connected, but by 1988 what had come to be called the Internet connected more than 50,000 host computers.

Electronic mail had not been on the minds of defense officials when they developed packet switching, but it quickly surpassed all other forms of traffic on ARPANET. It was much faster than "snail mail," the scornful term computer users applied to mail sent via the postal service, and it was much cheaper than long-distance telephone conversations. Moreover, two people could communicate on the same day without having to be at their phones at the same time, and they could do so easily across different time zones.

As ownership of personal computers spread, people not only exchanged e-mail but also began to put entire documents on the Net. Two key inventions helped users to find and retrieve such material. In 1991, researchers at the University of Minnesota launched a retrieval system called "gopher," a slang term for one who fetches things and also the university's mascot. Then came the World Wide Web, first proposed in 1989 by researchers at a physics institute in Geneva, Switzerland. Through the Web, users gained access to billions of documents connected to each other by hyperlinks, which take the user from one text to another.

The Internet and Web were central to what journalist Thomas Friedman calls "the democratization of information." Dictatorships could no longer keep their subjects ignorant of what was going on in the rest of the world or restrain dissidents from communicating with one another. As President Bill Clinton asserted in 1998, "In this global information age, when economic success is built on ideas, personal freedom is essential to the greatness of any modern nation." The Internet carried the potential to empower people even in democratic nations: Organizers of the protests against globalization carried out much of their mobilization via the Internet, and the high speed and low cost of communication enabled international movements to organize around other issues much more easily than ever before. In the United States, "distance learning" via the Internet began to breach geographical and financial barriers to formal education, and the Internet became a popular recruitment and campaigning tool during the 2004 presidential race.

By offering nearly instant, cheap communication around the globe, the Internet tremendously facilitated the growth of a global economy. It quickly spread capital around the world, made it easier for companies to manage operations abroad, and even enabled employees to work together while thousands of miles separated them. In 1997, for example, computer programmers in Beijing developing a project for IBM sent their work at the end of the day via the Internet to IBM workers in Seattle, who built on it and then passed it on to programmers in Belarus and Latvia, who did the same and relayed it on to counterparts in India, who passed it on to the Beijing group, who started the process all over again until the project was finished. According to IBM executive John Patrick, "It's like we've created a forty-eight-hour day through the Internet."

Although the Internet has enabled people to exchange news, knowledge, photographs, music, and money rapidly, it is not without critics. Some observers worry that the Internet is taking the place of human relationships. A 2000 survey found that 20 percent of the people who went online five or more hours a week spent less time with family and friends or at social events than they had spent before gaining access to the Net. Respondents had even more sharply reduced their time devoted to reading the newspaper or watching television. The availability of pornography on the Web and the exposure of users' personal and financial information are also concerns,

The Internet Links the World

By the end of the twentieth century, even the poorest countries had some access to the Internet, the network that links millions of computers throughout the world. President Bill Clinton displayed his fervent faith in the promise of technology to encourage democracy, claiming that "when over 100 million people in China can get on the Net, it will be impossible to maintain a closed political and economic society." In Iran, where the theocratic government tightly restricted women, young girls turned to the Internet for discussions about sex and marriage. As a seventeen-year-old declared, "What else can we do when we cannot have a normal social life?" These Buddhist monks stand outside an Internet café in the Cambodian capital of Phnom Penh in December 2000.

© Bettmann/Corbis.

along with the daily irritation of an electronic mailbox filled with spam, or junk e-mail.

Other critics have pointed to the disparate access to information technology, a "digital divide" across class and racial lines. As costs of hardware and software plummeted during the 1990s, computers and access to the Internet grew dramatically but unevenly. By 2000, more than 50 percent of all U.S. households had computers, and 41 per-

cent could log on to the Internet, in contrast to fewer than 25 percent of African American and Latino households. Even so, the Internet is well on its way to becoming as ubiquitous as television but with a much greater and varied impact. A computer software engineer who helped develop the Internet remarked, "It has already changed everything we do and changed it for good."

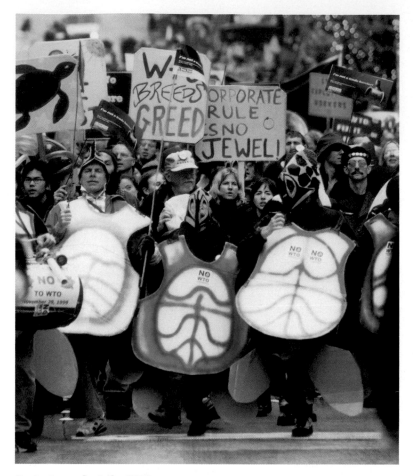

Protests against the WTO
Environmentalists and animal protection advocates were among the varied groups demonstrating against the World Trade Organization when it attempted to meet in Seattle, Washington, in November 1999. These activists dressed as sea turtles to protest WTO agreements permitting economic actions that they believed threatened the survival of the animals.
Wide World Photos, Inc.

wanted trade treaties requiring other countries to enforce decent wage and labor standards. Environmentalists similarly wanted countries seeking increased commerce with the United States to adopt measures that would eliminate or reduce pollution and prevent the destruction of endangered species.

Globalization controversies often centered on relationships between the United States, which dominated the world's industrial core, and the developing nations on the periphery, whose cheap labor and lax environmental standards attracted investment. United Students Against Sweatshops, for example, attacked the international conglomerate Nike, which paid Chinese workers $1.50 per pair to produce shoes that sold for more than $100 in the United States. Yet many leaders of developing nations actively sought foreign investment and manufacturing jobs for their workers, insisting that wages deemed pitiful by American standards offered people in poor nations a much better living than they could otherwise obtain. At the same time developing countries often pointed to the hypocrisy of the United States in advocating free trade in industry while heavily subsidizing its own agricultural sector. "We are kept out of the world market," complained John Nagenda, a farmer in Uganda. "When countries like America, Britain and France subsidize their farmers, we get hurt."

The demonstrations in Seattle, and the protests that followed in Washington, D.C., Prague (capital of the Czech Republic), Genoa, Italy, and Mexico City, targeted international financial institutions such as the WTO and the International Monetary Fund (IMF). Protesters charged that the WTO and IMF forced devastating regulations on developing nations, which had little voice in trade policy decisions. For example, the IMF often required poor nations to privatize state industries, deregulate their economies, and cut government spending for social welfare in order to obtain loans. While globalization's cheerleaders argued that in the long run everyone would benefit, critics focused on the short-term victims and destruction of traditional cultures that accompanied economic modernization. "International trade and global financial markets are very good at generating wealth," conceded American businessman George Soros, "but they cannot take care of other social needs, such as the preservation of peace, alleviation of poverty, protection of the environment, labor conditions, or human rights."

and say, 'We want rules for workers' rights to be integrated into the global economy.'" At the WTO demonstrations and elsewhere, U.S. labor unions emphasized the flight of factory jobs to developing nations as corporate executives sought cheaper labor to lower production costs. (See "Beyond America's Borders," page 1164.) For example, General Motors, one of the nation's largest manufacturers, produced its Pontiac Le Mans in South Korea, with parts manufactured in Japan, Germany, Taiwan, Singapore, Britain, Ireland, and Barbados. Critics linked globalization to the weakening of unions, the erosion of the safety net provided for workers since the 1930s, and the growing gap between rich and poor in the United States. Demanding "fair trade" rather than simply free trade, they

Liberalizing Foreign Trade

Building on steps taken by Presidents Reagan and Bush, Bill Clinton sought new measures to ease restrictions on international commerce. In November 1993, Congress approved the North American Free Trade Agreement (NAFTA), which eliminated all tariffs and trade barriers among the United States, Canada, and Mexico. Organized labor and other groups, fearing loss of jobs and industries to Mexico, lobbied vigorously against NAFTA. But proponents argued that all three trading partners would benefit from greater export opportunities, more jobs in the long run, and global clout. With 360 million people and a $6 billion economy, the NAFTA trio constituted the largest trading bloc in the world. A year later, the Senate ratified the General Agreement on Tariffs and Trade (GATT), establishing the WTO to enforce substantial tariff reductions, elimination of import quotas, and other provisions of the treaty.

The China trade bill of 2000, which added China to the vast majority of countries that enjoyed normal trade relations with the United States, aroused another controversy over free trade. Conservatives attacked the deal with Communist China as "selling out the very moral and spiritual principles that made America great," while liberals expressed concerns about Chinese labor standards and human rights violations. In contrast, supporters of the bill argued that increased trade would promote human rights and humane working conditions. Clinton himself advocated trade not just for its economic benefits but as a means of promoting international peace and security. Opening China to outside competition, he asserted, would "speed the information revolution there . . . speed the demise of China's huge state industries . . . spur the enterprise of private-sector involvement . . . and diminish the role of government in people's daily lives."

Although advocates of globalization prevailed on NAFTA, GATT, and the China bill, in 2000 opponents won an executive order from President Clinton requiring an environmental impact review before the signing of any trade agreement. And globalization's critics had an impact beyond the United States. In September 2000, officials from the World Bank and IMF along with representatives from wealthy nations promised to provide poor nations more debt relief and a greater voice in decisions about loans and grants. According to World Bank president James D. Wolfensohn, "Our challenge is to make globalization an instrument of opportunity and inclusion—not fear."

The Internationalization of the United States

Globalization was typically associated with the expansion of American enterprise and culture to—or its imposition on—other countries, yet the United States itself experienced the dynamic forces creating a global economy. Already in the 1980s, Japanese, European, and Middle Eastern investors had purchased American stocks and bonds, real estate, and corporations, such as Firestone, Brooks Brothers, and 20th Century Fox. By the twenty-first century, the Royal Bank of Scotland owned more than fifteen U.S. banks, and the German media giant Bertelsmann had acquired the publisher Random House. Local communities welcomed foreign capital, and several states outdid themselves in recruiting foreign automakers to establish plants within their boundaries. American non-union workers began to produce Hondas in Marysville, Ohio, and BMWs in Spartanburg, South Carolina. By 2002, the paychecks of nearly 4 million American workers came from European-owned companies.

Globalization was transforming not just the economy but American society as well, as the United States experienced a tremendous surge of immigration in the late twentieth century. (See "Historical Question," page 1156, and appendix, page A-51.) By 2002, one out of every ten Americans was an immigrant. Sixteen million foreign-born arrived between 1980 and 2000, surpassing immigration during the first two decades in the twentieth century, when Colin Powell's parents had come to America, and exhibiting a striking difference in country of origin. Eighty-five percent of the previous immigrants had come from Europe; by the 1980s, almost half of the new arrivals were Asians and nearly 40 percent came from Latin America and the Caribbean. Consequently, immigration changed the racial and ethnic composition of the nation. By 2002, the Asian and Pacific Islander population had grown to 13 million, and the number of Latinos increased to nearly 39 million. At 13 percent of the popula-

> Although the Clinton administration sometimes seemed uncertain about the use of military force, it moved energetically on the economic side to speed up the growth of a "global marketplace."

Jobs in a Globalizing Era

In November 2001, Paul Sufronko, a supervisor at Rocky Shoes and Boots in the small town of Nelsonville, Ohio, handed out final paychecks to the company's last sixty-seven employees in the United States, ending a process of outsourcing jobs that had begun in the 1980s. His own job was not quite over. Before receiving his last check, he traveled to Rocky plants in Puerto Rico and the Dominican Republic to complete the transfer of production and to train a local worker to do his job. Asked about his job loss, the thirty-six-year-old said, "I had other plans. Things just didn't work out."

Many Americans did not take the loss of their jobs to foreign workers so philosophically. One, a son of Mexican American sharecroppers, who had been laid off when Chrysler shut down its Jeep production in Kenosha, Wisconsin, in 1988, saw his fifteen years on the assembly line as "a habit that's your life" and mourned the loss of "pride in being an autoworker." One of his coworkers believed that "greed" drove the shutdown, pointing out that Chrysler had "plants down in Mexico" where workers were "making $1.25 a day." Another assembler agreed that "corporations are looking for a disposable workforce. . . . No commitment to community; no commitment to country."

In 1960, American workers made 96 percent of shoes bought in the United States; by 2000, as the number of American workers in the industry plummeted from hundreds of thousands to fewer than 25,000, nearly all shoes came from abroad.

The globalizing process was not a new experience for Julio Lopez, a temporary beneficiary of Rocky's transfer of labor abroad. Born in Puerto Rico, he went to New York as a young man to work in a toy factory, until it moved its operations overseas. Returning to Puerto Rico, he spent twenty-three years making shoes and boots for another company but lost his job when it sought cheaper labor elsewhere. In 2001, he found work at Rocky's Puerto Rico plant at the minimum wage of $5.15 an hour, less than half of what the company had paid Nelsonville workers. Lopez hoped that the factory would stay there for eight more years. "Then I will be 62, and I can retire." His hopes were not unusual, and his concerns were not unfounded. Lillian Chaparro, the plant manager, spoke about the perpetual motion of jobs: "It's like a chain, you know? The jobs leave the U.S. They come here. Then they go to the Dominican, to China. That's why I push people—we have to be able to compete."

Construction of a single pair of Rocky hiking boots in 2001 illustrates the web of connections that define the global economy. Leather produced in Australia was shipped to the Dominican Republic, where the uppers were cut and sewed and then sent to Puerto Rico. Puerto Rican workers like Julio Lopez assembled those materials along with outsoles that had been purchased in China and Gore-Tex waterproofing material made in the United States. Finally, the finished boots were transported to Rocky's warehouse near Nelsonville, Ohio.

The athletic shoe manufacturer Nike was one of the first companies to exploit the advantages of production abroad. Nike first turned to Japan, in the 1960s, but when labor costs there began to rise, it began to sign contracts with South Korean businessmen, who by the 1990s were turning out 4 million pairs of shoes. When South Korean workers began to demand higher wages and better working conditions, Nike moved production to China, Indonesia, and Thailand. Nike did not employ foreign workers directly but contracted their labor through local entrepreneurs, who in Indonesia, for example, paid workers as little as fifteen cents an hour as they churned out 70 million pairs of shoes in 1996.

Charles Seitz, who lost his job at Eastman Kodak in Rochester, New York, when the company moved some operations to China and Mexico, was not entirely wrong when he said, "There's nothing made here anymore." In the 1950s, one-third of all American workers were employed in manufacturing; by the twenty-first century just 10 percent produced goods. Of course, not all the job losses resulted from the transfer of work overseas. At Kodak, for example, a machine took the place of fourteen workers who previously had mixed film-making ingredients. In the 1980s and 1990s, American corporations devoted intense energy to increasing production so that they could downsize their workforces, in addition to looking abroad as a way of cutting labor costs. Moreover, some companies decided to build plants abroad in order to be close to burgeoning markets there, as foreign automakers had done when they began operations in the United States. Because so many companies, like Nike, contracted out production to foreign companies

U.S. Products Made Abroad

This woman, who is working on a mechanical part at a *maquiladora* (assembly plant) in Tijuana, Mexico, is part of one process by which manufacturing jobs left the United States. The Mexican government allowed foreign-owned companies to establish operations in Mexico, where they could take advantage of low labor costs, lax environmental protection measures, and close proximity to U.S. consumers. Beginning in the 1960s, but especially in the 1980s and 1990s, home appliance, electronics, automobile, and other U.S. manufacturers took advantage of these conditions to locate assembly plants in Mexico near the U.S. border. In 2002, more than 3,500 plants employed nearly one million workers. For Mexico, the program proved an important source of employment, but it also contributed to environmental degradation by enormously increasing population in the borderland area and encouraging the dumping of hazardous wastes. The manufacturing labels illustrate the global dispersal of garment manufacturing as the number of apparel jobs in the United States was cut in half between 1994 and 2003.

Worker: © Annie Griffiths Belt/Corbis; labels: Picture Research Consultants & Archives.

rather than employing foreign workers directly, statistics on the number of U.S. jobs lost through outsourcing do not exist.

The outsourcing of work for U.S. companies did not end with manufacturing jobs. By 2003, many corporations were relying on workers abroad, and especially in India, for a wide range of service and professional work. For example, 1,700 engineers and scientists conducted research for General Electric in Bangalore, India, which became the South Asian equivalent of California's Silicon Valley. Avis employed East Indians to manage its online car rentals; technology experts in Bangalore provided telephone help for customers flummoxed by their Dell computers; and the business consulting firm Accenture employed more than 4,000 workers in India, China, Russia, and the Philippines.

An executive in a research firm outlined the rationale: "You can get crackerjack Java programmers in India right out of college for $5,000 a year versus $60,000." Pointing to the power of technology to overcome distance, she asked, "Why be in New York City when you can be 9,000 miles away with far less expense?" An executive of IBM, which employed hundreds of researchers and developers in Haifa, Israel, agreed, adding, "Our competitors are doing it and we have to do it." Others worried about not just the immediate loss of jobs at home but also the long-term consequences for the American economy. "If we continue losing these jobs," argued the head of a computer software company, "our schools will stop producing the computer engineers and programmers we need for the future."

The flight of jobs has not been entirely one-way. Seeking to move production closer to its market, in 1982 Honda became the first Japanese company to manufacture cars in the United States, hiring more

(continued)

(continued)

than 150,000 American workers by 2003. Other automakers followed—South Carolinians began making BMWs, and Toyota opened a plant in Kentucky. Pointing to a factory in Lafayette, Indiana, college professor John Larson remarked that "in the 1950s, it was America that was doing all the outreaching. We did all the globalizing. But when the Japanese car people were looking for a site for the Subaru factory, they came in here the way Americans go into India." In all, about 5 percent of all American workers in 2003 received their paychecks from foreign companies operating in the United States.

Nonetheless, the vast majority of jobs moved in the opposite direction. In 2003, one of the most distinctive American products rolled off a U.S. production line for the last time. The blue jeans company founded in 1853 by Levi Strauss, a Bavarian immi-

grant, closed its last plants in the United States, contracting out its work to suppliers in fifty other countries from Latin America to Asia. The company's president refused to see any significance in the move. "Consumers are used to buying products from all over the world," he said. "The issue is not where they're made." But Clara Flores, who had sewn hems for twenty-four years and headed her union local in San Antonio, Texas, wondered, "Where are we ever going to find something like this?" Marivel Gutierez, a side-seam operator, acknowledged that workers in Mexico and elsewhere would benefit, suggesting the globalization of the American dream. "But, what happens to our American dream?" Workers like these stood as stark reminders that as the benefits of the free flow of economic enterprise

across national borders reached many, globalization left multitudes of victims in its wake.

BIBLIOGRAPHY

Jefferson Cowie, *Capital Moves: RCA's Seventy-Year Quest for Cheap Labor* (1999).

Jefferson Cowie and Joseph Heathcott, eds., *Beyond the Ruins: The Meanings of Deindustrialization* (2003).

Kathryn Marie Dudley, *The End of the Line: Lost Jobs, New Lives in Postindustrial America* (1994).

Bennett Harrison and Barry Bluestone, *The Great U-Turn: Corporate Restructuring and the Polarizing of America* (1988).

Walter LaFeber, *Michael Jordan and the New Global Capitalism* (1999).

Theodore H. Moran, *Beyond Sweatshops: Foreign Direct Investment and Globalization in Developing Countries* (2002).

Ellen Israel Rosen, *Making Sweatshops: The Globalization of the U.S. Apparel Industry* (2002).

tion, Latinos outnumbered African Americans for the first time.

The racial composition of the new immigration revived the century-old wariness of the native-born toward recent arrivals. Pressure for more restrictive policies stemmed from beliefs (generally unfounded) that immigrants took jobs from the native-born and fears that immigrants would erode the dominant culture and language. Americans expressed particular hostility to immigrants who entered the country illegally, even though the economy depended on their cheap labor. Estimated to number as many as 6 million by 2001, undocumented immigrants were primarily Latin Americans fleeing civil war and economic deprivation. The Immigration Reform and Control Act of 1986, which penalized employers who hired undocumented aliens but also granted amnesty to some two million illegal immigrants who had been in the country before 1982, did little to stem the tide. In California, with the largest numbers of illegal immigrants, voters passed an initiative denying public schooling to their children. Nor were legal immigrants immune from **nativist** policy. In 1996, Congress denied food stamps, Medicaid, and other benefits to those who had not become citizens.

The new immigration was again making America an international, interracial society, and not just along the coasts. American culture reflected growing diversity: Tortillas rivaled white bread in total sales, sushi bars and Thai food restaurants appeared in midwestern cities, cable TV companies added Spanish-language stations, Latinos became the largest minority in major league baseball, and a truly international sport, soccer, soared in popularity. Mixed marriages displayed a growing fusion of cultures, recognized by the Census Bureau in 2000 when it let Americans check more than one racial category on their forms. Demographers predicted that by 2050 the American population would be just over 50 percent white, 16 percent black, 24 percent Hispanic, and 9 percent Asian.

Like their predecessors a hundred years earlier, the majority of post-1965 immigrants were unskilled and poor. They took the lowest-paying jobs, providing farm labor, yard work, child and elder care, and cleaning services. Yet a significant number were highly skilled workers, sought after by burgeoning high-tech industries. For example, in 1999 about one-third of the scientists and engineers who worked in California's Silicon Valley had been born abroad. One small 31-person biotech company seeking cures for prostate diseases employed two Vietnamese, two Canadians, one Pole, two Lebanese, three Chinese, one Korean, one Indian, one Israeli, one Scot, one English, and two Latinos. Emphasizing American society's unique multiculturalism at the turn of the twenty-first century, the company's owner boasted, "I cannot think of another country in the world where you could so easily put such a team together."

President George W. Bush: Conservatism at Home and Radical Initiatives Abroad

The second son of a former president to gain that office himself, George W. Bush pushed an agenda that in many respects resembled Ronald Reagan's more than it did his father's, George H. W. Bush. The second Bush got Congress to pass tax cuts that helped send the federal budget into a huge deficit, and he reduced environmental protections. As Islamist terrorism replaced communism as the primary threat to U.S. security, the Bush administration launched a war in Afghanistan in 2001 and expanded government's powers to monitor, investigate, arrest, and detain individuals. In distinct contrast to his father's multilateral and cautious approach in

The New Immigration

These employees at UroGenesys, Inc., in Santa Monica, California, provide one example of America's increasingly diverse workforce at the start of the twenty-first century, the result of the highest immigration rates in a hundred years and of the economy's increasing need for a technologically skilled workforce. This biotechnology company conducts research aimed at discovering and developing therapeutic and diagnostic products for urological cancers, especially prostate cancer.

Courtesy UroGenesys. Photo by Deidre Davidson.

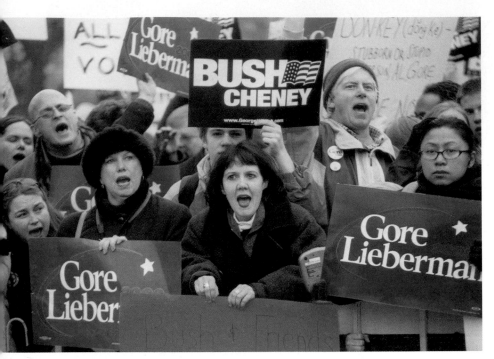

The Disputed Election

While attorneys representing presidential candidates George W. Bush and Al Gore pursued lawsuits over the counting of ballots that would determine who won Florida's 25 electoral college votes, partisan supporters took to the streets. Here backers of both sides rally outside the Supreme Court in Washington, D.C., on Monday, December 11, 2000, a day before the Court issued its five-to-four ruling that ended the hand recounts of ballots and consequently secured the presidency for Bush. Critics charging that the five justices who voted to stop the recounts had applied partisanship rather than objectivity to the case pointed out that the decision went against those justices' custom of preferring state over federal authority.

Wide World Photos, Inc.

foreign and military policy, George W. Bush adopted a policy of unilateralism and preemption by going to war against Iraq in 2003.

The Disputed Election of 2000

Even though the Clinton administration ended with a flourishing economy, Democratic candidate Vice President Albert Gore failed to retain the White House for his party in the election of 2000. His choice of running mate, Connecticut senator Joseph Lieberman, the first Jew to run on a major party ticket, was popular, and polls indicated that a majority of Americans agreed with the Democratic nominees on most issues. Yet Gore's personal style appeared stiff to many voters, and he seemed too willing to change his positions to gain political advantage. The Clinton administration scandals also burdened Gore's election campaign.

Texas governor George W. Bush emerged as the Republican nominee from a series of hard-

fought primaries financed with the most money ever raised in a presidential campaign. The oldest son of former president George H. W. Bush had attended Yale and Harvard and then worked in the oil industry in Texas and as managing partner of the Texas Rangers baseball team. In 1994, Texans elected him governor. Criticized for his lack of Washington and international experience and his unfamiliarity with certain policy issues, Bush chose for his running mate a seasoned official, Richard B. Cheney, who had served in the Nixon, Ford, and first Bush administrations.

Both candidates ran cautious campaigns, accommodating their positions to what polls indicated voters wanted. Bush's strategy mirrored Clinton's in 1992. Calling himself a "compassionate conservative," he separated himself from the extreme right wing of his party and tried to co-opt Democratic issues such as education. Like Republicans before him, he promised a substantial cut in taxes and federal spending.

Many observers predicted that the amazingly strong economy would give Gore the edge in the close race, and he did surpass Bush by more than a half million votes. Once the polls closed, however, it became clear that whoever won Florida's 25 electoral college votes would capture the election. Bush's margin was so tiny in that state, where his brother served as governor, that it prompted an automatic recount of the votes, which eventually gave Bush an edge of 537 votes.

Meanwhile, the Democrats asked for hand-counting of Florida ballots in several heavily Democratic counties where machine errors may have left hundreds of votes unrecorded. The Republicans, in turn, went to court to try to stop the hand-counts. As the dispute unfolded, Americans discovered that some counties used voting systems that were especially prone to error. Punch-card ballots were most unreliable, and they were used more in counties with large numbers of minority and poor voters.

The outcome of the 2000 election hung in the balance for more than a month as court cases went all the way up to the Supreme Court. Finally, a bitterly divided Supreme Court ruled

The Stability of American Constitutionalism
A week after the Supreme Court stopped the recount of votes in Florida and Gore conceded the presidency to Bush, the two met in Washington, D.C., at the vice president's residence. Their public handshake in the snow symbolized Americans' willingness to abide by the rules governing their political institutions even when the electoral process was flawed and bitterly contested.
Wide World Photos, Inc.

Although Bush had campaigned as a "compassionate conservative," his policies were more conservative than compassionate, at least in terms of who benefited. He claimed that the tax cuts would promote economic growth and jolt the economy out of a recession that had begun in 2001 and had sent the unemployment rate above 6 percent in 2003. But opponents stressed that the tax cuts favored the rich and pointed to a mushrooming federal deficit that reached some $500 billion in 2004, the highest in U.S. history. According to Senator Joseph Lieberman, Bush's tax cuts were "giving the most to those who need it least, piling more debt on the backs of our children and robbing Social Security and Medicare to pay for it." Republicans had traditionally railed against budget deficits, but some now saw them as a way to limit the size of the federal government. Representative Sue Myrick from North Carolina, for example, came to Congress in 1996 as a vigorous critic of deficits; six years later she said, "Anything that will help us stop spending money, I'm in favor of. And if there's a deficit, that may help us."

> Gore conceded the presidency to Bush on December 13, 2000. For the first time since 1888, a president who failed to win the popular vote took office.

five to four against further recounts of the Florida vote, and Gore conceded the presidency to Bush on December 13, 2000. For the first time since 1888, a president who failed to win the popular vote took office (Map 31.3). Despite the lack of a popular mandate, the Bush administration set out to make dramatic policy changes.

The Domestic Policies of a "Compassionate Conservative"

Bush moved quickly to implement his domestic agenda. He signed two tax-cut measures, one in 2001 reducing taxes over the following ten years by $1.35 trillion, followed by a 2003 bill slashing another $320 billion. The laws reduced income taxes, phased out estate taxes, cut rates on capital gains and dividends, provided benefits for married couples and families with children, provided deductions for college expenses, and gave immediate relief to all taxpayers through rebates of up to $300 each. House Majority Leader Dick Armey of Texas crowed over the bill: "The party is over. . . . We're no longer going to get stoned on other people's money."

MAP 31.3 The Election of 2000

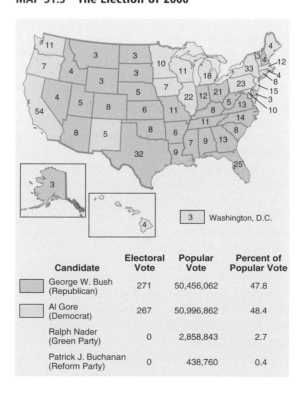

Candidate	Electoral Vote	Popular Vote	Percent of Popular Vote
George W. Bush (Republican)	271	50,456,062	47.8
Al Gore (Democrat)	267	50,996,862	48.4
Ralph Nader (Green Party)	0	2,858,843	2.7
Patrick J. Buchanan (Reform Party)	0	438,760	0.4

As Clinton had done, Bush altered environmental policy by issuing regulations that did not require congressional approval. But whereas Clinton had moved in the direction of greater controls, Bush subordinated environmental protection to larger goals of reducing government regulation, promoting economic growth, and increasing energy production. The Senate blocked Bush's efforts to allow drilling for oil in the Arctic National Wildlife Refuge, but elsewhere the administration withdrew 200 million acres of public land from consideration for wilderness protection, opening the way to mining, oil, and timber industries. Bush relaxed requirements of the Clean Air Act and issued new rules under the Clean Water Act that allowed coal companies to dump waste into rivers and streams. He imposed new restrictions on diesel pollutants but rejected higher standards for carbon dioxide emissions and, to worldwide dismay, withdrew from the Kyoto Protocol on global warming, signed in 1997 by 178 nations to reduce greenhouse gas emissions. While environmentalists pushed for measures to limit American energy consumption, the administration called for more rapid development of energy resources.

In contrast to the partisan conflict that attended tax and environmental policy, Bush mobilized bipartisan support behind his education initiative, the "No Child Left Behind" law of 2002, which marked the greatest change in federal education policy since the 1960s. Promising to end, in Bush's words, "the story of children being just shuffled through the system," the law required every school to meet annual testing standards and publish the results, provided penalties for—including the eventual closing of—failing schools and allowed parents to transfer their children out of them, and authorized a 20 percent increase in federal aid aimed primarily at the poorest districts.

One of the few critics of the education bill, Senator Paul Wellstone of Minnesota, asked, "How can you reach the goal of leaving no child behind on a tin cup budget?", a query that anticipated problems that states would face in implementing the legislation, since just 7 percent of their education budgets came from the federal government. Democratic senator Edward M. Kennedy, who had helped pass the law, complained that the administration was underfunding it: The Bush budget "may provide the resources to test our children," he said, "but not enough to teach them." By 2004, most states were straining to meet the demands of the new

education standards as they struggled with severe budget crises brought on in part by the recession.

The Bush administration's second major domestic effort to co-opt Democratic Party issues constituted what the president hailed as "the greatest advance in health care coverage for America's seniors" since Medicare was established in 1965. In December 2003, he signed a bill that for the first time would provide prescription drug benefits to the elderly and at the same time expanded the role of private insurers in the Medicare system. Most Democrats opposed the bill, warning that it left big gaps in coverage, subsidized private insurers with federal funds to compete with Medicare, banned imports of cheaper drugs from abroad, and prohibited the government from negotiating with drug companies to reduce prices. Legislators of both parties worried about the cost of the new drug benefit, estimated to surpass $500 billion after it took effect in 2006. Fiscal concerns mounted as the federal budget deficit mushroomed, the result of Bush's huge tax cuts, the recession, two wars, and an urgent new need to protect domestic security.

The Globalization of Terrorism

Immigrants and citizens from sixty nations shared the fate of more than 2,000 Americans killed on the morning of September 11, 2001, when U.S. civilian airplanes crashed into the twin towers of the World Trade Center in lower Manhattan and the Pentagon in Washington, D.C. In the most deadly and shocking attack ever launched on American soil, nineteen members of Osama bin Laden's Al Qaeda international terrorist organization had hijacked four planes and flown three of them into the buildings, the fourth crashing in a field in Pennsylvania. The nation, indeed the world, was stunned. As one commentator observed in the days immediately following the events, "It took hours to comprehend their magnitude; it is taking days for the defensive numbness they induced to wear off; it will take months—or years—to measure their impact and meaning."

The attacks, organized from Osama bin Laden's sanctuaries in Afghanistan, where the radical Muslim Taliban government had taken control after the Soviet departure (see chapter 30), related to globalization in several ways. The spread of Western goods, culture, and values into the Muslim world, along with the 1991 Gulf

War against Iraq and the stationing of American troops in Saudi Arabia, bin Laden's homeland, enraged Islamic extremists. Acting on a distorted interpretation of one of the world's great religions, bin Laden sought to rid the Middle East of Western influence and install puritanical Muslim control. High levels of poverty ignored by undemocratic and corrupt governments provided bin Laden a pool of disaffected young Muslims who saw the United States as the evil source of their misery and the supporter of Israel's oppression of Palestinian Muslims. The technological advances accompanying globalization and people's increased mobility facilitated bin Laden's worldwide coordination of his Al Qaeda network and eased the hijackers' entrance into and activities in the United States.

In the wake of the September 11 attack, President George W. Bush sought a global alliance against terrorism and won at least verbal support from most governments. On October 11, the United States and Britain began bombing Afghanistan, and American special forces aided the Northern Alliance, the Taliban government's main opposition. By December the Taliban were routed, but bin Laden had not been captured and numerous Al Qaeda forces had escaped or remained in hiding throughout the world. Although 12,000 U.S. troops were still stationed in Afghanistan three years later, economic stability and physical security for its people remained out of reach.

Afghanistan

At home, the balance between **liberty** and security tilted as authorities arrested more than 1,000 Arabs and Muslims, holding more than 300 on immigration violations for months even though they had not been charged with any crimes related to the attacks. As one security official stated, "It doesn't mean we're going to profile Arabs, but we are going to look at people who come from a certain culture with a certain background." An internal study by the Justice Department later reported that many people with no connections to terrorism spent months in jail denied their rights. "I think America overreacted . . . by singling out Arab-named men like myself," said Shanaz Mohammed, who was jailed for eight months for an immigration violation. Throughout the country, anti-immigrant

sentiment revived, and anyone appearing to be Middle Eastern or practicing Islam was likely to arouse suspicion.

"The smoke was still coming out of the rubble in New York City when we passed the law," said Republican representative from Idaho C. L. Otter, referring to the USA Patriot Act, which Congress approved by huge margins in October 2001. The law gave the government new powers to monitor suspected terrorists and their associates, including the ability to pry personal information about suspected individuals from libraries, universities, businesses, and the like, while allowing more exchange of information between criminal investigators and those investigating foreign threats. It soon provoked calls for revision from both conservatives and liberals. One hundred fifty cities and three states passed resolutions objecting to the Patriot Act. Ann Arbor councilwoman Kathleen MacKenzie explained that "as awful as we feel about September 11 and as concerned as we were about national safety, we felt that giving up [rights] was too high a price to pay." But a security official countered, "If you don't violate someone's human rights some of the time, you probably aren't doing your job."

The government also sought to protect Americans from future terrorist attacks by a major reorganization of the executive branch, the biggest since 1948. In November 2002, Congress authorized a new Department of Homeland Security combining 170,000 federal employees from 22 agencies through which responsibilities for different aspects of domestic security had been dispersed. Chief among the duties of the new department were intelligence analysis; overseeing immigration and border security; chemical, biological, and nuclear countermeasures; and emergency preparedness and response.

> On many international issues, the Bush administration adopted a go-it-alone approach, shattering a fifty-year-old tradition of multilateralism.

Unilateralism, Preemption, and the Iraq War

In contrast to the administration's search for a collective action against the Taliban, on many other international issues the Bush administra-

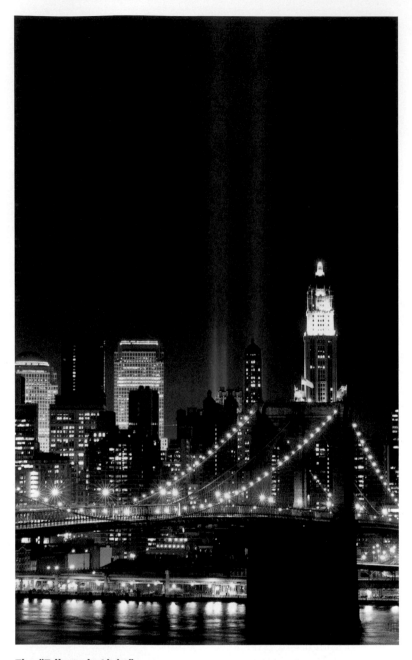

The "Tribute in Light"
Twin pillars of light, projected by 88 searchlights in the place where the World Trade Center twin towers had stood, soared as a monument to the victims of the terrorist attacks of September 11, 2001. Sharon Weicman, who worked as a volunteer for a month on the site of the destruction, was drawn by the illumination, remarking, "The closer I got, the more at peace I felt." Turned on at the six-month anniversary of the attack, the "Tribute in Light" was dimmed one month later.
Daniel Derella/AP/Wide World Photos, Inc.

the space-based missile-defense system—SDI—first proposed by Ronald Reagan. Bush also withdrew the United States from the UN's International Criminal Court, arguing that it would make U.S. citizens vulnerable to politically motivated prosecution. And the United States rejected an agreement to enforce bans on development and possession of biological weapons that was signed by all its European allies.

Nowhere was the new policy of unilateralism more striking than in a new war against Iraq, a war pushed by Vice President Dick Cheney and Secretary of Defense Donald H. Rumsfeld but not Secretary of State Colin Powell. In his State of the Union message in January 2002, Bush identified Iraq, Iran, and North Korea as constituting an "axis of evil," alarming leaders of European and Asian nations alike, who insisted that these three nations posed entirely different challenges. Bush's opponents in Europe and Asia preferred to emphasize diplomacy rather than confrontation, and they objected to America's unilateral decisions about what countries constituted the greatest threats to world order. Nonetheless, addressing West Point graduates in June, President Bush proclaimed a new policy for American security that scuttled a defense strategy based on containment for one based on preemption.

According to the president, "Traditional concepts of deterrence will not work against a terrorist enemy whose avowed tactics are wanton destruction and the targeting of innocents; whose so-called soldiers seek martyrdom in death and whose most potent protection is statelessness." Because nuclear, chemical, and biological weapons enabled "even weak states and small groups [to] attain a catastrophic power to strike great nations," it was necessary for the United States to "be ready for preemptive action." Even though the United States had intervened militarily and unilaterally in the affairs of small nations for a century, it had not gone to war except to repel aggression against itself or its allies. Claiming the right of the United States to start a war defied many Americans' understanding of their nation's ideals and distressed most of its great-power allies.

Nonetheless, the Bush administration moved deliberately to apply the doctrine of preemption to Iraq, whose dictator Saddam Hussein had violated UN resolutions from the 1991 Gulf War requiring Iraq to destroy and stop further development of nuclear, chemical, and biological

tion adopted a go-it-alone approach, shattering a fifty-year-old tradition of multilateralism. In addition to withdrawing from the Kyoto Protocol on global warming, it scrapped the 1972 Antiballistic Missile Treaty in order to develop weapons. In November 2002, the United States got the UN Security Council to pass a resolution requiring Iraq to disarm or face "serious consequences." When Iraq failed to comply fully with new UN inspections, the administration decided on war. Claiming that Hussein had links to Al Qaeda and harbored terrorists and that Iraq possessed weapons of mass destruction, Bush insisted that the threat was immediate and great enough to justify preemptive action. Despite opposition from the Arab world and most major nations—including France, Germany, China, and Russia—which preferred to give inspections more time, the United States and Britain invaded Iraq on March 19, 2003, supported by what the administration called the "coalition of the willing" (see Map 31.2). That coalition represented some thirty nations, including Australia, Italy, Japan, and Spain, but few major powers or traditional allies. Although Saddam Hussein remained at large until December 2003, the coalition forces won an easy and decisive victory, and Bush declared the end of the war on May 1.

The Bush administration believed that destroying the regime of Saddam Hussein would create a model for democracy and freedom throughout the Middle East, but while Arabs were glad to see the end of Hussein, many did not welcome American troops. As the publisher of a Lebanese newspaper put it, "They [Iraqis] have to choose between the night of tyranny and the night of humiliation stemming from foreign occupation." Moreover, the damage from U.S. bombing and the massive looting resulting from the inability of U.S. and British forces to secure order and provide basic necessities once the regime had fallen left Iraqis wondering how much they had gained. "With Saddam there was tyranny, but at least you had a salary to put food on your family's table," said a young father from Hussein's hometown of Tikrit. Tha'ar Abdul Qader, who worked at a children's hospital in Baghdad, complained, "They can take our oil, but at least they should let us have electricity and water."

By September 2003, three months after Bush had declared the war over, the United States had 150,000 troops in Iraq and was spending $3.9 billion a month. Iraqis still lacked basic necessities such as water and electricity; oil production, on which the administration had counted to help pay for the occupation, remained at a near standstill; and the dearth of security forces subjected Iraqis to crime and violence. "Yes, of course we are free," conceded Hisham Abbas, an unem-

ployed laborer, but "what good is freedom if we do not feel safe?" One defense official commented on the increasing Iraqi resentment of the U.S. occupation: "To a lot of Iraqis, we're no longer the guys who threw out Saddam, but the ones who are busting down doors and barging in on their wives and daughters."

American forces came under attack almost daily from remnants of the Hussein regime, religious extremists, and foreign terrorists now entering the chaotic country. As the American death toll surpassed 900 in July 2004, six times as many soldiers had been killed during the occupation as during the war. Terrorists launched deadly assaults on other targets, such as the UN mission in Baghdad, Red Cross headquarters, and a major Shiite mosque in Najaf, seeking to divide Iraqis and undermine the occupation. Some observers spoke of **guerrilla warfare** and "quagmire," evoking comparisons with the U.S. experience in Vietnam. By September 2003, the enormity of the task of reconstructing Iraq was apparent. "There is suddenly a new appreciation

---

The Iraq War

"The Americans did a great thing when they got rid of that tyrant," rejoiced Hassan Naji, a Shiite Muslim who worked at a hospital in southern Iraq. While he acknowledged that the occupation's inability to provide steady electricity increased the infant death rate at his hospital, he still insisted, "Things could even get worse here and I would still feel that way." Most Iraqis shared that initial jubilation, but the disorder and bloodshed that followed the defeat of Saddam Hussein's government threatened the Bush administration's plans to bring democracy and stability to the Middle East. In the first days of the American invasion, many Iraqis joined U.S. soldiers in removing Hussein's omnipresent image throughout the country. "We wanted to send a message that Saddam is done," reported U.S. marine major David Gurfein as he tore down a poster in the southern town of Safwan. Chris Hondras/Getty Images.

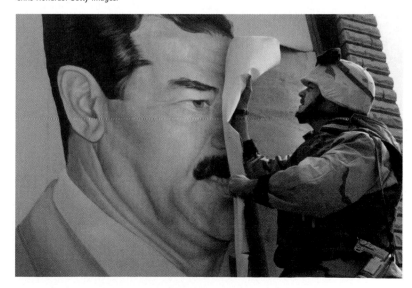

for alliances around here," said one foreign policy official as the Bush administration turned away from unilateralism and began to seek help from the very nations that had opposed the invasion.

The president's father, George H. W. Bush, had refused to invade Iraq at the end of the 1991 Gulf War. He, Colin Powell, and other advisers had believed that "unilaterally exceeding the United Nations' mandate would have destroyed the precedent of international response to aggression that we hoped to establish." The first Bush administration resisted making the nation "an occupying power in a bitterly hostile land," refusing to incur the "incalculable human and political costs" that such an invasion would produce.

Whether his son's decisions in the second Iraq war would serve American interests remained in question. To be sure, the U.S. military had felled a brutal dictator supported by few anywhere in the world. Yet coalition forces did not find the weapons of mass destruction that administration officials had insisted made the war necessary. The administration failed to prove its case that Iraq was linked to the terrorism of Osama bin Laden. In the war-induced chaos, more than a thousand terrorists entered Iraq—the place, according to one expert, "for fundamentalists to go . . . to stick it to the West." Although the war and occupation took relatively few American lives, they bore a steep price, not in dollars alone but also in U.S. relations with the other great powers and the nation's credibility and image in the world, especially among Arab nations. The war and occupation not only swelled the budget deficit but also diverted energies from the stabilization of Afghanistan and elimination of bin Laden and Al Qaeda and from dealing with the threat posed by North Korea's development of nuclear weapons. How quickly and how effectively Iraq became the model of democracy and freedom that President Bush had promised would determine whether the cost was worth it.

Conclusion: Defining the Government's Role at Home and Abroad

On March 21, 2003, some 225 years after the birth of the United States, Colin Powell referred to the unfinished nature of the American promise when he declared that the question of America's role in the world "isn't answered yet." In fact, the end of the cold war, the rise of international terrorism, and the George W. Bush administration's radically new doctrines of preemption and unilateralism sparked new debates over the long-standing question of how the United States should act beyond its borders.

Nor had Americans set to rest questions about the role of government at home. In a population so greatly derived from people fleeing oppressive governments, Americans had debated for more than two centuries what responsibilities the government could or should shoulder, and what was best left to private enterprise, families, churches, and other voluntary institutions. Far more than other democracies, the United States had taken the path of private rather than public obligation, individual rather than collective solutions. In the twentieth century, Americans had significantly enlarged the federal government's powers and responsibilities, but the last three decades of the twentieth century had seen a decline of trust in government's ability to improve people's lives, even as a poverty rate of 20 percent among children and a growing gap between rich and poor survived the economic boom of the 1990s.

The shifting of control of the government back and forth between Republicans and Democrats from 1989 to 2004 revealed a dynamic contestation over the role of the government in domestic affairs. The protections enacted for people with disabilities during the first Bush administration and Bill Clinton's incremental reforms built on a deep-rooted reform tradition that sought to realize the American promise of justice and human well-being. Those who demonstrated at Seattle and elsewhere against the ravages of globalization worked internationally for what the **populists** and **progressives**, the **New Deal** reformers, and many activists of the 1960s had sought for the domestic population— protection of individual rights, curbs on laissez-faire capitalism, assistance for victims of rapid economic change, and fiscal policies that placed greater responsibility on those best able to pay for the collective good. The second Bush administration, however—with a few exceptions such as the Patriot Act—pushed the pendulum back to a more limited role for the federal government.

As it entered the twenty-first century, the United States became ever more deeply embedded in the global economy as products, information, and people crossed borders with amazing speed and frequency. While the end of the cold war brought about unanticipated cooperation between the United States and its former enemies, globalization also contributed to international instability and the threat of deadly terrorism to a nation unaccustomed to foreign attacks within its own borders. In response to those dangers, the second Bush administration began to chart a departure from the multilateral approach to foreign policy that had been built up by Republican and Democratic administrations alike since World War II. Yet as the United States became mired in reconstruction efforts in Iraq, Americans continued to debate how the nation could best maintain domestic security while still exercising its economic and military power on a rapidly changing planet.

FOR ADDITIONAL FIRSTHAND ACCOUNTS OF THIS PERIOD, see Chapter 31 in Michael Johnson, ed., *Reading the American Past*, Third Edition.

TO ASSESS YOUR MASTERY OF THE MATERIAL IN THIS CHAPTER, see the Online Study Guide at bedfordstmartins.com/roark.

FOR WEB LINKS RELATED TO TOPICS IN THIS CHAPTER, see "HistoryLinks," "DocLinks," and "PlaceLinks" at bedfordstmartins.com/roark.

CHRONOLOGY

1988
- Republican Vice President George H. W. Bush elected president.

1989
- Communism collapses in eastern Europe; Berlin Wall falls.
- United States invades Panama and arrests dictator Manuel Noriega.

1990
- Bush and Congress agree to tax increase because of mounting federal deficit.

1991
- United States commits more than 400,000 troops to oust Iraqi army from Kuwait in Persian Gulf War.
- Clarence Thomas becomes second African American to sit on U.S. Supreme Court.
- Congress passes Americans with Disabilities Act, protecting people with disabilities from discrimination.

1992
- Democrat William Jefferson (Bill) Clinton elected president.

1993
- Israeli prime minister Yitzhak Rabin and PLO leader Yasir Arafat sign peace accords.
- Eighteen U.S. soldiers killed in UN peacekeeping operation in Somalia.
- Congress approves North American Free Trade Agreement (NAFTA).
- Clinton announces "don't ask, don't tell" policy for gays in military.
- Congress passes gun control and anticrime bills.
- Clinton signs Family and Medical Leave Act.

1994
- U.S. troops oversee peaceful return of Haitian president Jean-Bertrand Aristide to power.
- Senate ratifies General Agreement on Tariffs and Trade (GATT).
- Republicans recapture House and Senate in congressional elections.

1995
- Domestic terrorists bomb federal building in Oklahoma City.
- U.S. leaders broker peace accords, temporarily ending civil war in former Yugoslavia.

1996
- Clinton signs Personal Responsibility and Work Opportunity Reconciliation Act, replacing the Aid to Families with Dependent Children (AFDC) federal welfare program with state grants and two-year limits on payments.
- Clinton elected to a second term.

1997
- Clinton signs largest tax cut since 1981.

1998
- United States bombs terrorist sites in Afghanistan and Sudan in retaliation for embassy bombings.
- United States bombs Iraq for failure to comply with 1991 agreement to destroy chemical, germ, and nuclear weapons.
- Federal budget shows surplus for first time since 1969.
- President Clinton impeached for perjury and obstruction of justice in the Monica Lewinsky case.

1999
- Senate trial fails to approve articles of impeachment.
- United States, with NATO, bombs Serbia for more than two months to force an end to Serbian atrocities against ethnic Albanians in Kosovo.
- U.S. Senate defeats ratification of UN comprehensive nuclear test ban treaty.
- Protesters disrupt meeting of the World Trade Organization in Seattle.

2000
- Congress approves China trade bill, normalizing trade relations.
- Republican George W. Bush becomes president in disputed election.

2001
- **September 11.** Terrorists fly airplanes into World Trade Center buildings in New York City and the Pentagon in Washington, D.C., killing nearly 3,000 people.
- United States attacks Afghanistan, driving out its Taliban government, which had harbored terrorists involved in the September 11 attacks.
- USA Patriot Act gives government new powers to investigate suspected terrorists and their associates.
- Congress passes $1.3 trillion tax cut.

2002
- "No Child Left Behind" Act requires all public schools receiving federal funding to meet achievement standards.
- Newly created Department of Homeland Security effects comprehensive reorganization of federal government's units dealing with domestic security.

2003
- United States attacks Iraq, driving out the regime of Saddam Hussein.
- Congress enacts major revision of Medicare.

BIBLIOGRAPHY

Domestic Politics and Policies

Sidney Blumenthal, *The Clinton Wars* (2003).

Frank Bruni, *Ambling into History: The Unlikely Odyssey of George W. Bush* (2002).

James MacGregor Burns and Georgia Sorenson, *Dead Center: The Clinton-Gore Leadership and the Perils of Moderation* (1999).

Alan M. Dershowitz, *Supreme Injustice: How the Supreme Court Hijacked the Election of 2000* (2001).

Greg J. Duncan et al., eds., *For Better and for Worse: Welfare Reform and the Well-Being of Children and Families* (2002).

David Frum, *The Right Man: An Inside Account of the Bush White House* (2003).

Colin Gordon, *Dead on Arrival: The Politics of Health Care in Twentieth-Century America* (2003).

John Robert Greene, *The Presidency of George Bush* (2000).

Haynes Johnson, *The Best of Times: America in the Clinton Years* (2001).

Joe Klein, *The Natural: The Misunderstood Presidency of Bill Clinton* (2002).

Bruce D. Meyer and Douglas Holtz-Eakin, *Making Work Pay: The Earned Income Tax Credit and Its Impact on America's Families* (2002).

Herbert S. Parmet, *George Bush: The Life of a Lone Star Yankee* (1997).

Gerald Posner, *Citizen Perot: His Life and Times* (1996).

Richard A. Posner, *An Affair of State: The Investigation, Impeachment, and Trial of President Clinton* (1999).

Richard A. Posner, *Breaking the Deadlock: The 2000 Election, the Constitution, and the Courts* (2001).

Richard K. Scotch, *From Good Will to Civil Rights: Transforming Federal Disability Policy* (rev. ed., 2001).

Jeffrey Toobin, *A Vast Conspiracy: The Real Story of the Sex Scandal That Nearly Brought Down a President* (2001).

Jeffrey Toobin, *Too Close to Call: The Thirty-Six-Day Battle to Decide the 2000 Election* (2001).

The Domestic Economy

Martin Campbell-Kelly and William Aspray, *Computer: A History of the Information Machine* (1996).

John Cassidy, *Dot.con: How America Lost Its Mind and Money in the Internet Era* (2003).

Alfred D. Chandler Jr., *Inventing the Electronic Century: The Epic Story of the Consumer Electronics and Computer Science Industries* (2001).

Roger Lowenstein, *Origins of the Crash: The Great Bubble and Its Undoing* (2004).

Maggie Mahar, *Bull!: A History of the Boom, 1982–1999* (2003).

David K. Shipler, *The Working Poor: Invisible in America* (2004).

Beth Shulman, *The Betrayal of Work: How Low-Wage Jobs Fail Thirty Million Americans and Their Families* (2003).

Joseph E. Stiglitz, *The Roaring Nineties: A New History of the World's Most Prosperous Decade* (2003).

A Multicultural Society

Frank D. Bean and Gillian Stevens, *America's Newcomers and the Dynamics of Diversity* (2003).

George J. Borjas, *Heaven's Door: Immigration Policy and the American Economy* (1999).

Juan Gonzalez, *Harvest of Empire: A History of Latinos in America* (2001).

Andrew Hacker, *Two Nations: Black and White, Separate, Hostile, Unequal* (1992).

S. Mitra Kalita, *Suburban Sahibs: Three Immigrant Families and Their Passage from India to America* (2003).

Sarah J. Mahler, *American Dreaming: Immigrant Life on the Margins* (1995).

David M. Reimers, *Still the Golden Door: The Third World Comes to America* (rev. ed., 1992).

David M. Reimers, *Unwelcome Strangers: American Identity and the Turn against Immigration* (1998).

Al Santoli, *New Americans: An Oral History* (1988).

Peter Skerry, *Mexican Americans: The Ambivalent Minority* (1993).

Roberto Suro, *Strangers among Us: Latinos' Lives in a Changing America* (1999).

Ronald Takaki, *Strangers from a Different Shore: A History of Asian Americans* (1989).

Sanford J. Ungar, *Fresh Blood: The New American Immigrants* (1995).

William Wei, *The Asian American Movement* (1993).

Helen Zia, *Asian American Dreams: The Emergence of an American People* (2001).

Foreign Policy after the Cold War

Michael R. Beschloss and Strobe Talbott, *At the Highest Levels: The Inside Story of the End of the Cold War* (1993).

Ivo H. Daalder and James M. Lindsay, *America Unbound: The Bush Revolution in Foreign Policy* (2003).

Raymond I. Garthogg, *The Great Transition: America-Soviet Relations and the End of the Cold War* (1994).

David Halberstam, *War in a Time of Peace: Bush, Clinton, and the Generals* (2001).

Michael Hirsh, *At War with Ourselves: Why America Is Squandering Its Chance to Build a Better World* (2003).

Stanley Hoffmann, *World Disorders: Troubled Peace in the Post–Cold War Era* (1998).

Michael J. Hogan, ed., *The End of the Cold War: Its Meaning and Implications* (1992).

Robert L. Hutchings, *American Diplomacy and the End of the Cold War: An Insider's Account of U.S. Policy in Europe, 1989–1992* (1997).

William Hyland, *Clinton's World* (1999).

Robert Kagan, *Of Paradise and Power: America and Europe in the New World Order* (2003).

Richard Ned Lebow and Janice Gross Stein, *We All Lost the Cold War* (1994).

James Mann, *Rise of the Vulcans: The History of Bush's War Cabinet* (2004).

Joseph S. Nye Jr., *The Paradox of American Power: Why the World's Only Superpower Can't Go It Alone* (2002).

Clyde Prestowitz, *Rogue Nation: American Unilateralism and the Failure of Good Intentions* (2003).

James M. Scott, ed., *After the End: Making U.S. Foreign Policy in the Post–Cold War World* (1998).

The United States and Latin America

John Dinges, *Our Man in Panama: How General Noriega Used the United States and Made Millions in Drugs and Arms* (1990).

Frederick Kempe, *Divorcing the Dictator: America's Bungled Affair with Noriega* (1990).

W. Dirk Raat, *Mexico and the United States: Ambivalent Vistas* (1997).

Peter H. Smith, *Talons of the Eagle: Dynamics of U.S.–Latin American Relations* (2nd ed., 1999).

The United States and the Middle East

Rick Atkinson, *Crusade: The Untold Story of the Persian Gulf War* (1994).

Rick Atkinson, *In the Company of Soldiers: A Chronicle of Combat* (2004).

Richard Butler, *The Greatest Threat: Iraq, Weapons of Mass Destruction, and the Crisis of Global Security* (2000).

Lawrence Freedman and Efraim Karsh, *The Gulf Conflict, 1990–1991: Diplomacy and War in the New World Order* (1993).

Lawrence F. Kaplan and William Kristol, *The War over Iraq: Saddam's Tyranny and America's Mission* (2003).

Douglas Little, *American Orientalism: The United States and the Middle East since 1945* (2002).

Benny Morris, *Righteous Victims: A History of the Zionist-Arab Conflict, 1881–1999* (1999).

Williamson Murray and Robert H. Scales Jr., *The Iraq War: A Military History* (2003).

Donald Neff, *Fallen Pillars: U.S. Policy towards Palestine and Israel since 1945* (1995).

Todd S. Purdum, *A Time of Our Choosing: America's War in Iraq* (2003).

Elaine Sciolino, *The Outlaw State: Saddam Hussein's Quest for Power and the Gulf Crisis* (1991).

Milton Viorst, *In the Shadow of the Prophet: The Struggle for the Soul of Islam* (2001).

Globalization

Richard J. Barnet and John Cavanagh, *Global Dreams: Imperial Corporations and the New World Order* (1994).

Jeremy Brecher, Tim Costello, and Brendan Smith, *Globalization from Below* (2000).

Stephen Castles, ed., *Citizenship and Migration: Globalization and the Politics of Belonging* (2000).

Thomas L. Friedman, *The Lexus and the Olive Tree: Understanding Globalization* (1999).

Robert Gilpin and Jean M. Gilpin, *The Challenge of Global Capitalism* (2000).

John Gray, *The Delusions of Global Capitalism* (1999).

Evelyn Hu-Dehart, ed., *Across the Pacific: Asian Americans and Globalization* (1999).

Philippe Legrain, *Open World: The Truth about Globalization* (2004).

John R. MacArthur, *The Selling of "Free Trade": NAFTA, Washington, and the Subversion of American Democracy* (2000).

Douglas S. Massey, *Worlds in Motion: Understanding International Migration at Century's End* (1998).

Joseph E. Stiglitz, *Globalization and Its Discontents* (2002).

Terrorism

Peter L. Bergen, *Holy War, Inc.: Inside the Secret World of Osama bin Laden* (2001).

Yossef Bodansky, *Bin Laden: The Man Who Declared War on America* (1999).

Philip B. Heymann, *Terrorism, Freedom, and Security: Winning without War* (2003).

Bruce Hoffman, *Inside Terrorism* (1998).

James F. Hoge Jr. and Gideon Rose, *How Did This Happen? Terrorism and the New War* (2001).

Gilles Kepel, *Jihad: The Trail of Political Islam* (2002).

Walter Laqueur, *The New Terrorism: Fanaticism and the Arms of Mass Destruction* (2000).

Daniel Levitas, *The Terrorist Next Door: The Militia Movement and the Radical Right* (2002).

Paul R. Pillar, *Terrorism and U.S. Foreign Policy* (2001).

Gerald Posner, *Why America Slept: The Failure to Prevent 9/11* (2003).

Ahmed Rashid, *Taliban: Militant Islam, Oil, and Fundamentalism in Central Asia* (2000).

Simon Reeve, *The New Jackals: Ramzi Yousef, Osama bin Laden and the Future of Terrorism* (1999).

Richard A. Serrano, *One of Ours: Timothy McVeigh and the Oklahoma City Bombing* (1998).

Documents

For additional documents see the DocLinks feature at bedfordstmartins.com/roark.

THE DECLARATION OF INDEPENDENCE

In Congress, July 4, 1776,

THE UNANIMOUS DECLARATION OF THE
THIRTEEN UNITED STATES OF AMERICA

When in the course of human events, it becomes necessary for one people to dissolve the political bands which have connected them with another, and to assume, among the powers of the earth, the separate and equal station to which the laws of nature and of nature's God entitle them, a decent respect to the opinions of mankind requires that they should declare the causes which impel them to the separation.

We hold these truths to be self-evident, that all men are created equal; that they are endowed by their Creator with certain unalienable rights; that among these, are life, liberty, and the pursuit of happiness. That, to secure these rights, governments are instituted among men, deriving their just powers from the consent of the governed; that, whenever any form of government becomes destructive of these ends, it is the right of the people to alter or to abolish it, and to institute a new government, laying its foundation on such principles, and organizing its powers in such form, as to them shall seem most likely to effect their safety and happiness. Prudence, indeed, will dictate that governments long established, should not be changed for light and transient causes; and, accordingly, all experience hath shown, that mankind are more disposed to suffer, while evils are sufferable, than to right themselves by abolishing the forms to which they are accustomed. But, when a long train of abuses and usurpations, pursuing invariably the same object, evinces a design to reduce them under absolute despotism, it is their right, it is their duty, to throw off such government and to provide new guards for their future security. Such has been the patient sufferance of these colonies, and such is now the necessity which constrains them to alter their former systems of government. The history of the present King of Great Britain is a history of repeated injuries and usurpations, all having, in direct object, the establishment of an absolute tyranny over these States. To prove this, let facts be submitted to a candid world:

He has refused his assent to laws the most wholesome and necessary for the public good.

He has forbidden his governors to pass laws of immediate and pressing importance, unless suspended in their operation till his assent should be obtained; and, when so suspended, he has utterly neglected to attend to them.

He has refused to pass other laws for the accommodation of large districts of people, unless those people would relinquish the right of representation in the legislature; a right inestimable to them, and formidable to tyrants only.

He has called together legislative bodies at places unusual, uncomfortable, and distant from the depository of their public records, for the sole purpose of fatiguing them into compliance with his measures.

He has dissolved representative houses repeatedly for opposing, with manly firmness, his invasions on the rights of the people.

He has refused, for a long time after such dissolutions, to cause others to be elected; whereby the legislative powers, incapable of annihilation, have returned to the people at large for their exercise; the state remaining in the mean-time exposed to all the danger of invasion from without, and convulsions within.

He has endeavoured to prevent the population of these States; for that purpose, obstructing the laws for naturalization of foreigners, refusing to pass others to encourage their migration hither, and raising the conditions of new appropriations of lands.

He has obstructed the administration of justice, by refusing his assent to laws for establishing judiciary powers.

He has made judges dependent on his will alone, for the tenure of their offices, and the amount and payment of their salaries.

He has erected a multitude of new offices, and sent hither swarms of officers to harass our people, and eat out their substance.

He has kept among us, in times of peace, standing armies, without the consent of our legislature.

He has affected to render the military independent of, and superior to, the civil power.

He has combined, with others, to subject us to a jurisdiction foreign to our Constitution, and unacknowledged by our laws; giving his assent to their acts of pretended legislation:

For quartering large bodies of armed troops among us:

For protecting them by a mock trial, from punishment, for any murders which they should commit on the inhabitants of these States:

For cutting off our trade with all parts of the world:

For imposing taxes on us without our consent:

For depriving us, in many cases, of the benefit of trial by jury:

For transporting us beyond seas to be tried for pretended offences:

For abolishing the free system of English laws in a neighboring province, establishing therein an arbitrary government, and enlarging its boundaries, so as to render it at once an example and fit instrument for introducing the same absolute rule into these colonies:

For taking away our charters, abolishing our most valuable laws, and altering, fundamentally, the powers of our governments:

For suspending our own legislatures, and declaring themselves invested with power to legislate for us in all cases whatsoever.

He has abdicated government here, by declaring us out of his protection, and waging war against us.

He has plundered our seas, ravaged our coasts, burnt our towns, and destroyed the lives of our people.

He is, at this time, transporting large armies of foreign mercenaries to complete the works of death, desolation, and tyranny, already begun, with circumstances of cruelty and perfidy scarcely parallelled in the most barbarous ages, and totally unworthy the head of a civilized nation.

He has constrained our fellow citizens, taken captive on the high seas, to bear arms against their country, to become the executioners of their friends, and brethren, or to fall themselves by their hands.

He has excited domestic insurrections amongst us, and has endeavored to bring on the inhabitants of our frontiers, the merciless Indian savages, whose known rule of warfare is an undistinguished destruction of all ages, sexes, and conditions.

In every stage of these oppressions, we have petitioned for redress; in the most humble terms; our repeated petitions have been answered only by repeated injury. A prince, whose character is thus marked by every act which may define a tyrant, is unfit to be the ruler of a free people.

Nor have we been wanting in attention to our British brethren. We have warned them, from time to time, of attempts made by their legislature to extend an unwarrantable jurisdiction over us. We have reminded them of the circumstances of our emigration and settlement here. We have appealed to their native justice and magnanimity, and we have conjured them, by the ties of our common kindred, to disavow these usurpations, which would inevitably interrupt our connections and correspondence. They, too, have been deaf to the voice of justice and consanguinity. We must, therefore, acquiesce in the necessity which denounces our separation, and hold them as we hold the rest of mankind, enemies in war, in peace, friends.

We, therefore, the representatives of the United States of America, in general Congress assembled, appealing to the Supreme Judge of the world for the rectitude of our intentions, do, in the name, and by authority of the good people of these colonies, solemnly publish and declare, that these united colonies are, and of right ought to be, free and independent states: that they are absolved from all allegiance to the British Crown, and that all political connection between them and the state of Great Britain is, and ought to be, totally dissolved; and that, as free and independent states, they have full power to levy war, conclude peace, contract alliances, establish commerce, and to do all other acts and things which independent states may of right do. And, for the support of this declaration, with a firm reliance on the protection of Divine Providence, we mutually pledge to each other our lives, our fortunes, and our sacred honor.

The foregoing Declaration was, by order of Congress, engrossed, and signed by the following members:

JOHN HANCOCK

New Hampshire
Josiah Bartlett
William Whipple
Matthew Thornton

Massachusetts Bay
Samuel Adams
John Adams
Robert Treat Paine
Elbridge Gerry

Rhode Island
Stephen Hopkins
William Ellery

Connecticut
Roger Sherman
Samuel Huntington
William Williams
Oliver Wolcott

New York
William Floyd
Phillip Livingston
Francis Lewis
Lewis Morris

New Jersey
Richard Stockton
John Witherspoon
Francis Hopkinson
John Hart
Abraham Clark

Pennsylvania
Robert Morris
Benjamin Rush
Benjamin Franklin
John Morton
George Clymer
James Smith
George Taylor
James Wilson
George Ross

Delaware	North Carolina	Virginia	Georgia
Caesar Rodney	William Hooper	George Wythe	Button Gwinnett
George Read	Joseph Hewes	Richard Henry Lee	Lyman Hall
Thomas M'Kean	John Penn	Thomas Jefferson	George Walton
		Benjamin Harrison	
Maryland	**South Carolina**	Thomas Nelson, Jr.	
Samuel Chase	Edward Rutledge	Francis Lightfoot Lee	
William Paca	Thomas Heyward, Jr.	Carter Braxton	
Thomas Stone	Thomas Lynch, Jr.		
Charles Carroll,	Arthur Middleton		
of Carrollton			

Resolved, That copies of the Declaration be sent to the several assemblies, conventions, and committees, or councils of safety, and to the several commanding officers of the continental troops; that it be proclaimed in each of the United States, at the head of the army.

THE ARTICLES OF CONFEDERATION AND PERPETUAL UNION

Agreed to in Congress, November 15, 1777.
Ratified March 1781.

BETWEEN THE STATES OF NEW HAMPSHIRE, MASSACHU-SETTS BAY, RHODE ISLAND AND PROVIDENCE PLANTA-TIONS, CONNECTICUT, NEW YORK, NEW JERSEY, PENN-SYLVANIA, DELAWARE, MARYLAND, VIRGINIA, NORTH CAROLINA, SOUTH CAROLINA, GEORGIA.*

Article 1

The stile of this confederacy shall be "The United States of America."

Article 2

Each State retains its sovereignty, freedom and independence, and every power, jurisdiction, and right, which is not by this confederation expressly delegated to the United States, in Congress assembled.

Article 3

The said states hereby severally enter into a firm league of friendship with each other for their common defence, the security of their liberties and their mutual and general welfare; binding themselves to assist each other against all force offered to, or attacks made upon them, or any of them, on account of religion, sovereignty, trade, or any other pretence whatever.

---

* This copy of the final draft of the Articles of Confederation is taken from the *Journals,* 9:907–925, November 15, 1777.

Article 4

The better to secure and perpetuate mutual friendship and intercourse among the people of the different states in this union, the free inhabitants of each of these states, paupers, vagabonds, and fugitives from justice excepted, shall be entitled to all privileges and immunities of free citizens in the several states; and the people of each State shall have free ingress and regress to and from any other State, and shall enjoy therein all the privileges of trade and commerce, subject to the same duties, impositions, and restrictions, as the inhabitants thereof respectively; provided, that such restrictions shall not extend so far as to prevent the removal of property, imported into any State, to any other State of which the owner is an inhabitant; provided also, that no imposition, duties, or restriction, shall be laid by any State on the property of the United States, or either of them.

If any person guilty of, or charged with treason, felony, or other high misdemeanor in any State, shall flee from justice and be found in any of the United States, he shall, upon demand of the governor or executive power of the State from which he fled, be delivered up and removed to the State having jurisdiction of his offence.

Full faith and credit shall be given in each of these states to the records, acts, and judicial proceedings of the courts and magistrates of every other State.

Article 5

For the more convenient management of the general interests of the United States, delegates shall be annually appointed, in such manner as the legislature of each State shall direct, to meet in Congress, on the 1st Monday in November in every year, with a power reserved to each State to recall its delegates, or any of them, at any time within the year, and to send others in their stead for the remainder of the year.

No State shall be represented in Congress by less than two, nor by more than seven members; and no person shall be capable of being a delegate for more than three years in any term of six years; nor shall any person, being a delegate, be capable of holding any office under the United States, for which he, or any other for his benefit, receives any salary, fees, or emolument of any kind.

Each State shall maintain its own delegates in a meeting of the states, and while they act as members of the committee of the states.

In determining questions in the United States, in Congress assembled, each State shall have one vote.

Freedom of speech and debate in Congress shall not be impeached or questioned in any court or place out of Congress: and the members of Congress shall be protected in their persons from arrests and imprisonments, during the time of their going to and from, and attendance on Congress, except for treason, felony, or breach of the peace.

Article 6

No State, without the consent of the United States, in Congress assembled, shall send any embassy to, or receive any embassy from, or enter into any conference, agreement, alliance, or treaty with any king, prince, or state; nor shall any person, holding any office of profit or trust under the United States, or any of them, accept of any present, emolument, office or title, of any kind whatever, from any king, prince, or foreign state; nor shall the United States, in Congress assembled, or any of them, grant any title of nobility.

No two or more states shall enter into any treaty, confederation, or alliance, whatever, between them, without the consent of the United States, in Congress assembled, specifying accurately the purposes for which the same is to be entered into, and how long it shall continue.

No state shall lay any imposts or duties which may interfere with any stipulations in treaties entered into by the United States, in Congress assembled, with any king, prince, or state, in pursuance of any treaties already proposed by Congress to the courts of France and Spain.

No vessels of war shall be kept up in time of peace by any State, except such number only as shall be deemed necessary by the United States, in Congress assembled, for the defence of such State or its trade; nor shall any body of forces be kept up by any State, in time of peace, except such number

only as, in the judgment of the United States, in Congress assembled, shall be deemed requisite to garrison the forts necessary for the defence of such State; but every State shall always keep up a well regulated and disciplined militia, sufficiently armed and accoutred, and shall provide, and constantly have ready for use, in public stores, a due number of field pieces and tents, and a proper quantity of arms, ammunition and camp equipage.

No State shall engage in any war without the consent of the United States, in Congress assembled, unless such State be actually invaded by enemies, or shall have received certain advice of a resolution being formed by some nation of Indians to invade such State, and the danger is so imminent as not to admit of a delay till the United States, in Congress assembled, can be consulted; nor shall any State grant commissions to any ships or vessels of war, nor letters of marque or reprisal, except it be after a declaration of war by the United States, in Congress assembled, and then only against the kingdom or state, and the subjects thereof, against which war has been so declared, and under such regulations as shall be established by the United States, in Congress assembled, unless such State be infested by pirates, in which case vessels of war may be fitted out for that occasion, and kept so long as the danger shall continue, or until the United States, in Congress assembled, shall determine otherwise.

Article 7

When land forces are raised by any State for the common defence, all officers of or under the rank of colonel, shall be appointed by the legislature of each State respectively, by whom such forces shall be raised, or in such manner as such State shall direct; and all vacancies shall be filled up by the State which first made the appointment.

Article 8

All charges of war and all other expences, that shall be incurred for the common defence or general welfare, and allowed by the United States, in Congress assembled, shall be defrayed out of a common treasury, which shall be supplied by the several states, in proportion to the value of all land within each State, granted to or surveyed for any person, as such land and the buildings and improvements thereon shall be estimated according to such mode as the United States, in Congress assembled, shall, from time to time, direct and appoint.

The taxes for paying that proportion shall be laid and levied by the authority and direction of the legislatures of the several states, within the time agreed upon by the United States, in Congress assembled.

Article 9

The United States, in Congress assembled, shall have the sole and exclusive right and power of determining on peace and war, except in the cases mentioned in the 6th article; of sending and receiving ambassadors; entering into treaties and alliances, provided that no treaty of commerce shall be made, whereby the legislative power of the respective states shall be restrained from imposing such imposts and duties on foreigners as their own people are subjected to, or from prohibiting the exportation or importation of any species of goods or commodities whatsoever; of establishing rules for deciding, in all cases, what captures on land or water shall be legal, and in what manner prizes, taken by land or naval forces in the service of the United States, shall be divided or appropriated; of granting letters of marque and reprisal in times of peace; appointing courts for the trial of piracies and felonies committed on the high seas, and establishing courts for receiving and determining, finally, appeals in all cases of captures; provided, that no member of Congress shall be appointed a judge of any of the said courts.

The United States, in Congress assembled, shall also be the last resort on appeal in all disputes and differences now subsisting, or that hereafter may arise between two or more states concerning boundary, jurisdiction or any other cause whatever; which authority shall always be exercised in the manner following: whenever the legislative or executive authority, or lawful agent of any State, in controversy with another, shall present a petition to Congress, stating the matter in question, and praying for a hearing, notice thereof shall be given, by order of Congress, to the legislative or executive authority of the other State in controversy, and a day assigned for the appearance of the parties by their lawful agents, who shall then be directed to appoint, by joint consent, commissioners or judges to constitute a court for hearing and determining the matter in question; but, if they cannot agree, Congress shall name three persons out of each of the United States, and from the list of such persons each party shall alternately strike out one, the petitioners beginning, until the number shall be reduced to thirteen; and from that number not less than seven, nor more than nine names, as Congress shall direct, shall, in the presence of Congress, be drawn out by lot; and the persons whose names shall be so drawn, or any five of them, shall be commissioners or judges to hear and finally determine the controversy, so always as a major part of the judges who shall hear the cause shall agree in the determination; and if either party shall neglect to attend at the day appointed, without shewing reasons which Congress shall judge sufficient, or, being present, shall refuse to strike, the Congress shall proceed to nominate three persons out of each State, and the secretary of Congress shall strike in behalf of such party absent or refusing; and the judgment and sentence of the court to be appointed, in the manner before prescribed, shall be final and conclusive; and if any of the parties shall refuse to submit to the authority of such court, or to appear or defend their claim or cause, the court shall nevertheless proceed to pronounce sentence or judgment, which shall, in like manner, be final and decisive, the judgment or sentence and other proceedings begin, in either case, transmitted to Congress, and lodged among the acts of Congress for the security of the parties concerned: provided, that every commissioner, before he sits in judgment, shall take an oath, to be administered by one of the judges of the supreme or superior court of the State where the cause shall be tried, "well and truly to hear and determine the matter in question, according to the best of his judgment, without favour, affection, or hope of reward:" provided, also, that no State shall be deprived of territory for the benefit of the United States.

All controversies concerning the private right of soil, claimed under different grants of two or more states, whose jurisdictions, as they may respect such lands and the states which passed such grants, are adjusted, the said grants, or either of them, being at the same time claimed to have originated antecedent to such settlement of jurisdiction, shall, on the petition of either party to the Congress of the United States, be finally determined, as near as may be, in the same manner as is before prescribed for deciding disputes respecting territorial jurisdiction between different states.

The United States, in Congress assembled, shall also have the sole and exclusive right and power of regulating the alloy and value of coin struck by their own authority, or by that of the respective states; fixing the standard of weights and measures throughout the United States; regulating the trade and managing all affairs with the Indians not members of any of the states; provided that the legislative right of any State within its own limits be not infringed or violated; establishing and regulating post offices from one State to another throughout all the United States, and exacting such postage on the papers passing through the same as may be requisite to defray the expences of the said office; appointing all officers of the land forces in the service of the United States, excepting regimental officers; appointing all the officers of the naval forces, and commissioning all officers whatever in the service of the United States; making rules for the government and regulation of the said land and naval forces, and directing their operations.

The United States, in Congress assembled, shall have authority to appoint a committee to sit in the recess of Congress, to be denominated "a Committee of the States," and to consist of one delegate from each State, and to appoint such other committees and civil officers as may be necessary for managing the general affairs of the United States, under their direction; to appoint one of their number to preside; provided that no person be allowed to serve in the office of president more than one year in any term of three years; to ascertain the necessary sums of money to be raised for the service of the United States, and to appropriate and apply the same for defraying the public expences; to borrow money or emit bills on the credit of the United States, transmitting, every half year, to the respective states, an account of the sums of money so borrowed or emitted; to build and equip a navy; to agree upon the number of land forces, and to make requisitions from each State for its quota, in proportion to the number of white inhabitants in such State; which requisitions shall be binding; and thereupon, the legislature of each State shall appoint the regimental officers, raise the men, and cloathe, arm, and equip them in a soldier-like manner, at the expence of the United States; and the officers and men so cloathed, armed, and equipped, shall march to the place appointed and within the time agreed on by the United States, in Congress assembled; but if the United States, in Congress assembled, shall, on consideration of circumstances, judge proper that any State should not raise men, or should raise a smaller number than its quota, and that any other State should raise a greater number of men than the quota thereof, such extra number shall be raised, officered, cloathed, armed, and equipped in the same manner as the quota of such State, unless the legislature of such State shall judge that such extra number cannot be safely spared out of the same, in which case they shall raise, officer, cloathe, arm, and equip as many of such extra number as they judge can be safely spared. And the officers and men so cloathed, armed, and equipped, shall march to the place appointed and within the time agreed on by the United States, in Congress assembled.

The United States, in Congress assembled, shall never engage in a war, nor grant letters of marque and reprisal in time of peace, nor enter into any treaties or alliances, nor coin money, nor regulate the value thereof, nor ascertain the sums and expences necessary for the defence and welfare of the United States, or any of them: nor emit bills, nor borrow money on the credit of the United States, nor appropriate money, nor agree upon the number of vessels of war to be built or purchased, or the number of land or sea forces to be raised, nor appoint a commander in chief of the army or navy, unless nine states assent to the same; nor shall a question on any other point, except for adjourning from day to day, be determined, unless by the votes of a majority of the United States, in Congress assembled.

The Congress of the United States shall have power to adjourn to any time within the year, and to any place within the United States, so that no period of adjournment be for a longer duration than the space of six months, and shall publish the journal of their proceedings monthly, except such parts thereof, relating to treaties, alliances or military operations, as, in their judgment, require secrecy; and the yeas and nays of the delegates of each State on any question shall be entered on the journal, when it is desired by any delegate; and the delegates of a State, or any of them, at his, or their request, shall be furnished with a transcript of the said journal, except such parts as are above excepted, to lay before the legislatures of the several states.

Article 10

The committee of the states, or any nine of them, shall be authorized to execute, in the recess of Congress, such of the powers of Congress as the United States, in Congress assembled, by the consent of nine states, shall, from time to time, think expedient to vest them with; provided, that no power be delegated to the said committee, for the exercise of which, by the articles of confederation, the voice of nine states, in the Congress of the United States assembled, is requisite.

Article 11

Canada acceding to this confederation, and joining in the measures of the United States, shall be admitted into and entitled to all the advantages of this union; but no other colony shall be admitted into the same, unless such admission be agreed to by nine states.

Article 12

All bills of credit emitted, monies borrowed and debts contracted by, or under the authority of Congress before the assembling of the United States, in pursuance of the present confederation, shall be deemed and considered as a charge against the United States, for payment and satisfaction whereof the said United States and the public faith are hereby solemnly pledged.

Article 13

Every State shall abide by the determinations of the United States, in Congress assembled, on all questions which, by this confederation, are submitted to them. And the articles of this confederation shall be inviolably observed by every State, and the union shall be perpetual; nor shall any alteration at any time hereafter be made in any of them, unless such alteration be agreed to in a Congress of the United States, and be afterwards confirmed by the legislatures of every State.

These articles shall be proposed to the legislatures of all the United States, to be considered, and if approved of by them, they are advised to authorize their delegates to ratify the same in the Congress of the United States; which being done, the same shall become conclusive.

THE CONSTITUTION OF THE UNITED STATES*

Agreed to by Philadelphia Convention, September 17, 1787. Implemented March 4, 1789.

Preamble

We the people of the United States, in order to form a more perfect union, establish justice, insure domestic tranquility, provide for the common defense, promote the general welfare, and secure the blessings of liberty to ourselves and our posterity, do ordain and establish this Constitution for the United States of America.

Article I

Section 1 All legislative powers herein granted shall be vested in a Congress of the United States, which shall consist of a Senate and a House of Representatives.

Section 2 The House of Representatives shall be composed of members chosen every second year by the people of the several States, and the electors in each State shall have the qualifications requisite for electors of the most numerous branch of the State Legislature.

No person shall be a Representative who shall not have attained to the age of twenty-five years, and been seven years a citizen of the United States, and who shall not, when elected, be an inhabitant of that State in which he shall be chosen.

Representatives and direct taxes shall be apportioned among the several States which may be included within this Union, according to their respective numbers, *which shall be determined by adding to the whole number of free persons, including those bound to service for a term of years and excluding Indians not taxed, three-fifths of all other persons.* The actual enumeration shall be made within three years after the first meeting of the Congress of the United States, and within every subsequent term of ten years, in such manner as they shall by law direct. The number of Representatives shall not exceed one for every thirty thousand, but each State shall have at least one Representative; *and until such enumeration shall be made, the State of New Hampshire shall be entitled to choose three, Massachusetts eight, Rhode Island and Providence Plantations one, Connecticut five, New York six, New Jersey four, Pennsylvania eight, Delaware one, Maryland six, Virginia ten, North Carolina five, South Carolina five, and Georgia three.*

When vacancies happen in the representation from any State, the Executive authority thereof shall issue writs of election to fill such vacancies.

The House of Representatives shall choose their Speaker and other officers; and shall have the sole power of impeachment.

Section 3 The Senate of the United States shall be composed of two Senators from each State, *chosen by the legislature thereof,* for six years; and each Senator shall have one vote.

Immediately after they shall be assembled in consequence of the first election, they shall be divided as equally as may be into three classes. The seats of the Senators of the first class shall be vacated at the expiration of the second year, of the second class at the expiration of the fourth year, and of the third class at the expiration of the sixth year, so that one-third may be chosen every second year; *and if vacancies happen by resignation or otherwise, during the recess of the legislature of any State, the Executive thereof may make temporary appointments until the next meeting of the legislature, which shall then fill such vacancies.*

No person shall be a Senator who shall not have attained to the age of thirty years, and been nine years a citizen of the United States, and who shall not, when elected, be an inhabitant of that State for which he shall be chosen.

The Vice-President of the United States shall be President of the Senate, but shall have no vote, unless they be equally divided.

The Senate shall choose their other officers, and also a President *pro tempore*, in the absence of the Vice-President, or when he shall exercise the office of President of the United States.

The Senate shall have the sole power to try all impeachments. When sitting for that purpose, they shall be on oath or affirmation. When the President of the United States is tried, the Chief Justice shall preside: and no person shall be convicted without the concurrence of two-thirds of the members present.

Judgment in cases of impeachment shall not extend further than to removal from the office, and disqualification to hold and enjoy any office of honor, trust or profit under the United States: but the party convicted shall nevertheless be liable and subject to indictment, trial, judgment and punishment, according to law.

Section 4 The times, places and manner of holding elections for Senators and Representatives shall be prescribed in each State by the legislature thereof; but the Congress may at any time by law make or alter such regulations, except as to the places of choosing Senators.

The Congress shall assemble at least once in every year, and such meeting *shall be on the first*

---

*Passages no longer in effect are in italic type.

Monday in December, unless they shall by law appoint a different day.

Section 5 Each house shall be the judge of the elections, returns and qualifications of its own members, and a majority of each shall constitute a quorum to do business; but a smaller number may adjourn from day to day, and may be authorized to compel the attendance of absent members, in such manner, and under such penalties, as each house may provide.

Each house may determine the rules of its proceedings, punish its members for disorderly behavior, and with the concurrence of two-thirds, expel a member.

Each house shall keep a journal of its proceedings, and from time to time publish the same, excepting such parts as may in their judgment require secrecy; and the yeas and nays of the members of either house on any question shall, at the desire of one-fifth of those present, be entered on the journal.

Neither house, during the session of Congress, shall, without the consent of the other, adjourn for more than three days, nor to any other place than that in which the two houses shall be sitting.

Section 6 The Senators and Representatives shall receive a compensation for their services, to be ascertained by law and paid out of the treasury of the United States. They shall in all cases except treason, felony and breach of the peace, be privileged from arrest during their attendance at the session of their respective houses, and in going to and returning from the same; and for any speech or debate in either house, they shall not be questioned in any other place.

No Senator or Representative shall, during the time for which he was elected, be appointed to any civil office under the authority of the United States, which shall have been created, or the emoluments whereof shall have been increased, during such time; and no person holding any office under the United States shall be a member of either house during his continuance in office.

Section 7 All bills for raising revenue shall originate in the House of Representatives; but the Senate may propose or concur with amendments as on other bills.

Every bill which shall have passed the House of Representatives and the Senate, shall, before it become a law, be presented to the President of the United States; if he approve he shall sign it, but if not he shall return it with objections to that house in which it shall have originated, who shall enter the objections at large on their journal, and proceed to reconsider it. If after such reconsideration two-thirds of that house shall agree to pass the bill, it shall be sent, together with the objections, to the other house, by which it shall likewise be reconsidered, and, if approved by two-thirds of that house, it shall become a law. But in all such cases the votes of both houses shall be determined by yeas and nays, and the names of the persons voting for and against the bill shall be entered on the journal of each house respectively. If any bill shall not be returned by the President within ten days (Sundays excepted) after it shall have been presented to him, the same shall be a law, in like manner as if he had signed it, unless the Congress by their adjournment prevent its return, in which case it shall not be a law.

Every order, resolution, or vote to which the concurrence of the Senate and House of Representatives may be necessary (except on a question of adjournment) shall be presented to the President of the United States; and before the same shall take effect, shall be approved by him, or being disapproved by him, shall be repassed by two-thirds of the Senate and House of Representatives, according to the rules and limitations prescribed in the case of a bill.

Section 8 The Congress shall have power

To lay and collect taxes, duties, imposts, and excises, to pay the debts and provide for the common defense and general welfare of the United States; but all duties, imposts and excises shall be uniform throughout the United States;

To borrow money on the credit of the United States;

To regulate commerce with foreign nations, and among the several States, and with the Indian tribes;

To establish an uniform rule of naturalization, and uniform laws on the subject of bankruptcies throughout the United States;

To coin money, regulate the value thereof, and of foreign coin, and fix the standard of weights and measures;

To provide for the punishment of counterfeiting the securities and current coin of the United States;

To establish post offices and post roads;

To promote the progress of science and useful arts by securing for limited times to authors and inventors the exclusive right to their respective writings and discoveries;

To constitute tribunals inferior to the Supreme Court;

To define and punish piracies and felonies committed on the high seas and offences against the law of nations;

To declare war, grant letters of marque and reprisal, and make rules concerning captures on land and water;

To raise and support armies, but no appropriation of money to that use shall be for a longer term than two years;

To provide and maintain a navy;

To make rules for the government and regulation of the land and naval forces;

To provide for calling forth the militia to execute the laws of the Union, suppress insurrections and repel invasions;

To provide for organizing, arming, and disciplining the militia, and for governing such part of them as may be employed in the service of the United States, reserving to the States respectively the appointment of the officers, and the authority of training the militia according to the discipline prescribed by Congress;

To exercise exclusive legislation in all cases whatsoever, over such district (not exceeding ten miles square) as may, by cession of particular States, and the acceptance of Congress, become the seat of the government of the United States, and to exercise like authority over all places purchased by the consent of the legislature of the State, in which the same shall be, for erection of forts, magazines, arsenals, dock-yards, and other needful buildings;—and

To make all laws which shall be necessary and proper for carrying into execution the foregoing powers, and all other powers vested by this Constitution in the government of the United States, or in any department or officer thereof.

Section 9 The migration or importation of such persons as any of the States now existing shall think proper to admit shall not be prohibited by the Congress prior to the year one thousand eight hundred and eight; but a tax or duty may be imposed on such importation, not exceeding ten dollars for each person.

The privilege of the writ of habeas corpus shall not be suspended, unless when in cases of rebellion or invasion the public safety may require it.

No bill of attainder or ex post facto law shall be passed.

No capitation, or other direct, tax shall be laid, unless in proportion to the census or enumeration herein before directed to be taken.

No tax or duty shall be laid on articles exported from any State.

No preference shall be given by any regulation of commerce or revenue to the ports of one State over those of another; nor shall vessels bound to, or from, one State be obliged to enter, clear, or pay duties in another.

No money shall be drawn from the treasury, but in consequence of appropriations made by law; and a regular statement and account of the receipts and expenditures of all public money shall be published from time to time.

No title of nobility shall be granted by the United States: and no person holding any office of profit or trust under them, shall, without the consent of the Congress, accept of any present, emolument, office, or title, of any kind whatever, from any king, prince, or foreign state.

Section 10 No State shall enter into any treaty, alliance, or confederation; grant letters of marque and reprisal; coin money; emit bills of credit; make anything but gold and silver coin a tender in payment of debts; pass any bill of attainder, ex post facto law, or law impairing the obligation of contracts, or grant any title of nobility.

No State shall, without the consent of Congress, lay any imposts or duties on imports or exports, except what may be absolutely necessary for executing its inspection laws: and the net produce of all duties and imposts, laid by any State on imports or exports, shall be for the use of the treasury of the United States; and all such laws shall be subject to the revision and control of the Congress.

No State shall, without the consent of Congress, lay any duty of tonnage, keep troops, or ships of war in time of peace, enter into any agreement or compact with another State, or with a foreign power, or engage in war, unless actually invaded, or in such imminent danger as will not admit of delay.

Article II

Section 1 The executive power shall be vested in a President of the United States of America. He shall hold his office during the term of four years, and, together with the Vice-President, chosen for the same term, be elected as follows:

Each State shall appoint, in such manner as the legislature thereof may direct, a number of electors, equal to the whole number of Senators and Representatives to which the State may be entitled in the Congress; but no Senator or Representative, or person holding an office of trust or profit under the United States, shall be appointed an elector.

The electors shall meet in their respective States, and vote by ballot for two persons, of whom one at least shall not be an inhabitant of the same State with themselves. And they shall make a list of all the persons voted for, and of the number of votes for each; which list they shall sign and certify, and transmit sealed to the seat of government of the United States, directed to the President of the Senate. The President of the Senate shall, in the presence of the Senate and House of Representatives, open all the certificates, and the votes shall then be counted. The person having the greatest number of votes shall be the President, if such number be a majority of the whole number of electors appointed; and if there be more than one who have such majority, and have an equal number of votes, then the House of Representatives shall immediately choose by ballot one of them for President; and if no person have a majority, then from the five highest on the list said house shall in like manner choose the President. But in choosing the President the votes shall be taken by States, the representation from each State having one vote; a quorum for this purpose shall consist of a member or members from two-thirds of the States, and a majority of all the States shall be necessary to a choice. In every case, after the choice of the President, the person having the greatest number of votes of the electors shall be the Vice-President. But if there should remain two or more who have equal votes, the Senate shall choose from them by ballot the Vice-President.

The Congress may determine the time of choosing the electors, and the day on which they shall give their votes; which day shall be the same throughout the United States.

No person except a natural-born citizen, *or a citizen of the United States at the time of the adoption of this Constitution,* shall be eligible to the office of President; neither shall any person be eligible to that office who shall not have attained to the age of thirty-five years, and been fourteen years a resident within the United States.

In cases of the removal of the President from office or of his death, resignation, or inability to discharge the powers and duties of the said office, the same shall devolve on the Vice-President, and the Congress may by law provide for the case of removal, death, resignation, or inability, both of the President and Vice-President, declaring what officer shall then act as President, and such officer shall act accordingly, until the disability be removed, or a President shall be elected.

The President shall, at stated times, receive for his services a compensation, which shall neither be increased nor diminished during the period for which he shall have been elected, and he shall not receive within that period any other emolument from the United States, or any of them.

Before he enter on the execution of his office, he shall take the following oath or affirmation:—"I do solemnly swear (or affirm) that I will faithfully execute the office of the President of the United States, and will to the best of my ability preserve, protect and defend the Constitution of the United States."

Section 2 The President shall be commander in chief of the army and navy of the United States, and of the militia of the several States, when called into the actual service of the United States; he may require the opinion, in writing, of the principal officer in each of the executive departments, upon any subject relating to the duties of their respective offices, and he shall have power to grant reprieves and pardons for offenses against the United States, except in cases of impeachment.

He shall have power, by and with the advice and consent of the Senate, to make treaties, provided two-thirds of the Senators present concur; and he shall nominate, and by and with the advice and consent of the Senate, shall appoint ambassadors, other public ministers and consuls, judges of the Supreme Court, and all other officers of the United States, whose appointments are not herein otherwise provided for, and which shall be established by law: but Congress may by law vest the appointment of such inferior officers, as they think proper, in the President alone, in the courts of law, or in the heads of departments.

The President shall have power to fill up all vacancies that may happen during the recess of the Senate, by granting commissions which shall expire at the end of their next session.

Section 3 He shall from time to time give to the Congress information of the state of the Union, and recommend to their consideration such measures as he shall judge necessary and expedient; he may, on extraordinary occasions, convene both houses, or either of them, and in case of disagreement between them, with respect to the time of adjournment, he may adjourn them to such time as he shall think proper; he shall receive ambassadors and other public ministers; he shall take care that the laws be faithfully executed, and shall commission all the officers of the United States.

Section 4 The President, Vice-President and all civil officers of the United States shall be removed from office on impeachment for, and on conviction of, treason, bribery, or other high crimes and misdemeanors.

Article III

Section 1 The judicial power of the United States shall be vested in one Supreme Court, and in such inferior courts as the Congress may from time to time ordain and establish. The judges, both of the Supreme and inferior courts, shall hold their offices during good behavior, and shall, at stated times, receive for their services a compensation which shall not be diminished during their continuance in office.

Section 2 The judicial power shall extend to all cases, in law and equity, arising under this Constitution, the laws of the United States, and treaties made, or which shall be made, under their authority;—to all cases affecting ambassadors, other public ministers and consuls;—to all cases of admiralty and maritime jurisdiction;—to controversies to which the United States shall be a party;—to controversies between two or more States;—*between a State and citizens of another State;*—between citizens of different States;—between citizens of the same State claiming lands under grants of different States, and between a State, or the citizens thereof, and foreign states, citizens or subjects.

In all cases affecting ambassadors, other public ministers and consuls, and those in which a State shall be party, the Supreme Court shall have original jurisdiction. In all the other cases before mentioned, the Supreme Court shall have appellate jurisdiction, both as to law and fact, with such exceptions, and under such regulations, as the Congress shall make.

The trial of all crimes, except in cases of impeachment, shall be by jury; and such trial shall be held in the State where said crimes shall have been committed; but when not committed within any State, the trial shall be at such place or places as the Congress may by Law have directed.

Section 3   Treason against the United States shall consist only in levying war against them, or in adhering to their enemies, giving them aid and comfort. No person shall be convicted of treason unless on the testimony of two witnesses to the same overt act, or on confession in open court.

The Congress shall have power to declare the punishment of treason, but no attainder of treason shall work corruption of blood, or forfeiture except during the life of the person attainted.

Article IV

Section 1   Full faith and credit shall be given in each State to the public acts, records, and judicial proceedings of every other State. And the Congress may by general laws prescribe the manner in which such acts, records, and proceedings shall be proved, and the effect thereof.

Section 2   The citizens of each State shall be entitled to all privileges and immunities of citizens in the several States.

A person charged in any State with treason, felony, or other crime, who shall flee from justice, and be found in another State, shall on demand of the executive authority of the State from which he fled, be delivered up, to be removed to the State having jurisdiction of the crime.

No Person held to service or labor in one State, under the laws thereof, escaping into another, shall, in consequence of any law or regulation therein, be discharged from such service or labor, but shall be delivered up on claim of the party to whom such service or labor may be due.

Section 3   New States may be admitted by the Congress into this Union; but no new State shall be formed or erected within the jurisdiction of any other State; nor any State be formed by the junction of two or more States, or parts of States, without the consent of the legislatures of the States concerned as well as of the Congress.

The Congress shall have power to dispose of and make all needful rules and regulations respecting the territory or other property belonging to the United States; and nothing in this Constitution shall be so construed as to prejudice any claims of the United States, or of any particular State.

Section 4   The United States shall guarantee to every State in this Union a republican form of government, and shall protect each of them against invasion; and on application of the legislature, or of the executive (when the legislature cannot be convened), against domestic violence.

Article V

The Congress, whenever two-thirds of both houses shall deem it necessary, shall propose amendments to this Constitution, or, on the application of the legislatures of two-thirds of the several States, shall call a convention for proposing amendments, which, in either case, shall be valid to all intents and purposes, as part of this Constitution, when ratified by the legislatures of three-fourths of the several States, or by conventions in three-fourths thereof, as the one or the other mode of ratification may be proposed by the Congress; provided *that no amendments which may be made prior to the year one thousand eight hundred and eight shall in any manner affect the first and fourth clauses in the ninth section of the first article*; and that no State, without its consent, shall be deprived of its equal suffrage in the Senate.

Article VI

All debts contracted and engagements entered into, before the adoption of this Constitution, shall be as valid against the United States under this Constitution, as under the Confederation.

This Constitution, and the laws of the United States which shall be made in pursuance thereof; and all treaties made, or which shall be made, under the authority of the United States, shall be the supreme law of the land; and the judges in every State shall be bound thereby, anything in the Constitution or laws of any State to the contrary notwithstanding.

The Senators and Representatives before mentioned, and the members of the several State legislatures, and all executive and judicial officers, both of the United States and of the several States, shall be bound by oath or affirmation to support this Constitution; but no religious test shall ever be required as a qualification to any office or public trust under the United States.

Article VII

The ratification of the conventions of nine States shall be sufficient for the establishment of this Constitution between the States so ratifying the same.

Done in convention by the unanimous consent of the States present, the seventeenth day of September in the year of our Lord one thousand seven hundred and eighty-seven and of the Independence of the United States of America the twelfth. In witness whereof we have hereunto subscribed our names.

GEORGE WASHINGTON
PRESIDENT AND DEPUTY FROM VIRGINIA

New Hampshire
John Langdon
Nicholas Gilman

Massachusetts
Nathaniel Gorham
Rufus King

Connecticut
William Samuel
   Johnson
Roger Sherman

New York
Alexander Hamilton

New Jersey
William Livingston
David Brearley
William Paterson
Jonathan Dayton

Pennsylvania
Benjamin Franklin
Thomas Mifflin
Robert Morris
George Clymer
Thomas FitzSimons
Jared Ingersoll
James Wilson
Gouverneur Morris

Delaware
George Read
Gunning Bedford, Jr.
John Dickinson
Richard Bassett
Jacob Broom

Maryland
James McHenry
Daniel of St. Thomas
   Jenifer
Daniel Carroll

Virginia
John Blair
James Madison, Jr.

North Carolina
William Blount
Richard Dobbs Spaight
Hugh Williamson

South Carolina
John Rutledge
Charles Cotesworth
   Pinckney
Charles Pinckney
Pierce Butler

Georgia
William Few
Abraham Baldwin

AMENDMENTS TO THE CONSTITUTION WITH ANNOTATIONS
(including the six unratified amendments)

IN THEIR EFFORT TO GAIN Antifederalists' support for the Constitution, Federalists frequently pointed to the inclusion of Article 5, which provides an orderly method of amending the Constitution. In contrast, the Articles of Confederation, which were universally recognized as seriously flawed, offered no means of amendment. For their part, Antifederalists argued that the amendment process was so "intricate" that one might as easily roll "sixes an hundred times in succession" as change the Constitution.

The system for amendment laid out in the Constitution requires that two-thirds of both houses of Congress agree to a proposed amendment, which must then be ratified by three-quarters of the legislatures of the states. Alternatively, an amendment may be proposed by a convention called by the legislatures of two-thirds of the states. Since 1789, members of Congress have proposed thousands of amendments. Besides the seventeen amendments added since 1789, only the six "unratified" ones included here were approved by two-thirds of both houses and sent to the states for ratification.

Among the many amendments that never made it out of Congress have been proposals to declare dueling, divorce, and interracial marriage unconstitutional as well as proposals to establish a national university, to acknowledge the sovereignty of Jesus Christ, and to prohibit any person from possessing wealth in excess of $10 million.*

Among the issues facing Americans today that might lead to constitutional amendment are efforts to balance the federal budget, to limit the number of terms elected officials may serve, to limit access to or prohibit abortion, to establish English as the official language of the United States, and to prohibit flag burning. None of these proposed amendments has yet garnered enough support in Congress to be sent to the states for ratification.

Although the first ten amendments to the Constitution are commonly known as the Bill of Rights, only Amendments 1–8 actually provide guarantees of individual rights. Amendments 9 and 10 deal with the structure of power within the constitutional system. The Bill of Rights was promised to appease Antifederalists who refused to ratify the Constitution without guarantees of individual liberties and limitations to federal power. After studying more than two hundred amendments recommended by the ratifying conventions of the states, Federalist James Madison presented a list of seventeen to Congress, which used Madison's list as the foundation for the twelve amendments that were sent to the states for ratification. Ten of the twelve were adopted in 1791. The first on the list of twelve,

---

*Richard B. Bernstein, *Amending America* (New York: Times Books, 1993), 177–81.

known as the Reapportionment Amendment, was never adopted (see page A-15). The second proposed amendment was adopted in 1992 as Amendment 27 (see page A-24).

Amendment I

Congress shall make no law respecting an establishment of religion, or prohibiting the free exercise thereof; or abridging the freedom of speech, or of the press; or the right of the people peaceably to assemble, and to petition the government for a redress of grievances.

♦ ♦ ♦

The First Amendment is a potent symbol for many Americans. Most are well aware of their rights to free speech, freedom of the press, and freedom of religion and their rights to assemble and to petition, even if they cannot cite the exact words of this amendment.

The First Amendment guarantee of freedom of religion has two clauses: the "free exercise clause," which allows individuals to practice or not practice any religion, and the "establishment clause," which prevents the federal government from discriminating against or favoring any particular religion. This clause was designed to create what Thomas Jefferson referred to as "a wall of separation between church and state." In the 1960s, the Supreme Court ruled that the First Amendment prohibits prayer (see Engel v. Vitale, *online) and Bible reading in public schools.*

Although the rights to free speech and freedom of the press are established in the First Amendment, it was not until the twentieth century that the Supreme Court began to explore the full meaning of these guarantees. In 1919, the Court ruled in Schenck v. United States *(online) that the government could suppress free expression only where it could cite a "clear and present danger." In a decision that continues to raise controversies, the Court ruled in 1990, in* Texas v. Johnson, *that flag burning is a form of symbolic speech protected by the First Amendment.*

Amendment II

A well-regulated militia being necessary to the security of a free State, the right of the people to keep and bear arms shall not be infringed.

♦ ♦ ♦

Fear of a standing army under the control of a hostile government made the Second Amendment an important part of the Bill of Rights. Advocates of gun ownership claim that the amendment prevents the government from regulating firearms. Proponents of gun control argue that the amendment is designed only to protect the right of the states to maintain militia units.

In 1939, the Supreme Court ruled in United States v. Miller *that the Second Amendment did not protect the right of an individual to own a sawed-off shotgun, which*

it argued was not ordinary militia equipment. Since then, the Supreme Court has refused to hear Second Amendment cases, while lower courts have upheld firearms regulations. Several justices currently on the bench seem to favor a narrow interpretation of the Second Amendment, which would allow gun control legislation. The controversy over the impact of the Second Amendment on gun owners and gun control legislation will certainly continue.

Amendment III

No soldier shall, in time of peace, be quartered in any house without the consent of the owner, nor in time of war, but in a manner to be prescribed by law.

♦ ♦ ♦

The Third Amendment was extremely important to the framers of the Constitution, but today it is nearly forgotten. American colonists were especially outraged that they were forced to quarter British troops in the years before and during the American Revolution. The philosophy of the Third Amendment has been viewed by some justices and scholars as the foundation of the modern constitutional right to privacy. One example of this can be found in Justice William O. Douglas's opinion in Griswold v. Connecticut *(online).*

Amendment IV

The right of the people to be secure in their persons, houses, papers, and effects, against unreasonable searches and seizures, shall not be violated, and no warrants shall issue but upon probable cause, supported by oath or affirmation, and particularly describing the place to be searched, and the persons or things to be seized.

♦ ♦ ♦

In the years before the Revolution, the houses, barns, stores, and warehouses of American colonists were ransacked by British authorities under "writs of assistance" or general warrants. The British, thus empowered, searched for seditious material or smuggled goods that could then be used as evidence against colonists who were charged with a crime only after the items were found.

The first part of the Fourth Amendment protects citizens from "unreasonable" searches and seizures. The Supreme Court has interpreted this protection as well as the words search *and* seizure *in different ways at different times. At one time, the Court did not recognize electronic eavesdropping as a form of search and seizure, though it does today. At times, an "unreasonable" search has been almost any search carried out without a warrant, but in the two decades before 1969, the Court sometimes sanctioned warrantless searches that it considered reasonable based on "the total atmosphere of the case."*

The second part of the Fourth Amendment defines the procedure for issuing a search warrant and states the requirement of "probable cause," which is generally viewed as evidence indicating that a suspect has committed an offense.

The Fourth Amendment has been controversial because the Court has sometimes excluded evidence that has been seized in violation of constitutional standards. The justification is that excluding such evidence deters violations of the amendment, but doing so may allow a guilty person to escape punishment.

Amendment V

No person shall be held to answer for a capital, or otherwise infamous crime, unless on a presentment or indictment of a grand jury, except in cases arising in the land or naval forces, or in the militia, when in actual service in time of war or public danger; nor shall any person be subject for the same offence to be twice put in jeopardy of life or limb; nor shall be compelled in any criminal case to be a witness against himself, nor be deprived of life, liberty, or property, without due process of law; nor shall private property be taken for public use without just compensation.

♦♦♦

The Fifth Amendment protects people against government authority in the prosecution of criminal offenses. It prohibits the state, first, from charging a person with a serious crime without a grand jury hearing to decide whether there is sufficient evidence to support the charge and, second, from charging a person with the same crime twice. The best-known aspect of the Fifth Amendment is that it prevents a person from being "compelled . . . to be a witness against himself." The last clause, the "takings clause," limits the power of the government to seize property.

Although invoking the Fifth Amendment is popularly viewed as a confession of guilt, a person may be innocent yet still fear prosecution. For example, during the Red-baiting era of the late 1940s and 1950s, many people who had participated in legal activities that were associated with the Communist Party claimed the Fifth Amendment privilege rather than testify before the House Un-American Activities Committee because the mood of the times cast those activities in a negative light. Since "taking the Fifth" was viewed as an admission of guilt, those people often lost their jobs or became unemployable. (See chapter 26.) Nonetheless, the right to protect oneself against self-incrimination plays an important role in guarding against the collective power of the state.

Amendment VI

In all criminal prosecutions, the accused shall enjoy the right to a speedy and public trial, by an impartial jury of the State and district wherein the crime shall have been committed, which district shall have been previously ascertained by law, and to be informed of the nature and cause of the accusation; to be confronted with the witnesses against him; to have compulsory process for obtaining witnesses in his favor, and to have the assistance of counsel for his defence.

♦♦♦

The original Constitution put few limits on the government's power to investigate, prosecute, and punish crime. This process was of great concern to the early Americans, however, and of the twenty-eight rights specified in the first eight amendments, fifteen have to do with it. Seven rights are specified in the Sixth Amendment. These include the right to a speedy trial, a public trial, a jury trial, a notice of accusation, confrontation by opposing witnesses, testimony by favorable witnesses, and the assistance of counsel.

Although this amendment originally guaranteed these rights only in cases involving the federal government, the adoption of the Fourteenth Amendment began a process of applying the protections of the Bill of Rights to the states through court cases such as Gideon v. Wainwright *(online).*

Amendment VII

In suits at common law, where the value in controversy shall exceed twenty dollars, the right of trial by jury shall be preserved, and no fact tried by a jury shall be otherwise reexamined in any court of the United States, than according to the rules of the common law.

♦♦♦

This amendment guarantees people the same right to a trial by jury as was guaranteed by English common law in 1791. Under common law, in civil trials (those involving money damages) the role of the judge was to settle questions of law and that of the jury was to settle questions of fact. The amendment does not specify the size of the jury or its role in a trial, however. The Supreme Court has generally held that those issues be determined by English common law of 1791, which stated that a jury consists of twelve people, that a trial must be conducted before a judge who instructs the jury on the law and advises it on facts, and that a verdict must be unanimous.

Amendment VIII

Excessive bail shall not be required, nor excessive fines imposed, nor cruel and unusual punishments inflicted.

♦♦♦

The language used to guarantee the three rights in this amendment was inspired by the English Bill of Rights of

1689. The Supreme Court has not had a lot to say about "excessive fines." In recent years it has agreed that despite the provision against "excessive bail," persons who are believed to be dangerous to others can be held without bail even before they have been convicted.

Although opponents of the death penalty have not succeeded in using the Eighth Amendment to achieve the end of capital punishment, the clause regarding "cruel and unusual punishments" has been used to prohibit capital punishment in certain cases (see Furman v. Georgia, online) and to require improved conditions in prisons.

Amendment IX

The enumeration in the Constitution, of certain rights, shall not be construed to deny or disparage others retained by the people.

♦♦♦

Some Federalists feared that inclusion of the Bill of Rights in the Constitution would allow later generations of interpreters to claim that the people had surrendered any rights not specifically enumerated there. To guard against this, Madison added language that became the Ninth Amendment. Interest in this heretofore largely ignored amendment revived in 1965 when it was used in a concurring opinion in Griswold v. Connecticut (online). While Justice William O. Douglas called on the Third Amendment to support the right to privacy in deciding that case, Justice Arthur Goldberg, in the concurring opinion, argued that the right to privacy regarding contraception was an unenumerated right that was protected by the Ninth Amendment.

In 1980, the Court ruled that the right of the press to attend a public trial was protected by the Ninth Amendment. While some scholars argue that modern judges cannot identify the unenumerated rights that the framers were trying to protect, others argue that the Ninth Amendment should be read as providing a constitutional "presumption of liberty" that allows people to act in any way that does not violate the rights of others.

Amendment X

The powers not delegated to the United States by the Constitution, nor prohibited by it to the States, are reserved to the States respectively, or to the people.

♦♦♦

The Antifederalists were especially eager to see a "reserved powers clause" explicitly guaranteeing the states control over their internal affairs. Not surprisingly, the Tenth Amendment has been a frequent battleground in the struggle over states' rights and federal supremacy. Prior to the Civil War, the Democratic Republican Party and Jacksonian Democrats invoked the Tenth Amendment to prohibit the federal government from making decisions about whether people in individual states could own slaves. The Tenth Amendment was virtually suspended during Reconstruction following the Civil War. In 1883, however, the Supreme Court declared the Civil Rights Act of 1875 unconstitutional on the grounds that it violated the Tenth Amendment. Business interests also called on the amendment to block efforts at federal regulation.

The Court was inconsistent over the next several decades as it attempted to resolve the tension between the restrictions of the Tenth Amendment and the powers the Constitution granted to Congress to regulate interstate commerce and levy taxes. The Court upheld the Pure Food and Drug Act (1906), the Meat Inspection Acts (1906 and 1907), and the White Slave Traffic Act (1910), all of which affected the states, but struck down an act prohibiting interstate shipment of goods produced through child labor. Between 1934 and 1935, a number of New Deal programs created by Franklin D. Roosevelt were declared unconstitutional on the grounds that they violated the Tenth Amendment. (See chapter 24.) As Roosevelt appointees changed the composition of the Court, the Tenth Amendment was declared to have no substantive meaning. Generally, the amendment is held to protect the rights of states to regulate internal matters such as local government, education, commerce, labor, and business, as well as matters involving families such as marriage, divorce, and inheritance within the state.

Unratified Amendment

Reapportionment Amendment (proposed by Congress September 25, 1789, along with the Bill of Rights)

After the first enumeration required by the first article of the Constitution, there shall be one Representative for every thirty thousand, until the number shall amount to one hundred, after which the proportion shall be so regulated by Congress, that there shall be not less than one hundred Representatives, nor less than one Representative for every forty thousand persons, until the number of Representatives shall amount to two hundred; after which the proportion shall be so regulated by Congress, that there shall not be less than two hundred Representatives, nor more than one Representative for every fifty thousand persons.

♦♦♦

If the Reapportionment Amendment had passed and remained in effect, the House of Representatives today would have more than 5,000 members rather than 435.

Amendment XI
[Adopted 1798]

The judicial power of the United States shall not be construed to extend to any suit in law or equity, commenced or prosecuted against one of the United States by citizens of another State, or by citizens or subjects of any foreign state.

◆ ◆ ◆

In 1793, the Supreme Court ruled in favor of Alexander Chisholm, executor of the estate of a deceased South Carolina merchant. Chisholm was suing the state of Georgia because the merchant had never been paid for provisions he had supplied during the Revolution. Many regarded this Court decision as an error that violated the intent of the Constitution.

Antifederalists had long feared a federal court system with the power to overrule a state court. When the Constitution was being drafted, Federalists had assured worried Antifederalists that section 2 of Article 3, which allows federal courts to hear cases "between a State and citizens of another State," did not mean that the federal courts were authorized to hear suits against a state by citizens of another state or a foreign country. Antifederalists and many other Americans feared a powerful federal court system because they worried that it would become like the British courts of this period, which were accountable only to the monarch. Furthermore, Chisholm v. Georgia *prompted a series of suits against state governments by creditors and suppliers who had made loans during the war.*

In addition, state legislators and Congress feared that the shaky economies of the new states, as well as the country as a whole, would be destroyed, especially if loyalists who had fled to other countries sought reimbursement for land and property that had been seized. The day after the Supreme Court announced its decision, a resolution proposing the Eleventh Amendment, which overturned the decision in Chisholm v. Georgia, *was introduced in the U.S. Senate.*

Amendment XII

[Adopted 1804]

The electors shall meet in their respective States, and vote by ballot for President and Vice-President, one of whom, at least, shall not be an inhabitant of the same State with themselves; they shall name in their ballots the person voted for as President, and in distinct ballots the person voted for as Vice-President, and they shall make distinct lists of all persons voted for as President, and of all persons voted for as Vice-President, and of the number of votes for each, which lists they shall sign and certify, and transmit sealed to the seat of government of the United States, directed to the President of the Senate;—the President of the Senate shall, in the presence of the Senate and House of Representatives, open all the certificates and the votes shall then be counted;—the person having the greatest number of votes for President

shall be the President, if such number be a majority of the whole number of electors appointed; and if no person have such majority, then from the persons having the highest numbers not exceeding three on the list of those voted for as President, the House of Representatives shall choose immediately, by ballot, the President. But in choosing the President, the votes shall be taken by States, the representation from each State having one vote; a quorum for this purpose shall consist of a member or members from two-thirds of the States, and a majority of all the States shall be necessary to a choice. And if the House of Representatives shall not choose a President whenever the right of choice shall devolve upon them, before *the fourth day of March* next following, then the Vice-President shall act as President, as in the case of the death or other constitutional disability of the President.

The person having the greatest number of votes as Vice-President shall be the Vice-President, if such number be a majority of the whole number of electors appointed; and if no person have a majority, then from the two highest numbers on the list the Senate shall choose the Vice-President; a quorum for the purpose shall consist of two-thirds of the whole number of Senators, and a majority of the whole number shall be necessary to a choice. But no person constitutionally ineligible to the office of President shall be eligible to that of Vice-President of the United States.

◆ ◆ ◆

The framers of the Constitution disliked political parties and assumed that none would ever form. Under the original system, electors chosen by the states would each vote for two candidates. The candidate who won the most votes would become president, while the person who won the second-highest number of votes would become vice president. Rivalries between Federalists and Antifederalists led to the formation of political parties, however, even before George Washington had left office. Though Washington was elected unanimously in 1789 and 1792, the elections of 1796 and 1800 were procedural disasters because of party maneuvering (see chapters 9 and 10). In 1796, Federalist John Adams was chosen as president, and his great rival, the Antifederalist Thomas Jefferson (whose party was called the Republican Party), became his vice president. In 1800, all the electors cast their two votes as one of two party blocs. Jefferson and his fellow Republican nominee, Aaron Burr, were tied with 73 votes each. The contest went to the House of Representatives, which finally elected Jefferson after 36 ballots. The Twelfth Amendment prevents these problems by requiring electors to vote separately for the president and vice president.

Unratified Amendment

Titles of Nobility Amendment (proposed by Congress May 1, 1810)

If any citizen of the United States shall accept, claim, receive or retain any title of nobility or honor or shall, without the consent of Congress, accept and retain any present, pension, office or emolument of any kind whatever, from any emperor, king, prince or foreign power, such person shall cease to be a citizen of the United States, and shall be incapable of holding any office of trust or profit under them or either of them.

♦ ♦ ♦

This amendment would have extended Article 1, section 9, clause 8 of the Constitution, which prevents the awarding of titles by the United States and the acceptance of such awards from foreign powers without congressional consent. Historians speculate that general nervousness about the power of the emperor Napoleon, who was at that time extending France's empire throughout Europe, may have prompted the proposal. Though it fell one vote short of ratification, Congress and the American people thought the proposal had been ratified and it was included in many nineteenth-century editions of the Constitution.

The Civil War and Reconstruction Amendments (Thirteenth, Fourteenth, and Fifteenth Amendments)

In the four months between the election of Abraham Lincoln and his inauguration, more than 200 proposed constitutional amendments were presented to Congress as part of a desperate attempt to hold the rapidly dissolving Union together. Most of these were efforts to appease the southern states by protecting the right to own slaves or by disfranchising African Americans through constitutional amendment. None were able to win the votes required from Congress to send them to the states. The relatively innocuous Corwin Amendment seemed to be the only hope for preserving the Union by amending the Constitution.

The northern victors in the Civil War tried to restructure the Constitution just as the war had restructured the nation. Yet they were often divided in their goals. Some wanted to end slavery; others hoped for social and economic equality regardless of race; others hoped that extending the power of the ballot box to former slaves would help create a new political order. The debates over the Thirteenth, Fourteenth, and Fifteenth Amendments were bitter. Few of those who fought for these changes were satisfied with the amendments themselves; fewer still were satisfied with their interpretation. Although the amendments put an end to the legal status of slavery, it took nearly a hundred years after the amendments' passage before most of the descendants of former slaves could begin to experience the economic, social, and political equality the amendments had been intended to provide.

Unratified Amendment

Corwin Amendment (proposed by Congress March 2, 1861)

No amendment shall be made to the Constitution which will authorize or give to Congress the power to abolish or interfere, within any State, with the domestic institutions thereof, including that of persons held to labor or service by the laws of said State.

♦ ♦ ♦

Following the election of Abraham Lincoln, Congress scrambled to try to prevent the secession of the slaveholding states. House member Thomas Corwin of Ohio proposed the "unamendable" amendment in the hope that by protecting slavery where it existed, Congress would keep the southern states in the Union. Lincoln indicated his support for the proposed amendment in his first inaugural address. Only Ohio and Maryland ratified the Corwin Amendment before it was forgotten.

Amendment XIII

[Adopted 1865]

Section 1   Neither slavery nor involuntary servitude, except as a punishment for crime whereof the party shall have been duly convicted, shall exist within the United States, or any place subject to their jurisdiction.

Section 2   Congress shall have power to enforce this article by appropriate legislation.

♦ ♦ ♦

Although President Lincoln had abolished slavery in the Confederacy with the Emancipation Proclamation of 1863, abolitionists wanted to rid the entire country of slavery. The Thirteenth Amendment did this in a clear and straightforward manner. In February 1865, when the proposal was approved by the House, the gallery of the House was newly opened to black Americans who had a chance at last to see their government at work. Passage of the proposal was greeted by wild cheers from the gallery as well as tears on the House floor, where congressional representatives openly embraced one another.

The problem of ratification remained, however. The Union position was that the Confederate states were part of the country of thirty-six states. Therefore, twenty-seven states were needed to ratify the amendment. When Kentucky and Delaware rejected it, backers realized that without approval from at least four former Confederate states, the amendment would fail. Lincoln's successor, President Andrew Johnson, made ratification of the Thirteenth Amendment a condition for southern states to rejoin the Union. Under those terms, all the former Confederate states except Mississippi accepted the Thirteenth Amendment, and by the end of 1865 the amendment had become part of the Constitution and slavery had been prohibited in the United States.

Amendment XIV

[Adopted 1868]

Section 1   All persons born or naturalized in the United States, and subject to the jurisdiction thereof, are citizens of the United States and of the State wherein they reside. No State shall make or enforce any law which shall abridge the privileges or immunities of citizens of the United States; nor shall any State deprive any person of life, liberty, or property, without due process of law; nor deny to any person within its jurisdiction the equal protection of the laws.

Section 2   Representatives shall be appointed among the several States according to their respective numbers, counting the whole number of persons in each State, excluding Indians not taxed. But when the right to vote at any election for the choice of Electors for President and Vice-President of the United States, Representatives in Congress, the executive and judicial officers of a State, or the members of the legislature thereof, is denied to any of the male inhabitants of such State, being twenty-one years of age and citizens of the United States, or in any way abridged, except for participation in rebellion, or other crime, the basis of representation therein shall be reduced in the proportion which the number of such male citizens shall bear to the whole number of male citizens twenty-one years of age in such State.

Section 3   No person shall be a Senator or Representative in Congress, or Elector of President and Vice-President, or hold any office, civil or military, under the United States, or under any State, who, having previously taken an oath, as a member of Congress, or as an officer of the United States, or as a member of any State legislature, or as an executive or judicial officer of any State, to support the Constitution of the United States, shall have engaged in insurrection or rebellion against the same, or given aid or comfort to the enemies thereof. Congress may, by a vote of two-thirds of each house, remove such disability.

Section 4   The validity of the public debt of the United States, authorized by law, including debts incurred for payment of pensions and bounties for services in suppressing insurrection or rebellion, shall not be questioned. But neither the United States nor any State shall assume or pay any debt or obligation incurred in aid of insurrection or rebellion against the United States, or any claim for the loss or emancipation of any slave; but all such debts, obligations, and claims shall be held illegal and void.

Section 5   The Congress shall have power to enforce, by appropriate legislation, the provisions of this article.

◆ ◆ ◆

Without Lincoln's leadership in the reconstruction of the nation following the Civil War, it soon became clear that the Thirteenth Amendment needed additional constitutional support. Less than a year after Lincoln's assassination, Andrew Johnson was ready to bring the former Confederate states back into the Union with few changes in their governments or politics. Anxious Republicans drafted the Fourteenth Amendment to prevent that from happening. The most important provisions of this complex amendment made all native-born or naturalized persons American citizens and prohibited states from abridging the "privileges or immunities" of citizens; depriving them of "life, liberty, or property, without due process of law"; and denying them "equal protection of the laws." In essence, it made all ex-slaves citizens and protected the rights of all citizens against violation by their own state governments.

As occurred in the case of the Thirteenth Amendment, former Confederate states were forced to ratify the amendment as a condition of representation in the House and the Senate. The intentions of the Fourteenth Amendment, and how those intentions should be enforced, have been the most debated point of constitutional history. The terms due process *and* equal protection *have been especially troublesome. Was the amendment designed to outlaw racial segregation? Or was the goal simply to prevent the leaders of the rebellious South from gaining political power?*

The framers of the Fourteenth Amendment hoped Article 2 would produce black voters who would increase the power of the Republican Party. The federal government, however, never used its power to punish states for denying blacks their right to vote. Although the Fourteenth Amendment had an immediate impact in giving black Americans citizenship, it did nothing to protect blacks from the vengeance of whites once Reconstruction ended. In the late nineteenth and early twentieth centuries, section 1 of the Fourteenth Amendment was often used to protect business interests and strike down laws protecting workers on the grounds that the rights of "persons," that is, corporations, were protected by "due process." More recently, the Fourteenth Amendment has been used to justify school desegregation and affirmative action programs, as well as to dismantle such programs.

Amendment XV

[Adopted 1870]

Section 1   The right of citizens of the United States to vote shall not be denied or abridged by the United States or by any State on account of race, color, or previous condition of servitude.

Section 2   The Congress shall have power to enforce this article by appropriate legislation.

♦ ♦ ♦

The Fifteenth Amendment was the last major piece of Reconstruction legislation. While earlier Reconstruction acts had already required black suffrage in the South, the Fifteenth Amendment extended black voting rights to the entire nation. Some Republicans felt morally obligated to do away with the double standard between North and South since many northern states had stubbornly refused to enfranchise blacks. Others believed that the freedman's ballot required the extra protection of a constitutional amendment to shield it from white counterattack. But partisan advantage also played an important role in the amendment's passage, since Republicans hoped that by giving the ballot to northern blacks, they could lessen their political vulnerability.

   Many women's rights advocates had fought for the amendment. They had felt betrayed by the inclusion of the word male *in section 2 of the Fourteenth Amendment and were further angered when the proposed Fifteenth Amendment failed to prohibit denial of the right to vote on the grounds of sex as well as "race, color, or previous condition of servitude." In this amendment, for the first time, the federal government claimed the power to regulate the franchise, or vote. It was also the first time the Constitution placed limits on the power of the states to regulate access to the franchise. Although ratified in 1870, the amendment was not enforced until the twentieth century.*

The Progressive Amendments (Sixteenth–Nineteenth Amendments)

No amendments were added to the Constitution between the Civil War and the Progressive Era. America was changing, however, in fundamental ways. The rapid industrialization of the United States after the Civil War led to many social and economic problems. Hundreds of amendments were proposed, but none received enough support in Congress to be sent to the states. Some scholars believe that regional differences and rivalries were so strong during this period that it was almost impossible to gain a consensus on a constitutional amendment. During the Progressive Era, however, the Constitution was amended four times in seven years.

Amendment XVI

[Adopted 1913]

The Congress shall have power to lay and collect taxes on incomes, from whatever source derived, without apportionment among the several States, and without regard to any census or enumeration.

♦ ♦ ♦

Until passage of the Sixteenth Amendment, most of the money used to run the federal government came from customs duties and taxes on specific items, such as liquor. During the Civil War, the federal government taxed incomes as an emergency measure. Pressure to enact an income tax came from those who were concerned about the growing gap between rich and poor in the United States. The Populist Party began campaigning for a graduated income tax in 1892, and support continued to grow. By 1909, thirty-three proposed income tax amendments had been presented in Congress, but lobbying by corporate and other special interests had defeated them all. In June 1909, the growing pressure for an income tax, which had been endorsed by Presidents Roosevelt and Taft, finally pushed an amendment through the Senate. The required thirty-six states had ratified the amendment by February 1913.

Amendment XVII

[Adopted 1913]

Section 1   The Senate of the United States shall be composed of two Senators from each State, elected by the people thereof, for six years; and each Senator shall have one vote. The electors in each State shall have the qualifications requisite for electors of [voters for] the most numerous branch of the State legislatures.

Section 2   When vacancies happen in the representation of any State in the Senate, the executive authority of such State shall issue writs of election to fill such vacancies: Provided, that the Legislature of any State may empower the executive thereof to make temporary appointments until the people fill the vacancies by election as the Legislature may direct.

Section 3   This amendment shall not be so construed as to affect the election or term of any Senator chosen before it becomes valid as part of the Constitution.

♦ ♦ ♦

The framers of the Constitution saw the members of the House as the representatives of the people and the members of the Senate as the representatives of the states. Originally senators were to be chosen by the state legislators. According to reform advocates, however, the growth of private industry and transportation conglomerates during the Gilded Age had created a network of corruption in which wealth and power were exchanged for influence and votes in the Senate. Senator Nelson Aldrich, who represented Rhode Island in the late nineteenth and early twentieth centuries, for example, was known as "the senator from Standard Oil" because of his open support of special business interests.

Efforts to amend the Constitution to allow direct election of senators had begun in 1826, but since any proposal had to be approved by the Senate, reform seemed impossible. Progressives tried to gain influence in the Senate by instituting party caucuses and primary elections, which gave citizens the chance to express their choice of a senator who could then be officially elected by the state legislature. By 1910, fourteen of the country's thirty senators received popular votes through a state primary before the state legislature made its selection. Despairing of getting a proposal through the Senate, supporters of a direct-election amendment had begun in 1893 to seek a convention of representatives from two-thirds of the states to propose an amendment that could then be ratified. By 1905, thirty-one of forty-five states had endorsed such an amendment. Finally, in 1911, despite extraordinary opposition, a proposed amendment passed the Senate; by 1913, it had been ratified.

Amendment XVIII

[Adopted 1919; repealed 1933 by Amendment XXI]

Section 1   After one year from the ratification of this article the manufacture, sale, or transportation of intoxicating liquors within, the importation thereof into, or the exportation thereof from the United States and all territory subject to the jurisdiction thereof, for beverage purposes, is hereby prohibited.

Section 2   The Congress and the several States shall have concurrent power to enforce this article by appropriate legislation.

Section 3   This article shall be inoperative unless it shall have been ratified as an amendment to the Constitution by the legislatures of the several States, as provided by the Constitution, within seven years from the date of the submission thereof to the States by the Congress.

◆ ◆ ◆

The Prohibition Party, formed in 1869, began calling for a constitutional amendment to outlaw alcoholic beverages in 1872. A prohibition amendment was first proposed in the Senate in 1876 and was revived eighteen times before 1913. Between 1913 and 1919, another thirty-nine attempts were made to prohibit liquor in the United States through a constitutional amendment. Prohibition became a key element of the progressive agenda as reformers linked alcohol and

drunkenness to numerous social problems, including the corruption of immigrant voters. While opponents of such an amendment argued that it was undemocratic, supporters claimed that their efforts had widespread public support. The admission of twelve "dry" western states to the Union in the early twentieth century and the spirit of sacrifice during World War I laid the groundwork for passage and ratification of the Eighteenth Amendment in 1919. Opponents added a time limit to the amendment in the hope that they could thus block ratification, but this effort failed. (See also Amendment XXI.)

Amendment XIX

[Adopted 1920]

Section 1   The right of citizens of the United States to vote shall not be denied or abridged by the United States or by any State on account of sex.

Section 2   Congress shall have the power to enforce this article by appropriate legislation.

◆ ◆ ◆

Advocates of women's rights tried and failed to link woman suffrage to the Fourteenth and Fifteenth Amendments. Nonetheless, the effort for woman suffrage continued. Between 1878 and 1912, at least one and sometimes as many as four proposed amendments were introduced in Congress each year to grant women the right to vote. While over time women won very limited voting rights in some states, at both the state and federal levels opposition to an amendment for woman suffrage remained very strong. President Woodrow Wilson and other officials felt that the federal government should not interfere with the power of the states in this matter. Others worried that granting suffrage to women would encourage ethnic minorities to exercise their own right to vote. And many were concerned that giving women the vote would result in their abandoning traditional gender roles. In 1919, following a protracted and often bitter campaign of protest in which women went on hunger strikes and chained themselves to fences, an amendment was introduced with the backing of President Wilson. It narrowly passed the Senate (after efforts to limit the suffrage to white women failed) and was adopted in 1920 after Tennessee became the thirty-sixth state to ratify it.

Unratified Amendment

Child Labor Amendment (proposed by Congress June 2, 1924)

Section 1   The Congress shall have power to limit, regulate, and prohibit the labor of persons under eighteen years of age.

Section 2   The power of the several States is unimpaired by this article except that the operation of

State laws shall be suspended to the extent necessary to give effect to legislation enacted by Congress.

♦ ♦ ♦

Throughout the late nineteenth and early twentieth centuries, alarm over the condition of child workers grew. Opponents of child labor argued that children worked in dangerous and unhealthy conditions, that they took jobs from adult workers, that they depressed wages in certain industries, and that states that allowed child labor had an economic advantage over those that did not. Defenders of child labor claimed that children provided needed income in many families, that working at a young age developed character, and that the effort to prohibit the practice constituted an invasion of family privacy.

In 1916, Congress passed a law that made it illegal to sell goods made by children through interstate commerce. The Supreme Court, however, ruled that the law violated the limits on the power of Congress to regulate interstate commerce. Congress then tried to penalize industries that used child labor by taxing such goods. This measure was also thrown out by the courts. In response, reformers set out to amend the Constitution. The proposed amendment was ratified by twenty-eight states, but by 1925, thirteen states had rejected it. Passage of the Fair Labor Standards Act in 1938, which was upheld by the Supreme Court in 1941, made the amendment irrelevant.

Amendment XX

[Adopted 1933]

Section 1   The terms of the President and Vice-President shall end at noon on the 20th day of January, and the terms of Senators and Representatives at noon on the 3rd day of January, of the years in which such terms would have ended if this article had not been ratified; and the terms of their successors shall then begin.

Section 2   The Congress shall assemble at least once in every year, and such meeting shall begin at noon on the 3rd day of January, unless they shall by law appoint a different day.

Section 3   If, at the time fixed for the beginning of the term of the President, the President-elect shall have died, the Vice-President-elect shall become President. If a President shall not have been chosen before the time fixed for the beginning of his term, or if the President-elect shall have failed to qualify, then the Vice-President-elect shall act as President until a President shall have qualified; and the Congress may by law provide for the case wherein neither a President-elect nor a Vice-President-elect shall have qualified, declaring who shall then act as President, or the manner in which one who is to act shall be selected, and such person shall act accordingly until a President or Vice-President shall have qualified.

Section 4   The Congress may by law provide for the case of the death of any of the persons from whom the House of Representatives may choose a President whenever the right of choice shall have devolved upon them, and for the case of the death of any of the persons from whom the Senate may choose a Vice-President whenever the right of choice shall have devolved upon them.

Section 5   Sections 1 and 2 shall take effect on the 15th day of October following the ratification of this article.

Section 6   This article shall be inoperative unless it shall have been ratified as an amendment to the Constitution by the Legislatures of three-fourths of the several States within seven years from the date of its submission.

♦ ♦ ♦

Until 1933, presidents took office on March 4. Since elections are held in early November and electoral votes are counted in mid-December, this meant that more than three months passed between the time a new president was elected and when he took office. Moving the inauguration to January shortened the transition period and allowed Congress to begin its term closer to the time of the president's inauguration. Although this seems like a minor change, an amendment was required because the Constitution specifies terms of office. This amendment also deals with questions of succession in the event that a president- or vice president-elect dies before assuming office. Section 3 also clarifies a method for resolving a deadlock in the electoral college.

Amendment XXI

[Adopted 1933]

Section 1   The eighteenth article of amendment to the Constitution of the United States is hereby repealed.

Section 2   The transportation or importation into any State, Territory, or Possession of the United States for delivery or use therein of intoxicating liquors, in violation of the laws thereof, is hereby prohibited.

Section 3   This article shall be inoperative unless it shall have been ratified as an amendment to the Constitution by conventions in the several States, as provided in the Constitution, within seven years from the date of the submission thereof to the States by the Congress.

♦ ♦ ♦

Widespread violation of the Volstead Act, the law enacted to enforce prohibition, made the United States a nation of lawbreakers. Prohibition caused more problems than it solved by encouraging crime, bribery, and corruption. Further, a coalition of liquor and beer manufacturers, personal liberty advocates, and constitutional scholars joined forces to challenge the amendment. By 1929, thirty proposed repeal amendments had been introduced in Congress, and the Democratic Party made repeal part of its platform in the 1932 presidential campaign. The Twenty-first Amendment was proposed in February 1933 and ratified less than a year later. The failure of the effort to enforce prohibition through a constitutional amendment has often been cited by opponents to subsequent efforts to shape public virtue and private morality.

Amendment XXII

[Adopted 1951]

Section 1 No person shall be elected to the office of the President more than twice, and no person who has held the office of President, or acted as President, for more than two years of a term to which some other person was elected President shall be elected to the office of President more than once. But this article shall not apply to any person holding the office of President when this Article was proposed by the Congress, and shall not prevent any person who may be holding the office of President, or acting as President, during the term within which this Article becomes operative from holding the office of President or acting as President during the remainder of such term.

Section 2 This article shall be inoperative unless it shall have been ratified as an amendment to the Constitution by the legislatures of three-fourths of the several States within seven years from the date of its submission to the States by the Congress.

◆ ◆ ◆

George Washington's refusal to seek a third term of office set a precedent that stood until 1912, when former President Theodore Roosevelt sought, without success, another term as an independent candidate. Democrat Franklin Roosevelt was the only president to seek and win a fourth term, though he did so amid great controversy. Roosevelt died in April 1945, a few months after the beginning of his fourth term. In 1946, Republicans won control of the House and the Senate, and early in 1947 a proposal for an amendment to limit future presidents to two four-year terms was offered to the states for ratification. Democratic critics of the Twenty-second Amendment charged that it was a partisan posthumous jab at Roosevelt.

Since the Twenty-second Amendment was adopted, however, the only presidents who might have been able to seek a third term, had it not existed, were Republicans Dwight Eisenhower and Ronald Reagan, and Democrat Bill Clinton. Since 1826, Congress has entertained 160 proposed amendments to limit the

president to one six-year term. Such amendments have been backed by fifteen presidents, including Gerald Ford and Jimmy Carter.

Amendment XXIII

[Adopted 1961]

Section 1 The District constituting the seat of Government of the United States shall appoint in such manner as the Congress may direct: A number of electors of President and Vice-President equal to the whole number of Senators and Representatives in Congress to which the District would be entitled if it were a State, but in no event more than the least populous State; they shall be in addition to those appointed by the States, but they shall be considered for the purposes of the election of President and Vice-President, to be electors appointed by a State; and they shall meet in the District and perform such duties as provided by the twelfth article of amendment.

Section 2 The Congress shall have the power to enforce this article by appropriate legislation.

◆ ◆ ◆

When Washington, D.C., was established as a federal district, no one expected that a significant number of people would make it their permanent and primary residence. A proposal to allow citizens of the district to vote in presidential elections was approved by Congress in June 1960 and was ratified on March 29, 1961.

Amendment XXIV

[Adopted 1964]

Section 1 The right of citizens of the United States to vote in any primary or other election for President or Vice-President, for electors for President or Vice-President, or for Senator or Representative in Congress, shall not be denied or abridged by the United States or any State by reason of failure to pay any poll tax or other tax.

Section 2 The Congress shall have the power to enforce this article by appropriate legislation.

◆ ◆ ◆

In the colonial and Revolutionary eras, financial independence was seen as necessary to political independence, and the poll tax was used as a requirement for voting. By the twentieth century, however, the poll tax was used mostly to bar poor people, especially southern blacks, from voting. While conservatives complained that the amendment interfered with states' rights, liberals thought that the amendment did not go far enough because it barred the poll tax only in national elections and not in state or local elections. The amendment was ratified in 1964, however, and two years later, the Supreme Court ruled that poll taxes in state and local elections also violated the equal protection clause of the Fourteenth Amendment.

Amendment XXV

[Adopted 1967]

Section 1 In case of the removal of the President from office or of his death or resignation, the Vice-President shall become President.

Section 2 Whenever there is a vacancy in the office of the Vice-President, the President shall nominate a Vice-President who shall take office upon confirmation by a majority vote of both Houses of Congress.

Section 3 Whenever the President transmits to the President pro tempore of the Senate and the Speaker of the House of Representatives his written declaration that he is unable to discharge the powers and duties of his office, and until he transmits to them a written declaration to the contrary, such powers and duties shall be discharged by the Vice-President as Acting President.

Section 4 Whenever the Vice-President and a majority of either the principal officers of the executive departments or of such other body as Congress may by law provide, transmit to the President pro tempore of the Senate and the Speaker of the House of Representatives their written declaration that the President is unable to discharge the powers and duties of his office, the Vice-President shall immediately assume the powers and duties of the office as Acting President.

Thereafter, when the President transmits to the President pro tempore of the Senate and the Speaker of the House of Representatives his written declaration that no inability exists, he shall resume the powers and duties of his office unless the Vice-President and a majority of either the principal officers of the executive department[s] or of such other body as Congress may by law provide, transmit within four days to the President pro tempore of the Senate and the Speaker of the House of Representatives their written declaration that the President is unable to discharge the powers and duties of his office. Thereupon Congress shall decide the issue, assembling within forty-eight hours for that purpose if not in session. If the Congress, within twenty-one days after receipt of the latter written declaration, or, if Congress is not in session, within twenty-one days after Congress is required to assemble, determines by two-thirds vote of both Houses that the President is unable to discharge the powers and duties of his office, the Vice-President shall continue to discharge the same as Acting President; otherwise, the President shall resume the powers and duties of his office.

♦ ♦ ♦

The framers of the Constitution established the office of vice president because someone was needed to preside over the Senate. The first president to die in office was William Henry Harrison, in 1841. Vice President John Tyler had himself sworn in as president, setting a precedent that was followed when seven later presidents died in office. The assassination of President James A. Garfield in 1881 posed a new problem, however. After he was shot, the president was incapacitated for two months before he died; he was unable to lead the country, while his vice president, Chester A. Arthur, was unable to assume leadership. Efforts to resolve questions of succession in the event of a presidential disability thus began with the death of Garfield.

In 1963, the assassination of President John F. Kennedy galvanized Congress to action. Vice President Lyndon Johnson was a chain smoker with a history of heart trouble. According to the 1947 Presidential Succession Act, the two men who stood in line to succeed him were the seventy-two-year-old Speaker of the House and the eighty-six-year-old president of the Senate. There were serious concerns that any of these men might become incapacitated while serving as chief executive. The first time the Twenty-fifth Amendment was used, however, was not in the case of presidential death or illness, but during the Watergate crisis. When Vice President Spiro T. Agnew was forced to resign following allegations of bribery and tax violations, President Richard M. Nixon appointed House Minority Leader Gerald R. Ford vice president. Ford became president following Nixon's resignation eight months later and named Nelson A. Rockefeller as his vice president. Thus, for more than two years, the two highest offices in the country were held by people who had not been elected to them.

Amendment XXVI

[Adopted 1971]

Section 1 The right of citizens of the United States, who are eighteen years of age or older, to vote shall not be denied or abridged by the United States or by any State on account of age.

Section 2 The Congress shall have power to enforce this article by appropriate legislation.

♦ ♦ ♦

Efforts to lower the voting age from twenty-one to eighteen began during World War II. Recognizing that those who were old enough to fight a war should have some say in the government policies that involved them in the war, Presidents Eisenhower, Johnson, and Nixon endorsed the idea. In 1970, the combined pressure of the antiwar movement and the demographic pressure of the baby boom generation led to a Voting Rights Act lowering the voting age in federal, state, and local elections.

In Oregon v. Mitchell (1970), the state of Oregon challenged the right of Congress to determine the age at which people could vote in state or local elections. The Supreme Court agreed with Oregon. Since the Voting Rights Act was ruled unconstitutional, the Constitution had to be amended to allow passage of a law that would lower the voting age. The amendment was ratified in a little more than three months, making it the most rapidly ratified amendment in U.S. history.

Unratified Amendment

Equal Rights Amendment (proposed by Congress March 22, 1972; seven-year deadline for ratification extended June 30, 1982)

Section 1   Equality of rights under the law shall not be denied or abridged by the United States or by any State on account of sex.

Section 2   The Congress shall have the power to enforce, by appropriate legislation, the provisions of this article.

Section 3   This amendment shall take effect two years after the date of ratification.

◆ ◆ ◆

In 1923, soon after women had won the right to vote, Alice Paul, a leading activist in the woman suffrage movement, proposed an amendment requiring equal treatment of men and women. Opponents of the proposal argued that such an amendment would invalidate laws that protected women and would make women subject to the military draft. After the 1964 Civil Rights Act was adopted, protective workplace legislation was removed anyway.

The renewal of the women's movement, as a by-product of the civil rights and antiwar movements, led to a revival of the Equal Rights Amendment (ERA) in Congress. Disagreements over language held up congressional passage of the proposed amendment, but on March 22, 1972, the Senate approved the ERA by a vote of 84 to 8, and it was sent to the states. Six states ratified the amendment within two days, and by the middle of 1973 the amendment seemed well on its way to adoption, with thirty of the needed thirty-eight states having ratified it. In the mid-1970s, however, a powerful "Stop ERA" campaign developed. The campaign portrayed the ERA as a threat to "family values" and traditional relationships between men and women. Although thirty-five states ultimately ratified the ERA, five of those state legislatures voted to rescind ratification, and the amendment was never adopted.

Unratified Amendment

D.C. Statehood Amendment (proposed by Congress August 22, 1978)

Section 1   For purposes of representation in the Congress, election of the President and Vice-President, and article V of this Constitution, the District constituting the seat of government of the United States shall be treated as though it were a State.

Section 2   The exercise of the rights and powers conferred under this article shall be by the people of the District constituting the seat of government, and as shall be provided by Congress.

Section 3   The twenty-third article of amendment to the Constitution of the United States is hereby repealed.

Section 4   This article shall be inoperative, unless it shall have been ratified as an amendment to the Constitution by the legislatures of three-fourths of the several states within seven years from the date of its submission.

◆ ◆ ◆

The 1961 ratification of the Twenty-third Amendment, giving residents of the District of Columbia the right to vote for a president and vice president, inspired an effort to give residents of the district full voting rights. In 1966, President Lyndon Johnson appointed a mayor and city council; in 1971, D.C. residents were allowed to name a nonvoting delegate to the House; and in 1981, residents were allowed to elect the mayor and city council. Congress retained the right to overrule laws that might affect commuters, the height of federal buildings, and selection of judges and prosecutors. The district's nonvoting delegate to Congress, Walter Fauntroy, lobbied fiercely for a congressional amendment granting statehood to the district. In 1978, a proposed amendment was approved and sent to the states. A number of states quickly ratified the amendment, but, like the ERA, the D.C. Statehood Amendment ran into trouble. Opponents argued that section 2 created a separate category of "nominal" statehood. They argued that the federal district should be eliminated and that the territory should be reabsorbed into the state of Maryland. Although these theoretical arguments were strong, some scholars believe that racist attitudes toward the predominantly black population of the city was also a factor leading to the defeat of the amendment.

Amendment XXVII
[Adopted 1992]

No law, varying the compensation for the services of the Senators and Representatives, shall take effect, until an election of Representatives shall have intervened.

◆ ◆ ◆

While the Twenty-sixth Amendment was the most rapidly ratified amendment in U.S. history, the Twenty-seventh Amendment had the longest journey to ratification. First proposed by James Madison in 1789 as part of the package that included the Bill of Rights, this amendment had been ratified by only six states by 1791. In 1873, however, it was ratified by Ohio to protest a massive retroactive salary increase by the federal government. Unlike later proposed amend-ments, this one came with no time limit on ratification. In the early 1980s, Gregory D. Watson, a University of Texas economics major, discovered the "lost" amend-ment and began a single-handed campaign to get state legislators to introduce it for ratification. In 1983, it was accepted by Maine. In 1984, it passed the Colorado legislature. Ratifications trickled in slowly until May 1992, when Michigan and New Jersey became the thirty-eighth and thirty-ninth states, respectively, to ratify. This amendment prevents members of Congress from raising their own salaries without giving voters a chance to vote them out of office before they can benefit from the raises.

THE CONSTITUTION OF THE CONFEDERATE STATES OF AMERICA

In framing the Constitution of the Confederate States, the authors adopted, with numerous small but signifi-cant changes and additions, the language of the Con-stitution of the United States, and followed the same order of arrangement of articles and sections. The revi-sions that they made to the original Constitution are shown here. The parts stricken out are enclosed in brack-ets, and the new matter added in framing the Confed-erate Constitution is printed in italics.

Adopted March 11, 1861

WE, the People of the [United States] *Confederated States, each State acting in its sovereign and independent character,* in order to form a [more perfect Union] *permanent Federal government,* establish Justice, in-sure domestic Tranquillity [provide for the common defense, promote the general Welfare], and secure the Blessings of Liberty to ourselves and our Posterity, *invoking the favor and guidance of Almighty God,* do ordain and establish this Constitution for the [United] *Confederate* States of America.

Article I

Section I All legislative Powers herein [granted] *delegated,* shall be vested in a Congress of the [United] *Confederate* States, which shall consist of a Senate and House of Representatives.

Section II The House of Representatives shall be composed of Members chosen every second Year by the People of the several States, and the Electors in each State shall *be citizens of the Confederate States, and* have the Qualifications requisite for Electors of the most numerous Branch of the State Legislature; *but no person of foreign birth, and not a citizen of the Confederate States, shall be allowed to vote for any offi-cer, civil or political, State or federal.*

No Person shall be a Representative who shall not have attained to the Age of twenty-five Years, and [been seven Years a Citizen of the United] *be a citizen of the Confederate* States, and who shall not, when elected, be an Inhabitant of that State in which he shall be chosen.

Representatives and direct Taxes shall be ap-portioned among the several States which may be included within this [Union] *Confederacy,* according to their respective Numbers, which shall be deter-mined by adding to the whole Number of free Persons, including those bound to Service for a Term of Years, and excluding Indians not taxed, three-fifths of all [other Persons] *slaves.* The actual Enumeration shall be made within three Years after the first Meeting of the Congress of the [United] *Confederate* States, and within every subsequent Term of ten Years, in such Manner as they shall by Law direct. The Number of Representatives shall not exceed one for every [thirty] *fifty* Thousand, but each State shall have at Least one Representative; and until such enumeration shall be made, the State of [New Hampshire shall be entitled to choose three, Massachusetts eight, Rhode Island and Providence Plantations one, Connecticut five, New York six, New Jersey four, Pennsylvania eight, Delaware one, Maryland six, Virginia ten, North Carolina five, South Carolina five, and Georgia three] *South Carolina shall be entitled to choose six, the State of Georgia ten, the State of Alabama nine, the State of Florida two, the State of Mississippi seven, the State of Louisiana six, and the State of Texas six.*

When vacancies happen in the Representation from any State, the Executive Authority thereof shall issue Writs of Election to fill such Vacancies.

The House of Representatives shall choose their Speaker and other Officers; and shall have the sole Power of Impeachment; *except that any judicial or other federal officer resident and acting solely within the limits of any State, may be impeached by a vote of two-thirds of both branches of the Legislature thereof.*

Section III   The Senate of the [United] *Confederate* States shall be composed of two Senators from each State, chosen by the Legislature thereof, for six Years, *at the regular session next immediately preceding the commencement of the term of service;* and each Senator shall have one Vote.

Immediately after they shall be assembled in Consequence of the first Election, they shall be divided as equally as may be into three Classes. The Seats of the Senators of the first Class shall be vacated at the Expiration of the second Year, of the second Class at the Expiration of the fourth Year, and of the third Class at the Expiration of the sixth Year, so that one-third may be chosen every second Year; and if Vacancies happen by Resignation, or otherwise, during the Recess of the Legislature of any State, the Executive thereof may make temporary Appointments until the next Meeting of the Legislature, which shall then fill such Vacancies.

No Person shall be a Senator who shall not have attained to the Age of thirty Years, and [been nine Years a Citizen of the United] *be a citizen of the Confederate* States, and who shall not, when elected, be an Inhabitant of that State for which he shall be chosen.

The Vice President of the [United] *Confederate* States shall be President of the Senate, but shall have no Vote, unless they be equally divided.

The Senate shall choose their other Officers, and also a President *pro tempore,* in the Absence of the Vice President, or when he shall exercise the Office of President of the United States.

The Senate shall have the sole Power to try all Impeachments. When sitting for that Purpose, they shall be on Oath or Affirmation. When the President of the [United] *Confederate* States is tried, the Chief Justice shall preside: And no Person shall be convicted without the Concurrence of two-thirds of the Members present.

Judgment in Cases of Impeachment shall not extend further than to removal from Office, and Disqualification to hold and enjoy any Office of honour, Trust or Profit under the [United] *Confederate* States; but the Party convicted shall nevertheless be liable and subject to Indictment, Trial, Judgment and Punishment, according to Law.

Section IV   The Times, Places and Manner of holding Elections for Senators and Representatives, shall be prescribed in each State by the Legislature thereof, *subject to the provisions of this Constitution;* but the Congress may at any time by Law make or alter such Regulations, except as to the *times and* places of choosing Senators.

The Congress shall assemble at least once in every Year, and such Meeting shall be on the first Monday in December, unless they shall by Law appoint a different Day.

Section V   Each House shall be the Judge of the Elections, Returns and Qualifications of its own Members, and a Majority of each shall constitute a Quorum to do Business; but a smaller Number may adjourn from day to day, and may be authorized to compel the Attendance of absent Members, in such Manner, and under such Penalties as each House may provide.

Each House may determine the Rules of its Proceedings, punish its Members for disorderly Behaviour, and, with the Concurrence of two-thirds *of the whole number* expel a Member.

Each House shall keep a Journal of its Proceedings, and from time to time publish the same, excepting such Parts as may in their Judgment require Secrecy; and the Yeas and Nays of the Members of either House on any question shall, at the Desire of one-fifth of those Present, be entered on the Journal.

Neither House, during the Session of Congress, shall, without the Consent of the other, adjourn for more than three days, nor to any other Place than that in which the two Houses shall be sitting.

Section VI   The Senators and Representatives shall receive a Compensation for their Services, to be ascertained by Law, and paid out of the Treasury of the [United] *Confederate* States. They shall in all Cases, except Treason [Felony] and Breach of the Peace, be privileged from Arrest during their Attendance at the Session of their respective Houses, and in going to and returning from the same; and for any Speech or Debate in either House, they shall not be questioned in any other Place.

No Senator or Representative shall, during the Time for which he was elected, be appointed to any civil Office under the Authority of the [United] *Confederate* States, which shall have been created, or the Emoluments whereof shall have been increased during such time; and no Person holding any Office under the [United] *Confederate* States, shall be a Member of either House during his Continuance in Office. *But Congress may, by law, grant to the principal officers in each of the executive departments a seat upon the floor of either House, with the privilege of discussing any measures appertaining to his department.*

Section VII   All Bills for raising Revenue shall originate in the House of Representatives; but the Senate may propose or concur with Amendments as on other Bills.

Every Bill which shall have passed [the House of Representatives and the Senate] *both Houses,* shall, before it become a Law, be presented to the President of the [United] *Confederate* States; If he approve he shall sign it, but if not he shall return it, with his Objections to that House in which it shall have originated, who shall enter the Objections at

THE CONSTITUTION OF THE CONFEDERATE STATES OF AMERICA

large on their Journal, and proceed to reconsider it. If after such Reconsideration two-thirds of that House shall agree to pass the Bill, it shall be sent, together with the Objections, to the other House, by which it shall likewise be reconsidered, and if approved by two-thirds of that House, it shall become a Law. But in all *such* Cases the Votes of both Houses shall be determined by Yeas and Nays, and the Names of the Persons voting for and against the Bill shall be entered on the Journal of each House respectively. If any Bill shall not be returned by the President within ten Days (Sundays excepted) after it shall have been presented to him, the Same shall be a law, in like Manner as if he had signed it, unless the Congress by their Adjournment prevent its return, in which Case it shall not be a Law. *The President may approve any appropriation and disapprove any other appropriation in the same bill. In such case he shall, in signing the bill, designate the appropriation disapproved, and shall return a copy of such appropriation, with his objections, to the House in which the bill shall have originated; and the same proceedings shall then be had as in case of other bills disapproved by the President.*

Every Order, Resolution, or Vote to which the Concurrence of [the Senate and House of Representatives] *both Houses* may be necessary (except on a question of Adjournment), shall be presented to the President of the [United] *Confederate* States; and before the Same shall take Effect, shall be approved by him, or being disapproved by him, [shall] *may* be repassed by two-thirds of [the Senate and House of Representatives] *both Houses,* according to the Rules and Limitations prescribed in the Case of a Bill.

Section VIII   The Congress shall have Power

To lay and collect Taxes, Duties, Imposts and *Excises, for revenue necessary* to pay the Debts [and], provide for the common Defense [and general Welfare of the United States; but], *and carry on the government of the Confederate States; but no bounties shall be granted from the treasury, nor shall any duties, or taxes, or importation from foreign nations be laid to promote or foster any branch of industry; and* all Duties, Imposts and Excises shall be uniform throughout the [United] *Confederate* States;

To borrow Money on the credit of the [United] *Confederate* States;

To regulate Commerce with foreign Nations, and among the several States, and with the Indian Tribes; *but neither this, nor any other clause contained in this Constitution, shall ever be construed to delegate the power to Congress to appropriate money for any internal improvement intended to facilitate commerce; except for the purpose of furnishing lights, beacons, and buoys, and other aids to navigation upon the coasts, and the improvement of harbors, and the removing of obstructions in river navigation; in all such cases such duties shall be laid on the navigation facilitated thereby, as may be necessary to pay the costs and expenses thereof;*

To establish an uniform Rule of Naturalization, and uniform Laws on the subject of Bankruptcies throughout the [United] *Confederate* States; *but no law of Congress shall discharge any debt contracted before the passage of the same;*

To coin Money, regulate the Value thereof, and of foreign Coin, and fix the Standard of Weights and Measures;

To provide for the Punishment of counterfeiting the Securities and current Coin of the [United] *Confederate* States;

To establish Post Offices and post [Roads] *routes; but the expenses of the Postoffice Department, after the first day of March, in the year of our Lord eighteen hundred and sixty-three, shall be paid out of its own revenues;*

To promote the progress of Science and useful Arts, by securing for limited Times to Authors and Inventors the exclusive Right to their respective Writings and Discoveries;

To constitute Tribunals inferior to the supreme Court;

To define and punish Piracies and Felonies committed on the high Seas, and Offences against the Law of Nations;

To declare War, grant Letters of Marque and Reprisal, and make Rules concerning Captures on Land and Water;

To raise and support Armies, but no Appropriation of Money to that Use shall be for a longer Term than two Years;

To provide and maintain a Navy;

To make Rules for the Government and Regulation of the land and naval Forces;

To provide for calling forth the Militia to execute the Laws of the [Union] *Confederate States,* suppress Insurrections and repel Invasions;

To provide for organizing, arming, and disciplining the Militia and for governing such Part of them as may be employed in the Service of the [United] *Confederate* States, reserving to the States respectively, the Appointment of the Officers, and the Authority of training the Militia according to the Discipline prescribed by Congress;

To exercise exclusive Legislation in all Cases whatsoever, over such District (not exceeding ten Miles square) as may, by Cession of particular States, and the Acceptance of Congress, become the Seat of the Government of the [United] *Confederate* States, and to exercise like Authority over all Places purchased by the Consent of the Legislature of the State in which the Same shall be, for the Erection of Forts, Magazines, Arsenals, Dock Yards, and other needful Buildings;—And

To make all Laws which shall be necessary and proper for carrying into Execution the foregoing Powers, and all other Powers vested by this Constitution in the Government of the [United] *Confederate* States or in any Department or Officer thereof.

Section IX [The Migration or Importation of such Persons as any of the States now existing shall think proper to admit, shall not be prohibited by the Congress prior to the Year one thousand eight hundred and eight, but a Tax or Duty may be imposed on such Importation, not exceeding ten dollars for each Person.] *The importation of negroes of the African race from any foreign country other than the slaveholding States or territories of the United States of America, is hereby forbidden; and Congress is required to pass such laws as shall effectually prevent the same. Congress shall also have power to prohibit the introduction of slaves from any State not a member of, or territory not belonging to, this Confederacy.*

The Privilege of the Writ of Habeas Corpus shall not be suspended, unless when in Cases of Rebellion or Invasion the public Safety may require it. No Bill of Attainder or ex post facto Law, *or law denying or impairing the right of property in negro slaves,* shall be passed.

No Capitation, or other direct, Tax shall be laid, unless in Proportion to the Census or Enumeration herein before directed to be taken.

No Tax or Duty shall be laid on Articles exported from any State, *except by a vote of two-thirds of both Houses.*

No Preference shall be given by any Regulation of Commerce or Revenue to the Ports of one State over those of another; nor shall Vessels bound to, or from, one State, be obliged to enter, clear, or pay Duties in another.

No Money shall be drawn from the Treasury, but in Consequence of Appropriations made by Law; and a regular Statement and Account of the Receipts and Expenditures of all public Money shall be published from time to time.

Congress shall appropriate no money from the Treasury except by a vote of two-thirds of both Houses, taken by yeas and nays, unless it be asked and estimated for by some one of the heads of departments and submitted to Congress by the President; or for the purpose of paying its own expenses and contingencies; or for the payment of claims against the Confederate States, the justice of which shall have been officially declared by a tribunal for the investigation of claims against the Government, which it is hereby made the duty of Congress to establish.

All bills appropriating money shall specify in Federal currency the exact amount of each appropriation and the purposes for which it is made; and Congress shall grant no extra compensation to any public contractor, officer, agent or servant, after such contract shall have been made or such service rendered.

No Title of Nobility shall be granted by the [United] *Confederate* States; and no Person holding any Office of Profit or Trust under them, shall, without the Consent of the Congress, accept of any present, Emolument, Office, or Title, of any kind whatever, from any King, Prince or foreign State.

[*Here the framers of the Confederate Constitution insert the U.S. Bill of Rights.*]

Congress shall make no law respecting an establishment of religion, or prohibiting the free exercise thereof; or abridging the freedom of speech, or of the press; or the right of the people peaceably to assemble, and to petition the Government for a redress of grievances.

A well-regulated Militia, being necessary to the security of a free State, the right of the people to keep and bear Arms shall not be infringed.

No Soldier shall, in time of peace, be quartered in any house, without the consent of the Owner, nor in time of war, but in a manner to be prescribed by law.

The right of the people to be secure in their persons, houses, papers, and effects, against unreasonable searches and seizures, shall not be violated, and no Warrants shall issue, but upon probable cause, supported by Oath or affirmation, and particularly describing the place to be searched, and the persons or things to be seized.

No person shall be held to answer for a capital, or otherwise infamous crime, unless on a presentment or indictment of a Grand Jury, except in cases arising in the land or naval forces, or in the Militia, when in actual service in time of War or public danger; nor shall any person be subject for the same offence to be twice put in jeopardy of life or limb; nor shall be compelled in any Criminal Case to be a witness against himself, nor be deprived of life, liberty or property without due process of law; nor shall private property be taken for public use, without just compensation.

In all criminal prosecutions, the accused shall enjoy the right to a speedy and public trial, by an impartial jury of the State and district wherein the crime shall have been committed, which district shall have been previously ascertained by law, and to be informed of the nature and cause of the accusation; to be confronted with the witnesses against him; to have Compulsory process for obtaining Witnesses in his favour, and to have the Assistance of Counsel for his defence.

In Suits at common law, where the value in controversy shall exceed twenty dollars, the right of trial by jury shall be preserved, and no fact tried by a jury shall be otherwise reexamined in any Court of the [United] *Confederate* States, than according to the rules of the common law.

Excessive bail shall not be required, nor excessive fines imposed, nor cruel and unusual punishments inflicted.

Every law or resolution having the force of law, shall relate to but one subject, and that shall be expressed in the title.

Section X No State shall enter into any Treaty, Alliance, or Confederation; grant Letters of Marque and Reprisal; coin Money; [emit Bills of Credit;] make any Thing but gold and silver Coin a Tender in Payment of Debts; pass any Bill of Attainder, *or* ex post facto Law, or Law impairing the Obligation of Contracts, or grant any Title of Nobility.

No State shall, without the consent of the Congress, lay any Imposts or Duties on Imports or Exports, except what may be absolutely necessary for executing its inspection Laws: and the net Produce of all Duties and Imposts, laid by any State on Imports or Exports, shall be for the Use of the Treasury of the [United] *Confederate* States; and all such Laws shall be subject to the Revision and Control of the Congress.

No State shall, without the Consent of Congress, lay any Duty of Tonnage, *except on seagoing vessels, for the improvement of its rivers and harbors navigated by the said vessels; but such duties shall not conflict with any treaties of the Confederate States with foreign nations; and any surplus of revenue thus derived shall, after making such improvement, be paid into the common treasury; nor shall any State* keep Troops, or Ships of War in time of Peace, enter into any Agreement or Compact with another State, or with a foreign Power, or engage in War, unless actually invaded, or in such imminent Danger as will not admit of Delay. *But when any river divides or flows through two or more States, they may enter into compacts with each other to improve the navigation thereof.*

Article II

Section I [The executive Power shall be vested in a President of the United States of America. He shall hold his Office during the Term of four Years, and, together with the Vice President, chosen for the same Term, be elected, as follows:] *The executive power shall be vested in a President of the Confederate States of America. He and the Vice President shall hold their offices for the term of six years; but the President shall not be re-eligible. The President and Vice President shall be elected as follows:*

Each State shall appoint in such Manner as the Legislature thereof may direct, a Number of Electors, equal to the whole Number of Senators and Representatives to which the State may be entitled in the Congress; but no Senator or Representative, or Person holding an Office of Trust or Profit under the [United] *Confederate* States, shall be appointed an Elector.

The Electors shall meet in their respective States, and vote by ballot for President and Vice President, one of whom, at least, shall not be an inhabitant of the same State with themselves; they shall name in their ballots the person voted for as President, and in distinct ballots the person voted for as Vice President, and they shall make distinct lists of all persons voted for as President, and of all persons voted for as Vice President, and of the number of votes for each, which lists they shall sign and certify, and transmit sealed to the seat of the government of the [United] *Confederate* States, directed to the President of the Senate;—The President of the Senate shall, in the presence of the Senate and House of Representatives, open all the certificates and the votes shall then be counted;—The person having the greatest number of votes for President shall be the President, if such number be a majority of the whole number of Electors appointed; and if no person have such majority, then from the persons having the highest numbers not exceeding three on the list of those voted for as President, the House of Representatives shall choose immediately, by ballot, the President. But in choosing the President, the votes shall be taken by States, the representation from each State having one vote; a quorum for this purpose shall consist of a member or members from two-thirds of the States, and a majority of all the States shall be necessary to a choice. And if the House of Representatives shall not choose a President whenever the right of choice shall devolve upon them, before the fourth day of March next following, then the Vice President shall act as President, as in the case of the death or other constitutional disability of the President. The person having the greatest number of votes as Vice President shall be the Vice President, if such number be a majority of the whole number of Electors appointed, and if no person have a majority, then from the two highest numbers on the list the Senate shall choose the Vice President; a quorum for the purpose shall consist of two-thirds of the whole number of Senators, and a majority of the whole number shall be necessary to a choice. But no person constitutionally ineligible to the office of President shall be eligible to that of Vice President of the [United] *Confederate* States.

The Congress may determine the Time of choosing the Electors, and the Day on which they shall give their Votes; which Day shall be the same throughout the [United] *Confederate* States.

No Person except a natural-born Citizen [or a Citizen of the United States] *of the Confederate States, or a citizen thereof,* at the time of the Adoption of this Constitution, *or a citizen thereof born in the United States prior to the 20th of December, 1860,* shall be eligible to the Office of President; neither shall any Person be eligible to that Office who shall not have attained to the Age of thirty-five Years, and been fourteen Years a Resident within the [United States] *limits of the Confederate States, as they may exist at the time of his election.*

In Cases of the Removal of the President from Office, or of his Death, Resignation, or Inability to discharge the Powers and Duties of the said Office, the same shall devolve on the Vice President, and the Congress may by Law provide for the Case of Removal, Death, Resignation, or Inability, both of the President and Vice President, declaring what Officer shall then act as President, and such Officer shall act accordingly, until the Disability be removed, or a President shall be elected.

The President shall, at stated Times, receive for his Services, a Compensation, which shall neither be increased nor diminished during the Period for which he shall have been elected, and he shall not receive within that Period any other Emolument from the [United] *Confederate* States or any of them.

Before he enters on the Execution of his Office, he shall take the following Oath or Affirmation—"I do solemnly swear (or affirm) that I will faithfully execute the Office of President of the [United] *Confederate* States, and will to the best of my Ability, preserve, protect and defend the Constitution [of the United States] *thereof.*"

Section II   The President shall be Commander in Chief of the Army and Navy of the [United] *Confederate* States, and of the Militia of the several States, when called into the actual Service of the [United] *Confederate* States; he may require the Opinion, in writing, of the principal Officer in each of the executive Departments, upon any Subject relating to the Duties of their respective Offices, and he shall have Power to grant Reprieves and Pardons for Offenses against the [United] *Confederate* States, except in Cases of Impeachment.

He shall have Power, by and with the Advice and Consent of the Senate, to make Treaties, provided two-thirds of the Senators present concur; and he shall nominate, and by and with the Advice and Consent of the Senate, shall appoint Ambassadors, other public Ministers and Consuls, Judges of the supreme Court, and all other Officers of the [United] *Confederate* States, whose Appointments are not herein otherwise provided for, and which shall be established by Law: but the Congress may by Law vest the Appointment of such inferior Officers, as they think proper, in the President alone, in the Courts of Law, or in the Heads of Departments. *The principal officer in each of the executive departments, and all persons connected with the diplomatic service, may be removed from office at the pleasure of the President. All other civil officers of the executive department may be removed at any time by the President, or other appointing power, when their services are unnecessary, or for dishonesty, incapacity, inefficiency, misconduct, or neglect of duty; and when so removed, the removal shall be reported to the Senate, together with the reasons therefor.*

The President shall have Power to fill [up] all Vacancies that may happen during the Recess of the Senate, by granting Commissions which shall expire at the End of their next Session.

Section III   [He] *The President* shall from time to time give to the Congress Information of the State of the [Union] *Confederacy,* and recommend to their Consideration such Measures as he shall judge necessary and expedient; he may, on extraordinary Occasions, convene both Houses, or either of them, and in Case of Disagreement between them, with Respect to the Time of Adjournment, he may adjourn them to such Time as he shall think proper;

he shall receive Ambassadors and other public Ministers; he shall take Care that the Laws be faithfully executed, and shall Commission all the officers of the [United] *Confederate* States.

Section IV   The President, Vice President and all civil Officers of the [United] *Confederate* States, shall be removed from Office or Impeachment for, and Conviction of, Treason, Bribery, or other high Crimes and Misdemeanors.

Article III

Section I   The judicial Power of the [United] *Confederate* States shall be vested in one [supreme] *Superior* Court, and in such inferior Courts as the Congress may from time to time ordain and establish. The Judges, both of the supreme and inferior Courts, shall hold their Offices during good Behavior, and shall, at stated Times, receive for their Services a Compensation, which shall not be diminished during their Continuance in Office.

Section II   The judicial Power shall extend to all cases [in Law and Equity, arising under this Constitution], *arising under this Constitution, in law and equity,* the Laws of the [United] *Confederate* States, and Treaties made, or which shall be made, under their Authority;—to all Cases affecting Ambassadors, other public Ministers, and Consuls;—to all Cases of admiralty and maritime Jurisdiction;—to Controversies to which the [United] *Confederate* States shall be a Party;—to Controversies between two or more States;—between a State and Citizens of another State *where the State is plaintiff;*—*between* Citizens *claiming lands under grants* of different States,—[between Citizens of the same State claiming Lands under Grants of different States,] and between a State, or the Citizens thereof, and foreign States, Citizens or Subjects; *but no State shall be sued by a citizen or subject of any foreign State.*

In all Cases affecting Ambassadors, other public Ministers and Consuls, and those in which a State shall be Party, the supreme Court shall have original Jurisdiction. In all the other Cases before mentioned, the supreme Court shall have appellate Jurisdiction, both as to Law and Fact, with such Exceptions, and under such Regulations as the Congress shall make.

The Trial of all Crimes, except in Cases of Impeachment, shall be by Jury; and such Trial shall be held in the State where the said Crime[s] shall have been committed; but when not committed within any State, the Trial shall be at such Place or Places as the Congress may by Law have directed.

Section III   Treason against the [United] *Confederate* States shall consist only in levying War against them,

THE CONSTITUTION OF THE CONFEDERATE STATES OF AMERICA

or in adhering to their Enemies, giving them Aid and Comfort. No Person shall be convicted of Treason unless on the Testimony of two Witnesses to the same overt Act, or on Confession in open Court.

The Congress shall have Power to declare the Punishment of Treason, but no Attainder of Treason shall work Corruption of Blood, or Forfeiture except during the Life of the Person attainted.

Article IV

Section I Full Faith and Credit shall be given in each State to the public Acts, Records, and judicial Proceedings of every other State. And the Congress may by general Laws prescribe the Manner in which such Acts, Records and Proceedings shall be proved, and the Effect thereof.

Section II The Citizens of each State shall be entitled to all Privileges and Immunities of Citizens in the several States, *and shall have the right of transit and sojourn in any State of this Confederacy, with their slaves and other property; and the right of property in such slaves shall not be impaired.*

A Person charged in any State with Treason, Felony, or other Crime, who shall flee from Justice, and be found in another State, shall on Demand of the executive Authority of the State from which he fled, be delivered up, to be removed to the State having Jurisdiction of the Crime.

No *slave or* Person held to Service or Labor in [one State] *any State or Territory of the Confederate States* under the Laws thereof, escaping *or unlawfully carried* into another, shall, in Consequence of any Law or Regulation therein, be discharged from such Service or Labor, but shall be delivered up on Claim of the Party to whom such *slave belongs, or to whom such* Service or Labor may be due.

Section III [New States may be admitted by the Congress into this Union;] *Other States may be admitted into this Confederacy by a vote of two-thirds of the whole House of Representatives and two-thirds of the Senate, the Senate voting by States*; but no new State shall be formed or erected within the Jurisdiction of any other State; nor any State be formed by the Junction of two or more States, or Parts of States, without the Consent of the Legislatures of the States concerned as well as of the Congress.

The Congress shall have Power to dispose of and make all needful Rules and Regulations [respecting the Territory or other Property belonging to the United States; and nothing in this Constitution shall be so construed as to Prejudice any Claims of the United States, or of any particular State] *concerning the property of the Confederate States, including the lands thereof.*

The Confederate States may acquire new territory, and Congress shall have power to legislate and provide governments for the inhabitants of all territory belonging to the Confederate States lying without the limits of the several States, and may permit them, at such times and in such manner as it may by law provide, to form States to be admitted into the Confederacy. In all such territory the institution of negro slavery as it now exists in the Confederate States shall be recognized and protected by Congress and by the territorial government, and the inhabitants of the several Confederate States and territories shall have the right to take to such territory any slaves lawfully held by them in any of the States or Territories of the Confederate States.

[Section IV] The [United] *Confederate* States shall guarantee to every State [in this Union] *that now is, or hereafter may become, a member of this Confederacy*, a Republican Form of Government, and shall protect each of them against Invasion; and on Application of the Legislature, or of the Executive (when the Legislature [cannot be convened] *is not in session*) against domestic Violence.

Article V

[The Congress, whenever two-thirds of both Houses shall deem it necessary, shall propose Amendments to this Constitution, or on the Application of the Legislatures of two-thirds of the several States, shall call a Convention for proposing Amendments, which, in either Case, shall be valid to all Intents and Purposes, as Part of this Constitution, when ratified by the Legislatures of three-fourths of the several States, or by Conventions in three-fourths thereof, as the one or the other Mode of Ratification may be proposed by the Congress; Provided that no Amendment which may be made prior to the Year one thousand eight hundred and eight shall in any Manner affect the first and fourth Clauses in the Ninth Section of the first Article; and that no State, without its Consent, shall be deprived of its equal Suffrage in the Senate.]

Upon the demand of any three States, legally assembled in their several Conventions, the Congress shall summon a Convention of all the States, to take into consideration such amendments to the Constitution as the said States shall concur in suggesting at the time when the said demand is made; and should any of the proposed amendments to the Constitution be agreed on by the said Convention—voting by States—and the same be ratified by the Legislatures of two-thirds of the several States, or by Conventions in two-thirds thereof—as the one or the other mode of ratification may be proposed by the general Convention—they shall henceforward form a part of this Constitution. But no State shall, without its consent, be deprived of its equal representation in the Senate.

Article VI

The Government established by this Constitution is the successor of the Provisional Government of the

Confederate States of America, and all laws passed by the latter shall continue in force until the same shall be repealed or modified; and all the officers appointed by the same shall remain in office until their successors are appointed and qualified or the offices abolished.

All Debts contracted and Engagements entered into, before the Adoption of this Constitution, shall be as valid against the [United] *Confederate* States under this Constitution, as under the [Confederation] *Provisional Government.*

This Constitution and the Laws of the [United] *Confederate* States [which shall be] made in Pursuance thereof; and all Treaties made, or which shall be made, under the authority of the [United] *Confederate* States, shall be the supreme Law of the Land; and the Judges in every State shall be bound thereby, any Thing in the Constitution or Laws of any State to the Contrary notwithstanding.

The Senators and Representatives before mentioned, and the Members of the several State Legislatures, and all executive and judicial Officers, both of the [United] *Confederate* States and of the several States, shall be bound by Oath or Affirmation, to support this Constitution; but no religious Test shall ever be required as a Qualification to any Office or public Trust under the [United] *Confederate* States.

The enumeration in the Constitution, of certain rights, shall not be construed to deny or disparage others retained by the people *of the several States.*

The powers not delegated to the [United] *Confederate* States by the Constitution, nor prohibited by it to the States, are reserved to the States respectively, or to the people.

Article VII

The Ratification of the Conventions of [nine] *five* States shall be sufficient for the Establishment of this Constitution between the States so ratifying the same.

When five States shall have ratified this Constitution, in the manner before specified, the Congress under the Provisional Constitution shall prescribe the time for holding the election of President and Vice President; and for the meeting of the electoral college; and for counting the votes and inaugurating the President. They shall also prescribe the time for holding the first election of members of Congress under this Constitution, and the time for assembling the same. Until the assembling of such Congress, the Congress under the Provisional Constitution shall continue to exercise the legislative powers granted them, not extending beyond the time limited by the Constitution of the Provisional Government.

[Done in Convention by the Unanimous Consent of the States present, the Seventeenth Day of September in the Year of our Lord one thousand seven hundred and eighty-seven and of the Independence of the United States of America the Twelfth.] *Adopted unanimously March 11, 1861.*

Facts and Figures: Government, Economy, and Demographics

U.S. Politics and Government

PRESIDENTIAL ELECTIONS

Year	Candidates	Parties	Popular Vote	Percentage of Popular Vote	Electoral Vote	Percentage of Voter Participation
1789	**GEORGE WASHINGTON (Va.)***				69	
	John Adams				34	
	Others				35	
1792	**GEORGE WASHINGTON (Va.)**				132	
	John Adams				77	
	George Clinton				50	
	Others				5	
1796	**JOHN ADAMS (Mass.)**	Federalist			71	
	Thomas Jefferson	Democratic-Republican			68	
	Thomas Pinckney	Federalist			59	
	Aaron Burr	Dem.-Rep.			30	
	Others				48	
1800	**THOMAS JEFFERSON (Va.)**	Dem.-Rep.			73	
	Aaron Burr	Dem.-Rep.			73	
	John Adams	Federalist			65	
	C. C. Pinckney	Federalist			64	
	John Jay	Federalist			1	
1804	**THOMAS JEFFERSON (Va.)**	Dem.-Rep.			162	
	C. C. Pinckney	Federalist			14	
1808	**JAMES MADISON (Va.)**	Dem.-Rep.			122	
	C. C. Pinckney	Federalist			47	
	George Clinton	Dem.-Rep.			6	
1812	**JAMES MADISON (Va.)**	Dem.-Rep.			128	
	De Witt Clinton	Federalist			89	
1816	**JAMES MONROE (Va.)**	Dem.-Rep.			183	
	Rufus King	Federalist			34	
1820	**JAMES MONROE (Va.)**	Dem.-Rep.			231	
	John Quincy Adams	Dem.-Rep.			1	
1824	**JOHN Q. ADAMS (Mass.)**	Dem.-Rep.	108,740	30.5	84	26.9
	Andrew Jackson	Dem.-Rep.	153,544	43.1	99	
	William H. Crawford	Dem.-Rep.	46,618	13.1	41	
	Henry Clay	Dem.-Rep.	47,136	13.2	37	
1828	**ANDREW JACKSON (Tenn.)**	Democratic	647,286	56.0	178	57.6
	John Quincy Adams	National Republican	508,064	44.0	83	

*State of residence when elected president.

Year	Candidates	Parties	Popular Vote	Percentage of Popular Vote	Electoral Vote	Percentage of Voter Participation
1832	**ANDREW JACKSON (Tenn.)**	Democratic	687,502	55.0	219	55.4
	Henry Clay	National Republican	530,189	42.4	49	
	John Floyd	Independent			11	
	William Wirt	Anti-Mason	33,108	2.6	7	
1836	**MARTIN VAN BUREN (N.Y.)**	Democratic	765,483	50.9	170	57.8
	W. H. Harrison	Whig			73	
	Hugh L. White	Whig	739,795	49.1	26	
	Daniel Webster	Whig			14	
	W. P. Mangum	Independent			11	
1840	**WILLIAM H. HARRISON (Ohio)**	Whig	1,274,624	53.1	234	80.2
	Martin Van Buren	Democratic	1,127,781	46.9	60	
	J. G. Birney	Liberty	7,069		—	
1844	**JAMES K. POLK (Tenn.)**	Democratic	1,338,464	49.6	170	78.9
	Henry Clay	Whig	1,300,097	48.1	105	
	J. G. Birney	Liberty	62,300	2.3	—	
1848	**ZACHARY TAYLOR (La.)**	Whig	1,360,967	47.4	163	72.7
	Lewis Cass	Democratic	1,222,342	42.5	127	
	Martin Van Buren	Free-Soil	291,263	10.1	—	
1852	**FRANKLIN PIERCE (N.H.)**	Democratic	1,601,117	50.9	254	69.6
	Winfield Scott	Whig	1,385,453	44.1	42	
	John P. Hale	Free-Soil	155,825	5.0	—	
1856	**JAMES BUCHANAN (Pa.)**	Democratic	1,832,995	45.3	174	78.9
	John C. Frémont	Republican	1,339,932	33.1	114	
	Millard Fillmore	American	871,731	21.6	8	
1860	**ABRAHAM LINCOLN (Ill.)**	Republican	1,865,593	39.8	180	81.2
	Stephen A. Douglas	Democratic	1,382,713	29.5	12	
	John C. Breckinridge	Democratic	848,356	18.1	72	
	John Bell	Union	592,906	12.6	39	
1864	**ABRAHAM LINCOLN (Ill.)**	Republican	2,206,938	55.0	212	73.8
	George B. McClellan	Democratic	1,803,787	45.0	21	
1868	**ULYSSES S. GRANT (Ill.)**	Republican	3,012,833	52.7	214	78.1
	Horatio Seymour	Democratic	2,703,249	47.3	80	
1872	**ULYSSES S. GRANT (Ill.)**	Republican	3,597,132	55.6	286	71.3
	Horace Greeley	Democratic; Liberal Republican	2,834,125	43.9	66	
1876	**RUTHERFORD B. HAYES (Ohio)**	Republican	4,036,572	48.0	185	81.8
	Samuel J. Tilden	Democratic	4,284,020	51.0	184	
1880	**JAMES A. GARFIELD (Ohio)**	Republican	4,454,416	48.5	214	79.4
	Winfield S. Hancock	Democratic	4,444,952	48.1	155	
1884	**GROVER CLEVELAND (N.Y.)**	Democratic	4,879,507	48.5	219	77.5
	James G. Blaine	Republican	4,850,293	48.2	182	
1888	**BENJAMIN HARRISON (Ind.)**	Republican	5,439,853	47.9	233	79.3
	Grover Cleveland	Democratic	5,540,309	48.6	168	
1892	**GROVER CLEVELAND (N.Y.)**	Democratic	5,555,426	46.1	277	74.7
	Benjamin Harrison	Republican	5,182,690	43.0	145	
	James B. Weaver	People's	1,029,846	8.5	22	
1896	**WILLIAM McKINLEY (Ohio)**	Republican	7,104,779	51.1	271	79.3
	William J. Bryan	Democratic-People's	6,502,925	47.7	176	
1900	**WILLIAM McKINLEY (Ohio)**	Republican	7,207,923	51.7	292	73.2
	William J. Bryan	Dem.-Populist	6,358,133	45.5	155	

Year	Candidates	Parties	Popular Vote	Percentage of Popular Vote	Electoral Vote	Percentage of Voter Participation
1904	**THEODORE ROOSEVELT (N.Y.)**	Republican	7,623,486	57.9	336	65.2
	Alton B. Parker	Democratic	5,077,911	37.6	140	
	Eugene V. Debs	Socialist	402,283	3.0	—	
1908	**WILLIAM H. TAFT (Ohio)**	Republican	7,678,908	51.6	321	65.4
	William J. Bryan	Democratic	6,409,104	43.1	162	
	Eugene V. Debs	Socialist	420,793	2.8	—	
1912	**WOODROW WILSON (N.J.)**	Democratic	6,293,454	41.9	435	58.8
	Theodore Roosevelt	Progressive	4,119,538	27.4	88	
	William H. Taft	Republican	3,484,980	23.2	8	
	Eugene V. Debs	Socialist	900,672	6.1	—	
1916	**WOODROW WILSON (N.J.)**	Democratic	9,129,606	49.4	277	61.6
	Charles E. Hughes	Republican	8,538,221	46.2	254	
	A. L. Benson	Socialist	585,113	3.2	—	
1920	**WARREN G. HARDING (Ohio)**	Republican	16,143,407	60.5	404	49.2
	James M. Cox	Democratic	9,130,328	34.2	127	
	Eugene V. Debs	Socialist	919,799	3.4	—	
1924	**CALVIN COOLIDGE (Mass.)**	Republican	15,725,016	54.0	382	48.9
	John W. Davis	Democratic	8,386,503	28.8	136	
	Robert M. La Follette	Progressive	4,822,856	16.6	13	
1928	**HERBERT HOOVER (Calif.)**	Republican	21,391,381	58.2	444	56.9
	Alfred E. Smith	Democratic	15,016,443	40.9	87	
	Norman Thomas	Socialist	267,835	0.7	—	
1932	**FRANKLIN D. ROOSEVELT (N.Y.)**	Democratic	22,809,638	57.4	472	56.9
	Herbert Hoover	Republican	15,758,901	39.7	59	
	Norman Thomas	Socialist	881,951	2.2	—	
1936	**FRANKLIN D. ROOSEVELT (N.Y.)**	Democratic	27,751,597	60.8	523	61.0
	Alfred M. Landon	Republican	16,679,583	36.5	8	
	William Lemke	Union	882,479	1.9	—	
1940	**FRANKLIN D. ROOSEVELT (N.Y.)**	Democratic	27,244,160	54.8	449	62.5
	Wendell Willkie	Republican	22,305,198	44.8	82	
1944	**FRANKLIN D. ROOSEVELT (N.Y.)**	Democratic	25,602,504	53.5	432	55.9
	Thomas E. Dewey	Republican	22,006,285	46.0	99	
1948	**HARRY S. TRUMAN (Mo.)**	Democratic	24,105,695	49.5	303	53.0
	Thomas E. Dewey	Republican	21,969,170	45.1	189	
	J. Strom Thurmond	States'-Rights Democratic	1,169,021	2.4	38	
	Henry A. Wallace	Progressive	1,156,103	2.4	—	
1952	**DWIGHT D. EISENHOWER (N.Y.)**	Republican	33,936,252	55.1	442	63.3
	Adlai Stevenson	Democratic	27,314,992	44.4	89	
1956	**DWIGHT D. EISENHOWER (N.Y.)**	Republican	35,575,420	57.6	457	60.6
	Adlai Stevenson	Democratic	26,033,066	42.1	73	
	Other	—	—		1	
1960	**JOHN F. KENNEDY (Mass.)**	Democratic	34,227,096	49.9	303	62.8
	Richard M. Nixon	Republican	34,108,546	49.6	219	
	Other	—	—		15	
1964	**LYNDON B. JOHNSON (Texas)**	Democratic	43,126,506	61.1	486	61.7
	Barry M. Goldwater	Republican	27,176,799	38.5	52	
1968	**RICHARD M. NIXON (N.Y.)**	Republican	31,770,237	43.4	301	60.9
	Hubert H. Humphrey	Democratic	31,270,533	42.7	191	
	George Wallace	American Indep.	9,906,141	13.5	46	
1972	**RICHARD M. NIXON (N.Y.)**	Republican	47,169,911	60.7	520	55.2
	George S. McGovern	Democratic	29,170,383	37.5	17	
	Other	—	—		1	

Year	Candidates	Parties	Popular Vote	Percentage of Popular Vote	Electoral Vote	Percentage of Voter Participation
1976	**JIMMY CARTER (Ga.)**	Democratic	40,828,587	50.0	297	53.5
	Gerald R. Ford	Republican	39,147,613	47.9	241	
	Other	—	1,575,459	2.1	—	
1980	**RONALD REAGAN (Calif.)**	Republican	43,901,812	50.7	489	54.0
	Jimmy Carter	Democratic	35,483,820	41.0	49	
	John B. Anderson	Independent	5,719,722	6.6	—	
	Ed Clark	Libertarian	921,188	1.1	—	
1984	**RONALD REAGAN (Calif.)**	Republican	54,455,075	59.0	525	53.1
	Walter Mondale	Democratic	37,577,185	41.0	13	
1988	**GEORGE H. W. BUSH (Texas)**	Republican	47,946,422	54.0	426	50.2
	Michael S. Dukakis	Democratic	41,016,429	46.0	112	
1992	**WILLIAM J. CLINTON (Ark.)**	Democratic	44,908,254	42.3	370	55.9
	George H. W. Bush	Republican	39,102,282	37.4	168	
	H. Ross Perot	Independent	19,721,433	18.9	—	
1996	**WILLIAM J. CLINTON (Ark.)**	Democratic	47,401,185	49.2	379	49.0
	Robert Dole	Republican	39,197,469	40.7	159	
	H. Ross Perot	Independent	8,085,294	8.4	—	
2000	**GEORGE W. BUSH (Texas)**	Republican	50,456,062	47.8	271	51.2
	Al Gore	Democratic	50,996,862	48.4	267	
	Ralph Nader	Green Party	2,858,843	2.7	—	
	Patrick J. Buchanan	—	438,760	.4	—	

PRESIDENTS, VICE PRESIDENTS, AND SECRETARIES OF STATE

The Washington Administration (1789–1797)
Vice President	John Adams	1789–1797
Secretary of State	Thomas Jefferson	1789–1793
	Edmund Randolph	1794–1795
	Timothy Pickering	1795–1797

The John Adams Administration (1797–1801)
Vice President	Thomas Jefferson	1797–1801
Secretary of State	Timothy Pickering	1797–1800
	John Marshall	1800–1801

The Jefferson Administration (1801–1809)
Vice President	Aaron Burr	1801–1805
	George Clinton	1805–1809
Secretary of State	James Madison	1801–1809

The Madison Administration (1809–1817)
Vice President	George Clinton	1809–1813
	Elbridge Gerry	1813–1817
Secretary of State	Robert Smith	1809–1811
	James Monroe	1811–1817

The Monroe Administration (1817–1825)
Vice President	Daniel Tompkins	1817–1825
Secretary of State	John Quincy Adams	1817–1825

The John Quincy Adams Administration (1825–1829)
Vice President	John C. Calhoun	1825–1829
Secretary of State	Henry Clay	1825–1829

The Jackson Administration (1829–1837)
Vice President	John C. Calhoun	1829–1833
	Martin Van Buren	1833–1837
Secretary of State	Martin Van Buren	1829–1831
	Edward Livingston	1831–1833
	Louis McLane	1833–1834
	John Forsyth	1834–1837

The Van Buren Administration (1837–1841)
Vice President	Richard M. Johnson	1837–1841
Secretary of State	John Forsyth	1837–1841

The William Harrison Administration (1841)
Vice President	John Tyler	1841
Secretary of State	Daniel Webster	1841

The Tyler Administration (1841–1845)
Vice President	None	
Secretary of State	Daniel Webster	1841–1843
	Hugh S. Legaré	1843
	Abel P. Upshur	1843–1844
	John C. Calhoun	1844–1845

The Polk Administration (1845–1849)

Vice President	George M. Dallas	1845–1849
Secretary of State	James Buchanan	1845–1849

The Taylor Administration (1849–1850)

Vice President	Millard Fillmore	1849–1850
Secretary of State	John M. Clayton	1849–1850

The Fillmore Administration (1850–1853)

Vice President	None	
Secretary of State	Daniel Webster	1850–1852
	Edward Everett	1852–1853

The Pierce Administration (1853–1857)

Vice President	William R. King	1853–1857
Secretary of State	William L. Marcy	1853–1857

The Buchanan Administration (1857–1861)

Vice President	John C. Breckinridge	1857–1861
Secretary of State	Lewis Cass	1857–1860
	Jeremiah S. Black	1860–1861

The Lincoln Administration (1861–1865)

Vice President	Hannibal Hamlin	1861–1865
	Andrew Johnson	1865
Secretary of State	William H. Seward	1861–1865

The Andrew Johnson Administration (1865–1869)

Vice President	None	
Secretary of State	William H. Seward	1865–1869

The Grant Administration (1869–1877)

Vice President	Schuyler Colfax	1869–1873
	Henry Wilson	1873–1877
Secretary of State	Elihu B. Washburne	1869
	Hamilton Fish	1869–1877

The Hayes Administration (1877–1881)

Vice President	William A. Wheeler	1877–1881
Secretary of State	William M. Evarts	1877–1881

The Garfield Administration (1881)

Vice President	Chester A. Arthur	1881
Secretary of State	James G. Blaine	1881

The Arthur Administration (1881–1885)

Vice President	None	
Secretary of State	F. T. Frelinghuysen	1881–1885

The Cleveland Administration (1885–1889)

Vice President	Thomas A. Hendricks	1885–1889
Secretary of State	Thomas F. Bayard	1885–1889

The Benjamin Harrison Administration (1889–1893)

Vice President	Levi P. Morton	1889–1893
Secretary of State	James G. Blaine	1889–1892
	John W. Foster	1892–1893

The Cleveland Administration (1893–1897)

Vice President	Adlai E. Stevenson	1893–1897
Secretary of State	Walter Q. Gresham	1893–1895
	Richard Olney	1895–1897

The McKinley Administration (1897–1901)

Vice President	Garret A. Hobart	1897–1901
	Theodore Roosevelt	1901
Secretary of State	John Sherman	1897–1898
	William R. Day	1898
	John Hay	1898–1901

The Theodore Roosevelt Administration (1901–1909)

Vice President	Charles Fairbanks	1905–1909
Secretary of State	John Hay	1901–1905
	Elihu Root	1905–1909
	Robert Bacon	1909

The Taft Administration (1909–1913)

Vice President	James S. Sherman	1909–1913
Secretary of State	Philander C. Knox	1909–1913

The Wilson Administration (1913–1921)

Vice President	Thomas R. Marshall	1913–1921
Secretary of State	William J. Bryan	1913–1915
	Robert Lansing	1915–1920
	Bainbridge Colby	1920–1921

The Harding Administration (1921–1923)

Vice President	Calvin Coolidge	1921–1923
Secretary of State	Charles E. Hughes	1921–1923

The Coolidge Administration (1923–1929)

Vice President	Charles G. Dawes	1925–1929
Secretary of State	Charles E. Hughes	1923–1925
	Frank B. Kellogg	1925–1929

The Hoover Administration (1929–1933)

Vice President	Charles Curtis	1929–1933
Secretary of State	Henry L. Stimson	1929–1933

The Franklin D. Roosevelt Administration (1933–1945)

Vice President	John Nance Garner	1933–1941
	Henry A. Wallace	1941–1945
	Harry S. Truman	1945
Secretary of State	Cordell Hull	1933–1944
	Edward R. Stettinius Jr.	1944–1945

The Truman Administration (1945–1953)

Vice President	Alben W. Barkley	1949–1953
Secretary of State	Edward R. Stettinius Jr.	1945
	James F. Byrnes	1945–1947
	George C. Marshall	1947–1949
	Dean G. Acheson	1949–1953

The Eisenhower Administration (1953–1961)

Vice President	Richard M. Nixon	1953–1961
Secretary of State	John Foster Dulles	1953–1959
	Christian A. Herter	1959–1961

The Kennedy Administration (1961–1963)

Vice President	Lyndon B. Johnson	1961–1963
Secretary of State	Dean Rusk	1961–1963

The Lyndon Johnson Administration (1963–1969)

Vice President	Hubert H. Humphrey	1965–1969
Secretary of State	Dean Rusk	1963–1969

The Nixon Administration (1969–1974)

Vice President	Spiro T. Agnew	1969–1973
	Gerald R. Ford	1973–1974
Secretary of State	William P. Rogers	1969–1973
	Henry A. Kissinger	1973–1974

The Ford Administration (1974–1977)

Vice President	Nelson A. Rockefeller	1974–1977
Secretary of State	Henry A. Kissinger	1974–1977

The Carter Administration (1977–1981)

Vice President	Walter F. Mondale	1977–1981
Secretary of State	Cyrus R. Vance	1977–1980
	Edmund Muskie	1980–1981

The Reagan Administration (1981–1989)

Vice President	George H. W. Bush	1981–1989
Secretary of State	Alexander M. Haig	1981–1982
	George P. Shultz	1982–1989

The George H. W. Bush Administration (1989–1993)

Vice President	J. Danforth Quayle	1989–1993
Secretary of State	James A. Baker III	1989–1992
	Lawrence S. Eagleburger	1992–1993

The Clinton Administration (1993–2001)

Vice President	Albert Gore	1993–2001
Secretary of State	Warren M. Christopher	1993–1997
	Madeleine K. Albright	1997–2001

The George W. Bush Administration (2001–)

Vice President	Richard Cheney	2001–
Secretary of State	Colin Powell	2001–

ADMISSION OF STATES TO THE UNION

State	Date of Admission	State	Date of Admission
Delaware	December 7, 1787	Rhode Island	May 29, 1790
Pennsylvania	December 12, 1787	Vermont	March 4, 1791
New Jersey	December 18, 1787	Kentucky	June 1, 1792
Georgia	January 2, 1788	Tennessee	June 1, 1796
Connecticut	January 9, 1788	Ohio	March 1, 1803
Massachusetts	February 6, 1788	Louisiana	April 30, 1812
Maryland	April 28, 1788	Indiana	December 11, 1816
South Carolina	May 23, 1788	Mississippi	December 10, 1817
New Hampshire	June 21, 1788	Illinois	December 3, 1818
Virginia	June 25, 1788	Alabama	December 14, 1819
New York	July 26, 1788	Maine	March 15, 1820
North Carolina	November 21, 1789	Missouri	August 10, 1821

ADMISSION OF STATES TO THE UNION

State	Date of Admission	State	Date of Admission
Arkansas	June 15, 1836	Colorado	August 1, 1876
Michigan	January 16, 1837	North Dakota	November 2, 1889
Florida	March 3, 1845	South Dakota	November 2, 1889
Texas	December 29, 1845	Montana	November 8, 1889
Iowa	December 28, 1846	Washington	November 11, 1889
Wisconsin	May 29, 1848	Idaho	July 3, 1890
California	September 9, 1850	Wyoming	July 10, 1890
Minnesota	May 11, 1858	Utah	January 4, 1896
Oregon	February 14, 1859	Oklahoma	November 16, 1907
Kansas	January 29, 1861	New Mexico	January 6, 1912
West Virginia	June 19, 1863	Arizona	February 14, 1912
Nevada	October 31, 1864	Alaska	January 3, 1959
Nebraska	March 1, 1867	Hawaii	August 21, 1959

SUPREME COURT JUSTICES

Name	Service	Appointed by	Name	Service	Appointed by
John Jay*	1789–1795	Washington	Philip P. Barbour	1836–1841	Jackson
James Wilson	1789–1798	Washington	John Catron	1837–1865	Van Buren
John Blair	1789–1796	Washington	John McKinley	1837–1852	Van Buren
John Rutledge	1790–1791	Washington	Peter V. Daniel	1841–1860	Van Buren
William Cushing	1790–1810	Washington	Samuel Nelson	1845–1872	Tyler
James Iredell	1790–1799	Washington	Levi Woodbury	1845–1851	Polk
Thomas Johnson	1791–1793	Washington	Robert C. Grier	1846–1870	Polk
William Paterson	1793–1806	Washington	Benjamin R. Curtis	1851–1857	Fillmore
John Rutledge†	1795	Washington	John A. Campbell	1853–1861	Pierce
Samuel Chase	1796–1811	Washington	Nathan Clifford	1858–1881	Buchanan
Oliver Ellsworth	1796–1799	Washington	Noah H. Swayne	1862–1881	Lincoln
Bushrod Washington	1798–1829	J. Adams	Samuel F. Miller	1862–1890	Lincoln
			David Davis	1862–1877	Lincoln
Alfred Moore	1799–1804	J. Adams	Stephen J. Field	1863–1897	Lincoln
John Marshall	1801–1835	J. Adams	**Salmon P. Chase**	1864–1873	Lincoln
William Johnson	1804–1834	Jefferson	William Strong	1870–1880	Grant
Henry B. Livingston	1806–1823	Jefferson	Joseph P. Bradley	1870–1892	Grant
Thomas Todd	1807–1826	Jefferson	Ward Hunt	1873–1882	Grant
Gabriel Duval	1811–1836	Madison	**Morrison R. Waite**	1874–1888	Grant
Joseph Story	1811–1845	Madison	John M. Harlan	1877–1911	Hayes
Smith Thompson	1823–1843	Monroe	William B. Woods	1880–1887	Hayes
Robert Trimble	1826–1828	J. Q. Adams	Stanley Matthews	1881–1889	Garfield
John McLean	1829–1861	Jackson	Horace Gray	1882–1902	Arthur
Henry Baldwin	1830–1844	Jackson	Samuel Blatchford	1882–1893	Arthur
James M. Wayne	1835–1867	Jackson	Lucius Q. C. Lamar	1888–1893	Cleveland
Roger B. Taney	1836–1864	Jackson	**Melville W. Fuller**	1888–1910	Cleveland
			David J. Brewer	1889–1910	B. Harrison
			Henry B. Brown	1890–1906	B. Harrison
			George Shiras	1892–1903	B. Harrison
			Howell E. Jackson	1893–1895	B. Harrison

*Chief Justices appear in bold type.
†Acting Chief Justice; Senate refused to confirm appointment.

Name	Service	Appointed by	Name	Service	Appointed by
Edward D. White	1894–1910	Cleveland	Harold H. Burton	1945–1958	Truman
Rufus W. Peckham	1896–1909	Cleveland	**Frederick M. Vinson**	1946–1953	Truman
Joseph McKenna	1898–1925	McKinley			
Oliver W. Holmes	1902–1932	T. Roosevelt	Tom C. Clark	1949–1967	Truman
William R. Day	1903–1922	T. Roosevelt	Sherman Minton	1949–1956	Truman
William H. Moody	1906–1910	T. Roosevelt	**Earl Warren**	1953–1969	Eisenhower
Horace H. Lurton	1910–1914	Taft	John Marshall Harlan	1955–1971	Eisenhower
Charles E. Hughes	1910–1916	Taft	William J. Brennan Jr.	1956–1990	Eisenhower
Willis Van Devanter	1910–1937	Taft	Charles E. Whittaker	1957–1962	Eisenhower
Edward D. White	1910–1921	Taft	Potter Stewart	1958–1981	Eisenhower
Joseph R. Lamar	1911–1916	Taft	Byron R. White	1962–1993	Kennedy
Mahlon Pitney	1912–1922	Taft	Arthur J. Goldberg	1962–1965	Kennedy
James C. McReynolds	1914–1941	Wilson	Abe Fortas	1965–1969	L. Johnson
			Thurgood Marshall	1967–1991	L. Johnson
Louis D. Brandeis	1916–1939	Wilson	**Warren E. Burger**	1969–1986	Nixon
John H. Clarke	1916–1922	Wilson	Harry A. Blackmun	1970–1994	Nixon
William H. Taft	1921–1930	Harding	Lewis F. Powell Jr.	1972–1988	Nixon
George Sutherland	1922–1938	Harding	William H. Rehnquist	1972–1986	Nixon
Pierce Butler	1923–1939	Harding	John Paul Stevens	1975–	Ford
Edward T. Sanford	1923–1930	Harding	Sandra Day O'Connor	1981–	Reagan
Harlan F. Stone	1925–1941	Coolidge			
Charles E. Hughes	1930–1941	Hoover	**William H. Rehnquist**	1986–	Reagan
Owen J. Roberts	1930–1945	Hoover			
Benjamin N. Cardozo	1932–1938	Hoover	Antonin Scalia	1986–	Reagan
Hugo L. Black	1937–1971	F. Roosevelt	Anthony M. Kennedy	1988–	Reagan
Stanley F. Reed	1938–1957	F. Roosevelt			
Felix Frankfurter	1939–1962	F. Roosevelt	David H. Souter	1990–	G. H. W. Bush
William O. Douglas	1939–1975	F. Roosevelt			
Frank Murphy	1940–1949	F. Roosevelt	Clarence Thomas	1991–	G. H. W. Bush
Harlan F. Stone	1941–1946	F. Roosevelt			
James F. Byrnes	1941–1942	F. Roosevelt	Ruth Bader Ginsburg	1993–	Clinton
Robert H. Jackson	1941–1954	F. Roosevelt			
Wiley B. Rutledge	1943–1949	F. Roosevelt	Stephen Breyer	1994–	Clinton

SIGNIFICANT SUPREME COURT CASES

Marbury v. Madison (1803)

This case established the right of the Supreme Court to review the constitutionality of laws. The decision involved judicial appointments made during the last hours of the administration of President John Adams. Some commissions, including that of William Marbury, had not yet been delivered when President Thomas Jefferson took office. Infuriated by the last-minute nature of Adams's Federalist appointments, Jefferson refused to send the undelivered commissions out, and Marbury decided to sue. The Supreme Court, presided over by John Marshall, a Federalist who had assisted Adams in the judicial appointments, ruled that although

Marbury's commission was valid and the new president should have delivered it, the Court could not compel him to do so. The Court based its reasoning on a finding that the grounds of Marbury's suit, resting in the Judiciary Act of 1789, were in conflict with the Constitution.

For the first time, the Court had overturned a national law on the grounds that it was unconstitutional. John Marshall had quietly established the concept of judicial review: The Supreme Court had given itself the authority to nullify acts of the other branches of the federal government. Although the Constitution provides for judicial review, the Court had not exercised this power before and did not use it again until 1857. It seems likely that if the Court had waited until 1857 to use this power, it would have been difficult to establish.

McCulloch v. Maryland (1819)

In 1816, Congress authorized the creation of a national bank. To protect its own banks from competition with a branch of the national bank in Baltimore, the state legislature of Maryland placed a tax of 2 percent on all notes issued by any bank operating in Maryland that was not chartered by the state. McCulloch, cashier of the Baltimore branch of the Bank of the United States, was convicted for refusing to pay the tax. Under the leadership of Chief Justice John Marshall, the Court ruled that the federal government had the power to establish a bank, even though that specific authority was not mentioned in the Constitution.

Marshall maintained that the authority could be reasonably implied from Article 1, section 8, which gives Congress the power to make all laws that are necessary and proper to execute the enumerated powers. Marshall also held that Maryland could not tax the national bank because in a conflict between federal and state laws, the federal law must take precedence. Thus he established the principles of implied powers and federal supremacy, both of which set a precedent for subsequent expansion of federal power at the expense of the states.

Scott v. Sandford (1857)

Dred Scott was a slave who sued for his own and his family's freedom on the grounds that, with his master, he had traveled to and lived in free territory that did not allow slavery. When his case reached the Supreme Court, the justices saw an opportunity to settle once and for all the vexing question of slavery in the territories. The Court's decision in this case proved that it enjoyed no special immunity from the sectional and partisan passions of the time. Five of the nine justices were from the South and seven were Democrats.

Chief Justice Roger B. Taney hated Republicans and detested racial equality; his decision reflects those prejudices. He wrote an opinion not only declaring that Scott was still a slave but also claiming that the Constitution denied citizenship or rights to blacks, that Congress had no right to exclude slavery from the territories, and that the Missouri Compromise was unconstitutional. While southern Democrats gloated over this seven-to-two decision, sectional tensions were further inflamed and the young Republican Party's claim that a hostile "slave power" was conspiring to destroy northern liberties was given further credence. The decision brought the nation closer to civil war and is generally regarded as the worst decision ever rendered by the Supreme Court.

Butchers' Benevolent Association of New Orleans v. Crescent City Livestock Landing and Slaughterhouse Co. (1873)

The *Slaughterhouse* cases, as the cases docketed under the *Butchers'* title were known, were the first legal test of the Fourteenth Amendment. To cut down on cases of cholera believed to be caused by contaminated water, the state of Louisiana prohibited the slaughter of livestock in New Orleans except in one slaughterhouse, effectively giving that slaughterhouse a monopoly. Other New Orleans butchers claimed that the state had deprived them of their occupation without due process of law, thus violating the Fourteenth Amendment.

In a five-to-four decision, the Court upheld the Louisiana law, declaring that the Fourteenth Amendment protected only the rights of federal citizenship, like voting in federal elections and interstate travel. The federal government thus was not obliged to protect basic civil rights from violation by state governments. This decision would have significant implications for African Americans and their struggle for civil rights in the twentieth century.

United States v. E. C. Knight Co. (1895)

Also known as the *Sugar Trust* case, this was among the first cases to reveal the weakness of the Sherman Antitrust Act in the hands of a pro-business Supreme Court. In 1895, American Sugar Refining Company purchased four other sugar producers, including the E. C. Knight Company, and thus took control of more than 98 percent of the sugar refining in the United States. In an effort to limit monopoly, the government brought suit against all five of the companies for violating the Sherman Antitrust Act, which outlawed trusts and other business combinations in restraint of trade. The Court dismissed the suit, however, arguing that the law applied only to commerce and not to manufacturing, defining the latter as a local concern and not part of the interstate commerce that the government could regulate.

Plessy v. Ferguson (1896)

African American Homer Plessy challenged a Louisiana law that required segregation on trains passing through the state. After ensuring that the railroad and the conductor knew that he was of mixed race (Plessy appeared to be white but under the racial code of Louisiana was classified as "colored" because he was one-eighth black), he refused to move to the "colored only" section of the coach. The Court ruled against Plessy by a vote of seven to one, declaring that "separate but equal" facilities were permissible according to section 1 of the Fourteenth Amendment, which calls upon the states to provide "equal protection of the laws" to anyone within their jurisdiction. Although the case was viewed as relatively insignificant at the time, it cast a long shadow over several decades.

Initially, the decision was viewed as a victory for segregationists, but in the 1930s and 1940s civil rights advocates referred to the doctrine of "separate but equal" in their efforts to end segregation. They argued that segregated institutions and accommodations were often *not* equal to those available to whites, and finally succeeded in overturning *Plessy* in *Brown v. Board of Education* in 1954 (see below).

Lochner v. New York (1905)

In this case, the Court ruled against a New York state law that prohibited employees from working in bakeries more than ten hours a day or sixty hours a week. The purpose of the law was to protect the health of workers, but the Court ruled that it was unconstitutional because it violated "freedom of contract" implicitly protected by the due process clause of the Fourteenth Amendment. Most of the justices believed strongly in a laissez-faire economic system that favored survival of the fittest. They felt that government protection of workers interfered with this system. In a dissenting opinion, Justice Oliver Wendell Holmes accused the majority of distorting the Constitution and of deciding the case on "an economic theory which a large part of the country does not entertain."

Muller v. Oregon (1908)

In 1905, Curt Muller, owner of a Portland, Oregon, laundry, demanded that one of his employees, Mrs. Elmer Gotcher, work more than the ten hours allowed as a maximum workday for women under Oregon law. Muller argued that the law violated his "freedom of contract" as established in prior Supreme Court decisions.

Progressive lawyer Louis D. Brandeis defended the Oregon law by arguing that a state could be justified in abridging freedom of contract when the health, safety, and welfare of workers was at issue. His innovative strategy drew on ninety-five pages of excerpts from factory and medical reports to substantiate his argument that there was a direct connection between long hours and the health of women and thus the health of the nation. In a unanimous decision, the Court upheld the Oregon law, but later generations of women fighting for equality would question the strategy of arguing that women's reproductive role entitled them to special treatment.

Schenck v. United States (1919)

During World War I, Charles Schenck and other members of the Socialist Party printed and mailed out flyers urging young men who were subject to the draft to oppose the war in Europe. In upholding the conviction of Schenck for publishing a pamphlet urging draft resistance, Justice Oliver Wendell Holmes established the "clear and present danger" test for freedom of speech. Such utterances as Schenck's during a time of national peril, Holmes wrote, could be considered the equivalent of shouting "Fire!" in a crowded theater. Congress had the right to protect the public against such an incitement to panic, the Court ruled in a unanimous decision. But the analogy was a false one. Schenck's pamphlet had little power to provoke a public firmly opposed to its message. Although Holmes later modified his position to state that the danger must relate to an immediate evil and a specific action, the "clear and present danger" test laid the groundwork for those who later sought to limit First Amendment freedoms.

Schechter Poultry Corp. v. United States (1935)

During the Great Depression, the National Industrial Recovery Act (NIRA), which was passed under President Franklin D. Roosevelt, established fair competition codes that were designed to help businesses. The Schechter brothers of New York City, who sold chickens, were convicted of violating the codes. The Supreme Court ruled that the NIRA unconstitutionally conferred legislative power on an administrative agency and overstepped the limits of federal power to regulate interstate commerce. The decision was a significant blow to the New Deal recovery program, demonstrating both historic American resistance to economic planning and the refusal of the business community to yield its autonomy unless it was forced to do so.

Brown v. Board of Education (1954)

In 1950, the families of eight Topeka, Kansas, children sued the Topeka Board of Education. The children were blacks who lived within walking distance of a whites-only school. The segregated school system required them to take a time-consuming, inconvenient, and dangerous route to get to a black school, and their parents argued that there was no reason their children should not be allowed to attend the nearest school. By the time the case reached the Supreme Court, it had been joined with similar cases regarding segregated schools in other states and the District of Columbia. A team of lawyers from the National Association for the Advancement of Colored People (NAACP), led by Thurgood Marshall (who would later be appointed to the Supreme Court), urged the Court to overturn the fifty-eight-year-old precedent established in *Plessy v. Ferguson*, which had enshrined "separate but equal" as the law of the land. A unanimous Court, led by Chief Justice Earl Warren, declared that "separate educational facilities are inherently unequal" and thus violate the Fourteenth Amendment. In 1955, the Court called for desegregation "with all deliberate speed" but established no deadline.

Roth v. United States (1957)

In 1957, New Yorker Samuel Roth was convicted of sending obscene materials through the mail in a case that ultimately reached the Supreme Court. With a six-to-three vote, the Court reaffirmed the historical view that obscenity is not protected by the First Amendment. Yet it broke new ground by declaring that a work could be judged obscene only if, "taken as a whole," it appealed to the "prurient interest" of "the average person."

Prior to this case, work could be judged obscene if portions were thought able to "deprave and corrupt" the most susceptible part of an audience (such as children). Thus, serious works of literature such as Theodore Dreiser's *An American Tragedy*, which was banned in Boston when first published, had received no protection. Although this decision continued to pose problems of definition, it did help to protect most works that attempt to convey ideas, even if those ideas have to do with sex, from the threat of obscenity laws.

Engel v. Vitale (1962)

In 1959, five parents with ten children in the New Hyde Park, New York, school system sued the school board. The parents argued that the so-called Regents' Prayer that public school students in New York recited at the start of every school day violated the doctrine of separation of church and state outlined in the First Amendment. In 1962, the Supreme Court voted six to one in favor of banning the Regents' Prayer.

The decision threw the religious community into an uproar. Many religious leaders expressed dismay and even shock; others welcomed the decision. Several efforts to introduce an amendment allowing school prayer have failed. Subsequent Supreme Court decisions have banned reading of the Bible in public schools. The Court has also declared mandatory flag saluting to be an infringement of religious and personal freedoms.

Gideon v. Wainwright (1963)

When Clarence Earl Gideon was tried for breaking into a poolroom, the state of Florida rejected his demand for a court-appointed lawyer as guaranteed by the Sixth Amendment. In 1963, the Court upheld his demand in a unanimous decision that established the obligation of states to provide attorneys for indigent defendants in felony cases. Prior to this decision, the right to an attorney had applied only to federal cases, not state cases. In its ruling in *Gideon v. Wainwright*, the Supreme Court applied the Sixth through the Fourteenth Amendments to the states. In 1972, the Supreme Court extended the right to legal representation to all cases, not just felony cases, in its decision in *Argersinger v. Hamlin*.

Griswold v. Connecticut (1965)

With a vote of seven to two, the Supreme Court reversed an "uncommonly silly law" (in the words of Justice Potter Stewart) that made it a crime for anyone in the state of Connecticut to use any drug, article, or instrument to prevent conception. *Griswold* became a landmark case because here, for the first time, the Court explicitly invested with full constitutional status "fundamental personal rights," such as the right to privacy, that were not expressly enumerated in the Bill of Rights. The majority opinion in the case held that the law infringed on the constitutionally protected right to privacy of married persons.

Although the Court had previously recognized fundamental rights not expressly enumerated in the Bill of Rights (such as the right to procreate in *Skinner v. Oklahoma* in 1942), *Griswold* was the first time the Court had justified, at length, the practice of investing such unenumerated rights with full constitutional status. Writing for the majority, Justice William O. Douglas explained that the First, Third, Fourth, Fifth, and Ninth Amendments imply "zones of privacy" that are the foundation for the general right to privacy affirmed in this case.

Miranda v. Arizona (1966)

In 1966, the Supreme Court, by a vote of five to four, upheld the case of Ernesto Miranda, who appealed a murder conviction on the grounds that police had gotten him to confess without giving him access to an attorney. The *Miranda* case was the culmination of the Court's efforts to find a meaningful way of determining whether police had used due process in extracting confessions from people accused of crimes. The *Miranda* decision upholds the Fifth Amendment protection against self-incrimination outside the courtroom and requires that suspects be given what came to be known as the "Miranda warning," which advises them of their right to remain silent and warns them that anything they say might be used against them in a court of law. Suspects must also be told that they have a right to counsel.

New York Times Co. v. United States (1971)

With a six-to-three vote, the Court upheld the right of the *New York Times* and the *Washington Post* to print materials from the so-called *Pentagon Papers*, a secret government study of U.S. policy in Vietnam, leaked by dissident Pentagon official Daniel Ellsberg. Since the papers revealed deception and secrecy in the conduct of the Vietnam War, the Nixon administration had quickly obtained a court injunction against their further publication, claiming that suppression was in the interests of national security. The Supreme Court's decision overturning the injunction strengthened the First Amendment protection of freedom of the press.

Furman v. Georgia (1972)

In this case, the Supreme Court ruled five to four that the death penalty for murder or rape violated the cruel and unusual punishment clause of the Eighth Amendment because the manner in which the death penalty was meted out was irregular, "arbitrary," and "cruel." In response, most states enacted new statutes that allow the death penalty to be imposed only after a postconviction hearing at which evidence must be presented to show that "aggravating" or "mitigating" circumstances were factors in the crime. If the postconviction hearing hands down a death sentence, the case is automatically reviewed by an appellate court.

In 1976, the Court ruled in *Gregg v. Georgia* that these statutes were not unconstitutional. In 1977, the Court ruled in *Coker v. Georgia* that the death penalty for rape was "disproportionate and excessive," thus allowing the death penalty only in murder cases. Between 1977 and 1991, some 150 people were executed in the United States. Public opinion polls indicate that about 70 percent of Americans favor the death penalty for murder. Capital punishment continues to generate controversy, however, as opponents argue that there is no evidence that the death penalty deters crime and that its use reflects racial and economic bias.

Roe v. Wade (1973)

In 1973, the Court found, by a vote of seven to two, that state laws restricting access to abortion violated a woman's right to privacy guaranteed by the due process clause of the Fourteenth Amendment. The decision was based on the cases of two women living in Texas and Georgia, both states with stringent antiabortion laws. Upholding the individual rights of both women and physicians, the Court ruled that the Constitution protects the right to abortion and that states cannot prohibit abortions in the early stages of pregnancy.

The decision stimulated great debate among legal scholars as well as the public. Critics argued that since abortion was never addressed in the Constitution, the Court could not claim that legislation violated fundamental values of the Constitution. They also argued that since abortion was a medical procedure with an acknowledged impact on a fetus, it was inappropriate to invoke the kind of "privacy" argument that was used in *Griswold v. Connecticut* (see page A-43), which was about contraception. Defenders suggested that the case should be argued as a case of gender discrimination, which did violate the equal protection clause of the Fourteenth Amendment. Others said that the right to privacy in sexual matters was indeed a fundamental right.

Regents of the University of California v. Bakke (1978)

When Allan Bakke, a white man, was not accepted by the University of California Medical School at Davis, he filed a lawsuit alleging that the admissions program, which set up different standards for test scores and grades for members of certain minority groups, violated the Civil Rights Act of 1964, which outlawed racial or ethnic preferences in programs supported by federal funds. Bakke further argued that the university's practice of setting aside spaces for minority applicants denied him equal protection as guaranteed by the Fourteenth Amendment. In a five-to-four decision, the Court ordered that Bakke be admitted to the medical school, yet it sanctioned affirmative action programs to attack the results of past discrimination as long as strict quotas or racial classifications were not involved.

Webster v. Reproductive Health Services (1989)

By a vote of five to four, the Court upheld several restrictions on the availability of abortions as imposed by Missouri state law. It upheld restrictions on the use of state property, including public hospitals, for abortions. It also upheld a provision requiring physicians to perform tests to determine the viability of a fetus that a doctor judged to be twenty weeks of age or older. Although the justices did not go so far as to overturn the decision in *Roe v. Wade* (see at left), the ruling galvanized interest groups on both sides of the abortion issue. Opponents of abortion pressured state legislatures to place greater restrictions on abortions; those who favored availability of abortion tried to mobilize public action by presenting the decision as a major threat to the right to choose abortion.

Cipollone v. Liggett (1992)

In a seven-to-two decision, the Court ruled in favor of the family of Rose Cipollone, a woman who died of lung cancer after smoking for forty-two years. The Court rejected arguments that health warnings on cigarette packages protected tobacco manufacturers from personal injury suits filed by smokers who contract cancer and other serious illnesses.

Miller v. Johnson (1995)

In a five-to-four decision, the Supreme Court ruled that voting districts created to increase the voting power of racial minorities were unconstitutional. The decision threatens dozens of congressional, state, and local voting districts that were drawn to give minorities more representation as had been required by the Justice Department under the Voting Rights Act. If states are required to redraw voting districts, the number of black members of Congress could be sharply reduced.

Romer v. Evans (1996)

In a six-to-three decision, the Court struck down a Colorado amendment that forbade local governments from banning discrimination against homosexuals. Writing for the majority, Justice Anthony Kennedy said that forbidding communities from taking action to protect the rights of homosexuals and not of other groups unlawfully deprived gays and lesbians of opportunities that were available to others. Kennedy based the decision on the guarantee of equal protection under the law as provided by the Fourteenth Amendment.

Bush v. Palm Beach County Canvassing Board (2000)

In a bitterly argued five-to-four decision, the Court reversed the Florida Supreme Court's previous order for a hand recount of contested presidential election ballots in several counties of that battleground state, effectively securing the presidency for Texas Republican governor George W. Bush. The ruling ended a protracted legal dispute between presidential candidates Bush and Vice President Al Gore while inflaming public opinion: For the first time since 1888, a president who failed to win the popular vote took office. Critics charged that the Supreme Court had applied partisanship rather than objectivity to the case, pointing out that the decision went against this Court's customary interpretation of the Constitution to favor state over federal authority.

The American Economy

THESE FIVE "SNAPSHOTS" of the U.S. economy show significant changes over the past century and a half. In 1849, the agricultural sector was by far the largest contributor to the economy. By the turn of the century, with advances in technology and an abundance of cheap labor and raw materials, the country had experienced remarkable industrial expansion and the manufacturing industries dominated. By 1950, the service sector had increased significantly, fueled by the consumerism of the 1920s and the post–World War II years, and the economy was becoming more diversified. Note that by 1990, the government's share in the economy had grown to more than 10 percent and activity in both the trade and manufacturing sectors had declined, partly as a result of competition from Western Europe and Asia. Manufacturing continued to decline, and by 2001 the service and finance, real estate, and insurance sectors had all grown steadily to eclipse it.

Main Sectors of the U.S. Economy: 1849, 1899, 1950, 1990, 2001

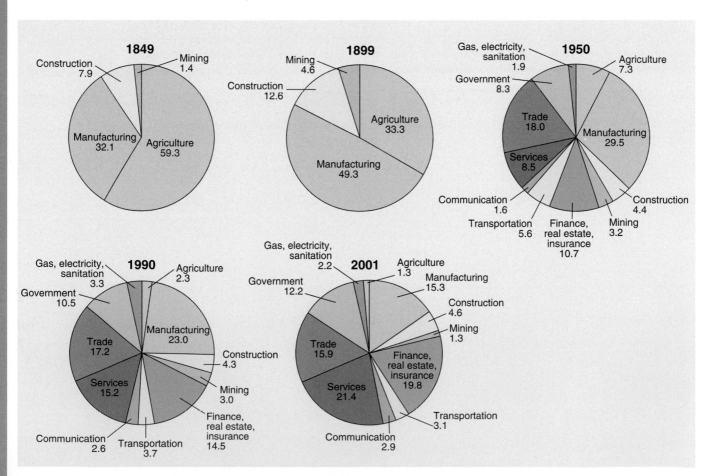

SOURCE: Data from *Historical Statistics of the United States, Colonial Times to 1970* (1975); *Statistical Abstract of the United States, 1998*; U.S. Bureau of Economic Analysis, *Industry Accounts Data, 2001*.

THE AMERICAN ECONOMY

FEDERAL SPENDING AND THE ECONOMY, 1790–2002

Year	Gross National Product (in billions)	Foreign Trade (in millions)		Federal Budget (in billions)	Federal Surplus/Deficit (in billions)	Federal Debt (in billions)
		Exports	Imports			
1790	NA	20	23	0.004	0.00015	0.076
1800	NA	71	91	0.011	0.0006	0.083
1810	NA	67	85	0.008	0.0012	0.053
1820	NA	70	74	0.018	−0.0004	0.091
1830	NA	74	71	0.015	0.100	0.049
1840	NA	132	107	0.024	−0.005	0.004
1850	NA	152	178	0.040	0.004	0.064
1860	NA	400	362	0.063	−0.01	0.065
1870	7.4	451	462	0.310	0.10	2.4
1880	11.2	853	761	0.268	0.07	2.1
1890	13.1	910	823	0.318	0.09	1.2
1900	18.7	1,499	930	0.521	0.05	1.2
1910	35.3	1,919	1,646	0.694	−0.02	1.1
1920	91.5	8,664	5,784	6.357	0.3	24.3
1930	90.4	4,013	3,500	3.320	0.7	16.3
1940	99.7	4,030	7,433	9.6	−2.7	43.0
1950	284.8	10,816	9,125	43.1	−2.2	257.4
1960	503.7	19,600	15,046	92.2	0.3	286.3
1970	977.1	42,700	40,189	195.6	−2.8	371.0
1980	2,631.7	220,600	244,871	590.9	−73.8	907.7
1990	5,832.2	393,600	495,300	1,253.2	−221.2	3,266.1
2000	9,848.0	1,070,054	1,445,438	1,788.8	236.4	5,701.9
2002	10,436.7	974,107	1,392,145	2,011.0	−157.8	6,255.4

SOURCE: *Historical Statistics of the U.S., Colonial Times to 1970* (1975), *Statistical Abstract of the U.S., 1996* (1996), *Statistical Abstract of the U.S., 1999* (1999), and *Statistical Abstract of the U.S., 2003* (2003).

A Demographic Profile of the United States and Its People

Population

FROM AN ESTIMATED 4,600 white inhabitants in 1630, the country's population grew to a total of just under 250 million in 1990. It is important to note that the U.S. census, first conducted in 1790 and the source of these figures, counted blacks, both free and slave, but did not include American Indians until 1860. The years 1790 to 1900 saw the most rapid population growth, with an average increase of 25 to 35 percent per decade. In addition to "natural" growth—birthrate exceeding death rate—immigration was also a factor in that rise, especially between 1840 and 1860, 1880 and 1890, and 1900 and 1910 (see table on page A-51). The twentieth century witnessed slower growth, partly a result of 1920s immigration restrictions and a decline in the birthrate, especially during the depression era and the 1960s and 1970s. The U.S. population is expected to reach almost 300 million by the year 2010.

POPULATION GROWTH, 1630–2000

Year	Population	Percent Increase	Year	Population	Percent Increase
1630	4,600	—	1820	9,638,453	33.1
1640	26,600	473.3	1830	12,866,020	33.5
1650	50,400	89.1	1840	17,069,453	32.7
1660	75,100	49.0	1850	23,191,876	35.9
1670	111,900	49.1	1860	31,443,321	35.6
1680	151,500	35.4	1870	39,818,449	26.6
1690	210,400	38.9	1880	50,155,783	26.0
1700	250,900	19.3	1890	62,947,714	25.5
1710	331,700	32.2	1900	75,994,575	20.7
1720	466,200	40.5	1910	91,972,266	21.0
1730	629,400	35.0	1920	105,710,620	14.9
1740	905,600	43.9	1930	122,775,046	16.1
1750	1,170,800	30.0	1940	131,669,275	7.2
1760	1,593,600	36.1	1950	150,697,361	14.5
1770	2,148,100	34.8	1960	179,323,175	19.0
1780	2,780,400	29.4	1970	203,302,031	13.4
1790	3,929,214	41.3	1980	226,542,199	11.4
1800	5,308,483	35.1	1990	248,718,302	9.8
1810	7,239,881	36.4	2000	281,422,509	13.1

Source: Historical Statistics of the U.S. (1960), Historical Statistics of the U.S., Colonial Times to 1970 (1975), Statistical Abstract of the U.S., 1996 (1996), and Statistical Abstract of the U.S., 2003 (2003).

A DEMOGRAPHIC PROFILE OF THE UNITED STATES AND ITS PEOPLE

Birthrate, 1820–2000

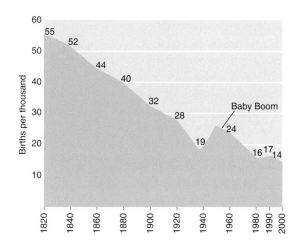

SOURCE: Data from *Historical Statistics of the U.S., Colonial Times to 1970* (1975) and *Statistical Abstract of the U.S., 2003* (2003).

Death Rate, 1900–2000

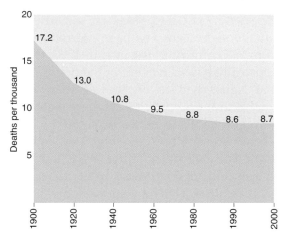

SOURCE: Data from *Historical Statistics of the U.S., Colonial Times to 1970* (1975) and *Statistical Abstract of the U.S., 2003* (2003).

Life Expectancy, 1900–2000

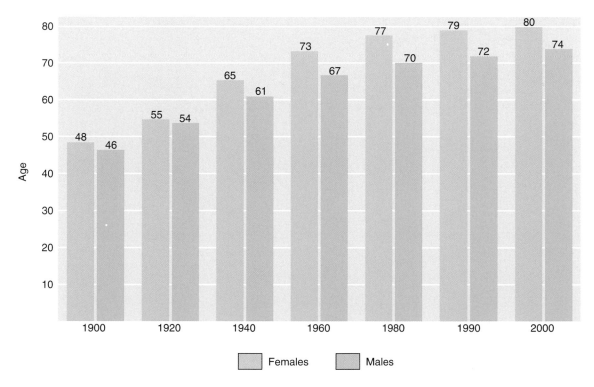

SOURCE: Data from *Historical Statistics of the U.S., Colonial Times to 1970* (1975) and *Statistical Abstract of the U.S., 2003* (2003).

MIGRATION AND IMMIGRATION

WE TEND TO ASSOCIATE INTERNAL MIGRATION with movement westward, yet equally significant has been the movement of the nation's population from the country to the city. In 1790, the first U.S. census recorded that approximately 95 percent of the population lived in rural areas. By 1990, that figure had fallen to less than 25 percent. The decline of the agricultural way of life, late-nineteenth-century industrialization, and immigration have all contributed to increased urbanization. A more recent trend has been the migration, especially since the 1970s, of people to the Sun Belt states of the South and West, lured by factors as various as economic opportunities in the defense and high-tech industries and good weather. This migration has swelled the size of cities like Houston, Dallas, Tucson, Phoenix, and San Diego, all of which in recent years ranked among the top ten most populous U.S. cities.

Rural and Urban Population, 1750–2000

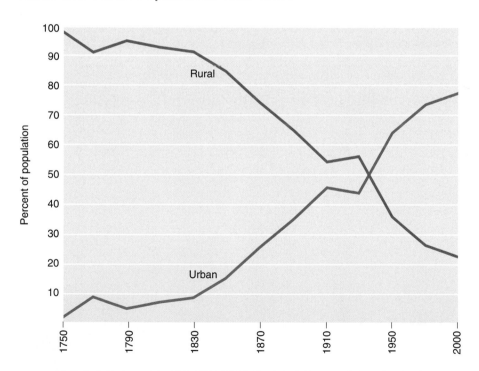

SOURCE: *Statistical Abstract of the U.S., 1991* (1991), *Statistical Abstract of the U.S., 2002* (2002).

MIGRATION AND IMMIGRATION

THE QUANTITY AND CHARACTER OF IMMIGRATION to the United States has varied greatly over time. During the first major influx, between 1840 and 1860, newcomers hailed primarily from northern and western Europe. From 1880 to 1915, when rates soared even more dramatically, the profile changed, with 80 percent of the "new immigration" coming from central, eastern, and southern Europe. Following World War I, strict quotas reduced the flow considerably. Note also the significant falloff during the years of the Great Depression and World War II. The sources of immigration during the last half century have changed significantly, with the majority of people coming from Latin America, the Caribbean, and Asia. The latest surge during the 1980s and 1990s brought more immigrants to the United States than in any decade except 1901–1910.

RATES OF IMMIGRATION, 1821–2002

Year	Number	Rate per Thousand of Total Resident Population
1821–1830	151,824	1.6
1831–1840	599,125	4.6
1841–1850	1,713,521	10.0
1851–1860	2,598,214	11.2
1861–1870	2,314,824	7.4
1871–1880	2,812,191	7.1
1881–1890	5,246,613	10.5
1891–1900	3,687,546	5.8
1901–1910	8,795,386	11.6
1911–1920	5,735,811	6.2
1921–1930	4,107,209	3.9
1931–1940	528,431	0.4
1941–1950	1,035,039	0.7
1951–1960	2,515,479	1.6
1961–1970	3,321,677	1.8
1971–1980	4,493,300	2.2
1981–1990	7,338,100	3.0
1991	1,827,167	7.2
1992	973,977	3.8
1993	904,292	3.5
1994	804,416	3.1
1995	720,461	2.7
1996	915,900	3.4
1997	798,378	2.9
1998	654,451	2.4
1999	646,568	2.3
2000	849,807	3.0
2001	1,064,318	3.7
2002	1,063,732	3.7

Source: Historical Statistics of the U.S., Colonial Times to 1970 (1975), Statistical Abstract of the U.S., 1996 (1996), Statistical Abstract of the U.S., 1999 (1999), 2002 Yearbook of Immigration Statistics (2002), and Statistical Abstract of the U.S., 2003. (2003).

Major Trends in Immigration, 1820–2000

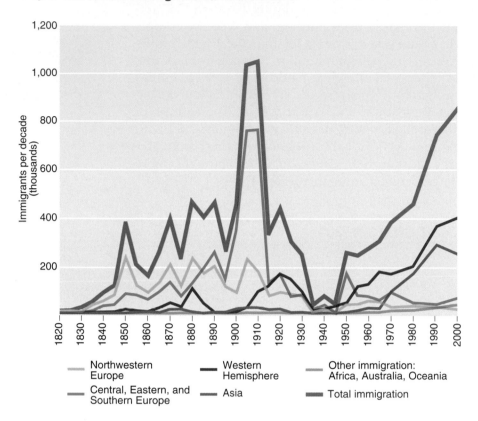

SOURCE: Data from *Historical Statistics of the U.S., Colonial Times to 1970* (1975), *Statistical Abstract of the U.S., 1999* (1999), and *Statistical Abstract of the U.S., 2003* (2003).

Research Resources in U.S. History

For help refining your research skills, finding what you need on the Web, and using it effectively, see "Other Resources at Bedford/St. Martin's" at bedfordstmartins.com/roark.

WHILE DOING RESEARCH IN HISTORY, you will use the library to track down primary and secondary sources and to answer questions that arise as you learn more about your topic. This appendix suggests helpful indexes, references, periodicals, and sources of primary documents. It also offers an overview of electronic resources available through the Internet. The materials listed here are not carried at all libraries, but they will give you an idea of the range of sources available. Remember, too, that librarians are an extremely helpful resource. They can direct you to useful materials throughout your research process.

Bibliographies and Indexes

American Historical Association Guide to Historical Literature. 3rd ed. New York: Oxford University Press, 1995. Offers 27,000 citations to important historical literature, arranged in forty-eight sections covering theory, international history, and regional history. An indispensable guide recently updated to include current trends in historical research.

American History and Life. Santa Barbara: ABC-Clio, 1964–. Covers publications of all sorts on U.S. and Canadian history and culture in a chronological/regional format, with abstracts and alphabetical indexes. Available in computerized format. The most complete ongoing bibliography for American history.

Freidel, Frank Burt. *Harvard Guide to American History.* Cambridge: Harvard University Press, Belknap Press, 1974. Provides citations to books and articles on American history published before 1970. The first volume is arranged topically, the second chronologically. Though it does not cover current scholarship, it is a classic and remains useful for tracing older publications.

Prucha, Francis Paul. *Handbook for Research in American History: A Guide to Bibliographies and Other Reference Works.* 2nd rev. ed. Lincoln: University of Nebraska Press, 1994. Introduces a variety of research tools, including electronic ones. A good source to consult when planning an in-depth research project.

General Overviews

Dictionary of American Biography. New York: Scribner's, 1928–1937, with supplements. Gives substantial biographies of prominent Americans in history.

Dictionary of American History. New York: Scribner's, 1976. An encyclopedia of terms, places, and concepts in U.S. history; other more specialized sets include the *Encyclopedia of North American Colonies* and the *Encyclopedia of the Confederacy.*

Dictionary of Concepts in History. New York: Greenwood, 1986. Contains essays defining concepts in historiography and describing how the concepts were formed; excellent bibliographies.

Encyclopedia of American Social History. New York: Scribner's, 1993. Surveys topics such as religion, class, gender, race, popular culture, regionalism, and everyday life from pre-Columbian to modern times.

Encyclopedia of the United States in the Twentieth Century. New York: Scribner's, 1996. An ambitious overview of American cultural, social, and intellectual history in broad articles arranged topically. Each article is followed by a thorough and very useful bibliography for further research.

Specialized Information

Black Women in America: An Historical Encyclopedia. Brooklyn: Carlson, 1993. A scholarly compilation of biographical and topical articles that constitute a definitive history of African American women.

Carruth, Gordon. *The Encyclopedia of American Facts and Dates.* 10th ed. New York: HarperCollins, 1997. Covers American history chronologically from 1986 to the present, offering information on treaties, battles, explorations, popular culture, philosophy, literature, and so on, mixing significant events with telling trivia. Tables allow for reviewing a year from a variety of angles. A thorough index helps pinpoint specific facts in time.

Cook, Chris. *Dictionary of Historical Terms.* 2nd ed. New York: Peter Bendrick, 1990. Covers a wide variety of terms—events, places, institutions, and topics—in history for all periods and places in a remarkably small package. A good place for quick identification of terms in the field.

Dictionary of Afro-American Slavery. New York: Greenwood, 1985. Surveys important people, events, and topics, with useful bibliographies; similar works include *Dictionary of the Vietnam War, Historical Dictionary of the New Deal*, and *Historical Dictionary of the Progressive Era.*

Knappman-Frost, Elizabeth. *The ABC-Clio Companion to Women's Progress in America.* Santa Barbara: ABC-Clio, 1994. Covers American women who were notable for their time as well as topics and organizations that have been significant in women's quest for equality. Each article is brief; there are a chronology and a bibliography at the back of the book.

United States Bureau of the Census. *Historical Statistics of the United States, Colonial Times to 1970.* Washington, D.C.: Government Printing Office, 1975. Offers vital statistics, economic figures, and social data for the United States. An index at the back helps locate tables by subject. For statistics since 1970, consult the annual *Statistical Abstract of the United States.*

Primary Resources

There are many routes to finding contemporary material for historical research. You may search your library catalog using the name of a prominent historical figure as an author; you may also find anthologies covering particular themes or periods in history. Consider also the following special materials for your research.

THE PRESS

American Periodical Series, 1741–1900. Ann Arbor: University Microfilms, 1946–1979. Microfilm collection of periodicals from the colonial period to 1900. An index identifies periodicals that focused on particular topics.

Herstory Microfilm Collection. Berkeley: Women's History Research Center, 1973. A microfilm collection of alternative feminist periodicals published between 1960 and 1980. Offers an interesting documentary history of the women's movement.

New York Times. New York: New York Times, 1851–. Many libraries have this newspaper on microfilm going back to its beginning in 1851. An index is available to locate specific dates and pages of news stories; it also provides detailed chronologies of events as they were reported in the news.

Readers' Guide to Periodical Literature. New York: Wilson, 1900–. This index to popular magazines started in 1900; an earlier index, *Poole's Index to Periodical Literature*, covers 1802–1906, though it does not provide such thorough indexing.

DIARIES, PAMPHLETS, BOOKS

The American Culture Series. Ann Arbor: University Microfilms, 1941–1974. A microfilm set, with a useful index, featuring books and pamphlets published between 1493 and 1875.

American Women's Diaries. New Canaan: Readex, 1984–. A collection of reproductions of women's diaries. There are different series for different regions of the country.

The March of America Facsimile Series. Ann Arbor: University Microfilms, 1966. A collection of more than ninety facsimiles of travel accounts to the New World published in English or English translation from the fifteenth through the nineteenth century.

Women in America from Colonial Times to the Twentieth Century. New York: Arno, 1974. A collection of reprints of dozens of books written by women describing women's lives and experiences in their own words.

GOVERNMENT DOCUMENTS

Congressional Record. Washington, D.C.: Government Printing Office, 1874–. Covers daily debates and proceedings of Congress. Earlier series were called *Debates and Proceedings in the Congress of the United States* and *The Congressional Globe.*

Foreign Relations of the United States. Washington, D.C.: Department of State, 1861–. A collection of documents from 1861, including diplomatic papers, correspondence, and memoranda, that provides a documentary record of U.S. foreign policy.

Public Papers of the Presidents. Washington, D.C.: Office of the Federal Register, 1957–. Includes major documents issued by the executive branch from the Hoover administration to the present.

Serial Set. Washington, D.C.: Government Printing Office, 1789–1969. A huge collection of congressional documents, available in many libraries on microfiche, with a useful index.

LOCAL HISTORY COLLECTIONS

State and county historical societies often house a wealth of historical documents; consider their resources when planning your research—you may find yourself working with material that no one else has analyzed before.

Internet Resources

The Internet has been a useful place for scholars to communicate and publish information in recent years. Electronic discussion lists, electronic journals,

INTERNET RESOURCES

and primary texts are among the resources available to historians. The following sources are good places to find historical information. You can also search the World Wide Web using any of a number of search engines. However, bear in mind that there is no board of editors screening Internet sites for accuracy or usefulness, and the search engines generally rely on free-text searches rather than subject headings. Be critical of all of your sources, particularly those found on the Internet. Note that when this book went to press, the sites listed below were active and maintained.

American Memory: Historical Collections for the National Digital Library Program. <http://rs6.loc.gov/amhome.html> An Internet site that features digitized primary source materials from the Library of Congress, among them African American pamphlets, Civil War photographs, documents from the Continental Congress and the Constitutional Convention of 1774–1790, materials on woman suffrage, and oral histories.

Douglass Archives of American Public Address. <http://douglassarchives.org> An electronic archive of American speeches and documents by a variety of people from Jane Addams to Jonathan Edwards to Theodore Roosevelt.

Historical Text Archive. <http://historicaltextarchive.com/> A Web interface for the oldest and largest Internet site for historical documents. Includes sections on Native American, African American, and U.S. history, in which can be found texts of the Declaration of Independence, the U.S. Constitution, the Constitution of Iroquois Nations, World War II surrender documents, photograph collections, and a great deal more. These can be used online or saved as files.

History Links from Yahoo! <http://dir.yahoo.com/arts/humanities/history/> A categorically arranged and frequently updated site list for all types of history. Some of the sources are more useful than others, but this can be a helpful gateway to some good information.

Index of Civil War Information on the Internet. <http://www.cwc.lsu.edu/cwc/civlink.htm> Compiled by the United States Civil War Center, this index lists everything from diaries to historic battlefields to reenactments.

Index of Native American Resources on the Internet. <http://www.hanksville.org/NAresources> A vast index of Native American resources organized by category. Within the history category, links are organized under subcategories: oral history, written history, geographical areas, timelines, and photographs and photographic archives. A central place to come in the search for information on Native American history.

Internet Resources for Students of Afro-American History and Culture. <http://www.libraries.rutgers.edu/rul/rr_gateway/research_guides/history/afrores.shtml> A good place to begin research on topics in African American history. The site is indexed and linked to a wide variety of sources, including primary documents, text collections, and archival sources on African American history. Individual documents such as slave narratives and petitions, the Fugitive Slave Acts, and speeches by W. E. B. Du Bois, Booker T. Washington, and Martin Luther King Jr. are categorized by century.

The Martin Luther King Jr. Papers Project. <http://www.stanford.edu/group/King> Organized by Stanford University, this site gives information about Martin Luther King Jr. and offers some of his writings.

NativeWeb. <http://www.nativeweb.org> One of the best organized and most accessible sites available on Native American issues, *NativeWeb* combines an events calendar and message board with history, statistics, a list of news sources, archives, new and updated related sites each week, and documents. The text is indexed and can be searched by subject, nation, and geographic region.

Perry-Castañeda Library Map Collection. <http://www.lib.utexas.edu/maps/index.html> The University of Texas at Austin library has put over seven hundred United States maps on the Web for viewing by students and professors alike.

Smithsonian Institution. <http://www.si.edu> Organized by subject, such as military history or Hispanic/Latino American resources, this site offers selected links to sites hosted by Smithsonian Institution museums and organizations. Content includes graphics of museum pieces and relevant textual information, book suggestions, maps, and links.

Supreme Court Collection. <http://supct.law.cornell.edu/supct/> This database can be used to search for information on various Supreme Court cases. Although the site primarily covers cases that occurred after 1990, there is information on some earlier historic cases. The justices' opinions, as originally written, are also included.

United States History Index. <http://www.ukans.edu/history/VL/USA> Maintained by a history professor and arranged by subject, such as women's history, labor history, and agricultural history, this index provides links to a variety of other sites. Although the list is extensive, it does not include a synopsis of each site, which makes finding specific information a time-consuming process.

United States Holocaust Memorial Museum. <http://www.ushmm.org> This site contains information about the Holocaust Museum in Washington, D.C., in particular and the Holocaust in general, and it lists links to related sites.

Women's History Resources. <http://www.mcps.k12 .md.us/curriculum/socialstd/Women_Bookmarks .html> An extensive listing of women's history sources available on the Internet. The site indexes resources on subjects as diverse as woman suffrage, women in the workplace, and celebrated women writers. Some of the links are to equally vast indexes, providing an overwhelming wealth of information.

WWW-VL History Index. <http://www.ukans.edu/ history/VL> A vast list of more than 1,700 links to sites of interest to historians, arranged alphabetically by general topic. Some links are to sources for general reference information, but most are on historical topics. A good place to start an exploration of Internet resources.

GLOSSARY OF HISTORICAL VOCABULARY

A Note to Students: This list of terms is provided to help you with historical and economic vocabulary. Many of these terms refer to broad, enduring concepts that you may encounter not only in further studies of history but also when following current events. The terms appear in bold at their first use in each chapter. In the glossary, the page numbers of those chapter-by-chapter appearances are provided so you can look up the terms' uses in various periods and contexts. For definitions and discussions of words not included here, consult a dictionary and the book's index, which will point you to topics covered at greater length in the book.

affirmative action Policies established in the 1960s and 1970s by governments, businesses, universities, and other institutions to overcome the effects of past discrimination against specific groups such as racial and ethnic minorities and women. Measures to ensure equal opportunity include setting goals for admission, hiring, and promotion, considering minority status when allocating resources, and actively encouraging victims of past discrimination to apply for jobs and other resources. (pp. 1023, 1106, 1144)

agribusiness Farming on a large scale, using the production, processing, and distribution methods of modern business. Farming became a big business, not just a way to feed a family and make a living, in the late nineteenth century as farms got larger and more mechanized. In the 1940s and 1950s, specialized commercial farms replaced many family-run operations and grew to an enormous scale. (pp. 652, 996)

alliance system The military and diplomatic system formulated in an effort to create a balance of power in pre–World War I Europe. Nations were bound together by rigid and comprehensive treaties that promised mutual aid in the case of attack by specific nations. The system swung into action after the Austrian archduke Francis Ferdinand was assassinated in Sarajevo on June 28, 1914, dragging most of Europe into war. (p. 793)

anarchist A person who rebels against established order and authority. An anarchist is someone who believes that government of any kind is unnecessary and undesirable and should be replaced with voluntary cooperation and free association. Anarchists became increasingly visible in the United States in the late nineteenth and early twentieth centuries. They advocated revolution and grew in numbers through appeals to discontented laborers. Anarchists frequently employed violence in an attempt to achieve their goals. In 1901, anarchist Leon Czolgosz assassinated President William McKinley. (pp. 687, 718, 759, 851)

antebellum A term that means "before a war" and commonly refers to the period prior to the Civil War. (p. 573)

archaeology A social science devoted to learning about people who lived in the past through the study of physical artifacts created by humans. Most but not all archaeological study focuses on the history of people who lived before the use of the written word. (p. 1086)

artisan A term commonly used prior to 1900 to describe a skilled craftsman, such as a cabinetmaker. (p. 682)

black nationalism A term linked to several African American movements emphasizing racial pride, separation from whites and white institutions, and black autonomy. Black nationalism gained in popularity with the rise of Marcus Garvey and the Universal Negro Improvement Association (1917–1927) and later with the Black Panther Party, Malcolm X, and other participants of the black power movements of the 1960s. (pp. 845, 1037)

bloody shirt A refrain used by Republicans in the late nineteenth century to remind the voting public that the Democratic Party, dominated by the South, was largely responsible for the Civil War and that the Republican Party had led the victory to preserve the Union. Republicans urged their constituents to "Vote the way you shot." (pp. 585, 616)

bracero **program** A policy begun during World War II to help with wartime agriculture in which Mexican laborers (*braceros*) were permitted to enter the United States and work for a limited period of time but not to gain citizenship or permanent residence. The program officially ended in 1964. (pp. 1001, 1156)

brinksmanship A cold war practice of appearing willing and able to resort to nuclear war in order to make an enemy back down. Secretary of State John Foster Dulles was the foremost proponent of this policy. (p. 991)

checks and balances A system in which the executive, legislative, and judicial branches of the government curb each other's power. Checks and balances were written into the U.S. Constitution during the Constitutional Convention of 1787. (p. 1109)

civil service The administrative service of a government. This term often applies to reforms following passage of the Pendleton Act in 1883, which set qualifications for U.S. government jobs and sought to remove such jobs from political influence. (pp. 585, 623) *See also* spoils system.

closed shop An establishment in which every employee is required to join a union. (p. 832)

cold war The hostile and tense relationship that existed between the Soviet Union on the one hand and the United States and other Western nations on the other from 1947 to 1989. This war was said to be "cold" because the hostility stopped short of armed (hot) conflict, which was warded off by the strategy of nuclear deterrence. (pp. 952, 985, 1067, 1114, 1142) *See also* deterrence.

collective bargaining Negotiation by a group of workers (usually through a union) and their employer concerning rates of pay and working conditions. (pp. 801, 883, 971, 997)

collective security An association of independent nations that agree to accept and implement decisions made by the group, including going to war in defense of one or more members. The United States resolutely avoided such alliances until after World War II, when it created the North Atlantic Treaty Organization (NATO) in response to the threat posed by the Soviet Union. (pp. 811, 833, 961) *See also* North Atlantic Treaty Organization.

colonization The process by which a country or society gains control over another, primarily through settlement. (pp. 731, 791, 1056)

communism (Communist Party) A system of government and political organization, based on Marxist-Leninist ideals, in which a single authoritarian party controls the economy through state ownership of production, as a means toward reaching the final stage of Marxist theory in which the state dissolves and economic goods are distributed evenly for the common good. Communists around the globe encouraged the spread of communism in other nations in hopes of fomenting worldwide revolution. At its peak in the 1930s, the Communist Party of the United States worked closely with labor unions and insisted that only the overthrow of the capitalist system by its workers could save the victims of the Great Depression. After World War II, the Communist power and aspirations of the Soviet Union were held to be a direct threat to American democracy, prompting the cold war. (pp. 814, 861, 868, 913, 951, 985, 1027, 1067, 1103, 1142) *See also* cold war.

conscription Compulsory military service. Americans were first subject to conscription during the Civil War. The Draft Act of 1940 marked the first peacetime use of conscription. (pp. 673, 798) *See also* draft.

conservatism A political and moral outlook dating back to Alexander Hamilton's belief in a strong central government resting on a solid banking foundation. Currently associated with the Republican Party, conservatism today places a high premium on military preparedness, free-market economics, low taxes, and strong sexual morality. (pp. 568, 610, 713, 762, 831, 870, 932, 978, 986, 1022, 1090, 1103, 1142)

consumer culture (consumerism) A society that places high value on and devotes substantial resources to the purchase and display of material goods. Elements of American consumerism were evident in the nineteenth century but really took hold in the twentieth century with installment buying and advertising in the 1920s and again with the postwar prosperity of the 1950s. (pp. 701, 844, 986)

containment The U.S. foreign policy developed after World War II to hold in check the power and influence of the Soviet Union and other groups or nations espousing communism. The strategy was first fully articulated by diplomat George F. Kennan in 1946–1947. (pp. 952, 985, 1051, 1068, 1155)

cult of domesticity The nineteenth-century belief that women's place was in the home, where they should create a haven for harried men of the household working in the outside world. This ideal was made possible by the separation of the workplace and the home and was used to sentimentalize the home and women's role in it. (pp. 692, 724) *See also* separate spheres.

de-industrialization A long period of decline in the industrial sector. This term often refers specifically to the decline of manufacturing and the growth of the service sector of the economy in post–World War II America. This shift and the loss of manufacturing resulting from it were caused by more efficient and automated production techniques at home, increased competition from foreign-made goods, and the use of cheap labor abroad by U.S. manufacturers. (p. 1123)

democracy A system of government in which the people have the power to rule, either directly or indirectly through their elected representatives. Believing that direct democracy was dangerous, the framers of the Constitution created a government that gave direct voice to the people only in the House of Representatives and that placed a check on that voice in the Senate by offering unlimited six-year terms to senators, elected by the state legislatures to protect them from the whims of democratic majorities. The framers further curbed the perceived dangers of democracy by giving each of the three branches of government (legislative, executive, and judicial) the ability to check the power of the other two. (pp. 578, 608, 654, 709, 758, 791, 871, 912, 953, 1071, 1114, 1155) *See also* checks and balances.

détente French for "loosening." The term refers to the easing of tensions between the United States and the Soviet Union during the Nixon administration. (pp. 1090, 1108)

deterrence The linchpin of U.S. military strategy during the cold war. The strategy of deterrence dictated that the United States would maintain a nuclear arsenal so substantial that the Soviet Union would refrain from attacking the United States and its allies out of fear that the United States would retaliate in devastating proportions. The Soviets pursued a similar strategy. (pp. 961, 1016)

domino theory The assumption underlying U.S. foreign policy from the early cold war until the end of the Vietnam conflict that if one country fell to communism, neighboring countries would also fall under Communist control. (pp. 959, 991)

doves Peace advocates, particularly during the Vietnam War. (p. 1085)

draft (draftee) A system for selecting individuals for compulsory military service. A draftee is an individual selected through this process. (pp. 798, 920, 961, 1080, 1115) *See also* conscription.

emancipation The act of freeing from slavery or bondage. The emancipation of American slaves, a goal shared by slaves and abolitionists alike, occurred with the passage of the Thirteenth Amendment in 1865. (pp. 559, 818)

evangelicalism The trend in Protestant Christianity stressing salvation through conversion, repentance of sin, adherence to Scripture, and the importance of preaching over ritual. During the Second Great Awakening, in the 1830s, evangelicals worshipped at camp meetings and religious revivals led by exuberant preachers. (pp. 622, 1117)

fascism An authoritarian system of government characterized by dictatorial rule, disdain for international stability, and a conviction that warfare is the only means by which a nation can attain greatness. Nazi Germany and Mussolini's Italy are the prime examples of fascism. (pp. 871, 908)

federal budget deficit The situation resulting when the government spends more money than it takes in. (pp. 1028, 1122, 1144)

feminism The belief that men and women have the inherent right to equal social, political, and economic opportunities. The suffrage movement and second-wave feminism of the 1960s and 1970s were the most visible and successful manifestations of feminism, but feminist ideas were expressed in a variety of statements and movements as early as the late eighteenth century and continue to be expressed in the twenty-first. (pp. 576, 779, 841, 1004, 1046, 1103, 1144)

flexible response Military strategy employed by the Kennedy and Johnson administrations designed to match a wide range of military threats by complementing nuclear weapons with the buildup of conventional and special forces and employing them all in a gradual and calibrated way as needed. Flexible response was a departure from the strategy of massive retaliation used by the Eisenhower administration. (p. 1069)

franchise The right to vote. The franchise was gradually widened in the United States to include groups such as women and African Americans, who had no vote when the Constitution was ratified. (pp. 577, 723) *See also* suffrage.

free labor Work conducted free from constraint and in accordance with the laborer's personal inclinations and will. Prior to the Civil War, free labor became an ideal championed by Republicans (who were primarily Northerners) to articulate individuals' right to work how and where they wished, and to accumulate property in their own name. The ideal of free labor lay at the heart of the North's argument that slavery should not be extended into the western territories. (p. 562)

free silver The late-nineteenth-century call by silver barons and poor American farmers for the widespread coinage of silver and for silver to be used as a base upon which to expand the paper money supply. The coinage of silver created a more inflationary monetary system that benefited debtors. (pp. 627, 713) *See also* gold standard.

frontier A borderland area. In U.S. history this refers to the borderland between the areas primarily inhabited by Europeans or their descendants and the areas solely inhabited by Native Americans. (pp. 663, 711)

fundamentalism Strict adherence to core, often religious beliefs. The term has varying meanings for different religious groups. Protestant fundamentalists adhere to a literal interpretation of the Bible and thus deny the possibility of evolution. Muslim fundamentalists believe that traditional Islamic law should govern nations and that Western influences should be banned. (pp. 852, 1115, 1142)

gender gap An electoral phenomenon that became apparent in the 1980s when men and women began to display different preferences in voting. Women tended to favor liberal candidates, and men tended to support conservatives. The key voter groups contributing to the gender gap were single women and women who worked outside the home. (pp. 1125, 1153)

globalization The spread of political, cultural, and economic influences and connections among countries, businesses, and individuals around the world through trade, immigration, communication, and other means. In the late twentieth century, globalization was intensified by new communications technology that connected individuals, corporations, and nations with greater speed at low prices. This led to an increase in political and economic interdependence and mutual influence among nations. (pp. 1090, 1142)

gold standard A monetary system in which any circulating currency was exchangeable for a specific amount of gold. Advocates for the gold standard believed that gold alone should be used for coinage and that the total value of paper banknotes should never exceed the government's supply of gold. The triumph of gold standard supporter William McKinley in the 1896 presidential election was a big victory for supporters of this policy. (pp. 629, 710) *See also* free silver.

gospel of wealth The idea that wealth garnered from earthly success should be used for good works. Andrew Carnegie promoted this view in an 1889 essay in which he maintained that the wealthy should serve as stewards and act in the best interests of society as a whole. (pp. 615, 750)

Great Society President Lyndon Johnson's domestic program, which included civil rights legislation, antipoverty programs, government subsidy of medical care, federal aid to education, consumer protection, and aid to the arts and humanities. (pp. 1021, 1104)

guerrilla warfare Fighting carried out by an irregular military force usually organized into small, highly mobile groups. Guerrilla combat was common in the Vietnam War and during the American Revolution. Guerrilla warfare is often effective against opponents who have greater material resources. (pp. 580, 661, 734, 992, 1068, 1173)

hawks Advocates of aggressive military action or all-out war, particularly during the Vietnam War. (p. 1084)

holding company A system of business organization whereby competing companies are combined under one central administration in order to curb competition and ensure profit. Pioneered in the late 1880s by John D. Rockefeller, holding companies, such as Standard Oil, exercised monopoly control even as the government threatened to outlaw trusts as a violation of free trade. (p. 605) *See also* monopoly; trust.

impeachment The process by which formal charges of wrongdoing are brought against a president, a governor, or a federal judge. (pp. 575, 888, 1110, 1150)

imperialism The system by which great powers gain control of overseas territories. The United States became an imperialist power by gaining control of Puerto Rico, Guam, the Philippines, and Cuba as a result of the Spanish-American War. (pp. 586, 710, 792, 962, 1056, 1159)

iron curtain A metaphor coined by Winston Churchill during his commencement address at Westminster College in Fulton, Missouri, in 1946, to refer to the political, ideological, and military barriers that separated Soviet-controlled Eastern Europe from the rest of Europe and the West following World War II. (pp. 954, 991, 1070, 1145)

isolationism A foreign policy perspective characterized by a desire to have the United States withdraw from the conflicts of the world and enjoy the protection of two vast oceans. (pp. 731, 812, 833, 909, 951)

Jim Crow The system of racial segregation that developed in the post–Civil War South and extended well into the twentieth century; it replaced slavery as the chief instrument of white supremacy. Jim Crow laws segregated African Americans in public facilities such as trains and streetcars and denied them basic civil rights, including the right to vote. It was also at this time that the doctrine of "separate but equal" became institutionalized. (pp. 582, 677, 783, 931)

jingoism (jingoes) Extreme nationalism marked by belligerent foreign policy, an attitude held by many late-nineteenth-century Americans. Jingoism was epitomized by Theodore Roosevelt, who believed that nations and individuals needed warfare to maintain their virility. (p. 737)

Keynesian economics A theory, developed by economist John Maynard Keynes, that guided U.S. economic policy from the New Deal to the 1970s. According to Keynesians, the federal government has a duty to stimulate and manage the economy by spending money on public works projects and by making general tax cuts in order to put more money into the hands of ordinary people, thus creating demand. (p. 900)

laissez-faire The doctrine, based on economic theory, that government should not interfere in business or the economy. Laissez-faire ideas guided American government policy in the late nineteenth century and conservative politics in the twentieth. Business interests that supported laissez-faire in the late nineteenth century accepted government interference when it took the form of tariffs or subsidies that worked to their benefit. Broader uses of the term refer to the simple philosophy of abstaining from interference. (pp. 615, 710, 748, 870, 1120, 1159)

land grant A gift of land from a government, usually intended to encourage settlement or development. The British government issued several land grants to encourage development in the American colonies. In the mid-nineteenth century the U.S. government issued land grants to encourage railroad development and through passage of the Land-Grant College Act (also known as the Morrill Act) in 1863 set aside public lands to support universities. (pp. 600, 648)

liberalism The political doctrine that government rests on the consent of the governed and is duty-bound to protect the freedom and property of the individual. In the twentieth century, liberalism became associated with the idea that the government should regulate the economy and ensure the material well-being and individual rights of all people. (pp. 714, 748, 824, 871, 932, 969, 987, 1023, 1103, 1144)

liberty The condition of being free or enjoying freedom from control. This term also refers to the possession of certain social, political, or economic rights such as the right to own and control property. Eighteenth-century American colonists evoked the principle to argue for strict limitations on government's ability to tax its subjects. (pp. 566, 794, 1171)

manifest destiny A term coined by journalist John O'Sullivan in 1845 to express the popular nineteenth-century belief that the United States was destined to expand westward to the Pacific Ocean and had an irrefutable right and God-given responsibility to do so. This idea provided an ideological shield for westward expansion and masked the economic and political motivations of many of those who championed it. (p. 731)

McCarthyism The practice of searching out suspected Communists and others outside mainstream American society, discrediting them, and hounding them from government and other employment. The term derives from Senator Joseph McCarthy, who gained notoriety for leading such repressive activities from 1950 to 1954. (p. 973)

military-industrial complex A term first used by President Dwight D. Eisenhower to refer to the aggregate power and influence of the armed forces in conjunction with the aerospace, munitions, and other industries that produced supplies for the military in the post–World War II era. (p. 995)

miscegenation The sexual mixing of races. In slave states, despite social stigma and legal restrictions on interracial sex, masters' almost unlimited power over their female slaves meant that liaisons inevitably occurred. Many states maintained laws against miscegenation into the 1950s. (pp. 620, 845)

monopoly Exclusive control and domination by a single business entity over an entire industry through ownership, command of supply, or other means. Gilded Age businesses monopolized their industries quite profitably, often organizing holding companies and trusts to do so. (pp. 592, 605, 651, 709, 759, 884, 945, 1121) *See also* holding company; trust.

Monroe Doctrine President James Monroe's 1823 declaration that the Western Hemisphere was closed to any further colonization or interference by European powers. In exchange, Monroe pledged that the United States would not become involved in European struggles. Although Monroe could not back his policy with action, it was an important formulation of national goals. (pp. 731, 767, 791)

nationalism A strong feeling of devotion and loyalty toward one nation over others. Nationalism encourages the promotion of the nation's common culture, language, and customs. (pp. 790, 993, 1071, 1142)

nativism Bias against immigrants and in favor of native-born inhabitants. American nativists especially favor persons who come from white, Anglo-Saxon, Protestant lines over those from other racial, ethnic, and religious heritages. Nativists may include former immigrants who view new immigrants as incapable of assimilation. Many nativists, such as members of the Know-Nothing Party in the nineteenth century and the Ku Klux Klan through the contemporary period, voice anti-immigrant, anti-Catholic, and anti-Semitic sentiments. (pp. 657, 752, 821, 850, 1166)

New Deal The group of social and economic programs that President Franklin Roosevelt developed to provide relief for the needy, speed economic recovery, and reform economic and governmental institutions. The New Deal was a massive effort to bring the United States out of the Great Depression and ensure its future prosperity. (pp. 713, 869, 909, 951, 985, 1028, 1135, 1174)

New Right Politically active religious conservatives who became particularly vocal in the 1980s. The New Right criticized feminism, opposed abortion and homosexuality, and promoted "family values" and military preparedness. (p. 1104)

New South A vision of the South, promoted after the Civil War by Henry Grady, editor of the *Atlanta Constitution*, that urged the South to abandon its dependence on agriculture and use its cheap labor and natural resources to compete with northern industry. Many Southerners migrated from farms to cities in the late nineteenth century, and northerners and foreigners invested a significant amount of capital in railroads, cotton and textiles, mining, lumber, iron, steel, and tobacco in the region. (pp. 560, 617)

North Atlantic Treaty Organization (NATO) A post–World War II alliance that joined the United States, Canada, and Western European nations into a military coalition designed to counter efforts to expand by the Soviet Union. Each NATO member pledged to go to war if any member was attacked. Since the end of the cold war, NATO has been expanding to include the formerly Communist countries of Eastern Europe. (pp. 952, 1131, 1145)

oligopoly A competitive system in which several large corporations dominate an industry by dividing the market so each business has a share of it. More prevalent than outright monopolies during the late 1800s, the oligopolies of the Gilded Age successfully muted competition and benefited the corporations that participated in this type of arrangement. (pp. 612, 640)

planters Owners of large farms (or more specifically plantations) that were worked by twenty or more slaves. By 1860, planters had accrued a great deal of local, statewide, and national political power in the South despite the fact that they represented a minority of the white electorate in those states. Planters' dominance of southern politics demonstrated both the power of tradition and stability among southern voters and the planters' success at convincing white voters that the slave system benefited all whites, even those without slaves. (pp. 562, 617)

Populism A political movement that led to the creation of the People's Party, primarily comprising southern and western farmers who railed against big business and advocated business and economic reforms, including government ownership of the railroads. The movement peaked in the late nineteenth century. The Populist ticket won more than one million votes in the presidential election of 1892 and 1.5 million in the congressional elections of 1894. The term *populism* has come to mean any political movement that advocates on behalf of the common person, particularly for government intervention against big business. (pp. 630, 710, 755, 1174)

progressivism (progressive movement) A wide-ranging twentieth-century reform movement that advocated government activism to mitigate the problems created by urban industrialism. Progressivism reached its peak in 1912 with the creation of the Progressive Party, which ran Theodore Roosevelt for president. The term *progressivism* has come to mean any general effort advocating for social welfare programs. (pp. 682, 713, 748, 790, 829, 872, 932, 1021, 1174)

Protestantism A powerful Christian reform movement that began in the sixteenth century with Martin Luther's critiques of the Roman Catholic Church. Over the centuries, Protestantism has taken many different forms, branching into numerous denominations with differing systems of worship. (pp. 616, 752, 850, 871, 1105)

reform Darwinism A social theory, based on Charles Darwin's theory of evolution, that emphasized activism, arguing that humans could speed up evolution by altering the environment. A challenge to social Darwinism, reform Darwinism condemned laissez-faire and demanded that the government take a more active approach to solving social problems. It became the ideological basis for progressive reform in the late nineteenth and early twentieth centuries. (p. 755) *See also* laissez-faire; social Darwinism.

scientific management A system of organizing work, developed by Frederick Winslow Taylor in the late nineteenth century, to increase efficiency and productivity by breaking tasks into their component parts and training workers to perform specific parts. Labor resisted this effort because it deskilled workers and led to the speedup of production lines. Taylor's ideas were most popular at the height of the Progressive Era. (pp. 755, 834)

separate spheres A concept of gender relations that developed in the Jacksonian era and continued well into the twentieth century, holding that women's proper place was in the private world of hearth and home (the private sphere) and men's was in the public world of commerce and politics (the public sphere). The doctrine of separate spheres eroded slowly over the nineteenth and twentieth centuries as women became more and more involved in public activities. (pp. 620, 692, 844) *See also* cult of domesticity.

social Darwinism A social theory, based on Charles Darwin's theory of evolution, that argued that all progress in human society came as the result of competition and natural selection. Gilded Age proponents such as William Graham Sumner and Herbert Spencer claimed that reform was useless because the rich and poor were precisely where nature intended them to be and intervention would retard the progress of humanity. (pp. 612, 676, 726, 755) *See also* reform Darwinism.

social gospel movement A religious movement in the late nineteenth and early twentieth centuries founded on the idea that Christians have a responsibility to reform society as well as individuals. Social gospel adherents encouraged people to put Christ's teachings to work in their daily lives by actively promoting social justice. (pp. 749, 873)

social purity movement A movement to end prostitution and eradicate venereal disease, often accompanied by censorship of materials deemed "obscene." (p. 749)

socialism A governing system in which the state owns and operates the largest and most important parts of the economy. (pp. 690, 713, 753, 805, 861, 873, 932, 960, 1046)

spoils system An arrangement in which party leaders reward party loyalists with government jobs. This slang term for *patronage* comes from the phrase "To the victor go the spoils." Widespread government corruption during the Gilded Age spurred reformers to curb the spoils system through the passage of the Pendleton Act in 1883, which created the Civil Service Commission to award government jobs on the basis of merit. (pp. 585, 615, 643) *See also* civil service.

states' rights A strict interpretation of the Constitution that holds that federal power over states is limited and states hold ultimate sovereignty. First expressed in 1798 through the passage of the Virginia and Kentucky Resolutions, which were based on the assumption that states have the right to judge the constitutionality of federal laws, the states' rights philosophy became a cornerstone of the South's resistance to federal control of slavery. (pp. 566, 773, 842)

strict constructionism An approach to constitutional law that attempts to adhere to the original intent of the writers of the Constitution. Strict construction often produces Supreme Court decisions that defer to the legislative branch and to the states and restrict the power of the federal government. Opponents of strict construction argue that the Constitution is an organic document that must be interpreted to meet conditions unimagined when it was written. (p. 1106)

suffrage The right to vote. The term *suffrage* is most often associated with the efforts of American women to secure voting rights. (pp. 561, 620, 709, 748, 790, 1056) *See also* franchise.

Sun Belt The southern and southwestern regions of the United States, which grew tremendously in industry, population, and influence after World War II. (pp. 999, 1105)

supply-side economics An economic theory based on the premise that tax cuts for the wealthy and for corporations encourage investment and production (supply), which in turn stimulate consumption. Embraced by the Reagan administration and other conservative Republicans, this theory reversed Keynesian economic policy, which assumes that the way to stimulate the economy is to create demand through federal spending on public works and general tax cuts that put more money into the hands of ordinary people. (p. 1121) *See* Keynesian economics.

temperance movement The reform movement to end drunkenness by urging people to abstain from the consumption of alcohol. Begun in the 1820s, this movement achieved its greatest political victory with the passage of a constitutional amendment in 1919 that prohibited the manufacture, sale, and transportation of alcohol. That amendment was repealed in 1933. (pp. 621, 723, 751)

third world Originally a cold war term linked to decolonization, "third world" was first used in the late 1950s to describe newly independent countries in Africa and Asia that were not aligned with either Communist nations (the second world) or non-Communist nations (the first world). Later, the term was applied to all poor, nonindustrialized countries, in Latin America as well as in Africa and Asia. Many international experts see "third world" as a problematic category when applied to such a large and disparate group of nations, and they criticize the discriminatory hierarchy suggested by the term. (pp. 962, 1057, 1068, 1104, 1157)

trickle-down economics The theory that financial benefits and incentives given to big businesses in the top tier of the economy will flow down to smaller businesses and individuals and thus benefit the entire nation. President Herbert Hoover unsuccessfully used the trickle-down strategy in his attempt to pull the nation out of the Great Depression, stimulating the economy through government investment in large economic enterprises and public works such as construction of the Boulder (Hoover) Dam. In the late twentieth century, conservatives used this economic theory to justify large tax cuts and other financial benefits for corporations and the wealthy. (p. 857)

Truman Doctrine President Harry S. Truman's assertion that American security depended on stopping any Communist government from taking over any non-Communist government—even nondemocratic and repressive dictatorships—anywhere in the world. Beginning in 1947 with American aid to help Greece and Turkey stave off Communist pressures, this approach became a cornerstone of American foreign policy during the cold war. (p. 952)

trust A corporate system in which corporations give shares of their stock to trustees who coordinate the industry to ensure profits to the participating corporations and curb competition. Pioneered by Standard Oil Company, such business practices were deemed unfair, were moderated by the Sherman Antitrust Act (1890), and were finally abolished by the combined efforts of Presidents Theodore Roosevelt and William Howard Taft and the sponsors of the 1914 Clayton Antitrust Act. The term *trust* is also loosely applied to all large business combinations. (pp. 604, 749, 891) *See also* holding company.

vertical integration A system in which a single person or corporation controls all processes of an industry from start to finished product. Andrew Carnegie first used vertical integration in the 1870s, controlling every aspect of steel production from the mining of iron ore to the manufacturing of the final product, thereby maximizing profits by eliminating the use of outside suppliers or services. (pp. 604, 654)

welfare capitalism The idea that a capitalistic, industrial society can operate benevolently to improve the lives of workers. The notion of welfare capitalism became popular in the 1920s as industries extended the benefits of scientific management to improve safety and sanitation in the workplace as well as institute paid vacations and pension plans. (p. 835) *See also* scientific management.

welfare state A nation or state in which the government assumes responsibility for some or all of the individual and social welfare of its citizens. Welfare states commonly provide education, health care, food programs for the poor, unemployment compensation, and other social benefits. The United States dramatically expanded its role as a welfare state with the provisions of the New Deal in the 1930s. (pp. 890, 987, 1024)

Yankee imperialism A cry raised in Latin American countries against the United States when it intervened militarily in the region without invitation or consent from those countries. (pp. 1070, 1115, 1147)

yeoman A farmer who owned a small plot of land sufficient to support a family and tilled by family members and perhaps a few servants. (pp. 578, 654)

Spot Artifact Credits

A note about the index:

Names of individuals appear in boldface; biographical dates are included for major historical figures.

Letters in parentheses following pages refer to:
(i)   illustrations, including photographs and artifacts, as well as information in picture captions
(f)   figures, including charts and graphs
(m)   maps
(b)   boxed features (such as "Historical Question")
(t)   tables

AAA (Agricultural Adjustment Act; 1933), 880, 885

AAA (Agricultural Adjustment Act; 1938), 901

Abernathy, Ralph D., 1016(i)

Abington School District v. Schempp (1963), 1031

ABMs (antiballistic missile systems), 1090, 1131

Abolitionists (abolitionist movement)
  Fifteenth Amendment and, 576
  Lincoln and, 561

Abortion, 1125(i)
  Nixon administration and, 1107
  opposition to the right to, 1055, 1058
  Roe v. Wade (1973), 1055, 1107, 1126

Abraham Lincoln Brigade, 912

Abstract expressionists, 1009

Acheson, Dean (1893–1971), 951, 952(i), 969, 973, 975, 1086
  aid to Greece and Turkey, 959–960
  containment policy, 952

Addams, Jane (1860–1935), 747, 748, 748(i), 750–752, 772, 776
  World War I and, 804, 807(b)

Administrative Reorganization Act (1938), 901

Advanced Research Projects Agency (ARPA), 1160(b)

Adventures of Huckleberry Finn, The (Twain), 598

Advertising
  in 1920s, 837–838
  in 1950s, 1004, 1007

AEF (American Expeditionary Force), 789, 797–800
  in 1918, 799(m)

AFDC (Aid to Families with Dependent Children), 1152

Affirmative action, 1023, 1036, 1053
  Lyndon Johnson administration and, 1036
  Nixon administration and, 1060–1061, 1106

Afghanistan, 1132, 1135, 1158, 1171(m)
  Soviet invasion of (1979), 1115
  Taliban government, 1170, 1171

AFL (American Federation of Labor), 690, 692, 718, 801, 891
  in 1930s, 860, 891–892
  merger with CIO (1955), 996–997
  Seattle strike and (1919), 813–814
  women workers and, 752, 803

Africa, 1155

African Americans, women, feminism and, 1054

African Americans (blacks). *See also* Civil rights movement; Free blacks; Desegregation; Integration; Racism; Reconstruction; Segregation; Slaves and slavery
  in 1920s, 844–846
  in 1930s, 862
  in 1960s, 1028
  in 1990s–2000s, 1151
  antilynching movement, 620, 621(i)
  in the armed services, 655(i)
    World War I, 820, 822–823(b)
    World War II, 920, 921
  art of, 845, 846(i)
  Buffalo soldiers, 655, 655(i)
  Clinton administration and, 1151
  education of
    colleges (1941–1961), 1003
    in the South, 577, 580, 582
  elected officials (1970s–1990s), 1038
  farmers
    Colored Farmers' Alliance, 711–712
    Populists and (1890s), 728
    sharecroppers, 583–584, 858, 862, 885, 885(i)
  income of, in 2001, 1155
  migration to cities, 676–677, 818–820, 819(i), 996, 999
  New Deal and, 894–895, 894(i)
  "New Negro," 845
  Nicodemus National Historic Site (Kansas), 590(b), 590(i)
  progressivism and, 782–784
  segregation, 784. *See also* Integration
    Jim Crow laws, 582, 677
    New Deal and, 901
    in Progressive era, 783
    residential, 680
    in schools, 969–970, 969(i), 1106

"separate but equal" doctrine, 783, 895, 1010, 1012
  Vietnam War and, 1080, 1086, 1087(i)
  voting rates (1940–1976), 1037(m)
  voting rights of, 577, 1038–1039(b)
    Civil Rights Act of 1875, 587
    Fifteenth Amendment and, 576
    Force Bill (1890), 627
    Fourteenth Amendment and, 571–574
    in Gilded Age (1870s–1890s), 620
    Ku Klux Klan Act (1871), 586–587
    Mississippi Freedom Summer Project (1964), 1035
    Populists and progressives, 782–783
    reconstruction and, 574, 586–587
    Voter Education Project (1961), 1034
    Voting Rights Act (1965), 1028, 1036, 1038, 1061
  in the West, 654–655, 1000
    cowboys, 650
  women
    in 1920s, 841
    antilynching movement, 620–621
    feminism and, 1054
    during Reconstruction, 560(i), 563, 577, 580, 583
    workers (1890s), 685
  World War I and, 819–820, 822–823(b)
  after World War II, 968
  World War II and, 930–931, 931(i)

African slaves. *See* Slaves and slavery

Afro style, 1040(i)

Agency for International Development (AID), 1071

Agent Orange, 1081, 1097

Agnew, Spiro T. (1918–1996), 1088, 1109

Agribusiness, 652, 996

Agricultural Adjustment Act (AAA; 1933), 880, 883(t), 885

Agricultural Adjustment Act (AAA; 1938), 901

Agricultural Marketing Act (1929), 857

Agriculture. *See also* Farmers and farms; Plantations; Planters; *and specific crops*
  1940–1960, 996
  1920–1940 income, 858(f)
  in Gilded Age (1870s–1890s), 652–654

Agriculture *(continued)*
    mechanization of, 652–653, 652(i), 998(i)
    Mexican laborers and (1910–1932), 820–821, 859
    New Deal and, 880–881
    sharecropping system of, 583–585
    technology
        1940–1960, 996, 998(i)
        mechanization of agriculture, 652–653, 652(i)
        mechanized cotton picking, 882(b), 882(i)
        World War II production, 930
Aguinaldo, Emilio, 740
AIDS (acquired immune deficiency syndrome), 1127
Aid to Families with Dependent Children (AFDC), 1028, 1152
AIM (American Indian Movement), 1042, 1044, 1044(i)
Air-conditioning, 838(b), 1000(m), 1001(b), 1001(i)
Air Quality Act (1965), 1030(t)
Alabama
    reconstruction and, 567, 589
    Selma-Montgomery march, 1035, 1035(i)
Alaska, purchase of, 586
Albright, Madeleine K., 1151
Alcatraz Island (San Francisco, California), 1043(b), 1043(i)
    Native American seizure of (1969), 1042
Alcohol consumption, after Prohibition, 842(b)
Alcoholics Anonymous (AA), 843
Aldrich, Nelson (1841–1915), 623, 771
Aldrin, Edwin E. ("Buzz"), Jr., 1070, 1070(i)
Algeciras (Spain), 1905 conference in, 769
Alger, Horatio (1832–1899), 678(b), 679(i)
Ali, Muhammad, 1083
Ali, Shareefeh Hamid, 1056
Alien Land Law (1913), 782
Allen, William V., 726
Allende, Salvador, 1090
Alliance for Progress, 1071
Al Qaeda, 1170, 1171, 1173, 1174
Altgeld, John Peter (1847–1902), 691, 722
Amalgamated Association of Iron and Steel Workers, 714, 715, 718
Amalgamation. *See* Miscegenation
Amendments to the U.S. Constitution. *See also* Bills of Rights; *and specific amendments*
American Bell, 607
American Communist Party, 817
    in 1930s, 861, 862, 887
    anti-Communist hysteria (1940s–1950s) and, 973, 974
American Equal Rights Association, 572
American Expeditionary Force (AEF), 789, 797–800
    in 1918, 799(m)
American Federation of Labor (AFL), 690, 692, 718, 801, 891
    in 1930s, 860, 891–892
    merger with CIO (1955), 996–997

Seattle strike and (1919), 813–814
    women workers and, 752, 803
American GI Forum, 969, 970
American Independent Party, 1088
American Indian Movement (AIM), 1042, 1044, 1044(i)
American Individualism (Hoover), 855
American Liberty League, 884, 893
American Medical Association, 844
American places
    Cripple Creek (Colorado), 642(b)
    East Texas Oil Museum (Kilgore, Texas), 836(b)
    Edison National Historic Site (West Orange, New Jersey), 614(b)
    Harry S. Truman Library (Independence, Missouri), 977(b)
    Hoover Dam (Nevada), 879
    Jane Addams Hull-House Museum (Chicago), 750–751(b)
    Lower East Side Tenement Museum (New York City), 681(b), 681(i)
    Nicodemus National Historic Site (Kansas), 590(b), 590(i)
    Rosie the Riveter/World War II Home Front National Historical Park (Richmond, California), 929(b)
American Railway Union (ARU), 721
American Revolution. *See also* Second Continental Congress
    American military forces in. *See also* Continental army; Militias, during Revolutionary War
    women and, 560
American Sugar Refining Company, 629
Americans with Disabilities Act (1991), 1143, 1144(i)
American Telephone and Telegraph (AT&T), 607
American Woman Suffrage Association (AWSA), 724
AmeriCorps, 1150
Ames, Adelbert, 589
Amputations, during Civil War, 571(i)
Amputees, artificial limbs for, 570–571(b)
Anarchists, 690
    Sacco and Vanzetti, 851–852, 851(i)
Anderson, John B., 1117
Angola, 1132
Animals. *See also* Hunting
Anthony, Susan B. (1820–1906), 572, 577(i), 621
    Fifteenth Amendment and, 576
    woman suffrage and, 724–725
Anthracite coal strike (1902), 760–761
Antiballistic missile systems (ABMs), 1090, 1131
Antiballistic Missile Treaty (1972), 1172
Anticommunism, Nixon administration and, 1090–1091
Anticommunist hysteria (1940s–1950s), 972–974
Anti-Drug Abuse Acts (1986 and 1988), 843
Antiforeign attitudes. *See* Immigration (immigrants), restrictions on; Nativism

Antilynching legislation, 901
Antilynching movement, 620, 620(i)
Antipoverty programs
    in 1960s, 1027, 1028
    Nixon administration and, 1059
Anti-Saloon League, 752, 842(b)
Anti-Semitism, 887, 910, 933
    Nazi, 934(b)
Antislavery movement. *See also* Abolitionists
Antitrust laws and suits
    Clayton Antitrust Act (1914), 775
    Northern Securities case (1902), 759–760
    Reagan administration and, 1121
    Theodore Roosevelt and, 760
    Sherman Antitrust Act (1890), 628–629, 759, 760, 1121
    Taft and, 772
    Wilson and, 775
Antiwar movement (1960s–1970s), 1046, 1081–1084, 1085(i), 1087–1088, 1088(i), 1093
Apache Indians, 658, 661–662
Apartments, 695–697
Apollo program, 1070
Appalachian Regional Development Act (1965), 1027
Appliances, 838–839(b)
Apprenticeship laws, 568
Arab League, 1148(m)
Arafat, Yasir, 1158
Arapaho Indians, 658
Arbenz, Jacobo, 993
Arctic National Wildlife Refuge, 1170
Area Redevelopment Act (1961), 1024
Aristide, Jean-Bertrand, 1155, 1158
Arizona Territory, 643, 661
Arkansas
    Reconstruction and, 561, 581(b), 589
Armey, Dick, 1169
Armstrong, Neil A. (1930–), 1070, 1070(i)
Army, U.S.
    in World War I, 797(i), 798–800, 800(i), 802(i), 820, 822–823(b)
    in World War II, 906(i), 920, 921(i)
Army of the Republic of Vietnam (ARVN), 992, 1074, 1075, 1086, 1092
Arnaz, Desi, 1006
ARPA (Advanced Research Projects Agency), 1160(b)
ARPANET, 1160(b)
Arthur, Chester A. (1829–1886), 624
Articles of Confederation. *See also* Confederation government
Artificial limbs, 570–571(b), 571(i)
Artisans, skilled. *See* Skilled workers and artisans
Arts, in 1950s, 1009
ARU (American Railway Union), 721
ARVN (South Vietnamese army), 992, 1073(t), 1074, 1075, 1086, 1092
Asia
    1940s–1950s, 962
    Taft's foreign policy, 772

Asian Americans. 1151, 1155, 1163.
    See also Chinese Americans;
    Japanese Americans
    immigrants, 677. *See also* Chinese
        immigrants; Japanese immigrants
    New Deal and, 896
    Truman's domestic policies and, 971
Assemblies, colonial. *See* Legislatures,
    colonial
Assembly-line manufacturing (mass
    production), 834–837
Assimilation of Native Americans, 636,
    660–661, 989(i), 990, 1042, 1061
    1940s–1950s, 989(i), 990
Aswan Dam (Egypt), 993
AT&T (American Telephone and
    Telegraph), 607
Atlanta Compromise (1895), 783
Atlanta Constitution, 617
Atlantic Charter, 916, 919(t)
Atomic bomb
    bombing of Hiroshima and Nagasaki
        (1945), 908–909, 908(i), 944–945,
        945(i)
    development of, 934–935(b), 944–945
    Soviet, 961
Atomic weapons, defense strategy and,
    960, 961
Auschwitz death camp, 936, 937
Austria, 810, 919(t)
Austria-Hungary, 793, 810
Automobile industry, 831(m)
    in 1920s, 834, 834(m), 855–856
    1945–1960, 996
Automobiles, 828(i), 1028
    in 1950s, 984(i)
AWSA (American Woman Suffrage
    Association), 724
"Axis of evil," 1172
Aztecs. *See* Mexica

"Back to Africa" movement, 845
Baer, George, 761
Baker, Ella, 1016, 1022(i), 1032
Baker, Newton D., 798
Baker v. Carr (1963), 1029, 1031
Bakke case (1978), 1106–1107
Balch, Emily Greene, 804
Balkans, 792, 810
Ball, Lucille, 1006
"Ballad of Pretty Boy Floyd, The," 860
Ballinger, Richard, 771
Baltimore and Ohio (B&O) Railroad,
    687–688
Bandanna handkerchiefs, 736(i)
Bank holiday (1933), 875
Banks (banking system)
    in 1920s, 833, 855, 856
    deregulation of, 1121
    failures (1932–1942), 877(f)
    farmers and, 711
    Federal Reserve Act (1913), 775
    New Deal and, 875–876, 877(f)
    Wilson and, 775
Banks, Dennis, 1042
Baptists, 563

Barbed wire, 650, 650(i)
Barrow plantation, 584(m)
Baruch, Bernard, 801
Baseball, 694, 968(i)
    in 1920s, 847, 848(f)
Bataan, Battle of (1942), 944(t)
Bataan Death March (1942), 925
Batista, Fulgencio, 992(i), 993
Bavaria, 816
Bay of Pigs invasion (1961), 1070
Beals, Melba Patillo, 1010
Beat generation, 1008–1009
Begin, Menachem, 1115
Belgium, 914
Bell, Alexander Graham (1847–1922),
    606–607
Belleau Wood, Battle for (1918), 799
Bentley, Elizabeth, 973
Berkeley, University of California at, free
    speech movement (1964), 1046
Berkman, Alexander, 718
Berlin
    1961 crisis, 1070–1071
    blockade and airlift (1949), 960, 960(i)
    capture of (1945), 940, 944(t)
    division of (1948), 960(m)
Berlin, Treaty of (1899), 734
Berliner, Emile, 702(b)
Berlin Wall, 1070, 1145, 1145(i)
Berry, Chuck, 1007
Bessemer, Henry (1813–1898), 602
Bethlehem Steel, 612, 814
Bethune, Mary McLeod (1875–1955),
    894(i), 895
B-52 bombers, 1079(i)
Bible, the, reading, in public schools, 1031
Bierce, Ambrose, 602(i)
"Big Bonanza" (1873), 640
Big business. *See also* Antitrust laws and
    suits; Corporations
    New Deal and, 874
    railroads as America's first, 599–602,
        601(m)
Bill of Rights (first ten amendments to
    the Constitution). *See also specific
    amendments*
Bimetalism, 629
Bin Laden, Osama, 1158, 1170, 1171, 1174
Birmingham (Alabama), integration
    campaign (1963), 1034
Birth control. *See also* Abortion
    in 1920s, 844
    movement for (1914–1920), 779–781
Birth of a Nation (film), 852
Bison (buffalo), decimation of herds,
    658–660
Black Americans. *See* African Americans
Black codes, 567–568, 567(i), 569
Black Elk, 663
Blackfeet Indians, 662
Black freedom struggle. *See* Civil rights
    movement
Black Friday (Laning), 856(i)
Black Hills (South Dakota), 658, 660
Black Muslims (Nation of Islam),
    1037–1038

Black nationalism, 845, 1036–1042
Black Panther Party for Self-Defense, 1040
Black power movement, 1039–1040
Blacks. *See* African Americans; Slaves
    and slavery
Black Star Line, 845
Black Thursday (1929), 856
Black Tuesday (1929), 856
Blackwell, Unita, 1038, 1039
Blaine, James G. (1830–1893), 596(i), 623,
    733
    1884 election, 624–626, 627(m)
    foreign policy, 733
Blair, Francis P., Jr., 588(i)
Blitzkrieg, 913, 914, 919(t)
"Bloody shirt, waving the," 585, 591, 616
Bolshevism, 814, 816–817(b)
Bonfield, John "Blackjack," 691
Bonus Marchers (Bonus Army; 1932),
    867–868, 868(i), 891
Bootblacks, 684, 684(i)
Bootlegging, 841
Borah, William (1865–1940), 812
Bork, Robert, 1109
Bosch, Juan, 1076, 1077(i)
Bosnia, 1158
Bosses, big-city, 698–700
Boston, 675
    busing in, for racial integration, 1106,
        1107(i)
    policemen's strike (1919), 814
Boston Public Library, 698
Boxer uprising (1900), 732–733
Boycotts
    of buses (1953, 1955), 1011, 1014–1015,
        1032
    of California grapes (1960s), 1045, 1045(i)
    of Pullmann cars (1894), 721
Boyer, LaNada, 1042
Bozeman Trail, 658
Bracero program, 1001, 1002(i), 1156
Bradley, Omar (1893–1991), 976
Brains Trust, 873–874
Brandeis, Louis (1856–1941), 754, 773,
    775, 776
Bray, Rosemary, 1028
Breaker boys, 761
Brest-Litovsk treaty (1918), 799
Briand, Aristide, 834
Briggs, Laura, 953
Brinksmanship, 991
Britain. *See* Great Britain
Britain, Battle of (1940), 914, 919(t), 944(t)
British Guiana, 733
British West Indies. *See* West Indies
Brooklyn Bridge, 668(i), 669–670, 670(i)
Brooks, Gwendolyn, 968
Browne, Oliver, 1010
Browne, Carl, 726(i)
Brown v. Board of Education of Topeka
    (1954), 1010, 1012(b)
Brunauer, Esther, 973
Bryan, William Jennings (1860–1925)
    1896 election, 729, 730
    1908 election, 770
    on expansionism, 741

Bryan, William Jennings (*continued*)
Scopes trial (1925) and, 852, 853
as secretary of state, 791, 795–796
Bryce, James, 699
Buchanan, Pat, 1059
Buchenwald death camp, 936
Buckley, William F., Jr., 1120
Buffalo (bison), decimation of herds, 658–660, 660(i)
Buffalo banner, People's (Populist) Party (1892), 708(i)
Buffalo Bill (William F. Cody; 1846–1917), 663, 664(i)
Buffalo soldiers, 655, 655(i)
Buffalo Telegraph, 625
Bulgaria, 953
Bulge, Battle of the (1944–1945), 940
Bull Moose Party (Progressive Party), 772–774
Bunche, Ralph J., 968
Burchard, Samuel, 626
Bureau of Indian Affairs (BIA), 658, 989, 989(i), 1042
occupation of (1972), 1044(i)
Burger, Warren E., 1106
Burger Court, 1106–1107
Burleson, Albert, 805
Burnham, Daniel, 700–701
Burnham, John, 701(i)
Bush, George H. W. (1924–), 1117, 1134, 1135, 1142, 1155, 1174
1992 election, 1149–1150
end of the cold war and, 1145–1146
gridlock in government and, 1143–1144
military conflicts and, 1147–1149
as president, 1143–1150
Bush, George W. (1946–), 1151, 1167–1174
2000 election, 1168–1169, 1168(i), 1169(i), 1169(m)
domestic policies of, 1169–1170
Iraq War and, 1172–1174, 1173(i)
terrorism and, 1171
Business (businesses; business interests). *See also* Big business; Capitalism
Coolidge and, 832–833
Harding and, 831–832
Hoover and, 854–855
New Deal and, 874, 884
Business consolidation, 610–612, 615
Busing for racial integration, 1106, 1107(i)
Butler, Nicholas Murray, 805
Byington, Margaret, 693
Byrnes, James F., 955

Cable cars (San Francisco), 697
Cadillac automobiles, 984(i)
Cahan, Abraham, 678(b)
California, 1105, 1132(b)
1934 election, 887
in 1950s, 999, 1000, 1002
agriculture, 651, 653, 654
anti-immigrant sentiment in (1990s), 1157
Chicano protest in (1960s), 1045–1046
Chinese Exclusion Act (1882), 651, 657, 677, 820

Chinese immigrants in, 651, 656–657, 657(i), 677
farmworkers' strike (1933), 861
Hiram Johnson, 759, 772, 782, 812
Hispanics in, 651, 655–656
hydraulic mining, 638–639(b), 639(i)
Japanese immigrants in, 770, 782
Johnson's administration (1911–1917), 759
land speculators, 648, 653
Mexicans and Mexican Americans in, 651, 820–821. *See also* Californios
migrant agricultural laborers, 651
Californios, 655, 656(i)
Calley, William, 1093, 1093(i)
Cambodia, 992
bombing and invasion of (1969–1970), 1092, 1092(m), 1093
Campaigns, electoral. *See* Election campaigns and elections
Campbell, E. Simms, 931(i)
Camp David accords (1979), 1115
Canada. *See also* New France
Canals, California's San Joaquin Valley, 653(i)
Cannon, Joseph (1836–1926), 763
Cantigny, Battle of (1918), 799
CAP (Community Action Program), 1026–1027
Capitalism (capitalist economy), 856
finance, 610–612
Franklin D. Roosevelt and, 873–874, 876, 886–887, 902
Stalin on, 954, 956
welfare, 835
Capone, Alphonse "Al," 841, 875
Caputo, Philip, 1077, 1080, 1096
Caribbean, U.S. involvement in (1895–1941), 792(m)
Carlisle Indian School (Pennsylvania), 636
Carmichael, Stokely, 1038–1039
Carnegie, Andrew (1835–1919), 599, 603(f), 603(i), 611–612, 617, 672, 686
Homestead lockout and strike (1892), 714, 715, 718
social Darwinism and gospel of wealth and, 615, 618(b)
steel industry and vertical integration, 602–604
Carnegie Endowment for International Peace, 804
Carnegie Steel, 603, 604, 612
Carpetbaggers, 558(i), 577
Carraway, Hattie, 889(i)
Carrier, Willis Haviland, 1001
Carrier Corporation, 1001(b)
Carson, Rachel, 1051
Carter, James Earl (Jimmy), Jr. (1924–), 1112–1116, 1112(i), 1130–1131
1976 election, 1111
foreign policy, 1113–1116, 1114(m)
human rights and, 1113–1115
Carter Doctrine, 1115
Casablanca conference, 927
Casey, William, 1134
"Cash-and-carry" policy, 911, 919(t)

Castro, Fidel (1927–), 992(i), 993, 1111
Catholicism. *See* Roman Catholic Church; Roman Catholics. *See also* Christianity; Missionaries
Catt, Carrie Chapman (1859–1947), 782, 803, 804
Cattell, James McKeen, 804–805
Cattle ranchers, 650
Cattle trails (1860–1890), 650
Cellular telephones, 1140(i)
Central America
in 1890s, 734
Reagan administration and, 1133
Centralia (Washington), 1919 events in, 818
Central Intelligence Agency (CIA), 961–962, 961(i), 1111
1953 coup in Iran, 993
Bay of Pigs invasion (1961) and, 1070
Chile and, 1090
Cuba and, 993, 1072
foreign policy in the 1950s and, 985, 992, 993
Nicaragua and, 1133–1134
Central Pacific Railroad, 656
Central Park (New York City), 697, 698
Central Park Lake (New York City), 697(i)
Chabot, Antoine, 638(b)
Chain gang system (labor gangs), 584, 676
Chamberlain, Neville, 912, 919(t)
Chamber of Commerce, 884
Chambers, Whittaker, 973
Chao, Elaine L., 1151
Chaplin, Charlie, 847
Chapman, Kathleen Welch, 718–719
Charleston, the (dance), 844(i)
Chase, Salmon P. (1808–1873), 563, 575
Chateau-Thierry, Battle of (1918), 799
Chavez, Cesar, 1045, 1045(i)
"Checkers speech" (1952), 979, 1006
Chemical weapons, in Vietnam War, 1084(i)
Cheney, Richard B. (Dick), 1168, 1172
Chesapeake Bay colonies. *See also* Virginia, colonial
Cheyenne Indians, 658
Chiang Kai-shek (1887–1975), 910, 940, 962
Chicago, 670–671, 675
1968 protests in, 1087–1088, 1087(i)
Haymarket rally and bombing (1886), 691–692, 692(i)
prohibition in, 841
skyscrapers, 695, 695(i)
World's Columbian Exposition (1893), 700–701, 701(i), 702–703(b)
Chicago Daily Tribune, 971
Chicago Tribune, 912
Chicago Women's Liberation, 1050(b)
Chicanos. *See* Mexicans and Mexican Americans
Child care, 1058, 1061, 1107
Child labor, 684–685, 684(i), 776(i), 777–778(b)
in Pennsylvania mines, 761(i)

Children. *See also* Education; Families;
Schools; Young people
black codes during Reconstruction and,
568
Great Depression (1930s) and, 858
welfare reform and, 1152–1153
Children's Aid Society (New York City),
684
Children's Bureau, 771, 858
Child Support Enforcement Amendments
Act, 1125
Chile, 1973 coup in, 1090–1091, 1090(m)
China, 811, 1114, 1146
Boxer uprising (1900), 732–733
civil war, 962
Communist revolution, 962
Japanese invasion of (1930s–1940s),
911, 916–917, 917(m)
Korean War (1950–1953) and, 976
missionaries in, 731–732, 732(i)
Nixon's visit to (1972), 1068, 1089, 1089(i)
Open Door policy, 734, 735(i), 768–769
Taft and, 772
trade bill (2000), 1163
Vietnam War and, 1078, 1079
World War II and, 940
China bloc, 962
Chinese Americans, 920. *See also* Chinese
immigrants
Chinese Exclusion Act (1882), 651, 657,
677, 820
Chinese Exclusion Act (1902), 782
Chinese immigrants
in California, 651, 656–657, 657(i), 677
Johnson-Reid Act (1924) and, 851
mining in the West and, 640
Chisholm, Shirley, 1108, 1108(i)
Chivington, John M., 658
Christian Coalition, 1120
Christianity, 1105, 1117, 1120. *See also*
Bible, the; Missionaries; Religion
Chrysler Corporation, 1113
Church Building (New York City), 696(b)
Churchill, Winston (1874–1965)
"iron curtain" speech (1946), 954–957(b)
after World War II, 953
during World War II, 914–916, 926,
927, 936, 937, 940, 941(i)
Church of Jesus Christ of Latter-Day
Saints. *See* Mormons
CIA (Central Intelligence Agency),
961–962, 961(i), 1111
1953 coup in Iran, 993
Bay of Pigs invasion (1961) and, 1070
Chile and, 1090
Cuba and, 993, 1072
foreign policy in the 1950s and, 985,
992, 993
Nicaragua and, 1133–1134
Cigarettes, 840(i)
Cisler, Lucinda, 1055
Cities
1870–1900, 670–681, 694–703
apartments, 695–697
government and big-city bosses,
698–700

leisure and amusements, 693–694,
694(i)
libraries, 698
migration to cities, 671–676
parks, 697, 697(i), 698
schools, 698
skyscrapers, 695, 695(i)
social geography, 680, 682
world's fairs, 702–703
in 1950s, 998–999
migration to
African Americans, 818–820, 819(i),
996, 999
Mexicans, 820–821
progressives' efforts to civilize, 749–752
Sun Belt (1920–1980), 1002(t)
Citizenship
Chinese immigrants and, 656
Fourteenth Amendment and, 571–573
male definition of, 619–620
Civilian Conservation Corps (CCC),
877–878, 878(i), 932
Civilian Conservation Corps Act (1933),
883(t)
Civil liberties, Red scare and (1919), 814,
818
Civil rights. *See also* Civil rights
movement; *and specific acts*
1960s legislation, 1028
Mexican American, 1002
Truman and, 969
Civil Rights Act (1866), 569, 576(t)
Civil Rights Act (1875), 576(t), 587
Civil Rights Act (1957), 1010
Civil Rights Act (1960), 1010
Civil Rights Act (1964), 1026, 1030(t),
1036, 1053
Civil Rights Act (1968), 1030(t), 1036
Civil rights movement. *See also specific
organizations and leaders*
in 1950s, 1009–1016
Brown v. Board of Education (1954), 1010
Montgomery (Alabama) bus boycott
(1955–1956), 1011, 1014–1016,
1014(i)
in 1960s, 1021–1023, 1031–1036
black nationalism and, 1036
Freedom Rides, 1033–1034, 1033(i),
1033(m)
Johnson administration and,
1035–1036
March on Washington (1963),
1034–1035, 1034(i)
nonviolence, 1033, 1037, 1040, 1041
sit-ins, 1032, 1032(i)
women's movement and, 1053
Civil Rights Restoration Act (1984), 1125
Civil Service Commission, 624
Civil service system, 623, 624, 625(i)
Civil unions, 1127
Civil Works Administration (CWA), 877
Claiborne, Liz, 1122
Clamshell Alliance, 1130
Clayton Antitrust Act (1914), 775
Clean Air Act (1970), 1052, 1170
Clean Air Act (1990), 1143

Clean Water Act (1972), 1060, 1170
Clemenceau, Georges (1841–1921), 799,
809, 810(i)
Clerical and service occupations, 686(i),
687, 997–998
Cleveland (Ohio), 680
progressive reform and, 755–758, 758(i)
Cleveland, Grover (1837–1908), 596(i)
1884 election, 624–626, 627(m)
1888 election, 626, 626(i)
1896 election, 728
as president (1885–1889 and
1893–1897)
foreign policy, 731, 733, 734
gold standard, 630
immigration, 677
Pullman strike (1894), 722
railroad regulation, 628
silver issue, 629–630
tariff issue, 627, 628
scandal involving, 625–626
Clinton, William Jefferson (Bill)
(1946–), 1132, 1150–1155
1992 election, 1149, 1149(i)
1996 election, 1153
apointment of women and minorities,
1151
domestic policies of, 1150–1152
economic boom and, 1154–1155
foreign policy, 1155, 1158–1160, 1161(i),
1163
impeachment of, 1153–1154, 1153(i)
rightward turn of, 1152–1153
trade policy, 1163
Clinton, Hillary Rodham, 1151
Closed shops, 832
Coal miners
1894 strike (Cripple Creek, Colorado),
718–719
1931 strike (Harlan County, Kentucky),
861, 861(m)
1943 strike, 924
anthracite coal strike (1902), 760–761
breaker boys, 761(i)
Truman and, 965
Cochrane, Charles, Jr., 1129(b)
Cody, William F. (Buffalo Bill;
1846–1917), 663, 664(i)
Coins, bimetalism system and, 629
Cold war, 1006. *See also* Containment
policy; John F. Kennedy, foreign
policy; Richard M. Nixon, foreign
policy
beginning of, 953–958(b), 958–959
Carter administration and, 1115–1116
Carter's approach to Nicaragua and,
1114
comic book, 950(i)
Eisenhower administration and, 985,
986
end of, 1145–1146
Truman administration and, 953–959
women's role and, 1005
Colfax, Schuyler, 585
Collective bargaining, 801, 883, 971, 997
Collective security, 961

Colleges and universities (higher education)
  democratization of (1940–1960), 1002–1004
  National Defense Education Act (1958), 994
  veterans in (after World War II), 965(i)
  World War I and, 804
Collier, John, 896, 896(i)
Colombia, Panama Canal and, 767
Colonies, Germany's, after World War I, 810–811
Colorado, 648
  woman suffrage in, 725
Colored Farmers' Alliance, 711–712
Colt, Mrs. William L., 804(i)
Columbia (female figure), 742(i)
Columbian Exposition (Chicago; 1893), 700–701, 701(i), 702–703(b), 703(i)
Columbia University (New York City), 1968 protests at, 1049–1050(b)
Comanche Indians, 658
Commerce. *See also* Merchants; Trade
Commission on Training Camp Activities, 798
Committee for a Sane Nuclear Policy, 995
Committee for Industrial Organization (CIO; later the Congress of Industrial Organizations), 892
Committee on Civil Rights, 969
Committee on Fair Employment Practices, 931
Committee on Public Information (CPI), 804, 806
Commodity Credit Corporation, 880
Common laborers, 682–683
Common Sense Book of Baby and Child Care (Spock), 1005
Commonwealth Edison Company, 838(b)
Commonwealth of Independent States (CIS), 1146
Communications
  telegraph, 600
  telephone, 606–607, 607(i)
Communist Party, 817
  in 1930s, 861, 862, 887
  anti-Communist hysteria (1940s–1950s) and, 973, 974
Communists (communism), 817(b)
  in 1930s, 897, 899
  Billy Graham on, 1006
  in China, 962
  collapse of, in Eastern Europe, 1145, 1146(m), 1158
  Kennedy's foreign policy and, 1067, 1069
  Red scare and (1919), 814–815, 818
Community Action Program (CAP), 1026–1027
Compromise of 1877, 591
Comstock Lode, mining on the, 637–643, 637(m), 641(i)
Coney Island (New York City), 694, 694(i)
Confederate flag dress, 569(i)
Conger, Sarah, 732

Congress, U.S. *See also* Election campaigns and elections; House of Representatives, U.S.
  Fourteenth Amendment, 571–574
  impeachment of Andrew Johnson, 574–576
  Military Reconstruction Act (1867), 574
  radical reconstruction and military rule, 573–574, 574(m)
  Reconstruction Acts of 1867, 574
  reconstruction and, 569–577. *See also* Congressional reconstruction
  Tenure of Office Act (1867), 575
Congressional reconstruction, 569–577, 585
  Fourteenth Amendment, 571–574
  radical reconstruction and military rule, 573–574, 574(m)
  Tenure of Office Act (1867), 575
Congress of Industrial Organizations (CIO), 892, 893
  merger with AFL (1955), 996–997
Congress of Racial Equality (CORE), 931, 1011, 1033
Conkling, Roscoe, 623
Connor, Eugene "Bull," 1034
Conscription (draft), 1080
  peacetime (1948), 961
  World War I, 797(i), 798
  World War II, 920
Conservation
  Civilian Conservation Corps (CCC), 877–878
  Taft and, 771
  Theodore Roosevelt and, 763–766, 766(i)
Conservatives (conservatism; the right), 1103
  in 1960s, 1022, 1027
  in 1980s, 1124–1125
  Clinton administration and, 1152–1153
  Eisenhower and, 986, 987
  federal courts and, 1124–1125
  George H. W. Bush and, 1143–1144
  grassroots conservative movement, 1105–1106, 1117
  Great Depression (1930s) and, 870–871
  Helsinki agreement (1975) and, 1090
  New Deal and, 900–902, 932
  New Right, 1104, 1105, 1116–1118, 1120, 1125
  Nixon and, 1104–1107
Consolidation, business, 610–612, 615
Constitutions, state, after Civil War, 561, 567, 568, 574, 578–579
Consumer borrowing, 1004
Consumer culture, 687, 701
  in 1920s, 836–839
  in 1950s, 986, 1004–1005
  Columbian Exposition and (1893), 703
  women and, 844
Consumer goods
  production of (1920–1930), 837
  after World War II, 965
Consumer prices. *See also* Inflation
  and farm income (1865–1910), 711(f)
Consumers' League of New York, 756(b)

Containment policy
  1952 election and, 978
  Eisenhower administration and, 985, 990–992
  Kennedy administration and, 1068
  Truman administration and, 952, 955, 958–960, 962
    Korean War (1950–1953), 976, 978, 980
  Vietnam and, 991–992
Contraception, 780, 781
Contras, 1133–1134
Convention on the Elimination of All Forms of Discrimination against Women (CEDAW), 1057–1058
Coolidge, Calvin (1872–1933), 814, 831, 832(i), 853
  1924 election, 833
  posing as a farmer, 833(i)
  as president, 832–833
Cooperatives, farmers', 712
Coral Sea, Battle of (1942), 925, 944(t)
Corliss, Alonzo B., 580(b)
Corn planter, mechanical, 652(i)
Corporations (corporate capitalism), 610, 1007. *See also* Big business
  consolidation of, 610–612, 615
  Fourteenth Amendment and, 615
Corregidor, Battle of (1942), 925, 944(t)
Corruption, 597–598
  big business and, 628(i)
  big-city bosses and, 698–700
  in Gilded Age (1870s–1890s), 623–624
  Grant administration and, 585
Costa Rica, 734, 768
Cotton Club (New York City), 846
Cotton-picking machine, 882(b), 882(i)
Cotton textile industry, in the New South, 617
Coughlin, Charles, 887
Coughlin, John, 699
Council of Economic Advisors, 964
Counterculture, 1960s, 1046–1047
Counterinsurgency strategy, 1072, 1073
Country Joe and the Fish, 1020(i)
County of London Orchestra, 915(i)
Courts, federal, conservative shift in, 1124–1125
Courtship, in urban industrial society, 693–694
Cowboys, 650–651
Cox, Archibald, 1109
Cox, Jacob D., 586
Cox, James M., 821
Coxey, Jacob S., 726
Coxey's army, 726–727, 726(i)
CPI (Committee on Public Information), 804, 806
Crazy Horse, chief (c. 1849–1877), 658, 660
Crédit Mobilier, 597–598
Creel, George, 804
Criminal justice system, Warren Court and, 1031
Cripple Creek (Colorado), 642(b)
  miners' strike in (1894), 718–719
Crocker, Charles, 656

Croly, Herbert, 773
Cronkite, Walter, 1086
Crook, George, 661
Crow Dog, Mary, 1042
Cuba, 910
    Bay of Pigs invasion (1961), 1070
    Kennedy administration and,
        1069–1070
    revolution (1959), 992(i)
    Spanish-American War (1898) and,
        734–740, 736(i)
Cuban missile crisis (1962), 1072–1073,
    1072(i), 1072(i), 1072(m)
Cuban refugees, 1157(i)
Cullen, Countee, 845
Culture(s)
    in 1950s, 1004–1009
        consumer culture, 1004–1005
        countercurrents, 1007–1009
        domesticity, 1005
    consumer, 687, 701
        in 1920s, 836–839
        in 1950s, 986, 1004–1005
    Columbian Exposition and (1893), 703
    women and, 844
    counterculture, 1960s, 1046–1047
    Gilded Age (1870s–1890s). See Gilded
        Age, politics and culture in
Cummings, Kate, 570(b)
Currency (money), gold standard, 629,
    629(i), 630
Custer, George Armstrong (1839–1876),
    660, 663, 664(i)
Czechoslovakia, 810, 912, 919(t), 953
    Communist takeover (1948), 960
Czech Republic, 1145
Czolgosz, Leon, 759

Daley, Richard J., 1087
Darrow, Clarence (1839–1876), 852, 853
Darwin, Charles (1809–1882), 613
Darwinism
    reform, 755
    social, 612–615, 618–619(b), 676, 726, 761
Davis, David, 591
Davis, Henry Winter, 561
Davis, James J., 683
Davis, John W., 833
Dawes, Charles, 834
Dawes Allotment Act (1887), 661
Dawes Plan (1924), 834
Dawidoff, Robert, 1127(i)
Dayton peace treaty (1995), 1158
D Day (June 6, 1944), 938, 938(i), 940,
    944(t)
Dean, John, 1109, 1110
Death camps, Allies' refusal to bomb,
    936–937(b)
Debs, Eugene V. (1855–1926)
    1912 election, 779(i)
    Pullman strike and (1894), 721–723
    Socialist Party and, 778–779
    during World War I, 805
Debt (borrowing)
    private
        in 1920s, 855

in 1950s, 1004
crop liens, 584
    by farmers (1880s–1890s), 712, 713
    by farmers (1930s), 881
    free silver issue, 629
    public (national; federal)
        Confederate war debts, 567
        under Reagan, 1122
Decade for Women, UN, 1057
Defense budget (military expenditures)
    Eisenhower's, 990, 994, 995
    Korean War and, 980
    Reagan administration, 1122
Defense of Marriage Act (1996), 1152
Defense strategy, Truman's, 960–962
Deficit, federal budget (deficit spending)
    in 1930s, 900
    Clinton administration and, 1151, 1154
    George H. W. Bush and, 1144
    George W. Bush administration and,
        1169
    Reagan administration and, 1122
De-industrialization, 1123
Democratic Party (Democrats)
    1868 election, 576, 588(i)
    1872 election, 586
    1874 election, 587
    1876 election, 591
    1896 election, 728–730
    1912 election, 772–773, 774(i)
    1916 election, 796
    1920 election, 821–822
    1928 election, 854
    1932 election, 871–872
    1936 election, 899
    1944 election, 932
    1948 election, 971
    1956 election, 990
    1968 convention in Chicago,
        1087–1088, 1087(i)
    1968 election, 1088
    1972 election, 1108
    1976 election, 1111
    1984 election, 1122
    1992 election, 1149
    in Gilded Age (1870s–1890s), 616, 617,
        620, 622, 624–629
    New York City, 698
    Nixon administration and, 1059
    in the South
        1932 election, 871
        1948 election, 971
        1968 elections, 1088
        Ku Klux Klan and, 581
        New Deal and, 887
        Nixon's southern strategy and, 1107
        reconstruction and, 579, 588, 589, 617
        Redeemers, 588, 617
        voting rights and, 782
        white supremacy and, 588, 589
Dempsey, Jack, 847–848
Denby, Charles, 733
Denmark, 914
Dennis, John Q. A., 564(b)
Dennis v. United States (1951), 974
Department stores, 687, 687(i)

Depression (economic panic)
    1893, 630
    1893–1897, 653, 731
        politics during, 725–730
    1907, 763
    1930s. See Great Depression
Deregulation, 1113, 1121, 1131, 1154
Desegregation
    in 1950s, 1010, 1011(i), 1012–1013(b)
    of armed services, 969
    Civil Rights Act (1964) and, 1036
Détente, strategy of, 1090, 1108, 1115
Deterrence, 961
Detroit, 859. See also Fort Detroit
    1943 race riot, 931
    1967 riot, 1037
    African Americans in, 820
    Pingree as mayor of, 699–700
Dewey, George (1837–1917), 737, 740(m)
Dewey, John (1859–1952), 755, 801
Dewey, Thomas E. (1902–1971), 932, 971
Díaz, Porfirio, 820
Dick, Deadwood, 663
Diem, Ngo Dinh (1901–1963), 992,
    1073(t), 1074, 1075
Dien Bien Phu, Battle of (1954), 991,
    1073(t)
Dime novels, 663
Dinkins, David, 1151
Disarmament, 911(i)
    Franklin D. Roosevelt and, 909
    nuclear, 1085(i), 1135(i)
    Washington Disarmament Conference
        (1921), 833
Dissent, in 1950s, 1007
Distribution of wealth
    in 1920s, 855
    New Deal and, 874
District of Columbia. See Washington, D.C.
Diversity, ethnic and cultural
    of labor force, 682–684
    in the West, 654–657, 676
Dixiecrats (States' Rights Party), 971
Dole, Robert (1923–), 1153
Dollar diplomacy, 772, 772(m)
Domesticity
    cult of, 692, 693, 724
    revival of, in 1950s, 1005
Domestic servants, 1870s–1890s, 693
Dominican Republic, 768, 772, 791
    1965 U.S. intervention in, 1076–1077,
        1077(i)
Domino theory, 959, 991
Donnelly, Ignatius (1831–1901), 709,
    716–717(b), 727
"Don't ask, don't tell" policy, 1152
Doolittle, James, 925
Double V campaign, 930–931
Douglas, Aaron, 845–846, 846(i)
Douglas, Helen Gahagan, 978
Douglass, Frederick (1817–1895), 572
Doves, Vietnam War, 1085
Draft (conscription), 1080
    peacetime (1948), 961
    World War I, 797(i), 798
    World War II, 920

Drake, Edwin, 604
Dred Scott decision (1857), 572
Dreiser, Theodore, 700
Drew, Daniel, 600
Drift and Mastery (Lippmann), 755
Droughts, Great Plains, 648
Du Bois, W. E. B. (1868–1963), 621, 784, 822, 823
    in 1920s, 845, 846(i)
Dulles, John Foster (1888–1959), 990–993
Dunkirk, Battle of (1940), 914, 919(t)
Dupree, Jack, 581(b)
Durkin, Martin, 987
Dust Bowl, 885(m), 886
Dutch East Indies, 916, 917, 925
Duties. *See* Tariffs and duties

Earned Income Tax Credit (EITC), 1150
Earth Day, first (1970), 1052
Eastern Europe
    1989–2002 events in, 1146(m)
    cold war and, 953–955, 958–960
    collapse of communism in, 1145, 1146(m), 1158
East Germany, 960, 1070, 1145
East St. Louis (Illinois), antiblack violence in (1917), 820
East Texas Oil Museum (Kilgore, Texas), 836(b)
Economic Development Act (1965), 1030(t)
Economic inequality. *See also* Wealth, distribution of
    1969–1998, 1123(f), 1154(f)
    in 1980s, 1123
    in 1990s, 1154
Economic Opportunity Act (1964), 1026, 1027, 1030(t)
Economic Recovery Tax Act (1981), 1121
Economy (economic policies). *See also* Agriculture; Business; Capitalism; Corporations; Depression; Manufacturing; Recession; Trade
    1920s, 836, 838, 855–856
    1930s, 857, 859, 873–878, 883, 883(t), 884, 890–891, 893–894, 900
    1950s, 995–996, 996(f), 1004
    1970s, 1060
    1990s, 1154–1155
    Clinton administration, 1150–1151
    under Hoover, 857
    Keynesian theory, 900
    laissez-faire, 615, 619(b), 622, 710, 748, 766, 854, 870, 1120, 1159
    Reagan administration and, 1121–1124
    southern, Republican governments (1870s) and, 582
    after World War I, 813–814
    after World War II, 953, 964, 965
    World War II and, 921, 924, 928(f)
Edelman, Marian Wright, 1152
Edison, Thomas Alva (1847–1931), 606, 607, 614(b), 838
    chemistry lab, 614(i)
Edison National Historic Site (West Orange, New Jersey), 614(b)

Education. *See also* Colleges and universities; Schools
    of blacks
        colleges (1941–1961), 1003
        in the South, 577, 580, 582
    George W. Bush administration and, 1170
    Indian schools, 635–636
    National Defense Education Act (1958), 994
    reconstruction and, 582
    of women, in colleges (1940–1960), 1003–1004
Efficiency, 755
Egypt
    Carter administration and, 1115
    Six-Day War (1967), 1091
    Suez crisis (1956), 993–994, 993(m)
Ehrlichman, John, 1060
Eighteenth Amendment, 802, 841
Eight-hour day movement, 690–692, 718, 719, 776, 813
Einstein, Albert (1879–1955), 934, 935(i), 961
Eisenhower, Dwight D. (1890–1969), 868(i), 1160
    1952 election, 978, 979(i)
    1956 election, 990
    domestic policies, 985–990
        civil rights, 1010
        Indian policy, 988–990
        Interstate Highway and Defense System Act (1956), 987, 988(m)
        social welfare, 987
    foreign policy
        domino theory, 991
        Latin America, 992–993
        Middle East, 993–994
        "New Look," 990–991
        nuclear arms race, 994–996
        Vietnam, 991–992
    Korean War and, 980
    McCarthy and, 986–987
    modern Republicanism and, 987–988
    in World War II, 927, 938
EITC (Earned Income Tax Credit), 1150
El-Alamein, Battle of (1942), 925–926, 944(t)
Elderly people
    Medicare and, 1027
    Social Security and, 893–894
Election campaigns and elections
    1866, 572–573
    1868, 576, 585–586, 585(m)
    1874, 587
    1876, 589, 591–592, 591(i), 592(m)
    1880, 623–624
    1884, 596(i), 624–626, 627(m)
    1888, 626, 626(i), 627
    1892, 626, 728(m)
    1896, 728, 729(i), 730(m)
    1904, 761
    1908, 770
    1912, 746(i), 772–774, 773(i), 773(m), 774(i), 779(i)
    1916, 776, 796

    1918, 808
    1920, 821–824, 824(m), 832(i)
    1924, 833
    1928, 853–854, 853(i), 854(m)
    1928–1932 electoral shift, 872(m)
    1932, 871–872, 872(m), 909
    1934, 889
    1936, 887, 897, 899
    1944, 932
    1946, 951, 970–971
    1948, 970(i), 971, 971(m)
    1952, 978, 1006
    1956, 990
    1960, 1023, 1023(m)
    1964, 1027
    1968, 1059(i), 1088, 1088(m)
    1972, 1107, 1108
    1976, 1111, 1111(m)
    1980, 1102(i), 1117, 1117(i)
    1984, 1122
    1992, 1149–1150
    1994, 1152
    1996, 1153
    2000, 1168–1169, 1168(i), 1169(i), 1169(m)
    television and, 1006–1007
Electricity, 607, 610, 610(i), 838–839(b)
    Rural Electrification Administration (REA), 881, 881(i)
Elementary and Secondary Education Act (1965), 1027, 1030(t)
Elevators, 695, 696(b), 696(i)
Elkins Act (1903), 760, 762
Ellis Island (New York), 677
Ellsberg, Daniel, 1093
El Salvador, 1133, 1134(m)
Emergency Banking Act (1933), 875, 883(t)
Emergency money, 876(i)
Emmons, Glenn, 988
Employment Act (1946), 964
Employment discrimination, 1036, 1127, 1143
Energy, Department of, 1113
Energy crisis (1973), 1060
England. *See* Great Britain
Enola Gay (B-29 bomber), 908–909
Entertainment (entertainment industry). *See also* Film industry
    1870s–1890s, 693–694, 694(i)
    in 1920s, 846–849
Environment, the (environmental policy). *See also* Agriculture; Conservation; Land; Mining
    1970s–1980s conflicts over environmental protections, 1130–1131
    Air Quality Act (1965), 1030(t)
    Clean Air Act (1970), 1052, 1170
    Clean Air Act (1990), 1143
    Clinton administration and, 1150
    Dust Bowl, 855(m), 886
    George W. Bush administration and, 1170
    hydraulic mining and, 638–639, 639(i)
    Johnson administration and, 1028, 1052
    national parks, 763, 766, 767(m)

Nixon administration and, 1051, 1052, 1060
solar energy, 1132(b)
sprawling urban and suburban settlement and, 1000
Theodore Roosevelt and, 763–766
Water Quality Act (1965), 1030(t)
Environmentalists, Nixon administration and, 1060
Environmental movement (environmentalism), 1047, 1050–1052
Environmental Protection Agency (EPA), 1052
Equal Employment Opportunity Commission (EEOC), 1053
Equal Pay Act (1963), 1053, 1056
Equal Rights Amendment (ERA)
1923, 843–844
1970s–1980s, 1055, 1118–1120(b), 1119(i), 1125, 1126(m)
Erie Railroad, 600–601
Ervin, Samuel J., Jr., 1109, 1118
Escobedo v. Illinois (1964), 1031
Espionage Act (1917), 805
Ethiopia, Fascist conquering of (1936), 919(t)
Ethnicity, urban development and, 680
Eugenics movement, 844
Europe
in 1990s, 1145
after World War I, 811(m)
after World War II, 955(m)
European theater
World War II (1939–1941), 926
World War II (1942–1945), 939(m)
Evangelical Protestants. *See also* Religious revivals
Reagan administration and, 1117
Evers, Medgar (1925–1963), 968, 1034
Executive Order 9066 (1942), 920
Executive Order 9835 (1947), 973
Executive Order 11246 (1965), 1030(t), 1036
Executive Order 11375 (1967), 1030(t)
"Exodusters," 651
Expansion (expansionism), 742(i). *See also* Imperialism
1890s, 731
to 1900, 741(m)
imperialism and, 739–742
Expertise, progressive reformers' emphasis on, 755

Fairbanks, Douglas, 846
Fair Deal, 964, 970–972
Fair Labor Standards Act (1938), 901
Fall, Albert, 832
Falwell, Jerry, 1118–1119
Families (family life)
in 1950s, 1005, 1007(i)
black southern (1870s), 583, 583(i)
economy of, 685
Great Depression (1930s) and, 859–860
the Internet and, 1161
Reconstruction and, 563

television and, 1006
during World War II, 930
Family and Medical Leave Act (1993), 1150
Farm Board, 857
Farm Credit Act (FCA), 881
Farmer, James, 1108(i)
Farmers' Alliance movement, 710–712, 712(i)
Farmers and farms. *See also* Agriculture; Rural areas
1870–1900, 710
consumer prices and farm income (1865–1910), 711(f)
Farmers' Alliance movement, 710–712, 712(i)
1940–1960, 996
black
Colored Farmers' Alliance, 711–712
Populists and (1890s), 728
sharecroppers, 583–584, 858, 862, 885, 885(i)
foreclosures (1932–1942), 877(f)
free silver issue and, 629
Great Depression (1930s) and, 861
Hoover administration and, 857
hydraulic mining and, 639
income
1920–1940, 858(f)
1929–1932, 880
1936, 881
New Deal and, 880–881, 901
Newlands Reclamation Act (1902) and, 766
as percentage of population (1870–1900), 651, 652(f)
railroad regulation and, 628
sharecropping, 583–585
westward migration (1870s–1890s), 651–654
Wilson and, 776
yeoman, reconstruction and, 578, 582
Farmers' cooperatives, 712
Farm Security Administration (FSA), 901
Father Knows Best (sitcom), 1007(i)
Fathers, in 1950s, 1005
Faubus, Orval, 1010
Federal Arts Program, 881(i)
Federal Bureau of Investigation (FBI), 920(i), 1111
Federal Deposit Insurance Corporation (FDIC), 875
Federal Election Campaign Act (1974), 1111
Federal Emergency Relief Administration (FERA), 877, 883(t)
Federal Housing Administration, 998
Federal Reserve Act (1913), 775
Federal Reserve Board, 775
Federal Trade Commission (FTC), 775
Feminine Mystique, The (Friedan), 1005
Feminism (feminist movement), 841, 1144. *See also* Woman's rights movement
1960s–1970s, 1046, 1052–1058
counter movement, 1055, 1057–1058
emergence of, 1052–1054

facets and achievements of, 1054–1055
in 1980s, 1125–1126
in other countries, 1056–1058(b)
Ferraro, Geraldine A., 1122
Fetterman, William, 658
Field, Stephen J., 615
Fiering, Henry, 964, 965
Fifteenth Amendment (ratified 1870), 576–577, 576(t), 587, 724
Film industry (movies)
in 1920s, 846, 847(i), 848(f)
in 1930s, 860
during World War I, 804, 805(i)
Finance capitalism, 610–612
Fireside chats, Franklin D. Roosevelt's, 866(i), 876, 916
Fish, Hamilton, 586
Fisk, James (1834–1872), 600
Fitzgerald, F. Scott (1896–1940), 849, 855
Five-Power Naval Treaty (1922), 833–834
Flappers, 844, 844(i)
Flash photography, 764–765(b)
Florida, 589
1876 election, 591(i)
2000 election, 1168–1169, 1169(i)
Flowers, Andrew, 581(b)
Foch, Marshal, 790, 799
Folk music, 1046–1047
Food Administration, 801
Food stamp program, 901, 1027, 1059, 1122, 1157, 1166
Football, 848
Ford, Edsel, 830(i)
Ford, Gerald R. (1913–), 1090, 1104, 1107, 1109
as president, 1110–1111
Ford, Henry (1863–1947), 828(i), 829–830, 830(i), 834, 839, 861
Ford Motor Co., 820
Ford Motor Company, 829, 893
violence against demonstrators (1932), 861
Fordney-McCumber tariff (1922), 831–832
Foreign policy
in 1890s, 731–734
in 1920s, 833–834
Carter's, 1113–1116, 1114(m)
Cleveland's, 731, 733, 734
Clinton's, 1155, 1158–1160, 1161(i), 1163
Eisenhower's
domino theory, 991
Latin America, 992–993
Middle East, 993–994
"New Look," 990–991
nuclear arms race, 994–996
Vietnam, 991–992
expansionism. *See* Expansion
Franklin D. Roosevelt's, 909–912
George W. Bush's, 1171–1173
Grant administration, 586
imperialism, 710, 739–742, 1147, 1159
mandate system and, 810–811
isolationism, 731, 812, 833, 915, 951
in 1930s and 1940s, 909–912
Kennedy's, 1067–1075

Foreign policy (continued)
  arms race, 1072–1073
  Berlin crisis (1961), 1070–1071
  Cuba, 1069–1070
  Cuban missile crisis (1962),
    1072–1073, 1072(m)
  Peace Corps, 1071, 1071(i)
  Soviet Union, 1068–1073
  third world, 1071–1072
  Vietnam War, 1068, 1073–1075
  Lyndon Johnson's, 1075–1081
    Latin America, 1076–1077
    Vietnam War, 1077–1081
  McKinley's, 739, 740
  Monroe Doctrine, 733–734
  Nixon's, 1088–1097
    anticommunism in the third world,
      1090–1091
    China, 1089–1090
    Middle East, 1091
    Soviet Union, 1090
    Vietnam War. See Vietnam War,
      Nixon administration and
  Reagan's, 1131–1135
    Iran-Contra scandal, 1134–1135
    militarization and interventions
      abroad, 1131–1134
    Soviet-American relations, 1134,
      1136(i)
  Taft's, 771–772
  Theodore Roosevelt's, 766–770
  Truman's, 952–962
    China, 962–963
    cold war, 953–959
    containment policy, 952, 955,
      958–960, 962
    defense strategy, 960–962
    Korean War, 974–978
    Marshall Plan, 959(i), 960
    Middle East, 963
    national liberation movements, 962
    national security, 960–962
    Point IV Program, 962
    Truman Doctrine, 959–960
  Wilson's, 790–796
Foreign trade. See Trade
Forrestal, James V., 953
Fortas, Abe, 1026(i)
Fort Laramie (Wyoming), Treaty of
  (1868), 658, 660
Fort Laramie Treaty (1868), 1042
Forty-niners, 637
"Four-Minute Men," 804, 806
Fourteen Points, Wilson's, 809–811
Fourteenth Amendment (ratified 1868),
  571–574, 576(t), 587, 724, 1010
  corporations and, 615
  Warren Court and, 1031
France, 833, 834
  Suez crisis and (1956), 993–994
  Vietnam and, 991–992
  World War I and, 792–794, 798–800,
    816(b)
    Paris peace conference (1919), 809–810
  World War II and, 914
    revised neutrality law, 915

Franchise. See Voting rights
Franco, Francisco, 911
Frankfurter, Felix, 937
Franz Ferdinand, Archduke, 793
Free blacks (freedmen), 582. See also
  Reconstruction
  Ku Klux Klan and, 580–581(b)
  westward migration, 651
Freedmen's Bureau, 562, 572, 575, 579
Freedmen's Bureau bill (1866), 569, 576(t)
Freedom Rides, 1033–1034, 1033(i),
  1033(m), 1036
Free silver, 629–630, 713, 728–730
Free speech movement (1964), 1046
Free trade, 627
Frémont, John C. (1813–1890), 643
French, Daniel Chester, 701(i)
Freud, Sigmund, 840
Frick, Henry Clay (1849–1919), 714,
  715(i), 718
Friedan, Betty, 1005, 1053
Friedman, Thomas, 1160
Frontier, the, 663, 711. See also West, the
  (American)
Fuel Administration, 801
Full-employment legislation, 964

Galbraith, John Kenneth, 996
García, Héctor Peréz, 969
Garfield, James A. (1831–1881), 573, 598,
  624
Garland, Hamlin, 700
Garment industry, 683–684
Garvey, Marcus (1887–1940), 845
Gary, Martin, 589
Gas mask, 788(i)
Gates, John "Bet a Million," 650, 650(i)
Gates, Merrill, 636
GATT (General Agreement on Tariffs and
  Trade), 1163
Gays and lesbians, (homosexuals)
  Clinton administration and, 1152
  McCarthyism and, 974
  rights movement, 1126–1130, 1127(m),
    1129(b)
  World War II and, 921
Gender gap, 1125–1126, 1153
Gender relations (gender roles)
  in 1920s, 841–842
  Equal Rights Amendment (ERA) and,
    1055
  politics between 1865 and 1900 and,
    619–620
  separate spheres, doctrine of, 620, 692,
    844
General Agreement on Tariffs and Trade
  (GATT), 1163
General Electric, 610, 838, 966
General Managers Association (GMA),
  721, 722
General Motors, 924(i), 984(i), 1162
  sit-down strike in Flint, Michigan
    (1937), 892–893, 892(i)
Geneva, 1955 summit conference, 994
Geneva Accords (1954), 991–992, 991(m),
  1073(t)

"Gentleman's Agreement" (1907), 770
Georgia
  1868 election, 581
  Ku Klux Klan in, 581(b)
  reconstruction and, 567, 588–589
German immigrants (German
  Americans), 812
  during World War I, 805, 805(i)
Germany
  in 1930s, 909–912
    anti-Semitism, 934
  Khrushchev and, 1070
  Samoan Islands and, 734
  unification of, 1145
  war reparation payments, 834
  World War I and, 792–797, 816
    Paris peace conference (1919), 810
  after World War II, 954
  World War II and, 912–914, 913(m),
    915, 927, 938, 940
    bombing raids, 933–936
    death camps, Allies' refusal to bomb,
      936–937(b)
    Holocaust, 932–933, 933(m)
    Panzers, 914(i)
    Poland, 912–914
Geronimo (1829–1909), 661, 662
Ghost Dance, 662–663, 662(i)
Gibbs, Lois, 1130
GI Bill (Servicemen's Readjustment Act;
  1944), 965, 968, 1003
GI Bill of Rights (1944), 932
Gideon v. Wainwright (1963), 1031
GI Forum, 969, 970
Gilded Age (1870s–1890s), 597–630. See
  also Cities, 1870–1900
  business consolidation in, 610–615
    J. P. Morgan and finance capitalism,
      610–612
    laissez-faire and the Supreme Court,
      615
    social Darwinism and the gospel of
      wealth, 612–615
  new and old industries in, 599–610
    oil industry, 604–606
    railroads, 599–601
    steel industry and vertical
      integration, 602–604
    the telephone and electricity,
      606–607, 610
  politics and culture in, 615–622
    big-city government and bosses,
      698–700
    depression politics (1893–1897),
      725–730
    gender, race, and politics, 619–621
    labor movement, 714–723
    political participation and party
      loyalty, 615–617
    presidential politics in, 622–626
    sectionalism and the New South,
      617–619
    women's activism, 723–725
    women's politics, 621–622
  in the West, 635–664
    clash of cultures, 654–664

Dawes Act and Indian land allotment, 660–661
dime novels, 663
final removal of the Indians, 657–660
Indian wars (1861–1890), 635, 657–660
land fever, 644–654
mining on the Comstock Lode, 637–643
territorial government, 643–644
Gilded Age, The (Twain and Warner), 597, 598(i), 692
Gilder, George, 1029
Gingrich, Newt, 1152
Ginsberg, Allen (1926–1997), 1009
Ginsburg, Ruth Bader (1933–), 1151
Gladden, Washington, 750
Glass-Steagall Banking Act (1933), 875, 883(t)
Glazer, Nathan, 1157
Glenn, John H., 1070
Glidden, Joseph F., 650, 650(i)
Globalization, 1159–1163
Global warming, 1170
Glover, Cathleen, 1152
Gold (gold mining)
   in the Black Hills of the Dakotas, 660
   hydraulic, 638–639(b)
Gold, Mike, 678(b)
Goldman, Emma (1869–1940), 779–780
   deportation of (1919), 815, 818, 818(i)
Goldmark, Josephine, 754, 757(b)
Goldmark, Pauline, 757(b)
Gold standard, 629, 629(i), 630
Goldwater, Barry M. (1909–1998), 1027, 1075, 1105
Gompers, Samuel (1850–1924), 690–692, 752, 775, 814
Gonzales, Rodolfo "Corky," 1045–1046
Goode, G. Brown, 703(b)
Good government, 699–700
Good neighbor policy, 910
Gorbachev, Mikhail (1931–), 1134, 1135, 1136(i), 1145, 1146
Gordon, John B., 580(b)
Gore, Albert, Jr. (1948–), 1168
   1992 election, 1149, 1149(i)
Gospel of wealth, 612–615, 618, 750
Gould, Jay (1836–1892), 599, 600, 600(i), 602
Gould and Curry Mine, 640
Government. *See also* States (state governments)
   city (1870–1900), 698–700
   good, 699–700
   territorial, 643–644
Government regulation. *See also* Antitrust laws and suits; Deregulation
   Coolidge administration and, 832
   Nixon administration and, 1060
   of railroads
      1870s–1880s, 628
      Elkins Act (1903), 760, 762
Grady, Henry, 617
Graham, Billy (1918–), 1005–1006, 1006(i), 1008, 1031

Grange
   the, 711
   the (Patrons of Husbandry), 628
Grange, Harold "Red," 848
Grant, Ulysses S. (1822–1885), 575
   1868 election, 581, 585–586, 588(i)
   corruption, 586(i)
   as president, 585–586
   retreat from reconstruction, 587
Great American Desert, 648
Great Britain, 833
   Civil War and, 586
   military assistance to Greece and Turkey after World War II, 959
   Suez crisis and (1956), 993–994
   woman suffrage in, 782
   World War I and, 792–794, 796, 798, 816
      Paris peace conference (1919), 810
   World War II and, 914, 926–927, 930
      Lend-Lease Act (1941), 916
      revised neutrality law, 915
Great Depression (1930s), 857–862
   human toll of, 858–860
   stock market crash of 1929 and, 856
Greater East Asia Co-Prosperity Sphere, 916
Great Northern Railroad, 600, 760(i)
Great Plains, 648
Great Railroad Strike of 1877, 687–690, 688(i), 689(m)
Great Society programs, 1021–1022, 1027–1030, 1030(t)
   War on Poverty, 1028–1029, 1042
Great Southwestern Strike (1886), 712
Great White Fleet, 770
Greece, 810, 959
Greeley, Horace (1811–1872), 586, 646(b), 670
Green, William, 860
Greenback Labor Party, 711
Green Berets, 1072, 1074
Greensboro (North Carolina), sit-in (1960), 1032
Grenada, 1132
Grey, Edward, 794
Griffith, D. W., 805(i), 852
Grinnell, Julius S., 691
Grove City v. Bell (1984), 1125
Guadalcanal, Battle for (1942–1943), 941, 944(t)
Guam, 739, 740
Guatemala, 734
   Eisenhower administration and, 992–993
Guerrilla warfare, 992
Guiteau, Charles, 624
Gulf of Tonkin Resolution (1964), 1073(t), 1075, 1093
Gulf Oil Company, 835(i)
Gulf War (1991), 1147–1149, 1147(i), 1148(m)
Gun control legislation, 1144, 1150, 1152
Guthrie, Woody, 860, 897
Gutierrez, José Angel, 1046

Haganah, 963(i)

Haight-Ashbury (San Francisco), hippie community, 1046
Haiti, 791, 910
   in 1990s–2000s, 1155, 1158
Half Breeds, 623
Hallidie, Andrew Smith, 697(i)
Hamer, Fannie Lou (1917–1977), 1021, 1022(i)
Hamilton, Grant, 736(i)
Hampton Pageant (1892), 635, 636(i)
Hancock, Winfield Scott, 624
Hanna, Mark (1837–1904), 730, 736, 761, 783
Hanson, Ole, 813–814
Happiness of Womanhood (HOW), 1119
Harding, Warren Gamaliel (1865–1923), 831–834
   1920 election, 822–824, 832(i)
   Five-Power Naval Treaty (1922), 833–834
Harlan County (Kentucky), 1931 coal miners strike, 861, 861(m)
Harlem (New York City), 820
   in 1920s, 845–846
Harlem Renaissance, 845
Harrington, Michael, 1025
Harris, David Golightly, 559, 583, 588
Harrison, Benjamin (1833–1901), 626, 663
   tariff issue, 627
Harrison, Carter, 691
Harry S. Truman Library (Independence, Missouri), 977(b)
Hawaii, annexation of, 731, 739
Hawks, Vietnam War, 1084
Hawley-Smoot tariff (1930), 857
Hay, John (1838–1905), 689, 732
   Open Door policy, 734, 735(i)
   Spanish-American War (1898), 735
Hayden, Casey, 1053–1054
Hayden, Tom, 1159
Hayes, Rutherford B. (1822–1893)
   1876 election, 591, 591(i), 592, 592(m), 617(i)
   Great Railroad Strike of 1877 and, 689
   as president, 623
Haymarket rally and bombing (1886), 691–692, 692(i)
Haywood, William Dudley "Big Bill," 779
Health, Education, and Welfare, Department of, 987
Health care
   Clinton administration and, 1151
   George W. Bush administration and, 1170
   Great Society programs (1960s), 1027
Hearst, William Randolph (1863–1951), 735, 738
Heide, Wilma Scott, 1118
Heidt, Wesley and Edward, 918(i)
Helicopters, military, 1082–1083(b), 1083(i)
Helms, Jesse, 1107
Helsinki agreement (1975), 1090
Hemingway, Ernest (1899–1961), 849
Hendricks, Thomas A., 587
Henry Street settlement (New York City), 749

Hepburn Act (1906), 762
Hernandez, Aileen, 1054
Hernandez v. Texas, 1002
Herndon, Angelo, 895
Hetch Hetchy Valley, 764–765, 766(i)
Higher education. *See* Colleges and
    universities
Higher Education Act (1965), 1027, 1030(t)
Highways
    1930–1970, 988(m)
    Interstate Highway and Defense
        System Act (1956), 987, 988(m)
Highway Safety Act (1966), 1030(t)
Hill, Anita, 1144
Hill, James J., 600, 760(i)
Hillman, Sidney, 892
Hinds, J. M., 581
Hippies, 1046–1047
Hirohito, Emperor (1901–1989), 917
Hiroshima, atomic bombing of (1945),
    908–909, 908(i), 944(t), 945
Hispanic-American Alliance, 895(i)
Hispanic Americans (Latinos), 1166. *See
    also* Mexicans and Mexican
    Americans
    in 1950s, 1001–1002
    1960s struggles for justice, 1044–1046
    in California, 651, 655–656, 1001–1002
    in Clinton administration, 1151
    in the Gilded Age West, 654, 655–656
    income, in 2001, 1155
    New Deal and, 895–896
    population of, in 2002, 1163–1166
    after World War II, 969–970
Hiss, Alger, 973
Hitler, Adolf (1889–1945), 910, 912, 919,
    934, 940
Hobby, Oveta Culp, 987
Hoboes, 858
Ho Chi Minh (1890–1969), 991, 992,
    1074
Hoffman, Abbie, 1087
Holding companies, 605
Hollywood (California), 846, 860. *See also*
    Film industry
Holmes, Oliver Wendell, Jr. (1841–1935),
    570, 818
Holocaust, 932–933
Home front, World War II
    African Americans, 930–931
    Double V campaign, 930–931
    the economy, 921, 924, 928(f), 930
    the Holocaust, 932–933, 933(m)
    politics and the 1944 election, 932
    riots (1943), 931
    security, 919–920
    women and families, 928–930
Homeland Security, Department of, 1171
Homelessness, 1123–1124, 1124(i)
Homes, 1870s–1890s, 692–693
Homestead (Pennsylvania), 693
    lockout and strike (1892), 714–715,
        715(i), 718
    steelworks, 613(i)
Homestead: The Households of a Mill Town
    (Byington), 693

Homestead Act (1862), 644
Homesteaders, 644–650
    areas settled before 1862, 649(m)
    women, 645, 646–647(b)
Homosexuality. *See* Gay and lesbian
    rights; Gay and lesbian rights
    movement
Honduras, 734, 772
Hood, John B. (1831–1879), 571
Hoover, Herbert (1874–1964)
    1928 election, 853, 853(i), 854
    1932 election, 871
    individualism and, 855, 857–858
    as president, 854–857, 860
        Bonus Army (1932), 867–868
        after stock market collapse (1929), 857
    as secretary of commerce, 832, 841,
        854
    during World War I, 801
Hoover, J. Edgar (1895–1972), 815
Hoover Dam (Nevada), 878, 879(b), 879(i)
Hoovervilles, 860
Hopkins, Harry (1890–1946), 873, 877
Horowitz, Carl F., 1129(b)
House Un-American Activities
    Committee (HUAC), 974
Housing, 1027
    National Housing Act (1937), 901
    National Housing Act (1968), 1028,
        1029
Housing Act (1949), 971
Housing and Urban Development
    (HUD), Department of, 1030(t)
Howard University students, demands of
    (1968), 1048–1049(b)
Howl (Ginsberg), 1009
How the Other Half Lives (Riis), 680,
    764–765
HUAC (House Un-American Activities
    Committee), 974
Huerta, Dolores, 1045
Huerta, Victoriano, 791
Hughes, Charles Evans (1862–1948), 796,
    831, 833, 899
Hughes, Langston (1902–1967), 845
Hull, Cordell (1871–1955), 910
Hull House (Chicago), 747, 748, 748(i),
    749(i), 752
Human rights, Carter administration
    and, 1113–1115
Humphrey, Hubert H. (1911–1978), 1088
Humphrey, Richard Manning, 711
Hungary, 810, 816, 953, 1145
    1956 revolt, 991
Hunt, H. L., 836
Hurston, Zora Neale, 845
Hussein, King of Jordan (1935–1999),
    1158
Hussein, Saddam (1937–), 1158, 1172,
    1173, 1173(i)
    Persian Gulf War and (1991),
        1147–1149
Hydraulic mining, 638–639(b), 639(i)

ICBMs (intercontinental ballistic
    missiles), 994, 1072

ICC (Interstate Commerce Commission),
    628, 762
Idaho, woman suffrage in, 725
Illegal immigrants (undocumented
    migrants), 1001–1002, 1002(i), 1166
I Love Lucy (television show), 1006
IMF (International Monetary Fund), 1162,
    1163
Immigration (immigrants)
    1870–1900, 671–683, 671(i), 674(m),
        676(i)
        "old" and "new" immigration,
            672–675
        racism and, 676–677
        restrictions on immigration, 677
    1870–1910, 675(f)
    in 1920s, 850–851
    in 1980s–2000s, 1163, 1166, 1167, 1167(i)
    Chinese
        in California, 651, 656–657, 657(i), 677
        Johnson-Reid Act (1924) and, 851
        mining in the West and, 640
    Democratic Party and, 617
    German, 812
        during World War I, 805, 805(i)
    illegal, 1001–1002, 1002(i), 1166
    mining in the West and, 639–640
    Nationality Act (1965), 1028
    restrictions on
        1870–1900, 677
        in 1980s and 1990s, 1157
        Al Smith and, 853
        Chinese Exclusion Act (1882), 651,
            657, 677, 820
        Chinese Exclusion Act (1902), 782
        Johnson-Reid Act (1924), 851
        McCarran-Walter Act (1952), 971
        after World War II, 1156–1157(b)
Immigration and Nationality Act (1965),
    1030(t), 1156
Immigration Reform and Control Act
    (1986), 1157, 1166
Impeachment
    of Andrew Johnson, 574–576
    of Clinton, 1153–1154, 1153(i)
    of Nixon, 1110
Imperialism, 710, 739–742, 1147, 1159
    mandate system and, 810–811
Import duties. *See* Tariffs and duties
Income. *See also* Wages and salaries
    in 1950s, 1004
    in 1990s, 1154–1155
    farm
        1920–1940, 858(f)
        1929–1932, 880
        1936, 881
    manufacturing and agricultural
        (1920–1940), 858(f)
    national (1929–1933), 858
    per capita (1945–1970), 996
Income tax, 771, 775
India, 962, 1146
Indian Claims Commission, 988–989
Indian Reorganization Act (1934), 661, 988
Indian Reorganization Act (IRA), 896,
    896(i)

Indians. *See* Native Americans
Indian Territory, 649
Indian wars (1861–1890), 635, 655(i), 657–660
Individualism, Hoover and, 855
Indochina, 962
Industrialization (industrial growth). *See also* Manufacturing
1865–1900, 598–599, 672(m)
interconnected economic regions of the world (1870s–1890s), 671–672, 673(m)
Industrial Workers of the World (IWW), 779
Industry (industrial production). *See also* Manufacturing; *and specific industries*
in Gilded Age (1870s–1890s), 599–610
oil industry, 604–606
railroads, 599–601
steel industry and vertical integration, 602–604
the telephone and electricity, 606–607, 610
New Deal and, 881, 883
in the South, 617
Industry, 1945–1960, 996
Inequality, economic. *See also* Wealth, distribution of
1969–1998, 1123(f), 1154(f)
in 1980s, 1123
in 1990s, 1154
Inflation
1865–1910, 711(f)
1896 election and, 730
1919–1920, 813
in 1930s, 900
1969, 1060
after World War II, 964
Information technology, 1154, 1161
Insull, Samuel, 838
Integration. *See also* Desegregation
civil rights movement and, 1032, 1034
of schools
1950s–1960s, 1010, 1011(i), 1012–1013(b)
in 1970s, 1060
busing for, 1106, 1107(i)
Nixon administration, 1106
southern manifesto on, 1012(b)
Intelligence (gathering of information), 961(i)
Inter-American Conference (1933), 910
Intercontinental ballistic missiles (ICBMs), 994, 1072
Intermediate-range nuclear forces (INF) agreement, 1135
International Alliance of Women, 1056
International Criminal Court, 1172
Internationalization of the United States, 1163, 1166, 1167
International Ladies' Garment Workers Union (ILGWU), 752–753, 753(i)
International Monetary Fund (IMF), 1162, 1163

International Women's Year (1975), 1056, 1057(i)
International Workers of the World (IWW), 813, 814
Centralia (Washington) events (1919), 818
Internet, the, 1160–1161(b), 1161(i)
Interstate Commerce Act (1887), 628
Interstate Commerce Commission (ICC), 628, 762
Interstate Highway and Defense System Act (1956), 987, 988(m)
Inventions, notable American (1865–1899), 606(t)
Iran, 953, 1172
1953 coup, 993
hostage crisis (1979–1980), 1115, 1116(i)
Iran-Contra scandal, 1134–1135
Iran-Iraq War, 1134
Iraq
2003-2004 American invasion and occupation of, 1148(m)
Clinton administration and, 1158
Persian Gulf War and (1991), 1147–1149, 1147(i), 1148(m)
war against, 1172–1174, 1173(i)
Irish immigrants (Irish Americans), 626, 812
mining in the West and, 640
Iron curtain, 991, 1070
Churchill's speech on(1946), 954–955
Isolationism, 731, 812, 833, 915, 951
in 1930s and 1940s, 909–912
Israel, 1149
Carter administration and, 1115
Eisenhower administration and, 993
events since 1989, 1158(m)
Nixon administration and, 1091
Six-Day War (1967), 1091, 1091(m)
Truman and, 963
Yom Kippur War (1973), 1060, 1091
Israel Defense Forces, 963(i)
Israeli-Palestinian conflict, 1114(m), 1115, 1158–1159, 1158(m)
Italian Americans, 812
Italian immigrants, 675, 678
Italy, 833
in 1930s, 911, 912
World War II and, 917, 927
Iwo Jima, Battle of (1945), 943, 944(t)

Jackson, Andrew (1767–1845), as president (1829–1837), Indian removal policy, 657
Jackson, Jesse (1941–), 1149
Jackson (Mississippi), 1963 sit-in, 1032(i)
Jackson State College (Mississippi), killing of students in (1970), 1093
James, Ronald M., 643
James, William, 755
Jane Addams Hull-House Museum (Chicago), 750–751(b)
Japan, 833
in 1930s, 910, 911
Theodore Roosevelt and, 770

World War I and, 794
after World War II, 963
World War II and, 916–919, 924–926, 925(i), 944(t)
atomic bombing of Hiroshima and Nagasaki (1945), 908–909, 908(i), 944–945, 944(t), 945(i)
attack on Pearl Harbor (1941), 918, 918(i), 918(m), 919(t), 944(t)
defeat, 940–941, 942(m), 943–946
surrender, 946
Japanese Americans, during World War II, 920, 921(m), 922–923(b)
Japanese immigrants, 657, 770, 782
Jazz, 846, 848–849
Jewish immigrants, 675–676
"making it" in America, 678–679(b)
Jews
Palestine and, 963
World War II and, 963
death camps, Allies' refusal to bomb, 936
the Holocaust, 932–933, 933(m)
Nazi anti-Semitism, 934(b)
Jews without Money (Gold), 678
Jim Crow laws, 582, 677, 783, 931
Job discrimination, 1036, 1127, 1143
Jobs, Steven, 1122
Johns, Barbara, 1010
Johnson, Albert, 1156
Johnson, Andrew (1808–1875), 563, 575(i)
as defender of slavery, 567
impeachment of, 574–576
personal background of, 566
reconstruction and, 566–570, 572–576. *See also* Reconstruction, presidential
Fourteenth Amendment, 572
Military Reconstruction Act vetoed (1867), 574
Johnson, Hiram (1866–1945), 759, 772, 782, 812
Johnson, James Weldon, 845
Johnson, Lyndon B. (1908–1973), 969, 1026(i), 1076
1960 election, 1023
1964 election, 1027
assumption of presidency, 1026
civil rights and, 1035–1036
the environment and, 1028, 1052
Great Society programs, 1021–1022, 1027–1030
Johnson, Tom, 755–758, 758(i)
Johnson-Reid Act (1924), 851
Jones, Cynthia, 1143
Jones, William "Billy," 685–686
Jordan, 1091
Jordan, Barbara, 1038
Jorgensen, Mary, 999
Joseph, Chief, 660
Josephson, Matthew, 609(b)
Jungle, The (Sinclair), 762(i), 763

Kamikaze, 943–944
Kansas, migration to, 648, 651
Kearney, Denis, 657

Keller, G. Frederick, 602(i)
Kelley, Florence (1859–1932), 754, 756–757, 777(b)
Kellogg, Frank, 834
Kellogg-Briand pact (1928), 834
Kenna, Michael "Hinky Dink," 699
Kennan, George F. (1904–), 955, 958
  on student protest movement (1967), 1051(b)
Kennedy, Anthony M., 1125
Kennedy, Edward M. (1932–), 1148, 1170
Kennedy, John F. (1917–1963), 1023–1026, 1024(i)
  1960 election, 1007
  antidiscrimination legislation and, 1036
  assassination of, 1025–1026
  foreign policy, 1067–1075
    arms race, 1072–1073
    Berlin crisis (1961), 1070–1071
    Cuba, 1069–1070
    Cuban missile crisis (1962), 1072–1073, 1072(m)
    Peace Corps, 1071, 1071(i)
    Soviet Union, 1068–1073
    third world, 1071–1072
    Vietnam War, 1068, 1073–1075
  funeral, 1025(i)
  women's rights and, 1053
Kennedy, Joseph P., 876
Kennedy, Robert F. (1925–1968), 1033, 1086
Kent, Rockwell, 839(i)
Kent State University (Ohio), killing of students in (1970), 1092–1093
Kerner Commission, 1037
Kerouac, Jack, 1009
Keynes, John Maynard (1883–1946), 858–859, 900
Keynesian theory, 900
Khmer Rouge, 1093
Khomeini, Ayatollah Ruholla, 1115
Khrushchev, Nikita (1894–1971), 994, 1069
  Kennedy administration and, 1070, 1072, 1073
  "kitchen debate" (1959), 985, 986(i)
Kikuchi, Charles, 923(b)
Kilpatrick, James J., 1120
Kim Il-sung, 974–975
King, Martin Luther, Jr. (1929–1968), 1016, 1033, 1068
  assassination of, 1041
  Birmingham (Alabama) campaign (1963), 1034
  birthplace, 1015(i)
  black power movement and, 1041
  at March on Washington (1963), 1034–1035, 1034(i)
  Montgomery bus boycott and, 1014, 1016(i)
  National Historic Site (Atlanta, Georgia), 1015(b)
  on Vietnam War, 1081
King, Mary, 1053–1054
King, Thomas Starr, 638(b)

Kinsey, Alfred, 1008
Kiowa Indians, 658, 659
Kissinger, Henry A. (1923–), 1089–1092, 1094
Klamath Indians, 989
Kleindienst, Richard, 1109
Knights of Labor, 690–692, 709, 712, 724
Korean War (1950–1953), 974–978, 975(m)
  containment policy and, 976, 978, 980
  effect on defense policy and spending, 980
  end of, 979–980
Korematsu decision (1944), 920
Kosovo, 1158, 1159(i)
Kreisler, Fritz, 805
Kubowitski, Leon, 937
Ku Klux Klan, 578, 580–581(b), 581(i)
  1868 election and, 585
  in 1920s, 852, 852(i)
Ku Klux Klan Acts of 1870 and 1871, 581(b), 586–587
Kuwait, Persian Gulf War (1991) and, 1147, 1147(i), 1148, 1148(m)
Ky, Nguyen Cao, 1081
Kyoto Protocol on global warming, 1170

Labor (labor force). *See also* Unemployment
  in 1950s, 996–998
  child labor, 684–685, 684(i), 776(i), 777–778(b)
    in Pennsylvania mines, 761(i)
  Clayton Antitrust Act (1914) and, 775
  in a globalizing era, 1164–1166(b)
  reconstruction and, 562, 568
  servants, domestic, 1870s–1890s, 693
  women in
    1870s–1890s, 683–687, 683(i)
    in 1920s, 844
    in 1930s, 859–860
    1940–1950, 964(f)
    in 1950s, 997–998, 1005
    progressives and, 752–755
    after World War II, 964–967(b), 966(i)
Labor gang system, 584, 676
Labor movement (labor unions). *See also* Strikes
  1870–1900, 687–691, 714–723
    Cripple Creek miners' strike (1894), 718–719
    eight-hour day movement, 690–692, 718, 719, 776, 813
    Haymarket rally and bombing (1886), 691–692, 692(i)
    Homestead (Pennsylvania) lockout and strike, 714–715, 715(i), 718
    Knights of Labor, 690–692, 709, 712, 724
    Pullman strike (1894), 721–723
  in 1920s, 832–833
  in 1950s, 996–997
  in 1980s, 1123
  American Federation of Labor (AFL), 690, 692, 718, 801, 891
    in 1930s, 860, 891–892
    merger with CIO (1955), 996–997

    Seattle strike and (1919), 813–814
    women workers and, 752, 803
  collective bargaining and, 801, 883, 971, 997
  Great Depression (1930s) and, 860–862
  New Deal and, 891–893
  Taft-Hartley Act (1947), 971
  women workers and, 965
  after World War I, 813–814
  World War I and, 801
  after World War II, 964
  World War II and, 921, 924
La Follette, Robert M. (1855–1925), 756, 759, 762, 763, 801
  1924 election, 833
La Guardia, Fiorello, 851
Laissez-faire, 615, 619, 622, 710, 748, 766, 854, 870, 1120, 1159
Lakewood (California), 1002
Lakota Sioux reservation, siege at (1972), 1042, 1044
Lakota vest, 634(i)
Land (landownership; landowners)
  Indian cession of lands, 1850–1890, 659(m)
  reconstruction and, 561–562, 583
Land grants, to railroads, 600, 648, 649(m)
Landon, Alf, 899
Land speculation, California, 648, 653
Laning, Edward, 856(i)
Lansing, Robert, 796, 810
Laos, 992
La Raza Unida, 1046
Latin America
  Eisenhower administration and, 992–993
  good neighbor policy, 910
  Johnson administration and, 1076–1077
  Kennedy administration and, 1071
  Roosevelt Corollary to the Monroe Doctrine, 768, 768(i), 768(m)
  U.S. military interventions in
    1895–1941, 792(m)
    1912–1916, 791
    1950s, 992–993
    1954–1994, 1069(m)
    1980s–1990s, 1132–1134, 1147
    Chilean coup (1973), 1090
    Dominican Republic (1965), 1076
    Franklin D. Roosevelt's nonintervention policy, 910
    Wilson's foreign policy, 791
Latinos (Hispanic Americans), 1166. *See also* Mexicans and Mexican Americans
  in 1950s, 1001–1002
  1960s struggles for justice, 1044–1046
  in California, 651, 655–656, 1001–1002
  in Clinton administration, 1151
  in the Gilded Age West, 654, 655–656
  income in 2001, 1155
  New Deal and, 895–896
  population of, in 2002, 1163–1166
  after World War II, 969–970

Lawson, James, 1033
Lazarus, Emma, 677
League of Nations, 809–812, 812(i),
    813, 833
    Franklin D. Roosevelt and, 909
League of United Latin-American
    Citizens (LULAC), 821, 969, 970
League of Women Voters, 843
League to Enforce Peace, 804
Leary, Timothy, 1046
Lease, Mary Elizabeth (1853–1933), 709,
    716(b), 727, 728(i)
Lebanon, 1132, 1134(i)
Lee, Robert E. (1807–1870), 569(i)
Left, the (radical groups and
    movements). *See also* Communists
    1870s–1900s, 690–692
    1900s–1920s, 778–781
    in 1930s, 861–862
    New Left and student protest
        movement (1960s), 1046–1047
    Red scare and, 814–815, 818
    student protest movement (1960s),
        1048–1051(b)
    women's liberation (1960s), 1053–1054
Leisure. *See* Entertainment
Lemlich, Clara, 752–753
Lend-Lease Act (1941), 916, 919(t)
Lenin, Vladimir Ilyich, 816
Lesbians, 1055
Levine apartment, 681(b), 681(i)
Levitt, William J., 998, 999(i)
Levittown (New York), 998, 999
Lewelling, Lorenzo, 717(b), 725, 727
Lewinsky, Monica, 1153
Lewis, John L. (1880–1969), 891, 892, 924
Lewis, Sinclair (1885–1951), 849
Leyte Gulf, Battle of (1944), 943, 944(t)
Liberalism
    in 1960s, 1023–1031
    Carter's retreat from, 1112–1113
    Nixon administration and, 1058–1061
Liberal Party (1872), 585–586
Liberty (freedom) of blacks, during
    reconstruction, 562, 564–565(b),
    566
Liberty League, 884, 893
Libraries, 698
Lieberman, Joseph, 1169
Lien merchants, 584, 585
Lin, Maya Ying, 1096, 1097
Lincoln, Abraham (1809–1865)
    death of (1865), 563
    Reconstruction and, 560, 561
    second inaugural address (1865), 561
Lindbergh, Charles (1902–1974), 848
Lippmann, Walter (1889–1974), 755, 801
Literacy (illiteracy), in the South, 582
Literature
    in 1920s, 849
    in 1950s, 1008–1009
    Harlem Renaissance, 845
Little Bighorn, Battle of (1876), 660
Little Rock (Arkansas), integration of
    Central High School in (1957),
    1010, 1011(i)

Lloyd, Henry Demarest (1847–1903),
    608(b), 623
Lloyd George, David (1863–1945), 809,
    810(i), 813
Locke, Alain, 845
Lodge, Henry Cabot (1850–1924), 627,
    677, 833
    Versailles treaty and League of
        Nations, 812–813
Lonely Crowd, The (Riesman), 1007
Long, Huey (1893–1935), 887–889(b),
    889(i)
Longoria, Felix, 969
Lon Nol, 1093
Los Angeles (California), 671
    1965 Watts riot, 1036, 1041(m)
Lost generation, 849
Louisiana
    1876 election, 591
    Huey Long, 888–889(b)
    reconstruction and, 561, 581(b), 589
Love Canal disaster (New York), 1130
Lowell, Josephine Shaw, 756(b)
Lower East Side Tenement Museum
    (New York City), 681(b), 681(i)
Loyalty program, Truman's, 973
Lozen, 661
Lucky Strike, 840(i)
LULAC (League of United Latin-
    American Citizens), 821, 969, 970
Luna Park (New York City), 694(i)
Lusitania (passenger liner), sinking of
    (1915), 795, 795(m), 796
Luxembourg, 914
Lynch, John R., 579(i)
Lynchings, 968, 1010
    in Gilded Age (1870s–1890s), 620–621
    after World War I, 820
Lynd, Robert and Helen, 837
Lyons, Maritcha, 621

MacArthur, Douglas (1880–1964)
    Bonus Army and (1932), 868, 868(i)
    in Korean War, 975, 976, 978
    in World War II, 925
McCarran-Walter Act (1952), 971
McCarthy, Eugene, 1087
McCarthy, Joseph R. (1908–1957), 972,
    973(i)
    Eisenhower and, 986–987
    McCarthyism, 973–974
McCloy, John J., 937
McClure's Magazine, 606, 606(i)
McCormick, Cyrus, Jr., 691
McDonald, "Country Joe," 1020(i)
McGovern, George S. (1922–), 1108
Machines, political, 698–700
McKay, Claude, 845
MacKenzie, Kathleen, 1171
McKinley, William (1843–1901)
    1896 election, 729–730, 729(i)
    assassination of (1901), 759
    foreign policy, 739, 740
    Spanish-American War (1898), 736,
        736(i), 737
    tariff, 627–628

McNamara, Robert S. (1916–), 1068,
    1076, 1085
Macune, C. W., 712
Maginot Line (France), 914, 919(t)
Mahan, Alfred Thayer (1840–1914), 731
Maine, prohibition in, 622
Maine (battleship), 736, 738–739(b), 739(i)
"Making it" in America, 678–679(b)
Malcolm X (1925–1965), 1037, 1038, 1040,
    1040(i)
Managers, 685–686
Manchuria, 910, 919(t)
Mandate system, 810–811
Mandela, Nelson, 1155
Manhattan Project, 935, 944
Manifest destiny, 731
Manila Bay, Battle of (1898), 737, 740(m)
Mann Act (1910), 751
Manpower Development and Training
    Act (1962), 1024
Manufacturing. *See also* Factories;
    Industry
    abroad, 1165(i)
    assembly-line (mass production),
        834–837
Mao Zedong (1893–1976), 962, 1089
Maquiladoras (assembly plants), 1165(i)
March on Washington (1963), 1034–1035,
    1034(i)
Marriage, Defense of Marriage Act
    (1996), 1152
Marshall, George C. (1880–1959), 960,
    973
Marshall, Thurgood (1908–1993), 1010,
    1144
Marshall Field (Chicago), 687(i)
Marshall Plan, 959(i), 960
Martin, Joseph W., Jr., 964
Martinez, Bob, 1151
Martinez, Mel, 1151
Martin Luther King Jr. National Historic
    Site (Atlanta, Georgia), 1015(b)
Mass culture, in 1920s, 846–849
Mass production (assembly-line
    manufacturing), 834–837
Mass transit, 680
Mathews, Mary McNair, 643
Matteson, Edward, 638
Matthews, Mark, 842
Matthews, Victoria Earle, 621
Meat Inspection Act (1906), 763
Meatpacking industry, 762(i), 763
Mechanization
    of agriculture, 652–653, 652(i), 998(i)
    of factory labor (1870s–1890s), 683–684
Medicaid, 1027, 1152
Medicare (Medical Care Act), 1027,
    1027(i), 1030(t), 1170
Mellon, Andrew (1855–1937), 831, 832
Memphis (Tennessee), riots (1866), 572,
    573(i)
Men. *See* Fathers; Gender relations
Mencken, H. L. (1880–1956), 842, 853(b)
Menominee Indians, 989
Merchants. *See also* Trade
    sharecroppers and, 584

Meredith, James H., 1036
Mergers, corporate, 610, 611, 611(f)
Methodists, 563, 616–617
Mexicans and Mexican Americans, 895(i).
    See also Hispanic Americans
    (Latinos)
    in 1950s, 1001–1002
    1960s political and economic struggles,
        1044–1046
    in California, 654, 651, 820–821,
        1001–1002. *See also* Californios
    deportation to Mexico (1930s), 859,
        859(i)
    immigration after World War I,
        820–821, 821(i), 851
    migrants in 1930s, 885, 895–896, 898(i)
    as ranchers, 650, 651
    after World War II, 969–970
    in World War II, 920
Mexico, 586
    maquiladoras (assembly plants) in, 1165
    Punitive Expedition into (1916, 1917),
        789, 791(b)
    revolution (1911), 772
    Wilson and, 791
    World War I and, 796
Middle class, 680
    African Americans, 563
    white women
        cult of domesticity, 692, 693
        domestic servants (1870s–1890s), 693
        feminism and, 1054
        secretarial work, 686
Middle East
    1948–1989, 1114(m)
    1989–2004 events in, 1148(m)
    Carter administration and, 1113, 1115
    Clinton administration and, 1158
    Eisenhower administration and,
        993–994
    Nixon administration and, 1091
    Persian Gulf War (1991), 1147–1149,
        1147(i), 1148(m)
    Reagan administration and, 1132,
        1134(i)
    Truman's foreign policy, 963
Middletown (Robert and Helen Lynd), 837
Midway, Battle of (1942), 925–926, 944(t)
Midwest, 1896 election, 729, 730
Migrant farm workers, 651, 653, 885–886
Migration. *See also* Immigration
    to cities
        1870–1900, 671–676
        1920–1930, 850(m)
    westward, 644–651
        commercial farming and industrial
            cowboys, 651–654
        homesteaders and speculators,
            644–650
        ranchers and cowboys, 650–651
        tenants, sharecroppers, and migrants,
            651
Miles, Nelson, 661, 662
Military, the, homosexuals in, 1152
Military alliances, regional, 961
Military Draft Act (1917), 798

Military expenditures (defense budget)
    Eisenhower's, 990, 994, 995
    Korean War and, 980
    Reagan administration, 1122
Military-industrial complex, 995
Military interventions by U.S. forces in
        Latin America
    1895–1941, 792(m)
    1912–1916, 791
    1950s, 992–993
    1954–1994, 1069(m)
    1980s–1990s, 1132–1134, 1147
    Chilean coup (1973), 1090
    Dominican Republic (1965), 1076
    Franklin D. Roosevelt's
        nonintervention policy, 910
Military Reconstruction Acts (1867), 574,
        576(t)
Milken, Michael, 1122
Miller, B. M., 861(i)
Miller, Washington, 563(i)
Miller & Lux, 653–654, 653(i)
Milliken v. Bradley (1974), 1106
Milosevic, Slobodan, 1158
Minek, Margaret, 1105
Miner, Luella, 732
Miners
    anthracite coal strike (1902), 760–761
    in the West, 637–643
Mineta, Norman Y., 1151
Minimum wage, 832–833
    1938, 901
Mining, in the West, 637–643, 637(m)
    1848–1890, 637(m)
    hydraulic mining, 638–639(b), 639(i)
Mining interests, free silver issue and, 629
Minneapolis, gay and lesbian rights in,
        1128(b)
Minow, Newton, 1007
Miranda v. Arizona (1966), 1031
Miscenegation (racial mixing;
        amalgamation), 620, 845
Miss America beauty pageant, picketing
        of (1968), 1054
Miss Black America contest, 1054
Missionaries, in 1890s, 731–732
Mississippi, 783
    reconstruction and, 567, 568, 582, 588, 589
Mississippi Freedom Democratic Party,
        1022(i), 1038
Mississippi Freedom Summer Project
        (1964), 1035
Mitchell, George, 1042, 1148
Mitchell, John, 761, 1110
Model Cities Act (1965), 1027, 1030(t)
Model T Ford, 828(i), 830(i)
Mohammad Reza Pahlavi, Shah, 993
Mohammed, Shanaz, 1171
Momyer, William W., 1079
Mondale, Walter F. (1928–), 1111, 1122
Money (currency), gold standard, 629,
        629(i), 630
Monopolies (monopolistic practices), 605.
        See also Trusts
    National Recovery Administration
        (NRA) and, 884

Monroe Doctrine, 733–735
    Roosevelt Corollary to the, 768, 768(i),
        768(m)
    Theodore Roosevelt and, 767
    Wilson and, 791
Montgomery (Alabama), 697
    bus boycott in (1955–1956), 1011,
        1014–1016, 1014(i)
Montgomery Improvement Association
        (MIA), 1014
Moody, Anne, 1032(i)
Moore, Alice, 1105–1106
Moore, Paul, 1128(b)
Moral Majority, 1120
Morgan, J. P. (1837–1913), 612(i), 615, 630
    1907 panic and, 763
    finance capitalism and, 610–612
    gold purchase scheme, 630
    Northern Securities case (1902) and,
        760, 760(i)
    Pujo committee and, 775
Mormons (Church of Jesus Christ of
        Latter-Day Saints), as oppressed
        group, 656
Morocco, 769
Morrow, E. Frederick, 1010
Mossadegh, Mohammed, 993
Moudy, Ross, 640–641
Mount Zion Baptist Church (Austin,
        Texas), 566(i)
Movies (film industry)
    in 1920s, 846, 847(i), 848(f)
    in 1930s, 860
    during World War I, 804, 805(i)
Ms. Magazine, 1053(i)
Muck, Karl, 805
Muckrakers, 762
Mugwumps, 623, 625
Muir, John (1838–1914), 764–765, 766(i)
Muller v. Oregon (1908), 754, 757(b)
Mullholland, Inez Hayes, 781(i)
Mumford, Lewis, 998
Munich agreement (1938), 912, 919(t)
Munn v. Illinois (1877), 628
Music
    jazz, 846, 848–849
    rock and roll, 1007–1008
Muslims, 1157, 1158
Mussolini, Benito (1883–1945), 910,
        913(m)
Myer, Dillon S., 989
My Lai massacre (1968), 1093, 1093(i)
Myrick, Sue, 1169

NAACP (National Association for the
        Advancement of Colored People),
        784, 820, 822, 969, 1144
    in 1920s, 845
    in 1950s, 1010
    Double V campaign and, 931
    after World War II, 968–969
NACW (National Association of Colored
        Women), 621
Nader, Ralph, 1028
NAFTA (North American Free Trade
        Agreement), 1163

Nagasaki, atomic bombing of (1945), 944(t), 945
Nanking, Japan's capture of (1937), 919(t)
NASA (National Aeronautics and Space Administration), 994
Nasser, Gamal Abdel, 993
Nast, Thomas, 586(i), 698–699
Nathan, Maud, 757(b)
National Aeronautics and Space Administration (NASA), 994
National American Woman Suffrage Association (NAWSA), 782, 803
National Arts and Humanities Act (1965), 1028, 1030(t)
National Association for the Advancement of Colored People (NAACP), 784, 820, 822, 969, 1144
  in 1920s, 845
  in 1950s, 1010
  Double V campaign and, 931
  after World War II, 968–969
National Association of Colored Women (NACW), 621
National Association of Manufacturers, 884
National Coalition of Labor Union Women, 1055
National Consumers' League (NCL), 754–755, 756–757(b)
National debt. *See* Debt, public
National Defense Education Act (1958), 994
National Farmers' Holiday Association, 861
National Housing Act (1937), 901
National Housing Act (1968), 1028, 1029
National Indian Youth Council (NIYC), 1042
National Industrial Recovery Act (NIRA; 1933), 883, 883(t)
Nationality Act (1965), 1028
National Labor Relations Act (NLRA), 891
National Labor Relations Board (NLRB), 891
National Liberation Front (NLF; Vietnam), 1074
National liberation movements
  Kennedy administration and, 1069, 1071–1072
  Truman administration and, 962
National Miners Union, 861
National Organization for Women (NOW), 1053, 1054, 1118, 1120
National parks, 763, 766, 767(m)
National Recovery Administration (NRA), 883, 884, 884(i), 885, 887
National Science Foundation (NSF), 1160
National security, Truman and, 960–962
National Security Act (1947), 961
National Security Council (NSC), 961
National Traffic and Motor Vehicle Safety Act (1966), 1030(t)
National Union for Social Justice (Union Party), 887
National Union Party, 572

National War Labor Policies Board, 801
National Woman's Party (NWP), 782, 843
National Woman Suffrage Association (NWSA), 621, 724
National Women's Conference (1977), 1057
Nation of Islam (Black Muslims), 1037–1038
Native Americans (Indians), 1036. *See also specific cultures and tribes*
  AIM (American Indian Movement), 1042, 1044, 1044(i)
  assimilation of, 636, 660–661, 989(i), 990, 1042, 1061
  1940s–1950s, 989(i), 990
  boarding schools, 635–636
  cession of lands by, 1850–1890, 659(m)
  Eisenhower administration and, 988–990
  Ghost Dance religion, 662–663, 662(i)
  mining in the West and, 639–640, 654
  New Deal and, 896
  protest movement (1960s), 1042, 1044
  relocation policy, 989–990, 989(m)
  removal policy
    Dawes Allotment Act (1887), 661
    decimation of bison herds and, 658–660, 660(i)
    Jackson administration (1829–1837), 657
    last acts of Indian resistance, 661–663
    in the West, 657–660
  reservations, 658, 660–661
  Sand Creek massacre (1864), 658
  termination policy, 989
  during World War I, 814(i)
  World War II and, 920
Nativism, 657, 752, 1166
  1914–1920, 821
  in 1920s, 842, 850
NATO (North Atlantic Treaty Organization), 961, 980, 1131, 1145
  Yugoslavian conflicts and, 1158, 1159(i)
Natural environment. *See* Environment, the
Nature reserves, preserves, and wildlife refuges, Maui, 1058
Navajo Indians, 658, 896
Naval Treaty, Five-Power (1922), 833–834
Navy, U.S., Great White Fleet, 770
NAWSA (National American Woman Suffrage Association), 782, 803
Nazi-Soviet nonaggression pact, 919(t)
NCL (National Consumers' League), 754–755, 756–757(b)
Nebraska farm family, 710(i)
Nebraska Territory, 648
  dugout in, 645(i)
Netherlands, the, 914
Neutrality
  in World War I, 794–796
  in World War II, 914–916
Neutrality acts (1935–1937), 911, 919(t)
Nevada
  admission to the Union, 643
  mining in, 637, 639–641, 641(i)

New Deal (1932–1939), 869, 872–902
  African Americans and, 895
  agricultural initiatives, 880–881
  Asian Americans and, 896
  banking and finance reform, 875–876, 877(f)
  "Brains Trust," 873–874
  challenges to the, 884–889
    agricultural processors and distributors, 885–886
    from the political fringes, 886–889
  conservatives and, 900–902
  economic reversals (1937–1938), 900
  farmers and, 880–881, 901
  foreign policy and, 909
  Hispanic Americans and, 895–896
  industrial recovery, 881, 883
  labor movement and, 891–893
  last reforms, 900–902
  major legislation of the first hundred days, 883(t)
  Native Americans and, 896, 896(i)
  needle book, 897(i)
  neglected Americans and, 894–897
  relief and conservation programs, 877–880
  Social Security, 893–894
  unemployment relief and, 890–891
  welfare state and, 889–897
New Deal coalition, 872
New Democrats, 1149
New Economic Policy, Nixon's, 1060
New Era, 830–839
New Freedom, 773, 776
New Guinea, 941
Newlands Reclamation Act (1902), 765–766
New Left, 1046
  feminism and, 1053–1054
"New Look" in foreign policy, Eisenhower's, 990–991
New Mexico
  Hispanics in, 656
  as territory, 643
New Nationalism, 773, 775
"New Negro," 845
New Orleans, mob violence in (1866), 572
New Right, 1104, 1105, 1116–1118, 1120, 1125
Newsboys, 684
New South, 560, 617–619
Newspapers, yellow journalism, 735
Newton, Huey, 1040
New York City, 859
  African Americans in, 845
  Central Park, 697, 698
  immigrants, 675–678, 681
  Tammany Hall, 698–699, 699(i)
New York Journal, 735, 738
New York state
  Temporary Emergency Relief Administration (TERA), 871
New York Stock Exchange, crash of 1929, 856
New York Times, 689, 1081, 1120
New York Tribune, 598

Nez Perce Indians, 658
Niagara movement, 784
Nicaragua, 772, 791, 910
  Carter administration and, 1114
  Reagan administration and, 1133–1134, 1134(m)
Nichols, H. D., 701(i)
Nicodemus (Kansas), 654–655
Nicodemus National Historic Site (Kansas), 590(b), 590(i)
Nicolas II, Czar, 816(b)
Nike, 1162
Nimitz, Chester W., 925
Nineteenth Amendment, 782, 803–804, 841
NIRA (National Industrial Recovery Act), 883
Nixon, E. D., 1011, 1014, 1014(i)
Nixon, Isaac, 968
Nixon, Richard M. (1913–1994), 1023, 1104
  1952 election, 978–979, 979(i)
  1960 election, 1023
  1968 election, 1059, 1088
  1972 election, 1107, 1108
  "Checkers speech" (1952), 979, 1006
  conservatism and, 1104–1107
  domestic policies of, 1106–1107
  the environment and, 1052
  farewell, 1110(i)
  foreign policy, 1088–1097
    anticommunism in the third world, 1090–1091
    China, 1089–1090
    Middle East, 1091
    Soviet Union, 1090
    Vietnam War (See Vietnam War, Nixon administration and)
  "kitchen debate" (1959), 985, 986(i)
  liberal policies of, 1058–1061
  pardoned (1974), 1111
  Watergate scandal, 1108–1110
NLRA (National Labor Relations Act), 891
NLRB (National Labor Relations Board), 891
Noble, Elaine, 1127
"No Child Left Behind" law (2002), 1170
Nonviolence, civil rights movement and, 1033, 1037, 1040, 1041
Noriega, Manuel, 1147
Norman, Henry C., 563(i)
Norris, Frank, 602(i)
North, the (northern states), migration of African Americans to northern cities, 676–677, 818–820, 819(i)
North, Oliver, 1134
North African campaign (World War II), 926–927
North American Free Trade Agreement (NAFTA), 1163
North Atlantic Treaty Organization (NATO), 961, 980, 1131, 1145
  Yugoslavian conflicts and, 1158, 1159(i)
North Carolina, 589
Northern Pacific Railroad, 660
Northern Securities Company, 759–760

North Korea, 1146, 1172
North Vietnam, 992, 1068, 1074–1079, 1093–1095
  bombing of, 1078–1079(b), 1086, 1088, 1094
Norton, Eleanor Holmes, 1022(i)
Norway, 914
NOW (National Organization for Women), 1053, 1118
NRA (National Recovery Administration), 883–885, 887
NRA codes, 883
NSC (National Security Council), 961
NSC 68 (1950), 980
NSF (National Science Foundation), 1160
NSFNET, 1160
Nuclear arms race, 991, 991(i), 994–996
Nuclear disarmament, 1085(i), 1135(i)
Nuclear energy, perils of, 1130
Nuclear Non-Proliferation Treaty (1968), 1089
Nuclear power (nuclear energy), Eisenhower administration and, 988
Nuclear test ban treaty, 1146–1147
Nuclear weapons (nuclear policy), anxiety over, 995(i)
Nurses, World War I, 802, 802(i)
Nye, Gerald, 910–911

Oakes, Richard, 1043
Oakland (California), 655
Oakley, Annie, 663
O'Brien, Tim, 1092
Occupational mobility, of immigrants, 678–679(b)
Occupational Safety and Health Act (OSHA), 1052
O'Connor, Sandra Day, 1125, 1126
O'Dell, Jack, 974
O'Donnell, Hugh, 715, 718
Office of Economic Opportunity, 1026
Oil companies (oil industry), 835(i)
"Okie" migrants, 886, 886(i)
Okinawa, Battle of (1945), 943, 944(t)
Oklahoma, 649–650, 886
Oklahoma City, bombing of a federal building in (1995), 1152
Old Age Revolving Pension, 887
Oligopolies, 612, 640
Olmsted, Frederick Law (1822–1903), 697–698, 697(i), 700, 701(i)
Olney, Richard B. (1835–1917), 722
Olympic Games (1980), 1115
"One person, one vote" principle, 1031
On the Origin of Species (Darwin), 613
On the Road (Kerouac), 1009
Open Door policy, 734, 735(i), 768–769
Operation Desert Storm (1991), 1148
Operation Rolling Thunder, 1073(t), 1076, 1078, 1081
Operation Wetback, 1001–1002
Opper, Fredrick Burr, 600(i)
O'Reilly, Leonora, 756(b)
Organization Man, The (Whyte), 1007
Organization of American States (OAS), 1076–1077, 1147

Orlando, Vittorio, 809
Ortega, Daniel, 1114, 1134
O'Sullivan, Mary Kenney, 752
Oswald, Lee Harvey, 1025
Other America, The (Harrington), 1025
Otis, Charles, 696
Otis, Elisha Graves, 695, 696(b)
Otter, C. L., 1171
Ottoman Empire, 810
Overlord, 937–938

Pacific theater, World War II, 924–926, 942(m)
Packard, Vance, 1007
Paige typesetting machine, 598
Pakistan, 1115, 1146
Palestine, 810
  Truman and, 963
Palestine Liberation Organization (PLO), 1158
Palmer, A. Mitchell (1872–1936), 815, 816, 818
Panama, 767
  1989 intervention in, 1147
Panama Canal, 767, 769(m), 1115
Panama Canal Zone, 1964 riots, 1076
Panic. See Depression
Pankhurst, Cristabel, 782
Pankhurst, Emmeline (1858–1928), 782
Pankhurst, Sylvia, 782
Paris, Treaty of (1898), 740
Paris accords (1973), 1094
Paris peace conference (1919), 809–811, 810(i)
Paris peace talks (1968), 1086
Parker, Lewis W., 777(b)
Parks, 697, 697(i), 698
Parks, Gordon, 969
Parks, Rosa (1913–), 1011, 1014(i)
Parsons, Albert, 690–691
Party loyalty, in Gilded Age (1870s–1890s), 615–616
PATCO (Professional Air Traffic Controllers Organization), 1121
Patrick, John, 1161
Patriot Act (2001), 1171
Patriotism, during World War I, 804
Patronage. See also Spoils system
  in Gilded Age (1870s–1890s), 615–616
Patton, George, 921
Paul, Alice (1885–1977), 782, 803
Payne-Aldrich tariff (1909), 771
PCSW (President's Commission on the Status of Women), 1053
Peace Corps, 1071, 1071(i)
Pearl Harbor, Japanese attack on (1941), 918, 918(i), 918(m), 919(t), 944(i)
Pendleton Civil Service Act (1883), 624
Pennsylvania Railroad, 600, 604
Penny sales, 861
Pentagon Papers, 1093–1094
People's Party (Populist Party), 708, 712–714, 727–730
  1892 convention (St. Louis), 709–710, 710(i), 727
  1892 election, 727

1928 election, 854
1944 election, 932
1946 election, 951, 970–971
1948 election, 971
1952 election, 978, 979, 979(i)
1956 election, 990
1968 election, 1088
1984 election, 1122
1994 elections, 1152
Eisenhower and modern
    Republicanism, 987
in Gilded Age (1870s–1890s), 616–617,
    622–624, 627, 628
Korean War (1950–1953) and, 975–976
Liberal Party and (1872), 585–586
New Deal and, 884
Nixon's southern strategy and, 1107
reconstruction and, 566, 568, 569
    Fifteenth Amendment, 576
    Fourteenth Amendment, 571–574
    Radicals, 573–574, 574(m)
    white supremacy, 588–589
    withering of northern resolve,
        586–588
Social Security and, 893
in the South, 617
    during Reconstruction, 577–582
Theodore Roosevelt and, 762, 763
Versailles treaty (1919) and, 812
women's rights and (1980s), 1125
during World War I, 805, 808
Republic Steel, 893
Reservations, Indian, 658, 660–661, 989(i)
Reston, James, 1026
Retirement Equity Act (1984), 1125
Reuther, Walter, 997
Revivals, religious, in 1950s, 1005–1006
Rhee, Syngman (1875–1965), 974, 980
Rice, Condoleezza, 1151
Richardson, Elliot, 1109
Richmond (California), 999(i)
Rickover, Hyman, 739
Ridgway, Matthew, 980
Ridgway, Matthew B., 976
Riesman, David, 1007
Right, the. *See* Conservatives
Riis, Jacob (1849–1914), 680, 684
    flash photography and, 764–765(b),
        765(i)
Riots and mob violence
    1868 election and, 585
    1943 race riots, 931
    1964–1968 urban riots, 1036–1037,
        1041(m)
    1968 "police riot" in Chicago,
        1087–1088, 1087(i)
    against blacks (1917–1918), 820
    Centralia (Washington; 1919), 818
    Great Railroad Strike of 1877, 688–689,
        688(i)
    Ku Klux Klan, 580–581(b)
    reconstruction and, 572, 573(i)
    during World War I, 805
Roaring Twenties, 840–849
Roberts, Owen, 899
Robertson, Pat, 1117, 1119, 1120

Robins, Margaret Dreier, 803
Robinson, Jackie, 968, 968(i), 1010
Robinson, Jo Ann, 1011, 1014
Rock and roll, 1007–1008
Rockefeller, Bill, 604
Rockefeller, John D. (1839–1937), 599,
    604–605, 606(i), 608–610(b), 680,
    750
    new world markets and, 731
Rockefeller, John D., Jr., 612
Rock music, 1046–1047
Rockne, Knute, 848
Roebling, Emily Warren, 670
Roebling, Washington, 670
Roe v. Wade (1973), 1055, 1107, 1126
Rogers, Will, 828(i)
Roman Catholic Church, 1055
    gay rights and, 1128(b)
Roman Catholics, 731
    Al Smith, 854
Rommel, Erwin, 926–927, 938
Roosevelt, Eleanor (1884–1962), 894(i),
    895, 1053, 1056
    Bonus Army and, 869
    New Deal and, 873
    women reporters and, 874(i)
Roosevelt, Franklin D. (1882–1945). *See
    also* New Deal
    1920 election, 821–822, 869
    1928 election, 870, 909
    1930 election, 870(i)
    1932 election, 909
    1936 election, 897, 899
    1944 election, 932
    on Bonus Army (1932), 868
    death of, 940
    early life and political career of,
        869–871
    first term as president (1933–1937),
        869
        banking and finance reform, 875–877
        Brains Trust, 873–874
        conservatives and, 871, 894, 895, 897
        critics and opponents, 884–887
        fireside chats, 866(i), 876
        Huey Long and, 889
        Hundred Days, 873, 883
        inaugural address (1933), 869, 872,
            876, 899, 910
        Social Security, 893–894
        Wagner Act (1935), 891
        welfare state and, 889–890
        work relief program, 890
    as governor (1928–1932), 870
    second term as president (1937–1941)
        court-packing scheme, 899–900
        foreign policy, 909–912
        good neighbor policy, 910
        last reforms, 900–902
        racial segregation, 901
        slowing the pace of the New Deal,
            900
    World War II and, 924, 926, 927, 936,
        937, 940
        African Americans, 930–931
        atomic bomb, 934–935

        the Holocaust, 932
        isolationism, 912
        Lend-Lease Act (1941), 916
        mobilization, 919–923
        neutrality, 914–916
        war economy, 921
        Yalta Conference (1945), 940, 941(i)
Roosevelt, Theodore (1858–1919), 662,
    869
    1912 election, 746(i)
    on birth control, 780
    as president (1901–1909), 759, 760(i)
        African Americans and, 783
        anthracite coal strike (1902), 761
        Booker T. Washington and, 783,
            783(i)
        conservation, 763–766, 766(i)
        foreign policy, 766–770
        Northern Securities case (1902),
            759–760
        Panama Canal, 767, 769(m)
        panic of 1907, 763
        as reformer, 762–763
        as trust-buster, 759–761, 760(i)
        Spanish-American War (1898),
            736–738, 737(i)
        Taft and, 771, 771(i), 772
        Venezuelan crisis and (1895), 733–734
        World War I and, 795
    Roosevelt Corollary to the Monroe
        Doctrine, 768, 768(i), 768(m)
Root, John Wellborn, 695
Root-Takahira agreement (1908), 770
Rose, Ernestine, 1056
Rosenberg, Ethel and Julius, 973
"Rosie the Riveter," 929(b), 929(i),
    966–967(b)
Rough Riders, 737, 738
Rubin, Jerry, 1087
Ruhr Valley, 834
Rumsfeld, Donald H., 1172
Rural areas. *See also* Agriculture; Farmers
        and farms; Plantations
    in 1920s, 849–850
        Ku Klux Klan, 852
        anti-immigrant attitudes, 851
        Great Depression (1930s) and, 858
        Hoover and, 857
    migration to cities from
        1870–1900, 671–676
        1920–1930, 850(m)
    population (1870–1900), 651, 652(f)
Rural Electrification Administration
    (REA), 881, 881(i)
Russell, Harold, 953
Russia. *See also* Soviet Union
    World War I and, 792, 793, 798
    Russian bolshevism, 814, 816–817(b)
    Russian Revolution (1917), 798, 816
    Russo-Japanese War, 770
    Rust cotton picker, 882(b), 882(i)
Ruth, George Herman "Babe," 847
Rwanda, 1155

Sacco, Nicola, 851–852, 851(i)
Sadat, Anwar, 1115

Saipan, 943(i)
Saleswomen, 687
SALT (Strategic Arms Limitation Talks), 1090
Salter, John, Jr., 1032(i)
Salt Lake City (Utah), 656
Samoan Islands, 734, 734(m)
Samuelson, Robert, 1004
San Carlos Reservation (Arizona Territory), 661
Sand Creek (Colorado), massacre at (1864), 658
Sandinistas, 1114
Sandoz, Jules, 663
San Francisco, 697
  Chinatown, 677
  Chinese immigrants, 677
Sanger, Margaret (1879–1966), 780–781, 780(i), 844
San Juan Hill, Battle of (1898), 737(i)
Santo Domingo, Grant's proposed annexation of, 586
Saturday Evening Post, The, 805, 841
Saudi Arabia, 1147
Savings and loan institutions (S&Ls), 1121–1122
Scalia, Antonin, 1125
Schenck, Charles, 818
Schenck v. United States, 818
Schlafly, Phyllis, 1055, 1103, 1104, 1104(i), 1105–1107, 1117–1119, 1119(i), 1120, 1125
Schneiderman, Rose, 753
Schools, 698
  desegregation (integration) of 1950s–1960s, 1010, 1011(i), 1012–1013(b)
    in 1970s, 1060
    busing for, 1106, 1107(i)
    Nixon administration, 1106
  Indian boarding, 635–636
  segregation in, 969–970, 969(i), 1106
Schreiber, Marie, 964–965
Schroeder, Patricia, 1121
Schurz, Carl, 559–560, 624
Schwartz, Edward, 1048(b)
Science. *See* Technology
Scientific management, 755, 834–835
SCLC (Southern Christian Leadership Conference), 1016
Scopes trial (1925), 852–853
Scott, Hugh D., 975–976, 1110
Scott, Tom, 602
Scottsboro Boys, 861(i), 862
SDI (Strategic Defense Initiative; "Star Wars"), 1131, 1172
SDS (Students for a Democratic Society), 1046, 1049–1050(b)
Seale, Bobby, 1040
SEATO (Southeast Asia Treaty Organization), 992, 1073(t)
Seattle, 1919 strike, 813
Seattle (Washington), 1999 anti-globalization protests, 1159, 1162, 1162(i)

Secession from the Union, Johnson's program of reconciliation and, 567
Secretaries, 686–687
Sectionalism, New South and, 617–619
Securities and Exchange Commission (SEC), 876
Sedition Act (1918), 805
Segregation, 784
  Jim Crow laws, 582, 677
  New Deal and, 901
  in Progressive era, 783
  residential, 680
  in schools, 969–970, 969(i), 1106
  "separate but equal" doctrine, 783, 895, 1010, 1012
Selective Service Act (1917), 798
Selective Service Act (1940), 920
Self-determination, principle of
  Franklin D. Roosevelt and, 910, 916, 940
  Truman and, 962
  Wilson and, 809, 810
Selma (Alabama), march for voting rights (1963), 1035, 1035(i)
Senators, election of, 623, 771
"Separate but equal" doctrine, 783, 895, 1010, 1012
Separate spheres, doctrine of, 620, 692, 844
September 11, 2001, terrorist attacks, 1170
Servants, domestic, 1870s–1890s, 693
Service industries, 997–998, 1123
Servicemen's Readjustment Act (GI Bill; 1944), 965, 968, 1003
Settlement house movement, 748, 749, 749(i), 750–751(b). *See also* Hull House
Settlement. *See also* Westward migration of trans-Mississippi West, 644
  areas settled before 1862, 648(m)
Sevara (Ute chieftain), 658(i)
Seventeenth Amendment, 771
Sewage systems, 696–697
Sewall, Arthur M., 729
Seward, William H. (1801–1872), 586
Sex and sexuality
  in 1950s, 1008
  in 1960s, 1047
  miscegenation, 620, 845
Sex discrimination, 1053, 1055, 1056, 1061, 1125
Seymour, Horatio, 585, 588(i)
Sha'arawi, Huda, 1056
Shafter, William, 740
Sharecroppers, 583–584, 858, 885, 885(i)
Sharecropping, 862
Share Our Wealth movement, 888–889(b)
Sheppard-Towner Act (1921), 841
Sheridan, Philip H. (1831–1888), 660
Sherman, William Tecumseh (1820–1891), 562, 658
  reconstruction and, 562
Sherman Antitrust Act (1890), 628–629, 759, 760, 1121
Sherman Silver Purchase Act (1890), 629, 630
Shipping Board, 801
Shultz, George, 1134

Sicily, in World War II, 927, 944(t)
Sigsbee, Charles Dwight, 738
Silent Spring (Carson), 1051
Silver, free, 629–630, 713, 728–730
Silver mining, 638
Silver Purchase Act (1890), 629–630
Simkhovitch, Mary Kingsbury, 757(b)
Simpson, John, 861
Sinclair, Upton (1878–1968), 762(i), 763, 887
Sioux Indians, 658, 659
  Ghost Dance religion, 662–663
Sirhan, Sirhan B., 1086
Sit-ins, 1032, 1032(i)
Sitting Bull, chief (c. 1834–1890), 658, 660, 663
Six-Day War (1967), 1091, 1091(m)
Sixteenth Amendment, 771, 775
Skilled workers and artisans, 682, 683
  American Federation of Labor (AFL), 691
Skyscrapers, 695, 695(i)
Slaughterhouse cases (1873), 587
Smith, Alfred E., 853–854
SNCC (Student Nonviolent Coordinating Committee), 1032–1035, 1035(i), 1038–1039(b)
Social Darwinism, 612–615, 618–619(b), 676, 726, 761
  reform Darwinism and, 755
Social engineering, 755
Social gospel, 749, 750–751
Socialism (socialists), 690
  in 1930s, 861–862, 886, 887, 897, 899
  Populism and, 713
Socialist Party, 723, 778–779
Social purity movement, 749, 751
Social Security, 893–894, 987, 1113
Social Security Act (1935), 893, 893(i)
Social welfare (welfare state)
  Eisenhower and, 987
  New Deal and, 889–897
  reform of, Clinton administration and, 1152–1153
Solar energy, 1132–1133(b), 1133(i)
Solomon Islands, 941
Somalia, 1155
Somme, Battle of the (1916), 798
Somoza, Anastasio, 1114
Sorensen, Theodore, 1072
Soros, George, 1162
Souls of Black Folk, The (Du Bois), 784
Souter, David, 1144
South, the (southern states). *See also* Civil War; Lower South; Reconstruction
  1896 election, 729, 730
  air-conditioning and, 1001(b)
  civil rights movement. *See* Civil rights movement
  grassroots conservatism in, 1105
  Jim Crow laws, 582, 677, 783, 931
  political realignment of (1984), 1122
  Populists in, 711–713, 727–728
  progressivism and, 783
  secession from the Union, Johnson's program of reconciliation and, 567

whites in. *See also* White supremacy
  landlords and black sharecroppers
    (1870s), 583–584
  reconstruction and, 567, 588–589
  Republican Party, 578
South Africa, 1133, 1155
South Carolina
  1876 election, 591
  reconstruction and, 567, 568, 579, 588,
    589
Southeast Asia Treaty Organization
    (SEATO), 992
Southern Christian Leadership
    Conference (SCLC), 1016
Southern Farmers' Alliance, 711, 712
Southern Farm Tenants Union, 885, 885(i)
Southern Pacific Railroad, 601, 602(i), 759
South Vietnam, 992, 1094, 1095
  evacuation of (1975), 1094(i), 1095
South Vietnamese army (ARVN), 992,
    1074, 1075, 1086, 1092
Soviet Union, 816, 909, 1145. *See also* Cold
    War
  Afghanistan and, 1115, 1132, 1135
  anti-Communist hysteria (1940s–1950s)
    and, 972–974
  China and, 1089
  containment policy toward. *See*
    Containment policy
  Cuba and, 993
  détente with, 1090, 1108, 1115
  Eisenhower administration and,
    994
  Kennedy administration and,
    1068–1073
  Korean War and, 974–976
  Nixon administration and, 1090
  nuclear arms race and, 994
  Reagan administration and, 1131–1132,
    1134
  Truman and, 953
  World War II and, 913, 916, 926, 927,
    930, 936–937, 940, 944(t)
Space exploration, 994, 1070(i)
  in 1960s, 1070
Spanish-American War (1898), 734–740,
    740(m)
  Maine (battleship), sinking of,
    738–739(b), 739(i)
Spanish Civil War (1936–1939), 911–912,
    911(m)
Spencer, Herbert (1820–1903), 613,
    618–619(b), 619(i)
Spies, August, 691
Spock, Benjamin, 1005
Spoils system, 585, 615, 616, 623, 624,
    643, 644
Sports, 847–848
Sputnik (satellite), 994
Square Deal, 761
Stagflation, 1060
Stalin, Joseph (1879–1953)
  Cold War and, 953, 954, 954(i), 955,
    956(b)
  during World War II, 926, 927, 936, 937,
    940, 941(i)

Stalingrad, Battle of (1942–1943), 933,
    944(t)
Stalwarts, 623
Standard of living, after World War II,
    964
Standard Oil Company, 604, 605(i), 606(i),
    623, 731
Stanton, Edwin M., 575
Stanton, Elizabeth Cady (1815–1902),
    572, 621
  Fifteenth Amendment and, 576
  woman suffrage and, 724–725
Starr, Kenneth, 1153
START (Strategic Arms Reduction Talks),
    1135, 1136(i)
Star Wars (Strategic Defense Initiative),
    1131
State constitutions, after Civil War, 561,
    567, 568, 574, 578–579
States (state governments)
  Fourteenth Amendment and, 571–574
  reconstruction and, 567–568, 574
States' rights, 773
  prohibition and, 842
  reconstruction and, 566, 568, 569
States' Rights Party (Dixiecrats), 971
Statue of Liberty (New York City), 677
Status Seekers, The (Packard), 1007
Steel industry, 611–612, 893
  1870–1895, 602–604, 603(f)
  1919 strike, 814
Steeplechase Park (New York City), 694
Steffens, Lincoln (1866–1936), 700, 758
Steichen, Edward, 612(i)
Stein, Gertrude, 849
Steinem, Gloria, 1053
Stephens, Alexander (1812–1883), 568
Stephens, Uriah, 690
Stephenson, David, 852
Stern, Edith, 1005
Stevens, Thaddeus (1792–1868), 573–574
Stevenson, Adlai E. (1900–1965), 978
  1956 election, 990
Stewart, Joseph Boyce, 581(i)
Stock market, regulation of, 876–877
Stock markets, crash of 1929, 856
STOP (Stop Taking Our Privileges) ERA,
    1119
Strategic Arms Limitation Talks (SALT),
    1090
Strategic Arms Reduction Talks (START),
    1135, 1136(i)
Strategic Defense Initiative (SDI; "Star
    Wars"), 1131, 1172
Streetcars, 680, 697, 757, 758(i)
Strict constructionists, 1106, 1125
Strikes
  coal miners'
    1931 (Harlan County, Kentucky), 861,
      861(m)
    anthracite coal miners (1902),
      760–761
  Cripple Creek (1894), 718–719
  Flint, Michigan (1937), 892, 892(i)
  garment workers (1909), 752–753,
    753(i)

  Great Railroad Strike of 1877, 687–690,
    688(i), 689(m)
  Great Southwestern Strike (1886), 712
  Knights of Labor and, 690
  May 1, 1886, general strike, 690–691
  Pullman (1894), 721–723
  steelworkers (1937), 893
  traffic controllers (1981), 1121
  after World War I, 813–814
  after World War II, 965
Student Nonviolent Coordinating
    Committee (SNCC), 1032–1035,
    1035(i), 1038–1039(b)
Student protest movement (1960s),
    1046–1051(b)
Students for a Democratic Society (SDS),
    1046, 1049–1050(b), 1081
Submarines (U-boats)
  in World War I, 795, 795(i), 796
  in World War II, 916, 919, 926
Substance abuse, 843
Subtreasury, 713
Suburbs, 680
  in 1950s, 998–999, 1003(i)
Sudan, 1158
Suez crisis (1956), 993–994, 993(m)
Suffrage. *See* Voting rights
Suffrage movement, 621
Sullivan, Louis, 695
Sumner, Charles (1811–1874), 572–574
Sumner, William Graham (1840–1910),
    613, 619
Sun Also Rises, The (Hemingway), 849
Sun Belt, 999–1002, 1002(t), 1000(m), 1105
Superfund, 1130–1131
Superpower rivalry, 962–963
Supply-side economics, 1121
Supreme Court, U.S. *See also specific cases*
  in 1960s (Warren Court), 1029, 1031
  2000 election and, 1169
  Clinton administration and, 1151
  Coolidge administration and, 832–833
  finance capitalism and, 610
  Franklin D. Roosevelt's court-packing
    scheme, 899–900
  George H. W. Bush and, 1144
  laissez-faire and, 615
  New Deal and, 884–885
  Nixon administration and, 1106–1107
  Reagan administration and, 1124–1125
  reconstruction and, 587–588
*Swann v. Charlotte-Mecklenburg Board of
    Education* (1971), 1106
Sweatshops, 683(i), 684
Syria, 1091
Szilard, Leo, 935

Taft, Robert A. (1889–1953), 959, 978
Taft, William Howard (1857–1930),
    770–773, 771(i)
  1912 election, 772, 773
  foreign policy, 771–772, 772(m)
  tariff and, 770–771
Taft-Hartley Act (1947), 971
Taft-Katsura agreement, 770
Taiwan, 962

Tammany Hall (New York City), 698, 699(i)
Tarawa, Battle of (1943), 941, 943
Tarbell, Ida M. (1857–1944), 606, 606(i), 608–609(b)
Tariffs and duties
in the 1880s, 627–628
Fordney-McCumber tariff (1922), 831–832
Hawley-Smoot tariff (1930), 857
Payne-Aldrich tariff (1909), 771
Reciprocal Trade Agreements Act (1934), 910
Taft and, 770–771
Underwood tariff (1913), 775
Wilson and, 774–775
Tarkington, Booth, 828(i)
Tatlock, John S. P., 806
Tax cuts and credits
in 1960s, 1024, 1026
Carter administration, 1113
Clinton administration, 1150, 1151
Eisenhower administration, 988
George W. Bush administration, 1169
Reagan administration, 1121
Tax Reform Act (1986), 1121
Tax Reduction Act (1964), 1030(t)
Taylor, Frederick Winslow (1856–1915), 755, 834
Taylor, Maxwell, 1073–1074
Taylorism, 755
Teapot Dome scandal, 832
Technology
agricultural
1940–1960, 996, 998(i)
mechanization of agriculture, 652–653, 652(i)
mechanized cotton picking, 882(b), 882(i)
air-conditioning, 1001(b), 1001(i)
artificial limbs, 570–571(b)
barbed wire, 650, 650(i)
electricity, 607, 610, 610(i), 838–839(b)
elevators, 695, 696(b)
flash photography and photojournalism, 764–765(b)
hydraulic mining, 638–639(b), 639(i)
the Internet, 1160–1161(b)
military, helicopters, 1082–1083(b), 1083(i)
solar energy, 1132–1133(b), 1133(i)
telephone, 606–607, 607(i)
Telegraph, railroads and, 600
Telephone, 606–607, 607(i)
Telephones, cellular, 1140(i)
Television
in 1950s, 1004, 1006–1007, 1007(i)
Vietnam War and, 1081
Temperance movement, 621–622, 723–724, 751–752. See also Prohibition
Temporary Emergency Relief Administration (TERA), 871
Tenant farmers, 885(i), 886(i)
Tennessee
during Reconstruction, 561
reconstruction and, 572, 589

Tennessee Coal and Iron Company, 763, 772
Tennessee Valley Authority (TVA), 878, 880, 880(m)
Tennessee Valley Authority Act (1933), 883(t)
"10 percent plan," 561
Tenure of Office Act (1867), 575
Termination policy, Native Americans and, 989
Terrell, Mary Church, 621
Territories
governments of, 643–644
Terrorism, 1173
in 1919, 814
in 1980s, 1132, 1134(i)
2001, 1157
Clinton administration and, 1158
globalization of, 1170–1171
Oklahoma City bombing (1995), 1152
Osama bin Laden and, 1158
Tet Offensive (1968), 1073(t), 1085–1086, 1086(i)
Texas
cattle ranchers and cowboys, 650
Farmers' Alliance movement in, 711, 712(i)
Hispanics in, 656
reconstruction and, 589
Textbooks, after the Civil War, 582(i)
Thieu, Nguyen Van, 1081
Third parties, 1936 election, 899
Third world, 962
Kennedy administration and, 1071–1072
Thirteenth Amendment (ratified 1865), 567, 576(t)
Thomas, Clarence, 1144
Thomas, Norman, 862
Thomas American Horse, 634(i)
Three Mile Island (Pennsylvania), 1130
Thurmond, J. Strom, 971, 1107
Tibbets, Paul, 907–908, 908(i), 945
Tientsin treaty (1858), 731–732
Tilden, Samuel J. (1814–1886), 591, 591(i), 592, 592(m)
Till, Emmett, 1010
Tillman, Benjamin "Pitchfork Ben," 728
Tilyou, George, 694
Title IX of the Education Amendments Act of 1972, 1055, 1061, 1125
Title VII of the Civil Rights Act (1964), 1036, 1053
Tojo, General Hideki, 917, 919(t)
Tokyo, 1942 raid on, 925
Townsend, Francis, 887
Trade. See also Merchants; Tariffs and duties
1870–1910 expansion, 733(f)
globalization and, 1159, 1162
Latin America, 910
liberalizing, 1163
Neutrality Act (1937) and, 911
during World War I, 794–795
Trade embargo (1941), 917
Trading with the Enemy Act (1917), 805

"Trail of Broken Treaties" caravan (1972), 1042
Transcontinental railroads, 599, 601(m), 645(i), 656
Transportation, Department of, 1030(t)
Treasury Department, U.S.
Morgan bailout of (1895), 630
prohibition and, 841
Triangle Shirtwaist Company (New York City)
fire (1911), 753, 754(i)
strike (1909), 752–753
"Tribute in Light," 1172(i)
Trickle-down economics, 857
Tripartite Pact (1940), 917, 919(t)
Triple Alliance, 792
Triple Entente (the Allies), 792
Trudell, John, 1043
Truman, Bess, 977
Truman, Harry S. (1884–1972), 932, 940
1946 election, 951
1948 election, 970
Acheson and, 951, 952(i)
atomic bomb and, 944–945
defense strategy, 960–962
domestic policies, 964–974
civil rights, 969
Eisenhower administration and, 985–986
labor unions, 965
reconversion and the postwar economic boom, 964–968
foreign policy, 952–962
China, 962–963
cold war, 953–959
containment policy, 952, 955, 958–960, 962
defense strategy, 960–962
Korean War, 974–978
Marshall Plan, 959(i), 960
Middle East, 963
national liberation movements, 962
national security, 960–962
Point IV Program, 962
Truman Doctrine, 959–960
superpower rivalry and, 962
Truman Doctrine, 959–960
Trumbull, Lyman, 569
Trusts, 604–605, 628–629. See also Antitrust laws and suits
Wilson and, 775
Tunney, Gene, 848
Turkey, 810, 959
Turner, Frederick Jackson, 663
Tuskegee Institute (Alabama), 783
Twain, Mark (Samuel Clemens; 1835–1910), 597, 598, 598(i), 639, 694
The Gilded Age, 597, 598(i), 692
on imperialism, 741
Tweed, William Marcy (1823–1878), 698
Twenty-fourth Amendment, 1030(t)
Typewriters (women workers), 686–687

U-boats. See Submarines
UFW (United Farm Workers), 1045

UMW (United Mine Workers), 761, 924
UN Convention on the Elimination of All
    Forms of Discrimination against
    Women (CEDAW), 1057–1058
UN Decade for Women, 1057
Underwood tariff (1913), 775
Unemployed, the
    1920, 831
    in 1930s, 857, 858, 859(i)
    1937–1940, 900
    in 1950s, 990
    1970, 1060
    1992, 1149
    2003, 1169
    Coxey's army (1894), 726–727, 726(i)
    depression of 1893–1897 and, 725, 726,
        726(i), 727
    New Deal and, 890–891
Unilateralism, George W. Bush's,
    1171–1172
Union Pacific Railroad, 598
Union Party (National Union for Social
    Justice), 887
Unions. *See* Labor movement
United Auto Workers (UAW), 892–893,
    892(i)
United Farm Workers (UFW), 1045
United Fruit Company, 734, 993
United Mine Workers (UMW), 761, 924
United Nations (UN), 940, 1172–1173
    Korean War (1950–1953) and, 975
    women's rights and, 1056–1058(b)
United Nations Charter, 940
United States Steel (USX), 612
United States v. Cruikshank (1876), 587
United States v. E. C. Knight Company, 629
United Students Against Sweatshops, 1162
Universal Negro Improvement
    Association (UNIA), 845
Universities. *See* Colleges and
    universities
Unsafe at Any Speed (Nader), 1028
Urban League, 819(i)
U.S. Steel Corporation, 763, 893
    antitrust suit against (1911), 772
USA Patriot Act (2001), 1171
Utah
    admission to the Union, 656
    woman suffrage in, 725
Utah Territory, 643
    Mormons in, 656
Ute Indians, 658
U-2 spy plane incident (1960), 994

Vail, Theodore N., 607
Valdez, Luis, 1045
Valentino, Rudolph, 846
Vandenberg, Arthur, 959
Vanderbilt, Alice, 682(i)
Vanderbilt, Alva, 680, 682
Vanderbilt, Cornelius (1794–1877),
    602, 680
Vanderbilt, William, 680, 682
Vanzetti, Bartolomeo, 851–852, 851(i)
Vaux, Calvert (1824–1895), 697, 697(i)
Venezuela, 1895 crisis, 733

Versailles, Treaty of (1919), 811–813, 911,
    919(t)
Vertical integration, 604
Veterans, Vietnam War, 1066(i), 1093, 1095
    Vietnam Veterans Memorial (Washington,
        D.C.), 1096–1097(b), 1097(i)
Veterans Administration, 998
Victory Gardens, 930
Vietcong, 1074, 1075, 1077, 1079, 1082,
    1085, 1094
Vietnam Veterans Memorial (Washington,
    D.C.), 1096–1097(b), 1097(i)
Vietnam Veterans Memorial Fund
    (VVMF), 1096
Vietnam War (1954–1975), 1067, 1068(i),
    1073–1076
    in 1950s, 991–992
    1964–1975, 1074(m)
    bombing of North Vietnam, 1073(t),
        1078–1079(b), 1086, 1088, 1094
    casualties, 1095, 1095(t)
    domestic opposition to, 1046, 1086–1087
    Johnson administration and, 1075–1081
    Kennedy administration and,
        1073–1075
    negotiations to end, 1086
    Nixon administration and, 1091–1105
        Cambodia, 1073(t), 1092, 1092(m),
            1093
        legacy of defeat, 1095–1097
        peace accords and the fall of Saigon
            (1972–1975), 1094–1095
        Pentagon Papers, 1093–1094
        Vietnamization of the war, 1092
        withdrawal of U.S. forces, 1092
    pro-war demonstrators, 1085(i)
    public opinion about, 1094(f)
    Tet Offensive (1968), 1085–1086
    U.S. involvement in, 1073(t)
    U.S. troops in (1962–1972), 1076(f)
    veterans, 1066(i), 1093, 1095
        Vietnam Veterans Memorial
            (Washington, D.C.), 1096–1097(b),
            1097(i)
    Vietnamization of, 1086, 1092
Villa, Francisco "Pancho" (1877–1923),
    789, 791–792, 791(i), 793(b),
Violence. *See* Political violence; Riots and
    mob violence
Violence against Women Act (1994), 1150
Virginia
    colonial. *See also* Chesapeake Bay
        colonies; Jamestown
    during Reconstruction, 561, 589
Virginia City (Nevada), 637, 639–643
VISTA (Volunteers in Service to
    America), 1026
Volunteers in Service to America
    (VISTA), 1026
Voter Education Project (1961), 1034
Voter registration drives, 1034, 1036,
    1038, 1039(i), 1045
Voter turnout
    1868–1900 and 1968–2000, 616(f)
    1896 election, 730
    African American (1940–1976), 1037(m)

Voting rights (suffrage)
    of blacks, 577, 1038–1039(b)
        Civil Rights Act of 1875, 587
        Fifteenth Amendment and, 576
        Force Bill (1890), 627
        Fourteenth Amendment and,
            571–574
        in Gilded Age (1870s–1890s), 620
        Ku Klux Klan Act (1871), 586–587
        Mississippi Freedom Summer Project
            (1964), 1035
        Populists and progressives, 782–783
        reconstruction and, 574, 586–587
        Voter Education Project (1961), 1034
        Voting Rights Act (1965), 1028, 1036,
            1038, 1061
    "one person, one vote" principle, 1031
    reconstruction and, 578
    universal white male suffrage, 578, 620
    of women
        Fifteenth Amendment and, 576
        Fourteenth Amendment and, 572
        in Gilded Age (1870s–1890s), 621
        movement for woman suffrage,
            724–725, 803
        Nineteenth Amendment, 782,
            803–804, 841
        before the Nineteenth Amendment,
            803(m)
        Washington suffrage parade (1913),
            781, 781(i)
        World War I and, 803–804
Voting Rights Act (1965), 1028, 1030(t),
    1036, 1038, 1061

Wabash v. Illinois (1886), 628
Waco (Texas), armed religious cult in
    (1993), 1152
Wade, Benjamin, 561
Wade-Davis bill (1864), 561
Wages and salaries
    1873–1893, 684
    1912–1920, 802(f)
    in 1920s, 855
    at Ford Motor Co., 839–840
    after World War II, 964, 965
Wagner, Robert, 891, 901
Wagner Act (1935), 891, 892
Wainwright, Jonathan, 925
Waite, Davis H., 718, 719
Wald, Lillian, 749
Wallace, George C. (1919–1998), 1088,
    1108
Wallace, Henry A. (1888–1965), 932,
    957–958(b), 958–959, 971
Wallace, Henry C., 831
Wallace, Lew, 643
Warburg, Paul, 775
Ware, Cellestine, 1054
War Industries Board, 808
War Industries Board (WIB), 801
Warner, Charles Dudley (1829–1900),
    597, 601, 692–693
War on Poverty, 1028–1029, 1042
War Powers Act (1973), 1095
War Production Board, 921

Warren, Earl (1891–1974), 1010, 1026, 1029, 1106
Warrior, Clyde, 1042
Warsaw Pact, 1145
Washington, Booker T. (1856–1915), 582(i), 783, 783(i), 784
Washington, D.C. (District of Columbia), minimum-wage law declared unconstitutional (1923), 832–833
Washington, George (1732–1799), as president (1789–1797), farewell address (1796), 731
Washington Disarmament Conference (1921), 833
Washoe basin (Nevada), 637
Watergate scandal, 1095, 1108–1110
Water Quality Act (1965), 1030(t)
Watson, Tom, 712, 728–730
Watt, James, 1130(i), 1131
WCTU (Woman's Christian Temperance Union), 622, 622(i), 723, 723(i)
Wealth, distribution of
  in 1920s, 855
  New Deal and, 874
Weaver, James B., 710(i), 727
Weinberg, Jack, 1046
Weinberger, Caspar, 1134, 1134(i)
Weiss, Carl Austin, 889
Welfare capitalism, 835
Welfare state (social welfare)
  Eisenhower and, 987
  New Deal and, 889–897
  reform of, Clinton administration and, 1152–1153
Wells, Ida B. (1862–1931), 620–621, 620(i)
Wellstone, Paul, 1170
West, the (American). See also Frontier, the; Westward migration; and specific states
  changing meaning of, 654
  in the Gilded Age (1870s–1890s), 635–664
    clash of cultures, 654–664
    Cripple Creek miner's strike, 718–719
    Dawes Act and Indian land allotment, 660–661
    dime novels, 663
    final removal of the Indians, 657–660
    Indian wars (1861–1890), 635, 657–660
    land fever, 644–654
    mining on the Comstock Lode, 637–643
    territorial government, 643–644
  grassroots conservation in, 1105
  Hollywood in the 1920s, 846, 860
  migrations into, 820–821, 851, 999–1002, 1000(m)
  and populist protest, 710–711, 712, 713, 728, 729, 730
  Sun Belt, 999–1002, 1000(m), 1005
  woman suffrage in, 725, 725(t), 803, 803(m)
  in the World War II era, 791–792, 793(b), 820–821, 851, 859

West Berlin, 1070
Western Electric, 607
Western Federation of Miners (WFM), 642(b), 718, 719
West Germany, 954, 960, 980, 1070, 1145
Westinghouse, 839(i)
Westinghouse, George W., 607
Westmoreland, William C., 1077, 1082, 1086
West Virginia, brakemen's strike (1877), 687–688
Westward migration, 644–651, 999–1002, 1000(m)
  of African Americans, 1000
  commercial farming and industrial cowboys, 651–654
  of Mexican Americans, 1001
  homesteaders and speculators, 644–650
  ranchers and cowboys, 650–651
  tenants, sharecroppers, and migrants, 651
Weyler, Valeriano, 735, 738, 739
What Social Classes Owe to Each Other (Sumner), 613
Wheat (wheat farming), 651
White, William Allen, 737
White Americans. See also Racism
  black power and, 1040
  middle-class white women
    cult of domesticity, 692, 693
    domestic servants (1870s–1890s), 693
    feminism and, 1054
    secretarial work, 686
  northern, in the South during Reconstruction, 577–578
  progressivism and, 781–784
  southern. See also Reconstruction; White supremacy
    landlords and black sharecroppers (1870s), 583–584
    reconstruction and, 567, 588–589
    Republican Party, 578
  in Sun Belt, 1002
White City (Chicago; 1893), 700–701, 701(i), 702–703(b)
White supremacy, 588(i)
  collapse of reconstruction and, 588–589
Whitewater land deals, Clinton administration and, 1153, 1154
Whitney, Richard, 856, 856(i)
Whyte, William H., Jr., 1007
Wilder, L. Douglas, 1151
Wilderness Preservation Act (1964), 1030(t)
Wilhelm II, Kaiser, 792, 794
Wilke, Harold, 1144
Wilkins, Roy, 1038
Willard, Frances (1839–1898), 709, 723–724, 723(i)
Williams, Juanita, 1035(i)
Williams, Nancy, 566(i)
Williams, Saundra, 1054
WILPF (Women's International League for Peace and Freedom), 804
Wilson, Charles (1890–1961), 990–992
Wilson, Edith, 803, 805(i)
Wilson, Edmund, 858

Wilson, Woodrow (1856–1924), 771, 773(i), 909
  1912 election, 772–773
  1916 election, 796
  death of, 813
  as governor of New Jersey, 773, 773(i)
  as president
    antitrust program, 775
    banking system, 775
    entry of the United States into World War I, 796–797
    foreign policy (before World War I), 790–796
    Fourteen Points, 809–811
    Latin American policy, 791–792
    League of Nations, 811–813, 812(i)
    neutrality policy, 794–796
    Paris peace conference (1919), 809–811, 810(i)
    peace aims, 809
    postwar politics, 821
    reforms, 774–775
    as reluctant progressive, 775–778
    suppression of dissent (1917–1918), 805
    Versailles treaty (1919), 811–813
    woman suffrage, 803, 804(i)
    World War I, 792–800, 816
Wisconsin, progressivism in, 759
Wittenmyer, Annie, 724
WKKK (Women of the Ku Klux Klan), 852(i), 852(i)
Wobblies, 779
Wolfensohn, James D., 1163
Womack, Bob, 642(b)
Woman's Christian Temperance Union (WCTU), 622, 622(i), 723, 723(i)
Woman's Crusade, 621, 622
Women. See also Families; Feminism; Gender relations; Marriage; Sex and sexuality; Woman's rights movement
  in 1920s, 841–844, 847(i)
    Women of the Ku Klux Klan (WKKK), 852(i)
  in 1950s, 1005
  abortion and, 1125(i)
    Nixon administration and, 1107
    opposition to the right to, 1055, 1058
    Roe v. Wade (1973), 1055, 1107, 1126
  African-American
    in 1920s, 841
    antilynching movement, 620–621
    during Reconstruction, 560(i), 563, 577, 580, 583
    workers (1890s), 685
  birth control, 779–781, 844
  civil rights measures of 1960s and, 1036
  Clinton administration and, 1150, 1151
  contraception, 780, 781
  education of, in colleges (1940–1960), 1003–1004
  gender gap, 1125–1126, 1153
  homesteading, 645, 646–647(b)
  in labor force
    1870s–1890s, 683–687, 683(i)
    in 1920s, 844

in 1930s, 859–860
1940–1950, 964(f)
in 1950s, 997–998, 1005
progressives and, 752–755
after World War II, 964–967(b), 966(i)
middle-class white
   cult of domesticity, 692, 693
   domestic servants (1870s–1890s), 693
   feminism and, 1054
   secretarial work, 686
mining in the West and, 640, 642–643
missionaries, in China, 732
politics and. *See also* Woman's rights
   movement
   in 1920s, 841–844
   Gilded Age (1870s–1890s), 621–622,
     723–725
during Reconstruction, 560
in reform movements (1870s–1890s)
   antilynching movement, 620, 620(i)
   settlement house movement, 749
   temperance movement (*See*
     Temperance movement)
rights of. *See also* Voting rights
   (suffrage, of women; Woman's
   rights movement)
servants, domestic, 1870s–1890s, 693
sex discrimination, 1053, 1055, 1056,
   1061, 1125
slave, miscenegation, 620, 845
southern white, black men as threat to,
   620
temperance movement and, 723–724
Vietnam War and, 1080
voting rights
   Fifteenth Amendment and, 576
   Fourteenth Amendment and, 572
   in Gilded Age (1870s–1890s), 621
   movement for woman suffrage,
     724–725, 803
   before the Nineteenth Amendment,
     803(m)
   Washington suffrage parade (1913),
     781, 781(i)
   World War I and, 803–804
World War I and, 802–804, 802(i), 804
World War II and, 928, 928(i), 929(b),
   930, 930(i)
Women of the Ku Klux Klan (WKKK),
   852(i)
Women's Bureau (Department of Labor),
   803
Women's International League for Peace
   and Freedom (WILPF), 804
Women's liberation movement, 1054
Women's Loyal Union, 621
Women's Peace Party, 804
Women's Political Council (WPC), 1011
Women's rights movement. *See also*
   Feminists (feminist movement)
   Fifteenth Amendment and, 576
   in Gilded Age (1870s–1890s), 621
   United Nations and, 1056–1058(b)
Women's Trade Union League (WTUL),
   752, 753, 753(i), 754, 803
Women Strike for Peace (WSP), 1085(i)

Wood, Leonard, 662
Woodstock Music Festival (1969), 1047(i)
Work. *See also* Labor (labor force);
   Workers
   in 1950s, 996
Workers (working class). *See also* Labor;
   Labor movement; Wages and
   salaries
   1870s–1890s, 682–691
     domestic servants, 693
     labor movement, 687–691
     leisure and amusements, 693, 694(i)
     managers and white-collar workers,
       685–686
     "typewriters" (women workers) and
       salesclerks, 686–687
   child labor, 684–685, 684(i), 776(i),
     777–778(b)
   in Pennsylvania mines, 761(i)
   Great Depression (1930s) and, 860–862
   New Deal and, 891–893
   progressives and, 752–755
   skilled, 682, 683
     American Federation of Labor (AFL),
       691
   welfare capitalism and, 835
   women
     1870s–1890s, 683–687, 683(i)
     in 1920s, 844
     in 1930s, 859–860
     1940–1950, 964(f)
     in 1950s, 997–998, 1005
     progressives and, 752–755
     after World War II, 964–967(b), 966(i)
     after World War I, 813–814, 815(i)
     World War II and, 931
Work gang system, 584, 676
Workingmen's Party (1876), 657
Work Projects Administration, 932
Work relief, 890
Works Progress Administration (WPA),
   890–891, 890(i)
World Bank, 1163
World's Columbian Exposition (Chicago;
   1893), 700–701, 701(i), 702–703(b),
   703(i)
World's fairs, nineteenth-century,
   702–703(b)
World Trade Center (New York City),
   September 11, 2001 attack on, 1170
World Trade Organization (WTO), 1159,
   1162, 1162(i)
World War I, 789–824
   African Americans and, 819–820,
     822–823(b)
   entry of the United States into,
     796–797
   Europe after, 811(m)
   European alliances after the outbreak
     of, 794(m)
   in France, 798–800
   national purpose and, 804–805, 808
   neutrality in, 794–796
   Nye committee and (1933), 910–911
   Paris peace conference (1919), 809–811,
     810(i)

poison gas warfare, 788(i)
progressive stake in, 801–802
propaganda during, 804, 806–808(b)
Russian revolution (1917), 816
submarines (U-boats) in, 795, 795(i),
   796
training and mobilization of U.S.
   forces, 798
woman suffrage and, 782
World War II, 907–909, 912–946. *See also*
   individual battles
   African Americans and, 930–931, 931(i)
   atomic bomb, 908–909, 908(i), 944–945,
     945(i)
   bombing raids in Germany, 933–936
   D Day, 938, 938(i), 940
   draft, 920
   European theater, 926, 939(m)
   Franklin D. Roosevelt and, 924, 926,
     927, 936, 937, 940
     African Americans, 930–931
     atomic bomb, 934–935
     the Holocaust, 932
     isolationism, 912
     Lend-Lease Act (1941), 916
     mobilization, 919–923
     neutrality, 914–916
     war economy, 921
     Yalta Conference (1945), 940, 941(i)
   gay Americans and, 921
   Germany and, 912–914, 913(m), 915,
     927, 938, 940
     bombing raids, 933–936
     death camps, Allies' refusal to bomb,
       936–937(b)
     Holocaust, 932–933, 933(m)
     Panzers, 914(i)
     Poland, 912–914
   home front, 927–933
     African Americans, 930–931
     Double V campaign, 930–931
     the economy, 921, 924, 928(f), 930
     the Holocaust, 932–933, 933(m)
     politics and the 1944 election, 932
     riots (1943), 931
     security, 919–920
     women and families, 928–930
   Japan and, 916–919, 924–926, 925(i)
     atomic bombing of Hiroshima and
       Nagasaki (1945), 908–909, 908(i),
       944–945, 945(i)
     attack on Pearl Harbor (1941), 918,
       918(i), 918(m), 919(t), 944(t)
     defeat, 940–941, 942(m), 943–946
     surrender, 946
   Japanese Americans during, 920,
     921(m), 922–923(b)
   Jews and, 963
     death camps, Allies' refusal to bomb,
       936
     the Holocaust, 932–933, 933(m)
     Nazi anti-Semitism, 934(b)
   major campaigns and battles of, 944
   mobilization for, 919–923
   Nazi aggression and, 912–914, 913(m)
   onset of, 912

World War II (continued)
  Pacific theater, 924–926, 942(m)
  racial discrimination and, 920–921
  road to, U.S., 919(t)
  submarines (U-boats) in, 916, 919, 926
World War II Home Front National Historical Park (Richmond, California), 929(b)
World Wide Web, 1160
Wounded Knee (South Dakota)
  massacre (1890), 635, 663
  siege at (1972), 1044
Wovoka (Paiute shaman), 662
WPA (Works Progress Administration), 890–891, 890(i)
WPC (Women's Political Council), 1011
Wright, Frank Lloyd, 999
WSP (Women Strike for Peace), 1085(i)

WTUL (Women's Trade Union League), 752, 753, 753(i), 754, 803
Wyoming, 658
  Teapot Dome scandal, 832
  woman suffrage in, 725

Yalta Conference (1945), 940, 941(i)
Yamamoto, Isoroku, 924
Yellow journalism, 735, 736(i)
Yeltsin, Boris, 1145–1146
Yeoman farmers (small farmers), reconstruction and, 578, 582
Yippies (Youth International Party), 1087
Yom Kippur War (1973), 1060, 1091
York (slave), 559
Yorty, Sam, 1031
Yosemite (California), 766(i)
Yosemite National Park, 764
Young, Andrew, 1038
Young, Brigham (1801–1877), 656

Young, Owen, 833
Young Americans for Freedom, 1050(b)
Young people (youth). See also Children; Colleges and universities; Education
  1870s–1890s, 693–694
  in 1950s, 1007–1008
  1960s counterculture, 1046–1047
  Great Depression (1930s) and, 858, 859, 859(i)
  student protest movement (1960s), 1046–1051(b)
Youth International Party (Yippies), 1087
Yugoslavia, 810
  breakup of, 1158, 1158(m)
Yuppies, 1122

Zimmermann, Arthur, 796
Zimmermann telegram (1917), 796

ATLAS OF THE TERRITORIAL GROWTH OF THE UNITED STATES

THE ORIGINAL THIRTEEN COLONIES IN 1776   M-2

THE UNITED STATES IN 1783   M-3

THE UNITED STATES IN 1819   M-4

THE UNITED STATES IN 1853   M-6

THE CONTEMPORARY UNITED STATES   M-8

Lake Superior

Lake Michigan

Lake Huron

Lake Ontario

Lake Erie

St. Lawrence R.

Connecticut R.

N.H.

MASS.

NEW YORK

Hudson R.

RHODE ISLAND

CONNECTICUT

PENN.

Delaware R.

Susquehanna R.

NEW JERSEY

DELAWARE

MARYLAND

Potomac R.

Chesapeake Bay

THE ORIGINAL THIRTEEN COLONIES

Proclamation Line of 1763

James R.

VIRGINIA

Missouri R.

Ohio R.

NORTH CAROLINA

Cape Fear R.

Cumberland R.

Tennessee R.

ATLANTIC OCEAN

Arkansas R.

SOUTH CAROLINA

Mississippi R.

Savannah R.

GEORGIA

THE ORIGINAL THIRTEEN COLONIES IN 1776

0	150	300 miles
0	150	300 kilometers

Gulf of Mexico

Lake Superior

Lake Huron

Lake Michigan

Lake Ontario

Lake Erie

St. Lawrence R.

N.H.

MASS.

NEW YORK

RHODE
ISLAND

CONNECTICUT

Connecticut R.

Hudson R.

PENN.

Delaware R.

Susquehanna R.

NEW JERSEY

DELAWARE

MARYLAND

Chesapeake
Bay

Missouri R.

Ohio R.

Potomac R.

James R.

VIRGINIA

**Gained by treaty
with Britain, 1783**

NORTH
CAROLINA

Cape Fear R.

Cumberland R.

Tennessee R.

Proclamation Line of 1763

THE ORIGINAL THIRTEEN COLONIES

ATLANTIC
OCEAN

Arkansas R.

SOUTH
CAROLINA

Mississippi R.

Savannah R.

GEORGIA

**THE UNITED STATES
IN 1783**

| 0 | 150 | 300 miles |

| 0 | 150 | 300 kilometers |

Gulf of Mexico

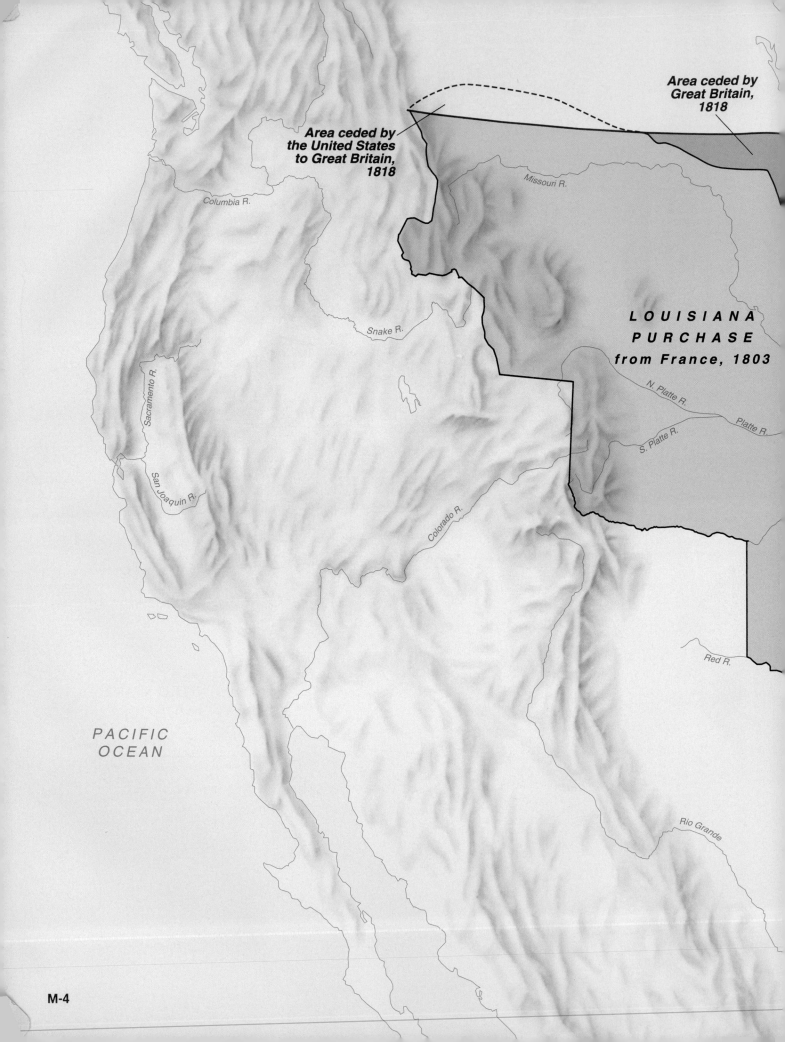

Area ceded by
Great Britain,
1818

Area ceded by
the United States
to Great Britain,
1818

Columbia R.

Missouri R.

Snake R.

**LOUISIANA
PURCHASE**
from France, 1803

Sacramento R.

N. Platte R.

Platte R.

S. Platte R.

San Joaquin R.

Colorado R.

PACIFIC
OCEAN

Red R.

Rio Grande

Lake Superior

(MICHIGAN TERRITORY)

Lake Huron

Lake Michigan

Lake Ontario

St. Lawrence R.

Maine (part of Mass.)

VERMONT (1791)

N.H. (1788)

Connecticut R.

Lake Erie

NEW YORK (1788)

MASS. (1788)

RHODE ISLAND (1790)

Hudson R.

CONNECTICUT (1788)

PENN. (1787)

NEW JERSEY (1787)

Susquehanna R.

THE ORIGINAL THIRTEEN COLONIES

Delaware R.

DELAWARE (1787)

OHIO (1803)

MARYLAND (1788)

Potomac R.

Chesapeake Bay

ILLINOIS (1818)

INDIANA (1816)

Proclamation Line of 1763

James R.

VIRGINIA (1788)

Ohio R.

KENTUCKY (1792)

Gained by treaty with Britain, 1783

Cape Fear R.

NORTH CAROLINA (1789)

Cumberland R.

Tennessee R.

TENNESSEE (1796)

Mississippi R.

SOUTH CAROLINA (1788)

ATLANTIC OCEAN

Savannah R.

MISSISSIPPI (1817)

ALABAMA (1819)

GEORGIA (1788)

LOUISIANA (1812)

THE UNITED STATES IN 1819

0   150   300 miles

0   150   300 kilometers

FLORIDA
Treaty with Spain, 1819

Areas taken from Spain in 1810, 1813

Gulf of Mexico

(1789)   Date of statehood

Area ceded by Great Britain, 1818

Area ceded by the United States to Great Britain, 1818

Missouri R.

Columbia R.

OREGON COUNTRY
Agreement with Britain,
1846

(OREGON TERRITORY)

Snake R.

LOUISIANA
PURCHASE
from France, 1803

N. Platte R.

Platte R.

S. Platte R.

Sacramento R.

(UTAH TERRITORY)

San Joaquin R.

MEXICAN CESSION,
1848

Colorado R.

CALIFORNIA
(1850)

(NEW MEXICO TERRITORY)

(Claim waived by
Texas, 1850)

Red R.

TEXAS
Annexed, 1845

PACIFIC
OCEAN

TEXAS
(1845)

GADSDEN PURCHASE
from Mexico, 1853

Rio Grande

Areas ceded by Britain, 1842
(Webster-Ashburton Treaty)

St. Lawrence R.

Lake Superior

MAINE
(1820)

VERMONT
(1791)

Connecticut R.

N.H.
(1788)

Lake Huron

Lake Ontario

NEW YORK
(1788)

MASS.
(1788)

(MINNESOTA
TERRITORY)

WISCONSIN
(1848)

MICHIGAN
(1837)

Lake Michigan

Hudson R.

RHODE
ISLAND
(1790)

CONNECTICUT
(1788)

Lake Erie

PENN.
(1787)

Susquehanna R.

Delaware R.

NEW JERSEY
(1787)

IOWA
(1846)

Missouri R.

OHIO
(1803)

Proclamation Line of 1763

DELAWARE
(1787)

THE ORIGINAL THIRTEEN COLONIES

Potomac R.

MARYLAND
(1788)

ILLINOIS
(1818)

INDIANA
(1816)

Chesapeake
Bay

James R.

VIRGINIA
(1788)

MISSOURI
(1821)

Ohio R.

KENTUCKY
(1792)

Gained by treaty
with Britain, 1783

NORTH
CAROLINA
(1789)

Cape Fear R.

Cumberland R.

Tennessee R.

TENNESSEE
(1796)

ARKANSAS
(1836)

Mississippi R.

SOUTH
CAROLINA
(1788)

ATLANTIC
OCEAN

(INDIAN
TERRITORY)

Savannah R.

MISSISSIPPI
(1817)

ALABAMA
(1819)

GEORGIA
(1788)

THE UNITED STATES
IN 1853

LOUISIANA
(1812)

FLORIDA
(1845)

0   150   300 miles

0   150   300 kilometers

FLORIDA
Treaty with Spain,
1819

Areas taken from Spain
in 1810, 1813

Gulf of Mexico

(1789)   Date of statehood

M-7

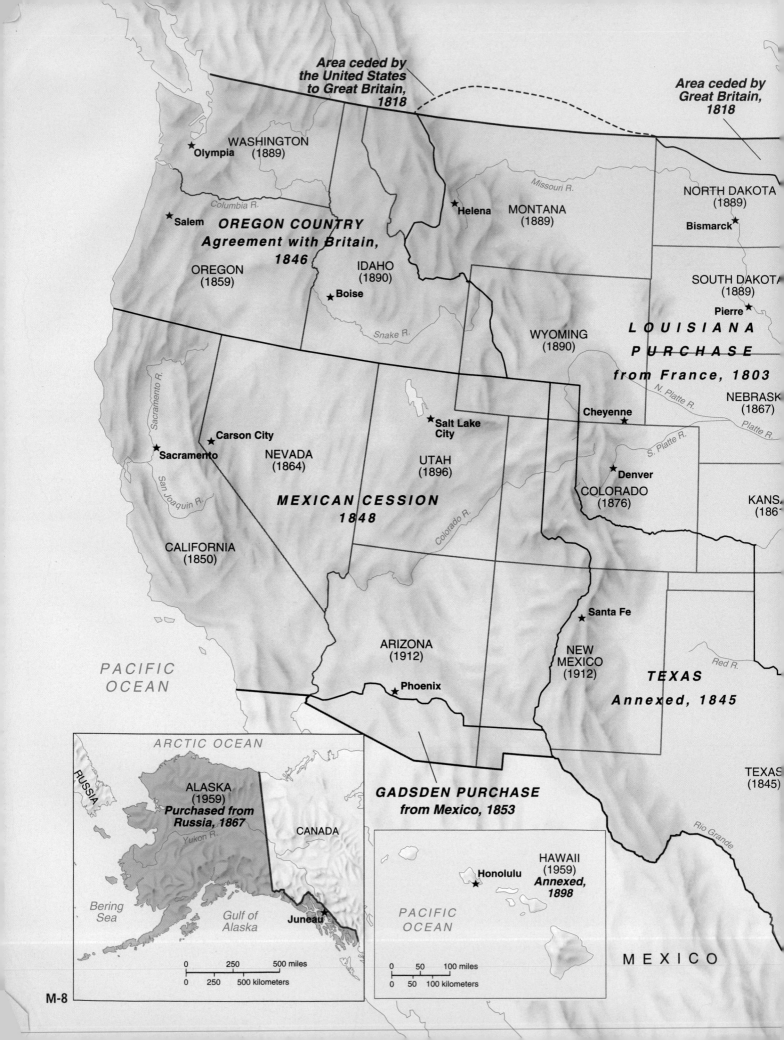

Area ceded by the United States to Great Britain, 1818

Area ceded by Great Britain, 1818

WASHINGTON (1889)
★ Olympia

★ Helena
MONTANA (1889)

Missouri R.

NORTH DAKOTA (1889)

Bismarck ★

Columbia R.

★ Salem
OREGON COUNTRY
Agreement with Britain, 1846

OREGON (1859)

IDAHO (1890)
★ Boise

Snake R.

WYOMING (1890)

SOUTH DAKOTA (1889)

Pierre ★

LOUISIANA PURCHASE
from France, 1803

N. Platte R.

NEBRASK (1867)

Platte R.

★ Salt Lake City

Cheyenne ★

★ Carson City

★ Sacramento

NEVADA (1864)

UTAH (1896)

Denver ★
COLORADO (1876)

S. Platte R.

KANS. (186

Sacramento R.

San Joaquin R.

MEXICAN CESSION
1848

Colorado R.

CALIFORNIA (1850)

PACIFIC OCEAN

ARIZONA (1912)

★ Phoenix

Santa Fe ★

NEW MEXICO (1912)

TEXAS
Annexed, 1845

Red R.

TEXAS (1845)

GADSDEN PURCHASE
from Mexico, 1853

Rio Grande

ARCTIC OCEAN

RUSSIA

ALASKA (1959)
Purchased from Russia, 1867

Yukon R.

CANADA

Bering Sea

Gulf of Alaska

Juneau ★

0   250   500 miles
0   250   500 kilometers

HAWAII (1959)
Annexed, 1898

Honolulu ★

PACIFIC OCEAN

0   50   100 miles
0   50   100 kilometers

MEXICO

M-8

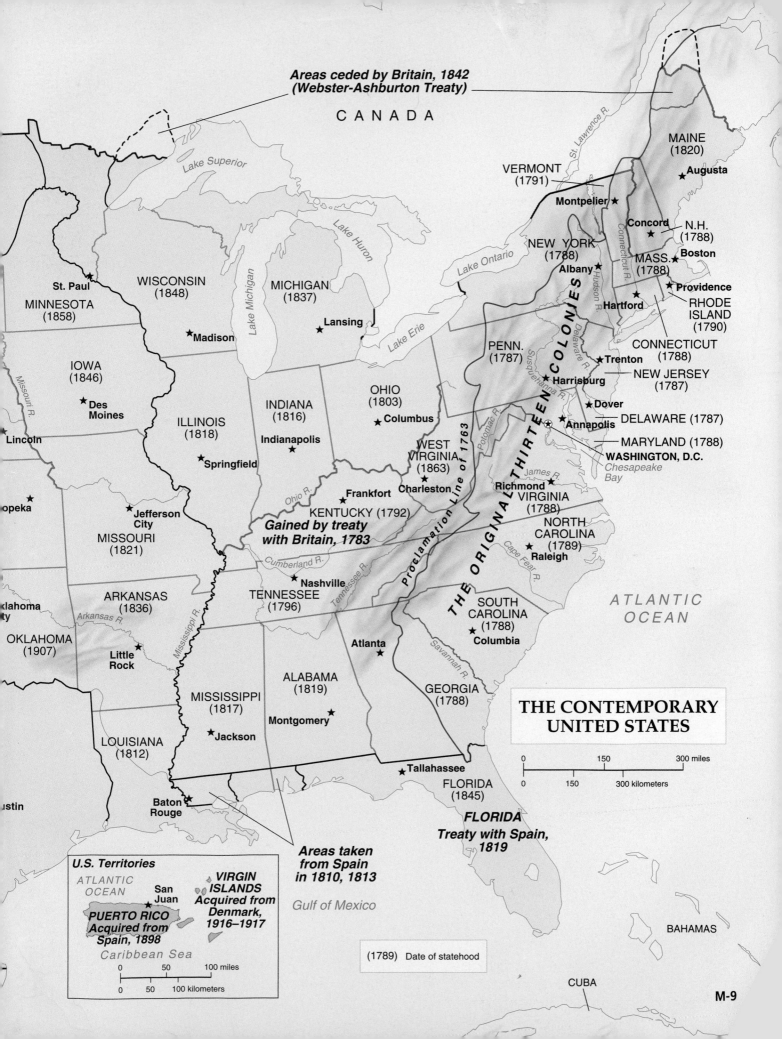

Areas ceded by Britain, 1842
(Webster-Ashburton Treaty)

C A N A D A

St. Lawrence R.

MAINE
(1820)
★ Augusta

VERMONT
(1791)

Lake Superior

Lake Huron

Lake Michigan

Montpelier ★

Concord
★
N.H.
(1788)

NEW YORK
(1788)
Albany ★

MASS.
(1788)
★ Boston

★ St. Paul

WISCONSIN
(1848)

MICHIGAN
(1837)

Connecticut R.

Hudson R.

Providence
★
RHODE
ISLAND
(1790)

MINNESOTA
(1858)

★ Madison

Lansing ★

Lake Ontario

Hartford ★

CONNECTICUT
(1788)

THE ORIGINAL THIRTEEN COLONIES

Lake Erie

PENN.
(1787)

Delaware R.

Trenton ★

★ Des
Moines

IOWA
(1846)

OHIO
(1803)

Harrisburg ★

NEW JERSEY
(1787)

Missouri R.

INDIANA
(1816)

★ Columbus

★ Dover

DELAWARE (1787)

★ Lincoln

ILLINOIS
(1818)

Indianapolis
★

WEST
VIRGINIA
(1863)

Proclamation Line of 1763

Potomac R.

Annapolis ★

WASHINGTON, D.C.

MARYLAND (1788)

*Chesapeake
Bay*

★ Springfield

★ opeka

★ Jefferson
City

MISSOURI
(1821)

Ohio R.

★ Frankfort

Charleston ★

KENTUCKY (1792)

**Gained by treaty
with Britain, 1783**

Richmond
★

James R.

VIRGINIA
(1788)

NORTH
CAROLINA
(1789)

ATLANTIC
OCEAN

Cumberland R.

★ Raleigh

Cape Fear R.

★lahoma
ty

OKLAHOMA
(1907)

ARKANSAS
(1836)

Arkansas R.

★ Nashville

TENNESSEE
(1796)

Tennessee R.

Mississippi R.

★ Little
Rock

Atlanta ★

SOUTH
CAROLINA
(1788)

★ Columbia

Savannah R.

★ustin

LOUISIANA
(1812)

MISSISSIPPI
(1817)

ALABAMA
(1819)

Montgomery ★

★ Jackson

GEORGIA
(1788)

THE CONTEMPORARY
UNITED STATES

| 0 | 150 | 300 miles |
| 0 | 150 | 300 kilometers |

★ Tallahassee

★ Baton
Rouge

**Areas taken
from Spain
in 1810, 1813**

FLORIDA
(1845)

Gulf of Mexico

FLORIDA
Treaty with Spain,
1819

U.S. Territories

ATLANTIC
OCEAN

San
Juan
★

*VIRGIN
ISLANDS*
**Acquired from
Denmark,
1916–1917**

PUERTO RICO
**Acquired from
Spain, 1898**

Caribbean Sea

| 0 | 50 | 100 miles |
| 0 | 50 | 100 kilometers |

(1789)   Date of statehood

BAHAMAS

CUBA

M-9

APPENDICES

I. Documents A-1

The Declaration of Independence A-1

The Articles of Confederation and Perpetual Union A-3

The Constitution of the United States A-7

Amendments to the Constitution with Annotations (including the six unratified amendments) A-12

The Constitution of the Confederate States of America A-25

II. Facts and Figures: Government, Economy, and Demographics A-33

U.S. POLITICS AND GOVERNMENT A-33

Presidential Elections A-33

Presidents, Vice Presidents, and Secretaries of State A-36

Admission of States to the Union A-38

Supreme Court Justices A-39

Significant Supreme Court Cases A-40

THE AMERICAN ECONOMY A-46

Main Sectors of the U.S. Economy: 1849, 1899, 1950, 1990, 2001 A-46

Federal Spending and the Economy, 1790–2002 A-47

A DEMOGRAPHIC PROFILE OF THE UNITED STATES AND ITS PEOPLE A-48

Population Growth, 1630–2000 A-48

Birthrate, 1820–2000 A-49

Death Rate, 1900–2000 A-49

Life Expectancy, 1900–2000 A-49

Migration and Immigration A-50

III. Research Resources in U.S. History A-53

Bibliographies and Indexes A-53

General Overviews A-53

Specialized Information A-53

Primary Resources A-54

Internet Resources A-54

Glossary of Historical Vocabulary G-1

Index I-1

Atlas of the Territorial Growth of the United States M-1

PREFACE

THIS NEW EDITION OF *The American Promise* is a cause for celebration, for it proudly announces the successful reception of earlier editions. Preparing this edition, however, allowed us the opportunity to revisit our original premises, evaluate our earlier efforts, take stock of what worked, and decide how to build on those successes. The result of our careful reexamination is a major revision of *The American Promise*. While the third edition rests securely on our original goals and draws on our continuing engagement with American history as classroom teachers, we have also benefited from the invaluable suggestions of many of our adopters. As our textbook established its place among introductory surveys of American history, an ever-growing community of book users informed our efforts to make this good text even better. We are grateful for their suggestions and are confident the result is a text that will be even more useful to students and instructors.

From the beginning, *The American Promise* has been shaped by our firsthand knowledge that the survey course is the most difficult to teach and the most difficult to take. Collectively, we have logged more than a century in introductory American history classrooms in institutions that range from small community colleges to large research institutions. Drawing on our practical experience, we set an ambitious goal, one that we continue to focus on in the third edition: to produce the most teachable and readable introductory American history textbook available.

Our experience as teachers informs every aspect of our text, beginning with its framework. Many survey texts emphasize either a social or a political approach to history, and by focusing on one, they inevitably slight the other. In our classrooms, we have found that students need **both** the structure a political narrative provides **and** the insights gained from examining social and cultural experience. To write a comprehensive,

balanced account of American history, we focused on the public arena—the place where politics intersects social and cultural developments—to show how Americans confronted the major issues of their day and created far-reaching historical change.

We also thought hard about the concerns most frequently voiced by instructors: that students often find history boring, unfocused, and difficult and their textbooks lifeless and overwhelming. Getting students to open the book is one of the biggest hurdles instructors face. We asked ourselves how our text could address these concerns and engage students in ways that would help them understand and remember the main developments in American history. To make the political, social, economic, and cultural changes vivid and memorable and to portray fully the diversity of the American experience, we stitched into our narrative the voices of hundreds of contemporaries—from presidents to pipefitters, sharecroppers to suffragists—whose ideas and actions shaped their times and whose efforts still affect our lives. By incorporating a rich selection of authentic American voices, we seek to capture history as it happened and to create a compelling narrative that captures students' interests and sparks their historical imagination.

Our title, *The American Promise*, reflects our emphasis on human agency and our conviction that American history is an unfinished story. For millions, the nation has held out the promise of a better life, unfettered worship, representative government, democratic politics, and other freedoms seldom found elsewhere. But none of these promises has come with guarantees. And promises fulfilled for some have meant promises denied to others. As we see it, much of American history is a continuing struggle over the definition and realization of the nation's promise. Abraham Lincoln, in the midst of what he termed the "fiery trial" of the Civil War, pronounced the

> We set an ambitious goal to produce the most teachable and readable introductory American history textbook available.

CHAPTER 28
Reform, Rebellion, and Reaction, 1960–1974   1021

OPENING VIGNETTE: *Fannie Lou Hamer leads grassroots struggles of African Americans for voting rights and political empowerment*   1021

Liberalism at High Tide   1023
The Promise and Substance of Kennedy's New Frontier *1023* • Assassination of a President *1025* • Johnson Fulfills the Kennedy Promise *1026* • Completing the Great Society Agenda *1027* • Assessing the War on Poverty *1028* • The Judicial Revolution *1029*

The Second Reconstruction   1031
The Flowering of the Black Freedom Struggle *1032* • The Response in Washington *1035* • Black Nationalism *1036*

HISTORICAL QUESTION: *What Difference Did Black Voting Rights Make?*   1038

A Multitude of Movements   1042
Native American Protest *1042* • Latino Struggles for Justice *1044* • Student Rebellion, the New Left, and the Counterculture *1046* • A New Movement to Save the Environment *1047*

AMERICAN PLACES: *Alcatraz Island, San Francisco, California*   1043

DOCUMENTING THE AMERICAN PROMISE: *Student Protest*   1048

The New Wave of Feminism   1052
A Movement Emerges *1052* • The Many Facets and Achievements of Feminism *1054* • A Counter Movement Arises *1055*

BEYOND AMERICA'S BORDERS: *Transnational Feminisms*   1056

The Persistence of Liberal Reform in the Nixon Administration   1058
Extending the Welfare State and Regulating the Economy *1059* • Responding to Demands for Social Justice *1060*

Conclusion: Achievements and Limitations of Liberalism   1061

Chronology 1062   •   **Bibliography** 1063

CHAPTER 29
Vietnam and the Limits of Power, 1961–1975   1067

OPENING VIGNETTE: *American GIs arrive in Vietnam*   1067

New Frontiers in Foreign Policy   1068
Meeting the "Hour of Maximum Danger" *1068* • New Approaches to the Third World *1071* • The Arms Race and the Nuclear Brink *1072* • Venturing into a Quagmire in Vietnam *1073*

Lyndon Johnson's War against Communism   1075
Toward an All-Out Commitment in Vietnam *1075* • Preventing Another Castro in Latin America *1076* • The Americanized War *1077*

HISTORICAL QUESTION: *Why Couldn't the United States Bomb Its Way to Victory in Vietnam?*   1078

THE PROMISE OF TECHNOLOGY: *The Military Helicopter*   1082

A Nation Polarized   1081
The Widening War at Home *1081* • 1968: Year of Upheaval *1084*

New Opportunities and Dangers in a Multipolar World   1088
Moving toward Détente with the Soviet Union and China *1089* • Shoring Up Anticommunism in the Third World *1090*

Nixon's Search for Peace with Honor in Vietnam   1091
Vietnamization and Negotiations *1091* • Nixon's War *1092* • The Peace Accords and the Fall of Saigon *1094* • The Legacy of Defeat *1095*

AMERICAN PLACES: *The Vietnam Veterans Memorial, Washington, D.C.*   1096

Conclusion: An Unwinnable War   1098

Chronology 1099   •   **Bibliography** 1100

CHAPTER 30

America Moves to the Right, 1969–1989   1103

OPENING VIGNETTE: *Phyllis Schlafly promotes conservatism*   1103

Nixon and the Rise of Postwar Conservatism   1104
The Emergence of a Grassroots Conservative Movement *1105* • Nixon Courts the Right *1106*

Constitutional Crisis and Restoration   1107
The Election of 1972 *1108* • Watergate *1108* • The Ford Presidency and the Election of 1976 *1110*

The "Outsider" Presidency of Jimmy Carter   1112
Retreat from Liberalism *1112* • Carter Promotes Human Rights *1113* • The Cold War Intensifies *1115*

Ronald Reagan and the Conservative Ascendancy   1116
Appealing to the New Right and Beyond *1116* • Unleashing Free Enterprise *1121* • Winners and Losers in a Flourishing Economy *1122*

HISTORICAL QUESTION: *Why Did the ERA Fail?*   1118

Continuing Struggles over Rights and the Environment   1124
The Conservative Shift in the Federal Courts *1124* • Feminism on the Defensive *1125* • The Gay and Lesbian Rights Movement *1126* • Conflicts over Environmental Protections *1130*

DOCUMENTING THE AMERICAN PROMISE: *Protecting Gay and Lesbian Rights*   1128

THE PROMISE OF TECHNOLOGY: *Solar Energy*   1132

Ronald Reagan Confronts an "Evil Empire"   1131
Militarization and Interventions Abroad *1131* • The Iran-Contra Scandal *1134* • A Thaw in Soviet-American Relations *1134*

Conclusion: Reversing the Course of Government   1135

Chronology 1137   •   **Bibliography** 1138

CHAPTER 31

The End of the Cold War and the Challenges of Globalization: Since 1989   1141

OPENING VIGNETTE: *Colin Powell adjusts to a post–cold war world*   1141

Domestic Stalemate and Global Upheaval: The Presidency of George H. W. Bush   1143
Gridlock in Government *1143* • The End of the Cold War *1145* • Going to War in Central America and the Persian Gulf *1147* • The 1992 Election *1149*

The Clinton Administration's Search for the Middle Ground   1150
Clinton's Promise of Change *1150* • Changing the Face of Government *1151* • The Clinton Administration Moves Right *1152* • Impeaching the President *1153* • The Booming Economy of the 1990s *1154*

The United States in a Globalizing World   1155
Defining America's Place in a New World Order *1155* • Debates over Globalization *1159* • Liberalizing Foreign Trade *1163* • The Internationalization of the United States *1163*

HISTORICAL QUESTION: *Still a Promised Land?*   1156

THE PROMISE OF TECHNOLOGY: *The Internet*   1160

BEYOND AMERICA'S BORDERS: *Jobs in a Globalizing Era*   1164

President George W. Bush: Conservatism at Home and Radical Initiatives Abroad   1167
The Disputed Election of 2000 *1168* • The Domestic Policies of a "Compassionate Conservative" *1169* • The Globalization of Terrorism *1170* • Unilateralism, Preemption, and the Iraq War *1171*

Conclusion: Defining the Government's Role at Home and Abroad   1174

Chronology 1175   •   **Bibliography** 1176

CHAPTER 24

The New Deal Experiment,
1932–1939   867

OPENING VIGNETTE: *The Bonus Army marches into Washington, D.C.*   867

Franklin D. Roosevelt: A Patrician in Government   869
The Making of a Politician *869* • The Election of 1932 *871*

Launching the New Deal   872
The New Dealers *873* • Banking and Finance Reform *875* • Relief and Conservation Programs *877* • Agricultural Initiatives *880* • Industrial Recovery *881*

AMERICAN PLACES: *Hoover Dam, Nevada*   879

THE PROMISE OF TECHNOLOGY: *Mechanized Cotton Picking Waits Out the Depression*   882

Challenges to the New Deal   884
Resistance to Business Reform *884* • Casualties in the Countryside *885* • Politics on the Fringes *886*

HISTORICAL QUESTION: *Huey Long: Demagogue or Champion of the Dispossessed?*   888

Toward a Welfare State   889
Relief for the Unemployed *890* • Empowering Labor *891* • Social Security and Tax Reform *893* • Neglected Americans and the New Deal *894*

The New Deal from Victory to Deadlock   897
The Election of 1936 *897* • Court Packing *899* • Reaction and Recession *900* • The Last of the New Deal Reforms *900*

Conclusion: Achievements and Limitations of the New Deal   902

Chronology 903   •   **Bibliography** 903

CHAPTER 25

The United States and the
Second World War,
1939–1945   907

OPENING VIGNETTE: *Colonel Paul Tibbets drops the atomic bomb on Hiroshima, Japan*   907

Peacetime Dilemmas   909
Roosevelt and Reluctant Isolation *909* • The Good Neighbor Policy *910* • The Price of Noninvolvement *910*

The Onset of War   912
Nazi Aggression and War in Europe *912* • From Neutrality to the Arsenal of Democracy *914* • Japan Attacks America *916*

Mobilizing for War   919
Home-Front Security *919* • Building a Citizen Army *920* • Conversion to a War Economy *921*

DOCUMENTING THE AMERICAN PROMISE: *Japanese Internment*   922

Fighting Back   924
Turning the Tide in the Pacific *924* • The Campaign in Europe *926*

The Wartime Home Front   927
Women and Families, Guns and Butter *928* • The Double V Campaign *930* • Wartime Politics and the 1944 Election *932* • Reaction to the Holocaust *932*

AMERICAN PLACES: *Rosie the Riveter/World War II Home Front National Historical Park, Richmond, California*   929

BEYOND AMERICA'S BORDERS: *Nazi Anti-Semitism and the Atomic Bomb*   934

HISTORICAL QUESTION: *Why Did the Allies Refuse to Bomb the Death Camps?*   936

Toward Unconditional Surrender   933
From Bombing Raids to Berlin *933* • The Defeat of Japan *940* • Atomic Warfare *944*

Conclusion: Allied Victory and America's Emergence as a Superpower   946

Chronology 947   •   **Bibliography** 948

CHAPTER 26
Cold War Politics in the Truman Years, 1945–1953   951

OPENING VIGNETTE: *Secretary of State Dean Acheson, President Truman's "good right hand"* 951

From the Grand Alliance to Containment 952
The Cold War Begins *953* • The Truman Doctrine and the Marshall Plan *959* • Building a National Security State *960* • Superpower Rivalry around the Globe *962*

DOCUMENTING THE AMERICAN PROMISE: *The Emerging Cold War* 956

Truman and the Fair Deal at Home 964
Reconversion and the Postwar Economic Boom *964* • Black and Mexican American Protest and the Politics of Civil Rights *968* • The Fair Deal Flounders *970* • The Domestic Chill: A Second Red Scare *972*

HISTORICAL QUESTION: *What Happened to Rosie the Riveter?* 966

The Cold War Becomes Hot: Korea 974
Korea and the Military Implementation of Containment *974* • From Containment to Rollback to Containment *975* • Korea, Communism, and the 1952 Election *978* • An Armistice and the War's Costs *979*

AMERICAN PLACES: *The Harry S. Truman Library, Independence, Missouri* 977

Conclusion: The Cold War's Costs and Consequences 980

Chronology 981   •   **Bibliography** 982

CHAPTER 27
The Politics and Culture of Abundance, 1952–1960   985

OPENING VIGNETTE: *Vice President Nixon and Russian premier Khrushchev debate the merits of U.S. and Soviet societies* 985

Eisenhower and the Politics of the "Middle Way" 986
The President and McCarthy *986* • Modern Republicanism *987* • Termination and Relocation of Native Americans *988* • The 1956 Election and the Second Term *990*

Liberation Rhetoric and the Practice of Containment 990
The "New Look" in Foreign Policy *990* • Applying Containment to Vietnam *991* • Interventions in Latin America and the Middle East *992* • The Nuclear Arms Race *994*

New Work and Living Patterns in an Economy of Abundance 995
Technology Transforms Agriculture and Industry *996* • Burgeoning Suburbs and Declining Cities *998* • The Rise of the Sun Belt *999* • The Democratization of Higher Education *1002*

THE PROMISE OF TECHNOLOGY: *Air-Conditioning* 1001

The Culture of Abundance 1004
A Consumer Culture *1004* • The Revival of Domesticity and Religion *1005* • Television Transforms Culture and Politics *1006* • Countercurrents *1007*

Emergence of a Civil Rights Movement 1009
African Americans Challenge the Supreme Court and the President *1009* • Montgomery and Mass Protest *1011*

DOCUMENTING THE AMERICAN PROMISE: *The* Brown *Decision* 1012

AMERICAN PLACES: *Martin Luther King Jr National Historic Site, Atlanta, Georgia* 1015

Conclusion: Peace and Prosperity Mask Unmet Challenges 1016

Chronology 1017   •   **Bibliography** 1018

Preface xii

CHAPTER 21

Progressivism from the Grass Roots to the White House, 1890–1916 747

OPENING VIGNETTE: *Jane Addams founds Hull House* 747

Grassroots Progressivism 749
Civilizing the City *749* • Progressives and the Working Class *752*

AMERICAN PLACES: *Jane Addams Hull-House Museum, Chicago, Illinois* 750

BEYOND AMERICA'S BORDERS: *Protecting the World's Workers: The Consumers' League* 756

Progressivism: Theory and Practice 755
Reform Darwinism, Pragmatism, and Social Engineering *755* • Progressive Government: City and State *755*

Progressivism Finds a President: Theodore Roosevelt 759
The Square Deal *759* • Roosevelt the Reformer *762* • Roosevelt and Conservation *763* • Roosevelt the Diplomat *766*

THE PROMISE OF TECHNOLOGY: *Flash Photography and the Birth of Photojournalism* 764

Progressivism Stalled 770
The Troubled Presidency of Taft *770* • Progressive Insurgency and the Election of 1912 *772*

Wilson and Progressivism at High Tide 774
Wilson's Reforms: Tariff, Banking, and the Trusts *774* • Wilson, Reluctant Progressive *775*

DOCUMENTING THE AMERICAN PROMISE: *The Issue of Child Labor* 777

The Limits of Progressive Reform 776
Radical Alternatives *778* • Progressivism for White Men Only *781*

Conclusion: The Transformation of the Liberal State 784

Chronology 785 • **Bibliography** 786

CHAPTER 22
World War I: The Progressive Crusade at Home and Abroad, 1914–1920   789

OPENING VIGNETTE: *General Pershing struggles to protect the autonomy of the American Expeditionary Force*   789

Woodrow Wilson and the World   790
Taming the Americas *791* • The European Crisis *792* • The Ordeal of American Neutrality *794* • The United States Enters the War *796*

AMERICAN PLACES: *Pancho Villa State Park, Columbus, New Mexico*   793

Over There   797
The Call to Arms *798* • The War in France *798*

The Crusade for Democracy at Home   801
The Progressive Stake in the War *801* • Women, War, and the Battle for Suffrage *802* • The Struggle over National Purpose *804*

DOCUMENTING THE AMERICAN PROMISE: *For and Against World War I*   806

A Compromised Peace   809
Wilson's Fourteen Points *809* • The Paris Peace Conference *809* • The Fight for the Treaty *811*

Democracy at Risk   813
Economic Hardship and Labor Upheaval *813* • The Red Scare *814* • The Great Migrations of African Americans and Mexicans *818* • Postwar Politics and the Election of 1920 *821*

BEYOND AMERICA'S BORDERS: *Bolshevism*   816

HISTORICAL QUESTION: *What Did the War Mean to African Americans?*   822

Conclusion: Troubled Crusade   824

Chronology 825   •   **Bibliography** 826

CHAPTER 23
From New Era to Great Depression, 1920–1932   829

OPENING VIGNETTE: *Henry Ford puts America on wheels*   829

The New Era   830
A Business Government *831* • Promoting Prosperity and Peace Abroad *833* • Automobiles, Mass Production, and Assembly-Line Progress *834* • Consumer Culture *836*

AMERICAN PLACES: *East Texas Oil Museum, Kilgore, Texas*   836

THE PROMISE OF TECHNOLOGY: *Better Living through Electricity*   838

The Roaring Twenties   840
Prohibition *840* • The New Woman *841* • The New Negro *844* • Mass Culture *846* • The Lost Generation *849*

HISTORICAL QUESTION: *Was Prohibition a Bad Idea?*   842

Resistance to Change   849
Rejecting the "Huddled Masses" *850* • The Rebirth of the Ku Klux Klan *852* • The Scopes Trial *852* • Al Smith and the Election of 1928 *853*

The Great Crash   854
Herbert Hoover: The Great Engineer *854* • The Distorted Economy *855* • The Crash of 1929 *856* • Hoover and the Limits of Individualism *857*

Life in the Depression   857
The Human Toll *858* • Denial and Escape *860* • Working-Class Militancy *860*

Conclusion: Dazzle and Despair   862

Chronology 863   •   **Bibliography** 864

The American Promise

A HISTORY OF THE UNITED STATES

Third Edition
Volume C: From 1900

James L. Roark
Emory University

Michael P. Johnson
Johns Hopkins University

Patricia Cline Cohen
University of California, Santa Barbara

Sarah Stage
Arizona State University West

Alan Lawson
Boston College

Susan M. Hartmann
The Ohio State University

BEDFORD/ST. MARTIN'S
Boston ◆ New York

FOR BEDFORD/ST. MARTIN'S

Executive Editor for History: Mary Dougherty
Director of Development for History: Jane Knetzger
Senior Developmental Editor: Heidi L. Hood
Senior Production Editor: Karen S. Baart
Senior Production Supervisor: Joe Ford
Senior Marketing Manager: Jenna Bookin Barry
Editorial Assistant: Elizabeth Harrison
Production Assistants: Amy Derjue, Anne E. True
Copyeditor: Patricia Herbst
Text Design and Page Layout: Wanda Kossak Design
Photo Research: Pembroke Herbert/Sandi Rygiel, Picture Research Consultants & Archives, Inc.
Indexer: Maro Riofrancos
Cover Design: Donna Lee Dennison
Cartography: Mapping Specialists Ltd.
Composition: TechBooks
Printing and Binding: R.R. Donnelley & Sons Company

President: Joan E. Feinberg
Editorial Director: Denise B. Wydra
Director of Marketing: Karen Melton Soeltz
Director of Editing, Design, and Production: Marcia Cohen
Managing Editor: Elizabeth M. Schaaf

Library of Congress Control Number: 2004102163

Manufactured in the United States of America.

9 8 7 6 5
f   e   d   c   b   a

For information, write: Bedford/St. Martin's, 75 Arlington Street, Boston, MA 02116 (617-399-4000)

ISBN: 0–312–40687–8 (combined edition) EAN: 978–0–312–40687–5
ISBN: 0–312–40688–6 (Vol. I) EAN: 978–0–312–40688–2
ISBN: 0–312–40689–4 (Vol. II) EAN: 978–0–312–40689–9
ISBN: 0–312–44956–9 (Vol. A) EAN: 978–0–312–44956–8
ISBN: 0–312–44957–7 (Vol. B) EAN: 978–0–312–44957–5
ISBN: 0–312–44955–0 (Vol. C) EAN: 978–0–312–44955–1

Cover Art: Elizabeth Eckford turned away from entering Central High School in Little Rock by Arkansas National Guard troops under orders from Governor Orval Faubus in September 1957. Francis Miller/Time Life Pictures/Getty Images.